CONTENTS

17 THE NORTHEASTERN AEGEAN ISLANDS 623

18 PLANNING YOUR TRIP TO GREECE 651

19 THE GREEK LANGUAGE 678

LIST OF MAPS

ABOUT THE AUTHORS

John S. Bowman has been a freelance writer and editor for more than 35 years. He specializes in nonfiction ranging from archaeology to zoology, baseball to biography. He first visited Greece in 1956 and has traveled and lived there over the years. He is the author of numerous guides to various regions in Greece. He currently resides in Northampton, Massachusetts.

Peter Kerasiotis, a native Athenian, currently lives in New York City, where he works as a web developer and editor. He is also a contributing author to Frommer's *Greek Islands.*

Sherry Marker majored in classical Greek at Harvard, studied archaeology at the American School of Classical Studies in Athens, and did graduate work in ancient history at the University of California at Berkeley. The author of a number of guides to Greece, she has also written for the *New York Times, Travel + Leisure,* and *Hampshire Life.* When not in Greece, she lives in Massachusetts.

Heidi Sarna is a freelance writer who has sailed on more than 100 cruise ships of all shapes and sizes all over the world, usually with her twin sons and agreeable husband in tow. Co-author of *Frommer's Cruises & Ports of Call* as well as author of *Frommer's Singapore Day by Day,* Heidi is a contributor to several other guidebooks, and she also writes regular travel columns for Frommers.com and *Porthole* magazine. She's written for countless magazines, newspapers, and websites on travel and cruising and also covers diverse topics from relationships to charities, artists, and nutrition.

HOW TO CONTACT US

In researching this book, we discovered many wonderful places—hotels, restaurants, shops, and more. We're sure you'll find others. Please tell us about them, so we can share the information with your fellow travelers in upcoming editions. If you were disappointed with a recommendation, we'd love to know that, too. Please write to:

Frommer's Greece, 8th Edition
John Wiley & Sons, Inc. • 111 River St. • Hoboken, NJ 07030-5774
frommersfeedback@wiley.com

ADVISORY & DISCLAIMER

Travel information can change quickly and unexpectedly, and we strongly advise you to confirm important details locally before traveling, including information on visas, health and safety, traffic and transport, accommodation, shopping and eating out. We also encourage you to stay alert while traveling and to remain aware of your surroundings. Avoid civil disturbances, and keep a close eye on cameras, purses, wallets and other valuables.

While we have endeavored to ensure that the information contained within this guide is accurate and up-to-date at the time of publication, we make no representations or warranties with respect to the accuracy or completeness of the contents of this work and specifically disclaim all warranties, including without limitation warranties of fitness for a particular purpose. We accept no responsibility or liability for any inaccuracy or errors or omissions, or for any inconvenience, loss, damage, costs or expenses of any nature whatsoever incurred or suffered by anyone as a result of any advice or information contained in this guide.

The inclusion of a company, organization or website in this guide as a service provider and/or potential source of further information does not mean that we endorse them or the information they provide. Be aware that information provided through some websites may be unreliable and can change without notice. Neither the publisher or author shall be liable for any damages arising herefrom.

FROMMER'S STAR RATINGS, ICONS & ABBREVIATIONS

Every hotel, restaurant, and attraction listing in this guide has been ranked for quality, value, service, amenities, and special features using a **star-rating system.** In country, state, and regional guides, we also rate towns and regions to help you narrow down your choices and budget your time accordingly. Hotels and restaurants are rated on a scale of zero (recommended) to three stars (exceptional). Attractions, shopping, nightlife, towns, and regions are rated according to the following scale: zero stars (recommended), one star (highly recommended), two stars (very highly recommended), and three stars (must-see).

In addition to the star-rating system, we also use **seven feature icons** that point you to the great deals, in-the-know advice, and unique experiences that separate travelers from tourists. Throughout the book, look for:

Special finds—those places only insiders know about

Fun facts—details that make travelers more informed and their trips more fun

Kids—best bets for kids and advice for the whole family

Special moments—those experiences that memories are made of

Overrated—places or experiences not worth your time or money

Insider tips—great ways to save time and money

Great values—where to get the best deals

The following **abbreviations** are used for credit cards:

AE	American Express	**DISC**	Discover	**V**	Visa
DC	Diners Club	**MC**	MasterCard		

TRAVEL RESOURCES AT FROMMERS.COM

Frommer's travel resources don't end with this guide. Frommer's website, **www.frommers. com**, has travel information on more than 4,000 destinations. We update features regularly, giving you access to the most current trip-planning information and the best airfare, lodging, and car-rental bargains. You can also listen to podcasts, connect with other Frommers.com members through our active-reader forums, share your travel photos, read blogs from guidebook editors and fellow travelers, and much more.

THE BEST OF GREECE

Greece is, of course, the land of ancient sites and architectural treasures—the Acropolis in Athens, the amphitheater of Epidaurus, and the reconstructed palace at Knossos among the best known. But Greece is much more: It offers age-old spectacular natural sights, for instance—from Santorini's caldera to the gray pinnacles of rock of the Meteora—and modern diversions ranging from elegant museums to luxury resorts.

It can be bewildering to plan your trip with so many options vying for your attention. Take us along and we'll help you figure it out. We've explored the archaeological sites, visited the museums, inspected the hotels, reviewed the tavernas and ouzeries, and scoped out the beaches. Here's what we consider the best of the best.

THE best TRAVEL EXPERIENCES

o **Making Haste Slowly:** Give yourself time to sit in a seaside taverna and watch the fishing boats come and go. If you visit Greece in the spring, take the time to smell the flowers; the fields are covered with poppies, daisies, and other blooms. Even in Athens, you'll see hardy species growing through the cracks in concrete sidewalks—or better yet, visit Athens's Ancient Agora, which will be carpeted with a dazzling variety of wildflowers. See chapter 6, "Exploring Athens."

o **Island-Hopping in the Cyclades:** Though the Cyclades are bound by unmistakable family resemblance, each island has a unique personality. Distances between islands are small, making travel by ferry logistically straightforward (at least in principle). Whether you are traveling in the off season, when you do not need hotel reservations, or in high season, when hotel reservations are a must, we suggest that you prepare to be flexible—which is a tactful way of preparing you for the unexpected in island boat schedules! See chapter 10, "The Cyclades."

o **Leaving the Beaten Path:** Leave the main routes and major attractions behind, and make your own discoveries of landscape, villages, or activities. For instance, seek out a church or monastery such as **Moni Ayios Nikolaos** outside Metsovo—you may be rewarded by a moving encounter with the church and its caretaker. When you visit the

Cycladic Islands, consider a base on Tinos or Siros. Both are popular with Greeks but attract hardly any foreigners. See chapter 10, "The Cyclades."

o **Exploring the Naturalists' Greece:** There is a Greece beyond the columns and cafes—a land of rugged terrain and wildflowers and birds and other natural phenomena. Sign up for a special tour (see chapter 2, "Greece in Depth"), or go it alone with one of the several beautifully illustrated handbooks available, such as Oleg Polunin's *Flowers of Greece and the Balkans* (Oxford University Press) or Paul Sterry's *Birds of the Mediterranean* (Yale University Press). And don't forget your binoculars!

o **Sunrise, Sunset, Siesta:** Get up a little earlier than usual to see the sun rise (preferably from the Aegean, illuminating the islands). Then watch it sink over the mountains (anywhere in Greece, but try not to miss the sunsets that change the Ionian Sea from the deepest blue to a fiery red). And, in between Sunrise and Sunset, don't forget to have a siesta—most Greeks do, especially in the summer

THE best OF ANCIENT GREECE

o **The Acropolis** (Athens): No matter how many photographs you've seen, nothing can prepare you for watching the light change the colors of the marble buildings, still standing after thousands of years, from honey to rose to deep red to stark white. If the crowds get you down, think about how crowded the Acropolis was during religious festivals in antiquity. See p. 157.

o **Nemea** (Peloponnese): This gem of a site has it all: a beautifully restored stadium, a handsome museum, even picnic tables with a view of the romantic Doric temple. Look for the three long-standing columns—and several newly restored and re-erected ones. If you're lucky, you may see Nemea's archaeologists at work reconstructing and re-erecting more columns from the temple's north facade in their ambitious restoration project. See p. 259.

o **Olympia** (Peloponnese) **& Delphi** (Central Greece): Try to visit both Olympia, where the Olympic Games began, and Delphi, home of the Delphic Oracle. That's the only way you'll be able to decide whether Olympia, with its massive temples and shady groves of trees, or Delphi, perched on mountain slopes overlooking olive trees and the sea, is the most beautiful ancient site in Greece. See chapters 8 and 12.

o **Palace of Knossos** (Crete): A seemingly unending maze of rooms and levels, stairways and corridors, in addition to frescoed walls—this is the Minoan Palace of Knossos. It can be packed at peak hours, but it still exerts its power if you enter in the spirit of the labyrinth. King Minos ruled over the richest and most powerful of Minoan cities and, according to legend, his daughter Ariadne helped Theseus kill the Minotaur in the labyrinth and escape. See p. 302.

o **Delos** (Cyclades): This tiny isle, just 3.2km (2 miles) offshore of Mykonos, was considered by the ancient Greeks to be both the geographical and the spiritual center of the Cyclades; many considered this the holiest sanctuary in all of Greece. The extensive remains here testify to the island's former splendor. The 3 hours allotted by excursion boats from Mykonos or Tinos are hardly sufficient to explore this vast archaeological treasure. See chapter 10.

- **Vergina** (Northern Greece): In the brilliantly designed museum here, you can peek into what may have been the tomb of Alexander the Great's father, Philip of Macedon. Nearby, more than 300 burial mounds stretch for miles across the Macedonian plain. See p. 615.

THE best OF BYZANTINE & MEDIEVAL GREECE

- **Mistra** (Peloponnese): This Byzantine ghost town has streets lined with the remains of homes both humble and palatial, as well as some of the most beautiful churches in all of Greece. If you have the energy, climb to the top of the defense walls for the superb view over the plain of Sparta. Try to visit in spring, when Mistra is carpeted with wildflowers. See p. 266.
- **Church of Panagia Kera** (Kritsa, Crete): Even if Byzantine art seems a bit stilted and remote, this striking chapel in the foothills of eastern Crete will reward you with its unexpected intimacy. The 14th- and 15th-century frescoes are not only stunning but depict many familiar biblical stories. See p. 336.
- **The Churches of Thessaloniki** (Northern Greece). Thessaloniki's Byzantine churches are the finest not just in Greece but in the entire world. From tiny Osios David to towering Ayios Dimitrios, these churches boast mosaics and frescoes that give you astonishing glimpses of the artistic grandeur of the mighty Byzantine Empire. See chapter 16.
- **Nea Moni** (Hios, Northeastern Aegean): Once home to 1,000 monks, this 11th-century monastery high in the interior mountains of Hios is now inhabited by only a handful of monks and nuns. Try to catch one of the excellent tours sometimes offered by the monks. The mosaics in the cathedral dome are works of extraordinary power and beauty. Check out the small museum, and take some time to explore the monastery grounds. See p. 637.
- **Monemvassia** (Peloponnese): Long called "the Gibraltar of Greece," this rocky promontory crowned by a medieval citadel and church has only one real street (just wide enough for two donkeys to pass each other), no cars, cobbled lanes, beautifully restored stone houses (some of which are now hotels), and views that stretch seemingly forever over the sea. See p. 269.
- **A Clutch of Castles: Acrocorinth, Argos, Methoni, Koroni, Mistra & Nafplion** (Peloponnese): Some of these castles have ancient foundations; all were added onto by the Franks, Venetians, Byzantines, and Turks. Several were used as fortresses as recently as World War II; one, Koroni, has a convent and settlement within its walls. See chapter 8.
- **A Profusion of Byzantine Churches in the Cyclades:** The fertile countryside of the island of Naxos is dotted by well-preserved Byzantine chapels. Parikia, the capital of Paros, has the Byzantine-era cathedral of **Panagia Ekatondapiliani.** Santorini boasts the 11th- to 12th-century **Church of the Panagia** in the hamlet of Gonias Episkopi. See chapter 10.

THE best BEACHES

- **Arvanitia** (Nafplion, Peloponnese): After a vigorous and tiring day of sightseeing, this convenient little municipal beach can seem like the best in Greece. Handy changing rooms and showers make this a great place for a quick break between exploring the ruins at Mycenae and taking in a play at Epidaurus. See p. 245.

o **Chrissi Akti** and **Santa Maria** (Paros, Cyclades); Energetic beach lovers head to Santa Maria and Chrissi Akti for superb windsurfing; the less energetic will have plenty of action to watch, beach-side cafes and restaurants, and lots of lovely sand and surf. See p. 376.

o **Porto** and **Kolimbithra** (Tinos, Cyclades); Two long sand beaches, both with umbrellas, cafes, and restaurants. You can walk to Porto from Tinos town, but why bother? There's excellent bus service in summer. If you take the bus to Kolimbithra, you get to see a good deal of the island as a bonus en route. See p. 426.

o **Paradise** (Mykonos, Cyclades): Paradise is the quintessential party beach, known for wild revelry that continues through the night. An extensive complex built on the beach includes a bar, taverna, changing rooms, and souvenir shops. This is a place to see and be seen, a place to show off muscles laboriously acquired during the long winter months. See p. 400.

o **Lalaria Beach** (Skiathos, Sporades): This gleaming, white-pebble beach boasts vivid aquamarine water and white limestone cliffs with natural arches cut into them by the elements. Admittedly, Skiathos's famous Koukounaries Beach offers a more pleasant sandy beach and is more accessible and thus more popular, but Lalaria rewards one with its gorgeous and pristine environment. See p. 516.

o **Myrtos** (Kefalonia, Ionian Islands): Although remote enough to require you to come with your own wheels, this isolated sand-pebble beach has long charmed countless visitors. It does lack shade and it offers limited refreshments—perhaps bring a picnic—but the setting makes up for these deficiencies. See p. 574.

o **Vroulidia** (Hios, Northeastern Aegean): White sand, a cliff-rimmed cove, and a remote location at the southern tip of the island of Hios combine to make this one of the most exquisite small beaches in the Northeastern Aegean. The rocky coast conceals many cove beaches similar to this one, and they rarely become crowded. See p. 638.

THE best ISLANDS

o **Hydra** (Saronic Gulf Islands): Old-timers keep waiting for Hydra, with its handsome stone mansions overlooking a picture-postcard harbor, to be spoiled. After all, even before Mykonos and Santorini, Hydra was one of the first Greek islands to be "discovered." So far, so good: Donkeys still outnumber motorcycles, and the daytrippers who blitz through the appealing harborside shops leave at twilight. That means that except in August you can almost always find the table you want at one of Hydra's pleasant small restaurants. See p. 222.

o **Crete:** Whether for its rugged mountains or its countless beaches, its ancient remains or its ultramodern hotels, its layered history or its intense people, Crete cannot be denied. It is not just a distinctive Greek island—it is a world unto itself. See chapter 9.

o **Santorini** (Cyclades): This is undoubtedly one of the most spectacular islands in the world. The streets of **Fira** and **Ia** are carved into the face of a high cliff, overlooking the circular caldera left by an ancient volcanic eruption and now filled with the deep-blue waters of the Aegean. The site of **Akrotiri** offers a unique glimpse into life in a Minoan city, frozen in time by the eruption 3,600 years ago. Add to this the Fira nightlife scene, and you'll see why this is one of the most popular (and overcrowded) summer vacation spots in the Aegean. See p. 340.

o **Siros** (Cyclades): This tiny island has it all: a vivacious, cosmopolitan capital town; thriving beach resorts; and a starkly beautiful region of farming communities, archaeological remains, and remote beaches to the north. Siros is also one of the centers of *rembetika,* a form of Greek traditional music with roots in Asia Minor. See p. 430.

o **Tinos** (Cyclades): The island often called the "Lourdes of Greece," because of the church, **Panagia Evangelistria** (Our Lady of Good Tidings) with its healing icon, also has Venetian dovecotes; farm fields set off with handsome stone boundary walls; fine sand beaches; and Pirgos, the village of marble with a superb Museum of Marble Crafts. See chapter 10.

o **Rhodes** (Dodecanese): The island of Rhodes has everything a visitor could want— dazzling ancient and medieval ruins, great food, spectacular beaches, and some of the hottest nightlife outside of Athens—the one drawback being that everyone knows it. See chapter 11.

o **Skyros** (Sporades): Winding roads and remote beaches, one main town and a few villages, some ancient legends and 20th-century tales: Skyros's charms remain perhaps the most elusive of the four northern Sporades. But though the island remains a bit difficult to access and not overstocked with touristy amenities, Skyros also offers both a living local culture and some natural wildness. See chapter 13.

o **Corfu** (Ionian Islands): With lush vegetation, some still-undeveloped interior and unspoiled coast, ancient sites and a 19th century presence, a dash of Italy and a dose of the cosmopolitan, Corfu is a Greek island like no other. Tourism may be rampant, but Corfu's attractions have survived worse. See chapter 15.

o **Hios** (Northeastern Aegean): You'd think that an island with such gorgeous beaches, exquisite medieval towns, and remarkable scenery wouldn't remain a secret for long. Despite the qualities that attract a small group of devotees year after year, Hios remains surprisingly quiet. If you like the idea of getting away from the tour buses, being alone on a beach to rival any in the Cyclades, and exploring towns that preserve the contours of medieval life, Hios is for you. See chapter 17.

o **Sifnos** (Cyclades): Sifnos is a green island of ravines, mountaintops, and pristine beaches. Sifnos is small enough that a hardy walker can explore the entire island on foot, following well-maintained foot and donkey paths from church to church and village to village. Each village has its own very distinct character. In the capital, **Apollonia,** houses are cheek-by-jowl, with tiny gardens. **Artemona** has startling neoclassical mansions and **Ex Ambela** has low houses with unusually large gardens. The village of **Kastro** (castle), on its seaside rock, is the medieval locus of the island, whereas **Platis Yialos** is a bustling beach resort. Don't visit in August, when the island is mobbed with vacationing Athenians. See chapter 10.

THE best PLACES TO GET AWAY FROM IT ALL

o **National and Zappeion Gardens** (Athens): It's all too easy to overlook this oasis of calm and cool in the heart of Athens. You'll discover shady benches, a small cafe, the excellent Aegli/Cibus cafe and restaurant in the adjacent Zappeion Gardens, and lots of opportunities to enjoy watching Greek families out for a stroll. Keep an eye out for the balloon sellers on weekends. See p. 178.

o **Mount Likavitos, aka Mount Lycabettus** (Athens): Walk up Likavitos at dawn and enjoy the sunrise over the hills that surround Athens. Come back for a spectacular sunset, with the city laid under your feet like a sparkling map, the sounds of its ferocious traffic pleasantly distant. See p. 178.

o **Folegandros** (Cyclades): Most visitors to Greece once sailed past the formidable Folegandros cliffs en route from the mainland to Santorini and other islands; they'd catch a glimpse of the whitewashed kastro walls perched 300m (984 ft.) above the sea. The beauty of Hora, the fine beaches, and the great walking trails are no longer secrets, but if you arrive during the off season, Folegandros still offers a restful retreat. Largely free of the commercialism that has engulfed so many Aegean isles, Folegandros is now appearing on insider lists as *the* new place to visit. See p. 357.

o **Milia** (Crete): Here is a true retreat from not only the hustle and bustle of mass tourism but of most modern distractions: a once-abandoned village off in the mountains of western Crete where you live in a renovated stone house and spend your days hiking, enjoying the wildlife, eating simple meals, and just plain relaxing. See p. 314.

o **Zagori & Vikos Gorge** (Western Greece): If the 40-some tiny villages linked by roads lined with spectacular terrain are not enough, you can venture into at least a section of one of the most spectacular gorges in Europe. Greeks and some Europeans have long appreciated this undeveloped corner of northwestern Greece known as the Zagoria. See p. 550.

o **The Road Not Taken** (Greece): Don't fret if you take a wrong turn in Greece. Go with it! This may be the highlight of your trip—the Athenian shop-owner who shows you pictures of his aunt's family in Chicago when you stop to ask for directions; the *yiayia* (granny) next to you on that boat that you caught after the boat you wanted to catch had left; the schoolchild who quizzes you about why you came to Greece when you bump into him at an ancient site; the little village you chance upon because you stumbled onto the road you did not mean to take.

THE best MUSEUMS

o **Acropolis Museum** (Athens): Athens' newest high-profile museum is also its most stunning. This impressive five-story building handsomely displays the riches that adorned the Acropolis in its heyday: stunning sculptures, statues, free-standing objects, and 36 of the original 115 frieze panels that remain in Greece. On the lower levels, visitors can peer through glass panels at the ongoing excavations of an ancient Athenian neighborhood and an early Christian settlement. See p. 165.

o **National Archaeological Museum** (Athens): This stunning collection has it all: superb red- and black-figured vases, bronze statues, Mycenaean gold, marble reliefs of gods and goddesses, and the hauntingly beautiful frescoes from Akrotiri, the Minoan site on the island of Santorini. See p. 167.

o **Museum of Popular Greek Musical Instruments** (Athens): Life-size photos of musicians beside their actual instruments and recordings of traditional Greek music make this one of the country's most charming museums. On our last visit, an elderly Greek gentleman listened to some music, transcribed it, stepped into the courtyard, and played it on his own violin! See p. 167.

- **Archaeological Museum of Iraklion** (Crete): Few museums can boast of holding virtually all the important remains of a major culture. This museum can do just that with its Minoan collection, including superb frescoes from Knossos, elegant bronze and stone figurines, and exquisite gold jewelry. The museum also contains Neolithic, Archaic Greek, and Roman finds from throughout Crete. See p. 301.

- **Archaeological Museum of Chania** (Crete): Let's hear it for a truly engaging provincial museum, not one full of masterworks but rather of representative works from thousands of years, a collection that lets us see how many people experienced their different worlds. All this, in a former Italian Renaissance church that feels like and is a special place. See p. 315.

- **Archaeological Museum of Thessaloniki & Museum of Byzantine Culture** (Northern Greece): These side-by-side museums showcase the art and architecture of Thessaloniki and Northern Greece from the earliest days to the Byzantine era and its legacy. See p. 588 and 589.

- **The Bank of Piraeus** has sponsored a number of absolutely superb museums (some with rather clunky names!) throughout Greece, including the **Museum of Marble Crafts** on Tinos; the **Museum of the Olive and Greek Olive Oil** in Sparta; the **Open-Air Water Power Museum** in Dimitsana, Arkadia; the **Rooftiles and Brickworks Museum** in Volos; and the **Museum of Industrial Olive Oil Production on Lesbos.** Check www.piop.gr for more information on these terrific interactive and educational small museums.

THE best RESORTS & HOTELS

- **AVA Hotel & Suites** (Athens): With an excellent location, clean and spacious grounds and a highly personable and helpful staff, the AVA has stolen our hearts. This no-smoking hotel is in actuality 46 self-contained apartments all equipped with their own kitchenettes and balconies—several of them (on the higher floors) are quite large and feature jaw-dropping city and Acropolis views. See p. 123.

- **Grande Bretagne** (Athens): Back for a return engagement and better than ever, Athens's premiere hotel still overlooks the best view in town if you have the right room: Syntagma Square, the Houses of Parliament, and, in case you wondered, the Acropolis. See p. 129.

- **Malvasia** (Monemvassia, Peloponnese): The Malvasia brought the concept of the boutique hotel to the Peloponnese. Each room in the Malvasia is different, with some of the best overlooking the sea; all are tastefully furnished with hand-loomed rugs and antiques. A visit here gives you the illusion of staying in the home of wealthy Greek friends who have enormously good taste—and who just happen to be away and have left the staff behind to tend to your needs. See p. 272.

- **Lato Boutique Hotel** (Iraklion, Crete): There may be more luxurious hotels in Crete, but few can beat the Lato's attractions: a central location, modern facilities, views over a busy harbor, and perhaps most important, the always helpful staff. With its newly renovated bathrooms, Wi-Fi throughout, and a superb restaurant attached, this modestly sized hotel can now stand with the best. See p. 306.

- **ASTRA Suites** (Santorini, Cyclades): This small hotel with 27 handsomely appointed suites and an excellent restaurant looks like a miniature whitewashed village—and has spectacular views over Santorini's famous caldera. The sunsets are not to be believed, the staff is incredibly helpful, and the village of Imerovigli itself offers an escape from the tourist madness that overwhelms the island each summer. This is a spot to get married at—or celebrate any special occasion.

o **Anemomilos Apartments** (Folegandros, Cyclades, p. 360) and **Castro Hotel** (Folegandros, Cyclades; p. 361): The small island of Folegandros has two of the nicest hotels in the Cyclades, both with cliff-top locations. The Anemomilos has all the creature comforts, traditional decor, and a good location (it's just out of town), with a pool and sea views that seem to stretch forever. The Castro, built into the walls of the 12th-century Venetian castle that encircles the village, has lots of character; it closed for a complete renovation in 2011, but promises to be back in 2012.

o **Hotel Dina** (Parikia, Tinos): This cozy little eight-room hotel combines traditional Greek hospitality with up-to-date comforts (air-conditioning, minifridge flatscreen TV, good bathrooms). Step from busy Market Street into the Dina's courtyard and you can feel yourself relax as you inhale the aroma of gardenias, roses, and pine trees. The Patelis, who run the Dina, are courteous, helpful, and delightful.

o **Hotel Nireus** (Simi, Dodecanese): Perfect island, perfect location, unpretentious, and tasteful: The views from the sea-facing rooms, framed by the fluid swirls of the wrought-iron balcony, define the spell of this little gem of an island. You'll never regret one more night on Simi, and here's the place to spend it. See p. 462.

o **White Rocks Hotel & Bungalows** (Kefalonia, Ionian Islands): For those who appreciate understated elegance, this is a shady retreat from all that sunshine, a private beach, and quiet but attentive service, this hotel, 3.2km (2 miles) outside Argostoli, can be paradise. See p. 571.

o **Mediterranean Palace Hotel** (Thessaloniki). This hotel has it all: location (overlooking the harbor, in the trendy Ladadika district) and luxury. The lobby is, as you might expect, seriously glitzy—but the really pleasant surprise is the comfort and elegance of the guest rooms. The service is usually excellent. The two restaurants are good enough to tempt you to dine here at least 1 night rather than explore the hot spots of Ladadika. See p. 604.

THE best RESTAURANTS

o **Spondi** (Athens): *Athinorama*, the weekly review of the Athenian scene, has chosen Spondi several years running (2001–07, 2011) as the best place in town. Exceptional cuisine, setting (a beautiful 19th-c. town house with a stone courtyard covered with bougainvillea) and service, this winner of two Michelin stars for exceptional dining is considered by many to be the finest restaurant in Greece. See p. 154.

o **Fish Taverna Takis to Limeni** (Limeni, Mani, Peloponnese): Visitors to Greece dream of finding the perfect open-air fish taverna perched by the sea, serving fish that were swimming in the sea earlier the same day. Here it is—with some of the fish still swimming in the underwater storage cages they're plopped into from the fishing boats. Everything here is fresh and delicious. See p. 277.

o **Selene** (Santorini, Cyclades): The best restaurant on an island with lots of good places to eat, Selene, which moved from congested Fira to charming Pyrgos in 2010, is one of the finest restaurants in Greece. Owner George Haziyannakis constantly experiments with local produce to turn out innovative versions of traditional dishes. Even better, there are cooking classes where you can see how dishes are made—and then eat them! The new Selene also has a cafe/patisserie/wine bar. See p. 356.

- **Well of the Turk** (Chania, Crete); p. 320): Set back in a quiet square in Chania's old Venetian quarter, this restaurant offers both a delightful ambience and a novel selection of dishes. The proprietress and her staff make dining here a special experience. See p. 320.
- **Petrino** (Kos, Dodecanese): When royalty comes to Kos, this is where they dine. Housed in an exquisitely restored, century-old stone *petrino* (private residence), this is hands-down the most elegant taverna in Kos, with cuisine to match. This is what Greek home cooking would be if your mother were part divine. See p. 471.
- **Venetian Well** (Corfu, Ionian Islands): A bit severe in its setting at the edge of a small enclosed square in Corfu town, with no attempt at the picturesque, this restaurant gets by on its more esoteric, international, and delicate menu. It's for those seeking a break from the standard Greek scene. See p. 564.

THE best NIGHTLIFE

- **Theater Under the Stars** (Athens and Epidaurus, Peloponnese): If you can, take in a performance of whatever is on at Odeion of Herodes Atticus theater in Athens or the Theater at Epidaurus. You'll be sitting where people have sat for thousands of years to enjoy a play beneath Greece's night sky. See chapters 6 and 8.
- **Mykonos** (Cyclades): Mykonos isn't the only island town in Greece with nightlife that continues through the morning, but it was the first and still offers the most abundant, varied scene. Year-round, the town's labyrinthine streets play host to a diverse crowd—Mykonos's unlimited ability to reinvent itself has assured it of continued popularity. Spring and fall tend to be more sober and sophisticated, whereas the 3 months of summer are for unrestrained revelry. See chapter 10.
- **Rhodes** (Dodecanese). From cafes to casinos, Rhodes has not only the reputation but also the stuff to back it up. A good nightlife scene is ultimately a matter of who shows up—and this, too, is where Rhodes stands out. It's the place to be seen, and if nobody seems to be looking, you can always watch. See chapter 11.
- **Skiathos** (Sporades): With as many as 50,000 visitors packing this tiny island during the high season, the many nightspots in Skiathos town are often jammed with the mostly younger set. If you don't like the music at one club, cross the street. See chapter 13.
- **Corfu** (Ionian Islands): If raucous nightspots are what you look for on a holiday, Corfu offers probably the largest concentration in Greece. Most of these are beach resorts frequented by young foreigners. More sedate locales can be found in Corfu town. Put simply, Corfu hosts a variety of music, dancing, and "socializing" opportunities. See chapter 15.

THE best SHOPPING

- **Traditional Arts & Crafts:** So many places in Greece pride themselves on their needlework that it is hard to single out even a few, but among those few would be Crete, Rhodes, and Skyros. Two places in Athens deserve mention: **The Center of Hellenic Tradition** (59 Mitropoleos and 36 Pandrossou) and the **National Welfare Organization** (6 Ipatias and Apollonos). The center offers ceramics, woodcarvings, prints—and one of the finest views of the Acropolis in Athens. The National Welfare Organization contains hand-loomed rugs and silk embroidery done by village women, as well as excellent copper work and ceramics.

- **Jewelry:** It now seems that half of Greece's retail stores sell jewelry, so shop around. Much of it is really no different than what can be found in cities all over the world, but Athens does have major, internationally known jewelers such as LALAoUNIS and Zolotas. Try Chania, Crete, and Ioannina, northwest Greece, for sophisticated local artisans' work. Islands such as Hydra, Mykonos, Paros, Santorini, Skiathos, and Rhodes have scores of stores appealing to the tourist trade, many with the work of local jewelers.

- **Rugs/Weavings:** Crete probably offers the largest variety of rugs and weavings. Metsovo has some distinctive textiles. If you like rag rugs, look for *kourouloudes* on sale at small shops as you travel the Peloponnese.

- **Wood:** Corfu seems to be the center of olive-wood products—carving boards, bowls, and utensils. Rethymnon, Crete, also has a selection. In the Peloponnese, woodcarvings and utensils are often found in the villages of Arcadia. The islands of Paros, Syros, Chios, and Mitilini also boast wood-carving traditions.

- **Icons, Ecclesiastical Books & Religious Items:** On the streets around the Greek Orthodox Cathedral (Metropolitan) in Athens, you'll find many shops selling votive offerings, candles, and reproductions of icons. In Thessaloniki, **Apostolic Diakonta Bookstore** (p. 600) has a wide selection of religious items. Many of the most important religious shrines, such as Panagia Evangelistria on Tinos, and many convents and monasteries, including most of the Meteora monasteries, sell reproductions of icons and other religious items. On Crete, the Petrakis couple in Elounda paints internationally sought traditional icons.

- **Natural Products:** In the last few years, Greece has begun to produce organic and natural products, including olive oil, honey, jams, and cosmetics. Keep an eye out for food products with the Peloponnese, Gaea, Milelia, Nefeli, Yiam, and Stater labels in groceries and delis.

GREECE IN DEPTH

By Sherry Marker & Peter Kerasiotis

ook up at the crowded apartment buildings that line so many streets in Athens, and you'll probably see pots of basil on most balconies. Travel through the isles of Greece and almost every whitewashed island house has at least one pot of basil on its doorstep. And, what's tucked behind the ear of that truck driver gesturing furiously at you to get out of his way as he speeds along the Athens-Thessaloniki highway? A sprig of basil for him to sniff from time to time to banish the highway's miasmic exhaust fumes. No wonder that the 19th-century Greek politician Ion Dragoumis said, "A pot of basil may symbolize the soul of a people better than a play of Aeschylus."

In fact, the pot of basil, lovingly clipped to a perfect sphere, may be the only item In Greece that outnumbers the cellphone *(kineto)* The 11 million–plus Greek citizens have at least 12 million cellphones, with many adults wielding at least one for business and another for personal calls. One May Day, I watched families deep in the Arcadian mountains gather wildflowers to make traditional May Day wreaths, stopping only to dance age-old circle dances—all the while snapping photos of each other and sending them to distant friends on their ubiquitous cellphones! The wreaths, the dances, many of the words the dancers spoke, would all have been familiar to the ancient Greeks. Only the cellphones were new.

Most Greeks are besotted with all that is new; in fact, a common greeting is *Ti nea?* (What's new?). Still, most Greeks are fiercely proud of those longtime attractions that attract visitors: Greece's mind-boggling physical beauty and its glorious past. Certainly, for most of us, to leave Greece without seeing the big three from antiquity—Athens's Acropolis; Olympia, the birthplace of the modern Olympic Games; and Delphi, the most beautiful ancient site in all Greece—would be, as Aeschylus himself might have said, tragic. As for Greece's physical beauty, it is so stunning that it traps you into spouting clichés. Palamas, the poet who wrote the words to the Olympic Hymn, was reduced to saying of his homeland, "Here, sky is everywhere."

Of course, Palamas was right: The Greek sky, the Greek light, the Greek sea are all justly famous. This is especially obvious on the islands.

Just how many islands there are depends on what you call an island, an islet, or a large rock. Consequently, estimates of the number of Greek islands range from 1,200 to about 6,000. In any event, almost all of the approximately 200 inhabited islands are ready and waiting to welcome visitors; more than half the hotels in Greece are on islands. Each year, more and more Greek hotels aspire to be boutique hotels, with Wi-Fi, spas, cocktails by the pools (fresh and saltwater), and restaurants serving sushi as well as souvlaki. Still, on the islands and on the mainland, throughout the countryside, picture-postcard scenes are around every corner. Shepherds still urge flocks of goats and sheep along mountain slopes, and fishermen still mend nets by their caiques. In Greece's two largest cities, Athens and Thessaloniki, where cars seem to outnumber residents, the country makes its presence known in the city in neighborhood street markets that sell cheese from flocks of sheep that graze on distant mountains and fish from far out to sea.

If this sounds romantic and enticing, it is. But remember that the Greek love of the new includes a startling ability to adjust to the unexpected. Everything—absolutely everything—in Greece is subject to change. The boat that you board in Piraeus, to visit the island of Tinos, may steam past Tinos to Mykonos, and then wander back to Tinos via several unscheduled stops at unidentified islands. Ask anyone on board—including the captain—why this happened and you'll see that most Greek of all gestures: the face and shoulder shrug. Then, you'll probably hear that most Greek of all remarks: *"Etsi einai e zoe,"* which literally means "That's life," but might better be translated as "Whatchya gonna do?" With luck, you'll learn the Greek shrug, and come to accept—even enjoy—the unpredictable as an essential part of life in Greece.

Recently, the unpredictable has become almost the only thing that is predictable in Greece. Greece's massive debts, the government's unpopular attempts to restructure the economy, involving tax hikes and salary and pension reductions, led to strikes and demonstrations in 2010 and 2011. At press time, serious questions remain as to how Greece will solve its problems. Tourism—which makes up from 15% to 20% of Greece's annual income—was significantly down, as word of strikes closing museums and archaeological sites and disrupting travel persuaded many potential visitors to go elsewhere. Most Greeks are deeply concerned about the future, worried at the decline in tourism—yet convinced they will weather this storm as they have weathered so many others since the dawn of history.

GREECE TODAY

Greece today is in the midst of a nervous breakdown. After 15 years of unprecedented growth—growth that continued even after the 2004 Olympics—being a "model E.U. member" and the 27th largest economy in the world, Greece saw its finances crumble in a very public and to many Greeks a very humiliating way, leading the country to ask for help from the E.U. and subsequently the IMF after it was clear the E.U. had no backup plan for a member state in crisis.

Public bickering among E.U. officials and a battering for Greece in the global media led to a bailout package in May 2010 to calm the global markets, ease the public's fear, and give the banks holding Greek stock enough time to figure out what to do. On the home front, however, the bailout meant a slashing of all government spending and an extreme austerity package that promised to dismantle the Byzantine labyrinthlike public sector—the main reason behind the country's growing debt.

Curiously enough, a year later the public sector had remained mostly untouched, whereas the private sector had taken all the beatings it could, leaving foreign investments and companies fleeing the country and unemployment soaring to nearly 17%. As expected by most first-semester economics students, but strangely not by any government or E.U./IMF official, austerity is hardly a recipe for growth and the shaky economy had retreated even further going from a recession to a near depression. Many Greeks had to accept these tough measures that brought with them job losses and wage and pension cuts, hoping it was the way out of the darkness.

A year later when the country found itself in the exact same (if not) worse position, most Greeks were up in arms as their hardships and sacrifices had amounted to nothing. Most Greeks felt frustrated and hopeless as they realized the first bailout had mostly gone to German, French, and Greek banks holding Greek stocks and there would have to be another bailout to avoid bankruptcy and/or default, which could only mean even more austerity measures with no leadership or vision in sight from either the E.U. or the Greek government on how to put the economy back on track.

Inside the country, the tension had created a toxic atmosphere. Protests and strikes became part of daily life in the first half of 2011. Unemployment was high, jobs scarce, wages shockingly low, and the cost of living remained high, the illegal migrant population had swelled to out-of-control numbers, crime was up, the suicide rate had spiked, and the younger people were looking for employment in other countries, much as the older generations before them had had to do after World War II. This wasn't the future anybody had anticipated in bright and sparkling 2004 Olympic Athens.

In 2011, most Greeks felt their country had been occupied once again, as it had been so many times during its turbulent history—this time by the E.U. and the IMF. Unable to devalue its currency, Greece had to give up much of its sovereignty in order to accept the second bailout, along with new even harsher austerity measures. As other E.U. economies collapsed in and required assistance in 2011, some hoped that the E.U. has finally realized that austerity is not the way to growth, and the new bailout does include suggestions and some hopeful ways for Greece to get back on its feet.

"Closed" occupations need to be opened; private investments need to be encouraged by easing the country's notorious red tape and the public sector needs to be scaled down and made more efficient. Greece owns the largest maritime fleet in the world as shipping, along with tourism, account for the two biggest sectors of its economy (tourism was up in 2009—19.3 million visitors, up from 17.6 million in 2008, but then the economic collapse had its impact and numbers were down in 2010 with 16 million visitors); Greece has untapped oil reserves in its sea and gold in its land and ought to become a major player in renewable energy in the near future.

And yet, much as they did in antiquity, all roads in Greece lead to Athens. Many Greeks are just now beginning to realize that Athens—with its enviable location, large port, archaeological treasures, and state-of-the-art infrastructure—might well be the key to lead the country back into the light. Obvious tourism industry hopes aside, the Chinese government has recently made a multibillion-euro deal with the Greek government to use the port of Athens in Piraeus as the gateway to Europe, the Balkans, and Africa for its products and businesses. The government of Qatar is hoping the Greek government will accept its multibillion-euro offer for investment in the former Athens airport in Hellenikon. Their ambitious plans for this much-sought-after seafront property include a large park and the city's new business, residential, commercial, arts, entertainment and leisure center, and many other offers and developments are taking place all over the ancient city. Many refer to Athens as the "sleeping giant" of Greece's economy. It is our hope someone wakes her up sooner rather than later.

LOOKING BACK: GREEK HISTORY

Greece has a long history, indeed. Here is a brief introduction to some of the main periods in Greek history, along with some suggestions as to where you can see some of Greece's most memorable monuments. I'm going to use the term "Greece" throughout, even though today's country did not come into being until the 19th century. Still, long before that, the people who lived here regarded themselves as unified by a common language and many shared traditions and beliefs.

Stone Age

Greeks were delighted when a Neanderthal skull found in 1960 in the Petralona cave in Chalkidiki, Macedonia, pushed their history back as far as 700,000 B.C. There are signs of human habitation in Greece from the Paleolithic (ca. 7000 B.C.) and Neolithic (ca. 6000–3000 B.C.) eras, and you can walk the narrow streets of astonishingly well-preserved Neolithic sites at Lerna (in the Argolid) and Dimini and Sesklo (in Thessaly). The Archaeological Museum in Thessaloniki and Volos are two places that bring daily life in Greece's oldest civilizations to life with displays of useful pottery and tools, and ornamental necklaces and rings. Some of the oldest known representational sculpture in Greece come from this period, often small, well-endowed clay figurines of women. Some believe that these figures represent a mother goddess who was honored before Zeus and the Olympians became popular.

Bronze Age

In Greece, the Bronze Age seems to have lasted from around 3000 B.C. to 1500 B.C. By around 3000 B.C., people in much of Greece seem to have learned how to craft bronze; this meant that they no longer had to fashion weapons and tools out of stone and obsidian, but could make the sharp knives, swords, and heavy shields on view in so many Greek museums. What the Bronze Age inhabitants of Greece thought is more mysterious, in the absence of written records of anything except lists of the

DATELINE

700,000–160,000 B.C.	Human remains, including a Neanderthal skull, suggest long habitation of Petralona Cave, Chalkidiki peninsula.
40,000 B.C.	Signs of human habitation appear in several caves in the Louros Valley, Epirus.
7000–3000 B.C.	People begin to live together in small villages, such as Sesklo and Dimini in Thessaly and Lerna, in the Argolid.
4000 B.C.	Neolithic settlement on Athens Acropolis.
3000 B.C.	Waves of invaders from Anatolia (today's Turkey) introduce bronze working and an early form of Greek to Crete, the Cyclades, and the mainland, beginning the Bronze Age.
1700 B.C.	A massive earthquake on Crete destroys the great Minoan palaces at Knossos and Phaestos. Undeterred, Minoans rebuild more luxurious digs.
1600–1100 B.C.	The Mycenaean civilization rises and abruptly collapses, sending Greece into centuries of

pots, pans, shields, and swords kept in palaces. Archaeologists and historians have identified three different civilizations or cultures that flourished in different parts of Greece during the Bronze Age: Cycladic, Minoan, and Mycenaean. Historians think that all these civilizations spoke a form of Greek. Only the Mycenaeans seem to have used early forms of writing, Linear B and Linear A, to keep inventories. No one seems to have used writing to send a note or write a poem.

The Cycladic civilization takes its name from the Cycladic islands where it flourished. Although architectural remains are sparse, you can see elegant Cycladic figurines, crafted from island marble, at the National Archaeological Museum in Athens, the Goulandris Museum in Athens, and the Archaeological Museum on Naxos. Unfortunately, even the world's leading experts on Cycladic figurines are not sure whether the figurines were, or were not, representations of deities or people. Almost everyone is startled by how "modern" these spare figurines are.

The Minoan civilization was centered at the Palace of Knossos on Crete, but fanned out to nearby islands and onto the mainland. Visitors to Crete can visit the Palace of Knossos, while visitors to Santorini will have to wait until the Minoan town of Akrotiri, currently undergoing restoration, reopens. Alas, the protective roof over Akrotiri's partially excavated site collapsed in 2005, and it has been closed since then.

Much of Santorini was destroyed in 1500 B.C. in an unimaginably powerful earthquake which also destroyed settlements on Minoan Crete, 63 nautical miles away, and led to its decline. On mainland Greece, the Mycenaean civilization, named after its center at Mycenae in the Peloponnese, flourished during many of these same years. The extensive remains of Mycenae, with its defense walls, palace, and enormous beehive tombs, demonstrates the architectural skill and political power of the Mycenaeans. The National Archaeological Museum in Athens is a showcase for the famous gold of Mycenae, whereas the Archaeological Museum at Mycenae itself tries to reconstruct how people here lived and to suggest what they may have believed and how they may have worshipped. Mycenae's museum also reminds us of that city's maritime empire that may have extended from the Black Sea to the Atlantic. In the *Iliad*, Homer commemorated the Greek expedition to recapture the beautiful Helen

strife and cultural isolation. The Dorian Invasion from the north contributes to instability.

1450 B.C. A volcanic eruption on Santorini (Thira)—one of the most violent on record—buries ancient Akrotiri, causes destruction as far away as Crete, and helps speed Minoan decline.

1000–600 B.C. Glints of Greece's resurrection appear in the form of city-states. Homer and Hesiod initiate the first great age of Greek poetry.

776 B.C. The first Olympic Games are held.

700–500 B.C. Black figure pottery spreads throughout Greece from Corinth; red figureware spreads from Athens. Geometric statues of *kouroi* (youths) and *korai* (maidens) are widely produced. Athens and most Greek city-states are ruled by tyrants.

525–485 B.C. The birth of "Athenian democracy" under Cleisthenes. The great playwrights Aeschylus, Sophocles, and Euripides are born. Classical sculpture in marble and bronze flourishes.

continues

that was led by Mycenae's best known king, Agamemnon. The *Iliad* ends with the fall of Troy to the Greeks; Mycenae's own decline seems to have begun not long after, and is sometimes blamed on the mysterious invaders known as the Dorians.

The Geometric & Archaic Periods

These two terms are both used to describe Greece during the years from around 1000 B.C. until the dawn of the classical era, around 500 B.C. The Geometric period takes its name from the figured pottery that started to be made around 800 B.C., on which bodies are often shown as simple triangles and borders are created from rows of meanders and cross hatchings. The Archaic period began around 700 B.C., when the first monumental human sculpture was made in Greece. The National Archaeological Museum in Athens has superb collections of both geometric pottery and archaic sculpture.

After the decline of the Mycenaeans in mainland Greece, things were a bit murky for several hundred years—hardly surprising, as we have no contemporary written sources of this period. Gradually, it seems that people living on mainland Greece, and in the islands, began to live in the sort of towns we would recognize today, rather than in small, scattered settlements. Many of the cities that are still prominent in Greece today developed during this period, Athens and Sparta, Argos and Corinth among them. The growth of independent city-states—many ruled by powerful tyrants—was important, as was the spread of trade and invention of coinage, but the emergence of writing, using an early but still recognizable form of the Greek alphabet, was even more important.

The city-states were fiercely independent. This is a serious understatement: Each city-state had not only its own dialect, but its own calendar, system of weights and measures, and important deities. Still, when the Persians from adjacent Asia Minor invaded Greece in 490 and 480 B.C., many of the Greeks—led by Athens and Sparta—stood together and turned back the Persians. You can read about the conflict in Herodotus, and visit the battlefields of Marathon and Thermopylae and see the bust of the Spartan hero Leonidas in the Archaeological Museum at Sparta. If Persia

---

490–480 B.C. The First and Second Persian Wars. Xerxes, emperor of Persia, invades Greece, burning Athens and the Acropolis. Greeks get revenge on land at Marathon and Plataea, and at sea near Salamis and Mycale.

461–429 B.C. Under Pericles, Athens begins to rebuild the Parthenon and ornament it with the sculptures now known as the Parthenon (or Elgin) Marbles.

431–404 B.C. Peloponnesian War leads to the fall of Athens and its empire. In 430–428, the Great Plague kills thousands, including Pericles.

399 B.C. Socrates is tried for heresy and sentenced to death. Given the chance to escape, he declines and drinks hemlock potion. Plato immortalizes him in *The Apology*.

338 B.C. At the Battle of Chaironeia, Philip of Macedon defeats the Greek armies and unifies Greece under Macedonian rule.

336–323 B.C. Philip's son Alexander the Great establishes reign over a kingdom that stretches as far as Egypt and India.

323 B.C. Alexander dies in Babylon. His successors squabble among

had conquered Greece, our history of Greece might well end now, before the classical era and the birth of Greek democracy.

The Classical Era

Brief and glorious, the Classical era lasted from the 5th century to the rise of Philip of Macedon, in the mid–4th century. This is when Pericles led Athens and when the Parthenon—and nearly every other ancient Greek monument, statue, and vase most of us are familiar with—was created. This is when Greek democracy was born in Athens: All male citizens, but no women, resident aliens, or slaves, could vote. Very quickly, Athenian democracy morphed into an aggressive empire, which "liberated" Greek city-states in Asia Minor from Persia—and then turned those Greek cities into Athenian client states. Greece's other major power, Sparta, saw its own influence threatened, and Athens and Sparta fought on and off from 431 to 404 B.C., by which time Athens had exhausted its resources and surrendered to Sparta. The historian Thucydides wrote an account of these Peloponnesian Wars. For the next 50 or so years, Athens, Sparta, and Thebes alternately united and fought with each other. This left all three cities weakened and unable to stop Philip of Macedon, when he moved south to conquer Greece.

The Hellenistic Era

The Hellenistic era is usually said to run from the 4th to the late 1st centuries B.C. and includes the rise of Philip of Macedon, the triumphs of his son Alexander the Great, and the several centuries of rule by Alexander's heirs and successors. Philip of Macedon conquered Greece in 338 B.C. and died only 2 years later. During his brief reign, Philip endowed a number of quite spectacular buildings at important Greek sanctuaries, including the Philippeion at Olympia, which he modestly named after himself. The royal tombs at Vergina, with their gold ornaments and frescoes, are lasting proof of Macedon's wealth.

Alexander became king of Macedon when he was only 23 and marched from his base camp at Dion all the way to India, conquering everything in his path. At that

themselves, squandering great parts of his empire.

146 B.C. After a series of wars, Rome crushes Greece, renaming the northern parts Macedonia, the southern and central parts Achaea.

50–200 A.D. New Testament is written in Greek dialect, *koine*. Local author John of Patmos gets the last word, in the Book of Revelation.

A.D. 328 Roman emperor Constantine the Great moves his capital to Byzantium (Constantinople), initiating the focus on the East that results in the Byzantine Empire.

476 Rome falls to the Goths; Greece is no longer a world power in any sphere, political or cultural.

1204 Fourth Crusade (led by the Western powers) sacks Constantinople and divides up much of the Byzantine Empire.

1453 Constantinople falls to Sultan Mehmet II, initiating more than 350 years of Turkish domination of most of the Byzantine Empire, including Greece.

continues

point, his soldiers virtually turned him around and pointed him back toward Macedonia. Alexander died under mysterious circumstances (Poison? Too much wine?) en route home in 334 B.C., leaving behind the vast empire that he had conquered but had not had time to organize and administer. Alexander's leading generals divided up his empire, and declared themselves not just rulers but, in many cases, divine rulers.

Alexander's conquests, which included much of Asia Minor and Egypt, made the Greek language the administrative and spoken language of much of the world. Within Greece itself, powerful new cities, such as Thessaloniki, were founded. Old cities, such as Athens, were revivified and ornamented with magnificent new civic buildings, such as the 2nd-century-B.C. Stoa of Attalos, which contained shops and offices. Today, this Hellenistic building, restored by American archaeologists in the 20th century, is the most conspicuous building in the Athenian agora.

The Roman Conquest

Along with most of Europe, North Africa, and Asia Minor, Greece was ruled by Rome from the 2nd century B.C. to the 3rd century A.D. As part of their eastward expansion, the Romans conquered Macedon in 168 B.C. and turned the once-powerful kingdom into the Roman province of Macedonia. In 147 B.C., Rome grabbed most of the rest of Greece and called it the province of Achaea. Still, the Romans honored the Greeks for their literature and art, and a tour of Greece was the equivalent of a gap year for many well-born Roman youths. As occupations go, the Roman occupation was benign and the Greeks participated in what has become known as the *Pax Romana*, the several centuries of general peace and calm in the Roman Empire. By the late 3rd century A.D. the Roman Empire was so vast that it was divided into eastern and western empires, each with its own emperor. One lasting legacy of the Roman occupation: the sprawling bath complexes that are often the most visible remain at many ancient Greek sites, from Dion in Macedonia to Corinth in the Peloponnese.

The Byzantine Empire

In various forms, in various countries, the Byzantine Empire lasted from the 4th to the 15th century. In 324 B.C., the Roman emperor Constantine the Great took control

1571 Turkish fleet destroyed by a Western coalition led by Sicilian, Italian, and Spanish fleets at Lepanto (Naupaktos), Greece.	**1833** Greece imports Prince Otto of Bavaria as its first king.
1687 A Venetian shell blows up the Parthenon, which was being used by the Turks to store gunpowder.	**1863–1913** Reign of George I sees Greece regain much of its lost territory.
	1896 Revival of the Olympic Games in Athens.
1801–05 Lord Elgin ships Parthenon Marbles to England, beginning a long battle between England and Greece for their possession.	**1913** King George I is assassinated at Thessaloniki.
	1917 Greece enters World War I aligned with Britain and France.
1821–1829 Greeks fight War of Independence, enlisting Britain, Russia, and France as allies.	**1919** Greece occupies Izmir; Mustafa Kemal (Atatürk) rises from ranks of military to champion Turkish nationalism.

of the entire empire, moved its capital from Rome to the Greek city of Byzantium on the Bosporus, and renamed his capital Constantinople (Constantine's City). This move effectively remade the Roman Empire (which included Greece) and was now firmly based in the east. In another bold move, Constantine reversed the prosecutions of Diocletian, changing the religious character of his vast empire. The monasteries of Mount Athos and the Meteora, of Osios Loukas in Central Greece, the icons on view in the Byzantine Museums in Athens and Thessaloniki, and the countless chapels in use everywhere in Greece today all speak to Christianity's deep and lasting influence.

It took a new people, the Ottoman Turks, to overturn the Byzantine Empire; in Greece, most people privately continued to speak the Greek language and remained devout Orthodox Christians. The official end of the empire came when Constantinople fell to the Turks, led by Mehmed the Conqueror, on Tuesday, May 29, 1453; to this day, Tuesday is considered an unlucky day in Greece.

The Occupation(s) & Independence

The Greeks celebrate Independence Day on March 25. On that day in 1821, Bishop Germanos of Patras raised a blue and white flag at the monastery of Ayia Lavra near Patras and the struggle for Greek independence officially began. In 1827, the so-called Great Powers (primarily the English, French, Italians, and Russians) finally backed Greek independence. In 1832, those same Great Powers declared that Greece was to be an independent country, ruled by a king, and dispatched a Bavarian princelet, Otto, to be king of the Hellenes.

This put an end to the long period of occupation (1453–1832), when Greece was ruled by a bewildering and often overlapping series of foreign powers: Venetians and Franks from the West, and Turks from the East. Castles and fortresses at Nafplion, Koroni, Methoni, and Argos in the Peloponnese are imposing reminders of the foreign occupiers. Today, the Catholic churches and considerable Catholic population of many Cycladic islands (including Tinos and Naxos) are a testament to the days when the Venetians ruled these islands. Another reminder: today's roofless Parthenon. In

1923 The Greco-Turkish War ends in disaster for Greece, with a compulsory exchange of populations between Greece and Turkey. Greece takes in more than a million Greek refugees from Turkey.

1924–1928 Greece declares itself a republic, but political upheaval leads to 11 military coups.

1936–1944 Dictator George Metaxas takes over, modeling his Greece on the examples of Mussolini and Hitler.

1940–1941 Italy invades Greece, followed by more determined German forces.

1944 Greece is liberated; civil war soon breaks out in Athens and the north.

1949 Civil war ends.

1952 Greek women gain the right to vote.

1967–1973 A military coup; King Constantine goes into exile; Operation Prometheus establishes military junta known as "the Colonels"; civil liberties are suspended. Performances of certain classical dramas, especially *Electra*, are forbidden as subversive.

continues

1687, a shell lobbed by the Venetians hit the Parthenon, which the Turks were using as a storehouse for gunpowder.

Throughout Greece, almost every village has at least one monument to the War of Independence, and Athens's Benaki Museum has superb displays of paintings, flags, costumes, and weapons documenting the struggle for Greek independence.

2 Greece Since Independence

By the end of the 19th century, Greece's capital was in Athens, but most of today's country was still held by the Turks and Italians. The great Greek leader from Crete, Eleftherios Venizelos (after whom Athens International Airport is named) led Greece in the Balkan Wars of 1912–1913. When the wars were done, Greece had increased its territory by two-thirds, and included much of Epirus, Macedonia, and Thrace in the north and the large islands of Samos, Chios, and Crete.

At the end of World War I, Greece invaded Turkey in an attempt to reclaim Constantinople and much of Aegean Turkey. Initially, the invasion went well, but the Turks, led by their future leader Mustafa Kemal (Atatürk), rallied and pushed the Greeks back to the sea. There, in 1922, in Smyrna (Izmir) and other seaside towns, the Greeks were slaughtered in what is still referred to in Greece as "The Catastrophe."

In the Treaty of Lausanne, Greece and Turkey agreed to an exchange of populations. The boundaries of Greece were fixed more or less as they are today. Some 1.5 million Greeks who lived in Turkey had to move to Greece, and about 500,000 Turks were sent from Greece to Turkey. Many spoke little or none of their ancestral language, and most were regarded with intense hostility in their new homelands. Thessaloniki, which doubled in size in less than a year, bore the brunt of the Greek population exchange. To this day, Greece is dotted with towns with names like Nea Smyrni and Nea Chios (New Smyrna and New Chios), reminders of this forced migration. A small Greek Muslim population still lives in Greece, primarily in Thrace.

Whatever stability and prosperity Greece gained after the population exchange of the 1920s was seriously undercut by the harsh German and Italian occupations during World War II. The famines of 1941 and 1942 were particularly harsh; in Athens, carts went around the city each morning to collect the corpses of those who had died

---

1974 Turkey invades Cyprus; the junta collapses and a democratic republic is established when a referendum abolishes the monarchy.

1981 Greece joins EC (Common Market); PASOK victory brings leftist Andreas Papandreou to power.

1989 Papandreou government collapses under corruption charges.

1993 After a 3-year hiatus, PASOK and Papandreou are victorious at the polls.

1996 Papandreou resigns and is succeeded by Costas Simitis.

1997 Athens is selected as the site for the 2004 Olympic Games.

1998 The European Council begins entry negotiations with Cyprus with a view toward its inclusion in the European Union.

1999 The growth rate of the Greek economy remains strong for a fourth consecutive year, and the minister of finance speaks of a "new Greece."

in the night. A bitter civil war (1944–49), between pro- and anticommunist forces, further weakened Greece. Recovery began slowly—assisted by the Marshall Plan—and did not take hold until well into the 1960s.

In the 1960s, Greece was discovered by travelers from western Europe and North America, who fell in love with the unspoiled—and cheap—country. In 1967, a right-wing junta of army officers, nicknamed the Colonels, seized power, ended the monarchy, and were themselves toppled, when democracy was restored in 1974.

In the years since then, Greek voters have alternated between favoring two parties: the conservative New Democracy and the left wing PASOK. For much of the time, New Democracy has been led by various members of the powerful Caramanlis family, while PASOK has been led by a series of Papandreous. In 1981, Greece was accepted into the European Union (Common Market) and began a period of initial prosperity (jump-started by EEC funding), followed by steady inflation. The euphoria of 2004 when Greece won the European soccer championship and hosted the wildly successful Athens Olympics lasted a year, and then fizzled, as did plans to turn the Olympic village into low-income housing. Soon, Greece, along with its Common Market neighbors, was trying to cope with the problems of illegal immigration, rising prices, an increasingly fragile ecosystem, and the economic recession that began to affect much of the world in 2008. In 2009, tourism—which brings in more than 15% of Greece's GDP—declined steeply in Greece (as detailed earlier in "Greece Today").

The ongoing global economic crisis has forced many holiday makers to give up their vacations, while many others have headed for Turkey—where prices for food and lodging are cheaper, service is often superior, and the strikes that so often disrupt public transportation and close museums and monuments in Greece are unknown.

GREECE'S ART & ARCHITECTURE

Many of the buildings we know best—from football stadiums to shopping malls—have Greek origins. The simple Greek **megaron** gave birth to both the temple and the

---

2000-2002 The Pan-Hellenic Socialist Movement, led by Costas Simitis, wins a third term. Greece applies to become the 12th member of the Eurozone in 2001.

2004 Conservative Kostis Karamanlis elected prime minister. Greece erupts in joy when the national team wins European Soccer Championship shortly before the 2004 Olympic Games are held in Athens.

2006-2009 Widespread summer forest fires, many set by developers, devour vast stretches of the Greek countryside, the Peloponnese and Attica, many islands, and around Thessaloniki.

2009-2011 As the world economy declines, and the Greek debt to the EEC (Common Market) grows, tourism drops steeply, adversely affecting the already vexed Greek economy.

basilica, the two building forms that many civic and religious shrines still embody. The **Greek temple,** with its pedimental facade, lives on in civic buildings, palaces, and ostentatious private homes throughout the world. Football and soccer are played in oval **stadiums,** the spectators now sitting on seats more comfortable than the stone slabs or dirt slopes they sat on in ancient Greek stadiums. Most theaters are now indoors, not outdoors, but the layout of stage, wings, and orchestra goes back to Greek theaters. The prototypes of shopping malls, with their side-by-side multiplicity of shops, can be found in almost every ancient Greek city. In fact, the mixture of shops and civic buildings, private homes,

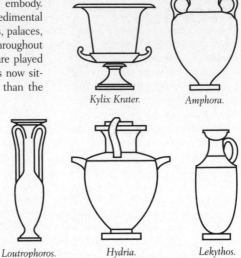

Kylix Krater.   *Amphora.*

Loutrophoros.   *Hydria.*   *Lekythos.*

and public parks is one that most ancient Greeks knew very well. And, whenever we can look inside those ancient buildings, we see pots and pans in shapes many of which are familiar today (round-lidded casseroles and long-handled frying pans, to name just two of the most common). Many elegant homes still emulate the frescoed walls and pitched red-tile roofs of classical Greek antiquity.

In short, Greece was not just the "cradle of democracy," but the nursery of much of Western art and architecture. The portrait busts and statues of heroes that ornament almost every European city have their origins in ancient Greece. Both the elaborate vaulted funerary monuments and the simple stone grave markers of today can be found throughout ancient Greece. Much of Greek art and architecture was dedicated to one or more of the Greek gods, many of whose names are unfamiliar today. The section below has a handy list of the better-known Greek gods and goddesses and some illustrations of some of the better-known elements of Greek art and architecture.

THE GODS & GODDESSES

As you travel around Greece, you'll notice that many of the monuments you see were dedicated to one or another of the Greek gods. For the ancient Greeks, the world was full of divine forces, most of which were thought to be immortal. Death, sleep, love, fate, memory, laughter, panic, rage, day, night, justice, victory—all of the timeless, elusive forces confronted by humans—were named and numbered among the gods and goddesses with whom the Greeks shared their universe. The most powerful of the gods lived with Zeus on Mount Olympos and were known as the Olympians. To make these forces more familiar and approachable, the Greeks imagined their gods to be somehow like themselves. They were male and female, young and old, beautiful and deformed, gracious and withholding, lustful and virginal, sweet and fierce.

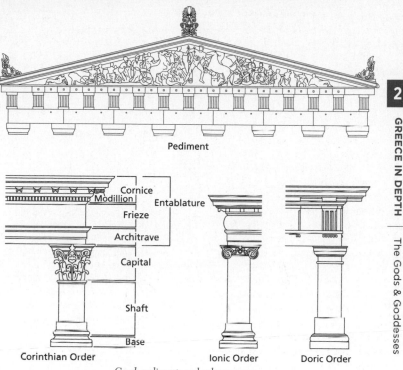

Greek pediments and column types.

As told by the ancient poets, the lives of the Olympians had elements of an eternal soap opera. Sometimes generous, courageous, insightful, the gods are also notoriously petty, quarrelsome, spiteful, vain, frivolous, and insensitive. And how could it be otherwise with the Olympians? Not made to pay the ultimate price of death, they need not know the ultimate cost of life. Fed on *ambrosia* ("not mortal") and *nektar* ("overcoming death"), they cannot go hungry, much less perish. When life is endless, everything is reversible.

Principal Olympian Gods & Goddesses

Greek Name	Latin Name	Description
Zeus	Jupiter	Son of Kronos and Rhea, high god, ruler of Olympus. Thunderous sky god, wielding bolts of lightning. Patron-enforcer of the rites and laws of hospitality.
Hera	Juno	Daughter of Kronos and Rhea, queen of the sky. Sister and wife of Zeus. Patroness of marriage.
Demeter	Ceres	Daughter of Kronos and Rhea, sister of Hera and Zeus. Giver of grain and fecundity. Goddess of the mysteries of Eleusis.

Greek Name	Latin Name	Description
Poseidon	Neptune	Son of Kronos and Rhea, brother of Zeus and Hera. Ruler of the seas. Earth-shaking god of earthquakes.
Hestia	Vesta	Daughter of Kronos and Rhea, sister of Hera and Zeus. Guardian of the hearth fire and of the home.
Hephaestos	Vulcan	Son of Hera, produced by her parthenogenetically. Lord of volcanoes and of fire. Himself a smith, the patron of crafts employing fire (metalworking and pottery).
Ares	Mars	Son of Zeus and Hera. The most hated of the gods. God of war and strife.
Hermes	Mercury	Son of Zeus and an Arcadian mountain nymph. Protector of thresholds and cross-roads. Messenger-god, patron of commerce and eloquence. Companion-guide of souls en route to the underworld.
Apollo	Phoebus	Son of Zeus and Leto. Patron-god of the light of day, and of the creative genius of poetry and music. The god of divination and prophecy.
Artemis	Diana	Daughter of Zeus and Leto. Mistress of animals and of the hunt. Chaste guardian of young girls.
Athena	Minerva	Daughter of Zeus and Metis, born in full armor from the head of Zeus. Patroness of wisdom and of war. Patron-goddess of the city-state of Athens.
Dionysos	Dionysus	Son of Zeus and Semele, born from the thigh of his father. God of revel, revelation, wine, and drama.
Aphrodite	Venus	Born from the bright sea foam off the coast of Cyprus. Fusion of Minoan tree goddess and Near Eastern goddess of love and war. Daughter of Zeus. Patroness of love.

EATING & DRINKING

The other day, while waiting to have a haircut in the Peloponnesian village where I spend most of my time in Greece, I eavesdropped on the other customers. If I had not known some Greek, I would have thought that the gaggle of grandmotherly women were having a fierce argument. Voices were raised and disapproving fingers were shaken. What was the topic? That day's lunch, and how best to prepare it. The women were comparing, in minute detail, the way each would prepare her stuffed eggplant, her chicken stew, or her bean soup. Voices were raised over the precise amount of dill to use, the variety of onion best suited for the stew, and whether the season's first tomatoes were worthy of taking their place in a salad, or still to be used only for sauce.

Greeks take what they eat, and how it is prepared, very seriously. Whereas many non-Greeks go to a restaurant in the hopes of getting something different from home cooking, in Greece it is always high praise to say that a restaurant's food is *spitiko* (homemade). Here are some tips on places to eat in Greece and what to eat there.

As to prices in restaurants and cafes, throughout the guide we try to tell you the best —and best value— inexpensive, moderate, and expensive places in each "Where to Eat" section. Keep in mind that the prices at the most expensive place in a country hamlet could be an amazing bargain in Athens. As for prices on Mykonos and Santorini, if you sit down at a popular cafe and have a coffee or a glass of wine, you'll find out just how expensive even simple pleasures can be in Greece's most popular tourist destinations!

Meals & Dining Customs

Although you may find many of the same dishes and drinks in different kinds of places, it's useful to know what's out there. Almost every village has at least one **kafeneion** (coffeehouse), and usually two. It would take a team of anthropologists working with a team of sociologists to figure out how most Greeks choose their favorite local kafeneion. When I asked a friend why she always went to the kafeneion in the main square in our village, she replied that she could not remember why, but thought it had to do with a disagreement a friend of hers had had several decades earlier with the owner of the other kafeneion. Often clients chose their kafeneion based on political ideology or profession (whether white or blue collar). Families, and women on their own, usually sit at tables outside. Indoors, the kafeneion is still an almost exclusively male establishment and often functions as a clubhouse. Men stop by, play a hand of cards or *tabli* (backgammon), and nurse a coffee or an ouzo for hours.

Greeks almost never drink without eating something, if only some chunks of feta cheese, a few olives, and perhaps some cucumber and tomato slices. This is an especially wise custom, especially when drinking fiery and potent **ouzo,** which turns a deceptively milky hue when diluted with water. An **ouzeri** is usually similar to a kafeneion, but with the emphasis more on ouzo, and the food often a bit heartier, often including grilled sausage or octopus. Thessaloniki is famous for its ouzeries, which are often filled wall to wall with both the beautiful people and the passers-by.

It is perfectly possible, and very satisfying, to make a full meal from a selection of **mezedes** (appetizers) at an ouzeri. Two recent additions to the scene include the *Fastfooddadiko* and the lounge bar. The fastfooddadiko, as its name suggests, serves snacks, either to go or to munch at the counter. Souvlaki joints usually stick to souvlaki and gyro, with or without pita bread. The lounge bar, an offspring of the disco, is usually a cafe with elaborate decor (mirrors, reflecting globes, massive flatscreen TVs), where full meals may be served and whiskey usually flows. The important thing at the lounge bar is to see and be seen and to survive the assault of the amplified music.

Restaurants serving full meals fall into a number of categories: a **psistaria** usually specializes in grilled meat, sometimes the *koukouretsi* (entrails) that are especially popular in Larissa and Lamia, while a **psarotaverna** serves mainly fish. As for the **estiatorio,** I'm still trying to figure out the real difference between a taverna and an estiatorio. At both, as at an ouzeri, you can make a full meal from mezedes. In theory, the taverna is more down home, the estiatorio more prone to certain refinements. There was a time when you could tell which was which by checking to see if the tablecloth was paper or cloth, but now, many chic places are deliberately casual and use paper cloths, while many simple places have a paper cloth on top of a cloth cover. Still, a taverna is usually a bit less formal, with less choice on the menu, than an estiatorio. Both usually have *magireio,* vegetable or meat stews prepared in advance, usually tastier at lunch than in the evening, by which time they have been sitting around for a while. Greeks think that some dishes, such as the vegetable stew called *briam,* benefit from this process, with the flavors getting extra time to mingle. Foreigners usually think the veggies get overcooked and soggy as the day goes on.

Many Greek restaurants do not serve dessert, and Greeks often troop off after a meal to a pastry shop (the tongue-twisting **zacharopolasteion**). In recent years, many tavernas and estiatoria have started to serve a free dessert, ranging from simple apple slices with honey and cinnamon to ice-cream confections topped with sparklers. Cafes and coffee shops usually serve light snacks, and some people head to them for dessert.

A few suggestions that may come in handy wherever you eat: Greeks usually tend to skip breakfast, or have a light snack in midmorning. If you stay in a hotel that offers breakfast, you won't have to look for a place that serves some approximation of a familiar breakfast. Greeks make lunch their big meal of the day, and eat it between 2 and 3pm. Especially in summer, Greeks often head to a cafe for some ice cream around 8pm. Dinner is often a light meal, seldom eaten earlier than 9pm, but when Greeks do go out to dinner, they usually don't think of eating before 10pm. If you want to be sure of a table, try for the off hours—and be prepared to have the place to yourself and other foreigners.

Menus are usually in Greek and English, but if not, just ask for help from your waiter, who is probably fluent in restaurant English. He may even take you into the kitchen to eye what's available. Often, the printed menu has little bearing on what is available, and it never hurts to ask what's special that day. As to water, if you want tap water, not bottled, ask for it from the *vrisi* (tap). If you want the house wine, ask what their own wine is *(to diko sas krasi),* lest you be guided to much more expensive bottled wine. Increasingly, however, the house wine is not local, but just a cheap, mass-produced wine, perhaps "decanted" surreptitiously from a large cardboard container hidden away in the kitchen.

Service is included in the bill, but it is customary to leave your waiter another 10% at a simple place, and 15% at a fancy place. Some Greeks do and some do not tip in family owned and operated places. If you go out with Greek friends, prepare to go late and stay late and to put up a losing fight for the bill. Greeks frown on bill splitting; usually, one person is host, and that is that. And, if you are invited to a Greek home for a meal, assume that everything will run hours late and that you will be offered an unimaginable amount of food. This is especially true on holidays, particularly Easter, when families spend most of their time preparing and eating roast lamb and all the fixings from the time that the Holy Saturday service ends at midnight until sunset on Easter day.

Another thing: Greeks do not waste food. The traditional *margeritsa* soup that breaks the Lenten fast includes the entrails of the lamb that makes up the Easter dinner. Easter is *the* big feast day of the year, with feasting continuing on Easter Monday. The week after Easter, most newspapers carry supplements on "How to Lose the Weight You Gained at Easter."

The Cuisine

Although fresh ingredients are vital, excellent **olive oil** is the one essential in Greek cuisine. Ineptly translated menus often offer "oilies," the vegetable stew that you may know better as *briam,* or ratatouille. The seriousness of the forest fires that have swept so much of Greece each summer since 2007 struck home when there were reports that Greece would have to do the unthinkable and import olive oil. Greeks consume more olive oil than any other nation (some 30 liters per person per year) and they want that oil to be not just Greek, but from specific regions, preferably from specific groves. The olives of the Peloponnese are especially admired, with Kalamata olives prized both for oil and eating. In 2010, the several infestations that threatened the Peloponnesian oil harvest were a staple of worried conversations there. In recent years, there has been a burst of interest in organic and virgin olive oil and you'll probably see shops in major tourist destinations such as Olympia, Delphi, and Nafplion with varieties of olive oil from around Greece, as well as olive oil products such as soaps, shampoos, and lotions.

Cheese is the other staple of the Greek diet. Some visitors to Greece leave thinking that feta is the only Greek cheese. They are wrong. Although a slab of feta, usually sprinkled with oregano, tops most Greek salads, there's a wide variety of cheeses. Most Greek cheeses, like feta, are made from sheep or goat's milk. Creamy *mizithra* is more delicate than feta, best when eaten fresh and soft, but useful when cured and grated on pasta. *Kefalotyri* and *graviera* are popular favorites, slightly bland, but with enough tang to be interesting.

Until recently, the standard Greek snack was a handful of olives, a chunk of bread, and a slab of cheese. Now, alas, potato chips are in the ascendency, as is childhood obesity. Still, fresh Greek fruit and vegetables in season are top notch and still make up a major part of the Greek diet. The first zucchini, peas, and green beans of the season are eagerly anticipated. Unfortunately, the widespread proliferation of hothouse gardening means that more and more fruit is picked before it has ripened. And, like the fruit in supermarkets almost everywhere else, more and more Greek peaches and apricots, melons and pears, look beautiful but taste, well, tasteless.

With oil, cheese, and fresh produce very popular throughout Greece, it's often said that there are few regional differences in Greek cuisine. While it is true that you can sit down to moussaka (veal in red sauce or stuffed eggplant) anywhere in Greece, each region is fiercely proud of its own version of the national favorites. The *revithadha* (chickpea) soup of Sifnos is famous throughout Greece, as are the almond cookies of Andros and Naupaktos. *Loukoumi* from Siros—to me indistinguishable from any other chewy piece of what the unwary visitor calls Turkish delight—is prized above all other loukoumi. The spread of supermarkets means that you can get loukoumi from Siros in supermarkets throughout Greece. Still, bringing home a souvenir box of loukoumi from Siros for the neighbors is as popular in Greece as bringing home maple syrup from Vermont is in the United States.

Here are a few dishes that have particular local associations to look for as you travel: In the Peloponnese, where the olive oil is plentiful and delicious, **vegetable stews** steeped in oil are almost always on the spring and summer menu. The slender **eggplant** of Leonidion in the southeast Peloponnese are so prized that they have their own celebratory festivals each May and August. Chefs vie to make the tastiest stuffed, baked, and puréed eggplant dishes. The **yogurt** from the Arcadian village of Vitina is famous throughout the Peloponnese and beyond. On Tinos, if you order an **omelet,** be prepared for some serious eating: The Tinian version includes potatoes, sausages, and just about anything else available. In Thessaloniki, where the food is spicier than anywhere else in Greece, **mussels** with pilaf are a local favorite. As to *loukanika* (sausages), almost every district has one or more local versions, ranging from quite sweet to fiery.

Wine

The Greek wine that almost every visitor to Greece has heard of is the one that almost no foreigner loves: **retsina.** It's the pine resin that's added to the brew to preserve the wine that gives the pungent taste. Most retsina is either white or rose, and most non-Greeks like theirs good and cold. In recent years, the Greek wine industry has taken off, with Boutari and Tsantali vintages becoming well known outside Greece. In general, reds from the Naoussa area of Macedonia and Nemea in the Peloponnese are excellent, as are whites (especially the prized *assyrtikos*) from Santorini and Crete. It's always a good idea to ask if the restaurant has a local wine. Another thing to remember: There's a wide variety of sweet Greek dessert wines. If you like sweet wines, you are in luck. If not, by all means avoid *mavrodaphne* and *vinsanto*—and don't even think about trying the syrupy Greek fruit liqueurs! For more on Greek wines, check out **www.greekwineworld.com**, or get a copy of Nico Manessis's *The Illustrated Greek Wine Book* (Olive Press).

WHEN TO GO

Just about everyone agrees that the best time to visit is Greece is spring and early summer (mid-Apr to mid-June) or autumn (Sept to mid-Oct). This way, you'll avoid the summer high season, with its inflated prices, hordes of tourists and high temperatures (heat waves of 100°F/+40C are routine). In fact, unless you *really* like scorching heat, crowds, and overbooked planes, ferry boats, and hotels, August is to be avoided. In the spring, you'll see more wildflowers than you could have imagined—and swim in a colder sea than you had hoped for! In the autumn, you will enjoy golden days with a still-warm seas to swim in. One drawback: Off-season there are fewer boats and flights to the islands, where some shops, hotels, and restaurants do not open until June and then close in October. Something to consider if you are coming to Greece in the spring: During Easter week, nearly every hotel room outside of Athens is booked well in advance by city Greeks who head to the country to celebrate Greece's most important holiday. Many sites and museums are closed Good Friday, Easter Saturday, and Easter Sunday, while many shops close on Good Friday and Easter Saturday. And when St. George's Day (usually celebrated Apr 23) falls in Lent, it is celebrated on the Monday after Easter Sunday, which just prolongs the Easter break. Also, the Feast of the Virgin on August 15 is an enormous holiday, especially on Tinos and Paros, but also on virtually every other Greek island and across the mainland.

Weather

I've been visiting Greece since the 1960s, and for the last decade I've spent about half the year in Greece, most of it in a village in the Peloponnese, south of Athens. The one thing I can swear to is that the weather is getting less predictable every year! When Greeks talk about the weather, increasingly they say that everything is *ano kato* (upside down). Villages where snow was almost unknown had blizzards in 2010/11. Areas where February always meant steady rain, saw hardly a drop all month. One thing everyone agrees on: the winters are colder (sometimes drier, sometimes wetter, sometimes with unusual bursts of warm weather). Summers are just plain hotter (and usually drier) than even 10 years ago. Even though our temperature chart for Athens reflects some sound statistics (this is the *average* daily temperature, not the daytime high), don't be surprised if you find deviations from it when you visit Greece. You'll find more on the weather patterns in different regions of Greece in each chapter of the guide. Our figures for Crete are based on Iraklion's temperature/precipitation.

Average Monthly Temperatures & Precipitation

		JAN	FEB	MAR	APR	MAY	JUNE	JULY	AUG	SEPT	OCT	NOV	DEC
Athens	Temp °F	50	50	54	59	67	75	81	81	75	67	59	53
	Temp °C	10	10	12	15	19	23	27	27	23	19	15	11
	Precip. (in.)	1.9	1.6	1.6	.9	.7	.3	.2	.3	.4	2.1	2.2	2.4
Crete	Temp °F	54	55	57	61	68	73	79	77	73	68	63	57
	Temp °C	12	13	14	16	20	23	26	25	23	20	17	14
	Precip. (in.)	3.5	2.7	2.3	1.1	0.6	0.1	0.1	0	.7	2.6	2.3	3.1

Holidays

Every day in Greece is sacred to one or more saints. That means that every day, at least one saint (and everyone named for that saint) is being celebrated. Tiny chapels that are used only once a year are opened for a church service followed by all-day wining and dining. If you're lucky, you'll stumble on one of these celebrations.

Greece Calendar of Events

For an exhaustive list of events beyond those listed here, check http://events.frommers. com, where you'll find a searchable, up-to-the-minute roster of what's happening in cities all over the world.

JANUARY

Feast of St. Basil (Ayios Vassilios). St. Basil is the Greek equivalent of Santa Claus. The holiday is marked by the exchange of gifts and a special cake, vassilopita, made with a coin in it; the person who gets the piece with the coin will have good luck. January 1.

Epiphany (Baptism of Christ). Baptismal fonts and water are blessed. A priest may throw a cross into the harbor and young men will try to recover it; the finder wins a special blessing. Children, who have been kept good during Christmas with threats of the kalikantzari (goblins), are allowed on the 12th day to help chase them away. January 6.

FEBRUARY

Carnival (Karnavali). Be ready for parades, marching bands, costumes, drinking, dancing, and general loosening of inhibitions, depending on the locale. Some scholars say the name comes from the Latin for "farewell meat," while others hold that it comes from "car naval," the chariots celebrating the ancient sea god Poseidon (Saturn, to the Romans). The city of Patras shows its support of the latter theory with its famous chariot parade and wild Saturnalia, private parties, and public celebrations. Masked revels are widely held

in Macedonia. On the island of Skyros, the pagan "goat dance" is performed, reminding us of the primitive Dionysiac nature of the festivities. Crete has its own colorful versions, whereas in the Ionian Islands, festivities are more Italian. In Athens, people bop each other on their heads with plastic hammers. Celebrations last the 3 weeks before the beginning of Lent.

MARCH

Independence Day and the Feast of the Annunciation. The two holidays are celebrated simultaneously with military parades, especially in Athens. The religious celebration is particularly important on the islands of Tinos and Hydra and in churches or monasteries named Evangelismos (Bringer of Good News) or Evangelistria (the feminine form of the name). March 25.

APRIL

Sound-and-Light Performances. These begin on the Acropolis in Athens and in the Old Town on Rhodes. Nightly through October.

Feast of St. George (Ayios Yioryios). The feast day of the patron saint of shepherds is an important rural celebration with dancing and feasting. Arachova, near Delphi, is famous for its festivities. The island of Skyros also gives its patron saint a big

Holy Week Celebrations

Orthodox Easter, a time of extraordinary festivities in Greece, usually falls one or more weeks after Easter in the West; inquire ahead! The Good Friday exodus from Athens is amazing, and you can remain and enjoy the deserted city or, if you're fortunate and have made reservations, because Greeks take up most of the travel facilities, you can be among the celebrants in any town or village. Holy Week is usually marked by solemn services and processions, and serious feasting on roasted lamb, the traditional *margaritsa* soup, and homemade wine. Dancing takes place, often in traditional costumes. In a unique celebration on Patmos, the Last Supper is reenacted at the Monastery of St. John the Divine. *Tip:* Tourists must dress appropriately during this special time. Shorts, miniskirts, and sleeveless shirts will not only offend Greeks, but will prohibit your entry to religious sites.

party on April 23. (If the 23rd comes before Easter, the celebration is postponed until the Mon after Easter.)

MAY

May Day. On this urban holiday, families have picnics in the country and pick wildflowers, which are woven into wreaths and hung from balconies and over doorways. May Day is still celebrated by Greek communists and socialists as a working-class holiday. May 1.

Hippocratic Oath. Ritual recitations of the oath by the citizens of Kos honor their favorite son, Hippocrates. Young girls in ancient dress, playing flutes, accompany a young boy in procession until he stops and recites in Greek the timeless oath of physicians everywhere. May through September.

Feast of St. Constantine *(Ayios Konstandinos).* The first Orthodox emperor, Constantine, and his mother, **St. Helen** *(Ayia Eleni),* are honored, most interestingly, by fire-walking rituals *(anastenaria)* in four villages in Macedonian Greece: Ayia Eleni, Ayios Petros, Langada, and Meliki. It's a big party night for everyone named Costa and Eleni. (Name days, rather than birthdays, are celebrated in Greece.) The anniversary of the Ionian reunion with Greece is also celebrated, mainly in Corfu. May 21.

JUNE

Athens Festival. Featured are superb productions of ancient drama, opera, orchestra performances, ballet, modern dance, and popular entertainers. The festival takes place in the handsome Odeum of Herodes Atticus, on the southwest side of the Acropolis. June to early October.

Folk-Dance Performances. The site of these performances is the theater in the Old Town of Rhodes.

Wine Festival. This festival is held annually at Daphni, about 10km (7 miles) west of Athens; wine festivals are also held on Rhodes and elsewhere.

Simi Festival. The 4-month feast features concerts, theater, storytelling, and dance, starring acclaimed Greek and international artists. With its epicenter on the tiny island of Simi, the events spill over onto seven neighboring islands: Astypalea, Halki, Kastellorizo, Karpathos, Kassos, Nissiros, and Tilos. June through September.

Lycabettus Theater. A variety of performances are presented at the amphitheater on Mount Likavitos (Lycabettus) overlooking Athens. Mid-June to late August.

Miaoulia. This celebration on Hydra honors Hydriot Admiral Miaoulis, who set much of the Turkish fleet on fire by ramming it with explosives-filled fireboats. Weekend in mid-June.

Aegean Festival. In the harbor of Skiathos town, the Bourtzi Cultural Center presents ancient drama, modern dance, folk music and folk dance, concerts, and art exhibits. June through September.

International Classical Musical Festival.
This annual festival takes place at Nafplion, in the Peloponnese. One week in June or July.

Midsummer Eve. The now-dried wreaths of flowers picked on May Day are burned to drive away witches, in a version of pagan ceremonies now associated with the birth of John the Baptist on June 24, Midsummer Day. June 23 to June 24.

Navy Week. The celebration takes place throughout Greece. In Volos, the voyage of the Argonauts is reenacted. On Hydra, the exploits of Adm. Andreas Miaoulis, naval hero of the War of Independence, are celebrated. Fishermen at Plomari on Lesvos stage a festival. End of June and beginning of July.

JULY

Puppet Festival. Hydra's annual festival has drawn puppeteers from countries as far away as Togo and Brazil. Early July.

Dodoni Festival. Classical dramas are presented at the ancient theater of Dodoni, south of Ioannina. For information, call ℂ **26510/20-090.** July through September.

Epidaurus Festival. Performances of classical Greek drama take place in the famous amphitheater. For information, contact the **Greek Festival Office,** 4 Stadiou (ℂ **210/322-1459** or 210/322-3111 to -3119, ext. 137). July to early September.

International Folklore Festival. At Naoussa, in northern Greece, both amateur and professional dance companies gather from all over the world. For information, call ℂ **23320/20-211** or e-mail cioff@nao.forthnet.gr. July.

Northern Greece National Theater. Classical drama is performed in the amphitheaters in Phillipi and on the island of Thasos. You will be able to see these productions without the hassles of Athens performances. For information, call ℂ **2510/223-504.** July and August.

Hippokrateia **Festival.** Art, music, and theater come to the medieval castle of the Knights of St. John, in the main harbor of Kos. July and August.

Dionysia Wine Festival. This is not a major event, but it's fun if you happen to find yourself on the island of Naxos. For information, call ℂ **22850/22-923.** Mid-July.

Wine Festival at Rethymnon, Crete.
Rethymnon hosts a wine festival as well as a **Renaissance Festival.** There are now wine festivals and arts festivals all over Greece, but among the more engaging are those held in Rethymnon. Sample the wines, then sample the Renaissance theatrical and musical performances. Mid-July to early September.

Feast of Ayia Marina. The feast of the protector of crops is widely celebrated in rural areas. July 17.

Feast of the Prophet Elijah *(Profitis Ellas).*
The prophet's feast day is celebrated in the hilltop shrines formerly sacred to the sun god Helios. The most famous shrine is on Mount Taygetos, near Sparta. July 18 to July 20.

AUGUST

Feast of the Transfiguration *(Metamorphosi).* This feast day is observed in the numerous churches and monasteries of that name, though they aren't much for parties. August 6.

Aeschylia Festival of Ancient Drama.
Classical dramas are staged at the archaeological site of Eleusis, home of the ancient Mysteries and birthplace of Aeschylus, west of Athens. August to mid-September.

The Aegina Music Festival takes place across the island in August; information from (ℂ **698/131-9332**).

Feast of the Assumption of the Virgin *(Apokimisis tis Panayias).* On this important day of religious pilgrimage, many come home to visit, so rooms are particularly hard to find. The holiday reaches monumental proportions in Tinos; thousands of people descend on the small port town to participate in an all-night vigil at the cathedral of Panagia Evangelistria, in the procession of the town's miraculous icon, and in the requiem for the soldiers who died aboard the Greek battleship *Elli* on this day in 1940. August 15.

Epirotika Festival. Ioannina presents theatrical performances, concerts, and exhibitions. August to early September.

Olympus Festival. Cultural events take place in several sites around Mount Olympus, in particular at the ancient theater of Dion and in the Venetian castle of Platamonas. Throughout August.

SEPTEMBER

Feast of the Birth of the Virgin (*Yenisis tis Panayias*). Another major festival, especially on Spetses, the anniversary of the **Battle of the Straits of Spetses** is celebrated on the weekend closest to September 8 with a reenactment in the harbor, fireworks, and an all-night bash.

Feast of the Exaltation of the Cross (*Ipsosi to Stavrou*). This marks the end of summer's stretch of feasts, and even Stavros has had enough for a while. September 14.

Thessaloniki Film Festival and Festival of Popular Song. That lively and sophisticated city continues to live it up. End of September.

Aegina honors its famous nut, the pistachio, with the **Pistachio Festival** every September (**www.aeginagistikifest.gr**).

OCTOBER

Feast of St. Demetrius (*Ayios Dimitrios*). Particularly important in Thessaloniki, where he is the patron saint, the Demetrius Festival features music, opera, and ballet.

New wine is traditionally untapped. October 26.

Ochi Day. General Metaxa's negative reply (*ochi* is Greek for no) to Mussolini's demands in 1940 conveniently extends the feast-day party with patriotic outpourings, including parades, folk music and folk dancing, and general festivity. October 28.

NOVEMBER

Feast of the Archangels Gabriel and Michael (*Gavriel and Mihail*). Ceremonies are held in the many churches named for the two archangels. November 8.

Feast of St. Andrew (*Ayios Andreas*). The patron saint of Patras provides another reason for a party in this swinging city. November 30.

DECEMBER

Feast of St. Nikolaos (*Ayios Nikolaos*). This St. Nick is the patron saint of sailors. Numerous processions head down to the sea and to the many chapels dedicated to him. December 6.

Christmas. The day after Christmas honors the Gathering Around the Holy Family (*Synaksis tis Panayias*). December 25 and 26.

New Year's Eve. Children sing Christmas carols (*kalanda*) outdoors while their elders play cards, talk, smoke, eat, and imbibe. December 31.

LAY OF THE LAND

Ask a Greek what his country's greatest natural wonder is and he often simply replies "Greece itself." What he really means is that what is most unique about Greece is simultaneously what is most common in Greece: the stunning combination of the mountains and the sea.

That said, if I were asked to name some individual sights not to miss, here's my short list: First, the **isles** of Greece. There are few things more wonderful than sitting on an island boat, slipping between the seemingly endless chain of marble and limestone mountained Greek islands, almost each one with an absurdly picturesque little harbor. You've got lots of islands to chose from, with the best known forming the Cyclades, Saronic Gulf, Sporades, Ionian, Dodecanese and Northeastern Aegean islands. And, of course, there's Crete, so large that the Greeks call it "the Great Island," and the Cretans think of it as a land unto itself.

At the risk of offending many Greek islanders, I'll just mention one "don't miss" island experience: Ask anyone who has sailed at dawn into the deep harbor of Santorini what it was like. Most will be at a loss for words. Go there, and you'll see why, as you bend over nearly backwards to see to the top of the red and black lava cliffs that were created when a volcano blasted the center out of the island about 1500 B.C. Second, leaving the islands for the mainland, try to see the bizarre rock formations of the Meteora in Central Greece, that rise hundreds of feet out of the flat plain of Thessaly. Look up at the strange, twisted rocks and what do you see on top? Monasteries, built centuries ago on what appear to be totally inaccessible perches. Third, go to Olympia, set in its magical pine-clad valley and to Delphi, perched high on the slopes of Mount Parnassus. Then try to decide which is the most beautiful ancient site in Greece.

Wherever you go in Greece, you'll be constantly reminded that this is a land of mountains and sea. Over a fifth of the Greek landmass is islands, numbering thousands if you count every floating crag—and nowhere in Greece will you find yourself more than 96km (60 miles) from the sea. It should come as no surprise, then, that the sea has shaped the Greek imagination, as well as its history.

So, too, have the **mountains.** The Pindos range stretches from the Balkans deep into Greece, where the Parnon and Taygetus ranges continue south to the tip of the Peloponnese. Greece's highest peak is **Mount Olympus,** the seat of the gods, nearly 3,000m (10,000 ft.) above sea level. Eighty percent of the Greek mainland is mountainous, as you will discover whether you make your way on foot or on wheels. And because of all those mountains, and all those twisting mountain roads, you will almost certainly make your way much more slowly in Greece than you anticipated. In short, Greece is the perfect place to make haste slowly.

Greece is a southern extension of the Balkan mountain range, albeit one with some 8,500km (5,280 miles) of serrated, irregular mainland coastline, and 7,500km (4,660 miles) of island coastlines. No place in Greece is more than 100km (62 miles) from the sea. In addition to the variety of landscapes within a few miles almost anywhere in Greece, there are some real regional differences. In the north, the mountains of Macedonia and Epirus are close cousins to the Alps, the rivers are broad and deep, and the forests are home to the last brown bears and most of the wild boars in Greece.

With the possible exception of the flat, often dusty, plains of Thrace and Thessaly, there is no part of Greece where you can drive very long without seeing something that takes your breath away. Even Thrace and Thessaly have the cliffs of the Meteora and vast stretches of wetlands that make Greece a birder's paradise. As for Attica, Athens has almost devoured the gentle plain that once produced the grapes for almost all of Greece's pungent retsina wine. The mountains that flank Athens— Hymettos, Parnes, and Pentelicon—seldom turn the violet hues that the ancient poets described. In fact, the ring of mountains is now often blamed for trapping Athens's nasty summer *nefos* (smog) within the city. Many days, the Acropolis of Pindar's "violet-crowned Athens" is barely visible through the beige smog. It's often a relief to leave Athens behind and head, for example, to mountain villages such as Delphi and Arachova, on the Parnassos range. It has to be admitted that the ski industry is busily covering much of Parnassos with chalets, ski lifts, and boutique hotels. Still, the sweeping views down from Parnassos to the Gulf of Corinth and the Peloponnese remain virtually unchanged.

I have to admit to being prejudiced in favor of the beauties of the Peloponnese, which really does have it all: the Parnon and Tayegetus mountain ranges, the lush valleys of Arcadia, crescent sand beaches tucked below seaside cliffs, and a tantalizing sprinkle of off-shore islands.

RESPONSIBLE TRAVEL

Greece has a population of about 11.3 million. Between 10 million and 14 million tourists visit most years—the figures were on the low side in 2010–11. Each year, visitors use a veritable Niagara of water by flushing hotel toilets, standing under long, restorative showers, and chugging down bottles of water. And of late, several water-hungry golf courses have been built in Greece, a country in which until recently the only broad swath of grass was the lawn of the American Embassy in Athens.

Along with most of the rest of the world, Greece has not rushed to encourage responsible travel, either among themselves or from their foreign visitors. Greeks hate to be told what to do and that includes being told where to park or how to recycle. As I was trying to inch precisely between the lines marking off a small parking space in a municipal parking lot in the Peloponnese recently, a car zipped ahead of me and parked lengthwise across two parking places, blocking the exit for two already properly parked cars! I've seen families ostentatiously dump beer cans and plastic bottles feet from recycling containers—to demonstrate that no one could tell them what to do. Add to this all those foreign visitors, many of whom have no idea of the severe water shortages that perpetually plague Greece, and you begin to get an idea of how important it is to travel responsibly in Greece. Here are some hints on how to protect Greece's natural resources and make the Greeks you meet hope you come back again.

HELPING TO CREATE A SUSTAINABLE GREECE   Be sure that any match, cigarette, or flammable material that you dispose of is completely out. Summer forest fires consume thousands of acres of Greek forests every year.

Few Greek hotels ask you to conserve water and reuse bath towels because almost all hotels are afraid of antagonizing their guests. It's up to visitors to remember that the entire country, but especially the islands, face chronic severe water shortages.

Be sure to turn off all lights and the air-conditioning in your hotel room when you go out. I know more than one small island hotel that has resorted to disconnecting its air conditioners and pretending all season that they are "temporarily" out of order. "What can I do?" one proprietor asked me. "If the tourists can use the air conditioners, they leave them on high while they are out sightseeing all day."

Finally, if you want to help create a greener Greece, you can make a contribution to the **Plant Your Roots in Greece Foundation,** which will use your money to help reforest the denuded hills of Greece. For information, check out the website **www. plantyourrootsingreece.org.** And if you want to help preserve Greek wildlife, the **Hellenic Wildlife Hospital** (www.ekpazo.gr) on Aegina treats wounded and injured wildlife, including many of the sea turtles that are injured each year by jet skis.

Minding Your Local Manners

BEING A WELCOME GUEST IN GREECE: Dress Codes   Most Greeks wear bathing suits only on the beach and do not go into restaurants, cafes, or shops without putting something over their swimsuits. Also, most Greeks consider bare feet off the beach seriously odd and quite rude. And almost no Greek man would go into a church in shorts and virtually no Greek woman would go into church in a sleeveless top or shorts. Slacks for women are now acceptable almost everywhere, except in the most traditional churches and monasteries.

Saying Hello and Goodbye　Few Greeks go into a bakery and say "Loaf of bread, please," and then pay and leave. Almost all encounters begin with a greeting: *"Kali mera"* (Good day) is always acceptable, but on Monday, you'll hear *"Kali ebdomada"* (Good week) and on the first of the month *"Kalo mena"* (Good month). Sprinkle your requests on how to find the Acropolis or where to buy a bus ticket with *"Sas para kalo"* (Excuse me, please) and *"Eucharisto"* (Thanks) and you'll help to make Greeks reconsider all those things they've come to believe about rude tourists! And on that topic, although most Greeks don't mind having their photo taken, always ask first. If you are traveling with your dog, know that most Greeks do not regard dogs as house pets, but as outdoor watchdogs. Except in chic city cafes, don't sit down with your dog without asking permission.

TOURS/SPECIAL-INTEREST TRIPS

You can find a wide variety of tours, special-interest trips, classes, and workshops available when you travel to Greece, focusing on everything from antiquities to wine tasting. In addition, there are a number of organized possibilities for volunteerism, whether on excavations or on farms. Here are some suggestions.

Educational Trips & Language Classes

Want to arrive in Greece knowing how to say more than "Sorry, I don't speak Greek"? Check out the **Dartmouth College Rassias Center** (**www.rassias.dartmouth. edu**) language program in modern Greek. This very popular 10-day total-immersion session should have you arriving ready to amaze and delight Greeks with your command of their glorious and tricky language. If you can't go to the Rassias Center but find yourself staying on in Greece and wanting to learn the language, the **Athens Center,** 48 Archimidou, Mets., 11636 Athens (**www.athenscenter.gr**), has been around since 1969 and offers modern Greek classes year-round.

Many colleges and universities offer tours of Greece, led by scholars at the institution sponsoring the tour. Most of these tours are serious, but very comfortable—and not cheap. Some of these tours are open only to graduates of the institution, others welcome all comers, so you'll probably want to check out a few university and college websites to find what interests you.

Archaeological Tours, 271 Madison Ave., Suite 904, New York, NY 10016 (🕾 866/740-5130; www.archaeologicaltrs.com), offers tours led by expert guides; typical tours might be to classical Greek sites or to Cyprus, Crete, and Santorini. **FreeGate Tourism,** 585 Stewart Ave., Suite 310, Garden City, NY 11530 (🕾 888/ 373-3428; www.freegatetours.com), also specializes in guided trips in Greece. **The Aegean Center for the Fine Arts** (**www.aegeancenter.org**), based on the island of Paros, offers courses in painting, photography, music, creative writing, and modern Greek. Most of the students are college-age Americans; the instructors are Greek, American, and international.

The American-run **Island Center for the Arts** conducts classes in painting, photography, and Greek culture on the island of Skopelos between June and September (© 617/623-6538; www.islandcenter.org). As it is affiliated with the Massachusetts College of Art, some educational institutions grant credits for its courses.

The popular **Road Scholar** program (formerly Elderhostel; © 800/454-5768; www.roadscholar.org) is a learning experience for adults (with some intergenerational programs) that offers a couple dozen trips to Greece and the surrounding area each year, ranging from cruises on smaller ships that explore the history and culture of the Aegean Islands, to overland road trips where participants explore the art, architecture, and archeology of the region.

Adventure & Wellness Trips

Trekking Hellas (**www.trekking.gr**) offers white-water rafting excursions in the Peloponnese and northern Greece. Although plenty of beginners (including many macho Greek guys) go on these trips, most foreign participants have had some rafting experience. Trekking Hellas also organizes hiking tours (see "Walking Tours," below).

The **Ashtanga Yoga Retreat** (**www.yogapractice.net/mani**) in the remote, austere, and beautiful Mani peninsula, offers 1-week retreats in the summer.

Eumelia (**www.eumelia.com**), in the Peloponnese south of Sparta, has five rental houses, a staff of three, and never more than 25 guests on its organic farm outside the hamlet of Gouves. Eumelia (the name means "melody") focuses on agrotourism and the manufacture and sale of organic produce (olive oil, herbs, and so on). There are frequent workshops and seminars (in 2011 workshops included a "raw vegan cooking seminar" and a tango workshop); Eumelia aims for "100% self-sufficiency" and all its buildings are built with great attention to environmental issues—and have TV and Internet access. Prices are reasonable: 120€ per night for two people sharing a two-bedroom cottage in 2011.

Limnisa (Creative Holidays by the Sea; **www.limnisa.com**) offers silent retreats, writing retreats, and workshops by the sea near Methana, in the east Peloponnese, near the island of Poros.

Skyros Center (**www.skyros.com**) offers yoga and holistic holidays (as well as writing holidays and singles holidays) on the island of Skyros. This British operation has a year-round office on the Isle of Wight.

Food & Wine Trips

If you're heading for Santorini and want to learn about Greek cuisine, the island's best restaurant, **Selene** (**www.selene.gr**), offers cooking classes with the most varied and fresh local ingredients each summer. Diane Kochilas (**www.dianekochilas.com**), a Greek-American expert on Greek foods, offers a variety of activities, including cooking classes in Athens and on Ikaria, and culinary tours in Athens or throughout Greece. **Aglaia Kremezi** (**www.aglaiakremezi.com**), an American-educated Greek authority on Greek food, and her husband, Costas Moraitis, run a cooking school on the island of Kea. And Nikki Rose (**www.cookingincrete.com**), a Cretan-American professional chef, operates seminars on Crete that combine some travel with cooking lessons and investigations of Crete's diet.

Want to mix seeing where the Olympic games began with some cooking, creative writing, or painting? Check out the website of the **Hotel Pelops** (**www.hotel pelops.gr**), where co-owner Susanna Spiliopoulou offers 3- and 4-day workshops a short walk from the pine groves of ancient Olympia.

Guided Tours

Organized and guided **bus tours** focusing on the glories of ancient Greece are widely available. Escorted tours are structured group tours, with a group leader. The price usually includes everything from airfare to hotels, meals, tours, admission costs, and local transportation. Single travelers are usually hit with a "single supplement" to the base price for package vacations and cruises, while the price of a single room is almost always well over half that for a double. **CHAT Tours** (**www.chattours.gr**), founded in 1953, is the oldest and most experienced provider of a wide selection of bus tours led by highly articulate guides. Its main office is at 9 Xenofontos St., Athens 10557 (✆ **210/323-0827**). Recently, a close friend of mine who went on a CHAT tour thought the pace was just about right, although she could have used a bit more free time. Be sure to ask how many will be on your tour, as a large group usually results in a more regimented and much less personal tour.

Fantasy Travel, 19 Filelinon (✆ **210/ 331-0530**; www.fantasytravel.gr), is one of our favorite travel agencies in Athens. Two other long-standing Greek tour organizers are **Homeric Tours** (✆ **800/223-5570**; www.homerictours.com) and **Tourlite International** (✆ **800/272-7600**; www.tourlite.com). Such tours fall into the "moderate" category in pricing and accommodations, and both companies carry the risk of all charter flights — that is, delays. Both offer some variety—often these tours provide local guides and include short cruises as part of the entire stay.

A more upscale agency is **TrueGreece** (✆ **800/817-7098** in North America, 203/026-1176 in the U.K., or 210/612-0656 in Greece; www.truegreece.com), which says it is an "innovative luxury vacation travel company," that escorts small groups on customized and more intimate tours to selected destinations.

If you'd like to take a day tour of Athens, or a week-long tour of Greece that focus on Greece's **Jewish heritage,** check out **www.jewishtours.gr**.

For more information on escorted general-interest tours, including questions to ask before booking your trip, see **www.frommers.com/planning**.

Volunteer & Working Opportunities

Many Greek Orthodox churches in the United States and in Great Britain can offer suggestions for volunteer work in Greece, although many opportunities assume a fluency in Greek. **GoGreeceabout.com** lists many volunteer possibilities in Greece, including chances to help sea turtles on Zakynthos or donkeys on Corfu. **www.nmp-zak.org**, the website of the National Marine Park of Zakynthos, also accepts volunteers. Other possibilities include The **World Wide Opportunities on Organic Farms** organization (**www.wwoof.org**), which offers listings for volunteers in several locations in Greece, including Mount Pelion.

On Chios, **Masticulture and Ecotourism Activities** (**www.masticulture. com**) has a range of tours and activities letting visitors participate in the mastic and wine harvests and learn about local pottery, cooking, and customs.

Walking Tours

Trekking Hellas (**www.trekkinghellas.gr**), based in Athens at 10 Rethimnou, 10682 Athens (© **210/331-0323**), is the best-known outfit offering guided hiking tours of the Greek mainland, Crete, and several Cycladic islands. If you don't want to be with a group, but do want some pointers, Trekking Hellas will help you plan an itinerary and book you places to stay along the way.

In the United States, **Appalachian Mountain Club,** 5 Joy St., Boston, MA 02108 (© **800/372-1758;** www.outdoors.org), often organizes hiking tours in Greece. **Ecogreece,** P.O. Box 2614, Rancho Palo Verdes, CA 90275 (© **877/838-7748;** www.ecogreece.com), conducts tours in Greece centered around activities such as hiking, sailing, hiking, diving, or riding.

SUGGESTED GREECE ITINERARIES

Greece is so small—the size of the state of Alabama—you might think it's easy to see most of the country in a short visit. There are two reasons why that's not true and they are the same two reasons that make travel here so beautiful: the mountains and the sea. Greece's mountainous terrain almost always makes mainland travel take much longer than you'd expected when you just figured out the distance on your map. As to island travel, often you can see your next island destination from the island you are on—only to find out that getting there requires an infuriatingly time-consuming, roundabout sea journey with either nerve-wrackingly tight connections or unwanted—sometimes totally unscheduled—stopovers on other islands. Last year, I tried three times to get from the port of Rafina to Tinos. The first time, a ferry strike canceled all sailings for several days. The second time, heavy seas canceled my sailing. The third time I made it as far as the neighboring island of Andros where, thanks to heavy seas, I spent the next 2 days—in sight of my destination, Tinos. Still, with advance planning, some good luck, and a willingness to be flexible, you can see what you set out to visit in Greece. And don't be surprised if your most lasting memories are of unexpected sights and unanticipated delights en route to your planned destinations.

If you'd like a little less of the unexpected on your Greek holiday, you might want to sign up for one of the standard cruises that stop at several of the major islands and often take in mainland highlights such as Delphi and Olympia (described in detail in chapter 4). Another alternative is to sign up for a bus tour, from 3 to 7 days, that visits the major mainland sites (we recommend some escorted tours in chapter 2).

The itineraries suggested below require from 8 to 16 days on the ground in Greece. Most make sure that you get to at least one of the Greek islands and see at least one of the big three ancient Greek sites: the Acropolis in Athens, Delphi, and Olympia. All of the itineraries end up in Athens, and in theory you'll have 24 hours of leeway to allow for any unanticipated travel delays. On most itineraries, you'll take a mixture of buses, trains, cars, ships, and planes. Keep in mind that strikes often make travel in Greece *very* tricky when airports close and buses and ferry boats stop running. When everything works, travel by bus and ferry is terrific—and a great way to meet Greeks. Driving your own car is much more isolating—but frees you from worry about most strikes (gas stations, after all, can go on strike!). If you choose to drive, you'll find out that most Greeks drive with hair-raising flair, passing on the right, using sidewalks as extra lanes, and almost never signaling before turning. And, yes, the traffic-accident rate in Greece is one of the highest in the world.

Because these itineraries include islands, they work best in the summer, May through September. Off season, the weather is not dependable, many hotels and restaurants close, and airline and ferry schedules to some of these places become extremely limited. Of course, in summer, you can travel more easily from island to island—but you may find yourself sleeping rough unless you have a reservation. Off season, you can luxuriate in feeling the natural rhythm of uncrowded island villages—but may find the best restaurants closed until next summer.

Speaking of seasonal schedules and closings, Greece often keeps to its own, frequently mysterious, schedule. On any given day, a museum or archaeological site may be closed without notice. Call in advance to make sure that a destination will be open while you're traveling, and double-check your reservations, especially during special occasions such as Greek Easter week and the August 15 Assumption of the Virgin. If you can, avoid the most crowded travel times. And now, as you set off for Greece, *Kalo taxidi* (Have a good trip)!

The Regions in Brief

Greece is a land of sea and mountains. Over a fifth of the Greek landmass is islands, numbering several thousand if you count every floating crag—and nowhere in Greece will you find yourself more than 96km (60 miles) from the sea. Mainland Greece is a great vertebrate, with the Pindos range reaching from north to south, and continuing, like a tail, through the Peloponnese. The highest of its peaks is Mount Olympus, the seat of the gods, nearly 3,000m (10,000 ft.) above sea level.

ATHENS Chances are you'll land in Athens when you arrive in Greece. The city is not always pleasant and is sometimes exhausting—just to be clear, it's the noise level and traffic—yet it's unavoidable. Its **archaeological sites** and its **museums** warrant a couple of days of exploration. Between visits to the sites, a stroll in the **National Garden** will prove reviving. Then, after dark as the city cools, the old streets of the **Plaka** district at the foot of the Acropolis offer you chances to stroll, shop, and have dinner with an Acropolis view. The central square, pedestrianized side streets, and residential streets of **Kolonaki** are where fashionable Athenians head to see and be seen—and to do some shopping. **Piraeus**, as in antiquity, serves as the port of Athens and the jumping-off point to most of the islands. Athens is a great base for day trips and overnight excursions, to the Temple of Poseidon at **Cape Sounion**, the slopes of **Mount Hymettus (Imittos)**, the Monastery of **Kaisariani (Kessariani)**, the Byzantine Monastery of **Daphni**, the plains of **Marathon**, or the ruins of **Eleusis**, place of ancient mysteries.

THE SARONIC GULF ISLANDS Cupped between Attica and the Peloponnese, in the sheltering Saronic Gulf, these islands offer both proximity and retreat for Athenians who, like their visitors, long for calming waters and cooler breezes. In high season, the accessibility of these islands on any given day, especially on weekends, can be their downfall. **Aegina,** so close to Athens it can be a daily commute, is the most besieged island, yet it possesses character and charm. The main port town of Aegina is picturesque and pleasant, while across the island to the east, set atop a pine-crested hill, stands the remarkably preserved Temple of Aphaia, a Doric gem. **Poros,** the next island in line proceeding south, is convenient to both Athens and the Peloponnese.

Its beaches and lively port are each a draw, with the picturesque rubble of an ancient, scenically situated temple thrown in. Still farther south lies vehicle-free **Hydra,** remarkable for its natural beauty and handsome stone mansions built by sea captains. The port of Hydra has a lot to offer and knows it, all of which is reflected in the prices. It's a great place for pleasant strolls, views, and a swim off the rocks. **Spetses,** the farthest of these islands from Athens, offers glades of pine trees and fine beaches—and a great many hotels catering to package tours from Europe.

THE PELOPONNESE Crossing the narrow Isthmus—less than 6.5km (4 miles) across at its narrowest point—from the mainland onto the southern peninsula of Greece is a move you will never regret. The Peloponnese retains a sense of separation from the north and from the rest of Greece. Its often barren landscape is studded with stunning archaeological remains: **Mycenae,** the mountain citadel of Agamemnon; **Olympia,** birthplace of the Olympic Games; **Sparta,** home of Helen and Menelaus; the palace of Nestor at **Pylos;** the magnificent and still-used theater of **Epidaurus;** the temple and stadium at **Nemea;** and the Bema at **Corinth,** where St. Paul addressed the Corinthians. The small but stately port of **Nafplion** provides a convenient base from which to explore surrounding sights. The mountain and seaside roads of the Peloponnese are unrivaled in Greece. There are several spectacular routes we suggest you take. The vertiginous route from **Sparta** to Kalamata passes the Byzantine ghost town of **Mistra** and continues on through the twists and turns of Langada Pass, one of Greece's most beautiful routes. Follow the excellent road from Tripolis to **Olympia** that cuts through some of the most beautiful mountain scenery in Arcadia, passing traditional villages that are among the region's loveliest. And allow yourself a day or two to head to **The Mani,** the southernmost region of the Peloponnese, where tower-villages dot the hillsides, and coastal roads wind high above the sea.

CRETE The largest of the Greek islands, birthplace of the painter El Greco (and

Zeus, they claim!), possesses a landscape so diverse, concentrated, and enchanting that no description is likely to do it justice. Especially if you rent a car and do your own exploring, a week will pass like a day. More or less circling the island on the national highway (don't imagine an interstate), you'll drive a line of inviting ports like **Iraklion,** the capital, **Chania, Rethymnon,** and **Ayios Nikolaos.** Venturing into the heartland of Crete—not far, since Crete's width ranges from 12 to 56km (7½–35 miles)—you'll find the legendary palaces of the Minoans: **Knossos, Phaestos,** and **Ayia Triadha,** to mention a few. Other excursions might include the **Lasithi Plain** or the **Amari Valley,** and for the energetic, the **Gorge of Samaria** is indispensable. Crete is a culinary mecca. For thousands of years its wines were sent all over the ancient world. Today, they complement the wonderful fresh local goat cheese and olives.

THE CYCLADES In antiquity, the *Cyclades*—the "encirclers" or "circling islands"—had at their center the small island of **Delos,** where mythology tells us that Apollo and his sister Artemis were born. Declared a sanctuary where both birth and death were prohibited, Delos was an important spiritual, cultural, and commercial hub of the Aegean. Today, its extensive remains remind visitors of its former importance. It's easy to make a day trip here from **Mykonos,** whose white, cubelike houses and narrow, twisting streets began to attract first a trickle and then a flood of visitors in the 1960s. Today, almost every cruise ship puts in at Mykonos for at least a few hours, so that visitors can take in the cafes, restaurants, and shops. Those who spend a few days can stay in boutique hotels, sip martinis in sophisticated bars—or head inland to the island's less-visited villages. The island of **Paros** (sometimes called "the poor man's Mykonos"), is the transport hub of the Cyclades, with a gentle landscape, appealing villages, good beaches, and opportunities for windsurfing. From here you can get to **Tinos,** home to perhaps the most revered of Greek Orthodox churches; **Naxos,** whose fertile valleys and high mountains lure hikers and campers; **Folegandros,** much of whose capital Hora is built within the walls of a medieval *kastro* (castle); and **Santorini,** which some believe to be the lost Atlantis. On Santorini you'll find a black lava beach, the impressive remains of the Minoan settlement at Akrotiri, chic restaurants, boutique hotels—and the most spectacular sunsets in all of Greece.

THE DODECANESE This string of islands, named "the 12" despite the fact that they number more than that, nearly touch the Turkish shoreline. Except for Rhodes and Kos, the Dodecanese are deforested, bare bones exposed to sun and sea. But what bones! Far to the north lies **Patmos** (already in the 5th c. nicknamed "the Jerusalem of the Aegean"), a holy island where the Book of Revelation is said to have been penned and where the Monastery of St. John still dominates the land. Far to the south basks **Rhodes,** "City of the Sun," with more than 300 days of sunshine per year. For obvious reasons, it's the most touristed of the islands. Rhodes has it all: history and resorts, ruins and nightlife. There's even peace and quiet—we'll tell you where to find it. Between these two lie an array of possibilities, from the traditional charm of tiny **Simi** to the ruins and well-known beaches of **Kos.** And with Turkey so close, you may want to consider an easily arranged side trip.

CENTRAL GREECE Central Greece, for our purposes, stretches from the Corinth Canal to Mount Olympus. Its landscape is vastly diverse, from the fertile Boetian plains to the snowy peaks of **Parnassus** and **Olympus.** Also here are the legendary battlegrounds of **Thermopylae** (where the Spartans under Leonidas delayed the Persian invasion in 480 B.C.) and **Chaironeia** (where Philip of Macedon defeated the Greeks in 338 B.C.). Central Greece's best-known site is the sanctuary of **Delphi,** whose imposing ruins and spectacular mountainside location dazzle visitors. Farther north, in Thessaly, the monasteries on the lofty heights of **Meteora** offer glimpses into the Byzantine and modern Greek world of the Orthodox Church. If you have a less austere retreat in mind, the

traditional villages on the lush, gentle slopes of **Pelion**—where centaurs once roamed—are ideal places to relax under chestnut trees.

THE SPORADES Whether by air, ferry, or hydrofoil, the Sporades, strewn north and east of the island of **Evvia** (Euboea), are readily accessible from the mainland and offer verdant forest landscapes, gold-sand beaches, and crystalline waters. That's the good news. The bad news is that they are no secret. **Skiathos** is the most popular. **Skopelos,** whose lovely port is one of the most striking in Greece, is more rugged and remote, with more trails and fewer nightclubs. Relatively far-off **Skyros** is well worth a visit, offering fishing and diving, sandy beaches, and luminously clear waters.

WESTERN GREECE Northwestern Greece, or **Epirus,** is predominantly mountainous and mostly cut off from the sea. It is unlikely that you will encounter many tourists. Nature lovers and trekkers venture here to challenge themselves hiking **Vikos Gorge** and the mountainous **Zagori** region. Epirus is not, however, without amenities and attractions. **Ioannina,** on the shores of Lake Pamvotis, is the largest and most appealing city in the region; it is one of the few places in Greece where evidence of the long Muslim occupation is still visible. The mountain village of **Metsovo,** several thousand feet high in the Pindos Mountains, offers a number of local attractions and hikes with vistas. Only 32km (20 miles) from Ioannina lie the ruins of one of the most famous of ancient shrines, the Oracle of Zeus at **Dodona,** where the voice of the great lord of Olympus was believed to speak through the rustling leaves of a sacred oak tree.

THE IONIAN ISLANDS Across centuries, these islands have been the apple of more than one empire's eye. Lush, temperate, blessed with ample rain and sun, and tended like architectural gardens, they are splendid. **Corfu,** the most noted and ornamented, is a gem, and is sought after accordingly. **Ithaka** needs no introduction for readers of the *Odyssey.* With adjustments for the nearly 3,000 years that have elapsed, Homer's descriptions of the island still hold their own. If you can do without name recognition, **Kefalonia** has a lot to offer: picturesque traditional villages, steep rocks plunging into the sea, fine beaches, and excellent local wine.

THESSALONIKI & NORTHERN GREECE

Just as it once was the urban understudy of Constantinople, **Thessaloniki** is modern Greece's second city. With less than 20% of Athens's population, however, it is not a close second. Even so, among Greece's major cities, it may be second to none in visual appeal and international flair. Among the city's attractions are the legendary White Tower and its archaeological and Byzantine museums. As a home base, it offers proximity to many of Macedonia's major sites. **Macedonia** is Greece's largest geographical region—rich in natural beauty, soaked in history, and mostly removed from the epicenters of the tourist explosion that, in places, has almost leveled the diverse traditions and cultures of Greece. Besides Thessaloniki, Macedonia is home to three major archaeological sites associated with Alexander and his father— **Pella, Vergina,** and **Dion**—as well as the independent religious state of **Mount**

Athos. This mountaintop theocracy, off-limits to women since the year 1060, may be viewed from cruise ships (departing from Thessaloniki) or visited with special permission—but only by men.

THE NORTHEASTERN AEGEAN ISLANDS

The four major islands comprising this group form Europe's traditional sea border with the East. Beyond their strategic and richly historic location, they offer a taste of Greece that is less compromised by tourism and more deeply influenced by nearby Asia Minor and modern Turkey. **Samos,** unique among the islands in the extent to which it is covered with trees, produces excellent local wine. Its archaeological sites and opportunities for outdoor activities make it a congenial and interesting destination, and it is an ideal place from which to enter and explore the northwestern Turkish coast. **Hios** is unspoiled and welcoming, offering isolated and spectacular beaches, as well as the stunning monastery of Nea Moni and some of Greece's most striking village architecture. The remaining islands of **Lesvos** and **Limnos** have their ways of inviting and rewarding those who explore them.

GREECE IN 1 WEEK

Ideally, everyone should have a whole summer for Greece. But let's face it, most people leave home on a Friday evening and then fly back to work the next Sunday. That's 8 full days on the ground. We've included 2 weekends, but any 8 days will work. Keep in mind that travel in Greece on summer weekends is always more difficult and hotels are almost always more expensive than during the week.

Day 1: Athens & the Acropolis

Arrive in Athens and get settled in your hotel. Especially if you've had a long flight, stretch your legs with a walk to the **Acropolis ★★★** (p. 157) to see the **Parthenon.** If you'd like to combine culture and coffee, head for the **Acropolis Museum** (art-course sculptures and a great cafe). On the way, you'll get a glimpse of the **Theater of Dionysos ★★**, the ground zero of Greek drama. After that long flight, and long walk (and, perhaps, a short nap!), how about a stroll along Adrianou (Hadrian) Street, the main drag in Plaka (where all too many "Greek" souvenirs are made in China) and dinner under a shady plane tree at the long-time favorite, the **Platanos Taverna ★★** (p. 142). If you like tortoises, you might spot one in the adjacent garden of the **Museum of Popular Greek Music Instruments.**

Day 2: Athens & Santorini

Check out the gold masks, jewelry, and sculptures, at the **National Archaeo-logical Museum** ★★★ (p. 167). Then head to the **Ancient Agora** ★★ (p. 162) to experience the Temple of Theseus and the business and political hub of ancient Athens. En route, you'll also experience a good deal of the hubbub of souvenir peddlers (knock-off handbags and watches, bizarre rubber tomatoes and fried eggs) who hang out along Adrianou Street. There are lots of cafes where you can grab a cold drink, but keep an eye on your purse and camera: this is a favor-ite haunt of pickpockets. Perhaps lunch at **Oraia Ellada** ★★—great Acropolis views, snacks, reproductions of folk art—in the Plaka (p. 148). You may want to do a circuit of **Syntagma Square** (p. 129), and have a look at the House of Parliament and National Gardens. Take the evening flight or overnight ferry to Santorini. If you take the ferry, set your alarm clock as early as necessary to be on deck when your ship sails past Santorini's drop-dead amazing cliffs. Get a taxi to **Oia** (Ia) and, after checking in at a hotel there, try **Skala** ★ for dinner (p. 356).

Days 3 & 4: Santorini & Crete

If **ancient Akrotiri** ★★★ (p. 344) has reopened, you must see it—how many chances will you ever have to walk down ancient streets and peer into frescoed homes last occupied some 3,500 years ago? If Akrotiri is still closed, head for ancient **Thira** ★★ (p. 340), a mountaintop settlement with 360-degree views over the island and beyond. Spend the rest of the day at Kamari beach, where the pebbles and sand are jet black and there are plenty of cafes for snacks. Have lunch on the beach at **Camille Stefani** (p. 355). Later, in Oia, take in sunset and then dinner at the **Restaurant-Bar 1800** ★★ (p. 356), a restored sea captain's mansion. On Day 4, perhaps visit a winery and keep an eye out for the low-growing vines near the island's typical cave houses hollowed into the solidi-fied ash (p. 348) Then you can fly via Athens or take the ferry to Iraklion, **Crete** (p. 294). Check into your hotel, stroll around, and grab a patio table for a meal at **Loukoulos** ★ (p. 308).

Days 5 & 6: Crete

Go early to visit the heavily—too heavily, many archaeologists say—restored palace of **Knossos** ★★★ (p. 302). Then, have a look at some of the palace's treasures, including the graceful figurines of snake goddesses and carved vases and frescoes the **Archaeological Museum** ★★★ (p. 315).and then have lunch at the **Pantheon** (p. 308) in the center of the market. After a siesta, take the walking tour of **Iraklion** (p. 298) before treating yourself to a meal at the **Brillant Gourmet** ★★ (p. 307). With only 1 day left, it's decision time: relax-ing on a beach, or seeing more of Crete. You could spend Day 6 touring the charming port town of **Chania** ★★, with its relatively intact Venetian-Turkish old town (p. 311); or **Phaestos** ★★, the second most ambitious Minoan palace (p. 310). Eat lunch at the restaurant above the Phaetos site, or along Chania's harbor at the **Amphora** (p. 320). Either trip involves a lot of driving—easily 5 hours round-trip—which may make a relaxed beach day pretty irresistible! Take an evening flight back to Athens.

Day 7: Athens or Delphi?

You may prefer to spend a leisurely day taking in more of Athens. Otherwise, why not take a day trip to **Delphi** ★★★ (177km/110 miles), one of Greece's most

breathtaking ancient sites. At Delphi, in addition to major attractions such as the **Sanctuary of Apollo ★★★** and the **Delphi Museum ★★★** (p. 489), you'll be treated to glorious mountain scenery with vistas off to the Gulf of Corinth. If Delphi seems like too long a day trip, have a relaxing morning and then head off for a swim near the **Temple of Poseidon ★★** at Sounion (p. 204). Stay for sunset before heading back to Athens. Whatever you've chosen to do, treat yourself to a leisurely dinner when you get back to Athens; if you want to admire the Acropolis while you eat, try a rooftop table at **Strofi Tavern ★** (p. 154).

GREECE IN 2 WEEKS

From the must-see ancient monuments (the Acropolis in Athens, the stadium in Olympia, and the site of the Delphic Oracle on the slopes of Mount Parnassus) to the famous isles (Mykonos, with its snow-white houses and trendy all-night bars, and volcanic Santorini, with its amazing harbor and sheer cliffs) to less famous places that not all visitors know about when they come to Greece (but fall in love with when they discover them)—we're going to show you how to see all this—and also keep some time for discoveries of your own. Here's how to do it in 2 weeks.

Day 1: Athens & the Archaeological Parkway

Settle into your hotel, then go for a walk along the **Archaeological Park,** which runs from Syntagma Square around the **Acropolis** ★★★; the new Acropolis Museum; past ancient Athens's shopping and civic center, the **Agora** ★★; and into the **Plaka,** the heart of old—and touristy—Athens (p. 109). Do what the Athenians do and stop for cappuccino, pastries, cheese, or yogurt at **Oraia Ellada** ★★ (p. 148), a Plaka shop with a restaurant that offers a drop-dead-gorgeous Acropolis view. Browse through the old and new Greek folk art on view before continuing your walk past, endless shops selling T-shirts, olive oil soap, and refrigerator magnets and night lights in the shape of the Parthenon. For lunch, sit under the plane tree as you enjoy roast lamb at **Platanos Taverna** ★★ (p. 142), or grab a souvlaki at **Thanasis** ★★ (p. 144). Feeling revived? Stop at the little **Museum of Popular Greek Musical Instruments** ★★ (p. 167), just a few feet away. Listen to recordings of Greek music and enjoy the peaceful garden. The slumbering tortoises there may remind you it's siesta time. Go to your hotel for a nap before you head out again for a nighttime stroll back to the Acropolis (even if it's closed, it's great at night when it's usually illuminated). For dinner, if you had a big lunch, you could just have a bite at one of the many fast-food cafeterias on Syntagma Square. Point to what you want and leave your phrase book in your pocket. If you're feeling energetic and missed it at lunch, head into the Plaka to eat at one of our suggestions for old-time "authentic" tavernas above.

Day 2: Museums & Mount Likavitos

Visit the **National Archaeological Museum** ★★★ to see sculptures, gold, and other impressive artifacts and—if you get there just as the doors open—as few tour groups as possible (p. 167). Then head to the Acropolis, but first grab a snack at one of the kiosks on the slopes (fresh orange juice and a cheese pie anyone?). Spend the rest of the day enjoying the sprawling **National Gardens** (p. 178) and watching elderly women feeding stray cats, courting couples, and children chasing each other along shady paths. Then have dinner at **Aegli** ★★ (p. 148). Or ride the cable car up **Mount Likavitos** (p. 178) before walking back down for drinks in Kolonaki Square. Try dinner a short walk away at **To Kafeneio** ★★ (p. 150), a great place to enjoy the bustle of Athens's most fashionable neighborhood.

Day 3: Mykonos & Paradise

By plane or ship, go to Mykonos. Settle into your hotel, then take a bus to one of the beaches outside town. **Paradise** ★ (p. 400) attracts partiers who love loud music with their sun and sand, while **Ornos** is a quieter beach preferred by families (p. 400). There are plenty of cafes on either beach for lunch. Back in town, get lost along winding streets and ogle the window displays of jewelry, cutting-edge clothes, and sling-back shoes. Perhaps end up at **Caprice** in Little Venice for a dry martini and good people-watching (p. 415). Before dinner, walk to Mykonos's three waterside windmills. You won't be alone, but even with a crowd, this is a great spot to take in the view back across the harbor. You'll see Little Venice's chic, chicer, and chicest bars, perched vertiginously over the sea. If you want to alternate chic with casual, try the fish at **Kounelas** ★ on the harbor (p. 411), where you'll vie for a table with locals—and longtime Mykonos visitors.

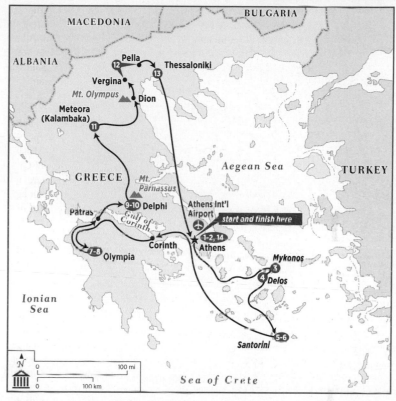

Greece in 2 Weeks

MACEDONIA

BULGARIA

ALBANIA

Pella

Thessaloniki

Vergina

Mt. Olympus

Dion

Meteora
(Kalambaka)

GREECE

Mt.
Parnassus

Aegean Sea

TURKEY

Patras

Delphi

Athens Int'l
Airport

start and finish here

Gulf of
Corinth

Corinth

Athens

Olympia

Mykonos

Delos

Ionian
Sea

Santorini

Sea of Crete

N

0   100 mi

0   100 km

Day 4: Mykonos & Delos

Take an early boat from Mykonos to **Delos** ★★★ (p. 416). Remember to bring
sunscreen and a wide-brimmed hat so you can spend several hours admiring
the acres of marble ruins in this ancient religious site and market. There's a
snack bar by the museum, but you'll do better bringing your own food and
picnicking in a patch of shade cast by the ancient monuments. When you get
back to Mykonos, enjoy some shopping. Don't miss the fabulous jeweler's
LALAoUNIS ★ shop here (p. 404). For dinner, sample the *mezedes* and grilled
fish (or meat) at the **Sea Satin Market ★★**, past the windmills at Kato Myli,
overlooking the sea (p. 413). If you want to see the sun come up, there are lots—
and lots—of bars, cafes, and hangouts where you can spend the hours until dawn.

Day 5: Santorini & Akrotiri

Head to **Santorini ★★★** next, by plane or ship (p. 340). If you go by ship, you'll
sail into the deep harbor with its high cliffs streaked with lava from the volcanic
eruption that tore the island in half around 1450 B.C.—this is one of the world's
great travel experiences. Check into your hotel and rent a car, or sign up for a tour
of the ancient site of **Akrotiri ★★★**, often called the "Pompeii of Greece," if it

has reopened (p. 344). If not, go to ancient Thira, perched on a mountaintop (see below). Then take in the **Boutari Winery** ★, where the tour usually includes enough snacks and samples of local wines for a light lunch (p. 346). In the evening, do what everyone does in Fira: Wander along the narrow streets before having drinks and dinner. For an inventive, memorable meal in a beautiful setting, make reservations at one of the best restaurants in all of Greece: **Selene** ★★★ (p. 356).

Day 6: Ancient Thira & Kamari

Explore the island by car, tour, or the extensive local bus system. See the cliff-top site of **ancient Thira** ★★ (p. 345) before heading down to the famous black-sand beach at Kamari for a swim and lunch at **Camille Stefani taverna** (p. 355). Back in Fira, see the reproductions of the beautiful Minoan wall paintings of Akrotiri in the **Thira Foundation** ★★ (p. 346). In the evening, while tour buses take hordes of tourists to see the sunset at Oia, head to the village of **Imerovigli** (p. 352) and watch the sunset over a medieval fortress. Then, head on to Oia and try **Katina's** ★ an excellent fish place in Ammoudi, Oia's minuscule port (p. 356).

Day 7: Athens to Olympia

Return early by plane or hydrofoil to Athens, and pick up your rental car. (You'll drop it off in Thessaloniki.) Head across the isthmus of Corinth into the Peloponnese for a night in **Olympia.** En route, consider a detour to **ancient Corinth** for a glimpse of the **Temple of Apollo** and a snack (p. 237). Back on the road, stop for a swim; the beaches at **Rio,** outside Patras, have better-than-usual parking. After your long drive, check in at Olympia's **Hotel Pelops** ★★★ or the larger **Hotel Europa** ★★★; both have excellent restaurants (p. 288).

Day 8: Ancient Olympia

Have the buffet breakfast at the hotel. Spend the day seeing the site of **ancient Olympia** ★★★ and the three superb museums, the little **Museum of the History of the Excavations in Olympia** ★, with its 19th-century photos documenting the temple's discovery (p. 287); the **Archaeological Museum** ★★★ (p. 285); and the astonishing wealth of bronze dedications now on view in the new **Museum of the History of the Olympic Games in Antiquity** ★★★ (p. 287). The evening meal at either the Europa or Pelops (by prearrangement) will be better than any served at the mostly tourist-trap places in the village of Olympia.

Day 9: Olympia to Delphi

Try to revisit Olympia's majestic sprawl once more in the early morning before driving from Olympia past the bridge that soars across the Gulf of Corinth, then head inland to **Delphi** ★★★ (p. 484). Along the way, pick one of the beaches on either side of the Gulf of Corinth for lunch and a swim. In Delphi, stroll past the ancient site and enjoy the view across the olive groves to the sea, but save your exploring for tomorrow. For dinner, head to the **Epikouros Restaurant** (p. 493) on the main drag or to the village of Arachova to sit outdoors and enjoy the succulent grills at **Taverna Karathanassi** or **Taverna Dasaryiris** (p. 494). Both are by the cafes in the main square with its lovely freshwater springs.

Day 10: Sanctuary of Apollo

At Delphi, you'll see the **Sanctuary of Apollo** ★★★, with the massive temple of Apollo and a well-restored stadium and theater, and the **Delphi Museum** ★★★, stuffed with some of antiquity's greatest treasures. After a full day's exploration, drive north toward Kalambaka, site of the monasteries of the **Meteora** ★★★ (p. 504). If you want to break up your journey, spend the night en route; lively Lamia, about halfway between Delphi and Meteora, has decent hotels and lots of ouzeries and grill restaurants.

Day 11: The Meteora & Dion
The monasteries of the Meteora give a glimpse of what monastic life must be like—in a setting of incredible natural beauty. The buildings seem to grow from the craggy rocks that soar up to 300m (984 ft.). Don't miss the frescoes of the Garden of Eden in the 14th-century monastery of **Ayios Nikolaos Anapaphsas** ★ (p. 507). Drive to Dion and stay in the modest Hotel Dion or the more sybaritic **Dion Palace Resort Hotel** ★ (p. 504) on the beach at Litochoro. The **Dionysos** restaurant is a good choice for lunch or dinner (p. 619). Then, visit the site of **Dion** ★★, in the foothills of Mount Olympus, where Philip and Alexander trained their armies (p. 618). There are lots of shady trees for a picnic lunch.

Day 12: Vergina & Pella
Drive from Dion to **Thessaloniki** ★★★, stopping at the royal tombs at **Vergina** ★★★ and **Pella** ★, former Macedonian capital and birthplace of Philip of Macedon and his son Alexander the Great (p. 614). The museum at Vergina exhibits the gold items found in the royal tombs. When you get to Thessaloniki (p. 581), drop off your rental car. Having one here is a real inconvenience! Enjoy a drink in **Aristotelous Square** and a stroll along the harbor. Settle into your hotel, then head out for home-style cooking at **Thanasis** ★★★ (p. 609).

Day 13: Thessaloniki
Spend the day strolling the city's streets, taking in the famous **White Tower** ★, ancient monuments, and **Byzantine churches** ★★★ (p. 592). Make a visit to the **Archaeological and Byzantine museums** ★★★, located next to each other (p. 588). Take a bus or cab up to **Ano Poli** ★★★, the old Turkish quarter above the modern city (p. 594). Enjoy the restored houses, the little churches, and the views over the city and out to sea. Stop for lunch in a cafe before strolling back down to the harbor. For dinner, try **Krikelas** ★★, one of the trendy places in the Ladadika district, where old warehouses are boutiques, cafes, and restaurants (p. 608). If you like night life, you're in luck: Thessaloniki's cafes and discos go all night.

Day 14
Fly back to Athens. End your trip with a final stroll beneath the Acropolis.

GREECE WITH A FAMILY

This itinerary works well for families with kids between 7 and 15 years old. We tried to balance the adults' reasons for coming all the way to Greece (seeing the glories of Greece) with the children's desires (swimming in hotel pools). As for food? The varied Greek menu should provide something for everyone's taste. And for better or worse, fast food is increasingly available all over Greece. Heat, especially in high season, should be a concern for travelers of all ages. Stay out of the midday sun, especially on the beach. Most forms of transportation offer reduced rates for kids 11 and under, as do most hotels, museums, and archaeological sites. Our itinerary assumes that you will rent a car for touring the Greek mainland. We also recognize that children wilt faster while traveling than adults do.

Days 1 & 2: Athens

After you arrive in Athens, cool off by getting a day pass to the **Athens Hilton** pool (p. 132). Later, stroll over to the **Acropolis** ★★★ (p. 157). Before and after dinner at **Taverna Sigalas** (p. 144), walk around the **Plaka/Monastiraki** district (p. 109). On Day 2, visit the **National Archaeological Museum** ★★★ (p. 167)—forget the vases and go straight to the gold objects and the statues! Have lunch at the museum's outdoor cafe, or head to the **National Garden** with its cool paths, small zoo, and outdoor dining (p. 178). Later, take in the changing of the guard at the **Tomb of the Unknown Soldier** on Syntagma Square. If no one in your group is flagging, check out **Attica Zoological Park** ★★ (p. 179), which is open until 7pm, or the **Hellenic Cosmos** museum (p. 169) and its interactive exhibits (hours vary). After a rest at your hotel, ride the cable car up Mount Likavitos. Treat yourself to a traditional Greek dinner at the **Rhodia** ★ (p. 150).

Day 3: Mycenae & Nafplion

Rent a car and drive via the Corinth Canal to Nafplion. Early risers with kids might stop at **Water Fun,** a water park near the canal. Otherwise, take at least an hour's detour to visit the **Citadel and the Treasury of Atreus** ★★★ (p. 254) at Mycenae. Tell the kids about the Trojan War, so they can appreciate the tombs here. Plan to eat at **La Petite Planete** ★ (p. 256). At Nafplion, settle in, then perhaps visit the impressive fortress before a swim at the town's Arvanitia beach (p. 245).

Day 4: Epidaurus & Luna Park

Drive to the **Theater at Epidaurus** ★★ (p. 257) and amaze your kids by demonstrating its excellent acoustics. For lunch, **Leonidas** on the approach road (p. 258) is a good bet. Return to Nafplion to swim, then take time to walk around before or after dinner at the reliable **Hellas Restaurant** ★, right on the main square (Plateia Syntagma; p. 250). There are usually lots of children running up and down and young people hanging out at the square. The best ice cream in the Peloponnese is just around the corner at the **Antica Gelateria di Roma.**

Day 5: Olympia

Set off across the interior highway via Tripolis to **Olympia** ★★★, the site of the original Olympic Games (p. 283). Stop for lunch at one of the many small restaurants along the way (the villages of Vitina and Langadia have quite a few). Check into the **Hotel Europa** ★★★ (big pool) in Olympia, or the beachside **Grecotel Olympia Riviera Resort** ★★ (p. 288); for a swim before (and after, too!) visiting ancient Olympia. If the stadium is open, cheer your children on if they want to run the dash along the original Olympic Stadium. After such a long day, it might make sense to dine at your hotel.

Day 6: Delphi & the Sanctuary of Apollo

Spend some time at Olympia before setting off along the coast road to Rio, with its spectacular bridge across the Gulf of Corinth, and continue to Delphi. If you want a pool, check into **Amalia Hotel** ★; or, head for the excellent **Acropole**

or **Varonos** hotels (p. 492). In the cool of the evening, take a walk down to the **Sanctuary of Apollo ★★★** (p. 490). Make a note to be back early to walk along the 2,000-year-old marble path, the Sacred Way. For dinner, try the excellent **Epikouros ★★★**, with its varied menu, or the traditional **Taverna Skala ★** (p. 493).

Day 7: Delphi & Crete

Spend the morning exploring Delphi and its museum. Take a late-afternoon flight from Athens to **Iraklion.** Hit the beach after checking into the **Candia Maris Resort and Spa ★** (p. 307); it's right out the door. The kids can swim or play basketball and tennis. Dine at the hotel or, go into Iraklion for an early dinner at **Ippocampus** (p. 308). With a front-row seat for activity along the harbor, the kids should love the fried zucchini and potato slices. You'll like the seafood.

Day 8: Knossos & Water City

Your hotel can arrange a visit to the Minoan **Palace of Knossos ★★★** (p. 302), one of the great archaeological sites of the world. Kids will appreciate the sheer diversity of the site. After, head for the hotel's beach or **Cretaquarium** p. 303), a water park at Kokkini Hani, just along the highway from the

Xenia-Helios hotel. If they find that too childish, visit the **Cretaquarium** (p. 303), 3.2km (2 miles) further east along that coast road. That night, try dinner at the **Pantheon** (p. 308) in Iraklion's famous Dirty Alley—no longer "dirty" but still atmospheric.

Day 9: Matala/Chania

In a rental car, drive to the caves and bluff-enclosed cove beach at **Matala ★★** (p. 310), once a major hippie destination. Then take the midisland route, with its spectacular scenery, to the **Hotel Porto Veneziano ★** (p. 317) along the harbor of **Chania** and dine at **Amphora ★** (p. 320). But be sure you have made arrangements with a travel agency or through the hotel for the daylong trek through the Samaria Gorge (see below) or the 2-hour *Aphrodite* boat excursion (p. 314).

Day 10: Samaria Gorge

Get up early and don good hiking shoes before you take the bus to undertake the 18km (11-mile) excursion through **Samaria Gorge ★★** (p. 322). It's a long day, and you should make sure your children have hiked before (and that you know their limits). Carry water and snacks, although tavernas await at the end of the gorge. A boat makes the leg from the gorge to a bus that will return you to your hotel. You will probably be too exhausted to dine anywhere except at the hotel. Or, if all this seems too demanding, head to the glass-bottomed boat, the *Aphrodite* (p. 314), for a tour of this area's underwater life. While on the harbor, be sure to visit the replica of an ancient Minoan boat in one of the old Venetian arsenali (p. 315).

Day 11: Santorini

Take the ferry to Santorini (a 5-hr. trip). Check in at a hotel at **Kamari,** if you prefer a beach (p. 349), or at **Oia (Ia),** if you prefer a spectacular view (p. 347). If you have a great view, any meal will be memorable, but if you want something quick and casual, try any of the fast-food places.

Days 12 & 13: Akrotiri & Fira

If it is open, visit the excavated ancient city (nicknamed the "Minoan Pompeii") at **Akrotiri ★★★**: Even jaded kids will be impressed by the three-story, 3,500-year-old houses (p. 344). If it remains closed, enjoy the spectacular site and ruins of **ancient Thira ★★** (p. 345). Then snorkel (or relax) at the beach at **Kamari** (p. 349); or take in the sights of **Fira** (p. 346). On Day 13, take the excursion to the volcanic islet in the caldera—it will probably be your only chance to walk on an emerging volcano (p. 348)! You should also have time to take the cable car from Fira town down to the shore and then come back up by donkey (p. 356) before flying to Athens in the early evening.

Day 14: Athens

For your final day, you have many choices—strolling, window-shopping, perhaps the National Gardens for the kids to have a chance to run around. For lunch, there are plenty of casual places on Syntagma Square, plus a chance to see the changing of the guards in front of the Parliament building. If you want to sit down, try the wide selection of mezedes (snacks) at **Tzitaikas kai Mermigas** on Mitropoleos Street. If you're up to renting a car again, head to the **Temple of Poseidon** at Sounion **★★** for the day and for the sunset (p. 204). Or stay in Athens to rest or sightsee. Top off your stay with dinner at **Thanasis ★** (p. 144) in the Plaka.

CRUISING THE GREEK ISLANDS

by Heidi Sarna

There are few truly perfect cruise-ship destinations in the world, and the Greek isles are one of them. Who can argue with jagged islands crowned by whitewashed villages and harbors of stunning blue sea lapping up against charming beaches and ancient city walls? The sea approach to places like Santorini and Rhodes is really hard to beat. Cruising in Greece is all about gorgeous scenery, ancient historic sites, delicious Mediterranean food, and lots of local culture. You don't have to worry about ferry schedules, driving a car, or changing hotel rooms. You get on the ship, you unpack once, and the vessel is your floating hotel. It's your familiar retreat after a long day of touring or a place to kick back and bask in the Greek sun. Among the most beautiful regions to cruise in all the world, the seas are relatively calm and the islands are individual in character, offering travelers a satisfying mix of local culture, stunning scenery, and ancient and medieval ruins to explore.

Most Greek island itineraries highlight the region's history with optional guided **shore excursions** that take in the major sights, spicing up the vacation brew with other, less history-minded excursions such as visits to beaches, meals at local restaurants, and fishing or sailing excursions.

Of course, you can choose to get off the ship at each port of call and head off on your own to explore the sights, hit the beach, or check out the local color at the nearest taverna. Solo is often the best way to go.

If cruising sounds like a good deal to you, fares can be low due to the worldwide economic downturn (though you may find the airfare to Europe can be high). The region has many cruising options. You can go ultraluxe on a small, yachtlike ship like the *SeaDream I* or übercasual on the *easyCruise Life*. You can choose a classic vessel or a modern megaship. You can choose from cruise lines making new inroads into Greece; other companies build on their current offerings and add new ports.

THE RIGHT CRUISE FOR YOU

In choosing your cruise, you need to think about what you want to see and at what level of comfort you want to see it.

We recommend you first decide **what you want to see.** Are you looking to visit the most popular islands—Mykonos, Santorini, and Rhodes—or are you interested in places off the beaten path? Whichever it is, you'll want to make sure your itinerary allows you enough time to experience the place or places that take your fancy. Some ships visit a port and spend the full day, while others visit two ports in 1 day, which limits your sightseeing time in each (but gives you more overall visits to different places).

Many Greek islands cruises either begin or end their itineraries elsewhere, often Venice or Istanbul, so you'll have to consider which embarkation and disembarkation points in making your decision.

Greece is also visited by ships as part of European itineraries where Greece is one of several countries visited. Most cruise lines like to give their passengers a bit of variety, which means the Greek isles itinerary you're considering might include a day in Alexandria, Egypt, or Dubrovnik, Croatia. This chapter focuses on cruises that spend the better part of the itinerary in Greece and Turkey, but there are lots of other options for Mediterranean cruises that include some Greek ports among a more varied lineup.

You'll also want to think about **what you want out of the cruise experience.** Is the purpose of your cruise to see as much as you can of the islands, or to relax by the ship's pool? And what level of comfort, entertainment, onboard activities, and so forth do you require? Some ships spend a day or more at sea, meaning they don't visit a port at all that day, and while some experienced cruisers enjoy those days the most, treasuring the opportunity they offer for real relaxation, they won't do you much good if your goal is seeing as much of Greece as you can.

Next, consider **how long you want to spend** cruising the islands—3 days, a week, 2 weeks? If you have the time, you may want to consider a **cruise tour,** which combines a cruise to the islands with a guided tour of important sights on the mainland. This is made easy in Greece with some lines offering cruises of only 3 or 4 days, which you can combine with a land tour into a 1-week vacation, and 1-week cruises you can combine with a land tour to make a 2-week vacation.

Also consider **when you want to cruise.** Most of the action on the islands takes place in the warmer months, late May through October; traveling in early spring and late fall has its own special charms, including the fact it allows you to avoid the tourist crush (although some visitor facilities may be closed in the off season) and the hottest months (in July and Aug, temperatures can reach 100°F/38°C). For the record, August is the month the islands are most crowded with vacationers (expect beaches, bars, and discos to be either lively or packed, depending on your point of view). April and November are the rainiest months. May and October are relatively problem-free, making them particularly nice times to sail in Greece.

Choosing Your Ship

The onboard experience changes dramatically depending on how many people and amenities you can fit onto your ship. You can choose anything from a 16-deck, 3,000-passenger ship with a three-story restaurant, ice-skating rink, and minigolf course, to a yachtlike ship for 100 or 200 people where the idea of entertainment is an open sun deck, a novel, and an attendant who drops by periodically with a glass of champagne and some jumbo shrimp. Which you choose has a lot to do with your personality and vacation goals.

MEGASHIPS & LARGE SHIPS Cruises aboard these vessels focus as much on onboard activities as they do on their destination. They are floating resorts—sometimes glitzy—offering American-style luxury and amenities along with attentive service.

These ships, which tend to be newer, feature Las Vegas–style shows, lavish casinos, big spas and gyms, plenty of bars and restaurants, extravagant meals, and lots of daytime activities from water slides and mini golf to goofy pool-side contests. You or your children can take part in games, contests, cooking lessons, wine tastings, and sports tournaments—although generally few ethnic Greek activities are offered.

CLASSIC & MIDSIZE SHIPS   Ships in this category include older, classic vessels as well as newer ships. Destination is more a focus than on the bigger ships, and itineraries may be very busy, with the ship visiting an island a day, or sometimes two. This leaves little time for onboard daytime activities, although some will be offered. In the Greek market, some of these ships feature Greek crews and cuisine, and service tends to be a big area of focus. Because some of these ships are often sold heavily in the European markets, you may hear many languages spoken onboard. The ships offer a variety of bars and lounges, at least one swimming pool and a small casino, a spa and gym, and plenty of open deck space. Entertainment is generally offered in a main show lounge; some ships show films in their cinemas. Some of the ships in this category fall in the luxury camp and offer upscale restaurants, modern spas and cabins with lavish touches, and big, private balconies; other ships are older and definitely more modest.

SMALL & YACHTLIKE SHIPS   These tend to offer a more relaxed pace and may seek itineraries that focus on smaller, alternative ports, which they can get into because of their small size and shallow draft (the amount of ship that rides beneath the waterline). They may offer "soft-adventure" cruise experiences focused on nature- and outdoor-oriented activities; or they may offer an experience more like that of a luxury yacht. Some feature Greek crews and Greek cuisine. On these small ships, there will typically be more interaction with fellow passengers than on larger ships—there's fewer faces to keep track of. There will be fewer entertainment options compared with the big ships, and there may or may not be a swimming pool, casino, spa, or gym. Both cabins and public rooms range from small and serviceable to large and luxurious, depending on the ship. Some ships are fully engine-powered while others are sailing vessels (though these sails are typically more for show than for power).

In addition to the small ships we mention in depth later in this chapter, you may want to look into even smaller yachts, especially if you're seeking a charter or a truly private yachtlike experience. We'll explore this option later in the chapter.

CALCULATING THE COST

Cruises in the Greek islands range from 3 nights to 2 weeks, with starting prices per day ranging from around $100 to more than $800 per person, double occupancy, and going up from there. These days, you can almost always get a rate that's substantially **less than brochure and/or cruise-line website prices.** Like new-car sticker prices, brochure rates are notoriously inflated, so that's why we've listed rates here from a pair of real travel agents, Sherrie and Charlie Funk, owners of **Just Cruisin' Plus** (© **800/888-0922;** www.jcp.travel). Depending on economic conditions and the age-old tenets of supply and demand, you may get a good price, as well a shot at the best cabins, if you book early; alternatively, if you're flexible with the cabin category you might be able to get a good price if you wait until the last minute, when the lines are trying to top up their sailings (cruise ships almost always sail full).

Travel agencies and Web-based agencies, as opposed to booking directly through the cruise lines, will typically offer the best overall deal (see "Booking Your Cruise," below). Depending on demand, you may snag a two-for-one deal or free airfare or onboard credits or hotel stays. No matter what price you end up paying, rates include three meals a day (with a couple of exceptions, which we've noted in the ship reviews), accommodations, most of the onboard activities and entertainment, and, if you book your airfare through the cruise line, a transfer from the airport to the ship. Some rates even include airfare (the inclusion of airfare is more common on European cruises than Caribbean cruises), and in rare cases the fare may include tips, shore excursions, and/or pre- and/or postcruise hotel stays. Some cruises are packaged as cruise tours, meaning the price includes both hotel stays and land tours. With the exception of a handful of high-end lines, don't expect alcoholic beverages to be included in the rates; almost never included are charges for spa and beauty treatments, Internet access, shore excursions, and tips for the crew.

Port charges can run anywhere from around $60 to upwards of $500 per person, depending on the length of your cruise and which ports you visit. These charges will be part of your total cruise fare, but be aware when you're pricing your cruise that although some lines include these charges in the initial base price, some do not. Government taxes and fees are usually excluded from the base rate but will be assessed when your final payment is due.

Cruise prices are based on two people sharing a cabin. Most lines have **single supplement** prices for solo passengers who want their own cabin. The "supplement," in this case, goes to the cruise line as their compensation for not getting two passenger fares for the cabin. At the opposite end, most lines offer highly discounted rates for a third or fourth person sharing a cabin with two full-fare passengers.

Seniors may be able to get extra savings on their cruise. Some lines will take 5% off the top for those 55 and over, and the senior rate applies even if the second person in the cabin is younger. Membership in groups such as AARP is not required, but such membership may bring additional savings.

If your package does not include **airfare,** you might want to consider booking air transportation through the cruise line. While the rates offered by the lines may or may not be as low as you can find on your own, booking through the line allows the cruise company to keep track of you if, for instance, your flight is delayed. In this case, the ship may be able to wait for you, and if it can't wait, it will arrange transportation for you to the next port of call. The cruise lines also negotiate special deals with hotels at port cities if you want to come in a few days before your cruise or stay after it.

In the past several years whenever the price of oil surges, some lines add a **fuel surcharge** on to your tab, which typically ranges from $5 to $10 per person, per day. Be sure to ask when you book.

BOOKING YOUR CRUISE

Today, everybody has a website, and the difference between so-called **Web-based cruise sellers** and more **traditional travel agencies** is that the former rely on their sites for most of their actual bookings, while the latter use theirs as advertising space to promote their offerings and do most of their actual business in person or over the phone. As far as cruise prices go, there's no absolutely quantifiable difference between the live travel agents and Internet-based cruise sellers. Sometimes one or the other, due to them buying or reserving cabins in bulk, can offer you perks like free onboard credits, a bottle of champagne or cabin upgrades. Though there are some loopholes, these days the major cruise lines tout a level playing field, where everybody gets the same price and agents aren't allowed to advertise discounted rates.

In deciding how to book your cruise, consider the value of your time, and your level of experience as a cruiser and as an Internet user. Most websites give you a menu of ships and itineraries to select from, plus a basic search capability that takes into account destination, price, length of trip, and date; some sites aid your search with sophisticated options such as interactive deck plans and ship reviews. If you've cruised before and know what you want, no problem. If, on the other hand, you have limited experience with cruising or with booking on the Web, or your time could be better used elsewhere, it may be better to go through a traditional agent (such as Just Cruisin Plus, who supplied the rates for this book), who can help you wade through the choices and answer your questions, from which cabins have their views obstructed by lifeboats to information on dining, tuxedo rentals, onboard kids programs, and cuisine.

A travel agent can also help you book airfare to and from the ship, and hotels and sightseeing trips before or after your cruise. No matter which way you wind up booking your cruise, you may want to first check out the cruise-line websites and browse the Internet for ship reviews, virtual tours, chats, and industry news.

To find an agent, rely on referrals from trusted friends and colleagues. Some agents (such as Just Cruisin Plus), really know the business—they travel themselves to sample what they sell and can reel off the differences between cabins on Deck 7 and Deck 8 down to where the towel racks are placed—while others are not much more than order-takers. Start looking as soon as you can, which can result in early booking rates and the best cabin choices.

Choosing a Cabin

One of your biggest decisions is what type of cabin you need. Will you be happy with a slightly cramped space without a window (the most budget-minded choice); a cabin with a private balcony; or a suite with a dining room, hot tub, and a personal butler?

Obviously, price will determine your choice. If you don't plan to spend time in your cabin except to sleep, shower, and change clothes, an **inside cabin** (one without a porthole or window) might do just fine. If you get claustrophobic; or if you insist on sunshine first thing in the morning; or if you intend to hole up in your cabin for extended periods, pay a bit more and take an **outside cabin,** which have windows—or pay a bit more and take one with a **private balcony,** where you can open the door and feel the sea breezes. On smaller or older ships, your choice might be limited to inside and outside cabins, some with the old-style porthole windows. Newer ships will have balconies on the majority of cabins, making them more affordable than ever.

One concern if you do go the window route is **obstructed views.** This isn't an issue with newer ships because the lifeboats are housed on the decks containing the public spaces like restaurants and lounges; the passenger cabins are either above or below those decks. But check to make sure none of the cabins in the category you've selected have windows that directly face lifeboats or other objects that may block your view of the clear blue sea. You can determine this by looking at a diagram of the ship (included in the cruise brochure or found online) or by consulting with your travel agent.

Most ships offer cabins for two with private bathroom and shower. (Bathtubs are considered a luxury on most ships and are usually offered only in the most expensive cabins.) These days, most ships have a double bed, or twin beds that may be convertible to a queen. Other variations are cabins with bunk beds (referred to as "upper and lower berths"), cabins designed for three or four people, and connecting cabins for families. Many lines—including Oceania, Holland America, and Regent—feature fluffy mattresses and soft down duvets.

Cabin amenities vary by line, and often include TVs (with a closed system of programmed movies and features and the occasional news channel), DVD players, hair dryers, safes, and minirefrigerators. If any of these are must-haves, let your agent know. Cruise lines tend to one-up their amenities pretty often, so it's possible your cabin may have a flat-panel LCD TV, a powerful hair dryer, brand-name toiletries, and fresh flowers or fruit awaiting you on arrival.

Usually the higher on the ship the cabin is located, the more expensive it is. But upper decks also tend to be rockier in rough seas than the middle or lower parts of the ship, a factor to consider if you're prone to seasickness.

The **size of a cabin** is determined by square feet. Keep in mind that ship cabins are generally smaller than the equivalent hotel rooms you'd find on land. As a rough guide, 11 sq. m (120 sq. ft.) is low end and cramped, 17 sq. m (180 sq. ft.) is midrange and fairly roomy, and 23 sq. m (250 sq. ft.) and larger is suite size and very comfortable.

If noise bothers you, pick a cabin far from the engine room and nowhere near the disco.

4 Mealtimes: Early, Late, or Anytime

Dining on cruise ships has undergone a revolution in the past decade or so. Traditionally, guests ate in the large dining room, at the same time and at the same table every night. Today, you can still dine the traditional way—many ships offer that as the default preference (if not the only preference). But there are several variations on the mealtime theme now, from complete open seating to separate restaurants specializing in seafood or steaks to proper en suite dining.

For traditional dining, because most ship dining rooms are not large enough to accommodate all passengers at one dinner seating, dining times and tables are assigned. When you book your trip, you will also indicate your preferred mealtime. Early, or "main," seating is usually at 6 or 6:30pm, late seating at 8 or 8:30pm. Lines catering to a majority of European clientele may offer seatings an hour or so later than these. Some of the bigger lines offer four staggered seatings, which gives you more choice and eliminates some of the crowding at the dining room door.

There are advantages to both times. **Early seating** is usually less crowded, and it's the preferred time for families and older passengers who want to get to bed early. Since the waiters know that the second wave is coming, they may be rushed. On the other hand, early diners get first dibs on nighttime entertainment venues, and might be hungry enough in a few hours to take advantage of a midnight buffet. **Late seating** allows time for a nap or late spa appointment before dinner, especially if you're returning to the ship from a full day in port. Service is slower paced, and you can linger with after-dinner drinks, then catch the late show at 10pm.

When choosing a mealtime, you also need to consider **table size** (on most ships, you can request to be at a table for 2, 4, 8, 10, or 12), though sometimes it's tough to snag a table for two since they're usually in great demand. On the other hand, many cruisers appreciate the fun that comes from sitting around a big table and talking up your adventures of the day. Most dining rooms are **nonsmoking,** so there's generally no need to request a smoking or nonsmoking table. You can request a different table when you get onboard, too.

If your ship has **open-seating** arrangements, you can dine at any hour the restaurant is open. You also choose your dinner partners, or you can ask the maitre d' to sit you with other guests. Open seating can feel more casual and less regimented. Open seating arrangements are typically offered on the smaller and/or most upscale lines, although now some of the majors offer this option as well. The pioneer in the big-ship category is Norwegian Cruise Line, which now builds its ships with up to 10 different restaurants. Princess Cruises, Celebrity Cruises, and Holland America Line, for example, have a hybrid dining policy: Passengers choose whether they want the traditional seating or the open plan, and then show up at the restaurants accordingly.

Most ships now also have at least one or two restaurants separate—in location, cuisine, and atmosphere—from the main dining room. These so-called **specialty restaurants** or **alternative restaurants** are open seating, so you can choose your dinnertime and dining companions. If you'd like to try an evening or two at these restaurants, make reservations in advance. A per-person cover charge, typically in the $20 to $30 range, often applies, so you should check in advance.

On most ships, **breakfast** and **lunch** are open seating. Most vessels also have buffet restaurants, where you can choose to have both meals at any time during open hours.

Inform the cruise line at the time you make your reservations if you have any **special dietary requests.** Kosher menus, vegetarian, low fat, low salt, low carb, "spa," and sugar-free are some of the options available.

Deposits, Cancellations & Extras

After you've made your decision about what ship you will vacation on, you will be required to put down a deposit if you're booking 2 or more months in advance (with the remaining fare usually paid no later than 2 months in advance of your departure date); or you must pay the entire fare if you're booking within 60 or 70 days of your sailing date.

Note: Cruise lines have varying policies regarding cancellations, and it's important to look at the fine print in the brochure or agency website to make sure you understand the policy. Most lines allow you to cancel for a full refund on your deposit and payment any time up to about 70 days before the sailing, after which you have to pay a penalty (a few lines charge an administrative fee if you cancel your cruise less than 120 days before departure, and some levy a cancellation fee once the deposit is made regardless of the sailing date). If you cancel at the last minute, you likely will lose the entire fare you paid, unless you bought trip-cancellation or -interruption insurance.

An agent will discuss with you optional **airline arrangements** offered by the lines, **transfers** from the airport to the pier, and any pre- or postcruise **hotel or tour programs.** Some lines also let you purchase **shore excursions** in advance (for more on shore excursions, see the section later in this chapter). And you may also be able to prebook certain onboard spa services.

If you are not booking airfare through the cruise line, make sure to allow several hours between the plane's arrival and the time you must board the ship. To reduce anxiety, it may be best to fly in the day before and spend the night in a hotel.

CRUISE PREPARATION PRACTICALITIES

About 1 month before your cruise and no later than 1 week before, you should receive your **cruise documents,** including your airline tickets (if you purchased them from the cruise line), a boarding document with your cabin number and sometimes dining choices on it, boarding forms to fill out, luggage tags, and your prearranged bus-transfer vouchers and hotel vouchers (if applicable). Some lines offer some or all of these documents and forms online. You'll save time checking in at the cruise terminal if you've filled out your boarding documents online.

There will also be information about **shore excursions** and additional material detailing things you need to know before you sail. Most lines also list excursions on their websites and allow you to book shore excursions in advance of your sailing online, which will give you first dibs at popular offerings that may sell out later.

Read all of this pretrip information carefully. Make sure your cabin category and dining preferences are what you requested, and that your flight and arrival times are what you were told. If there are problems, call your agent immediately. Make sure there is enough time so you can arrive at the port no later than an hour before departure.

You will be required to have a passport for your trip (see chapter 18 for more on this). If you are flying into Istanbul, you will also be required to have a Turkish visa, which can be easily obtained upon arrival at Istanbul airport for about $20.

Confirm your flight 3 days before departure. Also, before you leave for the airport, tie the tags provided by the cruise line onto your luggage and fill in your boarding cards. This will save you time when you arrive at the ship.

Cash Matters

You already paid for a good portion of your vacation when you paid for your cruise, but you will still need a credit card and perhaps bring along some cash, to handle your **onboard expenses** such as bar drinks, dry cleaning and laundry, e-mail, spa services, salon services, photos taken by the ship's photographer, babysitting, wine at dinner, souvenirs, shore excursions, specialty restaurant charges, and tips (see below for more on tipping). On most lines, you'll use your cabin key card as a charge card. Prepare to spend at least $200 and easily $600 to $800 per person on a weeklong cruise for "extras"—or more, depending on how much you drink, shop, love massages, and spend in the casino, and how many shore excursions you purchase during the cruise.

Some ships (but not all) will take a personal check for onboard expenses. If you want to pay in cash, you will be asked to leave a deposit. Some ships have ATMs, and some (but not all) offer currency-exchange services.

We suggest you keep careful track of your onboard expenses to avoid an unpleasant surprise at the end of your cruise. You can get this information at the purser's office or guest-relations desk.

You will want to have some cash in hand when going ashore for expenses, including taxis, snacks or meals, drinks, small purchases, and tips for guides.

Packing

Generally, ships describe their **daily recommended evening attire** as casual, informal, and formal, prompting many people to think they'll have to bring a steamer trunk full of clothes. Not true; you can probably get along with about half of what you think you need. Almost all ships offer laundry and dry-cleaning services, and some have coin-operated self-serve laundries, so you have the option of packing less and having your clothes cleaned midway through your trip.

During the day, the onboard style is casual, but keep in mind that some ships do not allow swimsuits or tank tops in the dining room. If your ship operates under the "traditional" dress codes, you can expect two formal dinners and two informal nights during a 5- to 7-day cruise, with the rest casual (or more typical these days, 1 or 2 formal nights and all the rest casual). There will usually be proportionally more formal nights on longer cruises.

The daily bulletin delivered to your cabin each day will advise you of the proper dress code for the evening. **Formal** means a tux or dark suit with tie for men and a cocktail dress, long dress, gown, or dressy pantsuit for women. **Informal** is a jacket with or without a tie, and dress slacks or a light suit for men and a dress, skirt with blouse, or pants outfit for women. **Casual** means different things to different people. Typically it means a sports shirt or open dress shirt with slacks for men; women can wear skirts, dresses, or pants outfits. Jeans and shorts are usually frowned upon.

Check your cruise documents to determine the number of formal nights (if any) during your cruise. Men who don't own a tuxedo might be able to rent one in advance through the cruise line's preferred supplier (who delivers the tux to the ship). Information on this service often is sent with your cruise documents. Also, some cruises offer **theme nights,** so you may want to check your cruise documents to see if there are any you'll want to bring special clothes for. (For instance, Greek Night means everyone wears blue and white—the Greek national colors.)

Having said all this about formal and informal, you might not even need to know about it: A few lines, especially the smaller, more casual ships, have an all-casual policy, meaning slacks and sundresses at night are as dressy as you need to be; others are "formal-optional," which gives you the option of dressing up (or not). If you're one of those people who refuses to wear a tie on vacation, consider that many lines also offer a casual alternative during formal evenings, such as dining in the buffet restaurant or in your cabin.

If you want to bring the crown jewels, be careful. If you're not wearing them, leave them either in your in-room safe (if there is one) or with the purser.

In general, during the day in Greece you're best off packing loose and comfortable cotton or other lightweight fabrics. You'll also want to pack a swimsuit, a sun hat, sunglasses, and plenty of sunscreen—the Greek sun can be intense. Adjust your wardrobe depending on when you plan to travel. Even if you're traveling in August, though, you should bring a sweater, as you'll be in and out of air-conditioning. And don't forget an umbrella.

For shore excursions, good walking shoes are a must, as some excursions involve walking on stone or marble. Also, some tours may visit religious sites that have a "no shorts or bare shoulders" policy, so it's best to bring something to cover up with. (If you're taking the tour through the cruise line, you'll be advised of this before you go.)

If you plan on bringing your own hair dryer, electric razor, curling iron, or other electrical device, check out the ship's electric current in advance. An adapter may be required. Because of the risk of fire, items like irons are prohibited; ask your cabin steward about pressing services or bring a portable steamer.

EMBARKATION

Check-in is usually 2 to 3 hours before sailing. You will not be able to board the ship before the scheduled embarkation time. You have up until a half-hour (on some ships it's 1 hr.) before sailing to embark.

At check-in, your boarding documents will be checked and your passport will likely be taken for immigration processing. You will get it back sometime during the cruise. (Make a photocopy and carry that as backup.) Depending on the cruise line, you may establish your **onboard credit account** at this point by presenting a major credit card or making a deposit in cash or traveler's checks. On other ships you need to go to the purser's office onboard to establish your account.

You may be given your **dining-room table assignment** in advance of your sailing (on your tickets) or as you check in, or find a card with your table number waiting for you in your stateroom. If you do not receive an assignment by the time you get to your stateroom, you will be directed to a maitre d's desk. This is also the place to make any changes if your assignment does not meet with your approval.

DEALING with SEASICKNESS

If you suffer from seasickness, plan on packing **Bonine** or **Dramamine** in case your ship encounters rough seas. Keep in mind that with both these medications, it is recommended you not drink alcohol; Dramamine in particular can make you drowsy. Both can be bought over the counter. Ships stock supplies onboard, either at the purser's office, at the medical center, or in the gift shop.

Another option is the **Transderm patch,** available by prescription only, which goes behind your ear and time-releases medication. The patch can be worn for up to 3 days, but it comes with all sorts of side-effect warnings. Some people have had success in curbing sea-sickness with **ginger capsules** available at health-food stores. You might also try the **acupressure wristbands** available at most pharmacies. When set in the proper spot on the wrist, they effectively ease seasickness, although if the seas are particularly rough they may have to be supplemented with medication.

Once you're aboard, a crew member will show you to your cabin and, on the smaller high-end lines, will probably offer to carry your hand luggage. No tip is required for this service, though feel free to slip the steward a few bucks if you're feeling generous.

In your cabin, you will find a **daily program** detailing the day's events, mealtimes, and so forth, as well as important information on the ship's **safety procedures** and possibly its **deck plan.** Deck plans and directional signs are posted around the ship, generally at main stairways and elevators.

Tip: If you plan to use the ship's **spa services,** it's best to stop by as soon as you board the ship to make appointments so you can get your preferred times. (The best times, particularly the slots during the days at sea, go fast, and some popular treatments sell out.) Ditto dropping by the **shore excursions desk** if you plan to purchase an excursion. Even better, some lines allow you to prebook shore excursions or spa treatments online before you board the ship.

Note: The ship's casino and shops are always closed when the ship is in port, and the fresh- or saltwater swimming pool(s) could be covered.

Some lines offer **escorted tours** of the public rooms to get you acquainted with the ship. Check the daily program in your cabin for details.

Lifeboat/Safety Drill

Ships are required by law to conduct safety drills the first day out. Most do this either right before the ship sails or shortly thereafter. At the start of the drill, the ship will broadcast its emergency signal. You will then be required to return to your cabin (if you're not there), grab your **life jacket** (which you're shown as soon as you arrive in your cabin), and report to your assigned muster station—outside along the promenade deck, or in a lounge or other public room. A notice on the back of your cabin door will list the procedures and advise you as to your assigned **muster station** and how to get there. You will also find directions to the muster station in the hallway. You will be alerted as to the time of the drill in both the daily program and in repeated public announcements (and probably by your cabin steward as well). If you hide out in your cabin to avoid the drill, you'll likely get a knock by the cabin steward reminding you to please join the others.

If you're **traveling with children,** make sure your cabin is equipped with special children's life jackets. If not, alert your steward.

END-OF-CRUISE PROCEDURES

Your shipboard account will close in the wee hours before departure, but prior to that time you will receive a preliminary bill in your cabin. If you are settling your account with your credit card, you don't have to do anything except make sure all the charges are correct. If there is a problem, report it to the purser's office.

If you are paying by cash or traveler's check, you will be asked to settle your account either during the day or night before you leave the ship. This will require a trip to the purser's office. A final invoice will be delivered to your room before departure.

Tips

You can bet you'll find tipping suggestions in your cabin on the last day of your cruise. These are only suggestions, but since service personnel make most (or all) of their salaries through tips, we don't recommend tipping less—unless, of course, bad service warrants it. (On some very upscale lines, acceptance of tips is strictly forbidden.)

Most cruise lines now **automatically add gratuities** to your shipboard account; and other lines will add gratuities to your bill on a request basis. It typically adds up to about $12 per person, per day. This takes a little of the personal touch out of tipping, but then again, you don't have to worry about running around with envelopes of cash on the last night of your vacation. Check with your cruise line to see if they offer automatic tipping. If you prefer to tip the crew in person or in cash, your ship should be able to cancel the automatic tips. There's also nothing wrong with tipping your cabin steward or waiter on top of the automatic tips.

If you do decide to tip the crew on your own, the cruise line will provide suggested minimums. Generally, each passenger should usually tip his or her cabin steward and waiter about $4 per day each, and the assistant waiter about $2. That minimum comes to about $70 for a 7-day cruise. You are, of course, free to tip more. On some European ships, the suggested minimums are even less. The reason: Europeans aren't us used to tipping as Americans. On some ships you are encouraged to tip the maitre d' and headwaiter. You may also encounter cases where tips are pooled: You hand over a suggested amount and it's up to the crew to divide it among themselves. Bar bills often automatically include a 15% tip, but if the wine steward, for instance, has served you exceptionally well, you can slip him or her a bill, too. If you have spa or beauty treatments, you can tip that person at the time of the service (though make sure a tip was not already automatically added on to the bill before you write one in).

Don't tip the captain or other officers. They're professional, salaried employees.

The porters who carry your bags at the pier will expect a tip.

Packing Up

Because of the number of bags being handled, big ships require guests to pack the night before departure and leave their bags in the hallway, usually by midnight. (Be sure they're tagged with the cruise line's luggage tags, which are color-coded to indicate deck number and disembarkation order.) The bags will be picked up overnight and removed from the ship before passengers are allowed to disembark. (Don't pack bottles or other breakables; luggage is often thrown from bin to bin as it's being off-loaded.) You'll see them again in the cruise terminal, where they'll most likely be arranged by deck number. **Reminder:** When you're packing that last night, be sure to leave at least one extra change of clothing, as well as necessary toiletries, in the cabin with you.

Tip: Pack all your purchases in one suitcase. This way you can easily retrieve them if you're stopped at Customs.

LARGE & MIDSIZE SHIPS

In this section, we describe the ships offering cruises with predominantly Greek islands itineraries; that is, itineraries where at least half of the port calls are in Greece and Turkey. We've broken the offerings up into two categories, based on ship size: Mega- and midsize ships (more than 400 passengers), and small and yachtlike vessels (anywhere from 40 to 400 passengers).

The lines are listed alphabetically within each category. Working with travel agents Sherrie and Charlie Funk, owners of Just Cruisin' Plus ($\textcircled{C}$ 800/888-0922; www.jcp. travel), we present a sample of the *actual prices* people are paying for cruises aboard all the ships in this chapter (as opposed to the often-inflated **brochure** or cruise-line website fares). We priced summer 2012 cruises in June 2011, and fares are based on two people sharing a cabin, unless otherwise noted. With a few exceptions, most of these rates were quoted in U.S. dollars.

The **itineraries** we list are also for the 2012 season unless otherwise stated. Both prices and itineraries are subject to change.

We've listed the **sizes of ships** in two ways: **passenger capacity** and **gross registered tons (GRTs).** Rather than describing actual weight, the latter is a measure of interior space used to produce revenue on a vessel. One GRT equals 100 cubic feet/2.83 cubic m) of enclosed, revenue-generating space.

Note that we've listed Athens as a port of call for many cruises, but in most cases you'll actually be calling in **Piraeus,** the port city for Athens. Other popular embarkation ports include Istanbul, Turkey; Venice, Italy; and Civitavecchia, Italy, about an hour's drive from Rome.

AZAMARA CLUB CRUISES

1050 Caribbean Way, Miami, FL 33132. $\textcircled{C}$**877/999-9553.** www.azamaracruises.com.

Azamara and its two midsize gems, *Azamara Journey* (built in 2000; 710 passengers, 30,277 GRTs) and sister *Azamara Quest* (built in 2000; 710 passengers, 30,277 GRTs), were originally built for now-defunct Renaissance Cruises. The twins straddle the mainstream and luxury segments of the cruise biz—somewhere between Celebrity and Crystal or Regent, though closer to the luxury end and geared to adults (there is no formal kids programming). Fares include complimentary house wines at lunch and dinner, free gratuities, free specialty coffees and bottled wines, and a good number of overnights in port and high-end excursions. The mood is casually elegant. On the Pool Deck, enjoy a quiet jazz trio and a harpist plays in the cafe, and overall, service is tops, from the butlers who attend to all cabins to little touches such as the cold towels offered at the gangway after a hot day in port. Dining feels high end and is open seating at the ships' three restaurants for optimal flexibility. Activities run from the usual (bingo, napkin folding, team trivia) to the unusual, including poetry reading/writing get-togethers and seminars on etiquette and art. Evenings, catch a cabaret, comedy or magic act, or enjoy a late-night movie or drinks and conversation.

Azamara Club Cruises Itineraries & Rates

SHIP	ITINERARY
Azamara Quest	**Seven-day round-trip Athens** cruise calls at Ephesus/Kusadasi (Turkey), Kos, Rhodes, Santorini, Chania, Nauplion. July 8. Rates: From $1,999. **Seven-day Athens to Istanbul** cruise calls at Hydra, Santorini, Mykonos (overnight), Patmos, Lesbos, Istanbul (overnight). July 15. Rates: From $1, 999. **Eleven-day Athens to Venice** cruise calls at Ephesus/Kusadasi (Turkey), Mykonos, Santorini, Chania, Olympia/Katakolon, Corfu, Kotor (Montenegro), Dubrovnik (Croatia), Hvar (Croatia), Venice (overnight). Rates: From $2,899.
Azamara Journey	**Eleven-day Rome (Civitavecchia, Italy) to Athens** cruise calls at Sorrento (Italy, overnight), Capri (Italy, overnight), Amalfi (Italy), Taormina (Sicily, Italy), Siracusa (Sicily, Italy), Santorini, Ephesus/Kusadasi (Turkey), Mykonos, Athens (overnight). October 4. Rates: From $2,699. **Eleven-day round-trip Athens** cruise calls at Nazareth/Galilee (Haifa, Israel), Jerusalem/Tel Aviv (Ashdod, Israel, overnight), Cairo/Giza (Alexandria, Egypt, overnight), Rhodes, Ephesus/Kusadasi (Turkey), Mykonos. October 15. Rates: From $2,699. **Ten-day Athens to Sokhna** (Egypt) cruise calls at Ephesus/Kusadasi (Turkey), Kos, Rhodes, Paphos, Nazareth/Galilee (Haifa, Israel), Jerusalem/Tel Avia (Ashdod, Israel, overnight), Cairo/Giza (Alexandria, Egypt), Suez Canal. October 26. Rates: From $2,299.

Celebrity Cruises

1050 Caribbean Way, Miami, FL 33132. © **800/437-3111.** www.celebrity.com.

Celebrity's got some of the industry's most stylish and chic ships, vessels that successfully marry innovation (from real grass lawns up on deck to glass blowing studios, art collections and craft beer bars) with gorgeous design, all for a decent price. Considered a premium U.S. operator (along with Holland America and Princess), Celebrity offers eastern Mediterranean itineraries that for the most part operate on *Equinox* (built in 2009; 2,850 passengers; 122,000 GRTs) and newer sister *Silhoutte* (built in 2011; 2,850 passengers; 122,000 GRTs). The pair are part of the line's newest and biggest class of ship; a sophisticated mix of ultramodern and classic, spacious, and sleek, but not superflashy. Both are outfitted in muted woods, beiges, and artistically applied bold color accents. The ships have panoramic ocean views on nearly every cabin, and most staterooms have a veranda. The ships have plenty of spots in which to relax, including the lawn, spa, elegant bars and lounges, or the Oasis pool, with its retractable roof. If you're splurging, book a Sky Suite on Deck 12 for their extra large, 17 sq. m (179-sq.-ft.) balconies. The *Constellation* (built in 2002; 1,950 passengers; 91,000 GRTs) is a smaller but equally attractive ship, recently renovated and it now offers a new **Tuscan Grille** steakhouse, martini bar, bistro and a martini bar with a permafrost bar top. Also, don't miss a gourmet meal in the **Ocean Liners** restaurant, a classic alternative dining venue that boasts artifacts from a variety of historic liners.

Service and cuisine are key with Celebrity. Little luxuries include chilled towels when you return from a day of port exploration and once per cruise, complimentary sorbets at poolside. The line, long known for its culinary focus, offers several specialty restaurants on its ships as well as a main dining room where you can choose to dine in the traditional early or late paradigm, or take advantage of a flexible program, where you can make a reservation for the time that suits your party best.

Celebrity Cruises Itineraries & Rates

SHIP	ITINERARY
Celebrity Silhouette	**Thirteen-day Rome (Civitavecchi) to Venice** cruise calls at Naples/Capri (Sorrento, Italy), Catania (Sicily, Italy), Valletta (Malta), Mykonos, Athens, Ephesus/Kusadasi (Turkey), Rhodes, Santorini, Chania, Venice (Italy, overnight). May 5, July 17. Rates: From $1,749. **Twelve-day Rome (Civitavecchia) to Venice** cruise calls at Naples/Capri (Sorrento, Italy), Catania (Sicily, Italy), Mykonos, Athens, Ephesus/Kusadasi (Turkey), Rhodes, Santorini, Chania, Venice (Italy, overnight). June 12. Rates: From $1,849.
Celebrity Equinox	**Ten-day round-trip Civitavecchi** cruise calls at Messina (Sicily, Italy), Athena, Ephesus/Kusadasi (Turkey), Rhodes, Santorini, Mykonos, Naples/Capri (Sorrento, Italy). May 11. Rates: From $1,299. **Ten-day round-trip Rome** (Civitavecchia) cruise calls at Chania, Santorini, Athens, Rhodes, Ephesus/Kusadasi (Turkey), Mykonos, Naples/Capri (Sorrento, Italy). June 1, June 22; July 13; August 3, August 24; September 14, October 5, October 26; November 16 Rates: From $1,119.
Celebrity Constellation	**Twelve-day round-trip Istanbul** cruise calls at Istanbul (Turkey, overnight), Ephesus/Kusadasi (Turkey), Marmaris (Turkey), Rhodes, Bodrum (Turkey), Rhodes, Mykonos, Athens, Santorini, Chania. September 19. Rates: From $1,459. **Twelve-day round-trip Istanbul** cruise calls at Istanbul (Turkey, overnight), Ephesus/Kusadasi (Turkey), Bodrum (Turkey), Marmaris (Turkey), Rhodes, Santorini, Athens, Mykonos, Chania. October 1, October 13. Rates: From $1,279.

Costa Cruise Lines

Venture Corporate Center II, 200 S. Park Rd., Hollywood, FL 33021. ℭ **877/88-COSTA** (882-6782). www.costacruises.com.

Fun and full of passion, Costa is an Italian line tracing its origins from 1860 and the Italian olive-oil business. Today it's among the most modern lines out there. These days Costa is owned by Carnival Corporation, parent of Carnival Cruise Lines, and you may recognize the colorful, flamboyant interiors. Many of both lines' ships were designed by interior designer Joe Farcus. However, aboard a Costa ship, Italy shows through in nearly everything, from the food to the Italian-speaking crew (although many are not from Italy), to the mostly Italian entertainers.

The line's ships represent one of the newer fleets in the industry, sporting blue-and-yellow smokestacks emblazoned with a huge letter C. And the fleet is growing fast: the past decade has seen seven new ships. The product is popular in the U.S./Caribbean market but is not designed strictly for a North American audience, and therein lies the charm. In Europe, the ships attract a good share of Italian and French passengers, so don't be surprised if your tablemates speak limited English.

Entertainment includes Italian cooking and language classes. The line also offers an activities program for kids and teens.

Costa Classica (built in 1991; 1,308 passengers; 53,000 GRTs) is a downright cozy breath of fresh air in the mega-world of giant ships, with public rooms and decks inspired by and named after iconic elements of Italian heritage.

Costa Deliziosa (built in 2009; 2,260 passengers; 92,000 GRTs) is an exciting ship with avant-garde style interiors incorporating marble, wood, mother-of-pearl, Murano glass and lots of art. High-tech features include a 4-D cinema, in-line skating track, golf simulator with putting green, and a Grand Prix race-car simulator.

CostaFortuna (built in 2004; 2,720 passengers; 105,000 GRTs) is a glitzy, modern cruise vessel that offers cabins with balconies; multiple bars, lounges, and eateries; swimming pools; a large kids' play area; and a themed decor—in this case, the great Italian ocean liners of yore. Public rooms are named after legendary Italian ships, such as the Rex Theater and the Restaurant Michelangelo. Check out the miniature fleet of Costa ships affixed to the ceiling of the bar in *Fortuna*'s atrium.

Costa Magica (built in 2004; 2,672 passengers; 102,587 GRTs) is the sister ship with similar appointments.

Costa Mediterranea (built in 2003; 2,114 passengers; 85,619 GRTs) was designed to reflect Italy's 17th- and 18th-century *palazzai* and castles, and it does feel palatial.

Costa Pacifica (built in 2009; 3,000 passengers; 114,147 GRTs) manages to be elegant and opulent without going over the top. It offers an abundance of bars and lounges all with a musical theme. Some unusual amenities include a music studio, Grand Prix simulator, and Virtual World that offers PlayStation games.

Costa Romantica (built in 1993; 1,356 passengers; 53,000 GRTs) is the sister ship of Costa Classica with similar appointments.

Costa Serena (built in 2007; 2,930 passengers; 114,500 GRTs), a sister of the *Pacifica*, is flamboyant with a fun space-age design that's whimsically merged with every architectural theme in the book, then candy coated with a hodgepodge of rainbow hues that make Antoni Gaudi seem conservative.

Costa Cruises Itineraries & Rates

SHIP	ITINERARY
Costa Classica	**Seven-day round-trip Trieste** cruise calls at Ancona (Italy), Mykonos, Athens, Corfu, Dubrovnik (Croatia). May 19, May 26, June 2, June 9, June 16, June 23, June 30, July 7, July 14, July 21, July 28, August 4, August 11, August 18, August 25, September 1, September 8, September 15, September 22, September 29, October 6, October 13, October 20, October 27, November 3, November 10, November 17. Rates: From $649.
Costa Deliziosa	**Eight-day round-trip Civitavecchia** (Italy) cruise calls at Savona (Italy), Olympia/Katakolon, Athens, Valletta (Malta), Tunis (Tunisia). December 20. Rates: From $959. Eight-day round-trip Savona (Italy) cruise calls at Olympia/Katakolon, Athens, Valletta (Malta), Tunis (Tunisia), Rome (Civitavecchia, Italy). December 21. Rates: From $879. **Eight-day round-trip Civitavecchia** (Italy) cruise calls at Savona (Italy), Naples/Capri (Italy), Tunis (Tunisia), Olympia/Katakolon, Athens. December 28. Rates: From $1,139. Eight-day round-trip Savona (Italy) cruise calls at Naples/Capri (Italy), Tunis (Tunisia), Olympia/Katakolon, Athens. December 29. Rates: From $1,099.
Costa Fortuna	**Ten-day round-trip Savona** (Italy) cruise calls at Naples/Capri (Italy), Messina (Sicily, Italy), Cairo/Giza (Alexandria, Egypt), Limassol (Cyprus), Marmaris (Turkey), Santorini, Olympia/Katakolon. September 12, September 22; October 2, October 12, October 22; November 1, November 11. Rates: From $1,029.
Costa Magica	**Ten-day round-trip Marseilles** (France) cruise calls at Florence/Pisa (Livorno, Italy), Palermo (Sicily, Italy), Athens, Izmis (Turkey), Rhodes, Valletta (Malta). April 21; May 1, May 11; September 13, September 23; October 3, October 13, October 23; November 2. Rates: From $1,299.

SHIP	ITINERARY
Costa Mediterranea	**Eleven-day round-trip Civitavecchia** (Italy) cruise calls at Olympia/Katakolon, Athens, Izmir (Turkey), Jerusalem/Tel Aviv (Ashdod, Israel), Cairo (Port Said, Egypt), Cairo/Giza (Alexandria, Egypt). April 3; May 30; July 15; August 6, August 28; October 24; November 15. Rates: From $979. **Thirteen-day round-trip Rome** (Civitavecchia, Italy) cruise calls at Savona (Italy, Olympia/Katakolon, Mykonos), Izmir (Turkey), Constanta (Romania), Odessa (Ukraine), Yalta (Ukraine), Athens. May 17. Rates: From $1,999. **Eleven-day round-trip Rome** (Civitavecchia, Italy) cruise calls at Savona (Italy), Olympia/Katakolon, Athens, Izmir (Turkey), Rhodes, Limassol (Cyprus), Cairo/Giza (Alexandria, Egypt). June 10. Rates: From $1,699. **Eleven-day round-trip Savona** (Italy) cruise calls at Olympia/Katakolon, Athens, Izmir (Turkey), Jerusalem/Tel Aviv (Ashdod, Israel), Cairo (Port Said, Egypt), Cairo/Giza (Alexandria, Egypt), Rome (Civitavecchia, Italy). April 4; May 31; July 16; August 6. Rates: From $1,259. **Thirteen-day round-trip Savona** (Italy) cruise calls at Olympia/Katakolon, Mykonos, Izmir (Turkey), Istanbul (Turkey), Constanta (Romania), Odessa (Ukraine), Yalta (Ukraine), Athens, Rome (Civitavecchia, Italy). May 18; July 3; September 9. Rates: From $1,969. **Eleven-day round-trip Savona** (Italy) cruise calls at Olympia/Katakolon, Athens, Izmir (Turkey), Rhodes, Limassol (Cyprus), Cairo/Giza (Alexandria, Egypt), Rome (Civitivecchia, Italy). June 11; September 22. Rates: From $1,579.
Costa Pacifica	**Eleven-day round-trip Savona** (Italy) cruise calls at Olympia/Katakolon, Athens, Izmir (Turkey), Jerusalem/Tel Aviv (Ashdod, Israel), Cairo (Port Said, Egypt), Rome (Civitavecchia, Italy). March 28; April 19, April 30; October 4, October 15, October 26; November 6, November 17. Rates: From $1,239. **Eleven-day round-trip Savona** (Italy) cruise calls at Olympia/Katakolon, Athens, Izmir (Turkey), Nazareth/Galilee (Haifa, Israel), Cairo (Port Said, Egypt), Cairo/Giza (Alexandria, Egypt), Rome (Civitavecchia, Italy). April 8; September 12, September 23. Rates: From $1,279. **Eleven-day round-trip Rome** (Civitavecchia, Italy) cruise calls at Savona (Italy), Olympia/Katakolon, Athens, Izmir (Turkey), Jerusalem/Tel Aviv (Ashdod, Israel), Cairo (Port Said, Egypt), Cairo/Giza (Alexandria, Egypt). April 18, April 29; October 3, October 14, October 25; November 5, November 16. Rates: From $1,239. **Eleven-day round-trip Civitavecchia** (Italy) cruise calls at Savona (Italy), Olympia/Katakolon, Athens, Izmir (Turkey), Nazareth/Galilee (Haifa, Israel), Cairo (Port Said, Egypt), Cairo/Giza (Alexandria, Egypt). April 7; September 22. Rates: From $1,279.
Costa Romantica	**Eleven-day round-trip Venice** (Italy) cruise calls at Bari (Italy), Olympia/Katakolon, Santorini, Izmir (Turkey), Istanbul (Turkey, overnight), Volos, Athens, Split (Croatia). April 15; May 15; June 21; July 25; August 28; October 1. Rates: From $1,599. **Twelve-day round-trip Venice** (Italy) cruise calls at Bari (Italy), Olympia/Katakolon, Athens, Yalta (Ukraine, Odessa (Ukraine), Constanta (Romania), Istanbul (Turkey), Corfu, Split (Croatia). May 29; July 13; August 16; September 19. Rates: From $2,019.
Costa Serena	**Eleven-day round-trip Civitavecchia** (Italy) cruise calls at Savona (Italy), Olympia/Katakolon, Jerusalem/Tel Aviv (Ashdod, Israel), Nazareth/Galilee (Haifa, Israel), Izmir (Turkey), Athens. January 7. Rates: From $869. Eleven-day round-trip Civitavecchia (Italy) cruise calls at Savona (Italy), Olympia/Katakolon, Athens, Izmir (Turkey), Jerusalem/Tel Aviv (Ashdod, Israel), Cairo (Port Said, Egypt), Cairo/Giza (Alexandria, Egypt). February 23; March 5, March 16.

SHIP	ITINERARY
Costa Serena *(continued)*	Rates: From $1,079. **Eleven-day round-trip Savona** (Italy) cruise calls at Olympia/Katakolon, Jerusalem/Tel Aviv (Ashdod, Israel), Nazareth/Galilee (Haifa, Israel), Izmir (Turkey), Athens, Rome (Civitavecchia, Italy). January 8. Rates: From $919. Eleven-day round-trip Savona (Italy) cruise calls at Olympia/Katakolon, Athens, Izmir (Turkey), Jerusalem/Tel Aviv (Ashdod, Israel), Cairo (Port Said, Egypt), Cairo/Giza (Alexandria, Egypt), Rome (Civitavecchia, Italy). February 13. Rates: From $1,019. **Eleven-day round-trip Savona** (Italy) cruise calls at Olympia/Katakolon, Nazareth/Galilee (Haifa, Israel), Jerusalem/Tel Aviv (Ashdod, Israel), Izmir (Turkey), Athens, Rome (Civitavecchia, Italy). March 6. Rates: From $1,199.

Crystal Cruises

2049 Century Park E., Suite 1400, Los Angeles, CA 90067. ℂ **310/785-9300.** www.crystalcruises.com.

Crystal offers a cultured, elegant atmosphere and unobtrusive service aboard its pair of midsize ships that afford passengers the best of everything—space and intimacy. Its parent company, NYK, is a Japanese firm, the cruise line itself is based in Los Angeles, and you can see a kind of upscale, tranquil, and elegant California-influenced design to these ships, especially in the feng shui–designed spas, the Japanese cuisine (chef Nobu Matsuhisa of Nobu restaurant fame designed the menus in the ship's sushi restaurants), and some of the more modern interior looks of the **Crystal Serenity** (built in 2003; 1,080 passengers, 68,000 GRTs).

This operator offers luxury, but on a slightly larger scale than lines like Silversea and Seabourn—and beginning in spring 2012, Crystal will begin including all alcoholic beverages in its fares as well as soft drinks. The line still preserves a traditional, two-seating dining pattern in its main restaurant and hosts formal nights. Crystal has invested heavily in education and enrichment. During the daytimes, passengers can take a financial planning class or pick up a new recipe or two. Cabins are spacious; the ship's upper-level penthouse suites (especially the top-of-the-line Crystal Penthouses) are top-notch.

Crystal Cruises Itineraries & Rates

SHIP	ITINERARY
Crystal Serenity	**Seven-day Civitavecchia** (Italy) to Athens cruise calls at Sorrento (Italy, overnight), Taormina (Sicily, Italy), Bodrum (Turkey), Mykonos. June 5. Rates: From $3,470. **Seven-day Athens to Venice** (Italy) cruise calls at Ephesus/Kusadasi (Turkey), Santorini, Corfu, Dubrovnik (Croatia), Venice (Italy, overnight). June 12. Rates: From $3,450. **Twelve-day Istanbul (Turkey) to Monte Carlo** (Monaco) cruise calls at Istanbul (overnight), Mykonos, Athens, Nauplion, Taormina (Sicily, Italy), Sorrento (Italy, overnight), Rome (Civitavecchia, Italy), Monte Carol (overnight). July 1. Rates: From $5,946. **Twelve-day Athens to Istanbul** (Turkey) cruise overnights in Athens and calls at Nauplion, Mykonos, Samos, Odessa (Ukraine, overnight), Yalta (Ukraine), Sochi (Russia), Istanbul (overnight). September 6. Rates: From $6,210. Twelve-day Istanbul (Turkey) to Venice (Italy) cruise overnights in Istanbul and calls at Mykonos, Athens, Nauplion, Corfu, Kotor (Montenegro), Zadar (Croatia), Venice (overnight). September 18. Rates: From $5,418. **Twelve-day Venice (Italy) to Athens** cruise overnights in Venice and calls at Ravenna (Italy), Kotor (Montenegro), Corfu (Greece), Mykonos, Istanbul (Turkey, overnight), Athens (overnight). September 30.

continues

SHIP	ITINERARY
Crystal Serenity (continued)	Rates: From $4,541. **Twelve-day Athens to Venice** (Italy) cruise calls at Santorini, Jerusalem/Tel Aviv (Ashdod, Israel, overnight), Cairo/Giza (Alexandria, Egypt, overnight), Corfu, Dubrovnik (Croatia), Venice (overnight). October 12. Rates: From $5,418. **Twelve-day Venice (Italy) to Istanbul** (Turkey) cruise overnights in Venice and calls at Dubrovnik (Croatia), Corfu, Cephalonia, Athens, Nauplion, Mykonos, Ephesus/Kusadasi (Turkey), Istanbul (overnight). October 24. Rates: From $4,541. **Twelve-day Barcelona (Spain) to Athens** cruise overnights in Barcelona and calls at Catania (Sicily, Italy), Santorini, Rhodes, Limassol (Cyprus), Beirut (Lebanon), Damascus (Syria), Athens (overnight). December 9. Rates: From $7,255. **Fourteen-day Athens to Barcelona** (Spain) cruise calls at Jerusalem/Tel Aviv (Ashdod, Israel, overnight), Cairo/Giza (Alexandria, Egypt, overnight), Valletta (Malta), Palermo (Sicily, Italy), Naples/Capri (Italy), Valencia (Spain), Barcelona (overnight). December 21. Rates: From $7,255.

Holland America Line

300 Elliott Ave. W., Seattle, WA 98119. ✆ **877/SAIL-HAL** (724-5425). www.hollandamerica.com.

Holland America is a premium-level line that offers a more traditional cruise flavor onboard new, modern cruise ships. The line takes pride in its Dutch heritage—the tradition of naming its ships with a "dam" suffix goes back to 1883—and in offering good service in a refined setting: teak deck chairs around the promenade deck, classical music in the Explorers Lounge after dinner, formal nights, and a collection of art and artifacts from around the world. Still, Holland America stays on the top of current trends as well. As part of the line's "Signature of Excellence" program, over the past few years the fleet has been enhanced with numerous fresh amenities, from culinary arts centers where passengers can go for cooking classes to bigger-than-ever children's facilities, a specialty Pinnacle Grill restaurant on every ship, big, comfortable internet cafe-cum-lounges that encompass computers, the library, game room, and specialty coffee shop.

The *Nieuw Amsterdam* (built in 2010; 2,104 passengers; 86,000 GRTs) is the latest and greatest Holland America beauty and features private cabanas on upper pool decks, a culinary arts center offering interactive cooking demonstrations, and a coffeehouse complete with an extensive library.

The *Noordam* (built in 2006; 1,848 passengers; 85,000 GRTs) is extraordinarily spacious, with large standard cabins, glamorous two-level dining rooms, and distinctive specialty restaurants. The best of old and new, the ship's decor mixes classic wine reds, dark blues, and earth tones with just a hint of zany, such as the silver-framed benches on the elevator landings and in the **Pinnacle Grill** and **Pinnacle Bar.**

Holland America Itineraries & Rates

SHIP	ITINERARY
Nieuw Amsterdam	**Twelve-day round-trip Venice** (Italy) cruise overnights in Venice and calls at Kotor (Montenegro, Athens), Istanbul (Turkey, overnight), Mykonos, Ephesus/Kusadasi (Turkey), Santorini, Split (Croatia). April 30; June 5; July 18; August 23, October 5. Rates: From $1,799.
Noordam	**Ten-day round-trip Rome** (Civitavecchia, Italy) cruise calls at Dubrovnik (Croatia), Corfu, Olympia/Katakolon, Santorini, Ephesus/Kusadasi (Turkey), Athens, Messina (Sicily, Italy). May 18; June 7, June 27; July 17; August 6, August 26; September 15; October 5. Rates: From $1,599.

Louis Cruise Lines

8 Antoniou Ambatielou St., Piraeus, Greece. ✆ **210/458-3400.** www.louiscruises.com.

The Cyprus-based Louis Group has been in the passenger shipping business for more than 75 years, with its Louis Cruise Lines division dedicating two ships to the Greek islands in 2012 for shorter 3- to 7-night cruises out of Athens.

The **Louis Majesty** (built in 1992; 1,800 passengers; 40,876 GRTs) and the recently acquired **Cristal** (built in 1992; 1,278 passengers; 25,661 GRTs) are the line's main ships in Greece for 2012.

The bulk of Louis's fleet consists of older, more classic-style vessels that have been rebuilt and refurbished. The ships aren't as flashy or as new as the ones used by the major U.S.-based cruise lines, so you won't find state-of-the-art amenities or rows of balconies, though the Cristal is a newer, more modern vessel. However, these cruises concentrate on the destination: The itineraries are port intensive, and the ships will sometimes visit more than one island in a day. Embarkations are somewhat flexible, as Louis permits cruisers to pick up the ships in Mykonos, or disembark early in order to stay a few days on Santorini or Crete. Its ships fly the Greek flag, and its officers are Greek, but Louis also is increasingly designing its ships, cuisine, and entertainment to appeal to an American market: 60% to 65% of its clientele is North American.

Tragedy struck in 2007 when Louis ship the **Sea Diamond** sank after scraping its side on a volcanic reef in Santorini; all passengers were evacuated except for two, who were reported missing and whose bodies were never found. The company, however, has continued its commitment to the Greece market, spending $49 million to acquire the Cristal as a replacement to the Sea Diamond and maintaining a two- or three-ship deployment to the region.

Louis Cruises Itineraries & Rates

SHIP	ITINERARY
Louis Majesty	**Three-day round-trip Athens** cruise calls at Istanbul (Turkey), Izmir (Turkey). March 16, March 23, March 30. Rates: From $429. **Four-day round-trip Athens** cruise calls at Mykonos, Ephesus/Kusadasi (Turkey), Patmos, Santorini. April 6, April 13, April 20, April 27; May 4, May 11, May 18, May 25; June 1, June 8, June 15, June 22, June 29; July 6, July 13, July 20, July 27; August 3, August 10, August 17, August 24, August 31; September 7, September 14, September 21, September 28; October 5, October 12, October 19, October, 26. Rates: From $446. **Four-day round-trip Athens** cruise calls at Mykonos, Ephesus/Kusadasi (Turkey), Patmos, Rhodes, Crete, Santorini. March 19; Marcy 26, April 2, April 9, April 16, April 23, April 30; May 7, May 14, May 21, May 28; June 4, June 11, June 18, June 25; July 2, July 9, July 15, July 23, July 30; August 6, August 13, August 20, August 27; September 3, September 10, September 17, September 24; October 1, October 8, October 15, October 22, October 29. Rates: From $639.
Louis Cristal	**Seven-day round-trip Athens** cruise calls at Istanbul (Turkey, overnight), Izmir (Turkey), Patmos, Mykonos, Rhodes, Heraklion, Santorini. March 30; April 6, April 13, April 20, April 27; May 4, May 11, May 18; May 25; June 1, June 8, June 15, June 22, June 29; July 6, July 13, July 20, July 27; August 3, August 10, August 17, August 24, August 31; September 7, September 14, September 21, September 28; October 5, October 12, October 19, October 26. Rates: From $1,223. **Three-day round-trip Athens** cruise calls at Istanbul (Turkey), Izmir (Turkey). November 2. Rates: From $429. Four-day round-trip Athens cruise calls at Mykonos, Ephesus/Kusadasi (Turkey), Patmos, Rhodes, Heraklion, Santorini. November 5. Rates: From $639.

MSC Cruises

6750 N. Andrews Ave., Fort Lauderdale, FL 33309. ℂ **800/666-9333.** www.msccruises.com.

MSC Cruises, a line with Italian heritage and a subsidiary of shipping giant Mediterranean Shipping Co., is one of the fastest-growing cruise lines. A few years ago MSC was an up-and-coming player, mixing a fleet of older, classic-style ships with mostly midsize vessels. These days the line is adding megaships to its fleet that compete on size and amenities with the biggest cruise companies, has made a big push into the U.S. market, and has established itself in the contemporary cruise market.

The line's "classic Italian cruising," focuses on service and on playing up its Italian ambience—Italian actress Sophia Loren is the godmother to four MSC Cruises ships. The line is trying to "Americanize" some aspects of the voyages in order to make the Continental vibe seem more familiar to U.S. passengers, such as offering coffee along with dessert (instead of afterward) and adding more items to the breakfast buffet. Still, the passenger mix is more international than many other lines. Itineraries are port-intensive, and the onboard experience friendly and fun.

The **MSC Magnifica** (built in 2010; 2,550 passengers; 89,600 GRTs) and sister **MSC Musica** (built in 2006; 2,550 passengers; 89,600 GRTs) are a good example of where MSC Cruises has been heading, hardware-wise: They've got room for a minigolf course, a sushi bar, an Internet cafe, a solarium, yoga classes, a wine bar, and a children's playroom in addition to all the usual activities you'll find on ships (a casino, gym, sauna, and so on). Nearly 830 of the 1,275 suites and cabins have private balconies. The **MSC Armonia** (built in 2001; 1,566 passengers; 58,625 GRTs) is a bit older and offers fewer amenities.

MSC Cruises Itineraries & Rates

SHIP	ITINERARY
MSC Musica	**Seven-day round-trip Venice** cruise calls at Bari (Italy), Corfu, Athens, overnights in Mykonos, Katakolon, Dubrovnik (Croatia). Musica cruises are offered weekly departing on Saturdays. April 4 through October 3. Rates: From $999.
MSC Armonia	**Seven-day round-trip Venice** (Italy) cruise calls at Ancona (Italy), Corfu, Santorini, Athens, Argostoli, Kotor (Montenegro). May 11, May 18, May 25; June 1, June 8, June 15, June 22, June 29; July 6, July 13, July 20, July 27; August 3, August 10, August 17, August 24, August 31; September 7, September 14, September 21, September 28; October 5. Rates: From $619. **Seven-day round-trip Ancona** (Italy) cruise calls at Corfu, Santorini, Athens, Argostoli, Kotor (Montenegro), Venice (Italy). May 12, May 19, May 26; June 2, June 9, June 16. June 23, June 30; July 7, July 14, July 21, July 28; August 4, August 11, August 18, August 25; September 1, September 8, September 15, September 22, September 29. Rates: From $799.
MSC Magnifica	**Nine-day round-trip Venice** (Italy) cruise calls at Bari (Italy), Rhodes, Nazareth/Galilee (Haifa, Israel, overnight), Athens. January 5, January 14, January·23; February 17, February 26; March 6, March 15. Rates: From $799. **Nine-day round-trip Bari** (Italy) cruise calls at Rhodes, Nazareth/Galilee (Haifa, Israel, overnight), Athens, Venice. January 6, January 15; February 18, March 7. Rates: From $799.

Norwegian Cruise Line

7665 Corporate Center Dr. Miami, FL 33126. ℰ **866/625-1166.** www.ncl.com.

Many mega–cruise lines operate with dinner seatings at set times and offer an alternative restaurant or two for a change of pace. Not so NCL; this company pushed the envelope a few years ago with a concept called Freestyle Dining: Pick one of several restaurants and make a reservation for dinner or stroll in whenever, just as you would at a shoreside restaurant. NCL started building its ships to take advantage of the Freestyle concept, and the result is a fleet of new ships that offer about 10 restaurant choices. Another difference: No required formal nights.

The *Norwegian Jade* (built in 2007; 2,380 passengers; 93,558 GRTs) is among the fleet's newest ships and among the most fun megaships today, offering a super-social atmosphere, creative decor, and onboard music and pop culture references tailored to folks in their 20s to folks in their 50s. The **Bliss Ultra Lounge** juxtaposes bordello decor with a four-lane, DayGlo bowling alley, while the nightclubs and atriums feature furniture out of *Alice in Wonderland*. The Jade's Garden Villas spread out up to an astonishing 500 sq. m (5,350 sq. ft.), and feature private gardens, multiple bedrooms with mind-blowing bathrooms, living rooms, full kitchens, and private butler service.

Norwegian Cruises Itineraries & Rates

SHIP	ITINERARY
Norwegian Jade	**Fourteen-day round-trip Venice** (Italy) cruise calls at Corfu, Santorini, Mykonos, Olympia/Katakolon, Venice (Italy), Dubrovnik (Croatia), Athens, Izmir (Turkey), Split (Croatia). April 28; May 12, May 26; June 9, June 23; September 8, September 22.Rates: From $1,379. **Fourteen-day round-trip Venice** (Italy) cruise calls at Dubrovnik (Croatia), Athens, Izmir (Turkey), Split (Croatia), Venice, Corfu, Santorini, Mykonos, Olympia/Katakolon. May 5, June 2, June 16; July 7; September 1, September 15, September 29. Rates: From $1,429. **Ten-day round-trip Rome** (Civitavecchia, Italy) cruise calls at Olympia/Katakolon, Athens, Izmir (Turkey), Cairo/Giza (Alexandria, Egypt, overnight). October 31; November 21; December 12. Rates: From $709.

Oceania Cruises

8300 NW 33rd St., Suite 308, Miami, FL 33122. ℰ **800/531-5619.** www.oceaniacruises.com.

This cruise line has grown quickly since its 2003 debut. It now boasts three ships, and it has orders in for two new 1,260-passenger ships. The current vessels are identical in layout, and their sizes, at 680 passengers each, make them cozy and intimate but able to stock a lot of amenities like multiple restaurants and big spas. Oceania straddles the line between the small luxury players and the larger, though less pricey, premium cruise lines. It tries to offer a reasonably priced yet intimate, casual, upscale experience.

Four ships hit the Greek Isles. The brand new *Marina* (built in 2011; 1,258 passengers; 65,000 GRTs) and sister *Riviera* (built in 2012; 1,258 passengers; 65,000 GRTs) are the line's newest and greatest, at twice the size of the *Regatta* and *Nautica* (built in 1998–2000; 684 passengers; 30,277 GRTs). The emphasis on all four of these ship is on casual, so you won't need to dress up (or even bring a tie or fancy dress). On Marina and Riviera, almost all of the cabins have balconies, while a good number also boast them on the older two ships. Public rooms, too, are of the big-but-not-too-big mold, and there are nice touches throughout the ships like teak decks and DVD players in the cabins. Private cabanas at the very top of the ship can be reserved for the day or for the whole cruise, and come with a dedicated attendant and food and beverage services. Alternative restaurants include the Polo steakhouse and Toscana Italian trattoria (plus two more, an Asian and a French venue, on the newer ships), fine complements to the main restaurant.

Oceania Cruises Itineraries & Rates

SHIP	ITINERARY
Marina	**Ten-day Venice** (Italy) to Athens cruise overnights in Venice and calls at Dubrovnik (Croatia), Kotor (Montenegro), Corfu, Monemvasia, Crete, Santorini, Ephesus/Kusadasi (Turkey), Delos, Mykonos. April 22. Rates: From $2,699. **Ten-day Athens** to Barcelona (Spain) cruise calls at Santorini, Ephesus/Kusadasi (Turkey), Taormina (Sicily, Italy), Amalfi (Italy), Rome (Civitavecchia, Italy), Florence/Pisa (Livorno, Italy, overnight), Marseille (France). May 2. Rates: From $2,549. **Ten-day Istanbul** (Turkey) to Athens cruise calls at Lesbos, Delos, Mykonos, Ephesus/Kusadasi (Turkey), Santorini, Marmaris (Turkey), Antalya (Turkey), Rhodes, Crete, Athens (overnight). October 12. Rates: From $2,949. **Ten-day Athens** to Istanbul (Turkey) cruise calls at Cairo/Giza (Alexandria, Egypt), Jerusalem/Tel Aviv (Ashdod, Israel), Nazareth/Galilee (Haifa, Israel), Limassol (Cyprus), Rhodes, Ephesus/Kusadasi (Turkey), Istanbul (overnight). October 22. Rates: From $2,749. **Seven-day Istanbul (Turkey) to Athens** cruise calls at Dikili (Turkey), Volos, Ephesus/Kusadasi (Turkey), Rhodes, Crete, Athens (overnight). November 1. Rates: From $2,199.
Nautica	**Ten-day Athens to Barcelona** (Spain) cruise calls at Santorini, Ephesus/Kusadasi (Turkey), Taormina (Sicily, Italy), Amalfi (Italy), Rome (Civitavecchia, Italy), Florence/Pisa (Livorno, Italy, overnight), Marseille (France). May 14. Rates: From $2,549. **Ten-day Barcelona** (Spain) to Athens cruise calls at Marseille (France), Florence/Pisa (Livorno, Italy, overnight), Rome (Civitavecchia, Italy), Amalfi (Italy), Taormina (Sicily, Italy), Ephesus/Kusadasi (Turkey), Santorini. October 26. Rates: From $2,749. **Ten-day Athens to Istanbul** (Turkey) cruise calls at Cairo/Giza (Alexandria, Egypt), Cairo (Port Said, Egypt), Jerusalem/Tel Avia (Ashdod, Israel), Nazareth/Galilee (Haifa, Israel), Limassol (Cyprus), Rhodes, Ephesus/Kusadasi (Turkey), Istanbul (overnight). November 5. Rates: From $2,424.
Regatta	**Ten-day Barcelona (Spain) to Athens** cruise calls at Marseille (France), Florence/Pisa (Livorno, Italy, overnight), Rome (Civitavecchia, Italy), Amalfi (Italy), Taormina (Sicily, Italy), Ephesus/Kusadasi (Turkey), Santorini. June 25. Rates: From $2,999. **Ten-day Istanbul (Turkey) to Athens** cruise calls at Lesbos, Ephesus/Kusadasi (Turkey), Delos, Mykonos, Santorini, Rhodes, Crete, Monemvasia, Olympia/Katakolon, Athens (overnight). July 17. Rates: From $2,849. **Twelve-day Athens to Istanbul** (Turkey) cruise calls at Cairo/Giza (Alexandria, Egypt), Cairo (Port Said, Egypt), Jerusalem/Tel Aviv (Ashdod, overnight), Nazareth/Galilee (Haifa, Israel), Alanya (Turkey), Rhodes, Patmos, Ephesus/Kusadasi (Turkey), Istanbul (overnight). July 27. Rates: From $3,399. **Twelve-day Istanbul (Turkey) to Athens** cruise calls at Ephesus/Kusadasi (Turkey), Patmos, Rhodes, Alanya (Turkey), Limassol (Cyprus), Nazareth/Galilee (Haifa, Israel), Jerusalem/Tel Aviv (Ashdod, Israel, overnight), Cairo (Port Said, Egypt). August 30. Rates: From $3,399. **Ten-day Athens to Istanbul** (Turkey) cruise calls at Nauplion, Olympia, Monemvasia, Crete, Rhodes, Santorini, Delos, Mykonos, Ephesus/Kusadasi (Turkey), Istanbul (overnight). September 11.

SHIP	ITINERARY
Regatta *(continued)*	Rates: From $3,199. **Twelve-day Athens to Istanbul** (Turkey) cruise calls at Cairo/Giza (Alexandria, Egypt), Cairo (Port Said, Egypt), Jerusalem/Tel Avia (Ashdod, Israel), Nazareth/Galilee (Haifa, Israel, overnight), Alanya (Turkey), Rhodes, Patmos, Ephesus/Kusadasi (Turkey), Istanbul (overnight). October 1. Rates: From $3,449. **Ten-day Istanbul (Turkey) to Rome** (Civitavecchia, Italy) cruise calls at Ephesus/Kusadasi (Turkey), Santorini, Athens, Valletta (Malta), La Goulette (Tunisia), Trapani (Sicily, Italy), Sorrento (Italy, overnight). October 13. Rates: From $2,749. **Ten-day Rome (Civitavecchia, Italy) to Athens** cruise calls at Monte Carlo (Monaco), Marseille (France), Florence/Pisa (Livorno, Italy, overnight), Sorrento (Italy), Messina (Sicily, Italy), Argostoli, Monemvasia, Ephesus/Kusadasi (Turkey). October 23. Rates: From $2,749. **Ten-day Athens to Barcelona (Spain)** cruise call at Olympia/Katakolon, Messina (Sicily, Italy), Naples/Capri (Italy), Rome (Civitavecchia, Italy), Florence/Pisa (Livorno, Italy), Monte Carlo (Monaco), Marseille (France), Barcelona (overnight). November 2. Rates: From $2,424.
Riviera	**Ten-day Barcelona (Spain) to Athens** cruise calls at Marseille (France), Florence/Pisa (Livorno, Italy, overnight), Rome (Civitavecchia, Italy), Amalfi (Italy), Taormina (Sicily, Italy), Ephesus/Kusadasi (Turkey), Santorini. April 14. Rates: From $3,799. **Twelve-day Athens to Istanbul** (Turkey) cruise calls at Santorini, Marmaris (Turkey), Nazareth/Galilee (Haifa, Israel), Jerusalem/Tel Aviv (Ashdod, Israel, overnight), Alanya (Turkey), Rhodes, Patmos, Ephesus/ Kusadasi (Turkey), Istanbul (overnight). April 24. Rates: From $3,149. **Ten-day Istanbul (Turkey) to Venice** (Italy) cruise calls at Lesbos, Sphesus/Kusadasi (Turkey), Mykonos, Athens, Argostoli, Corfu, Dubrovnik (Croatia), Split (Croatia), Venice (overnight). May 6. Rates: From $2,549. **Ten-day Venice (Italy) to Athens** cruise overnights in Venice and calls at Dubrovnik (Croatia), Kotor (Montenegro), Corfu, Monemvasia, Crete, Santorini, Ephesus/Kusadasi (Turkey), Delos, Mykonos. May 16, October 4. Rates: From $2,799. **Ten-day Athens to Barcelona** (Spain) cruise calls at Santorini, Ephesus/Kusadasi (Turkey), Taormina (Sicily, Italy), Rome (Civitavecchia, Italy), Florence/Pisa (Livorno, Italy, overnight), Marseille (France). May 26. Rates: From $2,549. **Ten-day Athens to Rome** (Civitavecchia, Italy) cruise calls at Ephesus/Kusadasi (Turkey), Monemvasia, Argostoli, Messina (Sicily, Italy), Florence/Pisa (Livorno, Italy, overnight), Marseille (France), Monte Carlo (Monaco). Rates: From $2,749.

Princess Cruises

24844 Ave. Rockefeller, Santa Clarita, CA 91355. ☏ **800/PRINCESS** (774-6237). www.princess.com.

Forever connected to its *Love Boat* past, American premium line Princess has grown up and evolved into a multidestination, multimegaship line that blends California-style casual with elegance and sophistication. Still, the line keeps the theme of love alive, with special promotions at Valentine's Day and occasional appearances by "Captain Stubing" (actor Gavin MacLeod).

Princess's signature vessels, the Grand-class ships, were so ahead of their time when they debuted in 1998 that the design of sister ships isn't significantly changed. Though the vessels give an impression of immensity from the outside, inside they're well laid out, easy to navigate, and surprisingly cozy. The "cozy" aspect carries over to public rooms like the dimly lit **Explorer's Lounge** and **Wheelhouse Bar,** whose traditional accents recall a grander era of sea travel. In the elegant three-story atriums, classical string quartets perform on formal nights and during embarkation. Throw in good-size kid and teen zones and a plethora of show lounges, bars, and pools, and you've got ships that can keep you busy for a week, never mind the destination.

Crown Princess (built in 2006; 3,080 passengers; 113,000 GRTs) and **Ruby Princess** (built in 2008; 3,080 passengers; 113,000 GRTs) are slightly larger versions of the original Grand-class concept, with amenities including the Sanctuary, an adults-only, top-deck hideaway of cabanas, healthy snacks and soothing music, plus an international cafe, a wine and seafood bar, a piazza-style atrium with a street-cafe vibe, a giant movie screen on deck, and a steak and seafood restaurant. The newer *Ruby Princess* added some fresh experiences: a British pub at lunch on sea days (no charge), a range of cheeses to go with the wine and seafood snacks available in Vines, and the Ultimate Ship tour, a truly behind-the-scenes look at how a ship operates.

Ocean Princess (built in 1999; 680 passengers; 30,277 GRTs) and **Pacific Princess** (built in 1999; 680 passengers; 30,277 GRTs) are small, but comfortable ships. They're traditional, sedate, and geared to adults, with an emphasis on intimate spaces—just like Princess's larger ships, but here it's the real thing. Like a European boutique hotel, they're decorated mostly in warm, dark woods and rich fabrics, and offer a small-scale, clubby feel that larger ships can only hope to mimic.

Princess Cruises Itineraries & Rates

SHIP	ITINERARY
Ruby Princess	**Twelve-day Barcelona (Spain) to Venice** (Italy) cruise calls at Monte Carlo (Monaco), Florence/Pisa (Livorno, Italy), Rome (Civitavecchia, Italy), Naples/Capri (Sorrento, Italy), Mykonos, Istanbul, Ephesus/Kusadasi (Turkey), Athens, Venice (overnight). May 30; June 23; July 17; August 10; September 3, September 27. Rates: From $1,990. **Twelve-day Venice (Italy) to Barcelona** (Spain) cruise overnights in Venice and calls at Athens, Epheusu/Kusadasi (Turkey), Istanbul (Turkey), Mykonos, Naples/Capri (Sorrento, Italy), Rome (Civitavecchia, Italy), Florence/Pisa (Livorno, Italy), Monte Carlo (Monaco). May 18; June 11; July 5, July 29; August 22; September 15. Rates: From $2,040.
Crown Princess	**Twelve-day Venice (Italy) to Rome** (Civitavecchia, Italy) cruise overnights in Venice and calls at Dubrovnik (Croatia), Corfu, Olympia/Katakolon, Athens, Mykonos, Ephesus/Kusadasi (Turkey), Rhodes, Santorini, Naples/Capri (Sorrento, Italy). May 24; June 17; July 11; August 4, August 28; September 21; October 15; November 8. Rates: From $1,790. **Twelve-day Rome (Civitavecchia, Italy) to Venice** (Italy) cruise calls at Monte Carlo (Monaco), Florence/Pisa (Livorno, Italy), Naples/Capri (Sorrento, Italy), Santorini, Athens, Mykonos, Olympia/Katakolon, Corfu, Split (Croatia), Venice (overnight). June 5, June 29; July 23; August 16; September 9; October 3. Rates: From $1,990. **Twelve-day Rome (Civitavecchia, Italy) to Venice** (Italy) cruise calls at Cairo/Giza (Alexandria, Egypt, overnight), Mykonos, Istanbul (Turkey), Epheusu/Kusadais (Turkey), Athens, Venice (overnight). October 27. Rates: From $1,790. Rome (Civitavecchia, Italy) to Venice (Italy) cruise calls at Naples/Capri (Sorrento, Italy), Santorini, Rhodes, Ephesus/Kusadasi (Turkey), Mykonos, Athens, Olympia/Katakolon, Corfu, Dubrovnik (Croatia), Venice (overnight). Rates: From $1,690.

SHIP	ITINERARY
Ocean Princess	**Fourteen-day Barcelona (Spain) to Athens** cruise calls at Carcassonne (Sete, France), Portofino (Italy), Florence/Pisa (Livorno, Italy), La Goulette (Tunisia), Naples/Capri (Sorrento, Italy), Rome (Civitavecchia, Italy), Itea, Argostoli, Santorini, Epheusu/Kusadasi (Turkey), Crete. September 2. Rates: From $2,598. **Twenty-one-day Barcelona (Spain) to Athens** cruise calls at Carcassonne (Sete, France), Portofino (Italy), Florence/Pisa (Livorno, Italy), La Goulette (Tunisia), Naples/Capri (Sorrento, Italy), Rome (Civitavecchia, Italy), Itea, Argostoli, Santorini, Epheusu/Kusadasi (Turkey), Crete, Athens, Mykonos, Olympia/Katakolon, Corfu, Dubrovnik (Croatia), Korcula (Croatia). September 2. Rates: From $4,347. **Seven-day Rome (Civitavecchia, Italy) to Athens** cruise calls at Itea, Argostoli, Santorini, Ephesus/Kusadasi (Turkey), Crete. September 9. Rates: From $1,399. **Fourteen-day Rome (Civitavecchia, Italy) to Venice** (Italy) cruise calls at Itea, Argostoli, Santorini, Epheusu/Kusadasi (Turkey), Crete, Athens, Olympia/Katakolon, Corfu, Dubrovnik (Croatia), Korcula (Croatia). September 9. Rates: From $2,498. **Seven-day Athens to Venice** (Italy) cruise calls at Mykonos, Olympia/Katakolon, Corfu, Dubrovnik (Croatia), Koper (Slovenia). September 16. Rates: From $1,299. **Seven-day Venice to Athens** cruise calls at Koper (Slovenia), Dubrovnik (Croatia), Corfu, Olympia/Katakolon, Mykonos. September 23. Rates: From $1,299. **Fourteen-day Venice (Italy) to Rome** (Civitavecchia, Italy) cruise calls at Koper (Slovenia), Dubrovnik (Croatia), Corfu, Olympia/Katakolon, Mykonos, Athens, Crete, Ephesus/Kusadasi (Turkey), Santorini, Argostoli, Itea. September 23. Rates: From $2,398. **Seven-day Athens to Rome** (Civitavecchia, Italy) cruise calls at Crete, Ephesus/Kusadasi (Turkey), Santorini, Argostoli, Itea. September 30. Rates: From $1,299.
Pacific Princess	**Twelve-day Venice (Italy) to Athens** cruise calls at Ravenna (Italy), Dubrovnik (Croatia), Patmos, Nazareth/Galilee (Haifa, Israel), Jerusalem/Tel Avia (Ashdod, Israel), Cairo (Port Said, Egypt), Cairo/Giza (Alexandria, Egypt), Ephesus/Kusadasi (Turkey). April 30; June 5; July 23; August 16. Rates: From $2,840. **Twelve-day Venice (Italy) to Athens** cruise calls in Split (Croatia), Istanbul (Turkey, overnight), Nesebur (Bulgaria), Constanta (Romania), Odessa (Ukraine), Yalta (Ukraine), Volos. June 29. Rates: From $3,090. **Twelve-day Athens to Rome** (Civitavecchia, Italy) cruise calls at Patmos, Santorini, Ephesus/Kusadasi (Turkey), Nazareth/Galilee (Haifa, Israel), Jerusalem/Tel Aviv (Ashdod, Israel), Cairo (Port Said, Egypt), Cairo/Giza (Alexandria, Egypt), Naples/Capri (Sorrento, Italy). May 12; October 3, October 27; November 20. Rates: From $2,740. **Twelve-day Athens to Venice** (Italy) cruise calls at Patmos, Ephesus/Kusadasi, Nazareth/Galilee (Haifa, Israel), Jerusalem/Tel Aviv (Ashdod, Israel), Cairo (Port Said, Egypt), Cairo/Giza (Alexandria, Egypt), Dubrovnik (Croatia), Ravenna (Italy). June 17; July 11; August 4. Rates: From $3,090. **Twelve-day Athens to Venice** cruise calls at Volos, Yalta (Ukraine), Odessa (Ukraine), Constanta (Romania), Nesebur (Bulgaria), Istanbul (Turkey, overnight), Korcula (Croatia). August 28. Rates: From $2,940. **Twelve-day Rome to Athens** cruise calls at Naples/Capri (Sorrento, Italy), Patmos, Ephesus/Kusadasi (Turkey), Nazareth/Galilee (Haifa, Israel), Jerusalem/Tel Avia (Ashdod, Israel), Cairo (Port Said, Egypt), Cairo/Giza (Alexandria, Egypt), Santorini. September 23; October 15; November 8. Rates: From $2,840.

Pullmantur Cruises

2 Mahonia St., Madrid, Spain 28043 (**092-09-5512.** www.pullmantur.es.

Built for Celebrity Cruises, the *Zenith* (built in 1992; 1,500 passengers; 47,255 GRTs) is now a part of the Spain-based Pullmantar fleet, whose parent company is Royal Caribbean. The ship is midsize with attractive tiered decks at the stern and everything you'll need for a cozy cruise of the Greek Isles, from a kids playroom for ages 3 to 11 to an elegant, one-level oceanview dining room, gym, spa and plenty of entertainment venues. Most guests will be European, the majority from Spain, with the languages spoken being Spanish, English, French and Portuguese; prices onboard are in Euros. Two seatings at dinner are offered, the early at 8pm and the late seating at 10:15pm. Fares include all meals and all alcoholic and soft drinks.

Pullmantur Cruises Itineraries & Rates

SHIP	ITINERARY
Zenith	**Seven-day round-trip Athens** cruise calls at Santorini, Marmaris (Turkey), Izmir (Turkey), Istanbul (Turkey), Mykonos. April 2, April 23; May 14; June 4, June 25; August 6, August 27. Rates: From $881. **Seven-day Athens to Ravenna** (Italy) cruise calls at Mykonos, Santorini, Olympia/Katakolon, Corfu, Dubrovnik (Croatia), Venice (Italy). April 9, April 30; May 21; June 11; July 2, July 23; August 13; September 3. Rates: From $642. Seven-day Ravenna (Italy) to Athens cruise calls at Venice (Italy), Dubrovnik (Croatia), Corfu, Olympia/Katakolon, Santorini, Mykonos. April 16; May 7, May 28; June 18; July 9, July 30; August 20; September 10. Rates: From $642.

Regent Seven Seas Cruises

1000 Corporate Dr., Suite 500, Fort Lauderdale, FL 33334. (**800/285-1835.** www.rssc.com.

Founded by Radisson Hotels Worldwide in 1992, Regent Seven Seas Cruises is one of the cruise industry's ultraluxury cruise lines. The *Seven Seas Mariner* (built in 2001; 708 passengers; 50,000 GRTs) was the first all-suite, all-balcony ship, followed by sister *Seven Seas Voyager* (built in 2003; 708 passengers; 46,000 GRTs). On both, many cabins have sizeable suites and bathrooms with a tub (unusual on a cruise ship). The spacious ships have an abundance of art on the walls and the decor successfully combines classic furnishings with modern accents. The ship's size means it's easy to get around to the different restaurants and bars. Outdoor deck furniture has a South Beach feel, and alcoholic beverages as well as all soft drinks are included in the rates. The four restaurants onboard both ships (five if you count the Pool Grill) include **Signatures,** operated by Le Cordon Bleu of Paris.

Regent Seven Seas Cruises Itineraries & Rates

SHIP	ITINERARY
Seven Seas Voyager	**Seven-day Athens to Istanbul** (Turkey) cruise calls at Santorini, Epheusu/Kusadasi (Turkey), Rhodes, Mykonos, Kavala/Philippi, Istanbul (overnight). April 16. Rates: From $3,399. **Ten-day Istanbul (Turkey) to Venice** (Italy) cruise calls at Ephesus/Kusadasi (Turkey), Santorini, Athens, Olympia/Katakolon, Corfu, Kotor (Montenegro), Dubrovnik (Croatia), Ancona (Italy), Venice (overnight). April 23. Rates: From $5,599. **Seven-day Istanbul (Turkey) to Athens** cruise calls at Kavala/Philippi, Mykonos, Ephesus/Kusadasi (Turkey), Rhodes, Crete/Heraklion, Santorini. October 17.

SHIP	ITINERARY
Seven Seas Voyager (continued)	Rates: From $3,899. **Seven-day Athens to Istanbul** (Turkey) cruise calls at Crete/Heraklion, Santorini, Rhodes, Ephesus/Kusadasi (Turkey), Kavala/Philippi, Istanbul (overnight). October 24. Rates: From $3,899.
Seven Seas Mariner	**Ten-day Istanbul (Turkey) to Venice** (Italy) cruise calls at Mykonos, Epheusu/Kusadasi (Turkey), Santorini, Athens, Zakynthos, Corfu, Kotor (Montenegro), Dubrovnik (Croatia) Venice (overnight). May 10. Rates: From $4,999. **Ten-day Rome (Italy) to Istanbul** (Turkey) cruise calls at Sorrento (Italy), Trapani (Sicily, Italy), La Goulette (Tunisia), Valletta (Malta), Athens, Santorini, Ephesus/Kusadasi (Turkey), Istanbul (overnight). June 16. Rates: From $6,499. **Seven-day Istanbul (Turkey) to Athens** cruise calls at Kavala/Phillipi, Mykonos, Ephesus/Kusadasi (Turkey), Rhodes, Crete/Heraklion, Santorini. June 26; July 13; August 23. Rates: From $4,799. **Seven-day Athens to Venice** cruise calls at Ephesus/Kusadasi (Turkey), Santorini, Olympia/Katakolon, Corfu, Dubrovnik (Croatia), Venice (overnight). July 20; August 30. Rates: From $4,799. Ten-day Barcelona (Spain) to Athens cruise calls at Marseille (France), Monte Carlo (Monaco), Florence/Pisa (Livorno, Italy), Rome (Civitavecchia, Italy), Taormina (Sicily, Italy), Santorini, Ephesus/Kusadasi (Turkey). September 26. Rates: From $5,999. **Fourteen-day Athens to Istanbul** (Turkey) cruise calls at Rhodes, Alanya (Turkey), Limassol (Cyprus), Nazareth/Galilee (Haifa, Israel), Jerusalem/Tel Aviv (Ashdod, Israel, overnight) Cairo (Port Said, Egypt), Cairo/Giza (Alexandria, Egypt), Santorini, Ephesus/Kusadasi (Turkey), Patmos, Istanbul (overnight). October 6. Rates: From $8,399.

Royal Caribbean International

1050 Caribbean Way, Miami, FL 33132. ☎ **877/202-1520** or 800/327-6700. www.rccl.com.

Heard about those megaships with the rock-climbing walls? Those are the vessels of Royal Caribbean International, which has made its unusual onboard features—ice-skating rinks and self-leveling billiards tables, for example—a benchmark for other cruise lines. Royal Caribbean sells a reasonably priced, big-ship, American-style experience. And they do it very well: The line's ships are consistent and well-run, and there are a lot of things to do, from wine tastings to climbing the ubiquitous rock wall. Royal Caribbean cultivates an active, fun image, most typified through advertising that urges would-be cruisers to "get out there."

The **Serenade of the Seas** (built in 2003; 2,100 passengers; 90,090 GRTs) is one of four Radiance-class ships, some of the most attractive vessels at sea. Sleek and spacious and a great size, the nine-story atrium is surrounded by glass for great views of the Greek Isles. The pleasing decor, a mix of dark-wood paneling, caramel-brown leathers, and deep-sea-blue fabrics and carpeting along with modern art and sculpture, is the backdrop for spaces like the **Viking Crown Lounge** up top to **Singapore Sling's** piano bar, **Champagne Bar** and many other attractive spaces. **Voyager of the Seas** (built in 1999; 3,114 passengers; 142,000 GRTs) was groundbreaking when it first launched, introducing amenities the world was shocked to see on a cruise ship, but which are now much more commonplace, from a full-sized ice-skating rink to an outdoor in-line skating track, mini golf, a full basketball court, and much more. The much smaller **Splendour of the Seas** (built in 1996; 1,802 passengers; 70,000 GRTs) is a Vision-class ship that can't hold a candle to her newer fleetmates, but if the price is right, amenities like the indoor-outdoor Solarium pool, nautically-themed **Schooner Bar,** 18-hole minigolf course and the **Viking Crown Lounge** observatory-cum-disco will do just fine.

Royal Caribbean International Itineraries & Rates

SHIP	ITINERARY
Serenade of the Seas	**Twelve-day round-trip Barcelona** (Spain) cruise calls at Cannes (France), Florence/Pisa (Livorno, Italy), Rome (Civitavecchia, Italy), Athens, Epheusu/Kusadasi (Turkey), Santorini, Naples (Salerno, Italy). May 5, May 29; June 22; July 16; August 9, September 2. Rates: From $1,119. **Twelve-day round-trip Barcelona** (Spain) cruise calls at Cannes (France), Florence/Pisa (Livorno, Italy), Rome (Civitavecchia, Italy), Ephesus/Kusadasi (Turkey), Mykonos, Naples (Salerno, Italy). October 3. Rates: From $1,299. **Twelve-day round-trip Barcelona** (Spain) cruise calls at Cannes (France), Florence/Pisa (Livorno, Italy), Athens, Ephesus/Kusadasi (Turkey), Chania, Naples (Salerno, Italy). October 27. Rates: From $1,099.
Splendor of the Seas	**Seven-day round-trip Venice** (Italy) cruise calls at Bari (Italy), Corfu, Mykonos, Athens, Dubrovnik (Croatia). May 19; June 2, June 16, June 30; July 28; August 11, August 25; September 8, September 22; October 6, October 20; November 3. Rates: From $549. **Seven-day round-trip Bari** (Italy) cruise calls at Corfu, Mykonos, Athens, Dubrovnik (Croatia), Venice (Italy). May 6, May 20; June 3, June 17; July 1, July 29; August 12, August 26; September 9, September 23; October 7, October 21; November 4. Rates: From $974. **Eight-day round-trip Bari** (Italy) cruise calls at Corfu, Santorini, Ephesus/Kusadasi (Turkey), Athens, Olympia/Katakolon, Venice (Italy). July 14. Rates: From $1,204.
Voyager of the Seas	**Ten-day round-trip Venice** (Italy) cruise calls at Dubrovnik (Croatia), Ephesus/Kusadasi (Turkey), Istanbul (Turkey, overnight), Athens, Chania. May 11; June 22; July 13; August 3, August 24; September 14; October 5. Rates: From $999. **Eleven-day round-trip Venice** (Italy) cruise calls at Dubrovnik (Croatia), Rhodes, Ephesus/Kusadasi (Turkey), Istanbul (Turkey, overnight), Athens, Chania. May 21; June 11; July 2, July 23; August 13; September 3, September 24. Rates: From $1,199.

SMALL & YACHTLIKE SHIPS
Seabourn Cruise Line

6100 Blue Lagoon Dr., Suite 400, Miami, FL 33126. © **800/929-9391.** www.seabourn.com.

The top of the line in the cruise world, Seabourn excels in many areas, including food, service, itineraries, and a luxurious and refined environment. These cruises are pricey, and the customers who can afford them are well-traveled sophisticates used to being doted on.

Although the ambience can be casual during the day, it becomes decidedly more formal in the evening, although new dining options with modern cuisine and an "always informal" option at the restaurant at the top of the ship go a way to making it feel more casual. There's an open-bar policy (all alcoholic and soft drinks are included in the fare) and lots of open, teak decks, which make these ships very yachtlike. The ships are all-suite with marble bathrooms, walk-in closets, plush software, stocked mini bars, elegant fine dining and more.

Nighttime entertainment is low key, though cabaret nights with themes like 1950s rock 'n' roll can get the audience going.

Seabourn has three nearly identical ships, and a trio of new larger ships. The *Seabourn Legend* (built in 1992; 208 passengers; 10,000 GRTs) and *Seabourn Pride* (built in 1991; 208 passengers; 10,000 GRTs) dip into the Greek Isles, though the newer larger *Seabourn Odyssey* (built in 2009; 450 passengers; 32,000 GRTs) and *Seabourn Quest* (built in 2011; 450 passengers; 32,000 GRTs) offer many more Greek itineraries.

All cabins on the *Seabourn Legend* and *Pride* are outside suites, many with French balconies—sliding doors you can open to let in the ocean breezes (the ships were built before full balconies were all the rage). The other cabins have 1.5m-wide (5-ft.) picture windows, plenty big enough to make the room bright and airy. Owner's suites are plush and offer private verandas.

The *Seabourn Odyssey* and *Quest* boast verandas on 90% of all staterooms. There is a main open-eating restaurant, two alternative venues, plus a poolside grille. Enjoy a two-level state-of-the-art gym and spa, which includes a pair of spa villas.

Seabourn Cruises Itineraries & Rates

SHIP	ITINERARY
Seabourn Odyssey	**Seven-day Athens-to-Istanbul** cruise calls at Mylos, Rhodes, Patmos, Khylos, Kusadasi (Turkey). May 8; July 3; August 21. Rates: From $5,135. **Seven-day Istanbul-to-Athens** cruise calls at Dikili (Turkey), Kusadasi (Turkey), Bodrum (Turkey), Santorini, Mylos, Nauplion. May 15; July 10, July 31, August 20. Rates: From $5,135. **Seven-day Venice-to-Athens** cruise calls at Sibenik (Croatia), Bari (Italy), Cephalonia, Katakolon, Gythion, Mykonos. May 29; June 26; August 14. Rates: From $5,530. Seven-day Athens-to-Istanbul, Istanbul-to-Athens and Venice-to-Athens, Athens-to-Venice cruises continue until October 23.
Seabourn Spirit	**Seven-day Civitavecchia-to-Athens** cruise calls at Sorrento (Italy), Lipari (Italy), Katakolon, Itea, Nafplion. May 8. Rates: From $4,260.

Sea Cloud Cruises

32–40 N. Dean St., Englewood, NJ 07631. ℂ **888/732-2568.** www.seacloud.com.

The flagship vessel *Sea Cloud* (built in 1931; 64 passengers; 2,532 GRTs) was built for heiress Marjorie Merriweather Post, who was involved in the design and construction of the sailing ship, planning the layout of the vessel down to where the antiques would be placed. At the time it was the largest sailing yacht to be built. The *Sea Cloud* served as a military support ship during World War II, was briefly owned by Dominican Republic dictator Rafael Trujillo, and sat tied up for 8 years before it was bought by a Hamburg-based group in the late 1970s and given a new, luxurious lease on life.

Guests can still see the care that Post originally put into it: Fireplaces in the cabins, antiques, marble, and shining wood. In the owner's suite, guests sleep in a Louis XIV–style bed next to a decorative marble fireplace; the bathroom alone is 9 sq. m (97 sq. ft.). The Category 5 cabins, on the other hand, are upper-and-lower berths, but Sea Cloud points out that since the cabins open to the promenade deck guests can sleep with the doors open to let in the sea air. Sailing buffs will be happy to gaze up at the 3,973 sq. m (32,000 sq. ft.) of sail—it has 36 separate sails, from the flying jib to the mizzen royal to the jigger gaff.

Sea Cloud is often chartered out by tour operators, who set their own itineraries for the ship; contact Sea Cloud for information on additional Greece cruises through tour operators. The company has a total of four vessels, including a riverboat.

Sea Cloud Cruises Itineraries & Rates

SHIP	ITINERARY
Sea Cloud	**Seven-day round-trip Athens** cruise calls at Crete, Mylos, Naxos, Siros, Nafplion. May 31. Rates: From $4,515. **Seven-day Athens-to-Istanbul** cruise calls at Mylos, Siros, Patmos, Kusadasi (Turkey), Dikili (Turkey), Lesbos. June 7; July 9. Rates: From $4,515. **Seven-day Athens-to-Istanbul** cruise calls at Mylos, Santorini, Marmaris, Rhodes, Patmos, Kusadasi (Turkey). July 31. Rates: From $4,515.

Seadream Yacht Club

2601 S. Bayshore Dr., Penthouse 1B, Coconut Grove, FL 33133. © **800/707-4911.** www.seadream yachtclub.com.

The owner and operator of SeaDream Yacht Club, Atle Brynestad, has a luxury-line pedigree as the founder of Seabourn Cruise Line. For more than 10 years, he has been carrying on the Seabourn tradition of luxury and elegance, on a smaller, more casual, yachtlike scale. SeaDream in 2001 purchased the *Sea Goddess I* and *Sea Goddess II* from Seabourn, and after renovations renamed them **SeaDream I** and **SeaDream II** (built in 1984; 116 passengers; 4,260 GRTs). Updated in 2009, the ships have all new bedding and one additional suite.

The company defines itself not as a cruise line but an ultraluxury yacht company whose vessels journey to smaller, less-visited destinations. Guests are offered an unstructured, casually elegant vacation (no formal nights) with plenty of diversions. Toys carried aboard include jet skis and mountain bikes. You can dine outdoors or indoors; there are enough tables to accommodate all the passengers in one outdoor lunch seating. None of the cabins have private balconies, but the line often urges guests to treat the teak decks as one large veranda where you can sprawl on bed-size Balinese loungers. With advanced reservations, they will even make the beds up for you with a turndown service so you can sleep under the stars. Another evening option is to meet for a drink at the **Top of the Yacht Bar**—SeaDream has an open-bar policy.

Seadream Yacht Club Itineraries & Rates

SHIP	ITINERARY
Seadream II	**Ten-day Venice (Italy) to Athens** cruise calls at Split (Croatia), Korcula (Croatia), Dubrovnik (Croatia, overnight), Kotor (Montenegro), Sarande (Albania), Delphi, Mykonos, Santorini, Hydra. May 30. Rates: From $6,999. **Seven-day round-trip Athens** cruise calls at Delos, Mykonos, Rhodes, Fethiye (Turkey), Gocek (Turkey), Bodrum (Turkey, overnight), Hydra. June 9. Rates: From $4,999. Seven-day round-trip Athens cruise calls at Hydra, Delphi, Olympia/Katakolon, Gythion, Elafonsios, Santorini. June 16. Rates: From $5,199. **Seven-day Athens to Istanbul** (Turkey) cruise calls at Hydra, Santorini, Paros Island, Patmos, Ephesus/Kusadasi (Turkey), Kepez (Turkey). June 23. Rates: From $5,199.

SHIP	ITINERARY
Seadream I	**Seven-day Dubrovnik (Croatia) to Athens** cruise calls at Parga, Delphi, Hydra Patmos, Ephesus/Kusadasi (Turkey), Santorini. July 21. Rates: From $5,199. **Seven-day Athens to Dubrovnik** (Croatia) cruise calls at Hydra, Delphi, Parga, Sarande (Albania), Kotor (Montenegro), Kotor (Montenegro), Dubrovnik (overnight). July 28. Rates: From $5,199. **Seven-day Rome (Civitavecchia, Italy) to Athens** cruise calls at Capri (Italy), Sorrento (Italy, overnight), Taormina (Sicily, Italy), Fiskardho, Delphi, Hydra. August 25. Rates: From $5,199. **Ten-day Athens to Istanbul** (Turkey) cruise calls at Hydra, Santorini, Lindos, Antalya (Turkey), Bodrum (Turkey), Patmos, Ephesus/Kusadasi (Turkey), Kepez (Turkey), Istanbul (overnight) Rates: From $6,999. **Seven-day Istanbul (Turkey) to Athens** cruise calls at Kepez (Turkey), Ephesus/Kusadasi (Turkey), Patmos, Bodrum (Turkey), Rhodes, Santorini. September 22. Rates: From $6,199. **Seven-day round-trip Athens** cruise calls at Santorini, Lindos, Gocek (Turkey), Bodrum (Turkey), Agadir (Morocco), Hydra. September 29; October 6. Rates: From $4,999.

Silversea Cruises

110 E. Broward Blvd., Fort Lauderdale, FL 33301. ℂ **800/722-9055.** www.silversea.com.

The luxurious *Silver Wind* (built in 1995; 296 passengers; 16,800 GRTs) and newer and larger *Silver Spirit* (built in 2009; 540 passengers; 36,000 GRTs) carry their guests in splendor and elegance. Passengers are generally well traveled and used to the good life. Fares include all alcoholic and nonalcoholic beverages along with tips.

Aboard both the *Wind* and the *Spirit,* all accommodations are outside suites with writing tables, sofas, walk-in closets, marble bathrooms, stocked minibars, and all the amenities you'd expect of top-of-the-line ships. Throughout, both vessels allot more space to each passenger than most other ships. Dine on some of the best cuisine at sea in open-seating restaurants that allow you dine when and with whom you desire. The larger *Spirit* boasts four restaurants, including **La Terrazza** for indoor or alfresco dining with breakfast and lunch buffets; **Le Champagne** for a six-course epicurean experience in an intimate atmosphere; **The Pool Grill** for lunch and dinner; the intimate **Seishin Restaurant** for a range of Asian-fusion menu items, from Kobe beef and spider lobster to caviar and lots of sushi choices (per-person degustation menu cost is $40); and the **Stars Supper Club,** where live music, dancing, and nightclub-style entertainment complement the innovative menus and provide a relaxed feeling.

Silversea Cruises Itineraries & Rates

SHIP	ITINERARY
Silver Wind	**Fourteen-day Barcelona (Spain) to Istanbul** (Turkey) cruise overnights in Barcelona and calls at Marseille (France), Monte Carlo (Monaco), Florence/Pisa (Livorno, Italy, overnight), Rome (Civitavecchia, Italy), Naples/Capri (Sorrento, Italy), Palermo (Sicily, Italy), Valletta (Malta), Crete, Athens. March 13 Rates: From $6,518. **Ten-day Istanbul (Turkey) to Athens** cruise calls at Canakkale (Turkey), Ephesus/Kusadasi (Turkey), Rhodes, Nazareth/Galilee (Haifa, Israel), Jerusalem/Tel Aviv (Ashdod, Israel), Cairo (Port Said, Egypt), Cairo/Giza (Alexandria, Egypt). March 27. Rates: From $4,678. **Eleven-day Athens to Barcelona** (Spain) cruise calls at Santorini, Valletta (Malta), Siracusa (Sicily, Italy), Palermo (Sicily, Italy), Cagliari (Sardinia, Italy), Alghero (Sardinia, Italy), Port Mahon (Menorca, Spain), Ibiza (Spain), Palma de Mallorca (Spain). April 6.

continues

Silver Wind *(continued)*	Rates: From $5,158. **Nine-day Istanbul (Turkey) to Athens** cruise calls at Ephesus/Kusadasi (Turkey), Patmos, Rhodes, Crete, Santorini, Hydra, Mykonos. May 26. Rates: From $5,678. **Nine-day Athens to Rome** (Civitavecchia, Italy) cruise calls at Mylos, Zakynthos, Itea, Corfu, Gallipoli (Italy), Sorrento (Italy, overnight). June 4. Rates: From $5,678. **Nine-day Istanbul (Turkey) to Athens** cruise calls at Canakkale (Turkey), Ephesus/Kusadasi (Turkey), Damascus (Syria), Beirut (Lebanon), Limassol (Cyprus), Rhodes, Santorini. July 20. Rates: From $5,678. **Nine-day Athens to Venice** (Italy) cruise calls at Mykonos, Crete, Itea, Corfu, Kotor (Montenegro), Hvar (Croatia), Venice (overnight). July 29. Rates: From $5,678. **Nine-day Venice (Italy) to Athens** cruise overnights in Venice and calls at Zadar (Croatia), Dubrovnik (Croatia, overnight), Brindisi (Italy), Agrostoli, Monemvasia, Nauplion. August 25. Rates: From $5,678. **Seven-day Athens to Istanbul** (Turkey) cruise calls at Mykonos, Santorini, Crete, Rhodes, Ephesus/Kusadasi (Turkey). September 3. Rates: From $4,118. **Seven-day Istanbul (Turkey) to Athens** cruise calls at Ephesus/Kusadasi (Turkey), Rhodes, Crete, Santorini, Mykonos. September 17. Rates: From $4,118. **Seven-day Athens to Venice** (Italy) cruise calls at Monemvasia, Corfu, Kotor (Montenegro), Split (Croatia), Venice (overnight). September 24. Rates: From $4,118. **Nine-day Istanbul (Turkey) to Athens** cruise calls at Canakkale (Turkey), Ephesus/Kusadasi (Turkey), Alanya (Turkey), Antalya (Turkey), Rhodes, Mykonos, Patmos. October 10. Rates: From $5,318. **Twelve-day Istanbul (Turkey) to Athens** cruise calls at Ephesus/Kusadasi (Turkey), Rhodes, Limassol (Cyprus), Nazareth/Galilee (Haifa, Israel), Jerusalem/Tel Aviv (Ashdod, Israel), Cairo (Port Said, Egypt), Cairo/Giza (Alexandria, Egypt), Crete, Nauplion. October 31. Rates: From $6,438.
Silver Spirit	**Seven-day Athens to Istanbul** (Turkey) cruise overnights in Athens and calls at Crete, Rhodes, Epheusu/Kusadasi (Turkey), Mykonos. October 1. Rates: From $5,318. Seven-day Istanbul (Turkey) to Athens cruise calls at Epheusu/Kusadasi (Turkey), Rhodes, Crete, Santorini, Mykonos. June 25; August 13; October 8. Rates: From $5,318. **Seven-day Athens to Venice** (Italy) cruise calls at Monemvasia, Corfu, Kotor (Montenegro), Split (Croatia), Venice (overnight). July 2; August 20. Rates: From $5,318. **Seven-day Venice (Italy) to Athens** cruise overnights in Venice and calls at Hvar (Croatia), Corfu, Itea, Olympia/Katakolon, Monemvasia. September 24. Rates: From $4,958. **Seven-day Athens to Rome** (Civitavecchia, Italy) cruise calls at Monemvasia, Valletta (Malta), Catania (Sicily, Italy), Palermo (Sicily, Italy), Sorrento (Italy). October 15. Rates: From $4,958.

Star Clippers

7200 NW 19th St., Suite 206, Miami, FL 33126. ☏ **800/442-0550.** www.starclippers.com.

Star Clipper (built in 1991; 170 passengers; 2,298 GRTs) is the name of the handsome old-timey vessel this three-ship line, named Star Clippers, is sending to Greece in 2012. It's a replica of the big 19th-century clipper sailing ships (or barkentines) that once circled the globe. Its tall square rigs carry enormous sails, are glorious to look at, and are a particular thrill for history buffs. And on this ship, the 3,345 sq. m (36,000 sq. ft.) of billowing sails are more than window dressing. The *Star Clipper* was constructed using original drawings and specifications of a leading 19th-century naval architect, but updated with modern touches so that today it is among the tallest (68m/226 ft.) and fastest clipper ships built.

The atmosphere onboard is akin to being on a private yacht rather than on a mainstream cruise ship. It's active and casual in an L.L. Bean sort of way, and friendly too. Cabins are decorated with wood accents; the top categories have doors that open up directly onto the deck. There is one owner's suite. The public rooms include an open-seating dining room, and an Edwardian-style library with a Belle Epoque fireplace and bookshelf-lined walls. There are two small swimming pools. Local entertainment is sometimes brought aboard and movies might be shown, plus you can always count on silly contests and games at the deck bar as part of the after-dinner offerings. Other activities on the ship tend toward the nautical, such as visiting the bridge, observing the crew handle the sails, and participating in knot-tying classes. Or you can just pad around the decks and lie in a deck chair underneath the sails. When seas are calm you can lie in the rigging.

StarClippers Itineraries & Rates

SHIP	ITINERARY
Star	**Seven-day round-trip Athens** cruise to the northern Greek islands calls at Camilimani (Turkey), Kusadasi (Turkey), Patmos, Amorgos, Mykonos, and Monemvasia. Once a month or so between May and October. Rates: From $2,075. **Seven-day round-trip Athens** cruise to the southern Greek islands calls at Rhodes, Bodrum (Turkey), Daylan River (Turkey), Santorini, Hydra. Once a month or so between May and October. Rates: From $2,075.

Swan Hellenic Cruises

Lynnem House, 1 Victoria Way, Burgess Hill, West Sussex, RH15 9NF. ℂ **800/257-5767** or 0844 871 4603. www.swanhellenic.com

This British company founded in 1954 excels in small-ship cruising and features the **Minerva** (built in 1996, 320 passengers; 12,500 GRTs). The line appeals to those who really want to learn something about a destination. Escorted shore excursions are included in the fares (and so are all tips) and impressive guest lectures speak about the islands' history and culture. Called a "country house at sea," the ship has two open-seating restaurants, two bars, a cinema, swimming pool, gym, spa, salon, and beautiful tiered decks and teak promenade offering plenty of vantage points for sightseeing. For some downtime, bring a book and your daydreams to the conservatory-style **Shackleton's Bar,** with its cane chairs and potted palms.

Swan Hellenic Cruises Itineraries & Rates

SHIP	ITINERARY
Minerva	**Fourteen-day Sharm-El-Sheikh (Egypt) to Athens** cruise overnights in Sharm-El-Sheikh and calls at Sokhna (Egypt, overnight), Cairo/Giza (Alexandria, Egypt), Damascus (Syria), Latakia (Syria), Antalya (Turkey), Fethiye (Turkey), Santorini, Athens (overnight). April 11. Rates: From $3,199. **Thirteen-day Athens to Rome** (Civitavecchia, Italy) cruise overnights in Athens and calls at Itea, Olympia/Katakolon, Argostoli, Preveza, Kotor (Montenegro), Korcula (Croatia), Dubrovnik (Croatia), Palermo (Sicily, Italy), Rome (overnight). April 25. Rates: From $2,499. **Fourteen-day Valletta (Malta) to Athens** cruise overnights in Valletta and calls at Dubrovnik (Croatia, overnight), Korcula (Croatia), Split (Croatia), Trieste (Italy), Venice (Italy), Pula (Croatia), Kotor (Montenegro, overnight), Sarande (Albania), Itea, Athens (two overnights). August 15. Rates: From $3,999. **Fourteen-day Athens to Istanbul** (Turkey) cruise overnights in Athens and calls at Souda Bay, Gythion,

continues

SHIP	ITINERARY
Minerva *(continued)*	Nauplion, Delos, Mykonos (overnight), Paros Island, Chios, Symi, Fethiye (Turkey), Ephesus/Kusadasi (Turkey, overnight), Istanbul (overnight). August 29. Rates: From $3,899. **Fourteen-day Izmir (Turkey) to Athens** cruise overnights in Izmir and calls at Thessaloniki, Kavala/Philippi, Rhodes, Antalya (Turkey), Tasucu (Turkey), Latakia (Syria), Damascus (Syria), Limassol (Cyprus), Syros, Athens (overnight). September 26. Rates: From $4,199.

Travel Dynamics International

132 E. 70th St., New York, NY 10021. ⓒ **800/257-5767.** www.traveldynamicsinternational.com.

This operator of small ships offers a number of interesting itineraries that include Greek ports, and no wonder: The cofounders of Travel Dynamics are two Greek brothers from the island of Rhodes. The journeys are tailored to be unique, visiting some of the smaller and lesser-known ports. Top-notch onboard educational programs complement the itineraries, and shore excursions are included in the cruise price. This line won't attract the budget-minded passenger or the folks who want to laze around. Itineraries are fast paced and educational. Each day has several components: a museum in the morning and an archaeological site in the afternoon, for example. The company's itineraries often include references to the nearby sites (Iraklion for Knossos or Gortyn, for example).

The cozy **Callisto** (built in 2006; 34 passengers; 499 tons) is adorned with rich fabrics, wood, polished brass, rare antiquities, and artwork, with cabins offering marble bathrooms, minibars, and fresh flowers. There's a swimming platform, hot tub, and library as well. The larger **Corinthian II** (built in 1992; 114 passengers; 4,200 GRTs) also has luxe touches including marble bathrooms, minifridges, and private balconies. An outdoor bar and cafe accommodates alfresco diners. The ship also has a gym, salon, sun deck with hot tub, and Internet cafe.

Travel Dynamics International Itineraries & Rates

SHIP	ITINERARY
Corinthian II	**Ten-day Venice (Italy) to Limassol** (Cyprus) cruise overnights in Venice and calls at Zadar (Croatia), Dubrovnik (Croatia), Kotor (Montenegro), Corfu, Pylos, Rethymnon, Chania, Anamur Limani (Turkey), Tasucu (Turkey). April 27. Rates: From $8,295. **Ten-day Limassla (Cyprus) to Istanbul** (Turkey) cruise calls at Tasucu (Turkey), Antalya (Turkey), Marmaris (Turkey), Ephesus/Kusadasi (Turkey), Delos, Platamonas, Thessalonica (overnight), Canakkale (Turkey). May 17. Rates: From $7,995. **Ten-day Istanbul (Turkey) to Athens** cruise calls at Canakkale (Turkey), Nauplion, Pylos, Valletta (Malta), Trapani (Italy), Naples (Italy), Messina (Sicily, Italy), Ithaca. May 27. Rates: From $7,995. **Eight-day Athens to Catania** cruise calls at Argostoli, Lipari (Sicily, Italy), Sorrento (Italy), Agropoli (Italy), Palermo (Sicily, Italy), Marsala (Sicily, Italy), Syracuse (Sicily, Italy), Catania (Italy). June 6. Rates: From $7,795. **Ten-day Rome (Civitavecchia, Italy) to Athens** cruise overnights in Rome and calls at Salerno (Italy), Olympia/Katakolon, Rethymnon, Santorini, Rhodes, Ephesus/Kusadasi (Turkey), Athens (overnight). June 22; July 10. Rates: From $7,695. **Ten-day Istanbul (Turkey) to Rome** (Civitavecchia, Italy) cruise calls at Chios, Santorini, Rethymnon, Valletta (Malta), Marsala (Sicily, Italy), Cagliari (Sardinia, Italy), Alghero (Italy), Bonifacio (Corsica, France). July 28. Rates: From $7,995. **Twelve-day Venice (Italy) to Istanbul** (Turkey) cruise calls

continues

SHIP	ITINERARY
Corinthian II *(continued)*	at Split (Croatia), Ploce (Croatia), Dubrovnik (Croatia), Kotor (Montenegro), Durres (Albania), Nafpaktos, Athens, Izmir (Turkey), Thessalonica, Constanta (Romania), Nessebur (Bulgaria). September 5. Rates: From $8,495. **Ten-day Istanbul (Turkey) to Venice** (Italy) cruise calls at Canakkale (Turkey), Ephesus/Kusadasi (Turkey), Rethymnon, Pylos, Syracuse (Sicily, Italy), Taranto (Italy), Vlore (Albania), Kotor (Montenegro), Dubrovnik (Croatia), Split (Croatia). September 17. Rates: From $7,985. **Eleven-day Venice (Italy) to Athens** cruise calls at Split (Croatia), Vlore (Albania), Taranto (Italy), Syracuse (Sicily, Italy), Gytheion, Agios Nikolaos, Fethiye (Turkey), Marmaris (Turkey), Bodrum (Turkey). September 27. Rates: From $8,495. **Twelve-day round-trip Athens** cruise overnights in Athens and calls at Santorini, Heraklion, Cairo/Port Said (Egypt), Jerusalem/Tel Aviv (Haifa, Israel), Limassol (Cyprus), Fethiye (Turkey), Marmaris (Turkey), Rhodes, Ephesus/Kusadasi (Turkey). October 7. Rates: From $9,395. **Fourteen-day Athens to Casablanca** (Morocco) cruise calls at Itea/Delphi, Saranda (Albania), Taranto (Italy), Calabria (Italy), Syracuse (Sicily, Italy), Valletta (Malta), Marsala (Italy), Tunis (Tunisia), Cagliari (Sardinia, Italy), Annaba (Algeria), Bejaia (Algeria), Tangier (Morocco). October 19. Rates: From $9,395.
Callisto	**Nine-day round-trip Athens** cruise calls at Nauplion, Gytheion, Rethymnon, Santorini, Rhodes, Patmos, Ephesus/Kusadasi (Turkey), Delos. April 17; May 23. Rates: From $8,995. **Nine-day round-trip Athens** cruise calls at Milos, Rethymnon, Santorini, Rhodes, Didyma, Ephesus/Kusadasi (Turkey), Delos, Palea Epidavros. September 8, September 26. Rates: From $8,995. **Nine-day round-trip Athens** cruise calls at Ithaca, Parga, Preveza, Assos, Pylos, Kalamata, Nauplion. June 10. Rates: From $8,995. **Nine-day round-trip Athens** cruise calls at Folegandros, Amorgos, Nisyros, Patmos, Chios, Skopelos, Limni, Kea. June 28; July 7, July 16. Rates: From $8,995. **Nine-day round-trip Athens** cruise calls at Rethymnon, Chania, Aghia Galini (overnight), Ierapetra, Aghia Nicolaos, Heraklion, Santorini. August 3. Rates: From $8,995. **Nine-day Kusadasi (Turkey) to Antalya** (Turkey) cruise overnights in Ephesus/Kusadasi and calls at Bodrum (Turkey), Cnidos (Turkey), Symi, Rhodes, Ekincik (Turkey), Fethiye (Turkey), Castellorizo, Kekova (Turkey). October 15, October 24; November 2, November 11. Rates: From $8,995.

Variety Cruises

494 Eighth Ave., 22nd Floor, New York, NY 10001. ✆ **800/319-7776.** www.varietycruises.com.

These line's Greek-flagged and -operated yachts might be just the ticket if you're looking for a casual, intimate experience with a more international flavor. Formerly known as Zeus Tours, the cruise portion of the company has been around since the mid-1960s when it chartered the yacht *Eleftherios;* it began scheduled weekly cruise service in 1973. Today, it divides its ships into three divisions. The more upmarket Variety Cruises division emphasizes a blend of cruising and yachting, relaxing, and exploring Greece's historical treasures. Ships in this fleet include the yacht *Harmony G* (built in 2001; 46 passengers; 490 GRTs).

There are sun decks but no pools except for the surrounding Mediterranean: passengers can swim off the side of the ship during swim stops. Fares include two meals a day, breakfast and then either lunch or dinner, depending on the itinerary, which gives guests the chance to eat and drink in port. There's no organized onboard entertainment *per se*, except for chatting with other guests in the saloon or while catching rays on deck. And with only a couple dozen other guests, you'll probably get to know everyone within a day. Open-seating dinner helps with the mingling.

Variety Cruises Itineraries & Rates

SHIP	ITINERARY
Harmony G	Seven-day round-trip Athens cruise call at Nauplion/Mycenae, Gythion, Pylos, Olympia/Katakolon, Delphi. February 17, February 24; March 2, March 9, March 16, March 23; April 13. Rates: From $1,071.

Voyages of Antiquity

Frensham House, Headley Road, Leatherhead, Surrey, KT22 8PT. ℂ **877/398-1460.** www.voyagesto antiquity.com.

The midsize *Aegean Odyssey* (built in 1973; 350 passengers; 11,563 GRTs) is a cozy boutique-style ship with classic lines and a retro feel. Built as a ferry, the ship was converted to a cruise ship in 1988 and extensively refurbished. Perfect for history buffs and class ship lovers, the *Aegean Odyssey* is an old-world gem, with two restaurants, six bars and lounges, a library, theater, Internet center, spa, and salon. Expert lecturers, often professors and historians, sail on board to educate guests about the region and fares include excursions; pre- and/or posthotel stays in Athens or Istanbul or Rome; all meals; free wine, beer, or soft drinks with the evening meal; and tips. Voyages of Antiquity is geared to sophisticated travelers looking to be immersed in the destination and the focus is on education and learning.

Voyages of Antiquity Itineraries & Rates

SHIP	ITINERARY
Aegean Odyssey	**Fourteen-day Athens to Rome** (Civitavecchia, Italy) includes 2-night precruise hotel stay in Athens; cruise calls at Nauplia, Monemvasia, Heraklion, Rethimnon, Syracuse (Sicily, Italy), Valletta (Malta), Trapani (Sicily, Italy), Palermo (Sicily, Italy, overnight). March 19. Rates: From $3,795. **Fifteen-day Venice (Italy) to Istanbul** (Turkey) includes 2-night postcruise hotel stay in Istanbul; cruise overnights in Venice and calls at Pula (Croatia), Split (Croatia, overnight), Korcula (Croatia), Dubrovnik (Croatia), Corfu, Monemvasia, Rethimnon, Santorini, Naxos, Lemnos. April 13. Rates: From $4,595. **Fourteen-day Istanbul (Turkey) to Athens** includes 2-night precruise hotel stay in Athens and 2-night postcruise hotel stay in Istanbul; cruise calls at Lemnos, Mount Athos, Skiathos, Izmir (Turkey, overnight), Delos, Mykonos, Santorini, Rethimnon, Nauplia. April 23; August 25. Rates: From $4,450. **Fifteen-day round-trip Athens** included 2-night precruise hotel stay; cruise calls in Nauplia, Monemvasia, Rethimnon, Rhodes, Delos, Mykonos, Samos, Ephesus/Kusadasi (Turkey, overnight), Istanbul (Turkey, overnight), Mount Athos, Skiathos. May 2; September 3; October 16. Rates: From $4,695. **Thirteen-day Athens to Venice** (Italy) includes 2-night precruise hotel stay in Athens; cruise calls at Nauplia, Monemvasia, Olympia/Katakolon, Ithaca, Corfu, Sarande (Albanic), Dubrovnik (Croatia, overnight), Split (Croatia), Zadar (Croatia), Venice (overnight). May 14. Rates: From $4,250.

continues

SHIP	ITINERARY
Aegean Odyssey *(continued)*	**Thirteen-day Venice (Italy) to Athens** includes 2-night postcruise hotel stay in Athens; cruise overnights in Venice and calls at Zadar (Croatia), Split (Croatia, overnight), Korcula (Croatia), Dubrovnik (Croatia), Corfu, Preveza, Olympia/Katakolon, Nauplia. June 23; October 7. Rates: From $4,250. **Fourteen-day Athens to Istanbul** (Turkey) includes 2-night precruise hotel stay in Athens and 2-night postcruise hotel stay in Istanbul; cruise calls at Nauplia, Rethimnon, Santorini, Delos, Mykonos, Izmir (Turkey, overnight), Skiathos, Lemnos. July 1; September 15. Rates: From $4,450. **Seventeen-day Istanbul (Turkey) to Rome** (Civitavecchia, Italy) includes 2-night precruise hotel stay in Istanbul and 2-night postcruise hotel stay in Rome; cruise calls at Lemnos, Izmir (Turkey), Delos, Mykonos, Athens, Nauplia, Taormina (Sicily, Italy), Palermo (Sicily, Italy, overnight), Sorrento (Italy, overnight). July 22. Rates: From $4,995. **Seventeen-day Rome (Civitavecchia, Italy) to Istanbul** (Turkey) includes 2-night precruise hotel stay in Rome and 2-night postcruise hotel stay in Istanbul; cruise calls at Sorrento (Italy, overnight), Palermo (Sicily, Italy, overnight), Taormina (Sicily, Italy), Nauplia, Athens, Delos, Mykonos, Izmir (Turkey), Lemnos. August 13. Rates: From $4,995. **Fifteen-day Istanbul (Turkey) to Venice** (Italy) included 2-night precruise hotel stay in Istanbul; cruise calls at Mount Athos, Thessalonica, Volos, Patmos, Athens, Monemvasia, Preveza, Corfu, Dubrovnik (Croatia), Korcula (Croatia), Ravenna (Italy). September 24. Rates: From $4,750. **Twelve-day Athens to Limassol** (Cyprus) cruise overnights in Athens and calls at Nauplia, Santorini, Rethimnon, Heraklion, Rhodes, Fethiye (Turkey), Antalya (Turkey), Tasucu (Turkey). October 30. Rates: From $3,750.

Windstar Cruises

2101 Fourth Ave., Suite 1150, Seattle, WA 98121. (C) **87-STAR-SAIL** (877/827-7245). www.windstarcruises.com.

Although they look like sailing ships of yore, **Wind Star** and **Wind Spirit** (built in 1986 and 1988; 144 passengers; 5,350 GRTs) and their bigger sister **Wind Surf** (built in 1990; 312 passengers; 14,745 GRTs) are more like floating luxury hotels with the flair of sailing ships. These vessels feature top-notch service and cuisine, yet have a wonderful casual vibe. Million-dollar computers operate the sails, and stabilizers allow for a smooth ride.

Windstar deploys its two smaller vessels, *Wind Spirit* and *Wind Star,* in the Greek islands. Casual, low-key elegance is the style. There's no set regime and no dress code above "resort casual." Most of the passengers are well heeled; the ships appeal to all ages except children. (There are no dedicated kids' facilities onboard the ships.)

None of the roomy outside cabins have balconies, but they do have large portholes. The top-level owner's cabins are slightly bigger. Refurbishments in 2009 include flatscreen TVs and DVD players; new mattresses, bedding, carpet, and curtains for the cabins; an expanded gym; and an updated spa.

A watersports platform at the stern allows for a variety of activities when the ships are docked. Entertainment is low key and sometimes includes local entertainers brought aboard at ports of call. Most of the onboard time revolves around the sun deck, plunge pool, and outdoor bar. The ships also have small casinos.

4

CRUISING THE GREEK ISLANDS | Small & Yachtlike Ships

SHIP	ITINERARY
Wind Spirit	**Seven-day Rome (Civitavecchia, Italy) to Athens** cruise calls at Ischia (Italy), Lipari (Italy), Taormina (Sicily, Italy), Gythion, Monemvasia. April 28. Rates: From $2,496. **Seven-day Athens to Istanbul** (Turkey) cruise calls at Mykonos, Santorini, Rhodes, Bodrum (Turkey), Epheusu/Kusadasi (Turkey). May 5, May 19; June 2, June 16; July 14, July 28; August 25; September 8, September 22, October 6. Rates: From $2,949. **Seven-day Istanbul (Turkey) to Athens** cruise calls at Ephesus/Kusadasi (Turkey), Rhodes, Bodrum, Santorini, Mykonos. May 12, May 26; June 9, June 23; July 21; August 4; September 1, September 15, September 29; October 13. Rates: From $3,431. **Seven-day Athens to Valletta** (Malta) cruise calls at Gythion, Argostoli, Butrint National Park (Albania), Siracusa (Sicily, Italy), Gozo (Malta). June 30; August 11; October 20. Rates: From $2,948. **Seven-day Valletta to Athens** cruise calls at Gozo (Malta), Siracusa (Sicily, Italy), Butrint National Park (Albania), Argostoli, Gythion. July 7; August 18; October 27. Rates: From $3,091. **Eight-day Athens to Rome** (Civitavecchia, Italy) cruise calls at Monemvasia, Gythion, Taormina (Sicily, Italy), Lipari (Italy), Sorrento (Italy), Ischia (Italy). November 3. Rates: From $2,379.
Wind Star	**Seven-day Istanbul (Turkey) to Athens** cruise calls at Ephesus/Kusadasi (Turkey), Rhodes, Bodrum (Turkey), Santorini, Monemvasia. June 2, June 16, June 30; August 25; September 8, September 15, September 22, September 29; October 6, October 20. Rates: From $3,431. **Seven-day Athens to Istanbul** (Turkey) cruise calls at Mykonos, Santorini, Rhodes, Bodrum (Turkey), Ephesus/Kusadasi (Turkey). June 9, June 23; August 18; September 1, September 15, September 29, October 13. Rates: From $3,431. **Eight-day Athens to Rome** (Civitavecchia, Italy) cruise calls at Monemvasia, Gythion, Taormina (Sicily, Italy), Lipari (Italy), Sorrento (Italy), Ischia (Italy). July 7; October 27. Rates: From $2,756. **Seven-day Rome (Civitavecchia, Italy) to Athens** cruise calls at Ischia (Italy), Lipari (Italy), Taormina (Sicily, Italy), Gythion, Monemvasia. August 11. Rates: From $2,496.

BEST SHORE EXCURSIONS IN GREECE

Shore excursions are designed to help you make the most of your limited time in port by transporting you to sites of historical or cultural value, or of natural or artistic beauty. The tours are usually booked online in advance or on the first or second day of your cruise; are sold on a first-come, first-served basis; and are nonrefundable. Some lines—but not many—include shore excursions in their cruise fares.

Generally, shore excursions that take you beyond the port area are the ones most worth taking. You'll get professional commentary and avoid hassles with local transportation. In ports where the attractions are within walking distance of the pier, you may be best off touring on your own. In other cases, it may be more enjoyable to take a taxi to an attraction and skip the crowded bus tours; many lines offer private cars and vans for those who want to tour solo (or you can walk into the port and find a taxi, probably cheaper, on your own).

A few tips on choosing the best shore excursion for you, as you look through your cruise line's shore excursion information: See if the description includes sites of interest to you. Check the activity level of the tour: a "level 1" or "moderate" tour means minimal walking; a "level 3" or "strenuous" marker means you may be climbing steep steps or walking long distances—especially true in Greece, as some tours of sites and ruins require a lot of walking up steps or over uneven ground. And check the tour's length and price tag—the longer and/or more expensive the tour, in general, the more comprehensive it tends to be.

When touring in Greece, remember to wear comfortable walking shoes and bring a hat, sunscreen, and bottled water to combat the effects of the hot sun. Most lines offer bottled water for a fee as you disembark.

Also, keep in mind that some churches and other religious sites require modest attire, which means shoulders and knees should be covered.

Cruise lines tend to set shore excursion pricing and options closer to the sail date. We've included 2011 prices to give you a general idea of how much each tour will cost. Shore excursions are a revenue-generating area for the cruise lines, and the tours may be heavily promoted aboard the ship. They aren't always offered at bargain prices.

Below are selected shore excursion offerings at the major cruise ports. Keep in mind that not all the tours will be offered by every line, and prices will vary. The tour may also show up on different lines with a few variations and a different name. For more information on many of these ports, consult the relevant chapters in this book.

CORFU (KERKIRA)

See chapter 15 for complete sightseeing information.

The Achilleion & Paelokastritsa (4½ hr., $64): Visit the hilltop town of Paleokastritsa on the western side of Corfu, punctuated with olive, lemon, and cypress trees and bays and coves. Stop at the 13th-century Monastery of the Virgin Mary, on the edge of a promontory as well as Achilleion Palace, built in the late 19th century as the home of Empress Elizabeth of Austria. The palace, now owned by the Greek government, has been renovated and guests can visit the home and the gardens, which boast views of the island. The tour includes time for shopping in old Corfu Town before heading back to the ship.

Mountain Bike Expedition (4 hr., $149): Travel from the port by coach to the town of Dassia, where you'll pick up your bike. The bike tour starts with an uphill ride to Kato Korakiana, where you'll stop at a coffee shop. Bike through a narrow, paved alley to get to the town of St. Marcos, with stone houses and a Byzantine chapel. Stop here for a Greek snack and then bike downhill.

IRAKLION & AYIOS NIKOLAOS (CRETE)

See chapter 9 for complete sightseeing information.

Knossos & the Minotaur (3 hr., $75): Knossos was once the center of the prehistoric Minoan civilization; it is thought to be the basis for the mythological Minotaur's labyrinth. Today it is one of the great archaeological sites. What remains are portions of two major palaces, plus several restorations made between 2000 B.C. and 1250 B.C.; parts of the palace were rebuilt in the 20th century. Visit the excavation of the palace of King Minos; view the royal quarter, the throne room, and the queen's quarters, with its dolphin frescoes above the door. Other sites include the house of the

BOOKING YOUR PRIVATE yacht CHARTER

Do you imagine yourself cruising the Greek isles on a boat built for two? Or six? Maybe you fancy taking a more active role in itinerary planning? Do you love the idea of requesting that you cruise for a few hours and stop in a secluded cove for swimming? Or do you relish the thought of stepping off your 24m (80-ft.) sailing vessel in the marina and heading off to a nearby beachfront restaurant for dinner?

Greece is a great place for a private yacht charter. Altogether, there are about 6,000 isles and islands in Greek territory. You're as free as a bird; you can cruise to an island and stay as long as you like (as long as the captain says it's okay). And although yacht cruising can be expensive, it doesn't have to be. But there are a few things to keep in mind.

You could go through a travel agent who's familiar with yacht chartering, or you could find a **yacht charter broker.** Yacht charter brokers are a link between yacht owners and you—they're the ones who know the boats and the crew, the ones who will guide you through the process and take your booking. Charter brokers go to boat shows around the world to check up on yachts and companies and crew; they might have personally sailed within the area you want to go to (or know someone who has).

For more information about charter brokers, visit the **Charter Yacht Brokers** Association at **www.cyba.net**. The site

has a page for prospective clients to request more information by describing their plans for a charter. Other associations for charter brokers include the **Mediterranean Yacht Brokers Association** and the **American Yacht Brokers Association.** The Greek Tourism Organization (www.gnto.gr) can also be a resource.

The yacht broker should ask questions and listen as you describe what you're looking for in a vacation. How many people are you traveling with? What are their ages—are there kids involved? Where are you interested in cruising, and when? Do you care more about visiting Greek towns and historic sites, or do you want to kick back on the boat and relax? Do you want to go ultraluxe, or are you on a tight budget? Do you want a power yacht, which is faster, or a sailing yacht, which burns less fuel? All these questions will help them plan the best route for you.

Here are a few tips:

- Be reasonable in your **itinerary planning.** A yacht probably won't be able to get you comfortably from Athens to Mykonos to Rhodes and back in a week. Generally speaking, you'll want to stick to nearby groups of islands, such as the Ionian, Dodecanese, Cyclades, and Sporades. If you're sailing from Athens, the Saronic Gulf and the Cyclades are close cruising areas.

high priest and the "small palace." Some tours include a visit to the archaeological museum, which includes artifacts from the Minoan civilization, or a stop in the town of Iraklion.

Windmills & Lassithi Plateau (4½ hr., $79): This tour takes participants up Mount Dikti to the Lassithi plateau. On the way you'll stop at the monastery of Kera, which houses Byzantine-era icons. The plateau boasts views of nearby mountains and the sailclothed windmills that irrigate the land. The tour includes about 2 hours of walking and standing, and there's considerable climbing involved. The tour includes a stop at a local restaurant.

Many yachts are based in Athens, but sometimes you can have a yacht sent up to an island group, as long as you're willing to pay a relocation fee, plus fuel, in order to get it there.

○ Who's driving? There are two basic types of charters. **Crewed** means there's a crew onboard. How many crew depends on the size of the boat, as well as your own personal needs. You'll need a captain and maybe a cook, a hostess, and/or a guide. A **bareboat** charter means there's no crew, and you'll do the sailing or provide your own crew.

○ Champagne and caviar? Well, that's all part of the provisioning and the charter's costs. Different charters work differently. Some vessels work on a **half-board** basis; in other words, breakfast and lunch are included in the cost, under the assumption that passengers will want to venture off the boat for dinner and nightlife. Another way of determining costs is an **advance provisioning amount,** or APA. The APA is an amount of money paid upfront for costs associated with the charter, and it's on average about 30% of the base rate for the charter. The APA could include fuel, crew costs,

food and beverages, marina fees, Corinth Canal fees, and other extras. At the end of the cruise, the costs are tallied and the passenger either gets money back or has to pay a little more. In either case, crew gratuity is not included. Be sure to work out with your charter broker exactly what's included and what's not.

○ Party of eight (or more)! You can rent a yacht for a cozy party of two, or bring a group of friends onboard—typically, the more people onboard the cheaper the cruise price works out per person. However, you're more limited in the choice of vessel once you go beyond 12 people. One solution for a big party: Charter two yachts and split up the party (or if you have *lots* of friends, think about chartering one of the cruise ships listed in this chapter).

○ What vessel **style**? You can get a 12m (40-ft.) yacht or a 30m (100-ft.) yacht, in as modest or luxurious style as you can imagine (and afford). Another consideration is whether you want a sleek, graceful sailing vessel or a modern, upscale power boat. Whatever you decide, there's probably a yacht out there that suits your style.

ITEA (DELPHI)

See chapter 12 for complete sightseeing information.

The Mythology of Delphi (4 hr., $79): Delphi was the ancient home of the Oracle, where pilgrims came to ask questions of the Greek god Apollo. Visit the Sanctuary of Apollo to see the Temple of Apollo, where one of three Pythian priestesses gave voice to Apollo's oracles; the well-preserved amphitheater; and the Castalian Spring and the Sacred Way. Be sure to visit the museum as well. The tour includes time to shop in the village of Delphi.

KATAKOLON (OLYMPIA)

See chapter 8 for complete sightseeing information.

Ancient Olympia & Archaeological Museum (3 hr., $74): Visit the site of the original Olympic Games, held from 776 B.C. to A.D. 393 (and most recently used in the 2004 Olympics). View temples and altars, including the Temple of Zeus, which once housed the gold-and-ivory statue of Zeus that was one of the Seven Wonders of the Ancient World; and the original stadium, which could seat 20,000. Also included is the temple of Hera, the shrine of Pelops, the Treasuries, the gymnasium, and the Council House, where athletes took the Olympic Oath. You'll spend about an hour in the museum, viewing artifacts and sculpture and conclude the tour with a visit to the village of Olympia. Some tours feature a folkloric show or snacks in Katakolon.

MYKONOS & DELOS

See chapter 10 for complete sightseeing information.

A Visit to Delos (4 hr., $65): Delos is the uninhabited island just off the coast of Mykonos where, according to mythology, the gods Apollo and Artemis were born. The island was a religious center. Excavations have uncovered the city of Delos, and the tour explores the site, which includes marble lions, three temples dedicated to Apollo, the theater district, and the Sacred Lake, which dried up in 1926.

Historic Walking Tour of Mykonos (2½ hr., $55): A downhill walking tour of Mykonos town takes in the Archaeological Museum, the Maritime Museum, and Lena's Traditional House, which re-creates the home of a 19th-century Mykonos family.

NAFPLION

Mycenae & Palamidi Castle (4 hr., $99): The area is rich with the remains of the ancient Mycenaean civilization. Drive by the ancient sites of Tiryns and come to the ruins of the ancient city of Mycenae, where excavation work begun in the 19th century eventually exposed the Lions Gate, the entrance to the city. Visit the Beehive Tomb, which gets its name from its shape. Take a shopping break at Fithia Village, then return to Nafplion and to the Palamidi Castle, which was built as a fortress by the Turks and Venetians (and later used as a prison). The castle offers views of the Argolic Gulf. *Note:* The path up consists of nearly 1,000 steps (buses can drive up to the gate).

PATMOS

See chapter 11 for complete sightseeing information.

St. John's Monastery & Cave of the Revelation (3 hr., $54): Depart the Port of Scala and travel by bus to the village of Chora and the 900-year-old, fortresslike Monastery of St. John, which overlooks the main harbor and is enclosed by fortified walls. You'll see the main church and the ecclesiastical treasures in the church and museum, including Byzantine icons, 6th-century Gospels, and frescoes in the chapel. Continue on by bus to the Cave of the Apocalypse. Niches in the wall mark the stone pillow and ledge used as a desk by St. John, said to have written the Book of Revelations here; a crack in the wall was said to have been made by the Voice of God. Refreshments are served in Scala. Visitors to the monastery must cover their shoulders; shorts are not allowed.

PIRAEUS/ATHENS

See chapter 6 for complete sightseeing information.

Athens & Cape Sounion (8 hr., $132): This tour visits the Acropolis, Athens's most prominent historical and architectural site, in the morning; after lunch, the tour continues to Cape Sounion (about a 1½–2 hr. drive from Athens), the most southern tip of the European landmass. Participants can explore the Temple of Poseidon, which is located at the top of a 60m (200-ft.) cliff and offers a panoramic view of the Saronic Gulf and the Cyclades.

Ancient Corinth and Canal Cruise (7 hr., $90): Drive past the coves of the Saronic Gulf to Isthmia, where you'll transit the Corinth Canal, a slim (30m/90-ft.-wide) waterway blasted through sheer rock in the 19th century. After cruise, explore ancient Corinth. Including the Apollo Temple, Fountain of Glauke, Spring of Periander and the remains of 25-ft wide Lechaion Road. Lunch is included in the tour.

RHODES

See chapter 11 for complete sightseeing information.

Filerimos Local Mezes & Wine Outing (3¾ hr., $63): Participants get a look at Rhodes Town before being driven to Filerimos, where hills are dotted with cypress, oaks, and pines. Visit Moni Filerimou and Lady of Filerimos, an Italian reconstruction of the Knights of St. John's 14th-century church, and ruins of the Temple of Athena. The tour continues to Kalithea Resort, where the thermal water was, according to story, once recommended by Hippocrates for its healing qualities; today the springs have dried up, but the area is known for swimming and scenery. There will be some time for shopping in Kalithea before you stop by a seaside taverna for local food and wine.

Walking Tour of Historic Rhodes (3½ hr., $52): Rhodes, which boasts one of the oldest inhabited medieval towns in Europe, is a great city for walking. This tour takes guests through the Old Town. You'll see churches, the Jewish quarter, the Inns of the Knights, and other spots; you'll tour the rebuilt Palace of the Grand Masters and the Hospital of the Knights, now a museum. And you'll walk down the cobblestoned Street of the Knights, an old pathway leading from the Acropolis of Rhodes down to the port and lined with medieval towers and architecturally interesting facades.

SANTORINI (THIRA)

See chapter 10 for complete sightseeing information.

Village of Oia & Santorini Island (3½ hr., $72): Another whitewashed hilltop town is Oia, the town where so many postcard-perfect photos are taken of blue-domed, whitewashed buildings and the blue sea beyond. There are small cobblestone streets to explore; pop in at shops and cafes. A wine tasting is offered to tourgoers, as well as a walk to the cable car station at the top of Fira.

SETTLING INTO ATHENS

by Peter Kerasiotis

This is Athens: Exciting and exasperating, worldly and oh so hot, a city that attacks the senses and stirs the spirit as only the cradle of Western civilization can. Homeland to gods, goddesses and some of the history's greatest philosophers and athletes, Athens boasts glorious ancient temples such as the Acropolis and its iconic Parthenon, and beautiful beaches. Best of all, Athens has the Athenians, who welcome progress, feed on the latest trends and, true to their hedonistic roots, party with Olympian stamina.

5

THINGS TO DO   While you'll be itching to see the Acropolis, majestically crowned by the Parthenon, take a siga, siga (slowly, slowly) approach to sightseeing. Go on an architectural dig in the Acropolis Museum, explore the ancient Agorá's marketplace, where democracy was born. For cool respite, head to the National Gardens and for gorgeous sunsets, perch on the peak of Lycabettus Mountain.

SHOPPING   Style-conscious Athenians browse for high-street fashion along pedestrian **Ermou** and for couture and designer jewelry in **Kolonaki** before brunch on Kolonaki Square. Skip the tourist kitsch in **Plaka** and **Monastiraki** in favor of poet/shoemaker **Stavros Melissonos'** handmade leather sandals. It's all early morning action in the 19th-century glass-and-steel **Central Market,** where stalls are laden with fresh fruit, nuts, and mounds of Aegean seafood.

NIGHTLIFE & ENTERTAINMENT   Athens is as hedonistic as its mythology suggests. **Psirri, Karitsi Square,** and **Panormou** street are pulsating districts; **Kolonaki** has fashionable bars, and born-again industrial zone **Gazi** is nightlife central. Summer means beach to Athenians— dress up for seafront cocktails and dancing in **Glyfada** and **Voula.**

RESTAURANTS & DINING   Whether it's creative Mediterranean cuisine in Michelin-starred **Spondi** or a take-out **souvlaki**—good food is taken for granted in Athens. Views of the Acropolis might distract you from the menu in **Plaka** and **Monastiraki,** where tavernas dish up Greek classics. Venture to the **Microlimano** harbor for fresh fish by the water's edge, and **Kolonaki's** trendy restaurants for a cosmopolitan feel.

ATHENS TODAY

Not too long ago, Athens used to be the city Greeks loved to hate. It had a reputation as expensive, polluted, and overcrowded, with more than five million inhabitants—over 40% of the country's population. Preparations for the 2004 Olympics brought forth many changes, and the successful staging of the games imbued the ancient city and its residents with a newfound confidence that acted as a catalyst for more evolution. As they were in Barcelona, the Olympics were just what Athens needed to get its groove back. The city feels young again. Forever the city of 1,000 contradictions, Athens is one of the few ancient cities in the world where the cutting edge, the hip, and the modern can suddenly coexist so harmoniously with the classical.

Athens today is sophisticated and cosmopolitan but no matter how fascinating its current renaissance, keep in mind this is a city that has gone through countless transformations in its long and turbulent history. The city continues its urban renewal despite massive headaches. Athens saw its illegal migrant population swell to over two million (in just 10 years!), altering the demographics of several inner city neighborhoods, spiking up petty crime and creating an anti-immigrant sentiment just as the economy collapsed, the IMF moved in and unemployment rose to over 16%.

The economic crisis and the government's austerity measures that have ushered in a recession, the constant fear of default and bankruptcy and the persistent rumors of a return to the old currency, have darkened the mood in the usually festive metropolis. Athens is struggling to find its footing, but Europe's oldest city shows no signs of slowing down.

The dawn of the 21st century found the ancient city with a multitude of much-needed improvements: since the turn of the century, the city has created a vast new infrastructure; a sparkling and expanding new Metro, with immaculate stations, many of which display the artifacts found during its construction; a new international airport; miles of new roads and a beltway that has eased the city's infamous traffic and has reduced the city's equally infamous smog.

The ancient sites have been linked together by a promenade, a sort of "boardwalk" around classical Athens, with antiquities on one side and modern-day sidewalk cafes, galleries, renovated mansions, and outdoor art installations on the other. All in all, 10 miles of downtown Athens's streets have been pedestrianized, transforming what had been one of the most pedestrian-unfriendly cities in the world into a more charming, accessible, and enjoyable city. The coastline has also been revived with a dizzying selection of cafes, restaurants, promenades, beaches, pedestrian shopping districts, and open-air nightclubs by the sea—accessible by a short tram ride from downtown.

The city's hotel scene has also gone through a renewal, with classic hotels restored to their former glory and boutique hotels continuing to pop up. The economic crisis might mean better deals can be found not only during the off-season, but year-round.

Greek cuisine continues its renaissance at the hands of talented new chefs, making Athens a haven for foodies; museums are being renovated and expanded, while several new and exceptional smaller museums have joined the impressive lineup. Galleries and art and exhibition centers continue to spring up—many housed in former warehouses and factories. The numerous industrial-to-art conversions have led to the rebirth of formerly run-down neighborhoods. Following the lead of Psirri and Thissio—two ancient neighborhoods once neglected, now the hippest downtown destinations—Gazi and Kerameikos have also risen from the ashes, going from gritty to urban chic.

As you explore Athens, try to make the city your own. Walk its streets; take in its scents; linger in its sidewalk cafes, courtyard gardens, squares, and rooftop terraces; take in a show in an ancient open-air theater, or an avant-garde performance, concert, or art exhibition at one of the new multipurpose arts complexes; enjoy a movie under the stars. Climb its mountains, swim in its waters, visit its ancient temples and Byzantine churches, try its food and its nightlife, and see as many museums as you can. Explore its ancient districts and its most modern ones, to witness an ancient city discovering its modern soul in front of your very eyes.

Take the bad in stride as well—long-term problems have been addressed, not eradicated. The smog does return from time to time (especially during heat waves) and traffic can still be fierce—so feel free to yell at the taxi driver who refuses to stop for you in a torrential rain or packs you into his taxi with many other passengers in the stifling summer heat; to mutter obscenities to yourself for getting stuck in traffic when you could have easily taken the Metro instead; and to throw up your hands in exasperation as a strike threatens to ruin your holiday—a glimpse of the floodlit Parthenon or a glass of wine on a rooftop, in an ancient quarter, or by the sea will have you back to your old self in no time.

Long after you have gone, you may feel a certain nostalgia. It is Athens, calling you back like a siren, as she has done to so many of us who have tried to leave her. For anybody who has taken the time to truly get to know her, you will find yourself longing to return. Exciting and exasperating, beautiful and gritty, ancient and modern, sultry and restless, seductive and unforgettable—welcome to my Athens.

Strategies for Seeing the Region

For some good ideas on how to approach the city as part of a longer stay in Greece, take a look at the suggested itineraries in chapter 3.

From mid-March through May, the weather is almost always pleasant in Athens, although Greeks rightly say that the March wind has "teeth." Between June and August, the temperature usually rises steadily, making August a good month to emulate the Athenian practice of avoiding the city. If you do come here in August, you'll find that Athens, like Paris, belongs to the tourists: Some 60% of all Athenians take their summer holiday between the 1st and 15th of August. Stretches when it's well over 100°F (38°C) are not uncommon in August, when anyone with health problems such as asthma should be wary of Athens's *nefos* (smog). Because the city can be hot and exhausting, give yourself time off for a coffee or a cold drink in a cafe. After all, you're on vacation!

September is usually balmy, with occasional light rain, although it's not unknown for August heat to spill over well into September. October usually offers beautiful summer/autumn weather, although with rain and some wind likely. It might even be intermittently chilly.

Most rain falls between November and February, when Athens can be colder and windier than you might expect. Average daytime temperatures range from 52°F (11°C) in January to 92°F (33°C) in August.

ORIENTATION
Arriving & Departing
BY PLANE
The **Athens International Airport Eleftherios Venizelos** (✆ **210/353-0000;** www.aia.gr), 27km (17 miles) northeast of Athens at Spata, is usually called

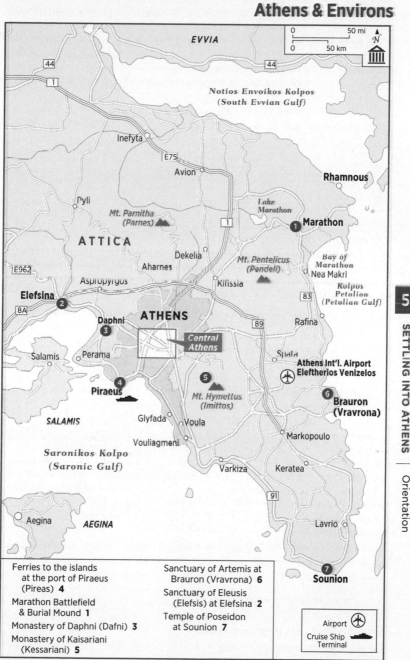

0 — 50 mi
0 — 50 km
N

EVVIA

Notios Envoikos Kolpos
(South Evvian Gulf)

44   44

1

Inefyta

E75

Avion   **Rhamnous**

Pyli   *Lake Marathon*

Mt. Parnitha (Parnes)   **Marathon** ❶

1

ATTICA   Dekelia   *Mt. Pentelicus (Pendeli)*   *Bay of Marathon*

Aharnes   Nea Makri

E962   Aspropyrgos   Kifissia   *Kolpos Petalion (Petalian Gulf)*

83

Elefsina ❷

8A   **Daphni** ❸   **ATHENS**   89   Rafina

Central Athens

Salamis   Perama   Spata

Athens Int'l. Airport Eleftherios Venizelos

❹

Piraeus   ❺   ❻ **Brauron (Vravrona)**

SALAMIS   *Mt. Hymettus (Imittos)*

Glyfada   Voula   Markopoulo

Saronikos Kolpo (Saronic Gulf)   Vouliagmeni

Varkiza   Keratea

91

Aegina   *AEGINA*

Lavrio

❼ **Sounion**

Ferries to the islands
  at the port of Piraeus
  (Pireas) **4**

Marathon Battlefield
  & Burial Mound **1**

Monastery of Daphni (Dafni) **3**

Monastery of Kaisariani
  (Kessariani) **5**

Sanctuary of Artemis at
  Brauron (Vravrona) **6**

Sanctuary of Eleusis
  (Elefsis) at Elefsina **2**

Temple of Poseidon
  at Sounion **7**

Airport ✈
Cruise Ship
Terminal ⛴

5

SETTLING INTO ATHENS | Orientation

"Venizelos" or "Spata," after the nearest town. Venizelos is a large, modern facility, with ample restrooms, interesting shops, and acceptable restaurants, but it is a serious slog from Athens; you no longer have the option of heading back into the city for a few extra hours of sightseeing if your flight is delayed, as visitors once did from the old airport. The airport has plenty to keep you busy, including a small museum with ruins found during the airport's construction and rotating art exhibits. Also, an Info-Point is available with excellent city brochures and guides, plus digital (iPads and flatscreen) tours of the city.

Here is a basic introduction to Athens's airport, based on information updated at press time.

ARRIVALS Most flights arrive at the main terminal, which has both an "A" and "B" area, but some flights—including most charter flights—arrive and depart from Spata's first of a projected cluster of satellite terminals. In addition, you may deplane down a steep flight of stairs onto the tarmac, where a bus will take you to the terminal. When planning what carry-on luggage to bring, remember that it can be quite a trek from your arrival point to the baggage claim area and Customs hall.

The baggage claim area has ATMs, telephones, restrooms, and luggage carts. Luggage carts cost 1€; if you see a cart attendant, he or she can make change for you. You can also use one of several free telephones in the baggage claim area to call for a porter.

If your suitcases do not greet you in the baggage claim area, proceed to a "baggage tracing" desk.

Signs in the baggage claim area indicate which route to use for Customs. Citizens of Common Market countries (EEC) do not have to go through Passport Control; citizens of non-EEC countries, such as the U.S. and Canada, must go through Passport Control.

If you are being met, you may want to rendezvous at the clearly marked Meeting Point (across from the Greek National Tourism Organization desk) between exits 2 and 3 in the main terminal Arrivals Hall.

The Pacific baggage storage (left luggage) facility is in the main terminal arrivals area; this service is officially open 24 hours a day and charges 2€ per piece per day.

Exits from the main terminal are signposted for taxi and bus connections into Athens.

GETTING INTO ATHENS Getting into post-Olympics Athens is an entirely different experience than what it used to be. The airport is linked to the city with a six-lane expressway **(Attiki Odos),** Metro, buses, and taxis. Public transportation to and from the airport is excellent and advised (especially the Metro because buses can be slow and get stuck in traffic during rush hour once they enter the city).

By Metro Line 3 of the Metro (www.amel.gr; 8€ one-way, 14€ round-trip—valid for 48 hr.; one-way fare for two people is 15€ and 20€ for three) is more convenient, less expensive, and faster than any other way of getting from the airport to downtown or vice versa. Unless you have a lot of luggage the Metro is an excellent, good-value option. Metro **line 3** serves the **city center** (where you can switch to the other lines at either Monastiraki or Syntagma stations) from the airport. The trip takes roughly 40 minutes and trains run every half-hour from 6:30am to 11:30pm. From the city to the airport (leaving from Syntagma and Monastiraki), trains run from 5:50am to 10:50pm. To get to Piraeus, switch at Monastiraki station to line 1; total travel time is about 1 hour. The airport ticket is valid for all forms of public transportation for 90 minutes; if you're approaching 90 minutes and are still in transit, simply revalidate your ticket by having it punched again. The Metro runs from 5:30am to midnight Sunday through Thursday and until 2am on Friday and Saturday.

By Suburban Railroad   The suburban railroad (**www.trainose.gr/en**) runs to and from the Larissa station, Doukissis Plakentias, with a connection to Metro line 1 at Nerantziotissa (at the Athens Mall in Marousi near the Athens Olympic Complex) and from the airport to the port of Piraeus. It might not be as convenient as line 3 to get downtown but it is more comfortable, not as crowded, and runs longer hours. Trains to the airport run from 4:30am to midnight, while the trains from the airport to the city run from 5am to 1:20am. The suburban railroad has the same pricing as the Metro; the only difference is that the return ticket is valid for a month. This is the best option to get from the airport to the port of Piraeus. Total travel time: 65 minutes.

By Bus   Buses (**www.oasa.gr**) are far slower than the Metro but they run 24 hours, and can reach areas the Metro does not, such as the coast. If you want to take a bus from the airport into central Athens, be prepared for what may be a long wait and a slow journey.

Several bus lines travel to and from the airport to destinations throughout the city. All buses depart from the designated area outside the Arrivals Hall of the main terminal building (doors 4 and 5). Bus service from the airport to Syntagma Square (X95) or to Piraeus (X96) costs 5€. The X95 runs every 10 minutes from 7am–10pm and every half-hour from 10pm–7am. The X96 runs every 20 minutes from 7am–10pm and every 40 minutes from 10pm–7am.

You can buy the ticket from a booth beside the bus stop or on the bus, and you must validate your ticket by punching it in the machine within the bus. And it's always a good idea to double-check where your bus is going by asking the driver before boarding.

By Taxi   The easiest way to get to town, you would assume, would be to take a taxi from the terminal. This is not as simple as it sounds: Greeks regard waiting in line with amusement, and getting a cab as a fiercely competitive sport. The City of Athens has created a **flat rate** from the airport to downtown Athens (Omonia Sq. and the Plaka/Makrigianni districts). Once you are in the taxi, make sure the meter is set on the correct tariff (tariff 1 is charged 5am–midnight; tariff 2 midnight–5am). For Omonoia, the price is 32€ (tariff 1); and 42€ (tariff 2); each rate **includes all additional charges** such as tolls and luggage. If you're heading for the Plaka/Makrigianni districts (at Hadrian's Gate), the rate is daytime 35€ and nighttime 50€. Depending on traffic, the cab ride can take under 30 minutes or well over an hour—something to remember when you return to the airport. Most likely you will not encounter any problems aside from city traffic. For more information check out the **Athens Taxi Info** site at **www.athenstaxi.info**. For other destinations, be sure to discuss your destination before getting into the taxi, either with an airline official or a policeman, to get the official flat rate price to your specific destination. If there's a problem with the taxi driver, you may threaten to call the police (© **100**).

By Car   Even though post-Olympics Athens is a radically different city—with the Metro, the railroad, and a new network of ring roads that have eased the city's notorious traffic—make no mistake, it is not an easy city to drive in, and if you're unfamiliar with the streets, it can be downright horrific. We recommend that you do not drive in Athens. If you still choose to drive into Athens, you'll pass through the region known as **Mesogeia** (the Inland). Until the new airport was built, this was one of the

If you plan to travel by air in Greece or elsewhere in Europe, keep in mind that the luggage allowance for most flights within Greece and Europe is 20 kilos (44 lb.). This is much less than most international weight allowances from the U.S. or Canada.

loveliest sections of Athens, with vineyards stretching for miles, sleepy country villages, and handsome chapels. Much of the area constituted the protected Attic Park; now, the once-protected wetlands and vineyards are being turned into new towns, subdevelopments, malls—and more roads. Numerous exits serve the most important areas of Athens.

If you plan to rent a car and head north or south, avoiding the city altogether, it's easier to do thanks to the new **National Highway.** If you're headed for Peloponnese, simply follow the signs for Elefsina. If you're headed toward northern Greece (including the city of Thessaloniki), get off at the Lamia exit.

DEPARTURES　If you are taking a taxi to the airport, ask the desk clerk at your hotel to reserve the car for you well in advance of your departure. Many taxis refuse to go to the airport, fearing that they will have a long wait before they get a return fare. Allow a minimum of an hour for the ride plus 2 hours for check-in for an international flight. Or, you can hop on Metro line 3 at Syntagma or Monastiraki, or take line 1 at Monastiraki and switch at Nerantziotissa for the suburban railroad.

For information on taxi fares to the airport, see above under "Getting into Athens."

For information on bus service to the airport from Syntagma, Ethniki Amyna, and Piraeus, see above under "Arrivals." For precise details on where to catch the airport bus from Athens to the airport, check with your hotel, the Greek National Tourism Organization, or—if you are very well organized and not too tired!—at an information desk when you arrive at the airport.

The flight information screens should indicate where you check in and what departure gate to go to. Make sure that the information on your boarding pass agrees with the information on the flight information screen. There have been frequent complaints that adequate information on arrivals, departures, cancellations, delays, and gate changes is not always posted. Nonetheless, it is important to check these screens and ask at the information desks, as there are **no** flight announcements.

Last-minute changes in your departure gate are not unknown; arrive at your gate as early as possible. Your best chance of finding out about a change is at the original gate.

CONNECTING FLIGHTS　The airport authority advises you to allow a minimum of 45 minutes to make a flight connection; this should be adequate if you arrive and depart from the main terminal and do *not* have to clear Customs. Allow at least an hour (1½ hr. is even better) if you have to clear Customs or if you arrive or depart from the satellite terminal. At present, many charter flights use the satellite terminal.

AIRPORT FACILITIES　The airport has about 35 shops, ranging from chic boutiques to Travel Value to duty-free shops. There are 10 restaurants and cafes, including a food village with seven food "hubs" in the main departure lounge. A McDonald's overlooking the runways perches on the upper level of the main terminal building. As with airports around the world, both food and goods are overpriced, although the prices of books, newspapers, and magazines are reasonable.

Duty-free shops have different regulations for Intra-Schengen and Extra-Schengen passengers. In short, **Intra-Schengen** refers to flights **within the EEC; Extra-Schengen** refers to flights **outside the EEC.** If you are flying from Athens to a country outside the EEC, you may find it worthwhile to check out the duty-free prices on perfumes and spirits.

The **Greek National Tourism Organization** (abbreviated GNTO in English-speaking countries and EOT in Greece) has an information desk in the Arrivals Hall.

Hertz, Avis, and Alamo rental cars are available at the airport. *Note:* All these companies levy a steep surcharge (at least 10%) if you pick up your car at the airport rather than at their in-town offices.

Both short-term (3€ per hr.) and long-term (12€ per day) parking is available at the airport. Much of the long-term parking is a serious walk from the main terminal. If you have the proper change (unlikely), you can use a machine to pay for your ticket; otherwise, join the queue at the payment booth.

Useful telephone numbers at Athens International Airport include: Information ✆ **210/353-0000;** Customs ✆ **210/353-2014;** Police ✆ **210/663-5140;** and First Aid ✆ **166** (from airport courtesy phones and information desks) and ✆ **210/353-9408** (from pay phones)

TRAVELING BETWEEN THE AIRPORT & PIRAEUS (PIREAS) The suburban railroad takes 50 minutes to reach the port of Piraeus—it is the best option. Taking the Metro from the airport to Piraeus (1 hr.) requires a change at Monastiraki, so this is not recommended if you have a lot of luggage. The taxi flat rate from the airport to Piraeus is 35€ (5am–midnight) and 50€ (midnight–5am). It's important to know that boats to the islands leave from several *different* Piraeus harbors. Most ferryboats and hydrofoils (Flying Dolphins) for Aegina leave from the **Main Harbor.** Hydrofoils for other islands leave from **Marina Zea,** a vigorous half-hour walk from the Main Harbor. If you don't know which harbor your boat is departing from, tell your taxi driver your final destination and he can probably find out which harbor and even which pier you are leaving from.

In theory, buses leave the airport for Piraeus every hour (5€). The bus usually leaves passengers in Karaiskaki Square, several blocks from the harbor. The official daily schedule is as follows: **Spata-Piraeus** (E96): Every 20 minutes from 5am to 7pm; every 30 minutes from 7pm to 8:30pm; every 40 minutes from 8:30pm to 5am.

AIRLINE OFFICES Some international carriers still have ticket offices in or near Syntagma Square, but many have moved to other areas in the city. Double-check the location of your airline's Athens office before you leave, as these offices can move without warning. **Air Canada** is at 10 Ziridi, Marousi (✆ 210/617-5321-3206).

The Attica Zoological Park

If you find yourself with 2 or more hours' layover at Venezelios Airport at Spata, consider taking a taxi (12€) to the nearby **Attica Zoological Park** ★ (www.atticapark.com) in Spata. It's open daily from 10am to 5pm October through April, and 9am to 7:30pm May through September. Admission is 8€ adults, 4€ children.

Hotels near the Airport

Have an early flight out of Spata? You might consider spending the night before at **Hotel Avra** (☎ **22940/22-780**; www.hotelavra.gr), 30 to 45 minutes by taxi from the airport on the waterfront in the nearby port of Rafina. The Avra was remodeled in 2004 and has a decent restaurant (sometimes with live music). Or, you can stroll to one of Rafina's harborside restaurants and watch the fishing boats and ferries come and go as you enjoy fresh seafood. Doubles start at 100€. If you want to be at the airport itself for an early flight or late arrival, the 345-room **Sofitel Athens Airport Hotel** (☎ **210/681-0882**; www.sofitel.com), offers such creature comforts as its own restaurants, fitness club, and swimming pool. Rates are from 140€ to 220€ double.

American Airlines is at 15 Panepistimiou (☎ 210/331-1045 or 210/331-1046). **British Airways** is at 1 Themistokleous, at 130 Leoforos Vouliagmenis, Glyfada (☎ 210/890-6666). **Delta Air Lines** is at 4 Othonos (☎ 800/4412-9506). **Lufthansa Airlines** is at 10 Ziridi, Marousi (☎ 210/617-5244). **Qantas Airways** inquiries are handled by British Airways (see address above; ☎ 801/115-6000). **Turkish Airlines** is at 19 Filellinon (☎ 210/324-6024).

Olympic Air (☎**210/355-0500**; www.olympic.gr) and Aegean Airlines (**www.aegeanair.com**)—the nation's top carriers—both have their hubs in Athens International Airport. Aegean Airlines's headquarters is at 31 Viltanioti, Kifissia (☎ **210/626-1700**).

BY CAR

If you arrive by car from **Corinth** (to the southwest), the signs into Athens will direct you fairly clearly to Omonia Square, which you will enter from the west along Ayiou Konstantinou. In Omonia, signs *should* direct you on toward Syntagma Square and other points in central Athens (signs in Omonia disappear mysteriously). If you arrive from **Thessaloniki** (to the north), the signs pointing you into central Athens are few and far between. It is not a good idea to attempt this for the first time after dark. If this happens, your best bet is to look for the Acropolis and head toward it until you pick up signs for Omonia or Syntagma squares.

BY BUS

Before you start out on any bus trip, check with the **tourist police** (☎ **210/171**) or the **Greek National Tourism Organization** (EOT) office (☎ **210/870-0000**; www.visitgreece.gr) for current schedules and fares. As the Metro continues to open new stations, bus routes and fares are always changing. It's best to double-check all routes and to be prepared for fare increases. If possible, get someone to write down the name and address of your bus station in Greek; this will be a great help when you take a taxi or bus. Keep in mind that many buses run both with and without a "0" prefix (024 and 24, for example).

There are two main stations for **KTEL** (www.ktel.org), the national bus company. **Terminal A,** 100 Kifissou (☎ **210/512-9233**), off the road out of Athens toward Corinth, handles buses to and from **the Peloponnese** and parts of **Northern Greece.** A taxi here from Syntagma Square should cost 8€ to 16€; if traffic is light, the journey is less than 20 minutes, but it can take an hour. If you don't have much to carry, take public bus no. 051 to the terminal (1.20€). It leaves from the corner of

Zinonos and Menandrou, several blocks off Omonia Square; you can catch the same bus at the terminal for the trip into town.

Terminal B (*©* **210/831-7096**) handles buses to and from **Central Greece** (including Delphi, Thebes, Evvia, and Meteora) and some destinations **to the north and east of Athens.** The GNTO, for reasons known best to itself, lists the address for Terminal B as 260 Liossion; this is where the bus for the terminal stops. To get to the terminal itself after you get off the bus, turn right onto Yousiou and you will see the terminal at the end of the street. Bus no. 024, which stops at Leoforos Amalias in front of the entrance to the National Gardens (a block south of Syntagma Sq.), will take you to and from the terminal for 1.20€. If you take this bus, tell the driver you want to get off at the bus terminal and then head right to Yousiou to reach the terminal. The **Mavromateon terminal** at Patission and Alexandras, a few hundred meters north of the Archaeological Museum, handles buses for most destinations in **Attica.**

BY TRAIN

Trains **from the south and west,** including Eurail (www.eurail.com) connections via Patras, arrive at the **Peloponnese station** (**Stathmos Peloponnisou;** *©* **210/513-1601**), about a mile northwest of Omonia Square on Sidirodromeon. Trains **from the north** arrive at **Larissa station** (**Stathmos Larissis;** *©* **210/529-8837**), just across the tracks from the Peloponnese station on Deligianni. The Larissa station has both an exchange office (daily 8am–9:15pm) and luggage storage (daily 6:30am–9pm).

To get to the train stations, you can take the **Metro** to Larissa (line 2), close to both stations. A taxi from the center of town should cost about 10€. The Metro runs from Omonia, Syntagma, and Koukaki to the Larissa Metro station, which is near the train stations. The most central place to catch the Metro is the stop in front of the Parliament building on Syntagma Square.

You can purchase train tickets just before your journey at the train station (running the risk that all seats may be sold); at the Omonia Square ticket office, 1 Karolou (*©* **210/524-0647**); at 17 Filellinon, off Syntagma Square (*©* **210/323-6747**); or from most travel agents. Information (in theory in English) on timetables is available by dialing *©* **145** or 147.

BY BOAT

Piraeus, the main harbor of Athens's main seaport, 11km (7 miles) southwest of central Athens, is a 15-minute Metro ride from Monastiraki, Omonia, and Thissio Metro stations. The subway runs from about 5am to midnight and costs 1.40€. The

---

Shopping near Spata

The **MacArthurGlen Athens Designer Outlet mall** (Block E71, Gialou, 19004, Spata. *©* **210/663-0840**; www.mcarthurglenathens.gr) is a site for some serious shopping, offering over 125 designer and high-end brands at discounted prices. Free shuttle buses run every half-hour (Mon–Fri 10am–9pm; Sat 10am–8pm) from Doukissis Plakentias metro stop and via Athens Walking Tours (www.athenswalkingtours/Shopping-Tour) as part of its shopping tours package, there is a bus to and from Syntagma Square three times a day. A shuttle bus to the mall will also be added to and from the airport in the near future.

A word about making air connections after an island trip: It is unwise—even foolhardy—to allow anything less than 24 hours between your return to Piraeus by island boat and your departure by air, as rough seas can significantly delay the trip.

far slower bus no. 040 runs from Piraeus to central Athens (with a stop at Filellinon, off Syntagma Sq.) every 15 minutes between 5am and 1am and hourly from 1am to 5am for 1.20€. To get to Athens International Airport, you can take the X96 bus (5€), the Suburban Railroad (8 €) or the metro which will require a change at Monastiraki station to line 3 (8 €).

You may prefer to take a **taxi** to avoid what can be a long hike from your boat to the bus stop or subway terminal. Be prepared for serious bargaining. The normal fare on the meter from Piraeus to Syntagma should be about 15€ to 20€, but many drivers offer a flat fare, which can be as much as 30€. Pay it if you're desperate; or walk to a nearby street, hail another taxi, and insist that the meter be turned on.

If you arrive at Piraeus by hydrofoil (Flying Dolphin), you'll probably arrive at **Zea Marina** harbor, about a dozen blocks south across the peninsula from the main harbor. Even our Greek friends admit that getting a taxi from Zea Marina into Athens can involve a wait of an hour or more—and that drivers usually drive hard (and exorbitant) bargains. To avoid both the wait and big fare, you can walk up the hill from the hydrofoil station and catch bus no. 905 for 1.20€, which connects Zea to the Piraeus Metro (subway) station, where you can complete your journey into Athens. You must buy a ticket at the small stand near the bus stop or at a newsstand before boarding the bus. **Warning:** If you arrive late at night, you may not be able to do this, as both the newsstand and the ticket stand may be closed.

If you've disembarked at the port of **Rafina** (about an hour's bus ride east of Athens), you'll see a bus stop up the hill from the ferryboat pier. Inquire about the bus to Athens; it runs often and will take you within the hour to the **Areos Park bus terminal,** 29 Mavromateon, near the junction of Leoforos Alexandras and Patission. The Areos Park terminal is 1 block from the Victoria Square Metro stop and about 25 minutes by trolley from Syntagma Square. From the bus terminal, there are buses to Rafina every half-hour.

The port of **Lavrion** (🕿 **22920/25-249**), 52km (32 miles) southeast of Athens, has taken over some of the itineraries from the port of Piraeus, including daily ferries and speedboats to Agios Efstratios, Alexandroupoli, Andros, Folegandros, Ios, Katapola, Kavala, Kea, Kythnos, Limnos, Milos, Mykonos, Naxos, Paros, Sikinos, Siros, and Tinos. The port's official website, www.oll.gr, is in Greek only, so check the GNTO site (see below) for more info. A taxi to Lavrio port from downtown Athens has a flat rate of 38€ (5am–midnight) and 55€ (midnight–5am). You can also get to the port by bus: Use the express lines of the interurban buses (KTEL) "Koropi station–Porto Rafti/Avlaki" or the urban buses of the area to reach the port. The price of the ticket is 5€. Also, there is a bus that can transfer you from the following Metro and suburban railway stations directly to the port: Pallini, Kantza, and Koropi.

Visitor Information

The **Greek National Tourism Organization** (**EOT** or **GNTO**) is at 7 Tsochas St., Ambelokipi (🕿 **210/870-0000;** www.visitgreece.gr; Metro: Ambelokipi). The office is officially open Monday through Friday, 8am to 3pm, and is closed on weekends. The GNTO information desk office is at 18–20 Dionissiou Aeropagitou St. (© **210/331-0392;** Metro: Acropolis; Mon–Fri 9am–7pm; Sat–Sun 10am–4pm). An information desk (© **210/345-0445**) and an Info-Point (© **210/325-3123;** www.atedco.gr) are also located at the airport. Two Info-Points are in the city in the Makrigianni district on the corner of Amalias Avenue and Dionisiou Aeropagitou Street (near the Acropolis metro station and the Acropolis Museum) and in the port of Piraeus. Both have excellent brochures and city maps, plus digital tours of the city. All Info-Points operate daily from 9am–9pm. Information about Athens, free city maps, transportation schedules, hotel lists, and other booklets on many regions of Greece are available at the office in Greek, English, French, and German.

Available 24 hours a day, the **tourist police** (© **210/171**) speak English as well as other languages, and will help you with problems or emergencies.

City Layout

As you begin to explore, you may find it helpful to look up to the **Acropolis,** west of Syntagma Square, and to **Mount Likavitos (Lycabettus),** to the northeast. From most parts of the city, you can see both the Acropolis and Likavitos, whose marble lower slopes give way to pine trees and a summit crowned with a small white church.

Think of central Athens as an almost perfect equilateral triangle, with its points at **Syntagma (Constitution) Square, Omonia (Harmony) Square,** and **Monastiraki (Little Monastery) Square,** near the **Acropolis.** The area bounded by Syntagma, Omonia, and Monastiraki squares is defined as the commercial center, from which cars are banned except for several cross streets. At one time **Omonia Square**—Athens's commercial hub—was considered the city center, but nowadays, most Greeks think of it as **Syntagma Square,** site of the House of Parliament. The two squares are connected by parallel streets, **Stadiou** and **Panepistimiou,** and where you will find the **Neoclassical University Trilogy.** (Panepistimiou is also known as Eleftheriou Venizelou.)

Flanking the Parliament building is one of Athens's most beautiful parks, the **National Gardens.** Right adjacent is the **Zappeio Hall and gardens,** another beautiful oasis in the center of the city. West of Syntagma Square, **Ermou** and **Mitropoleos** lead slightly downhill to **Monastiraki Square,** home of the city's famous flea market. From Monastiraki Square, **Athinas** leads north back to Omonia past the modern Central Market. The old warehouse district of **Psirri**—now the home of many chic galleries, cafes, and restaurants—is between Athinas and Ermou.

If you stand in Monastiraki Square and look south, you'll see the Acropolis. At its foot are the **Ancient Agora (Market)** and the **Plaka,** Athens's oldest neighborhood, many of whose street names honor Greek heroes from either classical antiquity or the Greek War of Independence. The twisting labyrinth of streets in the Plaka can challenge even the best navigators. Don't panic: The Plaka is small enough that you can't go far astray, and its side streets with small houses and neighborhood churches are so charming that you won't mind being lost. An excellent map may help (see "Street Maps," below, for info). Also, many Athenians speak some English, and almost all are helpful to direction-seeking strangers—unless you happen to be the 10th person in as many minutes to ask where the Acropolis is when it is clearly visible!

FINDING AN ADDRESS If possible, have the address you want written out in Greek so you can show it to your taxi driver, or ask for help from pedestrians. Most street signs are given both in Greek and a transliteration, which is a great help. Most taxi drivers carry a good Athens street guide and can usually find any destination. Increasingly, however, some Athenian cabbies are newcomers themselves to the capital and may have trouble with out-of-the-way addresses.

STREET MAPS The free maps handed out at branches of the **Greek National Tourism Organization** have small print and poor-quality paper. You may prefer to stop at a newspaper kiosk or bookstore to pick up a copy of the Greek Archaeological Service's *Historical Map of Athens* (with maps of the Plaka and of the city center showing the major archaeological sites). The map costs about 4€. For other city map recommendations, see "Books" under "Shopping A to Z," in chapter 6.

Neighborhoods in Brief

Athens is a big city that's a collection of many different neighborhoods, each with its own distinctive flair. Here are some of the neighborhoods that await you. If you have the time, why not just stroll, get lost, and be pleasantly surprised when you discover that you're on a street where almost all of the shops sell only icons or sugared almonds (an essential gift for guests at weddings and baptisms), or where there's a little park with a bench where you can sit and watch the world go by. Don't forget to take in the Archaeological Promenade, the walkways that stretch from Hadrian's Gate past the Acropolis on Dionissiou Areopagitou to the Ancient Agora, past Thissio and on to the Kerameikos.

CENTRAL ATHENS

Commercial Center The commercial center (a bureaucratic name no one uses, and that appears on no map) lies between **Omonia, Syntagma,** and **Monastiraki** squares, and includes the **Plaka** and **Psirri** districts. Certain streets are designated pedestrian-only, but consider that many motorists and almost all motorcycle riders assume that pedestrian-only regulations do not apply to them.

Omonia Square My grandmother always used to tell me how beautiful **Omonia Square** used to be; a grand *plateia* (square) surrounded by neoclassical buildings and couples strolling along. I never got to see that. For me, Omonia was never a destination, but a place you couldn't avoid. There wasn't anything in particular to see (except some good Acropolis views); it was gritty, grungy and not pretty, but interesting to wander through. Omonia today is in its worst shape ever. The latest redesign is a disappointment, and though the pre-Olympic cleanup got rid of the unsightly billboards, restored buildings' neoclassical facades, and paved the way for trendy hotels, the area remains gritty and attracts less desirable elements at night—it's best avoided after 9pm. The government has promised to clean up and redo the square

once more, along with pedestrianizing the entire Panepistimiou Avenue. Athinas Street (or better yet, pedestrianized Aiolou—also spelled Eolou—with its charming cafes and shops) will lead you away from the grunge and into Monastiraki. For a look at grand old Athens of the 19th century, check out the beautifully restored **Kotzia Square** with its grand neoclassical buildings including the **Athens City Hall** designed in 1874 and the **National Bank of Greece Cultural Center.** In the middle of the square a large portion of an ancient road has been uncovered, and can be seen in a fenced-off area where several ancient tombs and small buildings are also visible. The square is even more beautiful at night when it is dramatically lit, so be sure to include it in an evening stroll. The area near the **Athens Stock Exchange** is now home to an Asian quarter and several Bangladeshi shops.

Athinas Street This street links Omonia and Monastiraki squares, and has Athens's **Central Market.** Here you can browse fish and meat halls, buy vegetables and fruit from all over Greece, sample cheeses from distant islands—or buy a pair of shoes or sunglasses from a street vendor. Across from the markets, formerly bleak **Varvakeios Square** is now landscaped, has several cafes, and offers an opportunity to take a break from the frenzy of the market. Another nearby square, **Klaftmonos** has been redesigned and from it you can see the **Neoclassical University Trilogy**—another glimpse at grand and elegant 19th-century Athens.

Syntagma (Constitution) Square The heart of Athens—Syntagma Square is the focal point of the city's political and civic life, from protest rallies to New Year's celebrations. This is also where you'll find the major banks, travel agencies, and several fine hotels, including the **Grande Bretagne,** the grande dame of Greek hotels. If you are not staying here, take a peek at the magnificent Beaux Arts lobby, head into the **Alexander bar** for a drink (dress smartly), and take in the old-world elegance and glamour. The excellent **GB** restaurant on the terrace has some of the most stunning views of the city, but to enjoy the sweeping view and tempting menu you will need a reservation and lots of money. You might want to reserve a seat at the terrace bar (if it's early enough) and enjoy the view over a drink.

The **central post office** is at the corner of Mitropoleos. For years, the sidewalk cafes here were popular places to spend time, but with the proliferation of the fast-food joints that attract younger Athenians and bands of student travelers, you may not want to linger. That said, beautifully restored Syntagma Square, the *plateia* in front of the Syntagma Metro, with two cafes across from one another, is a convenient meeting point. This square is even more beautiful at night when it is brilliantly lit.

Syntagma is the home of much of governmental Athens: The handsome neoclassical building at the head of the square is the **Greek Parliament building,** formerly the Royal Palace. The most impressive thing about this grand building is its stone and how it changes color throughout the day: from off-white to gold to a light blush mauve before it is lit dramatically at night. During the day this is where you'll see the **Changing of the Guard** several times a day and may hear a band playing on Sunday around 11am. The soldiers who march in front of the Parliament building and the **Tomb of the Unknown Soldier** often wear the *evzone* uniform (frilly white skirts and pom-pommed red shoes) of their ancestors who fought to gain Greece's freedom during the War of Independence (1821-28). (Be sure to spend some time in the National and Zappeion Gardens adjacent to the Parliament.) Tucked away off Stadiou Street, across the street from the **National Historical Museum,** you will find a cobblestone oasis known as **Karitsi Square** with some of downtown's funkiest eateries, galleries and multipurpose cafe/bars spilling over onto Kolokotroni Street. This is where Athens' indie heart beats. South of Syntagma Square, **Monastiraki Square** and the **Plaka** area are Athens's two main tourist destinations.

Plaka Right below the Acropolis, Plaka is the most tourist-heavy neighborhood in the city. Its maze of narrow medieval streets twist their way through ancient sites, Byzantine churches, offbeat museums, and 19th-century homes. Restaurants and cafes line many streets of this pedestrian neighborhood that is rich in history and character and is atmospheric, romantic, and nostalgia inducing. Feel free to lose yourself in the labyrinthine streets. Maybe you will find the tiny village within a village of Anafiotika, a Cycladic town at the base of the Acropolis.

Monastiraki This neighborhood fringes the **Agora** and the **Roman Forum,** and the flea markets are open every day but are usually best—and most crowded—on Sunday. Many tavernas, cafes, and shops line the streets, but my favorite street by far is Adrianou, the street that links Monastiraki to beautifully restored Thissio, with restored houses as restaurants and cafes on one side and the Agora on the other—and Acropolis views as well.

Psirri Between Athinas and Ermou, Psirri was once derelict and forgotten; now it's one of the city's hottest destinations after dark. Slick warehouse conversions; restored neoclassical houses; trendy restaurants, bars, cafes, tavernas, and *mezedopoleia* (establishments offering "small plates") with live music, clubs, and galleries side by side with some still-remaining workshops and dilapidated buildings—this area comes alive in the late afternoon until the early morning hours, even though its outer pockets remain a bit gritty. Recently the neighborhood has taken a serious backseat to **Gazi** and is no longer the king of downtown urban chic or nightlife central as it used to be, though it still remains popular enough to have its own website: **www.psiri.gr**.

Back on the **Archaeological Promenade** (just cut across Ermou towards the Thissio Metro stop to get back on the Promenade), you will find the ancient neighborhood of **Kerameikos,** undergoing its own reinvention. The little-visited ancient Athenian cemetery is peaceful and green and a delight to visit, with many stunningly beautiful classical sculptures and part of the city's ancient walls. Psirri and Kerameikos are linked by yet another restored square: **Koumoundourou.**

The promenade ends right after Kerameikos, and across busy Pireos Avenue is **Technopolis** (Art City), better known as Gazi—once an industrial wasteland that spewed black gas fumes (thus the name Gazi, which means gas) from the foundry's smokestacks. When the factory closed in 1984, the area became an urban wasteland. But when the city of Athens bought the old foundry and turned it into a multipurpose art and exhibition center, it kickstarted a revival of the neighborhood. Today the old foundry's smokestacks are illuminated in neon red, and the streets are filled with the edgiest and hippest nightlife in the city and a real downtown vibe—arts spaces, fusion restaurants, galleries, theaters, bars, cafes, and a gay "village." The revival is beginning to spread beyond the neighborhood's borders into other long-forgotten urban areas, where closed factories are becoming the hottest clubs in town (due to their sheer size) or transformed into museums, multipurpose arts centers, and exhibition halls; this is the birthplace of 21st-century Athens.

A must-see here is the beautifully reimagined Technopolis center, which has retained much of its original industrial architecture while being converted to an arts complex for shows, festivals, and exhibitions. It also has a cafe and a courtyard used for concerts. The one permanent exhibition here is small **Maria Callas Museum.**

To understand the renaissance that Gazi started, apart from the many cutting-edge multiuse spaces and sophisticated dining and nightlife options, you must see the ripple effects it has had on the neighboring areas, creating new architectural landmarks. Within walking distance of Gazi (along **Pireos Ave.**) you will find the **School of Fine Arts** and the glossy **Foundation of the Hellenic World** (converted from an old warehouse and featuring interactive and virtual tours of ancient Greece) with its striking ribbed dome meant to evoke a Bronze Age beehive tomb. Farther along is the **Pantheon,** a concert and conference hall multiplex. Another new landmark is the **Benaki Museum** (called the Beautiful Red Box for reasons you will understand once you see it), which holds temporary exhibitions, film screenings, theater performances, and concerts in its internal courtyard. Farther down is the **Athinais,** a magnificent restoration of a former silk factory into a sophisticated arts complex. Here you will find the **Museum of Ancient Cypriot Art,** galleries, a concert hall, a theater and cinema. Nearby you will find the **Michael Cacoyannis Foundation,** a privately funded nonprofit institution founded by the acclaimed filmmaker (*Stella, Zorba the Greek, The Trojan Women*) that concentrates on the performing arts but also stages various exhibitions and has a wonderful cafe/restaurant on its top floor.

At night, be sure to take in the buzz of this lively neighborhood. Walk the streets and hop in and out of as many bars as you can, or join the locals as they enjoy their drinks out in the streets after bar capacity has reached its limit; the Kerameikos Metro station smack in the middle of **Gazi Square** is surrounded by some of the city's coolest bars and eateries and is where locals socialize (drink in hand) when the bars are full, creating a scene that can only be found in the most popular islands at the height of summer. Gazi is where Athens's modern heart beats to its own rhythm.

Back on the Archaeological Promenade, across Ermou from Psirri, is **Thissio**—my favorite downtown neighborhood. Right on the pedestrianized **Apostolou Pavlou,** Thissio with its restored neoclassical buildings, uninterrupted Acropolis views, the temple of Hephaestos, and some of the city's best places to hang out, is the place to be. It's charming and old-fashioned, modern and happening, with hip hangouts like **Stavlos**—the former royal stables now converted into an all-day cafe/bar/restaurant with indoor and outdoor seating, an internal courtyard, a terrace, a gallery, and an area for late-night dancing and live performances. Be sure to check out the grand **National Observatory,** a beautiful neoclassical mansion from the late 1800s.

Kolonaki Forever posh, elegant, and happening, this neighborhood tucked beneath the slopes of Lycabettus Mountain has long been the favorite address of the socialites. The streets (many pedestrianized) are packed with boutiques, designer houses, art galleries, and restaurants, cafes, and cooler-than-thou night and day spots. **Leof Vasiliss Sofias** is one of the most imposing streets in Athens, with beautiful neoclassical mansions that have been converted into museums (a few embassies as well), thus earning the nickname the Museum Mile (aka the Embassy District). Take your time soaking up all the urban chic you can before making your way to the top of Lycabettus mountain for an extraordinary sunset with Athens laid under your feet like a sparkling map. If you walk down, you'll pass through some of central Athens's nicest and greenest streets winding around Likavitos's lower slopes.

If you're in Kolonaki on a Saturday, don't miss the beautiful people and the wannabes promenading up and down the streets, thronging in front of favorite boutiques to ogle the latest fashions, and collapsing at street cafes to revive their spirits with cool drinks. There are more shoe stores per inch in Kolonaki than almost anywhere else in Greece.

Kolonaki gradually merges to the northwest with the university area, which is spread loosely between the 19th-century university buildings (the Neoclassical University Complex, or Trilogy) on Panepistimiou and the Polytechnic some 10 blocks to the northwest. Many publishers have their offices around here, and bibliophiles may enjoy the window displays of everything from children's books about Hercules to mathematical texts.

A few blocks from the Polytechnic—where countless students were killed in 1973 during a protest against the ruling junta—and near the excellent **National Archaeological Museum,** is **Exarchia.** Long before Gazi, this was the closest thing Athens had to an "alternative" neighborhood, ironically, next to the posh Kolonaki. This bohemian neighborhood—covering 50 city blocks—is a lively area to spend a few hours in, with excellent tavernas on a buzzing square and pedestrian streets, great lounges and bars, plus the city's finest rock clubs and live music venues. If you have the time, explore **Streffi Hill,** a little-visited area, green and lovely, which offers incredible views of the city and the Acropolis all the way to the Saronic Gulf once you reach its top. Across busy **Leoforos Alexandras** is central Athens's largest park, **Pedion Areos,** having just completed a 10-million-euro facelift and the results are stunning.

Koukaki & Makrigianni Once the working-class counterpart to Kolonaki, **Koukaki** has been thoroughly gentrified and is one of Athens's most desirable neighborhoods. The district lies at the base of **Lofos Filopappou (Filopappos Hill),** also known as the Lofos Mousseon (Hill of the Muses). A number of pleasant paths lead from streets at the base of Filopappos up through its pine-clad slopes, some ending at the **Dora Stratou Theater** or the observatory. Buses and trolleys run along Veikou, the main road through Koukaki, home to unpretentious cafes and restaurants as well as reasonably priced hotels. The arrival of the metro and the tram have made the area even more desirable for locals and tourists alike.

Makrigianni, the upscale neighborhood just north of Koukaki, at the southern base of the Acropolis, has a new lease on life with the arrival of the **Archaeological Promenade,** the **Acropolis Museum,** the Metro, the pedestrianization of Makrigianni street and its close proximity to the Plaka. You will also find several smaller museums, a few luxurious hotels, many wonderfully restored mansions and several good restaurants, including the popular **Strofi** and **Socrates's Prison** (also known as the Samaria). Stay here if you want to be as centrally located, but a bit out of the tourist maelstrom.

Pangrati & Mets Surrounding the reconstructed Athens Stadium known to the Greeks as **Kallimarmaro (Beautiful Marble),** where the first modern Olympics were held in 1896, you will find two lovely, lively residential areas with excellent dining and nightlife options. To the south of the stadium is the steep, beautiful street of **Markou Mousourou,** shaded by flowering trees, lined with neoclassical houses, and filled with the scent of jasmine and bougainvillea. Mets is a taste of old Athens, full of pre–World War II houses with tiled roofs and courtyards. It's one of the most beautiful neighborhoods to explore in the city, and the nightlife isn't bad either. To the south of the stadium is **Pangrati,** a residential area popular with those who can't afford Kolonaki.

If you enjoy baroque funerary monuments, don't miss the **First Cemetery,** where anybody who was anybody in 19th- and 20th-century Greece is buried among the tall cypress trees and exceptional century-old marble statues. Be sure not to miss the splendid *Koimomeni (Sleeping Girl),* considered by many to be a masterpiece by Ianoulis Halepas, a sculptor from Tinos, who battled mental illness most of his adult life and died in poverty during World War II. If you prefer your green spaces without tombs, explore Pangrati's green **park,** almost a miniforest in the heart of Athens. There are also lots of restaurants (the excellent **Spondi** for starters) and many charming traditional tavernas scattered in Pangrati.

The Embassy District Leoforos Vas. Sofias (Queen Sophia Blvd.) runs from Syntagma Square toward Athens's fashionable northeastern suburb of Kifissia. If you walk along Vas. Sofias and explore the side streets that run uphill into Kolonaki, you'll notice the national flags on elegant office buildings and town houses. This Embassy District stretches past the **Hilton,** where many embassy workers head for lunch or drinks after work—you should consider doing the same at least once for lunch or dinner at the excellent **Milos** seafood restaurant, or for a drink at around sunset on the rooftop's bar **Galaxy** with its great views of the city. The Embassy District is also known as the **Museum Mile** for the excellent museums found here just downhill from Kolonaki: The **Benaki Museum,** the **Goulandris Museum of Cycladic Art,** the **Byzantine Museum,** the **National War Museum,** and the **National Gallery.**

THE NORTHEAST SUBURBS

Much of Athens' expansion is to the northeast, in the valley between the mountains of **Penteli** to the east and **Parnitha** to the west. Going north on **Leoforos Kifissias,** you will pass by Kolonaki, **Ambelokipi** (with its many first-rate bar/restaurants such as **Vlassis, Baraonda, 48,** and **Balthazar**), popular **Panormou Street** (since the arrival of the Metro) and **Neo Psihiko** (with many first rate cafes, lounges, tea houses and restaurants), and you will find yourself in **Marousi** and **Kifissia.**

Marousi is home to Santiago Calatrava's **Athens Olympics Sports Complex,** the elegant, soaring modernist complex that stole the show during the 2004 Olympics and the stadiums that became the architectural landmarks of the new city; beautiful glass and steel arches over the main stadium; a velodrome; the **Athens Tennis**

Academy in a landscaped park lined with glass-covered walkways; and a steel arched agora.

The last stop on line 1 is elegant **Kifissia.** Cooler than downtown Athens, thanks to its elevation, Kifissia was fashionable enough for the royal family to have a villa here. Here you'll find 19th-century neoclassical mansions, outrageous 21st-century ones, graceful tree-lined streets, excellent shopping options, lovely parks, two good museums (the **Goulandris Museum of Natural History** and the **Gaia Center**), three of the city's most trendy hotels (the must-be-seen **Semiramis, 21,** and **Life Gallery**), and one of the best hotels, period, the **Pentillikon** with its Michelin-starred restaurant **Vardis.** Add these to countless bars, lounges, and clubs—and the open-air cinema dating from 1919—and you'll discover that Kifissia is a delight to spend some time in (if you've already spent some time in central Athens).

PIRAEUS (PIREAS)

The main port of Athens, Piraeus is a city very much in its own right—although even locals have trouble telling precisely where Athens ends and Piraeus begins. Piraeus prides itself on being rough and tough—a stronghold of communism, the home of *rembetika* (traditional Greek "blues" music, born out of the population exchange between Greece and Turkey in 1922). This is where you come to catch a boat to the islands from the **main harbor** (**Megas Limani** or **Great Harbor**), or from **Zea Marina,** also called Pasalimani. **Mikrolimano (Little Harbor),** also called Turkolimano (Turkish Harbor), is a picturesque harbor with eateries and cafes by the marina. Zea Marina also has countless cafes by the harbor and a bustling shopping center. Nearby is the pretty neighborhood of **Kastella,** with its neoclassical mansions and unbeatable views of the Saronic Gulf.

THE SOUTHERN SUBURBS— COASTAL ATHENS

The coastal avenue **Leoforos Poseidonos** begins where Syngrou ends—right by the sea. Easily accessible from downtown Athens via the tram (up to Voula) and farther via bus, this is where Athenians love to hang out and party during the hot summer months. Coastal Athens begins at the Metro line 1 stop Faliro and the tram stop SEF (Stadium of Peace and Friendship). Nearby, the revitalized yacht marina of **Flisvos** (at tram stop Trocadero) is a delight for strolling, with stores, restaurants, cafes, lounges, and bars where you can sit near the water and gaze at the gleaming yachts. There is also a lovely open-air cinema right by the surf. This is the marina where the **battleship *Averoff,*** which played a decisive role in the Balkan Wars, is berthed and operates as a museum. The coast is about to become even more high-profile as it is the site of two major new developments: First, the 550-million-euro **Stavros Niarchos Foundation Cultural Centre** (SNFCC) project, to be completed in 2015, that will include within a new cultural park right on the waterfront: the **National Library of Greece,** the **Greek National Opera,** and the **Greek National Ballet School,** all designed by acclaimed architect Renzo Piano. And the old airport **Hellinikon** (550 hectares/1,359 acres) is finally on the government's fast track, with a multibillion-euro investment planned that will create a large park, high-rises, business centers, marinas, five-star hotels, shopping, art and entertainment districts as well as multiple sports and recreational facilities.

As you continue down Leoforos Poseidonos, you'll find beaches (which consistently score high on the E.U.'s Blue Flag list of clean beaches), boardwalks, esplanades, marinas, multiplexes, and open-air mega-clubs. First-rate restaurants (**Matsuhisa Athens, Ithaki**) along with excellent shopping on pedestrian **Angelou Metaxa** in **Glyfada** and top hotels (such as the **Astir Palace,** the **Divani Athens Spa and Thalassio Centre,** the **Magri,** and **Grand Beach Lagonissi**), and many sports facilities and watersports options make the coast a fashionable and fun scene. Even if you're on a tight schedule try to at least have dinner or drinks in the city's most romantic venue: **Island.**

GETTING AROUND
By Public Transportation
BY METRO

The **Metro** (**www.amel.gr**) runs from 5:30am to midnight Sunday through Thursday; on Friday and Saturday, trains run until 2am. All stations are wheelchair accessible. Stop at the Syntagma station or go to the GNTO for a system map. To travel on the Metro, buy your ticket at the station, validate it in the machines as you enter, and hang onto it until you get off. A single ticket costs 1.40€; a day pass costs 4€. Make sure you validate your ticket as you enter the waiting platform, or you'll risk a fine. Metro and bus tickets are interchangeable, except for bus E22, that heads to the coast and costs 1.60€ more.

Even if you do not use the Metro to get around Athens, you may want to take it from Omonia, Monastiraki, or Thissio to Piraeus to catch a boat to the islands. (Don't miss the spectacular view of the Acropolis as the subway goes aboveground by the Agora.) The harbor in Piraeus is a 5-minute walk from the Metro station. Take the footbridge from the Metro and you're there.

BY BUS & TROLLEY BUS

Although you can get almost everywhere you want in central Athens and the suburbs by bus or trolley, it can be confusing to figure out which bus to take. This is especially true now, when many bus routes change as new Metro stations open. Even if you know which bus to take, you may have to wait a long time until the bus appears—usually stuffed with passengers. Check out the **Athens Urban Transport Organisation** (✆ **185**; www.oasa.gr) for directions, timetables, route details, and maps.

If you find none of this daunting, tickets cost 1.20€ each (or 1.40€ to be combined with the Metro, trolley, and tram for up to 90 min.) and can be bought from *periptera* (kiosks) scattered throughout the city. The tickets are sold individually or in packets of 10. Tickets are good for rides anywhere on the system. **Be certain to validate** yours when you get on. *Tip:* Hold on to your ticket. Uniformed and plainclothes inspectors periodically check tickets and can levy a basic fine of 5€ or a more punitive fine of 30€ to 60€ on the spot!

If you're heading out of town and take a blue A-line bus to transfer to another blue A-line bus, your ticket will still be valid for the transfer.

In central Athens, minibus nos. 60 and 150 serve the commercial area free of charge.

Buses headed to farther points of Attica leave from **Mavromateon** on the western edge of Pedion tou Areos Park, at the western end of Leoforos Alexandras.

BY TRAM

Athens's **tram** (**www.tramsa.gr**) connects downtown to the city's coast. Though it may not be the fastest means of transport, it takes a scenic route once it hits the coast and is handy for those wishing to visit the city's beaches and the coastline's attractions

> ### Cultured Commuting
>
> Allow extra time when you catch the Metro in central Athens: Three stations—**Syntagma Square, Monastiraki,** and **Acropolis**—handsomely display finds from the subway excavations in what amount to Athens's newest small museums. For more info, visit **www. amel.gr.**

and nightlife. The tram runs on a 24-hour schedule Friday and Saturday and 5am to midnight Sunday through Thursday; tickets are 1.20€ (1.40€ if you wish to continue your journey with the Metro, bus, or trolley bus for up to 90 min.) and **must be validated** at the platform or inside the tram. Trams are comfortable and air-conditioned. A ride from Syntagma Square to the current last stop in seafront Voula is a little over an hour.

By Taxi

It's rumored that there are more than 15,000 taxis in Athens, but finding an empty one is not easy. Especially if you have travel connections to make, it's a good idea to reserve a radio taxi (see below). Fortunately, taxis are inexpensive, and most drivers are honest men trying to wrest a living by maneuvering through the city's endemic gridlock. However, some drivers, notably those working Piraeus, the airports, and popular tourist destinations, can't resist trying to overcharge obvious foreigners.

When you get into a taxi during the day and up until midnight, check the **meter**. Make sure it is **turned on** and set to 1 (the daytime rate) rather than 2 (the night rate). The meter will register 1€. The meter should be set on 2 (double fare) only between midnight and 5am *or* if you take a taxi outside the city limits; if you plan to do this, negotiate a flat rate in advance. The "1" meter rate is .32€ per kilometer. There's a surcharge of 1€ for service from a port or from a rail or bus station. Luggage costs .32€ per 10 kg (22 lb.). Taxis to and from the airport to downtown have a flat rate of 35 € (5am–midnight) and 50€ (midnight–5am). Don't be surprised if the driver picks up other passengers en route; he will work out everyone's share of the fare. The minimum fare is 2.80€. These prices will almost certainly be higher by the time you visit Greece.

If you suspect that you have been overcharged, ask for help at your hotel or destination before you pay the fare.

Your driver may find it difficult to understand your pronunciation of your destination; ask a hotel staff member to speak to the driver directly or write down the address so you can show it to the driver. Carry a business card from your hotel, so you can show it to the taxi driver on your return.

There are about 15 **radio taxi** companies in Athens; their phone numbers change often, so check the daily listing in "Your Guide" in the *Athens News*. Some established companies include **Athina** (✆ 210/921-7942), **Express** (✆ 210/993-4812), **Parthenon** (✆ 210/532-3300), and **Piraeus** (✆ 210/418-2333). If you're trying to make travel connections or are traveling during rush hour, a radio taxi is well worth the 2.80€ surcharge. Your hotel can call for you and make sure that the driver knows where you want to go. Most restaurants will call a taxi for you without charge.

The GNTO's pamphlet *Helpful Hints for Taxi Users* has information on taxi fares as well as a complaint form, which you can send to the **Ministry of Transport and Communication,** 13 Xenophondos, 10191 Athens. Replies to complaints should be forwarded to the *Guinness Book of World Records*.

By Car

In Athens, a car is far more trouble than convenience. The traffic is heavy, and finding a parking place is extremely difficult. Keep in mind that if you pick up your rental car at the airport, you may pay a hefty (sometimes daily) surcharge. Picking up a car in town involves struggling through Athens's traffic to get out of town. That said, we do have some suggestions to follow.

Alamo, Avis, Budget, Dollar, Hertz, and National all have offices at Athens International Airport.

Tip: Renting a car from abroad is invariably cheaper than negotiating for one on the spot in Athens. In fact, the savings in the rental rate usually make it worth your while to telephone or e-mail a major car-rental firm in the U.S. from Greece, if you haven't made arrangements to rent a car before you left your home country.

If you decide to rent a car in Athens, you'll find many rental agencies south of Syntagma Square and in Athens International Airport. Some of the better agencies include **Avis,** 46–48 Leoforos Amalias (© 210/687-9600; www.avis.gr); **Budget Rent a Car,** 8 Leoforos Syngrou (© 210/898-1444; www.budget-athens.gr); **Eurodollar Rent a Car,** 29 Leoforos Syngrou (© 210/922-9672 or 210/923-0548); **Hellascars,** 148 Leoforos Syngrou (© 210/923-5353 to -5359); **Hertz,** 12 Leoforos Syngrou (© 210/922-0102 to -0104; www.hertz.gr) and 71 Leoforos Vas. Sofias (© 210/724-7071 or 210/722-7391); and **Thrifty Hellas Rent a Car,** 24 Leoforos Syngrou (© 210/922-1211 to -1213; www.thriftygreece.gr). Prices for rentals range from 50€ to 100€ per day. **Warning:** Be sure to take full insurance and ask if the price you are quoted includes everything—taxes, drop-off fee, gasoline charges, and other fees.

On Foot

Since most of what you'll want to see and do in Athens is in the city center, it's easy to do most of your sightseeing on foot. Fortunately, Athens has created pedestrian zones in sections of the **Commercial Triangle** (the area bounded by Omonia, Syntagma, and Monastiraki squares), the **Plaka,** and **Kolonaki,** making strolling, window-shopping, and sightseeing infinitely more pleasant. **Dionissiou Areopagitou,** at the southern foot of the Acropolis, was also pedestrianized, with links to walkways past the Ancient Agora, Thissio, and Kerameikos. Still, don't relax completely, even on pedestrian streets: Athens's multitude of motorcyclists seldom respect the rules, and a red traffic light or stop sign is no guarantee that vehicles will stop for pedestrians.

Wheelchair users will find Athens challenging even though the 2004 Paralympics brought some improvements. For one, the Acropolis is finally wheelchair accessible. Ramps and platforms have been added to bus stops, railway stations, and ports, while Metro stations and sports venues are wheelchair accessible. Some central Athens streets, sites, and Metro stations have special sidewalks for the visually impaired, but making the rest of the city accessible will be quite a task. For more information contact the **Panhellenic Union of Paraplegic & Physically Challenged,** 3–5 Dimitsanis, Moschato (© **210/483-2564;** www.pasipka.gr).

[FastFACTS] ATHENS

ATMs Automated teller machines are increasingly common at banks throughout Athens. The **National Bank of Greece** operates a 24-hour ATM in Syntagma Square.

Banks Banks are generally open Monday through Thursday, 8am to 2pm and Friday 8am to 2:30pm. In summer, the exchange office at the **National Bank of Greece** in Syntagma Square (© **210/334-0015**)

is open Monday through Thursday from 3:30 to 6:30pm, Friday from 3 to 6:30pm, Saturday from 9am to 3pm, and Sunday from 9am to 1pm. Other centrally located banks include **Citibank,** in Syntagma Square (☎ **210/322-7471**); **Bank of America,** 39 Panepistimiou (☎ **210/324-4975**); and **Barclays Bank,** 15 Voukourestiou (☎ **210/364-4311**). All banks are closed on the long list of Greek holidays. (See "When to Go," in chapter 2.) Most banks exchange currency at the rate set daily by the government. This rate is often more favorable than that offered at unofficial exchange bureaus. Still, a little comparison shopping is worthwhile. Some hotels offer better-than-official rates, though only for cash, as do some stores, usually when you are making a big purchase.

Business Hours Even Greeks get confused by their complicated, changeable business hours. In winter, shops are generally open Monday and Wednesday from 9am to 5pm; Tuesday, Thursday, and Friday from 10am to 7pm; and Saturday from 8:30am to 3:30pm. In summer, shops are generally open Monday, Wednesday, and Saturday from 8am to 3pm; and Tuesday, Thursday, and Friday from 8am to 2pm and 5:30 to 10pm. Most stores in central Athens, though, remain open all day.

Department stores and supermarkets are open 8am to 8pm Monday to Friday and 8am to 6pm Saturday.

Dentists & Doctors Embassies (see below)

may have lists of dentists and doctors. Some English-speaking physicians advertise in the daily *Athens News.*

Embassies & Consulates Australia, Level 6, Thon Building, corner Kiffisias & Alexandras, Ambelokipi (☎ 210/870-4000; www.greece. embassy.gov.au); **Canada,** 4 Ioannou Yenadiou (☎ 210/727-3400 or 210/725-4011; www.greece. gc.ca); **Ireland,** 7 Vas. Konstantinou (☎ 210/723-2771); **New Zealand,** 76 Kifissias Ave, Ambelokipi (☎ 210/692-4136); **South Africa,** 60 Kifissias, Maroussi (☎ 210/680-6645); **United Kingdom,** 1 Ploutarchou (☎ 210/723-6211; www.bhcc.gr); **United States,** 91 Leoforos Vas. Sofias (☎ 210/721-2951 or 210/729-4301 for emergencies; www.athens.us embassy.gov). Be sure to phone ahead before you go to any embassy; most keep limited hours and are usually closed on their own holidays as well as Greek ones. For a list of all embassies, log on to **www. embassy-finder.com.**

Emergencies In an emergency, dial ☎ **100** for the **police** and ☎ **171** for the **tourist police.** Dial ☎ **199** to report a **fire** and ☎ **166** for an **ambulance** and the **hospital.** Athens has a **24-hour** line for foreigners, the **Visitor Emergency Assistance** at ☎ **112** in English and French. If you need an English-speaking doctor or dentist,

try **SOS Doctor** (☎ **1016** or 210/361-7089). There are two medical hot lines for foreigners: ☎ **210/721-2951** (day) and 210/729-4301 (night) for U.S. citizens; and ☎ **210/723-6211** (day) and 210/723-7727 (night) for British citizens. The English-language *Athens News* (published Fri) lists some American- and British-trained doctors and hospitals offering emergency services. Most of the larger hotels can call a doctor for you in an emergency.

KAT, the emergency hospital in Kifissia (☎ **210/801-4411** to -4419), and **Asklepion Voulas,** the emergency hospital in Voula (☎ **210/895-3416** to -3418), have emergency rooms open 24 hours a day. **Evangelismos,** a centrally located hospital below the Kolonaki district on 9 Vas. Sophias (☎ **210/722-0101**), usually has English-speaking staff on duty. If you need medical attention fast, don't waste time trying to call these hospitals: Just go. They will see to you as soon as possible.

In addition, each major hospital takes its turn each day being on emergency duty. A recorded message in Greek at ☎ **210/106** tells which hospital is open for emergency services and gives the telephone number.

Internet Access Internet cafes, where you can check and send e-mail, have proliferated in Athens almost as fast as cellphones. Most midrange to top-end hotels have at least an "Internet corner," but for a current list of Athenian cybercafes, check out **www.athensinfoguide. com**. Also, several **Wi-Fi hot spots** can be found across the city, such as Syntagma Square, Kotzia Square, Flisvos marina, and the Thission; the airport and several cafes also offer free Wi-Fi.

Lost & Found If you lose something on the street or on public transportation, it is probably gone for good. If you wish, contact the police's **Lost and Found,** 173 Leoforos Alexandras (📞 **210/642-1616**), open Monday through Saturday from 9am to 3pm. For losses on the Metro, there is an office in Syntagma station (📞 **210/327-9630;** www. amel.gr; Mon–Fri 7am–7pm, Sat 8am–4pm). Lost passports and other documents may be returned by the police to the appropriate embassy, so check there as well. It's an excellent idea to travel with photocopies of your important documents, including passport, prescriptions, tickets, phone numbers, and addresses.

Luggage Storage & Lockers If you're coming back to stay, many hotels will store excess luggage while you travel. There are storage facilities at Athens International Airport, at the Metro stations in Piraeus

and Monastiraki, and at the train stations.

Newspapers & Magazines The *Athens News* is published every Friday in English, with a weekend section listing events of interest; it's available at kiosks everywhere. Most central Athens newsstands also carry the *International Herald Tribune,* which has an English-language insert of highlights from the Greek daily *Kathimerini,* and *USA Today.* Local weeklies include the *Hellenic Times,* with entertainment listings, and *Athinorama* (in Greek), which has comprehensive listings of events. *Athens Best Of* (monthly) and *Now in Athens* (published every other month) have information on restaurants, shopping, museums, and galleries, and are available free in major hotels and sometimes from the Greek National Tourism Organization.

Pharmacies *Pharmakia,* identified by green crosses, are scattered throughout Athens. Hours are usually Monday through Friday, 8am to 2pm. In the evenings and on weekends, most are closed, but each posts a notice listing the location of pharmacies that are open or will open in an emergency. Newspapers such as the *Athens News* list the pharmacies open outside regular hours.

Police In an **emergency,** dial 📞 **100.** For help dealing with a troublesome taxi driver, hotel staff,

restaurant staff, or shop owner, stand your ground and call the **tourist police** at 📞 **171.**

Post Offices The main post offices in central Athens are at 100 Eolou, south of Omonia Square; and in Syntagma Square, at the corner of 60 Mitropoleos. They are open Monday to Friday, 7:30am to 8pm, Saturday 7:30am to 2pm, and Sunday 9am to 1pm.

All post offices accept parcels, but the **Parcel Post Office** is at 4 Stadiou inside the arcade (📞 **210/322-8940**). It's open Monday through Friday from 7:30am to 8pm. It usually sells twine and cardboard shipping boxes. Parcels must remain open for inspection before you seal them at the post office.

You can receive correspondence in Athens c/o **American Express,** 2 Ermou, 10225 Athens, Greece (📞 **210/324-4975**), near the southwest corner of Syntagma Square, open Monday through Friday from 8:30am to 4pm and Saturday from 8:30am to 1:30pm. If you have an American Express card or traveler's checks, the service is free; otherwise, each article costs 2€.

Restrooms There are public restrooms in the underground station beneath Omonia and Syntagma squares and beneath Kolonaki Square, but you'll probably prefer a hotel or restaurant restroom. (Toilet paper is often not available, so carry tissue with you. Do not flush paper down the commode; use the receptacle provided.)

Safety Athens is among the safest capitals in Europe, and there are few reports of violent crimes. **Pickpocketing,** however, is not uncommon, especially in the Plaka and Omonia Square areas, on the Metro and buses, and in Piraeus. Unfortunately, it is a good idea to be wary of Gypsy children and super-friendly strangers. When in the Metro, always place your valuables in your front pockets. We advise travelers to avoid the side streets of Omonia and Piraeus at night. As always, leave your passport and valuables in a security box at the hotel. Carry a photocopy of your passport, not the original.

Taxes A VAT (value-added tax) of between 4% and 18% is added onto everything you buy. Some shops will attempt to cheat you by quoting one price and then, when you hand over your credit card, they will add on a hefty VAT

charge. Be wary. In theory, if you are not a member of a Common Market/E.U. country, you can get a refund on major purchases at the Athens airport when you leave Greece. In practice, you would have to arrive at the airport a day before your flight to get to the head of the line, do the paperwork, get a refund, and catch your flight.

Telephones Many of the city's public phones now accept only phone cards, available at the airport, newsstands, and the **Telecommunications Organization of Greece (OTE)** offices in several denominations, currently starting at 3€. Most OTE offices and **Germanos** stores (including the one in the airport) now sell cellphones and phone cards at reasonable prices; if you are in Greece for a month, you may find this a good option. Some kiosks still have metered phones; you pay what the meter records. North Americans can phone home directly by contacting **AT&T** (✆ **00/800-1311**), **MCI** (✆ **00/800-1211**), or **Sprint** (✆ **00/800-1411**); calls can be collect or

billed to your phone charge card. For reverse (collect) calls, dial 161. All visitors can call home (beware of hotel surcharges if you decide to call from your hotel room) by first dialing the **International Direct Dial Code, 00,** followed by the country's code (U.S.: 1, UK: 0044, Canada: 011, Ireland: 353, Australia: 61, New Zealand: 64), the area code, and then the number. You can send a telegram or fax from OTE offices. The OTE office at 15 Stadiou, near Syntagma, is open 24 hours a day. The Omonia Square OTE, at 50 Athinas, and the Victoria Square OTE, at 85 Patission, are open Monday through Friday 7am to 9pm, Saturday 9am to 3pm, and Sunday 9am to 2pm. Outside Athens, most OTEs are closed on weekends.

Tipping Athenian restaurants include a service charge in the bill, but many visitors add a 10% tip. Most Greeks do not give a percentage tip to taxi drivers, but often round up the fare; for example, you would round up a fare of 2.80€ to 3€.

WHERE TO STAY

Athens has a wide range of accommodations, from the luxurious and opulent landmarks such as the Grande Bretagne (dating from 1878), to designer chic boutique hotels, small pensions, and basic budget hotels and hostels. Nearly all hotels were renovated and updated with modern features and amenities at the very least in 2004, and new hotels appear all the time.

Athens Hotels

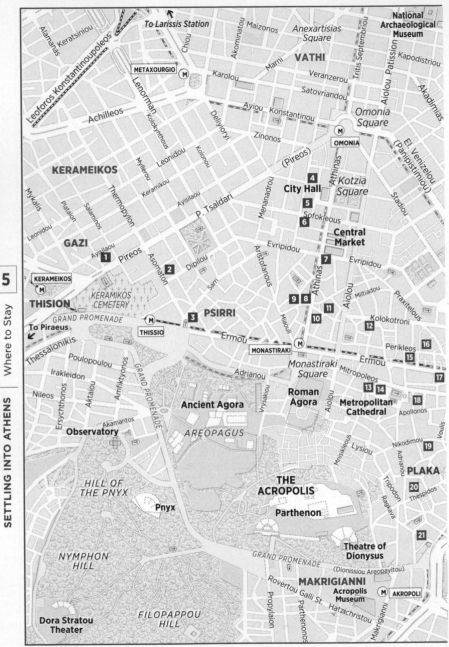

A is for Athens **9**
Acropolis House Hotel **24**
Athens Center
  Square Hotel **7**
Athens Cypria **15**
Athens Lycabettus Hotel **30**
Athens Plaza (NJV) **27**
Attalos Hotel **8**
AVA Hotel & Suites **21**
Baby Grand Hotel **4**
Cecil Hotel **10**
Central Hotel **19**
Economy Hotel **5**

Electra Hotel **17**
Electra Palace **20**
Fresh Hotel **6**
Grande Bretagne **29**
Hermes Hotel **18**
Hilton Athens **33**
Hotel Achilleas **16**
Hotel Adonis **25**
Hotel Carolina **12**
Hotel Dioskouros
  (Dioskouros
  Guest House) **22**
Hotel Eridanus **1**

Hotel Plaka **13**
Hotel Tempi **11**
Jason Inn Hotel **2**
King George Palace **28**
Magna Grecia **14**
New Hotel **26**
Ochre & Brown **3**
Periscope **31**
St. George Lycabettus
  Hotel **32**
Student and Traveller's
  Inn **23**

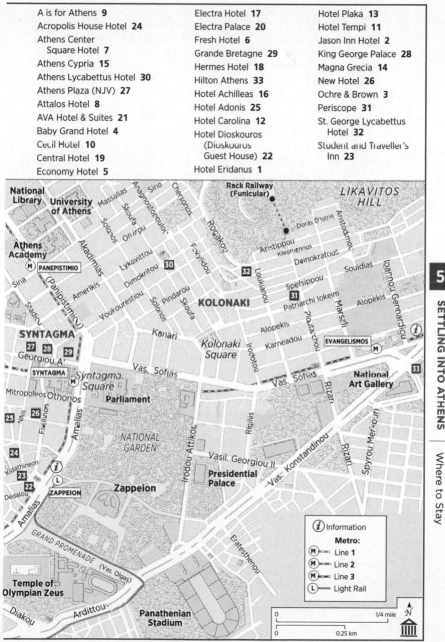

5

SETTLING INTO ATHENS | Where to Stay

It is *not* a good idea to rely on ATMs in Athens, since the machines are often out of service when you need them most, particularly on holidays or during bank strikes. If your PIN includes letters, be sure that you know their numerical equivalent, as Greek ATMs do not have letters.

Best Athens Hotel Bets

o **Best Historic Hotel:** Built as a private mansion in 1842 and converted into a hotel in 1874, the **Grande Bretagne** has housed royalty, movie stars, government officials, diplomats, spies, secret agents, and even Hitler—when it was the Nazi headquarters for 3 years—and managed to survive to whisper its tales to new generations of visitors. The Grande Bretagne, Syntagma Square and across the street from the House of Parliament, remains a firsthand eyewitness to modern Greek history as well as the capital's leading luxury choice. See p. 129.

o **Best for Business Travelers:** The concierge at the **Hilton Hotel** is one of the most skillful in Athens, well versed in procuring virtually anything a traveler could conceivably need during a trip to the Greek capital. There are 22 meeting rooms, ideal for conferences and events, and business function suites that can hold up to 1,300 delegates. See p. 132.

o **Best for a Romantic Getaway: The Margi**—it looks like a Moorish castle with its stone walls and outdoor arches—is stylish, atmospheric, and undeniably romantic with its colonial-style decor, spacious rooms, sea vistas, and wonderful beach. The Asian-style candlelit pool bar and restaurant add the final touch. See p. 137.

o **Best Splurge: The Astir Palace Hotel,** on the Athenian coast, is in a series of bungalows in three hotels on 30 pine-clad hectares (75 acres), with swimming pools, seven well-regarded restaurants (including Matsuhisa Athens), exceptional sea vistas, and a private beach. See p. 136.

o **Most Relaxing Hotel:** The **Divani Apollon** has picturesque gardens, towering palm trees, two large pools, a nice beach and a restaurant with seafront tables, and beautiful sea vistas from every room. See p. 136.

o **Best Location:** The **Athens Gate Hotel**—across from the Temple of Olympian Zeus and a stone's throw from the Plaka, the sites, and the Metro—has the best and most convenient location, plus spellbinding city and Acropolis views from its top-floor restaurant. See p. 132.

o **Best Budget Hotel: The Attalos,** near Monastiraki Square, has been housing Frommer's readers comfortably and well—for an affordable price—for years. In a convenient location, its clean rooms are comfortable, the staff is accommodating and warm, and the top-floor cafe has beautiful Acropolis views. See p. 126.

The Plaka

The **Plaka** district, below the Acropolis, is the most touristy—and picturesque—area of downtown Athens.

Best For: Travelers who want to be near the historic sites, to lose themselves in long walks around winding medieval streets and explore the city's oldest district.

Drawbacks: It's full of tourists—especially during high season.

Hotels & Restaurants South of the Acropolis

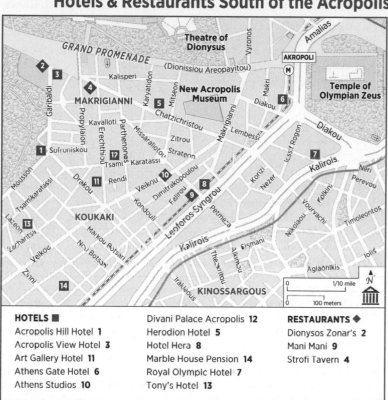

HOTELS ■
Acropolis Hill Hotel **1**
Acropolis View Hotel **3**
Art Gallery Hotel **11**
Athens Gate Hotel **6**
Athens Studios **10**

Divani Palace Acropolis **12**
Herodion Hotel **5**
Hotel Hera **8**
Marble House Pension **14**
Royal Olympic Hotel **7**
Tony's Hotel **13**

RESTAURANTS ◆
Dionysos Zonar's **2**
Mani Mani **9**
Strofi Tavern **4**

EXPENSIVE

AVA Hotel & Suites ★★   With its excellent location, clean and spacious grounds and a personable and helpful staff, the AVA has stolen our hearts. This smoke-free hotel is actually 46 self-contained apartments all equipped with kitchenettes. The executive apartments and suites are preferable not only because they are spacious enough for four guests (perfect for a family) but because they have a living room and a large balcony with Acropolis views. The standard rooms are fine, spacious for two guests, with modern furnishings, polished wood floors, and nice size bathrooms, but they only have a sitting room (not a separate living room) and their balconies are smaller.

9-11 Lysikratous, 10558 Athens. www.avahotel.gr. ✆ **210/325-9000.** Fax 210/325-9001. 46 units. 180€ double. 400€ executive apt./suite. Rates include breakfast buffet. AE, DC, MC, V. Metro: Acropolis. **Amenities:** Breakfast room; concierge; room service. *In room:* A/C, TV, hair dryer, kitchenette, minibar, Wi-Fi.

Electra Palace ★★   The Electra, a few blocks southwest of Syntagma Square on a quiet side street, is a modern and stylish hotel. The rooms on the fifth, sixth, and seventh floors are smaller than those on lower floors, but a top-floor room is where you want to be, both for the view of the Acropolis and to escape traffic noise. (Ask for a top-floor unit when you make your reservation. Your request will be honored "subject to availability.") Guest rooms here are pleasant and decorated in soft pastels

PRICE categories

Very Expensive	250€ and up
Expensive	150€–250€
Moderate	80€–150€
Inexpensive	Under 80€

and the rooftop pool is a great touch. The hotel restaurant (the **Electra Roof Garden**) is one of the best in town, with a view as sublime as the food.

18-20 Nikodimou, Plaka, 10557 Athens. www. electrahotels.gr. (℗ **210/337-0000.** Fax 210/324-1875. 106 units. 180€ double; 190€ triple. Rates include breakfast buffet. AE, DC, MC, V. Parking 12€ a day. Metro: Syntagma. About 2 blocks down on the left as you walk along Ermou with Syntagma Sq. behind you. **Amenities:** Restaurant; bar; gym; rooftop pool; indoor pool; spa. *In room:* A/C, pay TV, hair dryer, high-speed Internet, minibar.

MODERATE

Central ★★   This stylish hotel features wonderful sea grass or wooden floors, marble bathrooms, and excellent soundproofing. Family and interconnecting rooms are also available and the large roof has superb Acropolis views and a hot tub.

21 Apollonos, 10557 Athens. www.centralhotel.gr (℗ **210/323-4357.** 84 units. 100€–160€ double. AE, DC, MC, V. Private parking. **Amenities:** Bar; conference and meeting facilities; Jacuzzi; rooftop terrace; smoke-free rooms available upon request. *In room:* A/C, TV, hair dryer, Internet.

Hermes Hotel ★★   The Hermes Hotel has designer touches in every room, including polished wood floors, marble bathrooms, and balconies. Interconnecting rooms are also available. The rooftop terrace has excellent Acropolis views.

19 Apollonos, 10557 Athens. www.hermeshotel.gr. (℗ **210/323-5514.** Fax 210/322-2412. 45 units. 135€ double; 145€ triple. AE, MC, V. **Amenities:** Cafe/bar; rooftop terrace; smoke-free rooms. *In room:* A/C, TV.

Hotel Plaka ★★   This hotel is popular with Greeks, who prefer its modern conveniences to the old-fashioned charms of most other hotels in the area. It has a terrific location just off Syntagma Square. Most guest rooms have balconies; those on the fifth and sixth floors in the rear, where it's quieter, have views of the Plaka and the Acropolis (also visible from the roof-garden snack bar). Friends who stayed here recently were not charmed by the service, but enjoyed the location and the rooftop bar.

7 Mitropoleos and Kapnikareas, 10556 Athens. www.plakahotel.gr. (℗ **210/322-2096.** Fax 210/322-2412. 67 units, 38 with shower only. 135€ double; 145€ triple. Rates include breakfast. AE, MC, V. Follow Mitropoleos out of Syntagma Sq. past cathedral and turn left onto Kapnikareas. **Amenities:** Bar; roof garden. *In room:* A/C, TV, hair dryer, minibar.

Magna Grecia ★★   Inside a beautiful 19th-century neoclassical building in a hard-to-beat location (right on Mitropoleos Sq.), this is easily one of the best hotels in the Plaka. You'll find high ceilings, French doors, and hardwood floors. All front rooms have sweeping Acropolis views, and there is a pleasant and relaxing **rooftop bar/restaurant** (the Acropolis View Restaurant) that has become one of the most well-regarded restaurants in the city. Rooms are named after Ionian and Aegean islands.

54 Mitropoleos, 10563 Plaka. www.magnagreciahotel.com. (℗ **210/324-0314.** Fax 210/324-0317. 12 units. 120€–145€ double; 180€ triple. AE, DC, MC, V. **Amenities:** Cafe/bar; rooftop garden; room service. *In room:* A/C, TV, DVD/CD/MP3 player, hair dryer, Internet.

INEXPENSIVE

Acropolis House Hotel ★   This small hotel in a handsomely restored 150-year-old villa retains many of its original architectural details. It offers a central location—just off Kidathineon in the heart of the Plaka, a 5-minute walk from Syntagma Square—and the charm of being on a quiet pedestrian side street. Room nos. 401 and 402 have good views and can be requested (but not guaranteed) when making a reservation. The newer wing, only 60 years old, isn't architecturally special; each unit's spartan bathroom is across the hall.

6–8 Kodrou, 10558 Athens. www.acropolishouse.gr. (✆ **210/322-2344.** Fax 210/324-4143. 19 units, 15 with bathroom. 70€ double without bathroom, 80€ with bathroom; 104€ triple. 10€ surcharge for A/C. Rates include continental breakfast. V. Walk 2 blocks out of Syntagma Sq. on Mitropoleos and turn left on Voulis, which becomes Kodrou. *In room:* A/C, TV, Internet.

Hotel Adonis ★   Rather plain but efficient rooms (with tiny bathrooms) are highlighted by large balconies and breakfast in the unimaginative rooftop cafe/bar. You need only look over at the adjacent balcony for one of the most striking Acropolis views in the city. The hotel staff is a bit stern but very efficient.

3 Kodrou and Voulis, 10558 Athens. www.hotel-adonis.gr. (✆ **210/324-9737.** Fax 210/324-4143. 26 units. 80€ double; 108€ triple. No credit cards. **Amenities:** Cafe/bar; rooftop garden. *In room:* A/C, TV.

Hotel Dioskouros (aka Dioskouros Guest House)   As far as hostels go, this one is hard to beat. It's a small and intimate choice. There are no en suite bathrooms, but the place is clean and has a friendly staff, a peaceful garden, and an excellent location. Roughing it suddenly isn't so rough.

6 Pitakou, 10558 Plaka. www.hoteldioskouros.com. (✆ **210/324-8165.** Fax 210/321-9991. 12 units, all with shared bathrooms. 50€–60€ double; 60€–80€ triple. AE, MC, V. Free parking. **Amenities:** Bar; cooking facilities (Oct–May); garden; Internet; TV area. *In room:* A/C.

Student and Traveller's Inn   On a quiet pedestrian street on the outskirts of the Plaka, the inn features a charming, casual look with four- and eight-bed dorm rooms

---

WHAT YOU'LL really PAY

The prices quoted within this chapter are the hotel's rack rates, the maximum they can charge during the height of the season. Athens hotels have some of the lowest average room prices in Europe, so even during peak season you can often find good deals. Most hotels in town consider Easter through October high season; you can find discounts of 25% to 40% during low season. Interestingly enough, the opposite occurs with expensive and deluxe hotels downtown as upscale visitors tend to avoid Athens during the tourist rush of July and August, so you can find significant reductions in their prices during those 2 months. Deals can be found either by contacting the hotel directly, through online services such as **Priceline.com** or **Expedia.com**, or through a reputable local travel agency. The recent economic woes in Greece have thrown the hotel industry off balance as well. Not long ago, you wouldn't have found a double in the Baby Grand Hotel (for the summer season) available for as low as 80€ and even lower online. Whether it's a sign of the bad economy or the plethora of options remains to be seen.

The best way to getting what you want is to either contact the hotel directly and inform them of the prices you have found online and negotiate from there—most times they will match the online price.

Note: Quoted discount offers will seldom include breakfast, taxes, or resort fees.

with shared facilities, along with single, double, and triple rooms (some with en suite facilities) and a pleasant green courtyard, plus Internet access. What else do you need when you're young and on the go?

16 Kydathinaion, 10558 Athens. www.studenttravellersinn.com. © **210/324-4808.** Fax 210/321-0065. Private bathroom 65€ double, 78€ triple; shared bathroom 50€ single, 55€ double, 72€ triple. No credit cards. **Amenities:** Courtyard; Internet (shared terminals); vending machines; TV area. *In room:* A/C.

Monastiraki

The **Monastiraki** district is centrally located, close to all the sites, and busy 24 hours a day.

Best For: Travelers who want to be conveniently located but also in a "real" part of the city with all the frenzy, hustle and bustle of everyday city life. The area also has a large selection of inexpensive to moderate hotels to chose from.

Drawbacks: Surroundings get seedier the closer you get to Omonoia.

MODERATE

A for Athens ★👜 This funky, hip and modern arrival in Monastiraki has 35 rooms (apartments) with some of the best views in the city. The "Wide View" rooms (for one to three guests) all have windows facing bustling Monastiraki Square, the Plaka and the Acropolis, and are spacious with modern decor, hardwood floors and double-glazed windows while the "Comfy" rooms (for up to four guests) are just as nice, but face the backstreets of Psiri which are...well...not that pretty. The top floor **café** has some of the best city vistas around and has become a new favorite nighttime spot, particularly at sunset and after dark. The hotel has basic services but the rooms are spacious, bright and immaculate; its location is super convenient and the views are awesome. It's a wonderful new arrival.

20 Miaouli St, 10552 Athens. www.aforathens.com. © **210/324-4244.** 35 units. 95–150€ double. AE, MC, D, V. **Amenities:** *In room:* A/C, TV, hair dryer, minifridge, sofa. Metro: Monastiraki.

Athens Center Square Hotel ★ By the Central Market, this hotel with its rather unusual location and its bright colors (kiwi-blue-red-orange) is very clean and trendy with an efficient staff, small but comfortable rooms, good-size bathrooms, and a nice **rooftop bar** in summer. The front rooms (facing the Market) can be noisy so request a back room. Top floor suites have balconies and Acropolis views. Be warned, the Central Market is noisy during the day and somewhat seedy looking at night.

15 Aristogitonos St (corner Athinas), 10552 Athens. www.athenscentersquarehotel.gr. © **210/322-2706.** Fax 210/321-1800. 50 units. 95€ double. Rates include breakfast. AE, MC, V. Metro: Monastiraki. Leaving the Metro (exit Athinas St.), turn left on Athinas St. for 300m (984 ft.). Turn left again after the first traffic light at Aristogitonos street, the pedestrian street with the fruit market. **Amenities:** Luggage storage; smoke-free rooms. *In room:* A/C, TV, hair dryer, minifridge, Wi-Fi.

Attalos Hotel ★ 🍴 The six-story Attalos is well situated for visitors wanting to take in the daytime street life of the nearby Central Market and the downtown district's exuberant nighttime scene at the cafes and restaurants. Half of the plain yet pleasant rooms have balconies and 12 have Acropolis views. The roof garden also offers fine views of the city and the Acropolis. The Attalos (whose staff is very helpful) often gives Frommer's readers a 10% discount. This is a great budget hotel with excellent service in a central and convenient location, a 3-minute walk to the Metro.

29 Athinas, 10554 Athens. www.attalos.gr. © **210/391-2801.** Fax 210/324-3124. 80 units. 94€ double; 110€ triple; 134€ quad. AE, MC, V. Metro: Monastiraki. Exit from the Athinas St. exit and head 1 block north. **Amenities:** Luggage storage; smoke-free rooms. *In room:* A/C, TV, hair dryer.

Baby Grand Hotel ★ 🎒 The old Athens Grand Hotel underwent an extensive makeover in 2006 and reopened as Baby Grand, a "graffiti" hotel. Ten international artists were handpicked to decorate the 57 "graffiti" rooms with themes ranging from Japanese and Byzantine art to comic book art—check out the Spider-Man, Batman, and Smurfs rooms. The nongrafitti rooms are also spacious, comfortable, and contemporary. In the lobby, past the acid-green mirrors and the stainless-steel corridors, you will find the **Baby Grand Restaurant** with its reasonably priced menu and its glass floor that looks down to the pool. Be warned however, that the street the hotel is on can be seedy at night.

65 Athinas and Lycourgou, 10551 Athens. www.classicalhotels.com. ✆ **210/325-0900.** 76 units. 80 €–120€ double; 165€ suite. Breakfast 10€. AE, DC, MC, V. Metro: Omonia/Monastiraki. **Amenities:** Restaurant/bar; gym; indoor pool; smoke-free rooms; spa; rooms for those w/limited mobility. *In room:* A/C, TV, hair dryer, minibar, Wi-Fi.

Cecil Hotel ★ The Cecil offers reasonably priced rooms in a beautifully restored neoclassical town house with great architectural details—the rooms might be small but they all have polished wood floors, high ceilings, and are soundproof. Full breakfast is served and there's also a welcoming **roof garden restaurant.**

39 Athinas, 10554 Athens. www.cecil.gr. ✆ **210/321-7079.** Fax 210/321-8005. 36 units. 80€–90€ double; 115€ triple; 160€ suite. AE, MC, V. Metro: Monastiraki. **Amenities:** Restaurant/cafe, bar. *In room:* A/C, TV.

Fresh Hotel ★ What was once an undistinguished (well, ugly) hotel from the '70s has morphed into one of the coolest and most stylish designer hotels in the city. A black vertical fireplace in the reception area sets the tone for what is an ideal modern urban experience. The rooms aren't huge, but they are stylish and modern with many interesting choices, such as the armchairs that open into beds, blinds controlled from your bed, and funky colored glass dividers in the bathrooms. The **Magenta Restaurant** offers many healthy options during the day; on the ninth floor the **Air Lounge Bar** with its wooden deck and swimming pool has great city panoramas and good drinks. The only drawback is its location: a seedy street popular with the working girls at night.

26 Sofokleous and 2 Klisthenous, 10564 Athens. www.freshhotel.gr. ✆ **210/524-8511.** Fax 210/524-8517. 133 units. 110€–150€ double. AE, DC, MC, V. Parking 12€ per day. Metro: Omonia/Monastiraki. From Omonia Sq., head south along Athinas until you reach Sofokleus. From Monastiraki Sq., head north along Athinias until you reach Sofokleus. **Amenities:** Restaurant/bar; pool; minispa. *In room:* A/C, plasma TV, hair dryer, Wi-Fi.

Jason Inn Hotel ★ 🏊 On a dull street, just a few blocks from the Agora, the Plaka, and the Psirri district, this renovated hotel offers attractive, comfortable rooms with double-paned windows. If you don't mind walking the extra blocks to Syntagma, this is one of the best values in Athens, with an eager-to-help staff. If the Jason Inn is full, the staff may be able to find you a room in one of their other hotels: the similarly priced **Adrian Hotel,** on busy Hadrian in the Plaka.

12 Ayion Assomaton, 10553 Athens. www.douros-hotels.com. ✆ **210/325-1106.** Fax 210/523-4786. 57 units. 95€ double; 120€ triple. Rates include American-style buffet breakfast. AE, MC, V. Metro: Thissio. Turn right at Thissio Metro station to Ermou St., pass small belowground church, and bear left. **Amenities:** Breakfast room; bar. *In room:* A/C, TV, minibar.

INEXPENSIVE

Economy Hotel 🎒 The Economy offers just that: affordable rates in a central location (on a quiet street near the Old Town Hall), the clean, spacious, and cheery hotel is quite a find. The no-frills but comfortable rooms offer small balconies with not so nice views, and good-size bathrooms. You'll find excellent service in a convenient (Omonoia/Monastiraki Metro stops) location. The downside is that some of the back streets in the area are a bit seedy after dark—to be expected near Omonoia.

5 Klisthenous, 10552 Athens. www.economyhotel.gr. © **210/522-0520.** Fax 210/522-0640. 56 units. 65€ double; 78€ triple. AE, MC, V. Metro: Monastiraki/Omonoia. **Amenities:** Breakfast room (buffet); bar; luggage storage; Wi-Fi. *In room:* A/C, TV, minibar.

Hotel Tempi If you believe that location is everything, consider the three-story Tempi, which faces the flower market by the Church of Ayia Irini (St. Irene) on a pedestrian street. The Tempi has simply furnished rooms (bed, table, chair), the mattresses are overdue for replacement, and the plumbing can be a problem—hot water is intermittent and the toilets can smell. But you can see the Acropolis from 10 of its balconied rooms (if you lean). This hotel is popular with students and other spartan travelers able to ignore the Tempi's drawbacks and focus on its location, rates, and handy communal kitchen facilities.

29 Eolou, 10551 Athens. www.tempihotel.gr. © **210/321-3175.** Fax 210/325-4179. 24 units, 8 with bathroom. 64€ double with bathroom, 57€ (with shared bathroom); 78€ triple with bathroom. AE, MC, V. Metro: Monastiraki. *In room:* A/C, TV, Wi-Fi.

Psirri & Kerameikos

Psirri and **Kerameikos** are centrally located but a bit out of the tourist maelstrom and come alive as soon as the sun has set. **Gazi,** the undisputed king of downtown Athenian nightlife, is across the avenue from Kerameikos.

Best For: Travelers who want to be near some of the city's trendiest dining and nightlife options.

Drawbacks: Both areas are in the process of being gentrified. Outer pockets remain somewhat seedy.

EXPENSIVE

Hotel Eridanus ★ This very attractive boutique hotel (a former Athenian landmark house) feels and looks like an art gallery, with colors that alternate between shockingly bright and deeply soothing. The rooms have been tastefully furnished with modern designer touches, including funky furniture, luxurious dark green marble Indian bathrooms, original artwork, and huge beds. The well-known fish restaurant **Varoulko** next door is associated with the hotel. Some rooms have Acropolis views.

80 Piraeus, 10551 Athens. www.eridanus.gr. © **210/520-5360.** 38 units. 195€ double; 285€ double deluxe with Acropolis views; 180€ junior suite. AE, MC, V. Free parking. Metro: Thissio/Kerameikos. **Amenities:** Restaurant; breakfast room; bar. *In room:* A/C, Internet TV, minibar, Wi-Fi.

Ochre & Brown ★★ This trendy, small boutique hotel in the heart of Psirri has found its niche for fashion-conscious and experienced travelers looking for style, highly personalized service, high-tech amenities, and a chic urban experience. Some rooms have Thissio views, but the finest room is the junior suite with Acropolis views from its terrace. Rooms have stylish furnishings, large work desks, Wi-Fi access, and marble bathrooms with glass-enclosed showers. The hotel's **lounge/bar** and **restaurant** have become one of the city's favorite haunts.

7 Leokoriou, 10554 Athens. www.ochreandbrown.com. © **210/331-2950.** Fax 210/331-2942. 17 units. 120€–192€ double; 208€ junior suite. AE, MC, V. Metro: Monastiraki/Thissio. **Amenities:** Restaurant; lounge bar. *In room:* A/C, TV, Wi-Fi.

Syntagma

Syntagma Square is the center and heart of Athens. It's bustling, elegant and hectic with a wide selection of hotels from classic old-timers to trendy newcomers and everything in between.

Best For: People who want to stay in the center of things.

Drawbacks: It's not a spot for relaxing, as the area is busy night and day and sometimes (say, during protest demonstrations), it can be a little too "busy."

VERY EXPENSIVE/EXPENSIVE

Athens Plaza (NJV) ★★   Acres of marble adorn the lobby, and there's almost as much in some bathrooms, which have their own phones. Many of the guest rooms are larger than most living rooms, and many have balconies overlooking Syntagma Square. The service, although perfectly professional, lacks the personal touch.

Syntagma Sq., 10564 Athens. www.njvathensplaza.gr. *©* **210/335-2400.** Fax 210/323-5856. 207 units. 300€–400€ double. AE, DC, MC, V. Metro: Syntagma **Amenities:** 2 restaurants; 2 bars; free airport pickup; concierge; health club and spa w/Jacuzzi; room service; smoke-free rooms; 1 room for those w/ limited mobility. *In room:* A/C, TV, hair dryer, minibar, Wi-Fi.

Grande Bretagne ★★★   The Grande Bretagne, one of Athens's most distinguished 19th-century buildings, is back after a $70-million, 2-year renovation. The changes preserved the Beaux Arts lobby, made dingy rooms grand once more, and added indoor and outdoor swimming pools. From Winston Churchill to Sting, the guests who stay here expect the highest level of attention. The Grande Bretagne prides itself on its service; you are unlikely to be disappointed. Ask for a room with a balcony overlooking Syntagma Square, the Parliament building, and the Acropolis.

Syntagma Sq., 10564 Athens. www.grandebretagne.gr. *©* **210/333-0000.** Fax 210/333-0160. 328 units. 277€–285€ double. AE, DC, MC, V. Metro: Syntagma. **Amenities:** 2 restaurants; 2 bars; free airport pickup; concierge; health club and spa w/Jacuzzi; 2 pools (indoors and outdoors); room service; smoke-free rooms; 1 room for those w/limited mobility. *In room:* A/C, TV, hair dryer, Internet, minibar.

King George II ★★   Next door to the beautiful Grande Bretagne, the King George II is another of Athens's great historical hotels, opulent and classy. With only 102 rooms, it feels like a personalized boutique hotel rather than an Athenian landmark. Everything is immaculate from the antiques to the modern gym/health club. The rooms are individually designed with handmade furniture, silk and satin upholstery, and spacious, gray marbled bathrooms with sunken tubs and glass-encased showers. The **Tudor Bar** on the rooftop has excellent views of the city and its landmarks, while the power Greek-dining **Tudor Restaurant** is sublime. The infamous ninth-floor penthouse suite—whose occupants have included Aristotle Onassis, Maria Callas, Grace Kelly and Prince Rainier, Marilyn Monroe, and Frank Sinatra, among others—is said to be spectacular, and at the equivalent of $10,000 a night it should be! At press time, the hotel announced it was up for sale; most believe a new management will take over, but definitely keep an eye on the website and call ahead for details.

Vas Georgiou A2, Syntagma Sq., 10564 Athens. www.lux-hotels.com. *©* **210/322-2210** or 210/728-0350. Fax 210/325-0564 or 210/728-0351. 220€–260€ double. AE, DC, MC, V. Metro: Syntagma. **Amenities:** Rooftop bar/restaurant; bar; health club; indoor swimming pool; smoke-free rooms; spa; rooms for those with limited mobility. *In room:* A/C, TV, Internet.

EXPENSIVE

New Hotel ★ The "Yes" (Young Enthusiastic Seductive) hotel chain, responsible for some of the city's finest and trendiest hotels (Semiramis, Periscope, 21) has done it again and this time right in Syntagma Square and close to the Plaka, on the site of the former Olympic Palace Hotel. Designed by award-winning Brazilian architects and brothers Fernando and Humberto Campana, this super-trendy hotel—think jagged mirrors, nice-size rooms, contemporary furnishings from recycled materials, original art pieces throughout, and balconies with side street views—is a sophisticated newcomer. As with all the aforementioned hotels of the "Yes" chain, guests receive a 10% discount at the well-regarded Zouboulakis Art Gallery.

16 Fillelinon St., 10557 Athens. www.yeshotels.gr. ✆ **210/628-4565.** Fax 210/628-4640. 79 units. 160€–200€ double; **Amenities:** Breakfast room; bar; restaurant; gym; Internet; luggage storage. *In room:* A/C, TV, hair dryer, minibar, Wi-Fi.

MODERATE

Athens Cypria ★★ 👜 In a convenient location on a (usually) quiet street, the Cypria overlooks the Acropolis from unit nos. 603 to 607. With bright white halls and rooms, cheerful floral bedspreads and curtains, and freshly tiled bathrooms with new fixtures, the Cypria is a welcome addition to the city's moderately priced hotels. The breakfast buffet offers hot and cold dishes from 7 to 10am. The hotel can be infuriatingly slow in responding to faxed reservation requests.

5 Diomias, 10562 Athens. www.athenscypria.com. ✆ **210/323-8034.** Fax 210/324-8792. 115 units. 117€ double; 143€ triple. Reductions possible off season. Rates include buffet breakfast. AE, MC, V. Take Karayioryi Servias out of Syntagma Sq.; Diomias is on the left, after Lekka. **Amenities:** Breakfast room; bar; snack bar; luggage storage. *In room:* A/C, TV, hair dryer, Internet, minibar.

Electra Hotel ★ 🥄 On pedestrian Ermou, the Electra boasts a location that is quiet and central—steps from Syntagma Square. Most of the guest rooms have comfortable armchairs, large windows, and modern bathrooms. Take a look at your room before you accept it: Although most are large, some are quite tiny. The front desk is sometimes understaffed but the service is generally acceptable, although it can be brusque when groups are checking in and out.

5 Ermou, 10563 Athens. www.electrahotels.gr. ✆ **210/322-3223.** Fax 210/322-0310. 110 units. 140€ double; 260€ suite. Rates include buffet breakfast. AE, DC, MC, V. Metro: Syntagma. The Electra is about 2 blocks down on the left as you walk along Ermou with Syntagma Sq. behind you. **Amenities:** Restaurant; bar. *In room:* A/C, TV, hair dryer, minibar, Wi-Fi.

Hotel Achilleas The Achilleas (Achilles), on a relatively quiet side street near Syntagma Square, has good-size guest rooms that are bright and cheerful. Some rear rooms have small balconies; several on the fifth floor can be used as interconnecting family suites. The central location of Hotel Achilleas and its fair prices make it a good choice. If you want a room with a safe or hair-dryer ask at the main desk upon check-in.

21 Lekka, 10562 Athens. www.achilleashotel.gr. ✆ **210/323-3197.** Fax 210/322-2412. 34 units. 90€–120€ double. Rates include continental breakfast. AE, DC, MC, V. Metro: Syntagma. Take Karayioryi Servias out of Syntagma Sq. for 2 blocks and turn right onto Lekka. **Amenities:** Breakfast room; snack bar; Wi-Fi in lobby. *In room:* A/C, TV, hair dryer, minibar.

INEXPENSIVE

Hotel Carolina ★★ The friendly, family owned and -operated Carolina, on the outskirts of the Plaka, is a brisk 5-minute walk from Syntagma and has always been popular with students. In the last few years, the Carolina has undertaken extensive remodeling and now attracts a wide range of frugal travelers. Double-glazed windows and air-conditioning make the guest rooms especially comfortable. Many rooms have large balconies, and several (such as no. 308) with four or five beds are popular with families and students. The congenial atmosphere may be a bit too noisy for some.

55 Kolokotroni, 10560 Athens. www.hotelcarolina.gr. © **210/324-3551.** Fax 210/324-3350. 31 units. 90€ double; 110€ triple; 130€ quad. Rates include breakfast buffet. MC, V. Take Stadiou out of Syntagma Sq. to Kolokotroni (on left). **Amenities:** Breakfast room; bar; Internet cafe. *In room:* A/C, TV, Wi-Fi.

Kolonaki

Kolonaki has always been the posh section of downtown. Galleries, upscale shops, cafes, boutique hotels, and eateries line the trendy streets, many of them pedestrianized.

Best For: Travelers who want to be in a more cosmopolitan section of the city, ideal for shopping marathons and discovering some of the city's most eclectic dining and nightlife options. Also for those seeking to experience the city as locals do and away from most other tourists.

Drawbacks: The lack of budget accommodations and it's a bit away from the sites.

EXPENSIVE

St. George Lycabettus Hotel ★★ As yet, the distinctive, classy St. George does not get many tour groups, which contributes to its tranquil, sophisticated tone. The rooftop pool is a real plus, as is the excellently redesigned rooftop restaurant, **Le Grand Balcon,** much favored by wealthy Greeks for private events. Floors have differing decorative motifs, from Baroque to modern Italian. Most rooms look toward pine-clad Mount Likavitos; some have views of the Acropolis. Others overlook a small park or have interior views. This impeccable boutique hotel is steps from chic restaurants, cafes, lounges, and shops. Check out the **Frame** lounge in the hotel lobby after dark; this ultrahip lounge/bar is one of the hottest Athenian destinations.

2 Kleomenous, 10675 Athens. www.sglycabettus.gr. © **210/729-0711.** Fax 210/721-0439. 154 units. 148€–170€ double; 280€ suite. Continental breakfast 20€. AE, DC, MC, V. Parking 14€ per day. From Kolonaki Sq., take Patriarchou Ioachim to Loukianou and follow Loukianou uphill to Kleomenous. Turn left on Kleomenous; the hotel overlooks Dexamini Park. **Amenities:** 2 restaurants; 2 bars; concierge; pool; room service; smoke-free rooms; rooms for those w/limited mobility. *In room:* A/C, TV, hair dryer, minibar, Wi-Fi.

MODERATE

Athens Lycabettus Hotel ★ This stylish boutique hotel is on Valeoritou, a pedestrian street filled with trendy cafes, bars, restaurants, and lounges for the fashion-conscious crowd. Apart from its ideal location, the hotel has made a name for itself for its outstanding service. Rooms, though on the small side, are pleasant and bright with contemporary furnishings and nice-size marble bathrooms. The hotel also has a popular **bar/cafe restaurant.**

6 Valeoritou and Voukourestiou St., 10671 Athens. www.athenslycabettus.gr. © **210/360-0600.** 25 units. 110€–130€ double; 160€–200€ suite. Metro: Syntagma. **Amenities:** Restaurant/bar; Wi-Fi. *In room:* A/C, TV, hair dryer, minibar.

Periscope ★ The Periscope is a concept hotel with an unusual concept: surveillance. The 22 guest rooms, spread over six floors, are all black and white with large beds, industrial-style bathrooms, and ceilings decorated with aerial pictures of Athens taken from a helicopter. The penthouse suite has exclusive use of the rooftop deck with its Jacuzzi and breathtaking views of the city, including the Acropolis and Mount Lycabettus all the way to Piraeus. The **lobby bar** broadcasts live images of the city on huge flatscreen monitors—the images are shot from the **rooftop bar,** by a camera which is controlled by loungers in the lobby area. This has led to a lively bar scene. The neighborhood is upscale, with many posh boutiques, stylish cafes and eateries nearby. The hotel's restaurant (π) is one of the most popular in the city.

22 Haritos, 10675 Athens. www.yeshotels.gr. ℂ **210/623-6320.** Fax 210/729-7206. 22 units. 127€–136€ double; 204€suite. AE, DC, MC, V. **Amenities:** Cafe/bar; restaurant, gym; smoke-free rooms. *In room:* A/C, LCD TV, DVD player, minibar, Wi-Fi.

Embassy District (Museum Mile)

The **Embassy** district (or **Museum Mile**) near trendy Kolonaki, is home to some of the city's finest museums and galleries as well as the **Athens Music Hall.**

Best For: Travelers who want to be a bit out of the tourist frenzy but minutes away via Metro from the sites. It's also close to some of the city's finer smaller museums and the fashionable Kolonaki district.

Drawbacks: The lack of budget accommodations.

EXPENSIVE

Hilton Athens ★★★   The Hilton remains one of the best hotels in the city. Small shops, a salon, cafes, and restaurants surround the glitzy lobby. The guest rooms (looking toward either the hills outside Athens or the Acropolis) have large marble bathrooms and are decorated in the generic but comfortable international Hilton style, with some Greek touches. The Plaza Executive floor of rooms and suites offers a separate business center and a higher level of service. Facilities include a large outdoor pool, conference rooms, and a spa. Even if you're not staying here, you can dine at the superb **Milos** seafood restaurant and **Byzantinon** restaurant and have a drink around sunset at the **Galaxy** rooftop bar with its impressive city views. For 15€, visitors can use the pool for the day. Ask about special/promotional rates before booking.

46 Leoforos Vas. Sofias, 11528 Athens. www.hilton.com. ℂ **800/445-8667** in the U.S., or 210/728-1000. Fax 210/728-1111. 527 units. 179€–339€ single/double; 274€ triple. AE, DC, MC, V. Parking 27€ per day. Metro: Evangelismos. **Amenities:** 4 restaurants; 3 bars; free airport pickup; babysitting; concierge; health club and spa w/Jacuzzi; 2 pools (outdoor and indoor); room service; smoke-free rooms/floors; rooms for those w/limited mobility. *In room:* A/C, Internet TV, hair dryer, minibar, Wi-Fi.

Koukaki & Makrigianni (Near the Acropolis)

The **Makrigianni** district is home to the **Acropolis Museum** and a stone's throw away from the **Plaka** and the **Acropolis. Markigianni** and **Koukaki** have a wide variety of accommodations, are largely residential and centrally located to all the sites.

Best For: Travelers who want to be conveniently located to the sites, the **Plaka,** and the **Archaeologial Promenade** and still feel as if they're locals.

Drawbacks: The area is becoming very popular with tourists. This might be an advantage or a drawback for some.

MODERATE/EXPENSIVE

Athens Gate Hotel ★   This small boutique accommodation is stylish, elegant and close to the sights and the metro. The seven-floor hotel has 99 rooms; the front rooms on the busy Leof. Syngrou have Temple of Olympian Zeus views; you'll find a partial view of the Acropolis from the lower-floor back rooms (which are also quieter); the rooms on the seventh floor have spectacular Acropolis and city views. The rooms are comfortable and spacious with polished wood floors, modern furnishings, comfortable beds, and good-size bathrooms. The top floor **restaurant** with its spell-binding views is also a major plus.

10 Syngrou Ave., Makrigianni, 11742 Athens. www.athensgate.gr. © **210/923-8302.** Fax 210/237-4993. 99 units. 130€–185€ double; 195€ triple. Rates include breakfast buffet. AE, DC, MC, V. Metro: Akropolis. **Amenities:** Restaurant; 2 bars/cafe; concierge; room service; smoke-free rooms. *In room:* A/C, TV, hair dryer, Internet, minibar.

Divani-Palace Acropolis ★★ Just 3 blocks south of the Acropolis, in a quiet residential neighborhood, this place does a brisk tour business but also welcomes independent travelers. The bland guest rooms are large and comfortable, and some of the large bathrooms even have two washbasins. The cavernous marble-and-glass lobby contains copies of classical sculpture; a section of Athens's 5th-century-B.C. defensive wall is preserved behind glass in the basement by the gift shop. The breakfast buffet is extensive, the hotel's two restaurants are quite good (particularly the summer-only rooftop **Acropolis Secret Roof Garden**) and the outdoor pool is a nice touch.

19-25 Parthenonos, Makrigianni, 11742 Athens. www.divaniacropolis.gr. © **210/922-2945.** Fax 210/921-4993. 253 units. 110€–180€ double; 300€ suite. Rates include breakfast buffet. AE, DC, MC, V. Metro: Akropolis. **Amenities:** 2 restaurants; 2 bars; concierge; outdoor pool; room service; smoke-free rooms. *In room:* A/C, TV, hair dryer, Internet, minibar.

The Royal Olympic Hotel ★ The Royal Olympic has a lot going for it: tastefully decorated (marble, wood, and bronze) with clean, decent-size rooms and bathrooms, and there's a breathtaking city and Acropolis view from its top-floor restaurant, and an outdoor swimming pool. Of its 272 rooms, we were the most impressed with the **Athenian Panorama** rooms (45 in total) that command spellbinding views of the Temple of Zeus, National Gardens, and Lycabettus mountain; most of the hotel's standard rooms have views of the internal courtyard and the pool. For Acropolis views request a room above the third floor.

28-34 Athanasiou Diakou, 11743 Athens. www.royalolympic.com. © **210/928-8400.** Fax 210/923-3317. 272 units. 130€–187€ double; 359€ suite. Rates include breakfast buffet. AE, DC, MC, V. Metro: Acropolis. **Amenities:** Rooftop restaurant; 3 bars; concierge; gym (off-site); outdoor pool; room service; smoke-free rooms; spa. *In room:* A/C, TV, hair dryer, minibar, Wi-Fi.

MODERATE

Acropolis Hill ★ This boutique hotel, near the Filopappos Hill (Hill of the Muses), is pretty, spacious, clean, and in a quiet location. Here you'll find nice rooms with modern furnishings and polished wood floors, marble bathrooms, and many of the rooms on the top floor have balconies commanding Acropolis views. There's also a nice **rooftop restaurant/bar** and a small outdoor pool. It's up a rather steep hill, if that makes a difference to you.

7 Mouson, Filopappou, 11742 Athens. www.acropolishill.gr. © **210/923-5151.** Fax 210/924-7350. 36 units. 130€ double; 150€ triple. Rates include breakfast buffet. AE, DC, MC, V. Metro: Syngrou-Fix. From Syngrou-Fix station, ascend Drakou St. for a few blocks to Mouson St. and turn left. **Amenities:** 2 restaurants; 2 bars; concierge; outdoor pool; room service; smoke-free rooms. *In room:* A/C, TV, hair dryer, minibar, Wi-Fi.

Acropolis View Hotel ★ This nicely maintained hotel is on a residential side street off Rovertou Galli, not far from the Herodes Atticus theater. The quiet neighborhood, at the base of Filopappos Hill (a pleasant area to explore) is a 10- to 15-minute walk from the heart of the Plaka. Many of the small but appealing guest rooms are freshly painted each year. All units have good bathrooms as well as balconies.

Some, like no. 405, overlook Filopappos Hill, while others, like no. 407, face the Acropolis. A big plus is the **rooftop garden** with awesome Acropolis views.

Rovertou Galli and 10 Webster, 11742 Athens. www.acropolisview.gr. ✆ **210/921-7303.** Fax 210/923-0705. 32 units. 125€ double. Rates include buffet breakfast. Substantial reductions Nov–Mar. AE, MC, V. Metro: Akropolis. On Dionissiou Areopagitou, head west past Herodes Atticus theater to Rovertou Galli. Webster (Gouemster on some maps) is the little street intersecting Rovertou Galli btw. Propilion and Garabaldi. **Amenities:** Breakfast room; bar; roof garden. *In room:* A/C, TV, minibar.

Hera Hotel ★ 🏷 The Hera has a stunning indoor courtyard behind its breakfast room and great views of the Acropolis from its rooftop garden where the elegant **Peacock Lounge** has become one of the most popular bar/restaurants in the city—especially a little after sunset for its breathtaking views. The units are comfortable and tastefully furnished; the ones on the fourth floor and the suites on the fifth floor have the best views and large verandas.

9 Falirou, Makrigianni, 11742 Athens. www.herahotel.gr. ✆ **210/923-6682.** Fax 210/923-8269. 38 units. 135€ double; 180€ junior suite. AE, DC, MC, V. Free parking. Metro: Akropolis. **Amenities:** 2 cafe/bar/restaurants (1 on the rooftop); shared Internet terminal; smoke-free rooms; rooms for those w/limited mobility. *In room:* A/C, TV, hair dryer, Internet.

Herodion Hotel ★ This is an attractive hotel a block south of the Acropolis, near the Herodes Atticus theater. Rooms are a good size (with marble bathrooms) and many have balconies. The **rooftop terrace** is a major draw, with great views of the Acropolis and the Acropolis Museum, as well as two hot tubs. The lobby leads to a lounge and patio garden where you can have drinks and snacks under the trees.

4 Rovertou Gall, Makrigianni, 11742 Athens. www.herodion.gr. ✆ **210/923-6832** or 210/923-6836. Fax 210/921-6150. 90 units. 130€ double; 158€ triple. Rates include American buffet breakfast. AE, DC, MC, V. Metro: Akropolis. **Amenities:** Breakfast room; bar. *In room:* A/C, TV, Wi-Fi.

INEXPENSIVE

Art Gallery Hotel Once home to several artists, this small hotel in a half-century-old house maintains an artistic flair (and an old-fashioned cage elevator). Rooms are small and plain but comfortable, many with polished hardwood floors and ceiling fans. A Victorian-style breakfast room on the fourth floor is furnished with marble-topped tables and velvet-covered chairs. The top-floor **bar/lounge** has beautiful views of Filopappou Hill and the Acropolis.

5 Erechthiou, Koukaki, 11742 Athens. www.artgalleryhotel.gr. ✆ **210/923-8376.** Fax 210/923-3025. 22 units. 50€–80€ single; 70€–100€ double; 80€–100€ triple. 7€ buffet breakfast. AE, MC, V. Metro: Syngrou-Fix. *In room:* A/C, TV.

Athens Studios 🛏 You wouldn't realize that Athens Studios is a hostel if I hadn't told you. Located on Veikou street, down the Makrigianni pedestrian block from the Acropolis Metro station between a laundromat and the fun and affordable Athens Sports Bar, the studio apartments come with either two or four beds (some with six), and are bright, modern, and spacious, each with a kitchenette and balcony. The higher floor apartments have larger balconies and better views but all in all, this is a wonderful place in a great location with a warm homey feel to it that won't break the bank.

3a Veikou, Makigianni, 11742 Athens. www.athensstudios.gr. ✆ **210/923-5811.** 15 units. 60€–65€ double; 50€ quad AE, MC, V. Metro: Akropolis. *In room:* A/C, TV, Internet.

Marble House Pension ★ Named for its marble facade, which is usually covered with bougainvillea, this small hotel, whose front rooms offer balconies overlooking quiet Zinni Street, is famous among budget travelers (including many teachers) for its friendly staff. Over the last several years, the pension has been remodeled and redecorated, gaining new bathrooms and guest-room furniture (including small fridges). Two units have kitchenettes. If you're spending more than a few days in Athens, this is a homey base.

35 A. Zinni, Koukaki, 11741 Athens. www.marblehouse.gr. © **210/923-4058.** Fax 210/922-6461. 16 units, 12 with bathroom. 45€ double without bathroom, 49€ with bathroom. 9€ supplement for A/C. Monthly rates available off season. No credit cards. Metro: Syngrou-Fix. **Amenities:** 2 rooms for those w/limited mobility. *In room:* A/C (9 units), TV, minibar.

Tony's Hotel (aka Tony's Pension)   Travelers planning a longer stay in Athens should consider Tony's, which is popular with students and budget travelers. Located between Filopappos Hill and Leoforos Syngrou, Tony's has communal lounges, kitchens, and a roof garden with a barbecue grill. It's nothing fancy but it's friendly, charming, clean and homey. For a bit more, you can rent one of the studio apartments next door in the hotel's new building, all of which have balconies.

26 Zacharitsa, Koukaki, 11741 Athens. www.hoteltony.gr. © **210/923-5761.** 21 units, including 11 studio apts. 65€-85€ double. No credit cards. Metro: Syngrou-Fix. **Amenities:** Communal lounges; Wi-Fi; kitchens; roof garden w/barbecue grill. *In room:* A/C, TV, Wi-Fi.

Outside Central Athens: Worth the Journey

The following selections are most likely to appeal to travelers seeking a different kind of Athenian experience, away from the downtown scene but not too far from the city center. The northern suburbs—lush, aristocratic, and green—and the coastal suburbs with their beaches and buzzing summer nightlife are two excellent options, depending which time of year you are in Athens. Kifissia is a 40-minute train ride from downtown on Metro line 1, and the coast is accessible by tram (up to Voula) and farther out (from the center or Glyfada) either by bus or taxi.

Kifissia

Leafy, aristocratic Kifissia has long been the favorite destination of the rich and famous, and you'll enjoy its many elegant 19th-century neoclassical mansions found in tree-lined streets and squares, alongside modern mansions and apartment buildings.

Best For: Travelers seeking to bask in the elite Athenians' playground, shop all day, walk along tree-lined streets, wine and dine in posh and trendy surroundings with seldom another tourist in sight.

Drawbacks: It's a bit more of an effort to get to the major sites.

EXPENSIVE

Pentelikon ★★   Looking more like a private estate than a hotel—with its immaculately kept gardens—the Pentelikon, full of old-world glamour, was built in 1929 and features grand staircases and gigantic ballrooms of a long-gone era. The rooms are comfortable, clean, and nicely sized, as are the bathrooms if the overall look is a bit on the stuffy side, which these old-world glamour hotels tend to be. Rooms overlook either the gardens or the outdoor pool area. The pool itself is a refreshing treat. Elegance and impeccable style can be found around every corner, and to make it even more appealing, the hotel also houses the Michelin-starred restaurant **Vardis.**

66 Deligianni, 14562 Kifissia. www.hotelpentelikon.gr. © **210/623-0650.** Fax 210/801-0314. 101 units. 250€ double. AE, DC, MC, V. Free parking. Metro: Kifissia, then 5-min. taxi ride, 25-min. walk to Kefalari Sq. or Kefalari bus. **Amenities:** Restaurant; bar; outdoor pool. *In room:* A/C, TV.

Semiramis ★★   This is by far the most stunning of the designer hotels in Athens; if you approach the hotel at night, you might think you're in South Beach, when you behold the building dramatically lit in changing colors that include magenta, lime, orange, and yellow. New York–based British-Egyptian designer Karim Rashid has created a modern artistic masterpiece with original touches throughout: symbols on room doors instead of numbers, hallways that glow different colors, LCD displays outside the rooms, and a shoehorn-shaped pool. The hotel also has two popular **bars** and a great **restaurant.** The 51 units, which are bright with modern furnishings and decent-sized marble bathrooms, include five poolside bungalows overlooking a giant waterfall, while the suites command exceptional views from their terraces of the bustling city and nearby peaceful and serene Penteli mountain.

48 Harilaou Trikoupi, 14562 Kifissia. www.yeshotels.gr. ✆ **210/623-3521.** Fax 210/628-4499. 51 units. 190€ double; 260€ bungalow. AE, DC, MC, V. Metro: Kifissia, then 5-min. taxi ride, 25-min. walk to Kefalari Sq. or Kefalari bus. **Amenities:** Restaurant; 2 bars; gym; pool. *In room:* A/C, LCD/plasma/pay TV, Wi-Fi.

MODERATE/EXPENSIVE

Hotel 21 ★   Ultracool Hotel 21 features spacious rooms with giant beds and large glass-encased bathrooms for (relatively) moderate prices. Each of the 21 rooms features a segment of a painting by local artist Georgia Sagri (the painting in its entirety is featured—in miniature—in the reception area); split-level loft suites have sunroofs. Many guests come here for the scene at the outdoor cafe or bar inside the hotel.

21 Kolokotroni and Mykonou, 14562 Kifissia. www.yeshotels.gr. ✆ **210/623-3521.** Fax 210/623-3821. 21 units. 132€–160€ single/double; 200€–250€ loft suite. AE, DC, MC, V. Free parking. Metro: Kifissia then bus, taxi, or 25-min. walk to Kefalari Sq. **Amenities:** 2 restaurants/bars. *In room:* A/C, TV/DVD, Wi-Fi.

Along the Coast

Clear waters, nice restaurants and beautiful open-air clubs and bars by the sea, as well as excellent shopping options, make the Athenian coast irresistible during the summer.

Best For: Travelers seeking to bask, shop, wine, dine, and party in the sun and the surf without a care (or an itinerary) in the world.

Drawbacks: You might never want to make the time to visit the sites.

VERY EXPENSIVE

Astir Palace Resort ★★★   Tranquil and beautiful, with beautiful sea vistas and private pine-clad grounds, the Astir Palace is a series of secluded bungalows and two, soon to be three, different hotels (The Arion, the Westin Athens, and W Athens), with their own private beaches on 30 hectares (75 acres) with plenty of activity from windsurfing to Pilates classes. Seven well-regarded restaurants, including **Matsuhisa Athens,** are on-site. The Arion offers a more classical aesthetic, and its sea-view rooms are arranged in such a way so that even the bathtubs have prime water views; all rooms in the Westin have sea views while the rooms are elegant and modern, and the new W hotel is supposed to open in 2012, following a long, extensive renovation.

40 Apollonos, 16671 Vouliagmeni. www.astir-palace.com. ✆ **210/890-2000.** Fax 210/896-2582. 526 units. Arion: 380€–460€ double. Westin: 340€–410€ double. AE, DC, MC, V. Free parking. Tram to Glyfada, then either taxi or bus 114. **Amenities:** 7 restaurants; 7 bars; 3 pools; 3 tennis courts w/floodlighting. *In room:* A/C, TV, Internet, Wi-Fi.

EXPENSIVE/VERY EXPENSIVE

Divani Apollon Palace & Spa ★★   In a prime location on Kavouri beach with towering palm trees, picturesque gardens, and two large swimming pools, this is as close to a secluded island experience as you are likely to get in a large city. With sea views from every room, large balconies and green marble bathrooms, and a private beach, this one of the most romantic of Athens's hotels. Complementing the ambience is the well-regarded seafood restaurant, **Mythos tis Thalassas** (Legend of the Sea), with seafront tables, accessible for the guests of the hotel via an underground tunnel.

10 Agiou Nikolaou and Iliou, 16671 Vouliagmeni. www.divaniapollon.gr © **210/891-1100.** Fax 210/965-8010. 286 units. 220€ double; 340€ executive double; 1,600€ suite. AE, DC, MC, V. Free parking. Tram to Glyfada, then either taxi or bus 114. **Amenities:** 3 restaurants; bar; gym; 2 pools; spa; tennis court w/ floodlighting; free shuttle bus to Glyfada and/or Syntagma Sq. *In room:* A/C, TV, Wi-Fi.

Margi ★★   Wonderfully stylish and atmospheric with colonial-style decor, this 88-room hotel—which looks like a Moorish castle, complete with stone walls and outdoor arches—has spacious rooms where contemporary design and antiques blend seamlessly, gray marble bathrooms equipped with Bulgari products, and views overlooking either the pool, the sea, or the mountains. The Asian-style candlelit pool **bar and restaurant** is a major plus.

11 Litous, 16671 Vouliagmeni. www.themargi.gr. © **210/896-2061.** Fax 210/896-0229. 88 units. 240€ double; 600€ executive suite. AE, DC, MC, V. Free parking. Tram to Glyfada, then either taxi or bus 114. **Amenities:** Restaurant; 2 bars; pool. *In room:* A/C, TV, Wi-Fi.

Practical Hotel Information
THE BIG PICTURE
Athens hotel rooms come in basically the same size as most of their European counterparts and generally smaller than their U.S. ones. Athens has a large range of accommodations, from luxury historic hotels to designer boutiques and everything else in between, nearly all of them offer the same amenities, including at the very least an Internet corner if not Wi-Fi in the room, comfortable bathrooms (again on the small size), decent beds, a minibar, and a large number of the rooms have balconies.

On the whole Athens hotels are less expensive per average than the rest of Europe and bargains can be found even during peak season.

GETTING THE BEST DEAL
High season is considered from Easter to October with the height of the season between July and late September but deals can be found even then if you begin your search early enough. If you're making your plans last minute you can also find quite decent deals especially if you're willing to compromise and not stay in Makrigianni and the Plaka districts. At press time, the best deals were to be found in or near Omonoia Square, Metaxourgeio, and the National Archaeological Museum, all seedy parts of town that can get unpleasant, if not dangerous, after dark, so you should consider that when booking. Deals for all hotels can be found online, but it's best to contact the hotel personally and negotiate the online deal you have found or have a reputable local travel agency do the work for you. **Off-peak season** visitors will discover a cooler (temperature wise) Athens with less tourists, far less crowded sites and great deals.

Reservation Services: To get the best deals in town, you will need a reputable local travel agency that will do the hard work for you. Thankfully, Athens has many, but our three favorites are **Fantasy Travel,** 19 Filelinon (© **210/331-0530;** www.fantasytravel.gr); **CHAT Tours,** 4 Stadiou (© **210/323-0827;** www.chatours.gr); and **Key Tours,** 4 Kallirois (© **210/923-3166;** www.keytours.gr).

Alternative Accommodations: Athens has many hotel options (including the hostels recommended), but you can also rent or swap apartments if you're in town for a

PRICE categories

Very Expensive	100€ and up
Expensive	40€–100€
Moderate	20€–40€
Inexpensive	Under 20€

longer stay. In that case, popular websites to check out would be **www.expatriates.com**, **www.vacationrentals.com**, **www.craigslist.gr**, **www.homeaway.com**, and **www.worldhomeexchanges.com**. As always, proceed with care, and if a deal sounds too good to be true, it probably is.

WHERE TO EAT

Epicurian Athens is a foodie's delight, from the old-fashioned tavernas to the trendiest gourmet eateries; world cuisines are nicely represented as well. The plethora of dining options is dizzying and the settings range from city sidewalks, quiet courtyards and gardens, verandas with breathtaking Acropolis and city views to dining on the beach. A meal in Athens, particularly dinner, is to be relished, never rushed and preferably enjoyed alfresco.

Best Athens Restaurant Bets

- **Best Splurge:** Winner of two Michelin stars, **Spondi** is justly considered by many to be the finest restaurant in all of Greece. See p. 154.
- **Best Traditional Taverna:** The oldest taverna in Psiri, **Taverna tou Psiri** remains the best. See p. 145.
- **Best Contemporary Greek:** In a beautiful 1830s neoclassical house, **Daphne's** has been serving its delicious fare for many years, earning its well-deserved praise from local and visiting diners alike. See p. 139.
- **Best Regional Greek:** In Makrigianni, **Mani Mani** serves delicious traditional dishes from Mani (in the south of the Peloponnese) at affordable prices. See p. 153.
- **Best View:** Head up Lycabettus Mountain to **Horizons** to dine with the city laid under your feet like a sparkling map. See p. 149.
- **Best Seafood: Varoulko** is widely and justly considered the greater Athens area's finest seafood restaurant. See p. 145.
- **Best Grill House: To Steki tou Ilia** has the finest and most mouthwatering lamb chops in the city. See p. 148.
- **Best Mezedes:** At **Filistron** in Thissio, not only is the food exceptional but the views from its summer roof garden make everything even tastier. See p. 147.
- **Most Romantic: Ithaki** has exceptional seafood in an equally exceptional location on the coast, with tremendous sea vistas and an immaculate setting. See p. 155.
- **Best Meal on a Budget:** Internationally acclaimed **Melilotos** is ideal for affordable, delicious dishes. See p. 149.

The Plaka

Some of the most charming old restaurants in Athens are in the Plaka—as are some of the worst tourist traps. Here are a few things to keep in mind when you head off for a meal in the Plaka.

Some restaurants station waiters outside who pursue you with an unrelenting sales pitch. The hard sell is almost always a giveaway that the place caters to tourists. (That said, remember that announcements of what's for sale are not invariably ploys reserved for tourists. If you visit the Central Market, you'll see and hear stall owners calling out the attractions of their meat, fish, and produce to passersby—even waving particularly tempting fish and fowl in front of potential customers.)

In general, it's a good idea to avoid places with floor shows; many charge outrageous amounts (and levy surcharges not always stated on menus) for drinks and food. If you get burned, stand your ground, phone the **tourist police** (© **171**), and pay nothing before they arrive. Often the mere threat of calling the tourist police has the effect of causing a bill to be lowered.

MODERATE

Daphne's ★★ CONTEMPORARY GREEK Frescoes adorn the walls of this neoclassical 1830s home, which includes a shady garden courtyard displaying bits of ancient marble found on-site. Diners from around the world sit at Daphne's tables. The courtyard makes it a real oasis in Athens, especially when summer nights are hot. The food here—recommended by the *New York Times, Travel + Leisure,* and just about everyone else—gives you all the old favorites with new distinction (try the zesty eggplant salad), and combines familiar ingredients in innovative ways (delicious hot pepper and feta cheese dip). We could cheerfully eat the hors d'oeuvres all night. We have also enjoyed the *stifado* (stew) of rabbit in *mavrodaphne* (sweet-wine) sauce and the tasty prawns with toasted almonds. Live music plays unobtrusively in the background on some nights. The staff is attentive, endearing, and beyond excellent.

> **A Note on Credit Cards (or Bring Cash)**
>
> Many Athenian restaurants still do not accept credit cards, especially tavernas and "lower brow" places.

4 Lysikratous. ©/fax **210/322-7971.** www.daphnesrestaurant.gr. Reservations recommended. Main courses 30€–40€, with some fish priced by the kilo. AE, DC, MC, V. Daily 7pm–1am.

INEXPENSIVE

Damigos (The Bakaliarakia) ★★ GREEK/SEAFOOD This basement taverna, with enormous wine barrels in the back room and an ancient column supporting the roof in the front room, has been serving deep-fried codfish and eggplant, as well as chops and stews, since 1865. The wine comes from the family vineyards. There are few pleasures greater than sipping retsina (if you wish, you can buy a bottle to take away) while you watch the cook turn out meal after meal in his absurdly small kitchen. Don't miss the *skordalia* (garlic sauce), good with cod, eggplant, bread—well, you get the idea.

41 Kidathineon. © **210/322-5084.** Main courses 6€–18€. No credit cards. Daily 7pm to any time from 11pm–1am. Usually closed June–Sept. From Syntagma Sq., head south on Filellinon or Nikis to Kidathineon; Damigos is downstairs on the left just before Adrianou.

Giouvetsakia ★ TRADITIONAL GREEK Run by the same family since 1950, this traditional taverna at a bustling junction is perfect for people-watching in a scenic environment while enjoying some delicious, traditional fare. Try the Giouvetsi (stewed lamb in orzo-still the house's specialty and its namesake) and be sure to leave room for the complimentary fruit dish topped with cinnamon.

144 Adrianou and Thespidos. © **210/322-7033.** Main courses 6€–18€. MC, V. Daily 10am–2am.

Athens Restaurants

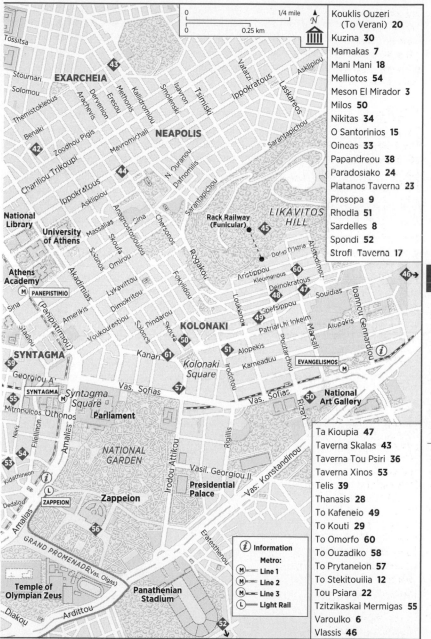

Kouklis Ouzeri
(To Verani) **20**
Kuzina **30**
Mamakas **7**
Mani Mani **18**
Melliotos **54**
Meson El Mirador **3**
Milos **50**
Nikitas **34**
O Santorinios **15**
Oineas **33**
Papandreou **38**
Paradosiako **24**
Platanos Taverna **23**
Prosopa **9**
Rhodia **51**
Sardelles **8**
Spondi **52**
Strofi Taverna **17**

Ta Kioupia **47**
Taverna Skalas **43**
Taverna Tou Psiri **36**
Taverna Xinos **53**
Telis **39**
Thanasis **28**
To Kafeneio **49**
To Kouti **29**
To Omorfo **60**
To Ouzadiko **58**
To Prytaneion **57**
To Stekitouilia **12**
Tou Psiara **22**
Tzitzikaskai Mermigas **55**
Varoulko **6**
Vlassis **46**

Kouklis Ouzeri (To Yerani) ★ GREEK/MEZEDES Besides Kouklis Ouzeri and To Yerani, Greeks call this old favorite with its winding staircase to the second floor the "Skolario" because of the nearby school. Sit down at one of the small tables and a waiter will present a large tray with about a dozen plates of *mezedes*—appetizer portions of fried fish, beans, grilled eggplant, *taramasalata* (fish roe dip), cucumber-and-tomato salad, olives, fried cheese, sausages, and other seasonal specialties.

14 Tripodon. ✆ **210/324-7605.** www.sholarhio.gr. Appetizers 5€–18€. No credit cards. Daily 11am–2am. From Syntagma Sq., head south on Filellinon or Nikis to Kidathineon; take Kidathineon across Adrianou to Thespidos and climb toward Acropolis; Tripodon is 1st street on right after Adrianou.

Paradosiako ★ TRADITIONAL GREEK Off the fringes of Plaka, removed from the tourist traps, is this great little place offering traditional fare (its name translates to "traditional"). We recommend the inexpensive and quite delicious whole grilled calamari and the baked chickpeas, but everything on the menu is quite tasty.

44A Voulis. ✆ **210/321-4121.** Main courses 7€–15€. No credit cards. Mon–Sat 10am–2am; Sun 10am–9pm.

Platanos Taverna ★★ TRADITIONAL GREEK In good weather, this taverna on a quiet pedestrian square puts its tables beneath a plane tree (*platanos* means plane tree). Inside, where locals usually congregate to escape the summer sun at midday and where tourists gather in the evening, you can enjoy the old paintings and photos on the walls. The Platanos has been serving good *spitiko fageto* (home cooking) since 1932, and has managed to keep its regulars happy while enchanting visitors. If artichokes or spinach with lamb are on the menu, you're in luck: They're delicious. The casseroles (either lamb or veal with spinach or eggplant) are especially tasty. The wine list includes a wide choice of bottled wines from many regions of Greece, although the house wine is tasty. Plan to come here and relax, not rush, through a meal.

4 Diogenous. ✆ **210/322-0666.** Fax 210/322-8624. Main courses 7€–15€. No credit cards. Mon–Sat noon–4:30pm and 8pm–midnight; also Sun in Mar–May and Sept–Oct noon–4:30pm. From Syntagma Sq., head south on Filellinon or Nikis to Kidathineon. Turn right on Adrianou, and take Mnissikleos up 1 block toward the Acropolis; turn right onto Diogenous.

Taverna Xinos ★ TRADITIONAL GREEK Hidden just off Plaka's main square, where it has been run for over 70 years by the same family, is this little gem, offering traditional, home-cooked meals specializing in lamb dishes. Try it fricasseed (with lemon sauce) or stewed with pasta (Giouvetsi) or grilled. According to family lore, this taverna is where my grandfather proposed to my grandmother as a strolling duo serenaded them with Greek love songs accompanied by the accordion. Though I am certain it isn't the same pair of musicians, a duo still serenades diners nightly with beautiful love songs of a long-gone but not quite forgotten era. In warm weather you can dine in the tree-lined courtyard; in winter, warm yourself by the coal-burning stove and admire the frescoes.

4 Geronta. ✆ **210/322-1065.** Main courses 6€–18€. No credit cards. Daily 8pm to any time from 11pm–1am; sometimes closed Sun. Usually closed part of July and Aug. From Syntagma Sq., head south on Filellinon or Nikis to Kidathineon; turn right on Geronta and look for the XINOS sign in the cul-de-sac.

Tou Psara ★ GREEK/SEAFOOD One of the few remaining places in the Plaka that remains a cut above its tourist-trap neighbors, this spot is tucked away in a quiet corner under blooming mulberry trees. This might just be the only seafood option in Plaka seriously worth considering. The marinated octopus is truly out of this world.

16 Erechtheos and 12 Erotokritou. ✆ **210/321-8733.** Main courses 7€–18€. No credit cards. Daily noon–2am.

Monastiraki

MODERATE

Abyssinia Cafe ★ TRADITIONAL GREEK   This small cafe in a ramshackle building sports a nicely restored interior featuring lots of gleaming dark wood and polished copper. It faces Abyssinia Square off Ifaistou, where furniture restorers ply their trade and antiques shops sell everything from gramophones to hubcaps. You can sit indoors or out with a coffee, but it's tempting to snack on Cheese Abyssinia (feta scrambled with spices and garlic), mussels and rice pilaf, the marinated anchovies, or wild boar *keftedes* (meatballs). Everything is reasonably priced, but it's easy to run up a tab, because everything is so good—especially the *mezedes* that are superior to the main courses. For a quieter experience, book a table on the mezzanine with its awesome views.

7 Kinetou, Plateia Abyssinia, Monastiraki. ℭ **210/321-7047.** Appetizers and main courses 10€–29€. MC, V. Tues-Sat 11am-midnight; Sun 11am-7pm. Closed mid-July to mid-Aug. Metro: Monastiraki. Abyssinia Sq. is just off Ifaistou (Hephaistos) across from Ancient Agora's entrance on Adrianou.

To Kouti ★ CONTEMPORARY GREEK   Located along Adrianou Street next to the Ancient Agora, this place is great for people-watching. To Kouti (the Box) looks like children decorated it with bright-colored crayons—even the menu is handwritten on brightly illustrated children's book covers. Beyond decor, To Kouti has an unusual but tasty menu: Try the beef in garlic and honey or the shrimp in carrots, or opt for some of its vegetarian dishes. The homemade bread is served in (of course!) boxes.

23 Adrianou, Monastiraki. ℭ **210/321-3229.** Main courses 15€–30€. AE, MC, V. Daily 1pm-1am. Metro: Monastiraki.

INEXPENSIVE

Bliss ★ MEDITERRANEAN/ORGANIC   Three levels in this extremely popular all day multiuse space include a wonderful cafe/restaurant that serves delicious organic fare: teas, coffee, smoothies, sandwiches, salads, and Greek taverna main courses; beginning with their first-rate breakfast. There's also yoga and alternative therapy rooms, a New Age bookstore, and gift shop.

24A Romvis St., Monastiraki. ℭ **210/325-0360.** www.purebliss.gr. Appetizers and main courses 5€–15€. MC, V. Daily 7am-2am. Metro: Monastiraki/Thissio

Dioskouri ★ GREEK MEZEDES   On busy Adrianou, ideal for its Acropolis, Agora and Temple of Hephaestus views, not to mention the countless passers-by, Dioskouri has been serving tasty *mezedes* at affordable prices for many years, becoming a favorite for locals and tourists alike. Good seafood and meat *mezedes*.

37 Adrianou, Monastiraki. ℭ **210/325-3333.** Appetizers 5€–15€. No credit cards. Daily 11am-1am. Metro: Monastiraki/Thissio

Diporto GREEK   This little place, sandwiched between olive shops, serves salads, stews, and delicious *revithia* (chickpeas) and *gigantes* (butter beans), both popular Greek winter dishes among stall owners, shoppers, and Athenians who make their way to the market for cheap and delicious food.

Central Market, Athinas. No phone. Main courses 8€–18€. No credit cards. Mon-Sat 6am-6pm. Metro: Monastiraki.

James Joyce Pub IRISH/AMERICAN   Yes, it's an Irish pub in downtown Athens, with excellent American-style buffalo wings, burgers, and stuffed potato skins; Irish dishes such as Connaught lamb chops and grilled salmon; great salads—and, of course, lots of beer. The James Joyce also has an excellent Irish breakfast and it's one of the few places where one can watch NFL football games and U.S. baseball as well as European soccer matches.

12 Astiggos, Monastiraki. © **210/323-5055.** www.jjoyceirishpubathens.com. Main courses 9€–19€. No credit cards. Daily 9am–2am. Metro: Monastiraki/Thissio.

Papandreou GREEK   The butcher, the baker, and the office worker duck past the sides of beef hanging in the Meat Hall and head to this hole in the wall for zesty tripe dishes. Don't like tripe? Don't worry: Their menu offers choices that don't involve it. Papandreou has a virtually all-male clientele during the daytime but it's infamous for its early morning after-club crowd.

Central Market, Athinas. © **210/321-4970.** Main courses 8€–18€. Daily 24 hr. Metro: Monastiraki.

Taverna Sigalas GREEK   This long-running Plaka taverna, housed in a vintage 1879 commercial building with a newer outdoor pavilion, boasts that it has been run by the same family for a century and is open 365 days a year. Huge old retsina kegs stand piled against the back walls; black-and-white photos of Greek movie stars are everywhere. After 8pm, Greek muzak plays. At all hours, both Greeks and tourists wolf down large portions of stews, moussaka, grilled meatballs, baked tomatoes, and gyros, washing it all down with the house red and white retsinas.

2 Plateia Monastiraki. © **210/321-3036.** Main courses 8€–19€. No credit cards. Daily 7am–2am. Across Monastiraki Sq. from the Metro station.

Thanasis ★ GREEK/SOUVLAKI   Thanasis serves terrific souvlaki and pita—and exceptionally good french fries—both to go and at its outdoor and indoor tables. As always, prices are higher if you sit down to eat. On weekends, it often takes the strength and determination of an Olympic athlete to get through the door and place an order here. It's worth the effort: This is both a great budget choice and a great place to take in the local scene, which often includes a fair sprinkling of Gypsies.

69 Mitropoleos (just off the northeast corner of Monastiraki Sq.). © **210/324-4705.** Main courses 6€–15€. No credit cards. Daily 9am–2am.

Psirri

EXPENSIVE/MODERATE

Godzilla ★ JAPANESE   For those late nights where drinking has left you ravenous but you can't stomach another souvlaki, Godzilla is the perfect option. Decorated like a Tokyo subway station, Godzilla is a great sushi bar whose popularity skyrocketed recently, but it remains reasonably priced and as tasty as ever. Sundays are a great deal for the hungry, with an all-you-can-eat lunch buffet for 27€ per person.

5 Riga Palamidou, Psirri. © **210/322-1086.** Main courses 30€–40€. MC, V. Daily 9pm–2:30am.

Kuzina ★★ CONTEMPORARY GREEK   With seating on busy, beautiful pedestrian Adriannou with its views of the Temple of Hephaestus, the Agora, and the Acropolis, this gem of contemporary Greek cuisine has exceptional dishes, impeccable service, and a roof garden terrace to die for. The impressive menu does no wrong—everything we tried was excellent. Steamed mussels, dumplings with feta cheese and pomegranate syrup, crab cakes, grilled pork chops, and the grilled salmon with fennel pie were all outstanding, but our favorite was the yellowfin tuna sashimi and the lobster tail over Greek noodles. The wine list is impressive and the views amazing. There also is an art gallery on the second floor.

9 Adriannou St, Psirri. © **210/324-0133.** www.kuzina.gr. Main courses 15€–35€. DC, MC, V. Daily 1pm–1am. Metro: Thissio/Monastiraki.

INEXPENSIVE

Nikitas ★★ TRADITIONAL GREEK Amid all the new and glitzy bars and bar/ restaurants of this hip area, Nikitas stands alone as an old-time, traditional taverna featuring its delicious classic fare all throughout the day The cuttlefish with spinach, the *horta* (boiled greens), cheese croquettes, and the stuffed tomatoes with oven-baked potatoes we had really hit the spot. This place is a must.

19 Agion Anargyron, Psirri. ☎ **210/325-2591.** Main courses 6€-18€. No credit cards. Daily 10am-7pm. Metro: Monastiraki/Thissio.

Oineas ★★ TRADITIONAL GREEK Delightful and delicious, this taverna in Psirri is popular with tourists and locals alike—the stamp of approval from both camps is deserved. The unusual appetizers (fried feta in light honey) may conspire to make you forget to order any main dishes, but don't—you can't go wrong in any of your selections here.

9 Aisopou. Psirri. ☎ **210/321-5614.** Main courses 8€-18€. DC, MC, V. Mon-Fri 7pm-2am; Sat-Sun noon-2am. Metro: Monastiraki.

Taverna Tou Psiri ★★ TRADITIONAL GREEK The oldest taverna in Psiri is still one of the best in the area. You'll find delicious traditional taverna fare (the lamb chops are particularly good), hearty salads, good house wine, live music, moderate prices, and a nice outdoor garden.

12 Eshylou, Psirri. ☎ **210/321-4923.** Main courses 8€-18€. DC, MC, V. Daily 10am-2am. Metro: Thissio/ Monastiraki.

Tellis ★ TRADITIONAL GREEK It lacks style and decor (to put it mildly), but the hordes of locals couldn't care less with such delicious fare in this extraordinary meaterie, which serves gigantic portions at budget prices. The grilled lamb chops with oven-roasted lemon potatoes are amazing. Salads are good, too.

86 Evripidou, Psirri. ☎ **210/324-2775.** Main courses 6€-15€. No credit cards. Mon-Sat 9am-1am. Metro: Monastiraki.

Gazi, Kerameikos, Thissio & Petralona
VERY EXPENSIVE

Varoulko ★★★ INTERNATIONAL/SEAFOOD This is widely considered the Athens area's finest seafood restaurant. We had one of our most memorable meals here—smoked eel; artichokes with fish roe; crayfish with sun-dried tomatoes; monk-fish livers with soy sauce, honey, and balsamic vinegar—and the best sea bass and monkfish we have eaten. Sweetbreads, goat stew, and tripe soup have joined seafood on the menu. In summer there's a rooftop terrace with a gorgeous view of the Acropolis.

80 Piraios, Athens. ☎ **210/522-8400.** www.varoulko.gr. Reservations necessary several days in advance. Dinner for 2 from about 120€; fish priced by the kilo. DC, MC, V. Mon-Sat about 8pm-midnight. Metro: Kerameikos.

EXPENSIVE

Funky Gourmet ★ CONTEMPORARY GREEK Housed in a beautiful neoclassical building, Funky Gourmet was a hit upon arrival. The gorgeous restaurant also has fine cuisine and as the name suggests, a playful menu. Highlights on a recent visit included the beef filet in tartar sauce with mashed potatoes, exceptional lobster with pasta, and duck with mushrooms and cashew nuts. The deserts were out of this world, particularly the Black Forest cake.

13 Paramythias and Salaminos, Kerameikos. ℂ 210/524-2727. www.funkygourmet.com. Reservations essential. Main courses 31€–39€. AE, DC, MC, V. Tues–Sat 8:30pm–midnight. Metro: Kerameikos.

MODERATE

Butcher Shop ★ GREEK GRILL   As the name suggests, this postmodern taverna/grill house, on the city's hippest street between Sardelles and Mamacas, is a haven for meat lovers: tender pork chops, steaks, *biftekia* (burgers), grilled and roasted (organic) chicken, a myriad of sausages (try the wild boar sausages), wonderful meat soups, and large salads—with a rich selection of cheeses from all over Greece (try the Kasseri from the island of Lesbos) and the freshest vegetables.

19 Persefonis, Gazi. ℂ **210/341-3440.** Main courses 15€–30€. No credit cards. Daily noon–1am. Metro: Kerameikos.

Chez Lucien ★ FRENCH/BELGIAN   Off pedestrian Apostolou Pavlou and tucked away in one of Thissio's many charming side streets (leading to Ano Petralona), you will find this popular French bistro with a small but excellent menu and a symposium-like atmosphere. They don't take reservations, so be prepared to wait and even share a table—it's worth the wait. Menu highlights include the French onion soup and the crème brûlée.

32 Troon, Petralona. ℂ **210/346-4236.** Main courses 15€–30€. No credit cards. Tues–Sat 8pm–2am. Metro: Petralona.

Dirty Ginger ★ CONTEMPORARY GREEK   In trendy Gazi, on an impossibly popular street lined with some of the city's hottest bars and restaurants, Dirty Ginger stood out from the get-go, thanks to its courtyard, the party mood that takes over after 10pm, and the sought-after seats on the tiny pavement in front where you can watch beautiful people come and go. The light Mediterranean fare is delicious, too. I had the most delicious chop suey I've ever eaten there. The Tinos french fries (served in a cone) are also first rate, as are the grilled eggplant with garlic and diced tomato, the grilled chicken with curry, the souvlaki (in a pita), and the mouthwatering veal and lamb chops. Eat, drink, and linger to watch and participate in the highly infectious nightly party. You won't want to or need to go anywhere else for the night.

46 Triptopolemou and Persefonis, Gazi. ℂ **210/342-3809.** www.dirtyginger.gr. Main courses 15€–25€. V, MC. Daily 8pm–2am. Metro: Kerameikos.

Mamacas ★★ GREEK   If any restaurant can be credited for kick-starting the transformation of Gazi from gritty to urban chic, it's Mamacas. A famous restaurant on the island of Mykonos, the city version of Mamacas has been irresistible to Athenians since 1998. With its modern, delicious twist on old favorites, whitewashed walls, chic clientele, and impossibly good-looking staff, Mamacas is still one of the best the ancient city has to offer. Check out the trays of cooked dishes (*magirefta*) and a range of dependable and delicious grills and appetizers (the spicy meatballs or *keftedakia* are a must!). After dinner, linger a little at the bar as it picks up heat after midnight, or watch the world go by outside in the hippest place in the city after dark.

41 Persophonous, Gazi. ℂ **210/346-4984.** www.mamacas.gr. Main courses 15€–35€. AE, MC, V. Daily 1:30pm–1:30am. Metro: Kerameikos.

Meson el Mirador ★ MEXICAN   After years of pseudo-Mexican fare, I finally had a genuine Mexican meal in Athens in the middle of Kerameikos, right off the ancient cemetery in a beautifully restored mansion. Top-notch enchiladas, quesadillas, and pork chops with beans—plus a vegetarian menu, excellent sangria, and margaritas—blow the would-be competitors out of the water. With the surroundings, food, and music in this atmospheric part of town, you can't go wrong. In summer the beautiful roof terrace with Acropolis views is open.

88 Agisilaou at Salaminas, Kerameikos. ℂ **210/342-0007.** www.el-mirador.gr. Main courses 15€–30€. MC, V. Mon–Fri 7:30pm–2am; Sat noon–2am; Sun noon–6pm. Metro: Thissio.

Prosopa ★ MEDITERRANEAN This little restaurant beside the train tracks on the outskirts of Gazi has plenty of atmosphere going for it in this once-forgotten section of the city. Wonderful Mediterranean fare, including a wide array of pasta and risotto entrees and some exceptional beef, chicken, and seafood dishes, make "Faces" a wonderful little place to discover. Leave enough room for the "trio of death"— cheesecake, chocolate brownie, and banana-cream pie.

4 Konstantinoupoleos and 52 Megalou Vassiliou, Gazi. ℂ **210/341-3433.** www.prosopa.gr. Main courses 25€–30€ No credit cards. Daily 8:30pm–2:30am. Metro: Kerameikos, then walk down to Konstantinoupoleos by the train tracks.

Sardelles ★ GREEK/SEAFOOD "Sardines" is a friendly and simple modern taverna specializing in delicious seafood *mezedes*. Try the fried shrimp, the grilled cuttlefish, and the grilled *sardeles* (sardines), plus the large, fresh salads.

15 Persefonis St., Gazi. ℂ **210/347-8050.** Main courses 15€–30€. No credit cards. Daily noon–1am. Metro: Kerameikos.

INEXPENSIVE

Filistron ★★ GREEK/MEZEDES Right on the Archaeological Promenade in Thissio, Filistron has a rooftop terrace with such awesome views of the dramatically lit Parthenon against the starry night sky, you won't want to leave. The delicious offerings will give you even more reason to linger. The menu is (mostly) *mezedes*, which means you can have many different dishes and try as many specialties as you'd like. And it's reasonably priced to boot. Begin with a glass of wine at dusk and watch the sky turn dark as the lights on the Acropolis come to life. After that, begin sampling the restaurant's many *mezedes*—my favorites are the island pies, the Byzantine salad, and the grilled potatoes with smoked cheese. If you like all things salty, order the salted sardines from Spain.

23 Apostolou Pavlou, Thissio. ℂ **210/346-7554.** www.filistron.com. Appetizers 7€–18€. DC, MC, V. Mon–Sat 8pm–1am; Sun 1:30–5pm. Reservations suggested for the rooftop. Metro: Thissio.

Gazohori ★ GREEK/MEZEDES "Gazi Village" has delicious fare (*mezedes*) at affordable prices, so its pretty courtyard is almost always packed with students. Festive, friendly, and fun, it also has live music. Try the hearty salads, the grilled meatballs and sausages, lemon potatoes, and slow-cooked eggplant.

2 Dekeloen, Gazi. ℂ **210/342-4044.** Appetizers 7€–15€. V, MC. Daily noon–1am. Metro: Kerameikos.

O Santorianios (The Man from Santorini) ★★ GREEK/MEZEDES Delicious fare from the island of Santorini is served at this little gem, open only in the evening. You'll get traditional cuisine from the island in an old Athenian home with a small garden, run by a family from Santorini. Try the impeccable fava dip, cherry tomato salad with chloro cheese, grilled octopus and red snapper, and their famous *tomatokeftedes* (tomato rissoles) paired with a fine wine from the island. You'll wish you were back there or planning a visit, but until then, you can always return here.

8 Doreion, Petralona. ℂ **210//345-1629.** Reservations strongly recommended Fri–Sat. Appetizers 8€–18€. No credit cards. Daily 8pm–midnight. Metro: Petralona.

QUICK BITES IN syntagma

In general, Syntagma Square is not known for good food, but the area has a number of places to get a snack. **Apollonion Bakery,** 10 Nikis, and **Elleniki Gonia,** 10 Karayioryi Servias, make sandwiches to order and sell croissants, both stuffed and plain. **Ariston** is a small chain of *zaharoplastia* (confectioners) with a location at 10 Voulis (just off Syntagma Sq.); it sells snacks as well as pastries and delicious cheese pies. For some of the best chocolate drinks in the city, stop by **Chocolate 56,** 56 Ermou St.

For the quintessentially Greek *loukoumades* (round doughnut hole–like pastries that are deep-fried, then drenched with honey and topped with powdered sugar and cinnamon), try **Doris,** 30 Praxitelous, a continuation of Lekka, a few blocks from Syntagma Square. If you're still hungry, Doris serves hearty stews and pasta dishes for low prices Monday through Saturday until 3:30pm. If you're nearer Omonia Square when you feel the need for *loukoumades* or a soothing dish of rice pudding, try **Aigaion ★,** 46 Panepistimiou.

Everest is another local chain worth trying; there's one a block north of Kolonaki Square at Tsakalof and Iraklitou. Also in Kolonaki Square, **Kotopoula Valsamakis** serves succulent grilled chicken to take out or eat in. In the Plaka, **K. Kotsolis Pastry Shop,** 112 Adrianou, offers excellent coffee and sweets; it's an oasis of old-fashioned charm in the midst of souvenir shops. **Oraia Ellada (Beautiful Greece) ★★,** a cafe at the Center of Hellenic Tradition, opens onto both 36 Pandrossou and 59 Mitropoleos near the flea market and has a spectacular view of the Acropolis. You can revive yourself here with a coffee and pastries. For the best espresso, cappuccino, Italian pastries, and brioche sandwiches in town, venture to **Alfiere Café ★** in Kolonaki, right behind the Italian Embassy at 5 Sekeri.

For delicious vegetarian and vegan dishes, head to **Avocado ★** at 30 Nikis.

To Steki Tou Ilia ★ TRADITIONAL GREEK GRILLHOUSE On a quiet pedestrian street away from the bustling cafes and bars of lively Thissio, you can find this popular grill house ("Ilias' hangout"). The house specialty is its irresistible *paidakia,* chargrilled lamb chops served the old-fashioned way, with grilled bread sprinkled with olive oil and oregano. A second location is at 5 Eptachalkou St., Thissio (℃ **210/345-8052**); that keeps the same hours (see below).

7 Thessalonikis, Thissio. ℃ **210/342-2407.** Main courses 8€–20€. No credit cards. Mid-June to mid-Sept Tues–Sat 8pm–1am, Sun 1:30–5pm (closed 2 weeks in Aug). Metro: Thissio.

Syntagma
EXPENSIVE

Aegli/Cibus ★★ INTERNATIONAL For years, the bistro in the Zappeion Gardens was a popular meeting spot; when it closed, it was sorely missed. Now it's back, along with a cinema, a hip and highly recommended outdoor bar/club, and a fine restaurant. Once more, chic Athenian families head here, to the cool of the Zappeion Gardens, for the frequently changing menu. Some of the specialties include foie gras, oysters, tenderloin with ginger and coffee sauce, profiteroles, fresh sorbets, strawberry soup, and yogurt crème brûlée. Tables indoors or outdoors by the trees offer places to relax with coffee. In the evening, take in a movie at the open-air cinema before dinner, or have a drink and a snack at one of the nearby cafes. In short, this is a wonderful spot to while away an afternoon or evening—and a destination for a special occasion.

Zappeion Gardens (adjacent to the National Gardens fronting Vas. Amalias Blvd.). © **210/336-9363.** Reservations recommended. Main courses 35€–53€. AE, DC, MC, V. Daily 10am–midnight. Sometimes closed in Aug. Metro: Syntagma.

MODERATE

Furin Kazan ★ JAPANESE Furin Kazan is continuously swarming with a mostly Japanese clientele—a sure stamp of approval. It's an ideal spot for lunch. Try the noodle and rice dishes, but it's best known for the sushi and sashimi.

2 Appolonos, Synatgma. © **210/322-9170.** www.furin-kazan.com. Main courses 15€–35€. AE, DC, MC, V. Mon–Sat 11:30am–11pm; Sun 2–11pm. Metro: Syntagma.

Izitzikas kai Mermigas ★★ GREEK The Greek translation of Aesop's fable of the "Cricket and the Ant" has come to the heart of Athens after being a suburban favorite for years. Try as many *mezedes* as you like; all are delicious—the cheese pies, shrimp with ouzo and cream, and spicy meatballs with mozzarella are just some of our favorites. The desserts and ice creams are also excellent.

12-14 Mitropoleos, Syntagma. © **210/324-7607.** www.tzitzikas-mermigas.gr. Main courses 15€–25€. MC, V. Mon–Sat 1pm–1am. Metro: Syntagma.

INEXPENSIVE

Melilotos ★★ MEDITERRANEAN/ORGANIC Inside the lobby of a commercial building by Syntagma Square, this isn't the kind of place you go to for ambience. What you will come here for, and I suspect more than once, is the delicious, meticulously prepared, and inexpensive meals cooked on the spot from the finest, freshest ingredients under the guidance of award-winning chef Konstantinos Siopidis. Everything here is excellent: green pies, fish (halibut and salmon), meat (beef), poultry (roasted chicken with potatoes), delicious soups, and salads; just leave enough room for the pastries prepared by the chef's mother-in-law, a recurring guest chef on Greek daytime TV. Come in, pick up your meal, and then head over to the National Gardens across the street for a wonderful picnic.

15 Xenofontos, Syntagma. © **210/322-2458.** Main courses 5€–13€. MC, V. Mon–Thurs 11am–7pm. Fri 11am–6pm.

Kolonaki, Ambelokipi

EXPENSIVE

Horizons ★★ MEDITERRANEAN For a table with a view, you can't do better than this. It sits on the top of Lycabettus hill, with the city laid under your feet like a sparkling map, and the view is sublime. The Mediterranean menu is very good. We started with the lobster salad gradine with Gorgonzola cheese, grilled vegetables, and the fried salmon with wasabi—all exceptional. The grilled shrimp, pasta risotto, and smoked pork tenderloin and lamb shank that followed were all top-notch too, as was the baklava dessert, but it was the view that stole the show. Arrive for sunset and enjoy.

Lycabettus Hill. © **210/722-7065.** Reservations recommended. Main courses 40€–60€. AE, MC, V. Daily 1pm–1am. Taxi or walk to the top of Lycabettus to Ploutarchou St. to take the funicular (6€ with return), or walk up from Dexamini Sq.

Milos ★★ SEAFOOD With two successful locations in Montreal and New York, Milos arrives at its birthplace and is better than ever. On the ground floor of the Hilton hotel, this place is a must for any seafood lover. The main draw is the freshness of the ingredients from all over the country, sent directly to the restaurant via airplane from the fishing boats. Lately, it has also added a nice selection of meat dishes to the menu, such as our new favorites, rib-eye steak and New York strip, which immediately joined our old-time favorites, such as the grilled Nova Scotia lobster, the oven-baked fish (in sea salt crust), and the tender fresh salmon over black tagliatelle. The prices are a bit high, but you'll get your money's worth.

Athens Hilton, 46 Vas Sofias, Ilissia. © **210/724-4400.** www.milosrestaurant.com. Main courses 40€–85€; prix-fixe dinner 7–9pm and midnight–1:30am 29€ for 3-course meal; family special 39€ for 5-course meal. AE, DC, MC, V. Daily noon–4:30pm and 7pm–1:30am. Metro: Evangelismos.

Ta Kioupia ★★ CONTEMPORARY/REGIONAL GREEK   After relocating from Kifissia to a neoclassical building in Kolonaki, this restaurant has ambience in spades and a menu to match, ranging from modern to traditional Greek cuisine from the islands and other regions. I suggest the tasting menu (25€–40€), which offers samplings from over 30 dishes. The *trahana* soup (with rooster and bulgur wheat), the warm eggplant and pine nut salad, and the lamb baked in vine leaves are delicious, as are the samplings slow cooked in clay pots (thus the name of the restaurant).

Dinokratous and 22 Anapiron Polemou. © **210/740-0150.** www.takioupia.com. Main courses 25€–54€. MC, V. Daily 1pm–1am. Metro: Evangelismos.

MODERATE

Filipou ★ TRADITIONAL GREEK   This longtime Athenian favorite almost never disappoints. The traditional dishes such as stuffed cabbage, stuffed vine leaves, vegetable stews, and fresh salads are consistently good. In the heart of Kolonaki, near the St. George Lykabettus Hotel, this is a place to head when you want good *spitiko* (home cooking) in the company of the Greeks and resident expats who prize the food.

19 Xenokratous. © **210/721-6390.** Reservations recommended. Main courses 12€–25€. No credit cards. Mon–Fri 8:30pm–midnight; Sat lunch 1–5pm. Metro: Evangelismos.

Jackson Hall ★ AMERICAN   On hip and popular Milioni Street in the heart of Kolonaki, Jackson Hall—with its grilled burgers, steaks, large salads, appetizers, and cocktails—packs them in all year-round. Hearty, generous-size dishes and delicious cocktails, especially the daiquiris, highlight the menu. The T-bone steak is top-notch, as is the Montana filet (pork filet with mushrooms sautéed with Madeira wine). Try the DI Siena risotto with chicken, and the surprisingly good cheesecake.

4 Milioni St. © **210/361-6098.** www.jacksonhall.gr. Main courses 15€–30€. AE, MC, V. Daily 10am–2am. Metro: Syntagma.

Rhodia ★ GREEK   This respected taverna is in a handsome old Kolonaki house. In good weather, tables are set up in its small garden—although the interior, with its tile floor and old prints, is equally charming. The Rhodia is a favorite of visiting archaeologists from the nearby British and American Schools of Classical Studies, as well as Kolonaki residents. Seriously, try the octopus in mustard sauce: it's terrific, as are the veal and *dolmades* (stuffed grape leaves) in egg-lemon sauce. The house wine is excellent, as is the halvah, which is both creamy and crunchy.

44 Aristipou. © **210/722-9883.** Main courses 8€–25€. No credit cards. Mon–Sat 8pm–2am. Metro: Evaggelismos, then climb Loukianou uphill to Aristipou, and turn right.

To Kafeneio ★★ GREEK/INTERNATIONAL   This is hardly a typical *kafeneion* (coffee shop/cafe). If you relax, you can easily run up a tab of 50€ for lunch or dinner for two. You can also eat more modestly yet elegantly. If you have something light, like the artichokes *a la polita,* leeks in crème fraîche, or onion pie (one, not all three!), accompanied by draft beer or the house wine, you can finish with profiteroles and not put too big a dent in your budget. I've always found this an especially congenial spot when I'm eating alone (perhaps because I love people-watching and profiteroles).

26 Loukianou. ✆ **210/722-9056.** Reservations recommended. Main courses 8€–25€. MC, V. Mon–Sat 11am–midnight or later. Closed most of Aug. Metro: Evangelismos.

To Ouzadiko ★★ GREEK/MEZEDES   This ouzo bar offers at least 40 kinds of ouzo and as many *mezedes,* including fluffy *keftedes* that make all others taste leaden. To Ouzadiko is popular with Athenians young and old who come to see and be seen while having a snack or a full meal, often after concerts and plays. A serious foodie friend of mine comes here for the wide variety of *horta* (greens), which she says are the best she's ever tasted. If you see someone at a nearby table eating something you want and aren't sure what it is, ask your waiter and it will appear for you—sometimes after a bit of a wait, as the staff here is often seriously overworked.

25–29 Karneadou (in the Lemos International Shopping Center). ✆ **210/729-5484.** Reservations recommended. Most *mezedes* and main courses 8€–25€. No credit cards. Tues–Sat 1pm–12:30am. Closed Aug. Metro: Syntagma. From Kolonaki Sq. take Kapsali across Irodotou into Karneadou. The Lemos Center is the miniskyscraper on your left.

To Prytaneion ★ MEDITERRANEAN   The bare stone walls here are decorated with movie posters and illuminated by baby spotlights. Waiters serve tempting plates of some of the city's most expensive, delicious and eclectic *mezedes,* including beef carpaccio, smoked salmon, bruschetta, and shrimp in fresh cream, as well as grilled veggies and that international favorite, the hamburger.

7 Milioni. ✆ **210/364-3353.** www.prytaneion.gr. Reservations recommended. Main courses 20€–35€. DC, MC, V. Daily 10am–1:30am. Metro: Syntagma.

Vlassis ★★★ TRADITIONAL GREEK   Greeks call this kind of food *paradisiako* (traditional), but paradisiacal is just as good a description. This reasonably priced food is fit for the gods: delicious fluffy vegetable croquettes, a unique eggplant salad, and hauntingly tender lamb in egg-lemon sauce.

l5 Meandrou, Ilissia. ✆ **210/725-6635.** Reservations recommended. Main courses 15€–30€. MC, V. Mon–Sat 1pm–midnight; Sun noon–5pm Closed much of June–Sept. Metro: Megaro Mousikis. Once you exit the Metro, cross the avenue and head down (adjacent the hospital) toward Michalacopoulou St. Meandrou is 1 block before. Across the street from the Crowne Plaza hotel.

INEXPENSIVE

To Omorfo (The Beautiful) ★ GREEK   And indeed it is beautiful! Tucked in a beautiful, tranquil section of Kolonaki on pretty Xenokratous Street, on the slopes of Lycabettus mountain, this quiet (lunch and early dinner) tavern has tons of old-world charm. The dishes (*mageirefta:* ready-cooked meals) change daily according to the freshest ingredients and catch of the day from the local markets. Their *stiffado* (rabbit stew), roasted chicken with baked lemon potatoes, and *giouvetsi* (stewed veal or lamb on orzo) are always on the money, as are their seasonal salads, and their cassaroles (either lamb or veal with spinach or eggplant) are especially tasty.

50 Xenokratous, Kolonaki. ✆ **210/722-6830.** Main courses 7€–15€. No credit cards. Mon–Sat 12:30–8:30pm. Metro: Evanggelismos. From Evanggelismos Metro station exit cross the avenue and walk up Marasli St. until you hit Xenokratous, 5 blocks away.

Omonia Square, Metaxourgeio & University Area (Near Exarchia Square)

EXPENSIVE

El Bandoneon ★ SOUTH AMERICAN   In a beautiful space, this fine Argentine restaurant, with its excellent meat selection, is dominated by a large central dance floor, where tango dancers spin to the music and offer the diners free lessons. Many well-known Argentine singers and dancers often perform here. It's lots of fun, with great food, and an exceptional bar. The *Bife Argentino*, a boneless veal steak, and the *Lomo Buenos Aires*, veal filet with Gorgonzola cheese and Bombon risotto, are our favorites.

7 Virginias Benaki, Metaxourgeio. ✆ **210/522-4346.** www.elbandoneon.com. Main courses 40€–60€. AE, DC, MC, V. Wed–Sat 8pm–1:30am; Sun 8pm–2am (operates only as a bar and offers tango lessons). Closed late May to early Sept. Metro: Metaxourgeio.

MODERATE

Archaion Gefsis (Ancient Flavors) ★★ ANCIENT GREEK CUISINE   It's a little on the kitschy side (columns, torches, and waitresses in togas), but a brilliant idea nonetheless. With recipes from Ancient Greece (recorded by the poet Arches-tratos), this is your one chance to dine like the ancients did. Offerings include cuttle-fish in ink with pine nuts, wild-boar cutlets, goat leg with mashed vegetables, and pork with prunes and thyme. Just remember: You may use a spoon and a knife, but no fork (!)—ancient Greeks did not use them. It's equally adored by locals, foodies, and tourists alike, and evenings here make for a unique dining experience.

22 Kodratou, Plateia Karaiskaki, Metaxourgeio. ✆ **210/523-9661.** www.arxaion.gr. Main courses 20€–33€. MC, V. Mon–Sat 8pm–1am. Metro: Metaxourgeio.

Giantes CONTEMPORARY GREEK/ORGANIC   With a charming location in a quaint, pretty garden by the open-air summer movie theater, Giantes has ambience and also serves tasty regional cuisine made with organic products. Many vegetarian dishes are on the menu, but our favorite was the chicken with honey, raisins, and coriander.

44 Valtetsiou, Exarchia. ✆ **210/330-1369.** Main courses 12€–27€. AE, DC, MC, V. Metro: Omonoia.

Ideal ★ TRADITIONAL GREEK   The oldest restaurant in the heart of Athens, today's Ideal has an Art Deco decor and lots of old favorites, from egg-lemon soup to stuffed peppers, and pork with celery to lamb with spinach. Ideal is a favorite of businesspeople, and the service is usually brisk, especially at lunchtime. It's not the place for a romantic rendezvous, but definitely for good, hearty Greek cooking.

46 Panepistimiou. ✆ **210/330-3000.** Reservations recommended. Main courses 8€–25€. AE, DC, MC, V. Mon–Sat noon–midnight. Metro: Omonia.

Kalliste Gefsis ★★ CONTEMPORARY GREEK   In a restored 19th-century house with polished wood floors and ornamental plaster ceilings, Kalliste manages to be both cozy and elegant and under its new management, seems to be bolder in its choices, yet always on the money. The constantly changing menu usually includes traditional dishes with a distinctive flair, such as lentil soup with pomegranate, and chicken with hazelnuts and celery purée. Even that old standby, crème caramel, is enlivened by the addition of rose liqueur.

137 Asklepiou, off Akadimias above the University of Athens. ✆ **210/645-3179.** Reservations recommended. Main courses 24€–30€. MC, V. Mon–Sat noon–2pm and 8pm–midnight. Metro: Panepistimio.

Kostoyiannis ★★ TRADITIONAL GREEK   Kostoyiannis has been doing everything right since the 1950s, serving a wide range of fresh seafood, grills, sweetbreads, and their signature *stifados* (rabbit or veal stews). Arriving here is a joy, as you walk past a display of what can be cooked for you. Inside the bustling restaurant, contented diners dig in to their choices. This is one of the nicest places in town to spend a leisurely evening watching more and more people arrive as concerts and theater performances let out across Athens.

37 Zaimi, Pedion Areos, behind the National Archaeological Museum. ☎ **210/822-0624.** Reservations recommended. Main courses 15€–25€; fish and shellfish by the kilo. No credit cards. Mon–Sat 8pm–midnight. Closed late July to Aug. Metro: Victoria.

INEXPENSIVE

Athinaikon ★★ GREEK/OUZERI   Not many tourists come to this favorite haunt of lawyers and businesspeople who work in the Omonia Square area. You can stick to appetizers (technically, this *is* an ouzeri) or have a full meal. Appetizers include delicious *loukanika* (sausages) and *keftedes;* pass up the more expensive grilled shrimp and the seafood paella. The adventurous can try *ameletita* (lamb's testicles). Whatever you have, you'll enjoy taking in the old photos on the walls, the handsome tiled floor, the marble-topped tables and bentwood chairs, and the regular customers, who combine serious eating with animated conversation.

2 Themistokleous. ☎ **210/383-8485.** Appetizers and main courses 8€–20€. No credit cards. Mon–Sat 11am–midnight. Closed Aug. Metro: Omonia. From Omonia Sq., take Panepistimou a block to Themistokleous; the Athinaikon is almost immediately on your right.

Taygetos ★ 🍴 GREEK/SOUVLAKI   This is a great place to stop for a quick meal on your way to or from the National Archaeological Museum. The service is swift and the souvlaki and fried potatoes are excellent, as are the chicken and the grilled lamb. The menu sometimes features delicious *kokoretsi* (grilled entrails).

4 Satovriandou. ☎ **210/523-5352.** Grilled lamb and chicken priced by the kilo. No credit cards. Mon–Sat 9am–1am. Metro: Omonia or Panepisitimio. From Omonia Sq. take Patision toward National Museum; Satovriandou is the 3rd major turn on your left.

Koukaki & Makrigianni (Near the Acropolis)

EXPENSIVE

Dionysos Zonar's ★ CONTEMPORARY/TRADITIONAL GREEK   In a picturesque location by Fillipapous Hill with Acropolis views, this all-day restaurant has great traditional fare (including the best moussaka we have had in a long time), as well as contemporary choices, including a wonderful risotto with cheese and a decent salmon, hearty salads, and good meat selections (the meat Stroganoff was good). But it was the made-on-site baklava (prepared on request, so it'll be a half-hour that's worth the wait) that stole our hearts. Along with the view from the outdoor terrace and a very personable (if at times slow) service staff, this is a great place to linger around. Arrive a few minutes before sunset (reservations are essential during summer) and enjoy.

43 Robertou Galli St, Makrigianni. ☎ **210/923-1936.** www.dionysoszonars.gr. Main courses 25€–100€. DC, MC, V. Daily 12pm–1am. Metro: Akropolis.

MODERATE

Mani Mani ★★ CONTEMPORARY/REGIONAL GREEK   Delicious and moderately priced, Mani Mani's menu is based on traditional dishes from Mani in the south of the Peloponnese. The rooster *bardouniotikos* (rooster stewed with feta) we had was exceptional as was the lamb shank, and their homemade pasta (*hilopites*). Appetizers include *siglino* (cured pork that is first salted, then smoked, and finally boiled) and grilled sausages. The salads are recommendable, and the service is wonderful.

10 Falirou, Makrigianni. ✆ **210/921-8180.** www.manimani.com.gr. Main courses 9.50€–17€. DC, MC, V. Tues–Sat 8pm–1am; Sun 2–5pm. Metro: Akropolis

Strofi Tavern ★ TRADITIONAL GREEK   The Strofi serves standard Greek taverna fare (the *mezedes* and lamb and goat dishes are especially good here), but the view of the Acropolis is so terrific that everything seems to taste particularly good. Keep this place in mind if you're staying south of the Acropolis, an area not packed with restaurants. Strofi is popular with the after-theater crowd that pours out of the nearby Herodes Atticus Theater during the Athens Festival.

25 Rovertou Galli, Makriyianni. ✆ **210/921-4130.** Reservations recommended. Main courses 8€–25€. DC, MC, V. Mon–Sat 8pm–2am. Metro: Akropolis. Located 2 blocks south of Acropolis.

Pagrati & Mets (Near the Old Olympic Stadium)

EXPENSIVE

Spondi ★★★ MEDITERRANEAN   *Athinorama,* the weekly review of the Athenian scene, has chosen Spondi several years running (2001–2007, 2011) as the best place in town. The menu features light dishes—the fresh fish, especially the salmon, is superb—as well as dishes you will find delightful (roast pork with *myzithra* cheese and a fig-and-yogurt sauce; sea bass in rose-petal sauce; hare and truffle *mille-feuille*). The setting, a 19th-century town house with a stone courtyard covered with bougainvillea, is lovely; the wine offers over 1,000 labels; the service is excellent; and the desserts, created with Paris-based patisserie Bristol, divine. You'll probably want to take a cab here, costing you (from Syntagma Sq.) around 6€. Spondi won its first Michelin star in 2002 and its second in 2008. It is considered by many to be the best restaurant in Greece.

5 Pyrronos, Pangrati. ✆ **210/752-0658.** www.spondi.gr. Reservations recommended. Main courses 45€–130€. AE, DC, MC, V. Daily 8pm–midnight. Closed Sun in Aug. Pyrronos runs btw. Empedokleous and Dikearchou, behind the Olympic Stadium.

MODERATE

Virinis ★ TRADITIONAL GREEK   This is one of the finest traditional tavernas in the city, always busy with locals and tourists in the know. You'll find simple, home-cooked fare at moderate prices, such as lamb or veal *giouvetsi* stewed over orzo, pastichio (baked macaroni with beef in a delicious béchamel sauce), grilled meats, fresh salads, and good barrel wine. In summer there's seating in the courtyard garden.

11 Archimidou, Pangrati. ✆ **210/701-2153.** Main courses 10€–22€. No credit cards. Daily 8pm–1:30am. Directly behind the old Olympic Stadium, 5-min. taxi ride from Syntagma Sq. to Plateia Plastira.

Outside Central Athens

Akanthus ★ GREEK/MODERN TAVERNA   Akanthus has a picturesque location inside the Asteras Glyfada beach complex—an easy, affordable tram ride from downtown. Begin with the *ouzokatastasi* (the ouzo situation) *mezedes* dish—a delightful combo of shrimp, smoked salmon, black caviar, and grilled octopus. The appetizers we tried—sashimi with feta and honey, and the minipizza slices topped with mozzarella, ham, and chicken—were delicious, as were the large shrimps and tender grilled chicken and veal filets (marinated in lemon juice and olive oil), but it was the *keftedes* that had us ordering multiple servings. The salads are large and delicious as well (try the Cretan Health Salad). Come for the scenery, the food, and the sunset over the sea, and stay on for the beach party.

58 Leoforos Poseidonas, Asteras Glyfada. ☏ **210/968-0800.** www.asterascomplex.com. Main courses 25€–30€. MC, V. May–Oct daily 8pm–1am. Tram to Plateia Glyfadas, then 5-min. walk along Leof. Poseidonos.

Ithaki ★★ SEAFOOD   Head here for exceptional seafood in an equally exceptional location on the coast, with tremendous sea vistas and an immaculate setting. With three levels of glass and wood, the restaurant opens onto a landscaped terrace set on a cliff. Between the views and the food, this is an ideal setting for a romantic dinner— definitely worth the 25km (15-mile) ride to the coast. Try the seafood pasta (particularly the lobster), smoked salmon (marinated in salt water with mango chutney and honey-and-ouzo vinaigrette), mouth-watering grilled octopus (cooked in wine), or choose from a variety of sushi and desserts (the best chocolate soufflé we've had).

28 Apollonos, Voulaigmeni. ☏ **210/896-3747.** www.ithakirestaurantbar.gr. Main courses 50€–70€. AE, MC, V. Daily 1pm–1:30am. Tram to Glyfada, then taxi from the square.

Matsuhisa Athens ★★★ JAPANESE   Set inside the Astir Palace Hotel Complex, with beautiful sea views, the restaurant is stunning—and the food is brilliant. The black codfish with sweet miso is melt-in-your-mouth good. The sushi is exceptional, as is the *Omakase* (chef's choice) menu (90€), a seven-course repast with Nobu Matsuhisa's signature dishes such as mixed sashimi salad with rice-paper-thin sliced vegetables and seared salmon piqued with a red onion, mustard, soy, and sesame oil sauce; Wagyu beef with a spicy Peruvian sauce; salad; and dessert. The Greek-style ceviche, featuring shrimp accompanied by cubes of feta, tomato, and cucumber, is a must. If the prices are out of your range, you can still enjoy cocktails at **Matsuhisa Bar** and nibble on the delicious finger food contents of the popular bento boxes.

40 Apollonos, Vouliagmeni. (at the Westin hotel in the Astir Palace Hotel Complex). ☏ **210/896-0510.** www.matsuhisaathens.com. Reservations required. Main courses 60€–105€. AE, DC, MC, V. Tues–Thurs noon–midnight; Fri–Sat noon–1am; Sun noon–5pm. Tram to Glyfada Sq., then taxi.

PRACTICAL INFORMATION

Dining in Athens will rarely come cheap at the quality restaurants and reservations are highly recommended, particularly on weekends. If you wish to dine with the locals, remember that most Athenians do not dine before 10pm. Your tip should be 10% to 15% of the bill (check to see if service is included). Menus can be found in both Greek and English (if not, the waiter will help you with suggestions.) The current E.U. nonsmoking law that went into effect in 2009 did not have a major effect on the city's countless warm season al fresco dining and drinking establishments.

EXPLORING ATHENS

by Peter Kerasiotis with Sherry Marker

t's likely that you'll arrive in Athens in the afternoon, groggy and disoriented after a long flight. The ride into town from the airport is unlikely to help your spirits. You'll whiz along an efficient but anonymous highway that could be anywhere, before being fed into Athens's ferocious traffic; or you'll be underground in the Metro, itching to get to your hotel. Somewhere, you know, not far away, must be the blue Aegean and the lofty Acropolis. But where?

When you get to your hotel, jump into the shower, take a nap, and then set off for an evening stroll through elegant **Syntagma (Constitution) Square** past the House of Parliament. Take a few minutes to explore Syntagma's handsome marble **Metro** station, with its display of finds from the excavations here. Sit on a bench or at one of the cafes and have a cup of coffee or a snack as you take in the city, its citizens, and your surroundings. (Syntagma Sq. has free Wi-Fi, so you have many reasons to return here and linger during your stay.)

If it's too warm out, escape into the shade of the **National Gardens**— an oasis of calm and cool in the heart of Athens. You'll discover shady benches; a small cafe; the excellent Aigli restaurant in the adjacent, wider, and more formal Zappeion Gardens; and lots of opportunities to watch Greek families out for a stroll. Keep an eye out for the shockingly well-preserved Roman Baths, have a seat and linger by the Zappeion's handsome fountain for a while, and then head into the **Plaka,** the old neighborhood on the slopes of the Acropolis that has more restaurants, cafes, and souvenir shops than private homes. If you get off the Plaka's main drags, Kidathineon and Adrianou, and follow one of the streets such as Thespidos that run up the slope of the Acropolis, you'll find yourself in **Anafiotika.** This district, built in the 19th century by immigrants from the Cycladic island of Anafi, retains much of its old village character. As you stroll, look up: You're bound to see the Acropolis, perhaps floodlit— the best reminder of why you came.

After you have had your first Greek meal, head for the **Archaeological Promenade,** stop by **Thissio** at the cafe/bar/restaurant **Athinaion Politeia** or the beautiful **Chocolat Café** for a glass of wine, and slowly head back to your hotel and get a good night's rest so that you'll be ready for your first real day in Athens.

The Ministry of Culture information site for archaeological sites, monuments, and museums is **www.culture.gr.** Four invaluable websites with a wealth of information and daily updates are **www. visitgreece.gr, www.cityofathens.gr, www.breathtakingathens.com,** and **www.athens24.com.**

THE TOP ATTRACTIONS

The Acropolis ★★★ ◙ The Acropolis is one of a handful of places in the world that is so well known, you may be anxious when you finally get here. Will it be as beautiful as its photographs? Will it be, ever so slightly, a disappointment? Rest assured: The Acropolis does not disappoint—but it *is* infuriatingly crowded. What you want here is time—time to watch the Parthenon's columns appear first beige, then golden, then rose, then stark white in changing light; time to stand on the Belvedere and take in the view over Athens (and listen to the muted conversations floating up from the Plaka); time to think of all those who have been here before you. *Tip:* There is no reason to head to the Acropolis during the day in summer; it's too crowded and hot. The best time to visit during the summer is after 5pm—the brilliant light of the late-afternoon hours will only enhance your experience.

When you climb the Acropolis—the heights above the city—you're on your way to see Greece's most famous temple, the **Parthenon.** People lived here as early as 5,000 B.C. The Acropolis's sheer size made it a superb natural defense, just the place to avoid enemies and to be able to see invaders coming across the sea or the plains of Attica. There was a spring here then, to provide water.

In classical times, when Athens's population had grown to around 250,000, people moved down from the Acropolis, which had become the city's most important religious center. The city's **civic and business center**—the **Agora**—and its **cultural center,** with several theaters and concert halls, bracketed the Acropolis. When you peer over the sides of the Acropolis at the houses in the Plaka, and the remains of the Ancient Agora and the Theater of Dionysos, you'll see the layout of the ancient city. Syntagma square, the heart of today's Athens, was well out of the ancient city center.

Even the Acropolis's superb heights couldn't protect it from the Persian assault of 480 B.C., when invaders burned and destroyed most of its monuments. Look for the immense column drums built into the Acropolis's walls. They are from the destroyed Parthenon. When the Athenian statesman Pericles ordered the Acropolis rebuilt, he had these drums built into the walls so that they would remember that they had rebuilt what they had lost. Pericles's rebuilding program began about 448 B.C.; the new Parthenon was dedicated 10 years later, but work on other monuments continued for a century.

You'll enter the Acropolis through **Beulé Gate,** built by the Romans and named for the French archaeologist who discovered it in 1852. You'll then pass through the **Propylaia,** the monumental 5th-century-B.C. entrance. It's characteristic of the Roman mania for building that they found it necessary to build an entrance to an entrance!

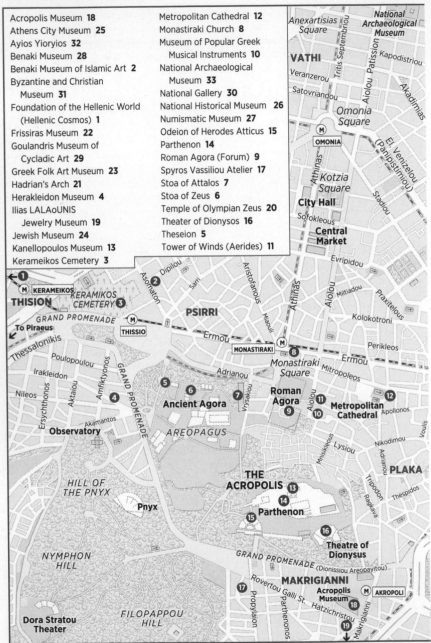

Acropolis Museum **18**
Athens City Museum **25**
Ayios Yioryios **32**
Benaki Museum **28**
Benaki Museum of Islamic Art **2**
Byzantine and Christian
  Museum **31**
Foundation of the Hellenic World
  (Hellenic Cosmos) **1**
Frissiras Museum **22**
Goulandris Museum of
  Cycladic Art **29**
Greek Folk Art Museum **23**
Hadrian's Arch **21**
Herakleidon Museum **4**
Ilias LALAoUNIS
  Jewelry Museum **19**
Jewish Museum **24**
Kanellopoulos Museum **13**
Kerameikos Cemetery **3**

Metropolitan Cathedral **12**
Monastiraki Church **8**
Museum of Popular Greek
  Musical Instruments **10**
National Archaeological
  Museum **33**
National Gallery **30**
National Historical Museum **26**
Numismatic Museum **27**
Odeion of Herodes Atticus **15**
Parthenon **14**
Roman Agora (Forum) **9**
Spyros Vassiliou Atelier **17**
Stoa of Attalos **7**
Stoa of Zeus **6**
Temple of Olympian Zeus **20**
Theater of Dionysos **16**
Theseion **5**
Tower of Winds (Aerides) **11**

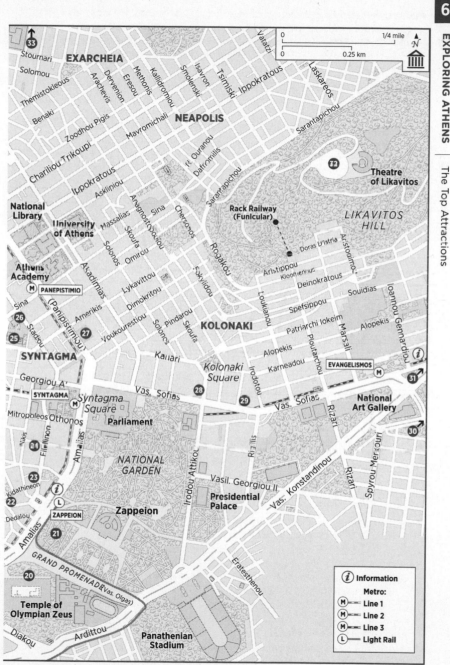

Just above the Propylaia is the elegant little **Temple of Athena Nike (Athena of Victory);** this beautifully proportioned Ionic temple was built in 424 B.C. and heavily restored in the 1930s. To the left of the Parthenon is the **Erechtheion,** which the Athenians honored as the tomb of Erechtheus, a legendary king of Athens. A hole in the ceiling and floor of the northern porch indicates where Poseidon's trident struck to make a spring gush forth during his contest with Athena to have the city named in his or her honor. Athena countered with an olive tree; the olive tree planted beside the Erechtheion reminds visitors of her victory—as, of course, does Athens's name.

Striking Out in Athens

Strikes can close museums and archaeological sites without warning. Decide what you most want to see, and go there as soon as possible after you arrive.

Give yourself time to enjoy the delicate carving on the Erechtheion, and be sure to see the original **Caryatids** in the Acropolis Museum. The Caryatids presently holding up the porch of the Erechtheion are the casts put there when the originals were moved to prevent further erosion by Athens's acid *nefos* (smog).

The **Parthenon** is dedicated to Athena Parthenos (Athena the Virgin, patron goddess of Athens) and is the most important religious shrine here. Visitors are not allowed inside, both to protect the monument and to allow restoration work to proceed safely. If you're disappointed, remember that in antiquity only priests and honored visitors were allowed in to see the monumental—about 11m tall (36 ft.)—statue of Athena designed by the great Phidias, who supervised Pericles' building program. Nothing of the huge gold-and-ivory statue remains, but there's a small Roman copy in the Acropolis Museum—and horrific renditions on souvenirs ranging from T-shirts to ouzo bottles. Admittedly, the gold-and-ivory statue was not understated; the 2nd-century-A.D. traveler Pausanias, one of the first guidebook writers, recorded that the statue stood "upright in an ankle-length tunic with a head of Medusa carved in ivory on her breast. She has a figure of Victory about 2.5m (8 ft.) high, and a spear in her hand and a shield at her feet, with a snake beside the shield, possibly representing Erechtheus."

Look over the edge of the Acropolis toward the **Temple of Hephaistos** (now called the **Theseion**) in the Ancient Agora, and then at the Parthenon, and notice how much lighter and more graceful the Parthenon appears. Scholars tell us that this is because Ictinus, the Parthenon's architect, was something of a magician with optical illusions. The columns and stairs—the very floor—of the Parthenon all appear straight, because all are minutely curved. Each exterior column is slightly thicker in the middle (a device known as *entasis*), which makes the entire column appear straight. That's why the Parthenon, with 17 columns on each side and 8 at each end (creating an exterior colonnade of 46 relatively slender columns), looks so graceful, while the Temple of Hephaistos, with only 6 columns at each end and 13 along each side, seems squat and stolid in comparison.

The other reason the Parthenon looks so airy is that it is, quite literally, open to the elements. In 1687, the Venetians, in an attempt to capture the Acropolis from the Turks, blew the Parthenon's entire roof (and much of its interior) to smithereens. A shell fired from nearby Mouseion Hill struck the Parthenon—where the Turks were storing gunpowder and munitions—and caused appalling damage to the building and its sculptures.

An Englishman, Lord Elgin, carted off most of the remaining sculptures to London—including one Caryatid—in the early 19th century, when Greece was part of the Ottoman Empire, to decorate his mansion. When he fell into bankruptcy, he sold what became known as the **Elgin Marbles** to the British government, which has had them on display in the British Museum since 1816, causing ongoing pain to generations of Greeks, who continue to press for their return. Things heated up again in the summer of 1988, when English historian William St. Clair's book *Lord Elgin and the Marbles* (Oxford University Press) was published. According to St. Clair, the British Museum "overcleaned" the marbles in the 1930s, removing not only the outer patina, but many sculptural details. The museum countered that the damage wasn't that bad—and that the marbles would remain in London. The Acropolis Museum—with stark-white reproductions of the missing Marbles in contrast to the originals, honey colored by the Attica sunlight—is the country's most eloquent and aggressive plea to Britain as of yet.

The Parthenon originally had sculptures on both of its pediments, as well as a frieze running around the entire temple. The frieze was made of alternating **triglyphs** (panels with three incised grooves) and **metopes** (sculptured panels). The east pediment showed scenes from the birth of Athena, while the west pediment showed Athena and Poseidon's contest for possession of Athens. The long frieze showed the battle of the Athenians against the Amazons, scenes from the Trojan War, and struggles of the Olympian gods against giants and centaurs. The message of most of this sculpture was the triumph of knowledge and civilization—that is, Athens—over the forces of darkness and barbarians. An interior frieze showed scenes from the Panathenaic Festival held each August, when citizens paraded through the streets with a new tunic for the statue of Athena. Only a few fragments of these sculptures remain in place.

On a smog-free and sunny day, you can see the gold and cream tones of the Parthenon's Pentelic marble at their most subtle. It may come as something of a shock to realize that in antiquity, the Parthenon—like most other monuments here—was painted in bright colors that have since faded, revealing the natural marble. If the day is a clear one, you'll get a superb view of Athens from the Belvedere at the Acropolis's east end.

Almost all of what you see comes from Athens's heyday in the mid–5th century B.C., when Pericles rebuilt what the Persians destroyed. In the following centuries, every invader who came built monuments, most of which were destroyed by the next wave of invaders. If you had been here a century ago, you would have seen the remains of mosques and churches, plus a Frankish bell tower. The archaeologist

Tourism Information in Athens

The **Greek National Tourism Organization (EOT**, also known as the Hellenic Tourism Organization) is at 18–20 Dionissiou Aeropagitou St. (② 210/870-0000; www.visitgreece.gr), near the Acropolis metro stop and the Acropolis Museum. The office is officially open Monday through Friday, 9am to 7pm and 10am–4pm on weekends. Two Info-Points (② 210/325-3123; www.atedco.gr) are available, apart from the one in the airport, one in the Makrigianni district (at Amalias and Dionissiou Aeropagitou sts.) and the other in the port of Piraeus. All three are open daily from 9am–9pm.

Ask about a discounted ticket if you are a student or a senior. Often these discounts apply only to members of Common Market countries. Also, ask for the handy information brochure available at most sites and museums; ticket sellers do not always hand it over unless reminded.

Heinrich Schliemann, discoverer of Troy and excavator of Mycenae, was so offended by the bell tower that he paid to have it torn down.

If you find the Acropolis too crowded, you can usually get a peaceful view of its monuments from one of three nearby hills (all signposted from the Acropolis): the **Hill of the Pnyx,** where the Athenian Assembly met; **Hill of the Areopagus,** where the Athenian Upper House met; and **Hill of Filopappos** (also known as the Hill of the Muses), named after the 2nd-century-A.D. philhellene Filopappos, whose funeral monument tops the hill. A visit to the sacred rock in itself however won't give you the complete picture of the temple's lavish past. The **Acropolis Museum** displays over 4,000 statues and artifacts that once adorned the temple—most of these treasures are being admired again for the first time in 200 years.

Dionissiou Areopagitou. ☏ **210/321-0219.** Admission 12€ adults; free Sun. Ticket, valid for 1 week, includes admission to the Acropolis, Ancient Agora, Theater of Dionysos, Karameikos Cemetery, Roman Forum, Tower of the Winds, and Temple of Olympian Zeus. Individual tickets may be bought (6€) at the other sites. Daily 8am–7pm. Ticket booth, small post office, and snack bar are located slightly below the Acropolis entrance. Metro: Acropolis. From Dionissiou Areopagitou, follow the marble path up to the Acropolis.

Ancient Agora ★★   The Agora was Athens's commercial and civic center. People used these buildings for a wide range of political, educational, philosophical, theatrical, and athletic purposes—which may be why it now seems such a jumble of ancient buildings, inscriptions, and fragments of sculpture. This is a pleasant place to wander, enjoy the views up toward the Acropolis, and take in the herb garden and flowers planted around the amazingly well-preserved 5th-century-B.C. Temple of Hephaistos and Athena (the Theseion).

Find a shady spot by the temple, sit awhile, and imagine the Agora teeming with merchants, legislators, and philosophers—but very few women. Women did not regularly go into public places. Athens's best-known philosopher, **Socrates,** often strolled here with his disciples, including **Plato,** in the shade of the Stoa of Zeus Eleutherios. In 399 B.C., Socrates, accused of "introducing strange gods and corrupting youth," was sentenced to death. He drank his cup of hemlock in a prison at the southwest corner of the Agora—where excavators centuries later found small clay cups, just the right size for a fatal drink. **St. Paul** also spoke in the Agora; he irritated many Athenians because he rebuked them as superstitious when he saw an inscription here to the "Unknown God."

The one monument you can't miss in the Ancient Agora is the 2nd-century-B.C. **Stoa of Attalos,** built by King Attalos of Pergamon in Asia Minor, and completely reconstructed by American archaeologists in the 1950s. (You may be grateful that they included an excellent modern restroom.) The museum on the stoa's ground floor contains finds from 5,000 years of Athenian history, including sculpture and pottery, a voting machine, and a child's potty seat, all labeled in English. The stoa is open Tuesday through Sunday from 8:30am to 2:45pm.

As you leave the stoa, take a moment to look at the charming little 11th-century Byzantine **Church of the Holy Apostles,** also restored by the Americans. The church is almost always closed, but its delicate proportions are a relief after the somewhat heartless—too new and too well restored—facade of the Stoa of Attalos.

Below the Acropolis at the edge of Monastiraki (entrance is on Adrianou, near Ayiou Philippou Sq., east of Monastiraki Sq., and on Ayiou Apostoli, the road leading down into Plaka from the Acropolis). 𝄐 **210/321-0185.** Admission (includes museum) 4€, or free with purchase of 12€ Acropolis ticket. Summer daily 8am–7pm; winter daily 8:30am–6pm (sometimes as early as 2:30pm). Metro: Monastiraki.

Hadrian's Arch ★ The Roman emperor Hadrian built a number of monuments in Athens, including this enormous triumphal arch with its robust, highly ornamental Corinthian columns. Although Hadrian was a philhellene (lover of things Greek), he didn't hesitate to use his arch to let the Athenians know who was boss: An inscription facing the Acropolis side reads THIS IS ATHENS, THE ANCIENT CITY OF THESEUS. On the other side it states THIS IS THE CITY OF HADRIAN, NOT OF THESEUS. Ironically, much more of ancient Athens is visible today than of Hadrian's Athens, and much of Roman Athens lies unexcavated under modern Athens. Hadrian's Arch is still a symbolic entrance to Athens: A number of times when demonstrations blocked traffic from the airport into central Athens, taxi drivers told us that they could get us as far as Hadrian's Gate, from which we'd have to walk into town.

On Leoforos Amalias, near Temple of Olympian Zeus, easily seen from the street. Free admission. Summer daily 8am–7pm; winter daily 8:30am–6pm (sometimes as early as 2:30pm). Metro: Acropolis.

Kerameikos Cemetery ★ Ancient Athens's most famous cemetery, just outside the city walls, is a lovely spot. Many handsome monuments from the 4th century B.C. and later line the Street of the Tombs, which has relatively few visitors. You can sit quietly and imagine **Pericles** putting the final touches on his **Funeral Oration** for the Athenian soldiers killed during the first year of fighting in the Peloponnesian War. Athens, Pericles said, was the "school of Hellas" and a "pattern to others rather than an imitator of any." Offering comfort to the families of the fallen, he urged the widows to remember that the greatest glory belonged to the woman who was "least talked of among men either for good or for bad"—which must have caused a few snickers, since Pericles's mistress, Aspasia, was the subject of considerable gossip.

Ancient Greek words often hide in familiar English words, and that's true of Kerameikos. The name honors the hero Keramos, who was something of a patron saint of potters, giving his name both to the ceramics made here and to the district itself. The Kerameikos was a major crossroads in antiquity, rather like today's Omonia Square. You can see remains of the massive **Dipylon Gate,** where most roads converged, and the **Sacred Gate,** where marchers in the Panathenaic Festival gathered before head-

---

✍ Acropolis Renovations

At press time, The **Temple of Nike** was scaffold-free and reassembled, having just completed an extensive 9-year renovation; the temple's **frieze,** however, is in the Acropolis Museum. Work continues on the Parthenon and a minor section of the Propylaia. The climb up to the Acropolis is steep; if you don't want to walk, an elevator has been installed and the sacred hill is now wheelchair accessible as well.

One of the great pleasures in Athens is strolling through what's been dubbed the **Archaeological Promenade** ★★★, Europe's longest and arguably prettiest pedestrian promenade. It takes visitors past the most important of the city's ancient monuments. In preparation for the 2004 Olympics, the city laid out walkways from Hadrian's Gate past the Acropolis on Dionissiou Areopagitou to the Ancient Agora, past the Acropolis Museum through Thissio to the temple of Hephaistus, and on to Kerameikos and Gazi to the west, veering north through Monastiraki to the Plaka. Athenians use the walkways for their evening *volta* (stroll); the promenade helped change central Athens from a traffic-ridden horror to a delight.

ing through the Ancient Agora and climbing to the Parthenon. What you can't see are the remains of **Plato's Academy,** which was in this district but has thus far eluded archaeologists. The well-preserved statue of a *kouros,* found in the Kerameikos in 2000, is in the Kerameikos Museum, along with photos showing its discovery.

The **Oberlaender Museum,** with a collection of finds from the Kerameikos, including terra-cotta figurines, vases, and funerary sculptures, is usually open when the site is. Be sure to see the handsome classical statue of a youth known as the *Kerameikos Kouros,* and the lion and sphinx pieces. You may also want to visit Athens's enormous **First Cemetery,** near Athens Stadium; it has acres of monuments, many as elaborate as anything you'll see at the Kerameikos.

148 Ermou. ✆ **210/346-3553.** Admission 2€, or free with purchase of 12€ Acropolis ticket. Summer Tues–Sun 8am–7pm; winter Tues–Sun 8:30am–6pm (sometimes as early as 2:30pm). Metro: Monastiraki or Thisio on line 1. Walk west from Monastiraki Sq. past Thisio Metro station on the Archaeological Promenade; cemetery is on the right.

Roman Agora (Forum) ★   One of the nicest things about the Roman Agora is that if you don't want to inspect it closely, you can take it in from one of the Plaka cafes and restaurants on its periphery. In addition to building a number of monuments on the Acropolis and in the Ancient Agora, Roman leaders, beginning with Julius Caesar, built their own agora, or forum, as an extension of the Greek agora. Archaeologists want to explore the area between the Greek and Roman agoras; Plaka merchants and fans of the district do not want more digging. At present, the Roman Agora is a pleasant mélange of monuments from different eras, including a mosque built here after the Byzantine Empire was conquered by Mehmet II in 1453.

The Roman Agora's most endearing monument is the octagonal **Tower of the Winds (Aerides),** with its relief sculptures of eight gods of the winds, including Boreas blowing on a shell. Like so many monuments in Athens—the Parthenon itself had a church inside it for centuries—the Tower of the Winds has had a varied history. Built by a 1st century-B.C. astronomer as a combination sundial and water-powered clock, it became a home for whirling dervishes in the 18th century. When Lord Byron visited Athens, he lodged near the tower, spending much of his time writing lovesick poetry to the beautiful "Maid of Athens."

You can usually find the remains of the Roman latrine near Tower of the Winds by following the sound of giggles to people taking pictures of each other in the seated position. The less-well-preserved remains of the enormous and once-famous **library of Emperor Hadrian** go largely unnoticed. Draw your own conclusions.

Enter from corner of Pelopida and Eolou. Admission 2€, or free with 12€ Acropolis ticket. Usually summer Tues–Sun 8am–7pm; winter Tues–Sun 8:30am–6pm (sometimes as early as 2:30pm). Metro: Monastiraki.

Temple of Olympian Zeus (Olympieion) ★★

Hadrian built this massive temple—or rather, finished the construction that began in the 6th century B.C. and continued on and off (more off than on) for 700 years. At 108m long and 43m wide (360×143 ft.), the **Olympieion,** also known as the **Kolonnes (Columns),** was one of the largest temples in the ancient world. The 17m-high (56-ft.) Pentelic marble columns that remain standing, as well as the one sprawled on the ground, give a good idea of how impressive this forest of columns must have been—although it may be more appealing as a ruin than it ever was as a contender for the title "mother of all temples." Inside, side by side, were once statues of Zeus and of Hadrian.

At Leoforos Vas. Olgas and Amalias, easily seen from the street. ✆ **210/922-6330.** Admission 2€. Summer Tues–Sun 8am–7pm; winter Tues–Sun 8:30am–6pm (sometimes as early as 2:30pm). Metro: Acropolis.

Theater of Dionysos & Odeion (Odeum) of Herodes Atticus ★★

This theater of Dionysos was built in the 4th century B.C. to replace and enlarge the earlier theater in which the plays of the great Athenian dramatists were first performed. The new theater seated some 17,000 spectators in 64 rows of seats, 20 of which survive. Most spectators sat on limestone seats—and probably envied the 67 grandees who got to sit in the front row on thronelike seats of handsome Pentelic marble. The most elegant throne belonged to the priest of Dionysos (god of wine, revels, and theater); carved satyrs and bunches of grapes appropriately ornament the priest's throne.

Herodes Atticus, a wealthy 2nd-century-A.D. philhellene, built the Odeion—also known as the Odeum or Irodio (Music Hall). It is one of an astonishing number of monuments funded by him. If you think it looks well preserved, you're right: It was reconstructed in the 19th century. Although your 2€ entrance ticket for the Theater of Dionysos allows you entrance to the Odeion, this is misleading. The Odeion is open only for performances. The best ways to see the Odeion are by looking down from the Acropolis or, better yet, by attending one of the performances staged here during the Athens Festival each summer. If you do this, bring a cushion: Marble seats are as hard as you'd expect, and the cushions provided are lousy.

Dionissiou Areopagitou, on the south slope of the Acropolis. ✆ **210/322-4625.** Admission 2€ (for both monuments), or free with purchase of 12€ Acropolis ticket. Theater of Dionysos: summer Tues–Sun 8am–7pm; winter Tues–Sun 8:30am–6pm (sometimes as early as 2:30pm). Odeion: open during performances and sometimes on performance day. Metro: Acropolis.

The Top Museums

The Acropolis Museum ★★★ 📷

Designed by Bernard Tschumi (and Michalis Fotiadis), the 21,000-sq.-m (226,000-sq.-ft.) glass-and-concrete museum is stunning. The treasures it displays (most of them in storage for almost 200 years) are breathtaking. At once awe inspiring and humbling, the museum has over 4,000 treasures on display (10 times more than the previous Acropolis museum), making this *the* must-see museum for anyone visiting Athens for the first time (it doesn't hurt that the museum's **restaurant** is top notch as well).

Ramps take visitors to the ongoing excavations in the museum's lower levels, where you can peer through glass panels at an ancient Athenian neighborhood (where houses, baths, workshops, and roads have been uncovered) and an early Christian settlement.

The artifacts, statues, sculptures, and free-standing objects that used to adorn the sacred rock (plus some little-known treasures from the Temple of Artemis Braurona) are all displayed throughout the first two floors, preparing visitors for the final moment when they ascend to the top floor, the **Parthenon Gallery.** The glassy gallery is different than the other floors. Rotated 23 degrees off its axis to mirror the layout of the Parthenon—visible throughout the gallery—it handsomely displays what remains in Greece of the original Parthenon sculptures and frieze—36 of the 115 original panels, alongside stark white plaster casts of the originals (The "Elgin Marbles") in London. This is where one gets the full picture; the grandeur of the past, the importance of this incredible legacy and the ugly truth that this is a work of art that has been looted. Even though fragments of the Parthenon frieze were returned in early 2009 from Italy, Germany, and the Vatican, they are but fragments of the whole of a spectacular work. The missing marbles break apart a poem carved in stone as a unity that tells a single story. There are also missing body parts, turning the splendid into the grotesque—the goddess Iris has her head in Athens and her body in London; Poseidon's rear is in Athens while his torso is in London, and so on and so forth.

As magnificent as the museum is, in its design and in its treasures, one cannot walk away without an even deeper appreciation of a glorious era in human history. Yet one also leaves with a sense of sadness knowing that this tremendous work of art has been looted, vandalized, and ravaged far too many times. We want to believe it is only a matter of time until the British Museum undoes the most recent wrong.

15 Dionisiou Aeropagitou. (℗ **210/900-0901.** www.theacropolismuseum.gr. Admission 5€. Tues–Sun 8am–8pm; Fri 8am–10pm. Metro: Acropolis.

Benaki Museum ★★
Housed in an elegant neoclassical mansion, the Benaki Museum was founded by art collector Antoni Benaki in 1931. This stunning private collection of about 20,000 small and large works of art includes treasures from the Neolithic era to the 20th century. The folk art collection (including magnificent costumes and icons) is superb, as are the two rooms from 18th-century Northern Greek mansions, ancient Greek bronzes, gold cups, Fayum portraits, and rare early Christian textiles. The museum shop is excellent. The **cafe** on the roof garden offers a spectacular view, as well as a 25€ buffet dinner on Thursdays. This is a pleasant place to spend several hours—as many Athenians do, as often as possible. After you visit the Benaki, take in its new branch, **Benaki Museum of Islamic Art** (p. 169).

1 Koumbari (at Leoforos Vasilissis Sofias, Kolonaki, 5 blocks east of Syntagma Sq.). (℗ **210/367-1000.** www.benaki.gr. Admission 6€; free Thurs. Mon, Wed, and Fri-Sat 9am–5pm; Thurs 9am–midnight; Sun 9am–3pm. Metro: Syntagma or Evangelismos.

Byzantine and Christian Museum ★★
If you love icons (paintings, usually of saints and usually on wood) this is the place to go. This museum is devoted to the art and history of the Byzantine era (roughly 4th–15th c. A.D.). You'll find selections from Greece's most important collection of icons and religious art, along with sculptures, altars, mosaics, religious vestments, Bibles, and a small-scale reconstruction of an early Christian basilica. The museum originally occupied the 19th-century Florentine-style villa overlooking the new galleries now used for special exhibits. Allow at least an hour for your visit; 2 hours are better if a special exhibit is featured, and 3 are even better. The small museum shop sells books, CDs of Byzantine music, and icon reproductions.

22 Vasilissis Sofias Ave. (℗ **210/723-1570.** www.byzantinemuseum.gr. Admission 4€. Tues–Sun 9am–3pm (Wed until 9pm). Metro: Evangelismos.

Greek Folk Art Museum ★★ This endearing museum showcases embroideries and costumes from all over the country. Seek out the small room with zany frescoes of gods and heroes done by the eccentric artist Theofilos Hadjimichael, who painted in the early part of the 20th century. We stop by every time we're in Athens, always finding something new—and always glad we weren't born Greek women 100 years ago, when we would have spent endless hours embroidering, crocheting, and weaving. Much of what is on display was made by young women for their *proikas* (dowries) in the days when a bride was supposed to arrive at the altar with enough embroidered linen, rugs, and blankets to last a lifetime. The museum shop is small but good.

17 Kidathineon, Plaka. © **210/322-9031.** www.culture.gr. Admission 2€. Tues–Sun 9am–2pm. Metro: Acropolis.

Museum of Popular Greek Musical Instruments ★★ Photographs show the musicians, while recordings let you listen to the tambourines, Cretan lyres, lutes, pottery drums, and clarinets on display. Not only that, but this museum is steps from the excellent **Platanos Taverna** (p. 142), so you can alternate the pleasures of food, drink, and music. When we were here, an elderly Greek gentleman listened to some music, transcribed it, stepped out into the courtyard, and played it on his own violin! The shop has a wide selection of CDs and cassettes and the courtyard hosts many musical performances throughout the summer.

1-3 Diogenous (around the corner from Tower of the Winds). © **210/325-0198.** Free admission. Tues and Thurs–Sun 10am–2pm; Wed noon–6pm. Metro: Acropolis or Monastiraki.

National Archaeological Museum ★★★ Considered one of the top 10 museums in the world, its collection of ancient Greek antiquities is unrivaled and stunning even to those who have been here quite a few times. The Akrotiri frescoes are on display again (after being damaged in the 1999 earthquake) as are many "new" items, recently returned to Greece from Los Angeles, Italy, Belgium, Britain, and Germany. In order to appreciate the museum and its treasures, try to be at the door when it opens, so you can see the exhibits and not the backs of other visitors. Early arrival, except in high summer, should give you at least an hour before most tour groups arrive; alternatively, get here an hour before closing or at lunchtime, when the tour groups may not be as dense. If you can come more than once, your experience will be a pleasure rather than a marathon. *Tip:* Be sure to get the brochure on the collection when you buy your ticket; it has a handy, largely accurate description of the exhibits.

The **Mycenaean Collection** includes gold masks, cups, dishes, and jewelry unearthed from the site of Mycenae by Heinrich Schliemann in 1876. Many of these objects are small, delicate, and hard to see when the museum is crowded. Don't miss the stunning **burial mask** that Schliemann misnamed the "Mask of Agamemnon." Archaeologists are sure that the mask is not Agamemnon's, but belonged to an earlier, unknown monarch. Also not to be missed are the **Vaphio cups,** showing mighty bulls, unearthed in a tomb at a seemingly insignificant site in the Peloponnese.

The museum also has a stunning collection of **Cycladic figurines,** named after the island chain. Although these figurines are among the earliest known Greek sculptures (about 2000 B.C.), you'll be struck by how modern the idols' faces look, comparable to those wrought by Modigliani. One figure, a musician with a lyre, seems to be concentrating on his music, oblivious to his onlookers. If you like these, visit the superb collection at the N. P. Goulandris Foundation Museum of Cycladic Art (p. 168).

The **Stathatos Gallery** has stunning jewelry, vases, figurines and objects from the middle Bronze Age to the post-Byzantine era. The **Egyptian Art Collection,** is

The Vases & Frescoes of Santorini

One of the museum's greatest treasures is its vast collection—not surprisingly, the finest in the world—of **Greek vases** and a wonderful group of **frescoes** from the Akrotiri site on the island of Santorini (Thira).

Around 1450 B.C., the volcanic island exploded, destroying not only most of the island but also, some say, the Minoan civilization on nearby Crete. Could Santorini's disappearance have created the myth of Atlantis? Perhaps. Fortunately, these beautiful frescoes survived and were brought to Athens for safekeeping and display.

Just as Athens wants the Elgin Marbles back, the present-day inhabitants of Santorini want their frescoes back, hoping that the crowds who come to see them in Athens will come instead to Santorini. There are as many theories on what these frescoes show as there are tourists in the museum on any given day. Who were the boxing boys? Were there monkeys on Santorini, or does the scene show another land? Are the ships sailing off to war, or returning home? No one knows, but it's impossible to see these lilting frescoes and not envy the people of Akrotiri who looked at such beauty every day.

considered one of the world's finest. Spanning more than 3,000 years from the pre-dynastic period to Roman times, this awe-inspiring collection's centerpiece is the **bronze statue** of princess-priestess **Takushit,** dating from around 670 B.C. She was found in Alexandria in 1880 and wears a crown covered in hieroglyphs.

The museum's staggeringly large sculpture collection invites you to wander, stopping when something catches your fancy. We stop for the **bronzes,** from the tiny jockey to the monumental figure variously identified as Zeus or Poseidon. Much ink has been spilled trying to prove that the god was holding either a thunderbolt (Zeus) or a trident (Poseidon). And who can resist the bronze figures of the handsome young men, perhaps athletes, seemingly about to step forward and sprint through the crowds?

44 Patission. ℂ **210/821-7724.** Fax 210/821-3573. www.namuseum.gr. Admission 6€, or 12€ with admission to the Acropolis. Mon 12:30–5pm; Tues–Fri 8am–5pm; Sat–Sun and holidays 8:30am–3pm. Metro: Panepistimio or Victoria. The museum is .5km (⅓ mile; 10 min. on foot) north of Omonia Sq. on the road named Leoforos 28 Octobriou, but usually called Patission.

N. P. Goulandris Foundation Museum of Cycladic Art ★★   Come here to see the largest collection of Modigliani-like Cycladic art outside the National Archaeological Museum. This handsome museum—the collection of Nicolas and Aikaterini Goulandris—opened its doors in 1986 and displays more than 200 stone and pottery vessels and figurines from the 3rd millennium B.C. This museum is as satisfying as the National Museum is overwhelming. It helps that the Goulandris does not get the same huge crowds, and that the galleries here are small and well lit, with labels throughout in Greek and English. The collection of Greek vases is small and exquisite—the ideal place to find out if you prefer black or red figure vases. The museum's elegant little shop has a wide selection of books on ancient art, as well as reproductions of items from the collection, including a pert Cycladic pig. When you've seen all you want to (and have perhaps refreshed yourself at the basement snack bar or courtyard cafe), walk through the courtyard into the museum's newest acquisition, the elegant 19th-century **Stathatos Mansion.** The mansion, with some of its original furnishings, provides a glimpse of how wealthy Athenians lived 100 years ago.

4 Neophytou Douka. ℂ **210/722-8321.** www.cycladic.gr. Admission 5€. Mon and Wed–Fri 10am–4pm; Sat 10am–3pm. Metro: Evangelismos.

MORE MUSEUMS & GALLERIES

The Athens City Museum ★   Modern Greece's first king, Otto, and his bride, Amalia, lived in this 19th-century Athenian town house while a more spacious royal palace (now the Parliament) was built. Poor Otto (a Bavarian princelet) attempted to ingratiate himself with his subjects by wearing the traditional *foustanella* (short pleated skirt); most thought him dotty. He and Amalia were sent packing in 1862 and Greece imported a new king, George I, from Denmark. The museum's collection of watercolors of 19th-century Athens includes works by English painter—and author of *The Owl and the Pussy-Cat*—Edward Lear. Amalia's piano is still here, along with portraits of the royal couple. A mini–throne room shows where they received visitors, and a model shows in detail the small town of Athens of 1842. Special exhibits, usually small and well done, focus on aspects of 19th- or 20th-century Athens.

7 Paparigopoulou (Klathmonos Sq., off Stadiou). ℂ **210/323-0168.** Fax 210/322 0765. www.athens citymuseum.gr. Admission 3€. Mon and Wed–Fri 9am–4pm; Sat–Sun 10am–3pm. Metro: Panepistimio.

Benaki Museum of Islamic Art ★★   The world-class collection, in a 19th-century neoclassical building complex, displays Islamic art (ceramics, carpets, woodcarvings, and other objects, plus two reconstructed living rooms from the Ottoman times and a 17th-century reception room from a Cairo mansion) that date from the 14th century to the present. Labels are in Greek and English.

22 Agion Asomaton and Dipylou, Psirri. ℂ **210/367-1000.** www.benaki.gr. Admission 5€. Tues and Thurs–Sun 9am–3pm; Wed 9am–9pm. Metro: Thissio.

Foundation of the Hellenic World ★★ ☺   Also known as the Hellenic Cosmos, this high-tech museum should spark kids' interest in history, with its interactive displays and virtual tours of Greece that allow visitors to call up and "see" moments in Greek history from ancient to modern times. Housed in a former factory, it also offers an Internet cafe and museum shop. Call ahead to make sure an English-speaking guide will be on duty. The museum frequently hosts visiting school groups. The ribbed dome—a high-tech reinterpretation of a Bronze Age beehive tomb—has a 3-D and virtual reality exploration of the Ancient Agora (among other things) that at 10€ might seem a little pricey but it is worth it. The **Kivotos** (arc) time machine has floor-to-ceiling 3-D screens taking you to ancient Miletus and Olympia.

254 Pireos, Tavros (near Kallithea Metro station). ℂ **210/483-5300.** www.fhw.gr. Admission 5€–10€ adults, 4€–8€ children. Dome admission 10€. Hours in flux; check before visiting. Metro: Kallithea.

Frissiras Museum ★   With over 3,5000 works on display, this immaculate collection has innovative and excellent special exhibits as well as a permanent private collection of 20th-century and later European art, with labels in English.

3-7 Moni Asteriou. ℂ **210/323-4678.** www.frissirasmuseum.com. Admission 6€. Wed–Fri 11am–7pm; Sat–Sun 11am–5pm. Small cafe. Metro: Akropolis.

Herakleidon Museum ★   Housed in a beautiful neoclassical mansion on the busy cafe strip of Thissio, this excellent private museum holds one of the world's biggest collections of M.C. Escher works, and also hosts various temporary exhibitions. It also has a great courtyard **cafe** and gift shop.

16 Iraklidon. ℂ **210/346-1981.** www.herakleidon-art.gr. Free admission. Daily 1–9pm; closed mid-Aug. Metro: Thissio.

Ilias LALAoUNIS Jewelry Museum ★ 🎒 The 3,000 pieces of jewelry on display are so spectacular that even those with no special interest in baubles will enjoy this glitzy museum, founded by one of Greece's most successful jewelry designers. The first floor contains a boutique and small workshop. The second and third floors display pieces honoring ancient, Byzantine, and Cycladic designs, as well as plants, animals, and insects. The shop carries copies of some of the displays, and jewelers in the museum's workshop take orders in case you want your own gold necklace inspired by insect anatomy.

12 Kalisperi (at Karyatidon). 𝄞 **210/922-1044.** Fax 210/923-7358. www.lalaounis-jewelrymuseum.gr. Admission 4€. Mon and Thurs-Sat 9am-4pm (free Sat 9-11am); Wed 9am-9pm (free 3-9pm); Sun 11am-4pm. Metro: Acropolis. Walk 1 block behind Acropolis Museum.

Jewish Museum ★★ Greece's Jewish community, a strong presence throughout the country and a dominant force in Thessaloniki, was essentially obliterated in the Holocaust. Heart-rending exhibits here include the wedding photograph of Yosef Levy and Dona Habif, who married in April 1944 and a month later were sent to Auschwitz, where they were killed. Articles of daily life and religious ceremony include children's toys and special Passover china. Perhaps the most impressive exhibit is the reconstruction of the Patras synagogue. Most exhibits have English labels. If you contact museum curator Zanet Battinou in advance, she will try to have a staff member take you through the collection. The small shop carries books and reproductions, including lovely note cards reproducing manuscripts and prints.

39 Nikis (on the left side of Nikis as you walk away from Syntagma Sq.). 𝄞 **210/322-5582.** Fax 210/323-1577. www.jewishmuseum.gr. Admission 5€ adult, 3€ children. Sun-Fri 10am-2pm. Metro: Syntagma.

Kanellopoulos Museum ★ This impressive private collection (6,000 antiquities), in a pretty 1884 mansion (renovated and expanded in 2010) with a wonderful position high on the slopes of the Acropolis, is another nice place to visit when you've had your fill of big museums. You'll see such items as superb red and black figure vases, stunning Byzantine and post-Byzantine icons, and even a few Mycenaean pottery baby bottles. The house itself, with some fine painted ceilings and a nice **cafe,** is a delight.

12 Theorias and Panos, Plaka. 𝄞 **210/321-2313.** Admission 3€. Tues-Sun 8:30am-3pm. Metro: Monastiraki.

National Gallery ★★ Greece's premier art gallery exhibits a stunning collection of over 9,500 paintings, sculptures, and engravings as well as miniatures and furniture, showcasing modern Greek art and hosting major international exhibits. Currently its prize exhibits are three El Greco masterpieces. The museum is currently being expanded—the new wing will more than double the size of the existing museum and will also include an amphitheater, educational facilities, a reception area and a gift shop—and is expected to be completed in 2013.

50 Vasileos Konstantinou. 𝄞 **210/723-5857.** www.nationalgallery.gr. Admission 6.50€. Mon and Wed-Sat 9am-3pm; 6-9pm; Sun 10am-2pm. Metro: Evangelismos.

National Historical Museum Housed in Greece's first Parliament building and featuring Greece's history since the fall of Constantinople (present-day Istanbul) in 1453 until the present. Exhibits include weapons, costumes, flags, and paintings, as well as Byzantine and medieval exhibits.

13 Stadiou, Plateia Kolokotroni. 𝄞 **210/323-7617.** www.nhmuseum.gr. Admission 3€, free on Sun. Tues-Sun 9am-2pm. Metro: Syntagma.

Numismatic Museum   Many Greek coins were works of art. You can see examples displayed in the magnificent 19th-century town house of the archaeologist Heinrich Schliemann. Until this museum opened in 1999, visitors could only imagine the decor behind the ornate facade. Lest anyone forget that he had discovered Troy, Schliemann emblazoned the inscription ILIOU MELATHRON (Palace of Troy) across the front of his house. The interior is equally impressive, as are the more than 60,000 ancient bronze, silver, and gold coins (many displayed with helpful magnifying lenses).

12 Panepistimiou. ℭ **210/364-3774.** www.nma.gr. Admission 3€; free Sun. Tues–Sun 8:30am–3pm. Metro: Syntagma.

The Spyros Vassiliou Atelier   In this museum and archive of one of the most important 20th-century Greek artists—painter and set designer Spyros Vassiliou (1902 1985), the artist's influential work is displayed in his former home, a beautiful building right around the block from the Acropolis.

5a Webster. ℭ **210/923-1502.** www.spyrosvassiliou.org. Admission 4€. Tues–Sun 10am–4pm; Wed noon–8pm. Metro: Acropolis.

Galleries

One of the great pleasures of visiting Athens is browsing in its small art galleries as well as its many warehouses converted to art and cultural centers that seem to pop up weekly in this city, and getting a sense of the flourishing contemporary Greek art scene (and possibly buying something to take home). Stop in at an opening, if you see a notice—most are free to the public. For listings, pick up complimentary copies of the quarterlies *Art and the City* and *The Athens Contemporary Art Map* (both in Greek and English), which are available in hotels and galleries and log on to www.breath takingathens.com. Here are some galleries to keep an eye out for.

In Plaka, the **Athens Gallery,** 14 Pandrosou St. (ℭ 210/324-6942; www.athensgallery.gr), features all major Greek artists, crafts, ceramics, jewelry, sculptures, and museum copies displayed over three floors in a 200-year-old neoclassical building. **Harma Gallery,** 10 Thespidos St. (ℭ 210/322-0040; www.athens-gallery.com), features excellent gifts, including replicas of ancient works and contemporary art. **Pandora,** 70 Adrianou St. (ℭ 210/331-4437; www.pandora.gr), has an excellent collection of modern and contemporary art, museum copies, sculptures and ceramics. Frequent shows are held at **Melina Mercouri Foundation,** 9–11 Polygnotou (ℭ 210/331-5601; www.melinamercourifoundation.org.gr).

In trendy Psirri, **About Gallery,** 18 Miaouli (ℭ 210/331-4480; www.about-art.gr), hosts exhibitions by contemporary artists and has a great bookstore. AD **Gallery,** 3 Pallados (ℭ 210/322-8785; www.adgallery.gr), focuses on modern and conceptual Greek art. **a.antonopoulou.art,** 20 Aristofanous (ℭ 210/321-4994; www.aaart.gr), is one of the most stunning art spaces in the city concentrating on Greek contemporary artists. **Els Hanappe Underground,** 2 Melanthiou (ℭ 210/325-0364; http://els.hanappe.com), showcases young international artists.

In Monastiraki, off Ermou Street, tucked inside a seemingly abandoned alley, you will find **TAF-The Art Foundation,** 5 Normanou (ℭ 210/323-8757; www.theartfoundation.gr), a renovated neoclassical building complex that now houses art exhibitions as well as theater and dance performances. The courtyard is occupied by a popular bar where you can have a drink and browse at your leisure.

In Thissio, **Bernier/Eliades Gallery,** 11 Eptachalkou, Thissio (ℭ 210/341-3936; www.bernier-eliades.gr), showcases Greek and international artists and stages group exhibitions, as does **Kappatos,** 12 Athinas (✆ **210/321-7931;** www.kappatos gallery.com). Frequent shows are held at **Melina Mercouri Cultural Center,** 66 Iraklidon and Thessalonikis (✆ **210/345-2150**).

In Gazi, **Gallery Kourd,** 2-4 Kassiani St. (✆ **210/642-6573;** www.gallerykourd. gr), has been in operation since 1922 and its collection is stunning, ranging from paintings and icons to ancient Islamic and Asian art. The latest arrival in Gazi is **The Hub,** 133 Pireos (✆ **210/341-1009;** www.thehubevents.gr), another former warehouse converted into a cultural space hosting exhibitions, galleries, screenings, conferences, performance arts, and fashion shows.

In Metaxourgeio, the neighborhood next in line to receive its own urban makeover, you will find the **Athens Municipal Art Gallery,** 32 Mylierou and Leonidou (✆ **210/324-3023;** Tues–Sat 10am–2pm and 5–9pm; Sun 10am–2pm) with its rich collection from 19th- and 20th-century Greek artists plus rotating exhibitions in a beautiful early-19th-century building designed by architect Hans Christian Hansen. Here you will also find art trailblazer **Rebecca Camhi,** 9 Leonidou (✆ **210/523-3049;** www.rebeccacamhi.com), and **the Breeder,** 45 Iasonos (✆ **210/331-7527;** www.thebreedersystem.com), which showcases some of the more interesting up-and-coming artists in solo shows, group shows, and gallery swaps and houses a popular and tasty restaurant: the Breeder Feeder.

The Athens House of Photography, 104 36 Eleusinon and Kerameon (✆ **210/522-8696;** www.phototheatron.com; Wed–Fri noon–8pm, Sat 10am–8pm, Sun 11am–6pm), is a space that includes photography exhibitions, a library and bookstore as well as seminars and workshops. The first gallery to set up shop in the neighborhood was **Gazon Rouge,** 8 Kikladon (✆ **210/883-7909;** www.gazonrouge. com), which along with being a gallery is also an art publishing house with a bookstore and cafe. It's since moved to Patission Avenue near Kypseli, which is becoming the next "in" neighborhood for artists. The recent arrival of **Salon de Vortex,** 24 Ithakis and Drosopoulou (✆210/825-9994; www.salondevortex.worldpress.com), a new space with exhibitions and artists' studios attests to that, as does the arrival of **The Apartment Gallery,** 29 Ithakis (✆ **210/321-5469;** www.theapartment.gr), from Syntagma Square to a pretty Kypseli neoclassical building.

The **National Museum of Contemporary Art** will one day move into its new Syngrou-Fix location, but until then, it is housed at the **Athens Conservatory,** 17–19 Vas. Georgiou (✆ **210/924-5200;** www.emst.gr; Tues–Sun 11am–7pm). The highway formerly known as the "industrial wasteland highway" Pireos Avenue, is gaining momentum as one of the city's main culture zones. The **Benaki Museum–Pireos Street Annexe,** 138 Pireos and Andronikou (✆ **210/345-3111;** www.benaki. gr), stages excellent exhibitions, as does the huge multipurpose space at **Technopolis,** 100 Pireos (✆ **210/346-0981;** www.technopolis.gr), while the **School of Fine Arts,** 256 Pireos (✆ **210/480-1315;** www.afsa.gr), stages exhibitions by new artists as well as retrospectives by top contemporary Greek artists. **Athinais,** 34–36 Kastorias (✆ **210/348-0000;** www.athinais.com.gr), the former silk factory restored into an arts center, also stages exhibitions and shows. The **Ileana Tounta Contemporary Art Center,** 48 Armatolon-Klefton, Ambelokipi (✆ **210/643-9466;** www.arttounta.gr), stages first-rate exhibitions.

The fashionable Kolonaki district is chockablock with galleries. A must-see is the **Gagosian Gallery,** 3 Merlin (✆ **210/364-0215;** www.gagosian.com), the contemporary art world eminent dealer's first Athens gallery. Nearby **Zoumboulakis Gallery,** 20 Kolonaki Sq. (✆ **210/360-8278;** www.zoumboulakis.gr), has exhibitions as well as a top-rate range of limited edition prints and posters by leading Greek artists.

Astrolavos Art Life, 11 Irodotou (© **210/722-1200;** www.astrolavos.gr), has excellent exhibitions from young and upcoming artists as well as established Greek and Greek-American artists. The **Fizz Gallery,** 9c Valaoritou St. (© **210/360-7598;** www.fizzgallery.gr), concentrates on contemporary Greek and international art: paintings, installations, videos, and photography. The **Kalfayan Galleries,** 11 Haritos St. (© **210/721-7679;** www.kalfayangalleries.com), showcase the work of many local and international artists and hosts events and art festivals in collaboration with museums. The **Medusa Art Gallery,** 7 Xenokratous (© **210/724-4552;** www. medusaartgallery.com), features emerging artists and showcases everything from video to photography, painting, and sculpture. Another gallery open year-round and well worth a visit (in part for its great cafe and shop) is **Deste Foundation for Contemporary Art ★,** 11 Filellinon (© **210/275-8490;** www.deste.gr). Deste, owned by collector Dakis Joannou, showcases cutting-edge works from the international scene. Farther north, in affluent Kifissia, it's worth checking out the excellent **Mihalarias Art Gallery,** Kifisias and Diligiani (© **210/623-0928;** www.mihalarias. gr), housed in a stunningly beautiful heritage-listed mansion. Also in Kifissia, it's a treat to visit the **Modern Sculpture Park,** 73 G. Lira St. ([**210/620-6437;** www. skironio.gr).

Also keep an eye out for what's going on at the **Onassis Cultural Center,** 107-109 Syngrou Ave. (© **210/178-0000;** www.sgt.gr), Athens's newest arrival is this stunning cultural space from the prestigious Onassis Foundation, that hosts events, exhibitions, and performances.

ANCIENT MONUMENTS

One small, graceful monument you might easily miss is the 4th-century-B.C. **Choregic Monument of Lysikrates,** on Lysikratous in the Plaka, located a few steps from the excellent **Daphne's** restaurant (p. 139). This circular monument with Corinthian columns and a domed roof bears an inscription stating that Lysikrates erected it when he won the award in 334 B.C. for the best musical performance with a "chorus of boys." A frieze shows Dionysos busily trying to turn evil pirates into friendly dolphins.

Three hills near the Acropolis deserve a respectful glance: **Areopagus, Pnyx,** and **Filopappos. Areopagus** is the bald marble hill across from the entrance to the Acropolis; it is so slippery, despite its marble steps, that it is never an easy climb, and it is treacherous in the rain. This makes it hard to imagine the Athenians who served on the council and court making their way up here. Still harder to imagine is St. Paul on this slippery perch thundering out criticisms of the Athenians for their superstitions.

From the Areopagus and Acropolis, you can see two nearby wooded hills. The one with the monument visible on its summit is **Filopappos (Hill of the Muses).** The monument is the funeral stele of the Roman consul after whom the hill is named. You can take pleasant walks on the hill's wooded slopes; view a Byzantine church, **Ayios Demetrios;** and see the **Dora Stratou Theater,** where you can watch folk dances being performed (p. 190). If you climb to the summit (at night, don't try this alone or wander here or on Pnyx hill) and face the Acropolis, you can imagine the moment in 1687 when the Venetian commander Morosini shouted "Fire!"—and cannon shells struck the Parthenon.

Pnyx hill, crowned by the Athens Observatory, is where Athens's citizen assembly met. As much as any spot in Athens—which is to say, anyplace in the world—it is the "birthplace of democracy." Here, for the first time, every citizen could vote on every matter of common importance. True, citizens did not include women, and there were far more slaves than citizens in Athens—as was the case in most of the world for a very long time after this democracy was born.

HISTORIC BUILDINGS

Athens was a small village well into the mid–19th century and did not begin to grow until it became capital of independent Greece in 1834. This fact is hard to believe when you look at today's traffic-clogged streets, but the recently restored and expanded **Byzantine and Christian Museum,** at 22 Vas. Sofias, occupies the Renaissance-style villa built by the Duchess of Plaisance as her country retreat in the 1840s. Syntagma Square is home to several other buildings from the same period, including **Parliament House** (the former royal palace); **Grande Bretagne Hotel** (a former mansion); and Schliemann's house, **Iliou Melathron** (see the Numismatic Museum, above). Many neoclassical 19th-century buildings fell in Athens's rapid expansion after World War II, but a large number of them survive all over the city from downtown into Kifissia. Watch for surviving buildings, described below, as you explore central Athens.

In the Plaka, several 19th-century buildings have survived, tucked between the T-shirt shops and restaurants at busy Adrianou (Hadrian) and Kidathineon. One of the oldest surviving prerevolutionary houses in Athens, **96 Adrianou** dates from the Turkish occupation. The nearby 19th-century **Demotic School** has a distinguished neoclassical facade. On Kidathineon is the house in which **King Ludwig** of Bavaria stayed when he visited Athens in 1835; there's no number on the house, but a small plaque identifies it. Several other former houses date from the same period.

Finally, if you climb through the Plaka to the **Anafiotika district** on the slopes of the Acropolis, you'll find yourself in a delightful neighborhood with many small 19th-century homes. This district is often compared to an island village, and small wonder: Most of the homes were built by stonemasons from the Cycladic island of Anafi, who came to Athens to work on the buildings of the new capital of independent Greece.

CHURCHES & SYNAGOGUES

As you stroll through Athens, you'll discover scores of charming churches. Many date from the Byzantine era of A.D. 330 to 1453—although almost nothing survives from the early centuries of that Christian empire. Alas, vandals and thieves have forced many churches to lock their doors, so you may not be able to go inside unless a caretaker is present. If you do go inside, **dress suitably:** Shorts, miniskirts, and sleeveless shirts are not appropriate. You can leave a donation in one of the collection boxes. Below we list a few churches to keep an eye out for.

Athens's 19th-century **Greek Orthodox (Metropolis)** on Mitropoleos gets almost universally bad press: too big, too new, too . . . well, ugly. It also suffers terribly in comparison with the adjacent 12th-century **Little Metropolis,** with the wonderful name *Panayia Gorgoepikoos* **(Virgin Who Answers Prayers Quickly).** Fragments of classical masonry (including inscriptions), built into the walls of this little church, create a delightful crazy-quilt effect.

The square in front of the cathedral is a great place to people-watch on summer weekends, when weddings often take place in the evening. As one bride leaves the church, the next bride (and her flowers, attendants, and guests) is poised to enter. It's

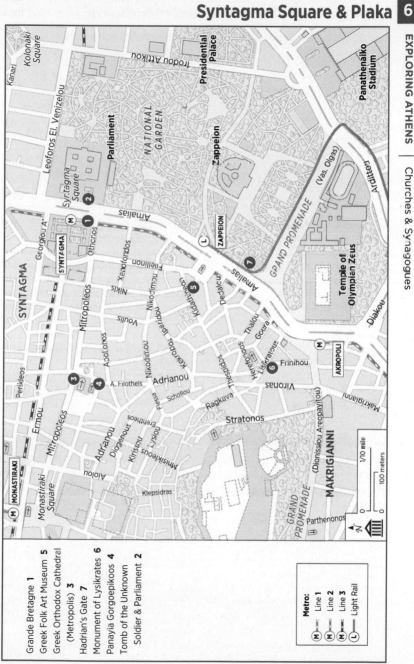

Grande Bretagne **1**
Greek Folk Art Museum **5**
Greek Orthodox Cathedral
(Metropolis) **3**
Hadrian's Gate **7**
Monument of Lysikrates **6**
Panayia Gorgoepikoos **4**
Tomb of the Unknown
Soldier & Parliament **2**

Metro:
Ⓜ Line **1**
Ⓜ Line **2**
Ⓜ Line **3**
Ⓛ Light Rail

0 — 1/10 mile
0 — 100 meters

SURF'S UP: ATHENS'S urban beaches

A string of popular beaches stretches along the Saronic Gulf from Athens to Cape Sounion; nearly all of them have been awarded the E.U. Blue Flag for clear waters. The beaches are easily accessible by bus, tram, and taxi. The tram reaches Voula, from there you can continue to the farther-away beaches via bus or taxi. *Tip:* To shorten your tram ride to the coast by 20 minutes, hop on Metro line 1 and get off at Faliro. Across the street is the tram stop, outside the Peace and Friendship Olympic Stadium Complex. From here you can just hop on the SEF tram line to Voula.

For beaches farther away from Voula, you can take a bus or taxi from Glyfada Square. The beaches are now run by private companies and charge admission, ranging from 6€ to 20€ per person per day. Entrance rates are always higher on weekends and holidays. Athens's privatized beaches resemble stylish clubs. For the admission price, you get a chair, umbrella, changing rooms, showers, and restrooms. Some have water parks, children's play areas, snack bars, lifeguards, beach volleyball, and racquetball areas—a few even have guest rooms in quaint bungalows for those wishing to have a siesta. Some of the best beaches along the coast are:

Agios Kosmas: Second Agios Kosmas tram stop. A little difficult to find, but worth it; it's a free, quiet beach, clean and well managed and perfect if you have little children.

Asteras Glyfada (www.asterascomplex. com): Take the tram to the Glyfada stop at "Palio Dimarheio," "Paralia," or "Plateia Katraki" and walk along the coast. Inside this complex is a clean and family friendly beach (admission weekdays 6€; weekends 7.50€) with clean grounds, a snack bar, cafe, children's playground, and watersport options. The admission to this complex also grants you admission to the **Balux House (www.balux cafe.com).** This glass-fronted beach house for all is a series of living rooms, with many intimate areas, a library, an indoor and outdoor playroom for children, TV sets with Xbox and PlayStation consoles, table games, a pool table, beanbags to curl up on, a restaurant cafe and lounge area, volleyball court, and gardens. After the sun has set, the house morphs into a fun, louder but still casual lounge-bar-club. Also on-site are the modern taverna **Akanthus** and the **B.E.D.** club.

Voula A: (www.thalassea.gr): The tram's last stop (Asklipeio Voulas) is right outside this beach (admission weekdays 6€, weekends 7€). Quiet, pretty, and clean,

a very Greek assembly line, with limousines pulling up, horns blaring, and everyone having a fantastic time.

Also on Mitropoleos, crouched on the sidewalk, is the minuscule chapel of **Ayia Dynamis,** where women who want to become pregnant light candles.

If you like spying (from a respectful distance) on weddings and baptisms, continue on to the 12th-century **Church of Ayia Aikaterini,** in the little square off Frinihou. The church sits well below ground level, an indication of how much Athens has grown over the centuries. You'll notice ancient columns strewn around the courtyard; you may even decide to sit on one to watch the comings and goings.

If you walk from Syntagma to Monastiraki Square, you can take in a few more churches. A few blocks from Syntagma Square, on Skouleniou, the little 11th-century **Church of St. Theodore** is also below street level. On Hrissopileotissis, the small with a water slide, ample space, and a snack bar, this beach is more for families seeking a quiet time, older folk, or anyone looking for a quiet, inexpensive, and clean beach.

Voula B: Here you'll find palm trees, a spacious beach, a cafe, self-service restaurant, sports facilities, and some great bungalows (admission 6€). Tram: Asklipeio Voulas then a 5-minute walk along coast.

Astir Beach (**www.astir-beach.com**): Take the tram to Glyfada, then bus no. 114 or 116. This, the most "in-crowd" beach of all (admission 15€ on weekdays, weekends vary), is nestled in a sheltered bay. The beach is clean and pleasant with many amenities (shops, cafe, restaurant, and sport facilities) and even ruins—a temple to Apollo.

Attica Vouliagmeni Beach: Take the tram to Glyfada, then bus no. 114 or 116. Set on an enormous stretch of sand on a beautiful coastline with playgrounds, tennis courts, basketball courts, all the usual beach amenities and a beautiful coastline, this is the best-value beach for your money (admission 6€).

Lake Vouliagmeni (✆ **210/896-2239**): You can also swim in the springs here, which are open year-round daily 7am–7:30pm (admission 7€, children 4 and

under free). Take the tram to Glyfada, then bus no. 114. The setting is strikingly beautiful (a huge cavelike rock) where the blue-green mineral water remains the same temperature year-round and is said to have many healing properties.

Varkiza Beach (✆ **210/897-2414**): Take the tram to Glyfada, then bus no. 116, 125, or 171. Varkiza Beach (admission 12€) is one of the fanciest beaches with pristine waters and is a lot of fun for both adults and children with beach bars, a water park, volleyball and tennis courts, and private cabanas. Though the beach gets busy during the weekends, it can be delightfully quiet weekdays. On your way back downtown from the beach, linger in **Glyfada** to explore this popular neighborhood. Pedestrian street **Metaxa** runs through central Glyfada alongside the tram line, and combined with its side streets offers shopping options, lively cafes, and fine restaurants. Walking down Metaxa, check out Zisimopoulou Street, with more upscale cafes than you could ever need, but ideal for a stop and take in the scene with a cool drink. Nearby is **George's Steakhouse,** 4-6 Konstantinoupoleos (✆ **210/894-2041;** www.georgessteak house.gr), a popular, affordable taverna serving delicious fare since 1951.

Church of the Virgin is a good place to buy incense from street vendors. Check out the flower market at the **Square of St. Irene,** off Eolou. On Monastiraki Square, **Church of the Pantanassa** is all that remains of a convent on this spot. A short walk away on Ermou, 11th-century **Kapnikarea Church** sits right in the middle of the road.

If you're walking along busy Leoforos Vas. Sofias, you may want to rest a bit in the courtyard of the **Church of Ayios Nikolaos.** A few blocks farther along on Gennadius, the 12th-century **Church of the Taxarchi** is set in a small park.

Beth Shalom, the Athens synagogue on Melidoni, stands in what was, before World War II, a vibrant Jewish neighborhood. Across the street from Beth Shalom's marble facade is the old synagogue it replaced. You can get information on synagogue visits and services from the **Jewish Museum,** 39 Nikis (✆ **210/322-5582**).

PARKS & GARDENS

In addition to the parks and gardens listed here, see "Especially for Kids," below.

The lush **National Gardens,** between Leoforos Amalias and Irodou Attikou, south of Vas. Sofias, was once the royal family's palace garden. Now a public park, the area combines a park; gardens; meandering paths; many quaint bridges over ponds and small lakes favored by ducks, swans, and peacocks; and a small zoo with shade trees and benches. Look for one of the several cafes tucked away in the gardens; you can also picnic here or stop by the elegant **Aigli** cafe/restaurant (p. 196). The large neoclassical exhibition/reception hall in the adjacent more orderly gardens were built by the brothers Zappas and so are known as the **Zappeion.** The National Gardens are open daily from 7am to 10pm. *Note:* At night, it becomes a spot for prostitutes, gay cruising, and pickups, but during daytime it is a wonderful little oasis in the city center.

Mount Likavitos (Lycabettus) dominates the city's northeast. It is a favorite retreat for Athenians, and a great place to get a bird's-eye view of the city as it spreads before you all the way to the Saronic Gulf. Even when the smog is bad, sunsets can be spectacular and the city beckoning from below is at its most seductive. A **Chapel of Ayios Yioryios (St. George)** sits at the top. Catch a summer performance at the Likavitos Theater. You can take the funicular (which leaves every 20 min. in summer) from the top of Ploutarchou (6€ with return), or walk up from Dexameni Square.

Pedion tou Areos (Plain of Mars) is central Athens's largest and most beautiful park, on busy Leoforos Alexandras and has never looked better thanks to a 2010–11 face-lift and redesign. Large trees, benches, gardens, fountains, lawns, and meandering paths offer escape from the bustling city. Near the park and across the busy avenue is the wonderful, little-visited **Lofos tou Strefi (Strefis Hill),** where a labyrinth of green paths lead you to the summit with spectacular vistas of the city and the Acropolis.

In the city center is **Fillopapou Hill** (also known as **Hill of the Muses**), a landscaped park with cypresses, pine trees, indigenous flora, joggers, dog walkers, lovers, and some important archaeological finds. It features the perfect vantage point from which to snap that postcard-perfect picture of the Acropolis. Along the way you will walk by ancient walls, a 16th-century church (Agios Dimitiros-St. Demetrios), and a cave dwelling thought to be Socrates's prison. The **Hill of the Pnyx** (the meeting place of the democratic assembly) also has vistas of the Acropolis and beyond. Farther to the west, there is a third hill, **Hill of the Nymphs,** said to be the location of William Shakespeare's *Midnight Summer's Dream.*

ESPECIALLY FOR KIDS

The **National Gardens** off Syntagma Square have a small **zoo,** several duck ponds, a playground, and lots of room to run around. There's also a **Children's Library** with books in English and some toys and coloring materials. The library is usually open Tuesday through Saturday from 8:30am to 3pm, and is closed in August. The National Gardens are open from sunrise to well after sunset.

Pedion Areos (Plains of Mars) is central Athens's largest and most beautiful park. With lawns, ponds, gardens, and fountains, it's the ideal park for the entire family to either stroll or bicycle through.

Among the many small parks and gardens scattered throughout Athens, the **National Gardens** (above) are the best for children. If you're staying in Kolonaki,

Serene Moments

Even though there are several cafes where you may enjoy a drink and/or a light snack by the surf, few are more scenic than **Moorings** ★, Marina Vouliagmenis (✆ **210/967-0659;** www.moorings.gr). On the Vouliagmeni marina, Moorings has a delicious menu, but it's also the ideal location to enjoy a drink as you take in the surroundings. It's off the beaten track, and only in-the-know locals hang out here. Take a seat on the deck overlooking the marina or the sea and enjoy. (Tram to Glyfada Square/Palio Dimarhio, and from there a 5-min. taxi ride to Vouliagmeni marina).

try **Dexamini Square,** which has a small playground and several cafes. (It's below the St. George Lycabettus hotel off Kleomenous.)

The impressive, privately operated **Attica Zoological Park** ★★ (✆ **210/663-4724;** www.atticapark.com) is home to more than 2,000 birds from some 320 species, a butterfly garden, and a small farm. The zoo is open daily from 10am to 7pm and charges 8€ admission for adults, 4€ for children. It's not far from the airport at Spata; you certainly could pay it a visit if you have some time before a flight.

The ride up **Mount Likavitos** on the cable-car railway (*teleferique*) is often a hit with kids. It operates every 20 minutes in summer (6€ round-trip). A cafe at the top sells ice cream, and kids can let off steam by running around on the paths.

The **Museum of Greek Children's Art** often hosts special activities and workshops (conducted in Greek). If your children might enjoy seeing what Greek kids like to draw, stop by 9 Kodrou, Plaka (✆ **210/331-2621;** www.childrensartmuseum.gr; admission 2€; Tues–Sat 10am–2pm, Sun 11am–2pm; closed Aug). This small museum has changing displays of children's art from throughout Greece. The **Children's Museum,** around the corner at 14 Kidathineon (✆ **210/331-2995;** www.hcm.gr; free admission), also runs workshops (the most popular one being the chocolate-making session) but has no exhibitions. In addition, sometimes **Karaghiozis Puppet Shows** (shadow theater) sets up a few doors away at the **Greek Folk Art Museum,** 17 Kidathineon. You don't have to understand Greek to appreciate the slapstick comedy of Karaghiozis.

In leafy and aristocratic Kifissia you will find two excellent museums that the entire family will enjoy. At the **Goulandris Museum of Natural History** ★, 13 Levidou, Kifissia (✆ **210/801-5870;** www.culture.gr; admission 5€ adults, 3€ children; Mon–Thurs and Sat 9am–2:30pm, Sun 10:30am–2:30pm; Metro line 1: Kifissia), you will find a flawlessly researched exhibit on Greece's wildlife, including mammals, birds, and reptiles. Down the street is the impressive **Gaia Center (Earth Center)** ★, 100 Othonos (✆ **210/801-5870;** admission 5€ adults, 3€ children; Mon–Thurs and Sat 9am–2:30pm, Sun 10:30am–2:30pm). The two museums are affiliated, so if you wish to visit them both on the same day you can purchase a combination ticket (at either museum) for 7€ adults, 4€ children. The Gaia Center features three floors of interactive video, computer, and tactile displays of our planet, our systems, how we have slowly damaged our planet, and how to prevent further damage.

The multimedia center **Hellenic Cosmos** ★★ (p. 169) is an excellent museum that offers interactive exhibits that focus on Greek history and culture through the ages. You can visit ancient Miletus via virtual reality, take a 3-D journey through the Agora in ancient Athens, visit ancient cities and civilizations, browse the Web in the Internet cafe, and in the more traditional way, view a collection of Greek costumes. The center was founded in 1998 by the **Foundation of the Hellenic World,** 254 Pireos, Tavros (© **210/342-2292** or 210/483-5300; www.fhw.gr; admission: 5€–10€ depending on exhibition; Mon–Tues and Thurs 9am–6pm, Wed and Fri 11am–9pm, Sat–Sun 11am–3pm; Metro: Kallithea). The "Dome" is 10€ for adults and 5€ for children, but is worth every penny. The nearest Metro station is a 10-minute walk away, so if you're bringing small children, you might want to take a taxi.

Another museum children and adults will enjoy is the **Hellenic Motor Museum** inside the Athenian Capital mall, 33-35 Ilouianou and 3rd Septembriou (© **210/727-9918;** www.hellenicmotormuseum.gr; admission: 8€ adults, 5€ children; Tues–Fri noon–8pm, Sat 10am–8pm; Sun 10am–6pm; Metro: Victoria). It features the impressive collection of Theodore Caragiannis, with 294 vehicles, including Paul Newman's Mercedes 300 SL Gullwing, Robert Plant's pink Chrysler Imperial and even a vehicle used in the film *The Flintstones.*

Athens has the world's finest, most modern, and well-equipped planetarium. The **New Eugenides Digital Planetarium ★**, 387 Syngrou Ave. (© **210/946-9641;** www.eugenfound.edu.gr. bus: B2, 550, E2, and E22 from Syntagma), is a 280-seat ultramodern auditorium with many shows daily and IMAX movies.

Allou Fun Park, Kifissou and Petrou Ralli, Rendi (© **210/425-6999;** www. alloufunpark.gr; Mon–Fri 5pm–1am; Sat–Sun 10am–2am; tram 21 from Omonoia [Kan Kan stop]), is a large amusement park and a fun way to spend a family evening. You can free-fall from a 40m (131-ft.) shock tower, ride roller coasters, and take in a view of the city from the Panorama Ferris wheel. Next door is another amusement park especially for younger children (up to 13) called **Kidom.**

If you want to spend a day on the beach or by the coast with the kids, many of the city's private beaches have children's play areas, watersports, and gaming (see "Athens's Urban Beaches," p. 176). If you want to linger by the coast with the kids, **Flisvos Marina ★** (© **201/987-1000;** www.flisvosmarina.com; tram: Trocadero) is the perfect option for lunch/dinner/strolling by the sea and where children can check out the *Averoff* battleship—now a museum (**www.bsaverof.com**). There's also an open-air cinema aptly named **Cine Flisvos.** You can also choose to walk along the waterfront—head south to the nearby Alimos seaside resort where you will find one of the biggest playgrounds in the Balkans right by the surf. Check the English-language daily *Athens News* (**www.athensnews.gr**) or the daily *Kathimerini* insert in the *International Herald Tribune* for listings of American **movies.** A couple of hours in an air-conditioned theater is not a bad way to pass a hot afternoon.

The "Scope" section's "Kids' Corner" in the weekly *Hellenic Times* lists activities of interest to children, including hiking excursions and day camps.

ORGANIZED TOURS

Some independent travelers eschew organized tours. Nonetheless, such a tour can be an efficient and easy way to get an overview of an unfamiliar city. We're impressed by the number of people we know who confess that they are glad they took a tour, which helped them get oriented and figure out which sights they wanted to see more thoroughly. Most tour guides must pass stiff tests to get their licenses.

The **CitySightseeing bus** (**www.city-sightseeing.com**; 18€ adults, 8€ children) is an open-top double-decker bus that begins and ends its journey at Syntagma Square. The ride through central Athens lasts 90 minutes, with stops at the Acropolis,

Temple of Zeus, Plaka, the university, Omonia Square, Kerameikos, Monastiraki, Psirri, Thission, the Benaki Museum, the National Gallery, the Central Market, and the Panathenaiko Stadium. Prerecorded commentaries are available in English, Greek, Spanish, French, German, Italian, Russian, and Japanese. Tickets are valid for 24 hours and buses depart every half-hour from 7am to 6pm. Also, **Hop in Sightseeing** (℗ **210/428-5500;** www.hopin.com) allows you to get on and off the bus tour over 2 days and even does hotel pickups.

Fantasy Travel, 19 Filelinon (℗ **210/331-0530;** www.fantasytravel.gr), is one of our favorite travel agencies in the city as they have splendid deals and can come up with excellent suggestions and ideas on the spot. They offer half-day and full-day tours of the city, an Athens Segway tour (which is a great way to get around the city), an "Athens by Night" tour for 62€ including dinner at the Mikrolimano harbor and great packages for the islands. Our other favorites are **CHAT Tours,** 4 Stadiou (℗ **210/323-0827;** www.chatours.gr), and **Key Tours,** 4 Kalliroïs (℗ **210/923-3166;** www.keytours.gr). To take any of these tours, you must book and pay in advance. At that time, you will be told when you will be picked up, or where you should meet the tour. **Athens Walking Tours** (℗ **210/884-7269;** www.athens walkingtours.gr) also has some nice packages, including a "shopping tour" and a very popular "food tour."

Each company also offers excursions from Athens. A visit to the popular **Temple of Poseidon at Sounion** costs about 60€ for a half-day trip, including swimming and a meal. A trip to **Delphi** usually costs about 110€ for a full day, and often includes stops at the Monastery of Osios Loukas and Arachova village. If you want to spend the night in Delphi (included are hotel, site, and museum admissions, as well as dinner, breakfast, and sometimes lunch), the price ranges from 50€ to 160€. Rates for excursions to the **Peloponnese,** taking in Corinth, Mycenae, and Epidaurus, are similar to those for Delphi. If your time in Greece is limited, you may find one of these day trips considerably less stressful than renting a car for the day and driving yourself.

If you want to hire a private guide, speak to the concierge at your hotel or contact the **Panhellenic Guides Federation,** 9a Apollonas (℗ **210/322-9705**). Expect to pay 90€for a 4-hour tour. Through **Athenian Days** (℗ **210/864-0415;** www. atheniandays.co.uk) you will have classicist Andrew Farrington lead you through tailor-made cultural and historical tours of the city for up to six people. **Rania Vassiliadou** (℗ **210/940-3932;** www.raniavassiliadou.virtualave.net) offers tours of Athens's archaeological sites and day trips for up to six people.

For the more adventurous, there are two ways of sightseeing that will offer you a unique perspective on the city—the first one is on the ground and the second above.

Pame Volta **(Let's Go for a Ride),** 20 Hadjichristou, Acropolis (℗ **210/922-1578;** www.pamevolta.gr; Wed–Fri 9am–5pm, Sat–Sun 11am–7pm), offers bicycles for rent and **bicycle tours** around the city. It's a unique and fun way to explore the city.

Much more expensive (with prices ranging from 1,800€–3,380€ for groups of up to five), but also much more spectacular is the **Helicopter Sightseeing Tour** of Athens by **Hop In Zinon Tours,** 29 Zanni St., Piraeus (℗ **210/428-5500;** www. hopin.com). Seeing Athens from above, especially at night when all the monuments are lit, is an unforgettable (if pricey) experience.

SPECTATOR SPORTS

The Greeks are devoted to soccer and basketball, and love to bet (it's legal) on sports. All sports events are listed in the Greek press and sometimes in the English-language

If you have the chance, see a concert or catch a match at the **Athens Olympic Sports Complex (OAKA;** 🖉 **210-683-4777; www.oaka.com.gr;** Metro: line 1 to Irini), do it. Otherwise, call to organize a tour (3€ admission). If you're traveling alone and want to see the complex and the showcase stadiums, e-mail **oakapre1@otenet.gr** with a request to join another tour. The complex is open daily 8am to 8pm, and there is no admission fee for those who wish to visit the grounds (not the inside of the stadiums). At press time, the grounds were being converted into a more "tourist-friendly" attraction, which will supposedly include a train on top of the Santiago Calatrava roof on the main showcase stadium.

daily *Athens News.* The concierge or desk clerk at your hotel should know what's on. The best known **soccer** teams are the fierce rivals **Olympiakos** (Piraeus) and **Panathanaikos** (Athens). Greece's Euro Cup Victory in 2004 brought the entire nation first to its feet and then to a halt for weeklong celebrations.

The Greek national **basketball** team endeared itself to the nation when it won the European Championship by defeating Russia in 1987. Celebrations went on all night. The championships take place in July or August at different venues in Europe. You may also be able to catch a game between Greek teams in Athens.

If you're in Greece when major international soccer or basketball events take place, you probably will be able to see them on Greek television or CNN. If you're in Greece during Wimbledon and not staying in a hotel with CNN or STAR cable service, you may have to settle for the BBC's live radio coverage.

SHOPPING

Your hotel room may have a copy of the monthly magazines *Athens Today* or *Now in Athens,* both of which have a shopping section.

You're in luck shopping in Athens, because much of what tourists want can be found in the central city, bounded by Omonia, Syntagma, and Monastiraki squares. You'll also find most of the shops frequented by Athenians, including a number of large **department stores** and malls.

Monastiraki has a **flea market,** which is especially lively on Sunday. Although there's a vast amount of tacky stuff, you can uncover real finds, including retro clothes and old copper. Many Athenians furnishing homes head here to pick up old treasures.

The **Plaka** has cornered the market on souvenir shops, with T-shirts, reproductions of antiquities (including antique imagery reproduced on obscene playing cards, drink coasters, bottle openers, and more), fishermen's sweaters (increasingly made in the Far East), and jewelry (often not real gold)—enough souvenirs to encircle the globe.

In the Plaka–Monastiraki area, shops worth seeking amid the endlessly repetitive souvenir shops include **Stavros Melissinos,** "the Poet-Sandalmaker of Athens," relocated after 50 years to his new location at 2 Agias Theklas (🖉 **210/321-9247; www.melissinos-poet.com**), where his son Pantelis has taken over; **Iphanta,** a weaving workshop, 6 Selleu (🖉 **210/322-3628**); the **Center of Hellenic Tradition,** 59 Mitropoleos and 36 Pandrossou (🖉 **210/321-3023**), which sells arts and crafts; and the **National Welfare Organization,** 6 Ipatias and Apollonos, Plaka

(© 210/325-0524), where a portion of the proceeds from everything sold (including handsome woven and embroidered carpets) goes to the National Welfare Organization, which encourages traditional crafts. **Amorgos,** 3 Kodrou (© **210/324-3836;** www.amorgosart.gr), has authentic Greek folk art, ceramics, embroideries, woodcarved furniture, and all sorts of collectibles; **Greece Is For Lovers,** 13a Kariatidon (© **210/924-5064;** www.greeceisforlovers.com), as kitsch as it might sound, has some fun stuff and **Koukos,** 21 Navarhou Nikodimou (© **210/322-2740**), has a great collection of antique ceramics, jewelry and all sorts of goodies. For more personalized gifts visit **www.kokicreations.gr**, an extremely successful online store that has taken Greece by storm. Even Oprah is a fan.

Kolonaki, on the slopes of Mount Likavitos, is boutique heaven. However, it's a better place to window-shop than to buy, since much of what you see here is imported and heavily taxed. During the January and August sales, you may discover bargains. If not, it's still fun to work your way up pedestrian Voukourestiou and along Tsakalof, Skoufa and Anagnostopoulou (with some of the most expensive boutiques in Athens) before you collapse at a cafe on one of the pedestrian streets in Kolonaki Square—perhaps fashionable Milioni. Then you can engage in the other serious business of Kolonaki: people-watching. Give yourself about 15 minutes to figure out the season's must-have accessory.

Pedestrianized **Ermou Street** is the prime shopping district in the city, with more stores than you will ever have the time to visit, but if you want to do all your shopping in one take, check our listings under "Department Stores" below.

Shopping A to Z
ANTIQUES

Warning: If you hope to take home an antique—perhaps an icon or a woodcarving—know that not everything sold as "antique" is genuine, and it's illegal to take antiquities more than 100 years old out of Greece without a hard-to-obtain export license.

If you're looking for first editions, prints showing 19th-century Athens, a silver sword, or amber worry beads, try **Antiqua,** 2 Leoforos Amalias, off Syntagma Square (© **210/323-2220;** www.antiqua.gr). This is one of Athens's oldest antiques stores, and perhaps the best. It also features handsome ancient coins and old icons—but take heed of the warning above.

Over in Monastiraki on Pandrossou street, **Martinos,** 50 Pandrossou (© **210/321-2414;** www.martinosart.gr), first opened in 1890 has Venetian and ancient glass, embroidery and kilims, swords, and side tables. Also in Monastiraki, check out **Byzantino,** 120 Adrianou (© **210/324-6605;** www.byzantino.com), for certified replicas of stunning, intricate gold designs of Byzantine and Hellenistic jewelry in addition to original works. In Kolonaki, the eponymous proprietor of **Argyriadis,** 42 Patriarchou Ioakim (© **210/725-1727**), specializes in 18th-century furniture, and a variety of more easily transported bibelots. **Mihalarias Art,** corner Kifisias and Diligianni (© **210/623-0928;** www.mihalarias.gr), in a heritage-listed Kifissia mansion, offers museum-quality furniture, paintings, and just about any bauble you can imagine. Visit the **Benaki Museum Gift Shop,** 1 Koumbari (© **210/367-1000;** www.benaki.gr), for prints, jewelry, ceramics, books, and replicas of Greek artifacts.

BOOKS
Eleftheroudakis ★, with its old quarters still open at 20 Nikis (© **210/322-9388;** www.eleftheroudakis.gr), has new eight-story headquarters at 11 Leoforos

Panepistimiou (☏ **210/325-8440**). It sells Athens's widest selection of English-language books and a good range of CDs, including Greek music. The cafe's staff doesn't mind when readers stop by here to rest, pick up a free newspaper or journal, or use the clean restrooms. The store is amazingly tolerant of tourists who read, but don't buy, the wide selection of books on Greece. Check the bulletin board by the cafe for readings by local authors (sometimes in English) or upcoming concerts.

Compendium, 5 Navarhou Nikodimou (corner Nikis; ☏ **210/322-1248**), on the edge of the Plaka near Syntagma Square, is a small but fine English-language bookstore, selling both new and used books, magazines and maps. Local writers sometimes hold readings here. For the best guidebooks and maps head to **Infognomon,** 14 Fillelinon (☏210/331-6036; www.infognomon.gr). Also check out **Kaufman,** 28 Stadiou (☏ **210/322-2160**) an old-world bookstore that has been in the same location since 1919, has an excellent selection of English, French, German, and Greek literature.

CRAFTS

There are lots of mass-produced "crafts" for sale in Athens, which is why it's good to know which shops offer quality work. The **Center of Hellenic Tradition,** 59 Mitropoleos and 36 Pandrossou in the Plaka (☏ **210/321-3023**), is a wonderful place for quality traditional Greek art, including icons, pottery, woodcarvings, embroideries, and prints. Best of all, you can take a break from shopping and look at the Acropolis while you have coffee and a snack at the **cafe.** While you are on and around Mitropoleos, named after Athens's Metropolitan cathedral, look for the shops where craftspeople still turn out decent reproductions of icons for the faithful.

On the fringes of the Plaka, the **National Welfare Organization (Ethnikos Organismos Pronias),** 6 Ypatias and Apollonos, just east of the cathedral (☏ 210/325-0524), has gorgeous embroideries, rugs, pottery, and icons. The **Greek Women's Institution,** 3 Kolokotroni (☏ **210/325-0524**), specializes in embroidery from the islands and copies of embroideries from the Benaki Museum.

DEPARTMENT STORES

The **Attica** department store in the CityLink building, 9 Panepistimiou (☏ **210/180-2500;** www.atticadps.gr; Metro: Syntagma), has the best window displays in the city and over 300 stores in its eight floors, with 800 different brands of clothing, accessories, cosmetics, and housewares. **Notos Galleries,** 2–8 Eolou (☏ **210/324-5811;** www.notosgalleries.gr; Metro: Omonia/Monastiraki), has seven floors of clothing, cosmetics, sportswear, and more. **Hondos Center,** 4 Platieia Omonias (☏ **210/323-3304;** www.hondoscenter.gr), in the middle of Omonia Square—and many other locations throughout the city—is reasonably priced and has just about everything you could want, plus a rooftop **cafe** with Acropolis views. For smaller shops, wander along **Ermou,** off Syntagma, where you'll find enough shoe shops to outfit the world. When you tire of shoes, explore the side streets, such as Mitropoleos, Voulis, and Praxitelous, where you can buy everything from chocolates and curtains, to doorknobs and wastebaskets, to buttons and baptism dresses.

Outside the center, coastal Glyfada and leafy Kifissia also offer excellent (but more high-end) shopping. **Athens Heart,** 180 Pireos (☏ **210/341-4105;** www.athensheart.gr; Metro: Petralona), **Athens Metro Mall,** 276 Leof. Vouliagmenis (☏ **210/976-9444;** www.athensmetromall.gr; Metro: Agios Dimitios), and **Athenian Capitol,**

Serious shoppers should look for the "Best of Athens" Issue of the English-language magazine *Odyssey.* Published in July or August and available at bookstores and kiosks, the issue is filled with shopping tips—and scoops on what's "in" in Athens.

3 Septembriou and Ilouanou (© **210/881-6187;** Metro: Victoria), are the latest malls to spring up in the city.

If you want to shop in a megamall with 15 movie theaters, 25 restaurants, and 300 shops, hop on Metro line 1 and get off at Nerantziotissa station, at **Athens Mall** (called the Mall Athens in Greece; Mon–Sat 9am–9pm, Sun 9am–8pm; www.themallathens.gr). When you're done shopping, go the top floor balcony and have a drink while you take in the view of northern Athens and the Athens Olympic Sports Complex.

FASHION

If you do any window-shopping, you'll see how expensive most things are, except during the January and August sales. Not surprisingly, Athens's most posh downtown clothing stores are in **Kolonaki.** Much of what you'll see is American or European and often carries a hefty import duty; the other selections are mostly Greek designer wear. Good streets to browse are **Voukourestiou** (where Baccarat, Prada, Louis Vuitton, Hermès, and Dolce & Gabana have boutiques), as well as Kanari, Milioni, Tsakalof, Patriarchou Ioakim, Skoufa, and Anagnostopoulou—where Versace, Ferre, Gucci, Lagerfeld, and Guy Laroche have boutiques, as do well-known Athenian designers such as Aslanis, Nikos, Filemon, and Sofos. If shoes are your thing, head for **Tsakalof,** with its heavy concentration of the shoe stores that most Athenians find irresistible.

A few individual shops near Kolonaki Square to check out: **LAK,** 25 Tsakalof (© **210/628-3260;** www.lak.gr), has hip Greek designer Lakis Gavalas men's and women's collection. Head to the **Bettina Boutique,** 40 Pindarou and 29 Anagnostopoulou (© **210/339-2094;** www.bettina.com.gr), for Greek designer Sophia Kokosalaki, whose sexy and edgy work has made her the toast of Paris. **Sofos,** 5 Anagnostopoulou (© **210/361-8713**), sells designer women's clothing. **Elina Lembessi,** 13 Irakleitou (© **210/363-1731**), has elegantly casual tops, bottoms, and accessories. Greek designer **Yiorgos Eleftheriades,** 13 Agion Anargiron (© **210/331-2622;** www.yiorgoseleftheriades.gr), well known in Greece and abroad for his casual yet elegant designs for both men and women, has moved his studio/store from Kolonaki to Psirri. It is well worth a visit. Back in Kolonaki, check out **Christos Veloudakis,** 22a Tsakalof (© **210/364-1764**), where long, red velvet curtains lead you into an impeccably stylish boutique for men and women right on Tsakalof street. Also keep an eye out for **Luisa,** 17 Skoufa (© **210/363-5600;** www.luisaworld.com) featuring the best international designers.

In pharmacies, look for the **Korres** line of natural beauty products, now being sold in smart shops abroad. The soaps and lotions make lovely gifts. If you want to visit Korres's flagship store, go to the corner of 8 Ivikou, near the Panathenaic Stadium (old Olympic Stadium; © **210/756-0600;** www.korres.com).

The **MacArthurGlen Athens Designer Outlet mall** (Block E71, Gialou, 19004, Spata; ☏ **210/663-0840;** www.mcarthurglenathens.gr) is a delight to stroll through and do some serious shopping amid the 125 designer and high-end brands at discounted prices. As part of their "shopping tour" package **Athens Walking Tours** (www.athenswalkingtours/Shopping-Tour) has a bus from Syntagma Square to the mall (which is a 15-min. drive away from the airport) and back, three times a day. If you would like to go solo, free shuttle buses run every half-hour (Mon–Fri 10am– 9pm; Sat 10am–-8pm) from Doukissis Plakentias Metro stop.

JEWELRY

All that glitters most definitely is not gold in Athens's myriad of jewelry shops. Unless you know your gold very well, you'll want to exercise caution when shopping here, especially in the Plaka and Monastiraki stores that cater to tourists.

Greece's best-known jewelry stores are **Zolotas,** with branches at 10 Panepistimiou (☏ **210/361-3782**) and at 9 Stadiou (☏ **210/331-3320;** www.zolotas.gr), and **LALAoUNIS,** 6 Panepistimiou (☏ **210/362-1371;** www.lalaounis.com). Both firms have gorgeous reproductions of ancient and Byzantine jewelry, as well as their own designs. You can see more of the LALAoUNIS designs at the LALAoUNIS museum (see "More Museums & Galleries," p. 169). Also, **Kanakis** at 17 Makrigianni (☏ **210/922-8297**) features a stunning range of ancient Greek motifs in original and contemporary gold designs.

For serious window-shopping for gold and silver, crisscross pedestrian **Voukourestiou,** which is dripping with jewelry shops. Then head to **Kolonaki Square** along Patriarchou Ioakim, where still more ornate and serious baubles are on display. Don't miss **J. Vourakis** at 8 Voukourestiou (☏ **210/322-1600;** www.vourakis.gr) and **Fanourakis** at 3 Patriiarchou Ioakeim (☏ **210/234-6624;** www.fanourakis.gr).

One of the best shops for silver is **Nisiotis,** 23 Lekka, just off Syntagma Square (☏ **210/324-4183**). Off Syntagma, but toward Plaka, **Pantelis Mountis,** 27 Apollonos (☏ **210/324-4574**), sells reproductions of Byzantine icons and religious medals.

We've been pleased with the quality and prices at Emanuel Masmanidis's small **Gold Rose Jewelry** shop, 85 Pandrossou (☏ **210/321-5662**). Others report satisfaction in dealings with **Stathis,** 2 Venizelou, Mitropoleos Square (☏ **210/322-4691**). For more moderate budgets, you might want to check out **Archipelagos** at 142 Adrianou in Plaka (☏ **210/323-1321**) for unique pieces in silver and gold; **Apriati** near Syntagma Square at 9 Pendelis (☏ **210/322-9020;** www.apriati.com) has great designs from local artists and a second store in Kolonaki at 29 Pindarou; **Folli Follie** at 37 Ermou (☏ **210/323-0601;** www.folli-follie.com) is an internationally successful Greek chain that has a wide range of goodies. Visit **Tonia Poulakis'** unique studio/store in Kolonaki at 1 Roma and Pindarou (☏ **210/364-8140;** www.toniapoulaki.com) for some excellent and unique pieces. Also in Kolonaki, **Petai Petai,** 30 Skoufa (☏ **210/362-4315**), has loads of beautiful designs from local designers. Acclaimed jewelry designer **Paul Sarz,** 4 Mavrokordatou (☏ **210/381-4144;** www.paulsarz.com), has beautiful vintage-inspired pieces. And be sure to check **Elena Votsi** at 7 Xanthou in Kolonaki (☏ **210/360-0936;** www. elenavotsi.com). Elena is the designer of the 2004 Olympic Games medals and is renowned worldwide for her striking designs using semiprecious stones.

MARKETS & GROCERIES

The **Central Market** ★ on Athinas is open Monday through Saturday from about 8am to 6pm. You may not want to take advantage of all of the bargain prices (two sheep's heads for the price of one is our all-time favorite), but this is a great place to buy Greek spices, herbs, cheeses, and sweets—and to see how Athens is fed. Every Friday from about 8am until 2pm, **Xenokratous** in Kolonaki turns into a street market selling flowers, fruits, and vegetables. This is a very different scene from the rowdy turmoil of the Central Market, although it's lively enough. Kolonaki matrons come here with their Filipino servants, who lug their purchases home while the ladies head off for shopping and light lunches (perhaps at fashionable **To Kafenio,** © 210/722-9056). Every neighborhood has a weekly market; if you want to take in a number of them, ask at your hotel. **Green Farm** (© 210/361-4001), also in Kolonaki, sells only organic produce.

In Plaka, **Mesogeia,** 52 Nikkis (© 210/322-9146), with organic produce, is one of a number of small "boutique" groceries springing up in Athens.

MUSIC

You won't have trouble finding **Metropolis,** 54 Panepistimiou and Tsakalof (© 210/361-1463; www.metropolis.gr), Athens's largest music store, as long as you follow the booming vibrations. They have six other locations including in the airport. The excellent bookstore **Eleftheroudakis** (see "Books," above) has a wide selection of CDs.

SHOES

If you walk along **Tsakalof** or **Patriarchou Ioakim** in Kolonaki, or along almost any street in central Athens, you'll get an idea of how serious Greeks are about their footwear. Sometimes the biggest crowds in town on a Saturday night are the window shoppers eyeing the shoes on **Ermou** off Syntagma Square. One good-quality store is **Kalogirou,** 4 Patriarchou Ioakim, Kolonaki (© 210/722-8804; www.lemonis.gr), housed in an elegant 19th-century mansion with four floors of shoes for women for all occasions (plus bags and accessories on the first floor) and a separate entrance for the men's store. Other good choices include **Mouriadis,** 4 Stadiou (© 210/322-1229); **Moschoutis,** 12 Voulis at Ermou (© 210/324-6504), **Spiliopoulos** at 63 Ermou (© 210/322-7590), **Prasini,** 7-9 Tsakalof (© 210/364-1590), and **Vassilis Zoulias Old Athens,** 30 Akadimias (© 210/722-5613), a haven for all serious shoe lovers.

SPIRITS/WINE

Cellier, 1 Kriezotou (© 210/361-0040), near Syntagma, has an excellent collection of some of Greece's best wines and liqueurs, with an enthusiastic, knowledgeable staff. The same can be said for **Fine Wine** in Plaka at 3 Lysikratous (© 210/323-0350).

SWEETS/ICE CREAM

You'll have no problem satisfying your sweet tooth in Athens. If anything, you'll come up gasping for air as you eat the seriously sweet sweets adored by most Greeks.

The long-established **Aristokratikon,** 9 Karayiorgi Servias, just off Syntagma Square (© 210/322-0546; www.aristokratikon.com), makes excellent chocolates, glazed pistachio nuts, and *loukoumia* (Turkish delight). Beware—even chocoholics may find the truffles coated with white chocolate too sweet. That said, **Chocolate 56,** 56 Ermou © 210/322-9919), serves some of the finest chocolate drinks in the city. **Karavan,** the hole-in-the-wall at 11 Voukourestiou (no phone), has the best Levantine delights in town. Serving excellent coffee and sweets, **K. Kotsolis Pastry Shop,** 112 Adrianou, is an oasis of old-fashioned charm in the midst of the Plaka.

Sermpetia of Psiri, 3 Aishilou (℗ **210/324-5862**), has some of the best desserts in the city, period.

Loukoumades are the Greek doughnuts with a difference—each is about the size of an American doughnut hole, drenched in honey, covered with cinnamon, and served hot. *Delicious!* If you're near Syntagma Square, try **Doris,** 30 Praxitelous (℗ **210/323-2671**). If you're nearer Omonia Square, try **Aigaion,** 46 Panepistimiou (℗ **210/381-4621**). Better yet, try both.

Looking for the best **gelato** in town? Venture into Psirri at **Gelatomania,** 21 Taki and Aisopou (℗ **210/323-0001**), for authentic homemade Italian ice cream and Makrigianni at **Gelatopoli** (Gelato City), 10 Makrigianni (℗ **210/321-7879**). For excellent frozen yogurt, try next door's **Fresko Yogurt Bar,** 3 Makrigianni (℗ **210/ 923-3760;** www.freskoyogurtbar.gr).

ATHENS AFTER DARK

Greeks enjoy their nightlife so much that they take an afternoon nap to rest up for it. The evening often begins with a leisurely *volta* (stroll); you'll see this in most neighborhoods, including the main drags through the Plaka and Kolonaki Square. Most Greeks don't think of dinner until at least 9pm in winter, 10pm in summer. Around midnight, the party may move on to a club for music and dancing.

Check the *Athens News* (published Fri) or the daily *Kathimerini* insert in the *International Herald Tribune* for listings of current cultural and entertainment events, including films, lectures, theater, music, and dance. The weekly *Hellenic Times* and monthly *Now in Athens* list nightspots, restaurants, movies, theater, and much more.

Festivals

New festivals spring up every year in Athens. You may want to check with the Greek National Tourism Organization to see what's new during your visit.

HELLENIC FESTIVAL   Early June through September, the Athens Festival (also known as the **Athens or Greek Festival**) features famous Greek and foreign artists from Elton John to Placido Domingo performing on the slopes of the Acropolis. You may catch an opera, concert, drama, or ballet here—and see the Acropolis illuminated over your shoulder at the same time. To enjoy the performance to the fullest, bring a cushion to sit on. Schedules are usually available at the **Hellenic Festival Office,** 39 Panepistimiou (in the arcade; ℗ **210/928-2900;** www.greekfestival.gr; Metro: Panepistimio). The office is usually open Monday through Saturday from 8:30am to 2pm and 5 to 7pm, Sunday from 10am to 1pm. You will have better luck if you come in person rather than try to reach the office by phone. If available—and that's a big *if*—tickets can be purchased at the **Odeion of Herodes Atticus** (℗ **210/323-2771** or 210/323-5582) several hours before the performance. Again, you will have better luck going to the ticket office than phoning, although if your hotel has a concierge, he or she may be able to obtain tickets (15€–50€) over the phone. Shows begin at 9pm.

ATHENS INTERNATIONAL DANCE FESTIVAL   Founded in 2003, this festival takes place during the first 2 weeks of July at the Technopolis arts complex, 100 Piraeus, Gazi. This is not the place to go for a traditional rendition of *Swan Lake;* groups performing here push the limits of contemporary dance. Schedule and ticket information is at ℗ **210/346-1589** or 210/346-7322 (www.greekfestival.gr).

THE festivals: ATHENS (HELLENIC), LYCABETTUS & EPIDAURUS

Tickets for the Athens, Lycabettus, and Epidaurus festivals are available at the **Hellenic Festival Box Office,** 39 Panepistimiou (in the arcade; ✆ **210/928-2900).** Hours are Monday through Friday 8:30am to 4pm, Saturday 9am to 2:30pm. (The name "Hellenic Festival" is an umbrella term for a number of summer festivals, including the Athens and Epidaurus festivals.) Advance booking for most events starts 3 weeks before each performance, 10 days before each event for the Lycabettus Festival. Ticket reservation and telephone booking (as above) are also possible by credit card, with the exact date and performance, number and category of tickets, and number and expiration date of the credit card. Tickets (if available) also go on sale at the **box offices** at each theater 2 hours before each performance. Events at the Odeion of Herodes Atticus on the slopes of the Acropolis are usually sold out by the day of the performance; for information, call ✆ **210/ 323-2771.**

Additional information is available at www.greekfestival.gr, www.athens24. com, and www.breathtakingathens.gr.

ATHENS INTERNATIONAL FILM FESTIVAL Over 100 features and shorts represent more than two dozen countries for 10 days in mid- to late September in various venues across the city (✆ **210/606-1963;** www.aiff.gr).

EPIDAURUS FESTIVAL 📷 From late June to late August, performances of ancient Greek tragedies and comedies (usually given in modern Greek translations) take place at Epidaurus, in Greece's most beautiful ancient theater. This makes for a long evening, but a memorable one. If you purchase bus service along with your ticket (about 2 hr. each way), the evening doesn't have to be exhausting. You may want to inquire as to whether the bus/boat excursion from Piraeus to Epidaurus offered in 2002 has been reinstituted; contact the **Greek National Tourism Organization,** the **Hellenic Festival Office** (see above), or the **Rex Theater** box office (✆ **210/330-1881**) on Panepistimiou just outside Spiromilios Arcade.

EUROPEAN JAZZ FESTIVAL Founded in 1999, this festival, usually held at the end of May, brings together Europe's best jazz musicians in the **Technopolis** center, 100 Pireos, Gazi (✆ **210/346-0981;** www.culture.gr.).

LYCABETTUS (LIKAVITOS) FESTIVAL The Pet Shop Boys, Buena Vista Social Club, and other pop musicians make appearances here at the outdoor amphitheater near the top of Likavitos during the summer. For information on music and special events, check with the **Hellenic Festival Office** (see above) or **Likavitos Theater** (✆ **210/722-7209**). Tickets may also be available at **Ticket House,** 42 Panepistimiou (✆ **210/618-9300** or 210/360-8366; www.tickethouse.gr).

ROCKWAVE FESTIVAL Popular groups and performers (Led Zeppelin, Metallica, Pearl Jam, the Killers, Moby, and others) from around the world perform each year at various venues in and around the city. For more information on what's taking place during your visit, check with the Greek National Tourism Organization, Ticket House (see above), or visit their website at **www.rockwavefestival.gr.**

The Performing Arts

The acoustically marvelous **Megaron Mousikis Concert Hall,** 89 Leoforos Vas. Sofias (© **210/729-0391** or 210/728-2333; www.megaron.gr; Metro: Megaro Mousikis), hosts a wide range of classical music programs that include operas symphonies, and recitals. On performance nights, the box office is open Monday through Friday from 10am to 6pm, Saturday from 10am to 2pm, and Sunday from 6 to 10:30pm. Tickets are also sold Monday through Friday from 10am to 5pm in the Megaron's convenient downtown kiosk in the Spiromillios Arcade, 4 Stadiou. Ticket prices run from 5€ to as much as 100€, depending on the performance. The Megaron has a limited summer season but is in full swing the rest of the year.

The **Greek National Opera** performs at **Olympia Theater,** 59 Akadimias St. (© **210/361-2461;** www.nationalopera.gr; Metro: Panepistimio). The indoor opera season runs from November to May. During the summer months the company plays at the **Odeon of Herodes Atticus** and occasionally tours the country and/or abroad.

Pallas Theater, 5 Voukourestiou (© **210/321-3100;** www.ticketshop.gr; Metro: Syntagma), hosts jazz and rock concerts, as well as some classical performances in a stunning space, restored to its former glory in the CityLink building. Prices vary from performance to performance, but you can get a cheap ticket from about 10€.

The **Hellenic American Union,** 22 Massalias between Kolonaki and Omonia squares (© **210/362-9886;** www.hau.gr; Metro: Panepistimio), often hosts performances of English-language theater and American-style music (tickets 10€ and up). If you arrive early, check out the art shows or photo exhibitions in the adjacent gallery.

The **Athens Center,** 48 Archimidous (© **210/701-8603;** www.athenscentre.gr), often stages free performances of ancient Greek and contemporary international plays in June and July. It is behind the Panethinaiko Stadium (old Olympic Stadium).

At the **National Theater,** 22–24 Agiou Konstantinou (© **210/522-3242;** www.n-t.gr; Metro: Omonia), you will find a variety of shows from classical theater to musicals in a beautiful neoclassical building. Tickets range from 15€ to 20€.

Since 1953, **Dora Stratou Folk Dance Theater** ★ has been giving performances of traditional Greek folk dances on Filopappos Hill. At present, performances take place May through September, Tuesday through Sunday at 9:30pm, with additional performances at 8:15pm on Wednesday and Sunday. You can buy tickets at the **box office,** 8 Scholio, Plaka, from 8am to 2pm (© **210/921-4650** after 5:30pm; www.grdance.org; Metro: Acropolis). Tickets are 15€. Tickets are also available at the theater before the performances. The program changes every 2 or 3 weeks.

The **Onassis Cultural Center,** 107–109 Syngrou Ave. (© **210/178-0000;** www.sgt.gr), hosts events, theater, visual art, and music performances.

The Club, Music & Bar Scene

Given the vicissitudes of Athens nightlife, your best bet is to have a local friend; failing that, you have this guide and you can always ask someone at your hotel for a recommendation. The listings in the weekly *Athinorama* (Greek) or in publications such as the English-language *Athens News,* the *Kathimerini* insert in the *Herald Tribune,* and hotel handouts such as *Best of Athens* and *Welcome to Athens,* can be very helpful. If you ask a taxi driver, he's likely to take you to either his cousin's joint or the place that gives him drinks for bringing you.

If you head to a large club, you're likely to face a cover charge of at least 10€ to 20€, which will likely include a drink. Thereafter, each drink will probably cost over

10€. It's best to go only to clubs with or recommended by someone *trustworthy* who knows the scene or that have come recommended from reliable sources (such as this guide). In large clubs, don't sit at a table unless you want to purchase a bottle of alcohol (100€), whether you want it or not. If you hear music you simply must have, **Metropolis** (p. 187) in Omonia Square has a wide choice of CDs of Greek music.

TRADITIONAL MUSIC

Walk the streets of the Plaka on any night and you'll find plenty of tavernas offering pseudo-traditional live music. As noted, many are serious clip joints, where if you sit down and ask for a glass of water, you'll be charged 100€ for a bottle of scotch. At most of these places, there's a cover of 10€. We've had good reports on **Taverna Mostrou,** 22 Mnissikleos (✆ **210/324-2441**), which is large, old, and best known for traditional Greek music and dancing. Shows begin around 11pm and can last until 2am. The cover of 30€ includes a fixed-menu supper. A la carte fare is available but expensive (as are drinks). Nearby, **Palia Taverna Kritikou,** 24 Mnissikleos (✆ **210/322-2809**), is another lively open-air taverna with music and dancing.

Tavernas offering low-key music include **Daphne's,** 4 Lysikratous (✆ **210/322-7971**); **Nefeli,** 24 Panos (✆ **210/321-2475**); **Dioyenis,** 4 Sellei (✆ **210/324-7933**); **Stamatopoulou,** 26 Lissiou (✆ **210/322-8722**); and favorites **Klimataria,** 5 Klepsidras (✆ **210/324-1809**), and **Xinos,** 4 Agelou Geronta ((✆ **210/322-1065**).

BARS/CLUBS

Greek nightlife has a reputation for just getting started when the rest of Europe has already gone to bed. It's true. The nightlife in Athens is sophisticated and varied. From large clubs by the beach to trendy lounges in **Kolonaki, Neo Psihiko,** and **Panormou** street, to indie and intimate bars in **Karitsi Square** and **Psirri** to clubs and red-hot bars in **Gazi,** this is a city that never sleeps. Apart from a few waterfront choices, visitors will find most places located in the center. For those wishing to visit the beach clubs, keep in mind the tram runs on a 24-hour schedule during the weekends, making getting to and from the coast easy and inexpensive. Some of the best lounges/bars in the city these days are in hotels. Don't forget to have a drink at the top-floor **Galaxy** bar at the **Hilton** hotel for an amazing city view. For the best Acropolis view head to the **Hera Hotel's Peacock Lounge;** for the most happening scene visit the **Frame Bar-Lounge** at **St. George Lycabettus Hotel** and **Ochre & Brown** lounge.

Plaka/Makrigianni

(For Plaka Metro: Syntagma/Acropolis. For Makrigiannni Metro: Acropolis)

Athens Sports Bar, 3a Veikou, Makrigianni (✆ **210/923-5811;** www.athens sportsbar.com), is just that, with snacks, projection screens, karaoke, and theme nights; happy hour is nightly 7–8pm. **Brettos Bar,** 41 Kydathineon, Plaka (✆ **210/323-2110;** www.brettosplaka.com), with its backlit wall of bottles, has been an Athenian landmark for over a century. **Chandelier,** 4 Benizelou, Plaka (✆ **210/631-6330**), is a cozy and laid-back lounge with a jazz soundtrack on the ground floor of a neoclassical building. **Duente Bar,** 2 Tzireon, Makrigianni (✆ **210/924-7069**), is an elegant old-world brasserie with a Rat Pack soundtrack, ideal for quiet evenings. **Melina Café,** 22 Lyssiou 22, Plaka (✆ **210/324-6501;** www.melinacafe.gr), is a charming cafe/bar that celebrates the life of Greek actress and politician Melina Mercouri and is popular with the French tourists. **Tiki Athens,**

15 Falirou, Makrigianni (✆ **210/923-6908;** www.tikiathens.com), as the name suggests, is a fun and funky place with '50s exotic decor, Asian-inspired cuisine, and
infectious good times.

Monastiraki
(Metro: Monastiraki)

Dude, 14 Kalamiotou (✆ **210/322-7130;** www.thedudebar.com), is named after
the cult-favorite character from *The Big Lebowski* and is a funky bar where the dude
himself would abide. **Gallery Café** (cafe/bar), 33 Adrianou (✆ **210/324-9080**), on
busy Adrianou, is a delightful and edgy cafe serving breakfast and snacks throughout
the day. At night, the lights dim and it morphs into an equally charming bar. When
electronica-loving hipsters bought **Inoteka,** 3 Plateia Avyssinias (✆ **210/324-
6446**), they redid the space into a funky bar. During the summer, the candlelit tables
spill out on the *plateia*—a great place to linger at all night long. **Keyser Soze,** 12
Avramiotou (✆ **210/323-4341**), is named for the enigmatic character from *The
Usual Suspects* and has an inspired and intriguing film noir theme: old detective
novels adorn the walls and there's even an outlined body on the floor as a rock
soundtrack and weekly theme parties add to the fun. **Magaze,** 33 Eolou (✆ **210/324-
3740;** www.magaze.gr), is an all-day cafe and laid-back evening bar with a mixed and
friendly crowd on pedestrian Eolou. **TAF—The Art Foundation** includes an art bar
at 5 Normanou (✆ **210/323-8757;** www.theartfoundation.gr). Off Ermou Street, in
a seemingly abandoned alley, the blink-and-you-missed-it door leads into a restored
neoclassical building complex from the 19th century that houses the Art Foundation,
a series of galleries, music, and theater showings. In the middle of the complex is the
lively courtyard bar.

Psirri
(Metro: Monastiraki)

Cantina Social, 6-8 Leokoreiou (✆ **210/325-1668**), is a bar directly across from
the "Ochre & Brown" boutique hotel, inside an old arcade. This unconventional bar
has flourished due to word of mouth, in a space (including a "courtyard") between
abandoned buildings. Old movies play on tarnished walls, the crowd is alternative and
friendly, the music fun and the drinks (5€–7€) a real find. **Cubanita** at 28 Karaiskaki
(✆ **210/331-4605;** www.cubanita.gr) offers, hands-down, one of the best nights to
be had in the city, where Latin beats and excellent Cuban cuisine combine to make
a great place to party until the early morning hours. On some nights there's live
Cuban music. **El Pecado,** a bar/restaurant/club at 11 Tournavitou (✆ **210/324-
4049;** www.elpecado.gr), came about from the unorthodox union of a medieval
Spanish-style church and erotic murals inspired by Bible themes. Confused? Don't
be. Follow the fun into this sinfully enjoyable venue (cover is 10€).

Thissio
(Metro: Thissio)

Athinaion Politeia (cafe/bar/restaurant), 30 Apostolou Pavlou and 1 Akamanthos
(✆ **210/341-3794;** www.athinaionpoliteia.gr), is in a grand restored building (a
grocery store in the 19th c.) right on the Promenade, with views of the Acropolis and
passersby. **Dust,** 3 Irakleidon, (✆ **210/342-6794**), is a wonderful all-day cafe and
cool bar at night with DJs, live performances, and weekly art events. **Loop,** 3 Plateia
Agion Asomaton (✆ **210/324-7666**), features industrial decor, rotating DJs, and a

fun crowd. **Stavlos** (multifunctional urban coolness), 10 Iraklidon (✆ **210/346-7206;** www.stavlos.gr), is off the Archaeological Promenade on pedestrian Iraklidon Street. It was the royal stables in the 1880s. Now it is a cafe during the day with an Italian restaurant and laid-back bar/club at night with outdoor seating in either the terrace, the tree-lined courtyard, or on the busy sidewalk.

Gazi
(Metro: Kerameikos)

And here we are: nightlife central. Trying to pick a place here is tricky because most of the bars and clubs in Gazi are good. For starters, take a stroll to scope out the scene. Walk down Persefonis Street and Triptopolemou in either direction: The Kerameikos Metro station is a landscaped *plateia* (Gazi Sq.) that covers an entire city block and is surrounded on either side by extremely popular bars, cafes and eateries. Once the bars reach full capacity, patrons head to the street and the *plateia,* drinks in hand.

There is always something cool going on at **Bios,** 84 Pireos (✆ **210/342-5335;** www.bios.gr), an art-space/cafe/bar/club, from avant-garde performances to exhibitions and foreign art film showings. A basement nightclub sways to a mostly rock soundtrack. An excellent place to begin the night is at **45 degrees,** 18 Iakhou, corner of Voutadhon (✆ **210/347-2729**). This rock bar/club has a rooftop terrace overlooking Gazi and the Acropolis. The oldest bar in Gazi **Gazaki,** 31 Triptopolemou (✆ **210/346-0901**), remains one of the best. The music is always excellent, as are the drinks. The no-pretense mixed crowd makes this a sure bet for any night of the week and the roof terrace is another plus.

Across from Gazaki, you will find **Dirty Ginger,** 46 Triptopolemou (✆ **210/342-3809;** www.dirtyginger.gr), a bar/restaurant with table seating on one of the most active streets in the city, a palm tree-lined garden, and excellent Mediterranean cuisine and pumping soundtrack. **Eighth Sin,** 141 Megalou Alexandrou (✆ **210/347-7048**), is a beautiful space, smartly decorated, with a mixed crowd and excellent cocktails based on, you got it, the seven deadly sins, plus an eighth one: the delicious and potent namesake's signature cocktail. **Gazarte,** 32–34 Voutadon (✆ **210/346-0347;** www.gazarte.gr), is a three-level urban chic space with various weekly art exhibitions, a good restaurant, and a lovely bar on the roof terrace with sweeping views. **Hoxton,** 42 Voutadon (✆ **210/341-3395**), is a hip bar with a seriously addictive rock/new wave soundtrack. At **Tapas Bar,** 44 Triptopolemou (✆ **210/347-1844**), the action begins with light snacks and a jazzy soundtrack that segues into Latin beats as patrons down the margaritas, mojitos, and rum-based drinks.

K44, 33 Leof. Konstantinoupolcos (✆ **210/342-6804;** www.k44.gr), is a multi-level warehouse that is a popular cafe/bar with live music performances on the ground floor and art exhibitions upstairs. **Nipiagogio (Kindergarten)** at Elasidon and 8 Kleanthous (✆ **210/345-8534**) is a former elementary school has been turned into one of the hottest bar/clubs in the city. On Saturday nights the former classrooms and playground stay hot until 6am! **Villa Mercedes,** Andronikou and 11 Jafferi (✆ **210/342-3606;** www.mercedes-club.gr), is an impressive nightclub with many rooms and an internal courtyard (plus a restaurant) that's always hopping. (Cover is 10€–15€.) *Tip:* Any night you're in Gazi, stop by **Mamacas** bar/lounge (inside the popular modern tavern; p. 146) and have a drink at the bar to check out the scene. Something interesting is always going on here.

Zappeio/Syntagma
(For Zappeio/Syntagma metro: Syntagma)

Banana Moon, 1 Adrittou (☎ 210/347-8716), is an all-day cafe and evening bar/club in the middle of Adrittou avenue (formerly "On the Road") across the street from the Old Olympic Stadium, with great music and decor and a wonderfully rowdy atmosphere. **Booze Coopertiva,** 57 Koloktroni (☎ 210/324-0944; www.boozecoopertiva.com), is an all-day hangout cafe with art exhibitions, screenings and performances, and lively bar at night. Inside the Aigli complex you will find the **Lallabai** lounge/club, 9 Zappeion (☎ 210/336-9340). Tastefully decorated, this is a great place to soak up the serene garden surroundings or the boisterous scene as the lounge turns into a club. (Cover is 10€.) **Six D.O.G.S.,** 6-8 Avramiotou (☎ 210/321-0510; www.sixdogs.gr), is an all-day cafe and gallery space, with live music performances and energetic bar in the evenings. **Kalua,** 6 Amerikis (☎ 210/360-8304), a bar near Syntagma Square, packs partiers into one of the city's most outrageously fun spots. **Stin Priza (Plugged In),** 1 Christou Lada. (☎ 210/324-4101), a popular bar on Karitsi Square (decorated in sockets—thus its name), is mellow during the day but picks up serious heat after 9pm and still manages to feel more like a friend's party than a bar. **The Gin Joint,** 1 Christou Lada. (☎ 210/321-8646), is a bar that explores a U.S. Prohibition-era "speakeasy" style, showcasing its bottles behind fenced windows and sways to a jazz and swing soundtrack. **The Seven Jokers,** 7 Voulis (☎ 210/321-9225), is a quiet cafe during the day, intimate bar in the early evening, and insanely busy after-hours bar with a serious crush on the Stones.

Exarheia
(Metro: Panepistimio)

Circus, 11 Navarinou (☎ 210/361-5255; www.circusbar.gr), is a bar on the border of Kolonaki and Exarheia, where posh meets bohemian. **Decadence,** 87 Emmanouil Benaki, Exarcheia (☎ 210/381-3685; www.decadence.gr), is a landmark Athenian rock club in a beautiful neoclassical mansion that used to belong to royalty. It's popular with all ages and touring bands that stop in after their shows. **Recital,** 64 Eressou (☎ 210/380-5556), is a club in an ivy-covered mansion that hosts live performances by Greek and foreign rock bands; you can also hang out on the terrace. Catch a rock concert at **Gagarin 205,** 205 Liossion (☎ 210/854-7601; www.gagarin205.gr), a large indoor space in Athens in the winter, or its other space on the coast in the summer.

Kolonaki/Ambelokipi
(Metro for Kolonaki: Syntagma or Evaggelismos; for Ambelokipi: Ambelokipi)

Balthazar, 27 Tsoha and Soutsou, Ambelokipi (☎ 210/644-1215; www.balthazar.gr), has been a favorite Athenian destination since the '80s, and has a fine restaurant, but it is the bar in the mansion's lantern-lit courtyard that's the nightlife spot. Show up late (after midnight) for drinks in this romantic location with the pretty people. **Baraonda,** 43 Tsoha, Ambelokipi (☎ 210/644-4308; www.baraonda.gr), features red velvet curtains, candles, stone and tiled walls, chandeliers, two bars, a VIP section, summer courtyard, a stylish clientele, and tasty Mediterranean cuisine. **Mike's Irish Bar,** 6 Sinopis, Ambelokipi (☎ 210/777-6797; www.mikesirishbar.gr), is a popular pub that's packed with expatriates and locals alike. **Mai Tai,** 18 Ploutarhou, Kolonaki (☎ 210/725-83062; www.mai-tai.gr), is an all-day hangout place, with a tasty menu, good drinks, and an attractive 30-plus crowd. **Mommy Open,** 4 Delfon,

Kolonaki (℗ **210/361-9682**), offers an impressive space—with a smart decor, art exhibitions, an excellent Mediterranean menu, and great drinks. It gets pumping after midnight, and also has an excellent Sunday brunch. **Scala Vinoteca,** 50 Sina, Kolonaki (℗ **210/361-0041**), is a beautiful, stylish wine bar/restaurant tucked between the stairs ascending to Lycabettus mountain, a perfect spot to begin the evening.

Seaside Clubs

Akrotiri Club Restaurant, Leof Vas Georgiou B5, Agios Kosmas (℗ **210/985-9147;** www.akrotirilounge.gr; tram to Elliniko stop), is a massive (capacity 3,000), beautiful and stylish open-air club next to the beach, with an elegant tropical decor, a huge pool, dance floors, deck seating by the beach, sea views, excellent (but pricey) Med-fusion cuisine (50€–70€), which has been popular since the '80s and shows no signs of stopping. (Cover, including a drink, 11pm–5am Mon–Thurs and Sun is 10€, Fri–Sat 15€.) **B.E.D.,** 58 Leoforos Poseidonos (℗ **210/894-1620;** tram to Plateia Glyfadas then 5-min. walk), is inside the Asteras Glyfada complex, and you can party right by the waves and the pool. (Cover, including drink Wed–Fri and Sun 11pm–5am is 10€; Fri–Sat 15€.) **Sea and City,** 14 Karamanli, Voula (℗ **210/895-9645;** tram to Plateia Glyfadas, then bus no. A2 or a taxi), is in a beautiful seafront mansion with a terrace right above the waves. It's a trendy cafe during the day that slowly morphs into a lounge/restaurant until its final reincarnation as a pumping club. Romantic **Island ★**, Limanakia Vouliagmenis (℗ **210/965-3563;** www.island clubrestaurant.gr; tram to Plateia Glyfadas and from there take a taxi or bus no. 114 and get off at Limanakia), is out of the way but worth the trip. Set on a cliff-top with sea vistas, where you can enjoy excellent finger food, sushi, and Mediterranean dishes, this is the quintessential Athenian summer nightspot. Things get louder after 1am. Show up early or make dinner reservations—prices are moderate to expensive (20€–70€)—or you can enjoy tapas at the bar. The door policy is annoying—if you arrive on foot you won't get in unless it's very early (10pm) or you have dinner reservations. (No cover with dinner reservations, 15€ without.)

REMBETIKA & BOUZOUKIA

Visitors interested in authentic *rembetika* (music of the urban poor and dispossessed) and bouzoukia (traditional and pop music featuring the bouzouki, a kind of guitar, today almost always loudly amplified) should consult their hotel concierge or check the listings in *Athinorama,* the weekly *Hellenic Times,* or *Kathimerini* (the daily insert in the *International Herald Tribune*). Another good place to ask is at the shop of the Museum of Popular Greek Musical Instruments (p. 167). *Rembetika* performances usually don't start until nearly midnight, and though there's rarely a cover, drinks can cost as much as 20€. Many clubs close during the summer.

One of the more central places for *rembetika* is **Stoa Athanaton,** 19 Sofokleous, in the Central Meat Market (℗ **210/321-4362**), which has been serving good food and live music since 1930 from 3 to 7:30pm and after 11pm. **Taximi,** 29 Isavron, Exarchia (℗ **210/363-9919**), is consistently popular. Drinks cost 12€. It's closed Sunday and Monday and during July and August. The downscale, smoke-filled **Rembetiki Istoria,** in a neoclassical building at 181 Ippokratous (℗ **210/642-4967**), features old-style *rembetika,* played to a mixed crowd of older regulars and younger students and intellectuals. The music usually starts at 11pm, but arrive earlier to get a seat. The legendary Maryo I Thessaloniki (Maryo from Thessaloniki), described as the Bessie Smith of Greece, sometimes sings *rembetika* at **Perivoli t'Ouranou,** 19 Lysikratous

(✆ 210/323-5517 or 210/322-2048), in Plaka. Expect to pay at least 10€ per drink in these places, most of which have a cover from 20€—except Rembetiki Istoria, which due to its student clientele is more affordable than most such places.

JAZZ

A number of clubs and cafes specialize in jazz, but also offer everything from Indian sitar music to rock to punk. The popular—and well thought of—**Half Note Jazz Club,** 17 Trivonianou, Mets (✆ 210/921-3310; www.halfnote.gr), schedules performers who play everything from medieval music to jazz; set times vary from 8 to 11pm and later. (Cover is 30€ with one drink.) In Gazi, at the **Art House,** 46 Konstantinoupoleos (✆ 210/461-1535; www.art-house-athens.gr), you can often hear jazz from 11pm. (Cover depends on event.) **Cabaret Voltaire,** 30 Marathonos, Metaxourgeio (✆ 210/522-7046; Metro: Metaxourgeio), has live jazz every Sunday. **Jazz n' Jazz,** 4 Deinokratous (✆ 210/725-8362; Tues–Sat 8pm–3am), a small, cozy and charming jazz museum/bar in Kolonaki, is a great place to take in the vibe and listen to their extensive jazz collection. If you're visiting in late May, check out the **European Jazz Festival** at **Technopolis,** 100 Pireos (✆ 210/346-0981; www. technopolis.gr). Also check out what's happening at the **Pallas Theater,** 5 Voukourestiou (✆ 210/321-3100; www.ticketshop.gr), which hosts frequent jazz concerts. Also, the beautiful **Athens Plaza Hotel** (www.njvathensplaza.gr) hosts weekly live jazz performances.

Movies

Athens has lots of air-conditioned theaters (mostly multiplexes) showing new-release Greek, American, and European films. Listings appear in the *Athens News,* in *Kathimerini* (the English-language insert in the *International Herald Tribune*), and in the weekly *Hellenic Times.*

If you're in Athens in summer, look for listings of neighborhood open-air cinemas; it's a pleasant way to pass an evening, although some old favorites have closed in recent years. Many of the open-air cinemas are family owned and run, and all are great places to watch Athenian families watching films—which is to say, talking to each other, pursuing runaway toddlers, munching snacks, and sipping cold drinks, all while keeping up a running commentary on the film. Admission will run you about 8€. We're fond of **Dexameni** in Dexameni Square, Kolonaki (✆ 210/362-3942), where there always seems to be a breeze on a hot evening. **Cine Paris,** on Kidathineon in the Plaka (✆ 210/322-2071), is one of the oldest in town—and has great views of the Acropolis, as does charming **Thission** on Apostolou Pavlou (✆ 210/342-0864), right on the Archaeological Promenade. **Aigli,** inside the Zappeion Gardens (✆ 210/336-9369), is the ideal place to enjoy a flick with a glass of wine. Shows begin after 9pm. If you want to watch a movie right next to the surf then head to **Cine Flisvos** (✆ 210/982-1256; tram: Parko Flisvou). For the more serious cinephiles, check out the **Greek Film Archive,** 48 Iera Odos and 134-136 Megalou Alexandrou, Gazi (✆210/360-9695; www.tainiothiki.gr), which has special screenings, various film festivals and an open-air summer rooftop cinema. If you're in Athens during the month of September, you might want to check out the **Athens International Film Festival** (✆ 210/606-1963; www.aiff.gr).

Gay & Lesbian Athens

There are lots of gay bars, cafes, and clubs in Athens, even though the gay male venues by far outnumber the lesbian ones. The scene used to be in Makrigianni and

Kolonaki, and the legendary gay bars and clubs of the past remain and are still popular but Gazi has taken over, with the hippest gay or gay-friendly scene. The weekly publications *Athinorama* and *Time Out* often list gay bars, discos, and special events in the nightlife section. You can also look for the Greek publication **Deon Magazine** (© 210/953-6479; www.deon.gr) or surf the Web at www.gaygreece.gr, www.greek gayguide.eu, www.gayathens.gr, or www.lesbian.gr. **Gay Travel Greece,** at 377 Syngrou Ave. in central Athens (© 210/948-4385; www.gaytravelgreece.com), specializes, as its name proclaims, in travel for gay and lesbian visitors.

Gay and lesbian travelers will not encounter difficulties at any Athenian hotel, but one with a largely gay and lesbian clientele is 41-room **Hotel Rio Athens** (© 210/522-7075; www.hotel-rio.gr), at 13 Odysseos off Karaiskaki Square in a restored neoclassical building. The popular Alexander Sauna has nice, clean apartments for rent above the bathhouse at affordable prices at **Alexander Apartments,** 134 Megalou Alexandrou and Iera Odos, Gazi (© 210/698-0282; www.alexander-apartments.gr). Below are some selections we have made of the city's more fun gay and lesbian bars/clubs. Also remember that **Athens Pride** (**www.athenspride.eu**) takes place in early June.

GAY & LESBIAN BARS/CLUBS

Alexander Sauna, 134 Megalou Alexandrou and Iera Odos, Gazi (© 210/698-0282; www.alexandersauna.com; Sun–Thurs 7pm–3am, Fri–Sat 7pm–8am; admission 9€–15€), is a very popular bathhouse with sauna, gym, Jacuzzi, private rooms, bar, garden, and many events and theme parties. **Bear Code Club,** 8 Konstantinoupoleos, Gazi (© 694/888-3241; www.bearcode.gr; Thurs–Sun 10pm–5am), is a bar/club with events and live performances for bears, cubs, and their admirers. **Blue Train,** 84 Konstantinoupoleos, Gazi (© 210/346-0677; www.bluetrain.gr; daily 8pm–4am), is right by the railway tracks on the edge of Gazi. The friendly scene here is a great place to begin the evening, preferably at a sidewalk table, where you can watch the trains and the boys go by, except on Fridays when the night belongs to the girls.

Group Therapy, 11 Lepenioutou, Psirri (© 210/323-4977; daily 10pm–4am), is an intimate, friendly, and sexy lesbian bar, popular with the beautiful, yet attitude-free girls and their friends. **Fou Club,** 8 Keleou, Gazi (© 210/346-6800; www.fouclub.gr; daily 10pm–5am), is a fun place with theme nights, special events, and an attitude-free crowd. **Kazarma,** first floor, 84 Konstantinoupoleos, Gazi (© 210/346-0667; Thurs–Sat midnight–5am), is above Blue Train, one of the best gay clubs in the city. During summer, the fun moves to the terrace (**El Cielo**). **Lamda Reloaded,** 15 Lembessi and 9 Syngrou, Makrigianni (© 210/922-4202; www.lamdaclub.gr; Thurs–Sun 11pm–5am), has been popular for so long, it has become an Athenian institution. The energy on the ground floor is mostly laid back, while things in the basement get far rowdier. **Mayo,** 33 Persefonis, Gazi (© 210/342-3066; daily 8pm–4am), is a quiet bar with a great inner courtyard and a rooftop terrace with a killer view. **Micraasia,** 70 Konstantinopoleos, Gazi (© 210/346-4851; daily 7:30pm–4am), whose name means "Asia Minor," has a decor with something of the Middle Eastern vibe of the old Greek world in that region (now Turkey). Red lighting, colored tiles, chaises, and belly dancers all contribute to making this an atmospheric venue (mostly for girls). There is also seating on its "secret" rooftop.

My Bar, 6 Kakourgiodikiou, Monastiraki (© 210/486-2161; www.mybar.gr; daily 11pm–4am), is a more intimate, less rowdy bar than its Gazi counterparts but just as energetic. The girls have made **Noiz,** 41 Evmolpidon and Konstantinoupoleos, Gazi (© 210/342-4771; www.noizclub.gr; Mon–Fri 10:30pm–4am, Sat–Sun

10:30pm–6am), into the most popular lesbian bar/club in town. With its good music and dynamic scene, Noiz offers the ultimate lesbian party. **Sodade,** 10 Triptopolemou, Gazi (© **210/346-8657;** Mon–Fri 10:30pm–4am, Sat–Sun 10:30pm–6am), was the first gay bar to open in Gazi, and it's become an institution, unbearably packed on weekends but always irresistible. **S'Cape,** Iera Odos and 139 Meg. Alexandrou, Gazi (© **210/345-2751;** www.s-cape-club.blogspot.com; Mon–Fri 10:30pm–4am, Sat–Sun 10:30pm–6am), is a large club with army bunks, military-style motif, and a sexy crowd; it's fun and very cruisy, but never takes itself too seriously. Monday is karaoke night, Thursday is Greek night.

RESTAURANTS/CAFES

Del Soul, 44 Voutadon, Gazi (© **210/341-8169**), is an all-day cafe, snacks, and late-night bar, along with **Magaze,** 33 Eolou, Monastiraki (© **210/324-3740;** www.magaze.gr). **Myrovolos,** 12 Giatrakou, Metaxourgeio (© **210/522-8806**), is a popular restaurant in a large piazza that opens at 11am daily as a cafe. It then becomes a very good restaurant before morphing into a busy bar for girls who love other girls, and their friends. **Kanella,** 70 Leof. Konstantinoupoleos, Gazi (© **210/347-6320**), is a good, moderately priced modern taverna with a mixed clientele. Everybody loves the cafe **Wunderbar,** 80 Themistokleous, Exarchia (© **210/381-85577**), especially the girls. The popular restaurants **Mamacas** (p. 146) and **Prosopa** (p. 147) are both mainstream but very gay friendly.

BEACH

Not a typical beach, as there is no sand, **Limanakia B** is a series of beautiful rocky coves. Nearby Limanakia A is far more popular, with a cafe/bar built right inside the rock and a rowdy, party crowd of teenagers and 20-somethings. Limanakia B is more forlorn and has no such features. Take the tram to Plateia Glyfadas then bus no. E22 to Limanakia (third stop), follow the steep trail down to the water and claim your own rock. The water is beautiful, and so are some of the visitors. Nudity and public sex are common, especially late in the day when men get to know each other in private caves.

BOOKSTORE

Even though **Colorful Planet,** 6 Antoniadou, Plateia Victoria (© **210/882-6600;** www.colourfulplanet.gr; Metro: Victoria), caters mostly to a Greek gay and lesbian clientele with many Greek and international works of gay literature, there is enough here for non-Greek readers to browse through, such as DVDs, calendars, gay foreign press, gay guides to Greece, and many other goodies.

PIRAEUS: ATHENS'S PORT

Piraeus has been the port of Athens since antiquity, and it is still where you catch most island boats and cruise ships. What's confusing is that Piraeus has **three harbors: Megas Limani (Main Harbor),** where you'll see everything from tankers to cruise ships; **Zea Limani (Zea Marina),** the port for most of the swift hydrofoils that dart to the islands; and **Mikrolimano (Little Harbor),** also called Turkolimano, or Turkish Harbor by the old-timers, one of the most charming and picturesque harbors in the Mediterranean, lined with a number of fish restaurants, cafes, and bars.

The absence of helpful signs at both the Main Harbor and Zea Limani, however, along with their constant bustle, means that this is not an easy place to navigate. To

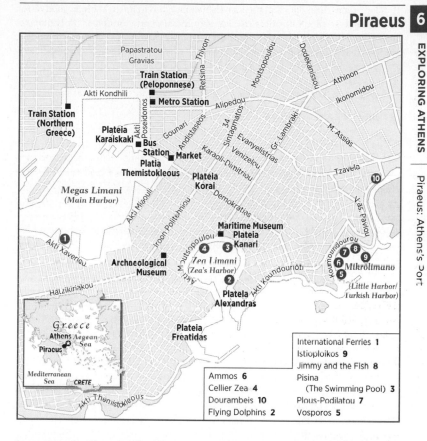

Map legend:

Ammos **6**	International Ferries **1**
Cellier Zea **4**	Istioploikos **9**
Dourambeis **10**	Jimmy and the Fish **8**
Flying Dolphins **2**	Pisina
	(The Swimming Pool) **3**
	Plous-Podilatou **7**
	Vosporos **5**

be on the safe side, even if you have your tickets, get there an hour before your ship is scheduled to sail—and don't be surprised if you curse this advice because your ship sails later than announced.

As in antiquity, today's Piraeus has the seamier side of a sailors' port of call as well as the color of an active harbor—both aspects, somewhat sanitized, were portrayed in the 1960 film *Never on Sunday* that made Melina Mercouri an international star. Piraeus also has a sprawling street market just off the Main Harbor, where you can buy produce that arrives each day on island boats, including bread baked that morning on distant islands. If you find yourself here with some time to spare, take a stroll along Mikrolimano, Zea Marina (otherwise known as Pasalimani, with countless cafes and shopping stores), and the pretty residential area of Kastella.

Essentials

These prices were accurate at press time and may have (and probably will have) gone up by the time you arrive here.

GETTING THERE   By Metro   The fastest and easiest way to Piraeus from central Athens is to take the Metro from Omonia Square, Monastiraki, or Thissio to the last stop (1.20€), then cross the footbridge to the domestic port.

By Bus   From Syntagma Square, take the (very slow) Green Depot bus no. 40 from the corner of Filellinon; it will leave you a block from the international port, about a 10-minute walk along the water from the domestic port. From the airport, bus no. X96 goes to Piraeus; the fare is 5€.

By Taxi   A taxi from Syntagma Square can cost up to 15€. The flat rate from Athens International Airport to the port is 35€ during the day and 50€ after midnight. For more info visit **www.athenstaxi.info**.

RETURNING TO ATHENS   The easiest way is to take the Metro to central Athens, to either Monastiraki, Thissio, or Omonia stations. Most taxi drivers waiting at the dock will try to overcharge tourists disembarking from the boats. They often offer a flat rate that's two or three times the legal fare. The options are to pay up, get a policeman to help you, or walk to a nearby street, hail a cab, and hope for a fair rate.

VISITOR INFORMATION   For boat schedules, transit information, and other tourist information 24 hours a day, dial ✆ **171** or 1441. The **Piraeus Port Authority** can be reached at ✆ **210/451-1311** to -1317 (www.olp.gr). The *Athens News* and the *Kathimerini* insert in the *International Herald Tribune* print major ferry schedules. The **Greek National Tourism Organization (EOT)** office (✆ **210/452-2591**) is inconveniently located on the street above Zea Marina (the hydrofoil port), on the second floor of a shopping arcade stocked with yacht supplies. It's open Monday through Friday from 9am to 2:30pm, but its limited resources probably won't warrant the 20-minute walk from the ferry piers. The small **tourist office** (✆ **210/412-1181**) in the Piraeus Metro station on Akti Poseidonos is open daily from 8am to 8pm. The numbers for the **harbor police** are ✆ **210/412-2501** or 210/451-1311. Most conveniently, an **Info-Point** (✆ **210/325-3123**; www.atedco.gr) is located at the port with city brochures, maps, and digital tours.

FAST FACTS   Several **banks** are along the waterfront. **National Bank,** on Ethniki Antistaseos, has extended hours in summer. A portable **post office** opposite the Aegina ferry pier offers currency exchange; it's open Monday through Saturday from 8am to 8pm and Sunday from 8am to 6pm. The **main post office** is on Tsamadoy; it's usually open daily from 8am to 4pm. There is also a substation in the Metro office on Akti Poseidonos. The **telephone office (OTE)** is a block away from the post office and is open 24 hours. There is another branch by the water, on Akti Miaouli at Merarchias, open daily from 7am to 9:30pm. You'll find secure **luggage storage** in the Metro station at the **Central Travel Agency** (✆ **210/411-5611**; www.athens-ferries.gr); hours are from 6am to 8pm. The website has all its info regarding departing and returning ferries to and from most major islands.

TICKETS TO THE ISLANDS   The quay of the Main Harbor is lined with **ticket agents,** many concentrated in Plateia Karaiskaki; some sell tickets for one or two lines or destinations only, some for more. A sign in the window should tell you what the agent sells. Almost every agent will tell you that you're getting a good deal; almost no agent will give you one.

FERRIES TO THE ISLANDS   You will be confused as to where to catch your boat; this is inevitable. Allow yourself plenty of time. Even the person you buy your ticket from may give you a bum steer. *Tip:* Information below may change at any moment. Sorry—but we thought you should know the truth!

Ferry tickets can be purchased at a ticket office up to 1 hour before departure; after that they can usually be bought on the boat. To book first-class cabins or buy advance-sale tickets, see one of the **harborside travel agents** (around Karaiskaki Sq. by the domestic ferries and along Akti Miaouli, opposite the Crete ferries). Most open at 6am, and some will hold your baggage for the day (but without security). The **Greek National Tourism Organization** publishes a list of weekly sailings. The **tourist police** (*©* **171**) or the **Port Authority** (*©* **210/451-1311** to -1317) can provide you with schedule information. Also check out the **Central Travel Agency** of Piraeus's website at **www.athensferries.gr** for schedules and info. As always it's the better and safer idea to book your tickets through a reputable local travel agency.

Boats for the eastern Cyclades (including Mykonos and Santorini) leave in the morning from Akti Tzelepi across from Plateia Karaiskaki. Aegina boats leave from Akti Poseidonos. Boats for Rhodes sail in the afternoon from Akti Miaouli. Boats for the western Cyclades (including Sifnos) sail in the early evening from Akti Kalimassioti near Plateia Karaiskaki. Boats for Crete sail in the early evening from Akti Kondyli. Many additional island boats leave from the quay opposite the Metro station. Boats heading out of Greece depart the quay on Akti Miaouli farthest away from the quays near the Metro and train stations. Boats for Aegina, Poros, Hydra, Spetses, Peloponnesian ports, and Kithira depart from Zea Marina, which is across the Piraeus peninsula and opposite the Main Harbor; the walk there takes 30 minutes.

What to See & Do

If you're stuck between boats, you may want to walk inland from the harbor on Demosthenous or Vas. Georgiou to Plateia Korai, which leads to a cafe where you can sit with a book. If you want to be by the sea, stroll or take the no. 904 bus (.50€) from the Main Harbor to Akti Themistokleous, where you can also find cafes.

If you're in Piraeus in the summer, a more energetic suggestion is an **open-air theatrical performance** at the Kastella Theater, a few blocks inland from Mikrolimano. In 2000, the first **Poseidon Festival,** with a wide range of concerts, took place in Piraeus; it's becoming an annual event. Get details at **Piraeus Municipal Theater,** Ayiou Konstantinou (*©* **210/419-4550**).

In the winter, performances are staged indoors, at the **Public Theater** on the green at Leoforos King Constantine. The Sunday **flea market** on and around Alipedou and Skylitsi is an equally crowded variation on the Monastiraki flea market, with generally lower-quality goods. The daily **street market** just off the Main Harbor is a good place to get **picnic supplies** for your boat trip.

The **Maritime Museum** *(Akti Themistokleous),* near the pier for hydrofoils (*©* **210/451-6264**), has handsome models of ancient and modern ships. Don't miss the classical warship *(trireme);* scholars still don't know how all those oarsmen rowed in unison. The museum is open Tuesday through Saturday from 9am to 2pm; admission is 3€. If you have time, stop by the **Archaeological Museum** ★, 31 Harilaou Trikoupi (*©* **210/452-1598**), to see three superb monumental bronzes, one depicting a youth (some say Apollo) and two of goddesses (some say Athena and Artemis). Museum hours are Tuesday through Sunday from 8:30am to 3pm; admission is 3€.

Where to Stay

Because Athens is so accessible by Metro, we don't recommend an overnight stay in Piraeus. However, if it makes sense in your travel plans, try one of these decent, moderately priced choices (usually no more than 100€): The 74-unit **Hotel Mistral,** 105 Vas. Pavlou, Kastella (www.mistral.gr; *©* **210/411-7150**), has a nice roof garden. The 31-unit **Ideal Hotel,** 142 Notara (www.ideal-hotel.gr; *©* **210/429-4050**) is clean and convenient. For something a bit nicer, try 32-unit **Hotel Castella,** 75 Vas. Pavlou (✆ **210/411-4735**), or **Piraeus Theoxenia Hotel,** 23 Karaoli and Dimitriou (www.theoxeniapalace.gr; ✆ **210/411-2550**), a five-star hotel with 76 rooms in a pretty neoclassical building. Frugal traveling friends who visit Greece every year always stay at 56-unit **Hotel Triton,** 8 Tsamadou (✆ **210/4173-4578**), which they praise for its quiet location—and double-glazed windows that cut down what noise there is.

Where to Eat

While there are some good restaurants in Piraeus, most of the places to eat along the harbor are mediocre at best. You'll do better if you walk a few blocks along Demosthenous to Plateia Korai, where the small cafes and restaurants are actually patronized by Greeks. If you decide on one of the seafood restaurants in central Piraeus or Mikrolimano, make sure you know the price before ordering; some of these places prey on the unwary. If the final tab seems out of line, insist on a receipt, phone the tourist police, and sit tight. Despite that warning, however, it would be a shame if such a postcard-perfect spot such as Mikrolimano had nothing to offer but ambience. Ignore the aggressive restaurant staff that try to get you to dine in their establishments (far worse than their Plaka counterparts) and try one of the restaurants listed below.

Ammos ★ SEAFOOD/MEZEDES   Reasonably priced, delicious seafood (with a large selection of *mezedes*) and a low-key island feel (great outdoor seating as well right on the marina), make this place popular with a younger crowd.

44 Akti Koumoundourou, Mikrolimano. ✆ **210/422-4633.** Appetizers and salads 10€–25€. Fish prices (by the kilo) change daily. MC. V. Daily noon–1am.

Dourambeis SEAFOOD   This taverna near the Delphinario theater in Piraeus is where many locals go when they want a good fish dinner. The decor is simple, the food excellent. The crayfish soup alone is worth the trip, but the whole point of going is for the excellent grilled seafood.

29 Dilaveri. ✆ **210/412-2092.** Reservations suggested. Fish prices (by the kilo) change daily. No credit cards. Mon–Sat noon–5pm and 8pm–1am.

Jimmy & the Fish ★★ SEAFOOD   In addition to its excellent location and great summer deck right by the marina, you will also find excellent food and impeccable service. The lobster spaghetti is out of this world, as is the octopus in red wine and virtually everything on the menu.

46 Akti Koumoundourou, Mikrolimano. ✆ **210/412-4417.** www.jimmyandthefish.gr. Reservations recommended. Main courses 35€–40€. MC, V. Daily noon–1am.

Margaro ★ 🍴 SEAFOOD   This fish taverna near the Main Harbor offers good value (along with excellent cooking) by keeping the menu simple: fish (large or small), crayfish, and salads. Service is brisk, although this place gets very crowded.

126 Hatzikyriakou. ✆ **210/451-4226.** Fish prices (by the kilo) change frequently. No credit cards. Mon–Sat 11am–midnight; Sun lunch only.

Plous Podilatou ★★ SEAFOOD   You'll find elegant dining on picturesque Mikrolimano in this pricey but excellent restaurant. The seafood and crab salads left us begging for more; the squid stuffed with feta cheese and seafood spaghetti are excellent, as are the three risottos (with chicken, shrimp, or leeks).

42 Akti Koumoundourou, Mikrolimano. ✆ **210/413-7910.** www.plous-podilatou.gr. Reservations recommended. Main courses 39€–46€. MC, V. Daily noon–1am.

Vassilenas ★ SEAFOOD/GREEK   Vassilenas has been serving its flat-fee menu for decades. Come here hungry, and even then you likely won't be able to eat everything in the more than 15 courses set before you. There's plenty of seafood, plus good Greek dishes. This is a great place to bring friends, so you can compare notes on favorite dishes or share them. Since Vassilenas is a fair hike from the waterfront, you may want to take a taxi.

72 Etolikou, Ayia Sofia. ℂ 210/461-2457. Reservations recommended Fri-Sat. Main courses 25€. No credit cards. Mon-Sat 8pm-midnight. Closed Aug.

Vosporos ★ GREEK   In the midst of the pretty marina and all the seafood restaurants, Vosporos specializes mostly in meat dishes, serving excellent souvlaki, gyros, burgers, and hearty salads in very generous portions at reasonable prices.

20 Akti Koumoundourou, Mikrolimano. ℂ 210/412-7324. Main courses 10€ – 22€. No credit cards. Daily noon-1am.

Hanging Out in Piraeus

Cellier Zea   Cellier Zea is a good restaurant, but its claim to fame is its multilevel neoclassical building overlooking Zea Marina, with superb views from the roof terrace, and a fine wine store on the first floor. Enjoy dinner (Mediterranean fare) on the roof terrace or a glass or two of their many wines while taking in the romantic view.

51 Akti Themistokleous, Zea Marina. ℂ 210/418-1049. www.cellier.gr. Main courses 18€-30€. AE, MC, V. Daily 8pm-2am.

Istioploikos   Surrounded by sailboats right on picturesque Mikrolimano, Istioploikos (named after the private Yacht Club of Greece) features delicious variations on classic Greek cuisine, but it is the cafe that steals the show with its incredible vistas. Later on in the night, the cafe turns into a bar.

Akti Mikrolomano. ℂ 210/413-4084. www.istioploikos.gr. Main courses 35€-40€. AE, DC, MC, V. Daily 10am-4am.

Pisina (The Swimming Pool)   Ultratrendy Pisina is centered around a large swimming pool (thus its name), offering amazing views of Zea Marina throughout the day and night. This is a great place to sit by the pool during the day, overlooking the yachts, and to dine and/or enjoy drinks by the candlelight at night.

Zea Marina. ℂ 210/451-1324. www.pisinacafe.gr. Main courses 22€-26€. AE, DC, MC, V. Daily 10am-4am.

DAY TRIPS FROM ATHENS

Although there are a number of tempting excursions from Athens, getting in and out of the city is so unpleasant that we suggest you visit most of the following places as you head off to the Peloponnese (Daphni and Eleusis are on the way) or to Central or Northern Greece (you can take in Marathon or Brauron). Nonetheless, two excursions—the **Monastery at Kaisariani** and the **Temple of Poseidon at Sounion**—can be more easily done as day trips from Athens.

These excursions take you into Attica—today, as in antiquity, the countryside around Athens. According to legend, the hero Theseus unified the 12 towns of Attica under Athens. The Attic countryside provided Athens with wine grapes, olives, honey, grains, fruit, marble from **Mount Pentelicus (Pendeli)** and **Mount Hymettus (Imittos),** and silver from the mines at Laurium, near Sounion. Today the Attic *mesogeion* ("the middle of the earth," or the Attic plain) is still known for its fine grapes, most often used in making white retsina.

Serious fires have raged through much of Attica every summer since 1995. Some forests on mounts Pentelicus and Hymettus have been destroyed, and many vineyards. In addition, the new roads constructed for the airport and the Olympics have accelerated the transformation of Attica into a spreading suburb of Athens.

Temple of Poseidon at Sounion ★★

One of the easiest and most popular day trips from Athens is to the 5th-century-B.C. Temple of Poseidon on the cliffs above Cape Sounion, 70km (43 miles) east of Athens (about 2 hr. by bus). This place is very popular at sunset—so popular that, if at all possible, you should not come on a weekend.

The easiest way to visit Sounion is on an **organized tour** (see "Organized Tours," earlier in this chapter). If you want to go on your own for far less money, take the Sounion **bus** leaving from Mavromateon along the west side of Pedion tou Areos Park (off the eastern end of Leoforos Alexandras). Buses leave about every half-hour, take 2 hours to reach Sounion, and cost 6€. To verify times, ask a Greek speaker to telephone the local **ticket office** (© 210/823-0179). Once you're in Sounion, you can catch a cab or walk the remaining kilometer to the temple. If you go to Sounion **by car,** heading out of Athens on Syngrou or Vouliagmenis boulevards, you'll probably fight your way through heavy traffic almost all the way, in both directions. If you can choose, take the bus that goes via Syngrou Avenue (it will eventually hit the coastal road) and get a seat on the right side of the bus.

Temple of Poseidon ★★   Cape Sounion is the southernmost point of Attica, and in antiquity, as today, sailors knew they were getting near Athens when they caught sight of the Temple of Poseidon's slender Doric columns. According to legend, it was at Sounion that Theseus's father, King Aegeus, awaited his son's return from his journey to Crete to slay the Minotaur. The king had told his son to have his ship return with white sails if he survived the encounter, and with black sails if he met death in the Cretan labyrinth. In the excitement of his victory, Theseus forgot his father's words, and the ship returned with black sails. When Aegeus saw the black sails, he threw himself, heartbroken, into the sea—forever afterward known as the Aegean. One of the reasons Sounion is so spectacular is that 15 of the temple's original 34 columns are still standing. A popular pastime here is trying to find the spot on a column where Lord Byron carved his name. After you find Byron's name, you may wish to sit in the shade of a column, enjoy the spectacular view over the sea, envy the solitude and quiet Byron found here, and recite these lines on Sounion from the poet's *Don Juan:*

> *Place me on Sunium's marbled steep,*
> *Where nothing, save the waves and I*
> *May hear our mutual murmurs sweep . . .*

There was also a Temple of Athena here (almost entirely destroyed); it's easy to think of Sounion as purely a religious spot in antiquity. Nothing could be more wrong: The entire sanctuary (of which little remains other than the Poseidon Temple itself) was heavily fortified during the Peloponnesian War because of its strategic importance overlooking the sea routes. Much of the grain that fed Athens arrived from outside Attica in ships that had to sail past Cape Sounion. In fact, Sounion had something of an unsavory reputation as the haunt of pirates in antiquity; it would be uncharitable to think that their descendants run today's nearby souvenir shops, restaurants, and cafes.

You can also swim in the sea below and grab a snack at one of the overpriced seaside restaurants, of which the **Akrogiali** (here since 1887), by the Aegeon Hotel, is a favorite and **Elias,** is just as good if not better. Or bring a picnic to enjoy on the beach. If you want to spend the night, the **Grecotel Cape Sounio** (✆ **22920/69-700;** www.grecotel.gr) has all the creature comforts for a minimum of 100€ a night.

Cape Sounion. ✆ **22920/39-363.** Admission 4€. Daily 10am–sunset.

Monastery of Kaisariani (Kessariani) & Mount Hymettus (Imittos)

Beautiful Kaisariani Monastery stands in a cool, bird-inhabited grove of pines and cypresses on the lower slopes of Mount Hymettus, famous for its marble and honey. In fact, the 4th-century-A.D. philosopher Synesius of Cyrene tells the story that the Sophists lured students to their lectures "not by the fame of their eloquence, but by pots of honey from Hymettus." This has long been a lovely place to escape the heat of Athens, especially after most of the bees left Hymettus and no longer vexed visitors. Keep in mind that the remaining pine groves here are a potential tinderbox. As always, be very careful if you smoke or use matches.

Kaisariani is 8km (5 miles) east of central Athens. The easiest way to visit is to take a **taxi** from Athens for about 20€ to 25€. Then, if you wish, you can return by bus, having spotted the bus stop on your way up to Kaisariani. If you want the cab to wait while you visit the monastery, negotiate a price in advance. Every 20 minutes, **bus no. 224** leaves from Plateia Kaningos on Academias and from Panepistimiou and Vas. Sofias, northeast of Syntagma Square, for the suburb of Kaisariani. If the day isn't hot, the monastery's wooded site is a pleasant 2km (1-mile) walk (follow the signs) up the road; or you can take one of the cabs by the bus stop.

> ### Kaisariani's Dress Code
>
> **Kaisariani is still an active church. Remember to dress appropriately. Shorts, miniskirts, and sleeveless or skimpy shirts are considered offensive.**

We suggest that you do not drive unless you want to explore Mount Hymettus, which is no longer the woodsy place fabled in antiquity, but which has become bleak after its recent fires. Kaisariani is poorly signposted so you may have trouble finding it, even with a good map.

Mount Parnitha, the most beautiful and largest national park in Athens (well known for its hiking trials, ski resort, and casino) was severely damaged during a fire that raged for days during a heat wave in June 2007. About a third of the forest (referred to as the "lungs of Athens") has either been destroyed or severely damaged.

Kaisariani Monastery ★   When a spot is holy in Greece, it has usually been holy for a very long time. Today's monastery occupies the site of an ancient temple to Aphrodite, probably built here because of the spring, part of the headwaters of the River Ilissos that flowed through Athens in antiquity. You'll see the water pouring through the open mouth of the marble goat's head at the monastery's entrance. This spring once supplied much of Athens with drinking water. Now, Greek brides who wish to become pregnant often journey here to drink from the spring, whose waters are believed to speed conception. The monastery was built in the 11th century over the ruins of a 5th-century Christian church, itself built over the temple. The monks supported themselves by keeping bees and selling the honey. The monastery's kitchen and refectory, which now house sculptural fragments, are on the west side of a paved, flower-filled courtyard. To the south, the old monks' cells and a bathhouse are being restored (exploration at your own risk is usually permitted). The well-preserved church, built like so many others in Greece in the shape of a Greek cross, has a dome supported by four ancient Roman columns. Most of the frescoes are relatively late, dating from the 17th and 18th centuries; the distinctive bell tower is from the 19th century.

Kaisariani. ☎ **210/723-6619.** Admission 4€. Tues–Sun 8:30am–3pm; often later in summer.

Sanctuary of Artemis at Brauron (Vravrona)

Most visitors do not come to this shrine to Artemis in the Attic hills. It's a lovely, tranquil spot—in danger of losing its peace to the proliferating roads and overhead noise from planes from the international airport. Brauron is 38km (24 miles) east of central Athens between Porto Rafti and Loutsa, on the east coast of Attica.

Take **bus no. 304** for the Zappion to the village of Loutsa, which is about 2km (about a mile) from the site. **By car,** from Athens, head toward Porto Rafti. In Porto Rafti, follow signs for Vravrona and Artemida. On the left, about 600m (1,968 ft.) before the site, are the remains of a 6th-century church. Traffic often backs up on the road between Stavrou and Markopoulo, particularly in Peania, so the trip will probably last the better part of an hour. You can also take the new highway from Athens to the airport and continue on to Rafina, where you can ask for directions to Brauron.

Sanctuary of Artemis ★ Just when you think that you're beginning to understand the ancient Greeks, you encounter something like the cult of Artemis at Brauron. According to legend, Agamemnon's ill-fated daughter Iphigenia served as a priestess here—and was buried here after her ritual sacrifice on the eve of the expedition to Troy. Little girls in modern times dress themselves as bear cubs for a quadrennial festival here to honor Iphigenia and Artemis. According to one story, the custom began when an epidemic broke out after a youth killed a bear that had attacked his sister. An oracle suggested that a purifying ceremony take place in which young girls dress like bears; this practice continued every 4 years throughout antiquity. As you sit on a shady slope, you may want to imagine the bearlike antics of the little girls as they parade here in bear masks and saffron-colored robes. To confuse matters further, these ceremonies were believed to assist women in childbirth.

The most striking structure at Brauron is the **stoa,** restored in 1961. The stoa was built in the shape of an incomplete Greek letter Ρ facing south toward the hill. Six rooms on the stoa's north side contained 11 small beds for the children, with stone tables by the beds. Four rooms on the stoa's west side may also have been used as bedrooms for the children. The foundations of the 5th-century **Temple of Artemis** are located here as well, along with a cave called the **Tomb of Iphigenia.** There's also a sacred spring and two chapels at this altogether delightful spot.

This small, well-lit **museum** has some charming displays, including marble portrait heads of the little girls, plus bear masks, handsome geometric vases from the nearby cemetery at Anavyssos, and grave markers found in the surrounding area.

Vraona. ☎ **22990/27-020.** Site and museum admission 4€. Tues–Sun 8:30am–3pm in winter; often later in summer.

Marathon

In 490 B.C., the vastly outnumbered Athenians and their allies from the little Boeotian town of Plataea defeated the invading Persian army on the plain of Marathon,

Forest Fires Create a Changing Landscape

During August 2009, Athens suffered terrible forest fires, continuing the destruction that began in 2007. In the greenest areas of Athens, fires raged for 3 nights and 4 days, aided by gale-force winds that kept many firefighting aircraft grounded and allowed the fires to swallow vast areas of pine trees and olive groves, leaving residents of the northern suburbs to fend for themselves. The destruction—though without human casualties—included 12,000 hectares (30,000 acres) of forest, fields, and olive groves, fully 50% of the capital's such areas.

and saved Athens and much of Greece (and, some say, much of Europe) from Persian rule. In honor of their valor, the 192 Athenians who fell here were buried on the battlefield in an enormous burial mound. Beyond that, there's little to see at Marathon, as there is little to see at Gettysburg and Runnymede, but such sites are moving because of the battles that shaped the course of history. When Lord Byron came to Greece to fight in the War of Independence, he visited Marathon and wrote:

The mountains look on Marathon,
And Marathon looks on the sea.
And musing there an hour alone,
I dreamed that Greece might still be free . . .

Alas, before he could fight to free Greece, Byron succumbed to fever in the boggy, cholera-infested town of Mesolongi, where he died on April 19, 1824.

Marathon is 42km (26 miles) northeast of Athens between the villages of Nea Makri and Marathona. **Buses** leave Athens from Mavromati along the east side of Pedion tou Areos Park every half-hour in the morning and every hour in the afternoon. The trip costs 4€ and takes 2½ hours. For departure times, call the **tourist police** (*© 171*) or ask a Greek speaker to call the local **ticket office** (*© 210/821-0872*). **By car,** drive north from Athens along Leoforos Kifissias, the more scenic route that circles Mount Pendeli through Dionissious to the sea at Nea Makri; or drive along the National Highway toward Thessaloniki, from where signs direct you to Marathon.

Marathon Battlefield & Burial Mound ★ By September of 490 B.C., the advancing force of Persia—then the most powerful empire in the world—reached Marathon, anchored its fleet in the bay, and made plans to attack Athens. The Athenians sent their swiftest runner, Pheidippides, to Sparta to ask for help, and marched their entire army of about 9,000 men north to Marathon. When Pheidippides reached Sparta (some say that it took him about a day and a half—clearly the gods were on his side), the Spartans said they would be delighted to join the Athenians, after the conclusion of an important Spartan religious festival observing the full moon. This was widely thought to be a delaying tactic, and Athens prepared to stand alone—and did, except for a small contingent of about 1,000 soldiers from the town of Plataea in Boeotia. The Persian force was at least 24,000 strong.

For some days, the two forces eyed each other, but neither attacked. Then, before dawn on September 12, the Athenians launched a surprise attack. As the Athenian right and left wings forged forward, the center gave way—but when the Persians pressed forward, the Athenian flanks surrounded them and the serious slaughter began. Many of the Persians tried to flee to the safety of their ships, anchored offshore, but were cut down in the marshy plain that lay between the battlefield and the sea. By nightfall, the victory was won, and Pheidippides was again dispatched, this time to run to Athens with news of the victory at Marathon. Pheidippides burst into the Athenian Agora, shouted, "We have won," and fell dead from exhaustion. Today's marathons commemorate Pheidippides's run. (If you want information on the annual rerunning of the Marathon in Nov, check out **www.athensmarathon.com**.)

Although the Athenians won the battle at Marathon, the Persian navy set sail for Athens. The weary Athenian army marched back to Athens and prepared to do battle again, but the Persians, after sailing up and down the coast of Attica, reversed course and returned to Asia Minor. Ten years later, they would be back—only to be defeated decisively in the Battle of Salamis.

The Athenian victory at Marathon, against such great odds, became the stuff of legend. Some said the Athenian hero Theseus himself fought alongside his descendants. Others said that the god Pan bewitched and confused the Persians, leading them to plunge to their deaths in the swamp—leading them, in short, to panic, the word derived from the god's name. According to one legend, Pan appeared to Pheidippides as he ran with news of the victory to Athens. Pointedly, Pan asked why the Athenians built so few shrines to him—a situation quickly rectified throughout Attica.

Although it was customary to bury war casualties in the Kerameikos cemetery in Athens, the 192 Athenian dead from this astonishing victory were cremated and buried together in the mound that still stands. When the Athenian mound was excavated in the late 19th century, quantities of ashes and burned bones were found.

Half a millennium after the battle, when the traveler Pausanias visited Marathon, he wrote, "Here every night you can hear the noise of whinnying horses and of men fighting." Indeed, there are those today who claim to have heard sounds of battle on moonlit nights at Marathon.

The excellent Marathon museum is several miles from the battlefield but is signposted both there and on the main road. The collection includes finds from the battlefield and other sites, including startling imitation Egyptian statues from a local shrine, possibly built by Herodes Atticus, the great 2nd-century-A.D. benefactor born near Marathon. Herodes Atticus, who owned a number of luxurious villas in Greece, seemed to be almost incapable of taking a day trip without building a fountain, shrine, or temple to commemorate his visit.

If you're not bothered by swimming near the marshy swamp where so many Persians drowned, you can take a dip and enjoy a bite at a taverna along the coast. Most tavernas close off season, although some open on the weekend. Nearby is the pristine beach of Schinias. Closer to Marathon is a very good, but busy, private beach called **The Boat** (**www.karavi.gr**). You can also visit the **Marathon Run Museum,** Junction of Marathonos Avenue and 25 March Street, Marathon Town (© **2294/67-617**; www.marathon.gr), opened in 2004, which chronicles the history of the Olympic marathon race, from Athens 1896 to the present day. Most of the photographs, posters, and drawings were provided to the museum by the International Olympic Committee from the Olympic Museum Lausanne. The Marathon Run Museum is open Tuesday through Sunday 9am to 9pm.

Marathonas. © **0294/55-155.** Admission of 3€ includes both the mound and the museum. Museum and battle site Tues–Sun 8:30am–3pm (often later in summer).

Monastery of Daphni (Dafni)

If you've never seen Byzantine mosaics and wonder what all the fuss is about, Daphni is the place to come. Daphni is one of the greatest masterpieces of the Byzantine

Open or Closed?

Be sure to check with the Greek National Tourism Organization (✆ 210/870-0000) or the Ministry of Culture website (**www.culture.gr**) to see whether Daphni, closed for some time, is open when you plan to visit.

Empire, which was founded by the first Christian emperor, Constantine, in the 4th century A.D. and conquered by the Turks in 1453. The great art historian of Byzantine Greece, Sir David Talbot-Rice, has called Daphni "the most perfect monument" of the 11th century—and this sober scholar was not given to hyperbole.

Unfortunately, getting here is an ordeal. If possible, see Daphni on your way to or from the Peloponnese. If you're driving, you can easily stop here; if you're traveling with a tour, most stop at Daphni. You could brave a taxi, but it's a very ugly ride—and the 9km (5½-mile) trip west of Athens can take an hour. Coming by bus involves numerous changes. It is best to take the Metro to the Daphni station and continue by bus or taxi. A visit to Daphni can be combined with a stop at Eleusis (see below).

If you're **driving,** follow the signs for Corinth out of Omonia Square. After you cross an overpass of the National Road that runs north to Thessaloniki (Salonika), the road rises for 5km (3 miles) to the gentle crest of a hill. There is a traffic light just over the crest and another traffic light approximately .5km (1,500 ft.) farther on. Turn left at the second light and then right along the parallel road about .3km (about 900 ft.) to the monastery. **Warning:** Due to the heavy traffic, turning off the National Road is not always easy, so allow yourself plenty of time to get to the left to make the turn.

Monastery of Daphni ★★ When you reach Daphni, you may want to take a few minutes to look at the church's lovely brickwork and think about the history of this sacred spot. There have been shrines here since antiquity, when there was a temple to Apollo. The temple is long gone (except for one column near the entrance), but the name Daphni (Greek for "laurel," Apollo's favorite plant) still honors that god.

In the 6th century, a small monastery was built here, later expanded in the 11th century. The monastic buildings have been almost entirely destroyed, but the domed church dedicated to the Virgin Mary remains. Over the centuries, Daphni has been repeatedly damaged by invaders and earthquakes, and repeatedly rebuilt. You'll see an example of that rebuilding in the twin Gothic arches in front of the church's west entrance. These were added by the Cistercian monks who turned Daphni into a Catholic monastery after the Crusaders captured Constantinople in 1204. During the long period of the Turkish occupation, there was no functioning monastery here—for a while, the buildings were used as army barracks. After the Greek War of Independence, Daphni was reclaimed by the Greek Orthodox church and restored.

A severe earthquake in the 1980s prompted another round of restoration in which the church was strengthened and its dazzling mosaic cycle repaired. Step inside and let your eyes become accustomed to the dark. On the **central dome** is the commanding mosaic of Christ *Pantocrator* (the Almighty). This image of Christ as an awesome judge is quite different from the Western image of Christ as a suffering mortal. If you're familiar with the Old and New Testaments, you'll be able to pick out familiar stories in the mosaics throughout the rest of the church. As is traditional in Greek Orthodox churches, the Annunciation, Nativity, Baptism, and Transfiguration are in the squinches supporting the dome, and the 16 major prophets are displayed between the windows of the dome. The Adoration of the Magi and the Resurrection are in the **barrel vault** inside the main (southern) entrance of the church, and the Entry into Jerusalem and the Crucifixion are in the **northern barrel vault.** Mosaics showing scenes from the life of the Virgin are in the **south bay** of the narthex (a passage between the entrance and nave). Even if you're not familiar with the stories, and even if you find the mosaic of Christ Pantocrator grim rather than awesome, you may well be enchanted by the charming details in scenes such as the Adoration of the Magi.

Daphni. ℂ **210/581-1558.** Admission 3€. Daily (except major holidays) 8:30am-2:45pm.

Sanctuary of Eleusis (Elefsis)

Although Eleusis was the site of the most famous and revered of all the ancient Mysteries, the present-day site is so grim (surrounded by the industrial city of Elefsina) that you'll need a keen interest in either archaeology, mystery cults, or oil refineries to enjoy a visit here. Eleusis is 23km (14 miles) west of Athens. To get here **by bus,** take no. A16, 853, or 862 from Eleftherias Square off Leoforos Pireos near Omonia. (This trip can be combined with a visit to Daphni Monastery.) Ask the driver to let you off at the Sanctuary (Heron), which is off to the left of the main road, before the center of town. If you're **driving,** take the National Road and exit at Elefsina. There are almost no signs for this important site; you may have to ask repeatedly for directions. You'll know you're close when you pass through a small, pleasantly wooded square with several restaurants and can catch a glimpse of the site off to the side.

Sanctuary of Eleusis ★ The unknown and the famous were initiated into the sacred rites here, yet we know almost nothing about the **Eleusinian Mysteries.** What we do know is that the Mysteries commemorated the abduction of Demeter's daughter, Persephone, by the god of the underworld, Hades (Pluto). Demeter was able to strike a bargain with the god, who allowed Persephone to leave the underworld and rejoin her mother for 6 months each year. The Mysteries celebrated this—and the cycle of growth, death, and rebirth of each year's crops.

Despite its substantial remains and glorious past—this was already a religious site in Mycenaean times—the sanctuary's present surroundings make it difficult to warm to the spot. Admittedly, there are the considerable remains of a **Temple of Artemis,** a 2nd-century-A.D. **Roman Propylaea (monumental entrance),** and **triumphal arches** dedicated to the Great Goddesses and to the emperor Hadrian. Hadrian's arch here, by the way, inspired the Arc de Triomphe on Paris's Champs-Elysées. Nearby is the **Telesterion,** the Temple of Demeter, where only initiates of the cult knew what happened at the sacred rites—and they kept their silence.

One poignant spot is **Kallichoron Well,** where the goddess Demeter wept over the loss of her daughter, whom Hades (Pluto) spirited away. The dark god may have dragged Persephone with him through the cave here known as **Ploutonion,** which was believed to be an entrance to the underworld. It seems ironic that modern Elefsina itself is so ghastly that it has become something of a hell on earth. If you're in luck, the small **museum** (closed since the 1999 earthquake but open intermittently of late) will be open. It contains finds from the site, including several **figures of Demeter** and a lithe **statue of Antinous,** the beautiful boy who won the emperor Hadrian's heart.

Elefsina. ℂ **210/554-6019.** Admission 3€; free Sun. Tues-Sun 8:30am-3pm (often later in summer).

THE SARONIC GULF ISLANDS

by Sherry Marker

The islands of the Saronic Gulf are so close to Athens that each summer Athenians flee there for some relief from the heat and the crowds. The summer of 2007 was the hottest in at least 90 years . . . until the summer of 2010! If these summer scorchers continue, more and more Athenians will try to escape the pulverizing heat of Athens on as many summer weekends as possible. These islands are also popular destinations for European and American travelers with limited time, who are determined not to go home without seeing at least one Greek island.

The easiest island to visit is **Aegina,** just 30km (17 nautical miles) from Piraeus. The main attractions—in addition to the ease of the journey—are the Doric **Temple of Aphaia,** one of the best-preserved Greek temples; several good beaches; and verdant pine and pistachio groves. That's the good news. The bad news is that Aegina is so close to Athens and Piraeus that it's become a bedroom suburb for Athens, with many of its 10,000 inhabitants commuting to work by boat. That said, Aegina town still has its pleasures, and the Temple of Aphaia and deserted medieval town of **Paleohora** are terrific. If you come here, try to avoid weekends and the month of August.

Poros is hardly an island at all; only a narrow (370m/1,214-ft.) inlet separates it from the Peloponnese. There are several decent beaches, and the landscape is wooded, gentle, and rolling, like the landscape of the adjacent mainland. Alas, Poros's pine groves were badly damaged by the summer fires of 2007, and still recovering. Poros is popular with tour groups as well as young Athenians (in part because the Naval Cadets' Training School here means that there are lots of young men eager to party). On summer nights, the waterfront is either very lively or hideously crowded, depending on your point of view.

Hydra (Idra), with its bare hills, superb natural harbor, and elegant stone mansions, is the most strikingly beautiful of the Saronic Gulf islands. One of the first Greek islands to be "discovered" by artists, writers, and bons vivants in the '50s, Hydra is not the place to experience traditional village life. The island has been declared a national monument, from which cars have been banished, but its relative quiet is increasingly being infiltrated by motorcycles. A major drawback: Few of the beaches are good for swimming, although you can swim from the rocks in and just out of Hydra town. **Spetses** has always been popular with wealthy

Booking Your Return Trip

With some of the hydrofoils and ferries that serve the Saronic Gulf islands, it is impossible to book a round-trip. If you cannot buy a round-trip ticket, head for the ticket office as soon as you arrive at your island destination, and book your return. If you do not do this, you may end up spending longer than you planned—or wished—on one or more of the islands. At press time, both Minoan Flying Dolphins and Ceres Flying Dolphins had been absorbed by **Hellenic Seaways (www.hellenicseaways.gr)**, the former Hellas Flying Dolphins, but there may be more ownership and name changes by the time you arrive.

Athenians, who built—and continue to build—handsome villas. If you like wooded islands, you'll love Spetses, although summer forest fires over the last few years have destroyed some of its pine groves.

You can make a **day trip** to any of the islands, and some day cruises out of Piraeus rush you on and off three of them, usually with quick stops at Hydra, Poros, and Spetses. If you plan to spend the night in summer, book *well* in advance. The website **www.windmillstravel.com** is a useful resource for all the islands. You can access a useful website for each of the Saronic islands Cyclades by typing **www.greeka.com/saronic** into your Web browser, followed by the name of the island; **www.openseas.gr** is a useful site for ferry schedules as is **www.gtp.gr**.

If you go to one of these islands on a day trip, remember that, unlike the more sturdy ferries, hydrofoils cannot travel when the sea is rough. You may find yourself an overnight island visitor, grateful to be given the still-warm bed in a private home surrendered by a family member to make some money. (I speak from experience.) *Greek Island Hopping*, published annually by Thomas Cook, is, by its own admission, out of date by the time it sees print. Still, it's a very useful volume for finding out where (if not when) you can travel among the Greek islands.

If possible, avoid June through August, unless you have a hotel reservation and think that you'd enjoy the hustle and bustle of high season. Also, mid-July through August, boats leaving Piraeus for the islands are heavily booked—often seriously overbooked. It is sometimes possible to get a deck passage without a reservation, but even that can be difficult when as many as 100,000 Athenians leave Piraeus on a summer weekend. Most ships will not allow passengers to board without a ticket.

And remember: Some hydrofoils leave from the Piraeus Main Harbor while others leave from the Piraeus Marina Zea Harbor—and some leave from both harbors! It's a good idea to arrive early, in case your boat is leaving from a different spot from the one you expect.

AEGINA

30km (17 nautical mi) SW of Piraeus

More travelers come to Aegina (Egina), the largest of the Saronic Gulf islands, than to any of the other Greek islands. Why? Location, location, location. Aegina is so close to Athens that it draws thousands of day-trippers. As the day-trippers arrive in the morning, many of the 10,000 who live on Aegina and commute daily to work in Athens depart. If you have only 1 day for one island, you may decide on Aegina, where you can see a famous temple (the Doric **Temple of Aphaia**), visit a romantic

The Saronic Gulf Islands

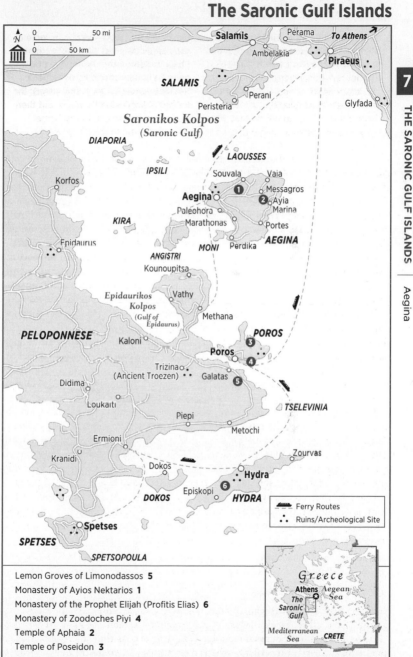

Lemon Groves of Limonodassos **5**
Monastery of Ayios Nektarios **1**
Monastery of the Prophet Elijah (Profitis Elias) **6**
Monastery of Zoodoches Piyi **4**
Temple of Aphaia **2**
Temple of Poseidon **3**

Avoiding the Aegina Crowds

If Aegina turns out to be too crowded for you, take a short ferry ride to little Angistri, where **Rosy's Little Village** (www.rosyslittlevillage.com; ☏ **22970/91-610**) is as charming as its name, with 16 whitewashed rooms tucked in a pine grove. The restaurant serves organic food, there's swimming in a rocky cove, and many guests meditate and relax, either on their own or in one of a number of holistic workshops; summer doubles start at 50€ and go to around 75€ in August.

medieval hill town **(Paleochora),** have lunch at one of the harborside tavernas in Aegina town, and munch the island's famous pistachio nuts as you sail back to Athens.

Most ships arrive and depart from the main port and capital of **Aegina town** on the west coast, though a few stop at the resort town of **Souvala** on the north coast and at the port of **Ayia Marina** on the east coast. Ayia Marina is charmless, but this port is your best choice, if your principal destination is the Temple of Aphaia.

Despite massive tourism and the rapid development devouring much farmland, the area still has its share of almond, olive, and especially **pistachio** orchards. In fact, the island has an endemic water problem because of the water necessary for the pistachio groves. Wherever you buy pistachios in Greece, the vendor may assure you that they are from Aegina to indicate their superior quality.

GETTING THERE **Car ferries** and **excursion boats** to Aegina usually leave from Piraeus's Main Harbor; **hydrofoils** leave both from the Main Harbor and from Marina Zea Harbor. Hydrofoil service is at least twice as fast as ferries and at least 40% more expensive (except to Aegina, for which the charge is only about 10% more). The sleek little hydrofoils are outfitted like broad aircraft with airline seats, toilets, and a minimum of luggage facilities. (The fore sections offer better views, but they're also bumpier.) The newer Super Cats are bigger, faster, and more comfortable, with food and beverage service. Reservations are vital on weekends. Often, in order to continue to another Saronic Gulf island by hydrofoil, you must return to Piraeus to transfer. Some ferries go from Aegina to the other Saronic Gulf islands. *Warning:* Schedules—and even carriers—can change, so double-check information you get— and then be prepared for last-minute schedule and carrier changes; **www.openseas. gr** is a useful site for ferry schedules as is **www.gtp.gr**.

Daily hydrofoil and ferry service to the Saronic Gulf islands is offered by **Hellenic Seaways** (☏ **210/419-9200;** www.hellenicseaways.gr). **Saronikos Ferries** (☏ **210/417-1190**) takes passengers and cars to Aegina, Poros, and Spetses; cars are not allowed to disembark on Hydra. **Euroseas** (☏ **210/411-3108**) has speedy catamaran service from Piraeus to Poros, Hydra, and Spetses. Boats often, but not always, leave from gates E8 and 9 in the main Piraeus harbor. You can usually visit any one of the Saronics for between 20€ and 65€ day-return; the faster the ship, the higher the price. Several cruises offer day trips to Hydra, Poros, and Aegina; for details, see chapter 4, "Cruising the Greek Islands."

For information on schedules for most Argo-Saronic ferries, try one of the numbers of the **Piraeus Port Authority** (☏ **210/422-6000,** 210/410-1480, or 210/410-1441), but phones are not always answered. On Aegina, try ☏ **22970/22-328.**

VISITOR INFORMATION The **Aegina Tourist Office** (℃ **22970/22-220**) is in the Town Hall. There's a string of travel agencies at the harbor, including the usually efficient **Aegina Island Holidays,** 47 Demokratias (℃ **22970/26-439;** fax 22970/26-430). To learn a little about Aegina's history, look for Anne Yannoulis's *Aegina* (Lycabettus Press), usually on sale at **Kalezis Boatokshop** on the harbor (℃ **22970/25-956**), which stocks foreign newspapers. Check the websites **www. aeginagreece.com** and **www.greeka.com/saronic/aegina** for info in English and pick up the handy free **Mini Guide,** published each year in English and Greek.

GETTING AROUND A left turn as you disembark takes you east to the **bus station** (℃ **22970/22-787**) on Plateia Ethneyersias. There's good service to most of the island, with trips every hour in summer to the Temple of Aphaia and Ayia Marina (3€); tickets must be purchased before boarding. Every Saturday and Wednesday in summer, **Panoramic Bus Tours** (℃ **22970/22-254**) offers a 3½-hour bus tour (6€) of the island, taking in the Temple of Aphaia, several beaches and villages, and the Wildlife Center and Hospital (℃ **22970/28-267;** www.ekpaz.gr) at Pachia Rachi. The tour has a commentary in Greek and English and is a great introduction to the island. **Taxis** are easy to find in Aegina town; if you want to take a taxi tour of the island, negotiate the fare before you set off. Your hotel can usually get you a decent price to rent either **bicycles** or **mopeds;** if you just show up at a rental place, the price is usually higher. An ordinary bike should cost about 12€ per day; mopeds, from 25€, except on summer weekends, when the sky is the limit. Motorcycle and moped agents are required to, but do not always, ask for proof that you are licensed to drive such vehicles and give you a helmet. Be sure to check the tires and brakes.

FAST FACTS The **National Bank of Greece** is one of four waterfront banks with currency-exchange service and ATMs; some travel agents, including **Island Holidays** (℃ **22970/23-333**), often exchange money both during and after normal bank hours, usually at less favorable rates. The island **clinic** (℃ **22970/22-251**) is on the northeast edge of town; for **first aid,** dial ℃ **22970/22-222.** The **police** (℃ **22970/23-343**) and the **tourist police** (℃ **22970/27-777**) share a building on Leonardou Lada, about 200m (656 ft.) inland from the port. The **port authority** (℃ **22970/22-328**) is on the waterfront. The **post office** is in Plateia Ethatneyersias, around the corner from the hydrofoil pier. The **telephone office (OTE)** is 5 blocks inland from the port, on Aiakou. There are several Internet cafes, including **Prestige** and **Nesant,** on and just off the waterfront. *Tip:* Try to pick up the useful

---

📎 Culture Calls

If you visit the islands of the Saronic Gulf in July and August, look for posters announcing exhibitions at local museums and galleries. There are often exhibits at the **Citronne Gallery** (℃ **22980-22-401**; www.citronne.com), on Poros, and at the **Koundouriotis Mansion** (℃ **22980/52-210**), on Hydra. In addition, many Athenian galleries close for parts of July and August, and some have shows on the islands. The **Athens Center,** 48 Archimidous (℃ **210/701-2268**; www.athenscentre. gr), sometimes stages plays on Spetses and Hydra. The center offers a modern-Greek-language summer program on Spetses in June and July.

guides *Essential Aegina* and *Mini Guide*, often available from travel agents, hotels, and the tourist police.

What to See & Do

EXPLORING AEGINA TOWN

Aegina town's neoclassical buildings date from its brief stint as the first capital of newly independent Greece (1826–28). Most people's first impression of this harbor town, though, is of fishing boats and the small cargo vessels that ply back and forth to the mainland. Have a snack at one of the little restaurants in the **fish market** (follow your nose!) just off the harbor. This is where the men who catch your snacks of octopus and fried sprats come to eat their catches. The food is usually much better here than the food at the harborfront places catering to tourists.

If you take a horse-drawn carriage or wander the streets back from the port, you'll spot neoclassical buildings, including the **Markelos Tower,** home of the island cultural center, where there are sometimes exhibits. The Cathedral of **Ayios Demetrios,** with its square bell towers, is nearby. Carriage ride prices fluctuate wildly, but are usually between 15€ and 25€. In 1827, the first government of independent Greece held sessions both in the tower and at the cathedral. Fans of Nikos Kazantzakis may want to take a cab to **Livadi,** just north of town, to see the house where he lived when he wrote *Zorba the Greek.* North of the harbor, behind the town beach, and sometimes visible from boats entering the harbor, is the lone worn Doric column that marks the site of the **Temple of Apollo** (known locally as Kolona), open Tuesday through Sunday from 8:30am to 3pm. The view here is nice, the ruins very ruined. The small museum (© **22970/22-637**) has finds from the site, notably pottery; it's open Tuesday through Sunday 8:30am to 3pm; combined admission is 3€.

About 4.8km (3 miles) out of Aegina town, the ruins of **Paleohora,** capital of the island from the 9th to the 19th centuries, sprawl over a steep hillside. During the centuries when pirate raids threatened seaside towns, the people of Aegina sensibly chose to live inland. Like the much larger "ghost town" of Mistra in the Peloponnese (p. 266), this is a wonderful spot to explore (be sure to wear sturdy shoes and a sun hat). You'll see ruined houses and a number of carefully preserved churches, and have fine views over the island. The bus to the beach resort of Ayia Marina makes a stop in Paleohora. If you come here, allow several hours for the excursion.

Lovers of wildlife will want to visit the **Wildlife Center and Hospital (www.ekpaz.gr)** in Pachia Rachi. The center is open daily from 9:30am to 7pm and cares for injured and abandoned birds and animals. The Wildlife Center welcomes volunteers as well as visitors.

If you're here in August, you can take some of the 20 or so concerts given by the **Aegina Music Festival** (© **698/131-9332**); offerings vary from classical to casual and take place by the Temple of Aphaia, in churches, and on beaches. If you show up in September, you can celebrate Aegina and Greece's most famous nut, the **pistachio** *(fistiki),* which has its own festival (**www.aeginafistikifest.gr**), usually held on a mid-September weekend.

SEEING THE TEMPLE OF APHAIA ★★

The 5th-century-B.C. **Temple of Aphaia,** on a pine-covered hill 12km (7½ miles) east of Aegina town (© **22970/32-398**), is one of the best-preserved and most handsome Greek temples. No one really knows who Aphaia was, although it seems that she was a very old, even prehistoric, goddess who eventually became associated

A Swim & a Snack

There's a small beach in the seaside village of **Perdika** (served by bus from Aegina town). This is also a good place to have a meal by the sea; **Antonis** (✆ **22970/61-443**) is the best-known and priciest place, but there are lots of other appealing (and cheaper) places nearby. If you visit Aegina with children, you may want to head to **Faros** (also served by bus from Aegina town) to the **Aegina Water Park** (✆ **22970/22-540**). There are pools, water slides, snack bars, and lots of overexcited children; on hot days, this is a popular destination for Athenian families.

both with Artemis and Athena. According to some legends, Aphaia lived on Crete, where King Minos, usually preoccupied with his labyrinth and Minotaur, fell in love with her. When she fled Crete, he pursued her, and she finally threw herself into the sea off Aegina to escape him. At some point in the late 6th or early 5th century B.C., this temple was built, on the site of earlier shrines, to honor Aphaia.

Thanks to the work of restorers, 25 of the original 32 Doric columns still stand. The pedimental sculpture, showing scenes from the Trojan War, was carted off in 1812 by King Ludwig of Bavaria. Whatever you think about the removal of art treasures from their original homes, Ludwig probably did us a favor by taking the sculptures to the Glyptothek in Munich: While he was doing this, locals were busily burning much of the temple to make lime and hacking up other bits to use in building their homes. Admission to the site is 4€; it's open Monday through Friday from 8:30am to 7pm, Saturday and Sunday from 8:30am to 3pm. Allow at least 4 hours for your visit, if you come here by the hourly bus from Aegina town; by taxi, you might do a visit in a couple of hours.

Where to Stay

In addition to the places mentioned below, you might consider two other appealing hotels in Aegina town: the **Hotel Brown** (www.hotelbrown.gr; ✆ **22970/22-271**), overlooks a sandy beach and is a short walk from the center of town. The stone building is a former sponge factory, converted into a hotel in 1959, and most recently updated in 2008. This stylish 28-room hotel has sea views from front rooms in the main building, its own restaurant, and a cluster of bungalow-like units in its garden; doubles from 75€. If you want a suite with a kitchenette, try the 11-unit **Rastoni** (www.rastoni.gr; ✆ **22970/270-39**), a 5- to 10-minute hike from the harbor, which has a lovely garden and sea views; many rooms have balconies (from 80€). All these places often have special offers, especially off-season and for long stays.

Eginitiko Archontiko ★★　This mansion near the cathedral, 60m (200 ft.) from the harbor, was built in the 1700s, expanded in the 1800s, and later renovations have preserved much original detail, including some walls and ceilings with paintings; the suite is charming. The small guest rooms are traditionally furnished, comfortable, and quiet (although motorcycle noise can be intrusive). The pleasant downstairs lobby retains much 19th-century charm, and the glassed-in sunroom is a delight. The owners care about this handsome building and make guests comfortable. This is not the place to stay if you want lots of modern conveniences; it is the place to stay if you want to imagine life 100 or so years ago in an elegant island townhouse. I would love to stay here in the winter, and just soak up the atmosphere.

Ag. Nikolaou and 1 Eakou, 18010 Aegina. www.lodgings.gr. ☏ **22970/24-968.** 12 units. 70€–90€ double; 120€ 2-room suite. AE, MC, V. **Amenities:** Breakfast room; communal kitchen; garden; sun room. *In room:* A/C.

Hotel Apollo ★ ☺   Large resort hotels are not my cup of tea and the resort of Ayia Marina leaves me cold. That said, friends with small children who stayed at this beach hotel were pleased with the large bathrooms and simple bedrooms, most with balconies. In short, if you're traveling with the kids, consider this place.

Ayia Marina, 18010 Aegina. www.apollohotel.gr. ☏ **22970/32-271.** 107 units. 100€–150€ double. Compulsory breakfast buffet 10€. Daily and weekly meal plans available. AE, DC, MC, V. Closed Nov–Mar. **Amenities:** Restaurant; bar; fresh- and saltwater pools; tennis; Wi-Fi. *In room:* A/C, TV, hair dryer, minifridge.

Where to Eat

Remember that fish is priced by the kilogram at most restaurants. The price varies from catch to catch, so it's a good idea to ask before you order. One place where the fish is always fresh is **Antonis** (☏ **22970/61-443**), harborside in Perdika. In Ayia Marina, **Kyriakakis** (☏ **22970/32-165**) has been packing them in since the 1950s; the fish is fresh, the veggie dishes tasty, and the french fries still homemade. If you don't mind being away from the fish and the sea, try **Vatsoula** (☏ **22970/22-711**) in Aegina town; any local can direct you there. Call ahead, as this place with the pleasant garden and tasty *spitiko* (home) cooking keeps idiosyncratic hours.

Maridaki ★ GREEK   This lively portside spot offers a wide selection of fish, grilled octopus, and the usual taverna fare of souvlaki and moussaka. The *mezedes* are usually very good, and you can make an entire meal of them. Come on a quiet evening, and you will have the sense of going back in time to an earlier Greece.

Demokratias. ☏ **22970/25-869.** Main courses 8€–20€; seafood priced by the kilo. DC, MC. Daily 8am–midnight.

Mezedopoleio To Steki ★★ MEZEDES   Locals and Athenians head to this little place by the fish market for its delicious *mezedes,* including succulent grilled octopus. You can make a meal of them here. If you eat as the Greeks do, wash it all down with ouzo. (If you're not used to ouzo, wash the ouzo down with lots of water.)

45 Pan Irioti. ☏ **22970/23-910.** *Mezedes* 6€–15€. No credit cards. Daily 8am–midnight.

Aegina After Dark

At sunset, the harbor scene gets livelier as everyone comes out for an evening *volta* (stroll). As always, this year's hot spot may be closed by the next season. As no one answers the phones at these places, we do not list phones. In Aegina town, **Avli** and **Perdikiotika,** in another one of Aegina's 19th-century houses, are durable favorites. On summer weekends, **En Egina** and **Kyvrenio** have live music and occasional traditional *rembetika* music—often from around midnight till dawn. On summer weekends, **Armida,** a bar/restaurant in a converted caique moored at the harbor, is open from breakfast until, well, breakfast. There are also several outdoor cinemas in town, including the **Olympia** and the **Faneromeni.** Young bloods and yachties rub shoulders after dark at the **Muzik Bar Café** on the Perdika beach. If you want some late-night ouzo and octopus in Aegina town, try **Tsias** or **Pelaisos** by the fish market.

POROS

55km (31 nautical miles) SW of Piraeus

Poros shares the gentle, rolling landscape of the adjacent Peloponnesian coastline, and has several good beaches, some decent tavernas, and lively summer nightlife. If that sounds like lukewarm praise, it may be. For me, Poros lacks the sense of being a world unto itself that makes most Greek islands so delicious to visit. And, in July and August, the island virtually sinks under the weight of day-trippers and tour groups.

As someone once said, "geography is destiny." Poros (the word means "straits" or "ford") is separated from the Peloponnese by a narrow channel only 370m (1,214 ft.). It's so easy to reach from the mainland that weekending Athenians and many tourists flock here each summer. A car ferry across the straits from Galatas to Poros town leaves about every 20 minutes in summer, which means there are a *lot* of cars here.

Technically, Poros is separated by a narrow canal into two islands: little **Sferia,** where Poros town is, and larger **Kalavria,** where everything else is. If you wish, you can use Poros as a base for visiting the nearby attractions on the mainland, including Epidaurus, ancient Troezen (modern Trizina), and the lemon groves of Limonodassos. In a long day trip, you can visit Nafplion (Nafplio) and Epidauros, in a very long day trip, you could also see Mycenae and Tiryns.

Essentials

GETTING THERE   Daily hydrofoil and ferry service to Poros and other Saronic Gulf islands is offered by **Hellenic Seaways** (© 210/419-9200; www.hellenicsea ways.gr). **Saronikos Ferries** (© 210/417/1190) takes passengers and cars to Aegina, Poros, and Spetses; cars are not allowed to disembark on Hydra. **Euroseas** (© 210/411-3108) has speedy catamaran service from Piraeus to Poros, Hydra, and Spetses. For information on schedules for most Argo-Saronic ferries, you can try one of the various numbers of the **Piraeus Port Authority** (© 210/422-6000, 210/410-1480, or 210/410-1441), but phones are not always answered. On Poros, try © 22980/22-274, www.greeka.com/saronic/poros; also, **www.openseas.gr** is a useful site for ferry schedules as is www.gtp.gr.

The other Saronic Gulf islands are easy to reach from Poros. In summer **Marinos Tours** (© 22980/22-297) offers excursions to Saronic and Cycladic islands.

VISITOR INFORMATION   The waterfront hotels are generally too noisy, so if you want to stay in town, we suggest you check with **Marinos Tours** (© 22980/22-297), which handles several hundred rooms and apartments, as well as many island hotels. We've had good reports of **Saronic Gulf Travel** (© 22980/24-555; www. saronicgulftravel.gr), which usually has an excellent free map of the island. To learn more about Poros, look for Niki Stavrolakes's enduring classic, *Poros* (Lycabettus Press), for sale on the island. The websites **www.poros.com.gr** and **www.greeka. com/saronic/poros** have information in Greek and English.

GETTING AROUND   You can walk anywhere in Poros town. The island's **bus** can take you to the beaches or to the **Monastery of the Zoodhochou Pigis** and the remains of the **Temple of Poseidon;** the conductor will charge you according to your destination. The **taxi station** is near the hydrofoil dock, or you can call for one at © 22980/23-003; the fare to or from the Askeli beach should cost about 14€. **Kostas Bikes** (© 22980/23-565), opposite the Galas ferry pier, rents bicycles for about 12€ per day, and mopeds from about 20€ per day, except on summer weekends, when the sky is the limit.

FAST FACTS   The **National Bank of Greece** is one of a handful of waterfront banks with an ATM where you can also exchange money. The **police** (© 22980/22-256) and **tourist police** (© 22980/22-462) are on the *paralia* (harbor). The **port authority** (© 22980/22-274) is on the harborfront. For **first aid**, call © 22980/22-254. The **post office** and **telephone office (OTE)** are also on the waterfront; their hours are Monday through Friday from 8am to 2pm. In summer, in addition to normal weekday hours, the OTE is open Sunday 8am to 1pm and 5 to 10pm. **Dionysus Internet Café** and **Kentrou Typou** (also a newsdealer with foreign newspapers) are both on the harborfront and offer Internet service for about 8€ per hour.

What to See & Do
ATTRACTIONS IN POROS TOWN

As you make the crossing, you'll see the streets of the island's capital, Poros town, which sprawls up a hill topped with a clock tower. The church of **Agios Yeoryios** (St. George) is well worth having a look at: the frescoes were created by a famous 20th-century Greek painter, Constantine Parthenis. As you wander, you'll realize that what you've read is true: Poros town is itself an island, joined to the rest of Poros by a causeway. The narrow streets along the harbor are usually crowded with visitors inching up and down past the restaurants, cafes, and shops. At night, the adjacent hills are, indeed, alive with the sound of music; the "Greek" music is often heavily amplified American rap.

Poros town has a **Naval Cadets' Training School**—which means that a lot of young men are looking for company here. Anyone wishing to avoid their attention should visit the small **Archaeological Museum** (© 22980/23-276), with finds from ancient Troezen. It's usually open daily from 9am to 3pm; admission is free. Lovers of seashells may want to visit the Public Library, where the Poros Shell Museum (©22980/22-936; www.poroshellmuseum.gr) is housed and may be visited Mon–Fri 9am–1pm and 5–8pm; no charge at present.

EXPLORING THE ISLAND

By car or moped, it's easy to make a circuit of the island in half a day. What remains of the 6th-century B.C. **Temple of Poseidon** is scattered beneath pine trees on the low plateau of Palatia, east of Poros town. The site is usually open dawn to dusk; admission is free. The ruins are scant, largely because the inhabitants of the nearby island of Hydra hauled away most of the marble to build their Monastery of the Virgin.

The Temple of Poseidon was the scene of a famous moment in Greek history in 322 B.C., when Demosthenes, the Athenian 4th-century orator and statesman, fled here for sanctuary from Athens's Macedonian enemies. When his enemies tracked him down, the great speechwriter asked for time to write a last letter—and then bit off his pen nib, which contained poison. Even in his death agonies, Demosthenes had the presence of mind to leave the temple, lest his death defile the sanctuary. It seems fitting that Demosthenes, who lived by his pen, died by the same instrument.

Those who enjoy monasteries can continue on the road that winds through the island's interior to the 18th-century **Monastery of the Zoodhochou Pigis (Monastery of the Life-Giving Spring),** south of Poros town. There are usually no monks in residence, but the caretaker should let you in from about 9am to 2pm and from 4 to 7pm. It's appropriate to leave a small donation. There's a little taverna nearby.

Poros's beaches are not enchanting. The beach easiest to visit after seeing the temple of Poseidon is Vagonia, one of the nicer ones. **Love Bay** and Monastiriou both have shade from pine trees and small restaurants. Both the sea and beach at **Megalo Neorio,** northwest of town, are sometimes polluted. Neorio has a string of places renting personal watercraft, water skis, and windsurfing equipment.

As you take in Poros, when you look out to sea, you may well see some of the naval cadets practicing rowing. The cadets have produced a number of world-class rowing teams, and you will often see them practicing close to shore.

A FESTIVAL, OLD TROEZEN & LEMON GROVES

If you're in Poros in mid-June, you might want to catch the ferry across to Galatas and take in the annual **Flower Festival,** with its floral displays and parades of floats and marching bands. (Lots of posters in Poros town advertise the festival.)

From Galatas, you can catch a bus the 8km (5 miles) west to **Trizina** (ancient Troezen), birthplace of the great Athenian hero Theseus. It's also where his wife, Phaedra, tragically fell in love with her stepson, Hippolytus. When the dust settled, both she and Hippolytus were dead and Theseus was bereft. There are the remains of a temple to Asclepius here—but again, these ruins are in bad shape.

About 4km (2½ miles) south of Galatas near the beach of Aliki, you'll find the olfactory wonder of **Limonodassos (Lemon Grove),** where more than 25,000 lemon trees fill the air with their fragrance each spring. Alas, many have been harmed by storms over the last decade or so, and the very hot summers in recent years damaged more. Some trees have survived, and more have been planted. Several cafes nearby serve freshly squeezed lemonade. When the trees aren't in bloom, there's not much point in visiting here!

Where to Stay

There are many places to stay on Poros; we suggest two appealing choices in Poros town. If you are interested in a longer stay, check out the **Villa Tryfon** (www.poros. com.gr/tryfon-villa; © **22980-25854**), which has six simply furnished apartment-like units up the hill, away from the harbor (but with great views down to the harbor), just off Plateia Georgiou; open year-round, prices by request.

Seven Brothers Hotel ★★ This small hotel with the handsome neoclassical facade was built in 1901 and converted into a hotel some 20 years ago. The simple, cheerful, and comfortable rooms have balconies, the hospitality is old-fashioned, and the tips on what to see and do are up to date. An excellent choice, it was charming when I first stayed there a number of years ago and is still charming today. This is not a full-service hotel, but the owners take care of you very well.

18020 Poros Island. www.7brothers.gr. © **22980/23-412.** 16 units. 80€ double. DC, V. **Amenities:** Breakfast. *In room:* A/C.

Sto Roloi ★★ Sto Roli is a 2-century-old town house well out of the hustle and bustle of the harbor, near the island's famous *roloi* (clock tower). The owner rents the building as two suites: a garden apartment and a terrace apartment. A separate garden studio is also available. Many of the original details of the building (tiles, woodwork) have been preserved, and a serious attempt has been made to furnish Sto Roloi with appropriate island furniture. This would be a good place to spend a week; you can take advantage of the substantial price reduction for a week's stay, watch performances at Epidaurus, tour the eastern Peloponnese, or simply relax (several units have a Jacuzzi). The owners will arrange caique excursions for guests and will help watersports enthusiasts hook up with Passage Watersports. In addition to the original three units in Sto Roloi they now have **Anenpone House** (with pool) and **Little Tower** and two nearby villas, with a shared pool (prices on request).

13 Karra, 18020 Poros, Trizinias. www.sto-roloi-poros.gr. ℂ **22980/25-808.** 16 units. 80€ studio; 150€ garden apt.; 180€ terrace apt. No credit cards. **Amenities:** Breakfast room; bar. *In room:* A/C, TV, mini-fridge, hair dryer, Wi-Fi.

Where to Eat

If you're willing to give up your view of the harbor, head into town, a bit uphill, and try one of the restaurants near the church of Ayios Yeorgios, such as **Platanos, Dimitris, Karavolos,** or **Kipos.** These places tend to draw a more Greek crowd than the harborside spots. Fish is usually priced by the kilogram; ask for prices before you order.

Caravella Restaurant GREEK   This portside taverna prides itself on serving organic homegrown vegetables and local (not frozen) fish. Specialties include traditional dishes such as snails, veal *stifado,* moussaka, souvlaki, and stuffed eggplant, as well as seafood and lobster.

Paralia, Poros town. ℂ **22980/23-666.** Main courses 8€–18€. AE, MC, V. Daily 11am–1am.

Taverna Grill Oasis ★ GREEK   This taverna has been here since the mid-1960s. Its harborside location, with indoor and outdoor tables, excellent fresh fish, and a cheerful staff, make it live up to its name as a pleasant oasis for lunch or dinner. One not-so-traditional item on the mènu: pasta with lobster.

Paralia, Poros town. ℂ **22980/22-955.** Main courses 8€–19€; seafood priced by the kilo. No credit cards. Daily 11am–midnight.

POROS AFTER DARK

There's endless evening entertainment in Poros town, including serious people-watching strolls up and down the harbor, past the solid bar/disco/restaurant territory. As always, this year's hot spot may be closed by the next season. As no one answers the phones at these places, we do not list phones. In town, **Symbosio** often has live bouzouki (stringed music instrument, resembling a mandolin), and **Cine Diana Café** has elaborate cocktails, background music, and views over the harbor. If you want to dance, try **Lithos, Orion,** in town, and **Poseidon,** about 2km (1¼ miles) out of town; all are popular discos. **Petros** at Megalo Neorio beach often has live Greek music late at night—or early in the morning, depending on your point of view!

HYDRA (IDRA)

65km (35 nautical miles) S of Piraeus

Hydra is one of a handful of places in Greece that seemingly can't be spoiled. Along with Mykonos, this was one of the first Greek islands to be "discovered" by the beautiful people in the '50s and '60s. Today, there are often more day-trippers here than "beautiful people," although when elegant Athenians flee their stuffy apartments for their Hydriote hideaway each summer, the harborfront turns into an impromptu fashion show. If you can, arrive in the evening, when most of the day visitors have left, and rejoice in the cool of the evening. Whatever you do, be sure to be on the deck of your ship as you arrive, so you can see Hydra's bleak and steep hills suddenly reveal its perfect horseshoe harbor overlooked by the 18th-century clock tower of the Church of the Dormition. This truly is a place where arrival is half the fun. But the best is yet to be when you step ashore.

Let's start with the cars—or, more precisely, their absence. With the exception of a handful of municipal vehicles, there are no cars on Hydra. You'll probably encounter at least one form of local transportation: the donkey. When you see Hydra's splendid 18th- and 19th-century stone *archontika* (mansions) along the waterfront and on the steep streets above, you won't be surprised to learn that the island has been declared a national treasure by the Greek government and the Council of Europe. You'll probably find Hydra town so charming that you'll forgive its one serious flaw: no top-notch beach. Do as the Hydriots do, and swim from the rocks at Spilia and Hydronetta, just beyond the main harbor, or hop on one of the caiques that ply from Hydra town to the relatively quiet island beaches.

Essentials

GETTING THERE   Daily hydrofoil and ferry service to Hydra and other Saronic Gulf islands is offered by **Hellenic Seaways** (*✆* **210/419-9200;** www.hellenic seaways.gr). **Saronikos Ferries** (*✆* **210/417/1190**) takes passengers and cars to Aegina, Poros, and Spetses; cars are not allowed to disembark on Hydra. **Euroseas** (*✆* **210/411-3108**) has speedy catamaran service from Piraeus to Poros, Hydra, and Spetses. For information on schedules for most Argo-Saronic ferries, try one of the numbers of the **Piraeus Port Authority** (*✆* **210/412/4585,** 210/422-6000, or 210/410-1480), but phones are not always answered. On Hydra, try *✆* **22980/52-279; www.openseas.gr** is a useful site for ferry schedules as is **www.gtp.gr**.

Reservations are a must in summer and on holiday weekends. *Tip:* Lots of porters, some with and some without mules, meet the boats. If you have enough luggage to require their services, agree on a price beforehand; be prepared to pay at least 14€.

VISITOR INFORMATION   The free publications *Holidays in Hydra* and *This Summer in Hydra* are widely available and contain much useful information, including maps and lists of rooms to rent; shops and restaurants pay to appear in these publications. **Hydra View,** available in print and online (**www.hydraview.gr**) is another useful resource. **Saitis Tours** (*✆* **22980/52-184**), on the harborfront, can exchange money, provide information on rooms and villas, book excursions, and help you make long-distance calls. For those wanting to pursue Hydra's history, we recommend Catherine Vanderpool's book *Hydra* (Lycabettus Press). You may also want to check **www.greeka.com/saronic/hydra** or **www.hydradirect.com**.

GETTING AROUND   Walking is the only means of getting around on the island, unless you bring or rent a donkey or a bicycle. **Caiques** provide water-taxi service to the island's beaches (Bilsi has extensive watersport facilities) and to the little offshore islands of Dokos, Kivotos, and Petasi, as well as to secluded restaurants in the evening; rates run from around 14€ to outrageously steep amounts, depending on destination, time of day, and whether or not business is slow.

FAST FACTS   The **National Bank of Greece** and **Commercial Bank** are on the harbor; both have ATMs. Travel agents at the harbor will exchange money from about 9am to 8pm, usually at less favorable rates. The small **health clinic** is signposted at the harbor; cases requiring complicated treatment are taken by boat or helicopter to the mainland. The police and tourist **police** (*✆* **22980/52-205**) share quarters on the second floor at 9 Votsi (signposted at the harbor). The **port**

Summer Festivals in Hydra

On a June weekend—often, but not always, the third weekend in June—Hydra celebrates the **Miaoulia,** which honors Hydriot Admiral Miaoulis, who set much of the Turkish fleet on fire in the Battle of Geronta in 1821. The plucky admiral rammed the Turkish fleet with explosives-filled fireboats; casualties on both sides were, understandably, considerable, with more Greek than Turkish ships left afloat. Celebrations include a reenactment of the sinking of a model warship; if you're not on Hydra for the festivities, you may see the fireworks light up the sky from other Saronic islands and the adjacent Peloponnesian mainland. In early July, Hydra has an annual **puppet festival** that in recent years has drawn puppeteers from countries as far away as Togo and Brazil. As these two festivals are not on set dates, check for schedules with the **Greek National Tourist Office (**✆ **210/870-0000;** www.gnto.gr) or the **Hydra tourist police (**✆ **22980/52-205).**

authority (✆ **22980/53-150**) is on the harborside. The **post office** is just off the harborfront on Ikonomou, the street between the two banks. The **telephone office (OTE),** across from the police station on Votsi, is open Monday through Saturday from 7:30am to 10pm, Sunday from 8am to 1pm and 5 to 10pm. For **Internet access,** try HydraNet (✆ **22980/54-150**), signposted by the OTE.

What to See & Do
ATTRACTIONS IN HYDRA TOWN

Why did all those "beautiful people" begin to come to Hydra in the '50s and '60s, and why is the island so popular today? As with the hill towns of Italy, the main attraction here is the architecture and setting of the town itself—and all the chic shops, restaurants, hotels, and bars that have taken up quarters in the handsome old stone buildings. In the 18th and 19th centuries, ships from Hydra transported cargo around the world and made this island very rich indeed. Like ship captains on the American island of Nantucket, Hydra's ship captains demonstrated their wealth by building the fanciest houses money could buy. The captains' lasting legacy: the handsome stone *archontika* (mansions) overlooking the harbor that give Hydra town its distinctive character. If you want to know more about Hydra's history, stop in at the harbor side **Historical Archives and Museum** (✆ **22980/52-355**; admission 4€; daily 9am–3pm and 7–8pm), which has old paintings, carved and painted ship figureheads, and costumes. There are sometimes exhibits of work by local artists in a gallery here.

One *archontiko* that you can hardly miss is the **Tombazi mansion,** which dominates the hill that stands directly across the harbor from the main ferry quay. This is now a branch of the School of Fine Arts, with a hostel for students, and you can usually get a peek inside. Call the mansion (✆ **22980/52-291**) or **Athens Polytechnic** (✆ **210/619-2119**), for information about the program or exhibits.

The nearby **Ikonomou-Miriklis mansion** (also called the **Voulgaris**) is not open to the public, but the hilltop **Koundouriotis mansion,** built by an Albanian family who contributed generously to the cause of independence, is now a house museum. The mansion, with period furnishings and costumes, is usually open from April until October, Tuesday to Sunday 10am to 4pm; 4€. If you wander the side streets this side of the harbor, you will see more handsome houses, some of which are being restored into private homes, while others are being converted into boutique hotels.

Hydra's waterfront is a mixed bag, with a number of ho-hum shops selling little of distinction—and a handful of jewelry shops and elegant clothing boutiques—one bold (or honest) enough to call itself **Spoiled!** (© **22980/52-363;** www.spoiled-shop.gr). Most of the elegant shops are either on side streets off the harbor, or in the area below the Tombazi mansion. Alas, the wobbly global economy has threatened a number of the nicest shops, and you may not find everything still there when you visit. **Elena Votsi (www.elenavotsi.com)** sells her original designs (including a graceful gravity-defying sterling silver clothes hanger for baby's first designer outfit) here and at her shop in Athens's Kolonaki district. **Hermes Art Shop** (© **22980/52-689**) has a wide array of jewelry, some good antique reproductions, and a few interesting textiles. **Domna Needlepoint** (© **22980/52-959**) has engaging needlepoint rugs and cushion covers, with Greek motifs of dolphins, birds, and flowers. **Vangelis Rafalias's Pharmacy** is a lovely place to stop in, even if you don't need anything, just to see the jars of remedies from the 19th century.

When you've finished with the waterfront, walk uphill on Iconomou (it's steep) to browse in more shops. **Meltemi** (© **22980/54-138**) sells original jewelry (including gorgeous earrings) and ceramics. Just about everything is borderline irresistible—especially the winsome blue ceramic fish. Across from Meltemi, **Emporium** (no phone) shows and sells works by Hydriot and other artists. If you want to take home a painting or a wood or ceramic model of an island boat, try here.

Hydra boasts that it has 365 churches, one for every day of the year. The most impressive, the mid-18th-century **Monastery of the Dormition of the Virgin Mary (E Kimisis tis Panagias)** is by the clock tower on the harborfront. This is the monastery built of the marble blocks hacked out of the (until then) well-preserved Temple of Poseidon on the island of Poros. The buildings here no longer function as a monastery, and the cells are now municipal offices. The church has rather undistinguished 19th-century frescoes, but the 18th-century marble *iconostasis* (altar screen) is terrific. Like the marble from Poros, this altar screen was "borrowed" from another church and brought here. Seeing it is well worth the suggested donation.

A MONASTERY, A CONVENT & BEACHES

If you want to take a vigorous uphill walk (with no shade), head up Miaouli past Kala Pigadia (Good Wells), still the town's best local source of water. A walk of an hour or two, depending on your pace, will bring you to the **Convent of Ayia Efpraxia** and **Monastery of the Prophet Elijah (Profitis Elias).** Both have superb views, both are still active, and the nuns sell their hand-woven fabrics. (**Note:** Both nuns and monks observe the midday siesta from 1–5pm. Dress appropriately—no shorts or tank tops.)

Unfortunately, most of Hydra's best **beach,** at **Mandraki,** a 20-minute walk east of town, is the private preserve of the Miramare Hotel. If you're on Hydra briefly, your best bet is to swim off the rocks just west of Hydra town at **Spilia** or **Hydronetta,** or head out to sandier (and fashionable) **Kaminia.** Still farther west are the pine-lined coves of **Molos, Palamida,** and **Bisti** (all three as sandy as it gets on Hydra), best reached by water taxi from the main harbor. The **Kallianos Dive Center** (**www. kallianosdivingcenter.gr**) offers PADI scuba lessons and excursions off Kapari island, near Hydra.

The island of **Dokos,** northwest off the tip of Hydra, an hour's boat ride from town, has a good beach and excellent diving conditions; it was here that Jacques Cousteau found a sunken ship with cargo still aboard, believed to be 3,000 years old. You may want to take a picnic with you, as the taverna here keeps unpredictable hours.

Where to Stay

Hydra has a number of small, charming hotels in restored 19th-century buildings. In addition to the following choices, you might try the 19-unit **Hotel Greco,** Kouloura (© **22980/53-200;** fax 22980/53-511), in a former fishing-net factory in a quiet neighborhood; the 20-unit **Misral Hotel** (© **22980/52-509**), a restored island home off the harbor; or the 27-unit **Hotel Leto** (www.letohydra.gr; © **22980/53-385**), which is airy and bright, with large bedrooms, a garden courtyard, and one wheelchair-accessible room. If you're traveling with friends, you might investigate the **Kiafa,** once a 19th-century sea captain's mansion, now a boutique hotel with a pool, in the Historic Hotels of Europe group, that rents to groups of up to nine people (www.yadeshotels.gr; © **210/364-0441**). In season, doubles start from 75€, with prices considerably higher on weekends and in August.

Hotel Angelica ★   The whitewashed Angelica complex, just off the main island road and just outside Hydra town, continues to expand its cluster of red tile–roofed buildings, offering accommodations ranging from the very nice ("Standard" VIP doubles and an apartment) to the luxurious ("Superior" VIP rooms and a villa, which share a pool). Almost all the rooms have high ceilings and a balcony or terrace, with rooms in the pension annex more simply furnished than the VIP units. If you stay here, try to splurge on the VIP quarters so that you are not tormented by the sounds of other guests splashing in that pool, while you stand under your shower or sink into your Jacuzzi to cool down. The breakfast buffet is highly praised.

42 Miaouli, 18040 Hydra. www.angelica.gr. © **22980/53-264.** 21 units. 140€–200€ double; villa from 300€. MC, V. **Amenities:** Breakfast room; VIP pool; garden. *In room:* A/C, TV, fridge, Wi-Fi.

Hotel Bratsera ★   The Bratsera, in a restored 1860s sponge factory that's a short stroll from the harbor, keeps turning up on everyone's list of the best hotels in Greece; this is a telling comment on the state of most Greek hotels. Throughout, there's lots of wood and stone, many Hydriot touches (paintings, engravings, ceramics), and units with antique four-poster beds. The small pool, with wisteria-covered trellises, is attractive; breakfast and meals are often served poolside in fair weather. We've had reports that room-service trays left in the hall after breakfast were not collected by dinnertime, and I know from personal experience that messages left for guests aren't always delivered—nor does staff express any surprise when this is brought to their attention. Still, many readers report having leaving here hoping they will be back soon. In short, for some the Bratsera produces memories of a relaxing stay in an charming hotel with a welcome pool and central Hydra town location; for others, cavalier service is their most lasting memory.

Tombazi, 18040 Hydra. www.bratserahotel.com. © **22980/53-971.** Fax 22980/53-626. 253 units. 165€–220€ double; from 280€ suite. Rates include breakfast. AE, DC, MC, V. Closed mid-Jan to mid-Feb. **Amenities:** Restaurant; bar; pool. *In room:* A/C, hair dryer, minibar, Wi-Fi.

Hotel Hydra ★★ ✆   This is one of the best bargains in town—if you don't mind the steep walk up to the beautifully restored two-story, gray-stone mansion on the western cliff, to the right as you get off the ferry. The guest rooms have high ceilings and are simply furnished; many have balconies overlooking the town and harbor.

8 Voulgari, 18040 Hydra. www.hydrahote.gr. ✆ **22980/52-102.** Fax 22980/53-330. 12 units, 8 with bathroom. 130€ double without view, from 160€ double with view. MC, V. **Amenities:** Breakfast room. *In room:* A/C. TV, hair dryer, Wi-Fi.

Hotel Miranda ★★   Once, when we were trapped for the night on Hydra by bad weather, we were lucky enough to get the last guest room at the Miranda. The unit was small, with a tiny bathroom and no real view—so it's a tribute to this hotel that we have wonderful memories. Most of the guest rooms are decent size, with nice views of the town and the Miranda's lovely garden courtyard (where breakfast is often served). The 1820 captain's mansion is decorated throughout with Oriental rugs, antique cabinets, wooden chests, marble tables, contemporary paintings, and period naval engravings. There's even a small art gallery—in short, this is a classy place. We're distressed and, frankly, surprised, at a recent report of indifferent service; let us know how you find things.

Miaouli, 18040 Hydra. www.mirandahotel.gr ✆ **22980/52-230.** Fax 22980/53 510. 14 units. 150€-225€ double. AE, V. Closed Nov-Feb. **Amenities:** Breakfast room. *In room:* A/C, TV, hair dryer, minibar, Wi-Fi.

Where to Eat

The harborside eateries are expensive and mostly not very good, although the views are such that you may not care. The cost of fish, priced by the kilogram at most restaurants, varies from catch to catch, so ask the price before you order. Two longtime favorites off the harbor are still going strong: **Manolis** (✆ **22890/29-631**) and **Kyria Sophia** (✆ **22980/53-097**), both with lots of vegetable dishes, as well as stews and grills. Kyria Sophia's is tiny, so it's vital to try to book a table. A number of cafes also lie along the waterfront, including **To Roloi (The Clock),** by the clock tower. **Omilos** (✆ **22980/53-800**), by Hydra town's rocky bathing spot, Hydronetta, has terrific salads, with a wide variety of hard-to-find greens and inventive dressings. Out on Kamini beach, **Castello** (✆ **22980/54-101**; www.castellohydra.gr) is open from early to late, serving snacks and full meals to elegantly casual young Athenians who like the mushroom-stuffed hamburgers and foreigners who toy with *mezedes* and Greek salads; there's a resident DJ, a master bartender (apple and pear martinis, anyone?), great views over the sea for sunset—or sunrise.

Marina's Taverna ★ GREEK   Several readers report that they have enjoyed both the food and the spectacular sunset at this seaside taverna, appropriately nicknamed Iliovasilema ("Sunset"). Perched on the rocks west of town, it's a 12€ water-taxi ride from town. The menu is basic, but the food is fresh and carefully prepared by Marina; her *klefltiko* (pork pie), an island specialty, is renowned.

Vlihos. ✆ **22980/52-496.** Main courses 10€-15€. No credit cards. Daily noon-11pm.

To Steki 🍴 GREEK   This taverna, a few blocks up from the quay end of the harbor, has simple food and reasonable prices. Inside, there are framed murals showing a rather idealized traditional island life. The specials, such as moussaka and stuffed tomatoes, come with salad, vegetables, and dessert. The fish soup is memorable.

Miaouli. ✆ **22980/53-517.** Main courses 7€-18€; daily specials 8€-15€; seafood priced by the kilo. No credit cards. Daily noon-3pm and 7-11pm.

Hydra After Dark

Hydra has an energetic nightlife, with restaurants, bars, and discos going full steam ahead in summer. In theory, bars close at 2am. As always, this year's hot spot may be closed by the next season. Portside, there are plenty of bars. As no one answers the phones at these places, we do not list phones. **The Pirate,** near the clock tower, is one of the longest living (since the 1970s) and loudest. **Veranda** (up from the west end of the harbor, near the Hotel Hydra) is a wonderful place to escape the full frenzy of the Hydra harbor scene, sip a glass of wine, and watch the sunset. **Hydronetta** tends to play more Western than Greek music—although the music at all these places is so loud that it's hard to be sure. Friends report enjoying drinks at the **Amalour,** just off the harbor, where they were surrounded by hip, black-clad 30-somethings and listened to jazz, rap, and vintage heavy metal. There are still a few local haunts left around the harbor; you'll be able to recognize them easily. You'll also easily spot the **Saronicos;** If you don't hear the music, just look for the fishing boat outside the front door.

SPETSES ★★

98km (53 nautical miles) SW of Piraeus; 3km (2 nautical miles) from Ermioni

Here's one real plus for visitors to Spetses: Cars are not allowed to circulate freely in Spetses town. This would make for admirable tranquillity if motorcycles were not increasingly endemic. Now, a closer look at the island.

Despite a series of dreadful forest fires, Spetses's pine groves still make this the greenest of the Saronic Gulf islands. Even in antiquity, this island was called Pityoussa (Pine-Tree Island). Over the centuries, many of Spetses's pine trees became the masts and hulls of the island's successive fleets of fishing, commercial, and military vessels. In time, Spetses was almost as deforested as its rocky neighbor Hydra is to this day.

In the early 20th century, local philanthropist Sotiris Anargyros bought up more than half the island and replanted barren slopes with pine trees. Anargyros also built himself one of the island's most ostentatious mansions, flanked by palm trees, which you can see off Spetses's main harbor, the Dapia. Amargyros also built the harborfront Hotel Poseidon to jump-start upper-class tourism. Then he built Anargyros College (modeled on England's famous Eton College) to give the island a first-class prep school; John Knowles taught here in the early 1950s and set his cult novel *The Magus* on Spetses.

Today, Spetses's pine groves and architecture are its greatest treasures: The island has an unusual number of handsome *archontika* built in the 19th and 20th centuries by wealthy residents, many of them shipping magnates, some now owned by their descendants or by well-heeled Athenians. Many Spetses homes have lush gardens and pebble mosaic courtyards; if you're lucky, you'll catch a glimpse of some when garden gates are ajar. Like Andros, another island beloved of wealthy Athenians, Spetses communicates a sense that there's a world of privilege that exists undisturbed by the rough and tumble of tourism, which—let's not mince words—means you and me.

Fortunately for attentive visitors, a number of Spetses's dignified villas have been converted into appealing small hotels, mostly based at Ayia Marina.

Essentials

GETTING THERE Daily hydrofoil and ferry service to Spetses and other Saronic Gulf islands is offered by **Hellenic Seaways** (© 210/419-9200; www.hellenicseaways.gr). **Saronikos Ferries** (© 210/417-1190) takes passengers and cars to Aegina, Poros, and Spetses; cars are not allowed to disembark on Hydra. **Euroseas**

(✆ 210/411-3108) has speedy catamaran service from Piraeus to Poros, Hydra, and Spetses. For information on schedules, you can try one of the various numbers of the **Piraeus Port Authority** (✆ **210/412-4585,** 210/422-6000, or 210/410-1480), but phones are not always answered. On Spetses, try ✆ **22980/72-245; www.open seas.gr** is a useful site for ferry schedules as is **www.gtp.gr.**

VISITOR INFORMATION The island's travel agencies include **Alasia Travel** (✆ **22980/74-098**) and **Spetses & Takis Travel** (✆ **22980/72-215**). Andrew Thomas's *Spetses* (Lycabettus Press), usually on sale on the island, is the book to get if you want to pursue Spetses's history. You can also check out **www.greeka.com/ saronic/spetses** and the helpful **www.spetsesdirect.com.**

GETTING AROUND The island's limited public transportation consists of several municipal **buses** and a handful of **taxis.** Motorcycle and moped agents are required to, but do not always, ask for proof that you are licensed to drive such vehicles and give you a helmet. Be sure to check the tires and brakes; mopeds start at 15€ a day, motorcycles start at 20€—except on summer weekends, when the sky is the limit. **Bikes** are also widely available, and the terrain along the road around the island makes them a good means of transportation; three-speed bikes cost about 12€ per day, while newer 21-speed models go for about 15€. **Horse-drawn carriages** can take you from the busy port into the quieter back streets, where most of the island's handsome old mansions are located. Take your time choosing a driver; some are friendly and informative, others are surly. Fares are highly negotiable.

The best way to get to the various beaches around the island is by **water taxi.** Locals call it a *venzina* (gasoline); each little boat holds about 8 to 10 people. Here, too, fares are negotiable. A tour around the island costs about 50€. Schedules are posted on the pier. You can also hire a water taxi to take you anywhere on the island, to another island, or to the mainland. Again, prices are highly negotiable.

FAST FACTS The **National Bank of Greece** is one of several banks on the harbor with an ATM. Most travel agencies (9am–8pm) will also exchange money, usually at less favorable rates than banks. The local health **clinic** (✆ **22980/72-201**) is inland from the east side of the port. The **police** (✆ **22980/73-100**) and **tourist police** (✆ **22980/73-744**) are to the left off the Dapia pier, where the hydrofoils dock, on Boattassi. The **port authority** (✆ **22980/72-245**) is on the harborfront. The **post office** is on Boattassi near the police station; it's open from 8am to 2pm Monday to Friday. The **telephone office (OTE),** open Monday to Friday from 7:30am to 3pm, is to the right off the Dapia pier, behind Hotel Soleil. **Internet access** is available at Delphina Net-Café on the harborfront for 5€ an hour.

What to See & Do

EXPLORING SPETSES TOWN (KASTELLI)

Spetses town (aka Kastelli) meanders along the harbor and inland in a lazy fashion, with most of its neoclassical mansions partly hidden from envious eyes by high walls and greenery. Much of the town's street life takes place on the main square, the **Dapia,** the name also given to the harbor where the ferries and hydrofoils now arrive. The massive bulk of the 19th-century Poseidon Hotel dominates the west end of the harbor. The Old Harbor, **Baltiza,** largely silted up, lies just east of town, before the popular swimming spots at **Ayia Marina.**

If you sit at a cafe on the Dapia, you'll eventually see pretty much everyone in town—who wants to be seen—passing by. The handsome black-and-white pebble mosaic commemorates the moment during the War of Independence when the first flag, with the motto "Freedom or Death," was raised. Thanks to its large fleet, Spetses played an important part in the War of Independence, routing the Turks in the Straits of Spetses on September 8, 1822. The victory is commemorated every year on the weekend closest to **September 8,** with celebrations, church services, and the burning of a ship that symbolizes the defeated Turkish fleet.

As you stroll along the waterfront, you'll notice the monumental bronze statue of a woman, her left arm shielding her eyes as she looks out to sea. The statue honors one of the greatest heroes of the War of Independence, **Laskarina Bouboulina,** the daughter of a naval captain from Hydra. Bouboulina financed the warship *Agamemnon,* oversaw its construction, served as its captain, and was responsible for several naval victories. She was said to be able to drink any man under the table, and strait-laced citizens sniped that she was so ugly, the only way she could keep a lover was with a gun. You can see where Bouboulina lived when she was ashore by visiting **Laskarina Bouboulina House** (© **22980/72-077;** www.bouboulinamuseum-spetses.gr), in Pefkakia, just off the port. It keeps flexible hours (posted on the house), but is usually open mornings and afternoons from Easter until October. An English-speaking guide often gives a half-hour tour. Admission is 5€. If the **Spetses Mexis Museum** (© **22980/72-994**), in the stone Mexis mansion (signposted on the waterfront), has reopened by the time you visit, you can see Bouboulina's bones, along with archaeological finds and mementos of the War of Independence. Check when you arrive for the new hours and fee. If you head east away from the Dapia, you'll come to the **Paleo Limani** (aka the Baltiza, or **Old Harbor**), where many yacht owners moor their boats and live nearby in villas hidden behind high walls. The **Cathedral of Ayios Nikolaos (St. Nicholas)** was built in the 17th century as the church of a monastery, now no longer functioning. The great moment here took place on April 3, 1821, when the flag of Spetses first flew from St. Nicolas's campanile as support for the War of Independence against the Turks. A bronze flag beside the church's war memorial commemorates this moment and a pebble mosaic commemorates the War of Independence (look for the figure of Bouboulina). While you're at the Old Harbor, have a look at the boatyards, where you can often see caiques being made with tools little different from those used when Bouboulina's mighty *Agamemnon* was built here.

Beaches

Ayia Marina, signposted and about a 30-minute walk east of Spetses town, is the best, and busiest, town beach. It has a number of tavernas, cafes, bars, including the locally famous **Paradise,** and discos. West of Spetses town, **Ayii Anaryiri** has one of the best sandy beaches anywhere in the Saronic Gulf, a perfect C-shaped cove lined with trees, and, increasingly, almost more bars and tavernas than trees. The best way to get here is by water taxi. **Paradise beach** is crowded, littered, and, for me at least, not very appealing. Now, I hate to mention this, as all of us travel writers try to keep some secrets, but **Zageria** is as undeveloped a beach as you will find here. If you are interested, ask around for directions. Whichever beach you pick, go early, as beaches here get seriously crowded by midday.

Fans of *The Magus* may want to have a look at the beach at **Ayia Paraskevi,** which is bordered by pine trees. Located here are a cantina and **Villa Yasemia,** residence of the Magus himself. West over some rocks is the island's official nudist beach.

Where to Stay

The former **Hotel Poseidonion** (www.poseidonion.com; C **22980/74-553**), now justifiably called the **Poseidon Grand Hotel,** situated on the harbor and impossible to miss, reopened in 2009 after renovations so extensive that they constituted rebirth. It's not, repeat *not,* cheap, but what a great splurge to stay in this glorious 55-room grand hotel, now merging modern luxury and convenience with Belle Epoque elegance. Of course, there's a spa, a trendy Japanese restaurant, and what the hotel describes as a "lavish" breakfast buffet. High season doubles start from 240€, suites from 562€; "super" high season (Aug. and holidays) doubles start from 300€, suites from 711€; excellent off-season prices are often available.

Economou Mansion ★★   Small and elegant, this 19th-century sea captain's mansion has mosaics with sea motifs in the garden, and views far out to sea from most rooms. Unlike many boutique hotels, the Economou Mansion rooms are cozy and elegant, but never pretentious. The owners are attentive, but never intrusive. The breakfast buffet is extensive and delicious. Friends who had never been particularly enamored of Spetses stayed here in 2006, returned in 2010, and report that the hotel made them fall in love with the island itself.

Kounoupitsa, Spetses town 18050 Spetses. www.spetsestravel.gr. C **22980/73-400.** 8 units. 200€ double; 220€ studio; 280€ deluxe suite. DC, MC, V. **Amenities:** Breakfast room; pool; Wi-Fi. *In room:* Fridge in rooms, kitchens in suites.

Hotel Nissia ★   If you're planning a lengthy stay, check out the Nissia, which is open all year. In an increasingly popular trend in Greece, the Nissia has restored a 1920s industrial building and made it the main building of a boutique hotel. Don't be dubious—it works. The Nissia has a wide range of accommodations, including double rooms, maisonettes, studios, and flats clustered around a pool to simulate traditional village residences. The hotel is a 10-minute walk from the center of Spetses town. When you get there, you can sink into the very welcome pool.

Kounoupitsa, 16675. 18050 Spetses. www.nissia.gr. C **22980/75-000.** 77 units. From 220€ double. AE, MC, V. Amenities: Bar/lounge; room service; pool. In room: A/C, TV, minibar.

Orloff Resort ★★   This elegant resort, about a 10-minute walk from the Old Harbor, was built in 1975, renovated in 2004, and won a place in *Odyssey* magazine's selection of the best hotels in Greece in 2007. The complex, with a swimming pool and sea and garden views, occupies the land and some of the buildings of the 1865 Orloff estate. Accommodations range from rooms, suites, and maisonettes (some with kitchenettes), to a self-contained house. The decor is simple, but not stark, with red accents perking up the pristine white and understated grays and beiges. If you play tennis and pull a muscle, not to worry: aromatherapy and massage are available.

18050 Spetses. www.orloffresort.com. C **22980/75-444.** 22 units. 210€–250€ double; 400€ suite; 500€ maisonette for 4; 1,200€ house. Rates include breakfast. DC, MC, V. **Amenities:** Restaurant; bar; babysitting; pool; spa facilities; tennis. *In room:* A/C, TV, minibar.

Star Hotel ⚲   We are talking good value here. This blue-shuttered, five-story hotel—the best in its price range—is flanked by a pebble mosaic, making it off-limits to vehicles. Almost all guest rooms have balconies, the front ones with views of the harbor. Each large bathroom has a tub, shower, and bidet. The rooms are simple and could use sprucing up. The staff is not terribly attentive. Breakfast is available, a la carte, in the lobby. The rates make the place recommendable.

Plateia Dapia, 18050 Spetses. © **22980/72-214** or 22980/72-728. Fax 22980/72-872. 37 units. From 75€ double. No credit cards. **Amenities:** Breakfast room. *In room:* A/C, TV.

Where to Eat

Spetses's restaurants can be packed with Athenians on weekend evenings, so you may want to eat unfashionably early (about 9pm) to avoid the crush. Count on spending at least 25€ at any of these places—unless you are careful. If the price of your fish is not on the menu, ask for it; fish is usually expensive and priced by the kilogram. **Liotrivi** (© **22980/72-269**), in the Old Harbor, is a great place for simple grilled fish or *makaronada tou psara* (fish, tomato sauce, and pasta) or *mayiatiko a la Spetsiate* (fish stewed with tomatoes and herbs).

For standard Greek taverna food, including a number of vegetable dishes, try the rooftop taverna **Lirakis,** Dapia, over the Lirakis supermarket (© **22980/72-188**), with a nice view of the harbor. **To Kafeneio,** a long-established coffeehouse and ouzo joint, on the harborfront, is a good place in which to sit and watch the passing scene, as is **To Byzantino.** Or try **Orloff,** on the road to the Old Harbor, which has a wide variety of *mezedes.* The island's popularity with tour groups seems to have led to a decline in the quality of restaurant fare.

Spetses has some of the best **bakeries** in the Saronic Gulf; all serve a Greek specialty beloved on the islands: *amygdalota,* small, usually crescent-shaped almond cakes, flavored with rosewater and covered with powdered sugar. It's usually served with a tall glass of cold water; you'll realize why when you bite into all that powdered sugar!

The Bakery Restaurant GREEK/CONTINENTAL This restaurant is on the deck above one of the island's more popular patisseries. There are a few ready-made dishes, but most of your choices are prepared when you order them. The chef obviously understands foreign palates and offers smoked trout salad, grilled steak, and roasted lamb with peas, in addition to the usual Greek dishes.

Dapia. No phone. Main courses 8€–20€. MC, V. Daily 6:30pm–midnight.

Lazaros Taverna ★ GREEK Another traditional place, Lazaros caters less to the yachties than Exedra does and more to locals. Lazaros is decorated with potted ivy, family photos, and big kegs of homemade retsina lining the walls. It's popular with locals (always a good sign), who come here for the good, fresh, reasonably priced food. The small menu features grilled meats and daily specials, such as goat in lemon sauce.

Dapia. No phone. Main courses 7€–14€. MC, V; cash preferred. Daily 6:30pm–midnight. Closed mid-Nov to mid-Mar. Inland and uphill about 400m (1,312 ft.) from the water.

Spetses After Dark

Spetses has plenty of bars, discos, and bouzouki clubs from the Dapia to the Old Harbor to Ayia Marina, and even to the more remote beaches. For bars, try golden oldies **Bratsera** or **Stavento,** in the heart of Dapia. For discos, there's **Figaro,** with a seaside patio and international funk until midnight; afterward, the music switches to Greek, and the dancing follows suit, often until dawn. The **1800 Bar & Internet Café,** in Kounoupitsa, Spetses town, is the place to go if you want to listen to music, keep an eye on a TV, check your e-mail, and take in the *narghile* lounge, where you can smoke a water pipe, with some flavored tobacco, for 2 hours (10€). **Fox** often has live Greek music and dancing; obvious tourists are encouraged to join the dancing.

THE PELOPONNESE

by Sherry Marker

What's special about the Peloponnese? It's tempting to answer, "Everything." Virtually every famous ancient site in Greece is in the Peloponnese—the awesome Mycenaean palaces of kings Agamemnon and Nestor at Mycenae and Pylos (Pilos); the mysterious thick-walled Mycenaean fortress at Tiryns; the magnificent classical temples at Corinth, Nemea, Vassae, and Olympia; and the monumental theaters at Argos and Epidaurus, still used for performances today.

But the Peloponnese isn't just a grab bag of famous ancient sites. This peninsula, divided from the mainland by the Corinth Canal, is studded with great beaches, boutique hotels, fine restaurants, and two of Greece's most impressive mountain ranges: Taygetos and Parnon. Tucked away in the valleys and hanging from the mountainsides are the villages that are among the Peloponnese's greatest treasures. This is especially true deep in the Mani peninsula and in the mountains of Arcadia, where traditional Greek hospitality hasn't been eroded by busloads of visitors. An evening under the plane trees in Andritsena, where the sheep bells are usually the loudest sounds at night, and where oregano and flowering broom scent the hills, is every bit as memorable as a visit to one of the famous ancient sites. Even the most avid travelers do not live by culture alone, and one of the great delights of seeing the Peloponnese comes from the quiet hours spent in seaside cafes, watching fishermen mend their nets while Greek families settle down for leisurely meals. *Leisurely* is the word to remember in the Peloponnese. And what better place to watch shepherds on the hills or fishing boats on the horizon as you wait for dinner?

Peloponnesian culinary favorites include *kouneli stifado* (rabbit stew) with a surprising hint of cinnamon; and fish *a la Spetsai* (baked with tomato sauce). In summer—when it seems that every tree on the plain of Argos hangs with apricots and every vine is heavy with tomatoes—Peloponnesian food is at its freshest and best. If you're here in spring, look for fresh artichokes and delicate little strawberries. The fresh lettuce grown here during the winter months is superb, and Greek hothouses produce excellent tomatoes year-round. Don't forget to sample the local wines; the vineyards at Nemea, Patras, and Mantinia are famous. You can find out more about local cuisine at **www.kerasma.gr** and wines at **www.greekwinemakers.com** and **www.greekwine.gr**.

A few suggestions for your trip to the Peloponnese: While many of the islands sag under the weight of tourists from May until September, the Peloponnese is still relatively uncrowded, even in midsummer. That doesn't mean that you're going to have Olympia all to yourself if you arrive at high noon in August, but it does mean that if you get to Olympia early in the morning, you may have a relatively quiet hour under the pine trees. It used to be that if you were traveling with a car and could set your own pace, you could avoid the crowds at the most popular tourist destinations of Corinth, Mycenae, Epidaurus, and Olympia by visiting early in the morning or late in the afternoon. Now, lunch time or late in the afternoon is best—unless you really are there just before the site opens sprint in while the tour groups are finishing their breakfasts.

So, *kalo taxidi* (bon voyage) on your trip to the Peloponnese, the most beautiful and historic—and fun—part of Greece.

STRATEGIES FOR SEEING THE REGION

Whether you decide to tour the Peloponnese clockwise (starting with Corinth and ending with Olympia) or counterclockwise, at some point you'll probably head inland, either to see the Byzantine ghost town of **Mistra** outside ancient **Sparta,** or to take in some of the mountain villages of Arcadia and the **Temple of Vassae** dedicated to Apollo. Here's one suggested itinerary if you have your own car and are setting out from Athens. If you're traveling by public transportation, you'd be wise to double the time allowed. Even if you do have a car, don't let yourself be deceived by the short distances between what you want to see in the Peloponnese. You'll be astonished at how long even a short drive on a winding mountain road can take—especially when you have to stop repeatedly to let goats cross that road!

If you have 2 days, head from Athens to **Corinth,** have a look down at the canal, and visit the ancient site with its impressive temple as well as **Acrocorinth,** the sugarloaf mountain that looms over the plain of Corinth. Head on to **Mycenae** to see the citadel and chamber tombs before spending the night in **Nafplion,** which just about everyone calls *oraia* (beautiful). Refresh yourself with a swim at the public beach, some window-shopping along the pedestrianized streets, maybe even a museum or two followed by an evening stroll around town and dinner. In the morning, spend more time exploring Nafplion's boutiques, museums and monuments, and then drive to **Epidaurus** to see the famous theater before heading back along the coast to Athens.

> ### Walking Tours
>
> The respected British agency **Filoxenia** (www.filoxenia.co.uk) offers weeklong walking tours of the Peloponnese.

If you have a few more days to spend, you can head from Nafplion to **Olympia,** taking in some of the Arcadian mountain villages, including **Andritsena,** with the **Temple of Vassae.** Then you can head back to Athens along the **Gulf of Corinth,** which offers lots of chances for lunch and a swim at seaside resorts such as **Xylokastro.** There's lots more to see in the Peloponnese—if you have a week to spend here and can take in **Sparta** and Byzantine **Mistra** and the fortress (and chic hotels) of **Monemvassia** and the tower house villages of the **Mani.** And remember: If you are heading from the Peloponnese into Central Greece, the **Rio-AntiRio** suspension bridge (13€) makes a journey from, for example, Olympia to Delphi, much easier than the old ferry did. **Tip:** If you just want to drive back and forth over this spectacular 2,252m-long (7,388 ft.) cable suspension bridge that links the Peloponnese with the mainland, get the 14€ round-trip ticket.

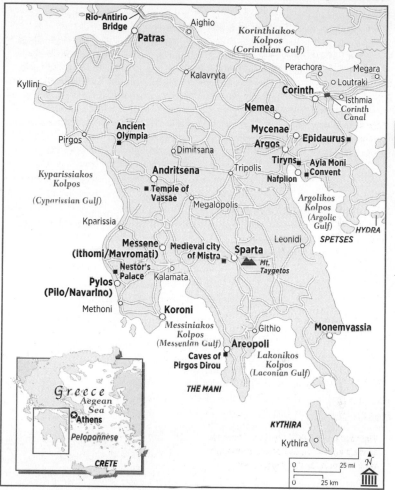

Rio-Antirio Bridge
Patras
Aighio
Korinthiakos Kolpos (Corinthian Gulf)
Perachora
Megara
Loutraki
Kyllini
Kalavryta
Corinth
Isthmia Corinth Canal
Nemea
Ancient Olympia
Mycenae
Epidaurus
Pirgos
Argos
Dimitsana
Tiryns
Ayia Moni Convent
Kyparissiakos Kolpos
Andritsena
Tripolis
Nafplion
(Cyparissian Gulf)
Temple of Vassae
Megalopolis
Argolikos Kolpos (Argolic Gulf)
HYDRA
Kparissia
Leonidi
SPETSES
Messene (Ithomi/Mavromati)
Medieval city of Mistra
Sparta
Nestor's Palace
Kalamata
Mt. Taygetos
Pylos (Pilo/Navarino)
Methoni
Koroni
Messiniakos Kolpos (Messenian Gulf)
Githio
Monemvassia
Areopoli
Lakonikos Kolpos (Laconian Gulf)
Caves of Pirgos Dirou
THE MANI

Greece
Aegean Sea
Athens
Peloponnese
CRETE

KYTHIRA
Kythira

0   25 mi
0   25 km
N

CORINTH ★★

89km (55 miles) W of Athens

Today, as in antiquity, Corinth, along with Patras, is one of the two major gateways to the Peloponnese. And, like most gates, Corinth offers no real temptations to linger. An earthquake destroyed much of ancient Corinth and the charming 19th-century town that sprawled around it. Today, modern Corinth (pop. 26,000) is a thicket of undistinguished concrete buildings, built to withstand future quakes, but the ancient site still has much to offer, including acres of the ancient commercial center and the spectacular **Temple of Apollo.**

Stop to see the ships slipping through the narrow **Corinth Canal** that cuts across the isthmus, then head straight for ancient Corinth, in the hamlet of Archaia

Building the Corinth Canal

The French engineers who built the Corinth Canal between 1881 and 1893 used dynamite to blast through 86m (285 ft.) of sheer rock to make this 6.4km-long (4-mile), 27m-wide (90-ft.), 90m-deep (300-ft.) passageway. This revolutionized shipping in the Mediterranean: Ships that previously had made their way around Cape Matapan at the southern tip of the Peloponnese could now dart through the canal. The journey from Brindisi, Italy, to Athens was shortened by more than 320km (200 miles).

Although it took modern technology to build the canal, the Roman emperors Caligula and Nero had tried, and failed, to dig a canal with slave labor. Nero was obsessed with the project, going so far as to lift the first shovelful of earth with a golden trowel. That done, he headed back to Rome and left the real work to the 6,000 Jewish slaves he had brought from Judea.

Korinthos (Old Corinth), bypassing the unappealing modern city. When you've seen ancient Corinth, head for Mycenae or Nafplion, both less than an hour away and both with excellent hotels and restaurants.

A LOOK AT THE PAST   Much of Corinth's ancient power and prosperity came from its strategic location overlooking the sea and land routes into the Peloponnese. No enemy could sneak across the isthmus without being spotted by the soldiers stationed on Corinth's towering acropolis, **Acrocorinth,** standing 566m (1,855 ft.).

During the 8th and 7th centuries B.C., Corinth controlled much of the trade in the Mediterranean and founded colonies as far away as Syracuse in Sicily. This was when Corinth made and exported the distinctive red-and-black figured pottery decorated with lively animal motifs, examples of which are on display in the excavation museum. Great sailors, the Corinthians were credited with refining the design of the **trireme,** the standard warship in Greek antiquity. The only obstacle Corinth couldn't overcome was the isthmus itself: there were only two ways for ships to get around the Peloponnese. Either they were dragged between the ports of Kenchreai on the east and Lechaion on the west, or they sailed around the entire Peloponnese.

Although Corinth's greatest period of prosperity was between the 8th and 5th centuries B.C., most of the ancient remains here are from the Roman period. Razed and destroyed when the Romans conquered Greece in 146 B.C., Corinth was refounded by Julius Caesar in 44 B.C. and began a second period of wealth and prosperity. When St. Paul visited here in A.D. 52, he found Corinth too sophisticated, and chastised the Corinthians for their wanton ways.

By the 2nd century A.D., with some 300,000 citizens and 500,000 slaves, Corinth was much larger and more powerful than Athens—and much larger than any city in the Peloponnese today. As one Greek proverb had it, "See Corinth and die," suggesting that there was nothing to look forward to after visiting its monuments (and fleshpots).

Essentials

GETTING THERE   By Train   I've always thought that only devoted train buffs should travel by train in the Peloponnese. Now, extensive work is being carried out on the rail system from Athens to the Peloponnese and within the Peloponnese itself. For up-to-date information on schedules and fares, call ⓒ **210/529-8735** or

210/323-6747 (**www.ose.gr**). It remains to be seen whether the renovations will produce a speedier and more efficient rail system.

By Bus   Prepare to be confused by almost any information involving Corinth and buses! There are at least 15 buses a day, taking 2 to 2½ hours, from the **Stathmos Leoforia Peloponnisou** (Bus Station for the Peloponnese) in Athens, 100 Kifissou (© **210/512-4910;** www.ktel.org), to the main bus terminal at the isthmus of Corinth (© **27410/83-000**), where you can catch a bus for the 30-minute trip to Archaia Korinthos. This bus sometimes goes via a stop at Dimokrates Street in modern Corinth. For general information on Athens-Peloponnese schedules and fares, call © **210/512-4910,** or check **www.ktel.org**.

Confusingly, many buses for destinations in the Peloponnese leave Corinth either from the main bus stop at the isthmus of Corinth, or from one of two badly signposted stations: one at the corner of Kolokotroni and Koilatsou (© **27410/24-444**) and the other at the corner of Ethnikis Konstantinou and Aratou (© **27410/24-403**). For most destinations in the Peloponnese beyond Tripolis, you'll find yourself changing buses at Tripolis.

By Car   The **National Highway** runs from Athens to Corinth. The highway, which has been widened over the last decade, still contains some nasty three-lane stretches. The highway now sweeps over the Corinth Canal; if you want to stop here, look for the signs indicating the Canal Tourist Area. Shortly after the canal, you'll see signs for Corinth (the modern town and ancient site), Isthmia (site of the Isthmian Games), and Patras. Allow about 1¼ hours for the journey from the Athens airport and a good deal longer if you leave from heavily trafficked central Athens.

What to See & Do

The new highway rushes you over the **Corinth Canal** very quickly, and unless you're vigilant you can miss the turnoff to the **Canal Tourist Area.** Before the new road was completed in 1997, almost everyone stopped here for a coffee, a souvlaki, and a look at the canal that separates the Peloponnese from the mainland. Now, traffic hurtles past, and the cafes, restaurants, and shops here are hurting. There's a small post office at the canal, along with a kiosk with postcards and English-language newspapers; most of the large souvlaki places have clean toilet facilities (but tough souvlaki). **Warning:** Be sure to lock your car door. This is a popular spot for thieves who prey on unwary tourists.

Ancient Corinth ★★   If you visit in summer, try to come here first thing in the morning or late in the afternoon: The sun on this virtually shadeless site will be less fierce, and fewer tourists will clog the area. Excavations continue at Corinth (you may see archaeologists at work) and since 1995, they have unearthed remains of an extensive Roman villa of the 4th century A.D. as well as imported English china of the 19th century A.D.—suggestions that Corinth's prosperity did not die in antiquity.

The most conspicuous—and most handsome—surviving building at ancient Corinth is the 6th-century-B.C. **Temple of Apollo,** which stands on a hill overlooking the remains of the **Roman Agora** (the Roman forum, or marketplace). Only 7 of the temple's 38 monolithic Doric columns are standing, the others having long since been toppled by earthquakes.

From the temple, ancient Corinth's main drag, a 12m (40-ft.) **marble-paved road** that ran from the port of Lechaion into the heart of the marketplace, is clearly visible. Pottery from Corinth was carried down this road to the ships that took it around the world; back along the same road came the goods Corinthian merchants bought in every corner of the Mediterranean. Everything made and brought here was for sale in countless shops, many of whose foundations are still clearly visible in the agora.

Two spots in the agora are especially famous: the **Bema** and the **Fountain of Peirene.** In the 2nd century A.D., the Roman traveler, philhellene (lover of Greeks), and benefactor Herodes Atticus rebuilt the original fountain house. Like most Romans, Herodes seemed to think that bigger was better: When he was done, the spring was encased in an elaborate two-storied building with arches and arcades and a 4.6-sq.-m (50-sq.-ft.) courtyard. Peirene was a woman who wept so hard when her son died that she finally dissolved into the spring that still flows here. As for the Bema, this was the public platform where St. Paul had to plead his case when the Corinthians, irritated by his constant harangues, hauled him in front of the Roman governor Gallo in A.D. 52.

> ### 📎 You Go First . . .
>
> If you want to bungee jump over the side of the 90m-deep (300-ft.) Corinth Canal, contact **Zulu Bungy** (𝒞 210/5470-51; www.zulubungy. com), which offers jumps from 60€.

Old Corinth. 𝒞 **27410/31-443.** Admission 6€, which includes the museum (see below). Summer daily 8am–8pm; winter daily 8am–3pm.

Acrocorinth ★★ A road twists from the ancient site to the summit of Acrocorinth, the limestone sugarloaf mountain that looms 566m (1,855 ft.) above the plain. This is a stiff climb; if you don't have a car, allow several hours for the ascent, or grab a taxi by the ancient site; it's about 15€ for the round-trip, with a half-hour wait—less if you decide to walk back. On a clear day, the views from the summit are splendid, although it's been a long time since the atmosphere was clear enough to spot the columns of the Parthenon on the Athenian Acropolis.

A superb natural acropolis, Acrocorinth was first fortified by the ancient Greeks. Everyone who came later—the Byzantines, Franks, Venetians, and Turks—added to the original walls. Today, there are three courses of outer walls; massive gates with towers; and a jumble of ruined houses, churches, and barracks. Alas, in 2011 the small cafe that used to sell cold drinks closed. Before you leave here, you may wish to reflect on the fact that there was a Temple of Aphrodite on this summit in antiquity, staffed by an estimated 1,000 temple prostitutes—some of whom worked the streets in town but others who worked here, awaiting those hardy customers who walked up from Corinth.

Old Corinth. 𝒞 **27410/31-966.** Admission 3€. Usually summer daily 8:30am–7pm; winter daily 9am–3pm.

The Archaeological Museum ★ As you'd expect, this museum has a collection of the famous Corinthian pottery that is often decorated with charming red-and-black figures of birds and animals. In addition, there are a number of statues of Roman worthies and several mosaics, including one in which Pan is shown piping away to a clutch of cows. When you visit, be sure to see the display of sculpture and vases stolen from the museum in 1990. In a bizarre happy ending, the treasures were found in 1998 packed in plastic containers in a fish warehouse in Miami and returned to Greece. The museum courtyard is a shady spot to sit; the toilet facilities are good.

Insider tip: The Archaeological Museum has an extensive collection of finds from the Shrine of Asclepius; because many of these are graphic representations of intimate body parts, they are kept in a room that is usually locked. If you express a scholarly interest, you may be able to persuade a guard to unlock the room for you.

Old Corinth, on the site of ancient Corinth. 𝒞 **27410/31-207.** Admission 6€, which includes admission to the site of ancient Corinth (see above). Summer daily 8am–8pm; winter daily 8am–3pm.

Where to Stay

In Old Corinth, 20-unit **Marinos Rooms** (© **27410/31-209**) has a great location, about 300m (984 ft.) from the ancient site, excellent home cooking, a garden, and *very* simple rooms from about 50€; reservations are vital in summer, when visiting archaeologists stay here.

Kalamaki Beach Hotel ★★ ☺ This beach resort, about 10km (6 miles) outside Corinth near Isthmia, is an excellent place for a family with children to combine sightseeing with relaxation. Many Greek families come here year after year with their children. The hotel is set in a nice garden, there's a small pool for children and good swimming in the sizable adult pool and in the Gulf itself. Meals are buffet style. The guest rooms are simply furnished, with tile floors, decent beds, good reading lamps, and roomy balconies and bathrooms. The floor-to-ceiling sliding glass doors that open onto the balconies allow you to take in the view; almost all rooms have at least a glimpse of the sea, but those over the garden facing the sea have by far the best views. If you take a stroll in the garden, keep an eye out for the remains of a Roman wall just beyond the hotel grounds. Most guests are tour groups or local families and if you are an independent traveler, you may be one of few singletons. When I stayed here alone in 2011, I enjoyed watching the Greek grannies watching over their grandchildren and the elegant young Athenian couples preening and Tweeting on poolside deck chairs

P.O. Box 22, 20100 Corinth. www.kalamakibeach.gr. (© **27410/37-653** or 210/323 5605 in Athens. Fax 27410/37-652 or 210/324-1092 in Athens. 80 units. 110€–180€ double. Rates include breakfast and dinner buffet. MC, V. Parking. **Amenities:** Restaurant; 2 outdoor pools (one for children); lifeguard; Ping-Pong; tennis. *In room:* A/C, TV, minibar, Wi-Fi.

Where to Eat

None of the cafes or restaurants along the Corinth Canal out of town or along the waterfront in town deserve to be singled out; most should be avoided. Similarly, the restaurants near the ancient site cater to tour groups and tend to have high prices and mediocre food. However, here are a couple suggestions if you find yourself hungry in Old Corinth (and can't wait until you get to Nafplion).

Locals speak well of the **Splendid** restaurant across from the site; a lunch or dinner of simple stews, chops, and salads costs around 15€. The **Ancient Corinth** and **Taverna Dionysos** on the main square offers much the same food at similar prices.

Side Trips from Corinth

LOUTRAKI & PERACHORA ★

Loutraki is the famous Greek spa whose springs churn out a good deal of the bottled water you'll see in restaurants. **Perachora** is a tiny seaside site with just enough remains of temples and shrines to give you something to admire while you enjoy being well off the touristic beaten track. To get to Loutraki from Corinth, cross the Corinth Canal. Once you're on the mainland, Loutraki will be signposted on your left. For Perachora, continue through Loutraki to Perachora, 32km (20 miles) or 30 minutes away by car on a peninsula hooking out into the Gulf of Corinth.

If possible, avoid visiting Loutraki on summer weekends when the town bursts at the seams with Athenian day-trippers and busloads of Russian visitors who gamble at the **Casino,** 48 Posidonos (© **27440/65-501;** open 24 hr.). If you come here, you might want to emulate Greek visitors and "take the waters" (and have a massage 45€) at the **Hydrotherapy Thermal Spa,** 24 G. Lekka (© **27440/22-215**), open Monday through Saturday from 7am to 2pm. Off season, the seaside promenades and leafy parks are charming; information is available at **www.loutraki.gr.**

Argos's confusing system of one-way streets and potentially lethal three-way intersections make getting through town almost as chaotic as the night in 272 B.C. when Pyrrus of Epirus stormed the city with a large force—including two war elephants, one of which overturned and blocked the main gate into the city. In short, drive with particular care here.

En route to Perachora from Loutraki is **Lake Vouliagmeni,** a saltwater inlet from the Gulf of Corinth. You'll find a number of seafood restaurants along the lake; make your choice depending on where the most Greeks are eating and what looks good in the kitchen. There's almost no shade here and it can be ferociously hot in summer.

Perachora ★ is at the end of the peninsula, around a tiny cove with a picturesque lighthouse chapel. The ancient Corinthians rather self-referentially named this place Perachora, which means "the land beyond"—in this case, the land beyond the gulf, as seen from Corinth. Views are superb south across the gulf of Acrocorinth and the mountains of the Peloponnese, and along the north coast to the mountains of Central Greece. Dilys Powell's memoir, *Perachora: An Affair of the Heart* (Efstatiadis Group, 1983), is an enchanting account of the excavations here and the prewar countryside.

Founded in the 8th century B.C., the **site of Perachora** had several temples to Zeus's wife, Hera; several stoas; and a number of useful water cisterns. Little was left standing after the Romans dismantled the temples and stoas and ferried the stones across the gulf to rebuild Corinth after they destroyed that city in 146 B.C. This is an ideal spot to spend a few lazy hours swimming and picnicking (but not on weekends, when lots of locals have the same idea). You may prefer to dangle your toes in the water and not swim in the cove, although the snorkeling is good. Sharks are not unknown just outside the harbor in the gulf.

The site is open daily in summer from 8am to 7pm, and in winter from 8am to 3pm. Admission is free.

ARGOS

48km (30 miles) S of Corinth

There should be lots of impressive remains to visit here, but because modern Argos (pop. 20,000) is built on top of the ancient city, there's little to see in town except the 4th-century theater, a hodgepodge of important, but not engaging, remains across from the theater, and the museum. Repeated earthquakes during the last century left modern Argos with an undistinguished agglomeration of flat-roofed concrete buildings, with only the occasional neoclassical house. Still, the central *plateia* (square) is lively and the street market on Wednesday and Saturday mornings is one of the largest in the Peloponnese. Still, it takes a vigorous imagination to visualize Argos as it was in its heyday in the 7th century B.C. Then, under the tyrant Pheidon, often credited with inventing coinage in Greece, Argos was the most powerful city in the Peloponnese. To this day, the fortifications on Argos's twin citadels, the Aspis and the Larissa—which include walls from the ancient, medieval, and modern eras—are impressive.

If your time in the Peloponnese is limited, you might consider saving Argos for a return trip. If you can spend a few hours here, have a look at the theater, stop by the museum, and try to drive up to the Larissa and Aspis citadels to take in the Venetian fortifications and the view over the plain. It's an easy side trip from Corinth.

Essentials

GETTING THERE By Train There are about five trains a day from Athens to Argos. Information on schedules and fares is available from Stathmos Peloponnisou (railroad station for the Peloponnese) in Athens (© **210/529-8735** or 210/323-6747), or at the Argos train station (© **27510/27-212**). Trains take at least 3 hours. The Argos train station, on Leoforos Vas. Sofias (© **27510/67-212**), is about 1km (½ mile) from the central square.

By Bus Five buses a day run to Argos from the Stathmos Leoforia Peloponnisou in Athens, 100 Kifissou (© **210/512-4910;** www.ktel.org), stopping, and sometimes involving a change of bus, at the Corinth canal. The bus ride usually takes just under 3 hours. Argos is also served by frequent buses from Nafplion (about 30 min.). Buses from Athens heading south into the Peloponnese usually stop in Argos by the **Sweet Corner** cafe (© **27510/23-162**) on Theatrou Street. Buses heading to Tripolis and the west usually leave from 24 Peithonos (© **27510/67-324**). In short, the bus connections in Argos are as confusing as the often unmarked and sometimes unexpectedly one-way streets! For general information on Athens-Peloponnese schedules and fares, call © **210/512-4910** or check www.ktel.org

By Car From Athens, take the **National Road** to Corinth, and then follow signs for Argos and Tripolis. The road divides just after the sign for Ancient Corinth. The speedy new Corinth-Tripolis toll road has green signposts with drawings of highways. Take the Argos exit and follow the exit road until it reaches an obvious main road (the old Corinth-Argos road). Turn right, cross the bridge, and you'll soon enter Argos. If you take the old road to Argos, it runs straight into the town. It's never easy to park in Argos, but you'll probably find a place on one of the side streets off the central square or by the ancient theater (except on Wednesdays and Saturdays when a street market draws shoppers from miles around).

FAST FACTS The **National Bank of Greece** and several others on the main square, Plateia Ayios Petros, all have ATMs. The **hospital** (© **27510/24-455**) is signposted on the main road into town from Athens. The **police** are at 10 Agelou Bobou (© **27510/67-222**). The **post office,** 16 Danaou, off the central square, is open Monday through Friday from 7am to 2pm. The **telephone office (OTE),** 8 Nikitara, is usually open Monday through Friday from 7am to midnight. **Café Net,** at 4 Oktavriou 28th, offers Internet access for 6€ per hour.

What to See & Do

The Larissa and the Aspis ★ Argos was famous in antiquity for its two citadels. The Greek word *aspis* means "shield," which is what the Argives thought this hill (98m/328 ft.) looked like. Now topped by a small chapel, the Aspis was Argos's first acropolis, abandoned when the higher (274m/905 ft.) Larissa was fortified in the 5th century B.C. You can still see some of the ancient blocks that were reused in Larissa's medieval battlements. There's an inner and outer system of walls, with several towers and the ruins of a church. The view's the thing here, and you get a bird's-eye view of the Aspis; the convent of Panaghia tou Vrakou (Virgin of the Rocks) on the lower slopes of the Larissa; Argos itself, with its fertile encircling plain; and the blue waters of the Gulf of Nafplion. The climb from Argos's ancient theater to the Larissa and Aspis is steep and shadeless; allow several hours and take water. If you drive, ask for

One of Greece's most distinguished ouzos, **Mavrakis,** has been made in Argos since 1864 and can be purchased in handsome metal bottles in the original shop (with many of its original furnishings) at 20 Vas. Konstantinou on the main *plateia,* Plateia Ayiou Petrou.

directions to the kastro, or castle, as the Larissa is called, at the theater, the Archaeological Museum, or the police station, as Argos roads are in a constant state of flux. Not many visitors come here, and you may have the place to yourself.

Free admission. Usually sunrise–sunset.

The Museum at Argos ★ This small museum has a handful of superlative pieces, including the fragment of a 7th-century-B.C. clay *krater* (vessel) showing a determined Ulysses blinding the one-eyed Cyclops Polyphemus. Nearby are a lyre made from a tortoise shell, and a stunning late geometric bronze helmet and suit of body armor. Downstairs, in the Lerna Room, the tiny, stout Neolithic clay figure of a woman or goddess found at Lerna is one of the oldest known sculptural representations of the human body yet found in Europe. Nearby is a handsome pitcher in the shape of a bird with its head thrown back in song—and ornamental breasts on its chest.

Outside, in the museum's shady courtyard, are some terrific Roman mosaics showing the god Dionysos and the seasons. The figures in the mosaics are bundled up in cloaks and leggings in the cold months, and casually dressed in light tunics and filmy cloaks in the summer months. If you visit the museum (which has a welcome icy-cold water fountain and clean toilets) on Wednesday or Saturday morning, don't miss the **street market** that runs for several blocks to your left as you leave. This is the place to get anything from water glasses, baseball caps, and farm implements to live chickens and every possible seasonal fruit and flower. If you're here on a nonmarket day and need supplies, there's a large **supermarket** just off the main square.

Elgas St. (no street number), off the main square, Plateia Ayiou Petrou. ✆ **27510/68-819.** Admission 2€; joint admission to theater, agora, Heraion, Archaeological Museum 6€. Tues–Sun 8:30am–3pm.

The Theater at Argos ★ If you've already seen the theater at Epidaurus, you'll find it hard to believe that Argos's 4th-century theater was not just larger, but probably the largest in classical Greece. Twenty-thousand spectators could sit here, in 89 tiers of seats, many of which were carved from the hillside itself. The thronelike seats in the front rows were added by the Romans and reserved for visiting bigwigs, including the Roman emperor. The Romans remodeled the theater, so that the orchestra (stage) could be flooded and mock naval battles staged. Fortunately, they had a genius for building the aqueducts needed to channel enough water to create a temporary inland sea. There was enough water left over to service the baths, whose remains are next to the theater. Across the street are the minimal remains of the ancient agora, as yet largely unexcavated, as it lies beneath today's Argos. That said, excavations in the last few years have revealed much more of the agora and the excavators have put up markers identifying many of the otherwise elusive remains.

✆ **27510/68-819.** Admission 3€; joint admission to theater, agora, Heraion, Archaeological Museum 6€. Summer Tues–Sat 9am–6pm, Sun 10am–3pm; often open in winter as well. Sometimes closed unexpectedly (but clearly visible from the Argos-Tripolis rd.).

Where to Stay & Eat

With Nafplion just down the road, there's really no reason to stay overnight in Argos unless you prefer the bustle of this crowded Greek market town to Nafplion's more sybaritic pleasures. If you do stay here, the **Mycenae** (*C* **27510/68-754**) and the **Morfeas** (*C* **27510/68-317**), on the main square, Plateia Ayiou Petrou, cater to businesspeople and are your best bets, with air-conditioning, central heating, and TV. Doubles cost from 40€ to 60€. None of the small cafes and restaurants in Argos are really worth seeking out, but the conveniently located **Aigle,** on the main square, has the usual chops, salads, and souvlaki, as well as pizza and veal in lemon sauce (*moskari lemonato*). Lunch or dinner costs from 15€ with beer or wine.

NAFPLION ★★★

145km (90 miles) SW of Athens

Nafplion is the most charming town in the Peloponnese, with stepped streets overhung with balconies dripping with bougainvillea, handsome neoclassical buildings, enticing shops, restaurants, cafes, and two fine museums. You could spend several enjoyable days simply exploring the port town, but you'll probably want to use Nafplion as your base for day trips to the ancient sites at Argos, Nemea, Mycenae, Tiryns, Epidaurus, and—if you didn't see it already—Corinth. Keep in mind that *lots* of Athenians come here year-round on weekends. It's important to reserve your hotel in advance.

Nafplion (pop. 10,000) brings you face to face with the beginnings of modern Greece. For several years after the Greek War of Independence (1821–28), this was Greece's first capital. Although the palace of Greece's young King Otto—a mail-order monarch from Bavaria—burned down in the 19th century, you can see the former mosque off Plateia Syntagma (Constitution Sq.) where Greece's first Parliament met. Another legacy of those years is the impressive number of commemorative statues of revolutionary heroes in Nafplion's squares and parks.

All this would be reason enough to visit this port on the east coast of the Gulf of Argos, but Nafplion also has two hilltop Venetian fortresses, a miniature castle on an island in the harbor, shady parks, some boutique hotels and shops, *and* the best ice cream in the entire Peloponnese (see Antica Gelateria di Roma, p. 251)!

Hair Today, Corinth Tomorrow

Female travelers might like to know that several of the staff at **AD Hair Studio** (*C* **27520/24-861**), at the corner of Ypsilanti and 5 Kotsonopoulou, speak English and do good work.

Essentials

GETTING THERE By Car From Athens, head south to the Corinth Canal. If you want to stop at Epidaurus en route, turn left just after the canal at the sign for Epidaurus. If you want to stop at Mycenae en route, take the winding old Corinth-Argos road and the signposted Mycenae bypass. If you want to stop at Nemea en route, take the new Corinth-Tripolis road to the Nemea exit. If you want to get to Nafplion as quickly as possible, take the new Corinth-Nafplion road to the Argos exit. Follow the signs first into Argos itself, about 10km (6 miles) from the exit, and thence on to Nafplion. You will almost certainly get lost at least once in Argos, which has an abysmal system of directional signs. Allow at least 3 hours for the drive from Athens to Nafplion, including a brief stop at the Corinth Canal and some time thrashing around in Argos. When you reach Nafplion, leave your car—and be sure to lock it—in the large municipal **parking lot** (no charge) by the harbor.

By Train   Extensive work is being carried out on the entire rail system from Athens to the Peloponnese and within the Peloponnese itself. It remains to be seen whether the renovations will produce a speedier and more efficient rail system. For information, call ℭ **210/529-8735** or 210/323-6747 (**www.ose.gr**).

By Bus   There are at least a dozen buses a day to Nafplion from the Stathmos Leoforia Peloponnisou in Athens, 100 Kifissou (ℭ **210/512-4910;** www.ktel.org). The trip is a slow one (about 4 hr.) because the bus usually stops at the isthmus of Corinth and often goes into both Corinth and Argos before reaching the Nafplion station on Syngrou Street, by Plateia Kapodistrias (ℭ **27520/28-555**). For general information on schedules and fares, call ℭ **210/512-4910** or go to **www.ktel.org**.

VISITOR INFORMATION   The **Municipal Tourist Office** is at 25 Martiou (ℭ **27520/24-444**), diagonally across from the bus station. It's usually open Monday through Friday from 9am to 1pm and 5 to 8pm (but is often mysteriously closed during work hours). Ask for the useful brochure *Nafplion Day and Night*. The website **www.nafplion.gr** is helpful—when functioning. Information and tickets for special events, such as the concerts in the June **Nafplion Music Festival,** are sometimes available from the Town Hall (Demarkeion) in the old high school building on Iatrou Square (ℭ **27520/23-332**); you can also check at **www.nafplionfestival.gr**. There are a number of travel agencies in Nafplion, such as **Staikos Travel,** by the harbor (ℭ **27520/27-950**), and **Yiannopoulos Travel,** on Plateia Syntagma (ℭ **27520/28-054**), where you can get information on car rentals and day trips from Nafplion.

FAST FACTS   The **National Bank of Greece,** on Plateia Syntagma (Constitution Sq.), has an ATM and currency exchange, as do most other banks in town. The **hospital** (ℭ **27520/27-309**) is at Kolokotroni and Asklipiou streets. The **police** (ℭ **27520/27-776**) and **tourist police** (ℭ **27520/98-729**) are now also on Asklipiou, just outside the town center. The **post office,** on Plateia Kapodistrias, and the **telephone office (OTE),** on 25 Martiou flanking Plateia Kapodistrias, are both signposted from the bus station. **Internet access** is available at many hotels and a number of cafes, including Echorama, 9 Alexandrou (ℭ **27520/26-050**), and the Diplo-Internet Cafe, 43 Bouboulinas (ℭ **27520/21-280**). Both charge 5€ an hour.

What to See & Do

Nafplion is a stroller's delight. One of the great pleasures here is to forget about maps and museums and just wander through parks (Kolokotronis and Kapodistrias parks run into each other), up and down the stepped side streets, and along the harbor, discovering unexpected Turkish fountains, small churches, and tempting cafes. Don't make the mistake of ending your harborside stroll when you come to the Five Brothers, five cannons beyond the cluster of large seaside cafes facing the miniature island fortress known as the Bourtzi. If you continue, you can watch fishing boats putting in at the pier, explore several cliff-side chapels (or seaside cafes), and wind your way past the small beach on a cliff-side path under the Acronafplia. Nafplion is so small that you can't get seriously lost, so have fun exploring. Below are some suggestions on how to take in the official sights after you've had your initial stroll.

Take a Dip or a Sail

The best place to swim is at **Arvanitia Beach** beneath the Palamidi. With the Bourtzi on your right, walk south along the quay until you come to the beach, which has changing facilities and chairs and great views of the sunset. If you'd rather be out on the sea looking back at the shore, contact **Captain Aris,** whose sailing ship is usually moored near where the shuttle runs to the Bourtzi. Captain Aris ((*C*) **69443/53-200**) gives day sails, with instruction and lunch and opportunities to swim and snorkel from about 80€ per person. The captain speaks fluent English and gets high praise from his novice sailors for his patience. You can take a day trip down the coast to Monembassia on the Alkyonis (run by Pegasus Cruises), which sometimes departs from Nafplion, sometimes from nearby Tolon. Information is available at **www.pegasus-cruises.gr** or on harborside posters.

ACRONAFPLIA & PALAMIDI ★

Nafplion's two fortifications, the **Acronafplia** and the **Palamidi,** dominate the skyline and, as usual with fortresses, are most impressive when seen from afar. It's a stiff climb to either, and you may prefer to take a taxi up (around 6€) and walk back down.

As you'll realize when you visit these fortresses, whoever held the heights here could keep a close watch on both the gulf and the plain of Argos. The Greeks began to fortify Acronafplia and Palamidi, and the Romans, Byzantines, Venetians, Franks, and Turks added a wall here and a turret there, with the results you see today. If you're here in the summer, try to visit the fortresses in the relative cool of either morning or evening, the sunsets are usually spectacular. If you're in Nafplion during the June **Music Festival,** find out if any evening concerts are being held at the **Palamidi,** which is open in summer, Monday through Friday from 8am to 7pm, and Saturday and Sunday from 8am to 3pm; in winter, hours are daily from 8am to 3pm. Admission is 3€.

If you're not in the mood to climb the 800-plus steps from Polyzoidhou Street to the **summit of Palamidi,** you can take a taxi up and then walk down. The Venetians spent 3 years building the Palamidi, only to be conquered the next year by the Turks in 1715. You'll enter the fortress the way the Turkish attackers did, through the main gate to the east. Once inside, you can trace the course of the wall that encircled the entire summit and wander through the remains of the five defense fortresses that failed to stop the Turkish attack. Kolokotronis, the hero of the Greek War of Independence who later tried to subvert the new nation and seize power for himself, was held prisoner for 20 months in **Fort Miltiades,** the structure to your right as you enter the Palamidi.

Compared to huffing and puffing up all those steps to the **Palamidi,** the ascent of **Acronafplia** (not enclosed and no charge) can be a leisurely—if always higher!—stroll through the upper city. If this still seems like work, you can either take a taxi up or take the elevator that runs from Koustouros Street up through the cliff side and deposits you on the summit at the Nafplia Palace Hotel.

If you're walking, follow signs in the lower town to the **Church of St. Spyridon;** one wall has the mark left by one of the bullets fired when Ioannis Kapodistrias, the first governor of modern Greece, was assassinated here in 1831. From there, continue up to the Catholic **Church of the Transfiguration,** a fitting symbol of Nafplion's vexed history. Built by the Venetians, it was converted into a mosque by the Turks, and then reconsecrated as a church after the War of Independence. Inside, an ornamental doorway has an inscription listing philhellenes who died for Greece, including nephews of both Lord Byron and George Washington. Greece's first king, young Otto of Bavaria, worshipped here wearing the Greek national costume, known as the *foustanella* (short pleated skirt for men), which he adopted to show solidarity with his new subjects. Ironically, while Otto wore his foustanella, the more fashion-conscious of his subjects abandoned their Greek costumes and copied the Western clothes worn by most members of Otto's court.

As you continue to climb toward Acronafplia, you may see several **carvings of the winged lion** that was the symbol of St. Mark, the protector of Venice. The most important fortifications on Acronafplia were built during the first (1388–1540) and second (1686–1715) Venetian occupations. In the days before the birth of today's Greek historical preservation movement, both the Xenia and the Xenia Palace Hotels were built over the fortifications, one reason the original structures have been obscured.

THE BOURTZI ★

Everyone's favorite fortress—and perhaps the only one to evoke squeals of "how cute"—the miniature **Bourtzi Fortress** was built by Venetians in the 15th century to guard the entrance to Nafplion's harbor. Since then, it's served as a home for retired executioners in the 19th century and as a small hotel in the 20th century. Small boats ply back and forth between the harbor and the Bourtzi (from 6€ round-trip); usually, you can stay as long as you wish, explore, and return with the same or a different boat. Take something to drink and a snack with you, as the small cafe is often closed. *Warning:* There are no toilet facilities. On hot summer days, the shadeless, often-crowded Bourtzi is much more pleasant to look at from a harborside cafe than to visit.

MUSEUMS

Keep an eye out in museums, galleries, and hotels for the elusive brochure *Artspotting Nafplion,* billed as a "guide to the best art spots in Nafplion," which lists local museums, galleries, and shops. Two of the best are the **Nafplion Art Gallery,** 5 Vassileos Alexandrou St. (© **27520/25-385**), which features the work of Greek and foreign artists, and **the Art Shop,** 14 Ipsilandou St. (© **27520/29-546**), featuring clothing, jewelry, toys and books by Greek and foreign artists.

The Archaeological Museum ★ It's about time! The **Nafplion Archaeological Museum** reopened in 2009 after 5 years of renovations. The museum now has large, bright rooms with exhibits themed to demonstrate life in the area from Neolithic to Christian times. An excellent video (with English text) shows and explains the sites where most objects were found. The collection, from sites in the area, includes pottery, jewelry, and some terrifying Mycenaean terra-cotta idols as well as a handsome bronze Mycenaean suit of armor. The museum is in one of the best-looking buildings in town, the handsome 18th-century Venetian arsenal that dominates Plateia Syntagma. The thick walls make this a deliciously cool place to visit on even the hottest day. And there are good restrooms.

Plateia Syntagma (Constitution Sq.). © **27520/27-502.** Admission 4€. Tues–Sun 8:30am–1pm.

The National Gallery-Alexandros Soutzos Museum, Nafplion Annex ★
The National Gallery in Athens has begun an ambitious scheme to open branches throughout Greece. This one, in a former neoclassical 19th-century town house, has a permanent exhibit of paintings showing scenes from the Greek War of Independence, including young warriors lounging by classical remains and wounded veterans

begging alms. There are frequently changing temporary exhibits, sometimes featuring local artists, and a small shop.

23 Sidiras Merarhias St. (✆ **27520/21-915.** Admission 4€; free Mon. Mon and Thurs 10am–3pm; Wed and Fri 10am–3pm and 5–8pm; Sat 10am–2pm.

The Peloponnesian Folklore Foundation ★★★ This is one of the best and most enjoyable small museums in Greece. Shortly after it opened in 1981, it won the European Museum of the Year Award. The collection of Greek costumes rivals that of Athens' Benaki Museum. It occupies three full floors in an elegant 18th-century house with a shady courtyard, a snack bar and excellent shop. In 2005, the museum installed a new permanent exhibition focusing less on rural than on urban Greece, particularly Nafplion in the 19th and 20th centuries. Dioramas show elegant town-house parlors stuffed with marble-topped furniture, Persian carpets, and ornate silver and china bibelots. The ground floor often has special exhibitions of work by local artists

1 V. Alexandros. (✆ **27520/28-947.** Fax 27520/27-960. www.pli.gr. Admission 4€. Museum Wed–Mon 9am–3pm; shop most days 9am–2pm and 6–10pm. Closed Feb.

SHOPPING

Nafplion has not escaped the invasion of mass-produced souvenirs that threatens to overwhelm Greece, but you'll also find some genuinely fine handicrafts for sale here. No shop that I recommend is more than a 5-minute walk from the central square, **Plateia Syntagma.** As in most Greek towns heavily dependent on tourism, some of these shops close in winter. Year-round, the weekly Saturday **market** occupies most of the road alongside Kolokotronis Park, from around 7am to 1pm. You can buy every-thing from handsaws to garlic here.

For a wide range of handcrafted jewelry, try **Preludio,** 2 Vas. Konstantinou just off Plateia Syntagma (✆ **27520/25-277**). Almost everything here is made and designed by the helpful owners, who travel as far away as Afghanistan and Australia to find fine gemstones. Two doors away at 4 Vas. Konstantinou, Cleopatra Pomoni at **Morphes** sells handsome wooden chests, antique locks and keys, jewelry, and other objects d'art

You'll know that you've found **To Enotion,** on Staikopoulou Street (no phone and no street number), when you see a window filled with museum-quality reproductions of characters from the Greek shadow theater—from country bumpkins to damsels in distress. The smallest of the colorful marionettes begins at about 20€. A few doors along, **Nafplio tou Nafpliou,** 56A Staikopoulou (no phone), sells icons showing virtually every saint in the Greek Orthodox church.

The **Komboloi Museum,** 25 Staikopoulou (✆/fax **27520/21-618;** www.cs-net. gr/komboloi), is on the second floor of a shop selling *komboloi,* usually referred to as "worry beads" (and priced from a few to many thousand euros); museum admission is 2€. **Premier Jewelry,** at 19 Vas. Konstantinou (✆ **27520/22-324**), also has a wide selection of *komboloi.*

Konstantine Beselmes, 7 Ath. Siokou (✆ **27520/25-842**), offers magical paintings of village scenes, sailing ships, and idyllic landscapes. Although new, the paintings are done on weathered boards, which gives each a pleasantly aged look. A few doors away, **Agynthes,** 10 Siokou (✆ **27520/21-704**), has hand-loomed fabrics that look and feel wonderful; some are fashioned into throws, bags, and scarves.

The **Odyssey,** Plateia Syntagma (✆ **27520/23-4300**), has a wide selection of newspapers, magazines, and books in English, as well as a startling collection of pornographic drink coasters. This is also a good place to pick up a copy of Timothy Gregory's *Nafplion* (Lycabettus Press); although printed in 1980, this remains the best guide to the city's history and monuments.

The **Karonis Wine Shop,** 5 Amalias (℗/fax **27520/24-446;** www.karoniswine shop.gr), is an excellent place to head if you want to browse and learn about Greek wines and/or Cuban cigars from owner Dimitris Karonis. If your tastes run to honey, stop at **Nektar and Ambrosia,** 6 Pharmakopoulou (℗ **27520/43-001**), for a wide selection of delicious organic honey products and herbs.

Where to Stay

Nafplion has some of the best hotels in the Peloponnese, ranging from small boutique hotels to large luxury establishments. Be sure to make a reservation if you want a view of the harbor or if you will be here during a performance at Epidaurus, when tour groups reserve entire hotels. Otherwise, Nafplion has enough hotels that you can usually find a room, although you may end up on the outskirts in high season. **Warning:** Many hotels are up steep streets and have no elevators and no parking.

If you arrive without a reservation and have trouble finding a room, try the **Municipal Tourist Office,** 25 Martiou (℗ **27520/24-444**), across from the bus station. They can sometimes find rooms in small pensions. In addition to the hotels below, here are a few other possibilities. Nafplion's 172-room **Amalia (www.amalia hotels.com**) had declined dreadfully, so it's good to say that it is spruced up after a renovation in 2008. If you don't mind being outside of Nafplion itself and want to relax in a big swimming pool, think Amalia. Like all Amalia Hotels, this one has extensive gardens; large, comfortable rooms; large bathrooms; efficient, attentive service—and lots of tour groups and wedding parties. Doubles start from 150€.

If you feel like a splurge, check out the 42-unit **Amphitryon,** transformed from its down-at-the-heels days into a five-star member of the Leading Small Hotels of the World (www.amphitryon.gr, or www.helioshotels.gr; ℗ **27520/70-700**). The Amphitryon has gorgeous flower arrangements, enormous bathrooms with fiendishly clever showers, pool privileges up the hill at the Nafplia Palace Hotel, and promises "romantic moments in an ambience of privileged scenery." Doubles start at 250€.

If, like me, you'd prefer the ambience of the pleasant residential neighborhood around Ayios Spiridon church, try the 21-unit **Pension Acronafplia** (www.pension acronafplia.gr; ℗ **27520/24-481**). The pension occupies five restored town houses whose congenial accommodations range from simple (small room, no private bathroom) to elegant (large room, private bathroom, and balcony with harbor view). Doubles range from small and simple, with no view, 45€, to large, very comfortable, with a grand view over Nafplion, 130€. If you want to stay with trendy young Greeks, try the jointly owned very artsy **Amymone** and **Adiani** boutique hotels, with 15 rooms in two buildings just off the harbor. This is *the* place to try if you've always wanted to sleep in a bed with a giant fly or the Blues Brothers painted on the headboard (www.hotel-adiandi-com; ℗ **27520-22073,** doubles from 90€–200€).

EXPENSIVE

Hotel Ilion ★   This is not the place to stay if you have trouble climbing and travel with heavy suitcases. If you do check in, however, you'll be rewarded with a great view over Nafplion from many rooms. As to the rooms, you'll have to decide whether you find the decor in this boutique hotel (a member of the Historic Hotels of Europe) in a restored 19th-century townhouse engaging or overwhelming. Virtually every ceiling is painted (often with cupids), and wall frescoes with scenes from Greek mythology alternate with borders of fruits and flowers. Many walls are deep rose or gold. Windows and beds are draped with filmy hangings. The mattresses are excellent. The five studio apartments are in a nearby less-appealing building. Some guests (including several fastidious friends of mine) are wild about this place, while others report that they found the Illion overpriced, overly ornate, and understaffed.

4 Efthimiopoulou and 6 Kapodistriou sts., 21100 Nafplion. www.ilionhotel.gr. © **27520/25-114.** Fax 27520/24-497. 15 units. 120€–175€ double; 200€–300€ suite. Breakfast 10€. No credit cards. **Amenities:** Bar/breakfast room. *In room:* A/C, TV, minibar, Wi-Fi.

Hotel Nafsimedon ★   Near the harbor, set back from a busy street, but overlooking quiet Kolokotronis Park, this boutique hotel occupies a handsome mid-19th-century neoclassical house with a small garden with palm trees. The guest rooms, many done in shades of apricot and peach, have handsome chandeliers, marble-topped tables, some old paintings, and good-size bathrooms and beds with firm mattresses. The Nafsimedon's younger sister boutique hotel, the **Ippoliti** (**www.ippoliti.gr**), just around the corner, is giving it a run for the money: the Ippoliti is often quieter, has some rooms with harbor views, and a seriously small pool; doubles 140€–190€).

Nafsimedon, 9 Sidiras Merarhias (on Kolokotronis Park), 21100 Nafplion. www.nafsimedon.gr. © **27520/25-060.** Fax 27520/26-913. 13 units. 100€–125€ double. No credit cards. **Amenities:** Bar/ breakfast room; courtyard. *In room:* A/C, TV.

Nafplia Palace Hotel ♨   Atop Acronafplia, the Nafplia Palace (formerly the Xenia Palace Hotel) has the best view in town, not only of Nafplion, but across the bay to the mountains of the Peloponnese. That view and renovations in 1999 and 2005 earned the villas and suites high praise in *Odyssey* magazine's "Best Hotels" issues. Though the bungalow villas are glamorous, with bathrooms the size of battleships, throughout the hotel the service remains lax, the room decor bland, the lobby sterile, and the food ranges from tedious to pretentious. Still, it has a view to die for.

Acronafplia, 21000 Nafplion. www.helioshotels.gr. © **27520/28-981** or 27522/89-815. Fax 27520/28-783. 105 units, including 54 bungalows. From 300€ double; from 600€ bungalow. Significant off-season reductions possible. Rates include breakfast. AE, DC, MC, V **Amenities:** 2 restaurants; 2 snack bars; 2 pools. *In room:* A/C, TV, DVD, minibar, Wi-Fi.

MODERATE

Byron Hotel ★★   Again, a steep walk leads to a charming small hotel, in a quiet, breezy location overlooking the Church of Agiou Spiridona. The Byron was one of the first hotels in town to add individual charm and creature comfort to a pleasant location, and has many repeat guests. It's almost impossible to snag a room in July or August without a reservation, especially on weekends, when the entire hotel can be taken over by Athenians. Sitting rooms and guest rooms (refreshed annually and frequently redecorated) contain nice bits of Victoriana, as well as modern conveniences. The cheapest rooms are small with no view; usually, for another 15€, you'll get a view of Nafplion—and enough space that you won't feel a little too close to your roommate.

2 Platonos, Plateia Agiou Spiridona, 21100 Nafplion. www.byronhotel.gr. © **27520/22-351.** Fax 27520/26-338. 17 units. 90€–110€. AE, MC, V. **Amenities:** Breakfast room; terrace. *In room:* A/C, TV, minibar, Wi-Fi.

Hotel Leto ★ ♦   Your effort in climbing up to the Leto, perched under Acronafplia, is rewarded with fine views over Nafplion. Guest units are simply furnished, with decent-size bathrooms; ask for a room with a balcony. The staff here has been praised as very helpful.

28 Zigomala, 21100 Nafplion. © **27520/28-098.** Fax 27520/29-588. 15 units. 75€–95€ double. No credit cards. *In room:* A/C, TV, minibar.

King Otho I & II ★★   The King Otho I, a longtime favorite, was getting down at the heels before its successful renovation in 2000 and touch-ups since then. In 2002, the owners bought and restored another wonderful town house a few blocks up the hill on Staikopoulou. Now, Nafplion has two small hotels that contend for the honor of the most breathtaking curved staircase in the Peloponnese, and both are easily accessible on foot. Both have high ceilings (some with frescoes), wood floors, and period furniture, including marble-topped tables; many doubles are small. The newer Otho is more expensive, because every guest room has a view (of Nafplion, or of Nafplion and the harbor). Each hotel has a garden, a real plus for breakfast or a quiet hour's reading. Both sometimes close in winter.

King Otho I: 4 Farmakapoulou, 21100 Nafplion. www.kingothon.gr. ℂ **27520/27-585.** 12 units. 90€ double. Rates include continental breakfast. AE, MC, V. **Amenities:** Breakfast room. *In room:* A/C, TV, minibar. **King Otho II:** 21 Staikopoulou, 21100 Nafplion. www.kingothon.gr. ℂ **27520/97-790.** 10 units. 120€ double. Rates include continental breakfast. AE, MC, V. **Amenities:** Breakfast room. *In room:* A/C, TV, minibar, Wi-Fi.

INEXPENSIVE

Epidaurus Hotel ★ 🔖 Rooms here are small but acceptable, with good, firm beds, small bathrooms, and ample wooden hanging cupboards. The location, on a quiet street just off the main square, is excellent and usually quiet, although adjacent nightclubs, restaurants, and bars can make things noisy on summer weekends. Service here is rather unpredictable, ranging from very hospitable and efficient to cursory. The Epidaurus also operates the slightly less expensive and less appealing 12-room **Tiryns** nearby on Othonos Street and will try to get you a room there if the Epidaurus is full.

2 Kokkinou, 21100 Nafplion. ℂ/fax **27520/27-541.** 30 units, 25 with full bathroom. 60€–70€ double. No credit cards. **Amenities:** Bar.

Omorfi Poli Pension ★★ ☺ What a pleasant place! This small pension/hotel above the charming **cafe** by the same name (Greek for "beautiful city") has gone all out: The restoration of the building gives guests the sense that they are staying in a Nafplion home—but with privacy; when business is not brisk, you can sometimes get a suite at a double room price. The beds are good, the tile floors and prints on the walls are tasteful. Families will like the rooms with fridges and sleeping lofts for children as well as the breakfasts with freshly baked bread.

5 Sofroni, 21100 Nafplion. www.greek-tourism.gr/nafplio/omorfi-poli. ℂ **27520/21-565.** 9 units, all with shower only. 75€ double; 120€ family suite (for up to 5 persons). Rates include breakfast. No credit cards.

Where to Eat

Not all the restaurants in and just off Plateia Syntagma (Constitution Sq.) are the tourist traps you'd expect. Furthermore, you'll see a good number of Greeks at the harborside cafes on Akti Miaouli. In short, Nafplion has many good restaurants—and some excellent sweet shops, including the Antica Gelateria di Roma.

Hellas Restaurant ★ ☺ GREEK Children who normally squirm in restaurants will enjoy the Hellas: Between courses, they can join the Greek kids kicking soccer balls and racing up and down Plateia Syntagma. Shady awnings make this a cool spot to eat outdoors. Locals tend to congregate in the indoor dining room year-round. Reliable dolmades with egg-lemon sauce are usually on the menu, as well as stuffed tomatoes and peppers in season. Just about everyone in town passes through Plateia Syntagma, so this is a great spot to watch the world go by.

Plateia Syntagma. ℂ **27520/27-278.** Main courses 8€–15€. AE, MC, V. Daily 9am–midnight.

Karamanlis ★ 🔖 GREEK This simple harborfront taverna several blocks east of the cluster of cafes tends to get fewer tourists than most of the places in town. It serves good grills and several kinds of meatballs (*keftedes, sousoutakia,* and *yiouvarla-kia*). If you like the food here, you'll probably also enjoy **Arapakos, Kanares Taverna,** and **Hundalos Taverna,** also on Bouboulinas.

1 Bouboulinas. ✆ **27520/27-668.** Main courses 7€–15€; fresh fish priced by the kilo. AE, MC, V. Usually daily 11am–midnight.

Ta Phanaria ★ GREEK   A shaded table under Ta Phanaria's enormous scarlet bougainvillea makes for one of the prettiest places in the center of town for lunch or dinner. Ta Phanaria usually has several inventive vegetable dishes on the menu in addition to such standbys as moussaka. The stews and chops here are also good. In winter, hearty bean dishes are usually available. Like the Hellas, Ta Phanaria continues to attract steady customers, despite doing much of its business with tourists.

13 Staikopoulo. ✆ **27520/27-141.** Main courses 7€–15€. MC, V. Daily about noon–midnight.

Taverna Old Mansion (Paleo Archontiko) ★★ GREEK   Sometimes when it's snowing in New England, where I spend part of the year, I dream of spending a cozy evening here, enjoying the good food and lively local scene. In summer, when I'm in Nafplion, tables spill out along Siokou Street. The menu offers good traditional Greek *spitiko* (home) cooking: stews, chops, and usually several vegetarian choices. When live music is featured in the evening, tables are at a premium.

7 Siokou. ✆ **27520/22-449.** Main courses 8€–15€. MC, V. Daily 7pm–midnight; summer weekends noon–4pm.

OUZERIES, CAFES & SWEET SHOPS

Antica Gelateria di Roma ★★★ SWEETS/ICE CREAM/COFFEE/DRINKS   This is where I head first when I get to Nafplion and where I stop last before I leave. Marcello and Claudia Raffo make and sell the best ice cream and ices in the Peloponnese—perhaps in Greece! You can have anything from a banana split to a tiny cup with just a taste. Don't miss the hazelnut, lemon, mango, strawberry, chocolate—well, you get the idea. If you tire of ice cream, finish off with an espresso while getting up-to-the-minute news of Italian soccer.

3 Pharmakopoulou and Komninou. ✆ **27520/23-520.** Sweets and sandwiches 4€–12€. No credit cards. Daily about 10am–midnight.

Sokaki COFFEE/DRINKS/SNACKS/BREAKFAST   In the morning, tourists enjoy the full American breakfast here, while locals toy with tiny cups of Greek coffee. In the evening, young men lounge, some eyeing the women who pass by, others eyeing the men. In short, there's great people-watching and good margaritas.

8 Ethniki Antistaseos. ✆ **27520/26-032.** Drinks and snacks 5€–15€. No credit cards. Daily about 8am–8pm; summer daily 8am–midnight.

Nightlife

In Nafplion, the **Paleo Lichnari** bar/restaurant on Bouboulinas often has live Greek music, sometimes including *rembetika,* the once revolutionary, now increasingly nostalgic songs of the urban poor. There's music most summer weekends and often nightly in August, from midnight. A number of nightclubs and discos cluster around Nea Chios on the coast road from Nafplion to Muloi; all are serious clip joints, often charging 100€ for a bottle of inferior Scotch. These places are popular with the sailors who turn up in Nafplion, and with area 20- and 30-somethings who come here for a night on the town. Some of the better-known places (with garish decor that has to be seen to be believed) include **Shiva of Liquid Club, Liquid Live,** and the **Rusty Club.** There's no point in phoning ahead: No one answers the phones at these places.

Side Trips from Nafplion

TIRYNS ★★

From the moment that you see Tiryns, you'll understand why Homer called this Mycenaean citadel "well-walled." The **Archaeological Site of Tiryns** (✆ 27520/22-657) is usually open in summer, daily from 8am to 8pm; in winter, hours are Monday through Saturday from 8am to 3pm. Admission is 3€. Tiryns is 5km (3 miles) outside Nafplion on the Argos road. If you have a car, this is an easy drive; if you don't, take one of the frequent Argos-Nafplion buses and ask to be let off at Tiryns. Taxi drivers will take you to Tiryns and wait while you visit; expect to pay from 30€ for an hour visit. A small stand by the ticket booth sometimes has cold drinks and postcards and the useful guidebook *Tiryns* (8 €) by archaeologist Alkestis Papademetriou. Finds from Tirnys are on display in the Archaeological Museums in Nafplion and Athens.

Tiryns is a good deal better preserved—and much less crowded and more pleasant to visit—than Mycenae. Most scholars assume that Tiryns was a friendly neighbor to the more powerful Mycenae, and some have suggested that Tiryns was Mycenae's port. Today, Tiryns is a mile from the sea; in antiquity, before the plain silted up, it would have been virtually on the seashore.

Tiryns's citadel stands on a rocky outcropping 27m (89 ft.) high and about 300m (990 ft.) long and is encircled by the **massive walls** that so impressed Homer. Later Greeks thought that only the giants known as Cyclops could have positioned the wall's 13-metric-ton (14-U.S.-ton) red limestone blocks, and archaeologists still call these walls "cyclopean." Even today, Tiryns's walls stand more than 9m (30 ft.) high; originally, they were twice as tall—and as much as 18m (57 ft.) thick. Tiryns seems to have increased its fortifications around 1400 B.C., but they were destroyed around 1200 B.C., whether by an enemy or an earthquake is not known.

Once you climb the ramp and pass through the two gates, you'll find yourself in a series of **storage galleries and chambers** on the east side of the citadel. One long passageway with a corbeled arch has walls that were rubbed smooth by the generations of sheep sheltered here for centuries after Tiryns's fall. Few places offer such a graphic example of how the mighty can fall, than this palace that became a sheep fold.

The citadel is crowned by the **palace,** whose **megaron** (great hall) has a well-preserved circular hearth and the base of a putative throne. This room would have been decorated with frescoed walls; you can see the surviving frescoes, some with scenes of elegant women riding in a chariot, in the National Archaeological Museum in Athens. Lesser folk would have lived below the citadel on the plain. Two tunnels led from the lower slopes of Tiryns out into the plain to the large **subterranean cisterns,** which held the secret water supply that allowed Tiryns to withstand even lengthy sieges.

Insider Tip: If you're feeling frustrated to be so near, but not in, the sea when you visit Tiryns, take one of the side roads from the Nafplion-Argos road that Tirnys overlooks across to the Gulf of Argos. A sandy beach stretches almost all the way from the outskirts of Nafplion to the hamlet of Nea Chios, where there are fresh fish restaurants. The water is shallow enough that you can wade a long way out, which makes this an ideal spot for families with young children. The men wading about with long-handled nets are rooting around in the sand for mussels. The families hanging their washing out to dry on trees and bushes are Gypsies. As always at a public beach, it's a good idea to lock your car and keep an eye on valuables.

AYIA MONI CONVENT ★

This hillside convent is a 3km (1½-mile) drive outside Nafplion. Until recently, much of the drive was through countryside. Now, the road to the convent winds uphill through a fast-growing suburb, where houses and small apartment blocks are fast replacing the olive groves. Still, the convent itself remains peaceful. To get here by car, head out of Nafplion on the Epidaurus road. Turn right at the sign for Ayia Moni and continue on a partly bumpy road uphill to the convent. Ayia Moni is usually open from about 9am to 5pm in winter, later in summer, but usually closed during the afternoon siesta (about 1–4pm).

Ayia Moni was founded in the 12th century, and the church is a fine example of Byzantine church architecture, with nice brickwork. Many of the other buildings here are modern and were built after a series of fires destroyed much of the original convent. If the main door is closed, knock. The nuns sometimes have embroidery to sell and are usually more than willing to show you the church and garden and tell about the rich Greek-American benefactor who rebuilt the convent.

The spring that feeds a small pond just outside the convent walls is one of a number of springs in Greece identified as the place where Zeus's wife, Hera, took an annual bath to restore her virginity and renew Zeus's ardor. Today, the spring water is considered both holy and delicious; pilgrims often fill bottles to take home.

MYCENAE ★★★

50km (31 miles) S of Corinth, 115km (71 miles) SW of Athens

Nearly every visitor to the Peloponnese comes to Mycenae, which can make for bumper-to-bumper tour buses on the narrow roads to the citadel and wall-to-wall tourists inside the citadel itself. Why do they all come? As the English philhellene Robert Liddell once wrote: "Mycenae is one of the most ancient and fabulous places in Europe. I think it should be visited first for the fable, next for the lovely landscape, and thirdly for the excavations." Once you're through the majestic Lion Gate, you may want to remember Liddell's remark if—as is very likely—you don't find it easy to imagine Mycenae when it was a bustling settlement with a richly decorated palace.

According to Greek legend and the poet Homer, King Agamemnon of Mycenae was the most powerful leader in Greece at the time of the Trojan War. It was Agamemnon, Homer says, who led the Greeks from Mycenae, which he called "rich in gold," to Troy (around 1250 B.C.). There, the Greeks fought for 10 years to reclaim fair Helen, the wife of Agamemnon's brother Menelaus, from her seducer, the Trojan prince Paris. The Greeks won, Helen dutifully returned home to Sparta, and Agamemnon headed home to Mycenae. There, his wife, Clytemnestra, welcomed him home with a soothing hot bath, in which she stabbed him to death. Her motive? Revenge, for the death of their daughter Iphigenia, whom Agamemnon had sacrificed when he set off for Troy, to ensure that the gods provided a fair wind and safe journey. Like many Greek myths and legends, the story of Agamemnon and Clytemnestra makes the grisly Grimm Brothers' fairy tales (and Steven King's novels!) seem almost harmless.

The German archaeologist Heinrich Schliemann, who found and excavated Troy, began to dig at Mycenae in 1874. Did Schliemann's excavations prove that what Homer wrote was based on an actual event—and not myth or legend? Scholars are suspicious, although most admit that Mycenae could have been built to order from Homer's descriptions of Mycenaean palaces. Displays at the **site museum** help put flesh on the bones of the archaeological remains. Try to visit the museum the minute

Visit Mycenae as early as possible in the morning (to avoid the midmorning and midday tour groups) or during the hour or two before closing (when crowds thin out). Wear a hat and sturdy shoes. There's no shade at the site (except in the cistern and the beehive tombs), and the rocks are very slippery. Bring a flashlight if you plan to explore the cistern. And, if you are staying here at full moon, be sure to walk up to see Mycenae's walls gleaming in the moonlight.

it opens; it is small, and gets horribly crowded as the day goes on. At press time, museum tickets and guidebooks were sold only at the ticket booth for the site itself.

Essentials

GETTING THERE   By Car   From Corinth, take the new national highway toll road to the Nemea exit, where you will join the old Corinth-Argos highway, which has a clearly marked turnoff for Mycenae. If you prefer, you can shun the new highway and take the old Corinth-Argos road to the turn off either for the site of Mycenae or for the village of Mycenae. This takes longer and you may get stuck behind a bus or truck, but you will have a better sense of the countryside than on the elevated highway. Either way, Mycenae is about 90km (56 miles) south of Corinth. **From Nafplion,** take the road out of town toward Argos. When you reach the Corinth-Argos highway, turn right and then, after about 16km (10 miles), turn right again at the sign for Mycenae. A slightly complicated back way to Mycenae via Ayia Triada used to be very quiet and pretty, but is now heavily used by tour buses. If a local suggests this route to you, expect tour buses at every turn!

By Bus   There is frequent bus service from the Stathmos Leoforia Peloponnisou, at 100 Kifissou in Athens (**(C) 210/512-4910;** www.ktel.org), to Corinth, Argos, and Nafplion (allow 3–4 hr.). From any of these places you can travel on by bus to Mycenae (allow 1 hr.). The Athens-Argos bus is usually willing to drop Mycenae-bound travelers at the turnoff at Fihtia—but don't count on finding a taxi to take you the rest of the way (about 2km/1 mile). For general information on Athens-Peloponnese schedules and fares, call **(C) 210/512-4910** or check www.ktel.org.

FAST FACTS   You can buy stamps and change money at the **mobile post office** at the ancient site, Monday through Friday from 8am to 2pm. This office is sometimes open on weekends and after 2pm, but don't count on it. There is a **pay phone** (not always in service) near the mobile post office.

What to See & Do

The Citadel & the Treasury of Atreus ★★★   As you walk uphill to Mycenae, you begin to get an idea of why people settled here as long ago as 3000 B.C.: Mycenae straddles a low bluff between two protecting mountains and is a superb natural citadel. The site overlooks one of the richest plains in Greece, and whoever held Mycenae could control all the land between the narrow Dervenakia Pass to the north and the Gulf of Argos, some 16km (10 miles) to the south.

By about 1400 B.C., Mycenae controlled not just the Plain of Argos, but also much of mainland Greece, as well as Crete, many of the Aegean islands, and outposts in distant Italy and Asia Minor. Then, some unknown disaster struck Mycenaean Greece; by about 1100 B.C., the Mycenaeans were on the decline. By the time of the classical era, almost all memory of the Mycenaeans had been lost, and Greeks speculated that the massive walls of Mycenae and Tiryns had been built by the mythical Cyclops.

You'll enter Mycenae through just such a wall, passing beneath the arching **Lion Gate,** whose two lions probably symbolized Mycenae's strength. The door itself (missing, like the lions' heads) would have been of wood, probably covered with bronze for additional protection; cuttings for the door jambs and pivots are clearly visible in the lintel. Soldiers stationed in the **round tower** on your right would have shot arrows down at any attackers who tried to storm the citadel. Because soldiers carried their shields on their left arms, the tower's position made the attackers vulnerable to arrows aimed at their unprotected right sides.

One of the most famous spots at Mycenae is immediately ahead of the Lion Gate: the so-called **Grave Circle A,** where Schliemann found the gold jewelry now on display at the National Archaeological Museum in Athens. When Schliemann opened the tombs and found some 14 kilos (31 lb.) of gold, including several solid-gold face masks, he concluded that he had found the grave of Agamemnon himself. At once, Schliemann fired off a telegram to the king of Greece, saying, "I have looked upon the face of Agamemnon bare." More sober scholars have concluded that Schliemann was wrong, and that the kings buried here died long before Agamemnon was born.

From the grave circle, head uphill past the remains of a number of **houses.** Mycenae was not merely a palace, but a village with the palace at the crest of the hill and administrative buildings and homes on the slopes. The **palace** was considerably grander than these small houses and had several courtrooms, bedrooms, a throne room, and a large megaron (ceremonial hall). You can see the imprint of the **four columns** that held up the roof in the megaron, as well as the outline of a **circular altar** on the floor. And spare a glance for the palace's **little bathtub;** Schliemann thought this was the very bathtub where Agamemnon was stabbed to death by his wife, Clytemnestra.

If you're not claustrophobic, head to the northeast corner of the citadel and climb down the flight of stairs to have a look at Mycenae's enormous **cistern.** You may find someone here selling candles, but it's a good idea to bring your own flashlight. Along with Mycenae's great walls, this cistern, which held water channeled from a spring 500m (1,640 ft.) away, ensured Mycenae a water supply even during enemy sieges.

There's one more thing to see before you leave Mycenae: the massive tomb known as the **Treasury of Atreus,** the largest of the *tholos* (beehive) tombs found here. You'll see signs for it on your right as you head down the modern road away from Mycenae. This treasury may have been built around 1300 B.C., at about the same time as the Lion Gate, in the last century of Mycenae's real greatness. The enormous tomb, with its 107 metric-ton (118 ton) lintel, is 13m (43 ft.) high and 14m (47 ft.) wide. To build it, workers first cut the 35m (115-ft.) passageway into the hill and faced it with stone blocks. Then the tholos chamber was built, by placing slightly overlapping courses of stone one on top of the other until a capstone could close the final course. As you look up, you'll see why this is called a beehive tomb. Once your eyes get accustomed to the tomb's poor lighting, you can make out the bronze nails that once held hundreds of bronze rosettes in place. This tomb was robbed even in antiquity, so we'll never know what it contained, although the contents of Grave Circle A give an idea of what riches must have been here. If this was the family vault of Atreus, it's possible that Agamemnon himself was buried here—indeed, some still call this the Tomb of Agamemnon.

Admission 8€ including Treasury of Atreus and museum. Summer daily 8am–7pm; winter daily 8am–8pm.

Mycenae Archaeological Museum ★★★ The museum, which opened in 2004, has a low blocky exterior which suggests the outline of the citadel itself—a point reinforced by the model of the citadel inside the museum's entrance. Unfortunately, since the museum's galleries are quite small, both the displays and the labels (in Greek and English) are hard to see when the museum is crowded, which it often is.

Most objects are grouped with others found in the same area of the citadel in an attempt to show how people lived here. The so-called "Cult Center," for example, has alarming representations of snakes and wide-eyed figures found together. Still, it's an indication of how little is known of what went on at the Cult Center and that it is not certain whether the figurines represent deities who were worshiped or the mortals who worshiped them. Copies of the famous gold masks and jewels found in Grave Circle A (the originals are in the National Archaeological Museum in Athens) are reminders of the fabled wealth of Mycenae.

© **27510/76-585.** Admission 8€, including admission to site. Summer daily 8am–7pm; winter shorter hours.

Where to Stay & Eat

Most of the restaurants in Mycenae specialize in serving set, fixed-price meals to groups. You won't starve here, but you're likely to be served a bland meal. It's sometimes possible to avoid tour groups at the **Achilleus** (*©* **27510/76-027**) or **Mykinaiko** (*©* **27510/76-724**), on the main drag, where you can eat lunch or dinner from about 15€. If you stay here, be sure to drive or walk up to the ancient site at night, especially if the moon is full.

La Belle Helene The real reason to stay here is to add your name to that of Schliemann (and stay in his old room) and other luminaries in the guest book. Sentiment aside, this small hotel, one of the most famous in Greece, is usually reasonably quiet, although it does a brisk business with tour groups in its large restaurant. The rooms are very simple; this is not the place to stay if you need a private bathrooms or the standard (TV, Wi-Fi) comforts of most hotels.

Mycenae, 21200 Argolis. *©* **27510/76-225.** Fax 27510/76-179. 8 units, none with bathroom. 50€–65€ double, sometimes lower off season. Rates include breakfast. DC, V. **Amenities:** Restaurant.

La Petite Planete ★ This would be a nice place to stay even without its small swimming pool, which is irresistible after a hot day's trek around Mycenae. I've found it quieter here than at La Belle Helene, except on summer weekends, when the entire hotel can be taken over by wedding groups. *Warning:* If the wedding party is going elsewhere for dinner, the hotel restaurant often closes, but someone will usually rustle up a simple meal for you. The owners here are helpful and there are splendid views over the plain of Argos to the hills beyond (from the front rooms).

Mycenae, 21200 Argolis. *©* **27510/76-240.** 30 units. 70€ double. AE, V. Usually closed Jan–Feb. **Amenities:** Restaurant; bar; outdoor freshwater pool. *In room:* A/C, TV.

EPIDAURUS ★★

32km (20 miles) E of Nafplion; 63km (39 miles) S of Corinth

The **Theater of Epidaurus** is one of the most impressive sights in Greece. Probably built in the 4th century, the theater seated—and still seats—some 14,000 spectators. Unlike so many ancient buildings, including almost everything at the Sanctuary of Asclepius, the theater was not pillaged for building blocks in antiquity. As a result, it is astonishingly well preserved; restorations have been both minimal and tactful.

Some say that the theater's architect was Polykleitos, a native of nearby Argos, who gained fame as a sculptor and quite probably designed Epidaurus's round tholos. The entire sanctuary was dedicated to the healing god Aesculpius, and many of those who came here did so in hopes of a cure—or to give thanks for one.

The village of Palea Epidaurus, a beach resort 10km (6 miles) from Epidaurus, is confusingly sometimes signposted ANCIENT EPIDAURUS; the theater and sanctuary are poorly signposted, but there are some road signs saying ANCIENT THEATER.

To confuse things further, Palea Epidaurus has its own small theater and festival. If you want a swim, Palea Epidaurus is the nearest beach—but it is often quite crowded.

Essentials

GETTING THERE **By Car** If you're coming from Athens or Corinth, turn left for Epidaurus immediately after the Corinth Canal and then follow the coast road to Ancient Epidaurus (or Epidaurus Theater), not to Nea Epidaurus or Palea Epidaurus. From Nafplion, follow the signs for Epidaurus and keep an eye out for signs for the Theater. If you drive to Epidaurus from Nafplion for a performance, be alert: The road will be clogged with buses and other travelers driving the road for the first time.

By Bus Two buses a day run from the Stathmos Leoforia Peloponnisou, 100 Kifissou, Athens (© **210/512-4910;** www.ktel.org), to Epidaurus. The trip takes about 3 hours. There are three buses a day from the Nafplion bus station, off Plateia Kapodistrias (© **27520/27-323**), to Epidaurus, as well as extra buses when there are performances at the Theater of Epidaurus. This bus takes about an hour. For general information on Athens-Peloponnese schedules and fares, call © **210/512-4910,** or check www.ktel.org.

FAST FACTS The ancient site has both a **mobile post office** and a **pay phone** (not always in service).

What to See & Do

The Sanctuary, Museum & Theater at Epidaurus ★★ Although it's pleasant to wander through the shady **Sanctuary of Asclepius,** it's not easy to decipher the remains here. Recent restoration work and some new signage certainly helps. You can make out the **propylaia** (a monumental entranceway), the round **tholos** (a mysterious building of uncertain purpose), and the long **abaton** (the name means "not to be trod on"; the building was evidently used for the sacred mysteries). As at Olympia, the Asklepion had accommodations for visitors, several large bathhouses, civic buildings, a stadium, a gymnasium, and several temples and shrines. Despite the ongoing restoration work, many of the remains here are so meager that you may have to take much of this on faith. But keep an eye out to see if the ongoing work on restoring some of the 26 columns of the tholos's Doric colonnade is taking place when you visit. The tholos was designed by the famous 4th-century-B.C. architect Polykleitos, who built similar round buildings at Olympia and Delphi. If you wonder why the inner foundations of the tholos are so convoluted and labyrinthine, you're in good company: Scholars still aren't sure what went on here, although some suspect that Asclepius's allegedly healing serpents lived in the labyrinth.

Next to the tholos are the remains of the abaton, made up of two long **stoas,** where patients slept in the hope that Asclepius would reveal himself to them in a dream. Those who had dreams and cures dedicated the votive offerings and inscriptions now in the museum.

At the entrance to the site, the **Excavation Museum** helps put some flesh on the bones of the confusing remains. It has an extensive collection of architectural fragments from the sanctuary, including lovely acanthus flowers from the mysterious tholos. The terra-cotta body parts are votive offerings that show precisely what part of the anatomy was cured. The display of surgical implements and intimate body parts will send you away grateful that you didn't have to go under the knife here, although hundreds of inscriptions record the gratitude of satisfied patients.

If you climb to the top of the **ancient theater,** seating 14,000, you can look down over the 55 rows of seats, divided into a lower section of 34 rows and an upper section with 21 rows. The upper seats were added when the original theater was enlarged in the 2nd century B.C. The theater's acoustics are famous: You'll almost certainly see someone demonstrate how a whisper can be heard all the way from the round orchestra to the topmost row of seats. In 2007, researchers at the Georgia Institute of Technology demonstrated that the theater's superb acoustics are due to its limestone seats! The seats deaden the low-frequency murmurs of the audience while magnifying the higher-frequency voices of the actors. Just as the stadium at Olympia brings out the sprinter in many visitors, the theater at Epidaurus tempts many to step stage center and test the acoustics by reciting poetry or bursting into song. Still, there's a respectful silence here when a performance of a classical Greek play begins, as the sun sinks behind the orchestra and the first actor steps onto the stage (see "Epidaurus After Dark," below).

If you're a theater buff, be sure to take in the **Epidaurus Festival Museum,** near the entrance to the site, with its displays of props, costumes, programs, and memorabilia from past performances. It's usually open daily on days when there is a performance at the ancient theater and is sometimes open (when the site is open) from May until September; admission is free.

Be sure to check the opening hours as soon as you arrive, if not before; they change unpredictably.

Tip: Although the sanctuary is shady, the theater is not and it can be very hot under the summer sun at the Theater of Epicaurus. Watch for the benches almost hidden under the pine trees outside the theater near the stage. This is an especially pleasant spot to sit after sprinting (or huffing and puffing) to the top of the theater!

© **27530/23-009.** Combined admission 6€. Site and theater summer daily 8am–7pm; winter daily 8am–5pm. Excavation Museum Mon 11am–5pm; Tues–Sun 8am–5pm.

Where to Stay & Eat

We suggest that you stay in Nafplion when you visit Epidaurus, or at the beachside **Hotel Kalamaki** on the Gulf of Corinth (p. 238). It's about a 30- to 45-minute drive to either destination, unless you get stuck behind a convoy of tour buses. The drive to Nafplion is not wildly interesting; the drive to the Hotel Kalamaki takes in some terrific coastal scenery, with plenty of ups and downs on the winding mountain and seaside road. The small hotels closer to Epidaurus are usually booked by tour groups well in advance of theater performances and are not sufficiently charming to recommend. As to food, several kiosks sell snacks and cold drinks near the ticket booth at Epidaurus. In Nea and Palea Epidaurus, you'll find a number of restaurants, most of which cater to large groups. In other words, you won't starve, but there's no place worth seeking out, except **Leonidas** (© **27530/22-115**). This small restaurant with a garden on the main Epidaurus road is open for lunch and dinner year-round, has consistently good food, and attracts a post-theater crowd that often includes actors who relax here after performances.

Epidaurus After Dark

Classical performances at the **ancient theater** are usually given Friday and Saturday and sometimes Sunday at around 9pm June through September. Many productions are staged by the **National Theater of Greece,** some by foreign companies. Ticket prices at press time ranged from 20€ to 60€. For the latest ticket prices and other information, contact the **Hellenic Festival Box Office,** 39 Panepestimiou (in the arcade; ℂ **210/928-2900;** www.hellenicfestival.gr). You can sometimes buy tickets (if available) for that night's performance or future performances at the box office at the theater of Epidaurus (ℂ **27530/22-026**). Most of Nafplion's travel agencies sell tickets on the day of a performance. The ancient tragedies are usually performed either in classical or modern Greek; programs (6€) usually have a full translation or synopsis of the play. The excellent **Odyssey** bookstore in Nafplion (p. 247) usually has English-language translations of the plays.

If you are in Epidaurus in July, check out the delightful **Musical July Festival** at the **Little Theater** of Ancient Epidaurus, 7km (4½ miles) from Epidaurus. Performances in the past have ranged from chamber music to flamenco. Information on ticket prices and chartered bus and excursion-boat transportation from Athens is usually available by June from the **Athens Concert Hall (Megaron Mousikis),** 1 Kokkali and Vas. Sophias (ℂ **210/728-2000;** www.megaron.gr); the **Greek National Tourism Organization** (ℂ **210/870-7000;** www.gnto.gr); or the **Municipality of Palea Epidaurus** (ℂ **27530/41-250**).

NEMEA ★★

25km (15 miles) SE of Corinth; 35km (21 miles) N of Argos

Nemea is a gem of a site, with a restored stadium, a temple with standing columns, and the most appealing and helpful small museum in the Peloponnese. The more famous Panhellenic Games were held every 4 years at Olympia and Delphi, but there were also games every 2 years at Isthmia, near Corinth, and at Nemea, in a gentle valley in the eastern foothills of the Arcadian Mountains, from about 573 B.C. to 100 B.C. Around 100 B.C., Nemea's powerful neighbor Argos moved the festival from Nemea to Argos, putting an end to the Games here. But, thanks to the Society for the Revival of the Nemean Games, the Games were held here for the first time in 2,000 years on June 1, 1996, when 1,000 contestants from around the world, ranging in age from 12 to 90, participated. The 2000, 2004, and 2008 Games drew even larger crowds, and the next Games are planned for 2012. So, when you visit Nemea, you won't see just the stadium where athletes once contended, but also the site of the new Nemean Games. Contestants run barefoot, as in antiquity, but wear short tunics rather than run naked. If you want to know more about the Nemean Games, contact the **Society for the Revival of the Nemean Games** (ℂ **510/642-5924** in the U.S.; www.nemeagames.gr).

Two excellent site guides should be on sale at the museum: *Nemea* (10€) and *The Ancient Stadium of Nemea* (2€). You'll find shady spots to read them both at the site and at the stadium.

┃ *In Vino Veritas* in Nemea

Nemea is famous for its **wines**, especially its red wines, many known as the "blood of Heracles." Signs along local roads indicate wine routes. On the road between Ancient and New Nemea, several vineyards, including **Palivos** (**www.palivos.gr**), offer tours and tastings of the excellent local wines most days in summer. Also check out **www. greekproducts.com/nemea**.

Essentials

GETTING THERE   By Car   From Athens, take the **National Road** to Corinth and then follow signs for Argos and Tripolis. The road divides just after the sign for Ancient Corinth. The speedy new Corinth-Tripolis toll road has green signposts depicting a highway. Take the Nemea turnoff and follow signs to the site. If you take the old Corinth-Argos road, the turnoff for Nemea is signposted. Allow 30 minutes from Corinth to Nemea on the new road and an hour on the old road.

By Bus   There are about five buses a day from the Stathmos Leoforia Peloponnisou in Athens, 100 Kifissou (© **210/512-4910;** www.ktel.org), to Nemea, usually via Corinth. Allow about 3 hours for the trip and ask to be let off at the ancient site of Nemea (Ta Archaia) on the outskirts of the hamlet of Archaia Nemea, not in the village of Nea Nemea. For general information on Athens-Peloponnese schedules and fares, call © **210/512-4910** or check www.ktel.org.

FAST FACTS   Nea Nemea has both a **post office** and a **telephone office,** but it's unlikely that you'll want to go there. There's a **pay phone** by the ancient site.

What to See & Do

The Museum & Ancient Site ★★   The Nemea Museum, set on an uncharacteristically Greek green lawn, is one of the most charming small museums in Greece (labels are in Greek and English). You'll get an excellent sense of the history of the excavation of Nemea and the Nemean Games, as well as the early Christian village here, much of which was built from material pillaged from ancient Nemea.

A display map inside the museum's main gallery shows all the cities in the Greek world whose coins were found at Nemea and illustrates just how far people came to see these Games. Just as today, most fans sat together—coins from each city were usually found in the same area of the stadium. You'll see photographs of the excavations as well as photos of important finds, such as the small bronze figure of the infant Opheltes, in whose honor the Nemean Games may have been founded.

According to one legend, the Seven Theban Champions founded the Games in memory of the infant, who—not as agile as Heracles (Hercules)—was killed by a serpent. In honor of Opheltes, the judges wore black mourning robes, just as they do today at the revived Nemean Games. Another legend says that the Games were established not to honor Opheltes but to honor Heracles, who killed a fierce lion that had his lair in one of the caves in Evangelistria hill, just behind the stadium. Fortunately, lions are unknown in today's Greece.

While you're in the museum, be sure to look from one of the large picture windows that overlook the ancient site where the coins, vases, athletic gear, and architectural fragments on display were found. A raised stone path tactfully suggests the route from the museum to the site, passing a carefully preserved early Christian burial tomb and skirting a 4th century-B.C. bath complex and the large 5th-century Christian basilica before arriving at the Temple of Zeus.

This temple was built of local limestone around 330 B.C. on the site of an earlier temple, which may have burned down. When Pausanias came by here in the 2nd century A.D., he felt that the temple was worth seeing but complained that "the roof has collapsed." Sometime later, the columns followed suit, perhaps when early Christians used the temple as a handy quarry for building material for their 5th-century basilica. For perhaps 1,500 years, only 3 of the original 32 exterior Doric columns were left standing; the drums of the others lay scattered on the ground. In 1999, University of California archaeologist Stephen Miller initiated an ambitious plan to reerect a number of the fallen columns, starting with two columns at the temple's north end.

Joint admission to site, museum, and stadium 8€. Tues–Sun 8:30am–3pm; in summer, often until 7pm.

The Stadium ★★ To reach the stadium, leave the site and head back along the road that brought you into Nemea. *The Ancient Stadium of Nemea*, on sale at the ticket booth, contains a self-guided tour of the stadium. The dressing room just outside the stadium caused quite a stir when it was discovered in 1991, with few journalists able to resist cracks about what a locker room must smell like after 2,500 years.

Athletes would have stripped down in the room, oiled their bodies with olive oil, and then entered the stadium through the vaulted tunnel, just as football players today rush onto the playing field. Once you pass through the tunnel, you'll see where the judges sat while spectators sprawled on earthen benches carved out of the hillside itself. When they got thirsty, they could have a drink from the water carried around the racetrack in a stone channel. If you wish, walk down onto the 178m (584-ft.) racecourse and stand at the stone starting line where the athletes took their places for the footraces. Running naked and barefoot, the athletes kept their balance at the starting line by gripping the indentations in the stone with their toes.

ⓒ **27460/22-739.** Joint admission to site, museum, and stadium 8€. Tues–Sun 8:30am–3pm; in summer, often until 7pm.

Where to Eat

As yet, there's no hotel I'd recommend near the site. **Nemeios Dias** (ⓒ **27450/24-244**), a welcome cafe/restaurant signposted SNAK BAR/SOUVENIR, is usually open from 10am to midafternoon; local wines are a tempting souvenir here.

SPARTA (SPARTI) ★

248km (153 miles) SW of Athens; 58km (36 miles) S of Tripolis

Sparta always perks me up. It's an energetic town, with lively street markets and a broad main square flanked by restaurants, cafes, and shops where locals congregate and engage in the unofficial Greek national sport: talking politics, telling jokes, and trading tidbits of gossip. In short, it's an ideal spot for people-watching.

Few sights in the Peloponnese are more imposing than the immense bulk of **Mount Taygetos** towering above Sparta along the western horizon. There's often snow on Taygetos until well into the summer, and when the sun sinks behind the mountain, the temperature seems to plummet instantly. To the east, the more gentle Parnon range brackets the Spartan plain. The ancient Spartans boasted that they didn't need fortifications because the Taygetos and Parnon mountains acted as their defense walls. Today, all around Sparta, lush olive and citrus groves spread across the rich plain watered by the bottle-green Eurotas River. The ornamental orange trees planted along Sparta's main avenues bring the country right into town.

The ancient Spartans were as famous for courage as the Athenians were for intellectual bravado. Little Spartan boys were told to "come back with your shield, or on it"—that is, victorious or dead. The Spartans first earned their reputation for courage and military heroism in 580 B.C., when the Spartan general Leonidas and a band of only 300 soldiers faced down the invading Persian army at Thermopylae—an event featured in the 2007 blockbuster film *300*. From 431 to 404 B.C., Sparta and Athens fought the Peloponnesian War; Sparta finally won, but was exhausted by the effort. From then on, Sparta was a sleepy provincial town with its future behind it. Greece's first king, young Otto of Bavaria, paid tribute to Sparta's past by redesigning the city with the wide boulevards and a central square that still make it charming today.

In a famously accurate prediction, the 5th-century-B.C. Athenian historian Thucydides wrote that if Sparta were ever "to become desolate, and the temples and the foundations of the public buildings were left, no one in future times would believe that this had been one of the preeminent cities of Greece." With the exception of the beautifully situated Menelaion, outside town, the ancient remains here are not memorable. Not to worry. There's plenty to do: enjoy Spartan street life, eat Spartan *loukoumades* (hot honey-drenched doughnuts), take in the small archaeological museum and the new Museum of the Olive, and then head 8km (5 miles) down the road to the more impressive remains of the Byzantine city of Mistra. If you're here in summer, try to get to Mistra early; climbing up and down the steep slope is not fun at high noon. As for Sparta, you'll want to spend no more than an hour at each of the sights—which is to say, a day here can pass pleasantly (especially with a break for *loukoumades*).

Essentials

GETTING THERE   By Bus   From Athens, seven buses a day depart from the Stathmos Leoforia Peloponnisou, 100 Kifissou (*✆* **210/512-4910;** www.ktel.org), for the Sparta bus station on the east side of town at Lykourgou and Dafnou (*✆* **27310/26-441**). Buses run back and forth to Mistra frequently from the Sparta station. For general information on Athens-Peloponnese schedules and fares, call *✆* **210/512-4910** or check www.ktel.org.

By Car   From Athens, allow 5 hours; from Corinth, 3 hours; from Patras, 3 hours; from Tripolis, 2 hours. From Athens or Corinth, the new Corinth-Tripolis road is well worth taking for those not wishing to visit much en route.

VISITOR INFORMATION   It is usually possible to get visitor information in the **Town Hall,** on the main square (*✆* **27310/26-517** or 27310/24-852); hours are Monday through Friday from 8am to 3pm. Ask whether the English-language pamphlet *Laconia Traveller* is available.

FAST FACTS   Two **National Bank of Greece** branches on Paleologou exchange currency and have ATMs. The **hospital** (*✆* **27310/28-671**) is signposted in town. The **police** and **tourist police** are at 8 Hilonos (*✆* **27310/20-492** or 27310/89-583). Both the **post office,** on Kleombrotou, and the **telephone office (OTE),** at 11 Kleombrotou, are signposted. The **Cosmos Club Internet Café** (*✆* **27310/21-500**) at 34 Paleologou charges 4€ per hour of Internet access.

> **Go Organic on a Spartan Farm**

If you want to stay on an organic farm less than an hour's drive south of Sparta in the hamlet of Gouves and perhaps learn the tango or vegan cooking, check out **Eumelia (www.eumelia. com)**, which has five rental houses, a staff of three, and never more than 25 guests taking a wide variety of semi-nars and workshops. Eumelia aims for "100% self-sufficiency" and all its buildings are built with great attention to environmental issues (but they still have TV and Internet access). Prices are reasonable: 120€ per night for two people in a two-bedroom cottage in 2011.

What to See & Do

The Acropolis & Ancient Theater   The Acropolis is at the north end of town, just beyond the statue of Leonidas near the supposed site of his tomb. The grove of trees makes the Acropolis a pleasant place to sit at sunset, but you'll probably enjoy the view of Taygetos more than the remains of the 2nd-century-b.c. theater. Originally, this was one of the largest theaters in Greece, seating 16,000. The theater was dismantled and the blocks were carted off for reuse when the Franks built Mistra in the 13th century. The theater is sometimes used during the summer festival that, funding permitting, Sparta sometimes has.

Free admission. Usually Tues–Sun 8:30am–3pm.

The Archaeological Museum ★   The prize of this museum is a handsome 5th-century marble bust, believed to show Leonidas and to have stood on his tomb. The Spartans, however, were famous as soldiers, not as artists, and for the most part, the museum's collection reflects Sparta's lack of a lively artistic tradition. Still, a stop here is worthwhile to see the statue of Leonidas, several fine Roman mosaics, and a small collection of objects found at Mycenaean sites in the countryside near Sparta. The museum's rose garden, peopled with decapitated Roman statues, is a nice spot to sit and read. *Note:* This museum has no restrooms.

On the square btw. Ayios Nikolaos and Paleologou sts. ✆ **27310/28-575.** Admission 3€ Tues–Sat 8:30am–3pm; Sun 8:30am–12:30pm.

The Coumantaros Gallery   En route to the Acropolis, it's easy to stop in at this branch of the National Gallery, in a handsome early-20th-century neoclassical house. The gallery has a small permanent collection of western European 16th- to 20th-century painters and temporary exhibits, usually by contemporary Greek artists.

Corner of Palaiologou and Thermopylon. Free admission. Tues–Sat 9am–3pm; Sun 10am–2pm. Often closed in winter.

The Menelaion ★   To visit the Menelaion, take the Tripolis road north out of town and turn right immediately after the bridge; the Menelaion is signposted about 5km (3 miles) down the road. The shrine's three terraces of gray limestone blocks, in honor of Helen of Troy's long-suffering husband, Menelaus, is about a 10-minute walk uphill from the chapel, where you can park your car. Next to the shrine are the low remains of several Mycenaean houses, none of which seem remotely grand enough to have belonged to Menelaus and Helen. Again, as with the Acropolis of ancient Sparta, the real reason to come here is the view of the plain and Taygetos.

Free admission. Usually Tues–Sun 8:30am–3pm.

Mount Taygetos ★★★   The **Hellenic Alpine Club of Sparta,** 97 Gortsol-ogou, near the central square (© **27310/22-574**), has information on climbing Mount Taygetos and on local hikes. *Taygetos,* published by the Municipality of Sparta, is an invaluable guide (9€). **Trekking Hellas** (www.trekking.gr) offers a number of weekend and 1-week hikes in the Taygetos area.

Museum of the Olive and Greek Olive Oil ★★   This small museum, in a restored stone warehouse, opened in 2005 and focuses on the cultivation and use of the olive through the ages in Greece. Drawings and photographs of scenes on vases show how the olive was raised in antiquity, and exhibits of tools and machinery bring the story up to the present. One gallery often has special exhibits. The small shop sells the excellent **museum guide** (5€, English or Greek), lovely olive oil soap, post-cards, and posters; the **cafe** has coffee, soft drinks, and light snacks. This is one of several terrific industrial museums in Greece founded by the Bank of Piraeus (**www.piop.gr**); others include the Museum of Industrial Olive Oil Production on Lesbos, the Hydroelectric Power in Dimitsana, the Marble Museum on Tinos, and the Roof-tile and Brickworks Museum in Volos.

129 Odos Othonos-Amalias. © **27310/89-315.** www.piop.gr. Admission 3€. Mar–Oct 15 Wed–Mon 10am–6pm; Oct 16–Feb Wed–Mon 10am–4pm.

The Temple of Artemis Orthia   If you head out of Sparta on the Tripolis road, you'll see a small yellow sign for the Temple of Artemis Orthia, where little Spartan boys were whipped to learn courage and endurance. The site, which dates from the 10th century B.C. but was extensively remodeled by the Romans, is often crowded with Gypsy children aggressively begging for money. Consequently, this can be an unpleasant place to visit, especially alone.

Free admission. Usually Tues–Sun 8:30am–3pm.

Where to Stay in Sparta & Mistra

There's one very special place to stay here, the **Xenonas Pyrgos Mystras,** a seven-unit boutique hotel (see below), which is the antithesis of most large, impersonal Greek hotels. Most hotels here offer substantial reductions in the off season. Mistra is a tiny village, but because of the Byzantine site, it has a number of cafes and restaurants.

Hotel Byzantion ★   This family-owned and -operated hotel is a great place to stay if you want to be poised to visit Mistra first thing in the morning—and not the place to be, of course, if you want to be in the considerably more lively town of Sparta. Guest rooms and bathrooms are on the small side and somewhat Spartan (!). Rooms in the back escape any sounds of traffic and overlook a pleasant garden. The staff is exceptionally helpful and the breakfast buffet is ample. The village of Mistra has several small tavernas if you don't want to go to Sparta for dinner.

23100 Mistra, Laconia. www.byzantionhotel.gr. © **27310/83-309.** Fax 27310/20-019. 22 units. 60€–75€ double. MC, V. Usually closed Dec–Mar 15. **Amenities:** Breakfast room; garden. *In room:* A/C, TV.

Hotel Maniatis   Despite its central location at the corner of Paleologou and Lycourgou, Sparta's two main streets, the Maniatis is reasonably quiet (the rooms in back are smaller but quieter). The marble-and-glass lobby is considerably grander than the guest rooms, which, if not Spartan, are simple, with the pine paneling, functional bedside tables, straight chairs, and the small bathrooms endemic in Greek hotels. The food at the hotel restaurant, the **Dias,** is quite good, but the place is often

The weekly **market** in Sparta is on Saturday. **Lampropoulou** and **Liakos**, both on Paleologou, stock English-language guides, newspapers, magazines, and books. During the last week in August, farmers from across Laconia bring goods to sell at a lively street fair in Mistra.

filled with tour groups; unless you're too tired after your sightseeing, consider walking a couple blocks to the excellent **Diethnes** restaurant (see below).

72 Paleologou, 23100 Sparta, Laconia. www.maniatishotel.gr. (℃ **27310/22-665.** Fax 27310/29-994. 80 units. 80€–90€ double. MC, V. **Amenities:** Restaurant; bar. *In room:* A/C, TV.

Hotel Menelaion ★ This is a grand old hotel, completely renovated and modernized in 2010, in a very central location. In fact, the Menelaion's location is almost *too* central: despite double-glazed windows, rooms fronting Paleologou can get traffic noise as well as commotion from the main taxi stand. You may forgive the hubbub: the neoclassical building has a welcome swimming pool in its central courtyard. Rooms are good-size and bathrooms are large; throughout, the hotel is decorated in soothing browns, grays, and pastels.

1 Paleologou, 23100 Sparta, Laconia. www.menelaion.com. (℃ **27310/22-161.** 48 units. From 80€ double. Rates include breakfast. MC, V. **Amenities:** Restaurant; bar; pool. *In room:* A/C, TV, minibar

Xenonas Pyrgos Mystra ★★ This seven-room boutique hotel may be the only place in Greece where you can stay in a restored traditional mid-19th-century tower house with flatscreen television and DVD player in your room. Some rooms have fantastic views of Byzantine Mistras, others look out on the hotel's garden and the plain of Sparta. The units are painted in pastels and decorated with silks and other elegant fabrics, with armchairs and reading lights. The breakfast buffet is extensive and has fresh baked goods, local honey, eggs cooked to order, and an array of regional cheeses. The staff gets high praise from guests. Friends who decided to splurge and stay here one night found this such a haven that they stayed another 2 nights.

3 Manousaki, 23100 Mistra, Laconia. www.pyrgosmystra.com. (℃ **27310/20-970** or 27310/20 700. Fax 27310/20-774. 250€–400€ double and suite. AE, DISC, MC, V. **Amenities:** Breakfast room; garden. *In room:* A/C, TV, Internet.

Where to Eat

Diethnes ★★ GREEK On summer Saturdays, all of Sparta seems to eat lunch in the Diethnes's shady garden after shopping at the street market around the corner. If you're going to eat only one meal in Sparta, it should be here; in fact, unless you really don't like eating in the same place more than once, why go anywhere else? The grills (including local *loukanika* sausages) are excellent; the vegetables are drizzled, not drenched, in oil; the local wine is eminently drinkable; and the waiters move at the speed of light through the crowds. If the Diethnes is too crowded, try the similarly priced but less tasty **Elysee,** a few doors away at 113 Paleologou.

105 Paleologou. (℃ **27310/28-636.** Main courses 7€–12€. No credit cards. Daily about 8am–midnight.

The Stoa Cafeteria ★ SNACKS This little hole-in-the-wall next to a florist is the place to go for a Greek favorite: *loukoumades,* airy deep-fried puffs of pastry drenched in honey syrup. I always stop by when I'm in Sparta.

8

THE PELOPONNESE

Sparta (Sparti)

140 Lycourgou. ☎ **27310/23-237.** Coffee and *loukoumades* 6€. No credit cards. Mon–Fri 8am–evening; Sat 8am–noon.

Mistra ★★★

A LOOK AT THE PAST

In 1204, the Frankish leader William de Villehardouin chose this site as the headquarters for his Greek empire. De Villehardouin crowned Mistra with a fortress and defense walls, built himself a palace on the slopes below, and had 10 good years here until the Byzantine Greeks defeated him at the Battle of Pelagonia in 1259. According to legend, de Villehardouin would have escaped capture if a Greek soldier had not identified him by his famously protruding buckteeth.

Mistra's real heyday came under the Byzantine Greeks, when most of its churches and more than 2,000 houses, as well as the **Palace of the Despots,** were built. Some 25,000 people lived in Mistra—twice the population of Sparta today. Among them were the philosophers, writers, architects, and artists who made it an international center of culture.

Mistra was such an important city that many Byzantine emperors sent their heirs here for on-the-job training. After Constantinople and the Byzantine empire fell to the Turks in 1453, Mistra held out; the last emperor of Byzantium was crowned in the cathedral at Mistra, which finally fell to the Turks in 1460.

The Venetians captured Mistra from the Turks in 1687 and ruled here for a half century, during which time Mistra swelled to a city of more than 40,000, largely supported by a flourishing silk industry. When the Turks regained power, Mistra began its long decline into what it is today: Greece's most picturesque ghost town.

THE ARCHAEOLOGICAL SITE OF MISTRA

Be sure to bring water and wear a hat and sturdy shoes when you visit Mistra. If you start your tour at the top, you can orient yourself by taking in the fine view over the entire site from de Villehardouin's **Castle** (kastro). The **Palace of the Despots,** which has been undergoing restoration for some years, stands out clearly, surrounded by the roofs of Mistra's magnificent **churches.** Despite what one scholar described as Mistra's "picturesque incoherence," you should be able to make out the tall walls of the once-handsome townhouses of Mistra's nobility on the upper slopes; on the lower slopes are the remains of the more modest homes of laborers and shopkeepers. Here, and throughout the site, there are excellent information signs in Greek and English beside many monuments. As you head down, you'll begin to pass some of the churches, most of which have elaborate brickwork decoration, a multiplicity of domes, and superb frescoes. Give your eyes time to adjust to the poor light inside the churches. Once they do, you'll be able to pick out vivid scenes, such as the *Raising of Lazarus* and the *Ascension* in the 15th-century frescoes in the **Pantannasa**

 Mistra's Earthly Delights

If you are lucky enough to visit Mistra in the spring or early summer, you'll find it carpeted with fragrant wildflowers and echoing with sheep bells from the flocks that are enjoying the fresh spring vegetation. This is the perfect place to take a break, smell the flowers, and enjoy the view down over the green plain of Sparta and up to the snow-clad peaks of Mount Taygetos.

Monastery; the *Marriage of Cana* in the 14th-century **Panayia Hodegetria;** and the *Birth of Christ* in the 14th-century **Peribleptos Monastery.** The frescoes that decorated Greek churches have been described as the "Books of the Illiterate"; any devout Byzantine Greek could have "read" these frescoes and identified every New and Old Testament scene, just as their descendants can today. Try also to sit for a quiet moment or two in the garden courtyard of the **Metropolis** (cathedral) **of St. Dimitrios,** with its small museum, with exhibits on Mistra as a link between East and West. The site (☎ **27310/83-377**) is open most days from 8am to 3pm and sometimes later in summer. Admission is 5€.

Tip: If you're heading west from Sparta and Mistra, take the **Langada Pass,** which is signposted for Kalamata as you leave Mistra and the village of Trypi. The 70km (40-mile) pass winds (*lots* of hairpin bends) and climbs some 1,500m (5,000 ft.) through the heavily wooded Parnon range and then winds back down to the outskirts of Kalamata. From there, you can head north to the Mani or continue west to Pylos and Olympia. The mountain scenery is spectacular and there are plenty of places to pull over en route and listen to the silence. If you're lucky, you may even see an eagle circling overhead.

ANDRITSENA ★★ & VASSAE ★

45km (28 miles) from Megalopolis to Andritsena; 24km (15 miles) from Andritsena to Vassae

Andritsena, with the scent of oregano and the sound of sheep bells everywhere, is one of the most charming Peloponnesian mountain villages. After years with only the desultory Theoxenia Hotel, Andritsena now has several good places to stay and a number of small restaurants. The main street is punctuated by enormous plane trees, several of which have been fitted with pipes gushing forth the delicious local spring water. In the evening, villagers stroll the main street while sheep bells echo in the hills. If you want to get away from it all and spend the night in a Greek mountain village, make it Andritsena. If you can, plan to be in Andritsena on Saturday, when the main street is taken over by the weekly **market,** an excellent place to buy every manner of bell (for sheep, goat, or cow), as well as mountain tea and herbs.

Vassae is one of the most impressive 5th-century Greek temples, its gray granite columns the perfect complement to its remote mountain setting. Unfortunately, the temple, badly damaged by time and earthquakes, is hidden under a bizarre protective tent that looks rather like the Sydney opera house. In short, the main reason to visit Vassae these days is to see the charming neighboring village of Andritsena.

Essentials

GETTING THERE By Bus Buses for Andritsena leave from the Stathmos Peloponnisiou in Athens, 100 Kifissiou (☎ **210/512-4910;** www.ktel.org). There are several buses a day to Andritsena from Athens and from Argos, Tripolis, Olympia, and Megalopolis. General information on Athens-Peloponnese schedules is available at ☎ **210/512-4910** or www.ktel.org.

By Car All the routes to Andritsena go through spectacular mountain countryside. The roads are excellent, but each winding mile takes about twice as long to drive as you might have anticipated.

FAST FACTS Everything you might need—the **bus station, OTE, post office, bank, police**—is clearly signposted on or just off Andritsena's main street.

What to See & Do
THE TEMPLE OF VASSAE

Coming around the last turn in the road and suddenly seeing the gray limestone columns of this 5th-century Doric temple to Apollo used to be one of the great sights in the Peloponnese. It seemed almost impossible that such a staggeringly impressive building should have been built in such a remote location—and designed by Ictinus, the architect of the Parthenon. Evidently, the temple was built by the inhabitants of the tiny hamlet of Phigaleia, to thank Apollo for saving them from a severe plague.

If you saw the temple before it disappeared under its tent, cherish your memory and don't bother to visit now. The tent fits so snugly that the only way to get a sense of what the temple actually looks like is to buy a postcard.

Every year, the guard at Vassae says that he hopes that the temple will be mended and the tent removed "next year," a phrase that in Greek does not carry the specificity that its translation into English implies! In the summer of 2000, the Committee for the Preservation of the Temple announced government-funded plans to begin a 20-year restoration. Initially, the foundation along the temple's north end, along with 10 columns, will be restored. Of course, when this vital work begins—which it had not at press time—and while it goes on, the temple itself will be even less visible to visitors.

Visiting hours to the currently shrouded monument are usually daily from 8am to 7pm in summer, to 3pm in winter. Admission is 3€.

THE VILLAGE OF ANDRITSENA

Tiny Andritsena has one of the finest small libraries in Greece, the legacy of a 19th-century philhellene. If you like old books, check to see if the **Nikolopoulos Andritsena Library,** just off the main street, is open (irregular hours, excellent English video on the collection). If you can't visit the library, you can console yourself reading online at the **Club Mylos Internet Café** on the *plateia.*

The small **folk museum,** on the *plateia* below the main street, is usually locked, despite its posted hours. Admission is 2€; contributions are welcome. To see the endearing collection of local wedding costumes, rugs, farm tools, and family photographs, ask to be let in at the house nearest to the museum. If the people there don't have the keys, they'll phone Kyria Vasso at the Sigouri restaurant (see below).

Where to Stay

In addition to our recommendation, in a pinch, there's the 45-unit **Theoxenia** (© **26260/22-219**), which continues to need remodeling—as it has for several decades. Doubles begin around 50€ (but prices are often negotiable). The restaurant is to be avoided. Rental rooms can usually be found if you ask around in the main square.

Epikourias Apollon Hotel ★　Frequent travelers to Andritsena rejoiced when this five-room hotel on the main *plateia* opened in 2002. The simple rooms have pleasant views over the town. Kuria Maria, who is in charge here, could not be more helpful. Since there are only five rooms, you should make a reservation, lest you be forced back on the Theoxenia or find yourself driving on to Olympia, the nearest place with a good number of hotels.

Plateia, 27061 Andritsena, Eleia. © **26260/22-840.** 5 units. 65€ double without breakfast; 70€ double with breakfast. No credit cards. **Amenities:** Breakfast room. *In room:* Heating in winter.

Where to Eat

There are a number of pleasant places on and just off the main street, including **Andritsena Kafezakeroplasteion** (a coffee and sweet shop) and the Greek restaurants **Georgitsis** and **Trani Brisi.** Phone numbers are not useful for any of these— walk in and sit down. In addition, there is one place to seek out (see below).

Sigouri ★★ TRADITONAL GREEK   Kyria Vasso's *briam* (vegetable stew) is excellent, as are her stuffed tomatoes and barrel wine. A meal here consists of a salad, main course, and the local wine. If you like *kourouloudes* (rag rugs), ask to see the ones she makes and sells by the meter; from about 30€, you can take home a colorful hand-loomed bedside rug. Kyria Vasso also usually has the keys to the Folk Museum. She may even have a Frommer's sticker on her window!

Sofoklcos (across from the metalworker's shop above the main *plateia*), Andritsena. ℂ **26260/22-197.** Lunch or dinner from 12€–15€. No credit cards. Lunch and dinner served most days; usually closes by 10pm.

MONEMVASSIA ★★

97km (60 miles) S of Sparta; 340km (210 miles) S of Athens

In the Middle Ages, Monemvassia was nicknamed "the Gibraltar of Greece" because of its strategic importance overlooking the East-West sea routes. Centuries of decline followed and Monemvassia had become a virtual ghost town by the early 20th century, remembered largely for its once-famous sweet wine, Malmsey. (For some information on one of today's local vintners, check out **www.vatistas-wines.gr**.) Today, this rocky island just off the easternmost tip of the Peloponnese has a new lease on life: For some years, wealthy foreigners and Greeks have been buying and restoring old houses here. Furthermore, word is getting out that in addition to its medieval fortress, handsome churches, and beautiful sunsets, Monemvassia has several of the most stylish small hotels in the Peloponnese (and increasingly good restaurants). Consequently, Monemvassia draws visitors year-round; I've made several spur-of-the-moment midwinter trips here only to find both the hotels and restaurants crowded.

In addition to independent travelers, a number of round-the-Peloponnese bus tours stop here for an hour or two. Try to arrive in the late afternoon or evening, so that early the next morning you can have a swim, relax, and do your sightseeing before the first bus arrives. And try to pack light for your visit: no cars are allowed here and even wheeled suitcases are hard to transport on the uneven cobblestone lanes.

Although Monemvassia is an island, it's connected to the mainland by a causeway across which you can drive or stroll. Once you step through the massive Venetian Gate that is Monemvassia's only entrance (*mone emvasis* means "one entrance" in Greek), you're in a different world where everything you see was carried here either by people or on the backs of donkeys. The main street is just wide enough for two laden donkeys to squeeze past each other. Beware that the donkeys seem to enjoy letting tourists know who has the right of way here!

Essentials

GETTING THERE   By Bus   There is one direct bus a day from the Stathmos Leoforia Peloponnisou, at 100 Kifissou in Athens, to Gefyra (on the mainland directly across the causeway from Monemvassia); there are six daily buses via Sparta. Call

☎ 210/512-4910 (www.ktel.gr) for schedule information. General information on Athens-Peloponnese schedules is available at ☎ 210/512-4910 or www.ktel.org.

By Car Take the National Road from Athens-Corinth-Tripolis. Head south to Monemvassia via Sparta. Allow 6 hours for the trip.

By Boat At press time, Flying Dolphin (hydrofoil) service from Piraeus to Monemvassia had been suspended. For an update, try ☎ 210/419-9200 or 210/419-9000, or check **www.hellenicseaways.gr**. Information in Monemvassia itself is available at the Port Authority (☎ 27320/61-266).

FAST FACTS The **National Bank of Greece** in Gefyra (on the shore across the causeway from the old town) exchanges currency and has an ATM. You'll find the **post office** and the **OTE** in Gefyra. For **first aid,** call ☎ 27320/61-204. The **police** are at 137 Spartis (☎ 27320/61-210). The **Malvasia Travel Agency** (malvtrvl@otenet.gr; ☎ 27320/61-752; fax 27320/61-432) in Gefyra has several helpful English-speaking staff members.

What to See & Do
SIGHTSEEING & SHOPPING

Monemvassia is a great place to wander. Sure, you'll get lost in the winding lanes, but how lost can you get on an island 480m (1,600 ft.) long and half as wide? The answer (at least at night) is: pretty lost. It's a good idea to wear good walking shoes, bring a flashlight, and save the 240m (800-ft.) ascent of the citadel (the best path up is marked on Odos Ritsos, the main street) for daytime—preferably in the cool of the morning.

You might begin your visit at the **Momemvassia Archaeological Collection** (☎ 27320/61-403), in the former mosque on the Plateia Tsami (Square of the Mosque). It's open daily (except for Mon) from 8am to 3pm (sometimes later in summer); admission is free. The exhibits of local architecture and artifacts include some elegant old clay pipes; try to pick up a copy of the excellent guide *The Castle of Monemvasia* (3€), with its detailed map and explanations of the castle's elaborate fortifications.

From the **citadel,** there are truly spectacular views down to the red-tile roofs of Monemvassia, out across the sea and deep into the mountains of the Mani peninsula. While you're here, try to figure out how the 13th-century Church of Ayia Sophia (Holy Wisdom) was built not just on, but virtually over, the edge of the cliffs.

After exploring the citadel, you'll probably want a swim, so head down to the bathing jetty, signposted along the sea wall. En route, you'll probably pass through the main square again, with the church of Christos Elkomenos (Christ in Chains) across from a Venetian canon, as well as the Venetian chapel of Panagia Chryssafiotissa. The churches are sometimes locked; if locked, content yourself with the thought that the handsome stone houses lining Monemvassia's lanes are the real treat to see here.

The line of small shops along Ritsos Street, the main drag on "the rock," have thus far avoided the infestation of T-shirts and cheap museum reproductions so common elsewhere. **Ioanna Angelatou's shop** ★, next to the Byzantion hotel, has been here more than 20 years; it sells the deep-blue glassware made in Greece, jewelry, and well-done reproductions of antique woodcarvings and copper. Just inside Monemvassia's gate, **Costas Lekakis** has a good selection of books in English, including R. Klaus and U. Steinmuller's excellent guide *Monemvassia* (6€). **Kelari** has wines, including examples from the local Vatistas vineyards. Takis Papadakis at Kelari can often give you information on local rentals of rooms and small apartments (© 27320/61-695).

Where to Stay

I always want to stay on the rock—especially at full moon—so that I can enjoy wandering along the winding stone lanes in the evening. This is a very popular destination for both Greek and foreign visitors. If you arrive on a summer weekend without a reservation, count yourself lucky to find a wretched room for 200€. If at all possible, avoid weekends and arrive here early in the day to be sure to get your room. Records of reservations have been known to disappear, even after several phone calls to double-check. As always, try to get a written confirmation and hold on to it.

If you can't find a room on the rock, a number of new hotels on the mainland are in and around Gefyra, including the 23-unit **Flower of Monemvassia** (**Louloudi tis Monemvasias; © 27320/61-395;** fax 27320/61-391). Most of its rooms come with minifridges and with partial views (across a road) of the beach and of the rock; doubles from 60€. If you want serious luxury and a distant view of the rock, check out the 27-unit **Kinternia** (www.kinterniahotel.gr; © **2730/66-300**), which opened in the hamlet of Agios Stefanos, 7km (4⅓ miles) southeast of Monemvassia, in 2010. The Kinternia occupies a restored and greatly expanded 13th-century Byzantine mansion, whose cistern gives the hotel its name, and provides a gorgeous pool beside which you can dine. There are 16 hectares (40 acres) of vineyards and gardens, a full-service spa, an infinity pool, beds smothered with masses of chubby pillows, and towels so thick you need to do Pilates to pick them up. Doubles from 260€, suites from 450€.

Closer to the rock, the **Hotel Pramataris** (www.pramatarishotel.gr; © **27320/61-833**) is on the seashore, with 20 units, including two apartments, and has views of the rock; doubles from 70€; you probably won't remember your simple room here, but you will remember the views. On the causeway itself, the elegant 21-unit **Lazareto** (www.lazareto.gr; © **27320/61-991**) re-creates a traditional cluster of houses, with rooms with traditional weavings—and modern Jacuzzis. A large garden and vineyard behind the tall stone walls keep out most traffic noise and the spa should be finished by 2012. Rates for 2012 were not fixed at press time, but doubles probably run from 160€. The **Theophano Guesthouse** (www.theophano.gr; © **27320/61-212**), with efficiency apartments, now also operates the 16-room **Theophano Art Hotel** (doubles from 100€), which opened in 2011 with all the modern conveniences, all-organic breakfasts, and a quiet location. Next door is another Monemvasia newcomer, the new four-suite, 12-room **Likinia Hotel** (www.likinia.gr; © **27320/61-939**), spread through four stone buildings. Rooms have air-conditioning for the summer, goose-feather duvets for the winter, Molton-Brown toiletries, and the usual amenities; doubles from 120€. Some hotels on the rock have Wi-Fi, and some do not, so if this is important to you, be sure to check on availability. And remember: *All* prices go up on summer weekends.

Ardamis Castle ★ This boutique hotel in an 800-year-old townhouse, with a vast terrace overlooking the sea, had hardly opened when it started turning up on lists of the best hotels in Greece, heaped with adjectives like "romantic" and "distinctive." Units are furnished with antiques and embroideries (and ferociously energetic showers)—and most have sea views. According to the website, beds are said to have a "Special under layer with the attributes to detensify the body's static electricity"; for better or worse, I was not aware of any effects of this feature on my visit. I was aware that the staff is not always noticeably attentive—or even in evidence.

23070 Monemvassia. www.ardamis.gr. ✆ **27320/61-887.** 6 units. 180€–250€ double. DC, MC, V. **Amenities:** Breakfast room/bar. *In room:* A/C, TV.

Kellia ★ 🐾 It is nice to be able to recommend the Kellia again. This former convent, with a quiet location by the church of the Panagia Chrissafitissa, was (mis)managed as a hotel by the GNTO, but has perked up greatly now that it is operated privately. Kuria Athena is helpful, and the once-neglected rooms and garden are now well tended. Inquire about a discount if you are staying more than a night.

By the Panayia Chrysafiotissa Church, 23070 Monemvassia. kellia@otenet.gr. ✆ **27320/61-520.** 15 units. 80€–180€ double. DC, V. **Amenities:** Restaurant; garden. *In room:* A/C.

Malvasia ★★ Monemvassia's first "boutique" hotel, the Malvasia remains charming—although service can be haphazard. Over the years, the owners bought up a number of old houses, restored them, and furnished them with old copper pieces, hand-loomed rugs and bedspreads, and antique wood furniture. This would be a wonderful place to stay a week or even a month (long-term reduced rates are available). If you can't do that, at least stay for a night and splurge on a sea-view room with balcony in the Stellaki Mansion on the ramparts or in the hotel's original building on Ritsos. If you're here in winter, ask for a room with a fireplace. Some units have phones and refrigerators; some suites have full kitchens.

Headquarters on Ritsos, 23070 Monemvassia. www.malvasia-hotel.gr. ✆ **27320/61-113.** Fax 27320/61-722. 35 units. 90€–125€ double. MC, V. **Amenities:** Restaurant; breakfast room; gardens; Wi-Fi. *In room:* A/C, TV (in some rooms), hair dryer (in some rooms), kitchenette (in some rooms), minibar (in some rooms).

Where to Eat

There are a number of cafes and restaurants along Monemvassia's main drag, but it's hard to resist **Matoula's** (✆ **27320/61-660**), which has been serving good *spitiko fageto* (home cooking) since the early 1960s. A few doors away, **To Kanoni** (✆ **27320/61-387**) has a more varied menu, including a rich spaghetti carbonara. Both restaurants have indoor and outdoor tables and views over the town and sea. Depending on what season and what time of day you eat, you'll enjoy watching the chic young Athenians who flock here on weekends—or the less chic middle-aged Europeans. They're the ones studying guidebooks, while the Athenians snap photos of each other with their *kineta* (cellphones). Lunch or dinner with wine runs from 20€.

THE MANI ★★

Githio is 301km (186 miles) S of Athens and 45km (27 miles) S of Sparta; Areopoli is 32km (20 miles) W of Githio

The innermost of the Peloponnese's three tridentlike prongs, the Mani is still one of the least visited areas in Greece. That's changing fast, as word gets out about the fine beaches near Githio and Kardamili and the haunting landscape of the Inner Mani (the southernmost Mani). Good new roads mean that you can drive the circuit of the entire Mani in a day, but why rush? To get a sense of this remote and haunting region, try to spend at least a night here, perhaps in one of the restored tower-house hotels.

Whatever you do, eat at least one meal in Limeni, the port of Areopoli, at the superb **Fish Taverna Takis To Limeni** (p. 277).

The Inner Mani's barren mountains are dotted with tiny olive trees and enormous prickly pear cacti. It's hard to believe that 100 years ago, this was a densely populated area and almost every hillside was cultivated. If you look carefully, you can make out the stone walls and terraces built by farmers on the deserted hillsides.

Originally, the Maniotes chose to live in tower houses because they were easy to defend, an important consideration for these feuding Peloponnesians who spent much of their time until the early 20th century lobbing cannonballs at their neighbors. Fortunately, many tower houses survived. The towers of the sparsely populated villages of Koita and Nomia look like miniature skyscrapers from a distance.

When the Maniotes weren't trying to destroy their neighbors' homes, they seem to have atoned for their warfare by building churches: The area is dotted with tiny medieval chapels tucked in the folds of the hills. Keep an eye out for the stands of cypress trees that often mark the chapels, many of which have decorative brickwork and ornately carved marble doors. If you don't want to tramp around the countryside in search of chapels, at least take a look at the **Church of the Taxiarchoi (Archangels)** in Areopoli. Don't miss the droll figures of the saints and the signs of the zodiac carved on the church's facade. The square around the Taxiarchoi is now freshly paved, as are several nearby streets; the square and many streets around it are also pedestrian-only in summer from 8pm to 6am. There's a big celebration (bands, speeches, parade marchers in period costumes) here on March 17, the day that local hero Petrobey Mavromichaelis called on Maniotes to rise up against the Turks. Maniotes delight that this took place a good week before the Archbishop of Patras called on all the Peloponnese to rise up and fight for independence.

After World War II, when most Maniotes moved away to Athens or abroad in search of work, entire villages of austere gray-stone tower houses became deserted. In recent years, many of these handsome houses have been restored as vacation or retirement houses by Maniotes, other Greeks, and foreigners. Villages that were ghost towns 10 years ago are gaining new leases on life in this austere and beautiful region.

Tip: Longtime Mani resident Sir Patrick Leigh Fermor died at age 96 in 2011; his *Mani* remains one of the best books on Greece ever written. University of Herefordshire professor and longtime hellenophile John Chapman's excellent and beautifully illustrated *Mani: A Guide and History* is available online at **www.maniguide.info** or **www.zorbas.de/maniguide**.

Essentials

GETTING THERE   By Car   This is a long trip but not as tedious as the bus ride, which makes many stops. For the fastest route, take the National Road Athens-Corinth-Tripolis, and then head south to Githio (Gythion) and Areopoli via Sparta.

By Bus   It's possible to travel from Athens to the Sparta bus station (𝒞 **27310/26-441**), and from Sparta to the Githio bus station (𝒞 **27330/22-228**) or the Areopoli bus station (𝒞 **27330/51-229**), but this is a full-day trip. For schedule information, call 𝒞 **210/512-9233**, 210/512-9410, or the numbers above for the bus stations in Sparta, Githio, and Areopoli. For general information on Athens-Peloponnese schedules, try 𝒞 **210/512-4910** or www.ktel.org.

By Ship   At press time, Flying Dolphin (hydrofoil) service from Piraeus to Githio had been suspended. For an update, try 𝒞 **210/419-9200** or 210/419-9000, or check www.hellenicseaways.gr. There is service from Githio to the islands of Kythera and Crete. The **Rozakis Ship Brokers & Travel Agency,** 5 Vas. Pavlou, on the harborfront (© **27330/22-650;** fax 27330/22-229; rosakigy@otenet.gr), has information on sailings (including the Patras-Ancona Super Ferry service). The agency can make reservations and issue tickets.

GETTING AROUND Longtime visitors to Greece—including me—wax nostalgic about the days when they had to hoof it around the Mani. You can get around today by local bus, but by car is the most efficient way.

FAST FACTS Githio and Areopoli both have **banks** with ATMs. Don't count on finding banks elsewhere in the Mani. In Areopoli, most services are on or just off the main square: the **bank** (usually Mon–Fri 9am–noon), the **post office,** the **OTE,** the **bus station,** several **restaurants,** and an excellent small **bookstore** called Mani (© **27330/53-670**). At the bookstore you can pick up Patrick Leigh Fermor's enduring classic, *Mani,* and Bob Barrow's *Inside the Mani.* The **police** (© **27330/51-209**) are signposted on the main square in Areopoli.

What to See & Do

The Caves of Dirou (Glyfada & Alepotrypa) ★★ Here's the good news: The crystal-studded stalactites (the ones hanging from the ceilings like icicles) and stalagmites (the ones rising from the cave's floor) are spectacular, in shades of rose, green, amber, black, blood red, and purple.

The bad news: These caves, a popular vacation destination for Greeks, are mobbed in summer, so try to arrive as soon as they open. If you get here later in the day, buy your ticket immediately; usually visitors are taken in some kind of order. As wonderful as they are, these caves are not recommended for the claustrophobic. Guided tours through the Glyfada Cave take about 30 minutes. The largest of the cave's passageways is 100m (328 ft.) long; and although the trail is lit with multicolored lights, you are well aware that you are far underground. Guides pole small boats (each holding up to a dozen passengers) past the strange formations and call out the stalactites' and stalagmites' nicknames (ranging from the reverential to the obscene). The guides also delight in warning passengers not to trail their fingers in the cool subterranean waters that reach depths of 20m (98 ft.): Giant eels are rumored to live just below the surface. Visitors usually disembark from the boat for a short excursion on foot through a slippery segment of the cave. Greek women do this in high heels and sling-back sandals; I prefer sensible rubber-soled shoes or sandals.

The Pirgos Dirou Caves were discovered in 1955 by a dog that crawled through a hole into the caves and returned several days later coated in red clay. Fortunately, its owner, spelunker Anna Petroclides, was curious about the red clay and followed her dog when it next set off on explorations. What she found was a vast network of caves, of which some 5km (3 miles) have now been explored. The caves themselves are impressive, but what has made them famous is the Paleolithic and Neolithic remains found here. The Pirgos Dirou Caves are one of the oldest inhabited spots in Greece, and the pottery, bone tools, and even garbage found here have shed light on Greece's earliest history.

Before you leave Pirgos Dirou, see if the small **Neolithic Museum** (© **27330/52-233**), with displays of artifacts found in the caves, is open. Admission is 2€.

Pirgos Dirou. © **27330/52-222.** Fax 27330/52-223. Admission and tour 15€. Cave visiting hours vary; in general, daily 9am–5pm in summer, with shorter hours off season.

Where to Stay

Our recommendations below are in the Mani itself, but if you want to stay on the outskirts of the Mani, here are some suggestions. In Githio, harborfront choices offering doubles from 70€ include the venerable (and restored) **Aktaion** (✆ **27330/23-500;** fax 27330/22-294), my favorite with its seaside balconies and the **Gythion** (✆ **27330/23-452;** fax 27330/23-523), in a charming 19th-century former businessmen's club. In Messenian Mani, at the seaside hamlet of Kardamili, **Kalamitsi Hotel & Bungalows** (www.kalamitsi-hotel.gr; ✆ **27210/73-131;** fax 27210/73-135) has doubles in the main building from 115€; suites and bungalows are also available. In the Mani itself, at Gerolimenas, the posh 25-unit **Kyrimai** (www.kyrimai.gr or www.yadeshotels.gr; ✆ **27330/54-288**), a member of the Historic Hotels of Europe, looks like a miniature seaside tower hamlet—albeit one with Jacuzzis and a swimming pool; doubles start at 150€, suites at 300€. We've had disappointing reports on the food and service here and welcome readers' updates.

Akroyiali & Yerolimenas Hotels ★★ ☺   Great location, great range of accommodations, great restaurant. Unless you need serious luxury, a sand beach, and vibrant night life, this is a perfect base for exploring the Mani. Over the years, the helpful multilingual Theodorakis family has expanded its empire from the original harborside 12-room Akroyiani with its excellent restaurant that serves fresh seafood. Now, the 23-unit Gerolimenas, a stone building built in traditional Maniote style, stands beside the original hotel; uphill are 20 furnished apartments in yet another stone-faced building. The new units have air-conditioning, while the furnished apartments have TV and complete kitchenettes; many units have balconies. All these rooms are popular in summer with vacationing Greek and European families who come for a week or more. Ask about long-term rates if you plan to do the same and reserve ahead, especially if you'll be here July through August or on weekends. The small beach in Gerolimenas is shadeless and rocky, although some good beaches are nearby.

Gerolimenas, 23062 Lakonia, Mani. www.gerolimenas-hotels.com. ✆ **27330/54-204.** 55 units. 55€–85€ double; 65€–90€ 1- and 2-room apts. Rates include breakfast. No credit cards. **Amenities:** Restaurant. *In room:* A/C (in most), TV (in most), kitchenettes (in some).

Hotel Itilo ★ ☺ 🏊   For more than 30 years, this beachfront family-run hotel on the Gulf of Itilo, just north of Areopoli, has attracted lots of families, whose children enjoy the beachside playground. In 2008–10, the main building was completely redone. Gone is the simple hotel of yesteryear and in its place is a stone building with very nicely decorated rooms—lots of stone, wood, and marble and large bathrooms, with toiletry goodies. Many of the large guest rooms overlook the sea. The hotel food, which includes lots of fresh fish, is excellent but, as always with fish, expensive. Children love the ice-cream sundaes with little parasols and sometimes sparklers.

Neo Itilo, 23062 Lakonia, Mani. ✆ **27330/59-222.** Fax 27330/29-234. 26 units. 150€–200€ double. Rates include breakfast. Cash payment preferred; MC, V accepted. **Amenities:** Restaurant; children's play area. *In room:* A/C, TV, minibar, Wi-Fi.

Kapetanakou Tower Hotel ★   This is a wonderful place to stay to get an idea of what it was like to live in a Maniote tower. (Noisy, for one thing: When the wind blows, or other guests walk on the wooden staircase, you know it!) One of the first of the traditional settlement hotels managed by the Greek National Tourism Organization, and now privately owned, the 180-year-old Kapetanakou Tower stands in a walled garden just off the main street in Areopoli. Some of the rooms have sleeping lofts (reached by wooden ladders), several have balconies or little patios, and most have colorful rag rugs and locally handmade weavings. The hotel serves breakfast, and it's only a 5-minute stroll to Areopoli's restaurants.

Areopoli, 26062 Laconia, Mani. ℰ **27330/51-233.** 8 units, with 2 shared bathrooms on each floor. 70€–80€ double. No credit cards. **Amenities:** Breakfast room.

Limeni Village Hotel ★★ Before I stayed here, I regarded this hotel, built as a Maniote tower village, a glaring example of bringing coals to Newcastle. But after enjoying the swimming pool each day before and after sightseeing, and taking in the sunset over the sea below while sipping gin and tonics on the balcony, I was a convert. The guest rooms (two units to most bungalows; some bungalows rented as suites) are outfitted with rag rugs, stone floors, and balconies overlooking the Bay of Itilo. The breakfast buffet is fine, the restaurant is ordinary (but the superb Fish Taverna Takis To Limeni is minutes away; see below). Most guests here seem to be Greek families visiting the Mani. Reservations are essential in August and on summer weekends.

Limeni, Areopoli, 23062 Laconia, Mani. www.limenivillage.gr. ℰ **27330/51-111.** Fax 27330/51-182. 32 units. 125€ double (lower off season). Buffet breakfast included. AE, MC, V. **Amenities:** Restaurant; bar; pool. *In room:* A/C, TV, minibar.

Londas Tower Guesthouse ★★ This place is a delight—and the innkeepers Hans Kleimer and Iakovos are a big part of what makes this place so special. Just off Ayii Taxiarches Square, the Londas Guesthouse has three doubles and a triple in a restored 18th-century tower that once was the home of the War of Independence hero Petrobey Mavromichaelis. Each unit has an en suite bathroom, done with wonderful attention to detail. Throughout, there are paintings done by the innkeepers. There are views over the town from the rooms and their terraces. There's no air-conditioning (the winds here are so fierce that it is almost never needed) and, to ensure tranquillity, no TVs. The innkeepers are amazingly helpful, serve homemade preserves at breakfast, and have great suggestions on how best to enjoy the Mani. One of their suggestions alerted me to a great new taverna in town: the **Katoi** (see below).

Limeni, Areopoli, 23062 Laconia, Mani. www.londas.com. ℰ **27330/51-360.** 4 units. From 85€ double. Minimum stay 2 nights except Aug (4 nights). MC, V. **Amenities:** Breakfast room/bar.

Where to Eat

Lela's (ℰ **27210/73-5411**) has been *the* place to eat in **Kardamili** for a long time, indeed. The location by the sea is lovely and the food is fresh, tasty, and—in that highest of all Greek praises—*spitiko* (like good home cooking). When Lela's is closed, there's usually a sign posted with directions to another family-run place.

I've eaten at most of the seafood restaurants on the harbor in **Githio,** and find them pretty similar. You should get good, fresh fish at any one of these places, so you may want to make your choice based on other factors, such as atmosphere or noise level. If, like me, you like octopus, head for **Nautilia** (there are usually octopus strung up outside the restaurant). **O Potis** across from the islet of Marathonisi, has consistently good seafood. Just off the harborfront, by the traffic roundabout, are several ouzeries. **Korali** serves snacks and light meals at lower prices than the seafood places.

If you are in a hurry, you could try one of the three interchangeable restaurants on **Areopoli's main square,** which all serve basic meals featuring grilled meats and salads. Lunch or dinner at any one of these costs from about 12€.

Barba-Petros ★ GREEK   This little taverna on Areopoli's sinuous main street, which runs from the main square to the cathedral, has a pleasant small garden and the usual taverna fare (chops, stews, salads, and so forth). I hope that the new pedestrianization rules in town will make it more pleasant to sit here. In the past, youths on motorcycles used the street as a race track.

On the main street, Areopoli. ✆ **27330/51-205.** Main courses 7€–15€. No credit cards. Usually daily noon–11pm (often closed midafternoon).

Fish Taverna Takis To Limeni ★★★ SEAFOOD   The superb fresh fish at this small restaurant in Limeni, the port of Areopoli, draws customers from as far away as Kalamata, Tripolis, and Athens so be sure to make a reservation if you want a seaside table. This is not the place to eat if you are squeamish about seeing fish cleaned a few feet away. On the other hand, the seafood here is so good you may find yourself coming back for meal after meal. The seafood's price per kilo varies from day to day and is never cheap; be sure to ask for prices unless price is no object. The lobster diavolo (lobster with spaghetti in a tangy sauce with green peppers) is among the memorable "fancy" dishes, but a plain grilled fish is equally delicious.

Limeni, Areopoli. ✆ **27330/51-327.** Reservations recommended weekends. Fish and lobster priced by the kilo. No credit cards. Usually daily noon–midnight; sometimes closed during the week in winter.

Katoi ★★   This excellent restaurant has two beautifully renovated kamaras that now seat 70 inside, with tables for 25 outside in fair weather. Inside, the restaurant has the stone-paved arched roof rooms traditional in many Maniote houses. The food here, from the zesty carrot salad to the tender young goat and delicious veal or rooster in red sauce, is fresh and tasty, with daily specials to consider. There are always several vegetarian choices (my favorite stuffed zucchini in egg-lemon sauce, anyone?).

Across from the Church of the Taxiarchoi. ✆ **27330/51-201.** Main courses around 8€. No credit cards. Lunch and dinner in summer; dinner only off season, when closed Mon.

PYLOS (PILO/NAVARINO) ★

50km (31 miles) W of Kalamata; 108km (67 miles) W of Sparta; 317km (196 miles) SW of Athens

I spend as much time in Greece as I can, but I have to admit that all too often the modern village with a famous ancient name—Argos or Corinth, for example—is a disappointment. That's not the case at Pylos (also known as Navarino). Although the outskirts of the modern town are ungainly, the harbor area has considerable charm. The harborfront, the tree-shaded main square with its statues and cafes, and the cobblestoned side streets all make Pylos an appealing place to wander, especially in the cool of the evening when breezes blow from the sea.

In fact, it's so pleasant to sit at a harborside cafe it's hard to realize that Pylos's harbor has seen some bloody battles. The Athenians trapped a Spartan force on the offshore island of Sfaktiria in 424 B.C.; and in 1827, a combined French, Russian, and British armada defeated the Ottoman fleet here. More than 6,000 Ottoman sailors were butchered in what proved to be one of the critical battles of the Greek War of Independence. There's a monument to the three victorious admirals in Pylos's main square (called the Square of the Three Admirals), as well as lots of cafes that stay open late for after-dinner wanderers.

Some memorabilia from the battle, as well as archaeological finds from the area, are on view in the little **Antonopouleion Museum,** just off the main square (usually Tues–Sun 8:30am–3pm; admission 3€).

Ancient **Pylos,** site of the Mycenaean palace of old King Nestor, is about 17km (10 miles) north of the town on the hill of Englianos. Homer described Pylos as "sandy Pylos, rich in cattle," and the hilltop palace still overlooks sandy beaches flanked by rich farmland. Ancient Pylos seems to be a site that people take to—or don't. For every visitor who complains about the protective plastic roof over the site, another raves about the palace's idyllic setting. Some call the remains here "scanty," while others find this the perfect place to imagine Nestor telling his tall tales (yet again!) while his courtiers sighed and cast surreptitious glances across the gentle countryside.

Essentials

GETTING THERE   By Bus   There are several buses a day from the Stathmos Leoforia Peloponnisou in Athens, 100 Kifissou (© **210/512-9410;** www.ktel.org), to the Pylos station (© **27230/22-230**). For a general schedule of Athens–Peloponnese service, try © **210/512-4910** or www.ktel.org.

By Car   I'd call Pylos a full day's drive from Athens (although Greeks boast in doing it in 4 hr.), and 3 to 4 hours from either Patras or Sparta. The drive from Sparta to Pylos via the **Langada Pass** to **Kalamata** takes in one of the most beautiful mountain roads in the Peloponnese.

FAST FACTS   Both **banks** in the main square offer currency exchange and have ATMs. The **hospital** (© **27230/22-315**) is signposted in town. The **post office, telephone office (OTE), police** (© **27230/22-316**), and **tourist police** (© **27230/23-733**) are all signposted in the main square.

What to See & Do

Ancient Pylos (Nestor's Palace) & Museum ★★   The palace at Pylos belonged to Nestor, the old king who told stories and gave unsolicited advice while the younger warriors fought at Troy. The palace was rediscovered in 1939 by the American archaeologist Carl Blegen, who had the good fortune of discovering the palace archives on his first day of work here. Blegen uncovered some 600 clay tablets written in a mysterious language initially called **Linear B** and later shown to be an early form of Greek, used mainly to catalogue holdings of the palace—many tablets contain lists of containers of oil and so forth. The tablets and buildings found at Pylos are thought to date from the late 14th to 13th centuries B.C.; the fire that destroyed the palace around 1200 B.C. calcified and thus preserved the tablets. In 2010, yet another Linear B tablet was found, this one in an excavation at the nearby village of Iklaina. The little tablet seems to have been tossed into a rubbish heap. When the rubbish was burnt all those years ago, the tablet, like the ones at Pylos, was calcified and preserved. Its discovery seems to push the known use of writing on tablets back at least 100 years.

Unlike Mycenae and Tiryns, Pylos was not heavily fortified: You'll see a sentry box but no massive walls. The well-preserved royal apartments include a more-than-adequate bathroom with the tub still in place. Archaeologists have suggested that the

> **Taking a Boat Tour in Pylos**
>
> If you'd like to take a boat tour of the magnificent **Pylos harbor** and the island of **Sfaktiria,** look for signs advertising excursions, usually posted by the harbor. An hour-long trip should cost from about 12€ per person; the captain usually requires at least five passengers to make the trip. If the water is calm, you may see some of the ships that were sunk here during the Battle of Navarino in 1827.

small block beside the tub was a step, installed when the elderly King Nestor had trouble stepping into his bath. The palace, with its central courtyard, was originally two stories high and richly decorated with frescoes, some of which are on display at the small **archaeological museum** 1.5km (1 mile) away in the village of Hora.

Joint admission to site and museum 6€.. Tues–Sat 8:30am–3pm; Sun 9:30am 2:30pm. Head north out of Pylos on the main road and follow the signs for Hora. Both the site and museum are signposted.

Neokastro ★ The Turkish fortress above the harbor, known as Neokastro to distinguish it from an earlier fortress, now contains a small museum in a restored 19th-century barracks. The museum features the extensive collection of maps, prints, and watercolors of the French philhellene Rene Puaux, as well as a number of marvelously kitschy porcelain figurines of the English philhellene Lord Byron. Neokastro also contains a small church (clearly a former mosque), fortification walls, shade trees, beds of geraniums and roses, and views over the harbor. It's nice place to sit and relax.

Admission 3€. Daily 8am–7pm.

Where to Stay

The pleasant coast north of Pylos, with wetlands beloved of migrating birds, is changing. The enormous Westin Resort, **Costa Navarino** (www.starwoodhotels.com), has 445 rooms, a spa, and an 18-hole golf course. The smaller, more exclusive **Costa Navarino Resort** (www.romanoscostanavarino) has opened the 321-room **Romanos Resort** (pools, golf, spas) and by the time the resort is finished in 2020 will include 11 hotels, 7 golf courses, a number of spas, and hundreds of holiday villas. Doubles at either start at 400€. The Romanos made it into *Odyssey* magazine's best hotels issue in 2011, but it is difficult to be optimistic about the effect of so much construction and so many visitors on the nearby wildlife sanctuary at Voidhokilia. You may want to check on the progress of the construction before staying at either the Westin or the Romanos, or our more modest seaside recommendations, whose tranquillity may be affected by the ongoing construction of these large resorts

Hotel Zoe ★ ☺ This pleasant seaside hotel (now also called the Zoe Resort Hotel), was renovated in 2011. It's on a wonderful beach about 5km (3 miles) north of Pylos and is popular with Greek and German families. If you're traveling with children, the chance to begin and end a day of sightseeing with a swim might be the salvation of a family vacation. (There's also a pool, which is good for children on days when the sea is a bit rough.) The guest rooms and apartments are good sized, nicely furnished in pastels and muted browns and grays; the beds are terrific, the reading lamps are excellent, and the place is ferociously clean. The in-house **restaurant** serves lots of organic veggies from the Zoe's own garden. Ask about long-term rates.

Gialova, 24001 Pylos, Messenia. www.zoeresort.com ✆ **27230/22-025.** Fax 27230/22-026. 28 units in hotel, 16 apts. in resort building. 70€–100€ double and apt. No credit cards. **Amenities:** Restaurant. *In room:* A/C, TV, fridge (some units).

Karalis Beach Hotel With the best location in town—at the end of the harbor below the Turkish kastro, near a stand of pine trees, far from most traffic—this used to be a special place to stay. But at some point, the management became haphazard, housekeeping became casual, and the lobby became a hangout for chain-smoking buddies of the desk clerks. In short, the reason to stay here is the location, especially if you get one of the seaside rooms with a balcony. The hotel often overbooks and sends its overflow to the **Karalis Hotel,** Kalamateas 26 (✆ **27230/22-980**), which is under the same management. Resist if they try this on you: the rooms here are okay, but the place is a hike from the harbor and restaurants and there's lots of traffic noise.

Paralia, 24001 Pylos, Messenia. ✆ **27230/23-021.** Fax 27230/22-970. 14 units, 4 with shower only. 80€ double. MC, V. Usually closed Nov–Apr. **Amenities:** Breakfast room; bar; Internet. *In room:* TV (in some).

Navarone Hotel/Bungalows ★ Friends who stayed here report enjoying this new hotel and its pool, about 5km (3 miles) north of Pylos and a 5-minute walk from an excellent sand beach. Many of the rooms have seafront balconies, and most have good reading lights and handy desks. Remember that it gets lots of tour groups.

Petrochori, 24001 Pilias, Messenia. navaron1@otenet.gr. ✆ **27230/41-571.** Fax 27230/41-575. 58 units, including 41 bungalows. 70€–85€ double. DC, MC, V. **Amenities:** Restaurant; pool. *In room:* TV.

Where to Eat

Diethnes Taverna ★ GREEK/SEAFOOD   The Diethnes has been here forever, serving meals both indoors and at tables by the quay overlooking the harbor. As you'd expect from a restaurant on the sea and next to the fish-inspection station, the seafood here is very fresh. There are usually a number of chicken and meat dishes, as well as a good *briam* (vegetable stew). If you like the food and want to try different restaurants with similar menus, **Pende Adelphia** and **4 Epoches** are also along the harborfront.

Paralia. ✆ **27230/22-772.** Fish priced by the kilo. No credit cards. Mid-May to mid-Sept daily noon–11pm (and sometimes later).

Side Trips from Pylos: Methoni & Koroni ★★

Methoni 13km (8 miles) from Pylos; Koroni 30km (18 miles) from Pylos

Methoni and Koroni are two of the most impressive medieval fortresses in Greece and would be worth seeing for that reason alone. But that's not the only reason to come here: Methoni has one of the best restaurants in the Peloponnese, and the drive through the Messenian countryside between Methoni and Koroni is ravishing. The route from Pylos to Koroni via Longa is blissful; by contrast, the southerly seaside route takes in the village of Finikounda, a windsurfer's paradise, and can be heavily trafficked on summer weekends. In a day trip, you can drive from Pylos to the convent and fortress at Koroni, have a swim and a bite near Finikounda, head to Methoni for another fortress, another swim, and dinner at the **Taverna Klimataria** (see below), before heading back to Pylos. Try not to visit either fortress on summer weekends when they are crowded with locals eager to have a swim and a fish dinner.

   The fortress at **Koroni** encloses a number of whitewashed and pastel **village houses,** a **convent,** and several **cemeteries.** Although the main road in town leads uphill to the fortress gate, park in town, unless you'd enjoy backing up beside a sheer

A Little History of the Area

The Venetians built Methoni on the Ionian Sea and Koroni on the Gulf of Messenia in the 13th century to safeguard their newly acquired Greek empire. In some of the bloodiest fighting on record, the fortresses, almost immediately nicknamed "the twin eyes of empire," passed back and forth between various powers for the next several centuries: In 1500, the Turks slaughtered all 5,000 Venetian defenders at Methoni; in 1685, the Venetians wiped out the 1,500-man Turkish garrison at Koroni.

drop to the sea if you meet a car heading downhill! The grounds inside the fortress walls are planted with roses and shade trees; piles of cannonballs and the occasional cannon remind visitors of Koroni's bloody past. There's a string of seafood restaurants by the harbor below, but nothing to compare with Methoni's Klimataria, although **Kagelarios** (✆ **27250/22-648**) is a good fish place. Zaga beach is sandy and has umbrellas and lounge chairs for rent. The 14-room **Sofitel** (www.koroni-holidays.com; ✆ **27250/22-230**) is charmless, but an okay place to spend a night or two; doubles run from 60€.

The long, sandy **Methoni beach** has won several awards for its ecosensitivity, including Greece's Golden Starfish and the Common Market's Blue Flag. The seaside cafes and fish tavernas all have fine views of the fortress, which stands at the end of a low spit of land and covers enough ground to have contained a city of several thousand inhabitants during the Middle Ages. Methoni's **exterior walls** are stupendous, although little remains inside the fortress itself. Don't worry about being locked in here when the gates close at 7pm: An officious guard on a motorcycle rounds up any stragglers. The fortress is usually open from 8am to 7pm; admission is free. When it closes, you can head to the **Taverna Klimataria** (✆ **27230/31-544**), where the chef somehow manages to take standard Greek dishes (fried zucchini, eggplant salad, *briam*) and turn them into elegant delights. The Klimataria is popular with foreign visitors, especially the Germans and Italians who flock to the west coast of the Peloponnese each summer. If you want to stay the night, the 36-room family run **Amalia** (m-amalia@otenet.gr; ✆ **27230/31-129**), set in a shady garden with wonderful rose bushes, is on a seaside hill a 5-minute drive away; doubles are from 80€.

MESSENE (MAVROMATI) ★★

25km (16 miles) N of Kalamata; 60km (39 miles) E of Pylos

Even though ancient Messene's walls and towers outshine the remains at many better-known classical sites, not many visitors come here. That's a shame, because between 370 and 369 B.C., the great Theban general and statesman Epaminondas built the sprawling city of Messene, much of which remains to be seen at the village of Mavromati. Epaminondas hoped that its almost 9.5km (6 miles) of walls below Mount Ithomi would check Sparta's power. Today, the defense wall, with its two-story towers and turreted gates, is the best-preserved classical fortification in the Peloponnese, a startling sight standing alone in the lush Messenian countryside.

To get here by car from Pylos, Kalamata, or Tripolis, take the main Kalamata-Pylos road to the modern town of Messini, where the road to ancient Messene is

A rough, but adequate, road runs from the site of ancient Messene to the summit of **Mount Ithomi** (800m/2,624 ft.). The views of the districts of Messene and Lakonia are spectacular. At Ithomi's summit are remains of a **Temple of Zeus** and the small medieval **monastery** of Voulkanos. The monks are long gone and visitors are few, so this is a place to feel that the view is yours and yours alone. At sunset, there are few more spectacular spots in Greece. The summit is presently unfenced, and there is no admission charge; this will no doubt change soon, so try to go now.

(imperfectly) signposted. The site of ancient Messene (also called Ithomi) is in the village of Mavromati, approximately 20km (13 miles) north of Messini.

What to See & Do

Ancient Messene ★★ The most impressive stretches of the ancient wall are outside the site, north of the village of Mavromati. As you pass through Mavromati, pick up a copy of the excellent site guide at the postcard shop next to the village spring (5€). Even at a distance, the sheer size of the wall, with its towers and gates, makes most visitors gasp. The **Arcadian Gate** is especially well preserved; the grooves cut into the marble pavement by ancient chariot wheels are clearly visible. As you drive back toward Mavromati, you'll pass more of the defense wall and the site museum, which keeps irregular hours. Admission is 2€.

The excavated ruins of Messene are signposted past the site museum (officially open Tues–Sun 8:30am–3pm; free at press time, but probably not by the time you visit, when 3€ may be charged). This is a vast, sprawling site with a partially restored theater, an impressive **agora/forum** (marketplace), and a **Sanctuary of Asclepius** so large that it was originally thought to be the entire agora (city center and marketplace). The partially excavated **stadium,** with many of its marble benches well preserved, lies along the dirt road beyond the Asklepeion. A walk through the entire site takes a minimum of several hours, but it's possible to see just the Asklepeion in an hour. Keep an ear cocked for the tuneful frogs that live in several wells and cisterns on the site.

Admission 3€. Usually Tues-Sun 8am-3pm.

Where to Stay & Eat

I have not yet visited, but want to mention the **Likouros Apartments** (© **27240/51-297**), just out of town, which opened in 2009, with five units with TV, electric kettle, and minifridges. I'd call these accommodations more rooms than apartments, but an archaeologist friend who stayed there was pleased with her room, the management, and the view toward the site, and found it much quieter than my old standby, the **Pension Zeus** (see below); doubles from 60€.

Ithome Restaurant GREEK This simple restaurant has a terrific view over the ancient site and serves souvlaki, grills, salads, french fries, and the occasional vegetable dish. If it is crowded, there are other spots nearby. The Ithomi also has rooms for rent over the taverna. Prices charged foreigners, not unusually, are often higher than those charged to Greeks.

Mavromati-Ithome (across from the Klepsidra Spring). ☏ **27240/51-498.** Fax 2724/51-298. Lunch or dinner with a beer from 12€. No credit cards. Summer daily 11am–10pm; shorter hours in winter.

Pension Zeus This small, family run pension—which is about as far from the Greece of tour-group hotels as you can get—has several small guest rooms, some with balconies. The family is very helpful and nice. The only problem: You're on the one road through town, and from your room you will hear whatever traffic there is.

Mavromati-Ithome, 24200 Messenia. ☏ **27240/51-025** or 27240/51-426. 5 units, 3 with bathroom. 55€ double with bathroom. Rates include breakfast. No credit cards.

OLYMPIA ★★★

311km (193 miles) W of Athens; 90km (55 miles) S of Patras; 21km (13 miles) E of Pirqos

With its shady groves of pine, olive, and oak trees; the remains of two temples; and the stadium where the first Olympic races were run in 776 B.C., Olympia is the most beautiful major site in the Peloponnese. When you realize that both the archaeological museum and the new museum of the ancient Games are among the finest in Greece, you'll see why it's wonderful to have more than just a day here, especially if your hotel has a swimming pool. *Tip:* Check on the admission hours for both the site and museum as soon as you arrive. The actual open hours fluctuate from the official hours more than one would expect.

A Quick Visit to Kalamata

If, after you visit the nicely excavated market place and streets of ancient Messene, you long for some more lively city streets, head to **Kalamata,** only 31km (19 miles) to the south. On the beach a few miles out of Kalamata, the Mark Warner-operated **San Agostino Beach and Spa Resort (www.mark warner.co.uk)** has 63 units and more than 100 bungalows, is family-friendly, and offers sailing clinics; prices are available on request. Closer to town, the 193-unit **Filoxenia Hotel** has all the creature comforts, including swimming pools and restaurants (Navarinou St., 24100 Kalamata; www.grecotel.gr; ☏ **210-322-5891**); doubles start at 200€. In Kalamata itself, the seven-unit **Hibiscus Hotel** occupies a 19th-century neoclassical house, is furnished with antiques, and has its own peaceful garden (196 Faron St., 24100 Kalamata; www.traditionalhomes.gr; ☏ **27210/** 62-511); doubles begin at 80€. I have to say that although I usually love anything in a neoclassical building, I find the **Hotel Rex** (26 Aristomenous, 21400 Kalamata; www.rexhotel.gr; ☏ **27210/94-440**) seriously boring. The facade is wonderful, the public rooms are okay, but the rooms are, well, unimaginative. If you get to Kalamata, try to eat the famous local figs and olives, take in the old market area, and visit the excellent **Benakion Archaeological Museum,** founded by the same family that gave Athens its Benaki museums (Benaki and Papazoglou sts., 24100 Kalamata; ☏ **27210/26-209**; Tues–Sun 8:30am–3pm). The **Kalamata Dance Festival** (www.kalamatadancefestival.gr) attracts contemporary dance groups from around the world for 10 days of performances, seminars, and films each year in mid-July.

THE ANCIENT olympic GAMES

The 5-day Olympic festival was held every 4 years between 776 B.C. and A.D. 393 at full moon in mid-August or September, after the summer harvest. Participants came from as far away as Asia Minor and Italy, and the entire Greek world observed a truce to allow athletes and spectators to make their way to Olympia safely. During all the years that the Games took place, the truce was broken only a handful of times.

By the time the Olympic Games opened, thousands of people had poured into Olympia, and much of the surrounding countryside was a tent city. Women were barred from watching or participating in the Games, although they had their own Games in honor of Hera, Zeus's wife, in non-Olympic years. Any woman caught sneaking into the Olympic Games was summarily thrown to her death from a nearby mountain.

No one knows precisely what the order of events was, but the 5 days included footraces, short and long jumps, wrestling and boxing contests, chariot races, the arduous pentathlon (discus, javelin, jumping, running, and wrestling), and the vicious pankration (which combined wrestling and boxing techniques).

The 3rd-century-A.D. writer Philostratos recorded that participants in the pentathlon "must have skill in various methods of strangling." The most prestigious event was the *stade*, or short footrace, which gave its name to the stadium. Each Olympiad was named after the winner of the stade, and athletes like the 2nd-century-B.C. Leonidas of Rhodes, who won at four successive Olympics, became international heroes. In addition to the glory, each victor won a crown made of olive branches and free meals for life in his hometown.

A LOOK AT THE PAST   There's really no modern equivalent for ancient Olympia, which was both a religious sanctuary and an athletic complex where the Games took place every 4 years from 776 B.C. to A.D. 393. Thereafter, the sanctuary slipped into oblivion, and buildings were toppled by earthquakes and flooded by the Alfios and Kladeos rivers. When the English antiquarian Richard Chandler rediscovered the site in 1766, most of Olympia lay under 3m (10 ft.) of mud and silt. The Germans began to excavate here in 1852 and are still at it today.

Reports of the rediscovery of Olympia prompted the French Baron de Coubertin to work for the reestablishment of the Olympic Games in 1896. The first modern Olympic Games were held in Athens in 1896, and since then the Olympic torch has always been lit here. Athens hosted the 2004 Olympics, with the shot put finals taking place in Olympia's ancient stadium.

OLYMPIA TODAY   The straggling modern village of Olympia (confusingly known as Ancient Olympia) is bisected by its one main street, Leoforos Kondili. The town has the usual assortment of tourist shops selling jewelry, T-shirts, and reproductions of ancient pottery and statues, as well as more than a dozen hotels and restaurants. Two things worth visiting in town: the small **Museum of the Olympic Games** and the excellent **Galerie Orphee bookstore** (see below).

The ancient site of Olympia is a 15-minute walk south of the modern village, but if you have a car, you might as well drive: The road teems with tour buses and the walk is less than relaxing.

Essentials

GETTING THERE **By Train** There are several trains a day from Athens to Pirgos, where you change to the train for Olympia. Information on schedules and fares is available from the Stathmos Peloponnisou (train station for the Peloponnese) in Athens (© **210/513-1601**).

By Bus There are three buses a day to Olympia from the Stathmos Leoforia Peloponnisou in Athens, 100 Kifissou (© **210/512-4910;** www.ktel.org). There are also frequent buses from Patras to Pirgos, with connecting service to Olympia. In Patras, KTEL buses leave from the intersection of Zaimi and Othonos (© **2610/273-694**). For general schedule information for Athens-Peloponnese service, try **210/512-4910** or www.ktel.org.

By Car Olympia is easily a 6-hour drive from Athens, whether you take the coastal road that links Athens-Corinth-Patras and Olympia (lots of trucks, lots of accidents) or head inland to Tripolis and Olympia on the new Corinth-Tripolis road. Heavy traffic in Patras means that the drive from Patras to Olympia can take 2 hours.

VISITOR INFORMATION Olympia is a one-street town; the few things you do not find on **Praxitelous Kondili** will be just off it. The **tourist office,** on the way to the ancient site near the south end of the main street, is officially open daily, in summer from 9am to 10pm, and in winter from 11am to 6pm. Ask for maps of the site and town, and for information on accommodations (© **26240/23-100** or 26240/23-125).

FAST FACTS The **National Bank of Greece,** on Praxitelous Kondili (the main drag), exchanges currency and has an ATM. The **health clinic** (© **26240/22-222**) is signposted in town. The **police** (© **26240/22-100**) are at 6 Ethnossinelefseos. The **tourist police** (© **26240/22-550**) are located on a street behind the tourist office. Both the **post office** (on the main street) and the **telephone office** (just off the main street) are signposted.

What to See & Do

The Archaeological Museum ★★★ Even though you'll be eager to see the ancient site, you might want first to head across the road to the museum, which reopened after extensive renovations in 2004. The collection makes clear Olympia's astonishing wealth and importance in antiquity: Every victorious city and almost every victorious athlete dedicated a bronze or marble statue here, and the site was something of an outdoor museum of the finest bronze and marble sculpture. Most of the exhibits are displayed in rooms to the right and left of the main entrance and follow an essentially chronological sequence, from severe Neolithic vases to baroque Roman imperial statues, neither of which will probably tempt you from heading straight ahead to see the museum's superstars. Labels are in Greek, English, and German.

The monumental **sculpture from the Temple of Zeus** is probably the finest surviving example of Archaic Greek sculpture. The sculpture from the west pediment shows the battle of the Lapiths (Greeks who lived in Thessaly) and centaurs raging around the magisterial figure of Apollo, the god of reason.

Most scholars think that the message is the triumph of civilization (as represented by the Greek Lapiths) over barbarism—those brutish centaurs. On the east pediment, Zeus oversees the chariot race between Oinomaos, the king of Pisa, and

Pelops, the legendary figure who wooed and won Oinomaos's daughter by loosening his opponent's chariot pins. Pelops not only won his bride, but went on to have the entire Peloponnese named in his honor. At either end of the room, sculptured metopes show scenes from the Labors of Hercules, including the one he performed at Olympia: cleansing the foul stables of King Augeus by diverting the Alfios River.

Just beyond the sculpture from the Temple of Zeus are the 5th-century-B.C. **Winged Victory,** done by the artist Paionios, and the 4th-century-B.C. figure of Hermes and the infant Dionysos, known as the **Hermes of Praxiteles.** The Hermes has a room to itself—or would, if tourists didn't make a beeline to admire Hermes smiling with amused tolerance at his chubby half-brother, Dionysos. If you want to impress your companions, mention casually that many scholars think that this is not an original work by Praxitelous, but a Roman copy.

Admission to museum and site 9€. Summer Mon noon–6pm, Tues–Sat 8am–7pm; winter Mon noon– 6pm, Tues–Sat 8:30am–3pm.

The Ancient Site ★★★   In antiquity, every 4 years during the Olympic Games, so many people thronged here that it was said by the time the Games began, not even one more spectator could have wedged himself into the stadium.

Olympia's setting is magical. Pine trees shade the small valley, dominated by the conical Hill of Kronos that lies between the Alfios and Kladeos rivers. In July 2000, archaeologists excavating beside the Kladeos discovered a Mycenaean tholos tomb with more than 100 amphorae, and they expect to find more tombs as excavations continue. The discovery was a reminder of how much is yet to be discovered here.

The handsome temples and the famous stadium that you've come to Olympia to see are not immediately apparent as you enter the site. To the left are the low walls that are all that remain of the **Roman baths,** where athletes and spectators could enjoy hot and cold plunges. The considerably more impressive remains with the slender columns on your right mark the **gymnasium** and **palestra,** where athletes practiced their footracing and boxing skills. The gymnasium had a roofed track, twice the length of the stadium, where athletes could practice in bad weather. Still ahead on the right are the meager remains of a number of structures, including a **swimming pool** and the large square **Leonidaion,** which served as a hotel for visiting dignitaries until a Roman governor decided it would do nicely as his villa.

The **religious sanctuary** was, and is, dominated by two temples: the good-size Temple of Hera and the massive Temple of Zeus. The **Temple of Hera,** with its three standing columns, is the older of the two, built around 600 B.C. If you look closely, you'll see that the temple's column capitals and drums are not uniform. That's because this temple was originally built with wooden columns, and as each column decayed, it was replaced; inevitably, the new columns had variations. The **Hermes of Praxiteles** was found here, buried under the mud that covered Olympia for so long due to the repeated flooding of the rivers.

The **Temple of Zeus** once had 34 stocky Doric columns; one was reerected in honor of the 2004 Olympic Games. Built around 456 B.C, the entire temple—so austere and gray today—was anything but austere in antiquity. Gold, red, and blue paint decorated it, and inside stood the enormous gold-and-ivory statue of Zeus, seated on an ivory-and-ebony throne. The statue was so ornate that it was considered one of the Seven Wonders of the Ancient World—and so large that people joked that if Zeus stood up, his head would go through the temple's roof. In fact, the antiquarian

Philo of Byzantium suggested that Zeus had created elephants simply so that the sculptor Phidias would have the ivory with which to make the statue of Zeus.

Not only do we know that Phidias made the 13m-high (43-ft.) statue, we know where he made it: The **Workshop of Phidias** was on the site of the well-preserved brick building clearly visible west of the temple, just outside the sanctuary. How do we know that this was Phidias's workshop? Because a cup with "I belong to Phidias" written on it and artists' tools were found here—and are now on display in the Archaeological Museum.

Between the temples of Zeus and Hera, you can make out the low foundations of a round building; the three standing columns and their *stylobate* (base) were restored in honor of the 2004 Olympics. This is all that remains of the **shrine** that Philip of Macedon, never modest, built here after conquering Greece in 338 B.C.

Beyond the two temples, built up against the Hill of Kronos itself, are the curved remains of a once-elegant **Roman fountain** and the foundations of 11 **treasuries** where Greek cities stored votive offerings and money. In front of the treasuries are the low bases of a series of bronze **statues of Zeus,** dedicated not by victorious athletes but by those caught cheating in the stadium. These statues would have been the last things that competitors saw before they ran through the vaulted tunnel into the stadium.

Ancient tradition clearly shows that the Olympic Games began here, but it is less clear why they were held every 4 years. According to one legend, Herakles (Hercules) initiated the Games to celebrate the completion of his 12 labors. With the fetid Augean stables clean, Herakles paced off the stadium and then ran its entire length of 192m (600 ft.) without having to take a single breath.

Admission to site and museum 9€. Usually summer Mon–Fri 8:30am–7pm, Sat–Sun 8:30am–3pm; winter Mon–Fri 8am–5pm, Sat–Sun 8:30am–3pm.

Museum of the History of the Excavations in Olympia ★

This charming museum occupies one of the original houses used by the German excavators (imagine them warming up by the large fireplace). Photographs and journals document the history of the excavations from 1766, when Richard Chandler identified the site, to the present. Look for the 19th-century photograph showing the unearthing of the Temple of Zeus. The photo was taken as the structure was emerging from beneath 5m (16 ft.) of soil. Some of the shovels and whisk brooms used are on display.

© **26240/20-128.** Free admission. Summer Mon noon–7pm, Tues–Sun 8am–7pm; in winter the museum usually closes by 5pm.

The Museum of the History of the Olympic Games in Antiquity ★★★

The museum, which opened in 2004, occupies the neoclassical building that served as the site's original archaeological museum. The path to the museum is steep; it is sometimes possible to drive up and drop off passengers by the museum's entrance. The collection is superb; the text (Greek, English, German) posted on exhibits is extensive. Each of the 12 galleries has a theme, including "The Beginning of the Games," "Zeus and his Cults," "The Events," and games at other ancient sites (Nemea, Isthmia, Delphi). Exhibits document the growth of the Games from a sprint on 1 day to 5 days of events for hundreds of athletes from around the Greek world. In wrestling, while breaking fingers was forbidden, eye-gouging was permitted. In each event, there was only one winner; there were no runners-up. Displays include massive chariot wheels, musical instruments, statues of lithe athletes, and all manner of athletic gear.

A Great Place for Books & Music

Galerie Orphee, Antonios Kosmopoulos's shop on the main street in Ancient Olympia (✆ **26240/23-555**), has a wide selection of books, an extensive range of CDs of Greek music, plus displays of contemporary art. What a pleasant contrast to Olympia's other shops, which have all too many T-shirts, museum reproductions, and machine-made rugs and embroideries sold as "genuine handmade crafts." Watch for any shops on the main drag selling attractively presented (but expensive) honey, olive oil, and other local products. I'm not giving shop names because in this economic climate, these shops tend to open and close unpredictably.

✆ **26240/22-529.** Free admission (but a fee is planned). Summer Mon noon–7pm, Tues–Sun 8am–7pm; winter, the museum usually closes by 5pm.

The Museum of the Olympic Games ★   When you head back to town, try to set aside half an hour to visit this museum, which is signposted on the main drag. Not many tourists come here, and the guards are often glad to show visitors around. Displays include victors' medals, commemorative stamps, and photos of winning athletes, such as former king Constantine of Greece and the great African-American athlete Jesse Owens. There's also a photo of the bust of the founder of the modern Olympics, Baron de Coubertin. (The bust itself stands just off the main road east of the ancient site and marks the spot where de Coubertin's heart is buried.)

Admission 3€. Mon–Sat 8am–3:30pm; Sun and holidays 9am–2:30pm.

Where to Stay

Main street Olympia alternates hotels—more than 20 at last count—with restaurants and shops. This means that you can almost always find a room—although if tourism here returns to its pre-2009 glory days, and you arrive without a reservation in July or August, you probably won't get your first choice. As is often the case in major tourist centers, hotels here often unofficially raise or lower rates depending on the kind of season they're having. In winter, many hotels are closed. If you want to see ancient Olympia, but stay by the sea, in considerable luxury combined with child-friendly facilities, you can do it, but you will have to do some nasty driving on truck-infested main roads to commute between a seaside hotel and Olympia. If this does not deter you, try the elegant **Grecotel Olympia Riviera Resort** (www.grecotel.gr), 45 minutes away on its own beach in Kyllini, with three hotel complexes (Mandola Rosa is the fanciest), 200 hectares (500 acres) of gardens, six restaurants (one organic), seven pools, and just about everything else you'd want. If it's full, try the seaside 288-room **Aldemar Olympian Village Royal Olympian Spa Thalasso** (www.aldemarhotels. com) in Skfridia, with extensive sport, restaurant, beach, playground, and spa facilities. Neither is cheap; doubles start from about 200€.

Hotel Europa ★★★   The Europa is the best hotel in town—and one of the best in the Peloponnese. Part of the Best Western chain (managed by a helpful local family), it's a few minutes' drive out of town on a hill overlooking the modern village and the ancient site. Most units face the large pool and garden, and several have views of a bit of the ancient site. The rooms are large, with extrafirm mattresses and sliding glass doors opening onto generously sized balconies. The **taverna** in the garden (indoors in bad weather) serves tasty grills and stews; the indoor breakfast buffet is extensive.

27065 Ancient Olympia, Peloponnese. www.bestwestern.com. *C* **800/528-1234** in the U.S., 26240/22-650 or 26240/22-700. Fax 26240/23-166. 80 units. 110€ double. Reductions available for AAA, AARP members, and off season. Rates include breakfast. AE, DC, MC, V. **Amenities:** Restaurant; bar; pool. *In room:* A/C, TV, minifridge.

Hotel Olympia Palace ★ Frankly, I had looked forward to staying here again after the renovations and was disappointed. It's true that the Olympia Palace, which was completely remodeled for the 2004 Olympics, has been touched up since then, and is an excellent choice if you want to be poised on the main street in order to investigate the village. The guest rooms have good beds, cheerful prints on the walls, and nice rag rugs on the floor; the bathrooms are modern and good-size. However, street noise plagues the front rooms and a large parking lot flanks the side toward the ancient site; try for a rear room. Another problem: seriously ho-hum service.

2 Praxiteleous Kondili, 27065 Ancient Olympia. www.olympiapalace.gr. *C* **26240/23-101.** 58 units. 100€–130€ double. AE, MC, V. **Amenities:** Restaurant; bar. *In room:* A/C, TV, minibar.

Hotel Pelops ★★★ If you've heard how helpful Aussie expat Susanna Spiliopoulou and her Greek husband and children are, believe every word! Susanna and her family make this one of the most welcoming hotels in Greece. Rooms are good-size, cheerful, and very comfy. Check out their website to learn about their 3- and 4-day cooking, writing, and painting classes, usually offered in the off season. An added bonus: Guests here can use the pool at the Europa Hotel and order a **Pelops Platter** (a wide variety of Greek *mezedes*) for dinner. But the real bonus here is leaving the all-too-often anonymous world of hotels and entering a welcoming haven, in the center of town, but on a blissfully quiet street.

2 Varela, 27065 Ancient Olympia. www.hotelpelops.gr. *C* **26240/22-543.** 25 units. 75€–85€ double. MC, V. **Amenities:** Breakfast room. *In room:* A/C, TV.

Where to Eat

Olympia has almost as many restaurants as hotels. The ones on and just off the main street with large signs in English and German tend to have indifferent food and service; the **Aegean, Zeus,** and the **4 Epoxes (4 Seasons),** are consistently better than average. The two restaurants of the Hotel Europa (see above) are far superior to most restaurants in town, but check to see if the excellent **Kladeos** restaurant has reopened. If you have a car, the family-operated **Taverna Bacchus,** some 5km (3 miles) outside Olympia in the village of Miraka, has long offered excellent country cooking. Phone first (*C* **26240/22-498**) to make sure the Bacchus is open the night you want to go.

PATRAS (PATRA)

207km (128 miles) SW of Athens

Patras is the third-largest city in Greece and far and away the largest in the Peloponnese, Patras's unappealing urban sprawl now extends for miles north and south of the city center. Patras has always had a lively cafe, theater, and music scene, and sights worth seeing—the Cathedral of St. Andrew, the Archaeological Museum, a Roman Odeon (music hall) on the slopes of the ancient acropolis, and a medieval castle on the summit. Still, this remains a better place to live than to visit; unless you are arriving or departing here by ship, love commercial ports, or have lots of time on your hands, you'll probably want to skip Patras.

If you do plan to spend time in Patras, here are some suggestions: In July and August, the **Patras International Festival of the Arts** (© **2610/276-540** or 2610/279-008) brings performances of everything from ancient drama to popular music to the Roman Odeon and the Patras Municipal Theater (© **2610/623-730**) and a number of locations around the city. Patras also has a vigorous **carnival** that lasts nearly a month, with parades, costumes, and floats, ending the Monday before Lent (**www.carnivalpatras.gr**). Whenever you are here, you may choose to sample local wines at the **Achaia Clauss winery,** 8km (5 miles) southeast of town (© **2610/325-051**); check with the tourist office for directions, bus schedules, and hours.

Essentials

GETTING THERE   **By Train**   Extensive work is being carried out on the entire rail system from Athens to the Peloponnese and within the Peloponnese itself. For up-to-date information on schedules and fares, call © **210/529-8735** or 210/323-6747 (www.ose.gr). It remains to be seen whether the renovations will produce a speedier and more efficient rail system. If trains are running, you may want to know that the Patras train station, on Othonos and Amalias (© **2610/273-694**), is on the waterfront near the boat departure piers. If you're catching a ferryboat, keep in mind that Greek trains usually run late, and allow extra time for your journey.

By Bus   There are some 15 buses to Patras daily from the Stathmos Leoforia Peloponnisou in Athens, 100 Kifissou (© **210/512-4910;** www.ktel.org). The Patras bus station (© **2610/623-886**) is on Othonos and Amalias. For general Athens-Peloponnese schedule information, try © **210/512-4910** or www.ktel.org.

By Car   The drive on the National Highway from Athens to Patras takes about 5 hours. **Note:** In the Patras city center, the system of one-way streets, not always obviously marked, along with the profusion of foreign drivers who have just arrived from Europe by car ferry, means that you should drive with particular care.

If you're heading from Patras across the Gulf of Corinth into Central Greece, you'll probably want to take the spectacular new Rio-AntiRio Bridge, which opened in 2004 (13€). If you prefer—and if it has not been discontinued, as threatened—you can still take the Rio-AntiRio car ferry, which runs twice an hour from early morning until about 11pm (3€).

Tip: The bridge's official, and seldom-used name, is the Harilaos Trikoupis Bridge. Most people prefer to simply call it *e gefyra* (the bridge).

VISITOR INFORMATION   There is a good **tourist information** office (with Internet access) in an old factory building at Othonos and 6 Amalias; it's usually open Monday through Friday 8am to 8pm (© **2610/461-740;** www.patras.gr). The **tourist police** are at 53 Patreos (© **2610/220-902** or 2610/451-833). The website www.infocenterpatras.gr has some useful information.

FAST FACTS   A number of **banks** on the waterfront and on Plateia Georgiou exchange currency and have ATMs. The **post office** is signposted at the intersection of Mezonas and Zaimile. There is a **telephone office (OTE)** on the waterfront by the Customs sheds. Most of the **car-rental agencies** (Avis, Hertz, Kemwell) have clearly marked offices on the waterfront. The **hospital** (© **2610/22-3812**) is signposted in town. There is also an **emergency first-aid station** (© **2610/277-386**)

Patras

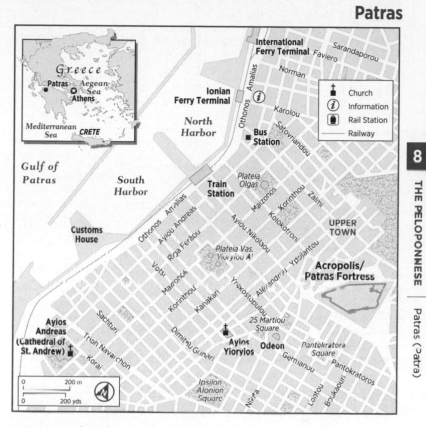

(Map of Patras)

Greece
Patras • Aegean Sea • Athens
Mediterranean Sea • CRETE

Gulf of Patras

South Harbor

North Harbor

International Ferry Terminal — Faviero — Sarandaporou
Norman

Ionian Ferry Terminal

Bus Station

Customs House

Train Station

Plateia Olgas

Plateia Vas. Yioryiou A'

UPPER TOWN

Acropolis/ Patras Fortress

25 Martiou Square

Ayios Andreas (Cathedral of St. Andrew)

Ayios Yioryios

Odeon

Pantokratora Square

Pantokratoros

Ipsilon Alonion Square

0   200 m
0   200 yds

Legend: † Church · ⓘ Information · 🚉 Rail Station · —— Railway

at the corner of Karolou and Ayiou Dionysion. For Internet access, try **Netp@rk,** 37 Gerokostopoulou (*©* **2610/279-699**); or try **Netrino Internet Café,** 133 Karais-kaki (*©* **2610/623-344**). Both charge 5€ per hour, and both are off the waterfront. English-language newspapers are available at kiosks along the waterfront.

What to See & Do

If you find yourself with a few hours, we suggest you head inland on Gerokostopoulou to **Plateia Yioryiou (George Sq.).** Sit at a cafe and take in the facades of the hand-some neoclassical theater and banks on the square. Patras was burned by the Turks during the War of Independence and has been hit repeatedly by earthquakes. These buildings are among the few that remain from the 19th century, when the city was famous for its arcaded streets and neoclassical architecture. Patras boasts other attractive squares: Plateia Olga and Plateia 25 Martiou have cafes, restaurants, and shops.

Then head down to the waterfront to the **Cathedral of St. Andrew.** Although the present (substantial, but undistinguished) church was built after World War II, the mosaics give a vivid picture of old Patras. It's important to dress appropriately to visit the cathedral, a major pilgrimage shrine thanks to the presence of St. Andrew's skull

8

THE PELOPONNESE | Patras (Patra)

291

The major ferry and shipping companies have offices on the waterfront. There is usually daily ferry service from Patras to the **Ionian islands** and **Corfu.** There are many daily services from Patras to the Italian towns of **Brindisi** and **Ancona.** The fastest service to Italy is the 18-hour **Super Ferry Crossing** from Patras to Ancona, offered by **Superfast Ferries** (✆ **2610/622-500,** or 210/969-1100 in Athens; www.super fast.com). In 2011, a cabin for two cost 350€, while a bunk in a shared four-bunk cabin cost 60€; bargaining is often possible on board.

in an ornate gold reliquary to the right of the altar. Visitors will find several pleasant cafes in the shaded park across from the cathedral.

The new **Archaeological Museum,** 44 Ethniki Odos (✆ **2610/220-829**), originally scheduled to open in 2006, when Patras was that year's European City of Culture, finally opened in July of 2009. The museum has startling architecture, including an entrance made of silver-hued titanium that is shaped like a flying saucer on steroids (or an enormous antacid tablet). In yet another attempt to lure the unwilling into museums, this one has what is described as an "aerial corridor," which will whisk visitors above the exhibits, as they give passing glances at whatever catches their fancy. If you go through the museum room by room, you'll see themed exhibits on private and public life from antiquity through the Byzantine epoch. Entire period houses have been reconstructed and a necropolis is on view. Shops and a cafe are promised. The hours are Tuesday through Sunday from 8:30am to 5pm; at press time, admission was free, but a fee was due to be charged sometime in 2011

If you're here on the weekend have a look at the **Roman Odeon** off Platia Martiou; at night, pedestrianized streets such as Gerokostopoulou around the *plateia* and the Odeon have lots of bars and cafes. There are also a number of cafes and restaurants in the streets leading up to the **Patras Fortress,** a medieval castle on the ancient acropolis that's open Saturday and Sunday from about 8am to 7pm; admission is free.

If you take the Rio-AntiRio bridge or ferry from the Peloponnese across to Central Greece, you can see another fortress, the 15th-century **Fortress of Rio.** The fortress is open daily from 8am to 7pm; admission is free.

Where to Stay

Prices are usually negotiable at these hotels, depending on how desperate customers without reservations look, the time of day, and the number of empty rooms to fill.

Astir Hotel   If you arrive too late to continue your journey or if you have an early morning boat to catch, this is a convenient hotel whose best feature is its roof garden with pool. The guest rooms are nothing special, and many seem to have been decorated by someone who couldn't decide which color would go with which and just used them all. Some units have harbor views, as does the rooftop terrace. For Patras, this is a quiet place to spend the night—which is to say that the street noise here is usually endurable.

16 Ayiou Andreas, 26223 Patras. www.hotelastirpatras.gr. ✆ **2610/277-502.** Fax 2610/271-644. 120 units. 90€–150€ double. MC, V. **Amenities:** Restaurant; bar; pool. *In room:* A/C, TV, minibar.

Grecotel Lakopetra Beach ★★ ☺   This resort hotel, with just about everything you would want after a long day of sightseeing, is set in extensive gardens a short walk from the beach. The guest rooms come with balconies or terraces, and the bathrooms are well appointed. If you are traveling with children, this could be the spot to compensate them for all those hours looking at what my own children called "those old things you want to see."

Kato Achaia, 25200 Achaia. www.grecotel.com. ℂ **26930/51-713.** Fax 26930/51-045. 192 units. 180€–350€ double. Rates include breakfast and either lunch or dinner. MC, V. **Amenities:** 2 restaurants; bar; fitness center w/sauna; pool. In room: A/C, TV, minibar, Wi-Fi.

Primarolia Art Hotel ★★   This boutique hotel with its own art gallery and trendy furniture occupies an elegantly restored 19th-century building. The Primarolia is popular with business travelers and with couples in search of a romantic spot to spend a few afternoon hours or the night before boarding a ship. If you have to spend the night in Patras and want to splurge, this is the place to stay. The guest rooms are stylish (especially those with balconies and sea views), have art (attractive, if not always distinguished) on display, and also have all the modern conveniences you'd expect.

33 Othonos and Amalias, 26223 Patras. www.arthotel.gr. ℂ **2610/624-900.** Fax 2610/623-559. 14 units. 100€–250€ double or suite. AE, DC, V. **Amenities:** Restaurant; bar; sauna. In room: A/C, TV, Wi-Fi.

Where to Eat

You can eat at any of these places for about 20€, as long as you don't have fish and stick to the house wine or a beer. The restaurants along the harbor serve mediocre food to the tourists arriving from and departing for Italy. If you are pressed for time, try **To Konaki,** across from the station; it serves good food. (Unfortunately, for most of the summer, To Konaki moves shop to the beach at Rio.) If you want an ouzo before dinner or a dessert afterward, head for the cafes on the main square, Plateia Yioryiou.

There are several old-fashioned tavernas along Ayiou Nikolaou, including the **Majestic** and **Nikolaras.** If you visit the kastro, you might have a meal at **Krini,** 57 Pandokratoros, which is usually open for lunch and dinner, has its own garden, and is popular with locals and Greek tourists; a simple lunch or dinner from 15€. If you want a leisurely and excellent meal in town, try **Mythos,** 181 Riga Ferrou Trion Navarchiou and (ℂ **2610/329-984**); in addition to the usual stews and grills, Mythos usually has local specialties on the menu.

One place I think of fondly is **Trikoyia,** 46 Otho and Amalias (no phone), a hole-in-the-wall taverna that serves excellent fresh fish and octopus. Chops and one or two other meat dishes are usually available as well. It's a 15-minute walk along the harbor from the main port; fish is priced by the kilo.

Next door at 48 Otho and Amalias (no street number) is **Pharos Fish Taverna** (ℂ **2610/336-500**). There are usually lots of locals here—always a good sign. Head inside first and choose your fish; if you arrive and sit at a table, the waiter will probably ignore you, thinking that you're waiting for friends. If these places are too crowded, you'll find lots of other tavernas on the harborfront, including **Dinos** at 102 Otho and Amalias and **Apameno** a few doors along at 107; as always, fish is priced by the kilo.

CRETE

by John S. Bowman

The birthplace of Zeus, the cradle of Minoan civilization, the site of Zorba's feats—Crete is steeped in at least 5,000 years of myth, history, and culture. Greece's largest island sometimes feels more like a country: You can go from the palm grove of Vai to the snowy heights of the White Mountains in a day. The Minoan palaces, the splendor of Venetian Rethymnon, the precipitous Samaria Gorge, the luxury beach resorts—if ever an island could claim it has something for everyone, it is surely Crete.

9

BEACHES With their sugar-fine sand and water the color of a tropical lagoon, you'll love **Elafonisi** at the southwest corner and **Vai** at the tip of the northeast. On the south coast, **Matala**'s crescent beach is embraced by promontories into which legendary chambers have been carved, while **Kommos Bay** attracts both nesting loggerhead turtles and nudists. But just driving along almost any stretch of coast will reveal beaches that can offer anything from complete solitude to a full menu of amenities.

THINGS TO DO Slip back to the Minoan world at the labyrinthine **Palace of Knossos,** legendary home of the Minotaur. View the treasures of the Minoan palaces in Iraklion's **Archaeological Museum.** Later Greek remains are at **Gortyna;** frescoed **Byzantine chapels** dot the land; see **El Greco**'s birthplace, Fodhele; and enjoy elegant **Venetian structures.** Then there are the **minarets** and **mosques** that remain from the 250 years of Ottoman Turkish rule. And then there are the villages that still host a traditional but vibrant way of life.

EATING & DRINKING Crete's cuisine is natural, straight from the land and sea. Although some restaurants now cater to more "cosmopolitan" tastes—Chania's **Well of the Turk,** for one—you can find traditional fare such as sautéed goat, snails, *marathopita* (fennel pie) in villages such as **Anoyia.** Have the fresh seafood special along **Rethymnon's Venetian harbor.** There are so many specialties to be sampled—try a *bougatsa* (sugar-sprinkled cheese turnover) in Iraklion's Fountain Square, but above all, indulge in tomatoes, strawberries, watermelons, cheese, and yogurt.

NATURE One of the great pleasures of traveling on Crete is seeing the gorgeous mountains that form its spine—and provide trails for hikes and peaks for climbs. **Mt. Idha** tops out at 2,456m (8,058 ft.). Then there's the **Samaria Gorge,** a deep rift about 16km (10 miles) long, that thousands of people explore annually. Bird lovers will have a chance to see

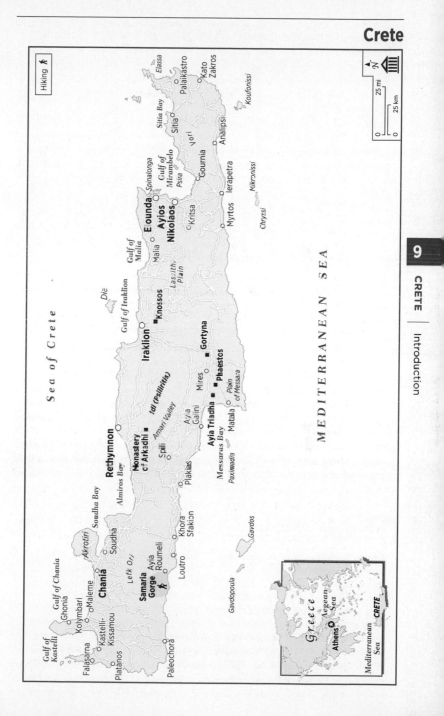

Crete

Hiking

25 mi

25 km

Sea of Crete

MEDITERRANEAN SEA

Elassa

Palaikástro

Kato

Zakros

Sitia Bay

Koufonissi

Sitia

Vori

Gulf of
Mirambelo

Análipsi

Spinalonga

Psira

Gournia

Ierapetra

E'ounda

Mikronissi

Ayios

Nikolaos

Kritsa

Myrtos

Chryssi

Gulf of
Malia

Malia

Lasith
Plain

Dia

Gulf of Iraklion

Knossos

Iraklion

Gortyna

Idi (Psiloritis)

Mires

Phaestos

Ayia
Galini

Plain
of Messara

Rethymnon

Monastery
of Arkadhi

Amari Valley

Ayia Triadha

Spili

Matala

Soudha Bay

Almiros Bay

Messaras Bay

Plakias

Paximadia

Akrotiri

Soudha

Khora
Sfakion

Gavdos

Gulf of Chania

Ghonia

Maleme

Lefk Ori

Ayia
Roumeli

Loutro

Kolymbari

Chania

Samaria
Gorge

Kastelli-
Kissamou

Falásarna

Platános

Gulf of
Kastelli

Gardopoula

Paleochóra

Greece

Aegean
Sea

Athens

CRETE

Mediterranean
Sea

295

many species, familiar and unfamiliar, and what everyone can enjoy will be the wild flowers and flowering bushes that bedeck the landscape.

Per square mile, Crete must be one of the most "loaded" places in the world—loaded, that is, in the diversity of its history, archaeological sites, natural attractions, tourist amenities, and just plain surprises. In a world where more and more travelers have "been there, done that," Crete remains an endlessly fascinating and satisfying destination.

An elaborate service industry has developed to please the many thousands of visitors to Crete each year. Facilities exist to suit everyone's taste, ranging from luxury resorts to guest rooms in villages that have hardly changed over the centuries. You can spend a delightful day in a remote mountain town where you're treated to fresh goat cheese and olives, then be back at your hotel within an hour, enjoying a cool drink on the beach.

To be frank, Crete isn't always and everywhere a gentle Mediterranean idyll—its terrain can be raw, its sites austere, its tone brusque. But for those looking for a distinctive destination, Crete never fails to deliver.

Strategies for Seeing the Island

If possible, go in June or September, even late May or early October, unless your goal is simply a sun-drenched beach: Crete has become an island on overload in July and August—and it's very hot! The overnight ferry from Piraeus is still the purist's way to go, but the 50-minute flight from Athens gives you more time for activities. The island offers enough to do to fill up a week, if not a lifetime of visits. By flying, you could actually see several major sites in 2 packed days. To make full use of your time, you can fly into Iraklion and out of Chania, or vice versa.

I recommend the following destinations, if you have 5 to 7 days. This mix of activities allows you time to collapse on a beach at the end of the day. Iraklion is a must, with its archaeological museum and nearby Knossos. An excursion to Phaestos, its associated sites, and the caves at Matala can occupy most of day 2. If you don't need to see that second Minoan palace, I recommend you move on at the end of the first day to overnight in Chania or Rethymnon—each or both can fill another day of strolling. Choose your route: The old road from Iraklion that winds through the mountains and villages has its charms, while the coastal expressway offers impressive vistas and a "tunnel" of flowering oleanders. If you set off in the morning, you could

---

📷 Crete's Wildflowers

Among the glories of Crete are its wildflowers: A walk in almost any locale outside the cities provides a glimpse of their loveliness. There are said to be at least 1,500 individual species, of which some 200 are endemic or indigenous to Crete. One need not be especially knowledgeable about flowers to appreciate them, although there are several guides in bookstores and stalls around the island. But there is a hitch: The greatest profusion is in the spring, which comes early on Crete—early March to early April is prime time. Those who cannot be there for the spring showing will be treated throughout much of the summer to the miles of blooming oleanders that line the national highway from Chania to Ayios Nikolaos.

stay on the coastal highway and just before Rethymnon take the side trip through the Amari Valley (p. 330).

Once in Chania, the walk through the famed Samaria Gorge requires one long day for the total excursion (p. 322). Those seeking less strenuous activity might prefer a trip east from Iraklion to Ayios Nikolaos and its nearby attractions—especially the many fine beaches along the way. Another alternative is a visit to the Lasithi Plain and the Dhiktaion Cave: This can be taken from either Iraklion or Ayios Nikolaos (p. 311). Various other side trips are described in the appropriate places. Although public transportation or tour groups are possibilities, you should really rent a car (although not for use in the cities or towns) so you can leave the overdeveloped tourist trail and explore countless villages, spectacular scenery, beaches at the ends of the roads, and lesser known archaeological, historical, and cultural sites.

A Look at the Past

Crete's diversity and distinction begin with a past that has left far more remains than the Minoan sites many people associate with the island. After being settled by humans around 6500 B.C.—claims of man-made tools dating as far back as 120,000 B.C. are not generally accepted—Crete passed through the late Neolithic and early Bronze ages, sharing the broader eastern Mediterranean culture.

Site & Museum Hours Update

If you visit Crete during the summer, check to see when major sites and museums are open. According to the tourist office, they should be open from 8am to 7:30pm, but some may close earlier in the day and all are usually closed 1 day a week.

Sometime around 3000 B.C., new immigrants arrived; by about 2500 B.C., there began to emerge a distinctive culture called Early Minoan. By about 2000 B.C., the Minoans were moving into a more ambitious phase, the Middle Minoan—the civilization that gave rise to the palaces and works of art that attract visitors to Crete every year.

Mycenaean Greeks appear to have taken over the palaces about 1500 B.C., but by about 1200 B.C., this Minoan-Mycenaean civilization had pretty much gone under. For several centuries, Crete was a relatively marginal player in the great era of Greek classical civilization.

When the Romans conquered the island in 67 B.C., they revived Knossos and other centers as imperial colonies. Early converts to Christianity, the Cretans slipped into the shadows of the Byzantine world, but the island was pulled back in 1204, when Venetians broke up the Byzantine Empire and took over Crete. The Venetians made it a major colonial outpost, revived trade and agriculture, and built elaborate structures.

By the late 1500s, the Turks were conquering the Venetians' eastern Mediterranean possessions; and, in 1669, they captured the last major stronghold on Crete, the city of Candia—now Iraklion. Cretans suffered considerably under the Turks, and although some of Greece finally threw off the Turkish yoke in the late 1820s, Crete was left behind. A series of rebellions marked the rest of the 19th century, resulting in a partly independent Crete.

Finally, in 1913, Crete, for the first time, was formally joined to Greece. Crete had yet another cameo role in history when the Germans invaded it in 1941 with gliders and parachute troops; the ensuing occupation was another low point. Since 1945, Crete has advanced amazingly in the economic sphere, powered by its agricultural products—particularly olives, grapes, melons, and tomatoes—as well as by its tourist industry. Not all Cretans are pleased by the impact of tourism, but all would agree that, for better or for worse, Crete owes much to its history.

IRAKLION (HERAKLION)

Iraklion is the gateway to Knossos, the most impressive of the Minoan palace sites, while the museum here is home to the world's only comprehensive collection of Minoan artifacts. Beyond that, the town has magnificent fortified walls and several other testimonies to the Venetians' time of power. Iraklion is also big enough (Greece's fifth-largest city) and confident enough to have its own identity as a busy modern city. It often gets bad press because it bustles with traffic and commerce and construction—the very things most travelers want to escape. At any rate, give Iraklion a chance. Follow the advice below, and you just may come to like it.

Essentials

GETTING THERE **By Plane** While many visitors fly in from European cities directly to Crete on charter/package tour flights, most will take the 50-minute flight from Athens to Iraklion or Chania on **Olympic Airways** (© 210/926-9111; www. olympicairlines.com) or **Aegean Airlines** (© 801/112-0000; www.aegeanair.com). Fares vary greatly depending on time of year and time of day, and can run from 130€ to 260€ round-trip. Olympic also offers at least one direct flight a week between Iraklion and Rhodes; and, in high season, the airline offers service between Athens and Sitia (in eastern Crete). Otherwise, flights between Crete and other points in Greece (such as Santorini, Mykonos, or Thessaloniki) go through Athens. Reservations are a necessity in high season.

Iraklion's airport is about 5km (3 miles) east of the city, along the coast. Major car-rental companies have desks at the airport. A taxi to Iraklion costs about 25€; the public bus, 4€. To get back to the airport, you have the same choices—taxi or public bus no. 1. You can take either from Plateia Eleftheria (Liberty Sq.) or from other points along the way. Inquire in advance at your hotel about the closest stop.

By Boat Throughout the year, there is at least one ship per day (and as many as two or three in high season) from Piraeus to Iraklion, and other ships to Chania and Rethymnon. Most trips take about 10 hours, but since 2007 there has been a "high-speed" service from Piraeus to Chania that is supposed to cut the trip to under 5 hours. Check online at **www.ferries.gr**. In the summer, **ANEK Lines** (www.anek. gr) operates traditional ferries about twice a week to and from Crete and Rhodes (and Karpathos, Kassos, and Khalki, the islands between the two) and Santorini and some of the other Cycladic islands en route to or from Piraeus. Occasional ferries also link Crete even to Thessaloniki and various Greek ports en route. In high season, occasional ships from Italy, Cyprus, and Israel put into Iraklion. Catamarans operated by **Hellenic Seaways** link Iraklion with several Cycladic islands (Santorini, Ios, Paros, Naxos, and Mykonos). These run daily in high season, four times weekly other times; check online (**www.greekislands.gr**), or contact their Athens office (© 210/419-9000). For information on all ships, inquire at a travel agency, search online (**www. gtp.gr**), or contact **Paleologos Agency** (www.ferries.gr).

Iraklion

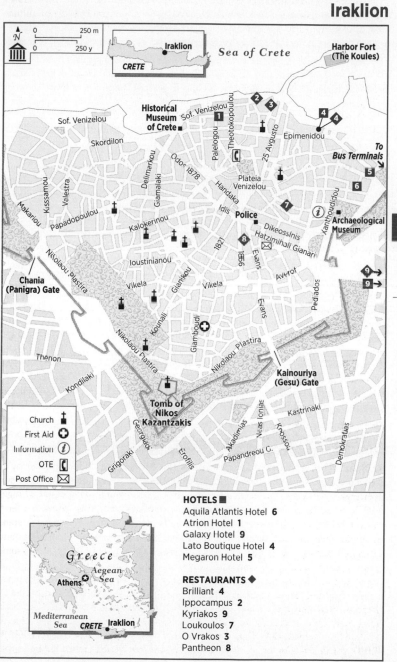

N

0 — 250 m
0 — 250 y

CRETE · Iraklion

Sea of Crete

Harbor Fort (The Koules)

Sof. Venizelou
Skordilon
Historical Museum of Crete
Sof. Venizelou
Theotokopoulou
Palelogou
25 Avgusto
Epimenidou
To Bus Terminals

Kissamou
Valestra
Makariou
Papadopoulou
Delimerkou
Giamalaki
Odos 1878
Handaka
Idis
Plateia Venizelou

Police
Dikeosinis
Hatzimihali Gianari
Archaeological Museum
Xanthoudidou

Kalokerinou
Ioustinianou
Vikela
Vikela
Gianikou
Kounali
1821
1866
Evans
Evans
Averof
Pediados

Chania (Panigra) Gate
Nikolaou Plastira
Giamboudi
Nikolaou Plastira

Thenon
Kondilaki
Nikolaou Plastira
Kainouriya (Gesu) Gate

Tomb of Nikos Kazantzakis
Georgiou
Grigoraki
Erofilis
Akadimias
Neas Ionias
Papandreou G.
Kastrinaki
Knossou
Demokratias

Church ✝
First Aid ✚
Information ⓘ
OTE 🄲
Post Office ✉

Greece
Aegean Sea
Athens
Mediterranean Sea
CRETE Iraklion

HOTELS ◼
Aquila Atlantis Hotel **6**
Atrion Hotel **1**
Galaxy Hotel **9**
Lato Boutique Hotel **4**
Megaron Hotel **5**

RESTAURANTS ◆
Brilliant **4**
Ippocampus **2**
Kyriakos **9**
Loukoulos **7**
O Vrakos **3**
Pantheon **8**

9

CRETE | Iraklion (Heraklion)

If you have arrived at Iraklion's harbor by ship, you'll most likely want to take a taxi up into the town, as it's a steep climb. Depending on where you want to go, the fare ranges from 8€ to 15€. Or you can take a bus from the depot.

By Bus   Visitors also come to Iraklion by public bus from other cities on the island. Where you arrive depends on where you've come from. Those arriving from points to the west, east, or southeast—Chania or Rethymnon, for instance, or Ayios Nikolaos or Sitia to the east—end up along the harbor. To get into the center of town, you must walk, take a taxi, or hop a public bus. The bus starts its route at the terminal where buses from the east and southeast stop; directly across the boulevard is the station for the Rethymnon-Chania buses. Visitors arriving from the south—Phaestos, Matala, and other towns—will end up at Chania Gate, on the southwest edge of town; walking may not appeal to most people, but you can take a public bus or taxi.

VISITOR INFORMATION   The **National Tourist Office** (© 2810/228-225; fax 2810/226-020) is at 1 Xanthoudidou, opposite the Archaeological Museum. Its hours are Monday through Friday 9am to 5pm. Maps and pamphlets are provided free, but the information is often a bit "general." For specifics you might do better to contact one of the more reliable travel agencies: **Creta Travel Bureau,** 49B Dikeossinis (© 2810/300-610; fax 2810/223-749), or **Arabatzoglou Travel,** 30 25th Avgusto (© 2810/301-398; fax 2810/301-399). For those interested in renting an apartment or villa on Crete, see the agencies listed in chapter 18, "Planning Your Trip to Greece."

GETTING AROUND   **By Bus**   You can see much of Crete by using the public bus system. The buses are cheap, relatively frequent, and connect to all but the most isolated locales. The downside: Remote destinations often have schedules that cater to locals, not tourists. The long-distance bus system is operated by **KTEL,** which serves all of Greece. Ask your travel agent, or call © 2810/221-765 to find out more about KTEL buses to Rethymnon-Chania and points west. For buses to Ayios Nikolaos, Sitia, Ierapetra, and points east, call © 2810/245-019. For buses to Phaestos and other points south, call © 2810/255-965.

By Car & Moped   A car gives you maximum flexibility in seeing the island. All the familiar car-rental agencies are available at the main centers of Crete, including the airports, and most travelers have their preferences. In Iraklion, aside from these, I recommend the locally owned **Motor Club,** 18 Plateia Agglon, at the bottom of 25th Avgusto, overlooking the harbor (© 2810/222-408; www.motorclub.gr). **Europrent,** with its home office in Chania, can also provide cars in Iraklion (© 28210/27-810; www.europrent.gr). If a moped or motorcycle looks tempting, be *very* sure you can control such a vehicle in chaotic urban traffic and on dangerous mountain roads (with few shoulders but lots of potholes and gravel). Try the Motor Club for rentals.

By Taxi   Taxis are reasonable if two or three people share a trip to a site; no place on Crete is more than a day's round-trip from Iraklion. Ask a travel agent to find you a driver who speaks at least rudimentary English; he can then serve as your guide as well. It might cost 100€ to tour the city and get out to Knossos, but for a party of three or four it is well worth it.

By Boat   Several excursion boats take day trips to offshore islands or to isolated beaches—occasionally even to Santorini; inquire at a travel agency.

FAST FACTS   The official **American Express** agency is Adamis Travel Bureau, 23 25th Avgusto (© 2810/346-202; fax 2810/224-717). There are numerous **banks**

Biking on Crete

In general, I am reluctant to encourage the casual visitor to Greece to rent and ride a bicycle—whether to get around cities or to set off for the countryside. In the former case, Greek drivers are not accustomed to bicycle riders, and their driving habits make it dangerous; in the latter case, the terrain is quite mountainous, roads are often not well maintained, and there is little shoulder. That said, Crete has become a major attraction for serious cyclists. Various specialized tour operators run bicycle tours on Crete—extending several days, with accommodations at each stopover; you could bring your own, but these firms also rent bikes. Some of the tours are described as requiring top-level conditioning, while others are less demanding, but all involve a lot of hills! (And in summer, any activity can be quite draining.) If you like to bike, try **Trekking Plan** (www.cycling.gr) to learn about some offerings. If you'd like to rent a bike to tour on your own, major tourist centers usually have some outfit that will rent a bike (usually a mountain bike); Trekking Plan, in Chania, will rent for the short term; in Iraklion, try **Blue Aegean Holidays** (www.blueaegean.com) or **MotoExpress** (www.motoexpress.gr). Note that many online sites that advertise bikes for rent are referring to motorbikes.

and **ATMs** (as well as several currency-exchange machines) throughout the center of Iraklion, with many along 25th Avgusto. The **British Consul** (© **2810/224-012**) is at 16 Papa Alexandrou, opposite the Archaeological Museum; there is no American consulate in Iraklion. **Venizelou Hospital** (© **2810/237-502**) is on Knossos Road. For general **first-aid** information, call © **2810/222-222**. For Internet access, try the InSpot Cafe, at 6 Korai, or the Cyberpoint Cafe, 117 Paraskiyopoulou. Both open midmorning and close at midnight. The access fee at both is now about 4€ per hour.

You can leave **luggage** at the airport for 5€ per piece per day; most hotels will hold luggage for brief periods. The **tourist police** are at 10 Dikeossenis, on the main street linking 25th Avgusto to Platcia Eleftheria (© **2810/283-190**); they are open daily from 7am to 11pm. The main **post office** (© **2810/289-995**) is on Plateia Daskaloyiannis and is open daily from 7:30am to 8pm. The **telephone office (OTE),** 10 Minotaurou (far side of El Greco Park), is open daily from 6am to 11pm.

What to See & Do
ATTRACTIONS
The Archaeological Museum ★★★ This—the world's premier collection of art and artifacts from the Minoan civilization—surprises most visitors, who are amazed by the variety of objects, styles, and techniques of the treasures inside. Many of the most spectacular objects are from Knossos; the rest, from other sites on the island. Among the most prized objects are **snake goddesses** from Knossos, the **Phaestos Disc** (with its still-undeciphered inscription), the **bee pendant** from Mallia, **carved vases** from Ayia Triadha and Kato Zakros, and objects depicting young men leaping over the horns of charging bulls. Upstairs you'll find the **original frescoes from Knossos** and other sites, their restored sections clearly visible (the frescoes now at Knossos are copies of these). Most displays have decent labels in English, but you may want to invest in one of the guidebooks for sale in the lobby.

📎 **Museum's Temporary Display**

When this edition went to press, Iraklion's Archaeological Museum was still closed for major renovations and additions, although it was claimed it would be open by the spring of 2012. However, they have installed a selection of all the major holdings in a new building at the rear of the museum. Its hours have been Tuesday to Sunday 8:30am to 5pm; Monday noon to 5pm. Admission is 4€; 2€ for students and E.U. seniors. To be frank, this reduced selection is probably enough for most visitors—all the notable pieces are on display. One drawback is that the floor space is limited, so try to visit there during off hours—very early in the morning or late in the day.

You will need at least 1 hour for even a quick walk-through. To avoid the tour groups in high season, plan to visit very early, late in the day, or on Sunday.

1 Xanthoudidou. ✆ **2810/226-092.** Admission 6€ adults, 3€ students with official ID and E.U. citizens 65 and over; free Sun Nov–Mar, and some Sun in summer. Combination ticket for museum and Palace of Knossos 10€. Apr to mid-Oct Tues–Sun 8am–8pm, Mon 12:30–8pm; late Oct to Mar Tues–Sun 8am–5pm, Mon 12:30–5pm. Far corner of Plateia Eleftheria. Parking in immediate area impossible—best to park below, along commercial harbor road.

Harbor Fort (the Koules)   You may feel as if you're walking through a Hollywood set—but this is the real thing. The harbor fort, built on the site of a series of earlier forts, went up between 1523 and 1540, and although greatly restored, it is essentially the Venetian original. Both its exterior and interior are impressive in their dimensions, workmanship, and details: thick walls, spacious chambers, great ramparts, cannonballs, and Lion of St. Mark plaques. It's well worth an hour's visit.

At breakwater on old harbor. ✆ **2810/288-484.** Admission 4€. Daily 9am–1pm and 4–7pm.

Historical Museum of Crete ★   This museum picks up where the Archaeological Museum leaves off, displaying artifacts and art from the early Christian era up to the present. You get some sense of the role the Cretans' long struggle for independence still plays in their identity. On display are traditional Cretan **folk arts;** the re-created study of **Nikos Kazantzakis,** Crete's great modern writer; and two paintings by **El Greco,** another of the island's admired sons. Even if you take only an hour for this museum, it will reward you with surprising insights about the island.

7 Lysimakos Kalokorinou (facing coast road, 450m/1,500 ft. west of harbor). www.historical-museum.gr. ✆ **2810/283-219.** Admission 5€ adults, 3€ students. Mar–Oct Mon–Sat 9am–5pm. Closed Sun and holidays.

The Palace of Knossos ★★★   This is one of the great archaeological sites of the world, yet until Arthur Evans began excavating in 1900, little was known about the ancient people who inhabited it. Using every possible clue and remnant, Evans rebuilt large parts of the palace—walls, floors, stairs, windows, and columns. Visitors must stay on a walkway, but you still get a good sense of the structure's labyrinthine nature. You are looking at the remains of two major palaces, plus several restorations made up to about 1250 b.c. This was not a palace in the modern sense, but a combination of a royal residence and the Minoans' chief religious/ceremonial center, as well as their administrative headquarters and royal workshops. Take the time for a guided tour; it's worth the expense (your hotel or a travel agency can arrange it). On your own, you'll need at least 2 hours for a walk-through. The latter part of the day and Sunday tend to be less crowded. And if time is an issue, splurge on a taxi, usually 12€ one way.

Knossos Rd., 5km (3 miles) south of Iraklion. © **2810/231-940.** Admission 6€, 3€ students with official ID and E.U. citizens 65 or over; free Sun Nov–Mar and some Sun in summer. Combination ticket for the Palace of Knossos and Archaeological Museum (see above) 10€. Apr to mid-Oct daily 8am–8pm; late Oct to Mar Mon–Fri 8am–5pm, Sat–Sun 8:30am–3pm. Frequent buses from center of Iraklion. Free parking down slope on left, 90m (300 ft.) before main entrance.

Venetian Walls & Tomb of Nikos Kazantzakis ★   These great walls and bastions were part of the fortress-city the Venetians called Candia. Two of the great city gates have survived fairly well: the Pantocrator or Panigra Gate, better known now as the Chania Gate (dating from about 1570), at the western edge; and the Gate of Gesu, or Kainouryia Gate (about 1587), at the southern edge. Walk around the outer perimeter of the walls to get a feel for their sheer massiveness. They were built by the forced labor of Cretans. On the Martinengo Bastion at the southwestern corner of the great walls is the grave of **Nikos Kazantzakis** (1883–1947), a native of Iraklion and author of *Zorba the Greek* and *The Last Temptation of Christ.* Here, too, is one of the best views to the south. Mount Iouktas appears in profile as the head of a man—some say the head of the buried god Zeus. A visit here requires a solid hour from the center of the city, especially if you want to see the Kainouryia Gate and a segment of the wall.

Tomb is on Martinengo Bastion, at southwestern corner of the walls, along Plastira. Free admission. Sunrise–sunset.

Cretaquarium ☺   It's hardly a world-class aquarium, but there's more than enough here to occupy your kids on a day when you need a break from the beach. On the edge of the former U.S. Air Force base, its several tanks house over 2,500 specimens from hundreds of Mediterranean and tropical species of fish and invertebrates—from hunter sharks to tiny sea horses to jellyfish. Various underwater terrains have also been replicated—it is definitely a professional operation. The whole complex, known as Thalassocosmos (Sea World), belongs to the Hellenic Center for Marine Research. A restaurant and souvenir shop are also on the premises.

At Gournes, 16km (10 miles) east of Iraklion. © **2810/337-788.** www.cretaquarium.gr. Admission 8€ adults; 6€ students, children 5–17, and seniors over 65. June–Sept daily 9am–9pm; Oct–May daily 10am–5:30pm. Bus from station at Iraklion port.

A STROLL AROUND IRAKLION

Start your stroll at **Fountain Square** (also known as Lions Sq., officially Plateia Venizelou), after trying a plate of *bougatsa* at one of the two cafes here serving this local pastry. Armenian Greeks introduced this cheese- or cream-filled delicacy to Crete. This square, long one big traffic jam, is now pedestrian-only. Francesco Morosini, Crete's Venetian governor, installed the **fountain ★** here in 1628. Note the fading but still elegant relief carvings around the basin. Across from the fountain is the **Basilica of St. Mark,** restored to its original 14th-century Italian style and used for exhibitions and concerts.

Proceeding south 50m (164 ft.) to the crossroads, you'll see the **market street** (officially from 1866); alas, it is increasingly taken over by tourist shops but is still a must-see, with its purveyors of fresh fruits and vegetables, meats, and wines.

At the far end of the market street, look for **Kornarou Square,** with its lovely Turkish fountain; beside it is the **Venetian Bembo Fountain** (1588). The modern statue at the far side of the square commemorates the hero and heroine of Vincenzo Kornarou's Renaissance epic poem *Erotokritos,* a Cretan-Greek classic.

Turning right onto Vikela, proceed (always bearing right) until you come to the imposing, if not artistically notable, 19th-century **Cathedral of Ayios Menas,** dedicated to the patron saint of Iraklion. Below and to the left, the medieval **Church of Ayios Menas** boasts old woodcarvings and icons.

At the far corner of the cathedral (to the northeast) is the 15th-century **Church of St. Katherine ★.** During the 16th and 17th centuries, this church hosted the Mount Sinai Monastery School, where it is alleged that Domenico Theotokopoulou studied before moving on to Venice and Spain; there he became known as **El Greco.** The church houses a small museum of icons, frescoes, and woodcarvings. It's open Monday through Saturday from 10am to 1pm, and Tuesday, Thursday, and Friday from 4 to 6pm. Admission is 5€.

Take Ayii Dheka, the narrow street that leads away from the facade of St. Katherine's, and you'll arrive at **Leoforos Kalokerinou,** the main shopping street for locals. Turn right and proceed up to the crossroads of the market street and 25th Avgusto—now set aside for pedestrians. Turn left to go back down past Fountain Square and, on the right, you'll see the reconstructed **Venetian Loggia,** originally dating from the early 1600s. Prominent Venetians once met here to conduct business affairs; it now houses city government offices.

A little farther down 25th Avgusto, also on the right, is the **Church of Ayios Titos,** dedicated to the patron saint of Crete (Titus of the Bible), who introduced Christianity to Crete. Head down to the **harbor,** with a side visit to **the Koules (harbor fort)** if you have time (see above), then pass on the right the two sets of great **Venetian arsenali**—where ships were built and repaired. (The sea at that time came in this far.) Climbing the stairs just past the arsenali, turn left onto Bofort and curve up beneath the **Archaeological Museum** to **Plateia Eleftheria (Liberty Sq.),** where you can pride yourself on having seen the main attractions of Irakion and reward yourself with a refreshing drink at one of the many cafes on the far side.

SHOPPING

Costas Papadopoulos, the proprietor of **Daedalou Galerie,** 11 Daedalou, between Fountain Square and Plateia Eleftheria (✆ **2810/346-353**), has been offering his tasteful selection of traditional Cretan-Greek arts and crafts for several decades—icons, jewelry, porcelain, silverware, pistols, and more. Some of it is truly old, and he'll tell you when it isn't.

Eleni Kastrinoyanni-Cretan Folk Art, 3 Ikarou, opposite the Archaeological Museum (✆ **2810/226-186**), is the premier store in Iraklion for some of the finest in embroidery, weavings, ceramics, and jewelry. The work is new but reflects traditional Cretan folk methods and motifs. Get out your credit card, and go for something you'll enjoy for years to come. It's closed October through February.

Stores that sell local agricultural products have sprung up all over Iraklion. Crete's olive oil—among the finest in the world—stands side by side with honey, wines and spirits, raisins, olives, herbs, and spices. One store is as good as the other.

Where to Stay

In recent years, tourism on Crete has led to a demand for beach hotels outside of the cities, but Iraklion still offers a range of hotels. Reservations are a must in high season.

INSIDE THE CITY

Our search for a good hotel tries hard to feature the criterion of "quiet." Iraklion lies under the flight patterns of many planes and the occasional Greek Air Force jet fighter. The noise factor probably adds up to less than 40 minutes every 24 hours, so the sounds of scooters and motorcycles at night will probably be more annoying. The city plans to build a new airport far inland, but it will take some years for this to happen. Meanwhile, closed windows and air-conditioning promise the best defenses.

Very Expensive

Megaron Hotel ★★★   The "grand hotel" of Iraklion was formerly an old and abandoned commercial/apartment building on the site of a bastion of the old Venetian walls and high above the harbor. In 2003, the new owners installed a hotel that is elegant in its decor, facilities, and service. All rooms have an exterior view, leaving the core of the structure as a great atrium. All the public areas bespeak understated luxury, and rooms are more generous than in many Greek hotels, as well as far more stylish. The various amenities and the service are of the highest standard. Special elements include a small library/reading area, plasma TV, free wireless Internet in public areas, private dining options, rooms for those with disabilities—even dogs will be welcomed. Convenient for walking to any place in the core of the city, the Megaron has undeniably seized the high ground of Iraklion's hotels in every sense of that phrase.

9 Beaufort, 71202 Iraklion (on street below Archaeological Museum). www.gdmmegaron.gr. © **2810/305-300.** 58 units. 164€–354€ double. Rates include full breakfast. AE, DC, MC, V. Private parking arranged. **Amenities:** Restaurant; 2 cafes (1 by pool); bar; airport pickup by arrangement; babysitting; health club and gym w/Jacuzzi, massage room, sauna, and steam bath; rooftop pool; room service; Wi-Fi; smoke-free rooms. *In room:* A/C, TV, fridge, hair dryer, Internet, minibar.

Expensive

Aquila Atlantis Hotel ★★ ☙   Although Iraklion now boasts a more luxurious hotel, the Atlantis is probably more than adequate for most. This Class A hotel is in the heart of Iraklion, yet removed from city noise (especially if you use the air-conditioning). The staff is friendly and helpful, and although the Atlantis is popular with groups—it has major conference facilities—individuals still get personal attention. Guest rooms (insist on smoke-free if that matters), although neither plush nor especially large, are comfortable. You can swim in the rooftop pool, send e-mail via your laptop, and within minutes can be out enjoying a meal or visiting a museum.

2 Iyias, 71202 Iraklion (behind the Archaeological Museum). www.aquilaatlantis-crete.com. © **2810/229-103.** 162 units. High season 155€ double; low season 140€ double. Rates include breakfast. Reduction possible for longer stays. Special rates for business travelers, and half board (breakfast and dinner) available. AE, DC, MC, V. Private parking arranged. **Amenities:** Restaurant; 2 bars; airport pickup by arrangement; babysitting; children's playground (across street); Jacuzzi; small indoor pool; room service; tennis court across street; smoke-free rooms. *In room:* A/C, TV, fridge, hair dryer, minibar, Wi-Fi.

Galaxy Hotel ★   With a reputation as one of the finer hotels in Iraklion, the Galaxy is classy once you get past its rather forbidding gray exterior. The interior was renovated in 2008. The public areas are striking if airport modern, and the Galaxy boasts (for now, at least) the largest indoor swimming pool in Iraklion. Guest rooms are stylish—international modern—but don't expect American-style size. Ask for an interior unit, as you lose nothing in a view and gain in quiet. The hotel also offers several suites, as well as rooms especially designed for those with limited mobility. Although a reader reported a less-than-gracious tone from desk staff, I have always found them courteous, if brisk. All in all, the Galaxy appeals most to travelers who prefer a familiar, international ambience to folksiness.

67 Leoforos Demokratias, 71306 Iraklion (about 1km/½ mile out main road to Knossos). www.ellada.net/ galaxy. ℂ **2810/238-812.** 127 units, some with shower, some with tub. High season 110€ double; low season 100€ double. Rates include buffet breakfast. AE, DC, MC, V. Parking on adjacent streets. Frequent bus to town center within yards of entrance. **Amenities:** 2 restaurants; bar; pastry shop; babysitting; health club; indoor pool; room service; sauna; Wi-Fi; smoke-free rooms. *In room:* A/C, TV, hair dryer, Internet, minibar.

Moderate

Atrion Hotel There's nothing spectacular here, but I have liked this hotel for years, if only for its location. It's in a quiet, seemingly remote corner that is in fact only a 10-minute walk to the center of town, and an even shorter walk to the coast road and the harbor. The adjacent streets are not that attractive, but they are perfectly safe; once inside the hotel, you can enjoy your oasis of comfort and peace. This hotel has well-appointed public areas—a lounge, a refreshing patio garden—and pleasant, good-size guest rooms. Guests often rave about the breakfast.

9 Chronaki (behind the Historical Museum), 71202 Iraklion. www.atrion.gr. ℂ **2810/229-225.** 60 units, some with shower, some with tub. High season 85€ double; low season 75€ double. Rates include buffet breakfast. Reductions for children. AE, MC, V. Parking on adjacent streets. Public bus within 200m (656 ft.). **Amenities:** Restaurant; bar; babysitting; room service; smoke-free rooms. *In room:* A/C, TV, hair dryer, Internet, minibar.

Lato Boutique Hotel ★ ✔ Long one of my favorites in Greece, the Lato provides value, a stylish environment, and warm hospitality. Renovations completed in 2011 have refurbished the public areas and transformed the rooms' decor and furnishings; by 2012 all will have new state-of-the art bathrooms. A few rooms are a bit small for more than one, five are suites, but all are adequate. The buffet breakfast is satisfying. A major plus is its location, convenient to the town's center while offering rooms with harbor views (just ask for one). A rooftop **restaurant** is also one of the attractions of this hotel, combining alfresco dining with a view. The hotel has its own luxury **restaurant** next door and in 2011 it opened a former hotel across the street as an annex. Valet parking eliminates parking aggravation, and the staff is always ready to help you make the most of your stay in Iraklion.

15 Epimenidou, 71202 Iraklion. www.lato.gr. ℂ **2810/228-103.** 58 units, some with shower only. High season 115€–125€ double; low season 100€–115€ double. Rates include buffet breakfast. 10% discount for Internet reservations; 50% discount for children 6-12. AE, DC, MC, V. Valet parking by desk staff. **Amenities:** 2 restaurants (see Brillant Gourmet, below); breakfast room; bar; Jacuzzi; minigym; room service; steam room; smoke-free rooms. *In room:* A/C, TV, hair dryer, Internet, minibar.

Inexpensive

Poseidon ✔ This is by no means for everyone, but in a contest among longtime Frommer's *Greece* guidebook loyalists for a favorite hotel in Iraklion, the Poseidon would probably win. And it's not just because of good value for the money. Owner/ host John Polychronides established a homey atmosphere, a tone maintained by the desk staff (fluent in English). The street is not especially attractive—but that's true at most of Iraklion's hotels, and few can match the fresh breezes and an unobstructed view over the port. Rooms are on the small side and showers are basic, but everything is clean and functional. The sound-insulated windows keep out most exterior noise, but overhead air traffic can be annoying. Frequent buses and cheap taxi fares let you come and go into Iraklion center, a 20-minute walk.

54 Poseidonos, Poros, 71202 Iraklion. www.hotelposeidon.gr. ℂ **2810/222-545.** 26 units, all with shower only. High season 75€ double; low season 65€ double. Rates include continental breakfast. For

e-mail reservations and cash payments, a 10% discount for 1–2 nights, 1%–5% discount for stays over 2 nights. AE, MC, V. Parking all around hotel. Frequent public buses, 180m (590 ft.) at top of street. About 2.5km (1½ miles) from Plateia Eleftheria, off the main road to the east. *In room:* A/C (8€ daily surcharge), TV, fridge.

OUTSIDE THE CITY

Assuming you want to be fairly close to Iraklion, stay on the coast, if you want to avoid city noise. If you just want to stay near a remote beach on Crete, such accommodations are described later in this chapter. Although the hotels below can be reached by public bus, a car or taxi will save you valuable time.

Expensive

Candia Maris Resort and Spa ★ ☺ After a couple of years under Swiss management, this hotel has returned to Greek ownership. It's on the western edge of Iraklion, and you have to pass through a rather dreary part to get here, but it's close enough to town to allow for easy excursions. Its beach makes it attractive to families with children, and it offers just about everything, from special Cretan Nights, with traditional music and dancing, to a squash court to the newest fad, thalassotherapy (seawater treatment). The exterior and layout are a bit severe, but the rooms are good-size and cheerful, the bathrooms up-to-date. Guests tend to praise the food and friendly staff. It was also one of the first hotels in Greece to offer accessibility for those with limited mobility.

Amoudara, Gazi, 71303 Iraklion. www.candiamaris.gr. ℂ **2810/377-000.** 285 units. High season 165€ double in hotel, 210€ bungalow. Closed Nov–Mar. Rates include buffet breakfast. Varied fees for extra person in room and for children; half-board plan (including breakfast and dinner) available for additional 30€. AE, DC, MC, V. Parking on grounds. Public bus every half-hour to Iraklion. On beach about 6km (4 miles) west of Iraklion center. **Amenities:** 4 restaurants; 4 bars; babysitting; basketball; bikes; billiards; bowling; children's programs; health club; minigolf; 7 pools (2 outdoor, 4 indoor, 1 children's); room service; spa; thalassotherapy; tennis and squash courts; volleyball; watersports; Wi-Fi in public areas for fee; rooms for those w/limited mobility. *In room:* A/C, TV, fridge, hair dryer, Internet (for fee), minibar.

Where to Eat

Avoid eating at Fountain Square or Liberty Square (Plateia Eleftheria), unless you want the experience of being at the center of activity—the food around here is, to put it mildly, nothing special. Save these spots for a coffee or beer break.

EXPENSIVE

Brillant Gourmet Restaurant ★★ INTERNATIONAL Since opening in 2007, this restaurant has offered the finest dining experience in Iraklion. The decor is striking but this would mean nothing if it were not matched by the menu and service, which are of the highest quality. The ingredients are basically Greek—even local Cretan—but prepared in unexpected combinations: Appetizers might include a tomato-brie puff pie and goat cheese with prosciutto, while entrees include tender filets of beef or pork, as well as chicken and fish dishes. The basic menu changes at least twice a year and specials are offered most nights. The wine list is equally special—trust the waiter to suggest a wine appropriate for your entree and you may be surprised at how good, say, one of the better Cretan wines can be. It is not cheap—a couple should be prepared to spend 90€ to 130€, depending on the number of courses and the choice of wine.

15 Epimenidou (adjacent to the Lato Boutique Hotel). www.brillantrestauarant.gr. ℂ **2810/334-959.** Reservations recommended for dinner in high season. Main courses 18€–25€ (lobster dishes extra). AE, DC, MC, V. Daily 7:30pm–12:30am. Lato Hotel can help with parking, but best just to walk here.

MODERATE

Kyriakos ★ GREEK   In recent years, this restaurant has gained the reputation of offering some of the finest cooking in Iraklion. The menu is essentially traditional Greek, but its specialties include artichokes with potatoes and lettuce, lamb fricassee, and eggplant stuffed with feta. Snails are another delicacy, and if that doesn't tempt you, come back at Christmas for the turkey. The wine choices are fine and expensive. Two people should expect to drop between 50€ and 75€ for the full works, but think what you'd pay at home for such a meal. Its location might disappoint some; it's on a busy boulevard and lacks Cretan "atmosphere." It's a bit stodgy, but if you're serious about what's on your plate, coming here is an occasion.

53 Leoforos Demokratias (about 1km/½ mile from center on the road to Knossos). ✆ **2810/224-649.** Reservations recommended for dinner in high season. Appetizers 4€–8€; main courses 6€–28€. AE, DC, MC, V. Daily noon–5pm and 7pm–1am. Closed Sun June 2–July 10. Frequent public bus service.

Loukoulos ★ ITALIAN/GREEK   Here's another restaurant that has gained a stylish reputation. It's in the heart of the city on a back street, crammed into a tiny patio with umbrellas shading the tables. The chairs are comfortable, the table settings lovely, and the selection of *mezedes* (appetizers) varied. The creative Italian menu features lots of pasta dishes, such as a delicious rigatoni with a broccoli-and-Roquefort cream sauce. Treat yourself at least once to Iraklion's "in" place.

5 Korai (1 street behind Daedalou). ✆ **2810/224-435.** Reservations recommended for dinner in high season. Main courses 6€–20€; fixed-price lunch about 18€. AE, DC, V. Mon–Sat noon–1am; Sun 6:30pm–midnight. Street closed to vehicles.

O Vrakos ★ GREEK   A once-modest taverna that has gained an enthusiastic following from both Greeks and foreigners, it has the added advantage of providing its diners a view over the old Venetian harbor and its fortress. Seafood is a specialty, but if you aren't looking to spend a lot, stick with the basic taverna fare. You could make a meal from their tasty *mezedes*, the appetizers—the fried zucchini, the lamb meatballs, and a Greek salad. The staff are hospitable and if you've spent for a full meal, you are apt to be served a complimentary dessert (and *raki* for an aperitif) after you've asked for the check.

1 Marinelli (at foot of street at the traffic circle at the harbor). ✆ **2810/243-243.** Main courses 6€–18€. Mon–Sat 11:30am–midnight; Sun 5:30pm–midnight. Parking on adjacent side streets.

INEXPENSIVE

Ippocampus MEZEDES   This is an institution among locals, who line up for a typical Cretan meal of appetizers. The zucchini slices, dipped in batter and deep fried, are fabulous. A plate of tomatoes and cukes, another of sliced fried potatoes, small fish, perhaps fried squid—that's it. A couple could assemble a meal for as little as 20€—but go early. Ippocampus is down along the coast road. You can sit indoors or on the sidewalk, a bargain either way.

3 Mitsotaki (along the waterfront, to left of traffic circle as you come down 25th Avgusto). ✆ **2810/282-081.** Appetizers 2.50€–8€. No credit cards. Mon–Fri 1–3:30pm and 7pm–midnight. Parking on adjacent side streets.

Pantheon ▣ GREEK   Anyone who spends more than a few days in Iraklion should take at least one meal in Dirty Alley, where this restaurant is a longtime favorite. Although it lost its rough-hewn atmosphere long ago, Dirty Alley still feels like an indigenous locale. The menu at Pantheon (much the same as the menus at the other Dirty Alley places) offers taverna standards—meat stews; chunks of meat, chicken, or fish in tasty sauces; and vegetables such as okra, zucchini, or stuffed tomatoes. These places are not especially cheap—the proprietors know to charge for the atmosphere—but the food's tasty. And if you sit in the Pantheon, on the corner of the market street, you'll get a choice view of the scene outside.

2 Theodosaki (Dirty Alley, connecting the market street and Evans). ℭ **2810/241-652.** Main courses 6€–16€. No credit cards. Mon–Sat 11am–11pm.

Iraklion After Dark

To spend an evening the way most Iraklians do, stroll and then sit in a cafe and watch others stroll by. The prime locations for the latter have been Plateia Eleftheria (Liberty Sq.) or Fountain Square, but the crowded atmosphere of these places—and some overly aggressive waiters—has considerably reduced their charm.

For a more relaxed atmosphere, go to **Marina Cafe,** at the old harbor (across from the restored Venetian arsenali). For as little as 2€ for a coffee or as much as 9€ for an alcoholic drink, you can enjoy the breeze as you contemplate the illuminated Venetian fort, which looks much like a stage set. Another possibility if you're looking to have a late meal and hang out with a younger crowd is to try the small cafe/restaurant right on the 1866 Street (the Market street), **Peninda-Peninda.**

An alternative is **Filos Sophias Roof-Garden Cafe** (ℭ 2810/222-333); enter through an interior staircase in the shopping arcade on Fountain Square. It attracts younger Iraklians, but travelers are welcome. The background music is usually Greek. You get to sit above the crossroads and, with no cover or minimum, enjoy anything from a coffee (2€) or ice cream (from 3€) to an alcoholic drink (from 4€).

There is no end to the number of **bars** and **discos,** featuring everything from international rock 'n' roll to Greek pop music, although they come and go from year to year. **Disco Athina,** 9 Ikarou, just outside the wall on the way to the airport, is an old favorite with the young; or try any of the clubs along Epimenidou—the **Villa Lokka** or **Privilege**—or **Vogue** or **Envy** along the seafront.

Most Class A hotels now host a **Cretan Night,** when performers dance and play **traditional music.** For more of the same, take a taxi to either **Aposperides,** out on the road toward Knossos, or **Sordina,** about 5km (3 miles) to the southwest of town.

During the summer, Iraklion's **arts festival** brings in world-class performers (ballet companies, pianists, and others), but mostly featured are ancient and medieval-Renaissance Greek dramas, Greek-themed dance, or traditional and modern Greek music. Many performances take place on the roof of **the Koules** (the Venetian fort in the harbor), **Kazantzakis Garden Theater,** or **Hadzidaksis Theater.** Ticket prices vary, but are well below what you'd pay at such cultural events elsewhere. Maybe you didn't come to Crete expecting to hear Vivaldi, but why not enjoy it while you're here? The festival begins in late June and ends in mid-September.

Side Trips from Iraklion

Travel agencies arrange excursions from Iraklion to nearly every point of interest on Crete, such as **Samaria Gorge** in the far southwest (p. 322). In that sense, Iraklion can be used as the home base for touring Crete. If you have only 1 extra day on Crete, I recommend the following trip.

GORTYNA, PHAESTOS, AYIA TRIADHA & MATALA ★★

If you have an interest in history and archaeology, and you've already seen Knossos and Iraklion's museum, this is the trip to make. The distance isn't that great—a round-trip of about 165km (100 miles)—but you'd want a full day to take it all in. A taxi or guided tour is advisable, if you haven't rented a car. Bus schedules won't allow you to fit in all the stops. (You can stay, of course, at one of the hotels on the south coast, but they're usually booked long in advance of high season.)

The road south takes you up and across the **mountainous spine** of central Crete. At about 40km (25 miles), you'll leave behind the **Sea of Crete** (to the north) and see the **Libyan Sea** to the south. You then descend onto the **Messara,** the largest plain on Crete (about 32km/20 miles × 5km/3 miles) and a major agricultural center. At about 45km (28 miles), you'll see on your right the **remains of Gortyna;** many more remnants lie scattered in the fields off to the left. Gortyna (or Gortyn or Gortys) first emerged as a center of the Dorian Greeks who moved to Crete after the end of the Minoan civilization. By 500 B.C., they had advanced enough to inscribe a code of law into stone. The stones were found in the late 19th century and reassembled here, where you can see this unique—and to scholars, invaluable—document testifying to the legal and social arrangements of this society.

After the Romans took over Crete (67 B.C.), Gortyna enjoyed another period of glory when it served as the capital of Roman Crete and Cyrenaica (Libya). Roman structures—temples, a stadium, and more—litter the fields to the left. On the right, along with the **Code of Gortyna ★,** you'll see a **Hellenistic Odeon,** or theater, as well as the remains of the **Basilica of Ayios Titos** (admission 5€; daily 8am–7pm high season, reduced hours off season). Paul commissioned Titos (Titus) to lead the first Christians on Crete. The church, begun in the 6th century, was later enlarged.

Proceed down the road another 15km (10 miles), turn left at the sign for Phaestos, and ascend to the ridge where the **palace of Phaestos ★★** sits in all its splendor (admission 6€; daily 8am–7pm high season, reduced hours off-season). Scholars consider this the second most powerful Minoan center; many visitors appreciate its setting on a prow of land that seems to float between the plain and the sky. Italians began to excavate Phaestos soon after Evans began at Knossos, but they decided to leave the remains much as they found them. The **ceremonial staircase** is as awesome as it must have been to the ancients, while the **great court** remains one of the most resonant public spaces anywhere. You can have a meal at the restaurant on the terrace overlooking the site.

Leaving Phaestos, continue down the main road 4km (2½ miles) and turn left onto a side road. Park here and make your way to pay your respects to a Minoan minipalace complex known as **Ayia Triadha.** To this day, scholars aren't certain exactly what it was—something between a satellite of Phaestos and a semi-independent palace. Several of the most impressive artifacts in the Iraklion Museum, including the painted sarcophagus (on the second floor), were found here.

Back on the road, follow the signs to **Kamilari** and then **Pitsidia.** Now you've earned your rest and swim, and at no ordinary place: the nearby **beach at Matala ★.** It's a cove enclosed by bluffs of age-old packed earth. Explorers found **chambers,** some with "bunk beds" that probably date back to the Romans (most likely no earlier than A.D. 100). Cretans long used them as summer homes, the German soldiers used them as storerooms during World War II, and hippies took them over in the 1960s. You can visit during the day; otherwise, they are off limits. Matala has become one more overcrowded beach in peak season, so after a dip, make your way back to Iraklion (via **Mires,** so you avoid the turnoff to Ayia Triadha and Phaestos).

LASITHI PLAIN ★

Here's an excursion that combines some spectacular scenery, a major mythological site, and an extraordinary view on a windy day. Long promoted as "the plain of 10,000 windmills," alas, the Lasithi Plain can no longer really boast of this: The many hundreds, if not thousands, of white-sailcloth-clad windmills have largely been replaced by gasoline-powered generator windmills (and wooden or metal vanes), but it is still an impressive sight as you come over the ridge to see these windmills turning.

What they are doing is pumping water to irrigate the crops that fill the entire plain: no buildings are allowed on this large plateau (some 40 sq. km/15 sq. miles) because its rich alluvial soil (washed down from the surrounding mountains) is ideal for cultivating potatoes and other crops. Having come this far—the plain is some 56km (35 miles) from Iraklion—you must go the next 16km (10 miles) to visit one of the major mythological sites of all Greece: the **Dhiktaion Cave**, regarded since ancient times as the birthplace of Zeus and the cave where he was hidden so that his father, Cronus, could not devour him.

Driving around the outer edge of the plain (via Tzermiadhes, Drasi, Ayios Constantinos, and Ayios Georgiios), you come to the village of **Psykhro** on the slopes on the southern edge of the plain. Psykhro and the cave are geared for tourists who come from all over the world (admission 1€). After you reach the tourist pavilion, you still face a steep climb to the cave; you are advised to take on one of the guides because the descent into the cave can be slippery and tricky (it's best to wear rubber-soled, sturdy footwear), and you will not know what you are looking at. Although long known as the cave associated with Zeus—it appears in numerous ancient myths and texts—it was not excavated until 1900, and successive "digs" in the decades since have turned up countless artifacts, confirming that it was visited as a sacred shrine for centuries. Other caves on Crete and elsewhere claim the honor of Zeus's birthplace, but the Dhiktaion Cave seems to have won out, and having visited it, you can claim to have been at one of the more storied sites of the ancient world.

Lasithi Plain can also be visited as a side trip from Ayios Nikolaos (see later in this chapter). You head back westward on the old road to Iraklion and, at about 8km (5 miles), turn left (signed DRASI); then climb another 25km (15 miles) up to the plain.

CHANIA (HANIA/XANIA/ CANEA) ★★

150km (93 miles) W of Iraklion

Until the 1980s, Chania was one of the best-kept secrets of the Mediterranean: a delightful provincial town between mountains and sea, a labyrinth of atmospheric streets and structures from its Venetian-Turkish era. Since then, tourists have flocked here, and there's hardly a square inch of the old town that's not dedicated to satisfying them. Chania was bombed during World War II; ironically, some of its atmosphere is due to still-unreconstructed buildings that are now used as shops and restaurants.

What's amazing is how much of Chania's charm has persisted since the Venetians and Turks effectively stamped the old town in their own images, between 1210 and 1898. Try to visit any time except July and August; whenever you come, dare to strike out on your own and see the old Chania.

Essentials

GETTING THERE **By Plane** **Olympic Airways** offers at least three flights daily to and from Athens in high season. (Flight time is about 50 min.) Flights to Chania from other points in Greece go through Athens. **Aegean Airlines** also offers several flights daily to and from Athens. See "Getting There," in the section on Iraklion, earlier in this chapter, for contact information. The airport is 15km (10 miles) out of town on the Akrotiri. Public buses meet all flights except the last one at night, but almost everyone takes a taxi (about 20€).

By Boat One ship makes the 10-hour trip daily between Piraeus and Chania, usually leaving early in the evening (**www.ferries.gr**). During tourist season **Hellenic Seaways** runs a once-daily high-speed catamaran between Piraeus and Chania that cuts the trip down to about 5 hours (**www.greekislands.gr**). All ships arrive at and depart from Soudha, a 20-minute bus ride from the stop outside the municipal market. Many travel agents around town sell tickets. In high season, if you're traveling with a car, make reservations in advance, or check with the **Paleologos Agency** (www.ferries.gr).

By Bus Buses run almost hourly from early in the morning until about 10:30pm, depending on the season, connecting Chania to Rethymnon and Iraklion. (Round-trip fare to Iraklion for example, is 25€.) There are less frequent, and often inconveniently timed, buses between destinations in western Crete. The main **bus station** to points all over Crete is at 25 Kidonias (© **28210/93-306**). Get there plenty early—it can be a madhouse in high season!

By Car All the usual agencies can be found in the center of town, but I've always had reasonable and reliable service with **Europrent**, at 87 Halidon (© **28210/27-810;** www.europrent.gr).

By Taxi It should be noted that in July 2009, the taxi drivers of Chania agreed to observe the posting of standard fares to some of the most frequented destinations in and around the city's center (such as the airport or points on the Akrotiri, or from one edge of the city to the other). These posting are supposed to be visible at major taxi pickup points, and although the actual charge cannot always be held to the exact penny (due, say, to traffic conditions that cause long waits), these posted costs should be useful in an appeal to the Tourist Police if you feel you have been grossly overcharged. Don't forget that taxi drivers are allowed a number of surcharges—late at night, extra luggage, and so on.

> ## A Taxi Tip
>
> To get a taxi driver who is accustomed to dealing with English speakers, call **Nikos,** at his cellphone (© **69774/45-585**). With Nikos, you get an informative guide as well as a driver.

VISITOR INFORMATION The official Tourist Information office is at 40 Kriari, off 1866 Square (© **28210/92-943**), but it keeps unreliable hours. You're better off turning to private travel agencies. I recommend **Lissos Travel,** Plateia 1866 (© **28210/93-917;** fax 28210/95-930), or **Diktynna Travel,** 6 Archontaki (© **28210/43-930;** www.diktynna-travel.gr); from your home abroad, try **Crete Travel,** in the nearby village of Monoho (© **28250/32-690;** www.cretetravel.com). A useful source of insider's information is **The Bazaar,** 46 Daskaloyiannis, on the main street down to the new harbor (to the right of the Municipal Market). This shop sells used

Chania

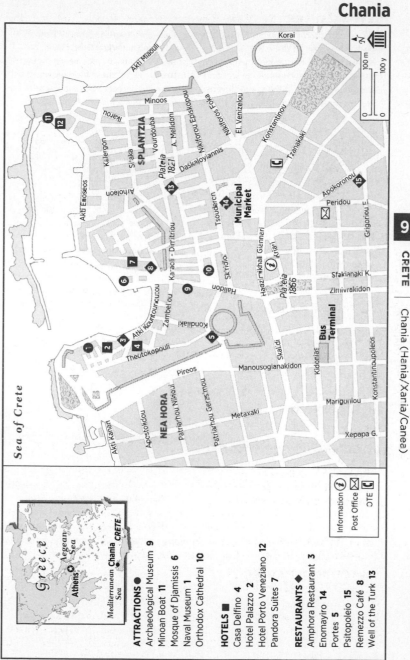

Korai

Akti Miaouli

Minoos

Ikarou

Karoin

SPLANTZIA

Kalergon

Siraka

Vourdouba

A. Melidoni

Plateia
1821

Daskaloyiannis

Nikiforou Episkopou

Nikolos Foka

El. Venizelou

Konstantinou

Tzanakaki

13

Arholeon

Akti Enoseos

Tsouderon

14

Municipal
Market

Apokoronou

15

Peridou

⊠

Grigoriou E

Karaoli - Dimitriou

7

8

Skridlo

Haazimihal Gianneri

Khari

ⓘ

Plateia
1866

Sfakianaki K.

Zimvrakidon

6

9

Halidon

Zambeliou

10

Akti Koundourioutou

Kondilaki

3

4

1

2

Theotokopouli

5

Skalidi

Bus
Terminal

Konstantinoupoleos

Sea of Crete

Pireos

Manousogianakidon

Kidonas

Marigoritou

NEA HORA

Apostolidou

Patriarhou Nikaou

Patriarhou Gerasmou

Metaxaki

Xepapa G.

Akti Kanari

100 m
100 y

9

CRETE | Chania (Hania/Xaria/Canea)

Greece

Aegean
Sea

Athens

Chania CRETE

Mediterranean
Sea

ATTRACTIONS ●
Archaeological Museum **9**
Minoan Boat **11**
Mosque of Djamissis **6**
Naval Museum **1**
Orthodox Cathedral **10**

HOTELS ■
Casa Delfino **4**
Hotel Palazzo **2**
Hotel Porto Veneziano **12**
Pandora Suites **7**

RESTAURANTS ◆
Amphora Restaurant **3**
Enomayiro **14**
Portes **5**
Psitopoleio **15**
Remezzo Café **8**
Well of the Turk **13**

Information ⓘ
Post Office ⊠
OTE 🅲

313

I am pleased to tell you about a couple of new ventures on Crete that should appeal to those who are into ecotourism. One is **Milia (www.milia.gr)**, a long-abandoned village in the mountains of western Crete that has been converted into a retreat for those willing to stay in old stone houses, do without modern hotel facilities (although there is electricity), and eat a limited but delicious natural diet. It is operated by native Cretans, and you are left pretty much on your own to enjoy the natural setting. I want to avoid guidebook superlatives, but I feel confident in predicting that if you are looking for a truly natural stay in Greece, no place beats this. The second is the **Dalabelos Estates (www.dalabelos.gr)**, with 10 houses (new and with all amenities), and is in the countryside outside Rethymnon; here you are on a working farm and, depending on the season, can participate in such activities as grape or olive picking or even sheep shearing. Both places require a vehicle to reach even though the proprietors would pick you up at a nearby bus station. Milia is a solid 2-hour drive from Chania and requires a willingness to travel the last miles up a rather scary dirt road; once there, you would probably want to take all your meals at the simple dining room. Dalabelos Estates is about a half-hour's drive from Rethymnon but not served by public transportation; in any case you would want a car to have the freedom to move about the island. For those wavering about which to take on, note that at Milia you have no view, but you step out of your cabin into a wooded area bursting with wildlife. The Dalabelos Estates is a bit more like a resort in that it offers both handsome accommodations and a selection of diversions.

foreign-language books and assorted "stuff." Owned and often staffed by non-Greeks, it maintains a listing of all kinds of helpful services.

GETTING AROUND   You can walk to most tourist destinations in Chania. Public buses go to nearby points and to all the major destinations in western Crete. But if you want to explore the countryside or more remote parts of western Crete, I recommend that you rent a car to make the best use of your time.

FAST FACTS   **Banks** in the new city have ATMs. For the **tourist police,** dial ☎ **171.** The **hospital** (☎ **28210/27-231**) is on Venizelou in the Halepa quarter. There are now several **Internet** cafes: I like the Vranas Studios Cafe, behind the cathedral and at the corner of Aghion Deka, or Cafe Santé (on the second floor at the far west corner of the old harbor). The **post office** is at 6 Peridou (an extension of Plastira that leads directly away for the municipal market); hours are Monday through Friday from 8am to 8pm, Saturday from 8am to noon. The **telephone office (OTE)** is on Tzanakaki (leading diagonally away from the municipal market); it is open daily from 7:30am to 11:30pm. **Foreign-language publications** are available at 8 Skalidi (main street heading west, at top of Halidon).

What to See & Do

In summer, several small **excursion ships** offer 1- to 5-hour trips to the waters and islets off Chania. These trips depart from the old and new harbors and include stops for swimming at one or another of the islets; some provide free snorkeling gear. On the glass-bottomed *Evangelos* and *Aphrodite,* you can see underwater life. The cost ranges from 10€ to 25€ adults; free for children 11 and under. Those more curious about the terrestrial environment might want to take an informative **walk through Old Chania** with Dr. Alexandra Ariotti, a local archaeologist. She can be contacted via e-mail at **alex@chania-oldtown-walks.gr**. The cost is 25€ and lower, depending on the number who go along. **Diktynna Travel Agency (www.diktynna-travel.gr)** sponsors a **day at a farm** outside Chania where you get lessons in cooking Cretan specialties, participate in cheese, wine, and olive tastings, and cap the day with a meal. And for those few who are looking for an adrenaline rush, there is now what is said to be the highest **bungee-jumping** site from a bridge in Europe at the Aradaina bridge, down near the south coast, just west of Khora Sfakion.

Archaeological Museum ★ Even short-term visitors should stop here, if only for a half-hour's walk-through. The museum, housed in the 16th-century Venetian Catholic Church of St. Francis, was carefully restored in the early 1980s and gives a fascinating glimpse of the different cultures that have played out on Crete, from the Neolithic through the Minoan and on to the Roman and early Christian. You'll come away with a sense of how typical people of these periods lived, as opposed to the elite classes featured in so many museums.

30 Halidon. © **28210/90-334.** http://odysseus.culture.gr. Admission 2€, 65 and over 1€. Tues-Sun 8:30am-3pm (but always subject to change). No parking.

The Minoan Ship ★ Here's something unique that has become a major attraction: a full-size replica (or at least an attempt at one) of a Minoan ship. It was constructed during 2 years leading up to the Athens Olympics of 2004, allegedly using only materials and tools available to the ancient Minoans (although one photo shows them using a modern pulley). Launched in December 2003, 22 oarsmen rowed it by stages to Piraeus where it was on display during the Olympics. Now part of the Maritime Museum annex in the Venetian arsenal at the far end of the new harbor, it is placed in the harbor once or twice a year to keep it seaworthy. There are many supporting displays including a video, but make sure you view the display board showing the ancient depictions (frescoes, vase paintings, and so on) used as sources for the reconstruction.

Akti Kountourioti. © **28210/91-875.** www.mar-mus-crete.gr. Admission 2€, 65 and over 1€. High season Mon-Sun 10am-2pm, 5-9pm; low season reduced hours. Parking behind arsenal.

A WALK AROUND OLD CHANIA

Start at **Plateia Venizelou,** the large clearing at the far curve of the old harbor—now distinguished by its marble fountain. Head along the east side to see the prominent domed **Mosque of Djamissis** (or of Hassan Pasha), erected soon after the Turks conquered Chania in 1645. Proceeding around the **waterfront** toward the **new harbor,** you'll come to what remains of the great **arsenali,** where the Venetians made and repaired ships; exhibitions are sometimes held inside. Go to the far end of this inner harbor and you can visit the Minoan ship (see above) In any case, you can walk out along the breakwater to the 19th-century lighthouse. Go back to the far corner of the long set of arsenali and Arnoleon, where you turn inland, and then proceed up Daskaloyiannis; on the left, you'll come to **Plateia 1821** and the **Orthodox Church of St. Nicholas.** Begun as a Venetian Catholic monastery, it was converted by the Turks into a mosque—thus its campanile and minaret! The square is a pleasant place to sit and have a cool drink. Go next to Tsouderon, where you turn right and, passing another minaret, arrive at the back steps of the great **municipal** market (ca. 1911)—worth wandering through, although and alas, it has been largely taken over by touristic shops.

If you exit at the opposite end of your entrance, you'll emerge at the edge of the **new town.** Turn right and proceed along Hadzimikhali Giannari until you come to the top of **Halidon,** the main tourist-shopping street. The stylish **Municipal Art Gallery,** at no. 98, sits at the top right side (hours posted). As you continue to make your way down Halidon, you'll pass on the right the famous **Skridlof,** with its leather workers; the **Orthodox Cathedral** or the Church of the Three Martyrs, from the 1860s; and on the left the **Archaeological Museum** (see above).

As you come back to the edge of Plateia Venizelou, turn left one street before the harbor, onto **Zambeliou.** Proceed along this street; you can then turn left onto any of the side streets and explore the **old quarter** (now, alas, also overwhelmed by modern tourist enterprises). If you turn up at Kondilaki, follow the signs and turn right at the alley that leads to the **Etz Hayyim Synagogue;** built in the 17th century (on site of still earlier synagogues) and destroyed in World War II, it has now been beautifully restored and is well worth a visit. Hours have been Monday to Friday 10am to 5pm. Check **www.etz-hayyim-hania.org** to learn about the history and activities of the synagogue. Back to Zambeliou, continue along, taking a slight detour to Moskhou to view **Renieri Gate,** from 1608. On Zambeliou again, you'll ascend a bit until you come to **Theotokopouli;** turn right here and take in the architecture and shops of this Venetian-style street as you make your way down to the sea.

At the end of the street, on the right, the recently restored **Church of San Salvatore** was converted into a fine little museum of Byzantine and post-Byzantine art (www.culture.gr; irregular hours; admission 2€). After the museum, you'll be just outside the harbor; turn right and pass below the walls of the **Firkas,** the name given to the fort that was a focal point in Crete's struggle for independence at the turn of the 20th century. The **Naval Museum** (✆ 28210/26-437) here has some interesting displays and artifacts (daily 10am–4pm; admission 5€); or you can take a seat for welcome refreshment at one of the cafes near the museum entrance.

SHOPPING

Jewelers, leather-goods shops, and souvenir stores are everywhere—but it's hard to find that special item that's both tasteful and distinctively Cretan. To help you, there's **Kaparakis** at 32 Portou (the street running below the Venetian wall, approached from the top of Kondolaki; ✆ 28210/99-205). Then there's **Carmela,** at 7 Anghelou, the narrow street across from the Naval Museum's entrance (✆ 28210/90-487), which has some elegant ceramics and jewelry—all original, but inspired by ancient works of art and even employing some of the old techniques.

Below, I point out some things you will not find anywhere else. And unless otherwise noted, these shops are open daily.

XPOMA (Chroma) at 42 Daskoloyiannis has a truly fine (and not cheap) selection of old prints and maps. The new **Notos Bookstore** (✆ 28210/86-771) at 10 Kondolaki has a surprisingly sophisticated (for its location) selection of books in several foreign languages. Call ahead if you have a special title in mind.

Step into **Cretan Rugs and Blankets,** 3 Anghelou (✆ 28210/98-571), to experience a realm not found elsewhere on Crete. It's an old Venetian structure filled with gorgeously colored rugs, blankets, and kilims. Prices range from 100€ to 2,000€. Or visit **Roka Carpets,** 61 Zambeliou (✆ 28210/74-736), where you can watch a traditional weaver at work. The carpets come in patterns, colors, and sizes to suit every taste; prices start at 20€. These are not artsy textiles, but traditional Cretan weaving.

There is no end of shops selling ceramics, trinkets and souvenirs of all kinds, for a more sophisticated selection of Greek handicrafts, try **Mitos** at 44 Halidon, opposite the Orthodox Cathedral (ⓒ **28210/88-862**). **Castello Vechio,** at the corner of Episkopi Chrysanthos, has a unusual selection of ceramics and woodware. For a varied selection by amateur Cretan artisans, visit the **Local Artistic Handicrafts Association** (ⓒ **28210/41-885**), located where the new harbor turns the corner into the old harbor.

Where to Stay
EXPENSIVE

Casa Delfino ★★   When did you last have the chance to stay in a 17th-century Venetian mansion, with fresh orange juice for breakfast? Its quiet neighborhood (also dating from the 1600s) is just a block from the harbor. The owners transformed the stately house into stylish suites and studios, whose tastefully decorated rooms are among the most elegant you will find on Crete. All have modern bathrooms (nine with Jacuzzi), and three have kitchenettes. But be warned: Several rooms have beds on a second level—little more than sleeping lofts—forcing you to go up and down stairs to get to the bathroom. (You should request other rooms unless the price differential deters you.) Especially attractive is the rooftop terrace, where light meals can be had. The reception desk may be informal, but the friendly staff will provide a wide range of services, from airport transport to tour arrangements.

8 Theofanous, 73100 Chania, Crete. www.casadelfino.com. ⓒ **28210/87-400.** 24 units. High season 200€–330€ double, 265€–335€ suite; low season 150€–220€ double, 210€–320€ suite. Rates include buffet breakfast. AE, MC, V. Free parking nearby. **Amenities:** Courtyard breakfast area; rooftop terrace cafe; bar; babysitting; Internet access; Jacuzzi; room service. *In room:* A/C, TV, hair dryer, minibar, Wi-Fi.

MODERATE

Doma ★★   Long regarded as one of the most distinctive hotels on Crete, the neo-classical, turn-of-the-20th-century Doma was once a fine mansion, former home of the Austrian consulate. Authentic Cretan heirlooms and historical pictures decorate its public areas. Bedrooms and bathrooms are not especially large but are perfectly adequate. The four suites are roomier. All the rooms are plainly decorated—even a bit severe, with muted wall colors and old-fashioned furniture. Front rooms have great views of the sea, but also the sounds of passing traffic. The third-story dining room offers fresh breezes and a view of old Chania; breakfast includes several homemade delights. An elevator provides access for those who can't take stairs. Among the hotel's special features is a museum-quality display of headdresses from all over the world. The Doma appeals to travelers who appreciate a discreet old-world atmosphere.

124 Venizelou, 73100 Chania, Crete. www.hotel-doma.gr. ⓒ **28210/51-772.** 25 units (22 with shower only). 140€ double; 190€–280€ suite. Rates include buffet breakfast. Special rates for more than 2 persons in suite; reduced rates for longer stays. AE, MC, V. Free parking on adjacent streets. Closed Nov–Mar. Bus to Chania center; can be reached on foot. 3km (2 miles) from the town center along the lower coastal road. **Amenities:** Restaurant; bar; smoke-free rooms. *In room:* A/C in suites, ceiling fan in rooms, TV, hair dryer, minibar.

Hotel Porto Veneziano ★   Thanks to the owner/manager "on the scene," this hotel combines the best of old-fashioned Greek hospitality with good, modern service. As a member of the Best Western chain, it has to maintain certain standards.

The tasteful bedrooms (standard international style) are relatively large; the bathrooms are modern but small. Many rooms have a fine view of the harbor. (Be warned—that can also mean harbor noise early in the morning!) Six suites offer even more space. At the far end of the old harbor (follow the quay from the main harbor all the way around to the east). There are many restaurants within a few yards of the hotel. Refreshments from the hotel's **Cafe Veneto** may be enjoyed in the garden or at the front overlooking the harbor. The desk personnel are genuinely hospitable and will make tour arrangements.

Akti Enosseos, 73100 Chania, Crete. www.portoveneziano.gr ⓒ **28210/27-100.** 57 units (48 with shower only). High season 120€–145€ double; low season 110€–130€ double. Rates include buffet breakfast. AE, DC, MC, V. Free parking nearby. **Amenities:** Breakfast room; cafe/bar; babysitting; Internet; room service. *In room:* A/C, TV, hair dryer, minibar.

Mistral Hotel ★ This is an unusual hotel—one designed expressly for mature singles. That "mature" is my characterization. The hotel's literature states that most guests are in their 30s to 50s, with others as young as 25 and others up to 70. But this is *not* a hotel for "swinging singles": if you are looking for all-night carousing, go over to Mallia or Chersonnisos. The Mistral is for the independent single traveler who has come to Crete to enjoy its special features. There are many excursions offered; bicycles for rent; early breakfast and packed lunches for those setting out on their own. Meanwhile the hotel offers all manner of in-house facilities and activities—such as classes in tai chi, watercolor, dance, cooking, and photography. The beach is about a 3-minute walk away; frequent buses take you to Chania. You can sit and read in the garden where much of their organic produce is grown to be used in their meals. There's still more—check out their website.

Maleme, 73100 (16km/10 miles west of Chania, left turn of coastal road). www.singlesincrete.com. ⓒ **28210/62-062.** 33 units. High season 90€–100€; low season 88€–97€. Rates include half board. AE, DC, MC, V. Free parking on grounds. **Amenities:** Breakfast room; bar; Internet; Jacuzzi; 2 swimming pools; spa; Wi-Fi. *In room:* A/C (5€ per day), fridge, hair dryer.

INEXPENSIVE

Eria Resort Hotel 👪 ★ Here is a distinctive establishment—probably unique in all Greece: A resort hotel designed, built, and operated for those with physical disabilities. The project of a Cretan pharmacist who has done well with a chain of medical supply stores, all of its public areas and rooms are accessible to those in wheelchairs. Specialist doctors can be seen by appointment and mechanized wheelchairs, bed hoists, and all kinds of equipment may be rented at reasonable rates. The swimming pool has a sloping ramp (and it provides waterproof chairs to allow entry into the water); it also offers special life jackets, a spa, physiotherapy; and special water games—some for an extra fee. The hotel has its own handicapped-accessible van to transport clients on excursions. Some clients have complained about the rough surfaces adjacent to the hotel grounds making it hard to leave the premises, but above all, the staff is sensitive to and prepared to serve those with physical disabilities.

Maleme 73104 (on coastal road some 21km/13 miles from Chania). www.eria-resort.gr ⓒ **28210/62-790.** 13 units, including 2 suites accommodating up to 4 adults (all with specially equipped bathrooms for those with limited mobility). High season 75€ double; low season 65€ double. Rates include buffet breakfast. Half board 23€, full board 38€ extra. MC, V. Parking on premises. **Amenities:** Restaurant; bar; gym w/modified equipment; physiotherapy; pool; spa; watersports equipment/rentals; boccie field; basketball; volleyball, Wi-Fi free in lobby. *In room:* A/C, TV, beds w/hoist bars, hair dryer, minibar.

Hotel Palazzo This Venetian town house, now a handsome hotel, delivers the feeling of old Crete without skimping on amenities. A fridge in every room, a TV in

The Botanical Park

It's rare to be able to come up with something new, different, and engaging after years of seeking out places of interest on Crete, but here is just such a place: Cretan brothers, having lost their olive grove to a forest fire in 2003, converted their mountain slopes into a botanical garden, with hundreds of species of trees, bushes, herbs, and flowers from all over the world. One walks along groomed paths up and down the slopes with most of the plants identified (in Greek and English) and their distinctive characteristics and uses (many are medicinal) described. There's a small collection of animals at the base—including Crete's famous wild goat. At a leisurely pace it can take 2 to 2½ hours; with shortcuts it can be done in half the time. The final ascent can be demanding but at the end you get to eat a meal prepared from local ingredients while sitting on the restaurant terrace and enjoying the spectacular view. The garden is about 19km (12 miles) southwest of Chania, just beyond the town of Fournes. Open April to October every day, 8am to 8:30pm. Admission is 4€ and includes a bottle of water and the use of a walking stick if desired. Children 12 and under enter free. See www.botanical-park.gr for more details.

the bar, and a roof garden with a view of the mountains and sea make this a comfortable hotel. There's nothing fancy about the rooms (furnishings are traditional Cretan rustic, knotty-pine style), but they are good size. Those at the front have balconies, so can be exposed to street and restaurant noise—perhaps a small price to pay for staying on Theotokopouli—the closest you may come to living on a Venetian canal. The owners speak English and will help you with all your needs, including laundry service, car rentals, and tours. You can drive up the street to unload and load but must park at a nearby square.

54 Theotokopouli, 73100 Chania, Crete. www.palazzohotel.gr. © **28210/93-227.** 11 units, some with shower, some with tub. High season 90€ double; low season 65€ double. Rates include breakfast. MC, V. Free parking 50m (164 ft.) away. Closed Nov–Mar (but will open for special groups). Within easy walking distance of all of Chania, around the corner from the west arm of harbor. **Amenities:** Breakfast room; bar; roof garden. *In room:* A/C, TV, fridge.

Pandora Suites   Centrally located, with views over the harbor, this hotel may seem a bit unpromising from its street-side entrance but inside is a quietly elegant hostelry, a renovated 17th-century Italian townhouse. All eight doubles and three suites (for four persons) have kitchenettes, but it should be said that the suites' beds are on an interior "second level" (see the website to get a clear sense of this). Two of the doubles have private balconies, and everyone is free to enjoy the rooftop terrace to take breakfast or an evening drink with a fabulous view of Chania's celebrated harbor. I think this is just the place for those who like a sort of old-world funkiness!

29 Lithinon, 73132 Chania, Crete. www.pandora-hotel.com. © **28210/43-588.** 11 units. High season 110€–115€ double; 155€ suite for 4. Rates include breakfast. MC, V. Parking on street or nearby streets. Closed Nov–Mar (but will open for special groups). Within easy walking distance of all of Chania, around the corner from the west arm of harbor. **Amenities:** Breakfast room; roof terraces; Wi-Fi. *In room:* A/C, hair dryer at front desk, kitchenette.

Where to Eat

Chania offers a wide variety of dining experiences, and all I can do is single out a few of them. At one extreme are places catering mainly to foreigners, such as the **Tamam,** at 49 Zambeliou (the main street behind and parallel to the old harbor); widely publicized, it's popular for its vaguely "fusion" cuisine and reasonable prices. Meanwhile, if you want a place more favored by Chania's own, seek out **Karnayio,** located in an open square abutting the *arsenali* on the new harbor. I'd pass up most of the restaurants on the old harbor but almost any of the restaurants at the far end of the new harbor—the **Antigone** for one—can be counted on for good meals and decent prices. But don't be afraid to take a chance here and there.

EXPENSIVE

Nykterida ★★ GREEK   Here is another restaurant where the location is a major part of the dining experience. It's on a high point with spectacular views of Chania and Soudha Bay—be sure to insist on a table with that view—so save it for when you can dine outdoors on a summer evening. An institution since 1933, its founder claims to have taught Anthony Quinn the steps he danced in *Zorba.* The cuisine is traditional Cretan Greek, but many of the dishes have an extra something. For an appetizer, try the *kalazounia* (cheese pie speckled with spinach) or the special *dolmades* (squash blossoms stuffed with spiced rice and served with yogurt). Any of the main courses will be well done, from the steak filet to the chicken with okra. Complimentary *tsoukoudia* (a potent Cretan liquor) is served at the end of the meal. Traditional Cretan music is played on Monday, Thursday, and Friday evenings until the end of October.

Korakies, Crete. ✆ **28210/64-215.** www.nykterida.gr. Reservations recommended for parties of 7 or more. Main courses 6€–22€. MC, V. Mon–Sat 6pm–1am. Parking on-site. Taxi or car required. About 6.4km (4 miles) from town on road to airport; left turn opposite NAMFI Officers Club.

MODERATE

Amphora Restaurant GREEK   At some point, almost everyone who spends any time in Chania will want to eat a meal right on the old harbor. Frankly, most of the restaurants there are undistinguished at best, but this old favorite still offers a decent meal at a reasonable price. As with any Greek restaurant, if you order fish or steak, you'll pay a hefty price, but you can assemble a good meal here at modest prices. To start, try the eggplant croquettes and the specialty of the house, a lemony fish soup. The restaurant belongs to the adjacent Amphora Hotel, and this is probably what has maintained its food and friendly service.

49 Akti Koundouriotou (near the far right, western curve of the harbor). ✆ **28210/71-976.** Main courses 6€–20€. AE, MC, V. Daily 11:30am–midnight. Closed Oct–Apr.

The Well of the Turk ★★ MIDDLE EASTERN/MEDITERRANEAN   Here's a restaurant that rises above others in Chania because of its unexpected menu, tasty cooking, and unusual setting. At the heart of the old Turkish quarter (Splanzia), in a historic building that contains a well, there is a quiet outside court where diners may sit in the summer. The chef's imaginative touches make the cuisine more than standard Middle Eastern. In addition to tasty kabobs, specialties include meatballs mixed with eggplant, and *laxma bi azeen* (a pita-style bread with a spicy topping). Middle Eastern musicians sometimes play here, and you can settle for a quiet drink at the bar.

1–3 Kalinikou Sarpaki (on small street off Daskaloyiannis). ✆ **28210/54-547.** Reservations recommended for parties of 7 or more. Main courses 7€–20€. No credit cards. Wed–Mon 7pm–midnight.

INEXPENSIVE

Enomayirio SEAFOOD   Here's a special treat for diners who can handle eating in a cramped, unstylish restaurant in the center of Chania's public market. The fish and other seafood come from stalls 3m (10 ft.) away. All the other ingredients come from the nearby stands. Food doesn't get any fresher than this. Sit and watch the world go by.

In the public market, at the "arm" with the fish vendors. Main courses 5€-18€; gigantic platter of mixed fish for 2 is 26€. No credit cards. Mon-Sat 9am-3:30pm.

Portes ★ GREEK/MEDITERRANEAN   Here's an unpretentious restaurant that offers a different menu, congenial service, and a setting off the beaten track. Perhaps it's because of the "hybrid" Irish and Greek proprietors, but since discovering Portes (and eating there several times) I've come to think of it as worth seeking out. Along with some traditional Greek fare, dishes such as roasted vegetable salad or spicy chicken livers make dining here a special experience. And although you're not on the harbor, a candle-lit table against the Venetian wall on a summer evening has its own cachet. And during the winter season, there is live music on the weekends.

48 Portu (the street against the Venetian wall btw. the tops of Kondolaki and Douka). *(C)* **28210/76-261.** Main courses 6.50€-9€. MC, V. Mon-Sat noon-1am; Sun 5pm-1am.

Psitopoleio (The Grill) GREEK   Known to the foreign community of Chania as The Meatery, this is not for the fainthearted (or vegetarians). Its clientele is almost 100% Cretan. I debated whether to include this place, but eventually decided that some travelers will appreciate its ambience. To call its decor "basic" is an understatement: It is a long, bare space, with the butcher's block at the rear and the grill at the front. Your meat course is butchered at the former and cooked at the latter. The specialties are lamb chops, pork chops, kidneys, spareribs, and sausages; excellent french fries, salads, both standard Greek and a cabbage version; soup; and *tzatziki*. House wine, beer, and soft drinks help you wash down the tasty, unforgettable food. Go for it!

48 Apokorono. *(C)* **28210/91-354.** Main courses 5€-14€. No credit cards. Daily noon-3pm and 7.30pm-1am. No parking nearby. With your back to the municipal market, walk along the main street leading diagonally away, off to the right.

Remezzo Cafe INTERNATIONAL   Sooner or later, we all say, "Enough Greek salads!" and want to indulge in a club sandwich or tuna salad. Remezzo, at the center of the action—Venizelou Square—on the old harbor, is a great choice for breakfasts and light meals (omelets, salads, and so on). It also offers a full range of coffee, alcoholic drinks, and ice-cream desserts. Sitting in one of the cushioned chairs as you sip your drink and observe the scene, you'll feel like you have the best seat in the house.

16A Venizelou (on corner of main square at old harbor). *(C)* **28210/52-001.** Main courses 5€-14€. No credit cards. Daily 7am-2am.

Chania After Dark

At night, instead of seeking out a packed club/bar/disco or walking around the harbor and old town, wander into Chania's back alleys to see the old Venetian and Turkish remains. Sit in a quayside cafe and enjoy a coffee or a drink, or treat yourself to a ride in a horse-drawn carriage at the harbor. At the other extreme, stroll through the new town; you might be surprised by the modernity and diversity (and prices) of the stores patronized by typical Chaniots.

Clubs come and go from year to year. Some popular spots include **El Mondo** and the **Happy Go Lucky,** both on Kondilaki (the street leading away from the center of the old harbor); **Idaeon Andron,** 26 Halidon; and **Ariadne,** on Akti Enoseos (around the corner, where the old harbor becomes the new). On Anghelou (up from the Naval Museum) is **Fagotta,** a bar that sometimes offers jazz.

Cafes are everywhere, but two stand out because of their locations. At **Pallas Roof Garden Cafe-Bar,** on Akti Tobazi (right at the corner where the new harbor meets the old harbor), you can sit high above the harbor, watch the lights, listen to the murmur of the crowds below, and nurse a refreshing drink or ice cream. However, you must climb 44 stairs to get here; as the sign says, IT'S WORTH IT. If you'd prefer to hear traditional Cretan songs, try **Cafe Lyriaka,** 22 Kalergon (behind the arsenali along the harbor).

The gay community in Chania does not seem to have any single gathering place, but the **DioLuxe** cafe, at 8 Sarpidonas (behind the Porto Veneziano hotel, on the new harbor), is reported to be gay friendly.

Movie houses around town—both outdoor and indoor—usually show foreign movies in their original language. The one in the public gardens is especially enjoyable. Watching a movie on a warm summer night in an outdoor cinema is one of life's simpler pleasures.

A **summer cultural festival** sometimes features dramas, symphonic music, jazz, dance, and traditional music. These performances take place from July to September at several venues: **Firka** fortress at the far left of the harbor; the **Venetian arsenali** along the old harbor; **East Moat Theater** along Nikiforou Phokas; or **Peace and Friendship Park Theater** on Demokratias, just beyond the public gardens. For details, inquire at one of the tourist information offices when you arrive in town.

A Side Trip from Chania: Samaria Gorge ★★

Everyone with an extra day on Crete—and steady legs and solid walking shoes—should consider hiking through the Samaria Gorge. The endeavor involves first getting to the top of the gorge, a trip of about 42km (26 miles) from Chania. Second comes the actual descent and hike through the gorge itself, some 18km (11 miles). Third, a boat takes you from the village of Ayia Roumeli, at the end of the gorge, to Khora Sfakion; from there, it's a bus ride of about 75km (46 miles) back to Chania. (Some boats go westward to Paleochora, approximately the same distance by road from Chania.)

Most visitors do it all in a long day, but you can put up for the night at one of the modest hotels and rooms at Ayia Roumeli, Paleochora (to its west), Souya (to its east), Khora Sfakion (main port to meet buses), and elsewhere along the south coast. I strongly advise signing up with one of the many travel agencies in Chania that get people to and from the gorge. This way, you are guaranteed seats on the bus (there and back) and on the boat. One agency I recommend is **Diktynna Travel,** 6 Archontaki St. (© **28210/41-458;** www.diktynna-travel.gr); it offers a day excursion—including all transportation to and from the Samaria George—for 65€ per person. In recent years, Samaria Gorge has been so successfully promoted as one of the great natural splendors of Europe that on the most crowded days, you can find yourself walking single file with several thousand other people. Starting very early is one way to beat the worst of the crowd; alternatively, start on in the afternoon and plan to spend the night in Ayia Roumeli. The gorge is open from about mid-April through mid-October (depending on weather conditions); the best chance for a bit of solitude means hiking near the beginning or end of the season. The hike is relatively taxing; and here and there, you will scramble over boulders. Bring water and snacks, and wear sturdy, comfortable shoes. Admission is 5€.

The gorge offers enough opportunities to break away from the crowds. You'll be treated to the fun of crisscrossing the water, not to mention the sights of wildflowers (but don't pick them!) and dramatic geological formations, the sheer height of the gorge's sides, and several unexpected chapels—it will all add up to a worthwhile experience, one that many regard as the highlight of their visit to Crete.

RETHYMNON (RETHIMNO)

72km (45 miles) E of Chania; 78km (50 miles) W of Iraklion

Whether you visit on a day trip from Chania or Iraklion or use it as a base in western Crete, Rethymnon can be a pleasant town—provided you pick the right Rethymnon.

The town's defining centuries came under the Venetians in the late Middle Ages and the Renaissance, then under the Turks from the late 17th century to the late 19th century. Its maze of streets and alleys is now lined with shops, its old beachfront is home to restaurants and bars, and its new beach-resort facilities (to the east of the old town) offer a prime (some might say appalling) example of how a small town's modest seacoast can be exploited. Assuming you have not come to see these "developments," we'll help you focus your attention on the old town—the side of Rethymnon that can still work its charm on even the casual stroller.

Essentials

GETTING THERE   Rethymnon lacks an airport but is only about 1 hour from the Chania airport and 1½ hours from the Iraklion airport.

By Boat   Rethymnon does have its own ship line, which offers direct daily trips to and from Piraeus (about 10 hr.).

By Car   Many people visit Rethymnon by car, taking the highway from either Iraklion (about 78km/50 miles) or Chania (72km/45 miles). The public parking lot at Plateia Plastira, at the far western edge, just outside the old harbor, is best approached via the main east-west road along the south edge of the town. But unless you plan to take some side trips en route to Rethymnon, taking the bus there might be the best way to go from either of those other cities.

By Bus   If you don't have your own vehicle, the bus offers frequent service to and from Iraklion and Chania—virtually every half-hour from early in the morning until midevening. In high season, buses depart Rethymnon as late as 10pm. The fare is about 15€ round-trip. The **KTEL** bus line (✆ 28310/22-212) that provides service to and from Chania and Iraklion is located at Akti Kefaloyianithon, at the city's western edge (so allow an extra 10 min. to get there).

VISITOR INFORMATION   The **National Tourism Office** (✆ 28310/29-148) is on Venizelou, the main avenue that runs along the town beach. In high season, it's open Monday through Friday from 8am to 2:30pm; off-season, its hours are unpredictable. But there are numerous private travel agencies that can arrange trips to anywhere on the island. Try **Ellotia Tours** at 155 Arkadhiou (**www.rethymnoatcrete.com**).

GETTING AROUND   Rethymnon is a walker's town. Bringing a car into the maze of streets and alleys is more trouble than it's worth—in fact, it's next to impossible. The sights you'll want to see around town are never more than a 20-minute walk.

To see the countryside of this part of Crete, unless you have unlimited time to use the buses, you'll need to rent a car. Among the many agencies with offices in Rethymnon are **Motor Club** (© 28310/54-253), **Budget** (© 28310/56-910), **Europeo** (© 28310/51-940), and **Hertz** (© 28310/26-286).

For Wine Lovers

Rethymnon's annual **wine festival** takes place for about 10 days starting near the end of July. It's centered on the public gardens, with music and dancing to accompany the samplings of local wines. The modest affair is a welcome change from larger, more staged festivals elsewhere.

FAST FACTS Several **banks** in both the old town and the new city have ATMs and currency-exchange machines. The **hospital** is at 7–9 Trantallidou in the new town (© 28310/27-491). For **Internet access,** try Caribbean Bar Cafe (behind Rimondi Fountain) or Alana Taverna (on Salaminas near Hotel Fortezza). The **tourist police** (© 28310/28-156) share the same building with the tourist office along the beach. The **post office** is east of the public gardens at 37 Moatsu (© 28310/22-571); its hours are Monday through Friday from 8am to 8pm, Saturday from 8am to noon. The **telephone office (OTE)** is at 40 Kountourioti; it's open daily from 7:30am to midnight.

What to See & Do
ATTRACTIONS
Archaeological Museum The exhibits here are not of great interest to any except specialists; rather, I recommend instead the Historical and Folk Art Museum, described below.

Near entrance to Venetian Fortezza. © **28310/29-975.** Admission 5€. Daily 8:30am–7pm. On foot, climb Katehaki, a fairly steep road opposite Hotel Fortezza on Melissinou; by car, ascend the adjacent Kheimara. Museum is in building just outside the fortress walls.

Historical and Folk Art Museum ★ Housed in a centuries-old and architecturally significant Venetian mansion, this small museum displays ceramics, textiles, jewelry, artifacts, implements, clothing, and other vivid reminders of the traditional way of life of most Cretans across the centuries. It's well worth a brief visit.

30 Vernardou.© **28310/23-398.** Admission 3€ adults, 1€ students, free for children. Mon–Fri 10am–2pm.

The Venetian Fortezza ★ Dominating the headland at the western edge of town, this massive fortress is the one site everyone should give at least an hour to visit. Built under the Venetians (but *by* Cretans) from about 1573 to 1580, its huge walls, about 1,130m (3,700 ft.) in perimeter, were designed to deflect the worst cannon fire of its day. In the end, of course, the Turks simply went around it and took the town by avoiding the fort. There's a partially restored mosque inside as well as a Greek Orthodox chapel. It's in this vast area that most of the performances of the annual **Rethymnon Renaissance Festival** take place (see below).

A STROLL THROUGH THE OLD TOWN
Rethymnon's attractions are best appreciated by walking through the old town. Start by getting a free map from the tourist office down along the beachfront, or follow the numbers on our Town Plan.

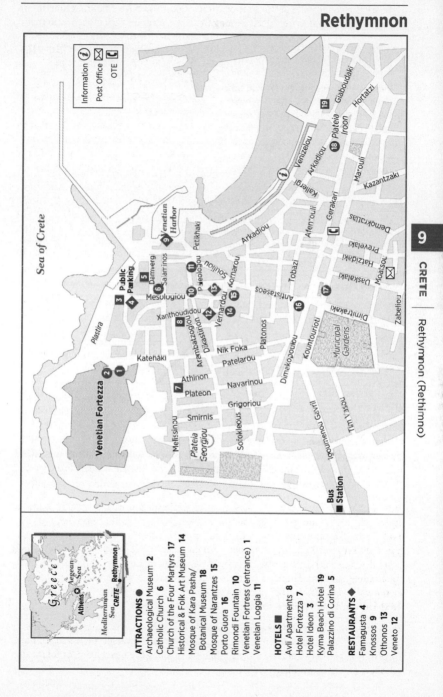

Rethymnon

Information *(i)*
Post Office ⊠
OTE ☎

Sea of Crete

Venetian Harbor **9**

Public Parking

3 **4**

Venetian Fortezza **2** **1**

Plastira

Katehaki

Athinon

Plateon **7**

Smirnis

Melissinou

Plateia Georgiou

Sotokleous

Grigoriou

Navarinou

Patelarou

Nik Foka

Platonos

Dimakopoulou

Igoumenou Gavril

Tim Vasou

Bus Station ■

Mesologiou **6** **5** Damverg.
Salaminos

10 Paleologou
11 Soutiou
13 Kornarou
Xanthoudidou
8 Arambatzoglou
Dikastirion **12** Vernardou **14** **15**

Petikhaki

Arkadiou

Kountourioti

Antistaseos **16**

Tobazi

17 Dimitrakaki

Municipal Gardens

Zabeliou

Kalleri
Afendouli
Gerakari **☎**
Prevelaki
Hatzidaki
Daskalaki
Moatsou ⊠

Venizelou
Arkadiou
18 Plateia Iroon **19**
Giaboudaki
Hortatzi
Marouli
Kazantzaki
Demokratias

(i)

9

CRETE | Rethymnon (Rethimno)

Greece
Aegean Sea
Athens ✪
Mediterranean Sea
CRETE Rethymnon

ATTRACTIONS ●
Archaeological Museum **2**
Catholic Church **6**
Church of the Four Martyrs **17**
Historical & Folk Art Museum **14**
Mosque of Kara Pasha/
Botanical Museum **18**
Mosque of Narantzes **15**
Porto Guora **16**
Rimondi Fountain **10**
Venetian Fortress (entrance) **1**
Venetian Loggia **11**

HOTELS ■
Avli Apartments **8**
Hotel Fortezza **7**
Hotel Ideon **3**
Kyma Beach Hotel **19**
Palazzino di Corina **5**

RESTAURANTS ◆
Famagusta **4**
Knossos **9**
Othonos **13**
Veneto **12**

325

Rethymnon's cultural festival offers mostly musical and theatrical events from July to early September. Productions range from ancient Greek dramas to more contemporary artistic endeavors (and now include folk and rock concerts). Most performers are Greek. The majority of performances are staged in the Fortezza itself; there's nothing like listening to 17th-century music or seeing a Renaissance drama in this setting. For details, inquire at the tourist information office.

If you have limited time, visit the **Venetian Fortress** (see the Rethmymnon map, above). If you have the time or inclination, look into the **Archaeological Museum.** Then make your way down to Melissinou and turn left and proceed to the **Catholic Church** at the corner of Mesologiou. Proceed down Salaminos to Arkadiou; make a left here to the western edge of the **old harbor.** Curving right down to the harbor is an unexpected sight: the wall of restaurants and bars that effectively obliterates the quaint harbor that drew them here in the first place. Making your way through this obstacle course, you'll emerge at the southeast corner of this curved harbor and come to a square that faces the town's long beach, its broad boulevard lined with even more restaurants and cafes. Turn right up Petikhaki, and at the first crossroads, you'll see the **Venetian Loggia** (ca. 1600)—for years the town's museum and now a Ministry of Culture gallery that sells reproductions of ancient Greek works of art. Continue up past it on Paleologou to the next crossroads. On the right is **Rimondi Fountain** (ca. 1623).

Leaving the fountain, head onto Antistaseos toward the 17th-century **Mosque of Nerantzes** (originally a Christian church) near the corner of Vernardou; you can climb the minaret Monday to Friday 11am to 7:30pm, Saturday 11am to 3pm (closed Aug). Again, if you have the time, proceed up Vernardou to the **Historical and Folk Art Museum.** If you follow Antistaseos to its end, you'll come to **Porta Guora,** the only remnant of the Venetian city walls.

Emerging at that point onto the main east-west road, opposite and to the right are the **municipal gardens.** On your left is the **Orthodox Church of the Four Martyrs,** worth a peek as you walk east along Gerakari. You then come to **Platei Iroon,** the circle that serves as the junction between the old town and the beachfront development.

Turning back into the old town on Arkadiou, you'll see on your left the restored **Mosque of Kara Pasha,** now converted to a botanical museum (daily 9am–6pm). Continue along Arkadiou, and in addition to the modern shops, note the surviving remains of the Venetian era—particularly the **facade of no. 154.** From here, you're on your own to explore the narrow streets, go shopping, or head for the waterfront for something cool to drink.

OUTDOOR PURSUITS

If you're interested in horseback riding, try the **Riding Center,** southeast of town at Platanias, 39 N. Fokas (© **28310/28-907**), or **Zoraida's Horse Riding** at Georgioupolis, midway between Chania and Rethymnon (© **28250/61-745**). Among the newer diversions offered in Rethymnon are the daily **excursion boats** that take people on day trips for **swimming** on the beach at either **Bali** (to the east) or **Marathi** (on the Akrotiri to the west). The price, which is about 40€ for adults, includes a midday meal at a local taverna as well as all the wine you care to drink. You can sign on at the far end of the harbor. **Manias Tours,** 5 Arkadiou (© **28310/56-400**), offers an **evening cruise** that provides a view of Rethymnon glittering in the night.

SHOPPING

Here, as in Chania and Iraklion, you may be overwhelmed by the sheer number of gift shops offering mostly souvenirs. Looking for something different? Try Nikolaos Papalasakis's **Palaiopoleiou,** 40 Souliou, which is crammed with some genuine antiques, old textiles, jewelry, and curiosities such as the stringed instruments made by the proprietor. At **Olive Tree Wood,** 35 Arabatzoglou, the name says it all—the store carries bowls, containers, and implements carved from olive wood. **Evangeline,** 36 Paleologlou, has a good selection of textiles, while **Haroula Spridaki,** 36 Souliou, has a nice selection of Cretan embroidery. **Talisman,** 32 Arabatzoglou, sells an interesting selection of blown glass, ceramics, plaques, paintings, and other handmade articles. And the AVLI Hotel's **Raki Baraki,** at 22 Xanthoudidou, has a large and varied selection of natural products from all over Greece.

Where to Stay

There is no shortage of accommodations in and around Rethymnon but it has become hard to find a place in town that offers location, authentic atmosphere, and a quiet night's sleep. Our choices try to satisfy the last-mentioned criterion first. Note that many places in Rethymnon shut down in winter.

EXPENSIVE

AVLI Lounge Apartments ★ This boutique hotel is a restored mansion dating from 1530, now loaded with elements from various centuries and cultures and with every possible modern convenience. The rooms are suites in the sense that they are large enough to assign areas to different functions—sleeping, working, relaxing—two even have working fireplaces. Clients are warned that some rooms are in a separate building across a narrow (pedestrian only) street and there are no elevators in either this or the main building. Rooms along the street are not well soundproofed and should be avoided by light sleepers. Also, because there are only seven units, you have little chance of switching. Insist on your room's location when making a reservation. Final word: You are paying a high price for more luxuries than you may need on Crete.

1622 Xanthoudidou, 74100 Rethymnon. www.avli.gr. © **28310/58-250.** 7 units. High season 190€–500€ double; low season 165€–210€ double. Rates include buffet breakfast. Surcharge for 3rd person sharing room; babies stay free. AE, DC, MC, V. Parking on public lot, 10-min. walk away. **Amenities:** Restaurant; bar; babysitting; pool; room service; yoga and massage. *In room:* A/C, TV, fridge, hair dryer, Internet, Jacuzzi, minibar.

Palazzino di Corina ★ Setting a new benchmark for stylish accommodations in Rethymnon, this boutique hotel is in a centuries-old Venetian mansion restored with taste and restraint. Each of the 21 rooms is named after one of the Greek gods or goddesses, and each has some distinctive configuration and appearance; size varies but all have comfortable beds and private bathrooms. A courtyard offers a delightful place to retreat from your city walks or wider excursions—plus a small pool in which to cool off. Its location offers closeness to the old town's center while providing a quiet night, but there is one drawback for some: There is no elevator and some rooms are on what Americans call a third floor; however, there is a room for travelers with limited mobility. It's definitely for those who appreciate subdued luxury and are willing to spend a bit more for such an environment.

7-9 Damvergi and A. Diakou, 74100 Rethymnon. www.corina.gr. © **28310/21-205.** 21 units. High season 130€–230€ double; low season 115€–180€ double. Rates include buffet breakfast. Surcharge for 3rd person sharing room; babies stay free. MC, V. Parking on public lot, 10-min walk away. **Amenities:** Restaurant; bar; babysitting; pool; room service. *In room:* A/C, TV, hair dryer, hydromassage, Internet, minibar.

MODERATE

Hotel Fortezza ★ Fortezza has long been one of the more popular hotels in Rethymnon, mainly because of its location and moderate prices, and since its total renovation in 2010-2011, it offers more pleasant accommodations and ambience. You're only a few blocks from the inner old town and then another couple of blocks to the town beach and the Venetian Harbor. It's convenient for driving and parking a car. The Venetian Fortezza rises just across the street. Guest rooms are decent size with modern bathrooms (some with shower, some with tub); most have balconies. It is essential, however, to ask for one of its inside rooms, which overlook the small but welcome pool—streetside rooms can be noisy. This hotel has become so popular that you must make reservations for the high season.

16 Melissinou, 74100 Rethymnon. www.fortezza.gr. © **28310/55-551.** 53 units. High season 85€–92€ double; low season 64€–76€ double. Family room for 4, high season 135€; low season 95€. Rates include buffet breakfast. Surcharge for 3rd person sharing room; babies stay free. AE, DC, MC, V. Free parking nearby. On the western edge of town, just below the Venetian Fortezza, which is approached by Melissinou. **Amenities:** Restaurant; bar; babysitting; pool; Wi-Fi. *In room:* A/C, TV, hair dryer, Internet.

Mare Monte Beach Hotel ★ ☺ If you stay at the Mare Monte, some 24km (15 miles) west of Rethymnon, you'll feel like you're living in a remote hideaway, with the sea before you and the mountains behind. This first-class resort hotel gets its highest ratings for its beautiful beach. Guest rooms are of moderate size with basic Greek hotel furnishings, but fully modern bathrooms. Some rooms are wheelchair accessible. Activities include minigolf, archery, and horseback riding by arrangement. Although it lacks the luxury of the grand resorts to the east of Rethymnon, the Mare Monte is a good alternative for those who want to focus their Cretan stay on Rethymnon, Chania, and western Crete, yet prefer to be based well away from a noisy town. The village of Georgioupolis is close enough for an evening stroll.

73007 Georgioupolis, Crete. www.mare-monte-beach.com. © **28250/61-390.** 200 units. High season 115€; low season 85€ double. Rates include breakfast but most guests take half-board. DC, MC, V. Parking on-site. Closed Nov–Mar. 25 min. west of Rethymnon, on the main road to Chania. **Amenities:** 2 restaurants; 2 bars; babysitting; children's playground; gym; 2 pools (adult and children's); room service; 2 night-lit tennis courts; extensive watersports equipment/rentals; Wi-Fi. *In room:* A/C, TV, hair dryer.

INEXPENSIVE

Hotel Ideon This longtime favorite is a solid choice for its location and price. It also boasts a pool with a sunbathing area. The friendly desk staff will arrange for everything from laundry service to car rentals. The guest rooms are the standard modern of Greek hotels—but insist on one away from the street, as an adjacent area is a popular gathering spot in summer. I like this place because it offers an increasingly rare combination in a Rethymnon hotel: It's near the active part of the old town and near the water (although it is several hundred feet to a swimming beach).

10 Plateia Plastira, 74100 Rethymnon. www.hotelideon.gr. © **28310/28-667.** 86 units, some with shower, some with tub. High season 85€ double; low season 60€ double. Rates include buffet breakfast. Reduced rates for 3rd person in room or for child in parent's room. AE, DC, MC, V. Parking on nearby lot. Closed Nov to mid-Mar. On coast road just west of the Venetian Harbor. **Amenities:** Restaurant; terrace cafe; 2 bars; babysitting; pool. *In room:* A/C, TV (in suites), kitchenette.

Kyma Beach Hotel This is a modern, city hotel—not a resort hotel—designed for people who want to take in Rethymnon and then retire to a stylish but no-nonsense hotel. It's close to the attractions of old town and to the beach. The somewhat austere gray exterior might put off some people, but in fact the hotel is well designed and has been totally renovated by 2011. Although rooms are hardly spacious, they are neatly furnished. Some have sleeping lofts, so if this doesn't appeal to you, speak up. Bathrooms are up-to-date. All rooms have balconies: ask for one with a sea view and insist on a higher floor to escape street noise. The outdoor cafe is a popular watering hole for locals; you won't feel as if you're in a foreigners' compound.

Agnostou Stratioti Sq. 74111 Rethymnon. www.kyma-beach.com.© **28310/55-503.** 35 units, some with shower, some with tub. High season 85€ double; low season 65€ double. Rates include continental breakfast. AE, MC, V. Parking on adjacent streets. Public buses nearby. At eastern edge of old town and its beach. **Amenities:** 2 restaurants; 2 bars; babysitting; Internet. *In room:* A/C, TV, minibar, Wi-Fi.

Where to Eat

Rethymnon may not have the choice of Iraklion or Chania in restaurants, but there is a choice for a range of budgets. For elegant dining and wining, try the above-described **AVLI Lounge**'s restaurant; it boasts of its wine selection and will also provide private dinners, special celebration dinners, wine-tasting evenings, and even cooking lessons. Or try the **Veneto,** a 600-year-old Venetian mansion at 4 Epimenidou (a small street halfway between Nerantzes Mosque and the Folk Museum). Either offers truly special cuisine but may be more expensive than most travelers are budgeting for.

EXPENSIVE

Knossos ★ GREEK/SEAFOOD   Visitors who appreciate dining in a 600-year-old taverna head for this small, charming family-owned restaurant along the old Venetian harbor. Specializing in fish as fresh as the day's catch, all meals are lovingly prepared by Maria Stavroulaki and her mother. You can't go wrong with the grilled whole fish with fresh vegetables, or baked lobster with pasta. Happiness is snagging the single table on the open second-floor balcony overlooking the blinking harbor lights.

40 Nearchou (the old port). © **28310/25-582.** Reservations recommended. Fish main courses 20€– 40€. MC, V. Daily 11am–midnight. Closed Nov–Mar.

MODERATE

Famagusta GREEK/INTERNATIONAL   This well-tested seaside restaurant is far from the hustle of the harbor yet convenient to the center's attractions. The menu offers Cretan specialties such as breaded, deep-fried zucchini with lightly flavored garlic yogurt or *halumi,* a grilled cheese. Grilled fish and filets are the core of the main courses, but the adventurous chef includes Chinese-style Mandarin beef and that old basic, chili con carne. Eating here makes you feel like you're at an old-fashioned seaside restaurant, not some touristic confection.

6 Plastira Sq., Rethymnon. © **28310/23-881.** Main courses 6€–18€. AE, DC, MC, V. Daily 10am–midnight. Closed Christmas through New Year's. Parking lot nearby. Near Ideon Hotel, on coast road just to west of Venetian Harbor.

Othonos GREEK   Just as Americans claim to trust a diner where the truckers are parked, you can trust a Greek restaurant where the locals gather, and the Othonos is such a place. It offers tasty taverna food and a front-row seat for the passing scene. Minor variations—such as a Roquefort dressing on a salad, cheese and ham pies, artichokes with the lamb dish—liven up the traditional fare such as rabbit *stifado* (stew). Just right for dropping in when you are on a walking tour of the town.

27 Pethihaki Sq., Rethymnon.© **28310/55-500.** Main courses 6€–20€. MC, V. Daily 10am–midnight. In center of old town, so park on edge of old town.

A Side Trip from Rethymnon: Monastery of Arkadhi

The events that took place here can help put modern Cretan history in perspective. The **Monastery of Arkadhi** sits some 23km (14 miles) southeast of Rethymnon and can be reached by public bus. A taxi might be in order if you don't have a car. If you ask the driver to wait an hour, the fare should total about 80€. What you'll see is a surprisingly Italianate-looking church facade, for although it belongs to the Orthodox priesthood, it was built under Venetian influence in 1587.

Like many monasteries on Crete, Arkadhi provided support for the rebels against Turkish rule. During a major uprising on November 9, 1866, many Cretan insurgents—men, women, and children—took refuge here. Realizing they were doomed to fall to the besieging Turkish force, the abbot, it is claimed, gave the command to blow up the powder storeroom. Whether it was an accident or not is debatable, but hundreds of Cretans and Turks died in the explosion. The event became known throughout the Western world, inspiring writers, revolutionaries, and statesmen of several nations to protest. To Cretans it became and remains the archetypal incident of their long struggle for "freedom or death." (An ossuary outside the monastery contains the skulls of many who died in the explosion.) Even if you never thought about Cretan history, a visit to Arkadhi can give you insight on the Cretan people.

An Excursion from Rethymnon: The Amari Valley

Everyone who has more than a few days to spend on Crete should try to make at least one excursion into the interior to experience three of the elements that have traditionally characterized the island: eons-old rugged mountains, age-old village life, and centuries-old chapels and monasteries. The Amari Valley, south of Rethymnon, offers just such an opportunity. It's not much more than a 161km (100-mile) round-trip, but given the mountainous roads and allowing for at least some stops to see a few villages and chapels, a full day should be budgeted. Your own vehicle or a rented taxi is a must (unless you get a travel agency to arrange a tour); if you go on your own, a good map of Crete is also a necessity. Heading east out of Rethymon, some 5km (3 miles) along at Platanias, you take the road south to Prassies and Apostoli, always climbing and zigzagging. At Apostoli, a turnoff to the left leads to Thronos and its Church of the Panayia, built on the mosaic floor of an early Christian church. Back on the main road, you proceed toward Monasteraki but take the turnoff to the left to visit the Monastery of Asomatos. Founded in the 10th century, its present building dates from the Venetian period; it served as a center of resistance and Greek culture under the Turks. Continue down to Fourfouras (a starting point for the ascent to Crete's highest peak, Psiloritis). Continue south to Nithavris and Ayios Ioannis, then head north via Ano Meros, Gerakari, Patsos, and Pantanassa until you rejoin the road where a left starts you back north and down to the coast. Along the way you will have passed through many other villages and be directed to other chapels, but best of all you will have spent an unforgettable day in the Cretan mountains.

AYIOS NIKOLAOS

69km (43 miles) E of Iraklion

Ayios Nikolaos tends to elicit strong reactions, depending on what you're looking for. Until the 1970s, it was a lazy little coastal settlement with no archaeological or historical structures of any interest. Then, the town got "discovered," and the rest is the history of organized tourism in our time.

For about 5 months of the year, Ayios Nikolaos becomes one gigantic resort town, taken over by the package-tour groups that stay in beach hotels along the adjacent coast and come into town to eat, shop, and stroll. During the day, Ayios Nikolaos vibrates with people. At night, it vibrates with music—the center down by the water is one communal nightclub.

Somehow, the town remains a pleasant place to visit, and it serves as a fine base for excursions to the east of Crete. And if you're willing to stay outside the center, you can take in only as much of Ayios Nikolaos as you want, and then retreat to your beach or explore the east end of the island. And anyone who's come as far as Ayios Nikolaos should get over to Elounda at least once: It's some 12km (8 miles), but in addition to taxis there are buses every hour back and forth. It's slower paced and less fashionable than Ayios Nikolaos, but all the more pleasant for being so.

Essentials

GETTING THERE **By Plane** Ayios Nikolaos does not have its own airport but can be reached in about 1 hour by taxi or bus (1½ hr.) from the Iraklion airport. During the high season, **Olympic Airways** offers a few flights weekly to Sitia, the town to the east of Ayios Nikolaos, but the drive from there to Ayios Nikolaos is also a solid 1½ hours, so you'd do just as well to fly into Iraklion.

By Boat At least during the summer season, several ships a week each way link Ayios Nikolaos and Piraeus (about 11 hr.); these ships usually run from Ayios Nikolaos to Sitia (just east along the coast) and on to Rhodes via the islands of Kassos, Karpathos, and Khalki. In summer, ships may link Ayios Nikolaos to Santorini (4 hr.), and then to Piraeus via several other Cycladic islands. Schedules and even ship lines vary so much from year to year that you should wait until you get to Greece to make specific plans, but you can try checking www.gtp.gr in advance.

By Bus Bus service almost every half-hour of the day each way (in high season) links Ayios Nikolaos to Iraklion; almost as many buses go to and from Sitia. The **KTEL** bus line (© **28410/22-234**) has its terminal in the Lagos neighborhood (behind the city hospital, which is up past the Archaeological Museum).

VISITOR INFORMATION The **Municipal Information Office** (© **28410/ 22-357;** gr_tour_ag_nik@acn.gr) is one of the most helpful in all of Greece, perhaps because it's staffed by young seasonal employees who have some energy and enthusiasm to them (mid-Apr to Oct daily 8am–10pm). In addition to providing maps and brochures, it can help arrange accommodations and excursions. (To the left, just around the corner, is a small Folklore Museum, open usually 10am–6pm; admission 3€.) Of several travel agencies in town, I recommend **Nostos Tours,** 30 R. Koundourou, along the right arm of the harbor (© **28410/26-383**).

GETTING AROUND The town is so small that you can walk to all points, although taxis are available. The KTEL buses (see above) serve towns, hotels, and other points in eastern Crete. If you want to explore this end of the island on your own, it seems as if car and moped/motorcycle rentals are at every other doorway. I found some of the best rates at **Alfa Rent a Car,** 3 Kap. Nik. Fafouti, the small street between the lake and the harbor road (© **28410/24-312;** fax 28410/25-639). I should point out that parking is such a problem in the center of town that you might like to know of a small **private parking lot** at the corner of Kyprou and Koziri, just off the square (signed) at the top of Koundourou, the main street leading up from the harbor.

FAST FACTS   Several **ATMs** and currency-exchange machines line the streets leading away from the harbor. The **hospital** (℅ **28410/22-369**) is on the west edge of town, at the junction of Lasithiou and Paleologou. For **Internet access,** try either the bookstore/cafe **Polychromos,** at 28 October, or the **Atlantis Café,** 15 Akti Atlantidos; they tend to be open daily in high season from 9am to 11pm (2€ an hour). The **tourist police** (℅ **28410/26-900**) are at 34 Koundoyianni. The **post office** is at 9 28th Octobriou (℅ **28410/22-276**). In summer, it's open Monday through Saturday from 7:30am to 8pm; in winter, Monday through Saturday from 7:30am to 2pm. The **telephone office (OTE),** 10 Sfakinaki, at the corner of 25th Martiou, is open Monday through Saturday from 7am to midnight, Sunday from 7am to 10pm.

What to See & Do

The focal point in town is the small pool, formally called **Lake Voulismeni,** just inside the harbor. You can sit at its edge while enjoying a meal or a drink. Inevitably, it has given rise to all sorts of tales—that it's bottomless (it's known to be about 65m/213 ft. deep); that it's connected to Santorini, the island about 104km (65 miles) to the north; and that it was the "bath of Athena." Originally it was a freshwater pool, probably fed by a subterranean river that drained water from the mountains inland. A 20th-century channel now mixes the fresh water with sea water.

Archaeological Museum ★   This is a fine example of one of the relatively new provincial museums that have opened up all over Greece—in an effort both to decentralize the country's rich holdings and to allow local communities to profit from the finds in their regions. It contains a growing collection of Minoan artifacts and art being excavated in eastern Crete. Its prize piece, the eerily modern ceramic **Goddess of Myrtos,** shows a woman clutching a jug; it was found at a Minoan site of this name down on the southeastern coast. The museum is well worth at least a brief visit.

74 Paleologou. ℅ **28410/24-943.** Admission 4€. Tues–Sun 8:30am–3pm. Closed all holidays (reduced hours possible in low season, so call ahead).

SHOPPING

Definitely make time to visit **Ceramica,** 28 Paleologou (℅ **28410/24-075**). You will see many reproductions of ancient Greek vases and frescoes for sale throughout Greece, but seldom will you have a chance to visit the workshop of one of the masters of this art, Nikolaos Gabriel. His authentic and vivid vases range from 25€ to 300€. He also carries a line of fine jewelry, made by others to his designs. Across the street, at no. 1A, **Xeiropoito** sells handmade rugs. **Pegasus,** 5 Sfakianakis, on the corner of Koundourou, the main street up from the harbor (℅ **28410/24-347**), offers a selection of jewelry, knives, icons, and trinkets—some old, some not. You'll have to trust the owner to tell you which is which. For something a bit different in women's clothing, step into **Vendemma,** 11 Koundourou.

For something truly Greek, what could be better than an icon—a religious or historic painting on a wooden plaque? The tradition is kept alive in Elounda at the studio/store **Petrakis Workshop for Icons,** 22 A. Papendreou, on the left as you come down the incline from Ayios Nikolaos, just before the town square (℅ **28410/41-669**). Georgia and Ioannis Petrakis work seriously at maintaining this art. Orthodox churches in North America as well as in Greece buy icons from them. Stop by and watch the artists at their painstaking work—you don't have to be Orthodox to admire or own one. The store also carries local artisans' jewelry, blown glass, and ceramics.

Ayios Nikolaos

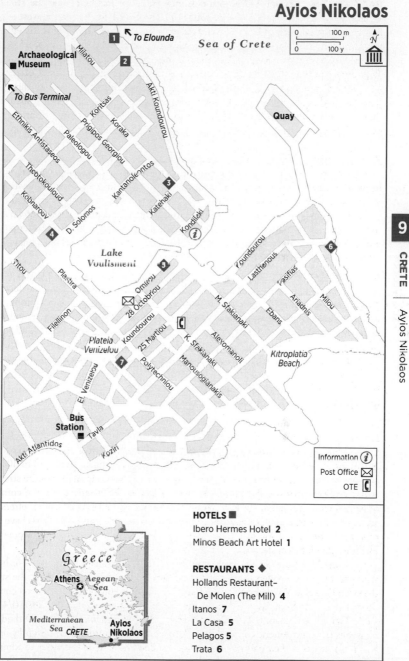

To Elounda

Archaeological Museum

To Bus Terminal

Sea of Crete

0   100 m
0   100 y

N

Quay

Miatou
Koritsas
Koraka
Prigipos Georgiou
Paleologou
Ethnikis Antistaseos
Theotokouloud
Kobnarovv
D. Solomos
Akti Koundourou
Kantanoleontos
Katehaki
Kondilaki

Lake Voulismeni

Ttou
Plastra
Filellinon
28 Octobriou
Omirou
Koundourou
25 Martiou
Plateia Venizelou
Polytechniou
K. Sfakianaki
Manousogianakis
El. Venizelou

Youndourou
Lasthenous
Vasifias
Ariadnis
Milou
Ebans
Alexomanoli
M. Sfakianaki

Kitroplatia Beach

Bus Station
Tavla
Koziri
Akti Atlantidos

Information 🛈
Post Office ✉
OTE 🄲

HOTELS ◼
Ibero Hermes Hotel **2**
Minos Beach Art Hotel **1**

RESTAURANTS ◆
Hollands Restaurant–
  De Molen (The Mill) **4**
Itanos **7**
La Casa **5**
Pelagos **5**
Trata **6**

Greece
Athens
Aegean Sea
Mediterranean Sea
CRETE
Ayios Nikolaos

Where to Stay

IN TOWN

Iberostar Hermes   Taken over by the Spanish international Iberostar hotel chain in 2011, the former Hotel Hemes remains the best choice if you want to stay close to the center of town. Yet the Hermes is just far away enough—around the corner from the inner harbor—to escape the nightly din. One drawback is that it requires at least half-board (breakfast and dinner), but this makes its rates relatively moderate—leaving you free to try local eateries now and then. Above all, it's a solid compromise between the deluxe beach resorts and the cheaper in-town hotels. Guest rooms are done in the standard style, and most enjoy views over the sea. There's a private terrace (not a beach) on the shore, just across the boulevard. The roof has a pool, with plenty of space to sunbathe. Probably not the town's best fit for adults with children.

If the Hermes is booked, you might try **Hotel Coral,** next door (✆ **28410/28-253**). It's almost as classy, and slightly cheaper.

Akti Koundourou, Ayios Nikolaos, 72100 Crete. www.iberostar.com/en/Creta. ✆ **28410/28-253.** 206 units. High season 125€ double; low season 85€ double. Rates include buffet breakfast; special rate for longer stays. AE, DC, MC, V. Parking on opposite seawall (but beware of spray). Closed Nov–Mar. On the shore road around from the inner harbor. **Amenities:** 2 restaurants; 2 bars; billiards; conference facilities; fitness center; swimming pool; sauna; video games. *In room:* A/C, TV, fridge on request, hair dryer.

Minos Beach Art Hotel ★★   I have to admit that I recommend this place out of loyalty to the first of the luxury beach-bungalow resorts in Greece. It remains a favorite among many returnees, but the common areas are not as well maintained as those at newer resorts, and its grounds now look a bit overgrown. But the individual accommodations are just fine, although as with almost all Greek hotels, the rooms and bathrooms are small (given the price). The hotel does have a civilized air, which is enhanced by the original, modern works of sculptors (several world famous) scattered around the grounds. It's a great place to enjoy complete peace and quiet not too far from Ayios Nikolaos. It will appeal to those who like a touch of the Old World when they go abroad and aren't looking for a lot of glitz.

Amoudi, Ayios Nikolaos, 72100 Crete. www.blugr.com. ✆ **28410/22-345.** 132 units. High season double-double/bungalow 285€–900€; low season double-double/bungalow 175€–765€. Rates include buffet breakfast. Special rates for children. AE, DC, MC, V. Parking on-site or nearby. Closed late Nov to late Mar. A 10-min. walk from center of Ayios Nikolaos. Frequent public buses to Ayios Nikolaos or Elounda. **Amenities:** 5 restaurants; 2 bars; airport transport arranged; babysitting; bike rentals; concierge; conference center; health club; Internet; saltwater pool; room service; sauna; table tennis; night-lit tennis court; TV room; watersports equipment/rentals. *In room:* A/C, TV, hair dryer, Jacuzzi (in some bungalows), minibar.

OUT OF TOWN

Istron Bay ★★   This beautiful and quiet beach resort, nestled against the slope on its own bay, has the atmosphere of a tropical paradise atmosphere that makes it a special place. Family owned, it maintains traditional Cretan hospitality; for example, newcomers are invited to a cocktail party to meet others. The comfortable guest rooms have modern bathrooms and spectacular views. If you can tear yourself away from here, you're well situated to take in all the sights of eastern Crete. The main dining room has a fabulous view to go with its award-winning cuisine; it takes special pride in offering choices based on the "Cretan diet," internationally recognized as especially healthy. The resort offers activities such as scuba diving at an authorized school, nature walks in the spring and autumn, wine tastings, fishing trips, and Greek lessons.

72100 Istro, Crete (12km/7 miles east of Ayios Nikolaos). www.istronbay.gr. ✆ **28410/61-347.** 145 units, including 27 bungalows. High season 145€–225€ double, 185€–310€ suite or bungalow; low season

105€–145€ double, 155€–210€ suite or bungalow. Rates include half-board with buffet breakfast. Special rates for extra beds in room, for children, for June, and for breakfast only. AE, DC, MC, V. Parking on premises. Closed Nov–Mar. Public buses every hour to Ayios Nikolaos or Sitia. **Amenities:** 3 restaurants; 2 bars; airport transport arranged; babysitting; billiards; children's program; concierge; conference facilities; seawater swimming pool and children's pool; room service; table tennis; night-lit tennis court; volleyball; watersports equipment/rentals. *In room:* A/C, TV, hair dryer, minibar.

Where to Eat

Ayios Nikolaos and nearby Elounda have so many restaurants that it's hard to know where to start or stop. Consider location and atmosphere; those factors have governed our recommendations below. If you're looking for just a basic taverna with traditional but tasty food, the **Trata,** on the Akti Pangalou overlooking the town's Kitroplatia Beach; standing at the port and facing the open sea, walk around the harbor to the right and then take a right onto Milou Street; follow that to the beach front and you will see the Trata on the right.

EXPENSIVE

Pelagos ★ GREEK/SEAFOOD Looking for a change from the usual touristy seafront restaurant—something a bit more cosmopolitan? Try Pelagos, in a handsome old house a block up from the bustle of the harbor. As its name suggests, it specializes in seafood and this is what makes it a bit more expensive. From squid to lobster (not really recommended in Greece), it's all done with flair. You can sit indoors in a subdued atmosphere or out in the secluded garden; either way you'll be served with style. This restaurant lets you get away from the crowd and share a more intimate meal. Parking on adjacent streets is impossible in high season.

10 Ketahaki (at corner of Koraka, a block up from the waterfront). ✆ **28410/25-737.** doxan45@hotmail.com. Reservations recommended in high season. Main courses 6€–20€; some fish by the kilo. MC, V. Daily noon–1am. Closed Nov–Feb.

MODERATE

Hollands Restaurant—De Molen (The Mill) DUTCH/INDONESIAN Looking for a change from the basic Greek menu? Aside from offering a (possibly) new experience for your palate, this place commands the most dramatic nighttime view of Ayios Nikolaos. Specialties include pork filet in a cream sauce. Vegetarian? Try the crepe with eggplant, mushrooms, carrots, and cabbage, tied up with leeks. I sampled the Indonesian dish *nasi goreng*—a plate heaped with rice, vegetables, and pork in a satay (peanut) sauce. Perhaps it's the setting, but everything seems to taste especially good.

10 Dionysos Solomos. ✆/fax **28410/25-582.** Main courses 6€–18€; combination plates offered. V. Daily 10am–11:30pm. Closed Nov–Mar. A taxi is your only choice, if you can't make it up the hill. It's the road at the highest point above the lake.

La Casa GREEK/INTERNATIONAL With its lakeside location, tasty menu, and friendly Greek-American proprietress, this might be many travelers' first choice in Ayios Nikolaos. You'll enjoy the fine meals Marie Daskaloyiannis cooks up, including such specialties as fried rice with shrimp, lamb with artichokes, and rabbit *stifado*. Or try the "Greek sampling" plate—moussaka, dolmades, stuffed tomato, meatballs, and other goodies Marie heaps on. There's always a slightly special twist to the food here.

31 28th Octobriou. ✆ **28410/26-362.** Main courses 6€–14€. AE, DC, DISC, MC, V. Daily 9am–midnight.

Vritomartes GREEK/SEAFOOD The 12km (8-mile) trip to get to this Elounda taverna takes a bit of effort, but a seat by the water makes it worthwhile. You can't beat dining at this old favorite—there's been at least a lowly taverna here long before the beautiful people and tour groups discovered the area. (In high season, come early or make a reservation.) The specialty, no surprise, is seafood. (You may find the proprietor literally "out to sea," catching that night's fish dinners.) If you settle for the red mullet and a bottle of Cretan white Xerolithia, you can't go wrong. The dining area itself is plain, but this is one place you won't forget.

On the breakwater, Elounda. 🌐 **28410/41-325.** Reservations recommended for dinner in high season. Main courses 6€–32€; 2-person fish-platter special 58€. MC, V. Daily 10am–11pm. Closed Nov–Mar.

INEXPENSIVE

Itanos GREEK   A now familiar story on Crete: A simple local taverna where you go to experience "authenticity" becomes overrun by tourists, changing the scene. But the fact is, the food and prices haven't changed *that* much. Standard taverna oven dishes are still served—grilled meats; no-nonsense chicken, lamb, or beef in tasty sauces; and hearty helpings of vegetables. The house wine comes from barrels. Low seasons and during the day, you sit indoors, where you'll experience no-nonsense decor and service. But at night during the hot months, tables appear on the sidewalk, a roof garden opens up on the building across the narrow street, and fellow travelers take over. Come here if you need a break from the harbor scene and want to feel you're in a place that still exists when all the tourists go home.

1 Kyprou. 🌐 **28410/25-340.** Reservations not accepted, so come early in high season. Main courses 6€–12€. No credit cards. Daily 10am–midnight. Just off Plateia Venizelos, at top of Koundourou.

Side Trips from Ayios Nikolaos

Almost everyone who spends any time in Ayios Nikolaos makes the two short excursions to Spinalonga and Kritsa. Each can easily be visited in a half day.

SPINALONGA

Spinalonga is the **fortified islet** in the bay off Elounda. The Venetians built one of their many fortresses here in 1579, and it had the distinction of being their final outpost on Crete, not taken over by the Turks until 1715. When the Cretans took possession in 1903, it was turned into a leper colony, but this ended after World War II. Now Spinalonga is a tourist attraction. In fact, there's not much to do except walk around and soak in the atmosphere and ghosts of the past. Boats depart from Ayios Nikolaos harbor and Elounda as well as from some hotels. It's not especially romantic, more like an abandoned site, so visitors are left to populate it with their own imaginations.

KRITSA ★

Although a walk through Spinalonga can resonate as a historical byway, if you have time to make only one of these short excursions, I advise taking the 12km (8-mile) trip into the hills behind Ayios Nikolaos to the village of Kritsa and its 14th-century **Church of Panagia Kera ★**. The church is architecturally interesting, and scholars regard its **frescoes,** dating from the 14th and 15th centuries, as among the jewels of Cretan-Byzantine art. They have been restored, but their impact still emanates from the original work. Scenes depict the life of Jesus, the life of Mary, and the Second Coming. Guides can be arranged at any travel agency or at the Municipal Information Office in Ayios Nikolaos. After seeing the church, visit the village of Kritsa itself and enjoy the view and the many fine handcrafted goods for sale.

THE CYCLADES

by Sherry Marker

When most people think of the isles of Greece, they're usually thinking of the Cyclades. This rugged, often barren, chain of islands in the Aegean Sea has villages with dazzling white houses that, from a distance, look like so many sugar cubes. The Cyclades got their name from the ancient Greek word meaning "to circle," or "surround," because the islands encircle Delos, the birthplace of the god Apollo.

Today, especially in the summer, it's the visitors who circle these islands, taking advantage of the swift boats and hydrofoils that link them. The visitors come to see the white villages, the blue-domed chapels, and the fiery sunsets over the cobalt blue sea. They also come to relax in chic boutique hotels, eat in varied and inventive restaurants, and to enjoy an ouzo—or a chocolate martini—in some of the best bars and cafes in Greece. When you visit the Cyclades, chances are that one island will turn out to be your favorite. Here are some of our favorites for you to shortlist when you set out to explore the islands that lie in what Homer called the "wine dark sea." We'll start in the north Aegean and make our way south, before circling back north.

Unlike many of the Cyclades, where you can easily hear more English, French, and German spoken in summer than Greek, almost everyone who comes to **Tinos** is Greek. The island is often nicknamed the "Lourdes of Greece" because its famous church of the Panagia Evangelistria is Greece's most important pilgrimage destination. Don't even think of coming here on the **Feast of the Assumption of the Virgin** (Aug 15) without a reservation unless you enjoy sleeping alfresco—with lots of company. Tinos is also famous for its villages ornamented with the ornate marble doors and carved window fanlights. Tinos also has intricate dovecotes that, from afar, can be mistaken for miniature villages perched on hills and hidden in valleys.

The "beautiful people" discovered **Mykonos** back in the 1950s and 1960s, drawn by its perfect Cycladic architecture—and, in those days, cheap prices. Today, despite seriously high prices, travelers still come to see the famous windmills and sugar-cube houses. Now, they also come for the boutique hotels, the all-night cafe life, and some serious shopping. In short, Mykonos—along with Santorini—is one of the Cyclades that just about everyone wants to see. If you come here in August, you'll think that just about everyone has arrived with you, and finding a hotel, or even a place at one of the chic, nouvelle-Greek-cuisine restaurants, will not be easy.

That's one reason some prefer **Paros,** which has something of a reputation as the poor man's Mykonos, with excellent windsurfing and restaurants and nightspots less pricey and crowded than those on its neighbor. Paros also has one preposterously picturesque seaside village—Naoussa—and the scenic inland village—Lefkes.

The largest and most fertile of the Cyclades, **Naxos** somehow has yet to attract hordes of summer visitors. You know what that means: Go there soon! The hills—sometimes green well into June—are dotted both with dovecotes and a profusion of endearing Byzantine chapels. The main town is crowned by a splendid kastro (castle) and a number of stately houses that the Venetians built between the 12th and 16th centuries; some of the houses are still lived in by the descendants of those very Venetians. Furthermore, although Naxos is a rich enough island that it does not have to woo tourists, there are some good small hotels and restaurants here.

Santorini (Thira) is famous from 1,000 travel posters, showing its black-lava pebble-and-sand beaches and sheer blood-red cliffs. Only a crescent-shaped sliver remains of the once-sizeable island that was blown apart in antiquity by the volcano that still steams and hisses. The first serious tourist invasion here began in the 1970s, as word got out about Santorini's deep harbor, framed by its sheer cliffs and its odd villages, cut out of the lava. The first travelers were willing to put up with the most modest of accommodations in local homes. (On my first visit, I was installed in a bed from which the owner's grandmother had just been ejected!) Today, Santorini gives Mykonos a serious run for the money as Boutique Hotel Central, with some of the best food in all Greece. Santorini also has one of the most impressive ancient sites: ancient Akrotiri, where you can walk down streets some 3,500 years old.

Folegandros is the perfect counterbalance to Santorini. As yet, this little island is not overwhelmed with visitors, but the helipad suggests that this generation's beautiful people have discovered this still-tranquil spot. Folegandros's capital—many say it's the most beautiful in the Cyclades—is largely built into the walls of a medieval kastro. Just outside the kastro is another reason to come here: the elegant cliff-side Anemomilos Apartments Hotel.

Sifnos, long popular with Athenians, is increasingly drawing other summer visitors to its whitewashed villages, which many consider to have the finest architecture in the Cyclades. In the spring, this is one of the greenest and most fertile of the islands. In summer, it's a place for the young at heart: In the capital, Apollonia, it's easier to count the buildings that have not (yet) been converted into shops, restaurants, and discos than those that have been.

Siros, on the other hand, is as "undiscovered" as a large Cycladic island can be. Its distinguished capital, Ermoupolis, has a number of handsome neoclassical 19th-century buildings, including the Cyclades's only opera house, modeled on Milan's La Scala. Ano Siros, the district on the heights above the port, has sugar-cube Cycladic houses and both Catholic and Orthodox monasteries. Like Tinos and Naxos, Siros welcomes, but does not depend on, foreign tourists.

If you wanted to describe the Cyclades in their entirety, you could do worse than to string together well-deserved superlatives: Wonderful! Magical! Spectacular! The sea and sky really *are* bluer here than elsewhere, the islands on the horizon always tantalizing. In short, the Cyclades are very "more-ish"—once you've visited one, you'll want to see another, and then another, and then, yes, yet another.

Tip: You can access a useful website for each of the Cyclades by typing **www.greeka.com/cyclades** into your Web browser, followed by the name of the island—for example, **www.greeka.com/cyclades/santorini**; **www.openseas.gr** is a useful site for ferry schedules as is **www.gtp.gr.**

The Cyclades

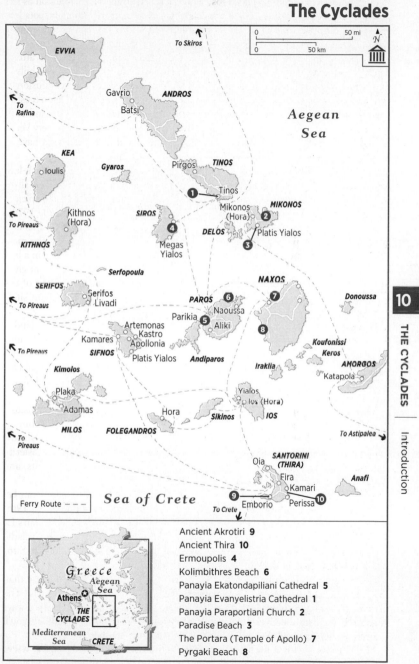

Ancient Akrotiri **9**
Ancient Thira **10**
Ermoupolis **4**
Kolimbithres Beach **6**
Panayia Ekatondapiliani Cathedral **5**
Panayia Evanyelistria Cathedral **1**
Panayia Paraportiani Church **2**
Paradise Beach **3**
The Portara (Temple of Apollo) **7**
Pyrgaki Beach **8**

Strategies for Seeing the Islands

As you might expect, the Cyclades are crowded and expensive during high season—roughly mid-June to early September—and high season seems to get longer every year. If summer crowds and prices don't appeal to you, visit during the off-season; the best times are mid-September through October or from mid-April to early June. April can still be cold in the islands and winter winds can be unremittingly harsh. Should you visit in winter or spring, keep in mind that many island hotels have minimal heating; find out if your hotel has genuine heat *before* you check in. Island boat service is much less frequent off-season, and many hotels, restaurants, and shops close for the winter (usually Nov–Mar). Whenever you visit, you'll discover that most hotels charge a **supplementary fee of 10%** for a stay of fewer than 3 nights. Finally, it's useful to remember that on most of these islands, the capital town has the name of the island itself. In addition, "Hora," or "Chora," meaning "the place," is commonly used for the capital. The capital of Paros, Parikia, for example, is also called Hora, as is Apollonia, the capital of Sifnos. Just to keep you on your toes, Apollonia/Hora is also called Stavri. When you're in island capitals, try to pick up the handy Sky Map, available at many travel agencies; there's a map for almost every Cycladic island. Although the businesses on these maps pay to be included, the maps are quite useful.

Although the Cyclades are bound by unmistakable family resemblance, each island is independent and unique, making this archipelago an island-hopper's paradise. Frequent ferry service makes travel easier—although changes in schedules can keep travelers on their toes (often on their toes as they pace harborside for ships to appear at unpredictable hours). Hydrofoils, in particular, are notoriously irregular, and even summer service is often canceled at the whim of the *meltemi* (blasting winds). Still, the growing fleet of catamarans is greatly facilitating travel between the ports of Piraeus and Rafina and the Cycladic islands.

Tip: If you haven't traveled here before, or for a while, here's some good news: you can now buy **interisland** transport tickets on almost any island. In the past, often you could only by a ticket from one port to the next: Tinos to Paros; then, on Paros, you could buy a ticket to Naxos; on Naxos, you could buy a ticket to Sifnos. And so forth. Ticket purchase is more streamlined now and you can also get many tickets online.

SANTORINI (THIRA) ★★★

233km (126 nautical miles) SE of Piraeus

Santorini is one of the most spectacular islands in the world. Greeks joke that there are foreigners who know where Santorini is—but are confused about where Greece is. While large ships dock at Athinios, many small ships arrive in Skala, a harbor that's part of the enormous **caldera** (crater) formed when a volcano blew out the island's center between 1600 and 1500 B.C., and which shapes the island today. Enjoy the famous sunsets over the caldera (the ramparts of the kastro and from the footpath between Fira and Oia have the best views).

BEACHES   Santorini's coastline is pure drama, from the steep cliffs that frame the caldera to the slopes of beaches whose pebbles come from long-ago explosion that rent the island in half. **Red Beach, White Beach,** and **Black Beach,** named for their distinctly colored pebbles, lie in the southwest. **Perissa, Agios Georgios,** and **Perivolos** are best for nightlife and watersports. Rock formations create a striking

Santorini

backdrop in family-friendly **Monolithos.** Descend the cliffs or hitch a donkey ride to one of **Oia**'s beaches with deep and startlingly blue water.

THINGS TO DO   **Akrotiri** was a Minoan town decimated by a volcanic eruption some 3,500 years ago, and preserved under lava until excavations began in 1967. If Akrotiri is closed, don't despair: you can visit the Greek, Roman and Byzantine ruins at **Ancient Thira.** The beautiful cliff-top capital **Fira** is rivaled only by **Oia**'s mosaic of white houses and blue church domes. For sheer beauty and tranquillity, **Imerovigli,** with its offshore islet crowned by a medieval kastro, bests its more famous neighbors.

EATING & DRINKING   In Fira, you can get acclaimed and inventive food (tiramisu with smoked eggplant mousse, anyone?) and a crater view at **Koukoumavlos.** At **Katina's** in Oia, postsunset relaxation goes well with the grilled fish and crisp white Assyrtiko wine from Santorini's volcanic vines. In the village of Pyrgos, you can dine at **Selene,** one of the best restaurants in all Greece, where the drop-dead gorgeous and delicious food uses the freshest of local ingredients.

NATURE   One of the biggest volcanic eruptions in history shook Santorini some 3,500 years ago and created its unique **caldera.** The best way to appreciate the views from its vertiginous cliffs is by **hiking** along the rim from Fira to Oia. Take a boat trip to see the **volcano** in all its steaming glory, stopping for a therapeutic dip in **sulfur** hot springs. The vineyards of **Megalohori** and **Pyrgos** produce volcanic wines such as dry white Assyrtiko and sweet, amber-hued Vinsanto.

Lay of the Land

The real wonder of Santorini is that it exceeds all glossy picture-postcard expectations. Like an enormous crescent moon, the island encloses the pure blue waters of its **caldera,** the core of an ancient volcano. Its two principal towns, **Fira** and **Oia** (also transliterated as **Ia**), perch at the summit of the caldera; as you approach by ship, bending back as far as possible to look up the cliffs, whitewashed houses look like a dusting of new snow on the mountaintop. Up close, you'll find that both towns' main streets have more shops (*lots* of jewelry shops), restaurants, and discos than private homes. If you come here off season—say in early May—you'll still find Fira's streets, shops, and restaurants crowded. In August, you'll experience gridlock.

Akrotiri is Santorini's principal archaeological wonder: a town destroyed by the volcano eruption, but preserved under layers of lava. As soon as you reach Santorini, check to see if Akrotiri is open; the site's protective roof collapsed in 2005, and it has been closed partially or totally since. If Akrotiri is closed, don't despair: If it weren't for Akrotiri, the site of **ancient Thira** would be the island's must-see destination. Spectacularly situated atop a high promontory, overlooking a black lava beach, the remains of this Greek, Roman, and Byzantine city sprawl over acres of rugged terrain. Ancient Thira is reached after a vertiginous hike or drive up to the acropolis itself.

Arid Santorini isn't known for the profusion of its agricultural products, but the rocky soil has long produced a plentiful grape harvest, and the local wines are among the finest in Greece. Visit one of the island **wineries** for a tasting; if you want to plan ahead, check out **www.santorini.com/wineries**. And keep an eye out for the tasty, tiny Santorini tomatoes and white eggplants—and the unusually large and zesty capers.

The best advice we can offer is to avoid visiting during the months of July and August. Santorini experiences an even greater transformation during the peak season than other Cycladic isles. With visitors far in excess of the island's capacity, trash collects in the squares, and crowds make strolling the streets of Fira and Oia next to impossible. *Tip:* Some accommodations rates can be marked down by as much as 50% if you come off season. Virtually all accommodations are marked up by at least as much for desperate arrivals without reservations in July and August.

Essentials

GETTING THERE   By Plane   Olympic Air (✆ **810/114-4444** or 210/966-6666, official Greek phone numbers never answer; www.olympicair.com) offers daily flights between Athens and the Santorini airport, **Monolithos** (✆ **22860/31-525**), which also receives European charters. There are frequent connections with Mykonos and Rhodes, and service two or three times per week to and from Iraklion, Crete. **Aegean Airlines** (✆ **810/112-0000;** www.aegeanair.com) also has several flights daily between Athens and Santorini. A bus to Fira (4€) meets most flights; the schedule is posted at the bus stop, beside the airport entrance. A taxi to Fira costs about 13€.

By Boat   Visit **www.gtp.gr** and **www.openseas.gr** for ferry schedules. Ferry service runs to and from Piraeus at least twice daily; the trip takes 9 to 10 hours by car ferry on the Piraeus-Paros-Naxos-Ios-Santorini route, or 4 hours by catamaran, if you go via Piraeus-Paros-Santorini. Boats are notoriously late and/or early; your travel or ticket agent will give you a rough *estimate* of times involved in the journeys. In July and August, ferries connect several times a day with **Ios, Naxos, Paros,** and **Mykonos;** almost daily with **Anafi** and **Siros;** five times a week with **Sikinos** and **Folegandros;** and twice weekly with **Sifnos.** Service to **Thessaloniki** (17–24 hr.) is offered four to five times per week. There is an almost daily connection by excursion boat with **Iraklion** in Crete, but because this is an open sea route, the trip can be an ordeal in bad weather and is subject to cancellation. Confirm ferry schedules with the Athens **GNTO** (© 210/870-0000; www.gnto.gr), the **Piraeus Port Authority** (© 210/451-1311, 210/451-1440, or -1441; phone not always answered), or the **Santorini Port Authority** (© 22860/22-239).

Almost all ferries dock at **Athinios,** where buses meet each boat and then return directly to Fira (one-way to Fira costs 3€); from the Fira dock, buses depart for many other island destinations. Taxis are also available from Athinios, at nearly five times the bus fare. Athinios is charmless; when you come here to catch a ferry, it's a good idea to bring munchies, water, and a good book.

The exposed port at **Skala,** directly below Fira, is unsafe for the larger ferries but is often used by small cruise ships, yachts, and excursion vessels. If your boat docks here, head to town either by cable car (5€), mule, or donkey (5€); or you can do the 15 minute uphill walk. Be prepared to share the narrow path with the mules. We recommend a mule up and the cable car down. If you suffer from acrophobia, try taking the cable car both ways with your eyes firmly shut.

VISITOR INFORMATION   Nomikos Travel (© 22860/23-660; www.nomikos villas.gr), **Bellonias Tours** (© 22860/22-469), **Pelican Travel** (© 22860/22-220; www.pelican.gr) and **Kamari Tours** (© 22860/31-390) are well established on the island. Bellonias, Nomikos and Pelican offer bus tours, boat excursions around the caldera, and submarine tours beneath the caldera. Expect to pay about 40€ for a bus tour to Akrotiri or ancient Thira, about the same for a day-trip boat excursion to the caldera islands, and about twice that for the submarine excursion.

GETTING AROUND   **By Bus**   The **central bus station** is just south of the main square in Fira. Schedules are posted here: Most routes are served every hour or half-hour from 7am to 11pm in high season. A conductor on board will collect fares, which range from 2€ to 5€. Destinations include Akrotiri, Athinios (the ferry pier), Oia, Kamari, Monolithos (the airport), Perissa, Perivolas Beach, Vlihada, and Vourvoulos. Excursion buses go to major attractions; ask a travel agent for details.

By Car   The travel agents listed above can help you rent a car Be sure to take full insurance. Of the better-known agencies, try **Budget Rent-A-Car,** at the airport (© 22860/33-290), or in Fira, a block below the small square that the bus station is on (© 22860/22-900); a small car in high season should cost about 60€ a day, with unlimited mileage. If you reserve in advance through Budget in the U.S. (© 800/527-0700), you should be able to beat that price.

Warning: If you park in town or in a no-parking area, the police will remove your license plates, and you, not the car-rental office, will have to pay a steep fine to get them back. There's free parking—often full—on the port's north side.

By Moped   The travel agents listed above can help you rent a moped. Many roads on the island are narrow and winding; add local drivers who take the roads at high speed, and visiting drivers who aren't sure where they're going, and you'll understand the island's high accident rate. If you're determined to use two-wheeled transportation, expect to pay about 25€ per day, less during off season. Greek law now requires wearing a helmet; not all agents supply the helmet.

Use caution when walking around Santorini, especially at night. Remember many drivers on the roads are newcomers to the island and may not know every twist and turn. Those who *do* know every twist and turn tend to take them at full throttle.

By Taxi   The taxi station is just south of the main square. In high season, book ahead by phone (✆ **22860/22-555** or 22860/23-951), if you want a taxi for an excursion; be sure that you agree on the price before you set out. For most point-to-point trips (Fira to Oia, for example), the prices are fixed. If you call for a taxi outside Fira, you'll be charged a pickup fee of at least 2€; you're also required to pay the driver's fare from Fira to your pickup point. Bus service shuts down at midnight, so book a taxi in advance if you'll need it late at night.

FAST FACTS   The **National Bank** (Mon–Fri 8am–2pm), with an ATM, is a block south of the main square, on the right, near the taxi station. The **health clinic** (✆ **22860/22-237**) is on the southeast edge of town, on Ayiou Athanassiou, immediately below the bus station and the new archaeological museum.

There are a number of **Internet** cafes on the main square, including **P.C. World** (✆ **22860/25-551**). The **police** (✆ **22860/22-649**) are several blocks south of the main square, near the post office. For the **port police,** call ✆ **22860/22-239.** The **post office,** open Monday through Friday from 8am to 1pm, is south of the bus station. The **telephone office (OTE)** is off Ipapantis, up from the post office; hours are Monday through Friday from 8am to 3pm.

The Top Attractions

The top attraction here is the island itself. It's far better to make haste slowly, linger on the black beach at Kamares, and stroll Thira in the early morning when the town belongs to its inhabitants, who are buying loaves sprinkled with sesame seeds at the bakery, and sweeping and washing the pavement outside all those jewelry stores. Most importantly, wherever you are, enjoy the view. There's nowhere else in the world, let alone in the Cyclades, with that caldera view. A great way to see the caldera is to take one of the **sunset cruises** offered by replica 18th-century sailing ships the *Thallasa* and the *Bella Aurora* (✆ **22860/24-024**). Some cruises include a light dinner. Most travel agents sell tickets from around 45€, or check out **www.santorini. com/sailing** and **www.santoriniyachting.com**.

Ancient Akrotiri ★★★   Akrotiri has been open only intermittently since the protective roof over the site collapsed in 2005. If even part of Akrotiri is open, go. If the entire site is closed when you want to visit, there's no point in coming here: Unlike many sites, Akrotiri is *not* visible from the road.

Since excavations began in 1967, this site has presented the world with a fascinating look at life in the Minoan period. Akrotiri—sometimes nicknamed the "Minoan Pompeii"—was frozen in time sometime between 1600 and 1500 B.C. by a cataclysmic eruption of the island's volcano. Many scholars think that this powerful explosion destroyed the Minoan civilization on Crete. Pots and tools still lie where their owners left them before abandoning the town; the absence of human remains indicates that the residents had ample warning of the town's destruction.

You enter the Akrotiri site along the ancient town's main street, on either side of which are the stores or warehouses of the ancient commercial city. *Pithoi* (large earthen jars) found here contained traces of olive oil, fish, and onion. In order to get the best sense of the scale and urban nature of this town, you should go to the triangular plaza, near the exit, where you'll see two-story buildings and a spacious gathering place. Imagine yourself 3,000 years ago, leaning over a balcony and spying on the passersby. As you walk along the path through town, look for the descriptive plaques in four languages. A few poor reproductions of the magnificent wall paintings are here; the best frescoes were taken to the National Archaeological Museum in Athens, although Santorini continues to agitate for their return. For now, you can see some originals in the **Museum of Prehistoric Thira** and a splendid re-creation in the **Thira Foundation.** As you leave the site, you may notice a cluster of flowers beside one of the ancient walls. This marks the burial spot of Akrotiri's excavator, Professor S. Marinatos, who died in a fall at Akrotiri. Allow at least an hour here.

Akrotiri. © **22860/81-366.** Admission 6€. Tues–Sun 8:30am–3pm.

Ancient Thira ★★ A high rocky headland (Mesa Vouna) separates two popular beaches (Kamari and Perissa), and at its top stand the ruins of ancient Thira. It's an incredible site, where cliffs drop precipitously to the sea on three sides and there are views of Santorini and neighboring islands. This group of ruins is not easy to take in because of the many different periods on view—Roman baths jostle for space beside the remains of Byzantine walls and Hellenistic shops. One main street runs the length of the site, passing first through two agoras. The arc of the theater embraces the town of Kamari, Fira beyond, and the open Aegean. Greeks lived here as early as the 9th century B.C., though most buildings are from much later and date from the Hellenistic era (4th c. B.C.). You may not decipher everything, but do take in the view from the large **Terrace of the Festivals.** This is where naked lads danced to honor Apollo (inadvertently titillating, some of the graffiti suggests, a number of the spectators).

You can reach the site by bus, car, or taxi or, if you wish, on foot, passing on the way a cave that holds the island's only spring (see "Walking," under "Outdoor Pursuits," below). Excursion buses for the site of Thira leave from Fira and from the beach at Kamari. Allow yourself at least 5 hours to view the site, if you walk up there and walk back down; if you come and go by transport, allow at least an hour at the site.

Kamari. © **22860/31-366.** Admission 4€. Tues–Sun 8am–2:30pm; site sometimes open later in summer. On a hilltop 3km (2 miles) south of Kamari by road.

Museum of Prehistoric Thira ★ Come here to see frescoes and other finds from ancient Akrotiri, along with objects from ancient Crete and the Northeastern Aegean Islands. Some of the pottery—cups, jugs, and *pithoi*—are delicately painted with motifs familiar to those of the wall paintings (see below). If possible, visit the museum and the archaeological site at ancient Akrotiri on the same day. Allow an hour here.

A Combination Ticket to the Ancient Sites

If you plan to visit the ancient sites and their associated museums, get the economical 10€ ticket good for the Archaeological Museum, ancient Akrotiri (if open), prehistoric Thira, and ancient Thira. Even if the price goes up (as it almost certainly will), and even if Akrotiri is closed (as it may be), this will be a good buy.

For information on a number of winery tours on Santorini, check out www. santonet.gr/wineries. **Boutari** (𝒞 **22860/ 81-011; www.boutari.gr**) is the island's largest winery, and Greece's best-known wine exporter. A variety of tours are offered at their winery in Megalochiri on the road to Akrotiri, from a simple tasting of three wines (6€) to the "Libation to Santorini," with four wines, serious appetizers, and a multimedia show. This is a pleasant way to spend an hour or so (but never on Sun, when the winery, like most on Santorini, is closed). If you want to sample other local wines, stop by the underground **Volcan Wine Museum** (𝒞 **22860/31-322; www.volcanwines.gr**), just outside Fira, on the mail road to Kamari. The museum, which occupies subterranean caves and tunnels, has an audio tour and reconstructions of the wine making process (6€). Volcan's once-a-week Greek Night, featuring dinner and belly dancers, is popular with large tour groups. Check the website of individual wineries for their varied hours.

Across the street from the bus stop in Fira; entrance is behind the Orthodox Cathedral. 𝒞 **22860/22-217**. Admission 5€. Tues–Sun 8:30am–3pm.

Thira Foundation: The Wall Paintings of Thira ★★ This exhibition created copies of the Akrotiri wall paintings, using a sophisticated technique of three-dimensional photographic reproduction that approximates the originals. The displays present some of the paintings in a re-creation of their original architectural context. The terrace in front offers an astonishing view toward Fira and Imerovigli. Allow an hour here. The center is also used for Thira's **Music Festival** each August and September.

Petros Nomikos Conference Center, Fira. 𝒞 **22860/23-016.** www.therafoundation.org. Admission 4€. Recorded tour 3€. On the caldera, 5 min. past the cable car, on the way to Firostephani.

Exploring the Island
FIRA

To put it (less than) mildly, Fira has a spectacular location on the edge of the caldera. Just when you think you've grown accustomed to the view down and out to sea and the offshore islands, you'll catch a glimpse of the caldera from a slightly different angle—and are awed yet again. If you're staying overnight on Santorini, take advantage of the fact that almost all the day-trippers from cruise ships leave in the late afternoon. Try to explore Santorini's capital, Fira, in the early evening, between the departure of the day-trippers and the onslaught of the evening revelers. As you stroll, you may be surprised to discover that, in addition to the Greek Orthodox cathedral, Fira has a Roman Catholic cathedral and convent, legacies from the days when the Venetians controlled much of the Aegean. The name "Santorini" is, in fact, a Latinate corruption of the Greek for St. Irene. **Megaron Gyzi Museum** (𝒞 **22860/22-244**), in a stately old house by the cathedral, has church and local memorabilia, an icon workshop, and before-and-after photographs of the island at the time of the devastating earthquake of 1956. It is open Monday to Saturday 10:30am to 1pm and 5 to 8pm, and Sunday 10:30am to 4:30pm. Admission is 4€.

Not surprisingly, Fira is Santorini's busiest and most commercial town. The abundance of **jewelry stores** is matched in the Cyclades only by Mykonos—as are the crowds in July and August. At the north end of Ipapantis (also known as "Gold Street," for all those jewelry stores), you'll find the **cable-car station.** The Austrian-built system, the gift of wealthy ship owner Evangelos Nomikos, can zip you down to the port of Skala in 2 minutes. The cable car makes the trip every 15 minutes from 7:30am to 9pm for 5€, and it's worth every euro, especially on the way up.

Up and to the right of the cable-car station is the small **Archaeological Museum** (© **22860/22-217**), which contains early Cycladic figurines, finds from ancient Thira, and erotic (or obscene, depending on the eye of the beholder) Dionysiac figures. It's open Tuesday through Sunday from 8:30am to 3pm. Admission is 4€. You can spend a day or more enjoying Fira, but don't count on getting much sleep: there's a wild all-night-every-night bar scene, with every bar seemingly competing for the award for attaining the highest decibel level with amplified music.

OIA ★

Oia gets most visitors' votes as the most beautiful village on the island. The village made an amazing comeback from the 1956 earthquake which left it a near-ghost town for decades. Several fine **19th-century mansions** survived and have been restored, including the elegant **Restaurant-Bar 1800** and the **Naval Museum** (see below). Much of the reconstruction continues the ancient Santorini tradition of excavating dwellings from the cliff's face, and the island's most beautiful cliff dwellings can be found here. The village has basically two streets: one with traffic, and the much more pleasant inland pedestrian lane, paved with marble and lined with an increasing number of jewelry shops, tavernas, and bars.

The **Naval Museum ★** (© **22860/71-156**) is a great introduction to this town where, until the advent of tourism, most young men found themselves working at sea and sending money home to their families. The museum, in a restored neoclassical mansion, was almost completely destroyed during the 1956 earthquake. Workers meticulously rebuilt the mansion using photographs of the original structure. The museum's collection includes ship models, figureheads, naval equipment, and fascinating old photographs. Its official hours are Wednesday through Monday from 12:30 to 4pm and 5 to 8:30pm, although this varies considerably. Admission is 3€.

The battlements of the ruined **kastro** (fortress), at the western end of town, are the best place to catch the famous Oia sunset. Keep in mind that many cruise ships disgorge busloads of passengers who come here just to catch the sunset; unless you are here on a rainy February day, you may prefer to find a more secluded spot (see "Imerovigli," later). Below the castle, a long flight of steps leads to the pebble beach at **Ammoudi,** which is okay for swimming and sunning, and has some excellent fish tavernas (see "Where to Eat," later in this chapter). To the west is the more spacious, sandy **Koloumbos Beach.** To the southeast, below Oia is the fishing port of **Armeni,** where ferries sometimes dock and you can catch an excursion boat around the caldera.

Santorini Below the Waterline

A different way to explore Santorini is the 1-hour **submarine tour** beneath the caldera's surface. It sinks 25 to 30m (82–98 ft.) below the surface and offers you a glimpse into the submerged volcanic crater. The trip costs 65€; information is available at most travel agents and at © **22860/28-900.**

OUT ON THE ISLAND: VARIOUS VILLAGES

It's easy to spend all your time in Fira and Oia, with excursions to the ancient sites and beaches, and to neglect other villages. Easy, but a shame, as there are some very charming villages on the island. As you travel, watch for the troglodytic **cave houses** hollowed into solidified volcanic ash. Another thing to look for: In many fields, you'll see what look like large brown circles of intertwined sticks neatly placed on the ground. What you're looking at is a vineyard. Santorinians twist the grape vines into wreaths that encircle the grapes and protect them from the island's fierce winds.

At the south end of the island, on the road to Perissa, is the handsome old village of **Emborio.** The town was fortified in the 17th century, and you can see its towers, a graceful marble statue of the muse Polyhymnia in the cemetery, and modern-day homes built into the ruins of the citadel.

Pirgos, a village on a steep hill just above the island's port at Athinios, is a maze of narrow pathways, steps, chapels, and squares. Until the mid–19th century, this hamlet hidden away behind the port was the island's capital. Near the summit of the village is the crumbling Venetian kastro, with sweeping views over the island. There is less tourism in Pirgos than in many island villages, and the central square, just off the main road, has just about all the shops and cafes. If you want a break, try the **Café Kastelli,** with tasty snacks, *glyka tou koutalou* (spoon sweets of preserved fruits), and fine views. If you want a sweet-and-sour treat, try the preserved *nerangi* (bitter orange).

In the hamlet of **Gonias Episkopi ★**, the Church of the Panagia is an astonishingly well-preserved 11th- to 12th-century Byzantine church. As is often the case, the builders pillaged classical buildings. You will see the many fragments they appropriated incorporated into the walls—and two ancient marble altars supporting columns. Among the frescoes, keep an eye out for the figure of a dancing Salome.

THE CALDERA ISLETS ★

These tantalizing **islands** in the caldera are part of the glory of Santorini's seascape, reminders of the larger island that existed before the volcano left today's crescent in the sea. Fortunately, you can visit the islands and get a view of Santorini from there.

Thirassia is a small, inhabited island west across the caldera from Santorini; a cliff-top village of the same name faces the caldera, and is a quiet(er) retreat from Santorini's summer crowds. You can reach the village from the caldera side only by a long flight of steep steps. Full-day **boat excursions** departing daily from the port of Fira (accessible by cable car, donkey, or on foot) make brief stops at Thirassia, just long enough for you to have a quick lunch in the village; the cost of the excursion—which includes Nea Kameni, Palea Kameni, and Ia—is about 50€ per person; check out **www.santoriniyachting.com** and **www.santoriniyacht.com** for some options. Another option is local **caiques,** which make the trip in summer from Armeni, the port of Oia; ask for information at your hotel or at one of the Fira travel agents (see "Visitor Information," earlier).

The two smoldering dark islands in the middle of the caldera are **Palea Kameni (Old Burnt),** the smaller and more distant one, which appeared in A.D. 157; and **Nea Kameni (New Burnt),** which began to appear sometime in the early 18th century. The day excursion to Thirassia (a far more enjoyable destination) often includes these two (unfortunately often litter-strewn) volcanic isles.

Outdoor Pursuits

BEACHES   Santorini's beaches may not be the best in the Cyclades, but the volcanic black and red sand here is unique in these isles—and gets very hot, very fast.

Kamari, a little over halfway down the east coast, has the largest beach on the island. It's also the most developed, lined by hotels, restaurants, shops, and clubs. In fact, Kamari is now so overrun with tour groups that I no longer recommend the string of hotels there. The natural setting is excellent, at the foot of cliffs rising precipitously toward ancient Thira, but the black-pebbled beach becomes unpleasantly crowded in July and August. **Volcano Diving Center** (© 22860/33-177; www.scubagreece. com) at Kamari, offers guided snorkel swims for around 25€ and scuba lessons from around 60€. Perissa, to the south, is another increasingly crowded beach resort, albeit one with beautiful black sand. The **Santorini Dive Center,** at Perissa, also has scuba and snorkel facilities and instruction (© 22860/83-190; www.divecenter.gr).

Red Beach (*Paralia Kokkini*), at the end of the road to ancient Akrotiri, gets its name from its small red volcanic pebbles; it is—but for how long?—usually less crowded than Kamari and Perissa. All three beaches have umbrellas and chairs to rent, cafes, and tavernas. If escaping the crowds is not on your beach agenda, head south to **Perivolos,** where the JoJo Beach Club was the place to be seen in 2011— although some people said that Sea Side gave JoJo a serious run for the money. Both beach bars teem with beautiful people (many topless) and a sprinkling of movie stars (sightings of Hugh Jackman reported in August).

BICYCLING Santorini's roads are in fairly good condition, it's the drivers you need to worry about. Local drivers know the roads with their eyes shut (and sometimes seem to drive that way), and visitors study maps as they drive. That said, you can rent high-quality suspension mountain bikes from 15€ per day from **Moto Chris** (© 22860/23-431), in Fira, and **Moto Piazza** (© 22860/71-055), in Oia. It's always a good idea to check the brakes and steering before you set off.

WALKING If it's not too hot, there are many walks you can enjoy. Here are a few:

○ **Fira to Oia ★★** The path from **Fira** to **Oia** (10km/6 miles) follows the edge of the caldera, passes several churches, and climbs two substantial hills along the way. Beginning at Fira, take the pedestrian path on the caldera rim, climbing past the Catholic Cathedral to the villages of Firostephani and Imerovigli. In Imerovigli, signs on the path point the way to Oia; you'll be okay so long as you continue north, eventually reaching a dirt path along the caldera rim that parallels the vehicular road. The trail leaves the vicinity of the road with each of the next two ascents, returning to the road in the valleys. The descent into Oia eventually leads to the main pedestrian street in town. Allow yourself at least 2 hours. If you end up at Oia around sunset, you'll feel that every minute of the walk was worth it.

○ **Imerovigli & Skaros ★★** In **Imerovigli,** a rocky promontory jutting into the sea is known as **Skaros.** From medieval times until the early 1800s, this small spot was home to the island's administrative offices. There is little to be seen of the Skaros castle now; it probably collapsed during a 19th-century earthquake. Skaros's view of the caldera is especially nice at sunset. Getting out on the promontory takes just enough effort that it is usually a tranquil haven from the crowds and bustle of the adjacent towns. The trail (signposted) descends steeply to the isthmus connecting Skaros with the mainland. The path wraps around the promontory, after a mile, reaching a small chapel with a panoramic view of the caldera. On the way, note the cliffs of glassy black volcanic rock, beautifully reflecting the brilliant sunlight. People used this rock to decorate many of the older buildings in Santorini.

○ **Kamari to Ancient Thira ★** The trail from Kamari to the site of **ancient Thira** is steep but doable. It passes the beautiful site of Santorini's only freshwater spring, which you will wish to drink dry. To reach the trail head from Kamari, take the road (in the direction of ancient Thira) past the Kamari beach parking, and turn right into the driveway of the hotel opposite Hotel Annetta, to the right of a minimarket. The trail begins behind the hotel. Climbing quickly by means of sharp switchbacks, the trail soon reaches a small chapel with a terrace and olive trees at the mouth of a cave. You can walk into the cave, which echoes with purling water, a surprising and miraculous sound in this arid place. Continuing upward, the trail rejoins the car road after a few more switchbacks, about 300m (984 ft.) from ancient Thira. The full ascent from Kamari takes a good hour.

Shopping

If you're interested in fine **jewelry,** keep in mind that many prices in Fira are higher than in Athens, but the selection is fantastic. Santorini's best-known jeweler, with lovely reproductions of ancient baubles, is **Kostas Antoniou** (✆ **22860/22-633**), on Ayiou Ioannou, north of the cable-car station. **Porphyra** (✆ **22860/22-981**), in the Fabrica Shopping Center, near the cathedral, also has impressive work. As signaled by its name, the **Bead Shop** (✆ **22860/25-176**), by the Archaeological Museum, sells beads. Most are carved from island lava. And there are plenty of shops between the two. Generally, the farther north you go, the higher the prices and the less certain the quality. In Firostephani, **Cava Sigalas Argiris** (✆ **22860/22-802**) stocks all the local **wines,** including their own. Also for sale are locally grown and **prepared foods,** often served as *mezedes: fava,* a spread made with chickpeas; *tomatahia,* small pickled tomatoes; and *kapari* (capers). The main street in Oia, facing the caldera, has many interesting stores, several with prints showing local scenes, in addition to the inevitable souvenir shops. **Replica** (✆ **22860/71-916**) is a source of contemporary statuary and pottery as well as museum replicas; it will ship purchases to your home at post office rates. Farther south on the main street is **Nakis** (✆ **22860/71-813**), which specializes in amber jewelry and, not surprisingly, has a collection of insects in amber.

Where to Stay

The summer of 2011 was not a good one for tourism in the Cyclades. Consequently, many hotels did not raise their prices. The minute that things improve, prices will go up, so be especially sure to double-check prices when you make your trip.

Santorini is stuffed to the gills with visitors in July and August; try to make a reservation with a deposit at least 2 months in advance; we consistently hear travelers' tales of miserable nights spent sitting up all night on those stiff wooden Greek cafe chairs. We also hear tales of hotels more than doubling the price on remaining rooms. Except in July and August, don't accept lodging offered at the port unless you're exhausted and don't care how meager the room is and how remote your lodging is from what you want to see when you wake up the next morning. Still, in July and August, be grateful for whatever you get if you show up without a reservation.

The island's **cave houses** have inspired many hotel designers. Barrel-vaulted ceilings and perhaps even a bathroom carved into the rock distinguish a typical **cave house.** Built for earthquake resistance and economy, some of the spaces may at first strike you as cramped; you'll soon see them as part of the island's special charm. The best of them are designed with high ceilings, airy rooms, and good cross-ventilation, because they are carved into the cliff face, they remain relatively cool throughout the summer.

Many apartments and villas have efficiency kitchens, but the facilities may be minimal. If you plan to do much cooking, check first to see what's in the drawers and cupboards, or you may find yourself frustrated if you try to prepare anything more elaborate than a cup of coffee.

For higher-end hotels, have a look at **www.santoriniluxuryhotels.com**; keep in mind that it is usual for hotels to pay a fee to be listed in these services.

FIRA

In addition to the choices below, we get good reports on the long-popular and usually quiet 25-room **Hotel Atlantis** (www.atlantishotel.gr; © **22860/22-232**), where guests can spend the sunset hours with a bottle of wine on the balcony overlooking the caldera. The tony eight-unit **Enigma Apartments** (www.enigmahotel.com) appeared in *Odyssey* magazine's "Best Hotels of 2009." Furnishings are elegantly simple; the views of the caldera and sunsets are spectacular. The Enigma is the sister hotel of another longtime entry in *Odyssey*'s best hotels list: **ASTRA Suites,** in Imerovigli. A perfect Santorini vacation would be divided between these two hotels: Enigma, in the island capital, and ASTRA, in one of Santorini's most perfect villages. For a (much) more modest place, consider **Loizos Apartments (www.loizos.gr)**; there's no caldera view, but it's a quiet Fira location and helpful owners.

Note: Due to the noise throughout Fira, you may want to consider staying in one of the villages out on the island, unless you stay in one of the quieter hotels we suggest.

Aigialos ★★   In a quiet caldera location, occupying 16 restored and expanded 18th- and 19th-century town houses, the Aigialos proclaims its intention to be a "Luxury Traditional Settlement." The oxymoron aside—few traditional settlements have had Jacuzzis, a swimming pool, and a counter-swim exercise pool—this is a nifty place. The units have all the modern conveniences and all the creature comforts. As the price goes up, you get more space (two bathrooms, not just one) and more privacy. Some units have their own garden and/or balcony, veranda, or terrace, while others share a garden, a veranda, or a terrace. (Aigialos presently calls its doubles "houses" and its suites "mansions" in much of its literature.) There's an extensive breakfast buffet and an in-house, guests-only highly-praised restaurant.

Fira, 84700 Santorini. www.aigialos.gr. © **22860/25-191.** 16 units. 16 units. 400€-600€ double; 800€-1200€ suites. Rates include breakfast. AE, DC, MC, V. Closed Nov-Mar. **Amenities:** Pool bar; 2 pools; room service. *In room:* A/C, TV, fridge, hair dryer, Wi-Fi.

Hotel Aressana ★★   This hotel (popular with Greek and foreign honeymooners) compensates for its lack of a caldera view with a large swimming pool and excellent location—tucked behind the Orthodox Cathedral in a relatively quiet setting. Most rooms have balconies or terraces; many have the high barrel-vaulted ceilings typical of this island. Unusual in Greece are the nonsmoking rooms. The breakfast room opens onto the pool terrace, as do most of the guest rooms; the elaborate buffet breakfast includes numerous Santorinian specialties. The Aressana also maintains seven nearby apartments facing the caldera, starting at 250€, which includes use of the hotel pool.

Fira, 84700 Santorini. www.aressana.gr. © **22860/23-900.** Fax 22860/23-902. 50 units,1 with shower only. 275€-350€ double; 350€-405€ suite. Rates include full breakfast. AE, DC, MC, V. Closed mid-Nov to Feb. Amenities: Snack bar; bar; freshwater pool; room service. In room: A/C, TV, hair dryer, minibar.

Hotel Keti ★★ ⚓   This simple little hotel offers one of the best bargains on the caldera. All of the (smallish) rooms have traditional vaulted ceilings, white walls, and coverlets, and open onto a shared terrace overlooking the caldera. The bathrooms, at the back of the rooms, are carved into the cliff face. Clearly, the Keti is doing something right: Not many places this modest make it into Alastair Sawday's *Special Places*. One drawback, if you have trouble walking: It's a steep 5- to 10-minute walk from the Keti's quiet cliffside location to Fira itself.

Fira, 84700 Santorini. www.hotelketi.gr. © **22860/22-324.** 7 units. 100€–150€ double. No credit cards. Closed Nov to mid-Mar. **Amenities:** Breakfast room; bar. *In room:* A/C, TV, fridge.

FIROSTEPHANI

This quieter and often less expensive neighborhood is just a 10-minute walk from Fira. The views of the caldera are just as good, if not better.

Tsitouras Collection ★   This is one of those places where if you have to ask what a room costs, you probably can't afford to stay there. This top-of-the-line luxury hotel will either dazzle or dismay you: Understatement is conspicuous by its absence, where antiques and reproductions jostle for space in five themed villas (including "House of Portraits" and "House of Porcelain"). The villa you stay in (decorated with art from the private collection of artist and mogul Demitris Tsitouras) is all yours, which ensures blissful privacy. Some spa services are available, and guests are encouraged to meet with the chef to discuss "constructing" a meal. A very expansive breakfast (and free copy of the *International Herald-Tribune*) is included in the room price. We've had almost as many criticisms for the indifferent service as we have had raves for the serious luxury and quiet location.

Firostefani, 84700 Santorini. www.tsitouras.gr. © **22860/23-747.** Fax 22860/23-918. 5 villas (for 4 or more). 500€–850€ 1-bedroom villa; 3,500€ 6-person villa. MC, V. **Amenities:** Restaurant; cafe. *In room:* A/C, TV/CD/DVD, hair dryer, kitchenette, wet bar, Wi-Fi.

IMEROVIGLI

The next village north along the caldera rim is named because it is the first place on the island from which you can see the rising sun. The name translates as "day vigil." By virtue of its height, Imerovigli also has the best views on this part of the caldera.

While everyone else is jostling for a place to see the sunset at Oia, head to Imerovigli and take the path over to the promontory of Skaros, with the picturesque remains of its medieval kastro. Amazingly, this deserted and isolated spot was the island's medieval capital. It's a blissful place to watch the sunset.

Imerovigli and Oia have a considerable number of attractive and comfortable places to stay. In addition to the places listed below, you might want to consider **La Maltese** (www.lamaltese.com; © **22860/24-701**), a member of Relais & Châteaux, in a restored sea captain's neoclassical mansion now fitted with indoor and outdoor pools, *hamam* and sauna, restaurant and piano bar, and of course, that caldera view.

ASTRA Suites ★★★   The 27-suite ASTRA is very special; although it looked perfect to me, ASTRA was completely renovated in 2010–11. Perched on a cliff, with spectacular views, this is one of the nicest places to stay in all of Greece. Other places nearby also have spectacular pools with spectacular views, but manager George Karayiannis is a large part of what makes ASTRA so special: He is always at the ready to arrange car rentals, recommend a wonderful beach or restaurant—or even help you plan your wedding and honeymoon here. The ASTRA Suites look like a tiny, whitewashed village (with elegant pools) set in the village of Imerovigli, which is still much less crowded than Fira or Oia. Nothing is flashy; everything is just right. The vibrant blue of the bed coverlets is echoed in the blue paint on the cupboards. Although each unit has its own kitchenette, breakfast can be served on your private terrace or balcony, and you can order salads and sandwiches from the bar day and night. There are spa services (massage, sauna, and Jacuzzi) and a Greek-Mediterranean full-service **restaurant** that emphasizes local cuisine. How about the Santorinian salad, with local cherry tomatoes, capers and caper leaves, fresh basil, onions and olives, chloro cheese, and barley croutons? After all that healthy and tasty virtue, it's on to Taliolina pasta with "fruits of the sea" marinara.

Imerovigli, 84700 Santorini. www.astrasuites.com. © **22860/23-641.** Fax 22860/24-765. 27 suites, 1 villa. 280€–800€ suite; from 1,500€ villa. MC, V. **Amenities:** Bar; restaurant; pool; spa services. *In room:* A/C, TV/CD/DVD, radio, hair dryer, kitchenette, Wi-Fi.

Chromata ★★ Along with Katikies (see below) this is one of a small group of luxury hotels (**www.katikies.com**) on Santorini. Here you'll get a wonderful view out over the island, an inviting pool, and excellent service. The rooms sport comfortable, stylish chairs and hand-loomed rugs. If it weren't that George Karayiannis makes its neighbor, ASTRA, so special, Chromata would be the place to stay. If ASTRA is full, you'll still be happy here. Some of the suites have small, private plunge pools.

Imerovigli, 84700 Santorini. www.chromata-santorini.com. © **22860/24-850.** 17 units. 200€–300€ double; 500€–800€ suite. AE, MC, V. **Amenities:** Bar; restaurant; Internet; pool. *In room:* A/C, TV, hair dryer, minibar.

KARTERADOS

About 2km (1 mile) southeast of Fira, this small village knows the tourist ropes, and has many new hotels and rooms to let. Buses stop at the top of Karterados's main street on their ways to Kamari, Perissa, and Akrotiri. Nevertheless, the location is somewhat inconvenient, not especially close to Fira or to the beach. Karterados beach is a 3km (2-mile) walk from the center of town. Get to Monolithos, a longer beach, by continuing south along the water's edge an additional 1km (½ mile).

Pension George ★ 🏊 With a small pool, simple wood furnishings, attractive and reasonably priced rooms, and helpful owners, the pension offers good value if you're on a budget. To save even more money, opt for a room without a balcony. If you want more space, ask about their five new apartments at Karterados beach. George Halaris and his English wife, Helen, will help you arrange car and boat rentals.

P.O. Box 324, Karterados, 84700 Santorini. www.pensiongeorge.com. © **22860/22-351.** 25 units. 60€–90€ double. No credit cards. **Amenities:** Breakfast on request; free transportation to airport or harbor. *In room:* A/C, TV (in some), fridge.

OIA

Oia's chic shops (check out **the Art Gallery** and **Art Gallery Oia** on Oia's meandering main drag), boutique hotels, and gorgeous sunsets make it an increasingly popular place to stay or to visit—especially for travelers who find Fira too frenetic.

If you're running low on reading material by the time you get to Santorini, head to **Atlantis Books** (© **22860/72-346;** www.atlantisbooks.org) in Oia, run by a group of expat Brits and Americans as well as several Greeks. You'll find everything from guidebooks and detective novels for the beach to poetry and philosophy.

Chelidonia ★ Chelidonia (the Greek name for the swallows that you'll see here) is a carefully restored and reconstructed slice of Oia that was destroyed in the 1956 earthquake. Most units are former homes, each with its unique layout—another unit was a bakery, yet another a stable. Rooms are large, the bathrooms luxuriously large, and the interiors simple, but elegant. Skylights illuminate many rooms from above. Most have truly private terraces, many with small gardens of flowering plants and herbs. All units enjoy the famous Oia view across the caldera toward Imerovigli, Fira, and the southern end of the island. If you want room service, this is not the place for you, but there is daily maid service, and the owner clearly understands what makes guests feel at home. There's usually a 3-night minimum for stays.

Ia, 84702 Santorini. www.chelidonia.com. ✆ **22860/71-287.** Fax 22860/71-649. 10 units. 185€ studio; 260 suite; 290€ villa. No credit cards. *In room:* A/C, TV, kitchenette.

Hotel Finikia ✦   This appealing hotel has a number of rooms with the domed ceilings traditional to Santorini architecture. Some rooms boast local weavings and artifacts. Most units have semiprivate balconies or terraces with views toward the sea—the hotel is on the east slope of the island, so the view is gentle rather than spectacular. The pool is good-size and the **restaurant/bar** is open almost all day. Irene and Theodoris Andreadis are helpful and friendly hosts. They have adjacent apartments for rent as well.

Finikia, 84702 Santorini. finikia@otenet.gr. ✆ **22860/71-373** or 210/654-7944 in winter. Fax 22860/71-118. 15 units. From 100€ double. Rates include breakfast. MC, V. Closed Nov–Mar. **Amenities:** Restaurant; bar; pool; Wi-Fi. *In room:* A/C, minibar.

Katikies ★★   Along with Chromata (see above), this is one of a small group of luxury hotels in Oia. The main pool—one of four—runs almost to the side of the caldera. You'll enjoy a world-class view. Katikies began as a small hotel, then added suites (some with their own plunge pools), and now has a seven-unit villa (with its own pool). The hotel's island-style architecture incorporates twists and turns, secluded patios, beamed ceilings, and antiques. If the people in the next room like to sing in the shower, you might hear them, but most people who stay here treasure the tranquility. The top-of-the-line honeymoon suite has its own Jacuzzi, in case you can't be bothered going to either outdoor pool. The new **White Cave** restaurant has only a handful of tables, so be sure to book ahead. Or head to one of Katikies' three other restaurants. A masseur is on call at the small spa on-site.

Oia, 84702 Santorini. www.katikies.com. ✆ **22860/71-401.** Fax 22860/71-129. 22 units. 540€ double; 610€–1,650€ suite. Rates include breakfast. MC, V. **Amenities:** 4 restaurants; bar; concierge; currency exchange; health club and spa; library; 4 pools. *In room:* A/C, TV, hair dryer, minibar, Wi-Fi.

Perivolas Traditional Settlement ★★   You could be forgiven for thinking that this is a pool with a nice hotel (with seriously splashy bathrooms) attached: The *Condé Nast Traveler* cover photo of Perivolas's pool meeting the edge of the sky and the lip of the caldera put this place on the jet-setters' map. The 17 houses that make up the hotel offer studios, as well as junior and superior suites. Price differences reflect the sizes; each unit has a kitchenette and a terrace. The superior suites have a separate bedroom; the other units are open plan. The architecture—wall niches, skylights, stonework—and some of the furnishings of these greatly enhanced cave dwellings are traditional. Everything is elegant—including the in-house library. The only downside: Few units have terraces with significant degrees of privacy, but that is true of almost every Santorini hotel—and certainly true of genuine traditional village settlements!

Ia, 84702 Santorini. www.perivolas.gr. ✆ **22860/71-308.** Fax 22860/71-309. 19 units. 520€ studio; 620€–950€ suite; 1,500€–2,000€ villa. Rates include buffet breakfast. No credit cards. Closed mid-Oct to mid-Apr. **Amenities:** Cafe; bar; pool. *In room:* A/C, TV, hair dryer, kitchen.

MEGALOHORI

Villa Vedema Hotel ★★   The sleepy village of Megalohori is not where you'd expect to find a luxury hotel, but Santorini is full of surprises. The hotel is a self-contained world, surrounded by a wall like a fortified town. A member of the Small

Luxury Hotels of the World group, the Vedema is justly proud of its attentive but unobtrusive service. The residences are set around several irregular courtyards, much like those found in a village. Each apartment is comfortable, with sink-into-them chairs and at least one huge marble bathroom. The restaurant is excellent, and the candlelit wine bar is located in a 300-year-old wine cellar. The principal disadvantage of a stay here is the location: Megalohori is not a particularly convenient base for exploring the island. But with this amount of luxury, you may not want to budge.

Megalohori, 84700 Santorini. www.vedema.gr. © **22860/81-796** or 22860/81-797. 45 units. 500€-750€ double/suite; 1,000€-3,600€ villa. Minimum 3-night stay. AE, DC, MC, V. Closed mid-Oct to mid-Apr. **Amenities:** Restaurant; bar; concierge; pool; room service. *In room:* A/C, TV/CD/DVD, hair dryer, minibar, Wi-Fi.

PYRGOS

Zannos Melathron ★★ The relatively uncrowded village of Pyrgos sits inland between Megalohori and Kamari. This 12-room boutique hotel, on one of the highest points on the island, occupies two adjacent former private mansions, one dating from the 18th century and one built in the early 19th century. Both are handsomely restored. The rooms mix antiques with modern pieces, the island views are lovely, the pool is welcoming, and some rooms have Jacuzzis. If you want nightlife, this is not the place; if you want a peaceful retreat and near-perfect service in—not outside—a village, this may be the spot. If you want a cigar bar, look no further. Something to consider: In 2011, most rooms here were available only for stays of three or more nights. The island's best restaurant, **Selene** (p. 356), moved to Pyrgos in 2011.

Pyrgos, 84700 Santorini. www.zannos.gr. © **22860/28-220.** 12 units. 250€-550€ double; 550€-1,000€ suite. MC, V required to make reservation; payment is cash only. **Amenities:** Restaurant; bar; airport pickup; concierge; Jacuzzi; pool; room service. *In room:* A/C, TV, hair dryer, minibar, Wi-Fi.

Where to Eat

FIRA

Restaurants in Fira range from blah to beatific; the island's best restaurant, Selene moved to Pyrgos in 2010. Some restaurants here let quality and service slide, because they know that most tourists are here today and gone tomorrow. The good places cater to the discriminating Greek and foreign visitors who come back again and again.

If all you want is breakfast or a fast cheap meal, try **Corner Crepes,** just off the main square (no phone). The popular taverna **Camille Stefani** (© **22860/28-938**), long in Kamari, is now in Fira, at the Fabrica shopping center. With a caldera view, **Lithos** (© **22860/23-203;** www.lithossantorini.com), turns out good *spitiko* (home-style) cooking at moderate prices.

Note: Many of the restaurants on the caldera and near the cable car fall into the forgettable category. In addition, some of them have been known to present menus without prices, and then charge exorbitantly for food and wine. If you are given a menu, make sure prices are listed.

Koukoumavlos ★★ GREEK The terrace at Koukoumavlos enjoys a caldera view, but unlike most caldera restaurants where the view compensates for mediocre food, here the view is a distraction from the inventive, even idiosyncratic, menu. Two examples: the grilled foie gras with raisin paste and ouzo jelly and the lobster and monkfish terrine with anchovy-caviar sour cream in a forest-fruit tea (tea blended with pieces of fruit) sauce. In short, you are likely to be either titillated or terrified by the combination of ingredients in most dishes. You'll definitely remember the food—

and probably find the prices equally memorable (salads start at around 20€). Despite the lofty character of the cuisine, the staff is usually both helpful and attentive.

Below the Hotel Atlantis, facing the caldera. ℂ **22860/23-807.** www.koukoumavlos.eu. Reservations recommended for dinner. Main courses 25€ and up and up. AE, MC, V. Daily noon–3pm and 7:30pm–midnight.

Taverna Nikolas ★ 🍴 GREEK   This is another one of the few restaurants in Fira where locals and tourists both turn up regularly—high praise, for a place that has been here forever. There aren't any surprises; you'll get traditional Greek dishes prepared very well. The lamb with greens in egg-lemon sauce is particularly tasty. The dining room is always busy, so arrive early or plan to wait.

Just up from the main square in Fira. No phone. Main courses 12€–15€. No credit cards. Daily noon–midnight.

OIA

If you want to be by the sea, head down to **Ammoudi,** Oia's port, hundreds of feet below the village, huddled between the cliffs and the sea. We recommend **Katina's** fish taverna there (see below). If you don't want to trek all the way down to the beach, stop along the way at **Kastro** (ℂ 22860/71-045), where you'll still have a fine view and can enjoy Greek dishes, pasta, or fresh fish. To get there, follow the stepped path down from the vicinity of Lontza Castle, rent a donkey (5€), or call a taxi. We recommend the walk down (to build an appetite) and a taxi or donkey up.

Katina's ★★ SEAFOOD   Fresh fish, grilled by the sea—what more could one ask for? Well, for one thing, a taxi back up the hill when it's time to leave. Just ask your waiter and a taxi will appear.

Ammoudi. ℂ **22860/71-280.** Fish priced by the kilo. No credit cards. Daily 10am–midnight (usually).

Restaurant-Bar 1800 ★★ MEDITERRANEAN   For many years recognized as the best place in Oia for a formal dinner, the 1800 has a devoted following among visitors and locals. Many items are Greek dishes with a difference, such as the tender lamb chops with green applesauce and the cheese pie, filled not just with feta, but with five cheeses. The restaurant, housed in a splendidly restored 19th century neoclassical captain's mansion, has romantic charm whether you eat indoors or on the amazing rooftop terrace. After you eat, you can decide whether the owner (an architect and chef) deserves more praise for his skill with the decor or with the cuisine. "Each plate resembles a canvas," this restaurant proclaims.

Odos Nikolaos Nomikos. ℂ **22860/71-485.** www.oia-1800.com. Main courses 18€–35€. AE, DC, MC, V. Daily 8pm–midnight.

Skala ★ 🍴 GREEK   Skala has fine taverna food, at prices that are less steep than at many other places here. All the staples of traditional Greek (if not local Santorini) food are good; the management is helpful and friendly. Veggies are not overcooked, and the grills and stews are tasty. If you've never tried rabbit stew (*stifado kouneli*), but are curious, this is a good place to see whether you agree that rabbit tastes a lot like, well, chicken.

Odos Nikolaos Nomikos. ℂ **22860/71-362.** Main courses 9€–20€. MC. Daily 1pm–midnight.

PYRGOS

Selene ★★★ 📷 GREEK   If you eat only one meal on Santorini, eat it here. This is the best restaurant on Santorini—and one of the best in Greece. Selene was in Fira from 1986 to 1910, when it moved to Pyrgos to continue to delight guests with what owner George Haziyannakis calls the "creative nature of Greek cuisine." The appetizers, often including a sea urchin salad on artichokes and fluffy fava balls with caper sauce, are famous. Entrees include *brodero* (seafood stew). The baked mackerel with caper leaves and tomato wrapped in a crepe of fava beans will convert even the most dedicated flesh eaters. The local lamb, quail, rabbit, and beef are all excellent. In short, everything—beautiful surroundings, perfect ambience and service—comes together to form the best imaginable setting for the delicious, inventive—but never coy—food. And, if you want something a little more casual, and less expensive, you can have an equally great meal at Selene's **bistro-cafe-patisserie-wine bar.** If you want to see how some of Selene's selections are made, check out the cooking classes at **www.selene.gr**, or come on a Tuesday, Thursday, or Saturday for the "Selene Experience" to learn about local cuisine and have a delicious 60€ fixed-price dinner.

Pyrgos. ℂ **22860/22-249.** Fax 22860/24-395. www.selene.gr. Reservations recommended. Main courses at restaurant 17€–30€. Snacks/drinks at the bistro from 6€; main courses from 12€. MC, V. Restaurant open daily 7–11:30pm, early Apr to Oct 30; bistro open daily noon–11pm, early Mar to Oct 30.

Santorini After Dark

The height of the tourist season is also the height of the music season in Santorini. If you are here in July, you may want to take in the annual **Santorini Jazz Festival** (**www.jazzfestival.gr**), which has been bringing international jazz bands and artists here since 1997. Many performances are on Kamari beach. In August and September, there's the 2-week **Santorini International Music Festival** (ℂ **22860/23-166**), with international singers and musicians, and performances of classical music at the Nomikos Centre, in Fira. Admission to most events starts at 15€.

Fira has all-night nightlife; as always on the islands, places that are hot one season are gone the next. I'm not listing phone numbers here because phones simply are not answered. If you want to kick off your evening with a drink on the caldera as you watch the spectacular sunset, **Franco's** and **Tropical** (both on Marinatou St.) are still the most famous spots for this magic hour; be prepared to pay 15€ and up (and up) for a drink. **Kira Thira** and **Koo** (two of the wall-to-wall places on Stavrou St.) pack people in later in the day (and through the night). If you are willing to forego the caldera view, you'll find almost too many spots to sample along the main drag and around the main square, including the inevitable Irish pub, **Murphy's. Kirathira Bar** plays jazz at a level that permits conversation, and the nearby **Art Café** offers muted music. And don't forget that the island's best restaurant, **Selene,** now in Pyrgos, has its own cafe bar for a quiet drink and snack.

Discos come and go, and you need only follow your ears to find them. **Koo** (see above), with at least five different bars, is the biggest; **Tithora** is popular with a young, heavy-drinking crowd. There's usually no cover, but the cheapest drinks at most places are at least 10€.

Out on the island, in Oia, **Zorba's** is a popular cliffside pub. The fine **Restaurant-Bar 1800** (see above) is a quiet, sophisticated place to stop in for a drink and a meal. Kamari Beach has lots of disco bars, including **Disco Dom, Mango's, Yellow Donkey,** and **Valentino's,** popular with the youngish tour groupers who grope about here.

FOLEGANDROS ★★

181km (98 nautical miles) SE of Piraeus

Tell people that you're off to Folegandros and you're likely to get one of two reactions: quizzical expressions from those who have not been here and envious glances from those who know the island. Folegandros has one of the most perfect capitals in the islands: More village than town, **Hora** huddles at the edge of cliffs some 250m (820 ft.) above the sea. As with so many Cycladic towns, this one was built far inland, to make it almost invisible to pirates. The town has a series of interlocked *plateias* (squares), whose streets are made of green and blue paving slates outlined in brilliant white. As you prowl the streets, you'll gradually realize that much of Hora is built into the walls of the kastro, a medieval castle. Small houses with steep front staircases and overhanging wooden balconies weighed with pots of geraniums line the narrow lanes.

Where's the Bank?

There's no bank here, and the ATM in Hora is not always reliable, so you may want to bring some extra cash. Most hotels and the travel agencies will change money for you (see "Fast Facts," below).

As for the main port, **Karavostasi:** If you didn't know about Hora and the island's beguiling interior landscape, you could be forgiven for continuing to the next port of call and not getting off. Karavostasi means "ferry stop," and the name sums up all there is to say about this desultory little port; although, in recent years, a sprinkling of cafes and jewelry shops have sprung up. Still, Karovostasi has little of architectural interest and few of the charms of most Cycladis ports.

If you want to explore Folegandros, you can do a good deal by local bus, but if you like to walk, this is a great place for it. Even if you rent a car, you'll have to leave it from time to time—no cars are allowed in Hora and several other villages. The island's paved roads are still fairly minimal and there is still an elaborate network of foot and donkey paths over beautiful terraced hillsides. Look closely and you'll see that some of these paths are paved with ancient marble blocks; others are hacked from the natural bedrock. Hills are crisscrossed with the stone walls that enclose the terraced fields that allow local farmers to grow barley on the island's steep slopes. Rocky coves shelter some appealing pebble beaches (best reached by caique). Try to allow at least a day and a night on Folegandros—and don't be surprised if you decide to stay a lot longer!

Essentials

GETTING THERE   By Boat   Check out **www.gtp.gr** and **www.openseas.gr** for ferry schedules. Three ferries a week stop at Folegandros on the Santorini-Folegandros-Sikinos-Ios-Naxos-Paros-Piraeus route; it's about 10 hours from Piraeus to Folegandros. Information is available at the **Piraeus Port Authority** (© **210/451-1311** or 210/451-1440 or -1441), which seldom answers the phone. Boats are notoriously late and/or early; your travel or ticket agent will give you an *estimate* of times involved in the following journeys. Several ferries per week stop on the Folegandros-Milos-Sifnos-Paros-Mykonos-Tinos-Siros hydrofoil run. During the off-season, infrequent service and bad weather can easily keep you here longer than you intend. **Folegandros Port Police** are at © **22860/41-530.**

VISITOR INFORMATION   Maraki Travel Agency (© **22860/41-273;** maraki@syr.forthnet.gr) and **Sottovento Travel** (© **22860/41-444;** www.sottovento.eu) exchange money, help with travel arrangements, sell maps of the island, and offer Internet facilities. Sottovento also serves as the local Italian consulate and its owner Flavio Facciolo runs the tasty Café del Viaggiatori in Hora, with Italian-style snacks and great espresso.

GETTING AROUND **By Bus** The bus (☎ **22860/41-425**) to Hora meets all ferries in peak season and most ferries during the rest of the year; it also makes eight or nine trips a day on the road running along the island's spine between Hora and Ano Meria at the island's northern end. The fare is 2€.

By Moped **Jimmy's Motorcycle** (☎ **22860/41-448**), in Karavostassi, and **Moto Rent** (☎ **22860/41-316**), in Hora, near Sottovento Travel, both rent mopeds. As always, check the brakes before you head off.

By Boat Mid-June through August, boat taxis or caiques provide transport to the island's southern beaches. From Karavostassi, boats depart for Katergo and Angali (10€ round-trip); another boat departs from Angali for Ayios Nikolaos, Livadaki, and Ambeli (10€ round-trip). There is a 7-hour tour of the island's beaches that departs from Karavostassi three times weekly in summer, and makes stops at five beaches; the cost is 30€ per person, including lunch. Reservations can be made at Diaplous or Sottovento Travel (see above); tickets must be purchased a day in advance.

By Taxi If you don't find a taxi at the port or in Hora, dial ☎ **22890/22-400** or 22860/41-048.

FAST FACTS Folegandros has neither bank nor ATM, but you can exchange money at travel agents and hotels. Commissions on money exchange can be steep, because you are something of a captive audience here. It may be wise to arrive with enough cash for your visit. The **post office** and **telephone office (OTE)** are right off the central square in Hora, open Monday through Friday from 8am to 3pm. The **police station** (☎ **22860/41-222**) is behind the post office and OTE.

What to See & Do

Unless you are determined to be by the sea, you won't want to linger in **Karavostassi,** perhaps the least enticing port in the Cyclades. Hop a bus and chug the 4km (2½ miles) up to Hora. If you do want to stay by the sea, the **Acolos Beach Hotel** (☎ **22860/41-205**), just outside Karavostassi, is across the road from the beach and has simple but perfectly okay studios (minifridge) from 85€ to 120€ in high season.

Cliffside **Hora ★★** is centered on five squares, closely connected by meandering streets lined with houses, restaurants, and shops. Even from the bus-stop square, the sheer drop of the cliff is an awesome sight. On the right in the next square, you'll find **the Kastro:** two narrow pedestrian streets connected by tunnel-like walkways, squeezed between the town and the sea cliffs, within the remaining walls of the Hora's medieval castle. One majestic church, **Kimisis Theotokou,** dominates the skyline of Hora. It's particularly beautiful at night, when it's illuminated. Built at the highest point in town—and with fine views over the island—the church stands on the foundations of the ancient Greek town. If you walk up here even once, your admiration for the ancient Folegandrians who lived here and did the walk up and down to their fields daily will soar! Today, townspeople parade through the village with the church's icon of the Virgin, with great ceremony, each Easter Sunday. The other church to see here is the deserted **Monastery of the Panagia,** north of town, also with lovely views.

OUT ON THE ISLAND

As you rush from island to island, checking in and out of hotels, it's not always easy to feel the rhythm of island life. One great way to do that is to visit Folegandros's small **Folk Museum,** in Ano Meria. If you want to see some countryside, head west from

Hora to the village of **Ano Meria.** This hamlet of scattered farms is the island's second-largest village. Some of the tools and household items in the museum have been used for generations, and you can see some still in use today. The museum (no phone; free admission, but donation appreciated) is open 5 to 8pm weeknights in July and August, and the bus can drop you a pleasant stroll away. If the museum turns out to be closed, console yourself that this, too, is an insight into the rhythms of island life!

BEACHES

You can swim at Karavostasi, or get a caique (10€ round-trip) to the island's best beach, **Katergo ★,** which is protected from the sometimes-fierce winds here by rocky headlands. You can also get by caique to **Angali,** the largest and most crowded fine-sand beach on the island. There are a few tavernas on the beach and rooms to let.

WALKING

The footpaths through the northern part of the island, for the most part, are well used and easy to follow. Numerous paths branch off to the southwest from the paved road through Ano Meria; the hills traversed by these trails, between the road and the sea, are particularly beautiful. Here's one walk you may enjoy; if you want to try more walks, check with someone at the Sottovento Travel agency for tips. There may even be a walker's map by the time you visit.

Ayios Andreas to Ayios Yeoryios   An easy path leads you from **Ayios Andreas** to the bay at **Ayios Yeoryios.** Take the bus to the next-to-last stop, at the northern end of Ano Meria; it will let you off by the church of Ayios Andreas. At the stop, the sign AG. GEORGIOS 1.5 points to the right. Follow the sign, and continue along a road that quickly becomes a path and descends steeply toward the bay. Follow the main path at each of several intersections; you'll be able to see the bay for the last 20 minutes of the walk. You'll find a small pebble beach at the bay of Ayios Yeoryios, but no fresh water, so be sure to bring plenty. Allow 2 hours for the round-trip.

Where to Stay

For some time there have been two special places to stay here: **Anemomilos Apartments** and the **Castro Hotel.** The Castro was closed for renovations during the 2011 season, but promises to be back in 2012. Since 2006, the 32-room **Chora Resort** (www.choraresort.com; ✆ **22860/415-90**), with spa facilities, a 500-sq.-m. (5,382-sq.-ft.) pool, and its own restaurant, has offered sybaritic pleasures and attractive package deals. If you want simpler accommodations, the 11-room **Meltemi Hotel** (www.greekhotel.com; ✆ **22860/41-425**), across from Anemomilos, is a good buy, with decent rooms, but no view or pool. The island's limited facilities are always fully booked in July and August, when advance reservations are essential; other times, reservations are recommended here.

Anemomilos Apartments ★★   This congenial place began to turn up on lists of the "best island retreats" soon after it opened in 1998—and made *Odyssey* magazine's best-of-the-year list again in 2007. Spectacularly situated at the edge of a cliff overlooking the sea, all but two of the units here have terraces; all units have either a full or partial sea view. A well-stocked kitchenette means you can actually cook here. If you don't want to make your own breakfast, Cornelia Patelis, who manages the hotel with her husband, Dimitris, makes a delicious sweet breakfast pie with local cheese. The hotel also serves breakfast and snacks throughout the day on the pool terrace. One apartment is accessible for travelers with disabilities. Transport to and from the port, arranged by the hotel, costs about 5€ per person one-way.

Hora, 84011 Folegandros. www.anemomilosapartments.com. ✆ **22860/41-309.** 22 units. 160€–240€ double. Breakfast 15€. V. Closed mid-Oct to Easter. Near the central bus stop. **Amenities:** Breakfast room/bar; pool. *In room:* A/C, TV, hair dryer, kitchenette, Wi-Fi.

Castro Hotel ★   The Castro was closed for renovations at press time, so I can't speak to what precisely you will find when this charming small hotel reopens in 2012. It will still have its wonderful location, in a Venetian castle dating from 1212; it's the oldest part of Hora, wedged against the cliffs and facing the Aegean 250m (820 ft.) below. I assume that the guest rooms will still be small, but even more comfortable than before. Seven rooms have phenomenal views. Even if you do not get a room with a balcony and view, you can enjoy the view from the shared rooftop terrace. The charming Mrs. Danassi, whose family has owned this house for five generations, will make you feel at home. And her homemade fig jam gets high praise.

Hora, 84011 Folegandros. www.hotel-castro.com. ✆ **22860/41-230** or 210/778-1658 in Athens. Fax 22860/41-230 or 210/778-1658 in Athens. 12 units. Prices for 2012 not available at press time. AE, V. Closed Nov–Apr.

Where to Eat

Main courses for all the restaurants listed run about 8€ to 20€; hours are generally from 9am to 3pm and 6pm to midnight.

The local specialty, *matsata*, is made with fresh pasta and rabbit or chicken. The best place to sample it is **Mimi's**, in Ano Meria (✆ **22860/41-377**), where the pasta is made on the premises. Look for two other restaurants in Ano Meria: **Sinandisi** (✆ **22860/41-208**), also known as Maria's, which has good *matsata* and swordfish (take the bus to the Ayios Andreas stop); and **Barbakosta** (✆ **22860/41-436**), a tiny room that serves triple duty as bar, taverna, and minimarket (the bus stop has no name, so ask the driver to alert you).

Hora has a number of tavernas, whose tables spill onto and partially fill the central squares. At the bus-stop square, **Pounda** (✆ **22860/41-063**) serves a delicious breakfast of crepes, omelets, yogurt, or coffee cake; lunch and dinner, including vegetarian dishes, are also available. **Silk** (✆ **22860/41-515**), on the *piatsa* (third) square, offers delicious variations on taverna fare, including numerous vegetarian options. **Piatsa** (✆ **22860/41-274**), also on the third square, is a simple taverna with tasty food. **O Kritikos** (✆ **22860/41-219**) is another local favorite, known for its grilled chicken. After dinner, if you want some nightlife, you'll find some bars and discos sprouting on the outskirts of the Kastro; **Greco Café Bar, Kolpo, Aquarius,** and **Ba-Raki** were popular in recent years.

SIFNOS ★★

172km (93 nautical miles) SE of Piraeus

Just about everyone thinks that Sifnos is the most beautiful of the western Cyclades. This island has long been a favorite of Greeks, especially Athenians; but now, in summer, it is an all-too-popular destination for European tourists. It's hectic in August, with rooms hard to find, cars impossible to rent, and the village buses sardine-can full.

The mountains that frame Sifnos's deep harbor, Kamares, are barren, but once you've left the port, you will see elegantly ornamented dovecotes above cool green hollows, old (no one really knows just how old) fortified monasteries, and watchtowers that stand astride the summits of arid hills. The beautiful slate and marble paths across the island are miracles of care, although an increasing number are now covered over with concrete and asphalt to accommodate motorcycles and cars. Nonetheless, Sifnos is a hiker's—even a stroller's—delight and astonishingly green, not only in spring but well into the summer. In addition, beaches along the southern coast offer long stretches of fine amber sand; several smaller rocky coves are also excellent for swimming.

Sifnos is small enough that any town can be used as a base for touring; the most beautiful are the **seven settlements** spread across the central hills—notably Apollonia (sometimes called Stavri) and Artemonas—and Kastro, a medieval fortified town atop a rocky pinnacle on the eastern shore. Buses now run from Cheronissos in the north to Vathi in the south, and the bus, combined with some walking, will take you to the island's top attractions: the acropolis at **Ayios Andreas,** the town of **Kastro** and its tiny but excellent **archaeological museum,** the southern **beaches,** the once-isolated beaches at **Vathi** and **Cheronisso,** and, for the ambitious, the walled **Monastery of Profitis Elias** on the summit of the island's highest mountain. Brown and gold signs in Greek and English now mark most places of archaeological and historical interest.

In Greece, Sifnos has long been famous for its ceramics, although fewer and fewer locals work as potters and fewer still use local clay. Some of the island's best potters are in Kamares and Platis Yialos. Sifnos is also famous for its olive oil and sophisticated cooking; in fact, "Tselementes," a slang term for a cookbook, is a tribute to the famous 20th-century Sifnian chef and cookbook writer, Nikos Tselementes.

Tip: If you find yourself waiting (and waiting) for your boat in Kamares, the **Emba K'Evas** (Come and Go) **Café** has tables and chairs by the water, good coffee, and ouzo and simple *mezedes* for a very reasonable 2€.

Essentials

GETTING THERE   By Boat   Weather permitting, there are at least four boats daily from Piraeus, including car ferries and HighSpeeds and SeaJets, some of which take cars. Check ferry schedules with a travel agency, or with the **Piraeus Port Authority** (© **210/451-1311,** -1440, or -1441; phone not always answered) or **Sifnos Port Authority** (© **22840/33-617**). Ferries travel on ever-changing schedules to other islands, including **Serifos, Kimolos Milos, Tinos, Paros,** and **Kithnos.** Boats are notoriously late and/or early; your travel or ticket agent will give you an estimate of times involved in above journeys. **www.openseas.gr** is a useful resource for boat schedules. If you have time to kill waiting for your boat, have a seat by the Poseidon Café, where an ouzo and *mezedes* were a reasonable 2€ in 2011.

VISITOR INFORMATION   The best place on the island for information and help getting a hotel room, boat tickets, car, or motorbike (and arranging hiking excursions) is **Aegean Thesaurus Travel and Tourism ★★**, with offices on the port (© **22840/ 32-152;** www.thesaurus.gr) and on the main square in Apollonia (© **22840/33-152**). Aegean Thesaurus handles tickets for all hydrofoils and ferries. Check at either office to get the helpful information packet on Sifnos for 2€. Just off the main square in Apollonia, **Xidis Travel** (© **22840/32-373;** www.xidis.com.gr) is another good travel agent.

GETTING AROUND   By Bus   Apollonia's central square, **Plateia Iroon** (which locals simply call the **Plateia** or **Stavri**), is the main bus stop for the island. Buses run regularly to and from the port at Kamares, north to Artemonas and Cheronisso, east to Kastro, and south to Faros, Platis Yialos, and Vathi. Pick up a schedule at Aegean Thesaurus Travel (see "Visitor Information," above).

By Car & Moped   Many visitors come to Sifnos for the wonderful hiking and mountain trails, but still want the convenience of a car or motorcycle. Reliable agencies include **Aegean Thesaurus** (© **22840/33-151**), in Apollonia and **Proto Moto Car** (© **22840/33-792;** www.protomotocar.gr), with a quayside office in Kamares and offices in Apollonia and Plati Yialos. In high season, you should reserve ahead. As always, exercise caution if you decide to rent a car or moped; many drivers, like you, will be unfamiliar with the island roads. The daily rate for an economy car with full insurance is from 30€; a moped rents from 20€.

By Taxi   Apollonia's main square is the island's primary taxi stand. There are about 10 taxis on the island, each privately owned, so you'll have to get their **mobile phone numbers** available at travel agents. Most hotels, restaurants, and shops will call a taxi for you; offer to pay for the call.

FAST FACTS   Visitor services are centered in or just off the main square in Apollonia. This is where you will find the **National Bank** (© **22840/31-317**), with an ATM; the **post office** (© **22840/31-329**); the **telephone office (OTE);** the **police** (© **22840/31-210**); for **medical emergencies** call © **22840/31-315.** The municipal website **www.sifnos.gr** is useful.

What to See & Do

In antiquity, Sifnos was a wealthy island, thanks to its gold deposits. If you've been to Delphi, you'll have seen the sculpture from the impressive treasury the Sifnians build there. When the island was an important center of shipping, pottery, and trade in the 19th century, wealthy Sifnians built the handsome houses you'll see across the island. After World War II, when shipping dried up, the island had some very lean years. Now, Sifnos's fortunes follow the fortunes of Greek tourism, although the island seems to have enough year-round Greek visitors to ward off more seriously lean years.

The capital town of the island, **Apollonia ★** (also called Hora and Stavri) is the name given jointly to the **seven settlements** on these lovely interior hills. It's 5km (3 miles) inland from Kamares; a local bus makes the trip hourly (from about 6am–midnight) every day in summer. The town's central square is the transportation hub of the island. All vehicle roads converge here, and this is where you'll find the bus stop and taxi stand. The small **Popular and Folk Art Museum** (great old photographs) cunningly does not post its hours, but is often open July 1 to September 15 from 10am to 1pm and 6 to 10pm (admission is 2€). From the square, pedestrian paths of flagstone and marble—lined with boutiques, restaurants, and cafes—wind upward through the beautiful town. If you stumble upon the Church of the Panagia, look for the carving of St. George besting the dragon, over the door, and the ancient marble column in the courtyard. The column was probably looted from a temple dedicated to Apollo, after whom Apollonia was named. As you go up and up the stepped-stone streets, once you get past the enormous cathedral, you'll find yourself in residential neighborhoods, with small courtyards, some with enormous caper and rose bushes. This is a great place to wander, admire the perfect whitewashed sugar-cube houses, get a bit lost, and hope you end up at the wonderful **Gerontopoulos** pastry shop for a restorative espresso and some sweet, dense chocolate pudding.

Tip: If you rent a car and have trouble finding a parking place in Apollonia—and you almost certainly will—head down the hill toward Kamares and turn right into the large municipal parking lot just out of Apollonia. From the parking lot, avoid walking up the main road by taking the side street that runs back up hill into the Main Square.

Kastro ★★ is one of the best-preserved medieval towns in the Cyclades, built on the dramatic site of an ancient acropolis. Until several decades ago, Kastro was almost entirely deserted; as tourists began to infiltrate the island, Kastro sprouted cafes, restaurants, and shops. The 2km (1-mile) walk from Apollonia is easy, except under the midday sun. Start out on the footpath that passes under the main road in front of Hotel Anthoussa, and continue through the tiny village of Kato Petali, finishing the walk into Kastro on a paved road, or the marked footpath. Whitewashed houses, some well preserved and others eroding, adjoin one another in a defensive ring abutting a sheer cliff. Venetian coats of arms are still visible above doorways of older houses. Within the maze of streets are a few tavernas and some beautiful rooms to let. The little **Archaeological Museum** (✆ 22840/31-022) here has a good collection of pottery and sculpture found on the island; it's often open Tuesday through Saturday from 9am to 2pm, Sunday and holidays from 10am to 2pm. Admission is free.

Artemonas ★, about 2km (1 mile) north of Apollonia, is a small village with streets lined with 19th-century mansions built by wealthy Siphnian ship owners. The walk from Apollonia in not-too-hot weather is lovely; if you drive, there is a good-size parking lot just as you come into town. When you get to Artemonas, you can have some homemade almond sweets (*amygdalia*) at any of the local sweet shops.

About 2km (1 mile) south of Apollonia, on the road to Vathi, is a trail leading to the hilltop church of **Ayios Andreas.** Until recently, this was an excursion to make simply for the amazing almost 360-degree view of Sifnos and neighboring islands. Since 2011 there has been another reason to visit here: the excavations of an **ancient acropolis,** and its excellent small site museum. Broad stone steps begin a long climb to the summit; count on at least 20 vigorous minutes to make the ascent. Having done this excursion previously on foot and on donkey back, I am happy to say that when I visited in 2011, I drove on the new road right up to the summit! People have lived on this spot from perhaps the 13th century B.C. until at least the 4th century B.C. The site was protected by massive walls that once stood some 6m (20 ft.) high and still reach more than 3.5m (11 ft.) in height. The walls encircled the settlement, with its sanctuary of Artemis, and small houses. Standing on the summit on a lovely early summer day it is hard to imagine how miserable life must have been here when winter winds whipped across the site and people huddled in their tiny dwellings. From the site, you can see the remains of some of Sifnos's more than 80 stone towers that were used for defense and for communication: bonfires could flash messages quickly across the island from tower to tower. All this and more is explained in the excellent museum, where everything is labeled both in Greek and English. The site and museum are usually open Tuesday to Sunday 8:30am to 3pm; entrance was free in 2011, but a fee is to be expected soon.

The pottery on display in the museum is a reminder that pottery making flourished on Sifnos well into the 1980s. Now, only a handful of potteries remain. The distinctive brown-and-blue glazed Sifnian pottery still being made has become something of a collector's item. If you fall for a piece, buy it—with more potteries closing down, you can't be sure you'll find this distinctive ware again. (See "Shopping," below.)

BEACHES

Sifnos has several really good beaches. You can reach many of them by caique shuttle services from Kamares; Aegean Thesarus Travel in Apollonia or Kamares can let you know the schedules. Not surprisingly, **Plati Yialos,** the island's longest sand beach, is easy to reach by taxi or public transportation. There are plenty of tavernas and cafes along the crescent sand beach where you can have a bite. (You can also hike from Platis Yialos to the Panagia tou Vounou monastery; see "Walking," below). Not surprisingly, Plati Yialos—which boasts that it is the longest beach in the Cyclades—can be crowded in summer. If you have time, you may want to explore some of the island's other beaches. Here are some suggestions.

From Platis Yialos, it's a half-hour walk east through the olive groves and intoxicating oregano and thyme patches over the hill to **Panagia Chrissopiyi,** a double-vaulted whitewashed church on a tiny island. There's good swimming at **Apokofto,** a cove with a long sand beach and several shade trees just beyond the monastery, where rocky headlands protect swimmers from rough water. **Pharos** and **Fasolou,** two other east-coast beaches (reachable from Platis Yialos on foot by the resolute), are easier to get to by taking the bus from Apollonia. The excellent **Dimitris taverna** (© **22840/71-493**) is by the sea at Fasolou.

Until 1997, the beach at **Vathi**—one of the best on the island—was accessible only on foot or by boat, but there's now a road and regular bus service. Sifnos's first posh resort, **Elies,** opened here in 2005. The beach does not have the dense development of the port of Kamares and Platis Yialos, but there's every sign that it may yet. Of the several tavernas here, my friends with houses on Sifnos praise To Livada (© **22840/71-123**). I couldn't agree more: great salads, grills, stews and a pleasantly cool spot to sit, just off the beach, surrounded by trees. The beach at **Cheronisso,** at the island's northern end, is a spectacular spot to watch the sun go down.

WALKING

More and more asphalt roads are appearing on Sifnos to accommodate wheeled vehicles, but you'll still be able to do lots of your walking on the island's distinctive flagstone and marble paths. You'll probably see village women whitewashing the edges of the paving stones, transforming the monochrome paths into elaborate abstract patterns. Throughout the island, you'll find dovecotes, windmills, and small white chapels in amazingly remote spots.

One wonderful walk on the island leads west from **Apollonia to Profitis Elias,** passing through a valley of extraordinary beauty to the summit of the island's highest mountain (wraparound amazing views). A short detour lets you also take in the church and ruined monastery at Skafis. Pick up a walking map at one of the local travel agencies. The 12th-century walled monastery of Profitis Elias is a formidable citadel, its interior courtyard lined with the monks' cells. The chapel has a fine marble iconostasis. Continue straight where the summit path branches right and walk through the next intersection. You'll soon reach the church of Skafis, within the ruins of an old monastery and overlooking a valley shaded by olive trees. Look for the remains of paintings on the walls of the monastery, in what must have been a chapel. Allow about 4 hours for the round-trip to Profitis Elias, with a half-hour for the detour to Skafis.

From Plati Yialos (see "Beaches," above), you can hike to the **Panagia tou Vounou** by following a paved road that leads off the main road to Plati Yialos; although the monastery (which has fine views) is signposted, it is best to have a good island map. The church here is usually unlocked in the morning, locked in the afternoons.

SHOPPING

Famed in antiquity first for its riches, then for its ceramics, Sifnos still produces some wonderful brown glaze pottery with minimalist white decorative swirls. As you crisscross the island, you'll see signs advertising pottery workshops, although the clusters of potters in Plati Yialos are, alas, gone. **Simos and John Apostolidis (© 22840/71-258)** are among the few potters who still have a workshop in Plati Yialos. In Kamares, **Antonis Kalogerou (© 22840/31-651)** sells folk paintings of island life and the pottery of Sifnos, which is manufactured in his showroom from the deep gray or red clay mined in the inland hill region. In Apollonia, Kastro, and Artemona a number of shops sell pottery, much of which is from neighboring Paros. You can spot the Parian pottery by its bright colors, shiny glazes, and scenes of fruit, flowers, and island life. For those in search of distinctive jewelry, Spyros Koralis's **Ble (© 22840/33-055)**, in Apollonia, does innovative work in silver and gold. I counted twenty jewelry shops in one short stroll recently in Apollonia, so you should find something you like here! Finally, here's something that you almost certainly did not come to Greece to find: a mall. It's in Apollonia and it's called **Cycladic Place (www.kikladonxoros.gr)**, a group of boutiques, cafes, and restaurants grouped around a garden. In short, as the Cycladic Place website says, a mall "especially designed for the Greek summer."

Where to Stay

If you feel like some indulgence, check out the **Elies Resort** (www.eliesresorts.com; **© 22840/34-000**), which opened in 2005 on a hillside stretching down to the beach in Vathi. Elies immediately won a regular place in *Odyssey* magazine's annual feature on the 50 best hotels in Greece. The glistening white (inside and out) resort, shaded by olive trees (*elies* is Greek for olive trees), is designed to look like a traditional Cycladic village—albeit a village with tennis courts, villas with private pools, and a spa. Doubles begin at 340€, suites at 550€, and villas at 950€. You may also want to check out the **Verina Complex (www.verina.gr)**, whose holdings, in addition to the Hotel Petali (see below), include the Verina Suites, at Plati Yialos; the Verina Astra Suites, in the village of Poulati; and a villa at Vathy. Many Sifnian hotels insist on a stay of more than 1 night in high season.

APOLLONIA

Apollonia is the most central place to use as a base on Sifnos. Buses depart from the central square to most island towns, and stone-paved paths lead to neighboring villages. Keep in mind that many Athenians vacation on Sifnos, particularly on summer weekends, when it can be virtually impossible to find a room, car, or, unless you start early, even a meal. If you plan to be here during the high season, be sure to make reservations by May. If you're here during off season, many hotels are closed, although some do remain open.

With advance notice, **Aegean Thesaurus Travel** (see "Visitor Information," above in this chapter) can usually place you in a rented room with your own bathroom, in a studio with a kitchenette, or in other, more stylish accommodations. A simple double in a place with no view can cost 100€ in high season.

Hotel Anthoussa　This hotel is above the excellent and popular Yerontopoulos cafe and patisserie (free Internet service), on the main road around Apollonia, less than a 5-minute walk from the main square. That sounds convenient, and is, but although streetside rooms offer views over the hills, they overlook both a main road and the late-night sweet-tooth crowd in the cafe/patisserie. It is usually very noisy here at night. Back rooms are somewhat quieter and overlook a beautiful bower of bougainvillea. In short, the very location is the problem here for an otherwise very appealing place.

Apollonia, 84003 Sifnos. © **22840/31-431.** 13 units. 90€ double. MC, V. **Amenities:** Breakfast room. *In room:* A/C, TV.

Hotel Petali ★★   Here's a quiet hotel with great views not far—but all uphill—from Apollonia's main square. The Petali is on a largely pedestrianized side street, with lovely views of the sea beyond the town's houses. After a day's sightseeing, it's nice to enjoy those views from the Petali's pool or poolside terrace. Each guest room has a large terrace, handsome and comfortable chairs, good beds, and modern bathrooms. A small restaurant serves delicious Sifnian specialties. Although the Hotel Petali does not accept credit cards, its managing office, **Aegean Thesaurus Travel Agency** (✆ **22840/32-152;** www.thesaurus.gr), accepts MasterCard and Visa. Like many island hotels, the Petali insists on a stay of at least 4 nights in high season.

Apollonia, 84003 Sifnos. www.hotelpetali.gr. ✆/fax **22840/33-024.** 11 units. 200€ double. No credit cards (see listing for details). **Amenities:** Restaurant; bar; Internet; Jacuzzi; pool; sauna. *In room:* A/C, TV, hair dryer.

Hotel Sifnos ★★   The hospitable owners here have tried hard to make their hotel reflect island taste, using local pottery and weavings in the smallish but cheerful rooms. The hotel **restaurant** offers good basic meals beneath a broad arbor; it's as popular with locals as it is with travelers and hotel guests. The restaurant makes this a good place to stay if you don't want to search out a place for dinner. Traffic and pedestrian noise can be a problem here.

Apollonia, 84003 Sifnos. ✆ **22840/31-624.** 9 units. 90€ double. AE, MC, V. **Amenities:** Restaurant; bar. *In room:* A/C, TV

ARTEMONA

There are several small hotels and rooms to rent in Artemona. Although the 25-room **Hotel Artemon** (www.hotel-artemon.com; ✆ **22840/31-303**) is just outside the village on the main road from Apollonia to Artemona, the road is usually not horribly noisy at night. The rooms (simple, but fine) at the back overlook a garden, all rooms have balconies, there's a very good **restaurant,** and the owners get high praise from the many guests who come back year after year; the Artemon is open year-round, which many island hotels are not. Doubles run from 80€ and fixed-price dinner 17€.

KASTRO

Aris Rafeletos Apartments   These traditional rooms and apartments are distributed throughout the medieval town of Kastro. Most have exposed ceiling beams, stone ceilings and floors, and the long narrow rooms typical of this fortified village. The two smallest units are somewhat dark and can be musty, but the three apartments are spacious and charming. All apartments have kitchenettes and terraces; three have splendid sea views. The largest apartment is on two levels and can comfortably sleep four. If the antiquity and charm of this hilltop medieval village appeals to you, and you don't want hotel service but a chance to experience village life, then these accommodations may be the perfect base for your exploration of the island.

Kastro. ✆/fax **22840/31-161.** 6 units. 85€–180€ apt. No credit cards. The rental office is at the village's north end, about 50m (164 ft.) past the Archaeological Museum. **Amenities:** Breakfast room/bar. *In room:* Kitchenette in some units.

KAMARES

The port of Kamares has the greatest concentration of hotels and pensions on the island, but has little of the beauty of Sifnos's traditional villages. Two moderately priced hotels are the 14-unit harborside **Hotel Stavros** (doubles from 80€) and the 18-unit **Hotel Kamari** (doubles from 60€), a 10-minute walk from the beach and harbor. Information is available on both, from Stavros and Sarah Kalogirou (www.sifnostravel.com; ✆ **22840/33-383**). This helpful couple (Sarah is English) also has

The History of Sweet Stuff in Sifnos

As you travel around Sifnos, you'll notice a lot of bakeries (a bakery is called a *furno* in Greece) and sweet shops. According to local lore, long ago a baker named Benios (pronounced *Ve*-ni-os) had 13 children (a baker's dozen)—and almost all the children and their children's children and successive generations of the Venios family became bakers. That's why many bakeries in Sifnos to this day are owned by one or another member of the Venios family. Many families and some restaurants send their *revithia* (chickpeas) in a Sifnian clay pot to a Venios bakery to be slow-cooked overnight for the traditional Sunday dinner.

a car-rental agency and the **Elonas** apartments to rent in Apollonia (units sleeping up to five, from 125€). They also run the **YaMas Internet Cafe Bar** in Kamares.

Hotel Boulis   This hotel, capably managed by two more members of the Kalogirou family, Lyn and Antonis, is right on the port's beach—you'll see it from the ferry as you approach Kamares. The large, carpeted rooms have balconies or patios, most with beach views; all have fridges and ceiling fans. The hotel has a spacious, cool, marble-floored reception area and a sunny breakfast room.

Kamares, 84003 Sifnos. www.hotelboulis.gr. ℂ **22840/32-122.** 45 units. 100€–130€ double. Rates include breakfast. AE. Closed Oct–Apr. Follow the main street 300m (984 ft.) from the ferry pier, turning left opposite the Boulis Taverna (operated by the same family). The hotel is on your left. **Amenities:** Breakfast room/bar. *In room:* Fridge.

PLATIS YIALOS

A busy beach resort on the island's south coast, Plati Yialos serves as a convenient base, especially if you are traveling with children. (I speak from happy experience at the Hotel Plati Yialos.) The town exists for tourism during high season. If Hotel Akti Platis Yialos is full, there are lots of other choices, including the attractive beachside 20 room **Hotel Efrosini** (www.hotel-efrosini.gr; ℂ **22840/71-353**), popular with Greek families, or the stylish **Verina** (www.verina.gr; ℂ **22840/71-525**), across from the beach, but with a lovely garden and big pool.

Akti Hotel Plati Yialos ★★ ☺   The island's oldest and most family-friendly beach hotel—completely renovated in 2010–11—overlooks the beach on the west side of the cove, set apart from the rest of the town's densely populated beach strip. The hotel is on an excellent sand beach that slopes gently into the sea. In short, it's an ideal location if you are traveling with young children—or, for that matter, on your own! Originally a government-owned Xenia hotel, its design follows the usual Xenia rectangle motel-like format, but the public rooms are now very bright and attractive, as are the guest rooms. The ground-floor guest rooms, with patios facing the garden and water, are especially desirable if you are traveling with children; rooms on the upper stories have balconies and better sea views. There are also two suites, one with its own Jacuzzi. Works of art by local artists are displayed throughout the hotel. The Platis Yialos's flagstone sun deck extends from the beach to a dive platform at the end of the cove. A **bar** and **restaurant** share the same Aegean views.

Platis Yialos, 84003 Sifnos. www.platys-gialos.gr. ℂ **22840/71-324** or 28310/22-626 in winter. 21 units, including 2 suites. 100€–200€ double; from 270€ small suite, from 320€ large suite. Rates include breakfast. No credit cards. Closed Oct–Mar. **Amenities:** Restaurant; bar. *In room:* A/C, TV, hair dryer, minifridge, Wi-Fi.

Where to Eat

APOLLONIA

If you want a sweet, head for the wonderful **Gerontopoulos Pastry Shop** (*©* 22840/32-220) in the Hotel Anthousa. I can vouch for their cookies, cakes, ice creams, and preserved fruits. Oh, yes, and the chocolate pudding is divine. For a snack, try **Veranda** or **Sifnos Café-Restaurant.** Both serve breakfasts and sweets all day—and, along with many other places, have the island specialty of *revithia* (chickpeas) most Sundays. My Sifnian friends told me that **Okyalos** (*©* 22840/32-650), on Apollonia's main drag, succeeds in its aim of serving "Mediterranean gourmet cuisine." When I ate there in 2011, I agreed: the food was beautifully displayed on the plate and very tasty, with lots of local touches (local cheese on the salad, fresh herbs galore). Dinner for two runs from 40 €. If you eat at the seriously upmarket **Elia & Kappari** (Olive and Kaper; *©* 22840/31-791; www.elia-kappari.gr), let us know what you thought. This restaurant in an old olive press, with a wide veranda with an even wider view, seems to be one of those places people either love or hate, and it had not opened for the season when I visited Sifnos recently.

Sunset (To Troullaki) ★ GREEK   This is a good place to go at sunset or any other time. About 8km (5 miles) out of Apollonia in a peaceful setting by the road to Cheronisso, this family-run taverna serves delicious island food. The sunsets here are spectacular. Much of the meat and vegetables is organic. The *Mastello,* melt-in-the-mouth lamb on vine leaves, is slowly baked in a (local, of course!) earthenware pot.

Apollonia. *©* **22840/31-970.** Main courses 7€–15€. No credit cards. Lunch and dinner most days.

ARTEMONAS & ENVIRONS

There are a number of sweet shops and cafes in Artemonas. On the main *plateia,* **Margarita's** (Margarita Chrysou's Snack Bar, *©* **22840-32-058**) is open virtually all day and has snacks, salads, and light meals. And, the Hotel Artemon's restaurant **Lambessis** (*©* **22830/31-303**), just outside Artenonas on the road to Apollonia, gets high praise from both locals and visitors.

Chrysso ★★ GREEK   Once you get to Artemonas, follow the small white signs with the blue arrow pointing on to "Chrysso." You'll pass neoclassical mansions and will be sure you're lost at least once until you come to the terrace with the wonderful view. The food is delicious: tender *paidakia* (lamb chops) grilled on charcoal, hearty stews, luscious salads. Maria the owner and cook does a wonderful job and most of my friends with homes on Sifnos say that this is their favorite place, both for the ambience and view, and for the food.

Apollonia. *©* **22840/31-322.** Main courses 8€–12€. No credit cards. Lunch and dinner most days. Sometimes closed in winter.

To Liotrivi (Manganas) ★ GREEK   We're still mentioning To Liotrivi because it has been an island favorite for a long time. Unfortunately, recent reports from readers and friends suggest that this place is resting far too heavily on its laurels. It was one of the first restaurants on the island to have a varied and inventive menu.

Artemona. *©* **22840/31-246.** Main courses 8€–10€. No credit cards. Daily noon–midnight. From Apollonia, follow the pedestrian street north from the main *plateia,* past Mama Mia and Hotel Petali; the walk takes a pleasant 10–15 min.

KAMARES

Boulis Taverna ★ GREEK   With an unexceptional location at the top of the town's busy main street, this isn't the place to go for a romantic evening, but it does offer some very good food. The taverna is operated by Andonis Kalogirou, of Hotel Boulis, who uses vegetables, cheeses, and meats raised on the family's organic farm. The walls of the vast interior room are lined with wooden wine casks. Outside, lamb, chicken, and steak cook on the grill.

At the top of the main street through town. ℂ **22840/31-648.** Main courses 7€–15€. No credit cards. Daily 11am–1am.

Kapitain Andreas ★ SEAFOOD   This place, with its sometimes gruff host, Andreas, who is both proprietor and fisherman, serves good food and grills.

On the town beach. ℂ **22840/32-356.** Main courses 8€–15€; fish priced by the kilo. No credit cards. Daily 1–5pm and 7:30pm–12:30am.

Poseidonas (Sophia's) ★★ GREEK   The first restaurant you pass after disembarking the ferry is easily the best place to eat in Kamares: Sophia Patriarke and her daughters are hospitable to strangers and serve tasty grills, truly fresh salads, and fabulous *rivithokeftedes rena* (chickpea croquettes).

ℂ **22840/32-362.** Fish priced by the kilo. No credit cards. Daily 1–5pm and 7pm–midnight.

KASTRO

To Astro ★ GREEK   Stews and chops, tomato salads in summer, and cabbage and carrot salads in winter served on a lovely shaded terrace with long views over the island on the outskirts of the picture-postcard perfect village of Kastro. Today, Kastro's winding lanes, houses with Venetian coats of arms, and classical sarcophagi unexpectedly popping up here and there are reminders that this was the main settlement of ancient Sifnos as well as the medieval capital of the island.

ℂ **22840/31-476.** Main courses 6€–10€. Irregular hours, but most days from 10am–midnight; no credit cards.

PLATIS YIALOS

To Steki ★★ GREEK   Platis Yialos's best restaurant for traditional Siphnian home-cooking taverna fare is also popular for its shady outdoor terrace.

At the beach's east end. ℂ **22840/71-202.** Main courses 8€–18€. No credit cards. Daily 8pm–1am.

Sifnos After Dark

My friends who have houses on Sifnos remind me that bars come and go with amazing rapidity; many don't last an entire season. I'm not listing phone numbers because phones simply are not answered. The main street of Apollonia vibrates to the sound

---

A Special Feast for the Prophet Elijah

Prophet Elijah's feast day (July 20–July 22) is one of the most important religious holidays on Sifnos, which has had a monastery dedicated to this saint for at least 800 years. The celebration begins with a mass outing to the monastery of Profitis Elias on the summit of the island's highest mountain, and continues through the night with dancing and feasting.

of music from virtually wall-to-wall bars all summer. Of these, the **Argo Bar** has been around for years; it plays European and American pop music with some Greek tunes thrown in.

In Kamares, there's another longtime survivor: the picturesque **Old Captain's Bar.** For classical music, the **Cultural Society of Sifnos** sometimes schedules summer concerts in Artemonas.

PAROS ★★

168km (91 nautical miles) SE of Piraeus

Paros is accurately (but hardly enticingly) known as the "transportation hub" of the Cyclades: Almost all island boats stop here en route to someplace else. As a result, Paros has suffered from the reputation of the place on the way to the place where you're going. At present, Paros is still cheaper than either Mykonos or Santorini—in fact, some call it the "poor man's Mykonos"—although rising prices are making that nickname anachronistic. Comparisons aside, Paros's good beaches and nightlife have made it a popular destination in its own right. Because of the absence of any single five-star attraction—there's no antiquity here to rival Santorini's ancient Akrotiri and nothing to rival the beauty of Mykonos's perfect Cycladic architecture—a lot of visitors come here simply to have a good time, windsurfing, sunbathing, and partying.

Still others—not necessarily opposed to having a good time—are drawn back to Paros because of its other attractions. Admittedly, if you come by ship, your first impression after docking at the main port and capital **Parikia** will be of the kitschy windmill on the quay, travel agents, cafes, and the fast-food joints lining the harborfront. Where, you'll wonder, is the town described as "charming"? Take a few steps inland, and you'll find it. **Parikia** has an energetic marketplace and the **Ekatondapiliani,** the 100-doored church designed in the 6th century by the famous architect Isodore of Miletus. Winding streets, the paving stones meticulously marked off with whitewash, lead off from the main square. One street meanders up and up, passing marble fountains and modest houses with elaborate door frames, to the remains of a medieval castle, built with chunks pillaged from various local ancient temples.

Parikia manages to be both cozy and cosmopolitan. The town has a lively cultural life: The **Archilochos Cultural Society** stages a winter film festival and hosts a summer music festival (**www.archilochos.gr**). This is also the home of the **Aegean Center for the Fine Arts,** which has exhibitions and lectures, and offers courses in painting and literature (**www.aegeancenter.org**). There are also lots of shops and galleries exhibiting and selling work by artists who spend all or part of the year here.

Out on the island, there's a scattering of appealing villages and two must-see spots: the hillside village of Lefkes in the interior, and the picture-postcard seaside hamlet of Naoussa. Paros also has enough good beaches to keep almost any visitor happy.

Paros is large enough that even if you're just here for a day, renting a car makes sense. If you're here in May or June, you can make an around-the-island tour that includes a morning visit to **Petaloudes (Valley of the Butterflies),** a visit to Lefkes, a stop for lunch in Naoussa, a swim at your beach of choice, and a night back in Parikia, where you visit the Byzantine Ekatondapiliana Cathedral and then shop and stroll the evening away. Other months, when the butterflies are not on Paros, you may want to spend more time visiting the cathedral, and taking in the archaeological museum, combined with a boat trip from Parikia or Pounta to the little island of Andiparos.

> ## It's Popular in Paros
>
> The **Feast of the Dormition of the Virgin** (Aug 15) is one of the most important religious holidays in Greece—and the most important, after Easter, in Paros. Pilgrims come here from throughout the Cyclades to attend services at the Panagia Ekatondapiliani, which is dedicated to the Virgin. If you come here then, make reservations well in advance, or you will probably find yourself sleeping rough. And, on the subject of dates: If you want to visit Paros to see its famous **butterflies,** remember that they come here in May and June.

Essentials

GETTING THERE   By Plane   The website of Athens International Airport, www.aia.gr, is a useful resource for domestic airline schedules. **Olympic Air** (© 810/114-4444 or 210/966-6666, official Greek phone numbers that are rarely answered; www.olympicair.com) offers daily flights between Athens and Paros, which also receives European charters. **Aegean Airlines** (© 810/112-0000; www.aegeanair.com) also has several flights daily between Athens and Paros. In Parikia, you can call © 22840/21-900 for flight information, but you'll do much better to use a local travel agent.

By Boat   The sites www.gtp.gr and www.openseas.gr are useful resources for ferry schedules. Paros has more connections with more ports than any other island in the Cyclades. The main port, Parikia, has connections at least once daily with Piraeus by ferry (5–6 hr.) and high-speed ferry (3–4 hr.). Confirm schedules with the Athens **GNTO** (© 210/327-1300 or 210/331-0562) or **Piraeus Port Authority** (© 210/926-9111). Boats are notoriously late and/or early; your travel or ticket agent will give you an *estimate* of times involved in the following journeys.

Daily ferry and hydrofoil service links Parikia with Ios, Mykonos, Santorini, and Tinos. Several times a week, boats depart for Folegandros, Sifnos, and Siros. There are daily excursion tours from Parikia or Naoussa (the north-coast port) to Mykonos. The high-speed services usually take half as long and cost twice as much as the slower ferries. There's also overnight service to Ikaria and Samos several times a week. (From Samos you can often arrange a next-day excursion to Ephesus, Turkey.) In high season, there's hourly caique service to Andiparos from Parikia and Pounda, a small port 6km (4 miles) south of Parikia, with regular connection by bus. The east-coast port of Piso Livadi is the point of departure for travelers heading to the "Little Cyclades." Ferries depart four times weekly for Heraklia, Schinoussa, Koufonissi, and Katapola.

For general ferry and other travel information, try **Santorineos Travel** (© 22840/24-245) or **Polos Tours** (© 22840/22-092), both on the harbor in Parikia. The **port authority** can be reached at (© 22840/21-240). Many agents around Mavroyenous Square and along the port sell ferry tickets; schedules are posted along the sidewalk.

VISITOR INFORMATION   There is a **visitor information office** on Mavroyenous Square, just behind and to the right of the windmill at the end of the pier. This office is often closed, but there are numerous travel agencies on the seafront, including **Santorineos Travel** and **Polos Tours** (see above). The municipality information office in the Parikia town hall can be reached at © 22840/22-078. The island has a number of helpful websites, including **www.parosweb.com** and **www.paroslife. com**. The quarterly English-language magazine *Paros Life and Naxos Life* (2€) is very useful and has a good calendar of upcoming events.

GETTING AROUND By Bus The cunningly unmarked **bus office and main station** (© 22840/21-395) in Parikia is on the waterfront, to the left as you face the windmill. There is often hourly service between Parikia and Naoussa, from 8am to midnight in high season. The other buses from Parikia run frequently, from 8am to 9pm, in two general directions: south to Aliki or Pounda, and southeast to the beaches at Piso Livadi, Chrissi Akti, and Drios, passing the Marathi Quarries and the town of Lefkes along the way. Schedules (not always up-to-date) are usually available at the Parikia bus office.

By Car & Moped Paros is large enough that renting a car makes sense. There are many agencies along the waterfront, and except in July and August, you should be able to bargain. **Iria Cars and Bikes** (© 22840/21-232), **Santorineos Travel** (© 22840/24-245), and **Stefanos** (© 22840/21-521) get praise from travelers. Expect to pay from 30€ per day for a car and from 15€ per day for a moped. Be sure to get full insurance and check the brakes.

By Taxi Taxis can be booked (© 22840/21-500) or hailed at the windmill taxi stand. Taxi fare to Naoussa with luggage should run about 15€. Be sure to agree on a fare before you set out.

FAST FACTS There are several **banks** with ATMs in Parikia on Mavroyenous, the main Square, and one on the square in Naoussa; their hours are Monday through Thursday from 8am to 2pm, and Friday from 8am to 1:30pm. The private **Medical Center of Paros** (© 22840/24-410) is to the north of the pier, across from the post office; the public **Parikia Health Clinic** (© 22840/22-500) is on the central square, down the road from the Ekatondapiliani Cathedral. Much of Paros now has **Wi-Fi,** but **Internet access** is available on the Wired Network (**www.parosweb. com**) at eight locations around the island; you can buy a "smart card" that stores your personal settings and provides access at any of these locations for about 6€ per hour. The main Wired Network location—often noisy and crowded—is in Parikia, on Market Street (© 22840/22-003). **Cyber Cookies** (© 22840/21-610), the cafe just past the square with the ficus tree and Distrato Cafe, on the street that runs from the cathedral into Market Street, is much nicer, with a very helpful multilingual manager.

For the Paraikia **police,** call © 22840/23-333; in Naoussa, call © 22840/51-202. The **post office** in Parikia (© 22840/21-236) is left of the windmill on the waterfront road, open Monday through Friday from 7:30am to 2pm, with extended hours in July and August. Parikia's **telephone office** (OTE; © 22840/22-135) is just to the right of the windmill; it's usually open daily in summer from 7:30am to

The Bus Stops Here?

Buses on Paros usually have no visible indication of their destination; the place where you are let off in, for example, Naoussa, is seldom the place you should be waiting to be picked up for the return trip. Try to get this useful information on which bus is yours and where you should be for your return trip from the bus office staff or bus driver. Be persistent.

📎 **A Semester Abroad in Paros**

The **Aegean Center for the Fine Arts** (www.aegeancenter.org) offers courses in painting, photography, music, creative writing, and other artistic endeavors, including two 3-month sessions. You'll see the mostly teen and 20-something students all over Parikia and out on the island.

2pm. (If the front door is closed, go around to the back, as wind direction determines which door is open.) A branch in Naoussa has similar hours. If you don't have your own phone, it is usually much easier to forget about the OTE office and make a phone call with a phone card, on sale at almost all kiosks.

What to See & Do
THE TOP ATTRACTIONS IN PARIKIA

Archaeological Museum   The museum's most valued holding is a fragment of the **Parian Chronicle,** an ancient chronology. The Ashmolean Museum at Oxford University has a larger portion of the chronicle, which is carved on Parian marble tablets. Why is it so important? Because it lists dates for actual and mythical events from the time of Cecrops until about 260 B.C. Cecrops was the legendary first king of Athens, whose dates—indeed, existence—cannot be proven. Just to confuse and irritate historians, the chronicle gives information about artists, poets, and playwrights—but doesn't bother to mention many important political leaders or battles. The museum also contains a number of sculptural fragments as well as a splendid running Gorgon (with a delicate incised border on its skirt) and a Winged Victory from the 5th century B.C. There's also part of a marble monument with a frieze of Archilochus, the 7th-century-B.C. lyric poet, known as the inventor of iambic meter and for his ironic detachment. ("What breaks me, young friend, is tasteless desire, lifeless verse, boring dinners.") The courtyard has lots of marble monuments (and excellent toilet facilities).

Parikia. ✆ **22840/21-231.** Admission 3€. Tues–Sun 8:30am–3pm. Behind the cathedral, opposite the playing fields of the local school.

Panagia Ekatondapiliani Cathedral ★★   According to tradition, the Byzantine cathedral of Panagia Ekatondapiliani (Our Lady of a Hundred Doors) was founded by **St. Helen,** the mother of Constantine the Great, the emperor whose conversion to Christianity led to its establishment as the official religion of the Roman Empire. St. Helen is said to have stopped on Paros en route to the Holy Land, where the faithful believe that she found the True Cross. Fragments of the Cross are revered relics in many a church. Helen's son fulfilled her vow to found a church here, and successive emperors and rulers expanded it—which may in part explain the church's confusing layout, an inevitable result of centuries of renovations and expansions, which include the six side chapels. The work has not stopped: The cathedral was extensively restored in the 1960s, and the large square in front was expanded in 1996 for the church's 1,700th birthday. The cathedral is hidden behind its high, thick wall, built to protect the shrine from pirates and other marauders. Cut into the wall are rows of monks' cells, some of which now house offices and a shop and ecclesiastical museum. After you step through the outer gate, the noise of the town vanishes, and you enter a garden with lemon trees and flowering shrubs. Ahead is the cathedral, its elegant arched facade a memento both of the Venetian period and of classical times (several of the columns were brought here from ancient temples).

Inside, the cathedral is surprisingly spacious. Almost every visitor instinctively looks up to the massive dome, supported on vaults ornamented with painted six-winged seraphim. Take time to find the handsome icons, including several set in the iconostasis (altar screen), side chapels, and an elegant little 4th-century baptistery, with a baptismal font in the shape of a cross. In the arcade, the museum contains a small but superb collection of 15th- to 19th-century icons, religious vestments, and beautiful objects used in Orthodox Church ceremonies. Everything is labeled in Greek and in English.

The small shop, also in the arcade, features religious books and memorabilia, as well as books on Paros. Panayotis Patellis's *Guide Through Ekatontapiliani* (4€) is both useful and charming. When you leave the cathedral precincts, turn left slightly uphill toward the Archaeological Museum for a fine view of the entire cathedral complex with its red-tile roofs.

Parikia. No admission fee for cathedral, although it is customary to leave a small offering. Daily 8am–8pm, but usually closed 2–5pm in winter. Museum: (*C*) **22840/21-243**. Admission 2€. Daily 10am–2pm and 6–9pm. On Parikia's central square, opposite and north of the ferry pier.

THE TOP ATTRACTIONS OUT ON THE ISLAND

Marathi Marble Quarries The inland road to Lefkes and Marpissa will take you up the side of a mountain to the marble quarries at Marathi, source of the famous Parian marble. Ancient sculptors prized Parian marble for its translucency and fine, soft texture, and they used it for much of their best work, including the *Hermes* of Praxiteles and the *Venus de Milo*. The turnoff to the quarries is signposted, and an odd, rather foolishly monumental, marble-paved path leads up the valley toward (but not to) a group of deserted buildings and the ancient quarries. The buildings, to the right of the path, once belonged to a French mining company, which, in 1844, quarried the marble for Napoleon's tomb; the company was the last to operate here. The quarry entrances are about 46m (150 ft.) beyond the marble path's end, on the left. The second, wide quarry on the left has a 3rd-century-B.C. relief of the gods at its entrance, encased in a protective cage. In Roman times, as many as 150,000 slaves labored here, working day and night to the flickering lights of thousands of oil lamps. There isn't much to see today inside the quarries, in which case you'll find it

---

🎁 **The Ancient Cemetery**

If you face Parikia's harborside windmill then turn and walk to your right, in about 15 minutes you will come to the ancient **cemetery**. If you want to go there from the Archaeological Museum, walk downhill to the sea, turn right, and you'll soon be there. Excavations since the 1980s have revealed much about the island's history between 11th century B.C. and the Roman period. Many of the graves contained the bones and weapons of warriors, often buried in ceramic jars and marble urns, some of which are on view at the Archaeological Museum. The cemetery, which still has a number of marble tombs, is sometimes illuminated at night. If you want to have a drink or meal and contemplate mortality, try the excellent harborside **Porphyra Seafood Restaurant** ((*C*) **22840/23-410**), which overlooks the cemetery.

As you visit the **Panagia Ekatondapil-iani Cathedral,** look for the two squat sculptured figures that support the columns of the monumental gate by the chapel of St. Theodosia, to the left of the main cathedral entrance. According to popular legend, the two figures are Isidore of Miletus, the best-known architect here, and his pupil Ignatius. As the story has it, Isodore was so envious of Ignatius's talent that he pushed him off scaffolding high inside the church's dome. As he fell, Ignatius grabbed onto Isidore and they both tumbled to their deaths. The sculptor has shown Isidore pulling on his beard (evidently a sign of apology) and Ignatius rubbing his head—perhaps in pain, perhaps as he cogitates on revenge. It's a nice story, but, in fact archaeologists think that the two figures come from a temple of Dionysos that stood here and represent two satyrs—yet another example of how often successive generations reused building materials and re-created appropriate legends.

irresistible to explore the deep caverns opened by the miners high above the valley. Bring a flashlight, wear appropriate clothing, and don't explore alone.

Marathi. Open site.

10 The Valley of Petaloudes & Convent of Christou Stou Dhassous ★ Another name for this oasis of plum, pear, fig, and pomegranate trees is **Psychopiani** (Soul Softs). The butterflies, actually tiger moths (*Panaxia quadripunctaria poda*), look like black-and-white striped arrowheads, until they fly up to reveal their bright red underwings. They have been coming here for at least 300 years because of the freshwater spring, flowering trees, dense foliage, and cool shade; they're usually most numerous in early mornings or evenings in June. Donkey or mule rides from Parikia to the site along a back road cost about 12€. You can take the Pounda and Aliki bus, which drops you off at the turnoff to the nunnery; you'll have to walk the remaining 2.5km (1½ miles) in to Petaloudes. Be sure to scowl at any visitors who clap and shout to alarm the butterflies and make them fly, often causing the fragile insects to collapse. A snack bar serves refreshments; men can wait here, while women visit the nearby Convent of Christos tou Dasou, which does not welcome male visitors. (Cooling their heels in the courtyard, the men can console themselves by thinking of visiting Mount Athos, which is forbidden to female visitors.)

Petaloudes. Admission 3€. Mid-May to mid-Sept daily 9am–1pm and 4–8pm. Head 4km (2½ miles) south of Parikia on the coast road, turn left at the sign for the nunnery of Christos tou Dasou, and continue another 2.5km (1½ miles).

BEACHES

Paros has some fine sand beaches. If you're really pressed for time, you can walk in less than 15 minutes from where the ferry docks past where the fishing boats and small pleasure boats are moored to sandy Livadia beach, which has cafes and umbrellas If you can visit a couple of out-on-the-island beaches, here are some suggestions. All have chairs and umbrellas to rent and lots of tavernas and cafes. **Chrissi Akti (Golden Beach)** ★, on the island's southeast coast, is 1km (½ mile) of fine golden sand (with umbrellas and chairs to rent, tavernas, and cafes), is generally considered the best beach on the island. It's also the windiest, although the wind is usually offshore. As a result, this has become the island's primary windsurfing center and has hosted the World Cup championship every year since 1993. **Aegean Diving College** (✆ **22840/43-347;** www.aegeandivingcollege.com) and the **Aegean Diving School** (**22840/92-071;** www.eurodivers.gr) offer scuba instruction and guided dives. There's frequent bus service here from both Parikia and Naoussa. If you're interested in kiteboarding, try (crowded, built-up) **Pounda** (see "Windsurfing & Scuba," below).

One of the island's best and most famous, picturesque **Kolimbithres** ★ is also served by bus from Parikia and Naoussa. It has smooth giant rocks that divide the gold-sand beach into several tiny coves—and appear on lots of island postcards. As at Golden Beach, there are umbrellas and chairs to rent and lots of places to have a bite.

There's bus and caique service from Naoussa to **Santa Maria beach** ★, one of the most beautiful on the island. It has particularly clear water and shallow dunes (rare in Greece) of fine sand along the irregular coastline. It also offers some of the best windsurfing on Paros. The **Santa Maria Surf Club** (✆ **22840/52-490**) provides windsurfing gear and a brief lesson for about 20€ per hour.

TOWNS & VILLAGES: NAOUSSA & LEFKES

If your time on Paros is limited, do try to see Naoussa and Lefkes. If you have more time, you'll enjoy rambling about the island discovering other villages. One to keep in mind is **Marpissa** and the nearby monastery of **Agios Antonios**, from which there are fine views over the island.

Until recently, the fishing village of **Naoussa** remained relatively undisturbed, with simple white houses in a labyrinth of narrow streets, but it's now a growing resort center with increasingly fancy restaurants, trendy bars, boutiques, and galleries. Most of the new building here is concentrated along the nearby beaches, but a multiplicity of boutiques and restaurants has infiltrated deep into Naoussa. Some of the shops are just great, with gorgeous summer togs, but if you want to get a sense of the village itself, walk inland and uphill until you get lost in the winding streets. Then, wander your way back to the harbor after seeing some of the charming houses and little tourist-shop-free squares Naoussa still has. In short, Naoussa retains its charm—but for how long? Local fishing boats jostle for space beside visiting yachts, and fishermen calmly go about their work on the docks, all in the shadow of a half-submerged ruined Venetian minifortress—and, increasingly, tour buses. A narrow causeway links the Venetian fortress with the quay; the little kastro is picturesque when illuminated at night. The best night of all to see the fortress is during the **festival** held on or about each **August 23,** when the battle against the pirate Barbarossa is reenacted by torch-lit boats converging on the harbor. Much feasting and dancing follows. On July 2, the **Festival of Fish and Wine** is celebrated here and elsewhere on Paros.

Studio Detour in Kostos

En route to or from Marathi, consider a detour to the nearby **Studio Yria** (✆ **22840/29-007;** www.yriaparos. com), signposted by the village of Kostos. A number of artists, including sculptors, painters, and potters, have set up shop here, and their wares are impressive. Many works draw on traditional Byzantine and island designs, whereas others are modern.

THE cave OF ANDIPAROS

Not long ago people went to Andiparos, the islet about a nautical mile (1.9km) off Paros, for two reasons: to see the famous cave and to get away from all the crowds on Paros. The cave is still a good reason to come here, but Andiparos is now on the tourist map. Tom Cruise cruised by here, other stars followed in their yachts, Madonna dropped in by helicopter, and the wannabes began to come by ferry. There's been a lot of charmless building to accommodate visitors, and it's hard to think of a reason to linger after you see the cave. Parikia and Naoussa eclipse Andiparos for people-watching, window-shopping, and good food.

The **cave** (4€) is open in summer from 11am to 3pm; excursion caiques run hourly from 9am from Parikia and Pounda to Andiparos (3€ one-way). A shuttle barge, for vehicles as well as passengers, crosses the channel between Paros's southern port of Pounda and Andiparos continuously from 9am; the fare is 2€ or 10€ with a car; you can take along a bicycle for free. Buses (1.50€) run back and forth from the port to the cave. Something to consider: Greeks have a soft spot for caves, and the Andiparos cave is often as crowded as an Athens bus.

Tourists once entered the cave by rope, but today's concrete staircase offers more convenient—if less adventurous—access. The cave is about 90m (300 ft.) deep, but the farthest reaches are closed to visitors. Through the centuries, visitors have broken off parts of the massive stalactites as souvenirs and left graffiti to commemorate their visits, but the cool, mysterious cavern is still worth exploring. As usual, Lord Byron, who carved his name into a temple column at Sounion, left his signature here. The Marquis de Nointel celebrated Christmas mass here in 1673 with 500 attendants; a large stalagmite served as the altar and the service was concluded with fireworks and explosions at the stroke of midnight.

There's frequent bus service from Parikia to Naoussa in summer. Signs along Naoussa's harbor advertise caique service to nearby beaches. Daily excursion tours from Naoussa to Mykonos are usually offered in summer; inquire at any of the travel agencies in Parikia, or here at any local travel agency, such as **Nissiotissa Tours** (© **22840/51-480;** fax 22840/51-189).

Hilltop **Lefkes** ★ is the medieval capital of the island. Its whitewashed houses with red-tile roofs form a maze around the central square, with its little *kafeneion* (coffeehouse) with its unexpectedly grand neoclassical facade. The *kafeneion;* a barbershop; a shop selling crafts; and a *plateia,* paved with stone slabs accented with fresh whitewash—this is surely the most perfect little *plateia* in the Cyclades, unless the *plateia* in Pyrgos on Tinos has a slight edge because of its fountain house. Like so many Cycladic hamlets, Lefkes was built in an inaccessible location and with an intentionally confusing pattern of streets to thwart pirates. Test your own powers of navigation by finding **Ayia Triada (Holy Trinity) Church,** whose carved marble towers are visible above the town. The Lefkes Village Hotel is one of the nicest places on the island to stay, although it's not easy to get a room there on summer weekends, when it is very popular with Greek families for wedding receptions.

OUTDOOR PURSUITS

WALKING   Paros has numerous old stone-paved roads connecting the interior towns, many of which are in good condition and perfect for walking. One of the best-known trails is the **Byzantine Road,** between Lefkes and Prodromos, a narrow path paved along much of its 4km (2½-mile) length with marble slabs. Begin in Lefkes, as from here the way is mostly downhill. There isn't an easy way to find the beginning of the Byzantine Road among the labyrinthine streets of Lefkes; we suggest starting at the church square, from which point you can see the flagstone-paved road in a valley at the edge of the town, to the west. Having fixed your bearings, plunge into the maze of streets and spiral your way down and to the right. After a 2-minute descent, you emerge into a ravine, with open fields beyond, and a sign indicates the beginning of the Byzantine Road. It's easy going through terraced fields, a leisurely hour's walk to the Marpissa Road, from which point you can catch the bus back to Parikia. Check the schedule and exact pickup point beforehand.

WINDSURFING & SCUBA ★★ The continuous winds on Paros's east coast have made it a favorite destination for windsurfers. Golden Beach has hosted the **Windsurfing World Cup** for the past 17 years. The best months are July and August, but serious windsurfers may want to visit earlier or later in the season to avoid the crowds. The free *Paros Windsurfing Guide* is available at most tourist offices in Parikia or Naoussa; **www.diving-greece.net** is also a good resource. On Golden Beach, the **F2 Windsurfing Center** (℗ **22840/41-878**) has lessons and sponsors the **Windsurfing World Cup.** The **Aegean Diving College** (℗ **22840/43-347;** www.aegeandivingcollege.com) offers scuba instruction; director and marine archaeologist Peter Nikolaides is also connected with the Aegean Center in Parikia. At the port town of **Pounda,** the **Paros Kite Pro Center** (℗ **22840/92-071;** www. paroskite-procenter.com) rents them from 25€ and gives kiteboarding and windsurfing lessons (from 25€ for 1 hr.).

SHOPPING

Market Street in Parikia is the shopping hub of the island, with lots of tempting jewelry, leather, pottery and—as always in Greece—shoe shops. This may not be a nation of foot fetishists, but it certainly is a nation of shoe lovers. The **Jewelry Workshop** (℗ **22840/24-359**) is precisely that, with the work of several local designers. If you're looking to decorate your home, have a look at **Yria Interiors** (℗**22840/24-359;** www.yriaparos.com), and Yvonne von der Decken's shop **Palaio Poleio** ★ (℗ **22840/21-909**), both on Market Street, both with pottery, home furnishings, and some old pieces from Greece and Europe. **Audiophile** (℗ **22840/22-357**) has an extensive collection of CDs of Greek and international music, at prices a bit higher than you might pay in Athens. On the harbor, **InterNews** (℗ **22840/22-513**) sells international newspapers, guidebooks, maps, and some novels.

Several shops that sell local produce, including cheeses, honey, and wine, all merit stars. **Pariana Proionta (Parian Produce)** ★ (℗ **22840/22-181**), run by the Agricultural Collective, is on Manto Mavroyennis Square; **Topika Proionta (Local Produce)** ★ (℗ **22840/24-940**) is on Market Street and **Paktia** (℗ **22840/21-029**) is just off Market Street, just around the corner from the tempting Dodona ice-cream parlor. (I have lost the card with the name of the shop adjacent to Paktia that has the island's most interesting silk-screened T-shirts. Don't worry: you'll spot the shop with the snowy-white T-shirts with scenes of scattered cafe chairs and beach umbrellas, starfish and constellations, flowers and herbs.) Further along the unsignposted street that leads from Market Street to the Cathedral the **Distrato Café** ★ (℗ **22840/24-789**), has its own shop with organic produce from Paros and elsewhere in the Cyclades.

Across the island, in the old part of Naoussa, **Metaxas Gallery** (℃ **22840/52-667**) holds exhibitions of paintings by local artists, which are sometimes for sale; you can also find locally crafted jewelry here. **Hera,** which is just down the lane from the **Naoussa Sweet Shop** (℃ **22840/53-566**), offers local pottery, jewelry, carpets from Greece and Turkey, and fine-arts books of local interest. Owner Hera Papamihail is a talented photographer whose prints are available for purchase. The **kiosk** on the main *plateia* has some international newspapers. **Paria Lexis Bookstore** (℃ **22840/51-121**) offers a selection of travel guides, maps, and novels.

In Lefkes, **Anemi** (℃ **22840/41-182**), by the *kafeneion* on the *plateia*, has hand-loomed and embroidered fabrics. In addition, nuns in several of the island's convents often sell crafts.

Where to Stay

PARIKIA

The port town has three basic hotel zones: **agora** (the market area), **harbor,** and **beach;** alas, all can be very noisy at night. As always in Greece, bring earplugs, in case people walking the streets talk louder than you'd wish after you've gone to bed.

Here are some suggestions for potentially quiet places to stay. In addition to the places listed below, the **Pandrossos** (www.pandrossoshotel.gr; ℃ **22840/22-903**); on a hill overlooking Parikia and the harbor, has a pool and a quiet location. Here's the problem: about half the people who tell me about their stay there were very happy. The others found the location and facilities fine, but the service dreadful. Let me know what you think if you stay here. If you want to be in town and on the beach, the 27-room **Parian Beach** (www.paros-accomodations-gr; ℃ **22840/23-187**) is about a 30-minute walk along the busy harborside road from the ferry dock. Doubles at either place from 100€. Most hotels here offer significant off-season discounts.

Captain Manolis Hotel ★   A tempting flower-covered entrance on Market Street, by the National Bank, leads into a passageway to this small hotel, which renovated its rooms in 2011. Rooms have balconies or terraces, the small lobby is comfy, and friends who have stayed here praise the staff and say that they were astonished at the tranquility of this hotel in the heart of Market Street. When I visited in 2011, my only concern was that, as with all hotels with balconies and terraces opening on a shared courtyard, noise can be a problem if a large party takes over a number of rooms. I should also mention that there have been some recent reports of lax housekeeping.

Market St., Parikia, 84400 Paros. ℃ **22840/21-244.** Fax 22840/25-264. 14 units. From 70€ double. No credit cards. **Amenities:** Breakfast room. *In room:* A/C, TV, fridge, hair dryer, Wi-Fi.

Hotel Dina ★★ 🍃   This is a charming place run by a charming couple. You reach the Dina through a narrow, plant-filled courtyard at the quiet end of Market Street. This is definitely a place to take time to smell the flowers, especially the gardenias in the courtyard. More pension than hotel, half the rooms and bathrooms were completely redone in 2010 (great new showers, reading lights, and some elegant brass bedsteads) and the rest are scheduled to be done in 2011. The room I stayed in was even nicer than I remembered—and I had remembered it as one of the nicest small hotel rooms I had ever been in. Three spacious rooms overlook Market Street; no. 2, with a balcony and brass bed calls out for a honeymoon couple. The balcony in room no. 8 (my favorite) looks onto a quintessentially Greek blue-domed church across a narrow lane; the other rooms face the garden courtyard. Dina Patellis has been the courteous and friendly proprietor for nearly 3 decades, and her personal touch keeps guests coming back year after year. Her husband wrote the excellent *Guide Through Ekatontapiliani,* available in local bookshops.

Market St., Parikia, 84400 Paros. www.hoteldina.com. ℭ **22840/21-325** or 22840/21-345. Fax 22840/23-525. 8 units. 50€–65€ double. No credit cards. Just off Market St., next to the Apollon Restaurant and across from the Pirate Bar. *In room:* A/C, TV, hair dryer, minifridge, Wi-Fi.

SOUTH OF PARIKIA

Yria Hotel Resort ★★ ☺ This resort complex is just the place, if you are traveling with children and want a great pool and beach for them and a spa for you. The beach is about 150m (492 ft.) away from the resort, whose architecture imitates the cluster of whitewashed Cycladic village houses. While not all rooms (most done in soft pastels, some with bright blue and white motifs) have a sea view, the grounds are so nicely landscaped that you won't feel deprived if your room faces inward. If you find the restaurant and bar too crowded, you can let it be known that you would like to be served in a private dining pavilion! The staff has been praised as helpful.

Parasporos, 84400 Paros. www.yriahotel.gr. ℭ **22840/24-154.** Fax 22840/21-167. 60 units. From 300€ double; from 370€ suite; from 550€ maisonette. Rates include full buffet breakfast. AE, DC, MC, V. Closed mid-Nov to Apr. Located 2.5km (1½ miles) south of the port. **Amenities:** Restaurant; bar; concierge; fitness center; freshwater pool; tennis. *In room:* A/C, TV, hair dryer, minibar, Wi-Fi.

NAOUSSA

In addition to the places listed below, you might consider the coyly named **Heaven Naoussa** (www.heaven-naoussa.com; ℭ **22840/51-549**), with four doubles, five suites, and two maisonettes (with shared pool). Doubles run from 120€, suites from 200€, and maisonettes from 1,600€ per week. Rates for rooms and suites, but not villas, include an extensive breakfast buffet. The architecture is, appropriately, Cycladic, the decor is eclectic and stylishly casual, and restaurants and the harbor are steps away. If you're unable to find a room in Naoussa, try **Nissiotissa Tours** (ℭ **22840/51-480**), just off the east (left) side of the main square.

Astir of Paros ★ The most luxurious hotel on the island is built like a self-contained Cycladic village within a garden, with a private beach, 3-hole golf course, pool, tennis court, gym, and a small art gallery. What the Astir does not have is something to make it really memorable. Double rooms are unexceptional, with simple beds, tables, and chairs. The spacious suites have a bit more personality, with armchairs, desks, and attempts at fancy window drapes. Four units are equipped for travelers with disabilities. Produce for the two hotel **restaurants** is grown on a nearby farm; the breakfast buffet (not included in the room rates) features more than 70 items. Some people come here and don't budge; if you want to see something of the island, Astir can arrange car rental.

Kolimbithres Beach, 84401 Paros. www.astirofparos.gr. ℭ **22840/51-976** or 22840/51-707. Fax 22840/51-985. 61 units. 200€–240€ double; 210€–450€ suite. Rates include continental breakfast. AE, DC, MC, V. Closed Oct 20–Easter. West of Naoussa, off the south end of the beach. **Amenities:** Restaurant; bar; concierge; 3-hole golf course; health club; freshwater pool; tennis; 4 rooms for those w/limited mobility. *In room:* A/C, TV/DVD, hair dryer, minibar, Wi-Fi.

Hotel Petres ★★ Clea and Sotiris Hatzinikolakis combine warm hospitality with helpful efficiency to meet the needs of their guests (they have many repeat guests from Germany and France). The large, comfortable rooms, with private terraces or balconies, cluster around the big pool. Throughout, antiques and paintings, many done by Clea herself, give the Petres the charm and comfort so sadly lacking in most Greek hotels. The extensive, inventive, and delectable buffet breakfast/brunch, served from

9 to 11:30am, may well be the highlight of your stay on Paros. Dinner is available on request, and most Saturdays in summer there's a barbecue at the poolside grill. The view is of farm fields, with the sea in the distance; if you want to get into Naoussa, the hotel offers a frequent, free minibus shuttle. The only drawback is that the temptation to relax by the pool may entice you to put off sightseeing until *aurio* (tomorrow).

Naoussa, 84401 Paros. www.petres.gr. © **22840/52-467**. Fax 22840/52-759. 16 units. From 125€ double. Rates vary depending on location and length of stay and include extensive buffet breakfast. DC, MC, V. Closed Nov–Mar. 3km (5 miles) from town. **Amenities:** Breakfast room/bar; airport/port pickup; Jacuzzi; freshwater pool; sauna; tennis; Wi-Fi. *In room:* A/C, TV, hair dryer, minibar.

LEFKES

The Lefkes Village Hotel is quite special, but if it is full when you visit, or if you want to spend less, the simple 14-unit **Pantheon** (© **22840/41-646**) is perfectly decent and a lot cheaper (doubles from 65€).

Lefkes Village Hotel ★★★ This handsome hotel out on the island, some 10km (6 miles) from Parikia, is designed to look like a small island village. It helps that Lefkes is probably the most charming inland village on the island. The spectacular views reach across the countryside to the sea. The pool is so nice that you may not mind not being on the sea. Guest rooms are light and bright, with good bathrooms; some have balconies with wonderful views. In addition, there's a small Museum of Popular Aegean Culture and a winery. This is a popular place for wedding receptions; some summer weekends, wedding parties take over the entire hotel, which means that you may listen to music, dancing, and toasts, until dawn.

P.O. Box 71, Lefkes Village, 84400 Paros. www.lefkesvillage.gr. © **22840/41-827** or 210/251-6497. Fax 2284/41-0827. 25 units. 200€–210€ double. MC, V. Rates include buffet breakfast. **Amenities:** Restaurant; bar; Jacuzzi; freshwater pool; Wi-Fi. *In room:* A/C, TV, hair dryer, minibar, Wi-Fi.

Where to Eat

A favorite standby on the harbor, below the kastro and especially nice at sunset time, **To Spitiko** (© **22840/24-956**) promises to serve "tasty answers to hungry questions"—just what you'd expect from a place whose name means home cooking; 20€ would let you eat lots here.

In addition to the places listed below, I want to mention several that were not yet open when I visited Parikia in the late spring of 2011. They are all places for which I have either good memories or good reports. On Market Street, as it bends toward the Ekatondapiliani Cathedral at the Dodona cafe, you'll find **Daphne** (© **22840/22-575**); **Tamarisko** (© **22840/24-689**) is just off Market Street. Both have nice gardens and excellent food. Daphne has elegant Mediterranean cuisine, while Tamarisko has a lighter touch (more salads and rice dishes). On the continuation of Market Street into town (as opposed to where it bends toward the Ekatondapiliani), **Franca Scala** (© **22840/24-407**) has a great rooftop terrace, possibly the best place in town for people watching. If I were sitting there with a glass of white wine, I might toy with an order of smoked salmon rolls with eggplant mousse. Dinner at Daphne, Tamarisko, or Franco Scala could run as little as 20€ or easily twice that, depending on your choices.

PARIKIA

Apollon Garden ★ GREEK THE PLACE TO GO, THE PLACE TO BE SEEN says the business card, and while that may be true, this is also a place with a lovely garden with flowers and palm trees and excellent food. You will find all the Greek standards here—stuffed vegetables in season, grills, stews—and the quality is consistently good.

Market St., Parikia. ✆ **22840/21-875.** Main courses 8€–20€. No credit cards. Daily 7pm–midnight. On Market St., just past the HOTEL DINA sign. Sometimes closed in winter.

Dionysos ★★ GREEK   The first thing you notice here is the palm tree that goes up and up and is draped with the fiery orange flowers of a trumpet vine. There's a nice garden and terrific food that is both elegant and hearty: pork fillet stuffed with sundried tomatoes, fresh basil and asparagus and duck breast with mango sauce are often on the menu, as well as a house favorite, spaghetti with lobster. Save room for dessert: and then try to decide between the chocolate fondant and the chocolate tiramisu.

Market St., Parikia. ✆ **22840/25-194.** Main courses 15€–40€. No credit cards. Daily in season 11am–3pm and 6pm–1am. Usually closed in winter.

Distrato ★★ GREEK/INTERNATIONAL   On the street that runs from the cathedral to Market Street, beneath the spreading branches of a ficus tree, this is as nice a place as any to spend an hour or two; some habitués seem to start the day with a coffee and croissant here and end it with wine and one of the tasty spaghettis. Distrato serves crepes, sandwiches, ice creams, pasta dishes, and inventive salads. If you're still hungry, the shop stocks nicely packaged organic Greek produce. If there are no tables at Distrato, try **Symposio,** a few steps away, with tasty snacks (great mozzarella and tomato baguette sandwich), but no shady tree.

Paralia. ✆ **22840/22-311.** Snacks and main courses 8€–15€. No credit cards. Daily 10am–midnight. Look for the big ficus tree as you walk from the cathedral to Market St.

Levantis ★★ GREEK/INTERNATIONAL   This place gets high praise for its offbeat dishes that combine local produce with international ingredients. Where else on the island will you find Thai dishes alongside stuffed eggplant? Owner-chef George Mavridis likes to cook and likes to talk food, so you can enjoy what you eat while learning about the kitchen. His daily specials are an indication of how much he enjoys trying out new dishes. The desserts are well worth saving room for, especially if you're a chocoholic. If you're too full for dessert, you can relax and enjoy the pleasant garden.

Paralia, on Market St. ✆ **22840/23-613.** Main courses 8€–22€. AE, V. Daily 7pm–midnight. Closed Nov–Easter.

Porphyra ★★ GREEK/FISH   Locals say Porphyra (overlooking the ancient Roman cemetery and the harbor) serves the best fish in town. It's small, and the nondescript, utilitarian service and decor are typical of your average taverna. The difference here is that the owner cultivates the shellfish himself, resulting in exceptional mussels *saganaki* (mussels cooked with tomato, feta, and wine) and a great fish soup. The *tzatziki* (cucumber-yogurt dip) and other traditional cold appetizers are also very good. The fish is fresh, and offerings vary with the season. The same owners operate the nearby **Art Café;** drinks and snacks are served at the small gallery and cafe, which sometimes features live music.

Paralia. ✆ **22840/22-693.** Main courses 8€–20€; fish priced by the kilo. AE, MC, V. Daily 6:30pm–midnight. Closed Jan–Feb. Past the cathedral, btw. the pier and the post office, just back from the waterfront, about a 10-min. walk from Market St.

NAOUSSA

Naoussa's restaurants are either harborside, or tucked away in town. Your best way to find the in-town restaurants is to ask. Streets are winding and street signs are virtually nonexistent. Don't worry: You'll get lost, but you'll find what you're looking for, often with the help of gaggles of giggling school children.

Barbarossa Ouzeri ★ GREEK/MEZEDES   This longtime local ouzeri is right on the port. Wind-burned fishermen and gaggles of chic Athenians sit for hours nursing their milky ouzo in water and their miniportions of grilled octopus and olives. If you want more of a meal, this is a fine fish restaurant. If you wonder what language the staff here is speaking, it's often Arabic or Russian—more evidence that the world is indeed becoming a global village.

Naoussa waterfront. ℰ **22840/51-391.** *Mezedes* 6€–15€. Fish priced by the kilo. No credit cards. Daily 1pm–1am.

Le Sud ★ GREEK/INTERNATIONAL   I happened to be on Paros when this small place opened in 2003. I must admit, I wondered if a new restaurant with serious French-influenced cuisine could lure diners away from the popular harborside tavernas. Le Sud, with its charming garden, has been a great success. There's often terrine of vegetables, bream with ginger, lamb with lemon and cardamom confit, and blinis. In short, although all the ingredients are fresh and almost all are local, the cuisine is somewhat eclectic. Try to reserve one of the handful of tables in the small garden; it's a good idea to call in advance in summer.

Off the harbor. ℰ **22840/51-547.** Main courses 15€–25€. No credit cards. Daily 7pm–midnight. About 200m (656 ft.) back from the port.

Mitsi's ★★ GREEK/SEAFOOD   This is the sort of seafood taverna you dream about finding. We stopped at this little place on the beach beyond the harbor one evening just to have an ouzo and watch the sun set—and left 4 hours later after a number of ouzos and a leisurely dinner of fresh greens, fresh fish, and something tasty that the *patron* called "grandmother's stew." When we sat down, we were the only customers; by the time we left, every table was taken, about half by locals, half by visitors. The retsina wine, which the engaging owner (Mitsi himself) makes, is terrific.

Harborside. ℰ **22840/51-302.** Main courses 8€–15€; fish priced by the kilo. No credit cards. Daily 7pm–midnight.

Papadakis ★ INNOVATIVE GREEK   Fresh fish is one of the specialties here, but be sure not to rush to the main course—the appetizers are admirable: The *tzatziki* with dill is delicious and refreshingly different; the traditionally prepared *melitzanosalata* (a cold eggplant salad, usually made with lots of garlic) is redolent of wood-smoked eggplant. The desserts are worth sampling, especially *kataifi ekmek,* a confection conjured from honey, walnuts, cinnamon, custard, and cream.

Naoussa waterfront. ℰ **22840/51-047.** Reservations recommended. Main courses 10€–30€. AE, V. Daily 7:30pm–midnight.

Pervolaria ★ GREEK/CONTINENTAL   There's something for everyone here. The restaurant is set in a garden, lush with geraniums and grapevines, behind a white stucco house decorated with local ceramics. There's pasta and pizza, and *schnitzel a la chef* (veal in cream sauce with tomatoes and basil). If you want to eat Greek, order the souvlaki and varied appetizers' special.

Off the harbor. ℰ **22840/51-598.** Main courses 7€–15€. MC, V. Daily 7pm–midnight. About 100m (328 ft.) back from the port.

Paros After Dark

Look for posters announcing concerts and art exhibits and check out the listings in the current issue of the quarterly *Paros Life* (2€). If you're on Paros in July and like jazz, check to see if the Greek International Jazz Summer School

Beware the *Bomba*

Several places on the strip in Parikia offer very cheap drinks or "buy one, get one free." What you'll get, most likely, is locally brewed alcohol that the locals call *bomba*. This speakeasy brew is made privately and often illegally. It's a quick way to get drunk—and to feel awful after you get sober.

(www.innovaros.com) is meeting and giving performances **Music-Dance Naoussa Paros** (*©* 22840/52-284; www.parosweb.com) often performs Greek dances; the group wears costumes and is quite good.

As on all the islands, what's a hot place this year is often forgotten by next year. You'll sense what the hot places are (they're the ones that are packed with customers and amplifiers). Here are a few durable favorites.

Just behind the windmill in Parikia is a local landmark, **Port Cafe,** a basic *kafenion* lit by bare incandescent bulbs and filled day and night with tourists waiting for a ferry, bus, taxi, or fellow traveler. The cafe serves coffee, pastry, and drinks; it's a good place for casual conversation.

Pebbles Bar ★ often has classical music and good jazz; as does the **Pirate Bar** ★, a few doors from Hotel Dina in the agora. Both are very congenial places, as popular with Greeks as with foreign visitors. **Alexandros,** in a restored windmill by the harbor, is awfully attractive and a perfect spot to enjoy being on an island, by the harbor, watching the passing scene. In Naoussa, check out **Agosta** or **Café del Mar** by the harbor or for an after-dinner drink. If you want to watch the sun rise after you see it set, head along the harbor to where the fishing boats are moored, and **Lindardo's** often goes all night. You'll find the serious discos on the outskirts of town and by the bus station (**Vareladikos,** by the bus station, often goes all night).

NAXOS ★★

191km (103 nautical miles) SE of Piraeus

Unlike many of its neighbors, whose prosperity depends on the summer tourist season, green, fertile Naxos is largely self-sufficient. This is the largest of the Cyclades, with wonderful groves of olives and fruit trees, wheat fields, and good grazing land for the cows, sheep, and goats whose milk goes into a wide variety of Naxian cheeses. Visitors here will find lots of blessings to count: for starters, there are rolling green hills and valleys with clusters of Byzantine churches, medieval towers, and villages with handsome neoclassical houses. There are long sand beaches, and a capital that has grown up in and around its own massive Venetian castle in the island's capital, Hora.

The Venetians ruled Naxos from 1207 until it fell to the Turks in 1566. The influence of **Venetian architecture** is obvious in Hora's kastro, some handsome mansions in Hora, and many of the *piryi* (fortified towers) that punctuate the hillsides. The presence on the island of descendants of the Venetians means that Naxos has both Catholic and Orthodox churches—sometimes side by side and even sharing a central wall, as at the **Bellonia Tower** (p. 390). Yet the glory of Naxos's church architecture is the abundance of small **Byzantine chapels,** many of which contain exceptional frescoes dating from the 9th to the 13th centuries. These chapels escaped destruction by Naxos's various overlords and remain to charm visitors today—if, that is, you can find them. Many are poorly signposted and elusive, which means that you will feel triumphant when you track them down. As always, Paul Hetherington's *Greek Islands* is an invaluable guide to the medieval and Byzantine monuments.

The island's mountain villages, on the lower slopes of Mount Zas, the highest mountain in the Cyclades, preserve the rhythms of agrarian life. The lush—for Greece—area known as the **Tragea** has plains of olive trees, upland valleys, and a cluster of villages, Venetian towers, and Hellenistic watchtowers. Just about everybody's favorite village is **Apiranthos,** with some marble-paved streets, a particularly handsome Venetian tower, and small shaded *plateias.*

The airport, good interisland ferry service, and high-speed ferries make Naxos easy to visit. New hotels have appeared in the port, and more hotels cluster on island beaches—which are among the best in the Cyclades. In short, tourism has arrived—but, as yet, in a way that makes visiting here easy and pleasurable. As always, it is handy to have a car, although the local bus service is good, if leisurely. If you just want to see Naxos town, a day will do you, but longer will let the charms of the little streets in the old fortress sink in. And, as you would expect of the largest of the Cyclades, there's lots to see out on the island. Unfortunately, some of what you see out on the island may still show signs of damage from severe summer forest fires in 2009.

Essentials

GETTING THERE By Plane The website of Athens International Airport, **www.aia.gr,** is a useful resource for domestic airline schedules. **Olympic Air** (✆ **810/114-4444** and 210/966-6666, official Greek phone numbers that are rarely answered; www.olympicair.com) offers daily flights between Athens and the Santorini airport Monolithos (✆ **22860/31-525**), which also receives European charters. **Aegean Airlines** (✆ **810/112-0000;** www.aegeanair.com) also has several flights daily between Athens and Naxos, Santorini. A bus meets most flights and takes passengers into Naxos town (2€).

By Boat The websites **www.gtp.gr** and **www.openseas.gr** are useful resources for ferry schedules. From Piraeus, there is at least one daily ferry (6 hr.) and one daily high-speed ferry (4 hr.). Check schedules at the Athens **GNTO** (✆ **210/870-0000;** www.gnto.gr), the **Piraeus Port Authority** (✆ **210/451-1311,** -1440, or -1441), or **Naxos Port Authority** (✆ **22850/22-300**). Boats are notoriously late and/or early; your travel or ticket agent will give you an *estimate* of times involved in the following journeys. There is at least a once-daily ferry connection with Ios, Mykonos, Paros, and Santorini. There is ferry connection several times weekly by high-speed ferry or hydrofoil with Siros, Tinos, and Samos, and somewhat less frequently with Sifnos and with Folegandros. For ferry tickets, try **Zas Travel** (✆ **22850/23-330**), on the *paralia* opposite the ferry pier.

VISITOR INFORMATION The privately operated **Naxos Tourist Information Center** (✆ **22850/22-993;** fax 22850/25-200), across the plaza from the ferry pier, is the most reliable source of information and help. (Don't confuse it with the small office on the pier itself, which is often closed.) The center, run by the owner of the **Chateau Zevgoli** (p. 395) provides ferry information; books charter flights between various European airports and Athens, accommodations, cars, and mopeds; arranges excursions; sells maps; exchanges money; holds luggage; assists with phone calls; and provides 2-hour laundry service.

Naxos has a helpful website, **www.naxosnow.com,** with maps and a photo tour of the island.

If you enjoy map reading, get a good map as soon as possible, as Hora (Naxos town) is old, large, and complex, with a permanent population of more than 3,000. The free *Summer Naxos* magazine has the best map of the city. Map or no map, prepare to get lost at least once in the little streets in and around the kastro. The *Harms-Verlag Naxos* is the best map of the island, but it's pricey at 7€. John Freely's *Naxos* (1976) remains delightful and helpful.

GETTING AROUND   By Bus   The bus station is on the harbor; bus schedules are often posted at the station, and free schedules are sometimes available. Regular bus service is offered throughout most of the island two or three times a day, more frequently to major destinations. In summer, there's service every 30 minutes to the nearby south-coast beaches at Ayios Prokopios and Ayia Anna. A popular day trip is to Apollonas, near the northern tip. In summer, the competition for seats on this route can be fierce, so get to the station well ahead of time.

In addition to the public buses, **Zas Travel** (*©* 22850/23-300) offers day excursions around the island in season, usually from 25€.

By Bicycle & Moped   Moto Naxos (*©* 22850/23-420), on Protodikiou Square, south of the *paralia,* has the best mountain bikes as well as mopeds for rent. A basic bike is about 15€ per day. For a moped, expect to pay from 30€ per day. Naxos has some major inclines that require a strong motor and good brakes, so a large bike (80cc or greater) is recommended (as is checking the brakes before you set off).

By Car   It's a good idea to inquire first about car rental at the Naxos Tourist Information Center (see "Visitor Information," above), which usually has the best deals. Car is the ideal mode of transport on this large island, and most travel agencies in Naxos town rent them, including the oddly named **Naxos Vision** (*©* **22850/26-2000;** www.naxosvision.com), **AutoTour** (*©* **22850/25-480**), **Auto Naxos** (*©* **22850/23-420**), and **Palladium** (*©* **22850/26-200**).

By Taxi   The taxi station (*©* 22850/22-444) is at the port. Taxi fares are slated to go up in 2012, but in 2011, a taxi trip within Naxos town cost around 4€. The fare to Ayia Anna Beach was about 8€; to the inland village of Apiranthos, 20€.

FAST FACTS   Commercial Bank, on the *paralia,* has an ATM. It and other banks are open Monday through Thursday from 8am to 2pm, Friday from 8am to 1:30pm. Naxos has a good 24-hour **health center** (*©* 22850/23-333) just outside Hora on the left off Papavasiliou, the main street off the port. The **police** (*©* 22850/22-100) are beyond Protodikiou Square, by the Galaxy Hotel. The **telephone office (OTE)** is at the port's south end; summer hours are daily from 7:30am to 2pm. The **post office** is south of the OTE by the basketball court; it's opposite the court on the left, on the second floor (Mon–Fri 8am–2pm).

The Top Attractions in Hora ★★

Kastro is the name both for the 13th-century Venetian kastro (castle), which is Hora's greatest treasure, and also for the neighborhood around it where the Venetian nobility lived from the 13th to the 16th century. You should allow yourself at least several hours to explore the Kastro area of Hora—preferably by meandering, getting a bit lost, and then being pleasantly surprised at the architectural treasures (and nice little cafes) that you happen upon. If you take in Kastro's two museums, it's nice to have at least half a day here. To get to Kastro, you have to climb up from the **harbor,** through **Bourgo,** Hora's lower town. This route goes from harborside, through Bourgo, to Kastro. This is a pleasant way to spend a day—or, if pressed, several hours.

The Portara and Myrditiotissa ★★   If you come here by sea, you'll see two of Naxos's most famous monuments as you sail into the harbor: the whitewashed **Myrditiotissa** chapel, on an islet off the quay, and the **Portara (Great Door),** connected

What's in a Name?

There are many churches in Greece called **Panagia Zoodochos Pigi** (Virgin of the Life-Giving Spring). Here, the name is especially appropriate: The church was built near the ancient Nymphaeum (fountain house). Much of the handsome marble in the cathedral was pillaged from ancient buildings both on Naxos and from neighboring islands, including Delos. Since Venetian times, this neighborhood has been known as Fontana, because of the spring that still flows here.

to the quayside by a causeway. The Myrditiotissa was built around 1207 by the Venetian Marco Sanudo, ruler of the Venetian Duchy of the Archipelago and a nephew of the doge of Venice. Sanudo also built much of the kastro (see below). The massive Portara entrance door is all that remains of a Temple of Apollo. A 6th-century tyrant, Lygdamis, began the temple; when he died, construction stopped and demolition began. Over the centuries, most of the temple was carted away to build other monuments and buildings, including parts of the Catholic and Orthodox cathedrals and much of the kastro. Fortunately, the massive posts and lintel of the Portara were too heavy. Each of the four surviving blocks weighs about 20 tons.

Some scholars have thought that this temple was dedicated to the god Dionysos, who spent some time in his youth on Naxos dallying with local nymphs. Many locals believed that this was the palace of Ariadne, the Cretan princess who taught Theseus the mysteries of the labyrinth and helped him to slay the Minotaur. Her reward was to be abandoned here by Theseus as he sailed back to Athens, an event commemorated by Strauss in his opera *Ariadne auf Naxos*. Dionysos took pity on the discarded princess and married her, which gave rise to the nice legend that this great door was the entrance to the bridal palace. Now, most scholars think that the temple was dedicated to Apollo, in part because of a brief reference in the Delian Hymns and in part because it directly faces Delos, Apollo's birthplace.

One of the nicest ways to see the Portara is at sunset, from a harborside cafe. If you feel like a swim, join the locals swimming off the rocks below the temple door.

Panagia Zoodochos Pigi Cathedral (Mitropolis) and Mitropolis Site Museum ★ As is so often the case in Greece, the modern town sits atop successive ancient settlements. Excavations undertaken around the Panagia Zoodochos Pigi Cathedral from 1982 to 1985 revealed a layered history of continuous occupation here from Mycenaean times to the present, with significant remains of the classical agora and the later Roman city. The cathedral is often locked; frustratingly, when I have seen a priest unlock a side door and go in, he has assured me that the cathedral is shut—and slammed the door in my face! The Mitropolis museum, in the square facing the cathedral, preserves the open space of the square while providing access to a segment of the archaeological site below. You'll want to spend at least half an hour here.

Hora. ✆ **22850/24-151.** Free admission. Tues–Sun 8am–2:30pm. Turn in from the *paralia* at Zas Travel and continue about 100m (328 ft.) until you see the Mitropolis Cathedral Sq. on your right.

Bourgo/Kastro/Archaeological Museum/Venetian Museum ★★★ In Venetian times, the grandees lived at the top of the hill, in Kastro, and the Greeks lived down the hill, in Bourgo. To get to the kastro, wend your way up through Bourgo, along one of the streets that snakes uphill. There's also a signposted lane leading up from the harborside, but almost any street going uphill will get you there, although perhaps not directly to one of the entrances through the kastro's thick walls.

The kastro had three main entryways, of which the most impressive today is the north entry, known as the **Trani Porta (Strong Gate),** signposted on Apollon Street. This narrow marble arched threshold marks the transition from the commercial bustle of Bourgo to the kastro's medieval world. Look for the incision on the right column of the arch, which marks the length of a Venetian yard, and was used to measure the cloth brought here for aristocratic Venetian ladies to consider purchasing. Exploring the kastro's byways, it's hard not to wish to be able to levitate up over the lofty walls and have a look inside one of these Venetian mansions, with their walled gardens and coats of arms carved over doorways. Fortunately, one typical aristocratic Venetian house, the 800-year-old Della Roca family home, just inside the Trani Porta, is open to the public. The 40-minute tour, offered in English and Greek, of the **Domus Venetian Museum** (✆ 22850/22-387; www.naxosfestival.com) is a wonderful chance to get an inside look at one of the surviving great Venetian homes; you'll see and learn about the reception rooms, chapel, and vaults, and end in a small shop with local produce and handicrafts A wide variety of concerts and Greek dance performances take place in the garden here during each summer's **Domus Naxos Festival** (✆ 22850/22-387; www.naxosfestival.com). Tours are not given when there is an evening concert.

At the center of the kastro is the perhaps-too-heavily restored 13th-century **Catholic cathedral,** with its brilliant marble facade. To the right, behind the cathedral, is the French School of Commerce and the former **Ursuline Convent and School,** where young ladies of the Venetian aristocracy were educated. The nearby French School has housed schools run by several religious orders, and among its more famous students was the (famous irreligious) Cretan writer Nikos Kazantzakis, who studied here in 1896. The school now houses the **Archaeological Museum ★.** One of the highlights here is the large group of the rare white marble Cycladic figurines. These are the often violin-shaped marble figurines (dating from as long ago as 3000 B.C.) whose stark outlines some have compared to figures painted by Modigliani. The museum also has an extensive collection of late-Mycenaean-period (1400 B.C.–1100 B.C.) pottery found near Grotta, a district in the northern part of Hora, including vessels with the octopus motif that still appears in local art. The museum has lousy lighting in many galleries, but a great view from its terrace and balconies to the hills of Naxos.

Hora. Archaeological Museum: ✆ **22850/22-725.** Admission 3€. Tues–Sun 8am–3pm; sometimes open evenings in summer. Venetian Museum: ✆ **22850/22-387.** Admission and tour 6€. Daily 10am–3pm and 6–9pm.

The Top Attractions Out on the Island

People who know Greece well often think that Naxos is both the most beautiful of the Cyclades and the nicest to visit—and revisit. The island has a magical landscape,

---

Reserve Early for the Domus Naxos Festival

Performances here are very popular and often sold out, as I recently found out to my sorrow. Naxos is now getting enough tour groups that all the tickets for a performance can be gobbled up well before a concert. If you want a ticket, try to book in advance (www. naxosfestival.com).

with somewhat mysterious valleys, fertile fields, and even the highest mountain in the Cyclades. That's **Mount Zas,** associated in antiquity with Zeus, who felt at home on lofty eminences. If you climb Mount Zas, you'll find out just how lofty it is. Naxos also has wonderful old chapels, some of the best tucked away in those valleys, absurdly picturesque villages, and—let's not mince words—often crowded beaches. You could spend a lifetime exploring this island. Here are just a few suggestions.

ANCIENT & MEDIEVAL MONUMENTS

In addition to the Temple of Demeter, Naxos has two unfinished *kouroi* (monumental statues of men) that are well worth seeing, in villages that are themselves worth seeing. See "The Villages," below, for the kouros of Apollonas and the kouros of Flerio.

Sangri and the Temple of Demeter ★

The village of Sangri is an agglomeration of several villages in a valley below Mount Profitias Elias. There's a deserted 16th-century monastery, **Timios Stavros,** on the mountain's lower slopes and the remains of a 13th-century Venetian kastro on its summit. The temple of Demeter is signposted (5km/3 miles) out of Stavri. Until about 10 years ago, the temple, built in the 6th century B.C., was in a state of complete ruin; it had been partially dismantled in the 6th century A.D. to build a chapel on the site, and what was left was plundered over the years. Then it was discovered that nearly all the pieces of the original temple were on the site, either buried or integrated into the chapel. A long process of reconstruction began. Most of the work has been completed, and it's possible to see the basic form of the temple—one of the few known square-plan temples. There's also a small site museum, often irritatingly closed.

Temple of Demeter at Ano Sangri. Free admission. Depart from Hora on the road to Filoti, and after about 10km (6 miles), turn onto the signposted road to Ano Sangri and the Temple of Demeter. From here it's another 3.5km (2 miles) to the temple, primarily on dirt roads (major turns are signposted).

THE BELLONIA, FRANGOPOULOS, ANGELOPOULOS & HIMARROS TOWERS ★

The Naxian countryside is dotted with the towers (some defensive, some dwellings) that the Venetians built here. If you visit island villages, you'll inevitably see some of the towers, such as the 17th-century Frangopoulos tower in the hamlet of Chalki, some 17km (10 miles) south of Hora. The easiest to see from Hora is the Bellonia, just 5km (3 miles) south of town, outside the village of Galando. The tower, once the residence of the Catholic archbishop of Naxos, is privately owned, but you can get a good look at the exterior without making the owners feel that they are under attack. The chapel beside the tower is really two chapels: one Catholic, one Orthodox; the arch between the chapels rests on an ancient column capital. About 10km (6 miles) north of Chora, a track road leads to the **Monastery of Our Lady Upsilotera** (Angelopoulos's Castle). This 17th-century fortified building has a small sign giving its open hours and is usually closed. There are sometimes turkeys wandering around the grounds.

Lovers of Hellenistic fortifications and of hiking may wish to see the 20m-tall (45-ft.) Hellenistic Himaros tower, outside the hamlet of Filoti; the tower is signposted in Filoti as Pirgos Himarou, but ask for supplementary directions locally and allow at least 3 hours to hike there and back from Filoti.

BYZANTINE CHURCHES ★★

You can easily spend a week seeing the Byzantine churches of Naxos, or you can see the handful mentioned below in a day. Getting to each one involves at least some walking and some luck: In order to see the interiors, you'll have to have the luck to find the caretaker. The churches are kept locked, due to increasing theft, although the caretaker often makes an early morning or early evening visit.

The remarkable numbers of small Byzantine chapels on Naxos mostly date from the 9th to the 15th centuries, many in or near some of the island's loveliest villages (see below). The prosperity of Naxos, during this period of Byzantine and Venetian rule, meant that wealthy patrons funded elaborate frescoes, many of which can still be seen on the interior walls of the chapels. Restoration has revealed multiple layers of frescoes and, whenever possible, the more recent ones have been removed intact during the process of revealing the initial paintings. Several frescoes removed in this way from the churches of Naxos can be seen at the Byzantine Museum in Athens. Anyone with an interest in Byzantine churches here and elsewhere would enjoy Paul Hetherington's *The Greek Islands: Guide to the Byzantine and Medieval Buildings and Their Art.*

Just south of Moni (23km/14 miles east of Hora), near the middle of the island, is the important 7th-century monastery of **Panagia Drossiani (Our Lady of Refreshment)** ★, which contains some of the finest—and oldest, dating from the 7th century—frescoes on Naxos (St. George and his dragon are easy to spot). Locals believe the icon of the Virgin ended a severe drought on the island shortly after the frescoes were painted. The church, with its huddled arched apses and domes, is all that survives of what we are told was an extensive monastery; what an appealing place for a contemplative life! Visits are allowed at all hours during the day; when the door is locked, ring the church bell to summon the caretaker (remember to dress appropriately). To get here, drive about 1km (½ mile) south from Moni and look for the low, gray, rounded form of the church on your left. Restoration work was going on in 2009, and one hopes that this does not end up among the many overly restored and tidied-up monuments of Greece.

About 8km (5 miles) from Hora along the road to Sangri, you'll see a sign on the left for the 8th-century Byzantine cathedral of **Ayios Mamas,** which fell into disrepair during the Venetian occupation but has recently been partly restored. The **view** from this charming church alone: *vaut le voyage!* Sangri (the Greek contraction of Sainte Croix) today is made up of three villages, and includes the ruins of a medieval castle. The church of Ayios Nikolaos, which dates to the 13th century, has well-preserved frescoes, with a lovely figure of the personified River Jordan. To view them, ask around to find out which villager has the keys.

THE VILLAGES ★★

Many of the nicest villages and churches are in the lush **Tragaea Valley** ★ at the center of the island. Each village is tempting, and you can easily spend several days, or several years, exploring them. The bus between Hora and Apollonas makes stops at each of the villages mentioned below, but you'll have considerably more freedom if you rent a car. You'll find cafes at all the villages, and restaurants in most.

Some Tragaea Valley Villages

The Tragaea is sometimes called a "little Mistra," which I find misleading. First, the Tragea is spread out across a good deal of central Naxos, unlike Byzantine Mistra in the Peloponnese, which is built on one steep hill. Secondly, Mistra's churches are the magnificent products of a wealthy center of the empire, all within walking distance of the ruler's palace. The Byzantine chapels of the Tragaea are largely appealing because they were built by locals in small villages between the 7th and 15th centuries. The Tragaea is green and charming, with appealing town squares in Halki and Filoti.

Halki, 16km (10 miles) from Hora, has a lovely central square shaded by a magnificent plane tree. Side streets have some grand 19th-century neoclassical homes. The 11th-century white church with the red-tiled roof, **Panagia Protothronos (Our Lady Before the Throne),** has well-preserved frescoes and is sometimes open in the morning. Turn right to reach the **Frankopoulos (Grazia) Tower.** The name is Frankish, but it was originally Byzantine; a marble crest on the tower indicates 1742, when it was renovated by the Venetians. Climb the steps for an excellent view of Halki and across to Filoti, one of the island's largest inland villages.

The brilliant white houses of **Filoti,** 2km (1 mile) up the road from Halki, elegantly drape the lower slopes of **Mount Zas,** the highest peak in the Cyclades. This is the largest town in the Tragaea, and the center of town life is the main square, shaded like Halki's square by a massive plane tree. There's a *kafenion* at the center of the square and two tavernas within 50m (164 ft.). In the town's center, the church of **Kimisis tis Theotokou (Assumption of the Mother of God)** has a lovely marble iconostasis and a Venetian tower. In the hamlet of Chalki, which has some wonderful neoclassical mansions and a shady *plateia,* the **Panagia Protothrone,** signposted down a pleasantly winding country path, has 13th-century frescoes and is usually open mornings.

Apiranthos ★, 10km (6 miles) beyond Filoti, the most enchanting of the mountain villages, is remarkable in that many of its buildings, streets, and even domestic walls are built of the brilliant white Naxos marble, others of a golden-hued local stone. Many of the narrow lanes are covered with arches that join houses. The people of Apiranthos were originally from Crete; they fled their homes during a time of Turkish oppression. Be sure to visit **Taverna Lefteris,** the excellent cafe/restaurant just off the main square; day tours of the island often stop here, so you may want to eat early or late. If you have time, have a look in the small folk museum signposted on the main square; it keeps irregular hours, but has some great old photos, farm implements, costumes, and a sweet wooden cradle. There's also a small archaeological museum that's sometimes open.

The Villages with the *Kouroi* ★

Apollon, at the northern tip of the island (54km/33 miles from Hora), is a small fishing village on the verge of becoming a wannabe resort. It has a sand cove, a pebbled beach, plenty of places to eat (tour groups come here to see the *kouroi*), rooms to let, and a few hotels. From the town, you can drive or take the path that leads about 1km (½ mile) south to the famous **kouros** (a monumental statue of a nude young man). The *kouros,* about 10m tall (33 ft.), was begun in the 7th century B.C. and abandoned, probably because the stone cracked during carving. Some archaeologists believe the statue was meant for the nearby temple of Apollo, but the *kouros's* beard suggests that it may be Dionysos.

Naxos's other *kouros* is in the village of **Flerio** (also known as Melanes), about 7km (4 miles) east of Naxos town. The 8m (26-ft.), probably 6th-century-B.C., *kouros* lies abandoned as though asleep in a lovely garden. Both *kouroi* sites are open to the public and free; in Flerio you can sip refreshments (including the local *kitron,* a lemon liqueur) served at the cafe run by the family that owns the garden and cares for the *kouros.* When you visit the National Museum in Athens, you can view a number of successfully completed *kouroi* statues.

BEACHES ★★

Naxos has the longest and some of the best beaches in the Cyclades, although you wouldn't know it from crowded **Ayios Yeoryios** beach just south of Hora.

Walking Tours of Naxos

If you're going to spend some time on the island, and want to explore on foot, try to pick up a copy of Christian Ucke's excellent guide, *Walking Tours on Naxos.* You can take an island bus to reach most of the start and finish points for the walks. It's available for 15€ at **Naxos Tourist Information Center** on the *paralia.* As with all off-the-beaten-track walks, be equipped with water, a hat, good shoes, sunblock, a map, a compass—and a good sense of direction.

Windsurfing equipment and lessons are available at Ayios Yeoryios from Naxos Surf Club (© **22850/29-170**). **Ayios Prokopios,** just beyond Ayios Yeorgios, is another sand beach, some of which is now dominated by the new Lagos Mare Hotel (see "Where to Stay," below). You can rent windsurfing gear at **Plaka Beach,** south of Ayios Prokopios, from **Plaka Watersports** (© **22850/41-264**). Continuing south, **Kastraki Beach** is 7km (4½ miles) long and has won awards for its clean waters.

SHOPPING

Hora is a fine place for shopping, both for value and variety. **Zoom** (© **22850/23-675**), on the waterfront, is the place to head for books and magazines. To the right and up from the entrance to the Old Market is **Techni** ★ (© **22850/24-767**), which has two shops within 20m (66 ft.) of each other. The first shop contains a good array of silver jewelry at fair prices; farther along the street, the second and more interesting of the two features textiles, many hand-woven (including some antiques) by island women. Nearby, **Loom** (© **22850/25-531**), as its name suggests, has hand-woven fabrics and garments.

On the *paralia,* next to Grotta Tours, is tiny **Galini** (© **22850/24-785**), with a collection of local ceramics. Also on the *paralia,* the venerable **Promponas Wines** (© **22850/22-258**) has been here since 1915; the local *kitron* liqueur is a house specialty, along with a wide variety of Naxian wines. If you want something to eat with your wine, head along the *paralia* to the OTE, turn left on the main inland street, Papavasiliou, and proceed up the left side of the street until your nose leads you into **Tirokomika Proïonda Naxou** ★ (© **22850/22-230**). This delightful old store is filled with excellent local cheeses (*kephalotiri,* a superb sharp cheese, and milder *graviera*), barrels of olives, local wines, honey and spices.

There are a lot of shops on the streets leading up to Kastro, and because the streets are winding and cross each other, and seldom have visible street signs, I'm just going to suggest that you wander and keep an eye out for these. As always in the Cyclades, there are a great many jewelry shops, many selling cheap trinkets imported from China, but some with local work. You'll see the difference. Near the main entrance to the kastro, **Paraporti** (© **22850/25-795**) has an appealing selection of local and off-island crafts. The **Byzantium Gallery** (© **22850/22-478**) has reproduction and original icons as well as a wide range of church art and gifts. **Techni** (© **22850/24-767**) has side-by-side shops selling traditional weaving and embroidery (understandably, because all is hand-done, is not cheap, but is lovely) done by Naxian women. In the kastro itself, **Antico Veneziano** ★ (© **22850/26-206**) has just that—antiques from the island's Venetian period—as well as glassware, woodcarvings, and old weavings from throughout Greece. This is a lovely place to browse; it's in a handsome Venetian-period house.

As you wander, look for **Elia** (🕾 22950/ 24-884), a delightful cafe/restaurant on the old market street up to the kastro. This is a lovely spot to break for a coffee and a snack. If you want to stop at the accurately described "highest elevated restaurant in town," head to

Oniro (🕾 22850/23-846; www.oniro-naxos.info). Oniro is perched outside the main entrance to kastro, and unless they only serve sawdust, I want to eat there soon. (They happened to be closed when I was last on Naxos.)

Where to Stay

Hora's harbor is too busy for quiet accommodations; the following hotels in Kastro and Bourgo are within a 10-minute walk of the port; hotels in Grotta are a bit farther away, and places in Ayios Yeoryios are just outside of Hora. Insect repellent is advised wherever you stay. In addition to the following, you might consider the 19-unit **Hotel Anixis** (www.hotel-anixis.gr; 🕾 22850/22-112), near the kastro's Venetian tower. Rooms are small, but about half have balconies, and the kastro location is appealing; as always with a kastro, the walk there is steep. If you want to be on a beach, consider Anixis's sister hotel, the seven-unit **Anixis Resort** (www.hotel-anixis.gr; 🕾 22850/26-475), a 10-minute walk from town, 30m (98 ft.) from Ayios Yiorgos Beach. The family management at both is highly praised; prices start at 70€. If you want to be in a quiet location, but near a number of Hora's night spots, including the disco **Soul,** as well as a supermarket, bus stop, and beach, check out **Margo Studies** (**www.naxos margot.com**), which has nine rooms, seven studios, two apartments, a nice garden terrace, and very helpful English-speaking owners; doubles from 50€, studios from 60€ apartments sleeping up to five for 90€.

KASTRO

Castro ★   Not quite a B&B, not quite self-catering flats, the two units here are rather fey studio apartments just inside Kastro, with a shared terrace and a view across town to the Portara and the sea—and that's quite a view! This is the sort of place that makes you have pleasant fantasies of holing up and writing a novel (or at least a novella) and spending enough time exploring the Kastro neighborhood that you would get lost only once a day. Try to get the top-floor unit with its own balcony so that you can watch the passing scene. Both units have wrought-iron beds and plenty of shelf space, with some interesting knickknacks; you can add to the collections of seashells if you wish. The Castro also rents several nearby apartments (usually by the week). The Castro, Apollon, and Chateau Zevgoli Hotels are associated.

Kastro, Hora, 84300 Naxos. www.naxostownhotels.com. 🕾 **22850/25-201.** 2 units. 80€–100€ studio; 110€–130€ apt. No credit cards. Closed Nov–Apr. *In room:* Kitchenette.

BOURGO

Apollon ★   What more appropriate spot to stay, on an island famous for its marble, than in a former marble workshop—although, I have to confess that if I had not been told this, I never would have guessed it. The Apollon has a both quiet and very convenient location a block from the waterfront shops and restaurants and steps from the Greek Cathedral. Rooms have verandas or balconies (always a big plus) and are simply furnished (twin beds, table, chair). Although there is no garden to speak of, there are plants everywhere. The breakfast room is pleasant and the staff attentive. Try to get one of the corner seaview rooms, which are especially nice.

Fontana, Hora, 84300 Naxos. www.apollonhotel-naxos.gr. ℂ **22850/22-468.** 13 units. 100€–150€ double. Rates include breakfast. DC, MC. **Amenities:** Breakfast room/bar; Internet. *In room:* A/C, TV, hair dryer, minifridge.

Chateau Zevgoli ★★   This small hotel, easily the most attractive in Naxos, lies at the foot of the 13th-century kastro walls. The Chateau is often fully booked months in advance; plan well ahead if you want to stay here. The energetic and helpful owner, Despina Kitini, decorated the lobby and dining area with antiques and family heirlooms. All guest rooms open onto a central atrium with a lush garden; there's also a roof terrace. The units are small but distinctively furnished with dark wood and drapes. Room no. 8, for example, features a canopy bed and a private terrace. Several rooms have views of the harbor. Kitini also rents four apartments in her house, also within the kastro walls, and only 100m (328 ft.) from the hotel. These share a large, central sitting room; throughout are handsome stone walls and floors. The honeymoon suite has a balcony overlooking the town and the sea. The owner also sometimes has studios for rent in town, often at excellent long-term rates.

Bourgo, Hora, 84300 Naxos. www.naxostownhotels.com. ℂ **22850/25-201** or 22850/22-993. Fax 22850/25-200. 14 units. 90€–120€ double. Hotel rates include breakfast. AE, MC, V. Closed Nov–Mar. **Amenities:** Breakfast room/bar; Internet. *In room:* A/C, TV, hair dryer, minifridge.

OUT ON THE ISLAND

Hora has plenty of charm and makes a pleasant base, but if you want to be near a pool or the sea, here are three places to check:

Ayios Prokopios Beach, about 5km (2 miles) out of Hora, has two good choices. The 42-unit **Lianos Village Hotel** (www.lianosvillage.com; ℂ **22850/26-362**) has a pool, snack bar, Internet cafe, and good views out toward the sea, and is a 15-minute walk from the beach (doubles from 130€). The fancier 30-unit **Lagos Mare** (www.lagosmare.gr; ℂ **22850/42-844**) opened in 2006, with two restaurants, two pools, spa facilities, Internet, children's playground, snorkeling lessons, and a beachside position (doubles 225€–275€). Some 18km (11 miles) out of Hora at Mikri Vigli Bay, **Orkos Beach Hotel** ★ (www.orkosbeach.eu, ℂ **22850/75-194**) is a 28-unit apartment complex (mostly bungalows) constructed beside a pool and across from the beach to suggest a segment of a Cycladic village.

Where to Eat

HORA

The Bakery, on the *paralia* (ℂ **22850/22-613**), sells baked goods at fair prices. Farther north, across from the bus station, **Bikini** (ℂ **22850/24-701**) is a good place for breakfast and crepes. **Meltemi** (ℂ **22850/22-654**) and **Apolafsis** (ℂ **22850/22-178**), on the waterfront, both offer all the Greek staples; Apolafsis's has a great view of the passing scene, great mussels in garlic sauce, and live music many summer nights.

The Old Inn ★★ GERMAN/INTERNATIONAL   Yearning for some homemade pâté or sausages? Dieter Ranizewski makes them at the Old Inn. The Germanic menu (this is one of relatively few places in the Cyclades where you can get jellied or smoked pork) offers a distinctive alternative to standard taverna fare. The food is hearty, abundant, and delicious, with lots of local touches. As for the decor, the courtyard offers a green haven from the noise and crowds of the *paralia*. The restaurant, once a small monastery, inhabits several buildings surrounding a courtyard. The wine cellar is situated in a former chapel. Another vaulted room houses an eclectic collection of old objects from the island and from Dieter's native Berlin. The chef often doubles as waiter so things can be leisurely here, especially if there is a German team playing soccer; on those occasions, a TV usually appears in the garden.

100m (328 ft.) in from the port off the street leading to the Apollon Hotel; it's well signposted. © **22850/26-093.** Main courses 8€–20€ No credit cards. Daily 6pm–2am. Sometimes closed in winter.

Popi's Grill ★ GREEK As the business card proclaims, this is the "oldest family tavern in Naxos," serving grills and stews since 1948. You sit under an awning to avoid sun or rain, watch Naxians belting down ouzo with their meals, and relax, perhaps over your own ouzo. The food is well-prepared Greek restaurant fare, the service is smooth, and the customers are mainly locals, which is always reassuring. If you like Popi's, you'll also like nearby **Nicos** (© **22850/23-153**), especially for fresh fish.

Paralia. © **22850/22-389.** No credit cards. Daily 11am–midnight or later. Main courses 7€–12€; fish priced by the kilo.

Taverna To Kastro ★ GREEK Just outside the kastro's south gate, you'll find small Braduna Square, which is packed with tables on summer evenings. There's an excellent view toward the bay and St. George's beach; at dusk, a pacifying calm pervades the place. The specialty here is rabbit stewed in red wine with onions, spiced with pepper and a suggestion of cinnamon. The local wines are light and delicious.

Braduna Sq. © **22850/22-005.** Main courses 7€–15€. No credit cards. Daily 7pm–2am.

APIRANTHOS

Taverna Lefteris ★★ GREEK One of the island's best restaurants is in Apiranthos, perhaps Naxos's most beautiful town. The menu features the staples of Greek cooking, prepared in a way that shows you how good this food can be. The dishes highlight the freshest of vegetables and meats, prepared with admirable subtlety; the hearty homemade bread is delicious. A marble-floored room faces the street, and in back is a flagstone terrace shaded by two massive trees. The homemade sweets are an exception to the rule that you should avoid dessert in tavernas—the trip here is worth making for the desserts alone. This place can be very crowded if a tour group has booked in.

Apiranthos. © **22850/61-333.** Main courses 7€–12€. No credit cards. Daily 11am–11pm.

Naxos After Dark

Naxos certainly doesn't compete with Mykonos and Paros for wild nightlife, but it has a lively and varied scene. As always on the islands, places that are hot one season are often closed the next year. For several years, a disco called **Soul** has been packed. Ask for directions, as it's a bit tricky to find, but only a 10-minute walk from the main dock. **Portara,** by its namesake at the far end of the harbor, is an excellent place to enjoy the sunset. Next, you can join the evening *volta* (stroll) along the *paralia.* **Fragile,** through the arch in the entrance to the Old Town, is one of the older bars in town and worth a stop. **Lakridi,** off the *paralia* and not easy to find (ask someone to point the way), often has jazz, classical, and other mellow selections. On the *paralia,* **Ocean Dance** and **Super Island** are reliably lively and usually go all night in summer. Ask for directions to the part of town called **Pigadakia,** in a bit from the *paralia,* and then follow the sounds of music to two neighboring bar/discos, **Jam** and **On the Rocks.** When you leave On the Rocks, I guess the next stop logically would be to head into the **Abyss,** in the part of town called Grotta.

MYKONOS (MIKONOS)

by Peter Kerasiotis

177km (96 nautical miles) SE of Piraeus

What is it about Mykonos that has captured the world's imagination for over 40 years and refuses to let go? Though it is an undeniably beautiful island, it isn't the prettiest Greek island, or even the prettiest in the Cyclades. It used to be the island's cosmopolitan lifestyle, luxury hotels, and nightlife drew crowds, but today many of the more popular islands claim to be able to compete with that. It used to be its title as the party capital of all Mediterranean islands that set it apart, yet today Spain's Ibiza shares that title. So what is it then?

It all began with the picture-perfect town of labyrinthine roads leading you in circles around the beautiful cubist Cycladic architecture that attracted the likes of Jackie Kennedy and Aristotle Onassis in the '60s. With their stamp of approval, Mykonos became *the* place to be for anybody who was anybody. Soon, in the hedonistic '70s, it became the island version of Studio 54, making world headlines on celebrity pages and magazines. The sheer contrast of a traditional Greek fishing village and the type of tourists it attracted—gay partiers, international jet-setters, celebrities, and models—made the island a unique place to visit, and it captured the world's imagination.

If this is your first visit, you'll find lots to enjoy—especially if you avoid mid-July and August, when it seems that every one of the island's million annual visitors is here. Then again, what is Mykonos if you can't experience some of its legendary nighttime vibe for yourself? I suggest (for first timers) an early July visit. It's busy enough so you can understand what all the fuss is about, but not choked with visitors like late July and August, when even finding a table at a restaurant can be difficult.

Keep in mind that **it's very important to arrive here with reservations in the high season,** unless you enjoy sleeping outdoors and don't mind being moved from your sleeping spot by the police, who are not charmed to find foreigners alfresco.

If you come in mid-September or October, you'll find a quieter Mykonos, with a pleasant buzz of activity, and streets and restaurants that are less clogged. Unlike many of the islands, Mykonos remains active year-round. In winter, it hosts numerous cultural events, including a small film festival. Many who are scared off by the summer crowds find a different, tranquil Mykonos during this off-season, demonstrating Hora's deserved reputation as one of the most beautiful towns in the Cyclades.

Essentials

GETTING THERE **By Plane** **Olympic Airways** (© **210/966-6666** or 210/936-9111; www.olympic-airways.gr) has several flights daily (once daily in off season) between Mykonos and Athens, and one flight daily from Mykonos to Iraklion (Crete) and Santorini. Book flights in advance and reconfirm with Olympic in Athens or on Mykonos (© **22890/22-490** or 22890/22-237). The Mykonos office is near the south bus station; it's open Monday through Friday from 8am to 3:30pm. Travel agencies on the port sell Olympic tickets as well. **Aegean Airlines** (© **210/998-8300** or -2888; www.aegeanair.com) has initiated service to Mykonos, daily in summer.

By Boat Mykonos now has two ports: the old port in Mykonos town, and the new port, north of Mykonos town, at Tourlos. Check before you travel to find out which port your boat will use. From Piraeus, the **Blue Star Ithaki** (**www.ferries.gr**) has departures once daily at 7:30am. The **Pegasus** has two afternoon departures during

Although some shops hand out maps of Mykonos town, you'll probably do better finding restaurants, hotels, and attractions by asking people to point you in the right direction—and saying *efcharisto* (thank you) when they do. Don't panic at how to pronounce *efcharisto;* think of it as a name and say "F. Harry Stowe." Most streets do not have their names posted. Also, maps do not always show lots of small, twisting, streets—and Mykonos has almost nothing but small, twisting, streets! The map published by **Stamatis Bozinakis,** sold at most kiosks for 2€, is quite decent. The useful **Mykonos Sky Map** is free at some hotels and shops.

summer at 7:30pm (Mon and Sat). The **High Speed** has two departures daily, one at 7:15am and 4:45pm; and the **Marina** has three departures weekly, at 11:50pm on Tuesdays, 5pm Thursday and Saturday. From Rafina, **the Super Ferry** has one departure daily at 8am; the **Super Jet 2** has two departures daily at 7:40am and 4pm. The **Aqua Jewel** has one departure daily at 5pm while the **Penelope** leaves at 7:35pm daily. **High Speed** boats line **2** and **3** have daily afternoon departures at 7:30pm and 4:30pm respectively. Schedules can be checked with the **port police** (© **22890/22-218**). There are daily ferry connections between Mykonos and Andros, Paros, Siros, and Tinos; five to seven trips a week to Ios; four a week to Iraklio, Crete; several a week to Kos and Rhodes; and two a week to Ikaria, Samos, Skiathos, Skyros, and Thessaloniki. **Hellenic Seaways** offers Flying Dolphin hydrofoil service from **Piraeus** (© **210/419-9100** or -9000; **www.hellenicseaways.gr**) in summer. From the port of Lavrio, the **Fly Cat 3** has an 11:15am departure daily to Mykonos.

On Mykonos, your best bet for getting up-to-date lists of sailings is to check at individual agencies. Or you can check with the **port authority,** by National Bank (© **22890/22-218**); **tourist police,** at the north end of the harbor (© **22890/22-482**); or **tourist office,** also on the harbor (© **22890/23-990;** fax 22890/22-229).

Hydrofoil service to Crete, Ios, Paros, and Santorini is often irregular. For information, check at **Piraeus Port Authority** (© **210/451-1311** or 210/422-6000; phone seldom answered), **Piraeus Port Police** (© **210/451-1310**), **Rafina Port Police** (© **22940/23-300**), or **Mykonos Port Police** (© **22890/22-218**).

Warning: Check each travel agency's current schedule, because most ferry tickets are not interchangeable. Reputable agencies on the main square in Mykonos (Hora) town include **Sunspots Travel** (© **22890/24-196;** fax 22890/23-790); **Delia Travel** (© **22890/22-490;** fax 22890/24-440); **Sea & Sky Travel** (© **22890/22-853;** fax 22890/24-753); and **Veronis Agency** (© **22890/22-687;** fax 22890/23-763).

VISITOR INFORMATION **Mykonos Accommodations Center,** at the corner of Enoplon Dhinameon and Malamatenias (© **22890/23-160;** www.mykonos-accommodation.com), helps visitors find accommodations. It also functions as a tourist information center. **Windmills Travel** ★ (© **22890/23-877;** www.windmills travel.com) has an office at Fabrica Square, where you can get general information, book accommodations, arrange excursions, and rent a car or moped. Look for the free *Mykonos Summertime* magazine, available in cafes, shops, and hotels throughout the island.

GETTING AROUND One of the best things to happen to Mykonos was the government decree that made Hora an architectural landmark and prohibited motorized traffic on its streets. You will see a few delivery vehicles, but the only ways to get around town are to walk or ride a bike or donkey. Many of the town's hotels ring the peripheral road, and a good transportation system serves much of the rest of the island.

By Bus Mykonos has one of the best bus systems in the Greek islands; the buses run frequently and on schedule. Depending on your destination, a ticket costs about .50€ to 4€. There are two bus stations in Hora: one near the Archaeological Museum and one near the Olympic Airways office (follow the helpful blue signs). At the tourist office, find out which station the bus you want to take leaves from, or look for schedules in hotels. Bus information in English is sometimes available from the **KTEL** office (© **22890/23-360**).

By Boat Caiques to Super Paradise, Agrari, and Elia depart from Platis Yialos every morning, weather permitting; there is also service from Ornos in high season (July–Aug) only. Caique service is highly seasonal, with almost continuous service in high season and no caiques October through May. Excursion boats to Delos depart Tuesday through Sunday between 8:30am and 1pm, from the west side of the harbor near the tourist office. (For more information, see a travel agent; guided tours are available.)

By Car & Moped Rental cars are available from about 50€ per day, including insurance, in high season; most agencies are near one of the two bus stops in town. **Windmills Travel** (see "Visitor Information," above) can arrange a car rental for you and get good prices. The largest concentration of moped shops is just beyond the south bus station. Expect to pay about 15€ to 30€ per day, depending on the moped's engine size. Take great care when driving. Island roads can be treacherous.

Warning: If you park in town or in a no-parking area, the police will remove your license plates. You—not the rental office—will have to find the police station and pay a steep fine to get them back.

By Taxi There are two types of taxis in Mykonos: standard **car taxis,** for destinations outside town, and tiny, cart-towing **scooters** that buzz through the narrow streets of Hora. The latter are seen primarily at the port, where they wait to bring new arrivals to their lodgings in town—a good idea, as most in-town hotels are a challenge to find. Getting a car taxi in Hora is easy: Walk to Taxi (Mavro) Square, near the statue, and join the line. A notice board gives rates for various destinations. You can also call **Mykonos Radio Taxi** (© **22890/22-400**).

FAST FACTS **Commercial Bank** and **National Bank of Greece** are on the harbor 2 blocks west of Taxi Square; both are open Monday through Friday from 8am to 2pm. ATMs are available throughout town. **Mykonos Health Center** (© **22890/23-994** or 22890/23-996) handles routine medical complaints; serious cases are usually airlifted to the mainland. The **tourist police** (© **22890/22-482**) are on the west side of the port near the ferries to Delos; the local **police** (© **22890/22-235**) are behind the grammar school, near Plateia Laka. The **post office** (© **22890/22-238**) is next to the police station; it's open Monday through Friday from 7:30am to 2pm. The **telephone office** (**OTE;** © **22890/22-499**) is on the north side of the harbor, beyond the Hotel Leto, and is open Monday through Friday 7:30am to 3pm. **Internet access** is expensive here: Mykonos Cyber Cafe, 26 M. Axioti, on the road between the south bus station and the windmills (© **22890/27-684**), is open daily 9am to 10pm and charges 16€ per hour or 5€ for 15 minutes. Angelo's Internet Cafe, on the same road (© **22890/24-106**), may have lower rates.

What to See & Do
BEACHES

The beaches on the island's **south shore** have the best sand, views, and wind protection. However, these days they are so popular that you'll have to navigate through a forest of beach umbrellas to find your square meter of sand. A few **(Paradise, Super Paradise)** are known as party beaches, and guarantee throbbing music and loud revelry until late at night. Others (**Platis Yialos** and **Ornos**) are quieter and more popular with families. **Psarrou** has gone from being a family beach to being perhaps the trendiest beach of them all (for visiting Athenians mostly). With all the south-coast beaches, keep in mind that most people begin to arrive in the early afternoon, and you can avoid the worst of the crowds by going in the morning. The **north-coast beaches** are less developed but just as beautiful. Because the buses and caiques don't yet make the trip, you'll have to rent a car or scooter; you'll be more than compensated for the trouble by the quiet and the lack of commercial development.

For those who can't wait to hit the beach, the closest to Mykonos town is **Megali Ammos (Big Sand)**, about a 10-minute walk south—it's very crowded and not particularly scenic. To the north, the beach nearest town is 2km (1 mile) away at **Tourlos;** however, because this is now where many ships dock at the new harbor, it's not a place for a relaxing swim. **Ornos** is popular with families; it's about 2.5km (1½ miles) south of town and has a fine-sand beach in a sheltered bay, with extensive hotel development along the shore. Buses to Ornos run hourly from the south station between 8am and 11pm.

With back-to-back hotels and tavernas along its long sandy beach, **Platis Yialos** is extremely easy to get to from the town and has pristine aqua-blue waters and a variety of watersports. Due to its proximity to town however, it is always crowded and lacks character. It's ideal for a swim if you're too hung over to make it to farther beaches. Here you can catch a caique to the more distant beaches of Paradise, Super Paradise, Agrari, and Elia as well as a small boat to Delos. The bus runs every 15 minutes from 8am to 8pm, then every 30 minutes until midnight. Nearby **Psarou** is the first stop on the bus from town to Platis Yialos and it is a much higher-brow version of its neighbor. It is actually a beautiful stretch of beach, with white sand and greenery, overlooked by the terraces of tavernas and hotels. The excellent **N'Ammos** restaurant is right here, as is the sublime hotel **Mykonos Blu,** of the Grecotel chain. A rowdy beach bar here has patrons dancing on whatever free inch of space they can find. During high season, and especially during the weekends when the trendy Athenians flock to this beach, even chaise longues require reservations. Psarou is also popular when the *meltemi* winds strike the island, as it offers protection in its bay to many yachts, boats, and swimmers. Its watersports facilities include **Diving Center Psarou,** water-skiing, and windsurfing. **Paranga,** farther east, is small and picturesque and can be reached easily on foot via an inland path from Platis Yialos; this small cove is popular for nude sunbathing and doesn't get too crowded, but is never too quiet either as the loud music from the neighboring beaches can be heard. From here you can take a hill path that will lead you to another beach, **Agia Anna (St. Anne).** Agia Anna is a pebbles beach with a beautiful landscape and sweeping views from the top of the hill.

Reach **Paradise** ★, the island's most famous beach, on foot from Platis Yialos (about 2km/1 mile), by bus, or by caique. The more adventurous arrive by moped on roads that are incredibly narrow and steep. Seeing how very few leave this beach sober, it is in your best interest (even if you have rented a moped) to get back to town by bus. This is the island's original nude beach, and it still attracts many nudists. A stand of small trees provides some shade, and the beach is well protected from the predominant north winds. Lined with bars, tavernas, and clubs, Paradise is never a quiet experience—it is the premier party beach of the island and shows no signs of stopping. The **Tropicana Beach Bar** and the **Sunrise Bar** are both havens for the party crowd that goes all day, long after the sun has set. On top of the hill, the popular and internationally known **Cavo Paradiso Club** is a large, open-air nightclub with rotating international DJs and doors that do not open until after 2am. In fact the "cool crowd" begins to arrive only after 5am. On the beach, Paradise Club is the club destination from 6pm to midnight, reopening from 2am to 6am. One beach party on Paradise you shouldn't miss is the **Full Moon Party,** once a month. The only other party that compares to it is the **Closing Party** every September that has become an island institution. As in most of the island, the water here is breathtakingly beautiful, but hardly anybody comes to Paradise for the sea.

Super Paradise (Plindri) is in a rocky cove just around the headland from Paradise; it's somewhat less developed than its neighbor, but no less crowded. You can get to the beach on foot, by bus, or by caique; if you go by car or moped, be very careful on the extremely steep and narrow access road. The left side of the beach is a nonstop party in summer, with loud music and dancing, while the right side is mostly nude and gay, with the exclusive **Coco Club** providing a relaxed ambience for its chic clientele until after 5pm, when things get rowdy and loud. On the right side, there are similar party bars for the straight crowd. The waters here are beautiful but very deep, so it isn't the best swimming option for families with small children. Farther east across the little peninsula is **Agrari,** a lovely cove sheltered by lush foliage, with a good little taverna and a beach that welcomes bathers in all modes of dress and undress.

Elia, a 45-minute caique ride from Platis Yialos and the last regular stop (also accessible by bus from the town), is a sand-and-pebble beach with crowds nearly as overwhelming as at Paradise, minimal shade and bamboo windbreaks. Nevertheless, this beautiful beach is one of the longest on the island. The beach is surrounded by a circle of steep hills, has an attractive restaurant/cafe/bar, and offers umbrellas, sun beds, and watersports. There is also a gay section to this beach that is clothing optional. Despite its popularity, there is no loud bar/club here, so the atmosphere is more sedate than the Paradise beaches. The next major beach is **Kalo Livadi (Good Pasture).** Located in a farming valley, this long, beautiful beach is about as quiet as a beach on Mykonos's southern coast gets. There's bus service from Mykonos town's

Mykonos Beach Notes

Activity on the beaches is highly seasonal, and the information here pertains only to the months of June through September. The prevailing winds on Mykonos (and throughout the Cyclades) blow from the north, which is why the southern beaches are the most protected and calm. The exception to this rule is a southern wind that occurs periodically during the summer, making the northern beaches more desirable for sunning and swimming. In Mykonos town, this southern wind is heralded by particularly hot temperatures and calm in the harbor. On such days, those in the know will avoid Paradise, Super Paradise, and Elia, heading to the northern beaches of Ayios Sostis and Panormos—or choose another activity for the day.

north station. Adjacent to the beach are a taverna and a few villas and hotels on the hills.

The last resort area on the southern coast accessible by bus from the north station is **Kalafatis ★**. This fishing village was once the port of the ancient citadel of Mykonos, which dominated the little peninsula to the west. A line of trees separates the beach from the rows of buildings that have grown up along the road. This is one of the longest beaches on Mykonos, and its days of being uncrowded are, alas, over. The waters are pristine, however, and the hotels offer water-skiing, surfing, and windsurfing lessons. Here you will also find a good beach restaurant and bar and many boats to take you to **Dragonisi,** an islet that has caves ideal for swimming and exploring. You might also catch a glimpse of rare monk seals at the islet; its caves are reportedly a breeding ground for them. Adjacent to Kalafatis in a tiny cove is **Ayia Anna** (not to be confused with the other beach of the same name, by Paranga beach), a short stretch of sand with a score of umbrellas. Several kilometers farther east, accessible by a good road from Kalafatis, is **Lia,** which has fine sand, clear water, bamboo windbreaks, and a small, exceptional, and shockingly low-priced taverna.

Most of the north-coast beaches are too windy to be of interest to anyone other than windsurfers and surfers. Though windsurfing has always been extremely popular in Greece, surfing is a relatively new sport here and Greece is a newly discovered destination for many surfers.

All over the country, from Athens to beach towns and villages that line both coasts and many islands, **surfers** are realizing Greece with its many coasts has more to offer than clear waters that aren't shark-infested. Though Mykonos doesn't appear in the top 10 list of favorite places to surf in Greece, it should; already many of the island's wind-battered north-coast beaches attract many European surfers in the know. When the north winds hit the island relentlessly, waves can swell up to impressive sizes and the lack of competition provides an uninterrupted haven for surfers and windsurfers alike. In order to enjoy this scene, however, you have to either have a car or a moped, as public transportation, regrettably or not, hasn't made it here yet.

Fokos is a superb sandy beach that has only recently begun to get noticed by tourists. The scenery is raw, wild, and beautiful, and there is a small taverna here that is quite good. Fokos was the first beach to get noticed by the surfers. The huge Panormos Bay has three main beaches. The one closest to town is **Ftelia,** and it is a long fine-sand beach, easily one of the best on the island, but for the force of the north wind, which has made it popular with surfers and windsurfers. There are, however, two well-sheltered northern beaches, and because you can only reach them by car or moped, they're much less crowded than the southern beaches. Head east from Mykonos town on the road to Ano Mera, turning left after 1.5km (1 mile) on the road to Ayios Sostis and Panormos. At **Panormos,** you'll find a cove with 100m (328 ft.) of fine sand backed by low dunes. Another 1km (¾ mile) down the road is **Ayios Sostis ★**, a lovely small beach that sits just below a village. There isn't any parking, so it's best to leave your vehicle along the main road and walk 200m (656 ft.) down through the village. An excellent small taverna just up from the beach operates without electricity, so it's open only during daylight hours. Both Panormos and Ayios Sostis have few amenities—no beach umbrellas, bars, or snack shops— but they do offer a break from the crowds. Ayios Sostis is wild, windswept, and beautiful, as are all north-coast beaches, offering a completely different landscape than their far more popular southern counterparts. When the *meltemi* winds are at their strongest, during July and August into September, the waves can be awesome and unrelenting and the water is filled with surfers. Ayios Sostis, however, is becoming the new "in" beach during the high season, when the visiting Athenians escape here when the winds aren't too strong.

Beaches to avoid on Mykonos because of pollution, noise, and crowds include **Tourlos** and **Korfos Bay.**

With so many sun worshipers on Mykonos, local merchants have figured out that they can charge pretty steep prices for suntan lotions and sunscreens. You probably want to bring some with you. If you want to try a Greek brand, the oddly named Carrot Milk is excellent.

DIVING

Mykonos is known throughout the Aegean as one of *the* places for diving. Scuba diving on many islands is prohibited to protect undersea archaeological treasures from plunder. The best month is September, when the water temperature is typically 75°F (24°C) and visibility is 30m (98 ft.). Certified divers can rent equipment and participate in guided dives; first-time divers can rent snorkeling gear or take an introductory beach dive. The best established dive center is **Mykonos Diving Centre,** at Paradise beach (②/fax **22890/24-808**), which offers 5-day PADI certification courses in English from about 500€, including equipment. **Psarou Diving Center** in Mykonos town (② **22890/24-808**) has also been around for a long time. As always, before you sign up for lessons, be sure that all instructors are PADI certified. The **Union of Diving Centers in Athens** (② **210/411-8909**) usually has up-to-date information. In general, certified divers can join guided dives from 50€ per dive; beginners can take a 2-hour class and beach dive from 60€. There's a nearby wreck at a depth of 20 to 35m (65–114 ft.); wreck dives run from 60€.

ATTRACTIONS

Ask anybody who has visited the Greek islands and they will tell you that apart from the beaches, nothing compares to the early evening stroll in the islands' towns. The light of the late hour, the pleasant buzz, the narrow streets filled with locals and tourists alike, and the romantic ambience in the air as you stroll along can lead you to anything from a modern restaurant, a pleasant taverna, a fortress, or an ancient, unassuming site.

Despite its commercialism and seething crowds in high season, Hora is still the quintessential Cycladic town and is worth a visit in itself. The best way to see the town is to venture inland from the port and wander. Browse the window displays, go inside an art gallery, a store, or an old church that may be open but empty inside. Keep in mind that the town is bounded on two sides by the bay, and on the other two by the busy District Road, and that all paths funnel eventually into one of the main squares: **Plateia Mantos Mavroyenous,** on the port (called **Taxi Square** because it's the main taxi stand); **Plateia Tria Pigadia;** and **Plateia Laka,** near the south bus station.

Hora also has the remains of a small **Venetian kastro** and the island's most famous church, **Panagia Paraportiani (Our Lady of the Postern Gate),** a thickly white-washed asymmetrical edifice made up of four small chapels. Beyond the Panagia Paraportiani is the **Alefkandra** quarter, better known as **Little Venice ★★,** for its cluster of homes built overhanging the sea. Many buildings here have been converted into fashionable bars prized for their sunset views; you can sip a margarita and listen to Mozart most nights at the **Montparnasse** or **Kastro Bar,** or check out the sunset and stay all night at **Caprice.** (See "Mykonos After Dark," later in this chapter.)

Another nearby watering spot is the famous **Tria Pigadia (Three Wells)** ★★. Local legend says that if a virgin drinks from all three, she is sure to find a husband, but it's probably not a good idea to test this hypothesis by drinking the brackish well water. After your visit, you may want to take in the famous **windmills of Kato Myli** and enjoy the views back toward Little Venice.

Save time to visit the island's clutch of pleasant small museums. **The Archaeological Museum** (② 22890/22-325), near the harbor, displays finds from Delos; it's open Wednesday to Monday 9am to 3:30pm. Admission is 3€ (free Sun). **Nautical Museum of the Aegean** (② 22890/22-700), across from the park on Enoplon Dinameon Street, has just what you'd expect, including handsome ship models. It's open Tuesday to Sunday 10:30am to 1pm and 6 to 9pm; admission is 3€. Also on Enoplon Dinameon Street, **Lena's House** (② 22890/22-591) re-creates the home of a middle-class 19th-century Mykonos family. It's usually open daily Easter through October; admission is free. **Museum of Folklore** (② 22890/25-591), in a 19th-century sea captain's mansion near the quay, displays examples of local crafts and furnishings. On show is a 19th-century island kitchen. It's open Monday to Saturday 4 to 8pm, Sunday 5 to 8pm; admission is free.

When you've spent some time in Hora, you may want to visit **Ano Mera,** 7km (4 miles) east of Hora near the center of the island, a quick bus ride from the north station. Ano Mera is the island's only other real town, and we especially recommend this trip for those interested in religious sites—the **Monastery of Panagia Tourliani** southeast of town dates from the 18th century and has a marble bell tower with intricate folk carvings. Inside the church are a huge Italian baroque iconostasis (altar screen) with icons of the Cretan school; an 18th-century marble baptismal font; and a small museum containing liturgical vestments, needlework, and woodcarvings. One kilometer (½ mile) southeast is the 12th-century **Monastery of Paleokastro,** in one of the island's greenest spots. Ano Mera also has the island's most traditional atmosphere; a fresh-produce market on the main square sells excellent local cheeses. This is the island's top choice for Sunday brunch.

SHOPPING

Mykonos has a lot of shops, many selling overpriced souvenirs, clothing, and jewelry to cruise-ship day-trippers. There are also a number of serious shops here, selling serious wares—at serious prices. **Soho-Soho,** 81 Matoyanni (② 22890/26-760), is by far the most well known clothing store on the island; pictures of its famous clientele (Tom Hanks, Sarah Jessica Parker, and so forth) carrying the store's bags have been in publications around the world. Maria will help the female clientele find the perfect outfit while just across the street, at the men's store, Bill will recommend the latest men's arrivals.

Luxury fashion boutique **Scoop NYC** (② 22890/25-122; www.scoopnyc.com) opened its first European location in the Belvedere Hotel. Its exquisite jewelry line by native Mykonian designer Ileana Makri sets this store apart from its New York counterpart. The finest jewelry shop on the island remains **LALAoUNIS** ★, 14 Polykandrioti (② 22890/22-444), associated with the famous LALAoUNIS museum and shops in Athens. It has superb reproductions of ancient and Byzantine jewelry as well as original designs. When you leave LALAoUNIS, have a look at **Yiannis Galantis** (② 22890/22-255), which sells clothing designed by the owner. If you can't afford LALAoUNIS, you might check out one of the island's oldest jewelry shops, the **Gold Store,** right on the waterfront (② 22890/22-397).

Delos Dolphins, Matoyanni at Enoplon Dimameon (© **22890/22-765**), specializes in copies of museum pieces; **Vildiridis,** 12 Matoyianni (© **22890/23-245**), also has jewelry based on ancient designs. Also be sure to check out **Karkalis,** 17 Matoyanni (© **22890/24-022**; www.gold.gr), the newest arrival in town, with striking original and contemporary designs. Mykonos is also well known for its house-designed sandals in many colors and styles; perhaps no better selection can be found in the entire island than at **Eccentric by Design,** 11 Fiorou Zouganelis St. (© **22890/28-499**), where you can even find sandals encrusted with Swarvoski crystals. For more traditional sandals, check out **Kostas Rabias,** on Matoyianni Street (© **22890/22-010**).

Mykonos has lots of art galleries, including some based in Athens that move here for the summer season. **Scala Gallery ★,** 48 Matoyianni (© **22890/23-407**; fax 22890/26-993; www.scalagallery.gr), is one of the best galleries in town. All the artists represented are from Greece, many of them quite well known. There is a selection of jewelry, plus an interesting collection of recent works by Yorgos Kypris, an Athenian sculptor and ceramic artist. Nearby on Panahrandou is **Scala II Gallery** (© **22890/26-993**), where the overflow from the Scala Gallery is sold at reduced prices. In addition, manager **Dimitris Roussounelos** (©/fax **22890/26-993**; scala@otenet.gr), of Scala Gallery, manages a number of studios and apartments in Hora, so you might find lodgings as well as art at Scala.

Mykonos was once world famous for its vegetable dyed hand-loomed weavings, especially those of the legendary Kuria Vienoula. Today, **Nikoletta** (© **22890/27-503**) is one of the few shops where you can still see the island's traditional loomed goods. Eleni Kontiza's tiny shop **Hand Made** (© **22890/27-512**), on a lane between Plateia Tria Pigadia and Plateia Laka, has a good selection of hand-woven scarves, rugs, and tablecloths from around Greece.

The best bookstore on Mykonos is **To Vivlio ★** (© **22890/27-737**), on Zouganeli, one street over from Matoyianni. It carries a good selection of books in English, including many works of Greek writers in translation, plus some art and architecture books and a few travel guides.

Works of culinary art can be found at **Skaropoulos** (© **22890/24-983**), 1.5km (1 mile) out of Hora on the road to Ano Mera, featuring the Mykonian specialties of Nikos and Frantzeska Koukas. Nikos's grandfather started making confections here in 1921, winning prizes and earning a personal commendation from Winston Churchill. Try their famed *amygdalota* (an almond sweet) or the almond cookies (Churchill's favorite). You can also find Skaropoulos sweets at **Pantopoleion,** 24 Kaloyerou (© **22890/22-078**), along with Greek organic foods and natural cosmetics; the shop is in a beautifully restored 300-year-old Mykonian house.

When you finish your shopping, treat yourself to another almond biscuit (or two or three) from **Efthemios,** 4 Florou Zouganeli (© **22890/22-281**), just off the harborfront, where biscuits have been made since the 1950s.

Where to Stay

In summer, reserve a room 1 to 3 months in advance (or more), if possible. Ferry arrivals are often met by a throng of people hawking rooms, some in small hotels, others in private homes. If you don't have a hotel reservation, one of these rooms may be very welcome. Otherwise, book as early as you can. Many hotels are fully booked all summer by tour groups or regular patrons. Keep in mind that Mykonos is an easier, more pleasant place to visit in the late spring or early fall. Off-season hotel rates are sometimes half the quoted high-season rate. Also note that many small hotels, restaurants, and shops close in winter, especially if business is slow.

Mykonos Accommodations Center (MAC), 10 Enoplon Dinameon (www.mykonos-accommodation.com; ☎ **22890/23-160** or 22890/23-408; fax 22890/24-137), is a helpful service, especially if you are looking for hard-to-find inexpensive lodgings. The service is free when you book a hotel stay of 3 nights or longer. If you plan a shorter stay, ask about the fee, which is sometimes a percentage of the tab and sometimes a flat fee.

IN HORA

Andronikos Hotel ★★ Beautiful, elegant, and right in town, this impeccably designed hotel offers spacious verandas or terraces with vistas of the sea and the town, a good **restaurant,** an edgy gallery, and a spa, at affordable (for Mykonos) prices.

Hora 86400, Mykonos. www.andronikoshotel.com. ☎ 22890/24-231. Fax 22890/24-691. 53 units. 180€–230€ double; 240€–290€ double with Jacuzzi; 310€–380€ suite. AE, DC, MC, V. **Amenities:** Restaurant; bar; gallery; gym; pool; spa. *In room:* A/C, TV/DVD, hair dryer, Internet, Jacuzzi (in some rooms), minibar.

Apanema Resort Hotel ★★ This intimate, pretty boutique hotel is ideally located a 10-minute walk from town. The young owner has decorated her hotel in impeccable taste, with personal touches throughout, such as handcrafted pottery and rugs, which create a homey feeling even amid the elegance. Another big plus (apart from the stunning view from the pool) is the hotel's ample and delicious American buffet breakfast, served from 7am to 2pm, for those who cannot get out of bed before 1pm. The on-site Mediterranean fusion restaurant, **Apanema,** is also another excuse to stay.

Hora, Tagoo 84600 Mykonos. www.apanemaresort.com. ☎ 22890/28-590. Fax 22890/79-250. 17 units. 179€–220€ double; 510€ suite. Rates include American buffet breakfast. Considerable off-season reductions. AE, MC, V. Free parking. **Amenities:** Restaurant; bar; pool; tennis court. *In room:* A/C, TV, hair dryer, Internet, minibar.

Apollon Hotel ✦ No-nonsense, no-frills hotels in Mykonos are hard to find. Rooms here are basic yet comfortable and well kept. The price seals the deal.

Hora, 84600 Mykonos. ☎ 22890/22-223. Fax 22890/2437. 10 units. 50€–65€ single or double with shower. No credit cards. *In room:* A/C, TV.

Belvedere Hotel ★★ The all-white oasis of the Belvedere, in part occupying a handsomely restored 1850s town house on the main road into town, has stunning views over the town and harbor, a few minutes' walk away. Rooms are nicely, if not distinctively, furnished. Stay here if you want many of the creature comforts of Mykonos's beach resorts but prefer to be within walking distance of Hora. The ultrachic poolside scene buzzes all night and day, in part due to Nobu Matsuhisa's only open-air restaurant, the impeccable **Matsuhisa Mykonos.** Also on site are the excellent Greek restaurant **Club Belvedere** and the wonderful **CBar Lounge**—ideal for its sunset views. In season, the hotel often offers massage, salon, and barber service. Off season, look for excellent specials; after a 4-night stay, this might mean a free Jeep for a day or a fifth night free. This is the Delano of Mykonos; stylish, always popular, and in a class of its own.

Hora, 84600 Mykonos. www.belvederehotel.com. ☎ 22890/25-122. Fax 22890/25-126. 48 units. 230€–460€ double; 650€ suite. Rates include American buffet breakfast. Considerable off-season reductions. AE, DC, MC, V. **Amenities:** 2 restaurants; bar/lounge; fitness center; Jacuzzi; pool; sauna. *In room:* A/C, TV, hair dryer, Internet, minibar.

Cavo Tagoo ★★ This exceptional hotel, set into a cliff, with spectacular views over Mykonos town, is hard to resist—and consistently makes it onto *Odyssey* magazine's list of 10 best Greek hotels. Cavo Tagoo's island-style architecture has won awards, and its marble floors, nicely crafted wooden furniture, queen- and king-size beds, and local-style weavings are a pleasure. An impressive redesign has left it better than ever. Elegantly minimalist with marble, spacious bathrooms and large balconies with sea vistas, Cavo Tagoo features suites with private pools, a spa center, lounge, and pool areas. Hora's harbor is only a 15-minute walk away, although you may find it hard to budge: A saltwater pool and a good **restaurant** are located at the hotel.

Hora, 84600 Mykonos. www.cavotagoo.gr. ℂ **22890/23-692** to -695. Fax 22890/24-923. 69 units. 225€–420€ double. Rates include buffet breakfast. AE, DC, MC, V. Closed Nov–Mar. **Amenities:** Restaurant; bar; gym; saltwater pool; sauna. *In room:* A/C, TV, hair dryer, Internet, minibar.

Elysium ★★ The smartest gay hotel on the island is located on a steep hillside right in the old town; a walk down the steep hill will have you back in town in 3 minutes. Gardens, a pool, great views, a gym, sauna, and a very relaxed atmosphere keep guests coming again and again.

Mykonos Old Town, 84600 Mykonos. www.elysiumhotel.com. ℂ **22890/23-952.** Fax 22890/23-747. 42 units. 101€ single; 180€ double; 246€ suite; 800€–1,126€ royal suite. AE, DC, MC, V. **Amenities:** Bar/cafe; gym; hydromassage; pool; sauna; spa. *In room:* A/C, TV, hair dryer, Internet.

Hermes Hotel ★ Atop a hill with vistas of the town, the port, the windmills, and the sea, Hermes Hotel has clean and comfortable rooms, a breakfast area, and a pool with breathtaking views. The 10-minute walk down the hill to town is effortless but the same walk back up can be exhausting—the only drawback to this charming hotel. However, the views and good value compensate for the extra calories burned.

Drosopezoula, Hora, 84600 Mykonos. www.greekhotel.com. ℂ **22890/24-242.** Fax 22890/25-640. 24 units. 72€–126€ single; 83€–147€ double; 98€–189€ triple. Rates include buffet breakfast. AE, MC, V. **Amenities:** Cafe/bar; pool. *In room:* A/C, TV.

Mykonos Theoxenia ★★ When the Mykonos Theoxenia reopened its doors in 2004 after an extensive makeover, it quickly became the talk of the town once again as it was in the '60s. With its stone-clad walls and orange and turquoise fabrics, the mood is already set before you venture beyond the reception. In the 52 rooms and suites, funky '60s-inspired furniture and loud colors dominate the decor with spacious bathrooms (stuffed with luxuries) enclosed in glass walls. The location, right by the windmills and impossibly romantic Little Venice, could not be any more ideal. A wonderful pool and restaurant are the perfect finishing touches. When you arrive at the hotel you will be treated to a welcoming drink, a fruit basket, and bottle of wine.

Kato Mili, Hora, 84600 Mykonos. www.mykonostheoxenia.com. ℂ **22890/22-230.** 52 units. 282€–420€ single/double, depending on balcony and view; 625€ junior suite; 830€ 2-bedroom suite. AE, DC, MC, V. Free parking. **Amenities:** Restaurant; bar; pool. *In room:* A/C, TV, hair dryer, Internet.

Mykonos View ★ With a view that can't be beat, the Mykonos View is ideally situated: On a hill above the town is a complex of apartments (studios, apartments, and maisonettes) all connected via cobblestone paths, giving you the sense of having your own island apartment, which is infinitely more alluring for some than feeling they are in a hotel. The swimming pool hangs over the Aegean and the town. The hotel's awesome **Oneiro Bar (Dream Bar)** has become an island-must sunset destination.

Hora, 84600 Mykonos. www.mykonosview.gr. ℂ **22890/24-045.** Fax 22890/26445. 30 units. 130€–160€ studio; 160€–220€ superior studio; 180€–250€ apt.; 200€–280€ maisonette. AE, DC, MC, V. **Amenities:** Restaurant; bar; pool. *In room:* A/C, TV, hair dryer, Internet.

Ostraco Suites ★   This mod-meets-island decor is ideal for young, hip couples or a group of young friends who are looking for something stylish (but not outrageously pricey or chic) and a 5-minute walk to town. It consists of five white villas, and manages to be affordable and trendy at the same time. Two of the suites were renovated by the late, renowned Greek interior designer Angelos Angelopoulos.

Drafaki, 84600 Mykonos. www.ostraco.gr. ✆ **22890/23-396.** Fax 22890/27-123. 21 units. 185€–230€ double; 305€–380€ suite. Rates include buffet breakfast. AE, DC, MC, V. **Amenities:** Restaurant; bar; cafe; pool; spa; sun deck. *In room:* A/C, TV/DVD, hair dryer, minibar.

Philippi Hotel   Each room in this homey little hotel in the heart of Mykonos town is different, so you might want to have a look at several before choosing yours. The owner tends a lush garden that often provides flowers for her son's restaurant, the elegant **Philippi** (p. 413), which can be reached through the garden.

25 Kaloyera, Hora, 84600 Mykonos. ✆ **22890/22-294.** Fax 22890/24-680. 13 units. 90€ double. No credit cards. **Amenities:** Restaurant.

Porto Mykonos ★   Just above the old port with vistas in every direction and an enviable location, this boutique hotel has minimalist rooms, new bathrooms, and great views from its front and side balconies (be sure not to get the back rooms, as they look into a parking lot). There is some noise here (as it is near the port), but you will be compensated by the comfortable rooms, a wonderful saltwater pool and Jacuzzi, and direct access to the action any time of the day and night. The very good *"A la Carte"* **restaurant** on-site is also another plus.

Palio Limani, Hora, 84600 Mykonos. www.portomykonos.gr. ✆ **22890/22-454.** 59 units. 226€ classic/ Greek double; 363€ suite. AE, DC, MC, V. **Amenities:** Restaurant; bar; cafe; gym; saltwater pool and Jacuzzi; spa. *In room:* A/C, TV, Internet.

Semeli Hotel ★   Named after the mother of Dionysos, the God of wine, Semeli has an enviable location in the middle of town and charm in spades. Once a stately home, the Semeli was turned into a four-star hotel without losing any of its distinctly Cycladic personality. The house's original furniture decorates the lobby and all the rooms abound with modern amenities. Rooms are bright and comfortable, with lovely verandas and large marble bathrooms. The Semeli's **restaurant** is also very good.

Lekka St, Hora, 84600 Mykonos. www.semelihotel.gr. ✆ **22890/27-466.** 45 units. 310€ double. AE, DC, MC, V. **Amenities:** Restaurant; bar; cafe; gym; pool; spa. *In room:* A/C, TV, Internet.

Tharraoe of Mykonos ★★   Built on top of a hill, this small boutique hotel has spacious rooms with stunning sea and town vistas from the balconies; clean-lined wooden furniture; colorful bathrooms with funky, spacious tubs; and a wonderful pool area overlooking the sea and town. The top-notch **Barbarossa** restaurant, the in-house salon, and the Ayurvedic Spa complete the picture.

Hora, 84600 Mykonos. www.tharroeofmykonos.gr. ✆ **22890/27-370,** ext. 4. Fax 22890/27-375. 24 units. 200€ double with island view; 226€ with /sea view; 380€–460€ suite. AE, DC, MC, V. Free parking. **Amenities:** Restaurant; bar; cafe; gym; pool; spa. *In room:* A/C, TV, hair dryer, Internet, minibar.

Zorzis Hotel   Confused by all the posh boutiques in town? Don't know quite what to choose? For a completely different experience, you might like to try this unique option. Zorzis is set inside a traditional 16th-century building in the center of town. The rooms have Casablanca ceiling fans, wooden antique furniture, and antique Louis XV beds; this is truly like taking a few stylish steps back in time.

30 Kalogear St., Hora, 84600 Mykonos. www.zorzishotel.com. ✆ **22890/22-167.** Fax 22890/24-168. 10 units. 200€ double with island view; 152€–460€ suite. AE, DC, MC, V. Free parking. **Amenities:** Restaurant; bar; cafe; gym; pool; spa. *In room:* A/C, TV, hair dryer, Internet, minibar.

OUT ON THE ISLAND

Although most visitors prefer to stay in Hora and commute to the beaches, there are some truly spectacular hotels on or near many of the more popular island beaches and many more affordable ones.

The beaches at Paradise and Super Paradise have private studios and simple pensions, but rooms are almost impossible to get, and prices more than double in July and August. Contact **Mykonos Accommodations Center** (✆ **22890/23-160**) or, for Super Paradise, **GATS Travel** (✆ **22890/22-404**), for information on the properties they represent. The tavernas at each beach may also have suggestions.

AT KALAFATI   The **Aphrodite Hotel** (www.aphrodite-mykonos.com; ✆ **22890/71-367**) has a large pool, two restaurants, and 150 rooms. It's a good value in May, June, and October, when a double costs about 100€. The hotel is popular with tour groups and Greek families.

AT ORNOS BAY   Elegant **Kivotos Club Hotel ★★**, Ornos Bay, 84600 Mykonos (www.kivotosclubhotel.gr; ✆ **22890/25-795**; fax 22890/22-844), is a small, superb luxury hotel about 3km (2 miles) outside Mykonos town. Most of the 45 individually decorated units overlook the Bay of Ormos, but if you don't want to walk that far for a swim, head for the saltwater or freshwater pool, the Jacuzzi and sauna, or the pool with an underwater sound system piping in music. Kivotos is small enough to be intimate and tranquil; the service (including frozen towels for poolside guests on hot days) gets raves from guests. If you're ever tempted to leave (and you may not be), the hotel minibus will whisk you into town. You can easily dine at the several restaurants on-site. The hotel also has a traditional sailing ship, at the ready for spur-of-the-moment sails. This popular honeymoon destination appears often on *Odyssey* magazine's annual list of the best hotels in Greece. Doubles run 290€ to 390€; suites are priced from 650€ to 1,000€.

The enormous **Santa Marina,** also at Ornos Bay (info@santa-marina.gr; ✆ **22890/23-200;** fax 22890/23-412), has 90 suites and villas on eight landscaped hectares (20 acres) overlooking the bay. If you don't want to swim in the sea, two pools and spa facilities are available at the hotel, which has its own **restaurant.** Suites with private pools are available from 1,500€. If you wish, you can arrive here by helicopter and land on the hotel pad. Doubles run from 395€ to 600€, suites and villas from 625€ to 2,400€. The more modest 25-unit **Best Western Dionysos Hotel** (✆ **22890/23-313**) is steps from the beach and has a pool, restaurant, bar, and air-conditioned rooms with fridges and TV; doubles from 190€. The even more modest 42-unit **Hotel Yiannaki** (✆ **22890/23-393**) is about 200m (656 ft.) from the beach and has its own pool and restaurant; doubles from 125€. Some have sea views and balconies.

Families traveling with children will find staying at one of the Ornos Bay hotels appealing. The beach is excellent and slopes into shallow, calm water. It's also not one of Mykonos's all-night party beaches. If your hotel does not have watersports facilities, several of the tavernas have surfboards and pedal boats to rent, as well as umbrellas. One minus: The beach is close to the airport, so you will hear planes come and go.

AT PLATI YIALOS   The large and comfortable rooms of the 82-unit **Hotel Petassos Bay,** Plati Yialos, 84600 Mykonos (✆ **22890/23-737;** fax 22890/24-101), all have air-conditioning and minibars. Doubles go for about 150€. Each has a balcony overlooking the relatively secluded beach, which is less than 36m (118 ft.) away. The hotel has a good-size pool, sun deck, Jacuzzi, gym, and sauna. It offers free round-trip transportation to and from the harbor or airport, safety-deposit boxes, and laundry service. The new seaside restaurant has a great view and serves a big buffet breakfast (a smaller continental breakfast is included in the room rate).

AT AYIOS IOANNIS **Mykonos Grand** is a 100-room luxury resort a few miles out of Hora in Ayios Ioannis, 84600 Mykonos (www.mykonosgrand.gr; ☎ **22890/25-555**). With its own beach and many amenities—pools, tennis, squash, Jacuzzis, a spa—this is a very sybaritic place. The Mykonos Grand regularly appears on *Odyssey* magazine's list of the 50 best hotels in Greece and is popular with Greeks, Europeans, and Americans. Doubles start at 225€. The **St. John Hotel,** Ayios Ioannis, 84600 Mykonos (www.saintjohn.gr; ☎ **22890/28-752; fax 22890/28-751**), has doubles from 310€ and suites from 590€. It's a breathtaking hotel, on a hillside over the Aegean, with spectacular sea vistas and a stunning infinity pool that has views over the cliff and into the sea. The St. John resembles a traditional blue-and-white village, complete with its own chapel. With 148 guest rooms and 9 suites, the rooms are huge, decorated in warm hues of deep peach, with simple and elegant furniture, marble bathrooms overflowing with products and their own Jacuzzi, and grand balconies with sea vistas as far as the eye can see. There's a superb **restaurant** and spa, three pools, and its own private beach.

AT AYIOS STEPHANOS This popular resort, about 4km (2½ miles) north of Hora, has a number of hotels. Most close from November to March. The 38-unit **Princess of Mykonos,** Ayios Stephanos beach, 84600 Mykonos (☎ **22890/23-806; fax 22890/23-031**), is lovely. The Princess has bungalows, a gym, a pool, and an excellent beach; doubles cost from 180€. **Hotel Artemis,** Ayios Stephanos, 84600 Mykonos (☎ **22890/22-345**), near the beach and bus stop, offers 23 units from 115€, breakfast included. Small **Hotel Mina,** Ayios Stephanos, 84600 Mykonos (☎ **22890/23-024**), uphill behind the Artemis, has 15 doubles that go for 80€.

   Mykonos Grace ★★, Ayios Stefanos, 84600 Mykonos (☎ **22890/26-690;** www.mykonosgrace.com), is an intimate yet undeniably stunning boutique hotel. Some of the hotel's 39 rooms might be on the small side, but the glass that separates the bathroom from the bedroom adds depth and the illusion of extra space, and huge balconies with stunning views more than compensate. Rooms range from standard to VIP suites, all with minimalistic design (230€–330€ double; 320€–420€ junior suite). Elegant and sophisticated, the Mykonos Grace won *Odyssey* magazine's "Best New Entry" award for 2007 and was singled out by the *London Sunday Times* as one of the hippest new hotels of 2007, after its complete face-lift that year. Guests can swim in the sea off Ayios Stephanos beach, or in one of several hotel pools, or soak in the spa Jacuzzis or their suite's hot tub. Decor, food, and privacy all get high marks—as do the prices, which are less extravagant than at some of Mykonos's other boutique hotels. It's only a 5-minute walk to town to boot.

AT PSARROU BEACH **Grecotel Mykonos Blu** ★★, Psarrou Beach, 84600 Mykonos (www.grecotel.gr; ☎ **22890/27-900; fax 22890/27-783**), is another of the island's serious luxury hotels with award-winning Cyclades-inspired architecture. Like Cavo Tagoo and Kivotos, this place is popular with wealthy Greeks, honeymooners, and jet-setters. The private beach, large pool, and in-house Poets of the Aegean restaurant allow guests to be as lazy as they wish (although there is a fitness club and spa for the energetic). Doubles run from 250€ to 450€.

Where to Eat

Camares Cafe (☎ **22890/28-570**), on Mavroyenous (Taxi) Square, has light meals and a fine view of the harbor from its terrace. It's open 24 hours and, for Mykonos, is very reasonably priced. Try the *strifwpita* or crispy fried *xinotiro* (bitter cheese) and the thyme-scented grilled lamb chops (9am–2am; no credit cards). As is usual on the islands, most of the harborside tavernas are expensive and mediocre, although **Kounelas ★**, on the harbor (no phone; no credit cards), is still a good value for fresh fish—as attested to by the presence of locals dining here.

Restaurants come and go here, so check with other travelers or locals as to what's just opened and is getting good reviews.

Antonini's GREEK   Antonini's is one of the oldest of Mykonos's restaurants. It serves consistently decent stews, chops, and *mezedes*. Locals eat here, although in summer they tend to leave the place to tourists.

Plateia Manto, Hora. ℂ **22890/22-319.** Main courses 9€–18€. No credit cards. Summer daily noon–3pm and 7pm–1am. Usually closed Nov–Mar.

Aqua Taverna ★★ MEDITERRANEAN/ITALIAN   Aqua, in Little Venice, has the ideal location, right by the sea with a view of the windmills and the sea. It's an impossible location to beat, picture perfect, romantic, and serene, so it's a surprise that this Mediterranean/Italian restaurant doesn't rely on its location but rather on its excellent food. Specials vary from day to day depending to the catch of the day; however, some dishes are staples. The spaghetti with lemon, olive oil, and Parmesan cheese; the seafood pasta; the lobster pasta; and the risotto and steamed mussels are all excellent. For a great meal during the island's stunning sunset, reserve a table on the terrace.

Little Venice, Hora. ℂ **22890/26-083.** Main courses 18€–35€. AE, DC, MC, V. Summer daily 7pm–1am.

Avra Restaurant (the Breeze) ★ GREEK/MEDITERRANEAN   You can dine in this wonderful restaurant on either its busy terrace, in its more intimate interior, or in its lovely private garden. Try the octopus in white sauce, the stuffed chicken (with cheese, vegetables, and apricots), the stuffed lamb (with cheese, vegetables, and mustard), or the salmon risotto—all are excellent choices.

Garden Kalogera St. (behind Alpha Bank, on Matoyanni St.), Hora. ℂ **22890/22-298.** Main courses 20€–40€. DC, V. Daily 7pm–2am. Closed Nov–Mar.

Casa di Giorgio ★ ITALIAN   Giorgio's grandson transformed his grandfather's old village house, located right behind the Catholic cathedral, into an exceptional Italian restaurant. Excellent risotto and linguine, traditional oven-baked thin-crust pizza, succulent sausages, and shrimp pasta are just the highlights.

1 Mitropoleos St., Hora. ℂ **69325/61-998.** http://casadigiorgio-mykonos.gr. Main courses 12€–25€. AE, DC, MC, V. Daily 11am–2am.

Chez Catrine ★★ GREEK/FRENCH   This is a pleasant place to spend the evening, enjoy a seafood soufflé or a seafood pasta, or try the chateaubriand. The candlelit dining room is so elegant that you won't mind being indoors. In addition to a wide variety of entrees, there is a range of excellent desserts. The feisty 70-year-old owner still makes her rounds night after night.

1 Nikiou St., Hora. ℂ **22890/22-169.** Reservations recommended July–Aug. Main courses 22€–44€. AE, DC, MC, V. Daily 7pm–1am.

Chez Marinas ★ GREEK   Formerly known as Maria's Garden, this is another longtime favorite, with a lovely, lantern- and candlelit garden full of bougainvillea and cacti, often animated by live music and fits of dancing. The vegetable dishes are always fresh and tasty, the lamb succulent, and the seafood enticing. In short, this is a place where ambience and cuisine come together to make a very successful restaurant. There's often a good-value set menu for around 25€.

27 Kaloyera, Hora. © **22890/27-565.** Reservations recommended July–Aug. Main courses 15€–30€. DC, V. Daily 7pm–1am.

Club Belvedere ★★ GREEK   Inside the ultratrendy Belvedere Hotel, across the lantern-lit pool from where Matsuhisa Mykonos is housed, this restaurant offers Greek cuisine with a twist, by Greek-Australian chef George Calombaris. The *kerasma* menu (treat menu, 80€) is a great way to sample some of the restaurant's finest offerings, including mussels, spinach pie, and *saganaki*. The bread is made daily and is served with locally made olive oil as well as black sea salt from Cyprus's volcanic salt beaches (something you must experience to appreciate). Grilled fish, vegetable and/or meat skewers, and the hearty and fresh salads are also top notch. Add to this impeccable service and sublime setting, and you have an ideal dining experience.

At the Belvedere Hotel, Hora. © **22890/25-122.** Reservations essential July–Sept. Main courses 35€–82€. AE, DC, MC, V. Daily 8pm–1am.

Danielle's Restaurant ★★ GREEK/MEDITERRANEAN   On the road from town to Ano Mera, this wonderful restaurant has excellent fare, combining traditional Greek island dishes with Mediterranean cuisine to stunning results. The salads are fresh and delicious, the pasta dishes are all excellent, and the wine is exceptional. Hands-down one of the best restaurants in Mykonos.

On the road to Ano Mera, Hora. © **22890/71-513.** Main courses 25€–40€. MC, V. Daily 7pm–1am. Closed Nov–Feb.

Edem Restaurant ★ GREEK/CONTINENTAL   This is one of the oldest restaurants in Hora, with a reputation for good food, built over 30 years. Tables are clustered around a courtyard pool—diners have been known to make a splash upon arrival with a preprandial swim—and the courtyard is a pleasant place to enjoy a leisurely dinner even if you aren't dressed for the water. Edem is known for its variety of lamb dishes and fresh fish—but the eclectic menu includes steak, pasta, and a variety of traditional Greek and Continental dishes. The service is good and the produce as fresh as you'll see on Mykonos.

Above Panachra Church, Hora. © **22890/23-355.** Reservations recommended July–Aug. Main courses 8€–30€; fish priced by the kilo. AE, DC, MC, V. Daily 6pm–1am. In off season, sometimes open for lunch. Walk up Matoyianni, turn left on Kaloyera, and follow the signs up and to the left.

El Greco/Yorgos GREEK/CONTINENTAL   Put aside your suspicions of a place called El Greco and be prepared to enjoy traditional recipes collected from various regions of Greece. The eclectic menu includes traditional dishes; from Kerkira, for example, *bourdeto* is a monkfish-and-shellfish stew in tomato-and-wine sauce. Many concoctions feature such local produce, such as mushrooms with Mykonian cheese. This place is doing something right: It's been here since the 1960s.

Plateia Tria Pigadia, Hora. © **22890/22-074.** Main courses 9€–30€; fish priced by the kilo. AE, DC, MC, V. Daily 7pm–1am.

Interni ★★ ASIAN FUSION   With its avant-garde space and fusion cuisine, Interni is one of the island's most fashionable restaurants. A happening bar scene is popular with affluent young Athenians, but the attraction is the cuisine. Try the marinated salmon and stir-fried seafood noodles, and you'll get what the fuss is about.

Hora, Matoyanni. © **22890/26-333.** www.interni.gr. Main courses 18€–40€. DC, V. Daily 8pm–2am.

Mamakas Mykonos ★★ GREEK/MODERN   This is a branch of the Mamakas that opened its second location in the down-at-the-heels area of Gazi, in Athens, in 1998, and helped transform the area from gritty to chic, while managing to start a new trend—traditional taverna fare with modern twists. This is where it all started, right by the Taxi Square, inside a lovely house built in 1845. You can dine in the courtyard (the terra-cotta planters were a gift from the Princess of Malta to the present owner's grandmother) or indoors. The meals are just as delicious and reasonably priced as ever. Check out the trays of cooked dishes (*magirefta*) and a range of dependable and delicious grills and appetizers—the spicy meatballs (*keftedakia*) are a must!

Hora, Mykonos. ℂ **22890/26-120.** www.mamakas.gr. Main courses 14€–30€. AE, MC, V. Daily 8pm–1:30am.

Matsuhisha Mykonos ★★ JAPANESE   Nobu Matsuhisa has extended his sushi empire to this, his only open-air restaurant, in the most happening hotel in town, the Belvedere. Right by the hotel's pool, with views of the sea and town, try the exceptional Japanese cuisine with Latin influences that will have you yearning for more, despite the high prices. Top-quality ingredients and sushi are flown in daily from Japan. Begin with a sakepirnha, the famous Brazilian cocktail made with sake instead of cachaça, and then continue to pick your way through the chef's choice tasting menu.

At the Belvedere Hotel, Hora. ℂ **22890/25-122.** Reservations essential July–Sept. Main courses 68€–82€. AE, DC, MC, V. Daily 8pm–1am.

Philippi ★ GREEK/CONTINENTAL   One of the island's most romantic dining experiences, Philippi is in a quiet garden. Old Greek favorites share space on the menu with French dishes and a more than usually impressive wine list. What this restaurant provides in abundance is *atmosphere,* and that's what has made it a perennial favorite.

Just off Matoyianni and Kaloyera, behind the eponymous hotel, Hora. ℂ **22890/22-294.** Reservations recommended July–Aug. Main courses 10€–25€. AE, MC, V. Daily 7pm–1am.

Sea Satin Market ★★ GREEK/SEAFOOD   Below the windmills, beyond the small beach adjacent to Little Venice, the *paralia* ends in a rocky headland facing the open sea. This is the location of one of Hora's most charming restaurants. Set apart from the clamor of the town, it's one of the quietest spots in the area despite the fact that the closing scene of *The Bourne Identity* was filmed here. On a still summer night, just after sunset, the atmosphere is all you could hope for. At the front of the restaurant, the kitchen activity is on view, along with the day's catch sizzling on the grill. You can make a meal on *mezedes* here, or let it rip with grilled *bon filet.* A couple of readers have recently mentioned "nonchalant" and "slow" service; let us know what you think.

Near the Mitropolis Cathedral, Hora. ℂ **22890/24-676.** Main courses 20€–45€. No credit cards. Daily 6:30pm–12:30am.

Sesame Kitchen GREEK/CONTINENTAL   This small, health-conscious taverna, which serves some vegetarian specialties, is next to the Naval Museum. Fresh spinach, vegetable, cheese, and chicken pies are baked daily. A large variety of salads, brown rice, and soy dishes are offered, as well as a vegetable moussaka and stir-fried veggies. Lightly grilled and seasoned meat dishes are available.

Plateia Tria Pigadia, Hora. ℂ **22890/24-710.** Main courses 8€–18€. AE, V. Daily 7pm–midnight.

Uno con Carme ARGENTINE   Set in the stunningly beautiful Art Deco space of a former open-air cinema, this fine restaurant also has an excellent bar and lounge for those wishing to take in the ambience with a drink. This steakhouse, apart from its excellent selection of meats (the T-bones are amazing) also has generously proportioned fresh salads, an excellent wine selection, and ambience to spare.

Panachra, Hora. © **22890/24-020.** Main courses 30€–60€. AE, DC, MC, V. Daily 8pm–1am.

Out-of-Town Delights

PSAROU

N'Ammos ★★ GREEK   On hip Psarou beach, N'Ammos, with its casual elegance and beachfront setting, is one of the island's finest restaurants. Wealthy Athenians stop by Mykonos just to have lunch here and taste the lobster-pumpkin risotto. Other highlights are the spicy Mykonian meatballs, the marinated anchovies, fresh fish, and T-bone steaks.

Psarou Beach. © **22890/22-440.** Main courses 25€–45€. AE, DC, MC, V. Daily 1pm–1am.

AYIOS SOSTIS

Kiki's Taverna GREEK   A small, delightful, unspoiled taverna (with no sign, telephone number, or electricity) is open only until sundown. Adjacent to the secluded Ayios Sostis beach, they serve island food the way it should taste. Meat and fish are grilled on a charcoal barbecue and served in the restaurant's shady courtyard. Be sure to try the tasty salads, too.

Ayios Sostis beach. No phone. Main courses 8€–18€. Daily 11am–6pm.

FOKOS BEACH

Fokos GREEK   On a secluded beach adored by surfers, Fokos serves excellent traditional Greek cuisine that's unpretentious and delicious. Fresh local meat, fish of the day, and vegetables flown in daily from the owners' garden on the island of Crete make the unpretentious meals here some of Mykonos's best.

Fokos Beach. © **22890/23-205.** Main courses 8€–18€. No credit cards. Daily 10am–7pm.

Mykonos After Dark

Once you arrive on Mykonos you will realize that the day has just as many party options as the night. As such, I've organized this section to give you party options for both day life and nightlife. Drinks in Mykonos are expensive; rarely less than 9€, but the good news is, if you are planning to head out at night, there are many supermarkets where you can buy a decent bottle of wine for no more than 6€ and begin your own party before hitting the town. As in previous sections, I do not give phone numbers or addresses for clubs and bars, as phones are never answered and the clubs and bars are located virtually on top of one another in Mykonos town.

DAY

Beach parties dominate the scene during the day. The most famous parties happen at Psarrou beach, where a hopping bar/club keeps the (mostly) Athenian crowd joyful. On Paradise beach, the **Tropicana Bar** and the **Sunrise Bar** cater to a more mixed crowd, and at Super Paradise, two loud bar/clubs on opposite sides of the beach cater to gay and mixed crowds, respectively. All three beaches have sunset parties, starting around 6pm, but it is Paradise Beach's **Paradise Club,** with its gigantic swimming pool in the middle of the club, that steals the show with its nightly fireworks and a wild party that lasts until midnight.

SUNSET

Back in town, things are less wild and more sophisticated around sunset. For over a quarter of a century, **Caprice** has been the island's sunset institution, with chairs lined along its narrow porch overlooking Little Venice, the windmills, and the sea. It is extremely popular with the Athenians (but it has caught on with the rest of the tourists as well). It isn't rare to come straight from the beach for the sunset and spend the entire night. The indoor area (set like a series of caves, with candlelit corners and a window opening up directly to the sea) is intimate and romantic.

Another must-visit sunset destination is the **Oneiro Bar** perched on a beautiful deck overlooking the sea. Coming here will also give you a chance to check out the bar scene at the Mykonos View hotel. The **CBar Lounge,** set in the Belvedere Hotel, offers breathtaking sunset vistas with menu, drinks, and decor by renowned wedding designer Colin Cowie. Back in Little Venice—or "Sunset Central," as it's sometimes called—**Kastro,** near the Paraportiani Church, is famous for its classical music and frozen daiquiris. This is a great spot to watch or join handsome young men flirting with each other. **Montparnasse** is cozier, with classical music and Toulouse-Lautrec posters. At night this becomes a very popular (mostly with a gay crowd) piano bar. **Veranda,** in an old mansion overlooking the water with a good view of the windmills, is as laid back as its name might imply. **Galeraki** has a wide variety of exotic cocktails (and customers); the in-house art gallery gives this popular spot its name, "Little Gallery." After dark, it turns into a loud and fun bar/club.

With sunset out of the way, most head back to their rooms for a quick shower and change of wardrobe before heading out to dinner and then for after-dark fun.

AFTER DINNER

Aroma bar is popular day and night, as it occupies one of the finest people-watching locations, right on busy Matoyanni Street. It's a great place for an after-dinner drink. **Astra** is a legendary bar and elegant lounge, with groovy modernist rooms with wonderful indoor and outdoor seating, and the perfect place to begin the night—or stay all night, as it morphs from a casual lounge to a pumping dance club when some of Athens's top DJs take over. Right in the entrance of town from the old harbor, the Athenian hot spot, Spanish restaurant/bar/club **El Pecado (The Sin),** moves to Mykonos in the summer and takes over the old space occupied by the infamous Remezzo. El Pecado has a great tapas bar and very good cuisine, but it is the sangria and the rum-based drinks, combined with the Latin beats (with some Greek as well), that make this such a fun place. Just follow the music.

Uno, a tiny bar on Matoyanni, is a popular destination for Athenians—peek inside to see why, or join in the fun. **New Faces,** formerly known as Down Under, is popular with a northern European and American crowd under 25, in large part because the happy hour extends from 9pm to midnight. On busy Matoyanni, **Pierro's (www.pierrosbar.gr)** is extremely popular with gay visitors and rocks all night long to American and European music. Adjacent **Icarus** is best known for its terrace and late-night drag shows. During the early evening hours, both bars are so popular that sometimes just walking by is difficult. In Taxi Square, another popular gay club, **Ramrod,** has a terrace with a view over the harbor and live drag shows after midnight. Even though the island used to have a loud and large gay club, it no longer does, so Pierro's (after 2am) is the closest you get, which quite frankly, is pretty close, as is **Yacht Club** (see below in "After Hours"). **Porta** (*©* **22890/27-807**), a popular gay cruising spot, is busy from 9pm onward.

The **Anchor** plays blues, jazz, and classic rock for its 30-something clients, as do **Argo, Stavros Irish Bar, Celebrities Bar,** and **Scandinavian Bar-Disco.** They draw customers from Ireland, Scandinavia, and quite possibly as far away as Antarctica. If you'd like to sample Greek music and dancing, try **Thalami,** a small club underneath the town hall. For a more intense Greek night out, head to **Guzel**—at Gialos, by the waterfront and near Taxi Square—the place to experience a super-trendy hangout, populated mostly by hip Athenians, with Greek and international hits that drive the crowd into a frenzy, with people dancing on the tables and on the bars. It's the sort of place that by the end of the night, you feel like you have partied with a group of close friends. Don't be intimidated if you aren't Greek. Go and have a blast! If you're looking for a club before 4am, try **Space Club,** by Lekka Square. It's extremely popular with the under-30 crowd, with a large dance floor and theme nights. The 10€ to 20€ entrance fee includes a drink.

If having a quiet evening and catching a movie is more your speed, head for **Cine Manto** (*C* 22890/27-190), in the Municipal Garden of Meletopoulou, a small oasis of green on this arid island. Films show nightly around 9pm. Many films are American; most Greek films have English subtitles.

AFTER HOURS

To continue late into the night, head for Paradise beach (take the bus from town), to either **Cavo Paradiso** (**www.cavoparadiso.gr**), on the hill (cover 25€–50€ depending on DJ and event; nightly 2–10am), or to **Paradise Club,** a large club by the beach (cover 15€–20€; nightly 2–6am). Both clubs are extremely popular, with rotating international DJs, theme nights, huge pools, and great views. If you last until they close, you can just go for a swim and begin the day all over again. After all, sunset is only a few hours away.

For those who want to continue their partying after 4am but don't want to go all the way to Paradise beach, there is **Yacht Club,** which is really the cafe by the old port that, for some reason, turns to a popular mixed bar/club after hours. Wild flirting, drinking, and dancing ensue—this is the perfect place to end the night and to finally get together with the object of your affection. Being a mixed place, there is something for everybody here.

If you're visiting between July and September, find out what's happening at **Anemo Theatre** (*C* 22890/23-944), an outdoor venue for the performing arts, in a garden in Rohari, just above town. A wide variety of concerts, performances, and talks are usually planned.

DELOS ★★★

There is as much to see at **Delos** as at Olympia and Delphi, and there is absolutely no shade on this blindingly white marble island covered with marble monuments. Just 3km (2 miles) from Mykonos, little Delos was considered by the ancient Greeks to be one of the holiest of sanctuaries, the fixed point around which the other Cycladic islands circled. It was Poseidon who anchored Delos to make a sanctuary for Leto, impregnated (like so many other maidens) by Zeus and pursued (like so many of those other maidens) by Zeus's aggrieved wife, Hera. Here, on Delos, Leto gave birth to Apollo and his sister, Artemis; thereafter, Delos was sacred to both gods, although Apollo's sanctuary was the more important. For much of antiquity, people were not allowed to die or give birth here, but were bundled off to the nearby islet of Rinia.

Delos

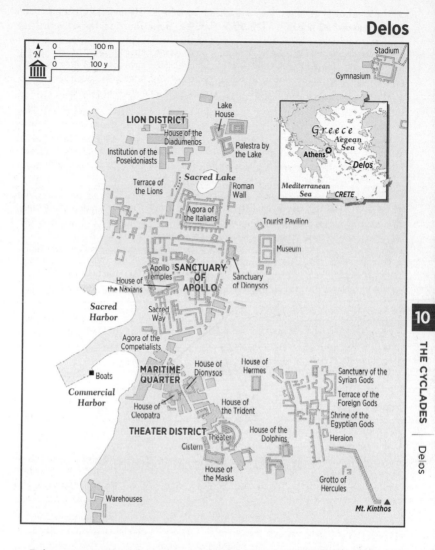

Delos was not exclusively a religious sanctuary: For much of its history, the island was a thriving commercial port, especially under the Romans in the 3rd and 2nd centuries B.C. As many as 10,000 slaves a day were sold here on some days; the island's prosperity went into a steep decline after Mithridates of Pontus, an Asia Minor monarch at war with Rome, attacked Delos in 88 B.C., slaughtered its 20,000 inhabitants, and sailed home with as much booty as he could carry in his fleet of ships.

The easiest way to get to Delos is by caique from Mykonos; in summer, there are sometimes excursion boats here from Tinos and Paros. Try not to have a late night before you come here, and catch the first boat of the day (usually around 8:30am). As the day goes on, the heat and crowds here can be overwhelming. On summer afternoons, when cruise ships disgorge their passengers, Delos can make the Acropolis look

Heavy seas can suddenly prevent boats docking at Delos. Follow the advice of the Roman poet Horace and *carpe diem* (seize the day). If you want to visit Delos, come here as soon as possible; if you decide to save your visit here for your last day in the area, rough seas may leave you stranded ashore.

shady and deserted. Sturdy shoes are a good idea here; a hat, water, munchies, and sunscreen are a necessity *Tip:* Bring water and a snack; the snack bar on Delos, minimal at best, is often closed. Toilet facilities are limited here.

Essentials

GETTING THERE From Mykonos, organized guided and unguided excursions leave starting about 8:30am about four times a day Tuesday through Sunday at the harbor's west end. Every travel agency in town advertises its Delos excursions (some with guides). Individual caique owners also have signs stating their prices and schedules. The trip takes about 30 minutes and costs about 10€ round-trip; as long as you return with the boat that brought you, you can (space available) decide which return trip you want to take when you've had enough. The last boat for Mykonos usually leaves by 4pm. The site is **closed** on Mondays.

Warning: If you're heading to Delos just to see the Avenue of the Lions, double-check to see if the lions are in place. Recent restoration activity and staff cutbacks have had caused some of the noble beasts to have to endure the indignity of being put into storage. Some replicas have been substituted on the site.

Exploring the Site

Entrance to the site and museum will cost 6€, unless this was included in the price of your excursion. At the ticket kiosk, you'll see a number of site plans and picture guides for sale; *Delos & Mykonos: A Guide to the History and Archaeology,* by Konstantinos Tsakos (Hesperos Editions), is a reliable guide to the site and the museum. Signs throughout the site are in Greek and French (the French have excavated here since the late 19th c.).

To the left (north) of the jetty where your boat will dock is the **Sacred Harbor,** now too silted for use, where pilgrims, merchants, and sailors from throughout the Mediterranean used to land. The commercial importance of the island in ancient times was due to its harbor, which made Delos an excellent stopping-off point between mainland Greece and its colonies and trading partners in Asia Minor.

The remains at Delos are not easy to decipher, but when you come ashore, you can head right, toward the theater and residential area, or left, to the more public area of ancient Delos, the famous avenue of the lions, and the museum. Let's head left, toward the **Agora of the Competialists,** built in the 2nd century B.C., when the island was a bustling free port under Rome. The agora's name comes from the *lares competales,* who were minor "crossroad" deities associated with the Greek god Hermes, patron of travelers and commerce. This made them popular deities with the Roman citizens here, mostly former slaves engaged in commerce. The agora dates from the period when Delos's importance as a port had superseded its importance as a religious sanctuary. To reach the earlier religious sanctuary, take the **Sacred**

Way—once lined with statues and votive monuments—north from the agora toward the Sanctuary of Apollo. Although the entire island was sacred to Apollo, during Greek antiquity this was where his sanctuary and temples were. By retracing the steps of ancient pilgrims along it, you will pass the scant remains of several temples (most of the stone from the site was taken away for buildings on neighboring islands, including Naxos, Mykonos, and Tinos). At the far end of the Sacred Way was the **Propylaea,** a marble gateway that led into the sanctuary. As at Delphi and Olympia, the sanctuary here on Delos would have been chockablock with temples, altars, statues, and votive offerings. You can see some of what remains in the **museum,** which has finds from the various excavations on the island. Admission to the museum is included in the site's entrance fee. Beside the museum, the remains of the Sanctuary of Dionysos are usually identifiable by the crowd snapping shots of the display of marble phalluses, many on tall plinths.

North of the museum and the adjacent tourist pavilion is the **Sacred Lake,** where swans credited with powers of uttering oracles once swam. The lake is now little more than a dusty indentation most of the year, surrounded by a low wall. Beyond it is the famous **Avenue of the Lions ★,** made of Naxian marble and erected in the 7th century B.C. There were originally at least nine lions. One was taken away to Venice in the 17th century and now stands before the *arsenali* there. The whereabouts of the others lost in antiquity remains a mystery; five were carted off to the museum for restoration some years ago and replaced by replicas. Beyond the lake to the northeast is the large square courtyard of the gymnasium and the long narrow stadium, where the athletic competitions of the Delian Games were held.

If you stroll back along the Sacred Way to the harbor, you can head next to the **Maritime quarter,** a residential area with the remains of houses from the Hellenistic and Roman eras, when the island reached its peak in wealth and prestige. Several houses contain brilliant **mosaics ★,** and in most houses the cistern and sewer systems can be seen. Among the numerous small dwellings are several magnificent villas, built around a central court and connected to the street by a narrow passage. The mosaics in the palace courtyards are particularly dazzling, and include such famous images as Dionysos riding a panther in the **House of the Masks,** and a similar depiction in the **House of Dionysos.** Farther to the south is the massive **Theater,** which seated 5,500 people and was the site of choral competitions during the Delian Festivals, an event held every 4 years that included athletic competitions in addition to musical contests. You may see donation boxes here: the Diazoma Organization, fearing that the Greek government has neither the funds nor the will to restore the theater, is attempting to finance the restoration privately. Behind the theater is a fine arched **cistern,** which was the water supply for the city. If you visit here in spring, the wildflowers are especially beautiful, and the chorus of frogs that live in and around the cisterns will be at its peak.

If you're not on a tour and have the energy, consider wrapping up your visit by getting an overview of the site—and of the Cyclades—from **Mount Kinthos ★,** the highest point on the island. On many days, nearby Mykonos, as well as Siros to the west, Tinos to the north, and Naxos and Paros to the south are easy to spot. On your way down, keep an eye out for the **Grotto of Hercules,** a small temple built into a natural crevice in the mountainside—the roof is formed of massive granite slabs held up by their own enormous weight.

10

THE CYCLADES | Delos

TINOS ★★

161km (87 nautical miles) SE of Piraeus

Tinos has some very good restaurants, some fine beaches, exquisite dovecotes, and handsome villages with houses decorated with locally carved marble doorways and window fanlights. But that's not why most people come here. Each year, thousands of pilgrims come here to pray before the icon of the Virgin Mary in the church of the **Panagia Evangelistria (Our Lady of Good Tidings)**—sometimes called the "Lourdes of Greece." Thousands of others come here to baptize their babies at Greece's holiest shrine. Although Tinos is the most important destination in all of Greece for religious pilgrims, it remains one of the least commercialized islands of the Cyclades—and a joy to visit for that reason. Don't let your first sight of Tinos's undistinguished harbor alarm you: behind the seaside sprawl of architecturally undistinguished restaurants, and cafes are lovely meandering lanes just waiting for you to get lost in them and discover their little courtyards and chapels.

From well out to sea, **Panagia Evangelistria**—illuminated at night—is visible atop a hill overlooking Tinos town. Almost any day of the year you can see people, particularly elderly women, crawling from the port on hands and knees up Megalocharis, the long, steep street that leads to the red-carpeted steps that are the final approach to the cathedral. Adjacent pedestrian-only Evangelistria is a market street, as well as a pilgrimage route for those who choose to walk it. The street is lined with stalls selling vials of holy water, incense, candles (up to 2m/7 ft. long), and mass-produced icons. There are also several jewelry and handicrafts shops, one or two cafes, groceries, old-fashioned dry-goods stores—and a surprising number of shops selling both incense and battery-powered kittens that roll over and meow.

Don't even think about arriving on Tinos without a reservation around **August 15** (Feast of the Assumption of the Virgin), when thousands of pilgrims travel here to celebrate the occasion. **March 25** (Feast of the Annunciation) is the second-most important feast day here, but it draws fewer pilgrims because it is harder to travel by sea in March. Pilgrims come here on **July 23** (the anniversary of St. Pelagia's vision of the icon) and on **January 30** (the anniversary of the finding of the icon). Remember that Tinos is a *pilgrimage place:* It is considered very disrespectful to wear shorts, short skirts, halters, or sleeveless shirts in the precincts of the Evangelistria (or any other church, for that matter). Photographing the pilgrims, especially those approaching the shrine on hands and knees, is not appropriate. On the other hand, photographing the joyful baptismal parties approaching or leaving the church is just fine.

Like Naxos, Tinos was ruled by Venice for several centuries and, like Naxos, Tinos still has a sizeable Catholic population. You'll see signs of Tinos's Venetian heritage in the number of fine old Venetian mansions (known as *pallada,* the word also used for the harborfront), on the streets off the harbor. Tinos town has a clutch of Catholic churches, including the harborfront churches of St. Anthony and St. Nicolas; out on the island, the **Church of the Virgin Mary Vrisiotissa,** near the village of Ag. Romanos, on the main Hora-Pirgos road, is an important Catholic pilgrimage shrine. The village of **Loutra** (see "Exploring the Island," below) has a folk-art museum in a Jesuit monastery, staffed by monks who come here from around the world.

The villages of Tinos are some of the most beautiful in the Cyclades. Many of the most picturesque are nestled into the slopes of **Exobourgo,** the rocky pinnacle crowned by a Venetian castle visible from the port. Many villages are connected by a network of walking paths that make this island a hiker's paradise. In these villages and

Looking for Dove . . .

Tinos is famous for its **dovecotes**, stout stone towers elaborately ornamented with slabs of the local shale, with ornamental perches and passageways for the doves. Venetians built the first dovecotes here. They brought with them the dovecote's distinctive miniature tower architecture. They used the doves' droppings as fertilizer, and the birds soon became an important part of the local diet. Locals still sometimes cook them, often in tomato sauce, as a winter dish. Some of the most elaborate of these birdhouses grace the towns of **Tarambados** and **Smardakito;** keep your eyes open. It is said that the island is home to 2,000 of them. Look for signs announcing detours to TRADITIONAL DOVECOTES as you explore the island.

dotting the countryside, you'll see the ornately decorated medieval *peristerionades* (**dovecotes**) for which the island is famous, as well as elaborately carved marble lintels, door jambs, and fan windows on village houses. According to one tradition, there are 365 churches scattered across the island, one for every day of the year; others boast that the island has 1,000 churches. The island's beaches aren't worthy of superlatives, but they are plentiful and uncrowded throughout the summer. All this may change if an airport is built here—all the more reason to visit Tinos now. If you want to do as the Greeks do, you'll spend a day or two here; do that once, and you may find that you keep coming back to this *very* Greek island.

Essentials

GETTING THERE   Several ferries travel to Tinos daily from Piraeus (5 hr.). Catamaran (1½ hr.) and ferry services (4 hr.) are available daily in summer from Rafina. Check schedules at the Athens **GNTO** (✆ **210/331-0562**); **Piraeus Port Authority** (✆ **210/459-3223** or 210/422-6000; phone seldom answered); or **Rafina Port Authority** (✆ **22940/22-300**). Several times a day, boats connect Tinos with nearby Mykonos (20–35 min.); there's daily service to Paros (and thence to many islands) in summer, and to and from Siros every day. Tinos has more winter connections than most Cycladic isles due to its religious tourism, which continues throughout the year.

There are three ports in Tinos harbor. Be sure to find out from which pier your ship will depart—and be prepared for last-minute changes. The small catamarans (Seajet, Flying Cat, and Jet One) dock at the old pier in the town center; the large and high-speed ferries use the new pier to the north, on the side of town in the direction of Kionia. **Tinos Port Authority** (not guaranteed to be helpful) can be reached at ✆ **22830/22-348.**

VISITOR INFORMATION   For information on accommodations, car rentals, island tours, and Tinos in general, contact Sharon Turner (sharon@thn.forthnet.gr) at **Windmills Travel ★★** (✆ **22830/23-398;** fax 22830/23-327; www.windmills travel.com). She is the friendly, helpful, and efficient Windmills Tinos representative, with unparalleled knowledge of Tinos and its neighboring islands. She sees clients at her office by appointment, but can solve almost any problem and supply information on Tinos, the Cyclades, and beyond by phone and email.

GETTING AROUND   By Bus   The **bus station** (✆ **22830/22-440**) is beside the Catholic church on the harbor, above the pier where the large island boats dock.

Schedules are usually posted or available here. There are frequent daily buses to most island villages. The local bus company also offers a tour of the island, which usually departs from the Tinos town station daily from late June to late September at 10am; it returns to Tinos town around 5pm, after stopping at a number of villages and for lunch and a swim at Panormos. The 15€ charge does not include lunch. It is an excellent way to get an initial sense of the island. If you speak Greek, or feel adventurous, do this tour simply by hopping on a variety of local buses.

By Car & Moped   Vidalis Car Hire on the harbor at 2 Trion Hierarchon, where taxis congregate (© 22830/15-670; www.vidalis-rentacar.gr), has a wide range of vehicles. Expect to pay from 40€ per day for a car, half that for a moped; prices lower off season.

By Taxi   Taxis hang out on Trion Hierarchon, which runs uphill from the harbor just before Palamaris supermarket and Hotel Tinion.

FAST FACTS   There are several **banks** on the harbor, open Monday through Thursday from 8am to 2pm and Friday from 8am to 1:30pm; all have ATMs. The **first-aid center** can be reached at © 22830/22-210. For **luggage storage,** try Windmills Travel (© 22830/23-398). The **police** (© 22830/22-348) are located just past the new pier, past Lito Hotel and Windmills Travel. The **post office** (© 22830/22-247), open Monday through Friday from 7:30am to 2pm, is at the harbor's south end, next to Tinion Hotel. The **telephone office (OTE),** open Monday through Friday from 7:30am to 12:30pm, is on the main street leading to the church of Panagia Evangelistria, about halfway up on the right (© 22830/22-399). The **Tinos Cultural Foundation** (© 22830/29-070) has a small permanent collection and temporary exhibitions; admission is sometimes charged for special exhibits. It's usually open Monday, Wednesday, and Friday 10am to 2pm and 7 to 9pm; weekend hours are 10:30am to 2pm and 7 to 9pm. It also has the cheapest Internet service in town, with a nearby cafe.

What to See & Do

Panagia Evangelistria Cathedral and Museums ★★★   Each year, the **Church of Panagia Evangelistria (Our Lady of Good Tidings)** draws thousands of pilgrims seeking the aid of the church's miraculous icon. According to local lore, in 1882 a nun named Pelagia dreamed that the Virgin appeared to her and told her where to find a miraculous icon. A modest woman, Pelagia could not believe the Virgin would appear to her, but when the dreams did not stop, Pelagia sought out the bishop of Tinos, whom she informed of her dreams. The bishop, convinced of her piety, ordered excavations to begin. Before long, the remains, first of a Byzantine church and then of the icon itself, were unearthed. As is the case with many of the most holy icons, this one is believed to be the work of St. Luke. The icon was initially housed in the chapel of the Zoodohos Pigi, under the present cathedral. Astonishingly on such a small and

---

Trying Your Hand at Marble Carving

Tinos has a long tradition of marble carving. If you want to try your hand, the **Dellatos Marble Sculpture School** (© 22830/23-664; www.tinosmarble. com), just outside Tinos town, in Spitalia, offers 1- and 2-week workshops, from May through October, for would-be marble workers.

A Swim, a Snack, an Ancient Site

If you're staying in Tinos town, the easiest place to take a dip is the beach at Kionia, about 3km (2 miles) west of Hora. Just across from the pebble-and-sand strand where you'll swim are the island's only excavated antiquities, the modest remains of the Temple of Poseidon and one of his many conquests, Amphitrite, a semidivine sea nymph (Tues–Sun 8:30am–3pm; admission 3€). When sheep or the custodians have trimmed the vegetation at the site, you can make out the foundations of the 4th-century-B.C. temple, and a large altar and long stoa, both built in the 1st century B.C. As usual with a site where Romans lived, there are the remains of a bath. Finds from the site are on display at the Tinos town Archaeological Museum (Tues–Sun 8:30am–3pm; admission 3€). When you head back to town, you can have a drink and a snack at the Mistral or Tsambia taverna, both on the main road near the site. Closer to town, also on the main road, you can check your e-mail at the Para Pende cafe. Depending on your mood, you can do this excursion on foot, by public bus, or taxi. If on foot, keep to the side of the road and don't expect the trucks and motorcycles to cut you much slack.

poor island, the Parians built the massive church of the Panagia in just 2 years. The church is made of gleaming marble from Paros and Tinos, with a tall slender bell tower and handsome black-and-white pebble mosaics in the exterior courtyard.

At the end of Evangelistria Street, a broad flight of marble stairs leads you up to the church. Inside, hundreds of gold and silver hanging lamps illuminate the icon of the Virgin, to the left of the entrance. The icon is almost entirely hidden by votive offerings of gold, silver, diamonds, and precious gems dedicated by the faithful. Even those who do not make a lavish gift customarily make a small offering and light a candle. Watch for the silver ship with a fish hanging beneath it. According to tradition, a fierce storm threatened to sink a ship, which was taking in water through a breach in its hull. When the captain and crew called out to the Virgin for help, the storm abated and the ship reached harbor safely. When it was brought ashore for repairs, an enormous fish was discovered plugging the hole in the hull.

Beneath the church is the crypt with the chapel where the icon was found, surrounded by smaller chapels. The crypt is often crowded with Greek parents waiting to have their (usually howling) toddlers baptized here. Others come to fill vials with holy water from the spring.

Keep in mind that to enter the cathedral, men must wear long pants and shirts with sleeves, and women must wear dresses or skirts and blouses with sleeves. If there is a church service while you are here, you will hear the beautiful, resonant chanting that typifies a Greek Orthodox service—but remember that it's not appropriate to explore the church during a service. Services are usually held just after the church opens, just before it closes, and at other times during the day. A schedule of services is usually posted outside the main entrance.

Within the high walls that surround the church are various museums and galleries, each of which is worth a quick visit: a gallery of 14th- to 19th-century religious art, a gallery of more modern Tinian artists, and a sculpture museum. Admission is sometimes charged at these places.

Hora, Tinos. Free admission. Cathedral daily 8am–7pm (off-season hours vary); galleries Sat–Sun (some weekdays during July–Aug) 8am–8pm (off-season usually noon–6pm).

Exploring the Island

If it's a clear day, one of your first sights of Tinos from the ferry will be the odd mountain with a bare summit that looks bizarrely like a twisted fist. This is **Exobourgo ★★**, a mountain eminence crowned by the remains of a Venetian kastro (castle) about 15km (9 miles) outside of Hora. Sheer rock walls surround the fortress on three sides; the only path to the summit starts behind a Catholic church at the base of the rock, on the road between Mesi and Koumaros. As you make the 15-minute ascent, you'll pass several lines of fortification—the entire hill is riddled with walls and hollowed with chambers. As you might expect, the view over the Cyclades is superb from the summit (565m/1,854 ft.). The fortress itself has long been in ruins—and was never as imposing as, for example, the massive Venetian fortress at Nafplion in the Peloponnese. The Turks defeated the Venetians here in 1714 and drove them from the island.

The village of **Kambos ★** is not far from Exobourgo; with a car, nothing in Tinos is very far from anything else. In 2011, the **Costas Tsoclis Museum** (*©* **22830/51-009;** tinos@tsoclismuseum.gr. Mon–Sun 9am–1pm and sometimes 6–9pm; entrance free at present, but that may change) opened here. The museum—more gallery than museum—showcases the work of the 20th-century Greek artist who was born in Athens, but had a home on Tinos. The museum occupies the former village school house, which had been abandoned when the village's population plummeted. Just outside the museum, you'll see Tsoclis's metal sculpture showing the long, writhing scaly tail of the dragon slain by St. George. Inside, some 45 of Tsoclis's works are on display; the most memorable is perhaps the fiery display *Prometheus Imprudent,* which typifies Tsoclis use of what he called "living painting"; the combination of painting and video projection which he helped to popularize.

A bus from Hora several times a day to the nearby **Convent of Kechrovouniou** (also known as the Monastery of Kurias Angellon/Our Lady of the Angels) **★★**, one of the largest in Greece—almost a town in its own right. It dates from the 10th century and was the home of Pelagia, the nun whose vision revealed the location of the island's famed icon; you can visit her cell and see a small museum of 18th- and 19th-century icons. The convent is usually closed from 1 to 4pm; if you arrive when the convent is closed, you can stroll outside the walls and visit the small deer park and the nearby chapel, with its impressive display of the skulls of deceased nuns and monks. If you have more time to spend, take in the hamlets of **Dio Horia, Arnados,** and **Triandaros,** all on the slopes topped by the convent; Arnados has a number of *stegasti,* tunnel-like streets formed by the overhanging second-floor rooms of village houses; Dio Hora has a wonderful village fountain, and Triandaros has several restaurants and nice side streets. Don't be surprised if you hear German spoken here: many Germans have bought homes in this area.

Loutra ★ is another especially attractive village with many *stegasti;* building houses with their second stories protruding over the street below was a clever way to have as much house as possible on a small amount of land. An imposing 17th-century Jesuit monastery contains a small museum of village life; implements for making olive oil and wine are on display alongside old manuscripts and maps. It's usually open mid-June to mid-September from about 10:30am to 3:30pm (no phone). If the door is locked, ring the cow bell at the entrance and hope for the door to open. From mid-July until the beginning of September, the Ursuline School is open for a fabulous tour that depicts the students' lives and studies, until the school closed in the 1950s. Admission is free at the museum and for the convent tour. Both places are usually closed during siesta time (3–5pm).

The **Museum of Traditional Pottery** ★ (admission 2€; open Apr 1–Oct 1, 10am–4pm; no phone or website at present), opened in 2009 in **Aetofolia,** one of the smallest and most charming Tinian villages. There are labels throughout in Greek and English and museum guide Lila Tsigkriki speaks excellent English. The museum showcases pottery made—or found—not only on Tinos, but on the neighboring island of Sifnos, as well as other Cyclades. The displays are delightful as is the traditional 19th-century island house which is now the museum, with its kitchen filled with locally made pottery. Don't miss the little pottery barbecue, called a "foufou," from the sound made when cooks blow on the coals.

After touring the museum's well-stocked kitchen, you may be thinking of food, so head for the village of **Volax** ★★, where tall trees shade the excellent family-run **Taverna Volax** (© 22830/41-021), one of the very best places on Tinos to eat, relax, and enjoy the passing scene. Don't miss the local *loukanika* (sausages), best accompanied with some Tinian wine. Volax is in a valley known for a bizarre lunar landscape of rotund granite boulders. On the theory of "if you have lemons, make lemonade," the villagers constructed a substantial stone amphitheater for theatrical productions; a schedule of summer performances is usually posted both in Volas and in Hora. Volax is also known for its local basket weavers, whose baskets are remarkably durable and attractive; you'll see signs pointing to their workshops. Be sure to visit the town spring, down a short flight of steps at the bottom of the village. Channels direct the water to the fields, and the basket weavers' reeds soak in multiple stone basins. From Volas, you may want to head on to **Koumaros,** a beautiful village on the road between Volax and Mesi, both of which have many of the arched *stegasti* passageways.

Pirgos ★★★, at the western end of the island, is one of Tinos's most beautiful villages, with an enchanting small plateia with enormous plane trees, a marble fountain, several cafes, and two tavernas, usually open for lunch and dinner in summer, less regularly off-season. Pirgos gets *lots* of visitors and, alas, the prices in the cafes and restaurants are high, the quality is mixed, at best, and the service is slow and often grumpy. Renowned for its school of fine arts, Pirgos is a center for marble sculpting, and many of the finest sculptors of Greece have trained here. In 2008, the superb **Museum of Marble Crafts** opened just outside Pirgos. On a terrace leading to the museum, huge marble blocks and quarry equipment recreate a Tinian marble quarry. Inside, the museum takes visitors into the lives of the sculptors and artisans of Tinos, with the help of photos and videos. Displays include examples of the more than 100 kinds of Greek marble, fanlight windows, doorway ornaments, and grave monuments done by Tinian artists—and a good selection of the tools used to make them. The museum has a cafe (great coffee, fresh orange juice, and, if you're not driving, fiery *tsiporo* liqueur and tasty *mezedes*) and an excellent shop, with the cheapest, most endearing and portable souvenir I have seen: a small white eraser, decorated with a traditional Tinian carved braid pattern (1€). The museum is open Wednesday to Monday 10am to 6pm in summer, 10am to 5pm off-season (admission 3€).

In Pirgos itself, the **Museum of Yiannoulis Chalepas** and **Museum of Panormian Artists** occupy adjacent houses, and give visitors a chance not only to see sculpture by local artists, but to step into an island house. After you see the small rooms on the ground floor, you'll be surprised at how large the cool, flagstone lower story with the kitchen is. The museums are located near the bus station, on the main lane leading toward the village. Both are open Tuesday through Sunday from 11am to 1:30pm and 5:30 to 6:30pm; admission is 2€.

Although you may be tempted by the sculptures you see on sale in local workshops, even a small marble relief is not easy to slip into a suitcase. In the hardware shop across from Pirgos's two museums, **Nikolaos Panorios** ★★★ makes and sells whimsical tin funnels, boxes, spoon holders, and dustpans, as well as dovecotes, windmills, and sailing ships. Each item is made of tin salvaged from olive oil and other containers, and every one is unique (some with scenes of Pallas Athena, others with friezes of sunflowers, olive gatherers, fruits, or vegetables). All these are delightful folk art; they cost from 15€. Nikolaos Panorios is usually in the shop mornings (✆ **22830/32-263**), from about 9am to 1pm.

BEACHES

The easiest place to take a dip from Tinos town is at **Kionia,** across from the site of the Temple of Poseidon, 3km/2 miles west of Tinos town (see "A Swim, a Snack, an Ancient Site" box, above). Another beach close to town lies 2km (1¼ miles) east of town, at busy **Ayios Fokas.** West of Tinos town, a series of hairpin-turn paved and unpaved roads lead down—and when we say "down," we mean "way down"—to beaches at Ayiou Petrou, Kalivia, and Giannaki. From Tinos, there's bus service on the south beach road (usually eight times a day) to the resort of **Porto,** 8km (5 miles) to the east. Porto offers several long stretches of uncrowded sand, a few hotel complexes, and numerous tavernas, several at or near the beach. The beach at Ayios Ioannis, facing the town of Porto, is okay, but you'd be better off walking west across the small headland to a longer, less popular beach, extending from this headland to the church or Ayios Sostis at its western extremity; you can also get here by driving or taking the bus to Ayios Sostis.

There are two beaches at **Kolimbithres,** on the north side of the island, which are easily accessed by car, although protection from the *meltemi* winds can be a problem. The smaller has more wind protection, beach umbrellas, a changing hut, and two tavernas. Just beyond Pirgos, the beach at **Panormos** is on the verge of turning into a holiday resort, but has a decent (usually windy) beach and several good fish tavernas, notably **Agoni Grammi** ★ (✆ **22830/31-689**). If you eat here, be prepared for cars and buses to come very close to your seaside table.

WALKING

Tinos is a walker's paradise, with a good network of paths and remote interior regions waiting to be explored. Some of the best walks are in the vicinity of **Exobourgo**— paths connect the cluster of villages circling this craggy fortress, offering great views and many places to stop for refreshment along the way. There isn't a current English-language guide to walks in Tinos, but most decent maps of the islands indicate the paths, many of which are the former donkey and footpaths that connected villages.

SHOPPING

In Hora, Megalocharis is the main street from the harbor up to the cathedral. My two favorite shops in town are on Megalocharis: **Enosis,** a few steps up from the harbor, is the shop of the local **agricultural cooperative,** where pungent capers, creamy cheeses, olive oil, and the fiery local *tsiporo* liqueur are on sale (✆ **22830/21-184**). If you like capers, stock up on a vacuum pack or two; I got mine safely back to Massachusetts and enjoyed them for months. Continue to 34 Megalocharis and you'll find **Nostos** (✆ **22830/22-208**). Everything here—the ceramics, wood work, jewelry, weavings—is handmade, and just about everything will make you start plotting how you can fit it into your suitcase. The owner, Litsa Malliari Toufekli, is a painter and many of her haunting scenes of Tinos, done on old wood panels, are on view.

Pedestrianized Evangelistria Street parallels Megalocharis Street. Shops and stalls lining Evangelistria Street sell icons, incense, candles, medallions, *tamata* (tin, silver, and gold votives), and various stuffed animals that nod, roll over, mew, and squeal. You'll also find local embroidery, weavings, and a delicious local nougat, as well as *loukoumia* (Turkish delight) from Siros.

Two fine jewelry shops stand side by side on Evangelistria: **Artemis,** 18 Evangelistria (✆ **22830/23-781**), and **Harris Prassas Ostria-Tinos,** 20 Evangelistria (✆ **22830/23-893;** fax 22830/24-568). Both have jewelry in contemporary, Byzantine, and classical styles; silverwork; and religious objects, including reproductions of the miraculous icon. Near the top of the street, on the left, in a neoclassical building, the small **Evangelismos Biotechni Shop,** the outlet of a local weaving school (✆ **22830/22-894**), sells reasonably priced table and bed linens, embroidered aprons, and rugs.

Weekdays, a **Marko's fish market** and a **farmers' market** set up in the square by the docks. Keep an eye out for the rather pink-plumed pelican (Marko himself) who lives at the fish market and usually takes a morning stroll from there through the farmers' market to St. Anthony's Catholic church and back. Once back, he often takes a dip in his pool outside the fish market. There's a Palamidis supermarket, on the harbor, and an even larger one is just outside Tinos town, on the road to Pirgos.

You can get English-language newspapers in the narrow street that parallels (to the extent that anything in Tinos runs straight enough to be said to parallel anything else!) restaurant row, with the Metaxi Mas, Palaia Pallada, and Aithrio restaurants).

Where to Stay

Unless you have reservations, avoid Tinos during important religious holidays, especially **March 25** (Feast of the Annunciation) and **August 15** (Feast of the Assumption). It is also not a good idea to come here without an advance reservation on summer weekends, when Greeks travel here by the thousands for baptisms and pilgrimages. Most high-season weekend rates start at 80€ a night; rates off-season, especially during the week, are considerably lower. Several hotels and apartment complexes have Wi-Fi, but check on this before booking. There are also cafes in town with Wi-Fi available, such **Sympsion** on Evangelistra St. (don't bother to call, as the phone is never answered); ask the price before you go online.

In addition to the following hotels, check out the good value **Asteria** (asteria hotel@otenet.gr; ✆ **22830/22-830**), perched above the harbor where the big boats dock. The Asteria remodeled in 2010 and its lobby, breakfast room, and, most important, guest rooms and bathrooms are now very comfortable. Doubles start from 65€. As with many Tinos hotels, the Asteria does a brisk business with Greek tour groups. If you are coming here for more than a night or two, consider the appealing **Tiniotissa Studios** (www.tiniotissa.gr, ✆ **22830/22-430**), on a quiet street off Megalocharis, between the Archaeology Museum and Grade School.

Oceanis Hotel ★   The Oceanis has a good quiet location, away from the main harbor hubbub, near where some of the fishing boats moor. Another plus: the Oceanis—formerly bland, shabby, and charmless—has spruced itself up. The lobby is positively cheerful and the rooms have been repainted; only the exterior, a somber gray, could use some livening up. Be sure to ask for a front room: the balconies provide a great view of the ships coming and going in Tinos's harbor, with views of Siros in the distance. The hotel is often taken over by Greek groups visiting the island's religious shrines. As an independent traveler, you may feel a bit like an outsider,

If you're lucky, while you're trying to decide what to have for lunch or dinner at a restaurant in Tinos, you'll become aware of family celebrations taking place at other tables. Why, you may wonder, is that young couple dancing on one of the tables and passing their screaming toddler from guest to guest? Why is everyone kissing him and pinching his cheeks? Families come from all over Greece to **baptize** their children at the Panagia Evangelistria Cathedral. After the ceremony, it's time to celebrate (which means lots of food, wine, and dancing). If you're lucky, you may get to kiss the baby and toast the occasion. Be sure to say *"Na sas zee-soun"* ("May he live for you") to the proud parents.

especially if you do not speak Greek or smoke. Don't bother with the restaurant, except for the breakfast buffet. The Oceanis stays open all year and has reliable heat in the winter.

Akti G. Drossou, Hora, 84200 Tinos. ☎ **22830/22-452.** Fax 22830/25-402. 47 units. From 70 € double. Rates include breakfast buffet. No credit cards. From the old harbor, walk south (right) along the *paralia* until you come to the Oceanis, whose large sign is clearly visible from the harbor. **Amenities:** Restaurant; bar. *In room:* A/C, TV, hair dryer, minifridge.

Porto Tango ★ ♨ I am only listing this place because it was once thought to be the breakthrough fancy place on the island. Porto Tango does have all the frills—restaurant, sauna, spa, health club, pool, and so forth. But the management seriously overbooks rooms, and then puts many arrivals elsewhere and tries to charge full price if guests use the hotel facilities. Did I mention that the beach is a 10-minute walk away, across a road? Or that the tennis court in June 2011 had weeds growing out of it? On the positive side, many rooms have balconies or terraces with sea views; some have both. In short, this is a place that has not got its act together, in either decor or service. See the Tinos Beach Hotel, below, for a much better choice.

Porto, 84200 Tinos. www.portotango.gr. ☎ **22830/24-411.** Fax 22830/24-416. 61 units. 150€ double; 450€ suite. Rates include breakfast buffet. AE, MC, V. **Amenities:** 2 restaurants; bar; health club; pool; spa. *In room:* A/C, TV, hair dryer, Internet, minibar.

Tinos Beach Hotel ★★ ☺ Despite a somewhat impersonal character, this is the best choice in a beachfront hotel. The decent-size rooms all have balconies, most with views of the sea and pool. The newly renovated superior doubles all face the sea and the suites are especially pleasant—large sitting rooms open onto poolside balconies. The pool is the longest on the island, and there's a separate children's pool as well. No one seems to praise either the ambience or the service here, but if you want to be near Tinos town, yet also on the beach, this is the place to be.

Kionia, 84200 Tinos. www.tinosbeach.gr. ☎ **22830/22-626** or 22830/22-627. Fax 22830/23-153. 180 units. 80€–100€ double. Rates include breakfast. Children 7 and under stay free in parent's room. AE, DC, MC, V. Closed Nov–Mar. 4km (2½ miles) west of Tinos town, on the coast road. **Amenities:** Restaurant; bar; children's pool; saltwater pool; tennis courts; watersports equipment rentals; Wi-Fi. *In room:* A/C, TV, hair dryer, minifridge.

Where to Eat

As usual, it's a good idea to avoid most harborfront joints, where food is generally inferior and service can be rushed—although, if you are catching a ferry and want a quick bite, the service can seem interminable. Be sure you know which quay your ferry is leaving from to avoid any last-minute dashes through crowds of embarking and disembarking passengers. One special place to try is **Etan Ena Mikro Karavi** ("There Was a Little Boat"; *C* **22830/22-818;** www.mikrokaravi.gr) in a narrow alleyway off Trion Hierarchon. This place is gorgeous, with a lovely garden, elegant indoor dining room, and inventive and delicious food (risotto with mushrooms, lamb with couscous, fresh fish, and for dessert a chocolate tart with homemade vanilla ice cream and caramel sauce). To my considerable distress, this place had not yet opened for the season when I was last on Tinos, and I had to make do with reading the menu and hearing from friends how very good everything is. Dinner for two starts at around 50€.

If, on the other hand, you just want a pizza (10€ and up), head to **Mesklies** (*C* **22830/22-151**) on the harbor. Mesklies also has some of the best pastry in town, at shops on the harbor and on Evangelistra Street. For the best coffee—and a full pot of it for only 2 €—try **Le Caffe,** also on the harbor. Le Caffe also has the best *loukoumades* (like doughnut holes, but drenched in honey, sprinkled with cinnamon, and if you wish, topped with ice cream).

Metaxi Mas ★ GREEK   The zest that made the cooking at this longtime distinctive *mezedopoleio* (hors d'oeuvres place) so wonderful for so many years is flagging again. In short, Metaxi Mas is having its ups and downs. The varied *mezedes* are still very good, especially the vegetable croquettes, fried sun-dried tomatoes, piquant fried cheeses, and succulent octopus. But they aren't quite as good as they were a few years ago, when it was clear that the food here was better than its nearby competition. There's a cozy interior dining room with a fireplace, for when it's chilly, and tables outside in the pedestrianized lane, for good weather.

Kontoyioryi, Paralia, Hora. *C* **22830/24-857.** Main courses 8€–20€. No credit cards. Daily noon–midnight. Off the harbor, in a lane btw. the old and new harbors. Look for the sign over the door. Sometimes a METAXI MAS banner is strung across the lane.

Palaia Pallada ★★ GREEK   Palaia Pallada, next to Metaxi Mas, is a bit more down home than Metaxi Mas, a bit less inventive, but more consistently good. There are fewer ruffles and flourishes, but the food (grills, stews, salads) in this family-run place is excellent, as is the local wine. You can eat indoors or outside. If you like Palaia Pallada, you'll also like **Aithrio** (*C* **22830/22-033**), the third restaurant on this restaurant row.

Kontoyioryi, Paralia, Hora. *C* **22830/23-516.** Main courses 7€–15€. No credit cards. Daily noon–midnight. Off the harbor, in a lane btw. the old and new harbors. Look for the sign over the door, and the sign that overhangs the lane.

To Koutouki tis Eleni ★ GREEK   There's usually no menu at this small taverna, known in town simply as To Koutouki. Basic ingredients are cooked into simple meals that remind you how delightful Greek food can be. Local cheese and wine, fresh fish and meats, delicious vegetables—these are the staples that come together so well in this taverna.

Paralia, Hora. *C* **22830/24-857.** Main courses 7€–15€. No credit cards. Daily noon–midnight. From the harbor, turn onto Evangelistria, the market street; take the 1st right up a narrow lane with 3 tavernas. Koutouki is the 1st on the left.

Tinos After Dark

As we've mentioned, Tinos is a place of pilgrimage, and there's less nightlife here than on many islands; as always on the islands, places that are hot one season are often gone the next. Two sweets shops, **Epilekto** and **Meskiles** (fantastic *loukoumades* with ice cream), both on the waterfront, stay open late.

In the streets beside restaurant row, where Palaia Pallada, Metaxi Mas, and Aithrio are located, there is a clutch of bars, with music, TV, and sometimes dancing, including **Koursaros, Kaktos, Volto,** and **Syvilla,** and, on the road toward Kiona, **Paradise.** If you want a late-night (or early morning) coffee, try **Iecaffe,** on the harborfront; instead of a cup, this place brings you a full pot of French filtered coffee. If you want to check your e-mail while you drink your coffee, try **Symposio,** which bills itself as a cafe/bar/restaurant. If you walk on the main road at night, watch out for the kamikaze motorcyclists.

SIROS (SYROS) ★★

144km (78 nautical miles) SE of Piraeus

Siros is very different from the other Cycladic islands. The capital, **Ermoupolis,** is not a cute Cycladic sugar-cube miniature town, nor a ramshackle port town, but the administrative capital of the Cyclades, with a large shipyard. If you live anywhere in the Cyclades and need a building permit, or a license, or a lawyer, you'll end up making at least one trip here. Consequently, Ermoupolis has a year-round businesslike bustle totally unlike any other town in the Cyclades.

Ermoupolis has been the most important town in the Cyclades almost since it was founded in the 1820s by a flood of refugees from Asia Minor and the eastern Aegean islands. The settlers named the town after Hermes, the god of merchants. The name seems to have been an excellent choice: Soon, this was the busiest port in Greece—far busier than Piraeus—and a center of shipbuilding. You'll see several still-functioning shipyards and dry docks along the harbor. Just inland are neighborhoods with handsome neoclassical mansions built by shipping magnates. When you walk into Plateia Miaoulis, the main square in town, you may find it hard to believe you're still in the Cyclades: The square is lined with truly grandiose public buildings, including a town hall that could hold its own beside any government building in Athens. Just off the Plateia is the **Apollon Theater,** a miniature of Milan's La Scala Opera House, with a summer music festival. Climb uphill from the Plateia Miaoulis and you'll find yourself in the oldest part of town, **Ano Syros,** which happens to be a little sugar-cube Cycladic neighborhood, albeit one with both a Capuchin and a Jesuit monastery. Although Ermoupolis saw a considerable period of decline in the 20th century, recent restoration efforts have brought back much of the city's glory; the entire town is now a UNESCO World Heritage Site.

I have to confess that Siros is one island where the capital town's pleasures are so considerable that I don't mind neglecting the island itself. That said, the north end of Siros is a starkly beautiful region of widely dispersed farms, multilayered terraced fields, and village-to-village donkey paths and footpaths. Some of the island's best beaches are here, many accessible only on foot or by boat. The south is gentler, with a number of villages with the 19th-century country villas of the wealthy shipping magnates who had both a town house and a summer retreat; the villages of Manna, Ano Manna, and Dellagrazia have especially impressive villas. Throughout the island, the San Mihali and *kopanisti* cheeses are made, and delicious thyme honey is produced.

The best months to visit Siros are May, June, and September; the worst month is August. That's when vacationing Greek families—many bringing with them at least two cars—pour into their villas here, with the overflow taking up virtually every hotel

Siros has two impressive summer festivals, the **Ermoupoleia** (www.syros-live.gr) and the **Festival of the Aegean** (www.festivaloftheaegean.com). The Ermoupoleia runs almost all summer and has indoor and open-air concerts, plays, and performances. The Festival of the Aegean, usually held in mid-July, stages many of its performances—including several operas—at the glorious Apollon Theater. And **Ano Siro,** the community clustered on a peak above Ermoupolis, has its own festival in July and August (**www.syros-live.gr**).

room on the island. If you want to tour the island, having a car is the best way to get around, although bus service to the more settled, southern part of the island is good.

Essentials

GETTING THERE   By Plane   The website of Athens International Airport, www.aia.gr, is a useful resource for domestic airline schedules. **Olympic Air** (🕿 810/114-4444 or 210/966-6666, official Greek phone numbers that are rarely answered; www.olympicair.com) offers daily flights between Athens and Siros, which also gets European charters. **Aegean Airlines** (🕿 810/112-0000; www.aegeanair.com) also plans to start service between Athens and Siros. Buses from the airport to nearby Ermoupolis run frequently (4€); a taxi costs about 10€. A bus from the airport meets most flights; the schedule is posted at the bus stop, beside the airport entrance. A taxi to Fira costs about 13€.

By Boat   The websites **www.gtp.gr** and **www.openseas.gr** are useful resources for ferry schedules. Ferries connect Siros at least once daily with Piraeus, Naxos, Mykonos, Paros, Tinos, and Santorini. The ferries connect once or twice weekly with Folegandros, Sifnos, Iraklion, Samos, and Thessaloniki (12–15 hr.). There is service in summer from Rafina. Boats are notoriously late and/or early; your travel or ticket agent will give you an *estimate* of times involved in the following journeys. Remember: You'll find numerous ferry-ticket offices on the harborfront: **Alpha Syros** (🕿 22810/81-185), opposite the ferry pier, and its sister company, **Teamwork Holidays** (🕿 22810/83-400; www.teamwork.gr), sell tickets for all the ferries (and also handle plane tickets and hotel reservations). Ferry information can be verified with the Ermoupolis **port authority** (🕿 22810/88-888 or 22810/82-690).

VISITOR INFORMATION   The **Hoteliers Association of Siros** operates an information booth at the pier in summer; it's open daily from 9am to 10pm. There is a phone, but it is never answered; you'll have to go there. Note that the list of hotels they offer includes only hotels registered with their service. **www.syros.com.gr** is also useful.

GETTING AROUND   By Bus   The **bus stop** in Ermoupolis is at the pier, where the schedule is posted. Buses circle the southern half of Siros hourly in summer (but never on Sun) between 8am and midnight. There is minimal bus service to the northern part of the island. **Teamwork Holidays** (🕿 22810/83-400; www.teamwork.gr) offers an excellent value **bus tour of the island** for 20€ on high-season Tuesdays, Thursdays, and Saturdays. Starting at 9am, it tours Ermoupoli, and then heads out on the island for a visit to some southern villages, lunch (a la carte), and a swim, then returns to town around 4:30pm. Teamwork also can arrange a day tour of Ermoupolis for 10€ and rents cars (insurance included) from 35€.

By Car & Moped   In addition to **Teamwork Holidays** (see above), **Gaviotis Travel** (✆ **22810/86-664;** info@gaviotis.gr), with two offices on the harbor, has mopeds and cars, and can provide ferry and plane tickets. A small car will cost from 35€ per day, including insurance. A 50cc scooter rents from 15€ per day.

By Taxi   The taxi stand is on the main square, Plateia Miaoulis (✆ **2810/86-222**).

FAST FACTS   Several **banks** on the harbor have ATMs. The Ermoupolis hospital (✆ **22810/86-666**) is the largest in the Cyclades; it's just outside town to the west near Plateia Iroon. For free **luggage storage,** ask at Teamwork Holidays (✆ **22810/ 83-400**). The **police** (✆ **22810/82-610**) are on the south side of Miaoulis Square. The **port authority** (✆ **22810/88-888** or 22810/82-690) is on the long pier at the far end of the harbor, beyond Hotel Hermes. The **post office** (✆ **22810/82-596**) is between Miaoulis Square and the harbor, on Protopapadaki; it's open Monday through Friday from 7:30am to 2pm. The **telephone office (OTE)** is on the east side of Miaoulis Square (✆ **22810/87-399**); it's open Monday through Friday from 7:30am to 3pm. You can get online in the main square, Plateia Miaoulis, at the Internet facility, on the ground floor of the Town Hall, or at **Bizanas,** a nearby Internet cafe on Plateia Miaoulis; **Multirama,** at 54 Ethnikis Antistasis, the main drag along the harbor, also has Internet facilities.

What to See & Do

MUSEUMS

Archaeological Museum ★   The highlight of this museum's small collection is a room containing finds, including pottery and several fine Cycladic figurines, from Halandriani and Kastri, prehistoric sites in the northern hills of Siros. There are also finds from the Greek and Roman city here, which lies under modern Ermoupolis. Because Ermoupolis is the capital of the Cyclades, the archaeological museum has holdings from the smaller Cycladic islands. Allow half an hour or so for your visit.

On the west side of the town hall, below the clock tower, Ermoupolis. ✆ **22810/86-900.** Admission 3€. Tues–Sun 8:30am–3pm.

Ermoupolis Industrial Museum ★★   Behind the cranes and warehouses of the Neorion Shipyard, at the southern end of the port, you'll find the Industrial Museum of Ermoupolis, which opened in a restored paint-works factory in 2000. If you have any fondness for industrial history, you're going to love this museum. There's an extensive collection of artifacts from the town's industrial past: weaving machines, metalworking tools, and items related to the town's famed shipyards (compasses, anchors, ship models). Also check out the collection of original drawings by the architects of Ermoupolis's neoclassical heyday, the old photographs and engravings depicting various aspects of island life, and the old maps of Siros and the Cyclades. The museum is a 20-minute walk or a short bus ride from the harbor. Allow an hour for your visit.

Ermoupolis. Just off Plateia Iroon and opposite the hospital. ✆ **22810/86-900.** Admission 3€; free on Wed. Tues–Sun 10am–2pm and 6–9pm.

EXPLORING ERMOUPOLIS ★★

If you arrive on Siros by boat, you'll be aware of the two steep hills that tower over Ermoupolis. Originally, the term **Ano Siros** (which means "the area above Siros") was used to describe the peaks of both hills. Today, the term Ano Siros describes the taller hill seen to the left as you enter the harbor. This was, and still is, the Catholic quarter of the town, settled by the Venetians in the 13th century. Much of the intricate maze of narrow streets from that period remains today; cars can drive up Ano Siros and park outside the gates (as residents here do), and then continue on foot, but cars are not allowed inside. There's a **Jesuit monastery** and a **Capuchin monastery,** as well as the elaborately decorated **Church of Ayios Yeoryios** (mass Sun at 11am), at the crest of the hill. The real joy of visiting Ano Siros comes from wandering along its narrow lanes, peeking surreptitiously into courtyards, and stumbling across a tiny shop or cafe. Needless to say, there are great views over Ermoupolis and the island. Omirou, one of the streets that run uphill, is probably your best bet for an assault on foot on Ano Siros

Ermoupolis's other hill, **Vrondado,** is crowned by the massive 19th-century blue-domed Greek Orthodox **Church of the Resurrection (Anastasi).** There's a fine view of Ermoupolis and the neighboring islands from the church's terrace. This area was built up as the town grew when Greeks from other islands, especially Chios, moved here at the time of the Greek War of Independence, in the 1820s. Narrow streets, marble-paved squares, and dignified pedimented mansions with elegant balconies make this neighborhood a quiet refuge from the bustling inner city.

Ermoupolis's central square, **Plateia Miaoulis,** and the elaborately elegant neo-classical **town hall** (designed by Ernst Ziller, who designed the Grande Bretagne Hotel in Athens) are conspicuous reminders of Ermoupolis's heyday. Ringed by high palm trees and facing the town hall, you really can't miss Plateia Miaoulis; if you do, go back to the harbor and head inland on Venizelou. This is the heart of Ermoupolis; this is where the island's most vigorous *volta* (promenade) takes place even if it takes place under umbrellas. Any of the cafes here is a nice place to sit, preferably with an elaborate ice-cream sundae, and watch the promenade.

A couple of blocks northeast of the town hall is the recently restored 19th-century **Apollon Theater ★**, a smaller version of Milan's La Scala, hence nicknamed "la piccola Scala." The theater is home to the **Festival of the Aegean** (www.festivalof theaegean.com), with its summer opera, classical, and pop music performances. Even if you can't go to a performance here, step inside to see the elaborate painted ceilings and crystal chandeliers (entrance fee 2€). To the northeast is the imposing Greek Orthodox church of **Ayios Nikolaos.** The green marble iconostasis and the touching monument to the Unknown Soldier, in the park across from the church, were both done by Vitalis, a famed 19th-century marble carver from Tinos. A short stroll beyond the church will bring you to the neighborhood called **Vaporia,** named after the steamships that brought it great prosperity. Many of the town houses are built on the edge of the rocks that plunge into the sea. One other church on nearby Omirou Street is worth seeing: the Cathedral Church of the Transfiguration (Metamorphosi), with its marble floors and precinct with wonderful pebble mosaics. This church, with its imposing arcade, is a grand tribute to the 19th-century prosperity of the Ermoupolis. One more church to visit: the Church of the Koimisis (Dormition), just off the harbor, a block or so from the casino. This 19th-century church, with a very cheerful blue and gold pulpit, houses (among much else) an icon of the Virgin, painted by Domenico Theotokopoulos, better known as El Greco. Exploring Ermoupolis is a very nice way to spend a day, or parts of any number of days.

BEACHES

Beaches are not the island's strongest suit, but there are a number of good places to swim and sun. **Mega Yialo,** as its name states, is the largest beach on the island and, not surprisingly, the most developed. Hotels there include the **Alexandra** (© **22810/42-540**). **Kini Berach,** on the west coast is rapidly turning into a beach resort, with more and more rent rooms and small hotels joining the restaurants and cafes.

On the west coast, **Galissas** (with its still charming village) has one of the best beaches on the island, a crescent of sand bordered by tamarisks. It also has a large campsite (for info, contact www.twohearts-camping.com) and a number of small hotels. Also on the west coast, **Finikas** has a slender beach and a cluster of hotels and restaurants. A few kilometers to the south, **Poseidonia** and **Agathopes** have sand beaches and less competition for a place in the sun. A bonus if you go to Poseidonia and Agathopes is that you can take in the charming village of Dellagrazia-Poseidonia, with its cluster of 19th-century villas.

Where to Stay

As you come off the ferry in Ermoupolis, you'll see the kiosk of the **Hoteliers Association of Siros,** which provides a list of island hotels. Note that hotels pay to become members of this association, so not all of the island's best lodgings are represented. In August, when vacationing Greeks pack the island, don't even think of arriving without a reservation. In addition to the following, you may want to consider the 16-unit **Syrou Melathron** (© **22810/85-963;** syroumel@otenet.gr), in a 19th-century town house. Only reports of indifferent service keep us from recommending this stylish little hotel wholeheartedly; doubles from 130€. One long-time favorite, the centrally-located 32-room **Hotel Palladion** (© **22810/86-400;** www.palladion-hotel-syros.gr) has good-sized, simply-furnished rooms with balconies over its quiet central courtyard; doubles from 100€. Also in a great location, just off Plateia Miaouli, the elegant and enticing little 13-room Apollonion Hotel (© **22810/89-056;** www.apollonionpalace.gr) opened in 2009 in a handsome 19th-century neoclassical mansion with sea views; doubles from 100€, suites from 150€.

Hotel Apollonos ★   This small hotel on the water in Vaporia is one of Ermoupolis's restored mansion hotels. Those looking for a fully authentic restoration might be disappointed—the furnishings and lighting are partly contemporary in style—but the overall effect works. The best guest rooms are the two facing the water at the back of the house: Both are quite spacious, and one has a loft sleeping area with sitting room below. Bathrooms are large, with tile and wood floors. A large common sitting room faces the bay, while a breakfast room faces the street. If you want 24-hour service, this is not the place for you.

8 Apollonos, Ermoupolis, 84100 Siros. www.xenonapollonos.gr. © **22810/81-387** or 22810/80-842. 3 units. 165€–200€ double. Rates include breakfast. No credit cards. **Amenities:** Breakfast room/bar. *In room:* A/C.

Hotel Ethrion ★ /   This small family-run hotel, with a quiet location in the heart of town, has rooms and studios (one with kitchenette) with terraces or balconies; five units have sea views from the balconies. The rooms are comfortably and pleasantly furnished (the ones on the top floors have fancier decor), the owners are very helpful (as is the website map), and the price is right. The more expensive rooms have a balcony and sea view. This is the sort of homey place that can tempt you to relax into getting to know Ermoupolis *siga, siga* (slowly, slowly).

24 J. Kosma, Ermoupolis 84100, Siros. www.ethrion.gr. © **22819/89-006.** 8 doubles, 4 studios (1 with kitchenette). 70€–85€ double. MC, V. **Amenities:** Internet. *In room:* A/C.

Hotel Hermes ★ /   The Hermes presents a bright, cheerful facade to busy Plateia Kanari at the harbor's east end. What you can't see from the street is that many of the better rooms face a quiet stretch of rocky coast at the back of the building. The functional, dull standard rooms have shower-only bathrooms and views of the street or a back garden. The rooms in the new wing are worth the extra money for their size, furnishings, and balconies that allow early risers to see the sunrise. If you get a room here on a summer weekend, be prepared to be the only guest not in a wedding party—and to see the sunrise from your balcony as the wedding reception winds down.

Plateia Kanari, Ermoupolis, 84100 Siros. *(*) **22810/83-011** or 22810/83-012. Fax 22810/87-412. 51 units. 100€ double. AE, DC, MC, V. **Amenities:** Restaurant; bar. *In room:* A/C, TV, hair dryer.

Hotel Omiros ★ The Omiros is in a restored neoclassical house, with comfortable and stylish public rooms—and much more simple guest rooms. The climb up to the hotel is steep and there is no elevator in the hotel. But, the location is quiet and the owners are helpful. If you are coming to Siros for a long stay, this quiet spot might feel like home. If you are here for a short stay, the walk up and down might be wearing.

43 Omirou, Ermoupolis, 84100 Siros. *(*) **22810/84-910** or 22810/88-756. Fax 22810/86-266. 13 units. From 90€ double. Continental breakfast 10€. MC, V. **Amenities:** Breakfast room; lounge. *In room:* A/C, TV.

Where to Eat

As you would expect of a town constantly visited by lawyers and businessmen, there are lots of excellent tavernas in and around Ermoupolis, but if you're only going to have one dinner here, head to **Thalami** (*(*) **22810/85-331**), in a 19th-century mansion with sea views and delicious food, especially seafood (great stuffed squid). Main courses run 8€ to 15€ and much more, of course, if you have the fresh fish. **Boubas Ouzeri** and **Yacht Club of Siros** are both known for ouzo and *mezedes.* In addition to the tavernas mentioned below, try the consistently good **Petrino Taverna** (*(*) **22810/84-427**), around the corner from To Arhontariki. Up in Ano Siros, try one of three places with great views: **Frangosiriani** (*(*) **22810/84-888**), down the street from the **Taverna Lilis,** or the nearby **Alithini** (*(*) **22810/88-253**), which specializes in rooster in wine sauce and *stifado,* a hearty stew with onions and veal or rabbit. Out on the island on one of the best sand beaches, you'll eat some of the best food on the island at Allou Yualou (*(*) **22810/71-196**). Look for the giant fish tank—and hope that the small fish don't know that many people at the nearby tables with pale pink tablecloths are eating their large relatives. In short, great fresh fish, inventive salads, and a dreamy seaside location. (The restaurant's name, a Greek expression, suggests daydreaming in a wonderful place.) True. Open from before Easter until, as the manager told me, "the weather is not so good," which many years means mid-October.

Taverna Lilis ★★ GREEK/SEAFOOD The view is to die for and the food is good. Lilis is one of the best of the tavernas in Ano Siros, the quarter cresting the high conical hill behind Ermoupolis. From the terrace, there's a view of Ermoupolis, the bay, distant Tinos and, even farther out, the shores of Mykonos. The food is better-than-average taverna fare—meats and fish are grilled on a wood fire, and the ingredients are reliably fresh. There's sometimes *rembetika* music here (see "Siros After Dark," below).

Ano Siros. *(*) **22810/88-087.** Reservations recommended in July–Aug. Main courses 8€–20€. No credit cards. Daily 7pm–midnight. Follow Omirou from the center of Ermoupolis, past the Hotel Omiros, and continue straight up the long flight of steps that leads to Taverna Lilis's brightly lit terrace. You can also call a taxi.

To Arhontariki ★ GREEK   This small place fills the narrow street with tables that are precariously perched on cobblestones, and it is probably the best of the tavernas in Ermoupolis center. It's easy to find—just plunge into the maze of streets at the corner of Miaoulis Square, between Pyramid Pizzeria and Loukas Restaurant, and weave your way left—it's 2 blocks or so in, between Miaoulis and the harbor. *Remember:* If you get lost, you can ask for directions, and any local knows this place. The menu is largely composed of specials (several vegetarian) that change daily.

Ermoupolis. (*)️ **22810/81-744.** Main courses 8€–18€. Daily noon–midnight.

Siros After Dark

Siros was among the most fertile grounds for *rembetika,* the haunting songs of the dispossessed underclasses that probably began in Asia Minor in the early 20th century. Markos Vambakaris, the Bob Dylan, as it were, of *rembetika,* was born on Siros, which still prizes his music. You can hear *rembetika* at **Xanthomalis** (no phone; closed in summer) and at **Taverna Lilis** (*)️ **22810/28-087**), in Ano Siros, which sometimes have late-night performances on the weekends; reservations are a must.

As always on the islands, places that are hot one season are often gone the next. Stick your head into any of the many bars along the waterfront to see which is playing music that suits your taste. **Liquid Bar** gets rave reviews from a taxi driver I talked to who likes his music very loud. You can also join in the evening *volta* (**stroll**) around Plateia Miaoulis, take a seat to watch it, or drop in at **Piramatiko, Agora,** or **Bizanas,** longtime music joints. The outdoor **Pallas Cinema,** east of the main square, has one nightly showing, often in English.

THE DODECANESE

by John S. Bowman

"The Dodecanese"—the very name suggests some-place exotic (in fact it is merely Greek for "Twelve Islands"), and these islands, if not exotic, certainly have been providing visitors for many, many centuries a range of extraordinary attractions and experiences.

Part of their appeal comes from the fact that the Dodecanese mostly hug the coast of Asia Minor, far from the Greek mainland. As frontier or borderline territories, their struggles to remain free and Greek have been intense and prolonged. Although they have been recognizably Greek for millennia, only in 1948 were the Dodecanese formally reunited with the Greek nation.

By the way, "the Twelve Islands" are in fact an archipelago of 32 islands: 14 inhabited and 18 uninhabited. But they have been known as the Dodecanese since 1908, when 12 of them joined forces to resist the revocation of the status they had long enjoyed under the Ottoman sultans.

The four islands selected for this chapter are certainly the most engaging of the Dodecanese. From south to north, they are **Rhodes, Simi, Kos,** and **Patmos.** Patmos and Simi are relatively arid in summer, while the interiors of Rhodes and Kos remain fertile and forested. Spectacular historical sights, such as ancient ruins and medieval fortresses, are concentrated on Patmos, Kos, and Rhodes; so are the tourists. Simi is the once-but-no-longer-secret getaway you will not soon forget.

Long accustomed to watching the seas for invaders, these islands now spend their time awaiting the tourists, who show up each spring and stay until October. The beginning of the tourist season sets into motion a pattern of activity largely contrived to attract and entertain outsiders. Such is the reality of island life today. As in the past, however, the islanders proudly retain their own character, even as they accommodate an onslaught of visitors.

Strategies for Seeing the Islands

In planning a visit to the Dodecanese, keep in mind that Rhodes has the longest tourist season. So if you're rushing into the season in April, begin in Rhodes; if you're stretching the season into October, end up in Rhodes. In any case, if you can, avoid the Dodecanese July and August, when they are so crowded that they nearly sink.

In high season, at least, you can travel easily from one to the other of the three principal islands described here—**Rhodes, Kos,** and **Patmos** (although the excursion to Patmos really requires a minimum of 2 days). From the mainland, all are best reached by air. Rhodes and Kos have airports; Patmos is a short jaunt by hydrofoil from Samos, which also has an airport. From Kos and Rhodes, you can get just about anywhere in the eastern Aegean, including nearby **Turkey,** which is worth at least a day's excursion. **Simi** can be reached by ferry from Piraeus, but most people will approach it by boat as an excursion from Rhodes.

RHODES (RODOS) ★★

250km (135 nautical miles) E of Piraeus

Selecting a divine patron was serious business for an ancient city. Most Greek cities played it safe and chose a mainstream god or goddess, a ranking Olympian—someone such as Athena or Apollo or Artemis, or Zeus himself. It's revealing that the people of Rhodes chose **Helios,** the sun, as their signature god.

Indeed, millennia later, the cult of the sun is alive and well on Rhodes, and no wonder: The island receives on average more than 300 days of sunshine a year. No wonder Rhodes has long been a destination for sun worshipers hailing from colder, darker, wetter lands around the globe.

But Rhodes gives visitors more than a mere tan. A location at the intersection of the East and West propelled the island into the thick of both commerce and conflicts. The scars left by its rich and turbulent history have become its treasures. Hellenistic Greeks, Romans, Crusader Knights, Turks, Italians—all invaders who brought some destruction but who also left behind fascinating artifacts.

Through it all, Rhodes has remained beautiful. Its beaches are among the cleanest in the Aegean, and its interior is still home to unspoiled mountain villages, rich fertile plains—and beautiful butterflies. Several days in Rhodes will allow you to appreciate its marvels, relax in the sun, and perhaps add a day trip to the idyllic island of Simi or to the coast of Turkey. If Rhodes is your last port of call in Greece, it will make a grand finale; if it is your point of departure, you can launch forth happily from here to just about anywhere in the Aegean or Mediterranean.

Essentials

GETTING THERE By Plane In addition to its year-round service between Rhodes and Athens and Thessaloniki, **Olympic Airways** offers summer service between Rhodes and the following Greek locales: Iraklion (Crete), Karpathos, and Santorini. The local Olympic office is at 9 Ierou Lohou (℡ **22410/24-57**). Flights fill quickly, so reserve in advance. **Aegean Airlines** (℡ **801/112-0000** in Greece; www.aegeanair.com), in addition to flights to Rhodes, offers at least high-season flights between Rhodes and Thessaloniki and Iraklion, Crete. Tickets for any flight in or out of Rhodes can be purchased directly from **Triton Holidays,** near Mandraki Harbor, 9 Plastira, Rhodes city (℡ **22410/21-690;** www.tritondmc.gr). Triton will either send your tickets to you or have them waiting for you at the airport.

The Rhodes **Paradissi Airport** (℡ **22410/83-214**) is 13km (8 miles) southwest of the city and is served from 6am to 10:30pm by bus. The bus to the city center (Plateia Rimini) is 6€. A taxi costs 22€. By the way, some taxi drivers resist taking passengers to hotels in the Old Town (because of the slow going in the old streets)—they will even claim they can't enter; note their number and threaten to report them,

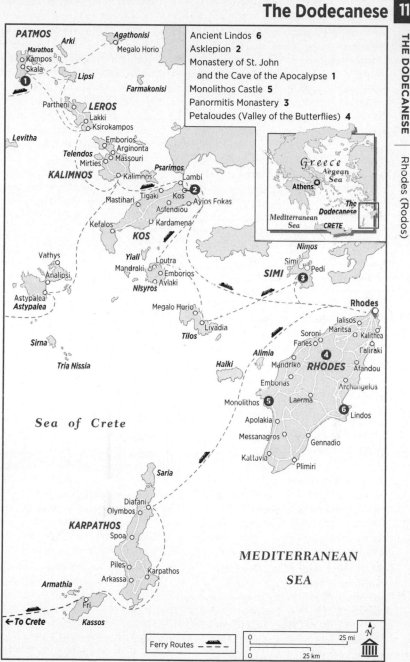

Ancient Lindos **6**
Asklepion **2**
Monastery of St. John
  and the Cave of the Apocalypse **1**
Monolithos Castle **5**
Panormitis Monastery **3**
Petaloudes (Valley of the Butterflies) **4**

and they will usually relent. Otherwise, make arrangements with your hotel to be met at one of the main gates.

By Boat Rhodes is a major port with sea links to Athens, Crete, and the islands of the Aegean, as well as to Cyprus, Turkey, and Israel. Service and schedules are always changing; check with the tourist office or a travel agency for the latest information.

In late spring and throughout the summer, there are daily sailings—some with high-speed hydrofoils or catamarans—from and to Rhodes and many of the Dodecanense and other islands in the eastern Aegean: Kos, Kalimnos, Kastellorizo, Leros, Nissiros, Patmos, Samos, Simi, and Tilos. The advantage of hydrofoils and catamarans is that they make the voyage in half the time, but when the wind blows, the sailings are canceled. Air quality is also poor, especially compared to that on larger open-deck excursion boats or ferries. For more detailed information about the most active ship line, **Dodekanisos Seaways,** see www.12ne.gr.

Wherever it is you want to go, whether by ferry, hydrofoil, catamaran, or excursion boat, schedules and tickets are available from **Triton Holidays** (see above). Although several agents in Rhodes city and island can issue air and sea tickets, Triton has had a "special relationship" with Frommer's people from the original "$5 a Day" guide!

VISITOR INFORMATION During the high season only, you'll find a helpful **Rhodes Municipal Tourist Office** at Plateia Rimini, facing the port taxi stand (© 22410/35-945). It dispenses information on local excursions, buses, ferries, and accommodations, and offers currency exchange as well. Its hours are Monday through Saturday from about 9am to 9pm, Sunday from 9am to 2pm. The above-recommended **Triton Holidays** is also willing to answer any traveler's question, free of obligation, and is sometimes open when the tourist offices are closed.

GETTING AROUND Rhodes is not an island you can see on foot. You need wheels of some sort: public bus, group-shared taxi, rental car, or organized bus tour for around-the-island excursions. Rhodes city is a different story. Walking is the only and most pleasurable mode of transport; you'll need a taxi only if you're going to treat yourself to a meal at one of the farther-flung restaurants. The fact is that even taxis are not allowed within the walls unless you have luggage and are arriving or leaving.

By Bus Public buses provide good service throughout the island; the tourist office should be able to help with a schedule of routes and times. Buses to points **east** (except for the eastern coastal road as far as Falilraki) leave from the East Side Bus Station on Plateia Rimini, whereas buses to points **west,** including the airport, leave from the nearby West Side Bus Station on Averof. Buses for the eastern coastal road as far as Falilraki also leave from the West Side Bus Station. Island fares range from 1€ within the city to 20€ for the most remote destinations. The city bus system also offers six different tours; details are available from the tourist office.

By Bicycle, Moped & Motorcycle Even where there are strips set aside for bicyclists, it can be risky cycling on Greek highways. You must have a proper license to rent anything motorized. We can recommend several outfits that rent motorbikes and bicycles: **Bicycle Center,** 39 Griva (© **22410/28-315**); **Mike's Motor Club,** 23 Kazouli (© **22410/37-420**); and **Moto Pilot,** 12 Kritis (© **22410/32-285**). Starting prices per day are roughly 15€ for a mountain bike, from 25€ for a moped, and 40€ to 70€ for a motorcycle.

By Taxi In Rhodes city, the largest of many taxi stands is in front of Old Town, on the harborfront in Plateia Rimini (© **22410/27-666**). There, posted for all to see, are

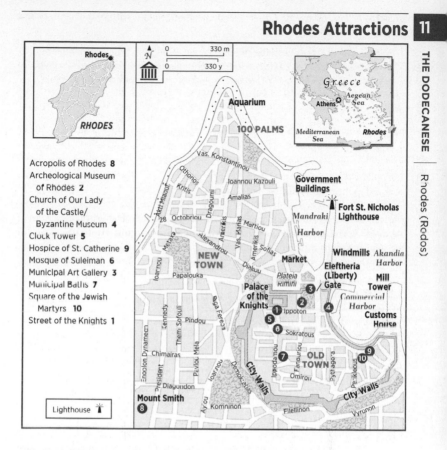

Rhodes

RHODES

Acropolis of Rhodes **8**
Archeological Museum
 of Rhodes **2**
Church of Our Lady
 of the Castle/
 Byzantine Museum **4**
Clock Tower **5**
Hospice of St. Catherine **9**
Mosque of Suleiman **6**
Municipal Art Gallery **3**
Municipal Baths **7**
Square of the Jewish
 Martyrs **10**
Street of the Knights **1**

the set fares for one-way trips throughout the island. (A sample fare to Lindos is 40€ one way; add at least another 20€ if the taxi waits for you.) Since many of the cabdrivers speak sightseer English, a few friends can be chauffeured and lectured at a reasonable cost. Taxis are metered, but fares should not exceed the minimum on short round-the-city jaunts. For longer trips, negotiate directly with the drivers. (I found Semis Limo Service to be reliable and friendly: semispa@yahoo.gr.) Better yet, **Triton Holidays** (see above), at no extra charge, will arrange for a private full- or half-day taxi with a driver who not only speaks fluent English, but will also respect your wishes regarding smoking or nonsmoking en route. For **radio taxis,** call ℭ **22410/69-800.** There is a slight additional pickup charge when you call for a taxi.

By Car   Triton Holidays agency (see above) can arrange for car rentals, both at the airport or in town. Apart from the array of international companies—among them **Alamo/National** (ℭ **22410/73-570**), **Avis** (ℭ **22410/82-896**), **Europcar** (ℭ **22410/21-958**), and **Hertz** (ℭ **22410/21-819**)—there are large numbers of local companies. The latter may offer the lowest rates but have only a handful of cars, so they may be unable to back you up, in the event of an accident. Be certain that you are fully covered, for all minor scrapes as well as major accidents, before signing anything. An established Greek company, with some 300 cars—reputedly the newest

The **Dodecanese Association for People with Special Needs** (📞 22410/73-109; cellphone 6940/463810) provides free minibus door-to-door service from the port, airport, and hotels—or even if you want to go out for coffee or a swim.

fleet on Rhodes—is **DRIVE Rent-a-Car,** now part of the **Budget** chain (📞 **22410/21-690;** www.driverentacar.gr). It has an excellent reputation for personal service, as well as low prices from about 40€ per day, depending on the season and demand. Keep in mind that some of the more remote roads on Rhodes require all-terrain vehicles, and Rhodian rental-car companies usually stipulate that their standard vehicles be driven only on fully paved roads.

By Organized Tour & Excursion Boats Several operators feature nature, archaeology, shopping, and beach tours. In Rhodes city, **Triton Holidays,** as one of the largest and most reliable agencies, specializes in trips designed for independent travelers. Triton offers day and evening cruises, hiking tours, and excursions in Rhodes, as well as in the other Dodecanese islands and in Mamaris in Turkey. We recommend the full-day guided tours, either the one to Lindos (50€) or the "Island Tour" (60€), which takes you to small villages, churches, and monasteries, and includes lunch in the village of **Embonas,** known for its local wines and fresh-grilled meat. There is also a fascinating half-day guided tour to Filerimos Monastery, Valley of the Butterflies, and the ancient city of Kamiros for 50€. Along Mandraki Harbor, you can find excursion boats that leave for **Lindos** at 9am and return around 6pm, costing about 50€, as well as daily excursions to **Simi** for 64€ round-trip. For an in-depth island experience, Triton Holidays also offers a combination package of car-rental and hotel accommodations in four small villages around the island (Kalavarda, Monolithos, Prasonisi, and Asklepion), ranging from 4 to 10 nights.

CITY LAYOUT Rhodes is not the worst offender in Greece, but it does share the country's widespread aversion to street signs and numbers. This means that you need a map marked with every lane, so that you can count your way from one place to another. My favorite is the map of Rhodes Town (Old and New) drawn by Mario Camerini; no longer widely available, I found it recently at a gift shop at 65 Socratous.

Rhodes city (pop. 50,000) is divided into two sections: the Old Town, dating from medieval days, and the New Town. Overlooking the harbor, the **Old Town** ★★ is surrounded by massive walls—4km (2½ miles) around and, in certain places, nearly 12m (40 ft.) thick—built by the Knights of St. John. The **New Town** embraces the old one and extends south to meet the **Rhodian Riviera,** a strip of luxury resort hotels. At its northern tip is the city beach, in the area called 100 Palms, and famed **Mandraki Harbor,** now used as a mooring for private yachts and tour boats.

FAST FACTS Numerous **banks** in the New Town will exchange currencies as will commercial **exchange offices,** but most everyone relies on the **ATMs** to be found not only on the banks' exteriors but at other locations frequented by tourists. For emergency care, call the **hospital** (📞 22410/80-000) or an **ambulance** (📞 166).

Internet cafes and **Wi-Fi cafes** are now found everywhere throughout Rhodes Town and there is no sense in singling out one over another: select the place that is most convenient at the time you need one—and of course you must purchase at least some beverage. **International Pharmacy,** 22 A. Kiakou in the New Town

(© 22410/75-331), is now but one of many pharmacies throughout the Old and New Towns. There are **public toilets** at 2 Papagou and across from 10 Papagou (the street leading up from Plateia Rimini); there is also one just outside the wall at the Marine Gate, by the Old Harbor. The **police** (© 22410/23-849) in the Old Town can handle any complaints from 10am to midnight. The **tourist police** (© 22410/27-423), on the edge of the Old Town, near the port, address tourists' queries, concerns, and grievances. The main **post office,** on Mandraki Harbor, is open Monday through Friday from 7am to 8pm.

What to See & Do in Rhodes City

Rhodes is blessed with first-rate sights and entertainment. As an international playground and a museum of both antiquity and the medieval era, Rhodes has no serious competitors in the Dodecanese and few peers in the eastern Mediterranean. Consequently, in singling out its highlights, we necessarily pass over sights and events that on lesser islands would be main attractions. Thus in late May and early June there is now a **Medieval Festival** with music, performances, and pageantry. In July there has been an **International Ecofilm Festival,** featuring films based on environmental themes.

EXPLORING THE OLD TOWN

Best to know one thing from the start about Old Town: It's not laid out on a grid—not even close. There are roughly 200 streets or lanes that have no name. Getting lost here, however, is an opportunity to explore. Whenever you feel the need to find your bearings, ask for **Sokratous,** the closest Old Town comes to having a main street.

Before setting out to visit Rhodes Old Town, there is at least one basic bit of history you should know: The great walls and the most impressive of the medieval buildings you will be seeing are the result of the occupation of the island by the Knights of St. John (aka Hospitallers), who were forced by the Muslims to abandon the Holy Land in 1309. These men—known more generally as Crusaders—were a mixed lot of western Europeans who established a combination of an occupation army and charity foundation wherever they settled. In 1522, after a 6-month siege, the Muslims forced the knights to surrender and retreat to Malta. But the magnificent structures we now see were built by the forced labor of the native Rhodians.

When you approach the walls of Old Town, you are about to enter arguably the most impressive continuously inhabited medieval town in Europe. It's a thrill to behold. Although there are many gates, we suggest that you first enter through **Eleftheria (Liberty) Gate,** where you'll come to **Plateia Simi,** containing ruins of the **Temple of Venus,** identified by the votive offerings found here, which may date from the 3rd century B.C. The remains of the temple are next to a parking lot (driving is restricted in the Old Town), which rather diminishes the impact of the few stones and columns still standing. Nevertheless, the ruins are a reminder that a great Hellenistic city once stood here and encompassed the entire area now occupied by the city, including the Old and New towns. The population of the Hellenistic city of Rhodes is thought to have equaled the current population of the whole island (roughly 100,000).

Plateia Simi is also home to the **Municipal Art Gallery of Rhodes,** above the Museum Reproduction Shop (generally Mon–Sat 8am–2pm); admission is 4€. Its impressive collection comprises mostly works by eminent modern Greek artists. The gallery now has a second beautifully restored venue in the Old Town (across from the Mosque of Suleiman) to house its collection of antique and rare maps and engravings

(Mon–Fri 8am–2pm). One block farther is the **Museum of Decorative Arts,** which contains finely made objects and crafts from Rhodes and other islands, most notably Simi (Tues–Sun 8:30am–3pm). Admission is 2€. Continue through the gate until you reach Ippoton, also known as the Street of the Knights. *Note:* If you are ready for serious sightseeing, purchase a ticket for 12€ that includes admission to the Museum of Decorative Arts, Archaeological Museum, Church of our Lady of the Castle, and Palace of the Knights. It's available at all of the museums.

Street of the Knights ★★ (Ippoton is its name on maps) is one of the best-preserved and most delightful medieval relics in the world. The 600m-long (1,968-ft.) cobble-paved street was constructed over an ancient pathway that led in a straight line from the Acropolis of Rhodes to the port. By the early 16th century, it became the address for most of the inns of each nation (and known as "tongues," because if the languages they spoke), which housed Knights who belonged to the Order of St. John. The inns were used as eating clubs and temporary residences for visiting dignitaries, and their facades reflect the architectural details of their respective countries.

Begin at the lowest point on the hill, at **Spanish House,** now used by a bank. Next door is **Inn of the Order of the Tongue of Italy,** built in 1519 (as can be seen on the shield of the order above the door). Then comes the **Palace of the Villiers of the Isle of Adam,** built in 1521, housing the Archaeological Service of the Dodecanese. The **Inn of France,** constructed in 1492, now hosts the French Language Institute. It's one of the most ornate inns, with the shield of three lilies (fleur-de-lis), royal crown, and the crown of the Magister d'Aubusson (the cardinal's hat above four crosses), which is off center, over the middle door. Typical of the late Gothic period, the architectural and decorative elements are somewhat asymmetrical, lending grace to the squat building.

Opposite these inns is one side of the **Hospital of the Knights,** now the **Archaeological Museum,** whose entrance is on Museum Square. The grand and fascinating structure is well worth a visit. (As with so many public buildings in Rhodes, its hours are subject to change, but summer hours are generally Tues–Fri 8am–7pm and Sat–Sun 8:30am–3pm.) Admission is 3€. Across from the Archaeological Museum is the **Byzantine Museum,** housed in the **Church of Our Lady of the Castle ★** (the Roman Catholic Cathedral of the Knights); it often hosts rotating exhibits of Christian art. Its hours vary but are generally Tuesday through Sunday from 8am to 7pm or later; admission is 3€.

The church farther on the right is **Ayia Triada** (open when it's open), next to the Italian consulate. Above its door are three coats of arms: those of France, England, and the pope. Past the arch that spans the street, still on the right, is the **Inn of the Tongue of Provence,** which was partially destroyed in 1856 and is now shorter than it once was. Opposite it on the left is the traditionally Gothic **Inn of the Tongue of Spain,** with vertical columns elongating its facade and a lovely garden in the back.

The culmination of this impressive procession should be **Palace of the Knights** ★★★ (also known as Palace of the Grand Masters), but it was destroyed in a catastrophic accidental explosion in 1856. What you see before you now is a grandiose palace built in the 1930s to accommodate Mussolini's visits and fantasies. Its scale and grandeur are more reflective of a future that failed to materialize than of a vanished past. Today it houses mosaics stolen from Kos by the Italian military as well as a collection of antique furniture. Hours vary, but, in summer, are Monday from 12:30 to 7pm, Tuesday through Sunday from 8am to 7pm. Admission is 6€.

The **Mosque of Suleiman** and the public baths are two reminders of the Turkish presence in old Rhodes. Follow Sokratous west, away from the harbor, or walk a couple of blocks south, from the Palace of the Knights; you can't miss the mosque, with its slender, though incomplete, minaret and pink-striped Venetian exterior.

The **Municipal Baths** (what the Greeks call the "Turkish baths") are housed in a 7th-century Byzantine structure and have been considerably upgraded since 2000. They merit a visit by anyone interested in vestiges of Turkish culture that remain in the Old Town, and cost less than the showers in most pensions. The *hamam* (most locals use this Turkish word for "bath") is in Plateia Arionos, between a large old mosque and the Folk Dance Theater. Throughout the day, men and women go in via their separate entrances and disrobe in private shuttered cubicles. A walk across cool marble floors leads you to the bath area—many domed, round chambers sunlit by tiny glass panes in the roof. Through the steam, you'll see people seated around large marble basins, chatting, while ladling bowls of water over their heads. The baths are open Tuesday through Saturday from 10:30am to 4pm. Their use costs 5€. Note that on Saturday, the baths are extremely crowded with locals.

The Old Town was also home to the Jewish community, whose origins date from the days of the ancient Greeks. Little survives in the northeast of Jewish Quarter of the Old Town other than a few homes with Hebrew inscriptions, the Jewish cemetery, and the **Square of the Jewish Martyrs** (**Plateia ton Martiron Evreon**, also known as Sea Horse Sq., because of the sea horse fountain). The square is dedicated to the 1,604 Jews who were rounded up here and sent to their deaths at Auschwitz. On Dosiadou, leading off just below the square (signed), is a lovely synagogue, where services are held on Friday night; it is usually open daily from 10am to 3pm. A surprisingly elegant and informative museum is attached to it (Apr–Oct Sun–Fri 10am–3pm; free admission). Those wishing to know more about this can e-mail **jcrhodes@otenet.gr**.

While at the Square of the Jewish Martyrs, be sure to visit the **Hospice of St. Catherine** ★ (Mon–Fri 8am–2pm; free admission). Built in the late 14th century by the Order of the Knights of St. John (Knights Hospitaller) to house and entertain guests, it apparently lived up to its mission; one such guest, Niccole de Martoni, described it in the 1390s as "beautiful and splendid, with many handsome rooms, containing many and good beds." The description still fits, though only one "good bed" can be seen today. The restored hospice has beautiful sea-pebble and mosaic floors, carved and intricately painted wooden ceilings, a grand hall and lavish bedchamber, and engaging exhibits. There's a lot here to excite the eyes and the imagination.

After touring the sites of the Old Town, you might want to walk around the **walls.** The fortification has a series of magnificent gates and towers, and is a remarkable example of a fully intact medieval structure. Much of the structure can be viewed by walking around the outside, but to walk along the top of the walls requires an admission fee of 4€ for adults, 2€ for students. The museum operates a 1-hour tour for 6€ Tuesday and Saturday at 3pm, beginning at the Palace of the Knights.

Another possibility is the so-called **Land Train,** a familiar attraction in many tourist towns, which takes people on a 50-minute ride through the main streets for 5€; you join it at the main market in the New Town.

EXPLORING THE NEW TOWN

The New Town is best explored after dark, as it houses most of the bars, discos, and nightclubs, as well as innumerable tavernas. In the heat of the day, its beaches—**Elli beach** and the **municipal beach**—are also popular. What few people make a point of seeking out, but also can't miss, are landmarks, such as **Mandraki Harbor** and the "neo-imperial" architecture (culminating in the Nomarhia or Prefecture) along the harbor, all of which date from the Italian occupation (1912–44). Other draws are the lovely park and ancient burial site at **Rodini** (2km/1¼ miles south of the city), and the impressive ancient **Acropolis of Rhodes,** on Mount Smith. There's also a fairly decent aquarium by the harbor.

The remains of the ancient Rhodian Acropolis stand high atop the north end of the island, above the modern city, with the sea visible on two sides. This is a pleasant site to explore with a picnic; there's plenty of shade. The restored stadium and small theater are impressive, as are the remains of the Temple of Pythian Apollo. Although just a few pillars and a portion of the architrave still stand, they are provocative and pleasing, giving fodder to the imagination. The open site has no admission fee.

SHOPPING

In Rhodes city, the Old Town is most interesting to shoppers. (*But note:* Most of these shops close at the end of Nov and don't reopen until Mar.) You'll find classic and contemporary **gold and silver jewelry** almost everywhere. The top-of-the-line Greek designer **Ilias Lalaounis** has a boutique on Plateia Alexandrou. **Chrisochos Jewelry,** at 13 Sokratous, offers a more modestly priced selection. For a good selection of antique and reproduction jewelry, as well as ceramics, silver, glass, and everything you'd expect to find in a bazaar, drop in at **Royal Silver,** 15 Apellou (off Sokratous).

For imported **leather goods** and **furs** (the former often from nearby Turkey, and the latter from northern Greece), stroll the length of Sokratous. Antiquity buffs should drop by the **Ministry of Culture Museum Reproduction Shop,** on Plateia Simi, which sells excellent reproductions of ancient sculptures, friezes, and tiles. True **antiques**—furniture, carpets, porcelain, and paintings—can be found at **Kalogirou Art,** 30 Panetiou, in a wonderful old building with a pebble-mosaic floor and an exotic banana-tree garden opposite the entrance to the Knights Palace.

Although most of what you find on Rhodes can be found throughout Greece, several products bear a special Rhodian mark. **Rhodian wine** has a fine reputation, and, on weekdays, you can visit two distinguished island wineries: **Cair,** at its winery 2km (1¼ miles) outside of Rhodes city, on the way to Lindo (www.cair.gr); and **Emery,** in the village of Embonas (www.emery.gr). Another distinctive product of Rhodes is a rare form of **honey,** made by bees committed to *thimati* (like oregano). To get this you may have to drive to the villages of Siana or Vati and ask if anyone has some to sell. It's mostly sold out of private homes, as locals are in no hurry to give it up. **Olive oil** is another local art, and again the best is sold out of private homes, meaning that you have to make discreet inquiries to discover the current sources.

Rhodes is also famed for handmade **carpets** and **kilims,** an enduring legacy from centuries of Ottoman occupation. Some 40 women around the island currently make carpets in their homes; some monasteries are also involved. There's a local carpet factory, known as **Kleopatra,** at Ayios Anthonias, on the main road to Lindos, near Afandou. In the Old Town, these and other Rhodian handmade carpets and kilims are sold at **Royal Carpet,** at 46 Aristotelos. Finally, there is "Rhodian" **lace** and **embroidery,** much of which, alas, now comes from Hong Kong. Insist on knowing the difference between what's local and what's imported.

SPORTS & OUTDOOR PURSUITS

Most outdoor activities on Rhodes are beach- and sea-related. For everything from **parasailing** to **jet skis** to **canoes,** you'll find what you need at **Faliraki beach** (see "Sights & Beaches Elsewhere on the Island," later in this chapter), if you can tolerate the crowds. If you've always wanted to try scuba diving, both **Waterhoppers Diving Schools** (☎/fax **22410/38-146;** www.waterhoppers.com) and **Dive Med** (☎ **22410/ 61-115;** www.divemedcollege.com) offer 1-day introductory dives for beginners, diving expeditions for experienced divers, and 4- to 5-day courses leading to various certifications. For wind- and kite-surfing, **Prasonisi beach** at the far southern end of Rhodes provides what has been described as a "surfer's heaven."

Or if you'd like to hike around the lesser-traveled parts of Rhodes, contact **Walking Rhodes** for guided excursions (☎ **69451/66-5850;** www.walkingrhodes.com).

No license is required for **fishing;** the best grounds are reputed to be off Kamiros Skala, Kalithea, and Lindos. Try hitching a ride with the fishing boats that moor opposite Ayia Katerina's Gate. For sailing and yachting info, call the **Yacht Agency Rhodes** (☎ **22410/22-927,** fax 22410/23 393), the center for all yachting needs.

Other sports are available at **Rhodes Tennis Club** (☎ **22410/25-705**) in the resort of Elli, or at **Rhodes-Afandu Golf Club** (☎ **22410/51-225**), 19km (12 miles) south of the port. A centrally located, fully equipped fitness center can be found at the **Fitness Factory,** 17 Akti Kanari (☎ **22410/37-667;** www.rodosnet.gr/ fitnessfactory).

If you want to get some culture as you get in shape, information on traditional Greek folk-dance lessons was long obtainable at the **Old Town Theater** (☎ **22410/ 29-085**). But since the world-famous Nelly Dimoglou troupe was forced to suspend its performances after 2010, this service is no longer guaranteed. Instead, contact the **Traditional Dance Center,** 87 Dekelias, Athens (☎ **210/251-1080**); they usually offer summer classes on dances from different regions of Greece.

Where to Stay in Rhodes City
IN THE OLD TOWN

Accommodations in the Old Town have an atmosphere of ages past, but character does not always equal charm. There are few attractive options here, and they are in considerable demand. One is that some hosts will hold you to the letter of your intent—so if you need or wish to cancel a day or more of your stay, they will do their best to extract every last cent. And there is some hedging, which means that the exact room agreed upon may be "unavailable" at the end of the day. Be explicit and keep a paper trail. And if any of this unsettles you, try booking a hotel through an agency such as Triton Holidays, which will go to bat for you in case of any problems.

Moderate
Marco Polo Mansion ★   Come here if you want a history lesson as well as a room with a touch of the exotic, but don't expect modern luxuries. What you will find, however, are extremely friendly and helpful proprietors and a comfortable environment. Featured in glossy fashion and travel magazines, the Marco Polo Mansion has captured attention with its stylish decor, its colors as if squeezed from tubes of ancient pigments and weathered in the bleaching sun. Each guest room is steeped in a history of its own and furnished with antiques and folk art. One was a harem, another a

447

hamam. The Imperial Room has six windows, whereas the Antika 2 room, lined with kilims, has a view of minarets. The smaller garden rooms, nestled in fragrant greenery, reflect the house's Italian period.

42 A. Fanouriou, 85100 Rhodes. www.marcopolomansion.gr. ℭ/fax **22410/25-562.** 7 units. 90€–160€ double. Rates include breakfast. AE, M, V. Free public parking with 10-min. walk. Closed Nov–Mar. **Amenities:** Restaurant, Wi-Fi. *In room:* A/C.

S. Nikolis Hotel and Apartments ★★

If you appreciate staying in a centuries-old building in a medieval town—which you really should do if you've come to experience Rhodes—this is the place. Proprietor and host Sotiris Nikolis has restored several medieval structures using the original stones, remaining as faithful as possible to the original style. The result is immensely pleasing. Many of the furnishings are antiques. Some rooms have sleeping lofts; some suites and studios have Jacuzzis; some studios have basic kitchenettes. A business suite comes with two bedrooms, two bathrooms, and a small office area with fax and computer (contact for rates). Breakfast and light meals are served in the rooftop garden. The S. Nikolis also has some less expensive, but equally pleasant, units—some with kitchens—in nearby annexes. In the hotel's enclosed garden are a small fitness center and a computer nook with Internet access. There is also a **cafe** at the far end and an adjacent **Ancient Agora Bar and Restaurant** where, in 1990, a 10-ton marble pediment dating from the 2nd century was found beneath the medieval foundations. Smoking is not permitted in these areas.

61 Ippodamou, 85100 Rhodes. www.s-nikolis.gr. ℭ **22410/34-561.** 16 units. 60€–120€ double; 110€–180€ suite. Complete breakfast 15€ per person. AE, MC, V. Parking on nearby streets. Call ahead Nov–Mar to see if hotel is open. **Amenities:** Restaurant (rooftop); bar; Internet. Wi-Fi. *In room:* A/C, TV, fridge, hair dryer, Jacuzzi in some suites, kitchenette in suites.

Inexpensive

Hotel Andreas This well-run hotel (under Belgian ownership) offers relief from the cardboard walls and linoleum floors that haunt many of the town's budget choices. Housed in a restored 400-year-old Turkish sultan's house, it offers attractive rooms, some with panoramic views of the town. Others have wooden lofts, which can comfortably sleep a family of four. The bedrooms (with firm beds) were once occupied by the sultan's harem, while the sultan held forth in room no. 11, a spacious corner unit with three windows and extra privacy. Breakfast is served on a shaded terrace that boasts gorgeous vistas of the town and the harbor—some of the best views in Old Town. The full **bar** has a wide-screen TV, and laundry service is provided. Room nos. 10 and 11 have the best views; room nos. 8 and 9 have private terraces.

28D Omirou (located btw. Omirou 23 and 20, *not* just before 29), 85100 Rhodes. www.hotelandreas. com. ℭ **22410/34-156.** 12 units, 6 with private bathroom. 55€–75€ double with private bathroom on corridor; 75€–110€ double with private bathroom in room. Breakfast 8€ per person extra. No credit cards. Public parking within 10-min walk. Closed Nov–Feb. **Amenities:** Wi-Fi. *In room:* A/C (in some rooms).

Spot Hotel Spotless would be a more suitable name for this small hotel. By Old Town standards, this building is an infant, barely 60 years old, but the proprietors have gradually added architectural enhancements that provide the hotel an island and medieval atmosphere more in keeping with its location. The garden and terrace sitting areas have also been enlarged. The rooms are simple and tasteful, if not especially bright. Guests enjoy a large communal fridge; access to a phone, for free local calls; free limited use of a PC for e-mail; and free luggage storage. Spot is near the harbor, right off Plateia Martiron Hevreon, so breakfast is available at nearby cafes.

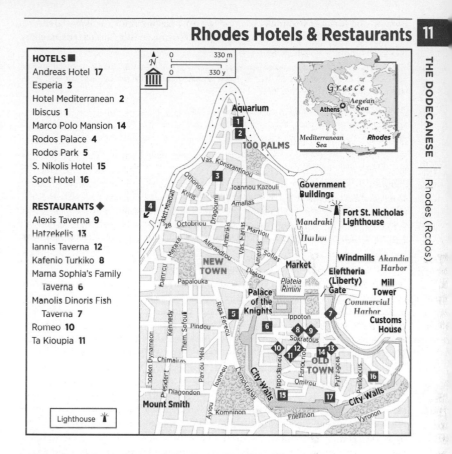

HOTELS ■
Andreas Hotel **17**
Esperia **3**
Hotel Mediterranean **2**
Ibiscus **1**
Marco Polo Mansion **14**
Rodos Palace **4**
Rodos Park **5**
S. Nikolis Hotel **15**
Spot Hotel **16**

RESTAURANTS ◆
Alexis Taverna **9**
Hatzekelis **13**
Iannis Taverna **12**
Kafenio Turkiko **8**
Mama Sophia's Family Taverna **6**
Manolis Dinoris Fish Taverna **7**
Romeo **10**
Ta Kioupia **11**

21 Perikleous, 85100 Rhodes. www.spothotelrhodes.gr. ☎ **22410/34-737.** 11 units. 70€–90€ double. Rates include continental breakfast. No credit cards. Parking on adjacent streets. **Amenities:** Wi-Fi for a fee. *In room:* A/C in some units, fridge, hair dryer.

IN THE NEW TOWN & ENVIRONS

Unlike the Old Town, the New Town doesn't prohibit new construction. You'll find a wild array of options, from boardinghouses to package-tour hotels to luxury resorts. Some are dazzling—take a look at the **Rodos Palace,** on the west-coast road running out of town, if your taste runs that way—but many are dull and indistinguishable. I've included a selection of those in different price ranges that stand out.

Very Expensive

Rodos Park Suites & Spa Hotel ★   This superb luxury hotel, with gleaming marble and polished wood interiors, enjoys a convenient yet secluded location. Guests are within a short stroll of the city's attractions—only a few minutes from the Old Town and Mandraki Harbor, yet close to the New Town shopping and dining areas. Some might regard the rooms as overdecorated, but they are certainly comfortable, with all the amenities you'd expect to find in a first-class hotel. This is not a beach resort—it's a fine city hotel open year-round. If you want a Jacuzzi in your room, opt for a suite, preferably one with a superb view of the Old Town walls. If you want to work off surplus calories from the in-house gourmet **restaurant,** head down to the fitness center or spa. A dip in the outdoor pool will offer the perfect finish to your regime.

12 Riga Fereou, 85100 Rhodes. www.rodospark.gr. ℂ **22410/89-700.** 59 units. High season 180€–210€ double, 310€–425€ suite. Rates include breakfast. AE, MC, V. Parking on adjacent streets. **Amenities:** 3 restaurants; 2 bars; babysitting; health club; pool; room service; spa. *In room:* A/C, TV, hair dryer, Internet, Jacuzzi (in suites), minibar.

Moderate
Hotel Mediterranean ★ ☺   Directly across from Kos beach and close to the aquarium, this is a great spot for kids. The year-round hotel's interior, from the common rooms to the private ones, is stylish and sophisticated. Doubles have adjoining twin beds, pullout sofas, and spacious tiled bathrooms. Rates vary according to the view; of the three exposures, the sea view far outshines the garden (pool and veranda) or side (city) view. All suites have sea views, sitting areas, and king-size beds. All units have balconies. Rooms for travelers with limited mobility are available upon request.

35 Kos Beach, 85100 Rhodes. www.mediterranean.gr. ℂ **22410/24-661.** 241 units. 135€–145€ double. Rates include breakfast. AE, DC, MC, V. Free parking arranged. Frequent public buses. **Amenities:** 2 restaurants; bar; babysitting; outdoor freshwater pool; room service; night-lit tennis court nearby; watersports equipment/rentals. *In room:* A/C, TV, hair dryer, Internet, minibar.

Ibiscus ★   The Ibiscus was a well-situated beachfront hotel when it underwent a makeover that took it from attractive to striking. The spacious marble entrance hall opens into a stylish cafe/bar; you can take your drinks out front to the beach or back onto the poolside garden veranda. (The pool is small, but most everyone goes to the beach across the road.) The large, tasteful, fully carpeted double rooms have king-size orthopedic beds, large wardrobes, ample desk areas, and tile and marble bathrooms. The suites are especially appealing, with their two bedrooms (one with a king-size bed and one with twin beds). Every unit has a balcony, many of which face the sea.

Kos Beach, 85100 Rhodes. www.rodos.com/ibiscus. ℂ **22410/24-421.** 205 units. 110€–150€ double. Rates include breakfast. AE, DC, MC, V. Free parking. Closed Nov–Mar. Frequent public buses. **Amenities:** Restaurant; bar; dipping pool. *In room:* A/C, TV, fridge, hair dryer.

Inexpensive
Esperia ✒   This hotel, open year-round, will appeal most to budget-conscious travelers. The guest rooms are nothing special but are tasteful and clean, most with a large balcony with pleasant views. New double-glazed sliding balcony doors effectively seal the rooms from most of the town's noise. TVs are available on request, at a small additional cost. The bar, lounge, and breakfast room are inviting, and the walled outdoor pool and poolside bar are well above average for a modest hotel. The hotel is located near the restaurant district and only a short walk from the beach.

7 Griva, 85100 Rhodes. www.rhodes-hotels.us (click on "Esperia" under "3 Star hotels"). ℂ **22410/23-941.** 187 units. 60€–80€ double. Rates include breakfast. AE, DC, MC, V. Parking within 10-min. walk. **Amenities:** Breakfast room; bar; babysitting; pool. *In room:* A/C, fridge, hair dryer.

Where to Eat in Rhodes City
IN THE OLD TOWN
The Old Town is thick with tavernas, restaurants, and fast-food nooks, all doing their best to lure you into places that might be where you would want to be. If not, the more brazen their overtures, the more adamant you must be in holding to your course. Don't imagine, however, that all Old Town restaurants are tourist traps. Many Rhodians come to this area for what they consider the island's best food, particularly fish. Don't even think of driving to these places; walk through an entrance to the Old Town.

Very Expensive

Alexis Taverna ★ GREEK/SEAFOOD   For some 70 years, this restaurant has been the one to beat in Old Town, but you do have to be prepared to abandon restraint (and your budget). The proprietors preserve the traditions established by their grandfather to devise a seafood feast for you, accompanied by the perfect wine from the cellar (which represents vineyards all over Greece). The fish is selected daily at the harbor and the proprietors have their own greenhouse on the outskirts of town to cultivate organic vegetables. Start with a bounteous seafood platter of delicately flavored sea urchins, fresh clams, and tender octopus carpaccio. Try the sargos, a sea-bream-type fish, chargrilled to perfection. In season, try the oysters. (At times they even have sushi.) The creamy Greek yogurt, with homemade green-walnut jam, is a perfect ending for a superb culinary experience. Every meal here begins with a chef's consultation and should end with applause.

18 Sokratous. **② 22410/29-347.** Reservations recommended. Individually prepared dinners without wine average 70€. AE, V. Mon–Sat 10am–4pm and 7pm–1am.

Manolis Dinoris Fish Taverna ★ GREEK/SEAFOOD   This restaurant, housed in the former stables of the 13th-century Knights of St. John's Inn, provides a unique setting to enjoy delicious fresh seafood delights. You can order either a la carte or from the set menu of Coquille St. Jacques, Greek salad, grilled prawns, swordfish, baklava, coffee, and brandy. In warm weather, the quiet side garden is delightful; in winter, a fire roars in the old stone hearth indoors.

14A Museum Sq. **② 22410/25-824.** Main courses 30€–65€; set menu 75€. AE, MC, V. Daily noon–midnight.

Expensive

Goniako Palati (Corner Palace) GREEK   The Goniako Palati may not be a palace, but it is on the corner—a busy corner you overlook once the food arrives. Great canvas awnings cover the seating area, raised above street level. The taverna menu is basic Greek, fresh and skillfully prepared in a slightly upscale environment at reasonable prices. This is one place local New Towners go for reliable, and then some, taverna fare. The grilled swordfish souvlaki, served with a medley of steamed vegetables, is tasty. The *saganaki* (grilled cheese) is a performance art, and delicious to boot.

110 Griva (corner of Griva and 28 Oktobriou). **② 22410/33-167.** Main courses 10€–28€. AE, MC, V. Daily 9am–midnight.

Ta Kioupia ★★ GREEK   Once rated by the *Guardian* as one of the world's 10 best restaurants, this unique place offers a true gourmet experience. Much-lauded Greek chef Michael Koumbiadis founded it in 1972, and he has preserved the true harmonies of traditional Greek cuisine, using the best local ingredients and village recipes. The meal might begin with a choice of soups, followed by an amazing array of appetizers and accompanied by home-baked breads. The main dishes are equally superb—broiled veal stuffed with cheese and sprinkled with pistachio nuts in yogurt sauce; or delectable pork souvlaki, with yogurt and paprika sauce on the side. For dessert, try the light crepes filled with sour cherries and covered with chocolate sauce and vanilla crème. Many of the foods are prepared in clay pots in a traditional wood-burning oven. **Warning:** The grand fixed-price meal requires fasting, devotion, and time (roughly 3 hr.).

22 Menekleos (off Sokratous; follow signs to Hammam Bath). **② 22410/91-824.** Reservations required. Main courses 25€–30€; fixed-price meals 40€–75€ per person, wine extra. MC, V. Mon–Sat 8pm–midnight; Sun noon–3pm.

Moderate

Hatzikelis ★ GREEK/SEAFOOD This delightful fish taverna enjoys a peaceful and pleasant setting in the midst of a small neighborhood park just behind the Church of Our Lady of the Burgh in the Square of the Jewish Martyrs. Although there is an extensive a la carte menu, the special dinners for two are probably the most appealing for many. The Fisherman's Plate consists of lobster, shrimp, mussels, octopus, squid, and a liter of wine, while the plates of traditional Rhodian dishes include specialties such as zucchini balls and shrimp *saganaki*. The portions are challenging, but the quality of the cuisine and the fact that you have until 2am to do your duty increase the odds in your favor. And top your meal off with some of their own pastries. Not so incidentally, Trivago Travel, a European rating outfit, named Hatzekalis the no. 1 restaurant in Rhodes and no. 6 in all of Greece

9 Alhadeff. www.hatzekalis.gr. ✆ **22410/27-215.** Main courses 9€–22€. No credit cards. Daily 11am–2am.

Mama Sophia's Family Taverna ★ GREEK/SEAFOOD/PIZZA Don't let the name fool you—although it is in fact a family institution—this is Greek taverna food and atmosphere at its best. From pizza to fresh seafood, *mezes* to steaks, everything comes to the table prepared to perfection. You could make a meal out of nothing but their fabulous appetizers—scallops on the half shell, *tyrokafteri* (feta lightly spiced with chili), marinated octopus. Seafood is their specialty and as always in Greece this can be a bit costly, depending on the variety chosen, but have you come all the way to Rhodes to save money? Also, the wine list offers some exceptional choices, from moderate to expensive. All this while you sit and watch the world go by at this choice location (also from a roof garden) and are served by Stavros and Yiannis, the sons of the founders.

Orfeos St. (behind the clock tower at top of Socratous). www.mamasofia.gr. ✆ **22410/24-469.** Main courses 8€–25€. AE, MC, V. Late Mar to early Nov. Daily 8am–midnight.

Romeo ★ GREEK/SEAFOOD/PIZZA Though under siege by tourists, many locals frequent the Romeo, as there is a good deal that's authentic within its walls (themselves some 500 years old). Beside the predictable taverna fare are the many local dishes on offer—including vegetarian options. Two house specialties are the mixed fish grill and the stuffed souvlaki. For the grill, you select your own fish from a generous array of fresh deep-sea options—the tender grilled octopus is especially good. The finely cut grilled souvlaki stuffed with melted cheese and tomatoes is a regional dish from the north end of the island. Their pizza is the thin-crust variety and quite tasty. The reasonably priced dry house wines go nicely with each entree. Set back in a quiet enclave, just off and out of the crush of Sokratous, Romeo offers courtyard and roof-garden seating, as well as tasteful, live traditional Greek music and song.

7–9 Menekleous (off Sokratous). www.romeo-restaurant.com. ✆ **22410/25-186.** Main courses 8€–26€. AE, MC, V. Daily noon–12:30am.

Inexpensive

Iannis Taverna ★ GREEK For a budget Greek meal, visit Chef Iannis's small place on a quiet back lane. The moussaka, stuffed vegetables, and meat dishes are flavorful and well prepared by a man who spent 14 years as a chef in the Greek diners of New York. His Greek plate is one of the best to be found in Rhodes, with a large variety of tasty foods. The breakfast omelets are a great deal. Portions are hearty and cheap, and the friendly informal service makes for a most enjoyable experience.

41 Platonos. ✆ **22410/36-535.** Main courses 6€–18€. No credit cards. Daily 9am–midnight.

Kafenio Turkiko GREEK/SNACKS Located in a medieval structure, this is the only authentic place left on touristy Sokratous, otherwise replete with Swatch, Body Shop, Van Cleef, and souvenir shops. Each rickety wooden table comes with a backgammon board for idling away the hours while you sip a Greek coffee or suck on a hookah pipe. The old pictures, mirrors, and bric-a-brac on the walls will enhance your feeling of bygone times.

76 Sokratous. No phone. Drinks/snacks 2€–9€. No credit cards. Daily 11am–midnight.

IN THE NEW TOWN & ENVIRONS
Moderate

Palia Historia (The Old Story) ★ GREEK If you're maxed out on run-of-the-mill Greek taverna fare, this is a good place to come—well worth a taxi ride from wherever you're staying. Most of the clientele is Greek, drawn by the subtle cuisine and lack of tourists. The marinated salmon and capers are worthy of the finest Dublin restaurant, and the broccoli with oil, mustard, and roasted almonds is inspired. As a main course, the shrimp *saganaki* leaves nothing to the imagination. With fish, the dry, white Spiropoulos, from Mantinia, is perfect. For a great finish, go for the banana flambé.

108 Mitropoleos (south in New Town, below modern stadium). ℂ **22410/32-421.** Reservations recommended. Main courses 12€–28€. AE, MC, V. Daily 7pm–midnight.

Rhodes City After Dark

During the high season, Rhodes claims one of the most active nighttime scenes in Greece outside of Athens. Granted, some of that energy is grounded in the resort complexes north of the city, but there is enough to go around.

Your own common sense is as good a guide as any in this ever-changing scene. In a city as compact as Rhodes, it's best to follow the lights and noise, and get a little lost. When you decide to call it quits, shout down a taxi (if you're outside the Old Town) to bring you back—just remember where you're staying.

As a rule of thumb, the younger foreign set will find the **New Town** livelier than the Old Town. **Cafe scenes** are located on the harbor, behind Academy Square, or on Galias near New Market. The **bar scene** tends to line up along Diakonou. In the Old Town, most of the clubs and bars are found along Miltiadhou—these tend to be more frequented by the local youth. There must be at least 100 **nightclubs** on Rhodes, so you're sure to find one to your liking.

Gambling is a popular nighttime activity in Greece. Rhodes, for many years, housed one of Greece's six legal casinos, a government-operated roulette and blackjack house adjoining the Grand Hotel. Now in private hands and known as the **Casino Rodos,** it is in the **Grande Albergo delle Rose,** in the New Town; admission costs 15€, and patrons must be at least 23 years old.

Unfortunately, the **sound-and-light** (*son et lumière*) production that for many years entertained and informed visitors with its dramatic presentation of the history of Rhodes was terminated in 2010 due to Greece's budgetary problems. We can only hope that it will be restored by the time this edition of the guide is in use. The public sat in the gardens just outside the walls adjacent to the Plateia Rimini in the New Town and it was one of the most pleasant diversions on a summer evening. Check at your hotel or any travel agency to learn if it has been revived (and if so, then be sure to check for the English-language performances). Admission was 6€ for adults, 2€ for youths, and free for children 10 and under.

Alas, too, the **Traditional Folk Dance Theater** of the Nelly Dimoglou Dance Company, was also terminated in 2010 for the same budgetary reasons. Located at

Adronikou, off Plateia Arionos, Old Town (© **22410/20-157**), this internationally acclaimed company has always been lively, colorful, and utterly entertaining. Spirited young men and women perform dances from many areas of Greece, often in embroidered flouncy costumes. Performances usually took place May through early October, on Monday, Wednesday, and Friday at 9:15pm. Admission was 12€ for adults. Ask at your hotel or travel agency to learn if this has been restored.

Exploring the Island

Sun, sand . . . and the rest is history. Nowhere is that more true than on Rhodes, where ruins and beaches lure visitors out of Rhodes city. For the best **beaches,** head to the island's east coast. Visitors also flock to archaeological sites identical to the three original Dorian city-states, all nearly 3,000 years old: **Lindos, Kamiros,** and **Ialisos.** Of these, Lindos was and is preeminent; it is by far the top tourist destination outside of Old Town. So we begin here with Lindos, and then go back to Rhodes town to explore the island counterclockwise.

LINDOS

Lindos is without question the most picturesque town on the island of Rhodes. Because Lindos has been designated a historic settlement, the Archaeological Society controls development in the village, and the traditional white-stucco homes, shops, and restaurants form the most unified, classically Greek expression in the Dodecanese. Be warned, however, that Lindos is often deluged with tourists, and your first visit may be unforgettable for the wrong reasons. Avoid it from mid-July to August, if possible.

Frequent public buses leave Plateia Rimini for a fare of 8€; a taxi will cost 40€ one-way. There are two entrances to the town. The first and northernmost leads down a steep hill to the bus stop and taxi stand, and then veers downhill again to the beach. (However, if you're driving, park in the lot above the town.) At this square, from April through October daily from 9am to 10pm, you'll find the **Tourist Information Kiosk** (© **22440/31-900;** fax 22410/31-288). Here, too, is the commercial heart of the village, with the acropolis looming above. The rural **medical clinic** (© **22410/31-224**), **post office,** and **telephone office (OTE)** are nearby. The second road into town leads beyond it and into the upper village, blessedly removed from the hordes. This is the better route for people more aesthetically minded. Follow signs to the acropolis. You'll pass a stand where, for 8€, you can ride a donkey (also known as a "Lindian taxi") all the way to the top. If you walk, the sides of the walkway are strewn with embroidery and lace for sale, which may or may not be the handiwork of local women. Embroidery from Rhodes was highly coveted in the ancient world. In fact, it is claimed that Alexander the Great wore a grand Rhodian robe into battle at Gaugemila; and, in Renaissance Europe, French ladies used to yearn for a bit of Lindos lace. Much of what is for sale in Lindos today, however, is from Asia.

Before you start the final ascent to the acropolis, be sure to inspect the famous **relief carving of a trireme ★**, or three-banked ship, dating from the 2nd century B.C. At the top, from the fortress ramparts, are glorious views of medieval Lindos below, where most homes date from the 15th century. To the south you can see the lovely beach at St. Paul's Bay—legend claims St. Paul put ashore here—along with Rhodes's less developed eastern coastline. Across to the southwest rises Mount Krana, where caves, dug out to serve as ancient tombs, are thought to have sheltered cults to Athena well into the Christian period.

The **acropolis ★** (© **22410/27-674**) is open Tuesday through Sunday from 8am to 7pm, Monday from 12:30 to 7pm. Admission is 6€ for adults and 3€ for students and children. This is one of three original Dorian acropolises in Rhodes. Within the much-later medieval walls stand the remains of the **Sanctuary of Athena Lindos,** with its large Doric portico from the 4th century B.C. St. John's Knights refortified the acropolis with turreted walls and built a church to St. John inside. Today, stones and columns are strewn everywhere as the site undergoes extensive restoration.

On your descent, as you explore the labyrinthine lanes of medieval Lindos, you will come to the exquisite late-14th- or early-15th-century **Byzantine Church of the Panagia** ★. Still the local parish church (admission 2€), its more than 200 iconic frescoes cover every inch of the walls and arched ceilings. Dating from the 18th century, all of the frescoes have been painstakingly restored at considerable expense and with stunning results. Be sure to spend some time here; many of these icons are sequentially narrative, depicting the Creation, the Nativity, the Christian Passover, and the Last Judgment. And, after you've given yourself a stiff neck from looking up, look down at the extraordinary floor, made of sea pebbles.

Adjoining the Church of the Panagia is the **Church Museum** (✆ **22440/32-020**), open April through October daily from 9am to 3pm, admission is 2€. The historical and architectural exhibits and collected ecclesiastical items, including frescoes, icons, texts, chalices, and liturgical embroidery, comprise a collection. Frankly, most people prefer to spend their time looking elsewhere around the village.

Then, of course, there's the inviting **beach** below, lined with cafes and tavernas.

Where to Stay in Lindos & Environs

In high season, Lindos marks the spot where up to 10,000 day-trippers from Rhodes city converge with 4,000 resident tourists. As hotel construction is no longer permitted, almost all of the old homes have been converted into pensions (called "villas," in the brochures), by English charter companies. **Triton Holidays** (www.tritondmc.gr; ✆ **22410/21-690**) books six person villas, including kitchen facilities (reservations are often made a year in advance). In peak season, the local **Tourist Information Kiosk** (✆ **22440/31-900;** fax 22440/31-288) has a list of homes that rent rooms. Plan to pay at least 60€ for a double and 90€ to 125€ for a studio apartment.

Atrium Palace Thalassos Spa Resort ★ ☺   Just over 6.4km (4 miles) out of Lindos, on the long beach of crystal-clear Kalathos Bay, this luxurious resort hotel features an eclectic architectural design—a neo-Greek, Roman, crusader, and Italian pastel extravaganza. The rooms are colorful and comfortable; the inner atrium is an exotic, tropical garden of pools and waterfalls. The landscaped outdoor pool complex is an alternative to the nearby beach, and the indoor pool, sauna, and fitness club will keep you busy and now there is a spa that offers sea water treatment. To fully entertain the family on the rainy days that seldom occur, there are game rooms, a miniclub for young children, and an arcade of shops. Despite the hotel's five-star status, the atmosphere is relaxed, unpretentious, and friendly, due to the excellent staff.

Kalathos Beach, 85107 Rhodes. www.atrium.gr. ✆ **22440/31-601.** 316 units. 120€–155€ double. Rates include breakfast. AE, DC, MC, V. Parking on premises. Closed Nov–Mar. Pets allowed. **Amenities:** Restaurant; bars; babysitting; children's center; fitness club; Internet; Jacuzzi; pools; room service; sauna; spa. *In room:* A/C, TV, minibar.

Lindos Mare ★   This small and classy cliff-side resort hotel is a prime site at which to drop anchor on the east shore. The rooms are a notch above those of comparable luxury hotels on the coast, and the views of the bay are glorious. A tram descends from the upper lobby, restaurant, and pool area to the lower levels of attractive Aegean-style bungalows, and continues onward down to the beach area (linked by a cable car), where you'll find umbrellas and watersports. The hotel is only a 2km (1¼-mile) walk or ride into Lindos, although you might want to stay put in the evenings to enjoy in-house social activities, such as barbecues, folklore evenings, or dancing.

Lindos Bay, 85107 Rhodes. www.lindosmare.gr. ℂ **22440/31-130.** 141 units. 210€–240€ double; 250€–420€ suite. Rates include breakfast. With half-board plan (breakfast and dinner) 260€–290€ double. AE, DC, MC, V. Parking on premises. Closed Nov–Mar. **Amenities:** 2 restaurants; 2 bars; children's playground; 2 pools; room service; watersports equipment/rentals. *In room:* A/C, TV, fridge, hair dryer, Internet.

Melenos Lindos Exclusive Studios ★   This boutique hotel admittedly will appeal only to those able to afford a pricey luxury retreat, but as such, it's a once-in-a-lifetime experience. It's in an authentically Lindian-style villa, with hand-painted tiles, local antiques, handcrafted lamps, fine linens—in short, traditional splendor combined with contemporary comforts and convenience. The terraces, landscaping, and views over the sea can make you forget that you are in the crowded Lindos, while you gaze up at the acropolis and muse about all the history that surrounds you.

Lindos Town, 85107 Rhodes. www.melenoslindos.com. ℂ **22440/32-222.** 12 units. 210€–310€ double; 230€–650€ suite. Rates include breakfast. AE, MC, V. Free parking nearby. **Amenities:** Restaurant; bar; room service. *In room:* A/C, TV, hair dryer, Internet, minibar.

Where to Eat in Lindos & Environs

You'll have a paralyzing array of restaurants and tavernas to choose from in Lindos. On the beach, the expansive **Triton Restaurant** gets a nod because you can change into your swimsuit in the bathroom, essential for nonresidents who want to splash in the gorgeous water across the way. The restaurant is also not as pricey as the others.

Argo Fish Taverna ★ GREEK/SEAFOOD   Haraki Bay is a quiet fishing hamlet with a gorgeous, crescent-shaped pebbly beach—and this excellent seafood taverna. Consider stopping here for a swim and lunch on a day trip to Lindos. You'll appreciate the freshness of the food, as well as a creative variation on a Greek salad that added mint, dandelion leaves, and other fresh herbs, served with whole-wheat bread. The lightly battered, fried calamari is tasty and a relief from the standard overbattered fare. Mussels, baked with fresh tomatoes and feta cheese, are also something special.

Haraki beach (10km/6 miles north of Lindos). ℂ **22440/51-410.** Reservations recommended. Main courses 13€–55€. AE, MC, V. Easter–Oct daily noon–1am.

Mavrikos ★ GREEK/FRENCH   There's no denying that this is the most celebrated restaurant in Lindos—arguably in all of Rhodes—as attested to by the rich and famous who have dined here in recent decades. It sometimes gets negative reviews but I find that most times it lives up to its reputation, combining elegant food with the rustic charm of the tree-shaded terrace. Brothers Michalis and Dimitri Mavrikos continue a now-70-year-old family tradition of fine Greek and French cuisine, such as their oven-baked lamb and nicely done beef filets, or the perfectly grilled and seasoned fresh red snapper. The food is distinguished by the subtle flavors provided by seasonings—butter beans in a sauce with carobs, beef in a casserole with bergamot, and tuna with fenugreek. Vegetarians will also find much on the menu to satisfy their palates. The brothers Mavrikos also run an ice-cream parlor **Geloblu,** serving homemade frozen concoctions and cakes. It's in the Old Town, near the church.

Main square, Lindos. ℂ **22440/31-232.** Reservations recommended. Main courses 10€–30€. V. Daily noon–midnight.

SIGHTS & BEACHES ELSEWHERE ON THE ISLAND

A tour around the island provides you with a chance to view the wonderful variations of Rhodes's scenery. The sights described below, with the exception of Ialisos and

Kamiros, are not of significant historical or cultural importance, but if you're tired of lying on the beach, they provide a pleasant diversion. The route outlined below traces the island counterclockwise from Rhodes city, with a number of suggested sorties to the interior. Even a cursory glance at a map of Rhodes will explain the many zigs and zags in this itinerary. Keep in mind that not all roads are equal; all-terrain vehicles are required for some of the detours suggested below.

Ialisos (Ialyssos) was the staging ground for the four major powers that were to control the island. The ancient ruins and monastery on Mount Filerimos reflect the presence of two of these groups. The Dorians ousted the Phoenicians from Rhodes in the 10th century B.C. (An oracle had predicted that white ravens and fish swimming in wine would be the final signs before the Phoenicians were annihilated. The Dorians, quick to spot opportunity, painted enough birds and threw enough fish into wine jugs that the Phoenicians left without raising their arms.) Most of the Dorians left Ialisos for other parts of the island; many settled in the new city of Rhodes. During the 3rd to 2nd centuries B.C., the Dorians constructed a temple to Athena and Zeus Polios, whose ruins are still visible, below the monastery. Walking south of the site will lead you to a well-preserved 4th-century-B.C. fountain.

When the Knights of St. John invaded the island, they, too, started from Ialisos, a minor town in Byzantine times. They built a small, subterranean chapel decorated with frescoes of Jesus and heroic knights. Their whitewashed church is built right into the hillside above the Doric temple. Over it, the medieval Italians constructed the **Monastery of Filerimos,** which remains a lovely spot to visit (and with a most impressive cross at the top). Finally, Suleiman the Magnificent moved into Ialisos (1522) with his army of 100,000 and used it as a base for his takeover of the island.

In summer, the site of Ialisos is open Monday through Saturday from 8am to 7pm; hours are irregular the rest of the year. Proper dress is required. Admission is 3€. Ancient Ialisos is 6km (3½ miles) inland from Trianda, on the island's northwest coast; buses leave from Rhodes frequently for the 14km (8½-mile) ride.

Petaloudes is a popular attraction because of the millions of black-and-white-striped **"butterflies"** (actually a species of moth) that overtake this verdant valley in July and August. When resting quietly on plants or leaves, the moths are well camouflaged. Only the wailing of infants and the Greek rock blaring from portable radios disturbs them. Then the sky is filled with a flurry of red, the moths' underbellies exposed as they try to hide from the summer crush. The setting, with its many ponds, bamboo bridges, and rock displays, is admittedly a bit too precious; and, the fact is, you cannot always be guaranteed of seeing the moths in flight. But it's worth at least a try. Petaloudes is 25km (16 miles) south of Rhodes and inland; it can be reached by bus but is most easily seen on a guided tour. It's open daily from 8:30am to 6:30pm; admission is 5€ from mid-June to late September, and 3€ the rest of the year.

The ruins at **Kamiros** are much more extensive than those at Ialisos, perhaps because this city remained an important outpost after the new Rhodes was completed in 408 B.C. The site is divided into two segments: the upper porch and the lower valley. The porch served as a place of religious practice and provided the height needed for the city's water supply. Climb to the top and you'll see two aqueducts, which assured the Dorians of a year-round supply of water. The small valley contains ruins of homes and streets, as well as the foundations of a large temple. The site is well enough preserved to visualize what life in this ancient Doric city was like more than 2,000 years ago. Think about wearing a swimsuit under your clothes: Across from the site is a good stretch of **beach,** where there are some rooms to let, a few tavernas, and the bus stop. The site is open Tuesday through Sunday from 8:30am to 3pm.

An Unexpected Delight: Kallithea Springs

Surely one of the pleasures of traveling is to come across a place that you never expected to find. Just such a place is the **Kallithea Springs** north of Faliraki (and about 10km/6 miles from Rhodes city). The thermal waters of Kallithea had been praised for their therapeutic qualities by Hippocrates and had attracted visitors through the Middle Ages. But by the 20th century the place had been forgotten and abandoned until in the 1920s, the Italians restored the site as a classic curative spa, erecting an exotic complex of buildings in what is best described in an Arabic/Art Deco style. After World War II the place was once again abandoned until in the late 1990s work began on a complete restoration of the site and its structures. This is what one sees today and possibly by the time this guide is in use, people will even be able to at least drink the water. Meanwhile, there is a small bay here where people come to swim and snorkel or just sit in the cafe and contemplate the history of such an unexpected place. Not a major destination, but well worth an afternoon's excursion—easily reached by frequent public buses.

Admission is 4€. Kamiros is 34km (21 miles) southwest of Rhodes city, with regular bus service.

Driving south along the western coast from Kamiros for about a mile, you'll come to the late-15th-century knights castle of **Kastellos (Kritinias Castle),** dominating the sea below. From here, heading south and then cutting up to the northeast, make your way inland to **Embonas,** the wine capital of the island and home to several tavernas famed for their fresh meat barbecues. This village is on the tour-group circuit, and numerous tavernas offer feasts accompanied by live music and folklore performances. If you then circle the island's highest mountain, **Attaviros** (1,196m/3,923 ft.), you come to the village of **Ayios Issidoros,** where devoted trekkers can ask directions to the summit. (It's a 5-hr., round-trip hike from Ayios Issidoros to the top of Mount Attaviros.) Otherwise, proceed to the picturesque village of **Siana,** nestled on the mountainside. From here, head to **Monolithos,** with its spectacularly sited crusader castle perched on the pinnacle of a coastal mountain.

If you now decide to head for the eastern coast, you retrace your path back through Siana and Ayios Issidoros and then proceed on to **Laerma,** where you might consider taking a 5km (3-mile) seasonal road to **Tharri Monastery,** the oldest functioning monastery on the island, with beautiful though weather-damaged frescoes. From Laerma, it's another 10km (6 miles) to Lardos and the eastern coastal road, where you can either head straight to **Lindos** (see above) or take another detour to **Asklipio,** with its ruined castle and impressive Byzantine church. The church has a mosaic-pebbled floor and gorgeous cartoon-style frescoes, which depict the 7 days of Creation (check out the octopus) and the life of Jesus.

The **beaches** south of Lindos, from Lardos Bay to Plimmiri (26km/16 miles in all), are among the best on Rhodes, especially the stretch between Lahania and Plimmiri. At the southernmost tip of the island, for those who seek off-the-beaten-track places, is **Prasonisi (Green Island),** connected to the main island by a narrow sandy isthmus, with waves and world-class windsurfing on one side and calm waters on the other.

Heading north from Lindos to Faliraki, there are a number of sandy, sheltered beaches with relatively little development. **Faliraki beach** is the island's most developed beach resort, offering every possible vacation distraction imaginable—from bungee jumping to laser clay shooting. For families with kids in tow, there is a **Water Park** and a sort of Disneyland-type amusement park, the **Magic Castle.** The southern end of the beach is less crowded and frequented by nude bathers. But for those who want to avoid the gigantic beach resort hotels, I can recommend the following:

Ladiko Bungalows Hotel Anthony Quinn obtained permission to build a retirement home for actors on this pretty little bay on the road to Lindos, 3km (2 miles) south of the swinging beach resort of Faliraki, but never realized his plans. But you can see why the location attracted him—it is both quiet and convenient. This friendly family-operated lodge has activities for nature lovers (swimming, fishing, and hiking to nearby ruins and beaches), but is just a 20-minute walk to noisy, bustling Faliraki. The terrace bar and dining area with a splendid view of Ladiko Bay provide lovely tranquil spots for a drink or a meal. The guest rooms are not exceptional, but they are quite comfortable. Fourteen rooms come with fridges.

Faliraki, P.O. Box 236, 85100 Rhodes. ℂ **22410/85-560.** Fax 22410/80-241. 42 units. 65€–105€ double. Rates include breakfast. MC, V. Parking on premises. Closed Nov–Mar. **Amenities:** Coffee shop; fitness center. *In room:* A/C, some w/fridge, hair dryer.

SIMI (SYMILES)

11km (7 miles) N of Rhodes

Tiny, rugged Simi is often called "the jewel of the Dodecanese." Arrival by boat affords you a view of pastel-colored neoclassical mansions climbing the steep hills above the broad, horseshoe-shaped harbor. Yíalos is Simi's port, and Horio its old capital. The welcome absence of nontraditional buildings is due to an archaeological decree that severely regulates the style and methods of construction and restoration of all old and new buildings. Simi's long and prosperous tradition of shipbuilding, trading, and sponge diving is evident in its gracious mansions and richly ornamented churches. Islanders proudly boast that there are so many churches and monasteries that you can worship in a different sanctuary every day of the year.

During the first half of this century, Simi's economy deteriorated as the shipbuilding industry declined, the maritime business soured, and somebody invented a synthetic sponge. Simiots left their homes to find work on nearby Rhodes or in North America and Australia (a startling 70% eventually returned). Today, the island's picture-perfect traditional-style houses have become a magnet for moneyed Athenians and Italians in search of vacation homes; and Simi is a highly touted off-the-beaten-path resort for European tour groups trying to avoid other tour groups. The onslaught of tourists for the most part arrives about 10:30am and departs by about 5pm.

In recent years, the **Simi Festival,** which goes on intermittently from July to September, has put Simi on the cultural map as an attractive seasonal contender, offering an eclectic menu of international music, theater, and cinema. Some of the performers have major international reputations.

By the way, Simi has no natural source of water—all water has to be transported by boat from nearby islands. Day visitors will scarcely be aware of this, but everyone is asked to conserve water. Simi is also one of the hottest places in Greece during the summer, so come prepared with everything from a hat to sunscreen.

Essentials

GETTING THERE Many (if not most) visitors to Simi arrive by boat from Rhodes. Several **excursion boats** arrive daily from Rhodes; schedules and itineraries for the boats vary, but all leave in the morning from Mandraki Harbor and stop at the main port of Simi, Yialos—some with an additional stop at Panormitis Monastery or the beach at Pedi—before returning to Rhodes later in the day. Currently, there are daily **car ferries** from Piraeus, and two **local ferries** weekly via Tilos, Nissiros, Kos, and Kalimnos. From late spring to summer, **hydrofoils** and a **catamaran** skim the waters daily from Rhodes to Simi, usually making both morning and afternoon runs. Round-trip fares run from 40€ to 64€, depending on the type (and speed!) of the ship. Most travel agencies could make arrangements; in Rhodes town, use **Triton Holidays** (© **22410/21-690;** www.tritondmc.gr).

VISITOR INFORMATION Check out the helpful website operated by Simi's delightful and informative independent monthly, *The Symi Visitor* (© **22460/71-785;** www.symivisitor.com). Through the site's e-mail option, you can request information on accommodations, buses, weather, and more. Don't ask them to recommend one hotel over another; explain exactly what you're looking for and they'll provide suggestions. Once you're on Simi, you'll find free copies of the latest *Symi Visitor* at tourist spots.

The long-established **Kalodoukas Holidays** (© **22410/71-077;** www.kalodoukas.gr) can help with everything from booking accommodations (often at reduced rates) to chartering a boat. Once you've arrived on Simi, drop by the office at the base of the stairway to Horio (where there is another office; Mon–Sat 9am–1pm and 5–9pm). In summer, this agency plans a special outing for every day of the week, from cruises to explorations of the island. Most involve a swim and a healthy meal.

A **tourist information kiosk** on the harbor keeps hours that remain a mystery. Information and a free pamphlet may also be obtained at the **town hall,** located on the town square behind the bridge.

GETTING AROUND Ferries and excursion boats dock first at hilly **Yialos** on the barren, rocky, northern half of the island. Yialos is the liveliest village on the island and the venue for most overnighters. The clock tower, on the right as you enter the port, is used as a landmark when negotiating the maze of car-free lanes and stairs. Another landmark used in giving directions is the bridge in the center of the harbor's inlet.

Simi's main road leads to **Pedi,** a developing beach resort one cove east of Yialos, and a new road rises to **Horio,** the old capital, which is now overshadowed by Yialos. The island's 4,000 daily visitors often take an excursion boat that stops at Panormitis Monastery or at Pedi beach. **Buses** leave every hour from 8am until 11pm for Pedi via Horio (1€). Taxis at the center of the harbor charge a set fee of 8€ to Horio and 10€ to Pedi. **Mopeds** are also available, but due to the limited network of roads, you'll do better relying on public transportation and your own two feet. **Caiques** (converted fishing boats) shuttle people to various beaches: Nimborios, Ayia Marina, Ayios Nikolaos, and Nanou; prices range from 15€ to 25€, depending on distance. You can rent sun beds at these beaches.

FAST FACTS For a **doctor,** call © **22410/71-316;** for a dentist, call © **22410/71-272;** for the **police,** © **22410/71-11.** The **post office** (© **22410/71-315**) and **telephone office** (**OTE;** © **22410/71-212**) are located about 50m (170 ft.) behind the clock tower on the waterfront; both open Monday through Friday from 7:30am to 3pm. Numerous cafes around the harbor now offer either **Internet access** or **Wi-Fi.**

What to See & Do

Simi's southwestern portion is hilly and green. Located here is the medieval **Panor-mitis Monastery,** dedicated to St. Michael, the patron saint of seafaring Greeks.

The monastery is popular with Greeks as a place of pilgrimage and of refuge from modern life; young Athenian businessmen speak lovingly of the monks' cells and small apartments that can be rented for rest and renewal. There is also an almshouse that provides shelter for the elderly. Call the **guest office** (✆ **22410/72-414**) to book accommodations, ranging from 40€ to 75€ for an apartment or house. All units are self-contained, with their own stove and fridge. The least expensive units have shared outdoor toilets. Most sleep at least four people.

The whitewashed compound has a verdant, shaded setting and a 16th-century gem of a church inside. **Taxiarchis Mishail of Panormitis** boasts icons of St. Michael and St. Gabriel adorned in silver and jewels, and a superb iconostasis. The combined folk and ecclesiastical museums are well worth the 2€ entrance fee, which goes to support the almshouse mentioned above.

The town of **Panormitis Mihailis** is at its most lively and interesting during the annual November 8 **Feast of Archangel Mihaili,** but it can be explored year-round via boats or bus tours from Yialos. The hardy can hike here—it's 10km (6 miles), about 3 hours from town—then enjoy a dip in the sheltered harbor and a meal in the taverna.

In Yialos, if you are sure you are up to it (no pun intended) you can climb the 375 or so stone steps, known as the **Kali Strata** (the **Good Steps**), that take you to **Horio**—but this is not recommended for everyone in the heat of midsummer. This wide stairway ascends to a picturesque community that reflects a Greece that is in many ways long departed. Old women sweep the whitewashed stone paths outside their homes, and occasionally a young boy or very old man can be seen retouching the neon-blue trim over doorways and shutters. Nestled among the immaculately kept homes, which date from the 18th century, are renovated villas now rented to an increasing number of tourists. And where tourists roam, tavernas, souvenir shops, and bouzouki bars soon follow but commercialization has yet to transform Horio.

Horio has an **Archaeological and Folklore Museum** that houses archaeological and folklore artifacts that the islanders consider important enough for public exhibition. You can't miss the blue arrows that point the way. It's open Tuesday through Saturday from 9am to 2pm. Admission is 2€. Also, if you walk through the town you will pass on your right an iron-gated building that retains an intact old pharmacy; if not open, you can peer through the windows and see the jars with their curatives. The **Maritime Museum** in the port costs 2€ and is open daily from 11am to 2:30pm.

Crowning Horio is the **Church of the Panagia.** The church is surrounded by a fortified wall and is therefore called the kastro (castle). It's adorned with the most glorious frescoes on the island, which can be viewed only when services are held (Mon–Fri 7–8am; all morning Sun).

Simi is blessed with many beaches, though they are not wide or sandy. Close to Yialos are two: **Nos,** a 15m-long (50-ft.) rocky stretch, and **Nimborios,** a pebble beach.

A bus to **Pedi,** followed by a short walk, takes you to **St. Nikolaos beach,** with shady trees and a good taverna, or to **St. Marina,** a small beach with little shade but stunning turquoise waters, as well as views of the St. Marina islet and its cute church.

The summertime cornucopia of outings provided by Kalodoukas Holidays has already been mentioned in "Visitor Information," above; but if you want to set out on your own, pick up a copy of *Walking on Symi: A Pocket Guide* or *Walks on Symi,* each available at Kalodoukas Holidays for about 7€. They describe numerous walks to help you discover and enjoy Simi's historic sites, interior forests, and mountain vistas.

LOCAL industries ON SIMI

One skill still practiced on Simi is **ship-building.** If you walk along the water toward Nos beach, you may see boats under construction or repair. It's a treat to watch the men fashion planed boards into graceful boats. Simi was a boat-building center in the days of the Peloponnesian War, when spirited sea battles were waged off its shores.

Sponge fishing is almost a dead industry in Greece. Only a generation ago, 2,000 divers worked waters around the island; today only a handful undertake this dangerous work, and most do so in the waters around Italy and Africa. In the old days divers often went without any apparatus. Working at depths of 50 to 60m (164–197 ft.), many divers were crippled or killed by the turbulent sea and too-rapid depressurization. The few sponges that are still harvested around Simi—and many more imported from Asia or Florida—are sold at shops along the port. Even if they're not from Simi's waters, they make inexpensive and lightweight gifts.

Where to Stay

Many travelers bypass hotels for apartments or houses. Between April and October, rooms for two, with shower and kitchen access, go for 45€ to 80€. More luxurious villa-style houses with daily maid service rent for 90€ to 150€. To find out more, contact Kalodoukas Holidays or the Simi website (see "Visitor Information," above).

Dorian Studios   In a beautiful part of town, only 10m (33 ft.) from the sea, this rustically furnished hotel offers comfortable lodging (orthopedic beds!) and a kitchenette in every room. Some of the studios have vaulted beamed ceilings as well as balconies or terraces overlooking the harbor, where you can enjoy your morning coffee or evening ouzo.

Yialos, 85600 Simi. www.symigreece.com/dorian. ☎ **22460/71-307.** 9 units. 55€–80€ double. MC, V. Parking on adjacent streets. Closed Nov to mid-Apr. Just up from the Akti Gennimata, at the Aliki Hotel. *In room:* A/C (in 5 units), kitchenette.

Hotel Aliki ★   This grand Italianate sea captain's mansion, dating from 1895, is one of the more elegant tourist hostelries on Simi. It has the atmosphere of a boutique guest house, intimate and charming, and offers tastefully styled accommodations furnished with Italian antiques. Four rooms and two separate large apartments (for four to six persons) have balconies. Several units enjoy dramatic waterfront views, and the roof garden provides a spectacular 360-degree vista of the sea, town, and mountains. It is right on the waterfront, yet not in the built-up section. Because the Aliki has become a chic overnight getaway from bustling Rhodes, reservations are absolutely required.

Akti Gennimata, Yialos, 85600 Simi. www.symi-greece.com. ☎ **22460/71-665.** 15 units. 120€–150€ double; 150€–180€ suite. Rates include breakfast. AE, MC, V. Parking on adjacent streets. Closed mid-Nov to Mar. *In room:* A/C, fridge.

Hotel Nireus ★   This beautifully maintained hotel on the waterfront is gracious and inviting, with its own shaded seafront cafe and restaurant, sunning dock, and swimming area. Its location, amenities, and price make it a favorite on Simi for foreigners and vacationing Greeks alike. The traditional Simiot-style facade has been preserved, while the spacious guest rooms are contemporary and comfortable. Ask for one of the 18 units that face the sea and offer stunning views; if you're fortunate, you might get one with a balcony. All four suites front the sea.

Akti Gennimata, Yialos, 85600 Simi. niraeus@rho.forthnet.gr. © **22460/72-400.** 35 units. 90€ double; 120€ suite. Rates include buffet breakfast. MC, V. Parking on adjacent streets. Closed Nov-Easter. **Amenities:** Restaurant; bar. *In room:* A/C, TV, fridge.

Hotel Nirides If you crave tranquil seclusion, this small cluster of apartments, on a rise overlooking Nimborios Bay and only minutes on foot from the one-taverna town of Nimborios, may be exactly what you're seeking. It's about 35 minutes from Yialos on foot and appreciably less by land or sea taxi. Each attractive and spotless apartment sleeps four (two in beds and two on couches) and has a bedroom, bathroom, salon, and kitchenette. Seven apartments have balconies, three have terraces, and all face the sea. The Nirides has its own small bar and rents bicycles for excursions to town or beyond. There's a small beach with pristine water just a few minutes down the hill.

Nimborios Bay, 85600 Simi. nirapart@otenet.gr. ©/fax **22460/71-784.** 11 units. 65€-90€ double. Rates include breakfast. MC, V. Parking on adjacent streets. Closed Nov-Mar. **Amenities:** Cafe/bar; bike rental. *In room:* A/C, TV, kitchenette.

Where to Eat

In Yialos, for traditional home cooking and a respite from the crowds, look for the **Family Taverna Meraklis,** at the top of Menoilkidi Street (the first right after the statue of the little fisher boy across the harbor inlet; © **22410/71-003**).

Hellenikon (The Wine Restaurant of Similes) ★ GREEK/MEDITERRANEAN If you have the impression that the Greek culinary imagination spins on a predictable wheel, you need a night at the Hellenikon. In addition to spectacular fare, this open-air restaurant on the Yialos town square often provides, by virtue of its location, free evening concerts, compliments of the Simi Festival. Start with one of the combination-appetizers plates. The chef's fish soup is spectacular, as are the grilled vegetables. In addition to a piquant array of traditional Greek entrees, you can select one of seven homemade pastas and combine it with one of numerous sauces. Meanwhile, host Nikos Psarros is a wine master, who has over 150 Greek wines in his cellar, all from small independent wineries, and he will help you select the perfect wine to complement your meal.

Yialos. © **22410/72-455.** psarrosn@otenet.gr. Main courses 12€-24€. MC, V. May-Oct daily 8pm-midnight.

La Vaporetta (The Steam Cloud) ★ GREEK/ITALIAN This new (since 2007) addition to Simi's fine dining is the offspring of the adjacent Hotel Aliki (see above) and equals it in its high standards. Located in an old mansion right on the harbor, its proprietors are in fact a mix of Greeks and Italians so the dishes are authentic on both sides of the menu. You can sit right on the water's edge or if it's too hot (or windy) inside to partake of any number of well prepared meals, from familiar Italian foods—various pasta dishes, of course—or traditional Greek foods, fresh seafood among them. Congenial, informal service makes for a most pleasant dining experience.

Akti Gemminati, Yialos. © **30-69479-72332.** www.hotelaliki.gr. Main courses 10€-20€. AE, MC, V. May-Nov daily noon-4pm and 7pm-midnight.

Nireus Restaurant ★ GREEK Michalis, the chef of this superior restaurant in the Nireus Hotel, on the waterfront, has gained quite a reputation in recent years. Kudos to his *frito misto*, a mixed seafood plate with tiny, naturally sweet Simi shrimp and other local delicacies. The savory filet of beef served with a Madeira sauce is also recommended. They say you can't eat the scenery, but the view from here is delicious. Yialos. ℭ **22410/72-400.** Main courses 8€–22€. MC, V. Easter–Oct daily 11am–11pm.

Taverna Neraida 🐟 SEAFOOD   Proving the rule that fish is cheaper far from the port, this homey taverna on the town square has among the best fresh-fish prices on the island, as well as a wonderful range of *mezedes.* Try the black-eyed-pea salad and *skordalia* (garlic sauce). The grilled daily fish is delicious, and the ambience is a treat. Yialos. ℭ **22410/71-841.** Main courses 7€–24€. No credit cards. Daily 11am–midnight.

KOS

370km (230 miles) E of Piraeus

Kos today is identified with and, at times, nearly consumed by tourism; but the island and its people have endured, and so will you, with a little initiative and independence. Almost three-quarters of the island's working people are directly engaged in tourism, and that tells you something about Kos's beauty and attractions.

Kos has been inhabited for roughly 10,000 years, and for a significant portion of that time, has been both an important center of commerce and a line of defense. Its population in ancient times may have reached 100,000, but today it is less than a third of that number. Across the millennia, the unchallenged favorite son of the island has been Hippocrates, the father of Western medicine, who has left his mark not only on Kos, but also on the world.

The principal attractions of Kos are its **antiquities**—most notably the Asklepion—and its **beaches.** You can guess which are more swamped in summer. But the taste of most tour groups is thankfully predictable and limited so the congestion can be evaded, if that's your preference.

Kos town is still quite vital. Because the island is small, you can base yourself in the town, in an authentic neighborhood if possible, and venture out from there. You'll get the most out of Kos by following the locals—especially when it comes to restaurants. If you think you're in a village and see no schools or churches, and no old people, chances are you're in a resort. Kos has many, especially along its coasts.

Essentials

GETTING THERE   By Plane   Kos is now serviced by both **Olympic Airways,** with a Kos town office at 22 Vas. Pavlou (ℭ **22420/28-331**), and **Aegean Airlines** (ℭ **22420/51-654**). Although Olympic has experimented with expanded service and may do so again, at present its only direct flights to Kos are from Athens and Rhodes. From **Hippocrates Airport** (ℭ **22420/51-229**), a public bus will take you the 26km (16 miles) to the town center for 8€, or you can take a taxi for about 25€.

By Boat   As a transportation hub of the Dodecanese, Kos offers (weather permitting) a full menu of options: car ferries, passenger ferries, hydrofoils (Flying Dolphins), excursion boats, and caiques. Though most schedules and routes are always in flux, the good news is that, with more or less patience, you can make your way to Kos from virtually anywhere in the Aegean. Currently, the only ports linked to Kos with year-round nonstop and at least daily ferry service are Piraeus, Rhodes, Kalimnos, and Bodrum. Leros and Patmos enjoy the same frequency but with a stop or two along the way. The Kos harbor is strewn with travel agents, who can assist you; or check current schedules with the Municipal Tourism Office (see below).

VISITOR INFORMATION The **Municipal Tourism Office** (☏ **22420/24-460;** fax 22420/21-111), on Vas. Yioryiou, facing the harbor near the hydrofoil pier, is your one-stop source of information in Kos. It's open May through October Monday to Friday 8am to 2:30pm and 5 to 8pm, Saturday and Sunday 9am to 2pm; November through April, hours are Monday to Friday 8am to 2:30pm. Hotel and pension owners keep the office informed of what rooms are available in the town and environs; however, you must book your room directly with the hotel. Be sure to pick up a free map of Kos. For a more extensive and detailed guide to Kos—beaches, archaeological sites, birds, wildflowers, tavernas, and much more—pick up a copy of *Where and How in Kos,* available at most news kiosks for 4€.

GETTING AROUND **By Bus** The **Kos town (DEAS) buses** offer service within roughly 6.4km (4 miles) of the town center, whereas the **Kos island (KTEL) buses** will get you nearly everywhere else. For the latest schedules, consult the **town bus office,** on the harbor at 7 Akti Kountourioti (☏ **22420/26-276**), or the **island bus station,** at 7 Kleopatras (☏ **22420/22-292**), around the corner from the Olympic Airways office. The majority of DEAS town buses leave from the central bus stop on the south side of the harbor.

By Bicycle This is a congenial island for cyclists. Much of Kos is quite flat, and the main road from Kos town to Kefalos has all but emptied the older competing routes of traffic. As bike trails are provided until well beyond Kos town, you can also avoid the east-end beach roads. But don't expect to pedal one-way and then hoist your bike onto a bus, because that won't work here. Rentals are available throughout Kos town and can be arranged through your hotel. Prices range from 10€ to 25€ per day.

By Moped & Motorcycle It's easy to rent a moped through your hotel or a travel agent. Or, as with bicycles, you can walk toward the harbor and look for an agency. Rentals range from 25€ to 40€. You can also call **Motoway,** 9 Vas. Yioryiou (☏ **22420/20-031**), for mopeds and motorcycles.

By Car It's unlikely that you'd need to rent a car for more than 1 or 2 days on Kos, even if you wanted to see all its sights and never lift a foot. Numerous companies, including **Avis** (☏ **22420/24-272**), **Europcar** (☏ **22420/24-070**), and **Hertz** (☏ **22420/28-002**), rent cars and all-terrain vehicles. Expect to pay as much as 95€ per day, including insurance and fuel. Gas stations are open Monday through Saturday from 7am to 7pm; there are also several stations open (in rotation) in Kos town on Sunday; ask your hotelier or the tourist office for directions.

By Taxi For a taxi, drop by or call the **harbor taxi stand** beneath the minaret and across from the castle (☏ **22420/23-333** or 22420/27-777). All Kos drivers are required to know English—then again, maybe you were once required to know trigonometry.

ORIENTATION Kos town is built around the harbor from which the town fans out. In the center are an **ancient city** *(polis),* consisting of ruins; an old city, limited mostly to pedestrians; and the new city, with wide, tree-lined streets. Most of the town's hotels are near the water, either on the road north to Lambi or on the road south and east to Psalidi. If you stand facing the harbor, with the castle on your right, **Lambi** is to your left and **Psalidi** on your right. In general, the neighborhoods to your right are less overrun and defined by tourists; this area, although quite central, is overall more residential and pleasant. The relatively uncontrolled area to your left (except for the occasional calm oasis, such as that occupied by the Pension Alexis) has been largely given over to tourism. Knowing this will help you find most of the

| 📷 | **The Oldest Tree in Europe?** |

From the Kos Museum, you might want to walk across to the **Municipal Fruit Market,** and then have a picnic at the foot of the oldest tree in Europe, only a short walk toward the harbor, at the entrance bridge to the castle. The bizarre-looking tree standing with extensive support is said to be the **Tree of Hippocrates ★,** where he once instructed his students in the arts of empirical medicine and its attending moral responsibilities. Botanists may not endorse this claim, but why not enjoy the legend!

tourist-oriented services by day and action by night, as well as where to find a bit of calm when you want to call it quits. Most recommended places to stay lie to your left, east of the castle.

FAST FACTS   Any of the major banks can exchange currency, but most people now use the ATMs at the banks' exteriors. The **hospital** is at 32 Hippokratous (✆ **22420/22-300**). **Del Mare Internet Cafe,** 4a Megalo Alexandrou (✆ **22420/ 24-244;** www.cybercafe.gr), is open daily from 9am to 2am. The **post office,** on Vas. Pavlou (at El. Venizelou), is open Monday through Friday from 7:30am to 2:30pm. Across from the castle, the **tourist police** (✆ **22420/22-444**) are available 24 hours to address any outstanding need or emergency, even trouble finding a room.

What to See & Do
ATTRACTIONS IN KOS TOWN

Dominating the harbor, the **Castle of the Knights** stands in and atop a long line of fortresses defending Kos since ancient times. What you see today was constructed by the Knights of St. John in the 15th century and fell to the Turks in 1522. Satisfying your curiosity is perhaps the only compelling reason to pay the 4€ admission fee. The castle is a hollow shell, with nothing of interest inside that you can't imagine from the outside, except when it serves as a venue for concerts. Best to stand back and admire from a distance this massive reminder of the vigilance that has been a part of life in Kos from prehistory to the present.

At the edge of town, at the intersection of Vas. Pavlou and E. Grigoriou, stands the **Casa Romana** (✆ **22420/23-234**), a Roman villa that straddles what appears to have been an earlier Hellenistic residence. The largest Roman villa in Greece (with 37 rooms), it was actually built and rebuilt over the centuries, and what you see today is the villa of the 3rd century A.D., one with lavish mosaics, marble paving, and fountains. It was closed to the public in 2005 for major restoration but reopened in 2009 (and there has been talk of using the villa's upper story as a museum for the villa's finds, now in Kos town's Archeological Museum). The villa is open Tuesday through Sunday from 8:30am to 3pm and costs 3€ for adults. Nearby, to the east and west of the Casa Romana, are a number of interesting open sites, comprising what is, in effect, a small archaeological park. Entrance is free. To the east lie the remains of a **Hellenistic temple** and the **Altar of Dionysos,** and to the west and south a number of impressive excavations and remains, the jewel of which is the **Roman Odeon,** with 18 intact levels of seats. The other extensive area of ruins is in the agora of the **ancient town,** just in from Akti Miaouli. Kos town is strewn with archaeological sites, opening like fissures and interrupting the flow of pedestrian traffic. Rarely is anything identified for passersby, so they seem like mere barriers or building sites.

The rich architectural tradition of Kos did not cease with the eclipse of antiquity—Kos is adorned with a surprising number of striking and significant structures, sacred and secular, enfolded unselfconsciously into the modern town. While you're strolling about town, note the **sculptures** by Alexandros Alwyn, in the Garden of Hippocrates, opposite Dolphins Square, down along the Old Harbor. An English painter and sculptor with something of an international reputation, Alwyn long maintained a studio in the village of Evangelistra, on Kos.

Asklepeion ★ Unless you have only beaches on the brain, Asklepeion is reason enough to come to Kos. On an elevated site with grand views of Kos town, the sea, and the Turkish coastline, this is the mecca of modern Western medicine, where Hippocrates—said to have lived to the age of 104—founded the first medical school in the late 5th century B.C. (In case your mythology is a bit rusty, Asclepius was the Greek god of healing.) For nearly a thousand years after his death, this was a place of healing, where physicians were consulted and gods invoked in equal measure. The ruins date from the 4th century B.C. to the 2nd century A.D. Systematic excavation of the site was not begun until 1902. Truth be told, this is one of those archaeological sites that work best for those who bring something to them—namely some associations, some knowledge, some respect for the history behind the ruins   in this case, a sense of the role of Hippocrates in our own lives.

Located 4km (2½ miles) southwest of Kos town. © **22420/28-763.** Admission 4€ adults, 2€ E.U. seniors and students, free for children 16 and under. Oct to mid-June Tues–Sun 8:30am–3pm; late June to Sept Tues–Fri 8:30am–7pm, Sat 8:30am–3pm.

Kos Archaeological Museum For a town the size of Kos, this is an impressive archaeological museum, built by the Italians in the 1930s to display mostly Hellenistic and Roman sculptures and mosaics uncovered on the island. Although there is nothing startling or enduringly memorable in the collection, it will remind visitors of the former greatness of this now quite modest port town. Look in the museum's atrium for the lovely 3rd-century mosaic showing how Hippocrates and Pan once welcomed Asclepius, the god of healing, to this, the birthplace of Western medicine.

Plateia Eleftherias (across from the municipal market). © **22420/28-326.** Admission 3€ adults, 2€ seniors and students, free for children 16 and under. Tues–Sun 8:30am–3pm.

SHOPPING

Kos town is compact, and the central shopping area all but fits in the palm of your hand, so you can explore every lane and see what strikes you. If you've grown attached to the traditional music you've been hearing since your arrival in Greece and want some help in making the right selection, stop by either of the **Ti Amo Music Stores,** 11 El. Venizelou and 4 Ipsilandou, where Giorgos Hatzidimitris will help you find traditional or modern Greek music. At either shop you may sit and listen before making a purchase.

Even if you're unwilling to pack another thing, you won't notice the weight of the unique handmade gold medallions at the jewelry shop of **N. Reissi,** opposite the museum at 1 Plateia Kazouli (© **22420/28-229**). Especially striking are the Kos medallions, designed and crafted by Ms. Reissi's father (60€–125€). Handcrafted rings, charms, and earrings are also on display. For unusual ceramic pieces, visit the shop of **Lambis Pittas,** at 6 Kanari (leading away from the inner harbor), or his factory at G. Papendreou (on the coast, leaving town for the southeast).

Another sort of treasure to bring home is a hand-painted Greek icon. **Panajiotis Katapodis** has been painting icons for over 40 years, both for churches and for individuals. His studio and home are on a hillside about 2km (1 mile) west of Kos center, at Ayios Nektarios, and visitors are welcome April through October, Monday through Saturday from 9am to 1pm and 4 to 9pm. The way is signposted from just east of the Casa Romana.

BEACHES & OUTDOOR PURSUITS

The beaches of Kos are no secret. Every foot of the 290km (180 miles) of mostly sandy coastline has been discovered. Even so, for some reason, people pack themselves together in tight spaces. You can spot the package-tour sites from afar by their umbrellas, dividing the beach into plots measured in centimeters. **Tigaki** and **Kardamena** epitomize this avoidable phenomenon. Following are a few guidelines to help you in your quest for uncolonized sand.

The beaches 3 to 5km (2–3 miles) east of Kos town are among the least congested, probably because they're pebbled rather than sandy. Even so, the view is splendid, and the nearby hot springs are worth a good soak. In summer, the water on the northern coast of the island is warmer and shallower than that on the south, though less clear due to stronger winds. If you walk down from the resorts and umbrellas, you'll find some relatively open stretches between **Tigaki** and **Mastihari.** The north side of the island is best for **windsurfing;** try Tigaki and Marmara, where everything you need can be rented on the beach. A perfect day at the northwestern tip of the island would consist of a swim at **Limnionas Bay,** followed by grilled red mullet at Taverna Miltos.

Opposite, on the southern coast, **Kamel beach** and **Magic beach** are less congested than **Paradise beach,** which lies between them. Either can be reached on foot from Paradise beach, a stop for the Kefalos bus. The southwestern waters are cooler yet calmer than those along the northern shore; and apart from Kardamena and Kefalos Bay, the beaches on this side of the island are less dominated by tour groups. Note that practically every watersport, including jet-skiing, can be found at **Kardamena.** The southwestern tip of the island, on the **Kefalos peninsula,** near Ayios Theologos, offers remote shoreline ideal for surfing. You can end the day watching the sunset at **Sunset Wave beach,** where you can also enjoy a not-soon-forgotten family-cooked feast at **Agios Theologos Restaurant,** which rents molded plastic surfboards as well.

For yachting and sailing, call the **Yachting Club of Kos** (☎ 22420/20-055) or **Istion Sailing Holidays** (☎ 22420/22-195; fax 22420/26-777). For diving, contact **Kos Diving Centre,** 5 Plateia Koritsas (☎ 22420/20-269 or 22420/22-782); **Dolphin Divers** (☎ 2940/548-149); or **Waterhoppers** (☎ 22420/27-815; cellphone 69440/130533).

As already outlined (see "Getting Around," above), the island is especially good for **bicycling,** and rentals are widely available. If horseback riding is your thing, you can arrange guided excursions through the **Marmari Riding Centre** (☎ 22420/41-783), which offers 1-hour beach rides and 4-hour mountain trail rides. **Bird-watchers** will be interested in the wild peacocks in the forests at Skala, and the migrating flamingos that frequent the salt-lake preserve just west of Tingaki.

EXPLORING THE HINTERLANDS

The most remote and authentic region of the island is comprised of the forests and mountains stretching roughly from beyond Platani all the way to Plaka in the south. The highest point is Mount Dikeos, reaching nearly 900m (3,000 ft.). The mountain villages of this region were once the true center of the island. Only in the last 30 years or so have they been all but abandoned for the lure of more level, fertile land and, since the 1970s, the cash crop of tourism.

There are many ways to explore this region, which begins little more than a mile beyond the center of Kos town. Trekkers will not find this daunting, and by car or motorbike it's a cinch, but peddling a mountain bike over the ups and downs may be a challenge. Regardless of which way you go, the point is to take your time. You could take a bus from Kos to Zia and walk from Zia to Pili, returning then from Pili to Kos town by bus. The 5km (3-mile) walk from Zia to Pili will take you through a number of traditional island villages. (Pili, by the way, celebrates Apr 23 with horse racing and traditional foods.) Along the way you'll pass the ruins of **old Pili,** a mountaintop castle growing so organically out of the rock that you might miss it. As your reward at day's end, have dinner in **Zia** at **Sunset Taverna,** where at dusk the view of Kos island and the sea is magnificent. Zia also has a ceramics shop and a Greek art shop to occupy you as you wait for your taxi. For those looking to get away from the crowds, an hour's drive from Kos town all the way to the southwest coast leads to **Sunset Wave beach,** below Ayios Theologos. There the Vavithis family, including some repatriated from North America, maintain a restaurant that makes for a most enjoyable setting and meal.

VENTURING OFFSHORE

Two interesting offshore options lie within easy reach of Kos. Hop one of the daily ferries from Kardamena and Kefalos to the small island of **Nissiros.** Nissiros, while not especially attractive, has at its center an active volcano, which blew the top off the island in 600 B.C. and last erupted in 1873. There are also daily ferries from Kos harbor to **Bodrum, Turkey** (ancient Halikarnassos). Note that you must bring your passport to the boat an hour before sailing so that the captain can prepare the necessary documents for the Turkish port police.

Where to Stay

Plan ahead and make a reservation well in advance. Most places are booked solid in summer and closed tight in winter.

EXPENSIVE

Kiprlotis Village Resort ★ ☺   Here's a resort hotel that will appeal to families willing to spend at least part of a vacation amid loads of fun-seeking Europeans with all the possible holiday facilities. Only 4km (2½ miles) from Kos town and right on the beach, it is constructed as a village of sorts, with its two-story bungalows and apartments surrounding its outdoor sports facilities (volleyball, basketball, tennis, minigolf). The attractive rooms vaguely suggest an Ikea-modern style with a Greek touch. Kids can take part in a full day of supervised activities. If you're here to soak up the sun, you'll never have to leave the premises; meals, however, as might be predicted for such a large institution, are not especially imaginative, but there is public transportation every 15 minutes into Kos town. While this place is relatively classy, it does tend to be booked by groups, so don't expect a cozy atmosphere.

P.O. Box 206, Psalidi beach, 85200 Kos (4km/2½ miles south of Kos town). www.kipriotis.gr. © **22420/ 27-640.** 512 units. 175€ double; 200€ bungalow for 2 (including breakfast). AE, MC, V. Closed mid-Oct to mid-Apr. Parking on premises. **Amenities:** 5 restaurants; 4 bars; babysitting; children's center; health center w/sauna; 2 pools (1 indoor heated); tennis; watersports equipment/rentals. *In room:* A/C (July-Aug only), TV, fridge, hair dryer, Internet.

MODERATE

Hotel Astron ★   This is the most attractive hotel on Kos town's harbor, yet only some 360m (1,180 ft.) from a swimming beach—although the hotel does have its own generous-size pool and pleasant patio. The entrance and lobby are striking and suggest an elegance that, in fact, does not extend to the rooms and suites. However, all units are tasteful and clean, with firm beds and balconies. The pricier rooms include extras such as harbor views and Jacuzzis. In the larger and more expensive suites, the extra space is designed to accommodate a third person and is wasted if you intend to use it as a sitting area. One extra that might be worth the money is a harbor view; but remember, by nighttime, you are facing the action. Kos is no retirement community: In summer, about 65% of the rooms are allotted to package-tour groups that come to live it up.

31 Akti Kountourioti, 85300 Kos. www.astron-hotel-kos.gr. © **22420/23-703.** 80 units. 125€ double; 150€ suite. Rates include breakfast. AE, MC, V. Parking on adjacent streets. **Amenities:** Restaurant; bar; Internet; Jacuzzi; 2 pools (1 children's); room service. *In room:* A/C, TV, fridge, hair dryer, minibar.

INEXPENSIVE

Hotel Afendoulis ✦   Nowhere in Kos do you receive so much for so little. Nestled in a gracious residential neighborhood a few hundred yards from the water and less than 10 minutes on foot from the center of Kos, Afendoulis offers the combination of convenience and calm. The rooms are clean and altogether welcoming, with firm beds. Nearly all units have private balconies, and most have views of the sea. Whatever room you have, you can't go wrong. Note that the hotel has an elevator. This is a long-established family-run place, and the Zikas family spares nothing to create a vacation community in which guests enjoy and respect one another. If you are coming to Kos to bask in luxury or raise hell, go elsewhere. Although this is likely to be many people's first choice in Kos, the family also owns the Pension Alexis (see below) several blocks away and can usually accommodate someone who shows up at the last minute.

1 Evrepilou, 85300 Kos. afendoulishotel@kos.forthnet.gr. © **22420/25-321.** Fax 22420/25-797. 23 units. 60€–75€. MC, V. Parking on adjacent streets. Closed mid-Oct to mid-Apr.

Hotel Yiorgos   This inviting, family-run hotel is a block from the sea and no more than a 15-minute walk from the center of Kos town. Although the immediate neighborhood is not residential, the hotel enjoys relative quiet year-round. Guest rooms are modest and clean. All units have balconies, most with pleasant but not spectacular views of either sea or mountains. Individually controlled central heating makes this an exceptionally cozy small hotel at the chilly edges of the tourist season. Convenience, hospitality, and affordability have created a place to which guests happily return.

9 Harmilou, 85300 Kos. www.yiorgoshotel.com. © **22420/23-297.** 35 units. 40€–65€ double. Rates include breakfast. No credit cards. Parking on adjacent streets. **Amenities:** Breakfast room; bar; Wi-Fi. *In room:* A/C, TV, fridge.

Pension Alexis   Ensconced in a quiet neighborhood only a stone's throw from the harbor, Pension Alexis feels like a home because it is one—or was, until it opened as a guesthouse. This is a gracious dwelling, with parquet floors and tasteful architectural touches. The expansive rooms have high ceilings and open onto shared balconies. Most have sweeping views of the harbor and the Castle of the Knights. Individual rooms are separated from the halls by sliding doors, and share three large bathrooms. Room no. 4 is a grand corner space with knockout views. In summer, the heart of the pension is the covered veranda that faces private gardens, where, in the morning, guests can enjoy breakfast and, at dusk, can share stories late into the night. You do have to share the hallway bathrooms with two or three other rooms—balance that against the price, location, and ambience.

9 Irodotou, 85300 Kos. ☏ **22420/28-798** or 22420/25-594. Fax 22420/25-797. 14 units. 40€–50€ double. Breakfast extra 7€. No credit cards. Parking on adjacent streets. Closed mid-Oct to mid-Apr. **Amenities:** Bar; Internet. *In room*: A/C or fans.

Where to Eat

In Kos, as at all popular Greek tourist destinations these days, there's a lot of routine food and even fast food. But there's no need to make eating on Kos a Greek tragedy; the key is to eat where the locals do. Along with your meals, you may want to try some of the local wines: dry **Glafkos,** red **Appelis,** or crisp **Theokritos** retsina.

EXPENSIVE

Petrino ★ GREEK   When royalty come to Kos, this is where they dine—so should you. Housed in an restored, century-old, two-story stone (*petrino*) private residence, this is the most elegant taverna in Kos, with food to match. In summer, sit outside on the three-level terrace overlooking the ancient agora; but be sure to take a look at the splendid architecture inside, especially upstairs. Although the menu focuses on Greek specialties, it is vast enough to include lobster, filet mignon, and other Western staples. But don't waste this opportunity to experience Greek traditional cuisine at its best (and not necessarily all that expensive). The stuffed peppers, grilled octopus, and *beki meze* (marinated pork) are perfection. More than 50 carefully selected wines, all Greek, line the cellar—this is your chance to learn why Greece was once synonymous with wine. The dry red kalliga from Kefalonia is exceptional.

1 Plateia Theologou (abutting agora's east extremity). ☏ **22420/27-251.** Reservations recommended. Main courses 10€–55 €. AE, DC, MC, V. Mid-Dec to Nov daily 5pm–midnight.

Platanos Restaurant ★ GREEK/INTERNATIONAL   Not only is Platanos in one of Kos's best locations, overlooking the Hippocrates Tree, it is in a handsome building, a former Italian officers' club replete with arches and the original tile floor. Try reserving a place on the upstairs balcony, with its impressive vista. Among the creatively prepared appetizers is chicken stuffed with dates in a spicy sauce. If you're tired of Greek salads, try the mixed vegetable salad. For a main course, try the souvlaki, a combination of chicken, lamb, and beef; or the duck Dijonnaise, served with a tasty sauce and a selection of seasonable vegetables. A generous selection of choice wines, live music, and gracious service makes for a splendid evening.

Plateia Platanos. ☏ **22420/28-991.** Main courses 12€–32€. AE, MC, V. Apr–Oct daily noon–11:30pm.

MODERATE

Taverna Mavromatis ★ GREEK   One of the best choices in town is this 40-year-old vine- and geranium-covered beachside taverna run by the Mavromati brothers. Their food is what you came to Greece for: melt-in-your-mouth *saganaki,* mint- and garlic-spiced *sousoutakia* (meatballs in red sauce), tender grilled lamb chops, moist beef souvlaki, and perfectly grilled fresh fish. In summer, the taverna spills out along the beach; you'll find yourself sitting only feet from the water watching the sunset and gazing at the nearby Turkish coast. A dinner here can be quite magical, something locals know very well, so arrive early to ensure a spot by the water.

Psalidi beach. ☏ **22420/22-433.** Main courses 6€–20€. AE, MC, V. Wed–Sun 11am–11pm. A 20-min. walk southeast of the ferry port, or accessible by the local Psalidi Beach bus.

INEXPENSIVE

Arap (Platanio) Taverna GREEK/TURKISH   Although this place requires a short walk or a taxi ride, it is worth the effort. Like the population of Platinos, the food is a splendid mix of Greek and Turkish. The spirit of this family restaurant is contagious. Whatever you order, it's impossible to go wrong. Although there are many meat dishes, vegetarians will have a feast. The roasted red peppers stuffed with feta and the zucchini flowers stuffed with rice are splendid, as is the *bourekakia* (a kind of fried pastry roll stuffed with cheese). For a really top-notch meal, put yourself in the hands of the Memis brothers and let them order for you. Afterward, you can walk across the street for the best homemade ice cream on Kos, an island legend since 1955.

Platinos-Kermetes. ☎ **22420/28-442.** Main courses 6€–16€. No credit cards. Apr–Oct daily 10am–midnight. Located 2km (1¼ miles) south of town on the road to the Asklepion.

Taverna Ampavris ★ GREEK   This is undoubtedly one of the best tavernas on Kos. It's just outside the bustling town center on the way to the Asklepion, down a quiet village lane. In the courtyard of this 130-year-old house, you can feast on local dishes from Kos island. The *salamura,* from Kefalos, is mouthwatering pork stewed with onions and coriander; the *lahano dolmades* (stuffed cabbage with rice, minced meat, and herbs) is delicate, light, and not at all oily. The *faskebab* (veal stew on rice) is tender and lean, while the vegetable dishes, such as the broad string beans cooked and served cold in garlic and olive-oil dressing, are out of this world.

Ampavris. ☎ **22420/25-696.** Main courses 8€–18€. No credit cards. Apr–Oct daily 5:30pm–1am. Take a taxi.

Taverna Ampeli ★ GREEK   This is as close as you come in Kos to authentic Greek home cooking. Facing the sea and ensconced in its own vineyard, Ampeli is delightful even before you taste the food. The interior is unusually tasteful, with high-beamed ceilings, and the outside setting is even better. The dolmades rate with the best in Greece. Other excellent specialties are *pliogouri* (gruel), *giouvetsi* (casserole), and *revithokefteves* (meatballs). Even the fried potatoes set a new standard. The house retsina is unusually sweet, almost like a sherry; the house white wine, made from the grapes before your eyes, is dry and light and quite pleasing—the red, however, is less memorable. If you're here on Saturday or midday on Sunday, the Easter-style goat, baked overnight in a low oven, is not to be missed.

Tzitzifies, Zipari village (8km/5 miles from Kos town). ☎ **22420/69-682.** Main courses 7€–20€. MC, V. Apr–Oct daily 10am–midnight; Nov–Mar daily 6–11pm. Closed Easter week and 10 days in early Nov. Off the beach road, 1km (½ mile) east of Tingaki. Take a bus to Tingaki and walk, or take a taxi.

Taverna Nikolas 🐟 GREEK/SEAFOOD   Known on the street as Nick the Fisherman's, this is one taverna in Kos that wasn't designed with tourists in mind. Off-season, it's a favorite haunt for locals, with whom you'll have to compete for one of eight tables. In summer, however, seating spills freely onto the street. Although you can order anything from filet mignon to goulash, the point of coming here is the seafood. If the Aegean has it, you'll find it here: grilled octopus, shrimp in vinegar and lemon, calamari stuffed with cheese, and mussels souvlaki, for example. The menu is extensive, so come with an appetite.

21 G. Averof. ☎ **22420/23-098.** Main courses 6€–20€; fixed-price dinners 12€–20€; 2-person seafood dinner 40€. No credit cards. Daily noon–midnight.

Kos After Dark

Kos nightlife is no more difficult to find than your own ears. Just go down to the harbor and follow the noise. Names change but the scene remains. The **portside cafes,** opposite the excursion boats to Kalimnos, are best in the early morning. **Apoplous** (on Psalidhi St., near Market) has live Greek music; **Platanos,** across from the

Hippocrates Tree, has live music, often jazz; and just across from Platanos is the beginning of **Bar Street,** which needs no further introduction. The lively **Fashion Club,** Kanari 2 Dolphins Sq., has the most impressive light-and-laser show. On Akti Zouroudi there are two popular discos, **Heaven** and **Calua** (with a swimming pool). If you want to hit the bar scene, try **Hamam Club,** on Akti Kountourioti, or **Beach Boys,** at 57 Kanari. Another option is an old-fashioned outdoor movie theater, Kos style, at **Open Cine Orfeas,** 10 Vasileos Yioryiou. Relatively recent films, often in English, cost 6€.

PATMOS ★

302km (187 miles) E of Piraeus

If a musician were to compose and dedicate a piece to Patmos, it might be a suite for rooster, moped, and bells (church *and* goat), for these are the sounds that fill the air. But just because Patmos is wonderfully unspoiled, don't imagine that it's primitive. In fact, in recent years, it has developed quite sophisticated tourist facilities and attracted a large following. The saving grace for those who come seeking a bit of quiet is that most visitors either come for a day or settle in a couple of beach resorts.

Architects sometimes speak of "charged sites," places where something so powerful happened that its memory must always be preserved. Patmos is such a place. It is where **St. John the Divine,** traditionally identified with the Apostle John, spent several years in exile, dwelling in a cave and composing the Book of Revelation, also known as the Apocalypse. From that time on, the island has been regarded as hallowed ground, reconsecrated through the centuries by the erection of more than 300 churches, one for every 10 residents.

Neither the people of Patmos nor their visitors are expected to spend their days in prayer, but the Patmians expect—and deserve—a dose of respect for their traditions. Patmos is a place for those seeking a "retreat," and by that, we do not mean a religious calling, but a more subdued, civilized alternative to major tourist destinations. Some guidebooks highlight the island's prohibitions on nude bathing and how to get around them—but if this is a priority for you, then you've stumbled onto the wrong island. Enjoy your stay on Patmos, by all means, but don't expect raucous nightlife.

Essentials

GETTING THERE By Plane Patmos has no airport, but it is convenient (especially by hydrofoil and catamaran in spring and summer) to three islands that do: Samos, Kos, and Leros. Rather than endure the all-but-interminable ferry ride from Piraeus, fly from Athens to one of these, then hop a boat or hydrofoil the rest of the way to Patmos. Samos is your best bet; with the right schedule, you can get from the Athens airport to Patmos in 3 hours via Samos.

By Boat Patmos, the northernmost of the Dodecanese Islands, is on the daily ferry line from Piraeus to Rhodes—confirm schedules with **Piraeus Port Authority** (© **210/417-2657** or 210/451-1310) or **Rhodes Port Authority** (© **22410/23-693** or 22410/27-695). Patmos has numerous sea links with the larger islands of the Dodecanese, as well as with the islands of the northeast Aegean. Options are limited from late fall to early spring, but Easter through September, sea connections with most of the islands of the eastern Aegean are numerous and convenient. With **Blue Star Line's** (**www.bluestarferries.com**) new high-speed ferries, the travel time from Piraeus has been reduced to about 7 hours.

VISITOR INFORMATION The **tourism office** (⏀ 22470/31-666) in the port town of Skala is directly in front of you as you disembark from your ship; it's open June through August daily from 9am to 10pm. It shares the Italianate "municipal palace" with the post office and the **tourist police** (⏀ 22470/31-303), who take over when the tourism office is closed. The **port police** (⏀ 22470/31-231), in the first building on your left on the main ferry pier, are very helpful for boat schedules and whatever else ails or concerns you; the building is open year-round, 24 hours a day. There is also a host of helpful information about Patmos at **www.patmosisland. com** or **www.travel-to-patmos.com**.

Apollon Tourist and Shipping Agency, on the harbor near the central square (⏀ **22470/31-724**; fax 22470/31-819), can book excursion boats and hydrofoils and arrange lodging in hotels, rental houses, and apartments throughout the island. It's open year-round from 8am to noon and 4 to 6pm, with extended summer hours.

GETTING AROUND **By Moped & Bicycle** Mopeds are definitely the vehicle of choice on the island, provided you have a proper license. At the shops that line the harbor, 1-day rentals start at around 25€ and go up to 50€. **Australis Motor Rent** (⏀ **22470/32-723**), in Skala's new port, is a first-rate shop; and you can usually rent at a discounted rate for rentals lasting less than a full day. You can also contact **Billis** (⏀ **22470/32-218**), on the harbor in Skala. Bicycles are hard to come by on the island, but **Theo & Georgio's** (⏀ **22470/32-066**) has 18-speed mountain bikes for 15€ per day.

By Car Two convenient car-rental offices, both in Skala, are **Patmos Rent-a-Car,** just behind the police station (⏀ **22470/32-203**), and **Avis,** on the new port (⏀ **22470/33-095**). Daily rentals in high season start about 50€. The island does not have many gas stations, so be sure you watch your gas tank gauge.

By Taxi The island's main taxi stand is on the pier in Skala Harbor, right before your eyes as you get off the boat. From anywhere on the island, you can request a taxi by calling ⏀ **22470/31-225.** As the island is quite small, it's much cheaper to hire a taxi than to rent a car.

By Bus The entire island has a single bus, whose current schedule is available at the tourist office and is posted at locations around the island. Needless to say, it provides limited service—to Skala, Hora, Grikos, and Kambos—so it's best to use another method to get around.

ORIENTATION Patmos lies along a north-south axis; were it not for a narrow central isthmus, it would be two islands, north and south. **Skala,** the island's only town of any size, is situated near that isthmus joining the north island to the south. Above Skala looms the hilltop capital of **Hora,** comprising a mazelike medieval village and the fortified monastery of St. John the Divine. There are only two other towns on Patmos: **Kambos,** to the north, and **Grikou,** to the south. While Kambos is a real village of roughly 500 inhabitants, Grikou is mostly a resort, a creation of the tourist industry.

Most independent visitors to Patmos, especially first-timers, will choose to stay in Skala (Hora has no hotels) and explore the north and south from there. Patmos is genuinely addicting, an island to which visitors, Greek and foreign, return year after year. So while it makes sense on your first visit to Patmos to be centrally located, you may wish to stay elsewhere during future visits.

FAST FACTS **Commercial Bank of Greece,** on the Skala harbor, and **National Bank of Greece,** on the central square, offer exchange services and ATMs. Both are open Monday through Thursday from 8am to 2pm and Friday from

8am to 1:30pm. You will also find an ATM where ferries and cruises dock at the main pier. For **dental or medical emergencies,** call © **22470/31-211;** for special **pharmaceutical needs,** call © **22470/31-500.** The **hospital** (© **22470/31-211**) is on the road to Hora. The **post office** on the harbor is open Monday through Friday 8am to 1:30pm. The **tourist police** (© **22470/31-303**) are directly across from the port.

For **Internet access,** the **Internet Cafe at Blue Bay** (Blue Bay Hotel) is open April through October daily, from 8am to 8pm. **Millennium Internet Cafe,** on the lane to Horio, near the OTE office, is open year-round daily, from 9am to 10pm. A short walk down toward the new port will bring you to

On Patmos: Don't Drink the Water!

One essential you need to know about Patmos from the outset is that tap water is not for drinking. *Drink only bottled water.*

Just Like Home (© **22470/33-170**), where a load of laundry costs 15€. It's open daily until 9pm September through June, and until 10pm in July and August.

What to See & Do
THE TOP ATTRACTIONS

What Patmos lacks in quantity, it makes up for in quality. Apart from its natural beauty and its 300-plus churches, to which we can't provide a detailed guide here, there are several extraordinary sights: the **Monastery of St. John ★★, Cave of the Apocalypse ★★,** and the medieval town of **Hora ★.** The latter is a labyrinthine maze of whitewashed stone homes, shops, and churches in which getting lost is the whole point. By the way, if you are so inclined, put off your visit till the end of September—beginning of October when there is a **Religious Music Festival** with concerts close to the Cave of the Apocalypse—a unique and moving experience. Another such experience is the Easter-time Holy Thursday **Service of the Washing of the Disciples' Feet** in the Monastery.

Off season, the opening days and times for the **cave** and the **monastery** are unpredictable, as they are designed to accommodate groups of pilgrims and cruise-ship tours rather than individual visitors. Neither place is public. The cave is enclosed within a convent, and the monastery is just that. It's best to consult the tourist office or the travel agent listed above for the open hours on the day of your visit (the times given below are for the peak season May–Aug). To visit both places, appropriate attire is required, which means that women must wear full-length skirts or dresses and have covered shoulders, while men must wear long pants.

The road to Hora is well marked from Skala, but if you're walking, take the narrow lane to the left just past the central square. Once outside the town, you can mostly avoid the main road by following the uneven stone-paved donkey path, which is the traditional pilgrims' route to the sanctuaries above. And if you have taken this much trouble to get to Hora, hang around awhile—it is really quite a delightful old town with many mansions from the 17th and 18th centuries.

Cave of the Apocalypse ★★ Exiled to Patmos by the Roman emperor Domitian in A.D. 95, St. John the Divine is said to have made his home in this cave, though Patmians insist quite reasonably that he walked every inch of the small island, talking with its people. The cave is said to be the epicenter of his earth-shaking dreams, which he dictated to his disciple Prochoros, and which has come down to present believers

Who Is This John?

Even non-Christians are at least vaguely aware that the fourth Gospel, or life of Christ, is attributed to a John; because of its literary associations, they may also be aware that the Book of Revelation is attributed to John; and well-informed Christians may also know that a John wrote the first three Epistles of the New Testament. Oh, yes—and there was a John who was among the 12 disciples. So how many Johns were there? Well, it is agreed that John the disciple was present at the trial and Crucifixion of Jesus, and it is also widely believed that this John wrote the fourth Gospel and those first three Epistles to the early Christian communities. But there is not solid agreement among scholars that this was the same John who wrote the Book of Revelation. Nevertheless, the religious community of Patmos does believe that the John who dictated the book in the cave here was the same as the other John and thus flatly proclaims their institution and site as that of St. John the Divine.

as the Book of the Apocalypse, or Revelation, the last book of the Christian Bible. The cave is now encased within a sanctuary, which, in turn, is encircled by a convent. A stirring brochure, written by Archimandrite Koutsanellos, superior of the cave, provides an excellent description of the religious significance of each niche in the rocks, as well as the many icons in the cave. Other guides are available in local tourist shops. The best preparation, of course, is to bone up on the Book of Revelation.

On the road to Hora. ℂ **22470/31-234.** Free admission. May–Aug Sun 8am–1pm and 2–6pm; Mon 8am–1:30pm; Tues–Wed 8am–1:30pm and 2–6pm; Thurs–Sat 8am–1:30pm. Otherwise, hours vary (as described above).

Monastery of St. John ★★ Towering over Skala and, for that matter, over the south island is the medieval Monastery of St. John, which looks far more like a fortress than a house of prayer. Built to withstand pirates, it is up to the task of deterring runaway tourism. The monastery virtually controls the south island, where the mayor wears a hat but the monastic authority wears a miter. In 1088, with a hand-signed document from the Byzantine emperor Alexis I Comnenus ceding the entire island to the future monastery, Blessed Christodoulos arrived on Patmos to establish what was to become an independent monastic state. The monastery chapel is stunning, as is the adjoining **Chapel of the Theotokos,** whose frescoes date from the 12th century. On display in the treasury is but a fraction of the monastery's exquisite Byzantine treasures—icons, vestments, rare books—which are second only to those of Mount Athos, a monastic state. One of the icons, by the way, is claimed to be by El Greco.

Hora. ℂ **22470/31-234.** Free admission to monastery; 4€ to treasury. May–Aug Sun 8am–1pm and 2–6pm; Mon–Sat 8am–1:30pm; Tues–Wed also 2–6pm.

OUTDOOR PURSUITS

The principal outdoor activities on Patmos are walking and swimming. The best **beaches** are highlighted below (see "Exploring the Island," below) and the best **walking trails** are the unmarked donkey paths which crisscross the island. You won't find jet-skis or surfboards on Patmos, although limited **watersports** are available. Paddleboats and canoes can be rented and water-skiing arranged at Helen's Place, on Agriolivada beach, while Elisabeth, on Kampos Beach, offers a variety of watersports (water-skiing, tubes, boards). Those intent on scuba diving should start at the **Blue Fin** store in Skala (ℂ **22470/31-251;** www.bluefincenterpatmos.com).

SHOPPING

Patmians are quick to lament and apologize for the fact that just about everything, from gas to toothpaste, is a bit more expensive here. Patmos doesn't even have its own drinking water, and import costs inevitably get passed along to the customer. Having said that, the price differences are much more evident to the locals than to tourists.

There are several excellent jewelry shops, such as **Iphigenia** (© **22470/31-814**) and **Midas** (© **22470/31-800**), on the harbor; though **Filoxenia** (© **22470/31-667**) and **Art Spot** (© **22470/32-243**), both behind the main square, in the direction of Hora, have more interesting contemporary designs, often influenced by ancient motifs. The Art Spot also sells ceramics and small sculptures, and is well worth seeking out. Farther down the same lane is **Parousia** (© **22470/32-549**), the best single stop for hand-painted icons and a wide range of books on Byzantine subjects. The proprietor, Mr. Alafakis, is quite learned in the history and craft of icon painting and can tell you a great deal about the icons in his shop and the diverse traditions they represent.

The most fascinating shop on Patmos may be **Selene** (© **22470/31-742**), across from the port authority office. The highly selective array of Greek handmade art and crafts here is extraordinary, from ceramics to hand-painted Russian and Greek icons to marionettes, some as tall as 1m (3 ft.). And be sure to notice Selene's structure, also a work of art. Built in 1835, it was once a storage space for sails and later a boat-building workshop. Look down at the shop's extraordinary floor, made of handmade stamped and scored bricks, quite special and traditional to Patmos.

Where to Stay in Skala

There are no hotels, only pensions in Hora, but you will find many in Skala and elsewhere around the island. Unless you plan to visit Patmos during Greek or Christian Easter or late July through August, you should not have difficulty finding a room upon arrival, though it's always safer to book ahead. Residents offering private accommodations usually meet ferries. If you're interested in renting an apartment or villa, contact the **Apollon Agency** (© **22470/31-724;** fax 22470/31-819).

EXPENSIVE

Porto Scoutari (Romantic) Hotel and Spa ★ ☺   High on a bluff overlooking Meloï Bay, this luxury hotel is seductively gracious, with the largest rooms and pool on the island. Ground-level suites are designed with families in mind, whereas upper-level suites, with four-poster beds and bathtubs, have "honeymoon" written all over them. Each bungalow-style studio has a kitchenette, year-round climate control, and a private balcony. The common areas—breakfast room, lounge, piano bar, and pool—are simultaneously informal and refined. This is the most ambitious "full-service" hotel on the island. If your stay on Patmos is brief, you probably wouldn't want to stay here, only because you're paying for facilities that you might not have time to use.

Scoutari, 85500 Patmos. www.portoscoutari.com. © **22470/33-123.** 30 units. 120€–280€ double; 260€–520€ studio or suite. Rates include full breakfast buffet. Discounts for paying in advance or booking for a week. MC, V. Parking on premises. Closed Nov–Easter. Note that this hotel overlooks, but is not in, Meloï Bay—so follow the signs to Kambos, not to Meloï Bay. It's less than 3km (2 miles) from the center of Skala. **Amenities:** Restaurant; bar; Internet and fax facilities; pool; room service; spa; smoke-free rooms. *In room:* A/C, TV, fridge, hair dryer.

MODERATE

Blue Bay Hotel ★   Two unique features distinguish this hotel (operated by a Greek-Australian couple): First, its stellar location on the southwest side of the harbor offers a rare fusion of convenience and quiet; second, guests are requested not to smoke anywhere in the hotel except on the private balconies. The bedrooms are spacious, immaculate, and comfortable. Room nos. 114 and 115 share a terrace the size of a tennis court overlooking the sea. The hotel emphasizes service and gracious hospitality. The new **Blue Bay Internet Cafe** offers Internet access at a reasonable rate.

Skala, 85500 Patmos. www.bluebay.50g.com. ✆ **22470/31-165.** 27 units. 110€ double; 150€–170€ suite. Rates include buffet breakfast. MC, V. Parking on adjacent streets. Closed Nov–Mar. **Amenities:** Breakfast room; bar; Internet. *In room:* A/C, minibar.

Castelli Hotel 🌶   Nothing fancy and with minimal amenities, this hotel's location and rates are what make it attractive. It's on a hillside overlooking the sea, and all rooms have balconies with a view. The hotel's striking sea vista can be enjoyed from cushioned wrought-iron chairs on each room's covered balcony or from a pleasant covered terrace/bar. The large, spotless rooms have white walls and beige tile floors. The lounge and lobby areas are filled with photographs, flower-print sofas, seashells, fresh-cut flowers from the surrounding gardens, and other knickknacks of seaside life. The price you pay for the view is a mildly challenging 5-minute climb from the harbor.

Skala, 85500 Patmos. ✆ **22470/31-361.** Fax 22470/31-656. 45 units. 85€–95€ double. Rates include breakfast. No credit cards. Parking on adjacent streets. **Amenities:** Breakfast room; bar. *In room:* A/C, TV, fridge.

Romeos Hotel   Of Skala's newer lodgings, this one, run by a Greek-American family from Virginia, is especially commodious, with a large pool and a quiet garden. The simply decorated, spotless rooms are built like semiattached bungalows on a series of tiers, with balconies offering views across the countryside to Mount Kastelli. Large honeymoon suites, with double beds, full bathtubs, and small lounges, are available. One downside to its otherwise attractive location is that the bungalows are on a fairly steep slope; for some, this might present a challenge.

Skala (in the back streets, behind the OTE), 85500 Patmos. romeos@greekhotel.com. ✆ **22470/31-962.** 60 units. 80€–95€ double; 110€ suite. Rates include breakfast. MC, V. Parking on adjacent streets. Closed Nov–Mar. Pets accepted. **Amenities:** Breakfast room; bar; 2 pools (1 large, 1 children's). *In room:* A/C, TV, hair dryer, minibar.

Skala Hotel   Tranquilly but conveniently situated well off the main harbor road, behind a lush garden overflowing with arresting pink bougainvillea, this comfortable hotel has become an established Skala favorite. Attractive features include a large pool with an inviting sun deck and bar, a large breakfast buffet, and personalized service. The three views to choose from are the sea, the western mountains, and the Monastery of St. John—and all are striking. If you want to stay here at Easter or in late July and August, you'll need advance reservations. The hotel describes itself as handicap accessible, but this might be a shade optimistic.

Skala, 85500 Patmos. skalahtl@12net.gr. ✆ **22470/31-343.** Fax 22470/31-747. 78 units. 90€ double. Rates include breakfast. MC, V. Parking on adjacent streets. Closed Nov–Mar. **Amenities:** Restaurant; 2 bars; babysitting; pool; room service. *In room:* A/C, TV, minibar, Wi-Fi.

INEXPENSIVE

Australis Hotel and Apartments ★   On the approach, you may have misgivings regarding this hotel's location, down a less-than-charming lane off the new port area. Your doubts will vanish when you enter the hotel compound, a blooming hillside oasis run by the hospitable Fokas family. The pleasant communal porch, where breakfast is served, offers delightful views of the open harbor. The guest rooms are bright, tasteful, and impeccably clean (and with firm beds). Within the same compound and enjoying the same floral and sea vistas, four apartments offer spacious homes away from home for families or groups of four to six people; these are fully equipped with kitchenettes, TVs, and heat for the winter months. In addition to these apartments, the Fokas family has three handsome studios over a house on the old road to Hora; each has a well-stocked kitchen and goes for 45€ to 65€ per day.

Skala (a 5-min. walk from the center), 85500 Patmos. ℂ **22470/32-562.** Fax 22470/32-284. 29 units. 75€ double; 165€ apt., depending on size and season. Rates include breakfast. No credit cards. Parking on adjacent streets. Closed Nov–Mar. *In room:* TV, fridge (in some).

Villa Knossos ♦   This small, white villa off the new port is set within an abundant garden of palms, purple and pink bougainvillea, potted geraniums, and hibiscus. The tasteful, spacious guest rooms have high ceilings (making them cool even in the summer's heat). All rooms but one have private balconies. The two units facing the back garden are the quietest, while room no. 7, in front, has a private veranda. Guests can use a comfortable sitting room.

Skala, 85500 Patmos. ℂ **22470/32-189.** Fax 22470/32-284. 7 units. 50€–75€ double. No credit cards. Parking on adjacent streets. Closed Nov–Mar. *In room:* Fridge.

Where to Eat in Skala & Hora

Skala and Hora may not have any standout restaurants, but there are many that will not disappoint. In Hora, on the path to the Monastery of St. John, you'll find **Pirgos; Balkoni** (with view of Skala Harbor); **Patmian House;** and (following signs from the monastery) **Vagelis,** in the central square (Vagelis enjoys views of the south island). Two favorites in Skala are recommended below, but you will want to browse for yourself. Alternatively, venture out to the north and south islands, which serve up some of Patmos's most enticing food. In particular, the restaurant at the Petra Hotel and Apartments (see "Exploring the Island") stands out.

Grigoris Grill GREEK   One of Skala's better-known eateries, this place was formerly the center of Patmian chic. Any of the grilled fish or meat dishes are recommended, particularly in the slow season, when more time and attention are lavished on the preparation. Well-cooked veal cutlets, tender lamb chops, and the swordfish souvlaki are favorites. Grigoris also offers several vegetarian specials. Both curbside seating and a more removed and quiet roof garden are available.

Opposite Skala car ferry pier. ℂ **22470/31-515.** Main courses 7€–16€. No credit cards. Easter–June and Sept–Oct 6pm–midnight; July–Aug 11am–midnight.

Pantelis Restaurant GREEK   Pantelis is a proven local favorite for no-frills Greek home cooking. The food here is consistently fresh and wholesome—the basics prepared so well that they surprise you. Daily specials augment the standard menu. Portions are generous, so pace yourself; and if you're not yet a convert to the Greek cult of olive oil, order something grilled. The lightly fried calamari, chickpea soup, swordfish kabob, and roasted lamb meet all expectations. In winter, the spacious dining hall with high ceilings makes this a relatively benign environment for nonsmokers.

Skala (1 lane back from the port). ℂ **22470/31-922.** Main courses 6€–19€. No credit cards. Daily 11am–11pm.

Vegghera Restaurant ★★ GREEK/MEDITERRANEAN   Vegghera has become the premier restaurant of Skala and deserves this status for its food, service, and ambience. In a handsome mansion, overlooking the marina, Vegghera carries this international flavor into its menu. George Grillis, proprietor and chef, combines traditional Greek fare with French-influenced Mediterranean cuisine, such as salmon smoked with rose sticks (rose-scented incense) or lobster with tagliatelle. Its specialties feature seafood from various regions, but the vegetables, pork, and rabbit are all raised by Grillis himself. The wine list is equally selective and desserts are to die for. It's not cheap, but once in a while, when you've come this far, you should just splurge. And you get a choice of eating on the shaded terrace or inside.

Nea Marina, Skala. © **22470/32-988.** Main courses 9€–34€. MC, V. Easter–Oct daily 7:30pm–1am.

Patmos After Dark

The nightlife scene on Patmos, while not ecclesiastical, is a bit subdued compared to some Greek islands. Clubs tend to open for a few weeks in season, then close like flowers. Up in Hora at Plateia Agia Lesvias, there's **Kafe 1673,** known as **Astivi,** where you can dance to whatever the DJ spins. In Skala, a standby—never fully "in" and never fully "out"—that survives each year's fads is **Consolato Music Club,** to the left of the quay. Skala also has the **Kahlua Club,** at the far end of the new port; and **Sui Generis,** behind the police station. Others recommended by visitors are **Pyrgos Bar, Kafe Aman, Café Arion, Isalos,** and **Celine.** On a more traditional note, **Aloni Restaurant,** in Hora, offers Greek music and dance performances in traditional costume a few nights each week in summer. Most clubs charge a modest admission and tend to stay open into the early hours of the morning. And for those who come for a more "ecclesiastical" experience, Patmos hosts a **Festival of Religious Music** in September, featuring music from the Balkans, Russia, and Turkey as well as Greece.

Exploring the Island

Apart from the seductive contours of the Patmian landscape, the myriad seascapes, and the seemingly countless churches, the **beaches** of Patmos draw most visitors beyond the island's core. Don't be tempted to think of the strand between the old and new ports in Skala as a beach. It's better and safer to take a shower in your bathroom. Most beaches have tavernas on or near them, as well as rooms to rent by the day or week. They're too numerous and similar to list here.

THE NORTH ISLAND

The nicest beaches in the north lie along the northeastern coastline from Lambi Bay to Meloï Bay. The northwestern coastline from Merika Bay to Lambi is too rocky, inaccessible, and exposed. The most desirable northern beaches are in the following bays (proceeding up the coast from south to north): **Meloï, Agriolivada,** and **Lambi.** Meloï has some shade and good snorkeling. **Kambos Bay** is particularly suitable for children and families, offering calm, shallow waters, rental umbrellas, and some tree cover, as well as a lively seaside scene with opportunities for windsurfing, paragliding, sailing, and canoeing. East of Kambos Bay, at Livada, it's possible to swim or sometimes to walk across to **Ayiou Yioryiou Isle;** be sure to bring shoes or sandals, or the rocks will do a number on your feet. The stretch of shoreline from **Thermia to Lambi** is gorgeous, with crystalline waters and rocks from which you can safely dive. The drawback here is that access is only by caique from Skala. Also, avoid the north coast when the *meltemi* (severe north summer winds) are blowing.

Where to Stay & Eat

Aspri GREEK   Poised on a north island headland just minutes by taxi from Skala, this dramatically situated restaurant enjoys splendid views of Meloï Bay, Aspris Bay, and Skala and Hora from its multiple terraces. In addition to the standard taverna fare offered throughout the islands, which Aspris prepares with great skill, the menu has unusual, enticing items such as cuttlefish with Patmian rice. The portions are generous and attention is paid to presentation in this quite stylish and widely recommended spot. Geranos Cape. ✆ **22470/32-240.** Main courses 8€–22€. MC, V. June–Sept daily 7pm–midnight.

Patmos Paradise Perched high above Kambos Bay, this is one of several upscale hotels on the island. The rooms are spacious and inviting, with private balconies that enjoy spectacular sea vistas (although in some cases broken by a power line)—room rates depend on the nature of your view! This unpretentious place is exceptionally pleasant and quite chic. Down below, Kambos Bay has a modest strand, a handful of shops and tavernas, and rental outlets for windsurfing boards, paddleboats, and canoes. A hotel minibus transports you to and from Skala Harbor when you arrive at or depart from Patmos. Highly recommended if you want to stay close to Skala.

Kambos Bay, 85500 Patmos. www.patmosparadise.com ✆ **22470/32-624.** 37 units. 110€–220€ double; 190€–375€ suite. Rates include buffet breakfast. MC, V. Parking on adjacent streets. Closed Nov–Easter. **Amenities:** Restaurant; 2 bars; large saltwater terrace pool; room service; sauna; indoor squash court; tennis court; Wi-Fi. *In room:* A/C, TV, fridge, hair dryer.

Taverna Leonida ★ GREEK At least one Patmian in the know claims "the best *saganaki* in the world" is served here. A taxi driver went further, calling this the "number-one taverna" as he dropped off his passengers on Leonida's pebble beach. The restaurant enjoys a dramatic location; at high tide, it's just a few yards from the clear water of Lambi Bay. If the wind is high, the waves come pounding in. The drama continues with the arrival of your flaming *saganaki*. Your next course should be the fresh catch of the day. But you can also order a steak, and there is a good selection of the standard Greek dishes.

Lambi Bay. ✆ **22470/31-490.** Main courses 8€–18€. No credit cards. Easter–Oct daily noon–11pm.

Taverna Panagos & Sarandin GREEK Eating here is an experience that goes beyond merely consuming food. Just above Kambos Bay sits the sleepy village of Kambos, and squarely on its pulse, directly across from the village church, sits the cafe-estiatorion-taverna Panagos. In this local hangout for everyone from children to cats to timeless, bent figures in black, the sea vistas are replaced by myriad glimpses into Patmian village life. The food is the same fare villagers eat at home, and the origins of the succulent daily specials are visible on the nearby hillsides: capons in wine, kid in tomato sauce, lamb in lemon sauce, Patmian goat cheese.

Kambos. ✆ **22470/31-570.** Main courses 7€–30€. No credit cards. Daily noon–midnight.

THE SOUTH ISLAND

The island's south end has two beaches, one at **Grikou Bay** and the other at **Psili Ammos.** Grikou Bay, only 4km (2½ miles) from Skala, is the most developed locale on Patmos and home to most of the package-tour groups. Psili Ammos is another story, an isolated fine-sand cove bordered by cliffs. Most people arrive by one of the caiques leaving Skala Harbor at 10am, and, on arrival (at 10:45am), do battle for the limited shade offered by some obliging tamarisks. The only way to ensure yourself of a place in the shade is to arrive before 10:30am; the best way to do that is to take a taxi to Diakofti for about 25€ and ask the driver to point the way to Psili Ammos, which is about a 30-minute trek on goat paths (wear real shoes). The caiques returning to Skala leave Psili Ammos around 4 to 5pm. At any given time, a range of caiques provide this service. Round-trip fare is about 30€ and 20€ one-way.

Another reason to head south is to dine at **Benetos** (see below), only a short taxi ride from Skala and known as the finest restaurant on the island.

Where to Stay & Eat

Benetos Restaurant ★ MEDITERRANEAN For fashionable, unpretentious, fine dining on Patmos, this Tuscan villa at the sea's edge is the place. Where else could you find light jazz filling the air, a fresh arugula salad with shaved Parmesan, shrimp baked in phyllo, and filet mignon, accompanied by an exclusively Greek wine list? Nowhere but Benetos, where the owners, Benetos and his American wife, Susan Matthaiou, have made it their goal to give Greeks and their visitors "a night out" from what they will find elsewhere on these islands. Their winning recipe begins with the freshest and finest local ingredients, mostly from their own organic garden and from nearby waters. The regular menu strikes Greek notes with its appetizers, and the occasional Asian note with its entrees; daily specials reflect the best fresh materials available. Only 12 tables are available, so you must reserve yours several days in advance during high season.

Sapsila. © **22470/33-089.** Reservations necessary in high season. Main courses 9€–26€. No credit cards. June–Sept Tues–Sun 7:30pm–1am.

Joanna Hotel-Apartments These comfortable, relatively spacious, and fully equipped apartments are just a few minutes on foot from the beach. Each has a balcony. Rooms with air-conditioning cost extra. The layout and feel of the one-bedroom apartments is better than that of the two-bedroom apartments, which have limited kitchen space. Room no. 15 has a private deck with a sea view, but it is usually reserved for friends, clients, and guests staying 2 to 3 weeks—still, there's no harm in asking. There's an attractive air-conditioned lounge with satellite TV and bar.

Grikos, 85500 Patmos. © **22470/31-031.** Fax 22470/32-031, or 210/981-2246 in Athens. 17 units. 65€–85€ double. Full hot breakfast 8€ extra. V. Parking on adjacent streets. Closed mid-Oct to Easter. **Amenities:** Bar. *In room:* A/C (5€ per day), fan, kitchenette.

Petra Hotel and Apartments ★★ ☺ Petra Hotel, true to its name, has long been a rock-solid sure thing, and with a series of major renovations since 2002, it has bolstered its position as one of the finest boutique hotels in Greece. The Stergiou family lavishes care on their stylish, spacious apartments. These one- and two-bedroom apartments come with handsome bathrooms. All except one unit have balconies that enjoy splendid views of Grikos Bay. It's a perfect family place, just a 2-minute walk from the beach. It's also ideal for couples, who can enjoy a drink on Petra's elegant, romantic main veranda. The Stergious provide an **intimate dining experience** as well, with a menu that includes both Greek standards and gourmet offerings. Advance reservations are advised, especially in August. And now they offer an elegant villa in Horio itself—it requires a short walk from your car and it is not cheap (975€–1,570€ per night), but it has four bedrooms (each with bathroom) so that four couples would find it quite reasonable for such a splendid locale.

Grikos, 85500 Patmos. www.petrahotel-patmos.com. © **22470/34-020** or ©/fax 210/806-2697 in Athens off season. 13 units. 175€–275€ double; 265€–580€ suite. Rates include breakfast. AE, MC, V. Parking on-site. Closed Oct–May. **Amenities:** Restaurant; bar; room service; smoke-free rooms; Wi-Fi. *In room:* A/C, TV, fridge, hair dryer, Internet, kitchenette.

Stamatis Restaurant GREEK Stamatis, serving reliable taverna fare since 1965, is a landmark in Grikou. On its covered terrace, practically at water's edge, diners enjoy drinks and consume prodigious amounts of fresh mullet, while watching yachts and windsurfers. This is a pleasant spot to unwind while you savor delicious island dishes.

Grikos beach. © **22470/31-302.** Main courses 6€–18€. No credit cards. Easter–Oct daily 10am–11pm.

CENTRAL GREECE

by Sherry Marker

M ost people today—just as in antiquity—come to Central Greece to visit Delphi, the home of the famous ancient oracle that is one of Greece's must-see destinations. Delphi has it all: a gravity-defying cliffside location with the remains of treasuries, small temples, a stadium, and a theater—not to mention the monumental temple of Apollo.

Mount Parnassus rises above the ancient site, and the site itself overlooks a plain of giant, gnarled olive trees. This forest of olive trees runs on and on across the plain below Delphi, stopping only when the plain itself is stopped by the blue waters of the Gulf of Corinth. Delphi is not just beautiful, it is awesome. The star of the Delphi museum is the famous bronze statue of the charioteer who raced his horses to victory in Delphi's stadium.

If you thought nothing else in Central Greece could rival Delphi's physical beauty, you were wrong. To the north, improbable sheer-sided rock formations rise up from the dusty plain of Thessaly.

For a thousand years, pilgrims and tourists have tried to figure out just how monks built the vertiginous monasteries of the Meteora atop these seemingly unscalable cliffs. Keep heading north and you'll pass through one of Greece's legendary beauty spots, the slender **Vale of Tempe**—now, alas, more the haunt of long-distance trucks than of the nightingales the poets once celebrated. Head over to **Mount Pelion** and you can explore a clutch of beautifully restored traditional villages set in wooded mountain slopes. Central Greece is also home to two of Greece's most famous and bloody ancient battle sites—Thermopylae and Chaironeia. Ahead stand the snow-topped peaks of Mount Olympus, once home to Zeus and the other Olympian gods, today a destination for mountain climbers, hikers, and nature lovers.

If you are a lover of vibrant nightlife, you may find that evenings in the neighborhood of the monasteries and ancient sanctuaries can be a bit tame. Don't despair, the mountain village of Arakova, 10km (6 miles) from Delphi, has a lively (and very chic) après ski scene in winter.

The term Central Greece (*Sterea Ellada*) dates from only 1821, when it was used as a shorthand term for the area of mainland Greece that had been liberated from the Turks. Today, most Greeks would agree that Central Greece stretches from the Gulf of Corinth in the south to Mount Olympus in the north.

DELPHI ★★★

Delphi is the big enchilada of Greek sites. Even more than Olympia, this place has it all: a long and glorious history, spectacular ancient remains, a superb museum, and a beautiful location on the slopes of Mount Parnassus. Look up and you see the cliffs and crags of Parnassus; look down, and Greece's most beautiful plain of olive trees stretches as far as your eyes can see, toward the town of Itea on the Gulf of Corinth.

Delphi is especially magical in the spring, when there's often both snow and wild-flowers on Parnassus—and fewer tourists tramping around the site than in summer. But whenever you visit, you'll understand why the ancient Greeks believed that Delphi was the center of the world, the spot Apollo chose as the home of his most famous oracle. The **Sanctuary of Apollo** is the main attraction here, although the smaller **Sanctuary of Athena** has Delphi's most photographed attraction, the mysterious round tholos (discussed later).

The modern village of Delphi's main drag is Vasileos Pavlou and Frederikis, also simply called Pavlou; sometimes, just to keep you on your toes, the street is called Karamanlis. Not to worry: this is obviously Delphi's main drag, usually clogged with herds of tour groups migrating from hotel to restaurant to the generally indifferent souvenir shops. It's the side streets, clinging to the slopes of Parnassus, that give a sense of village life.

A LOOK AT THE PAST Pilgrims came to Delphi from throughout the Greek world—and much of the non-Greek world—to ask Apollo's advice on affairs of state as well as small, personal matters. Unfortunately, the god's words were famously hard to interpret. "Invade and you will destroy a great empire," the oracle told Lydian King Croesus when he asked whether he should go to war with his Persian neighbors. Croesus invaded and destroyed a great empire: his own.

Delphi was also the site of the Pythian Games, the most famous festival in Greece after the Olympics. The Games commemorated Apollo's triumph over his oracular predecessor here, the snaky Python. Because Apollo was the god of music, the Pythian Games had more artistic contests than the Olympic Games. When you sit in the theater, you can imagine the flute and lyre contests and the dances and plays staged every 4 years throughout antiquity to honor Apollo.

Like so many ancient sites, Apollo's sanctuary at Delphi was first neglected, and then virtually forgotten during the Christian era. Kings and generals looted Delphi of its treasures; later, locals hacked up the buildings and used the blocks to build their own houses. The medieval and modern villages of Delphi sat atop the ancient site until the late 19th century, when the village began to be relocated just around the corner so that archaeologists could help Delphi reclaim its past.

◙ Delphi's Morning Scent

If you are an early riser, sniff deeply, follow your nose, and take a sunrise tour of Delphi's bakeries as the first loaves are coming out of the ovens.

Then, climb up to the Sikelanos Museum and enjoy some fresh bread and the view over the ancient site in the early morning light. *Bliss.*

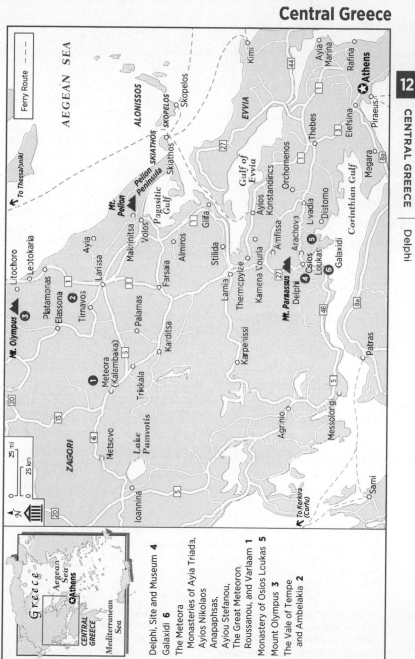

Ferry Route

AEGEAN SEA

To Thessaloniki

ALONISSOS

SKOPELOS

Skopelos

SKIATHOS

Skiathos

Pelion Peninsula

Mt. Pelion

Pagasitic Gulf

Volos

Makrinitsa

Ayia

Larissa

Litochoro

Leptokaria

Mt. Olympus 3

Platamonas

Elassona

Tirnavos 2

Farsaa

Palamas

Almiros

Glifa

Stilida

Lamia

Thermopylae

Kamena Vourla

Karpenissi

Agrinio

Messolargi

Sami

To Kerkira (Corfu)

Patras

Galaxidi

Delphi 4

Mt. Parnassus

Osios Loukas 5 6

Arachova

Amfissa

Ayios Konstandinos

Orchomenos

Livadia

Distomo

Gulf of Evvia

EVVIA

Kimi

Ayia Marina

Rafina

Athens

Piraeus

Elefsina

Megara

Thebes

Corinthian Gulf

Meteora (Kalambaka) 1

Trikala

Karditsa

Ioannina

Metsevo

ZAGORI

Lake Pamvotis

25 mi
25 km

N

Delphi, Site and Museum **6**

Galaxidi **6**

The Meteora
Monasteries of Ayia Triada,
Ayios Nikolaos
Anapaphsas,
Ayiou Stefanou,
The Great Meteoron,
Roussanou, and Varlaam **1**

Monastery of Osios Loukas **5**

Mount Olympus **3**

The Vale of Tempe
and Ambelakia **2**

Greece
Aegean Sea
Athens
CENTRAL GREECE
Mediterranean Sea

Essentials

GETTING THERE **By Bus** There are usually five buses daily to Delphi from the Athens bus station at 260 Liossion (℡ **210/831-7153** or 210/831-7096) in Athens, or 22650/82-317 in Delphi. **Warning:** Phones at information and ticket offices at the main Athens bus stations are seldom answered.

By Car If you're setting out from Athens, take the **National Road** toward Corinth and then the Thebes turnoff to take in the monastery of Osios Loukas and the sanctuary of Delphi; try to spend 2 nights in Delphi. Then, head north via Lamia to the Meteora for another night or two, before visiting Mount Pelion and Mount Olympus. Take the Athens-Corinth National Hwy. about 74km (46 miles) west of Athens to the Thebes turnoff. The frequently two-lane stretch of road between the National Highway and Thebes is heavily trafficked by trucks and buses. From Thebes, follow signs for Levadia and Delphi.

To get to Osios Loukas, take the Distomo turnoff and continue 9km (5½ miles). Be prepared to meet tour buses thundering along this road. At the fork in the road in the village of Distomo, bear left. After visiting Osios Loukas, return to Distomo and continue via Arachova 26km (16 miles) to Delphi. If you are approaching Delphi from the Peloponnese, cross over the Rio-Antirio Bridge to avoid the above drive, which can be seriously unpleasant between Athens and Thebes. Once across the bridge into Central Greece, the coastal road climbs upwards from Itea to Delphi (65km/40 miles). The road is spectacular, but with many curves and almost as many tour buses.

By Organized Tour Athens-based companies such as **CHAT,** 9 Xenophontos (℡ **210/322-2886;** www.chatours.gr), and **Key,** 4 Kallirois (℡ **210/923-3166;** www.keytours.com), offer 1-, 2-, and 3-day trips to Delphi. If possible, take the 2- or

---

A NICE break ON THE WAY TO DELPHI

If you approach Delphi by car along the northern shore of the Gulf of Corinth, you might want to take a lunch-and-swim break at the miniature port of **Galaxidi** (35km/22 miles southwest of Delphi). One thing to remember: on summer weekends, when Galaxidi's cobblestoned streets, boutiques, cafes, and restaurants are thronged with excursion-loving Athenians, it can be standing room only. In the 19th and 20th centuries, Galaxidi was a center of shipbuilding, and its harbor is flanked with the very good-looking stone homes of 19th-century ship captains and seafarers, many of which have been transformed into restaurants, cafes, and small hotels. **Tassos** (℡ **22650/41-291**) and **Omilos** (℡ **22640/42-111**) both have fresh fish. If you just want a snack, try the *amagdalopasta* (an almond sweet somewhere btw. a candy and a cookie). Almost every Greek island makes its own version of *amagdalopasta,* but some connoisseurs think Galaxidi does it best. Athenian friends of mine especially praise those on sale at **Mina** (℡ **22650/ 41-1117**), just off the waterfront. If you're tempted to stay the night, the eight-unit **Hotel Ganimede** (www.ganimede.gr; ℡ **22650/41-328**) is set in a 19th-century sea captain's house with lots of charm, a garden, and wonderful breakfasts with homemade jams and freshly baked bread (one of the two owners makes the jams, the other is the town baker!) doubles start at 70€; book directly with the hotel and mention Frommer's and you'll get a 10% discount.

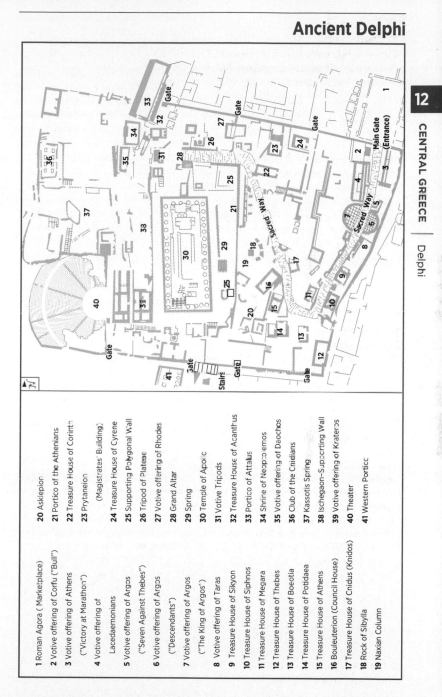

1 Roman Agora (Marketplace)
2 Votive offering of Corfu ("Bull")
3 Votive offering of Athens
  ("Victory at Marathon")
4 Votive offering of
  Lacedaemonians
5 Votive offering of Argos
  ("Seven Against Thebes")
6 Votive offering of Argos
  ("Descendants")
7 Votive offering of Argos
  ("The King of Argos")
8 Votive offering of Taras
9 Treasure House of Sikyon
10 Treasure House of Siphnos
11 Treasure House of Megara
12 Treasure House of Thebes
13 Treasure House of Boeotia
14 Treasure House of Potidaea
15 Treasure House of Athens
16 Bouleuterion (Council House)
17 Treasure House of Cnidus (Knidos)
18 Rock of Sibylla
19 Naxian Column

20 Asklepion
21 Portico of the Athenians
22 Treasure House of Corinth
23 Prytaneion
  (Magistrates' Building)
24 Treasure House of Cyrene
25 Supporting Polygonal Wall
26 Tripod of Plataea
27 Votive offering of Rhodes
28 Grand Altar
29 Spring
30 Temple of Apollo
31 Votive Tripods
32 Treasure House of Acanthus
33 Portico of Attalus
34 Shrine of Neoptolemos
35 Votive offering of Daochos
36 Club of the Cnidians
37 Kassotis Spring
38 Ischegaon-Supporting Wall
39 Votive offering of Krateros
40 Theater
41 Western Portico

Ride the Delphi Tram

If you want to tour today's Delphi as well as the ancient sanctuaries, check out the free tram that leaves from the Hotel Vouzas and gives 30-minute rides around the village of Delphi daily in the summer and on some off-season weekends.

3-day trip, which usually includes a bit of the Peloponnese or an excursion to the Meteora. Most tours leave Athens by 8am and arrive at Delphi by 3pm after a stop at Osios Loukas and Arakova. Day tours get back to Athens by 8pm, while longer trips give you most of your second day in Delphi before heading to their next destination. The price (including transportation, site and museum admissions, guide, hotel, and most meals) is from 100€for a day trip, from 160€ for a 2-day trip, and from 350€ for a 3-day trip (often including Meteora). Prices are for one person in a shared double room; prices are usually much lower in winter. Sometimes it is possible to get a single room at the same rate, but there is usually a 50€ supplement. An exceptionally well-traveled friend who was leery of the regimentation of a group tour had nothing but praise for her 2-day CHAT excursion, although she would have liked a bit more free time to enjoy the sites.

VISITOR INFORMATION   Most services, such as the post office, tourist office, and banks, are in the village of Delphi (pop. 2,500), on the main street. Like many streets in Greece, Delphi's main street has several names (King Paul and Queen Frederika, or Karamanlis), but directions are given by landmarks, not street names. The **tourist office** (© 22650/82-311; www.visitdelphi.gr), in the town hall, is usually open Monday through Friday from 8am to 2:30pm, and sometimes reopens from 6 to 8pm in summer, although staff may be of minimal help. (In 2010, staff assured me that the site, which was closed, was open.) The website, on the other hand, has useful information on outdoors activities (hiking, swimming) in the area. The museum and ancient site (signposted) are about 1km (½ mile) out of town, on the Arachova Road. If you want an English-speaking taxi driver for a tour of the area, or an English-speaking guide for your visit to the site and museum, inquire at your hotel or at the tourist office. Delphi native **Georgia Hasiotis** (© 69449/43-511; hasioti1@otenet.gr) will try to tailor her tour to your special interests.

GETTING AROUND   Parking spots are at a premium both in the village and at the site. If you can, park your car near your hotel and walk everywhere. If you have to drive to the site rather than walk the 5 to 10 minutes from town, be sure to set off early to get one of the few parking places. Whether you walk or drive, keep an eye out for the enormous tour buses that barrel down the center of the road. Traffic on the lower main street heads toward the site and Arachova; traffic on the upper main street heads out of Delphi toward Itea and the Gulf of Corinth.

FAST FACTS   Everything you need, including the **post office, telephone office,** and several banks with **ATMs,** including the **National Bank of Greece,** is on the main street. The **police** (© 22650/82-222) are in the town hall. For **first aid,** call © 22650/82-307.

What to See & Do

There's little in the modern village to tempt you away from the ancient site, but stopping at the museum first can help you put flesh on the bones of the sanctuary's remains. After all, in antiquity Apollo's sanctuary was something of an unofficial outdoor museum, crammed with goodies from around the world. As at Olympia, begin your visit here as early as possible and hold onto your 9€ ticket; it's good for admission to both the museum and the site. *Tip:* Both site and museum can be relatively uncrowded an hour before closing time or during the midday lunch break.

The Angelos and Eva Sikelianos Museum   The road that leads steeply uphill through the village of Delphi ends at the stone-and-brick Sikelianos home, now a museum commemorating the work of the eccentric 20th-century Greek poet Sikelianos and his equally eccentric American wife, Eva Palmer. The couple's attempts to revive the Pythian Games were not long lived, but their staging of Greek tragedies in Delphi's theater in the 1930s had lasting effects, as all who have seen plays performed here or at Epidaurus know. Few tourists visit this elegant home, which has spectacular views from most windows, a fine collection of Sikelianos-designed costumes, and possibly the nicest bathroom in town. It's a pleasant place to spend an hour.

© **22650/82-173.** Fax 22650/82 722. cpk@delfi@otenet.gr. Admission 2€. Wed Mon 8:30am 3pm.

The Delphi Museum ★★★   Almost everyone who was anyone in the ancient world sent gifts to Delphi. The gifts were meant to honor Apollo, often with the hope of winning his favor—and clearly intended to impress one's neighbors. As a result, this museum contains some of the finest works found in Greece, and a visit here is a connoisseur's tour of some of the very best that was made between around 1400 B.C. and the 4th century A.D. In addition, the masses of architectural sculpture on view, including pieces from the elegant **Siphnian** and **Athenian treasuries** and the majestic **Temple of Apollo,** bring us as close as we can get to seeing what pilgrims saw when they came here century after century to consult the Oracle of Delphi.

The star of the museum, with much of room 13 to himself, is the 5th-century-B.C. *Charioteer of Delphi,* a larger-than-life bronze figure that was originally part of a group that included a four-horse chariot. The Sicilian tyrant Polyzalos sponsored the winning charioteer and dedicated this near-monumental work to honor both his own generosity in sponsoring the winner and his victory. This is an irresistible statue: Don't miss the handsome youth's delicate eyelashes shading his wide-set enamel-and-stone eyes, the realistic veins that stand out in his hands and feet, and the little curls that graze his brow and neck. The graceful charioteer makes earlier statues on view here, such as the 6th-century- B.C. *kouroi* (monumental youths) Kleobis and Biton (room 3), look like muscle-bound hulks. That's not far from the truth: According to Herodotus, the boys' mother was a priestess at the Temple of Hera near Argos in the Peloponnese. On the morning of an important temple ceremony, the oxen went missing and it looked like the priestess would not make it to the temple on time. Kleobis and Biton hitched themselves to the oxen's yoke and pulled their mother's cart the 1.6km (10 miles) across the dusty plain of Argos to the Temple of Hera. As they reached the temple, the boys collapsed—earning both good deaths and immortal fame. The story is one of a number of Greek tales which show that death is a small price to pay for immortal glory.

Although the charioteer is the star of the collection, he's in good company. Don't miss the massive 6th-century-B.C. **gold-and-silver-plated bull,** flanked by delicate gold and ivory dedications (room 4). It's ironic that we don't know who gave this imposing statue to Apollo, since the donor must have wanted to impress everyone in the Greek world! Live bulls were the most expensive offering sacrificed to the gods on special occasions, and perhaps the donor wanted this statue to make the point that his sacrifice had spared no expense. A donor whose name we do know is the 2nd-century-A.D. Emperor Hadrian. Heartbroken at the death of his young lover Antinous, Hadrian commissioned statues of the boy to be erected throughout the Roman

Eggs & Eagles at the Earth's Center

At the museum, don't miss the 4th-century-B.C. **marble egg,** a copy of the yet older *omphalos* (egg) that symbolized Delphi's unique position as the center (or navel) of the world. According to legend, when Zeus wanted to determine the earth's center, he released two eagles from Olympus. When the eagles met over Delphi, Zeus had his answer. It's easy to see why the ancient Greeks thought that Delphi, straddling a cleft in the rocky slopes of the majestic Parnassus mountain range and looking out over the Corinthian gulf, was so spectacular that it must be the center of the universe. You may still see eagles in the sky above Delphi, but more often than not, the large birds overhead are the less distinguished Egyptian vultures.

Empire. One of the loveliest statues of this full-lipped sensual youth totally steals the thunder from its neighbor, a Roman victory monument (room 12). Don't miss the small photograph on the wall beside Antinous that shows the moment in 1893 when the archaeologists unearthed this delectable statue. The Delphi museum is a great place to browse slowly. It's all too easy, rushing to see the charioteer, to miss the delicate miniature bronze and clay statuettes and snarling bronze griffins in rooms 1 and 2. Spend as much time as possible here, treating yourself to coffee breaks at the cafe to stave off museum burnout. Since the cafe is usually packed, it's a good idea not to wait until exhaustion strikes. The cafe and gift shop are both just outside the museum itself.

Delphi. © **22650/82-312.** Admission 9€ to museum and site; site or museum only 6€. Summer Mon noon–6:30pm, Tues–Sun 8am–7:30pm; winter daily 9am–3pm. (Be sure to check these hours when you arrive in Delphi, as they can change without warning.)

The Sanctuary of Apollo ★★★   The Sanctuary of Apollo is immediately beyond and just above the museum. The less well-known Sanctuary of Athena on the lower slopes of Parnassus is a 10-minute walk past the museum. The Castalian Spring, whose waters the ancients thought inspired poets, is between the two sanctuaries. If you can't visit everything, spend your time at the Sanctuary of Apollo, stroll to the Castalian Spring, and then cross the Delphi-Arachova Road to take a peek down at the Sanctuary of Athena. When you see hatless visitors in sling-back sandals huffing and puffing here, you'll be glad to have good shoes, a sun hat, and a bottle of water.

As you enter the Sanctuary of Apollo, you'll be on the marble **Sacred Way,** walked by pilgrims and visitors for thousands of years. The road runs uphill past the remains of **Roman stoas** and a number of **Greek treasuries,** including the restored **Athenian treasury.** Cities built these small, templelike buildings at Delphi for several reasons: to impress their neighbors and to store riches and works of art dedicated to Apollo. Take a close look at the **treasury walls:** You'll see countless inscriptions. The Greeks have never been shy about using the walls of their buildings as bulletin boards.

So many recent visitors were bent on adding their names to the ancient inscriptions that the Greek archaeological service no longer allows visitors inside the massive 4th-century-B.C. **Temple of Apollo,** which was built after the 7th- and 6th-century-B.C. temples were destroyed. In antiquity, one of the three Pythian priestesses on duty gave voice to Apollo's oracles from a room deep within the temple. That much is known, although the details of what precisely happened here are obscure. Did the priestess sit on a tripod balanced over a chasm, breathing in the hallucinatory fumes that may well have escaped from fissures in the rocks the temple rested on? Did she chew various herbs, including the laurel leaf sacred to Apollo, until she spoke in tongues, while priests interpreted her sayings? Perhaps wisely, the oracle has kept its secrets.

From the temple, it's a fairly steep uphill climb to the remarkably well-preserved 4th-century-B.C. **theater** and the **stadium,** which was extensively remodeled by the Romans. In 1927, the Greek poet Angelos Sikelianos and his wife attempted to revive the ancient contests here (see the Sikelianos Museum, above). Today, the theater and stadium are used most summers for the **Festival of Delphi,** which has, on occasion, featured exceptionally nonclassical pop music. For several years now, both the stadium and theater have been closed to the public, except when there are special events here. This is a shame, because it means that most visitors can not actually stand and sit in the two places where the musical and athletic events in the Pythian festival took place.

Keep your ticket as you leave the Sanctuary of Apollo and head along the Arakova-Delphi road toward the Sanctuary of Athena (also called the Marmaria, which refers to all the marble found here). En route, you'll pass the famous **Castalian Spring,** where Apollo planted a laurel he brought from the Vale of Tempe. Drinking from the spring inspired legions of poets in antiquity; now, poets have to find their inspiration elsewhere, as the spring is off limits, purportedly to allow repairs to the Roman fountain facade. (Once an antiquity is closed in Greece, it often stays closed quite awhile.) Above are the rose-colored cliffs known as the **Phaedriades (Bright Ones),** famous for their reflection of the sun's rays.

North of the Castalian Spring, a path descends from the main road to the **Sanctuary of Athena,** the goddess of wisdom who shared the honors at Delphi with Apollo. Because the remains here are fragmentary, except for the 4th-century-B.C. **gymnasium,** you might want to wander about and enjoy the ruins without trying too hard to figure out what's what. The round 4th-century **tholos** with its three graceful Doric columns is easy to spot, though no one knows why it was built, why it was so lavishly decorated, or what went on inside. You can easily spend all day at Delphi; at the least, allow 3 hours and try to give yourself time to sit in a bit of shade and take in the view.

Sanctuary of Apollo, Castalian Spring, and Sanctuary of Athena Pronaia. © **22650/82-313.** Admission 9€ site and museum; 6€ site or museum only. Summer Mon 8am-6:30pm; Tues-Sun 8am-7:30pm; winter daily 9:30am-3pm. (Check hours as soon as you arrive at Delphi, as they can change without warning.)

Where to Stay

Delphi has no shortage of lodgings; you can usually find rooms even in July or August. When tourists are few, you can often improve on the rates below. Still, if you want to be sure that you get a room in a specific price category (or with a view or a pool), it's

---

The Festival of Delphi

Each summer (usually in June), the European Cultural Center of Delphi sponsors a **festival** featuring ancient Greek drama and works inspired by ancient drama. Tickets and schedules are available at the center's Athens office at 9 Frynihou, Plaka (© **210/331-2781**), and at the center's Delphi office (© **22650/82-731** or -732; www.eccd.eu), just out of town set back from the Itea road in a grove of trees.

best to make a reservation. With the growing popularity of skiing Parnassus, fewer of Delphi's hotels close for part of the winter, but summer is still high season here.

In addition to the following options, we've had good reports of **Hermes Hotel,** 29 Vasileos Pavlou (© **22650/82-318;** fax 22650/82-639); **Pan Hotel,** 53 Vasileos Pavlou (© **22650/82-294**); and its annex, the **Artemis,** 53a Vasileos Pavlou (www. panartemis.gr; © **22650/82-294**). The little **Odysseus Pension,** 1 Isea (© **22650/ 82-235**), has a garden and is a good budget choice (most rooms with shared bathroom). Three recently renovated, comfortable hotels, the **Delphi Palace,** just out of the village, with pool and gardens; the **King Iniohos,** on one of the upper streets, and the **Pythia Art Hotel,** on the nonview side of the main street, are jointly managed and share a website and a reservations number (www.delphi-hotels.com; © **22650/82-151**). Doubles at the Hermes, Artemis, Pan, and Odysseus from 50€; doubles at the Iniohos, Delphi, Iniohos, and Pythia from 70€. Despite its proximity to the site, and nice balconies, I no longer recommend the Hotel Vouzas, once *the* in-town hotel to stay at, because it has declined badly in recent years.

Tip: If you want a main street room with a view, be sure the hotel is on the side of the street overlooking the Gulf of Corinth and ask for a back room with a balcony that faces the gulf. You may not always see the water, but from your balcony you will almost always see the magnificent valley of olive trees that leads down to the gulf—and avoid the traffic noise of the main street.

Amalia Hotel ★ ☺ The pros: Like most of the Amalia chain hotels, the Delphi Amalia has good-size rooms with balconies and is in a quiet location outside town. If you are traveling with a car and have children, you may find the Amalia's garden and pool irresistible. The cons: Also like most Amalia hotels, this one is too far outside town for a walk to anything. Most guest rooms are large but rather anonymous, and the Amalia does most of its business with tour groups, many of whose members seem to find it impossible to resist shouting greetings from balcony to balcony.

Signposted on the Delphi-Itea road, 33054 Delphi. www.amalia.gr. © **22650/82-101.** Fax 22650/82-290. 185 units. 150€–200€ double. Rates include breakfast. AE, MC, V. **Amenities:** Restaurant; bar; pool; room service. *In room:* A/C, TV, hair dryer, Internet, minibar.

Hotel Acropole ★★ 🍴 One street below Delphi's main street, the 42-room Acropole has one of the quietest locations and best views in town over private houses, gardens, and the olive groves that stretch beneath Delphi to the sea. The Acropole stays open year-round and is owned and managed by the helpful Kourelis family. If the Acropole is full—it does get bus tours—the staff can usually find you a room at one of their other Delphi hotels, both on the main street: the slightly more modest and less expensive **Parnassos** (www.delphi.com.gr; © **22650/83-675**) and the appealing **Fedriades** (www.fedriades.com; © **22650/82-370**), which the Kourelis family purchased, renovated, and reopened in 2008. A 10% discount at all three is usually available to Frommer's readers. Check about special deals including a dinner plan at the excellent family-run **Epikouros** restaurant (see below).

13 Filellinon St., 33054 Delphi. www.delphi.com.gr. © **22650-82-675.** 42 units. 65€–95€ double. Rates include breakfast. Inquire about Frommer's discount. AE, MC, V. **Amenities:** Breakfast room; lounge w/ fireplace; Wi-Fi. *In room:* A/C, TV, fridge.

Hotel Varonos ★★★ 🍴 This excellent, inexpensive hotel is the best buy in town, with Delphi's famous views over the olive plain from most rooms. Make your reservation with the hotel and mention Frommer's and you will get a generous discount that brings the price of the standard single down to 45€, standard double to 60€, standard triple to 70€. Some 20 years ago, I arrived here with an ailing gardenia

Wining in Delphi

At Delphi and elsewhere in Central Greece, try some of the excellent wines from this region's **Hatzimichalis** vineyards. The chardonnay, Cabernet Sauvignon, and Merlot are widely available both in shops and restaurants.

plant, and the entire family pitched in to make sure it was well taken care of. In those days, the hotel was very simple, almost austere, but over the years, this has become one of the coziest and most comfortable small hotels in Greece. The guest rooms are comfortable, painted in soothing pastels, and the lobby is anything but austere, with lots of plants and a fire when it's chilly (and free Internet service). The view is still fantastic, the Varonos family could not be more helpful, and the breakfast buffet is unusually varied (four different kinds of juice and at least as many baked goods, along with yogurt, fresh fruits, eggs, cheese, and ham). Check out the family-owned shop next door with local honey, herbs, preserves, and other goodies.

25 Vasileos Pavlou, 33054 Delphi. www.hotel-varonos.gr. ⓒ/fax **22650/82-345.** 12 units, 11 with shower (1 with tub/shower). 65€–90€ double. Rates include breakfast. Inquire about the very generous Frommer's discount. MC, V. **Amenities:** Breakfast room; lounge w/fireplace; Internet. *In room:* A/C, TV, fridge.

Where to Eat

The problem with most of the Delphi restaurants that cater to tourists (most of them) is that the restaurateurs know that they aren't serving repeat customers. This does not inspire good service or loving food preparation. A happy exception to this rule is the excellent **Epikouros Restaurant** (see below). One other suggestion: If you have a car and are here any time but the winter, consider eating in **Arachova,** 10km (6 miles) east of Delphi, where the restaurants cater to a more local crowd. In winter, Arachova is teeming with the Athenians who come here to ski. Especially at night, the drive to and from Arachova, along a switchback mountain road, is best taken *siga, siga* (slowly, slowly), as the Greeks say.

Epikouros Restaurant ★★★ GREEK   This is easily the best restaurant with the best view in Delphi, with an extensive and varied menu, including tasty veggie fritters, local olives and formaella cheese, lamb with fresh tomato sauce, *keftedes* (grilled round meatballs), and *sousoutakia* (oval rice-and-meat balls, stewed in tomato sauce) and, in season, wild boar casserole with tomatoes, onions, and herbs. If you come early, you may be one of few diners not with a tour group; come after 10 pm and you may dine with Greek visitors and locals.

Vasileos Pavlou and Frederikis. ⓒ **22650/83-250.** Main courses 9€–18€. AE, MC, V. Daily lunch, dinner.

Taverna Skala ★ GREEK   This simple, but consistently good, year-round restaurant on the stepped street that runs uphill off the main drag attracts locals in the summer and skiers in the winter. The menu is typical Greek taverna fare (grills and stews), there's usually a wide variety of *mezedes.* Don't miss the black-and-white photos on the walls of Delphi in its pre–tour bus days.

Vasileos Pavlou and Frederikis. ⓒ **22650/82-762.** Main courses 7€–10€. No credit cards. Daily noon to around midnight.

Taverna Vakchos ★ 🍴 GREEK   This small taverna gets many of its customers from the youth hostel. This means that the prices are very reasonable, the clientele casual, and the food solid, basic, and tasty (although they sometimes serve game in winter). As you'd expect from a place whose name honors the god of wine, the local wines here are very good. The back room with its veranda has fantastic views over Delphi, across the plain of olives, and to the Corinthian gulf. If the Vakchos is full, try the neighboring **Taverna Lekaria,** which has a nice courtyard with flowering plants and usually serves local *loukanika* (sausages) for meat eaters and *briam* (a veggie stew steeped in olive oil) for those who prefer vegetables.

31 Apollonos.✆ **22650/83-186.** Main courses 7€–10€. No credit cards. Daily noon to around midnight.

Side Trips from Delphi

ARACHOVA ★★

Arachova clings to Mount Parnassus 950m (3,116 ft.) above sea level. For a long time, the adjective most often used to describe this tiny mountain village 10km (6 miles) east of Delphi, was "sleepy." In those days, Greek and foreign tourists paused here en route to and from Delphi to drink a coffee and buy the fluffy hand-loomed wool *flokates* (thick rugs and spreads) and *tagaria* (brightly colored wool bags) made from wool of the local sheep. A number of shops on the main street still sell authentic local crafts, including woodcarvings, copper, and weavings (some still sold by the weight of the wool used). Other shops have local honey, cheese, and herbs, including mountain tea. **Anemi** (✆ **22670/31-701**) often has nice antique reproductions.

That said, the development of the Mount Parnassos ski center has transformed Arachova into what might be thought of as a "boutique village." Nearly every one of the modest stone buildings in Arachova now conceals an après ski boutique, cafe, restaurant, or hotel—some with sauna facilities where a family's looms were once housed. If you come here in ski season, you can enjoy watching the beautiful people (many from Athens) lounging in cafes in their après ski togs—but if you want to spend the night, don't show up without a reservation!

Although winter is now Arachova's big season, when several tour buses choose the same moment to make a stop here in summer, this small village can be seriously overcrowded. Don't despair: Come back in the evening. The shops are still open, and the cafes and restaurants give you a chance to escape from the tour-group dominated world of Delphi to the village world of Greece. Locals often take to the streets in the evening for a *volta* (energetic stroll) on Delphon, the main street. If you climb the steep stairs to the upper town, you'll find yourself on quiet neighborhood streets, where children play and families sit in front of their homes.

For lunch or dinner, unless you just graze on some veggie dishes, you should be prepared to pay from 25€ wherever you eat—and the tab could easily go well above that, especially with alcohol. Try the simple family fare at **Taverna Karathanassi,** by the coffee shops in the main square with the lovely freshwater springs. *Brasto,* a rather bland broth with gray chunks of boiled goat meat, thought to be very restorative by many Greeks, is often on the menu. That may be why I often end up nearby at the venerable **Taverna Dasaryiris,** which specializes in *loukanika* (sausages), grills, and—are you ready?—delicious spicy *kokoretsi* (stuffed entrails). The homemade *chilopites* (tasty little square noodles) are terrific, as is the house red wine. If you want a meal with a view, head uphill on the stepped street and try either the **Panayiota** or **Kaplanis** restaurants, both with excellent *spitiko* cuisine (home cooking). **Emboriko** is another upscale restaurant very popular with Greeks; reservations at both Kaplanis and Emboriko are almost always necessary on weekends. If you're here in winter, try two fine places, **Fterolakka** or **Agnandi;** both are in the center of the village and are usually closed in summer—which certainly drives home the point that winter is *the*

St. George's Day in Arachova

Arachova's main feast day, April 23, honors **St. George,** the patron saint of shepherds. Locals and visitors celebrate by eating vast amounts of roast lamb washed down with the local red wines and dancing to folk music until the wee hours. (If Apr 23 falls during Lent, the feast day is observed the Mon after Easter.) Make a hotel reservation well ahead if you want to join them. Also be sure to wish everyone, especially anyone named George, *Chronia Polla* (Many more years).

time to be here for Greeks! Try something with the excellent *skordalia* (a garlic-potato sauce that the novice may suspect is almost 100% garlic). If you want to dance after you lounge, see what's going on at **Snow Me** (℃ 6944/341-317), a lively (and loud) disco cafe (often sporting a doorman, unusual in Greece). **Snow Me Petit** (same phone), an offshoot of Snow Me usually has almost all Greek music.

Low season for most Arachova hotels is summer; winter weekends, when nearly every hotel room is booked well in advance, is the most expensive time to stay here. For a room with a view, try the **Anemolia** (www.anemolia.gr; ℃ 22670/31-640; fax 22670/31-642), with 55 rooms, a restaurant, and a heated pool on a hill above the Delphi road just outside Arachova. Originally a member of the Best Western chain, with American-style bathrooms, it has large, comfortable rooms, many with balcony views down to Delphi and the Gulf of Corinth. Doubles go from 150€, chalet-style suites (fireplaces, balconies) from 300€, except on popular winter weekends when prices can be double that.

If you want to be in town and don't mind parking your car and then walking perhaps 10 minutes through Arachova's narrow lanes to your car, both the **Paradisiakos Xenonas Maria** (www.mariarooms.com; ℃ 22670/31-803) and the **Generalis Guesthouse** (www.generalis.gr; ℃ 22670/31-529) occupy handsomely restored 19th-century *arkontika* (town houses). Doubles at the Maria, which has seven rooms, start at 75€, although most are 150€ and up; doubles at the Generali, which has a subterranean indoor plunge-pool and sauna, start at 200€. The Maria gets consistent raves for friendly efficient service, which is not always the case with the Generalis.

If you want a room (or suite, or villa) with a Jacuzzi in a "boutique retreat" on the slopes of Parnassus that aims to re-create a "private village," with two pools, a spa, tennis courts, and fitness center, head for the **Santa Marina Arachova Resort and Spa** (www.generalis.gr; ℃ 22670/31-955); doubles start at 250€ in summer, 350€ winter weekends. Guest rooms are light, bright, and spacious. Their sister hotel, the **Santa Marina Arachova** (www.santa marina.gr; ℃ 22670/31-230) in the village, has doubles from 150€ (summer) to 280€ (winter). Rooms are perfectly comfortable but slightly somber, and could use some sprucing up. Guests here, including many Greeks and Germans, can use the resort hotel's spa facilities.

PARNASSUS (PARNASSOS) ★★

The good news is that you can drive 23km (14 miles) from Arachova to the **ski resort at Kelaria,** or 27km (17 miles) from Arachova to the **ski resort at Fterolakka,** in about an hour. Each resort is about 2,200m (7,216 ft.) up the mountain, whose highest peak rises to 2,459m (8,065 ft.); information is available at **www.parnassos-ski. gr.** The bad news is that the road and several incipient hamlets of ski lodges (the

Santa Marina Resort is one of the more tasteful developments) have eradicated much of the mountain's isolation and beauty. All in all, **Parnassus** is an odd mountain: It's difficult to see its highest peaks from either Delphi or Arachova, although if you approach from the north, you'll have fine views of its twin summits.

If you come in winter, you can rent ski equipment either in Arachova or at the resorts. Keep in mind that fog and high winds often sweep in suddenly. When this happens, the ski lifts close and the road down the mountain is often also closed, stranding day-trippers until it reopens. In fact, fog can close this road at almost any time, even in summer—something to consider if you decide to drive up for a look around. I was glad to have a bottle of water and cookies in the car when this happened to me one May afternoon and I had to pull over for several hours.

In summer, don't expect to find the shops, cafes, and restaurants (not to mention the dozen ski runs) open. If you want to hike Parnassus, there are two possibilities, both with trail markings. The **Hellenic Federation of Mountaineering and Climbing,** 5 Milioni, 10673 Kolonaki (© **210/364-5904;** www.sport.gov.gr), and the **Mountaineering Club** in Athens (© **210/323-4555**) have information on both routes. In Arachova, inquire about guides and weather conditions at the **town tourist office,** Plateia Xenias, open most days at least from 9am to 6pm (© **22670/31-630;** depta@arachova.gr). As always in the mountains, it's not a good idea to make such an excursion alone and it is always wise to check the local weather forecast.

If you begin your climb in Delphi, head uphill past the Sikelianos house and keep going, bearing left above the sanctuary and following the trail markers. Four hours will bring you to the upland meadows known as the **Plateau of Livadi,** where shepherds traditionally pasture their flocks. Want to keep going? Past the meadow is the **Corcyrian Cave** (known locally as Sarantavli, or Forty Rooms), where Pan and the Nymphs once were thought to live; beyond are the summits. It's also possible to begin your ascent from Arachova, where it is best to get directions locally. The Road Edition map of Parnassos (no. 42 in the mountain map series) is an excellent investment at 6€, as is Tim Salmon's *The Mountains of Greece* (Cicerone Press). However, nothing substitutes for a companion, especially one who knows the terrain well.

THE MONASTERY OF OSIOS LOUKAS ★★

You'll probably want to see Osios Loukas (**www.osiosloukas.gr**) en route to or from Delphi (see "Essentials," earlier in this chapter, for directions). You can also do the 96km (60-miles) round-trip via Arachova as a day excursion, although when I last did this, battling against steady phalanxes of tour buses in both directions, I vowed never to do so again. If you go to Osios Loukas via Levadia, pause at **Schiste (Triodos),** where three roads intersect. This is the spot where the ancients believed that Oedipus unknowingly slew his father.

The splendid mosaics of **Osios Loukas (Monastery of St. Luke)** are rivaled only by the mosaics at Daphne outside Athens and in the churches of Thessaloniki. Much of Osios Loukas dates from the 10th and 11th centuries and commemorates not the better-known St. Luke the Evangelist, but the Blessed Luke, a revered 10th-century hermit, perhaps born in nearby Delphi. Much more than a tourist destination, devout Greek Orthodox visitors consider it a holy spot. This is not the place for sleeveless shirts or shorts: The tomb of St. Luke in the **Katholikon (main church)** is an important pilgrimage destination and taking photos is usually discouraged.

Osios Loukas perches on a steep slope, with sweeping views over the surrounding countryside. The monastery's buildings are lavishly decorated with brick and a wide variety of jewel-like polychrome marbles. If you are lucky enough to be here when the

Katholikon isn't too crowded, enjoy the changing play of light and shadows on the marbles and mosaics. Mosaic scenes from the Bible, including the Nativity and Baptism, glow overhead. You may see visitors handing their family icons to a monk, who takes them off for a special blessing. Next, head to the smaller **Church of the Theotokos (Mother of God),** with a wall fresco showing Joshua as a warrior and a fine mosaic floor. If you have time, visit the fresco-adorned crypt, and then sit in the courtyard. Imagine what Osios Loukas was like when, rather than today's handful of monks, hundreds of monks lived and worshiped here. The monastery's former refectory (dining room) now serves as a small museum of sculpture and fragments of architectural ornament.

Admission to Osios Loukas is 3€. Summer hours are daily 8am to 2pm and 4 to 6pm; winter hours are 8:30am to 3pm. (Note that these are the posted times; they are not always observed.) A shop sells icons and other religious goods as well as local oil and honey; the small cafe (not always open) offers soft drinks, coffee, snacks, and local delicacies. Allow at least an hour for your visit.

THERMOPYLAE & CHAIRONEIA ★

Both these battlefields lie beside main highways and are easily visited with a brief stop. A seasonal *kantina* (snack shop) is sometimes open at both battlefields

Thermopylae

194km (120 miles) N of Athens on the Athens-Thessaloniki National Hwy.

One of the most famous battles in history was fought at Thermopylae in 480 B.C. when the Persian king Xerxes attempted to conquer Greece. To this day, historians speculate on how different the world might have been if Xerxes had succeeded and Greece had become a small part of the vast Persian Empire. If you find yourself on the Athens-Thessaloniki Highway, watch for signs alerting you to the larger-than-life **statue of the Spartan king Leonidas,** about halfway through the 6.4km-long (4-mile) Pass of Thermopylae that snakes between the mountains and the sea.

When Xerxes invaded Greece in 480 B.C. with about 100,000 men, soldiers from almost every city-state in south and Central Greece rushed to Thermopylae to try to stop the advancing Persian army. The pass is the only easy route from the north into Central and southern Greece, and if the Persians made it through the pass, Greece could be theirs. The statue of Leonidas—the man who did most to delay the Persian advance—marks the battlefield. The 6,000 or so Greek soldiers might have succeeded in holding the narrow pass of Thermopylae had not a traitor told the Persians of a secret mountain path that allowed a party of Persians to infiltrate the pass and outflank the Greeks. Ordering the main Greek force to retreat south, Leonidas and his 300 Spartans, along with several hundred other Greek soldiers—with the certain knowledge of immanent death—stood and fought a critical delaying action at Thermopylae. This gave the main Greek force time to retreat south to regroup, reinforce, and fight another day. When the fighting at Thermopylae was over, Leonidas and his men lay dead, but the Spartan king had earned immortal fame for his heroism. In 2007 the story was retold in the Hollywood film *300.*

The name *Thermopylae* (Hot Gates) refers to the warm springs that bubbled here in antiquity, when the pass was considerably narrower than it currently is, now that centuries of silt have built up the seashore. Many of Thermopylae's springs have been partly diverted to spas, such as Kamena Vourla. Unfortunately, overdevelopment has seriously undercut the former charm of the nearby seaside towns. If you want a quick look at some of the springs, look for plumes of smoke after you park near the statue of Leonidas. If you don't see plumes, follow your nose: The smell of sulfur is strong.

Chaironeia

132km (81 miles) NW of Athens on the Athens-Levadhia-Lamia Hwy.

Just north of Levadhia, the Athens-Lamia Highway passes an enormous **stone lion** that marks the site of the common grave of the Theban Sacred Band of warriors, who died here in the Battle of Chaironeia in 338 B.C. It was at Chaironeia that Philip of Macedon, with some 30,000 soldiers, defeated the combined forces of Athens and Thebes and became the most powerful leader in Greece. It was also at Chaironeia that Philip's 18-year-old son Alexander first distinguished himself on the battlefield. Young Alexander, soon to be called "Alexander the Great," led the attack against the superbly trained Theban Sacred Band, which fought to the last man. Philip's admiration for the Thebans' courage was such that he allowed them the unusual honor of being buried where they fell on the battlefield.

The stone lion itself, sitting on its haunches with a surprisingly benign expression on its face, was probably erected by Thebes to honor the Sacred Band sometime after the battle. Some scholars think that the Thebans waited tactfully until after Philip's death in 316 B.C. to erect the monument. With the passing of time, the winds blew soil from the plain almost entirely over the lion. In 1818, two English antiquarians stumbled upon the lion's head; from 1902 to 1904 the Greek Archaeological Service conducted excavations on the battlefield and restored the lion here on the dusty plain of Chaironeia. The small site museum keeps irregular hours.

VOLOS ★ & MOUNT PELION ★★

320km (200 miles) N of Athens

There comes a time on almost every trip when you need to take a brief vacation from your vacation. A stop at the port city of **Volos** and a visit to the rustic villages of **Mount Pelion** can banish museum-and-antiquities burnout. And, if you're doing the long (largely tedious) national highway drive from Athens to Thessaloniki, Volos, and Pelion are a perfect break from the motorway blues. Volos's seaside location (about 320km/200 miles north of Athens and 210km/130 miles south of Thessaloniki) is refreshing, and the wooded villages of Mount Pelion are relaxing. In short, Volos and Pelion offer the perfect contrasting combination of city energy and country leisure.

Legend has it that Jason and the Argonauts set sail from Volos when they began their search for the Golden Fleece. Today, many tourists pass through Volos en route to the villages of Mount Pelion or when they catch a ferry to one of the Sporades islands (see chapter 13). Too few stop here—a pity, because Volos has a terrific waterfront packed with cafes and restaurants, a fine archaeological museum, and is close to four important ancient sites. The **Volos Information Center** on Grigoriou Lambraki and Sekeri (© **24210/30-940**) is usually open 8am to 8pm weekdays, 9am to 4pm weekends, and has information on Volos, Mount Pelion, and the surrounding area.

If you want to be pampered, the 48-room **Domotel Xenia Volos,** 1 Plastira, on the waterfront to the east of central Volos (www.domotel.gr; © **24219/92-700**), has spa facilities, pool and big rooms with big bathrooms—and offers a choice of fluffy or firm pillows; doubles from 100€. **The Hotel Aegli,** 24 Argonauton, on the waterfront (www.aegli.gr; © **24210/24-471**), has rooms with balconies and seaside view from

100€. The nearby **Park Hotel,** 2 Deligiorgi (www.amhotels.gr; ℓ **24210/36-511**), is another good bet, with rooms from 120€. The Aegli is just steps away from excellent inexpensive restaurants, including **Apostolis,** 15 Argonauton (ℓ **24210/26-973**), and the **Ouzerie Iolkos,** 32 Argonauton (ℓ **24210/35-277**). Don't be surprised if you see customers sipping ouzo instead of wine or beer with their meals; Volos produces (and drinks) much of Greece's national drink. And if you think ouzo is strong, try the local *tsipouro,* a firewater so strong that that Greeks usually dilute it with lashes of water and tame it with lots of *mezedes* (snacks).

The **Archaeological Museum,** 1 Athanasaki (ℓ **24210/25-285**), has a unique collection of rare painted Hellenistic grave monuments. Paint is fragile, washes off in the rain and erodes easily when buried, and almost no painted monuments have survived from antiquity. The museum also has a rose garden with picturesque fallen columns and ancient statues. Just beyond the garden is a seaside park with replicas of several Neolithic houses. Some of the finds at the museum come from four nearby and relatively easy-to-find ancient sites: **Neolithic Dimini** and **Sesklo,** with the remains of some of Greece's oldest habitations, **Hellenistic Demetrias,** with the remains of a royal palace, theater and fortifications, and **Nea Anchialos** (ancient Pyrasos), which has Greek, Roman, and extensive early Christian remains. If you decide to spend part of a day visiting the ancient sites, try to end up at Nea Anchialos, which has a string of cafes and tavernas on the seashore a few blocks from the ancient site. This is a great spot to combine a swim with a snack at one of a number of seaside tavernas and cafes. Locals praise the taverna **Alexandros,** which is usually closed on Tuesday, which, alas, is the day I was last in town.

Before you head off to Mount Pelion, try to stop in at Volos's **Makris Folk Art Center** (ℓ **24210/37-119**), 1 Athanaski St., usually open daily until noonish, except for Saturday. The museum has a number of works of the early 20th century "primitive" painter Theophilos Hatzimichaelis, who fell for Pelion and painted for his supper as he traveled around. its villages. Theophilos's paintings are a lovely introduction to the magical world of Pelion. Theophilos was especially fond of painting scenes of gods and nymphs, and some of the half-human, half-horse centaurs who, in antiquity, were said to be especially fond of Pelion's green hills and valleys. Achilles himself was tutored on Pelion by the wise old centaur Chiron.

If you have a week to spend on Pelion, you won't regret it, but if you only have a day or two—or even just a day—you can see enough to vow to come back as soon as possible. I'll give some suggestions on where to stay and eat if you can linger here, but do remember that in summer and on winter weekends (when skiers head here), almost all rooms on Pelion are booked well in advance. If you're interested in renting a house here, check out **www.pelion.co.uk** or **www.pelion.org/mulberrytravel**.

Despite some good new roads, doing the full circuit of Pelion in one day, given some still-rough roads and the need to double back from time to time, is more exhausting than exhilarating. This is a place, if at all possible, to make haste slowly, so here are some tips on how to see just some of Pelion's highlights in a day excursion. I hope you'll decide to spend at **least** 1 night here. Less than 10km (6 miles) out of Volos, you come to the village of Portaria—and so do a lot of tour groups that stop here to see the famous plane trees on the shaded plateia and the chestnut trees that grow profusely on Pelion. Keep going, and you'll soon be in **Makrinitsa,** which has nicknamed itself the "Balcony of Pelion," because of its high perch on a mountain slope. At almost any time of the year, roses, hydrangeas and the inevitable geraniums are in bloom. Makrinitsa is so well-watered that it has more than 50 fountains—one for almost every family in town. Many of the stone houses have slate roofs and the projecting wooden upper stories characteristic of Pelion's architecture. Makranitsa is largely pedestrianized, and you can leave your car on the outskirts (try not to be outflanked by the tour buses, which take no notice of the needs of cars when they park). The 10-room **Sisilanou Archontiko** (© **24280/99-556**), like many hotels on Pelion, occupies a nicely restored village mansion (*archontiko* means mansion) and has rooms from around 60€ to 100€.

From Makrinitsa, head on to the village of Zagora; if you've been eating an apple a day while you've been in Greece, it probably was grown here. The 5-room **Archontiko Drakopoulou** (© **24260/21-566**) is one of a number of Pelion hotels run by a women's association devoted to maintaining Pelion's traditions while advancing the region's prosperity.

By now you may be wondering why this rural backwater has so many mansions. In the 19th century, Pelion was a center of the silk industry, and wealthy merchants and moguls built massive houses, many of which could function as a family fortress in a pinch. When the silk industry moved west, Pelion lost its prosperity. In an odd way, that's what saved so many of the handsome buildings people come to see today. Villagers either emigrated or just continued to live in their old houses, without the means to modernize them. This spared Pelion the post-WWII frenzy of tearing down much of the old and building the new that destroyed so much of Greece's traditional architecture. When prosperity returned in the 1980s, many deserted and run-down houses were restored as Greeks became nostalgic for the past. Pelion is one tourist destination where you are likely to encounter more Greek visitors than foreigners.

Near Zagora, in the hamlet of Kissos, the **Church of Agia Marina** has fine frescoes and, unusually for many rural Greek churches, is often open. By now you may be thinking that chestnut trees, shady plateias, wooden houses, and low, broad slate-roofed churches are all very well, but what you really want to hear is not the sound of water splashing in village fountains, but the sea lapping a sand beach. No problem.

Head down to the sea at the village of **Horefto** and enjoy a swim in what legend says was the centaur Chiron's home town. Who knows? Maybe Chiron taught Achilles to swim here. You can imagine the scene while you swim and have lunch at one of the seaside tavernas. Both Horefto and the nearby village of Ayios Ioannis have a number of small hotels, but nothing as charming as the restored archontika in the inland villages. Two nearby villages with especially charming inns are **Mouresi,** with the four-room **Old Silk Store** (**www.pelionet.gr/oldsilkstore**) and **Tsangarada,** with the eight-room **Lost Unicorn** (**www.lostunicorn.com**). The Old Silk Store is an amazing value, with its lovely garden and views down to the sea from Mouresi (doubles from 65€; 420€ per week); the English owner, Jill Sleeman, knows the area well, and is quite helpful. The Lost Unicorn, on Tsangarda's main plateia (doubles from 90€), has a great restaurant. Both consistently get rave reviews from visitors and both villages are in the running for the most picturesque on Pelion

At this point, if your time is limited, and you can resist more seaside time, head across the peninsula, and over to the west coast and its cluster of idyllic villages: **Milies, Vyzitsa,** and **Pinakates.** Each has massive plane trees, cobbled streets, and frescoed churches (Agios Taxiarches in Milies is especially fine). From here, you can return along the road that links Pelion's coast to Volos to the world beyond Pelion.

Tip: Steam train buffs are in luck on Pelion. **To Trenaki** is a restored 18th-century narrow-gauge steam train that chugs from the western village of Ano Leonia to the central village of Miles and back most weekends and holidays. Miles has a small museum, nice plateia with church, and good restaurants, especially the Taverna Panorama. You can get the up-to-date schedule and prices at the Volos Information Center (see above) or at 24210/24056.

THE VALE OF TEMPE & AMBELAKIA ★★

360km (223 miles) N of Athens; 27km (16 miles) N of Larissa

The Vale of Tempe, a steep-sided 8km (5-mile) wooded gorge between mounts Olympus and Ossa, has been famous since antiquity as a beauty spot. Unfortunately, since nearly all north-south traffic in Greece now passes through the Vale, this is no longer the sylvan spot that was once the haunt of nightingales. I'd even put it on the "overrated" list. It's hard to realize that this congested spot is—according to legend and myth—where Apollo caught a glimpse of the lovely maiden Daphne bathing in the Peneios River. When Apollo pursued Daphne, she cried out to the gods on nearby Olympus to save her from Apollo's ardor—which they did, by turning her into a laurel tree (*daphne* in Greek). Apollo, who didn't give up easily, plucked a branch from the tree and planted it at his shrine at Delphi. Thereafter, messengers from Delphi came to the Vale of Tempe every 9 years to collect laurel for Apollo's temple.

The narrow approaches to the Vale have caused many serious road accidents. Still, if you're lucky enough to be here off season, the sound of the gurgling river may be louder than tourists' footsteps on the suspension bridge over the gorge. River rafting is becoming popular here; for information contact **Olympos Trekking** (oltrek@ote. net.gr). If you park and walk into the Vale, allow an hour for your visit.

Keep an eye out for two medieval fortresses here: The remains of **Kastro tis Oreas (Castle of the Beautiful Maiden)** are on the cliffs inside the Vale; and **Platamonas Kastro** is at the northern end of the pass. You won't have any trouble spotting the souvenir stands throughout the Vale. There is also a small chapel deep in the gorge.

If you want a break from the popular tourist destinations such as the Vale of Tempe, take a detour to the mountaintop village of **Ambelakia ★★**, about 6km (4 miles) southeast of the Vale perched amid old oak trees on Mount Kissavos. Most of the village streets are cobblestone and massive plane trees grow beside springs near several of the frescoed churches. If you spend an hour or two here—better yet, a night or two—you can experience village Greece, inhale the crisp, clean mountain air; and enjoy the spectacular views of Mount Olympus.

Ambelakia, whose name means "vineyards" in Greek, is one of six villages in Greece that have come together to form the **National Network of Tradition, Culture, and Community Life.** Their mission is preserving local traditions and crafts—and boosting local economy Astonishingly, this tiny village produced most of the red cotton thread used throughout Europe in the 18th and 19th centuries, with offices in far-off London and Vienna. Today, little survives of Ambelakia's earlier wealth, but two museum houses give a glimpse of past glories. The late-18th-century **Schwartz House ★★** was built by the Schwartz brothers, two of Ambelakia's wealthiest merchants, who lived and worked in Austria, hence the name "Schwartz," a translation of their Greek name "Mavros." Their wooden house, with its overhanging balconies and elaborately frescoed interiors, is an absolute delight—and it is a great joy to see it so carefully restored and well cared for. Allow an hour for the guided tour of the house. (Its somewhat flexible hours are usually Tues–Sat 9am–3pm, Sun 9am–2:30pm; admission is 3€.) If you want to visit another restored mansion, take in the **Folk Art and Historic Museum** ★ in the 19th-century Mola mansion (© **24950/93-090;** usually open Mon–Fri 11am–3pm, Sat–Sun 11am–4:30pm; admission 3€). Dioramas recreate scenes of family life and photographs and frescoes show how generations of Ambelakians have lived. Again, this is a pleasant spot to spend an hour.

It's a good idea to make an advance reservation at the **Nine Muses Hotel** (also listed as **Ennea Musses** and **Nine Mouses;** h9mouses@hotmail.com; © **24950/93-405**), which has 12 rooms from 60€. The chalet-style hotel just off the main plateia is popular with visitors, and in summer all the rooms are often taken by Greek families. The Nine Muses has great views over Ambelakia and the countryside, which includes Mount Olympos; the proprietors, Georgios Machmoudies and son Kostas, are both very helpful. The 16-room **Hotel Kouria** (www.hotelkouria.gr; © **24950/93-33**), built on the outskirts of town in 2006, also has wonderful views of the countryside and large, comfortable rooms, but lacks local atmosphere; rooms from 85€. Both hotels serve breakfast and the Kouria has a restaurant and Internet service. Both hotels can be either blissfully quiet or quite noisy; the Kouria is a popular venue for wedding and baptisms receptions, and the Nine Muses is flanked by tavernas.

MOUNT OLYMPUS ★★★

390km (241 miles) N of Athens; 70km (43 miles) N of Larissa; 100km (62 miles) SW of Thessaloniki

Greece's most famous mountain range, home of the Olympian gods (see chapter 2, "Greece in Depth"), towers 2,919m (9,574 ft.) above the plains of Thessaly and Macedonia.

The first recorded successful ascent of Olympus's summit Mytikas—nicknamed "the Needle"—was in 1913, when two Swiss mountaineers and a local guide made it to the top. Today, for such an imposing mountain, Olympus is surprisingly easy to climb. A number of well-marked paths lead to the summit; climbers can rest or overnight in **shelters** at Stavros (944m/3,096 ft.) and at Spilios Agapitos (2,100m/6,888 ft.). In summer, these paths can be very heavily trafficked. Elegant Greek women have been known to make the ascent in high heels (not recommended).

Still, Olympus is a serious mountain, and no one should attempt it alone—or without water, provisions, and gear. From a distance, it's almost impossible to pick out the summit, although the massive, gnarled, snowcapped range is often visible from Thessaloniki (albeit less and less so, given the area's increasing pollution). Another of its main peaks (it has six), Stafani (2,909m/9,541 ft.), is called the "throne of Zeus."

As always in the mountains, weather conditions can change for the worse without warning. Well into May, severe snowstorms can hit the heights of Olympus—which helps explain why the area has been developed in recent years as a ski resort. The main town on the slopes, and the base camp for climbers, is Litochoro.

Essentials

GETTING THERE By Bus Four buses that stop at the Litochoro station (© **23520/81-271**) run daily from Athens to Katerini. Seven buses a day make the trip from Athens to Larissa; from there you'll find frequent service to Litochoro. All buses leave Athens from the station at 260 Liossion (© **210/831-7059** or 210/831-7153). At least eight buses a day leave from Thessaloniki for Litochoro.

By Train   Trains go daily from Athens to Larissa, and from Thessaloniki to Larissa. From Larissa, you can continue to Litochoro by bus. You can also take a train from Athens or Thessaloniki to the Litochoro station (© **23520/22-522**)—but the station is on the coast 9km (5½ miles) from town, and you'll have to continue on by bus or taxi. Only devoted train lovers will want to come this way.

By Car   Take the Litochoro exit on the Athens-Salonika Highway.

VISITOR INFORMATION   In Litochoro (www.litohoro.gr), the **tourist office** (© **23520/83-100**) faces the bus stop. Information on Olympus is available from the **Hellenic Federation of Mountaineering and Climbing,** 5 Milioni, 10673 Kolonaki, Athens (© **210/364-5904;** www.sport.gov.gr), and from the **Hellenic Mountaineering Club (EOS; © 210/323-4555** or 210/323-4555 in Athens, 231/ 278-288 in Thessaloniki, or 23520/81-944 in Litochoro; eos@olympus.gr). Olympus is best climbed from June 1 to October 1; before and after, snow falls and bad weather make this treacherous. The **Spilios Agapitos** refuge can be reached at © **23520/81-800.** Rates are flexible but are usually no more than 20€. Make your reservation at the refuge well in advance of your arrival and be sure to check when you must arrive by to hold your place (usually 8pm).

FAST FACTS   The **National Bank of Greece,** on Plateia Kentriki, offers currency exchange and has an ATM. The **clinic** (© **23520/22 222**), 5km (3 miles) outside Litochoro, is signposted; if you need medical care and it is not an emergency, try to get to Thessaloniki. The signposted **police station** (© **23520/81-110-1**) and the **telephone office (OTE)** are just off the central square, Plateia Kentriki, on the road up Olympus to Priona. The **post office** is on Plateia Kentriki.

Climbing Mount Olympus

If you plan to climb **Olympus,** check first with the EOS (see "Visitor Information," above) and get the excellent Road Edition map of Olympus (no. 31; 7€). If you can, also get a copy of Marc Dubin's *Trekking in Greece.* You should *not* attempt the climb alone; weather here can change in an instant from pleasant to life-threatening. Forest fires are common in summer—when there can also be heavy snows.

Purists will want to begin the ascent at the increasingly developed **ski resort of Litochoro,** while others may prefer to drive from Litochoro as far as **Prionia** (18km/11 miles) and begin the climb there. On foot, the journey from Litochoro to Prionia takes about 4 hours; by car, it's about an hour but seems longer on the twisting road. Reward yourself with a meal or even a stiff drink at the small **cafe** in Priona.

From Priona, it's at least a 3-hour climb, much of it over slippery schist slopes and knobby limestone outcroppings, to the **shelter at Spilios Agapitos.** Most climbers begin the final 3-hour ascent at dawn and then do the entire descent, arriving back in Litochoro before dusk. The **Monastery of Ayios Dionysos,** not far from Spilios Agapitos, is a good place to break your downward trek and enjoy the views. In short, your climb will take at least a day and you will probably want to stay overnight at one of the shelters.

Where to Stay & Eat

Most of the restaurant pickings in Litochoro are slim: a number of fast-food joints and so-so restaurants. If climbers are foodies, they'll be disappointed here, with one notable exception: **Gastrodromio en Olympo,** by the large church on the main square (© **23520/21-300;** www.gastrodromio.gr), has a varied menu including fresh fish and pasta cooked al dente (more than 200 wines and a cheese menu of 22 traditional Greek cheeses). Mountain-climbing friends who come here regularly eat at Gastrodromio and think that the **Hotel Xenos Dias,** also on Litochoro's main square (www.hotel-xeniosdias.gr; ✆ **23520/81-234;** fax 23520/81-423; doubles from 70€), is very comfortable, welcoming, and excellent value.

Dion Palace Resort Hotel ★ ☺   I would find this a tempting spot, if I were traveling with several children and wanted to see the scene at a Greek family resort hotel where I could alternate sightseeing with spa pampering and seaside relaxation. This sprawling beachfront resort, about 6km (4 miles) from Litochoro, includes the main hotel building, its disco, lots of cabanas, and some small "villas." The public rooms are seriously glitzy; guest rooms are large and comfortable (renovated in 2006 and 2009), if somewhat bland (as is almost always the case in Greece). In summer, Greek families from Thessaloniki flock here to relax by the pools and on the beach.

Litochoro Beach, Pierias, 60200 Macedonia. www.dionpalace.com. ✆ **23520/61-431.** Fax 23520/61-435. 187 units. Doubles from 150€. AE, DC, MC, V. Sometimes closed in winter. **Amenities:** 2 restaurants; 4 bars; children's playground; health club; 2 pools; spa; tennis;. *In room:* A/C, TV, hair dryer, minibar, Wi-Fi.

Villa Drossos ★★ ☺   The big plus here—which makes reservations in summer a necessity—is the swimming pool in the garden and the pleasant family atmosphere. In a quiet neighborhood, by a church, the Drossos uses bright pastels and floral prints in its furnishings, and all the guest rooms have balconies.

Litochoro, 60200 Macedonia. www.villadrossos.gr. ✆ **23520/84-561.** Fax 23520/84-563. 13 units. 60€–80€ double. MC, V. **Amenities:** Bar/breakfast room; pool. *In room:* A/C, TV, Wi-Fi.

THE METEORA ★★★

Kalambaka is 356km (220 miles) NW of Athens; the circuit of the Meteora monasteries is approximately 25km (15 miles)

As you drive across the plain of Thessaly, which can seem endless on a hot summer day, you'll suddenly see a cluster of gnarled black humps and peaks outside the town of Kalambaka. Some travelers have compared these crags to the mountains of the moon. The rock formations of the **Meteora** (the word means "in midair") are unique. Many geographers speculate that some 30 million years ago, all Thessaly was a vast inland sea; when the sea receded, sweeping the topsoil along, rock formations were left behind. Over the millennia, the Peneios River and the wind carved the rock into the weird, twisted shapes that now rise about 300m (984 ft.) above the plain. The Meteora is especially stunning in winter, when snow caps the Pindos range and mists swirl around the monasteries.

These bizarre rock formations would be attraction enough, but many are topped with substantial monasteries. Why did monks settle here, and how did they build anything larger than huts on the rocks atop these sheer, slippery, seemingly unscalable rocks that really do seem to hang in midair? Small wonder that many monks believe that St. Athanasios (founder of the first monastery here) did not scale these rocks, but was carried up by an eagle.

The first monks to live here were probably 10th-century ascetics who lived as hermits in caves and spent their days in prayer and meditation. In fact, the word "monk" comes from the Greek for "alone." Over the centuries, more and more hermits and monks seeking to lead the solitary life made their way to the Meteora until, in the 14th century St. Athanasios founded the Great Meteoron (Monastery of the Transfiguration). By 1500, there were 24 monasteries here. Six—the Great Meteoron, Varlaam,

Important Meteora Reminders

The visiting days and hours of the Meteora monasteries are unpredictable and changeable. Since May 2009, most monasteries have closed 1 day a week and been open other days from 9am to 4 or 5pm. In winter, most close 1 or 2 days a week and are open other days from 9am to 1pm (St. Nicholas), 9am to 2pm (Ayia Triada and Roussanou), 9am to 3pm (Varlaam), and 9am to 4pm (Great Meteoron); Ayiou Stefanos planned to be open 9:30am to 1pm and 3 to 5pm. This is a departure from the monasteries' former practice of all closing for several hours in the middle of the day for siesta. It remains to be seen if the many monasteries will continue to be open in the middle of the day or revert to their previous schedule. Sometimes the monasteries are much less crowded in the early evening, when tour groups have departed for their next destination. Ideally, you would be able to visit monasteries on two late afternoons. Failing that, start your visit as early in the day as possible, so you're not left cooling your heels if the monasteries revert to closing while the monks and nuns have their afternoon siestas. Try to allow at least a full day here—you don't want to rush your experience of the contemplative life! If you are on a tight schedule, you can visit several monasteries and then do a circuit of the others by car in an hour or so. Women should wear skirts, not slacks, and men should wear slacks, not shorts. If you come in winter, dress warmly, as many of the monasteries have little or no heat in the public rooms. Also in winter, many small restaurants and hotels in the area may be closed. In compensation, you might get to see the Meteora at its most beautiful: covered with snow and shrouded in mists.

Roussanou, Ayia Triada, Ayios Nikolaos Anapaphsas, and Ayiou Stefanou—are still inhabited and welcome visitors.

Touring the monasteries is not easy for those who suffer from severe acrophobia and downright impossible for those unable to climb the steep (sometimes slippery) flights of stairs cut into the rock's face. These vertiginous stepped paths are an improvement over what earlier visitors had to endure. When the English traveler Leake visited here in the 19th century, he was ferried up to the Great Meteoron in a net attached by a slender rope to a winch. Leake later wrote, "Visitors' morale was not helped by persistent rumors that the monks only replaced the homemade ropes which held the nets when they broke—usually in midair!"

Essentials

GETTING THERE By Train There are usually about five daily trains from Athens's Larissa station (© **210/821-3882**) to Larissa and then on to the Kalambaka station (© **24320/22-451**). Allow at least 8 hours for the Athens-Kalambaka trip.

By Bus Seven buses run daily to Trikkala from the Athens terminal at 260 Liossion (© **210/831-1434** or 210/831-7153). Allow at least 8 hours for the Athens-Kalambaka trip. Buses leave frequently from Trikkala (© **24310/73-130**) for Kalambaka (© **24320/22-432**). Several buses a day connect Kalambaka and the Meteora monasteries.

By Car From Athens, take the Athens-Thessaloniki National Highway north to Lamia; from Lamia, take the highway northwest to Kalambaka. From Delphi, take the

Lamia-Karditsa-Trikkala-Kalambaka Highway north. Allow at least 6 hours for the Athens-Kalambaka trip.

GETTING AROUND   If you don't have a car, you may want to hire a taxi to visit the Meteora monasteries. Expect to pay between 50€ and 100€ to visit the six monasteries usually open to the public. Your fee will vary depending on whether you want a drive-by tour with a brief stop at one or two monasteries, or a more thorough daytrip with stops at each. Be sure you are in agreement with your driver as to how much time you will have at each monastery. Most drivers are content to wait up to 30 minutes at each monastery, while some drivers will accompany you into each and act as guide (and expect a tip).

FAST FACTS   The **tourist office** (✆ 24320/77-734) on Plateia Riga Fereou, the main square (with the prominent fountain), is usually open Monday to Friday 9am to 1pm and 5 to 8pm in summer, with abbreviated winter hours. Information is also available at the Town Hall (✆ 24320/22-339). The **National Bank** and the **Ionian Bank,** also on Plateia Riga Fereou, exchange currency and have ATMs. The **clinic** in Kalambaka (✆ 24320/24-111), the **police** (✆ 24320/22-109), and the **tourist police** (✆ 24320/76-100) are about 1km (½ mile) outside town on the road to Ioannina. The **post office** and **telephone office (OTE)** are signposted off Plateia Riga Fereou. **Cafe Hollywood** (✆ 24320/24-964), on the main drag, Trikalon, and **Arena** (✆ 24320/77-999) on Plateia Dimoula, function as Internet cafes. Hang gliding in the Meteora became popular as a result of spectacular scenes in the 1981 James Bond movie *For Your Eyes Only.* If you're interested in rock climbing or hang gliding, see **www.meteoraclimbing.gr** or **www.kalambaka.gr**, allegedly soon to have its website available in English).

What to See & Do
THE METEORA MONASTERIES
The road from Kalambaka through the Meteora takes you past Ayios Nikolaos, Roussanou, the Great Meteoron, Varlaam, Ayia Triada, and Ayios Stephanos. Perhaps most impressive about the Meteora is the visual from the plain, as one approaches, of the bizarre and stunning visual melding of monasteries and cliffs. If you have time to visit only one monastery, it should be the **Great Meteoron.** You can chat with the monks and enjoy stunning views through the forest of rocks from monastery to monastery. You'll find souvenir stands and places to buy bottled water or soft drinks (but usually no food) outside most of the monasteries.

We've listed the individual phone numbers for each monastery below, but don't be surprised if no one answers: Telephones and the monastic life are not compatible, although an increasing number of monks have cellphones tucked in their monastic robes. There is a central number for the monasteries (✆ **24320/22-649**); again, do not be surprised if no one answers. And (sorry) also don't be surprised if you find one or more of the monasteries closed—usually the one you've just climbed a long series of rock-cut steps to reach.

Ayia Triada ★★   It's not easy to say which of the monasteries has the most spectacular position, but Ayia Triada would be near the top of the list. Perched on a slender pinnacle reached only by laboring up 140 steps, Ayia Triada really does seem to belong to another world. The one monk who lives here is usually glad to see visitors and show them around the **church, refectory,** and **courtyard.** Don't miss the **winch,** for years used to bring up supplies and visitors. If this monastery looks more familiar to you than the others, perhaps you remember it from the James Bond movie

For Your Eyes Only, which was filmed here. If you want to walk the 3km (2 miles) back to Kalambaka from here, ask to be pointed toward the footpath.

© **24320/22-220.** Admission 2€. Usually daily 9am–5pm. Sometimes closed Thurs and/or Fri.

Ayios Nikolaos Anapaphsas ★   This little 14th-century monastery, approached by a relatively gentle path, has splendid **frescoes** by the 16th-century Cretan painter Theophanes the Monk. Don't miss the delightful fresco of the Garden of Eden, with elephants, fantastic beasts, and all manner of fruits and flowers. A good painting of the death of St. Ephraim the Syrian shows scenes from the saint's life, including the pillar atop which he lived for many years in the Syrian desert.

In recent years, when I have visited Ayiou Nikolaos, no monks have been in residence; because tour buses often rush past here to get to the Great Meteoron, you may find that you have this spot all to yourself.

© **24320/22-375.** Admission 2€. Daily 9am–5pm. Often closed Fri and in winter.

Ayios Stefanos ★   Founded in the 14th century, Ayios Stefanos, now a nunnery, is almost on the outskirts of Kalambaka. A bridge from the main road makes it easy to get here. The nuns usually make you feel glad that you've come and sometimes sell reasonably priced embroideries. Ayios Stefanos was badly damaged in both World War II and the Civil War that followed. Many priceless frescoes were defaced and others were destroyed, but the monastery's most famous relic was saved: the **head of St. Charalambos,** whose powers include warding off illness. There's also a small **museum** here, with ecclesiastical robes and paraphernalia. Recently, the nuns have been restoring sections of the monastery that had been allowed to decline. Donations are always welcome.

© **24320/22-279.** Admission 2€. Usually Tues–Sun 9am–4pm.

The Great Meteoron ★★   Although the Great Meteoron was founded in the 14th century, most of what you see here was built in the 16th century by monks from the Holy Mountain of Mount Athos. The **church** here is especially splendid, in the form of a Greek cross inscribed on a square, topped by a **12-sided dome.** Once your eyes get accustomed to the darkness, you'll be able to enjoy the elaborate **frescoes.** If you look up to the dome, you'll see Christ, with the four evangelists, apostles, and prophets arranged below, the church fathers by the altar, and the liturgical feasts of the church year along the walls of the nave. There's also a rather bloodcurdling *Last Judgment* and *Punishment of the Damned* in the narthex. After visiting the church, you may wish to sit awhile in the shady courtyard before visiting the small **museum,** which has a collection of icons and illustrated religious texts. Don't miss the **wine cellar,** whose enormous wooden barrels suggest that monastic life is not all prayer and meditation.

© **24320/22-278.** Admission 2€. Wed–Mon 9am–5pm.

Roussanou ★   Roussanou is relatively accessible, thanks to its restored bridge. This 13th-century monastery is now a nunnery, whose inhabitants are usually much more jolly than the monks. If the nuns offer you sweets while you sit in the courtyard between the refectory and the octagonal-domed church, be sure to leave a contribution in the church collection box.

No phone. Admission 2€. Thurs–Tues 9am–5pm.

Varlaam ★★   A narrow bridge from the main road runs to this 16th-century monastery, which was named for a hermit who lived here in the 14th century and built a tiny chapel on this promontory. The **chapel,** considerably enlarged and decorated with **frescoes,** is now an annex of the main church. Varlaam's founders were two brothers from Ioannina, who considered Ioannina's monastery and lakeside scenery too sybaritic. Presumably the brothers found the Meteora's harsh landscape more to their liking: According to legend, they had to drive away the monster who lived in a cave on the summit before they could settle here. The nicest thing about Varlaam is its **garden;** the monks who sometimes sit here are often willing to chat with visitors.

© **24320/22-277.** Admission 2€. Sat–Wed 9am–4pm (and Fri in summer).

THE CATHEDRAL OF THE DORMITION OF THE VIRGIN & THE CENTER OF CONTEMPORARY ART

After visiting the monasteries of the Meteora, you may find it a relief to know that there's only one church to see back in Kalambaka: the 12th-century Cathedral of the Dormition of the Virgin, which is often locked. If it's open, take a look at the frescoes, which date from the 12th to the 16th centuries. Keep an eye out for the ancient marble blocks and column drums pilfered by this church's builders from the earlier Temple of Apollo. An admission fee of 2€ is sometimes charged.

For a complete change of subject and mood, head to the **Center of Contemporary Art,** 38 Patriarchou Dimitriou (*©* **24320/22-346**), which houses the extensive private collection of Leonidas Beltsios, the important contemporary Greek art collector. The museum is officially open daily 9am to 3pm and 5 to 9pm.

SHOPPING

A lot of tourist shops in Kalambaka (most of which close for the winter) sell the usual carved wooden canes and spoons, rugs, ceramics, and more rugs. One shop worth a look: **Kava Nikos,** on the main drag, 114 Trikalon (*©*/fax **24320/77-881**). This small liquor shop carries a good selection of wines both in the bottle and from the barrel, and also stocks local Macedonian and Thessalian *tsipouro,* a firewater that makes ouzo seem like a delicate aperitif. If you're lucky enough to be in Kalambaka on a Friday, you can join the crowd at the **farmers' market** that spills onto the streets off Kondyli. Many of the monasteries have small gift shops with religious items.

Where to Stay

For centuries, visitors have speculated on why monks and nuns chose to lead isolated lives high on the inhospitable cliffs of the Meteora. I'm beginning to think it was because they knew what was coming: In the last few years, **Kalambaka** has almost doubled in size, changing from a rather ho-hum small town to a rather ugly large town.

Kalambaka's best feature is still its three plateias, with their fountains, cafes, and restaurants, strung out along the main drag, **Trikalon.** Unfortunately, many pleasant stone buildings with tile roofs have been torn down and replaced with the architecturally tedious buildings that are infesting so much of Greece. The once-sleepy village of **Kastraki,** a few miles closer to the monasteries, has virtually been absorbed by Kalambaka's sprawl. That said, I still stay in Kalambaka or Kastraki when I visit, because I enjoy driving up to the monasteries early and late, when they are closed, and you can sit and enjoy the view the monks and nuns have before the tour buses arrive. Just out of Kalambaka itself, the low-key, family-run 16-unit **Pension Arsenis** (www.arsenis-meteora.gr; *©* **24320/23-500**) has a highly praised restaurant, wonderful views, helpful hosts, and well-cared-for simple rooms; doubles from 50€.

In Kastraki, the views at the 24-room **Doupiani House** (www.doupianihouse.com; *©* **24320/ 77-555**) are great and the prices reasonable (doubles officially start at 80€, but are often considerably less). Some visitors have praised the hosts and restaurant—while others have found the food mediocre and the hosts elusive. A lot can depend on whether your visit overlaps with the visit of a tour group, when things can become hectic. Most of the hotels here considerably lower prices off season and when tourists are few—although Japanese tour groups seem to flock here in winter months when, it must be said, the mists and fog around the cliffs are absolutely stunning.

Amalia ★★ This rather handsome hotel—with two restaurants, a souvenir shop, and a pool—looks almost like a small village from the road. The large guest rooms (most with balconies) are decorated in soft colors, and bathrooms have actual shower stalls. A couple of drawbacks: Like most other Amalia hotels, this one is located too far out of town to make walking back and forth on the main road appealing—or safe. Nonetheless, this is a very comfortable place to stay, although you may find yourself feeling like an outsider if tour groups or a large wedding party occupy all the other rooms. By the way, the website photo makes the pool look enormous. It is not.

Outside Kalambaka on the Meteora rd., 42200 Kalambaka. www.amalia.gr. ℂ **24320/72-216.** Fax 24320/72-457. 173 units. 110€–200€ double. Rates include breakfast buffet. Often significantly cheaper off season. AE, DC, MC, V. **Amenities:** Restaurant; bar; concierge; pool; room service. *In room:* A/C, TV, hair dryer, Internet, minibar.

Divani Motel ★★ In 2007, the Divani first appeared in *Odyssey* magazine's prestigious list of the best hotels in Greece, and has made several appearances since then. I still think that the Amalia's pool (flanked by a cafe and garden, as opposed to the parking lot) and general facilities give the more expensive Divani stiff competition. You may be swayed toward the Divani by its fine views toward the Meteora from the balconied rooms at the back. In addition to its gym, the Divani now boasts its own spa, with Jacuzzis, indoor pool, and steam baths. Like the Amalia, this is also a popular spot for wedding and baptism receptions, so you may get to spy on Kalambaka society.

Outside Kalambaka on the Meteora rd., 42200 Kalambaka. www.divanis.gr. ℂ **24320/23-330.** Fax 24320/23-638. 165 units. 120€–220€ double. Often significantly cheaper off season. AE, DC, MC, V. **Amenities:** Restaurant; bar; gym; pool; spa. *In room:* A/C, TV, hair dryer, minibar, Wi-Fi.

Hotel Meteora ★ ✦ The price is right, some rooms have balconies with Meteora views, the location is quiet, and the helpful managers, Niko and Kosta Gekas, make this a good budget choice. *Warning:* There is also a much larger, much more expensive Hotel Meteora (www.meteorahotels.com) in Kastraki. It's okay, but not a more cozy budget choice!

14 Ploutarchou, 42200 Kalambaka. gekask@otenet.gr. ℂ **24320/22-367.** Fax 24320/75-550. 20 units. 70€ double. Rates include breakfast. No credit cards. **Amenities:** Internet. *In room:* A/C, TV, fridge, hair dryer.

Where to Eat

I've never had a drop-dead wonderful meal in Meteora—maybe the influence of the monks inhibits exploration of haute cuisine. The places I suggest are perfectly fine but not memorable. One advantage of Kalambaka's recent growth: There are now plenty of cafes selling ice cream and sweets along Trikalon, Kalambaka's main street.

Gertzos (aka the Meteora) ★ GREEK This simple taverna (with good local wines) has been in Kalambaka for more than 50 years, serving standard Greek fare but also offering spicy meat and vegetable dishes that reflect the owner's Greek heritage in Asia Minor.

4 Economou, Plateia Dimarchiou. *©* **24320/22-316.** Main courses 7€–15€. No credit cards. Daily noon–
11pm, but sometimes only open for lunch off season and usually completely closed Jan–Feb. sometimes
longer.

Panellino GREEK When I was once here on a chilly but beautiful February visit
to the Meteora, Panellino (on Plateia Dimarchiou, across from the bus stop) was
resolutely open when many other places were closed. The menu consisted of the
usual chops and stews, as well as vegetable dishes.

Plateia Dimarchiou. *©* **24320/24-735.** Main courses 7€–14€. No credit cards. Usually open daily
noon–11pm.

Vakhos ★ GREEK If you've eaten at Vakhos before, don't go to the restaurant with
a small garden that you remember in the center of town. Instead, head out of Kalambaka as if you were going to the Meteora monasteries to the new Vakhos restaurant.
It does a serious business with tour groups and local weddings and baptisms and can
seat 700 inside and out. The menu has a wide range of traditional Greek dishes,
including sweets, so you don't have to search out a *zacheroplasteion* (sweet shop) for
dessert. The view of the Meteora cliffs is splendid and the restaurant's motto, "Gas-
tronomy has also its beauties," shows that the Vakhos is not relying on the view alone
to please customers.

Plateia Demetriou A. *©* **24320/24-678.** www.vakhos.gr. Main courses 8€–14€. No credit cards. Daily
noon–11pm. Open all year.

THE SPORADES

by John S. Bowman

With their excellent golden sand beaches, fragrant pine trees, and unspoiled villages, you might think that the Sporades ("Scattered") islands have always been major tourist magnets. But because these islands lack major archaeological remains and historical associations, foreigners traditionally headed elsewhere in Greece.

These days, however, the Sporades are no longer the natural retreats they once were. **Skiathos** becomes extremely crowded in high season—although in spring and fall it can be lovely and relaxing. Even in summer, it's worth a visit by those interested in a beach vacation, good food, and active nightlife. **Skopelos** is nearly as bustling as Skiathos in the high season, but isn't quite as sophisticated. Its beaches are fewer and less impressive, but Skopelos town is among the more attractive ports in Greece, and the island offers some pleasant excursions. These two most popular islands also have fine restaurants, fancy hotels, and an international (heavily British) following.

More remote **Skyros** hardly seems a part of the group, especially as its landscape and architecture are more Cycladic. But it has a few excellent beaches, as well as a colorful local culture, and it remains a fine destination for those who want to get away from the crowds. Although space limits do not allow us to describe Alinossos, the fourth of these islands, it might be attractive to those seeking a less popular, more natural island.

Strategies for Seeing the Islands

If you have only 1 to 3 days, plan on seeing just one of the Sporades. (Technically, by the way, these are the Northern Sporades.) If you have a bit more time, you will be able to get a ship directly from various ports (identified below) and a plane in the case of Skiathos and Skyros; if time is a factor, we strongly advise flying to Skiathos or Skyros and staying there. If you have more time, you can continue around the islands via hydrofoils (known as Flying Dolphins) or ferryboats. (**Note:** The frequency of all connections is cut back considerably between September and May.)

Museum & Site Hours Update

If you visit the Sporades during the summer, check to see when museums and sites are open. They do not always maintain the hours that are officially posted, and most will be closed at least 1 day a week.

SKIATHOS ★

108km (58 nautical miles) from Ayios Konstandinos, which is 166km (103 miles) from Athens

Skiathos, which remained isolated and agrarian until the early 1970s, has become a "package-tour" island, and during high season, Skiathos town can feel like a shopping mall. By the same token, it has some elegant shops, fine restaurants, and a lively nightlife. If you can, come off season when the town and beaches are less crowded.

Essentials

GETTING THERE   By Plane   Olympic Air has service daily (twice daily Apr–May, five times daily June–Sept) from Athens; contact **www.olympicair.com** or the Athens office (✆ **210/966-6666**) for information and reservations. At this time, Olympic does not maintain an office in Skiathos town, but can be reached at the nearby **airport** (✆ **24270/22-049**). Public bus service to and from the airport is so infrequent that everyone takes a taxi; expect to pay about 10€ depending on your destination.

By Boat   Skiathos can be reached by either ferryboat (3 hr.) or hydrofoil (1½ hr.) from Volos or Ayios Konstandinos. (Volos is at least a 4-hr. bus ride from Athens, Ayios Konstandinos a 3-hr. bus ride.) From Kimi on Evvia, there is also hydrofoil service (50 min.) and ferryboat service (4 hr.). In high season, there are frequent hydrofoils daily from Volos and from Ayios Konstandinos, as well as service from Thessaloniki (3 hr.). Hydrofoils also link Skiathos to Skopelos (30–45 min.), Alonissos (60–75 min.), and Skyros (2⅓ hr.).

In Athens, **Alkyon Travel,** 97 Akademias, near Kanigos Square (✆ **210/383-2545;** www.alkyontravel.com), can arrange bus transportation from Athens to Ayios Konstandinos, and hydrofoil or ferry tickets. Alkyon will not take phone reservations—in person sales only. The 3-hour bus ride costs about 20€ one-way.

For hydrofoil (Flying Dolphins) schedules and information, contact the **Hellenic Seaways,** Akti Kondyli and 2 Aitolikou, Piraeus (www.hellenicseaways.gr; ✆ **210/419-9000**). For ferryboat information from Piraeus, contact the **G.A. Ferries** line in Piraeus (www.ferries.gr/gaferries; ✆ **210/458-2640**). Ferry tickets can be purchased at travel agencies in Athens or on the islands. During high season, I recommend that you purchase your boat tickets in advance through the boat lines. While you may purchase tickets at Alkyon in person, they will not reserve ferryboat or hydrofoil tickets for you in advance, and these often sell out.

VISITOR INFORMATION   The town maintains an **information booth** at the western corner of the harbor; in summer, at least, it's open daily from about 9am to 8pm. Meanwhile, private travel agencies abound and can help with most of your requests. We highly recommend **Mare Nostrum Holidays,** 21 Papadiamandis (✆ **24270/21-463;** marenost@otenet.gr), which since 2009 has been part of the Heliotropio Travel Group. It books villas, hotels, and rooms; sells tickets to many around-the-island, hydrofoil, and beach caique (skiff) trips; books Olympic Air flights; exchanges currency; and changes traveler's checks without commission. The staff speak excellent English, are exceedingly well informed, and have lots of tips on everything from beaches to restaurants. The office is open daily from 8am to 10pm.

GETTING AROUND   By Bus   Skiathos has public bus service along the south coast of the island from the bus station on the harbor to Koukounaries (5€), with stops at the beaches in between. A conductor will ask for your destination and assess the fare after the bus starts moving. Buses run at least six times daily April through November; every hour from 9am to 9pm May through October; every half-hour from

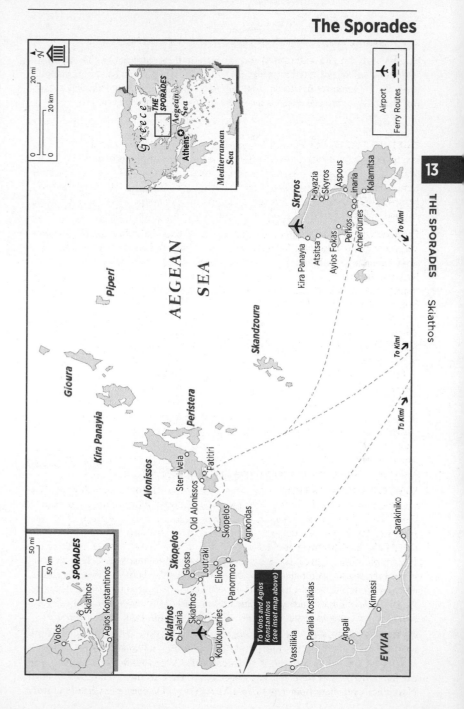

Airport
Ferry Routes

Skyros

Mavazia
Aspous
Inaria
Kalamitsa
Skyros
Pefkos
Atsitsa
Ayios Fokas
Acheroúnes
Kira Panayia

To Kimi

AEGEAN

SEA

Piperi

Skandzoura

Gioura

Kira Panayia

Peristera

Alonissos

Ster Vela
Fatitiri

Old Alonissos

Skopelos
Agnondas

To Kimi

To Kimi

Sarakiniko

Skopelos

Glossa
Loutraki
Ellos
Panormos

Skiathos

Lalaria
Skiathos
Koukounaries

To Volos and Agios
Konstantinos
(see inset map above)

Vassilikia
Paralia Kostikias
Angali
Kimassi

EVVIA

20 mi
20 km

Greece
THE
SPORADES
Aegean Sea
Athens
Mediterranean Sea

50 mi
50 km

SPORADES

Volos
Skiathos
Agios Konstantinos

8:30am to 10pm June through September; and every 20 minutes from 8:30am to 2:30pm and 3:30pm to midnight July through August.

By Car & Moped   Reliable car and moped agencies, all on the *paralia* (shore road), include **Avis** (☏ **24270/21-458**), run by the friendly Yannis Theofanidis; **Aivalioti's Rent-A-Car** (☏ **24270/21-246**); and **National-Alamo** (☏ **24270/23-308**). In high season, expect to pay 60€ to 100€ per day; weekly rates are significantly cheaper. Mopeds start at about 35€ per day.

By Boat   The north-coast beaches, adjacent islands, and historic kastro are most easily reached by caique; these smaller vessels, which post their beach and island tour schedules on signs, sail frequently from the fishing harbor west of the Bourtzi fortress. An around-the-island tour that includes stops at Lalaria Beach and the kastro will cost about 50€.

The Flying Dolphins agent, **Skiathos Holidays,** on the *paralia,* is open from 7am to 9:30pm; in high season there are as many as eight high-speed hydrofoils daily to Skopelos and Alonissos. (I feel the extra cost for the hydrofoils is worth it for traveling among the Sporades islands for the time saved.) There are also daily excursions to Skyros in high season. Call ☏ **24270/22-018** for up-to-date schedules. Note that even if you have a ticket, you must appear at the agent's ticket office at least 30 minutes before the scheduled sailing to get your ticket confirmed and seat assigned. **Vasilis Nikolaou** (☏ **24270/22-209**), the travel agent at the corner of the *paralia* and Papadiamandis, sells tickets for the ferryboats to the other islands.

FAST FACTS   The official **American Express** agent is Mare Nostrum Holidays, 21 Papadiamandis (☏ **24270/21-463;** marenost@otenet.gr), open daily from 8am to 10pm. There are many banks in town, such as the **National Bank of Greece,** Papadiamandis, open Monday through Friday from 8am to 2pm and 7 to 9pm, and Sunday from 9am to noon. The **hospital** (☏ **24270/22-040**) is on the coast road at the far-west edge of town. For **Internet access,** try Internet Zone Cafe, 28 Evangelistrias (zonecafe@hotmail.com).

The **police station** (☏ **24270/21-111**) is about 250m (820 ft.) from the harbor on Papadiamandis, on the left. The **tourist police** booth is about 15m (49 ft.) farther along on the right. The **post office** (☏ **24270/22-011**) is on Papadiamandis, away from the harbor about 160m (525 ft.) and on the right; it's open Monday through Friday from 7:30am to 2pm. The **telephone office** (**OTE;** ☏ **24270/22-135**) is on Papadiamandis, on the right, some 30m (98 ft.) beyond the post office. It's open Monday through Friday from 7:30am to 10pm, Saturday and Sunday from 9am to 2pm and 5 to 10pm.

What to See & Do

Skiathos is a relatively modern town, built in 1930 on two low-lying hills, then reconstructed after heavy German bombardment during World War II. The handsome **Bourtzi Fortress** (originally from the 13th c., but greatly rebuilt across the centuries) jutting into the middle of the harbor is on an islet connected by a broad causeway. Ferries and hydrofoils stop at the port on the right (east) of the fortress, while fishing boats and excursion caiques dock on the left (west). Whitewashed villas with red-tile roofs line both sides of the harbor. The small church of **Ayios Nikolaos** dominates the hill on the east side, as does the larger church of **Trion Ierarchon (Three Archbishops)** on the west side.

The main street leading away from the harbor and up through town is named **Papa-diamandis,** after the island's best-known son (see the Papadiamandis House, below). Here you'll find numerous restaurants, cafes, and stores, plus services such as Mare Nostrum Holidays, the post office, the telephone office, and the tourist police.

On the west flank of the harbor (the left as you disembark from the ferry) are outdoor cafes and restaurants, excursion caiques (for the north-coast beaches, adjacent islands, and around-the-island tours) and, at the far corner, the stepped ramp (above the Oasis Café) leading up to the town's next level. Mounting these broad steps will lead you to **Plateia Trion Ierarchon,** a stone-paved square around the town's most important church. The eastern flank, technically the New Paralia, is home to many tourist services as well as a few recommended hotels and many restaurants. At the far end, the harbor-front road branches to the right along the yacht harbor—an important nightlife area in summer, and to the left toward the airport and points of interest inland.

The Papadiamandis House Alexandros Papadiamandis (1851–1911) was born on Skiathos, and after his adult career as a journalist in Athens, he returned in 1908 and died in this house. His nearly 200 short stories and novellas, mostly about Greek island life, assured him a major reputation in Greece, but his rather idiosyncratic style and vernacular language make his work difficult to translate into foreign languages. His house is less a museum than a shrine containing personal possessions and tools of his writing trade. (A statue of Papadiamandis stands in front of the Bourtzi Fortress on the promontory at the corner of the harbor.) And if you want to read some of his stories, look for *Tales from a Greek Island* (Johns Hopkins University Press).

An alley to right of Papadiamandis (main street), 50m (164 ft.) up from harbor. (C) **24270/23-843.** Admission 3€. Tues–Sun 9:30am–1pm and 5–8pm.

Skiathos Riding Center ☺ This is the perfect place for a half-day excursion and activity, with or without children. It's just off the road to Koukounaries beach so could be combined with a visit to that beach. Nikos Drakos started the center in 1990 and continues to breed his own horses here. Anita Reize now operates it with him. The center offers guided walks for small groups (a maximum of four people) of different levels of riders on a selection of tours including an early morning beach walk. The horses, by the way, are of only medium size so novices will not feel intimidated. The center provides donkey rides for children and also maintains a small farm-zoo and playground.

On route to Koukounaries beach after crossroad to Ayia Eleni beach. (C) **24270/49-548.** www.skiathos-horse-riding.gr. Walks cost between 30€–45€; donkey rides are 5€; private lessons are 25€ for about 40 min.

BEACHES

Skiathos is famous for its beaches, and I'll cover the most important ones briefly, proceeding clockwise from the port. The most popular beaches are west of town along 12km (8 miles) of coastal highway. At most of them, you can rent an umbrella and two chairs for about 15€ per day.

The first, **Megali Ammos,** is the sandy strip below the popular package-tour com-munity of Ftelia. It's so close to town and so packed with groups it probably won't appeal to most. **Vassilias** and **Achladias** are also crowded and developed; **Tzane-rias** and **Nostos** are slight improvements. Farther out on the Kalamaki peninsula, south of the highway, **Kanapitsa** is good for fans of watersports; **Kanapitsa Water-Sport Center** ((C) **24270/21-298**) has water and jet skis, windsurfing, air chairs, sailing, and speedboat hire. Scuba divers will want to stop at **Dolphin Diving Center** ((C) **24270/21-599**) at the big Nostos Hotel.

Across the peninsula, **Vromolimnos (Dirty Lake)** is fairly attractive and relatively uncrowded, perhaps because of its unsavory name and the cloudy (but not polluted) water. The beach offers water-skiing and windsurfing. **Koulos** and **Ayia Paraskevi** are fairly well regarded. **Platanias,** the next major beach, isn't crowded, perhaps because the big resort hotels here have their own pools and sun decks. Past the next headland, **Troulos** is one of the prettiest beaches, due to its relative isolation, crescent shape, and the islets that guard the small bay. Nearby is **Victoria Leisure Center** (© 24270/49-467), which has rooms to rent, a pool, shops, and two tennis courts.

The last bus stop is at much ballyhooed **Koukounaries ★★,** 16km (10 miles) from Skiathos town. The bus chugs uphill past the Pallas Hotel luxury resort, then descends and winds alongside the inland waterway, Lake Strofilias, stopping at the edge of a fragrant pine forest. *Koukounaries* means "pine cones" in Greek, and behind this grove of trees is a half-mile–long stretch of fine gold sand in a half-moon-shaped cove. Tucked into the evergreen fold are some changing rooms, a small snack bar, and the concessionaires for beach chairs, umbrellas, and windsurfers. The beach can be extremely crowded but with an easy mix of families and singles. (There are several hotels near the beach, but because of the intense mosquito activity and construction, I recommend staying back in town or along the coast road.)

Ayia Eleni, a short but scenic walk from the Koukounaries bus stop (the end of the line) west across the island's tip, is a broad cove popular for windsurfing, as the wind is a bit stronger than at the south-coast beaches but not nearly as gusty as at the north. Across the peninsula, at the far right end of the beach, 15 to 20 minutes of fairly steep grade from the Koukounaries bus stop, is **Banana Beach ★** (sometimes called Krassa). It's slightly less crowded than Koukounaries, but with the same sand and pine trees. There's a snack bar or two, plus chairs, umbrellas, windsurfers, and jet skis for rent. One stretch of Banana Beach is the island's most fashionable nude beach.

Limonki Xerxes, also called Mandraki, north across the island's tip, a 20-minute walk up the path opposite the Lake Strofilias bus stop, is the cove where Xerxes brought in 10 triremes (galleys) to conquer the Hellenic fleet moored at Skiathos during the Persian Wars. It's a pristine and relatively secluded beach. **Elia,** east across the little peninsula, is also quite nice. Both beaches have small refreshment kiosks.

Continuing along the northeast coast from Mandraki, you arrive at **Megalos Aselinos,** a windy beach where free camping has taken root. It is linked to the southern coastal highway via the road that leads to the Panagia Kounistria monastery (see below). You must continue north when the main road forks off to the right toward the monastery. There's an official campsite and a good taverna. **Mikros Aselinos,** farther east, is smaller and quieter, and you can reach it via a dirt road that leads off to the left just before the monastery.

Skiathos's north coast is much more rugged and scenic, with steep cliffs, pine forests, rocky hills, and caves. Most of these beaches are accessible only by boat, and of these, one is well worth the effort: **Lalaria ★,** on the island's northern tip, is one of Greece's most picturesque beaches (although it is a pebble beach). One of its unique qualities is the **Tripia Petra,** perforated rock cliffs that jut into the sea on both sides of the cove. These have been worn through by the wind and the waves to form archways. You can lie on the gleaming white pebbles and admire the neon-blue Aegean and cloudless sky through their openings. The water at Lalaria is an especially vivid shade of aquamarine because of the reflective white pebbles and marble and limestone slabs that coat the sea bottom. The swimming is excellent, but the undertow can be quite strong; inexperienced swimmers should not venture far. There are several naturally carved caves in the cliff wall that lines the beach, providing privacy or shade for those who have had too much sun. Lalaria is reached by caique excursions from the port; the fare is about 40€ for an around-the-island trip, which usually includes a stop for lunch (not included in the fare) at one of the other beaches along the northwest coast.

Three of the island's most spectacular grottoes—**Skotini, Glazia,** and **Halkini**—are just east of Lalaria. Spilia Skotini is particularly impressive, a fantastic 6m-high (20-ft.) sea cave reached through a narrow crevice in the cliff wall just wide enough for caiques to squeeze through. Seagulls drift above you in the cave's cool darkness, while below, fish swim in the 9m (30-ft.) subsurface area. Erosion has created spectacular scenery and many sandy coves along the north and east coasts, though none are as beautiful or well sheltered from the *meltemi* (high winds) as Lalaria beach.

THE KASTRO & THE MONASTERIES

When you want a change from the beach, I recommend an excursion to the **Kastro ★,** the old fortress-capital on the northernmost point of the island, east of Lalaria beach. The kastro was built in a remote and spectacular site in the 16th century, when the island was overrun by the Turks. It was abandoned shortly after the War of Independence. Once joined to firm ground by a drawbridge, it can now be reached by cement stairs. The remains of the more than 300 houses and 22 churches have mostly fallen to the sea, but three of the churches, porcelain plates embedded in their worn stucco facades, still stand, and the original frescoes of one are still visible. From this citadel prospect there are excellent views to the **Kastronisia** islet below and the sparkling Aegean. Kastro can be reached by excursion caique (with a fairly demanding climb from the beach), overland by mule or donkey tour (available through most travel agencies), or by car via the road that leads northeast out of town, passing the turnoff to the Moni Evangelistrias (see below), and continuing on to the end near the church of Panagia Kardasi. From here it is a mildly demanding 2km (1-mile) walk.

Moni Evangelistrias ★ is the more rewarding of the two monasteries that draw many visitors. Public buses travel here sporadically, but with your own vehicle it can be easily visited in not much more than an hour from Skiathos town. (Driving will also allow you to stop and admire the views.) To get here, take the road out of the northeast end and pass by the turnoff to the airport. After less than a kilometer (½ mile), take the sharp right turnoff (signed) and climb about 3km (2 miles) to the monastery. Dating from the late 18th century, it has been completely (but authentically) restored; its architecture, icons, and woodcarvings make the trip worthwhile.

The other monastery, **Panagia Kounistria,** is approached from the coastal highway along the beaches (described above); just before Troulos Beach, take the right branch of the road (signed SELINOS) and climb about 4km (2½ miles) to the monastery. The 17th-century structure contains some fine icons (although its most important icon is now displayed in the Tris Ierarches Church in Skiathos town).

SHOPPING

Skiathos town has no shortage of shops, many offering standard wares but some with distinctive items. The highlight for Greek crafts and folk art is **Archipelago** (© 24270/22-163); adjacent to the Papadiamandis House, it offers a world-class assemblage of objects of art and folklore, both old and new, including textiles, jewelry, and sculpture. **Galerie Varsakis ★** (© 24270/22-255), on Trion Ierarchon Square above the fishing port, also has a nearly museum-quality collection of folk antiques, embroidered bags and linens, rugs from around the world, and other collectibles. Less stylish but full of curiosities is **Gallery Seraina** (© **24270/22-390**), at the first junction of Papadiamandis (opposite the alleyway to the Papadiamandis House); it has a selection of ceramic plates, jewelry, some textiles, and unusual glass lampshades.

Where to Stay

Between July 1 and September 15, it can be very difficult to find accommodations. Try calling ahead from Athens to book a room or book before you leave home. Note that many of the "luxury" hotels were thrown up quickly some years ago, and some have since been managed and maintained poorly—so if you plan an extended stay at a beach resort, we recommend you first check into one of the hotels in town and then look over the possibilities before you commit to an extended rental.

If you crave the restaurant/shopping/nightlife scene, or you've arrived without reservations at one of the resort communities, try setting up base in **Skiathos Town.** From here, you can take public buses to the beaches on the south coast or go on caique excursions to the spectacular north coast or other islands.

Families often prefer to stay in two- to four-bedroom villas outside of town or at hotels overlooking a beach, with only an occasional foray into town.

One of the most pleasant parts of Skiathos town is the quiet neighborhood on the hill above the bay at the western end of the port. Numerous **private rooms** to let can be found on and above the winding stairs/street. Take a walk and look for the signs, or ask a travel agent. All over the hillside above the eastern harbor are several "hotels," basically rooms to rent. You'll be surprised at which buildings turn out to be lodgings.

By the way, the in-town hotels (Alkyon excepted) cannot provide adjacent parking, but there are possibilities at the harbor's far eastern edge.

IN & AROUND SKIATHOS TOWN

In addition to the following options, consider **Hotel Athos,** on the "ring road" that skirts Skiathos town (©/fax **24270/22-4777**), which offers ready access to town without the bustle; and **Hotel Meltemi,** on the *paralia* (© **24270/22-493**), a comfortable, modern place on the east side of the harbor (the front units can be noisy).

Babis Hotel ★ ✦ A most appealing choice for those who want to stay in town, have a limited budget, and like to relax at their own pace. There's no bar or restaurant but half of the units have fully equipped kitchenettes (including microwave) and the others have the means for making coffee or tea. There is also a good-size terrace where with a barbecue stove and where you can sit and enjoy a fabulous view over the whole harbor and much of the town. A homey place—the proprietors will provide free transportation to and from the airport if you've kept them informed of your schedule. There are bicycles available for rent. There is a slight climb up from the harbor so the hotel is not really suitable for anyone with mobility problems. All in all, it's a true find.

On hill facing New Harbor (approached by steps) 37002 Skiathos. babispension@hotmail.com. © **24270/21-968.** 14 units. 65€ double. MC, V. Parking at edge of town. **Amenities:** Wi-Fi. *In room:* A/C, TV, fridge.

Bourtzi Boutique Hotel ★★★ This is a contemporary luxury hotel in the heart of Skiathos Town. Yes, and expensive by Greek island in-town standards but not by international standards, and so for some, well worth a few nights here. Aside from each room's stylish decor and amenities, the outdoor swimming pool, the furnished balconies, and the classy **cocktail bar** (which serves light snacks), what make this a true pleasure to come back to after a day on the island is the impeccable staff and service. You're close to everything in town but rooms are soundproofed, but while you're at it, ask for a room that faces the garden in the back.

8 Moraitou (just off and midway up Papadiamandis), 37002 Skiathos. www.hotelbourtzi.gr. © **24270/ 21-304.** 38 units. 145€–175€ double. Rates include breakfast. MC, V. Parking at edge of town. **Amenities:** Bar; outdoor swimming pool; free Wi-Fi in public areas. *In room:* A/C, TV, fridge, hair dryer.

Hotel Morfo   Looking for a slightly "atmospheric" offbeat hotel and not too fussy about creature comforts? Turn right off the main street opposite the National Bank, then left at the plane tree (there's a sign). You'll find this attractive hotel on your left on a back street in the center of town. You enter through a small garden into a festively decorated lobby. The rooms are comfortable if basic, but you can't beat the rates.

23 Anainiou, 37002 Skiathos. © **24270/21-737.** Fax 24270/23-222. 17 units. 40€ double. No credit cards. No parking. *In room:* A/C, fridge, hair dryer.

Hotel Orsa ★★   This is one of the most charming small hotels in town on the western promontory beyond the fishing harbor. To get here, walk down along the west port all the way past the fish stalls, proceed up two flights of steps, and watch for a recessed courtyard on the left, with handsome wrought-iron details. Rooms are standard in size but tastefully decorated; most have windows or balconies overlooking the harbor and the islands beyond. A lovely garden terrace is a perfect place for a tranquil breakfast. For advance booking, contact **Heliotropio Travel** on the harbor's east end (© **24270/22-430;** fax 24270/21-952; info@heliotropio.gr).

Plakes 37002 Skiathos. www.heliotropio.gr. © **24270/22-430.** 17 units. 75€ double. Rates include breakfast. Credit cards for reservation only; payment in cash. No parking. **Amenities:** Breakfast terrace. *In room:* A/C, fridge, hair dryer.

ON THE BEACH

Atrium Hotel ★★   This is one of the class acts of Skiathos hotels. Its location (on a pine clad slope overlooking the sea) plus amenities make the Atrium Hotel a most pleasant place to vacation. Admittedly, the shady beach is some 100m (330 ft.) below and across the road, but the hotel's beautiful pool sits on a plaza high above the Aegean. The rooms have balconies or terraces that offer views over the sea. The hotel has a popular **bar** and **restaurant;** if you like, you can enjoy your meal outdoors on the veranda. I've always found the desk personnel and staff most courteous and helpful, but both the staff and guests here do expect a certain level of style in dress and conduct.

Platanias (some 8km/5 miles along the coast road southeast of Skiathos town), 37002 Skiathos. www. atriumhotel.gr. © **24270/49-345.** 75 units. 200€–260€ double. Rates include buffet breakfast. MC, V. Parking on grounds. **Amenities:** Restaurant; bar; babysitting; billiards; fitness room; Ping-Pong; pool; watersports equipment. *In room:* A/C, TV, fridge, hair dryer, Wi-Fi.

Troulos Bay Hotel ✦ ☺   Though it's not exactly luxurious, this would be my first choice among the island's beach hotels for those looking for an unpretentious and laid-back vacation—and especially for families with small children. It's on handsomely landscaped grounds on one of the south coast's prettiest little beaches. Like many of Skiathos's hotels, it's used primarily by groups, but individual rooms are often available. Guest rooms are modest but comfortably furnished; most have a balcony overlooking the beach and the lovely wooded islets beyond it. Everyone who stays here reports that they find the staff refreshingly hospitable and helpful.

Troulos (9km/6 miles along the coast road southeast of Skiathos, down from the Alpha Supermarket), 37002 Skiathos. www.troulosbayhotel.gr. © **24270/49-390.** 43 units. 110€ double; 140€ for family of 4. Rates include breakfast. MC, V. Parking on grounds. **Amenities:** Breakfast room; bar. *In room:* A/C (July–Aug only), TV, fridge.

Where to Eat

As in most of Greece's overdeveloped tourist resorts, cafes, fast-food stands, and overpriced restaurants abound, but there are also plenty of good—even excellent—eateries in Skiathos town. Some of the best-regarded restaurants are above the west end of the harbor, around Trion Ierarchon church.

EXPENSIVE

Asprolithos ★ GREEK/INTERNATIONAL   An elegant ambience, friendly and attentive service, and superb meals of light, updated taverna fare make this one of our favorite places to dine on Skiathos. You can get a classic moussaka here if you want to play it safe, or try specialties like artichokes and prawns smothered in cheese. The excellent snapper baked in wine with wild greens is served with thick french fries that have obviously never seen a freezer. A handsome stone fireplace dominates the main dining room. You can sit at outdoor tables and catch the breeze.

Mavroyiali and Korai (up Papadiamandis a block past the high school and then turn right). ℂ **24270/ 21-016.** Reservations recommended. Main courses 8€–22€. MC, V. Daily 6pm–midnight. Closed late Oct to mid-Mar.

The Windmill Restaurant ★★ INTERNATIONAL   The town's most special dining experience is at an old windmill visible from the *paralia*. (You can approach it in several ways, but the signed route begins on the street between the back of the Akti and San Remo hotels at the eastern end of the harbor.) It is quite a climb, but well worth it.—and reservations are a must in high season You couldn't ask for a more romantic setting than on one of the terraces, where you can enjoy the sunset and then the lights of the town with your meal. The menu features a stylish version of basic dishes—fish, beef, lamb, pork, as well as vegetarian dishes. The desserts, too, are unusual, and there are many wines to choose from, including the best from Greece. A three-course meal with a modest wine will cost at least a 100€, but it's well worth it.

Located on peak east of Ayios Nikolaos church. ℂ **24270/24-550.** www.skiathoswindmill.gr. Reservations strongly recommended. Main courses 12€–25€. MC, V. Daily 7–11pm.

MODERATE

Carnayio Taverna TAVERNA/SEAFOOD   One of the better waterfront tavernas is next to Hotel Alkyon. Favorites over the years have been the fish soup, lamb *youvetsi* (lamb baked with pasta), and grilled fish. The garden setting is still special. If you're here late, you might be lucky enough to see a round of dancing waiters and diners.

Paralia. ℂ **24270/22-868.** Main courses 6€–18€. AE, V. Daily 8pm–1am.

Taverna Limanakia TAVERNA/SEAFOOD   In the style of its next-door neighbor Carnayio, the Limanakia serves some of the best taverna and seafood dishes on the waterfront. I always vacillate about which of the two neighbors I prefer, but always come away feeling satisfied after a meal at this reliable eatery.

Paralia (at far eastern end, past Hotel Alkyon). ℂ **24270/22-835.** Main courses 6€–18€. MC. Daily 6pm–midnight.

Taverna Mesoyia ★ TAVERNA   You'll have to exert yourself a bit to find some of the best authentic traditional food in town. This little taverna is in the midst of the town's most labyrinthine neighborhood, above the western end of the harbor, but there are signs once you approach it. Try an appetizer such as the fried zucchini balls, enjoy the evening specials, or go for fresh fish in season. (As all Greek restaurants are

A Local Favorite in Skiathos

I think the best-kept secret of Skiathos town is the **little outdoor cafe** at the tip of the promontory with the Bourtzi fortress, a 5-minute stroll from the harbor. Removed from the glitter of the town, you can sit and enjoy a (cheap) drink in the cool of the evening and watch the ships come and go: This is the Aegean lifestyle at its best.

supposed to, this one reveals when something is frozen—as some fish must be at certain times of the year, when they're illegal to catch.) You'll feel as though you're at an old-fashioned neighborhood bistro, not a large tourist attraction.

Grigoriou (follow the signs behind Trion Ierarchon, high above the western end of the harbor). ℭ **24270/21-440.** Main courses 8€–20€. No credit cards. Daily 7pm–midnight.

INEXPENSIVE

Kabourelia Ouzeri GREEK   Although it bills itself as an ouzeri—for drinks and snacks—this is really your standard taverna, and one of the most authentic eateries in town. Try the ouzo and octopus (which you can see drying on the front line) combo; or make a meal of the rich supply of cheese pies, fried feta, olives, and other piquant *mezedes*. It's a great place to sit and watch the activity along the waterfront while you linger over a modest but tasty meal.

Paralia (on harbor's western stretch). ℭ **24270/21-112.** Main courses 5€–15€. AE, MC, V. Daily 10am–1am.

Skiathos After Dark

The **Aegean Festival** takes place from late June to early October, offering occasional performances of ancient Greek tragedies and comedies, traditional music and dance, modern dance and theater, and visiting international troupes. Festival events take place in the outdoor theater at the **Bourtzi Cultural Center,** on the promontory on the harbor. (The center itself, open daily 10am–2pm and 5:30–10pm, hosts art exhibits in its interior.) Performances begin at 9:30pm and usually cost about 15€; call ℭ **24270/23-717** for information.

Although many may prefer to pass the evening with a *volta* (stroll) along the harbor or around and above the Plateia Trion Ierarchon, there is no denying that Skiathos town has a lively nightlife scene. I'll do my best to single out some of the more recently popular places, but I cannot be responsible for the frequent changes of names.

The main concentration of **nightclubs** is in the warren of streets west of Papadiamandis (left as you come up from the harbor). On Evangelistrias, the street opposite the post office is the **Blue Chips Club;** this street intersects with Polytechniou—also known as "Bar Street": you'll find **Destiny Bar,** the favorite—and lively—hangout for the gay crowd; the **Admiral Benbow Club,** which offers something a bit quiet; and the flashier **Spartacus.** At the next intersection south, you'll find **Kirki,** a more intimate bar. Wander back down Papadiamandis to find **Kentavros Bar,** on the left beyond the Papadiamandis House, which plays classic rock and jazz.

On the far west end of the harbor, if you want sports with your drinks, try **Oasis Cafe;** if there's a game of any sort going on, it'll be on the tube. Meanwhile, at the far eastern end of the harbor are a few clubs popular with the younger set—among them, **Remezzo** and **Rock 'n' Roll Bar.**

Movie fans might enjoy the open-air showings at **Attikon** (on Papadiamandis, opposite Mare Nostum Holidays) or at **Cinema Paradiso** (up along the "ring road"). Both have two shows nightly, the first around 8:30pm; tickets are 6€.

SKOPELOS

121km (65 nautical miles) from Ayios Konstandinos, which is 166km (103 miles) from Athens

Skopelos is nearly as bustling as Skiathos in the high season, but isn't quite as "sophisticated." Its beaches are fewer and less impressive, but Skopelos town is pleasant enough, and the island offers some pleasant excursions. It was inevitable that handsomely rugged Skopelos would eventually be "discovered" but it has happened at a slower pace and a bit more wisely than on Skiathos. (No coincidence, perhaps, that it was used for most of the Greek scenes in the hit movie *Mamma Mia!*) Skopelos is also known for keeping alive *rembetika* music, the Greek version of American blues, that can be heard in tavernas late in the evening.

Essentials

GETTING THERE **By Plane** Skopelos cannot be reached directly by plane, but you can fly to nearby Skiathos and take a hydrofoil or ferry to the northern port of Loutraki (below Glossa) or to the more popular Skopelos town.

By Boat If you're in Athens, take a boat or hydrofoil from Ayios Konstandinos to Skopelos (75 min.). **Alkyon Travel,** 97 Akademias, near Kanigos Square (℮ 210/ 383-2545), can arrange the 3-hour bus ride from Athens to Ayios Konstandinos (about 20€) and hydrofoil or ferry tickets.

Coming from Central or Northern Greece, depart for Skopelos from Volos (about a 2-hr. trip). For hydrofoil (Flying Dolphins) and ferryboat information, contact **Hellenic Seaways,** Akti Kondyli and 2 Aitolikou, Piraeus (℮ 210/419-9000; www. hellenicseaways.gr). For ferries from Piraeus, contact the **G.A. Ferries** line in Piraeus (℮ 210/458-2640; www.ferries.gr/gaferries). Ferry tickets can be purchased at travel agencies in Athens or on the islands. During high season, I recommend that you purchase your boat tickets in advance through the boat lines. Although you may purchase tickets at Alkyon in person, they will not reserve ferry or hydrofoil tickets for you in advance, and these often sell out.

From Skiathos, the ferry to Skopelos takes 90 minutes if you call at Skopelos town, or 45 minutes if you get off at Glossa/Loutraki; the one-way fare to both is about 12€. Ferry tickets can be purchased at **Vasilis Nikolaou** (℮ 24270/22-209), the travel agent at the corner of the Paralia and Papadiamandis. The Flying Dolphin hydrofoil takes 15 minutes to Glossa/Loutraki (four to five times daily; 15€), and 45 minutes to Skopelos (six to eight times daily, 17€). If you're on Skiathos, you can also take one of the many daily excursion boats to Skopelos.

There are infrequent ferryboat connections from Kimi (on Evvia) to Skopelos. Check with **Skopelos Port Authority** (℮ 24240/22-180) for current schedules, as they change frequently. As stated previously, I think hydrofoils are worth the extra expense for hopping around the Sporades.

In the port of Skopelos town, hydrofoil tickets can be purchased at the Hellenic Seaways agent, **Madro Travel,** immediately opposite the dock where ferries tie up. It also serves as the Olympic Air representative.

VISITOR INFORMATION The **Municipal Tourist Office** of Skopelos is on the waterfront, to the left of the pier as you disembark ((✆ **24240/23-231**); it's open daily from 9:30am to 10pm in high season. It provides information, changes money, and reserves rooms. If you want to call ahead to book a room, the **Association of Owners of Rental Accommodation** maintains an office on the harbor ((✆ **24240/24-567**).

Madro Travel, opposite the ferry dock ((✆ **24240/22-300;** www.madrotravel. com) is open all year; its knowledgeable and helpful staff know the island inside out and can provide information and make any arrangements you need. **Skopelorama Holidays,** about 100m (330 ft.) beyond Hotel Eleni on the left (east) end of the port ((✆ **24240/23-040;** fax 24240/23-243), can also can help you find a room, exchange money, rent a car, or take an excursion. It's open daily from 8am to 10pm.

GETTING AROUND **By Bus** Skopelos is reasonably well served by public bus; the bus stop in Skopelos town is on the east end of the port. There are four routes. Buses run the main route every half-hour in the high season beginning in Skopelos and making stops at Stafilos, Agnondas, Panormos, the Adrina Beach Hotel, Milia, Elios, Klima, Glossa, and Loutraki. The fare from Skopelos to Glossa is 3€.

By Car & Moped Rent a car or moped at one of the many shops on the port. A four-wheel-drive vehicle at **Motor Tours** ((✆ **24240/22-986;** motortours@skopelos. travel) runs around 55€, including insurance; expect to pay less for a Fiat Panda. A moped should cost about 20€ per day.

By Taxi The taxi stand is at the far end of the waterfront (left off the dock). Taxis will take you to almost any place on the island. Taxis are not metered—negotiate the fare before you get in. A typical fare, from Skopelos to Glossa, runs 40€.

By Boat To visit the more isolated beaches, take one of the large excursion boats; these cost about 70€ including lunch, and should be booked a day in advance in high season. Excursion boats to Glisteri, Gliphoneri, and Sares beaches operate only in peak season (about 20€). From the port of Agnondas, on the south coast, fishing boats go to Limnonari, one of the island's better beaches.

FAST FACTS There are several ATMs at banks around the harbor. The **health center** is on the road leading out of the east end of town ((✆ **24240/22-222**). The **police station** ((✆ **24240/22-235**) is up the narrow road (Parados 1) to the right of the National Bank, along the harbor. For **Internet access,** try Click & Surf (info@ skopelosnetcafe.com), just up from the police station—ask for Platanos Square— then proceed up past the supermarket. The **post office,** on the port's far east end (take the stepped road leading away from the last kiosk, opposite the bus/taxi station), is open Monday through Friday from 8am to 2:30pm. The **telephone office (OTE)** is at the top of a narrow road leading away from the center of the harbor; it's open Monday through Saturday from 8am to 5pm.

What to See & Do

The ferries from Alonissos, Skyros, and Kimi, and most of the hydrofoils and other boats from Skiathos, dock at both Glossa/Loutraki and Skopelos town. Most boats stop first at **Loutraki,** a homely little port near the northern end of the west coast, with the more attractive town of **Glossa** ★ high above it. Especially if this is your first visit, we suggest you stay onboard for the trip around the island's northern tip and along the east coast to the island's main harbor, Skopelos town. You'll understand the island's name—"Cliff" in Greek—when your boat pulls around the last headland into

Sporades National Marine Park

One of the most unusual attractions is the National Marine Park off the adjacent island of Alonissos. There you are guaranteed to see some of the dolphins that frequent this protected area, and if you are lucky, you may even see some Mediterranean monk seals, an endangered species protected within the marine park. Several travel agencies in the Sporades arrange for excursions to the park on licensed ships. The trips usually include a stop at the volcanic islet of **Psathoura,** with a chance to dive into a sunken city, a ride into the Blue Grotto of Alonissos, and a short walk to a Byzantine monastery. I recommend **Madro Travel** (www.madrotravel.com) in Skopelos; it provides a full-day trip (including noonday lunch) for 45€; 32€ for children). Meanwhile, check out their site, **www.alonissos-park.gr.**

a huge and nearly perfect C-shaped harbor, and you get your first glimpse of Skopelos town rising like a steep amphitheater around the port.

Skopelos town (also called Hora) is one of Greece's most treasured towns, on par with Hydra and Simi. It scales the steep, low hills around the harbor and has the same winding, narrow paths that characterize the more famous Cycladic islands to the south. Scattered on the slopes of the town are just a few of the island's 123 churches, which must be something of a record for such a small locale. The oldest of these is **Ayios Michali,** past the police station. The waterfront is lined with banks, cafes, travel agencies, and the like. Interspersed among these prosaic offerings are truly regal shade trees. Many of the shops and services are up the main street leading away from the center of the paralia. The back streets are amazingly convoluted (and unnamed); it's best that you wander around and get to know a few familiar landmarks.

The **Venetian Kastro,** which overlooks the town from a rise on the western corner, has been whitewashed. Built over an archaic Temple of Athena, it proved to be too strong for the Turks to capture during the War of Independence in the 1820s.

At the far eastern end of town is the **Photographic Center of Skopelos** (© 24240/24-121), which during the high season sponsors quite classy photography exhibitions in several locales around town.

SHOPPING

Skopelos has a variety of shops selling Greek and local ceramics, weavings, and jewelry. One of the most stylish is **Armoloi,** in the center of the shops along the harbor (© 24240/22-707). It sells only Greek jewelry, ceramics, weavings, and silver; some of the objects are old. The owners make most of the handsome ceramics. Another special store is **Ploumisti,** at a corner of an alley about midway along the paralia (© 24240/22-059; kalaph-skp@skt.forthnet.gr). It sells beautiful Greek rugs, blankets, jewelry, pottery, and crafts. Its friendly proprietors, Voula and Kostas Kalafatis, are full of information for visitors, especially about the *rembetika* music scene. **Nikos Rodios** (© 24240/22-924), whose gallery is between Hotel Eleni and Skopelorama Holidays agency, is from a Skopelos family who have made ceramics for three generations. Nikos makes each piece on a foot-pumped wheel and his elegant vessels, at once classical and modern, are a change from the usual pottery found around Greece.

EXPLORING THE ISLAND

The whole island is sprinkled with monasteries and churches, but five **monasteries** south of town can be visited by following a pleasant path that continues south from the beach hotels. The first, **Evangelistria,** was founded by monks from Mount Athos, but it now serves as a nunnery, and the weavings of its present occupants can be bought at a small shop; it's open daily from 8am to 1pm and 4 to 7pm. The fortified monastery of **Ayia Barbara,** now abandoned, contains 15th-century frescoes. **Metamorphosis,** very nearly abandoned, comes alive on August 6, when the feast of the Metamorphosis is celebrated here. **Ayios Prodromos** is a 30-minute hike farther, but it's the handsomest and contains a particularly beautiful iconostasis. **Taxiarchon,** abandoned and overgrown, is at the summit of Mount Polouki to the southeast, a hike recommended only for the hardiest and most dedicated.

There is basically a single highway on the island, with short spurs at each significant settlement. It runs south from Skopelos town, then cuts north and skirts the west coast northwest, eventually arriving at Glossa; it then runs down to Loutraki. The first spur leads off to the left to **Stafilos,** a popular family beach recommended by locals for a good seafood dinner, which you must order in the morning. About half a kilometer across the headland is **Velanio,** where nude bathing is common.

The next settlement west is **Agnondas,** named for a local athlete who brought home the gold from the 569 B.C. Olympic Games. This small fishing village has become a tourist resort thanks to nearby beaches. **Limnonari,** a 15-minute walk farther west and accessible by caique in summer, has a good fine sand beach in a rather homely and shadeless setting.

The road then turns inland again, through a pine forest, coming out at the coast at **Panormos.** With its sheltered pebble beach, this has become the island's best resort with a number of taverns, hotels, and rooms to let, as well as watersports facilities. The road then climbs again toward **Milia ★,** which is considered **the island's best beach.** You will have to walk down about half a kilometer from the bus stop, but you'll find a lovely light-gray beach of sand and pebbles, with the island of Dassia opposite and watersports facilities at **Beach Boys Club** (✆ **24240/23-995**).

The next town, **Elios (Neo Klima),** was thrown up to shelter the people displaced by the 1965 earthquake. It's become home to many of the locals who operate the resort facilities on the west coast, as well as something of a resort itself.

The main road proceeds on to **Glossa ★,** which means "tongue," and that's what the hill on which the town was built looks like from the sea. Most of it was spared during the earthquake, so it remains one of the most Greek and charming towns in the Sporades. Those tempted to stay overnight will find a number of rooms for rent, a good hotel, and a very good taverna. (The hotel is the **Avra;** ✆ **24240/33-550;** fax 24240/33-681.)

Most of the coastline here is craggy and has a few hard-to-reach beaches. Among the best places to catch some rays and do a bit of swimming is the small beach below the chapel of **Ayios Ioannis,** sitting high on a rocky prominence on the coast a few miles to the east of Glossa; it was at this site and chapel that the climax of *Mamma Mia!* takes place. (Bring food and water if you plan to swim here.) As for the port of **Loutraki,** it's a winding 3km (2 miles) down; we don't recommend a stay there.

That ends the road tour of Skopelos, but other sites can be reached from Skopelos town by caique. Along the east coast north of Skopelos is **Glisteri,** a small, pebbled beach with a nearby olive grove offering respite from the sun. It's a good bet when the other beaches are overrun in summer. You can also go by caique to the grotto at **Tripiti,** for the island's best fishing, or to the little island of **Ayios Yioryios,** which has an abandoned monastery.

The whole of Skopelos's 95 sq. km (38 sq. miles) is prime for **hiking** and **biking,** and the interior is still waiting to be explored. There's also **horseback riding, sailing** (ask at the Skopelos travel agencies), and a number of **excursions** to be taken from and around the island. Both Skopelorama Holidays and Madro Travel (see "Visitor Information" and "Getting There," above) offer a fine series of excursions, such as monasteries by coach, a walking tour of the town, and several cruises. Another possibility (spring or fall only) is a nature (or town) walk led by a longtime English resident, Heather Parsons (© **24240/24-022;** www.skopelos-walks.com); if you prefer to go it alone, you can buy her *Skopelos Trails Guide* (3rd edition) in shops around town.

One excursion that should appeal to many is on one of the licensed boats that take you to the waters around nearby Alonissos that make up the **National Marine Park** (p. 524); lucky visitors may spot Mediterranean monk seals, an endangered species protected within the park

Where to Stay

In high season, Skopelos is becoming nearly as popular as Skiathos. If you've arrived without reservations and need help, talk to the Skopelorama Holidays agency (see "Visitor Information," above) or to the officials at the town hall. Look at the room and agree on a price before you accept anything, or you may be unpleasantly surprised. To make matters confusing, there are few street names in the main, old section of Skopelos town, so you'll have to ask for directions to find your lodging.

IN SKOPELOS TOWN

Handsome, traditional-style **Hotel Amalia,** along the coast, 500m (1,640 ft.) from the port's center (© **24240/22-688;** fax 24240/23-217), is largely occupied by groups but should have spare rooms in spring and fall.

Hotel Denise　One of the most appealing hotels in Skopelos thanks to its premier location, clean facilities, and its own pool, the Hotel Denise stands atop the hill overlooking the town and commands spectacular vistas of the harbor and Aegean. A wide balcony rings each of the hotel's four stories. Most of the guest rooms—admittedly, rather small—have views that are among the best in town. The Denise is popular and open only in high season; before hiking up the steep road, call for a pickup and to check for room availability—or better yet, reserve in advance.

Skopelos town 37003. www.denise.gr. © **24240/22-678.** 25 units. 50€ double. Rates include continental breakfast. Credit cards accepted for deposit only. Parking on adjacent street. **Amenities:** Restaurant; bar; pool; Wi-Fi. *In room:* A/C, TV, fridge, Internet.

Hotel Eleni　Hotel Eleni is a modern hotel that can boast of location and convenience as it is set back from the coast and 300m (984 ft.) to the left (off the dock) from the harbor's center. After many years spent operating pizzerias in New York, Charlie Hatzidrosos returned from the Bronx to build this establishment. His daughter now operates the hotel and provides gracious service. All guest rooms have balconies.

Skopelos town 37003. © **24240/22-393.** Fax 2424/022-936. 37 units. 75€ double. AE, MC, V. Parking on adjacent street. **Amenities:** Snack bar. *In room:* A/C, TV, fridge.

Skopelos Village ★ ☺ Although Skopelos Village is more expensive than other Skopelos hotels, it offers a lot for the money. Guests here may want to settle in for a while so they can take advantage of this miniresort's amenities—or just enjoy the aromatic greenery of the surroundings. The buildings are tastefully constructed as "traditional island houses." Each bungalow is equipped with kitchen, private bathroom, and one or two bedrooms, and can sleep from two to six persons. Facilities include a breakfast room and snack bar. In the evening, the restaurant offers Greek meals accompanied by Greek music and dance. The hotel provides free transportation to the island's various beaches, although one is right in front of the hotel.

About a half-mile southeast of town center, Skopelos 37003. www.skopelosvillage.gr. ✆ **24240/22-517.** 36 units. High season studio or suite for 2 persons, with a kitchen 175€–195€; bungalow for up to 6 210€. Rates include buffet breakfast. MC, V. Free parking nearby. **Amenities:** 2 restaurants; babysitting; children's playground; pool; room service; tennis nearby; Wi-Fi. *In room:* A/C, TV, hair dryer, minibar.

IN PANORMOS

This pleasant little resort is on a horseshoe-shaped cove along the west coast, about halfway between Skopelos town and Glossa. Here you'll find several cafeteria-style snack bars and minimarkets. We recommend it as a base, especially because one of the best hotels on the island—Adrina Beach Hotel (see below)—is just above it. As for restaurants, a particularly lively taverna, **Dihta,** is right along the beachfront.

   Panormos Travel Office (✆ **24240/23-380;** fax 24240/23-748) has decent rooms to let; offers phone and fax services, exchanges money; arranges tours (including night squid fishing); and rents cars, motorbikes, and speedboats.

   If you can't get a room at the Adrina, try 38-unit **Afrodite Hotel** (✆ **24240/23-150;** www.afroditehotel.gr), a more modern choice about 100m (328 ft.) across the road from the beach at Panormos.

Adrina Beach Hotel and Resort & Spa ★ ☺ This traditional hotel on the beach outside Panormos has long rated as one of the better ones on the island, and with the opening of its adjacent grand Resort & Spa in 2011 it is even more impressive. The hotel's guest rooms are large and tastefully furnished in pastels, each with its own balcony or veranda. In addition to the main hotel's rooms, 22 villas are raked down the steep slope toward the hotel's private beach. The complex has a big saltwater pool with its own bar, a restaurant, a buffet room, a playground, and a minimarket. Conference facilities for 50 to 60 people can be provided. Meanwhile, the new facility offers in addition to 16 more villas, a spa, a gym, its own pool and playground, a beach volleyball court—and a monorail that transports guests up and down the slope from the villas and to the restaurant and beach.

About 500m (¼ mile) from Panormos, 37003 Skopelos. www.adrina.gr. ✆ **24240/23-373** or 210/682-6886 in Athens. 52 units. 75€–145€ double at hotel; 150€–250€ villa at resort accommodating up to 3 adults and 3 children. Rates include buffet breakfast. AE, DC, MC, V. **Amenities:** 2 restaurants; bar; children's playground; Jacuzzi; minimarket; pool; spa. *In room:* A/C, TV, fridge, hair dryer.

IN GLOSSA

There are approximately 100 rooms to rent in the small town of Glossa. Expect to pay about 40€ for single or double occupancy. The best way to find a room is to visit one of the tavernas or shops and inquire about vacancies. You can ask George Antoniou at **Pythari Souvenir Shop** (✆ **24240/33-077)** for advice. If you can't find a room in Glossa, you can take a bus or taxi down to Loutraki and check into a pension by the water; or you can head back to Panormos.

Where to Eat

IN SKOPELOS TOWN

Finikas Taverna and Ouzeri ★ GREEK   Tucked away in the upper back streets of Skopelos is a picturesque garden taverna/ouzeri dominated by a broadleaf palm. The Finikas offers what might be Skopelos's most romantic setting, thanks to its isolated and lovely garden seating. (You have to ask for directions here.) Among the many fine courses are an excellent ratatouille and pork cooked with prunes and apples, a traditional island specialty.

Upper back street of Skopelos town. *(C)* **24240/23-247.** Main courses 6€–14€. No credit cards. Daily 7pm–2am.

The Garden Restaurant GREEK   Some locals claim this is the best restaurant in town. Two young brothers operate what most people call "the Garden," for its setting and casual atmosphere. The food is tasty and often a bit different. We've enjoyed the mushrooms with garlic (an appetizer), and calamari with cheese (a main course).

At harbor's far eastern end, 1st left at corner of Amalia Hotel. *(C)* **24240/22-349.** www.skopelosweb.gr/kipos. Reservations recommended in high season. Main courses 6€–20€. MC, V. Daily 11am–midnight. Closed Oct to mid-June.

Platanos Jazz Bar SNACKS/BAR FOOD   For everything from breakfast to a late-night drink, try this pub. Breakfast in the summer starts as early as 5 or 6am for ferry passengers, who can enjoy coffee, fruit salad with nuts and yogurt, and fresh-squeezed orange juice for about 8€. Platanos is also pleasant for evening and late-night drinks. Music from the owners' phenomenal collection of jazz records accompanies your meal.

Beneath the enormous plane tree just to the left of the ferry dock. *(C)* **24240/23-661.** Main courses 5€–12€. No credit cards. Daily 5am–2am.

IN GLOSSA

Taverna Agnanti ★ TRADITIONAL SKOPELITIAN   Highly praised by numerous international travel magazines, this is the place to meet, greet, and eat in Glossa. The food is inexpensive, the staff friendly, and the view spectacular. The menu is standard taverna style, but the proprietors make a point of using the finest fresh products and wines. Specialties include herb fritters, fish *stifado* (rabbit and onions) with prunes, pork with prunes, and almond pie. Traditional music is occasionally played. The Stamataki family runs this and the nearby souvenir shop Pythari.

Glossa (about 200m/656 ft. up from the bus stop). *(C)* **24240/33-076.** agnanti-rest@agnanti-rest.gr. Main courses 6€–22€. No credit cards. Daily 11am–midnight.

Skopelos After Dark

The nightlife scene on Skopelos isn't nearly as active as on neighboring Skiathos, but there are still plenty of bars, late-night cafes, and discos. Most of the coolest bars are on the far (east) side of town, but you can wander the scene around Platanos Square, beyond and along the paralia: **Anemos, Karavia, Ntokos, Ionas, Mythos**—one of these places should satisfy. The best place for bouzouki music is **Metro,** and for *rembetika* try the **Kastro.** For live music with a spectacular view of the town, ask for directions to the **Anatoli Ouzeri.**

SKYROS (SKIROS) ★

47km (25 nautical miles) from Kimi; 182km (113 miles) from Athens

Fairly remote **Skyros** hardly seems a part of the Sporades group, especially as its landscape and architecture are more Cycladic. But it has several excellent beaches, as well as a colorful local culture, and it remains the perfect destination for those who want to get away from the crowds. Some of us, in fact, think Skyros's more meager tourist facilities and the stark contrast between the sea, sky, and rugged terrain make it all the more inviting. Also it can be the base for a day's excursion to Alinossos, the fourth of the Sporades, less popular than the other three but that much more natural.

Essentials

GETTING THERE   By Plane   In summer, **Olympic Air** has about three flights a week between Athens and Skyros and Thessaloniki and Skyros. Call the Olympic office in Athens (✆ **210/966-6666**) for information and reservations; the local Olympic representative is **Skyros Travel and Tourism** (✆ **22220/91-123**). A bus meets most flights and goes to Skyros town, Magazia, and sometimes Molos; the fare is 6€. A taxi from the airport is about 18€, but expect to share a cab.

By Boat   Skyros Shipping Company (www.sne.gr) offers the only ferry service to Skyros; it's operated by a company whose stockholders are all citizens of the island. In summer, it runs twice daily (usually early afternoon and early evening) from Kimi (on the east coast of Evvia) to Skyros, and twice daily (usually early morning and midafternoon) from Skyros to Kimi; the trip takes a little over 2 hours. Off season, there's one ferry each way, leaving Skyros early in the morning and Kimi in late afternoon. The fare is 12€ to 20€. For information, call the company's office either in Kimi (✆ **22220/22-020**) or Skyros (✆ **22220/91-790**). The Skyros Shipping Company's offices also sell bus tickets to Athens; the fare for the 3-hour ride is about 15€. In Athens, **Alkyon Travel,** 97 Akademia, near Kanigos Square (✆ **210/383-2545**), arranges bus transportation to Kimi and sells ferry tickets.

In the summer occasional ferries and hydrofoils link Skyros to the other Sporades as well as to ports on the mainland, but these links are either fairly infrequent or involve land transportation to ports that are not on most tourists' itineraries. If you're trying to "do" the Sporades and want to make connections at Kimi, the tricky part can be the connection with ferries or hydrofoils from the other Sporades islands. When they don't hold to schedule, it's not uncommon to see the Skyros ferry disappearing on the horizon as your ship pulls into Kimi. You might have to make the best of the 24-hour layover and get a room in Paralia Kimi. (We recommend **Hotel Korali,** at ✆ **22220/22-212**; or the older **Hotel Krineion,** at ✆ **22220/22-287.**)

From Athens, buses to Kimi and Ayios Konstandinos leave the Terminal B, 260 Lission, six times a day, though you should depart no later than 1:30pm; the fare for the 3½-hour trip is about 20€. At Kimi, you transfer to a local bus to the dock; ask the bus driver if you're uncertain of the connection.

On Skyros, the ferries and hydrofoils dock at **Linaria,** on the opposite side of the island from Skyros town. The island's only public bus will meet the boat and take you over winding, curving roads to Skyros town for 2€. On request, the bus will also stop at Magazia beach, immediately north below the town, next to Xenia Hotel.

VISITOR INFORMATION   The largest tourist office is **Skyros Travel and Tourism** (✆ **22220/91-123**; www.skyrostravel.com), next to Skyros Pizza Restaurant in the main market. It's open daily from 8am to 2:30pm and 6:30 to 10:30pm. English-speaking Lefteris Trakos offers assistance with accommodations, currency exchange, Olympic Air flights (he's the local ticket agent), phone calls, interesting bus and boat tours, and Hellenic Seaways Flying Dolphin tickets.

GETTING AROUND   By Bus   The only scheduled service is the Skyros-Linaria shuttle that runs four to five times daily and costs 3€. Skyros Travel (see above) offers a twice-daily beach-excursion bus in high season and daylong island excursions in a small bus with an English-speaking guide (50€); for many, this may be the best way to get an overview of the island.

By Car & Moped   A small car rents for about 70€ per day, including insurance. Mopeds and motorcycles are available near the police station or the taxi station for about 25€ per day. The island has a relatively well-developed network of roads.

By Taxi   Taxis can take you just about any place on the island at the standard Greek rates, but discuss the price before setting off; service between Linaria and Skyros costs about 20€.

On Foot   Skyros is a fine place to hike. The island map, published by Skyros Travel and Tourism, will show you a number of good routes, and it is pretty accurate.

FAST FACTS   The most convenient ATM on Skyros is at the **National Bank of Greece** in the main square of Skyros town. (Because Skyros's tourist services are relatively limited, we recommend bringing cash and/or traveler's checks for emergencies.) The **clinic** is near the main square (𝄢 **22220/92-222**). The **police station** (𝄢 **22220/91-274**) is on the street behind the Skyros Travel Center. The **post office** is near the bus square in Skyros town; it's open Monday through Friday from 8am to 2pm. The **telephone office (OTE)** is opposite the police station. It's open Friday only, from 7:30am to 3pm, but there are card phones in town.

What to See & Do

The Faltaits Historical and Folklore Museum   This is one of the best island folk-art museums in Greece. Located in an old house belonging to the Faltaits family, the private collection of Manos Faltaits contains a large and varied selection of plates, embroidery, weaving, woodworking, and clothing, as well as many rare books and photographs, including some of local men in traditional costumes for Carnival. Attached to the museum is a workshop where young artisans make lovely objects using traditional patterns and materials. The proceeds from the sale of workshop items go to the upkeep of the museum. The museum also has a shop, **Argo,** on the main street of town (𝄢 **22220/92-158**). It's open daily from 10am to 1pm and 6:30 to 11pm.

Plateia Rupert Brooke on the northeast edge of Skyros Town. 𝄢 **22220/91-327.** www.faltaits.gr. Admission 2€. Summer Tues–Sun 8:30am–3pm; off season, ring the bell and someone will probably let you in.

EXPLORING THE ISLAND

All boats dock at **Linaria,** a plain, mostly modern fishing village on the west coast, pleasant enough but not recommended for a stay. Catch the bus waiting on the quay to take you across the narrow middle of the island to the west-coast capital, Skyros town, which is built on a rocky bluff overlooking the sea. (The airport is near the northern tip of the island.) **Skyros town,** which is known on the island as Horio or Hora, looks much like a typical Cycladic hill town, with whitewashed houses built on top of one another. The winding streets and paths are too narrow for cars and mopeds, so most of the traffic is by foot and hoof. After you alight at the bus stop square, continue on up toward the center of town and the main tourist services.

Near the market, signs point to the town's **kastro.** The climb takes 15 minutes, but the view is worth it. On the way you'll pass the church of **Ayia Triada,** which contains interesting frescoes, and the monastery of **Ayios Yioryios Skyrianos.** The monastery was founded in 962 and contains a famous black-faced icon of St. George brought from Constantinople during the Iconoclastic controversy. From one side of the citadel, the view is over the rooftops of the town, and from the other the cliff drops precipitously to the sea. According to one myth, King Lykomides pushed Theseus to his death from here. (Skyros also happens to be where Neoptolemis, the son of Achilles, was living when he was sent to revenge his father' death at Troy.)

The terrace at the far (northern) end of the town is **Plateia Rupert Brooke,** where the English poet, who is buried on the southern tip of the island, is honored by a nude statue, *Immortal Poetry.* (Brooke died on a hospital ship off Skyros in 1915 while en route to the Dardanelles as an army officer.) The statue is said to have offended the local people when it was installed, but you're more likely to be amused (or annoyed) when you see how pranksters have chosen to deface the hapless bronze figure. (The Faltaits Historical and Folklore Museum, described above, is near this site, as is the not especially distinguished—and thus not recommended—archaeological museum.)

Local customs and dress are currently better preserved on Skyros than in all but a few locales in Greece. Older men can still be seen in baggy blue pants, black caps, and leather sandals with numerous straps, and older women still wear long head scarves. The **embroidery** you will often see women busily working at is famous for its vibrant colors and interesting motifs—such as people dancing hand in hand with flowers twining around their limbs and hoopoes with fanciful crests.

Peek into the doorway of many a Skyrian home and you're likely to see what looks like a room from a dollhouse with a miniature table and chairs, as well as **colorful plates**—loads of them—hanging on the wall. These displays are said to date from the Byzantine era, when the head clerics from Epirus sent 10 families to Skyros to serve as governors. They were given control of all the land not owned by Mount Athos and the Monastery of St. George. For hundreds of years, these 10 families dominated the affairs of Skyros. With Kalamitsa as a safe harbor, the island prospered, and consulates opened from countries near and far. The merchant ships were soon followed by pirates, with whom the ruling families went into business. The families knew what boats were expected and what they were carrying, and the pirates had the ships and bravado to steal the cargo—and then share with their informants. The pirates, of course, soon took to plundering the islanders as well, but the aristocrats managed to hold onto much of their wealth.

Greek independence reduced the influence of these ruling families, and during the hard times brought by World War I, they were reduced to trading their possessions to the peasant farmers for food. Chief among these bartered items were sets of dinnerware. Plates from China, Italy, Turkey, Egypt, and other exotic places became a sign of wealth, and Skyrian families made elaborate displays of their newly acquired trophies. Whole walls were covered, and by the 1920s local Skyrian craftsmen began making their own plates for the poorer families who couldn't afford the originals. This, at least, is the story they tell.

Skyros is also the home of a unique breed of **wild pygmy ponies,** often compared to the horses depicted on the frieze of the Parthenon and thought to be similar to Shetland ponies. Most of these rare animals have been moved to the nearby island of Skyropoula, though tame ones can still be seen grazing outside the town. Ask around and you might be able to find a local who will let you ride one.

Every July 15, the ponies of Skyros are assembled and rated as to their characteristics, and then young boys race some of the ponies around a small track.

BEACHES & OUTDOOR PURSUITS

The island is divided almost evenly by its narrow waist; the northern half is fertile and covered with pine forest, while the southern half is barren and quite rugged. Both

Skyros (Skiros)

THE FAMOUS carnival OF SKYROS

The 21-day **Carnival** celebration is highlighted by a 4-day period leading up to Lent and the day known throughout Greece as **Kathari Deftera** (Clean Monday). On this day, Skyros residents don traditional costumes and perform dances on the town square. *Lagana* (unleavened bread) is served with *taramosalata (fish roe spread)* and other meatless specialties. (Traditionally, vegetarian food is eaten for 40 days leading up to Easter.) Much of this is traditional throughout Greece, but Skyros adds its own distinctive element. Culminating on midafternoon of the Sunday before Clean Monday is a series of ritual dances and events performed by a group of weirdly costumed men. Some dress as old shepherds in animal skins with belts of sheep bells and masks made of goatskin. Other men dress as women and flirt outrageously. (Skyros seems to have an age-old association with cross-dressing: It was here that Achilles successfully beat the draft during the Trojan War by dressing as a woman, until shrewd Odysseus tricked him into revealing his true gender.) Other celebrants caricature Europeans. All behave outlandishly, reciting ribald poetry and poking fun at bystanders. This ritual is generally thought to be pagan in origin, and what you see has deep roots. Some of the elements might seem similar to parts from ancient Greek comedies, and the word "tragedy" means "goat song," so the goat-costume ceremonies may go way back also.

halves have their attractions, though the most scenic area of the island is probably to the south toward **Tris Boukes,** where Rupert Brooke is buried. The better beaches, however, are in the north.

To get to the beach at **Magazia,** continue down from Plateia Rupert Brooke. (If your load is heavy, take a taxi to Magazia, as it is a hike.) From Magazia, once the site of the town's storehouses (magazines), it's about a half-mile to **Molos,** a fishing village, though the two villages are quickly becoming indistinguishable because of development. There's windsurfing along this beach and, beyond Molos, windsurfing at fairly isolated beaches with nudist sections.

South of town, the beaches are less enticing until you reach **Aspous,** which has a couple of tavernas and rooms to let. **Ahili,** a bit farther south, is where you'll find the big new **marina,** so it's no longer much of a place for swimming. Farther south, the coast gets increasingly rugged and has no roadway.

If you head back across the waist of the island to **Kalamitsa,** the old safe harbor, 3km (2 miles) south of Linaria, you'll find a good beach. Buses run here in summer.

North of Linaria, **Acherounes** is a pretty beach. Beyond it, **Pefkos,** where marble was once quarried, is better sheltered and has a taverna that's open in summer. The next beach north, **Ayios Fokas,** is probably the best on the island, with a white pebble beach and a taverna open in summer. Locals call it paradise, and like all such places it's difficult to reach. Skyrians will suggest walking, but the hike is long and hilly. To get here from Skyros town, take the bus back to Linaria, tell the driver where you're going, get off at the crossroads with Pefkos, and begin your hike west from there.

North of Ayios Fokas is **Atsitsa,** another beach with pine trees, but it's a bit too rocky. It can be reached by road across the Olymbos mountains in the center of the island, and has a few rooms to let. It is also the location of a **holistic health-and-fitness holiday community,** which offers "personal growth" vacations, with courses in fitness, holistic health, creative writing, and handicrafts. For information on its activities, contact the **Skyros Center** in the United Kingdom at 9 Eastcliff Rd., Shanklin, Isle of Wight PO37 6AA (www.skyros.com; ✆ **01983/865566**). This same outfit runs the **Skyros Centre** at the edge of Skyros town; it differs from the one at Atsitsa in that it offers a more conventional touristic experience. A 15-minute walk farther north from Atsitsa, **Kira Panagia** is a sandy beach that's a bit better.

The northwest of the island is covered in dense pine forests, spreading down to the Aegean. The rocky shore opens onto gentle bays and coves. This area provides wonderful **hiking** for the fit. Take a taxi (40€ to **Atsitsa**), and arrange for it to return in 5 or 6 hours. Explore the ruins of the ancient mining operation at Atsitsa, then head south for about 7km (4½ miles) to **Ayios Fokas ★**, a small bay with a taverna perched right on the water where you can expect the meal of your trip: fresh fish caught that morning in the waters before you, vegetables plucked from the garden for your salad, and the house feta cheese and wine. Relax, swim in the bay, and then hike back to your taxi. The ambitious may continue south for 11 or 12km (7–8 miles) to the main road and catch the bus or hail a taxi. This part of the road is mainly uphill. In case you tire or can't pry yourself away from the secluded paradise of Ayios Fokas, Kali offers two extremely primitive rooms with the view of your dreams, but without electricity or toilets.

SHOPPING
Skyros is a good place to buy local crafts, especially embroidery and ceramics. **Ergastiri,** on the main street, is noted for its wood furniture **Yiannis Nicholau,** whose studio is next to Xenia Hotel, is known for his handmade plates. You can find good hand-carved wooden chests and chairs made from beech (in the old days it was blackberry wood) from **Lefteris Avgoklouris;** his studio (✆ **22220/91-106**) is on Konthili, around the corner from the post office. Another fine carver is **Manolios,** in the main market.

Where to Stay
The island has few hotels, so most visitors to Skyros take private rooms. The best are in the upper part of Skyros town, away from the bus stop, where women in black dresses accost you with cries of "Room! Room!" If you want to make arrangements before arriving, you could phone or fax the **Skyros Association of Hotels and Rooms** ((✆ **22220/92-095;** fax 22290/92-770). It is better to wait until you are on the scene and contact **Skyros Travel and Tourism** (see "Visitor Information," above). The island of Skyros is somewhat more primitive in its facilities than the other Sporades, so before agreeing to anything, check out the room to ensure that it's what you want.

IN SKYROS TOWN
Hotel Nefeli ★ The most ambitious—and arguably the best—in-town option is the Nefeli, designed and furnished in traditional Skyrian style. It is actually composed of three buildings, each with various room arrangements and amenities; there are even some with kitchenettes. The bedrooms and bathrooms are decent in size and well appointed; many units have fine views. The large downstairs lobby is a welcoming space. Reserve in advance, as the Nefeli is one of the favorite choices on Skyros.

Skyros town center, 34007 Skyros. www.skyros-nefeli.gr. ✆ **22220/91-964.** 16 units. 100€ double; 120€–180€ for larger units. Breakfast 6€ extra. AE, MC, V. Parking on premises. **Amenities:** Restaurant; bar; children's play area; Internet access; 2 pools (1 children's); smoke-free rooms. *In room:* A/C, TV, hair dryer, minibar.

IN MAGAZIA BEACH & MOLOS

Hotel Angela 🏊 This is among the most attractive and well-kept abodes in the Molos/Magazia beach area, near the Paradise Hotel complex. All rooms are clean and tidy with balconies, but because the hotel is set back about 150m (500 ft.) from the beach, it has only partial sea views. Nevertheless, the facilities and hospitality of the young couple running the Angela make up for its just-off-the-beach location, and it's your best bet for the money.

Molos, 34007 Skyros. anghotel@otenet.gr. 📞 **22220/91-764.** Fax 2222/92-030. 14 units. 90€ double. No credit cards. **Amenities:** Pool. In room: A/C.

Hydroussa Hotel With the best location on the beach at Magazia, the Xenia offers some of the nicest (if not cheapest) accommodations on Skyros. The guest rooms have handsome 1950s-style furniture and big bathrooms with tubs, as well as balconies and sea views. You can get all your meals here if you want. Perhaps the hotel's greatest drawback is the unsightly concrete breakwater that's supposed to protect the beach from erosion.

Magazia Beach, 34007 Skyros. 📞 **22220/92-063.** Fax 22220/92-062. 22 units. 115€ double. Rates include buffet breakfast. V. **Amenities:** Bar, free Internet (in lobby), parking. In room: A/C, TV, hairdryer, fridge.

Paradissos Hotel This pleasant lodging is at the north end of Magazia beach, in the town of Molos. The older part of the hotel has 40 rooms; these more basic units run considerably less. I'd recommend one of the newer section's 20 rooms, which are better kept and have much better light. The hotel is somewhat removed from the main town, but there is a taverna on the premises and another down the street.

Molos, 34007 Skyros. 📞 **22220/91-560.** Fax 22220/91-443. 60 units. 85€ double new building; 50€ double older building. Breakfast 6€ extra. No credit cards. **Amenities:** Restaurant; bar. In room: A/C, TV, fridge.

Pension Galeni 🏊 The small but pleasant Pension Galeni offers modest rooms, all with private bathrooms. Ask for one of the front, sea-facing rooms on the top floor for their (currently) unobstructed views. The Galeni overlooks one of the cleanest parts of Magazia beach.

Magazia beach, 34007 Skyros. 📞 **22220/91-379.** 13 units. 70€ double. No credit cards.

IN ACHEROUNES BEACH

Pegasus Apartments Nothing spectacular, these fully equipped studios and apartments were built by the resourceful Lefteris Trakos (owner of Skyros Travel). They are at Acherounes, the beach just south of the port of Linaria, on the east coast. One of the pluses of staying here is the chance to see (and ride, if you're 14 or under) Katerina, a Skyrian pony.

Acherounes Beach, 34007 Skyros. 📞 **22220/91-552.** 8 units. 60€ studio for 2; 130€ apt. for 3–5. MC, V. In room: Minibar.

IN YIRISMATA

Skiros Palace Hotel ★ If you want to get away from it all and enjoy upscale amenities, this is the place for you. This out-of-the-way resort—about 1.6km (1 mile) north of Molos, and 3km (2 miles) north of Skyros town—has some of the most ambitious facilities on the island. The plainly furnished but comfortable guest rooms come with large balconies. The beach across the road is sandy and inviting, but it can be windy and rocky—be very careful in the sea here. Facilities include a (saltwater) pool and bar, tennis and basketball courts, and a garden—not to mention a soundproof disco, the island's most sophisticated. A minibus heads into town twice a day.

Yirismata, 34007 Skyros. www.skiros-palace.gr. © **22220/91-994.** 80 units. 110€ double. Rates include breakfast. AE, DC, MC, V. Parking at hotel. **Amenities:** 2 restaurants; bar; basketball court; minibus to town; outdoor pool; sailboat for excursions; tennis; TV in lobby. *In room:* A/C and TV in some rooms.

Where to Eat

The food in Skyros town is generally pretty good and reasonably priced. **Anemos,** on the main drag (© **22220/92-155**), is a nice spot for breakfast, with filtered coffee, omelets, and freshly squeezed juice. Nearby **Skyros Pizza Restaurant** (© **22220/91-684**) serves tasty pies as well as other Greek specialties. For dessert, head to **Zaccharoplasteio** (the Greek word for sweet shop/bakery) in the center of town.

Linaria offers three decent tavernas: **Almyria, Filippeos,** and **Psariotos.**

Kristina's/Pegasus Restaurant ★ INTERNATIONAL   Come here if you need a break from standard Greek fare. Kristina's has been an institution in Skyros town for some years, but in 2000 it moved to the locale of the former Pegasus Restaurant, a neoclassical building (ca. 1890) in the center of town. The Australian proprietor/chef, Kristina, brings a light touch to everything she cooks. Her fricasseed chicken is excellent, her herb bread is tasty, and her desserts, such as cheesecake, are exceptional.

Skyros town. © **2222091-123.** Reservations recommended in summer. Main courses 7€-20€. No credit cards. Mon-Sat 7am-4pm and 7pm-1am. No parking.

Marvetes Grill GRILL   One of the oldest and best places in town, the Maryetes is a second-generation-run grill that's equally popular with locals and travelers. Go for the food, not the dining room, which is as simple as can be. We recommend anything grilled—fish, chicken, or meat. And sample one of the salads.

Skyros town. © **22220/91-311.** Main courses 6€-12€. No credit cards. Daily 1-3pm and 6pm-midnight. No parking.

Restaurant Kabanero 🍴 GREEK   One of the best dining values in town, this perpetually busy eatery serves the usual Greek menu: moussaka, stuffed peppers and tomatoes, fava, a variety of stewed vegetables, and several kinds of meat. The dishes are tasty and the prices somewhat lower than those at most other places in town.

Skyros town. © **22220/91-240.** Main courses 6€-14€. No credit cards. Daily 1-3pm and 6pm-midnight. No parking.

Skyros After Dark

Skyros is not the island for you if you've come to Greece looking for a lively bar and club scene. That said, during high season, there is enough to satisfy most people. As usual in such locales, names and atmospheres can change from year to year. But at last checking, the **Kastro Club,** in Linaria, was for dancing. **Skyropoula** on the way from Plateia Ruper Brooke to Magazia, and Linaria's **O Kavos** are other popular hangouts. Aside from these, you'll find few diversions other than barhopping on the main street of Skyros town. **Apocalypsis** draws a younger crowd. **Kalypso** attracts a more upscale set of drinkers. **Renaissance** is lively but can be loud. **Rodon** is best for actually listening to music, while **Kata Lathos (By Mistake)** has also gained a following.

WESTERN GREECE HIGHLIGHTS

by John S. Bowman

14

Want a change from those Greek islands, with their artifice and crowds? Looking for a holiday in a Greek environment that is, well, just naturally natural? I have just the place! Evergreen slopes and lush valleys, deep-set rivers and unspoiled lakes, towns that are lived in and villages of timbered houses, slate or tile roofs—it's the northwestern corner the Greeks know as Epirus. Plentiful rainfall, the rugged Pindos Mountains, and a generally more temperate climate—in places, it seems like Alpine country. And, in fact, it's one of the few regions in Greece where you'll be enjoying your travels away from the sea.

Epirus and its capital city, **Ioannina,** seem immune to the throngs who crowd the beaches and restaurants, the ferries and ancient sites of so many parts of Greece these days. It isn't the travel-poster Greece many expect, and it certainly hasn't organized itself around tourism and foreigners.

Although there are plenty of hotels and restaurants, the pace of life in Ioannina and other Western Greece cities, not to mention in the villages, is still governed by local customs. During the off season, for instance, places such as the post office and information offices may be closed all weekend. Museum hours are cut back, as are the hours of gift shops and many restaurants. And except for staff in the hotels, better restaurants, and visitor information and car-rental offices, few people speak English, although they may speak Italian, French, or German. You may find yourself sharing a hotel with Greek commercial travelers, and it will probably be harder to find your English-language newspaper or fresh-squeezed orange juice. In other words, this area is for those who enjoy traveling in an authentic foreign land. Try it—you may like it!

A Strategy for Seeing the Region

Visitors to this corner of Greece will come by ship from Italy or Corfu (via Igoumenitsou), by plane from Athens or Thessaloniki, or by car or bus from other parts of Greece. We recommend basing yourself in Ioannina, a city that offers a fine mix of natural attractions, historical associations, and modern amenities. You could rush around Ioannina and Metsovo in 2 to 3 days but I recommend a minimum of 4 days for Epirus—1½ days for

> **Travel Tip: When to Go**
>
> Visit Epirus between mid-June and early September, unless you don't mind slightly cooler weather. Then again, in the winter, you can come here to ski.

Ioannina (and remember you'll have evenings there), 1 day for Metsovo, and a half-day each for Dodona, the Perama cave, and the Zagori region.

A LOOK AT THE PAST In their history, Western Greece and Epirus in particular have often gone in different directions from the rest of the country. The early Greek-speaking communities here shared a common culture with the rest of Greece, worshiping many of the same gods. However, many non-Greeks also settled here and influenced day-to-day life. This, coupled with the region's remoteness, meant that the people here did not participate in the grand classical civilization. Social organization remained more tribal, led by small-time kings. The greatest of the Epirote kings, **Pyrrhus** (318–272 B.C.), was constantly waging war. The term "Pyrrhic victory" refers to his victories (over the Romans south of Rome), which came at great cost. Epirus itself was reduced to a Roman province after 168 B.C. Ioannina, its capital, is said to have been founded by the emperor Justinian around A.D. 527.

During the **Middle Ages,** Western Greece constantly fell prey to invaders. When the Crusaders conquered Constantinople in 1204, some Greeks decided to set up a new state with Ioannina as the capital, the so-called Despotate of Epirus. It never amounted to much and soon fell under outside control. In 1431 it was taken over by the Turks, who eventually controlled most of Greece (although the Venetians and various other western Europeans gained possession of parts of Western Greece).

Near the end of this 350-year phase, Epirus experienced its most dramatic historic moment. In 1788, **Ali Pasha,** the "Lion of Ioannina," established his own relatively independent domain with Ioannina its capital. Born in Albania, he rose to prominence fighting on behalf of the Ottoman sultan in Constantinople. An international celebrity in his day, visited by Byron among others, he was a cruel despot who boasted of killing 30,000 people, often in the most brutal fashion. The Ottomans tolerated Ali Pasha as long as they could, but in 1822 they sent a large force to capture him. He hid in a monastery on the islet off Ioannina but was tracked down, killed, and beheaded.

When the Greeks rose up against the Turks in the 1820s, the southern part of Western Greece, centered around Messolonghi, took an active role, but the bulk of Epirus did not join in. Arta, in the southwest, was freed from Turkish rule in 1881, but Epirus did not formally join Greece until after the Second Balkan War of 1913.

Epirus became a battleground twice more, against the invading Italians and Germans in World War II and then in the Greek civil war. Since then, it has enjoyed peace and quiet prosperity.

GETTING TO & AROUND EPIRUS
Getting There

BY PLANE **Olympic Air** (© 210/966-6666; www.olympicair.com) offers flights to Ioannina from Athens—usually two a day. Olympic flies at least once a day between Ioannina and Thessaloniki, but with a stopover in Athens.

BY BOAT **Igoumenitsou,** on the coast opposite Corfu, is the point of entry to northwestern Greece for many people. In summer, ferries connect hourly to Corfu (trip time 1–2 hr., depending on the ship) and less frequently to Kefalonia, Ithaka, and Paxi. A hydrofoil service also runs twice daily during high season, between Corfu and Igoumenitsou (allow about a half-hour). Numerous ferries and ships that put into Igoumenitsou go to and from ports in Italy—Ancona, Bari, Brindisi, and Venice; some of these connect with Patras or Piraeus in Greece or with even more distant ports such as Iraklion, Crete, or Cesme, Turkey.

In high season a ferry connects **Astakos**—on the Ionian coast south of Preveza and north of Messolonghi—to the offshore islands of Ithaka and Kefalonia.

The schedules are too complex to list here. For information in advance, go to **www. gtp.gr** or **www.ferries.gr**. When in Igoumenitsou and wanting to make plans to move on, contact **Thalassa Travel** at 20 Ethniki Antistasseos (© **26650/22-001**).

BY BUS   The **KTEL** line (© **210/512-5954** in Athens, or 26510/26-211 in Ioannina) enters northwestern Greece from points such as Athens (7½ hr.) or Thessaloniki (8 hr.).

BY CAR   **From Athens,** there are two main routes. One takes the inland route north via Livadia, Lamia, Karditsa, Trikkala, Kalambaka, and Ioannina. The second runs via Corinth and then along the southern coast of the Gulf of Corinth to Rio; from there, take the new bridge to Anti-Rio, and then drive north via Messolonghi, Agrinio, and Arta to Ioannina. Alternatively, head to the Ionian coast after Messolonghi, and go up to Igoumenitsou via Astakos, Preveza, and Parga.

From **Igoumenitsa** and **Thessaloniki** you now travel on the recently (2009) completed A-2 expressway—also referred to as the Egnatia Road (as it parallels the ancient Roman road of that name). **From western Europe,** you can drive through the former Yugoslavia (now independent nations)—either along the Dalmatian Coast or via the inland expressway—and enter northern Greece at Florina, from where you head south to Kastoria and Ioannina.

Getting Around

BY BUS   With enough time, you can see most of Western Greece by bus (add time for side trips); given the many mountainous roads and curves, you might prefer to let others do the driving. **KTEL** provides bus links between most towns in Western Greece. Buses leave for **Athens** and points **north, northwest,** and **northeast** (Igoumenitsou, Metsovo, Konitsa, Kastoria, and Thessaloniki) from Ioannina's **main bus terminal** at 4 Zosimadon (© **26510/26-211**). A smaller **bus terminal** in Ioannina, at 19 Vizaniou (© **26510/25-014**), handles travel to the **south** (Parga, Arta, Preveza, Astakos, Messolonghi, and Patras).

BY CAR   Having a car is probably the best way to experience Western Greece at its fullest. Trips take much longer than a map might suggest due to the many mountain roads. (Mopeds and motorcycles are not advised except for the most experienced riders.) Western Greece doesn't offer the choice in car rentals found in more touristed parts of Greece. We think **Budget** in Ioannina, at 109 Dodonis (© **26510/43-901**), is the best agency to deal with. This family affair is run by owner Angela Tsamatos, her son Stelios, and genial manager Paul Angelis. Don't

Museum & Sites Hour Update

If you visit Greece during the summer, check to see when major sites and museums are open. According to the official postings, they should be open from 8am to 7:30pm, but some may close earlier in the day and are often closed 1 day a week.

expect to haggle during high season—there are a limited number of vehicles for the influx of tourists.

BY TAXI   With all the switchbacks and hairpin roads, you might prefer to take a taxi. Agree on a fee before you set out. Each hour's drive into the countryside should cost about 40€, and each hour's waiting, about 10€, so that a full day's excursion would run about 150€—not all that much if divided among two or three people. Try to get a driver who speaks some English or a foreign language you understand, and you'll get a guide, too. Reward him in turn with a generous tip.

IOANNINA ★

106km (65 miles) E of Igoumenitsou; 452km (280 miles) N of Athens

Once a sleepy medieval town, Ioannina changed in 1204, when Greeks fleeing Constantinople (after its capture by the Crusaders) arrived and made it the capital of the Despotate of Epirus. The first despot, Michael I, started building the walls that over the next centuries would be enlarged and strengthened by various conquerors—Greeks, Italians, Serbs, and Turks—to become the magnificent walled old town and the lively contemporary city that appeals to many of us today.

Essentials

GETTING THERE   **By Car**   Ioannina is 8 hours from Athens by car.

BY PLANE   **Olympic Air** (www.olympicir.com; ✆ **26510/26-518**) flies to Ioannina from Athens, usually twice a day. At least once a day there are Olympic flights between Ioannina and Thessaloniki (but via Athens). Olympic's office in downtown Ioannina is in a building at the far side of the triangle of greenery at the top of the Central Square. Hours are Monday through Friday from 8am to 3pm; outside those hours, try the airport office at ✆ **26510/39-131.** The **airport** is about 4km (2½ miles) from the center of town; public buses (nos. 2 and 7) run frequently from the main square, but you will probably find it more convenient to take a taxi.

VISITOR INFORMATION   **Epirus Tourism Directorate** is at 39 Leoforos Dodonis, the main street exiting the top of the square (✆ **26510/41-868;** www.gtp.gr/cpirus-tourism). Summer hours are Monday through Friday from 7:30am to 2:30pm and 5:30 to 8:30pm, Saturday from 9am to 1pm; winter hours are Monday through Friday from 7:30am to 2:30pm.

In summer, the city also maintains an information booth down on the lake, to the left of the fortress and by the quay where you get the boats to the islet Nissi; it's open Monday through Saturday from 10am to 8pm.

Also helpful are the many travel agencies, particularly **Daskalopoulos Yiannis Tour World,** 13 28th Octobriou (✆ **26510/29-667;** www.daskalopoulos-travel.com).

FAST FACTS   There are numerous **ATMs** in the center of Ioannina (and also a couple in Metsovo); branches of the big national **banks** can handle all money exchanges. There is an internationally respected medical school and **hospital** at Dourouti, some 7km (4 miles) south of Ioannina. There is another hospital at Hatzikosta (2km/1 mile). There are several **Internet cafes**—the most central are at 17 Pirsinella and 105 Leoforos Dodonis. The **tourist police** are located at **Police Headquarters,** 13 28th Octobriou (✆ **26510/65-938**); it's open daily from 7am to 2am. The main **post office** is on 3 28th Octobriou (✆ **26510/26-437**). It's open Monday through Saturday from 7:30am to 8pm; in the off season, it's closed on Saturday. The telephone office (OTE) is at the rear (right) on 4 28th Octobriou, and is open daily from 7am to 10pm.

What to See & Do

Archaeological Museum ★ This fine little provincial museum showcases a few unique items, including the small lead tablets found at the **Oracle of Dodona** (see "Side Trips from Ioannina," later in this chapter). Other displays focus on items taken from graves and burial sites in Epirus, ranging from Paleolithic implements (including one of the oldest stone tools in Greece) through the Bronze Age to Roman times. Various bronze works—including a drinking cup, pitcher, vessels, and votive animals—are especially interesting, as is the superb Attic-style sarcophagus dating from the 2nd to 3rd century A.D., with carved scenes from the *Iliad*.

Plateia 25 Martiou (behind clock tower and Greek Army base on Central Sq.). ⓒ **26510/25-490.** Fax 26510/22-595. Admission 5€ adults, 2€ E.U. seniors over 65. Tues–Sun 8:30am–3pm. In central city so no need to drive.

A STROLL AROUND THE FROURIO: THE WALLED OLD TOWN & CITADEL ★

For many of the centuries that Ioannina fell under the occupation of foreign conquerors, city walls enclosed the most important structures. There's not much of historic or architectural importance outside the citadel except on the islet of Nissi. A moat—now filled in—separated the fortress from the mainland. An esplanade circles the lakeside below the walls, and there are several openings in the wall, but most people enter the walls from **Plateia Giorgio,** which is lined with tavernas and shops.

A left turn inside the Plateia Giorgio gate onto Ioustinianou leads (in about 2 blocks) to the **synagogue.** Dating from 1829, this white-walled synagogue remains locked. You must track down someone who can let you in—best is to ask at the **shop** of Mrs. Allegra Matsa, 18 Anexartisias (ⓒ **26510/27-008**). Continue around the inside perimeter of the walls until you come to a large clearing. From here, ascend a cobblestoned slope to **Aslan Pasha Cami,** a 17th-century school with cells for Islamic scholars. Its **mosque** now houses the **Municipal Popular Art Museum.** In summer, it's open daily from 8am to 8pm; in winter, hours are Monday through

---

Ioannina's Jewish Community

The oldest records of Jews in Ioannina date from the early 1300s, but it is generally accepted that they had been there since at least Roman times—and likely since the time of Alexander the Great. Having come directly from the Near East, they, like other such Jews in Greece, are known as **Romaniotes;** they spoke a dialect of Greek with some Hebrew and other elements and differed in various ways from the Sephardic Jews elsewhere in the Mediterranean. Over the centuries, Ioannina's community grew with infusions of Jews from around the Mediterranean, but many then emigrated abroad, so that by the mid–20th century there were only about 2,000 Jews in Ioannina. After the Germans occupied Greece in 1941, they rounded up Ioannina's Jews and sent them off to labor and extermination camps, where most perished. After the war about 175 returned; today barely 60 Jews live in Ioannina, but they manage to maintain their fine old synagogue. A small **Holocaust Memorial** is located just outside the citadel, on the corner of Karamanlis and Soutsou.

Ioannina

ATTRACTIONS ●
Boats to Island **4**
Byzantine Museum **8**
Folk Art Museum **12**
The Kastro **14**
Municipal Popular Art
  Museum **5**
Synagogue **7**
Turkish Bazaar **10**

HOTELS ■
Galaxy Hotel **15**
Hotel Kastro **6**
Hotel du Lac **16**
Hotel Olympic **13**
Hotel Palladion **11**

RESTAURANTS ◆
Gastra **1**
Pamvotis **4**
Propodes **4**
Stin Ithaki **2**
The Pharos **3**
To Mantelo **9**

ⓘ Information Ⅽ OTE ✉ Post Office

Friday from 8am to 3pm, Saturday and Sunday from 9am to 3pm. Admission is 4€. Aslan Pasha built the mosque in 1618 on the site of an Orthodox church he razed to punish the Christian Greeks for a failed revolt. The exhibits, which include traditional costumes, jewelry, weapons, documents, and household wares, are grouped around the three major religious-ethnic communities of Ioannina: Orthodox Greeks, Muslims, and Jews. When an adjacent minaret and the mosque are illuminated each night, the scene from the lake is captivating.

In the opposite and far corner of the walled town is the innermost citadel, known by its Turkish name, **Itz Kale.** Within it are the **Victory Mosque (Fethiye Camiles),** the remains of Ali Pasha's palace, and the alleged **tombs** of Ali Pasha and his wife (see "A Look at the Past," above, for more about him). The Greek army occupied this part of the citadel for years; its structures, now restored, include the **Byzantine Museum,** in the rebuilt **palace** and **harem.** The former houses icons and other church-related objects; the latter concentrates on silverwork. Hours are daily from 9am to 3pm; admission is 4€.

A STROLL AROUND MODERN IOANNINA

Ioannina has become a busy commercial center for all of northwestern Greece (pop. 100,000), and its streets can be crowded and noisy. One interesting retreat is the old **Turkish Bazaar,** near the walled town just off the main street, Averoff. In its tiny shops, you may see a few men practicing the old crafts—metalsmiths, jewelry makers, cobblers, tailors, and the like. Averoff leads into the edge of the Central Square with the **clock tower** on the left. Up behind this is the city's **Archaeological Museum** (see above). When you leave the museum, stroll across the broad, terraced gardens built over the site of what was once the **walled kastro,** where the Christians lived during the Turkish era. Returning to the main street, you are now on the **Central Square (Plateia Pyrros),** with its share of cafes and restaurants.

A BOAT TRIP TO THE ISLET OF NISSI (NISSAKI) ★★

If you have only a day in Ioannina, try to spend at least 2 to 3 hours (including a meal) visiting **Nissi,** the islet in Lake Pamvotis. Small boats leave from the quay below the fortress every half-hour in summer, from 6:30am to 11pm. In the off season, service is every hour—but note that the last boat leaves the island around 10pm. The fare is 1.50€. The lake has unfortunately become overgrown with algae and is so polluted that local restaurants do not serve the fish taken from it (or so we've been assured).

The boat ride takes barely 10 minutes and, day and night, provides a fine view of Ioannina. You get off near the lobby of three restaurants—each displaying a tank filled with seafood. Resist all until you are truly ready to eat. The specialties of these restaurants include eel, frogs' legs, carp, crayfish, trout, and other imported fish.

The small village here is said to have been founded in the 16th century by refugees from the Mani region of the Peloponnese, but your destination is the five monasteries that predate it. Take the narrow passage between the two restaurants; signs are posted to your left and right. Follow the signs to the left (east), and you will come to the restored **Monastery of Panteleimon.** Little of the original remains.

The monastery houses a **small museum** devoted to the infamous Ali Pasha; its numerous pictures and personal items include his clothing and water pipe. It's open daily, and an attendant will come if it's closed. Admission is 1€. In 1820, Pasha took refuge here, where he was eventually killed in 1822 by Turks. You may even be shown holes in the floor where it is alleged he was shot from below.

Directly beside this monastery is the **Monastery of the Prodromos (St. John the Baptist),** but most people will want to move on to the western edge of the islet, following the signs to **Moni Filanthropinon ★** (also known as the **Monastery of Ayios Nikolaos Spanos**). It's sometimes referred to as the "Secret School"; Orthodox priests supposedly maintained a clandestine school here during the Turkish occupation. Founded in the 13th century, it was rebuilt in the 16th century with magnificent frescoes. Seldom does the public get to view such an ensemble of Byzantine frescoes so close up. Although the dim light can be a problem (bring a flashlight), you should be able to recognize such subjects as the life of Christ on the walls of the apse, God and the Apostles in the central dome, and the many saints. Most unexpected, however, are the portrayals of famous ancient Greek sages on the wall of the narthex as you enter—Aristotle, Plato, Plutarch, Solon, and Thucydides. (There's no admission, but it's customary to leave a gratuity with the caretaker.)

About 100m (328 ft.) farther along the trail is **Ayios Nikolaos Dilios** (or **Moni Stratgopoulou**), the oldest monastery (dating from the 11th c.) on Nissi. Its 16th-century frescoes are also of some interest but are in poor condition. (A small tip to the caretaker is called for.) The fifth monastery, **Ayios Eleouses,** is closed to the public.

By now you have earned your meal on Nissi. Choose a restaurant (see **Pamvotis** under "Where to Eat," below).

SHOPPING

It seems as if every third store in old Ioannina sells jewelry, silverware, hammered copper, and embossed brasswork—the traditional crafts. Many of the jewelry stores sell modern work in gold and silver and/or precious and semiprecious jewels. Prices are probably lower than those in more cosmopolitan cities. However, be wary of "antiques" offered in some shops—they may not be all that old, and if they really do date earlier than 1830, you need an export license!

There's a cluster of jewelry and gift shops opposite the walled citadel. Typical selections of metalwork (and also water pipes) may be found at **Politis Douvflis,** 12 Plateia Yioryio; or at **Nikos Gogonis,** 13 Karamanlis. At 56 and 65 Averoff, **George Minos Moschos** offers a somewhat more unusual selection of silver, jewelry, and older secondhand objects ("antiques"). **Pospotikis Bothers,** 12 Ethnikis Antistaseos, has a fine selection of bronze objects, some antiques jewelry, and reproductions of older metal objects. Here and there you may see embroidered clothing or woven socks, but this region is not especially known for its needlework.

Where to Stay

EXPENSIVE

Hotel du Lac Congress Center and Spa ★ This has been Ioannina's prime hotel since 1998, and it remains highly recommended both for its accommodations and location. (The Epirus Lux Palace is equally luxurious but is out on the highway.) Its marble and woodwork and carpets may strike some as a bit pretentious, but most importantly, its service lives up to its image. The rooms are a bit larger than in many Greek hotels, and many enjoy a view across to the lake; ask for one. The buffet breakfast is almost excessive; the **restaurant's** meals are probably the most elaborate in town, although not especially Greek. Some might find its distance from the center (a 15-min. walk) a downside, but in return you get a quiet lakeside locale. The only negative: As its name suggests, it is often crowded with conference attendees.

Leoforos Andrea Miaouli and Ikkou (along the lake, 1km/½ mile right of the walled citadel), 45221 Ioannina. www.hoteldulac.gr. ✆ **26510/59-100.** Fax 26510/59-200. 170 units. High season 175€ double; low season 150€ double. Rates include buffet breakfast. AE, DC, MC, V. Free parking on grounds. **Amenities:** 2 restaurants; 2 bars; babysitting; children's playground and pool; concierge; outdoor pool; room service; smoke-free rooms; Wi-Fi in lobby. *In room:* A/C, TV, CD player, hair dryer, Internet, minibar.

MODERATE

Hotel Olympic If you like to step out of a hotel and be at the center of the action, such as it is in Ioannina—and don't need a lot of frills—the Olympic is your choice. It has long attracted members of the foreign diplomatic corps, government dignitaries, and such. All that means nothing, of course, if you aren't made to feel welcome and comfortable, and you can be assured of both. The lobby is modest, but the desk service and 24-hour room service are what count. All the corridors, guest rooms, and bathrooms have been renovated since 2004. Ask for an upper-story front room with a view of the distant lake.

2 Melanidi (1 block off Central Sq.), 45220 Ioannina. www.hotelolymp.gr. ✆ **26510/25-888.** Fax 26510/ 22-041. 54 units. High season 130€ double; low season 110€ double. MC, V. Free parking close to hotel. **Amenities:** Restaurant; bar; babysitting; room service, Wi-Fi. *In room:* A/C, TV, Internet, minibar.

Hotel Palladion 🔥   Maybe it's because it's the first hotel in Ioannina I happened to have stayed in, but I have always liked it for its combination of features: convenient yet quiet, helpful desk staff, no frills but good value, and the fact that everything works. Rooms of decent size and decor are insulated from most street noise by good windows. Bathrooms are standard issue. When I asked to move from one room because of cigarette odor, this happened instantly and with no questions. (The hotel has now set aside rooms for nonsmokers.) The Palladion often hosts small groups, but this should not interfere with your stay. A final advantage: The hotel has its own parking lot.

1 Botsari (off 28th Octobriou), 45444 Ioannina. www.palladionhotel.gr. ✆ **26510/25-856.** Fax 26510/ 74-034. 128 units. High season 110€ double; low season 75€ double. Rates include buffet breakfast. AE, DC, MC, V. Private parking lot. **Amenities:** 2 restaurants; bar; babysitting; smoke-free rooms. *In room:* A/C, TV, fridge, hair dryer.

INEXPENSIVE

Hotel Galaxy   There's not much else to say about this hotel except that the rooms are cheap and clean and it's centrally located. Rooms have tub showers but in return some rooms offer a view of the lake. Clearly only for those on a limited budget.

Plateia Pyrros (Central Sq.), 45221 Ioannina. ✆ **26510/25-432.** Fax 26510/30-724. 38 units. 60€ double. No credit cards. Parking in area. **Amenities:** Bar, room service. *In room:* A/C, TV, hair dryer

Hotel Kastro ★ 🔥   As the only hostelry inside the old walled city, this is arguably the most rewarding place to stay in Ioannina—and thus hard to get one of its seven rooms at the last minute. It's a 19th-century house, tastefully restored by the proprietors. Most visitors happily accept its lack of some amenities in return for the unique experience of being here. Visitors also report that outside noise can be annoying at night during the high season. Cheaper basement rooms look out onto street level; showers in the bathrooms are small; breakfast is basic. But for those who enjoy old inns or pensions, this will be a highlight of your visit to Ioannina.

57 Andronikou Paleologou (near the Byzantine Museum, approached from lakeside gateway), 45221 Ioannina. www.i-escape.com/hotel-kastro. ✆ **26510/22-866.** 7 units. High season 75€–90€ double. Rates include continental breakfast. MC, V. Parking outside on street. *In room:* Fan.

Where to Eat

MODERATE

Gastra Restaurant ★ GREEK REGIONAL   A must for those looking to try this regional specialty—food cooked in a *gastra:* A conical cast-iron lid is placed over the iron baking dish (similar to a clay pot) holding the food of choice (lamb, goat, pork, or chicken); it is placed in an outdoor oven heaped with red-hot embers. The meat roasts slowly, resulting in an especially succulent, delicious meal. The restaurant has other specialties as well; for an appetizer, try the *skordalia karithia* (walnut-garlic dip), and for dessert, the special crème caramel. In pleasant weather, sit in the garden and watch your meal cook in the open fireplace. On Sunday, you are advised to leave the restaurant to the citizens of Ioannina. (If it's too crowded and you need your *gastra,* proceed less than 2km/1 mile after taking the left turn signed to Igoumenitsou to another, similar restaurant, the **Diogenes**.)

16a Kostaki, Eleousa, along the Airport-Igoumenitsou Hwy. (7km/4 miles outside Ioannina; 3km/2 miles past airport entrance, just before turnoff to Igoumenitsou). ℂ **26510/61-530.** www.gastra.gr. Reservations recommended in high season on weekend evenings. Main courses 7€-19€. No credit cards. Tues-Sun 1-5pm and 8pm-1am. Bus: 2.

Pamvotis GREEK/SEAFOOD   If you can have only one meal in Ioannina, head to the islet in the lake. Ask around as to which restaurant is the best, and you'll get a different answer from each person. The choices serve similar dishes, so choose a location that appeals to you. I've always liked this one—near the dock where the ferries put in. You can pick your lobster, *karavides* (a cross btw. crayfish and shrimp), trout, or other fish out of holding tanks. If you're game, try one of the two local specialties: frogs' legs or eel. The white Zitsa Primus, a slightly sparkling white wine from the region, is a perfect accompaniment. For a more natural setting, try **Propodes Restaurant** next to Ayios Panteleimon Monastery. (See "A Boat Trip to the Islet of Nissi [Nissaki]," above.)

Nissi Ioannina (the offshore islet). ℂ **26510/81-081.** Fax 26510/81-631. Main courses 7€-18€. MC, V. High season daily 11am-midnight; low season daily 11am-10pm. Ferry from Ioannina's lakefront.

The Pharos GREEK   One of several restaurants set back from the lakefront, the Pharos offers good meals in a pleasant setting. In warm weather, you can sit under the awning in the square opposite. The menu is traditional but offers some variation. The fried peppers in garlic sauce make a delicious appetizer. For your main course, order whatever's being grilled that day, and get the pilaf instead of potatoes. Feeling flush? Go for the crab or trout. If you're there only for the location, opt for the fresh fruit-salad plate.

13 Plateia Mavili (down along lakefront—just walk here). ℂ **26510/26-506.** Main courses 6€-18€. No credit cards. Daily 9am-10pm. Closed mid-Oct to Mar. Bus from Central Sq., or a 10-min. walk.

Stin Ithaki ★ GREEK/MIDDLE EASTERN   Many consider this if not the best, then the most interesting of the restaurants along the waterfront. There's no explaining why and how the proprietors offer such a varied ethnic menu—Turkish, Cretan, Cypriot. Try some of the unusual *mezes*—many are from Anatolia. Various types of chicken dishes are among its specialties. They also serve some of the dishes of the region, including trout and frogs' legs. Portions are generous—save space for the desserts, especially the walnut cake. There's no denying its location makes everything that much tastier, so go here on an evening and be prepared to linger.

20a Stratigou Papagou (about .5km/¼ mile) from the boat landing on the lakefront. Parking on site. ℂ **26510/73-012.** Main courses 5€-18€. No credit cards. Daily 10am-1 am.

INEXPENSIVE

To Mantelo ♦ GREEK TAVERNA   Here's a no-frills, traditional Greek taverna that gives you a front-row seat on the square outside the old walled town, where all kinds of characters congregate. For an appetizer, try the marinated, fried peppers, squash, or eggplant. All of the grilled dishes—veal, chicken, lamb, and calves' liver— are good. Be sure to ask for the pilaf. The taverna can feel cramped when it's crowded, but that's what makes it Greek.

Plateia Georgio 15 (opposite the citadel's main entrance—just walk here). ℂ **26510/25-452.** Main courses 6€-12€. No credit cards. Daily 10am-2am.

SIDE TRIPS FROM IOANNINA

Dodona (Dodoni) ★

Even if you don't visit every classical ruin, this one offers a rare reward: a spectacular theater at one of the major oracles of the ancient world. In August, the theater produces classical Greek dramas; ask at a travel agency for specific information.

Dodona is only 22km (14 miles) from Ioannina. With a car, a round-trip visit should take about 3 hours. The bus service is inconvenient—basically there's only one bus very early in the morning, and then you're stuck at the site for hours. It's better to spring for a **taxi**—about 75€ for the round-trip, including an hour's wait. The first 7km (4 miles) are on a main highway due south (signed to Arta); the turn to the right at about 7km (4 miles) is signed Dodona; you proceed about 3km (2 miles) on a relatively flat road before the final 12km (7½ miles) on an ascending and curving road. You'll arrive at a plateau ringed by mountains. The trip becomes part of the experience—you get the sense that you're on a pilgrimage to a remote shrine. Admission to the sacred areas is 4€. In high season, the site is open daily from 8am to 8pm; off season, it's open Monday through Saturday from 10am to 3pm.

The **Oracle of Zeus** at Dodona traces its roots back to the early Hellenistic people who had arrived in northwestern Greece by about 2000 B.C. They probably worshiped Zeus, but at Dodona there was already an earth goddess cult with an oracle that might have based its interpretations on the flights of pigeons. In any case, by about 1400 B.C., it appears that the Zeus-worshiping Greeks had imposed their god on the site and turned the goddess into his consort, Dione.

By this time, too, the priests linked Zeus's presence to the rustling leaves of an oak tree at Dodona and interpreted these sounds as oracular messages. The Greeks set up a shrine around the tree—a simple, protective fence. Over the centuries they built more and more elaborate structures on the site.

Eventually, they established a temple to Zeus here in the 4th century B.C. At that time, the oracle spoke through the bronze statue of a youth with a whip. The wind stirred the whip so it would strike nearby metal cauldrons. Priests then interpreted the reverberations. Many ambitious structures, both religious and secular, were erected at Dodona, but the oracle effectively ceased functioning in the 4th century A.D.—about the time when, it is claimed by some, the original oak died. The oak now on the shrine's site is, of course, a recent planting.

Although the walls are all but destroyed, the magnificent **theater** survives, thanks to its reassembling in the 19th century. The first theater, built in the 3rd century B.C.,

---

✄ Ancient Greeks' Dear Abby

People from all stations of life came to Dodona with a request or a question for the oracle. Their desire or query was inscribed on a strip of lead and then submitted to the oracle. Some were quite practical: "Should I buy a certain property?" "Should I engage in shipping?" Others had a religious tinge: "To which god should we pray or sacrifice to get certain results?" But the most intriguing are also the most personal: "Shall I take another wife?" "Am I the father of her children?" These tablets—some now to be seen in the Ioannina Archaeological Museum—speak to us as do few remains from the ancient world.

Visiting with the Vlachs

One special inducement to visit Metsovo is that it's the center (in Greece) of the **Vlach people,** who claim descent from Latin-speaking Wallachians of what is now Romania. The Vlachs were originally shepherds who followed their flocks, and some still do just that; but over the centuries, many others settled down in Northern Greece and prospered in crafts, commerce, trade, and now tourism. Some wealthier Vlachs made their money dealing in wool. Because the Vlachs wrote little of their Latin-based language down and because it's not taught in the schools, it's in danger of being lost as the new generation marries and moves away. You'll find the Vlachs of Metsovo extremely congenial—and patient— when visitors ask them to say something in Vlach. (Don't expect your Latin to help much!) A declining number of older people wear traditional Vlach clothing every day, but fancier costumes come out on Sundays and holidays. If you want to see their **dances,** July 26 is the village's feast day, but be forewarned— the village will be jammed.

is said to have seated 17,000. It was destroyed, but another of the same size replaced it in the 2nd century B.C. Later, the Romans converted the theater into an arena for gladiator contests. The theater, one of the largest on the Greek mainland, has almost the same marvelous acoustics as the famous (but smaller) one at Epidaurus. Just to sit here is an evocative experience.

Perama Cave ★

Only about 5km (3 miles) north of Ioannina (the turnoff is past the airport), this cave is actually a series of caverns. It was discovered in 1941, during World War II, when people were combing the countryside in search of hiding places. Now thoroughly developed, with lights, steps, and handrails, it features a half-mile walk through a series of vast caverns and narrow passageways. In high season it's open daily from 8am to 8pm, and in winter daily from 9am to 5pm (✆ **26510/81-521**). Guided tours set out about every 15 minutes from the well-signed entrance in Perama village; the fee is 6€ (2.5€ for children). The guides often don't speak much English; they may only repeat the names assigned to the unusually shaped stalagmites and stalactites. They may also rush everyone through—but you can linger and join the next group. Perama may not live up to its boast as one of the most spectacular caves in the world, but it's worth a visit if you haven't been in many caves. **Warning:** Some stretches can be slippery. And at the very end, you must climb what seems like an endless number of steps to come out of the cave. But people of all shapes and ages have made it up and—you emerge into a cafe!

Metsovo ★★

This traditional mountain village has become so popular that at times its original appeal is in danger of being overwhelmed by tourism at its worst. Still, most visitors find it satisfying—some even find it magical. It's about a 1½-hour bus ride east of Ioannina. A couple of buses go to Metsovo in the morning, but only one returns from Metsovo in the late afternoon that allows for a day in the village. So either pay close attention to the always-changing bus schedule or, better still, rent a car. (Buses also come from Athens and Thessaloniki.)

Metsovo sits at about 1,000m (3,300 ft.) above sea level, nestled among peaks of the Pindos Mountains. In addition to day-trippers, serious nature lovers and hikers are drawn here from all over Greece and Europe. Overnight accommodations are often strained, especially during Greek holidays. And with ski slopes nearby, Metsovo is also a popular winter destination.

The village is renowned for its Alpine-style architecture—stone buildings with wooden balconies and slate roofs. Disneyland it ain't, but don't go to Metsovo thinking you're the first to come upon an undiscovered village—there's even a fairly ambitious conference center in town. To get some advance views of Metsovo, Google it and you'll find lots of photos posted.

Crafts—weaving, embroidery, and woodwork—are on display in many shops along the main street. Some is touristy kitsch, but some is authentically local and handsome. The best can be found at **Metsovo Folk Art Cooperative,** about 50m (164 ft.) from the Egnatia Hotel on the slope above it. Also representing the true Metsovo is the little **church of Ayia Paraskevi** on the main square, with its carved-wood altar screen, silver chandeliers, and copies of Ravenna mosaics.

The **Museum of Folk Art** is in the Arhondiko Tossizza (sometimes spelled Tositsa), a 17th-century mansion completely restored by Baron Michalis Tossizza, a wealthy Vlach living in Switzerland. With its paneled rooms, furniture, rugs, clothing, and crafts, it's a superb example of how a prosperous family might once have lived in Epirus. The museum, located on a road above the main street, is open Friday through Wednesday 8:30am to 1pm and 4 to 6pm in the summer, but hours are limited to 3 to 5pm only in the off season. Admission is 3€.

An unexpected and unusual attraction in Metsovo is the **Averoff Museum of Neohellenic Art,** founded in 1988 by a wealthy and prominent member of the town's premier Vlach family, Evangelos Averoff-Tossizza. The museum has a fine selection of Greek paintings, sculpture, and prints from the 19th and 20th centuries,

A Special Monastery

Some of the most memorable experiences in Greece come not from visiting major sites but from remote, unexpected encounters. There's one outside Metsovo—the restored 14th-century **Moni Ayios Nikolaos**—that rewards a little extra effort. It's not just that the church contains some spectacular 18th-century frescoes (lost to sight until the 1950s), a fine iconostasis, and some icons. It's that the resident caretaker is a lovely woman who, even if you don't know a word of Greek, somehow manages to communicate with you; beyond that, she weaves her own textiles in the Metsovo tradition and will sell them to you—but only if you are interested. Finally there is the monastery's location, high on a slope in a remote setting. There are two ways to get there. One is a half-hour walk down a rather steep and rough trail (and an hour-long walk back up). It's signed from the far corner of the main square; take the second left, head for the clock tower, and then follow the signs. But you can drive closer to it by taking the road out of the town square signed Ioannina; at about 1km (½ mile), turn left onto the asphalt road signed Anilio, and wind downward for another 3.5km (2 miles). You will spot the monastery on the hillside to your left, and after parking you have to scramble through a vineyard. Knock on the door—the caretaker will allow entry during reasonable hours (until 7:30pm in high season).

housed in a building erected for it (and located behind the Town Hall above the main street—it's signposted). Hours are Wednesday through Monday 10am to 6:30pm July 15 to September 14, and 10am to 4pm September 15 to July 14. Admission is 3€ for adults, 2€ for students; children 9 and under admitted free.

WHERE TO STAY

If you want to overnight in Metsovo, choosing a hotel is easy; all are relatively inexpensive, all offer acceptable accommodations, and all are to some degree decorated in the regional style. Those listed below stay open all year because of the winter sports in the area, so all offer central heating. If none of those listed can accommodate you, readers have also recommended the **Hotel Bitouni** near the town center (www.bitouni-metsovon.eurobokings.com; ✆ **26560/41-217**).

Galaxias ★ If you want to be at the center of things, then this should be your choice—but it's for travelers who appreciate the feeling of a country inn. The homey atmosphere emanates from the Barbayanni family, who run this hotel and restaurant (reviewed below). It's by no means fancy—the rooms are modest in size and decor, the bathrooms adequate. The decor, lots of wood and stone and textiles, is the traditional style for this region. Ask for a room in the front with a view of the distant mountains.

On a terrace above the main square. http://hotel-galaxias-metsovo.focusgreece.gr. ✆ 26560/41-202. Fax 26560/41-124. 10 units, with shower or with tub. High season 80€ double; low season 65€ double. Rates include continental breakfast. MC, V. Parking behind hotel. Pets allowed. **Amenities:** Restaurant; bar; roof garden; smoking room. In room: A/C, TV, fireplace, fridge, hair dryer.

Hotel Victoria ★ The Victoria, reminiscent of an Alpine inn, offers a little luxury in a natural setting on the edge of town. Natural materials, large functioning fireplaces, and hearty furnishings make the smallish guest rooms quite cozy; all have balconies and/or views. And because the Victoria is relatively new (from the late 1980s and completely renovated in 2007), its bathrooms are modern. The hotel maintains its own fine **restaurant** as well. However, you really come here for the isolation and the views. In winter, the Victoria is frequented mainly by skiers, but it's popular year-round with Greeks and other Europeans—reservations are advised. By the way, the proprietors are Vlach—here's your chance to learn a few words!

About 1km (½ mile) from the main square. www.victoriahotel.gr. ✆ 26560/41-771. Fax 26560/41-454. 37 units, with shower or with tub. 85€ double; Christmas and Easter seasons 110€ double. Rates include continental breakfast. MC, V. **Amenities:** Bar; swimming pool; sauna. In room: TV, fireplace, Jacuzzi.

Kassaros Hotel For a location away from the square (but not as far as the Victoria), try the Kassaros Hotel. This is the perfect place for an extended or active stay in Metsovo—the proprietor also runs a travel agency, Kassaros Travel, which rents out ski equipment and a snowmobile as well as its own buses for excursions throughout Epirus. There's nothing special about the rooms or facilities but all are first-rate.

About 90m (300 ft.) along road leading from main square back to Ioannina. ✆ 26560/41-800. Fax 26560/41-262. 31 units, with shower or with tub. High season 90€ double; low season 75€ double. Rates include continental breakfast. AE, DC, MC, V. **Amenities:** Bar; Jacuzzi; sauna. In room: TV.

WHERE TO EAT

Even if you spend only a few hours in Metsovo, you should try a meal at a restaurant that offers traditional Epirote fare. Along the main street, **Tositsa, Taverna Panormiko, Restaurant Toxotis,** and **Cafe Chroni Roof Garden** are all good.

Galaxias ★ GREEK/REGIONAL This is my favorite restaurant in Metsovo. In warm weather, you can sit outdoors; in cooler weather, sit in the handsome dining

trekking INTO vikos gorge

A trek into Vikos Gorge is a serious endeavor. Just to get to the gorge's beginning, you must do a rugged 4½- to 5-hour walk—not including the hike back up. The walk through the entire gorge—approximately 16km (10 miles)—is even more demanding. Do not attempt this without proper gear, supplies, and experience.

If you do go, Monodendri's lower square offers one of the most accessible approaches. The path down into the gorge is signed here. To take part in an organized expedition, join one of the groups put together by **Robinson Travel Agency,** at the edge of Ioannina on the main road to the airport, 10 8th Merarchias (© **26510/29-402**). More experienced trekkers might prefer to deal with the **Mountain Climbing Association of Ioannina** (© **26530/22-138**) or the **Mountain Climbing Association of Papingo** (© **26530/41-138**), based in one of the Zagori villages.

room warmed by a cheerful fire. Choose among local specialties: Begin with the *trachana* (bean soup) or a cheese pie with leek; move on to the spicy sausage or beef patties with leeks and celery baked in a pot. For dessert, try the baklava or yogurt, but be sure to save room for one of the local cheeses, either *metsovony* (smoked) or *vlachotiri* (mild). To accompany your meal, ask for the local red wine, Katoyi, or if that's in short supply, the house wine.

In the Galaxias Hotel, just above the main square. © **26560/41-202.** Main courses 6€–20€. MC, V. Daily noon–11pm. Parking up behind hotel.

Zagori (Zagoria/Zagorohoria) & Vikos Gorge

If you have limited time in northwestern Greece and prefer wilder nature to tourist destinations, you might opt to head here instead of Metsovo, Dodona, or Perama Cave. The Zagori is the mountainous area just north of Ioannina, a region of about 1,035 sq. km (400 sq. miles) now part of the **Greek National Park System.** About 45 villages here have remained almost unchanged through the centuries. *Note:* The mountainous roads make for slow going.

The region's most spectacular sight is **Vikos Gorge.** Do not attempt the hike without advance planning. (See the box "Trekking into Vikos Gorge," above.)

Getting around the Zagori without your own vehicle is all but impossible. The buses are too few and far between; on a day trip, you'd have time to visit only one destination. With a car, you can visit several villages, view Vikos Gorge from above, experience the scenery, and be back in Ioannina within 6 to 8 hours.

Take the main road north out of Ioannina toward Konitsa; turnoffs are clearly marked. For most first-time visitors, I'd recommend heading for **Monodendri;** after taking the highway north for 19km (13 miles), just past Metamorfosi, take the right turn signed Vikos Gorge. At about 5km (3 miles), a sign to the right indicates Kipi; the famous high-arched bridges are well worth the brief diversion (8km/5 miles). Regarded as old Turkish structures, they were most likely built in the 19th century for the convenience of packhorse caravans. The first, single-span bridge is Kokkoros; beyond that is three-arched Plakida Bridge. (If you have the time and inclination, another 11km/ 7 miles on through Kipi village leads to **Nigades,** with its strikingly handsome **Church of Ayios Yioryios,** built in 1795.) Returning to the main route, proceed about 39km (25 miles), where a sign indicates a turn right onto Monodendri's lower square.

Drive to the small parking lot at the edge of the village square. Proceed on foot from there, following the sign for Vikos Gorge (which directs travelers to Kato, or Lower Monodendri). It's about a 10-minute walk to the lovely little 15th-century **Monastery of Ayia Paraskevi ★,** perched on the edge of the gorge. The well-protected viewing areas here will be spectacular enough for most people. Only sure-footed and experienced hikers will want to get back on the narrow, unprotected trail above the monastery; there the next several hundred meters lead you to even more spectacular views of the gorge—as well as dramatic drops from the path.

Back at the parking lot, continue on the main road for about another half-mile, until you come to **Monodendri**'s upper square. (A short cobblestone path leads from the lower to this upper square.) The upper town has several modest hotels (I would recommend the **Monodendri Hotel; ☎ 26530-71-300;** www.monodendrihotel.com) and decent restaurants, but unless you seek such amenities, you need not go up there. If you want to have a meal, I recommend either **Katerina's Restaurant** (try her tasty chicken or meat pies) at the top of the square, or **To Petrino Dasos,** the little taverna on the right as you come up to the square. The **Oxio,** a hotel and restaurant opposite To Petrino Dasos, is another possibility but the food is nothing special.

To view the gorge from **Vikos Balcony,** drive up through the upper square and on for another 7km (4½ miles) along the road to Oxia. Leave your car and walk down a stone path to a spectacular view. Local signs claim that Vikos Gorge, at 900m (2,950 ft.), is "the world's deepest," but several places around the world might dispute that.

Next stop is **Papingo.** Drivers are usually advised to retrace their entire route back to the main Ioannina-Konitsa highway and then proceed north to the turnoff to Papingo (a 1½-hr. drive). If you're adventurous—and, more important, able to ask basic directions in Greek—you can take an asphalt road that cuts that time almost in half because it is a more direct route to the highway. You start down from Monodendri but at about 5km (3 miles), take the (signed) right turn and head across the flatland for Elafatopos; do not go up on to Elafatopos, however, but continue and take the left turn signed Kato Pedina. You then come to the main highway; turn right and proceed 4km (2½ miles) until a sign to the right indicates Papingo. The drive from this point on offers the kind of scenery best described by Simon, a young English traveler I once fell in with, who exclaimed, "It makes you want to stop the car and get out and applaud."

Of the two villages, **Megalo Papingo** and **Micro Papingo**—"Big" and "Little" Papingo—we recommend visiting at least the first. Many regard this as the archetypal Zagori village, with its terrain, streets, homes, roofs, public buildings, and everything else seemingly all made of the same stone. Megalo Papingo has several cafes and restaurants as well as modest hotels. You can always be sure of a meal in Papingo, but rooms may be booked up at various times of the year—such is the reputation of the Zagori in Greece and elsewhere in Europe. The most ambitious hotel is the **Papaevangelou** (☎ 26530/41-135; 120€ double); behind it is the **Saxonis Houses** (☎ 26530/41-615; 110€ double); more modest is the **Hotel Koulis** (☎ 26530/41-115; 65€ double); all include private bathrooms and breakfast.

If you drive on another 1.6km (1 mile) from Megalo Papingo, you'll come to Micro Papingo, which offers a view of the mountains from another angle. To really get away from it all, stay at the cozy **Dias Guesthouse** here, with its limited but tasty menu (☎ 26530/41-257; fax 26530/41-892). A double can be 75€, but that may be negotiable depending on the tourist traffic.

For those looking for a special place to stay, there is the **Aristi Mountain Resort ★★** (www.aristi.eu) in the village of that name. It is off the same road that leads from the main highway to the Papingo villages (see above) and is signposted. Built of local stone, this is a true spa resort, with an indoor heated swimming pool as well as a Jacuzzi, sauna, steam bath, and masseur. Rooms include A/C, TV, and Internet connection. The hotel's restaurant specializes in local produce. All of this doesn't come cheap—a double runs from 120€ to 140€ in high season. Whether you sit and admire the view or set out on daily walks, you cannot beat the location.

After all this, you are only about 60km (38 miles) from Ioannina. You can return knowing you've had a taste of the true Epirus.

THE IONIAN ISLANDS

by John S. Bowman

The Ionian Islands (which the Greeks know as the Heptanissi, or "Seven Islands") include Corfu (Kerkira), Paxos (Paxoi), Levkas (Lefkas, Lefkada), Ithaka (Ithaki), Kefalonia (Kefallinia, Cephalonia), and Zakinthos (Zakynthos, Zante); the seventh, Kithira (Cythera, Cerigo). Located off Greece's northwest coast (except for Kithera), the Ionians offer some of the country's loveliest natural settings, including beaches, a fine selection of hotels and restaurants, a distinctive history and lore, and some unusual architectural and archaeological remains.

Strategies for Seeing the Islands

The Ionian Islands are rainier, greener, and more temperate than other Greek islands, so the high season lasts a little longer, from late June to early September. In this chapter, we single out **Corfu** and **Kefalonia,** with a side trip to **Ithaka.** With a couple of weeks to spare, you can take a ship or plane to either Corfu, in the north, or Zakinthos, in the south; and then make your way by ship to several of the other Ionians (although outside high season, you will have to do considerable backtracking). If you have only a week, you should get to one of the larger islands the fastest way possible, and then use ships to get to, at most, a couple of the others. If it comes down to visiting only one, Corfu is a prime candidate, but if you want to get off the beaten track, consider Kefalonia or Ithaka. All the Ionians—especially Corfu—are overrun in July and August; aim for June or September, if you can.

A LOOK AT THE PAST In the fabric of their history, the Ionian Islands can trace certain threads that both tie and distinguish them from the rest of Greece. During the late Bronze Age (1500–1200 B.C.), a Mycenaean culture thrived on several of these islands. Although certain names of islands and cities were the same as those used today—Ithaka, for instance—scholars have never been able to agree on exactly which were the sites described in the *Odyssey.*

People from the city-states on the Greek mainland then recolonized the islands, starting in the 8th century B.C. The Peloponnesian War, in fact, can be traced back to a quarrel between Corinth and its colony at Corcyra (Corfu) that led to Athens's interference and eventually the full-scale war. The islands later fell under the rule of the Romans, then the Byzantine Empire. They remained prey to warring powers and pirates in this part of the Mediterranean for centuries. By the end of the 14th century, Corfu fell

15

📎 **Kerkira = Corfu**

Kerkira is the Modern Greek name for Corfu. Look for it on many schedules, maps, brochures, and other publications.

under Venice's control, and the Italian language and culture—including Roman Catholicism—became predominant.

When Napoleon's forces overcame Venice in 1797, the French took over and held sway until 1815. The Ionian Islands then became a protectorate of the British; although the islands experienced peace and prosperity, they were in fact a colony. When parts of Greece gained independence from the Turks, by 1830—due in part to leadership from Ionians, such as Ioannis Capodistrias—many Ionians became restless under the British. In 1864, British Prime Minister Gladstone allowed the Ionians to unite with Greece.

During World War II, Italians first occupied these islands, but when the Germans took over, the Ionians, especially Corfu, suffered greatly. Since 1945, the waves of tourists have brought considerable prosperity to the Ionian Islands.

CORFU (KERKIRA) ★★

32km (20 nautical miles) W of mainland; another 558km (342 miles) NW of Athens

Cast aside the package tour and you will find Homer's "rich and beautiful land" of olive groves and rugged mountains, 32km (20 miles) off the west coast of Greece. The sunny beaches and ouzo-fueled revelry are there if you want, but this island has a unique history and culture that rewards even the casual visitor. Wander Venetian Corfu Town as the grand fortress lights up in the evening, visit the beach associated with Odysseus, or relax while reading the works of Lawrence and Gerald Durrell, to get a feel for the real Corfu.

BEACHES   **Paleokastritsa** deserves its excellent reputation, with its several bays flanked by cave-riddled cliffs and bluer-than-blue sea. Moving south, **Liapades** has a sublime backdrop, while secluded **Myrtiotissa** attracts nudists. Families like **Sidari,** up on the north coast, with its sandstone formations, and **Ayios Georgios,** with its fine sand and shallow water. On the northeast coast, amid cypress and olive trees, is crescent-shaped **Kalami Bay,** where the Durrells spent their childhood. For watersports and partying, there's **Kavos** on the southern tip.

THINGS TO DO   With its Italianate buildings, French arcade, and English remains, **Corfu Town** provides a history lesson. Visit one of the great **fortresses** to be reminded that the island was long fought over, or the **Archaelogical Museum** to realize it was once important to Greek sculpture. Northeast is the deserted Byzantine town **Old Perithia,** on the slopes of **Mt. Pantocrator** from which **Albania** can be viewed. Leave time for shopping for **fine handicrafts** such as olive wood and needlework.

EATING AND DRINKING   Authentic Greek food, English breakfasts, gyros to go, fine Italian cuisine—you'll find it all in Corfu Town. In tavernas, you'll have your choice of local favorites such as **bourdetto,** spicy fish in a tomato sauce, or **pastitsada,** beef stewed in tomato sauce. Family-run tavernas serve simple but delicious **fresh fish.** So-called house wines are never that great in Greece, but Corfiots are particularly proud of their island wines; among the best are wines such as **Robola, Liapaditiko,** and **Theotaki.**

NIGHTLIFE AND ENTERTAINMENT   Do as the Corfiots do and begin your evening with a *volta* (stroll) under the **Liston's** elegant arcades in Corfu Town. The

Western Greece & The Ionian Islands

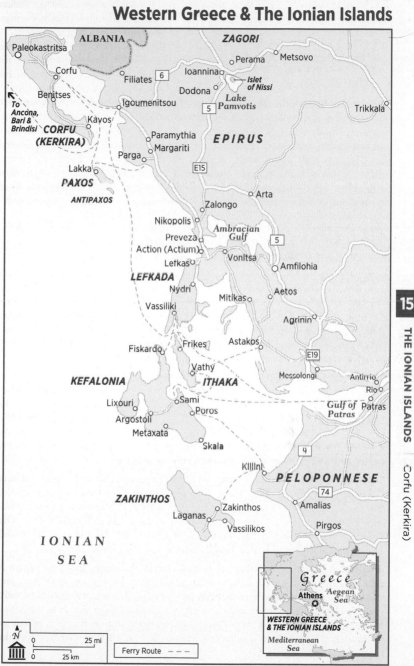

ALBANIA

ZAGORI

Paleokastritsa

Corfu

Benitses

To Ancona, Bari & Brindisi

CORFU (KERKIRA)

Kavos

Filiates   6

Ioannina

Perama   Metsovo

Dodona

Islet of Nissi

Igoumenitsou

Lake Pamvotis   5

Trikkala

Paramythia

EPIRUS

Margariti

Parga

Lakka

PAXOS

ANTIPAXOS

E15

Arta

Zalongo

Nikopolis

Ambracian Gulf

Preveza

Action (Actium)

Vonltsa

5

Lefkas

Amfilohia

LEFKADA

Nydri

Aetos

Vassiliki

Mitikas

Agrinin

Fiskardo

Frikes

Astakos

E19

Vathy

Messolongi

Antlrrlo

KEFALONIA

ITHAKA

Rio

Lixouri

Sami

Gulf of Patras

Patras

Argostoll

Poros

Metaxata

Skala

4

Klllln

PELOPONNESE

74

ZAKINTHOS

Amalias

Laganas

Zakinthos

Vassilikos

Pirgos

IONIAN SEA

Greece

Athens

Aegean Sea

WESTERN GREECE & THE IONIAN ISLANDS

Mediterranean Sea

N

0   25 mi

0   25 km

Ferry Route - - - -

younger set may prefer to join the revelers at one of the bars and clubs lining **Ethnikis Antistaseos.** Elsewhere on the island, at seaside towns such as **Ipsos, Roda,** and **Sidari,** you can find English pubs, karaoke bars, and "Greek nights" with fast-paced *sirtaki* dancing. Those whose holidays include some serious partying will want to try **Kavos,** at the island's lowest tip.

Corfu Town ★

There's Corfu the coast, Corfu the town, and Corfu the island, and they don't necessarily appeal to the same vacationers. Corfu the coast lures travelers who want to escape civilization and head for the water—whether an undeveloped little beach with a simple taverna and rooms to rent, or a spectacular resort. Then there's the more cosmopolitan **Corfu Town,** with its Greek, Italian, French, and British elements. Finally, there's a third and little-known Corfu: the interior, with its lush vegetation and gentle slopes, modest villages and farms, and countless olive and fruit trees. (It should be admitted that there's now a fourth Corfu—rather tacky beach resorts, crowded with package tourists from Western Europe, who can be extremely raucous.)

Whichever Corfu you choose, it should prove pleasing. It was, after all, this island's ancient inhabitants, the Phaeacians, who made Odysseus so comfortable. Visitors today will find Corfu similarly hospitable.

Essentials

GETTING THERE   By Plane   Olympic Air provides at least three flights daily from and to Athens, and three flights weekly from and to Thessaloniki (via Athens). Round-trip fare can vary between about 168€ to 286€. The Olympic Air office in Corfu town (✆ **26610/38-694**) is at 11 Polila, down from the Ionian Islands Tourism Office, but agents all over town sell tickets. **Aegean Airlines** also offers occasional flights (✆ **210/626-1000** in Athens, or 26610/27-100 in Corfu).

Corfu airport is about 4km (2½ miles) south of the center of Corfu town. Fortunately, the flight patterns of most planes do not bring them over the city. Everyone takes taxis into town; the standard fare should be 12€ but may fluctuate with destination, amount of luggage, and time of day.

By Boat   Many lines and ships link Corfu to both Greek and foreign ports. Ferries run almost hourly between Corfu and Igoumenitsou, directly across on the mainland (1–2 hr.), and several go weekly to and from Patras (about 7 hr.). At least during high season, there is a twice-daily hydrofoil express (about 30 min.) between Corfu and Igoumenitsou. Also in high season are daily ships linking Corfu to ports in Italy—Ancona, Bari, Brindisi, Trieste, Venice—or to Piraeus and/or Patras. The schedules and fares vary so much from year to year that it would be misleading to provide details here; work with a travel agent in your homeland or Greece; or check **www.ferries.gr**. The ship lines are: **Adriatica** (✆ 210/429-0487 in Piraeus), **ANEK Lines** (✆ 210/323-3481 in Athens), **Fragline** (✆ 210/821-4171 in Athens), **Hellenic Mediterranean Line,** or **HML** (✆ 210/422-5341 in Piraeus), **Minoan Lines** (✆ 210/414-5700 in Piraeus), **Strintzis Lines** (✆ 210/422-5015 in Piraeus), and **Ventouris Line** (✆ 210/988-9280 in Piraeus). In high season, the typical one-way cost from Brindisi to Corfu is about 320€ to 380€, for two people in a double cabin with a private bathroom, and with a standard-size vehicle.

By Bus   KTEL offers service from Athens or Thessaloniki; its ferry carries you between Corfu and Igoumenitsou, on the mainland opposite. Buses allow you to get

Corfu Town

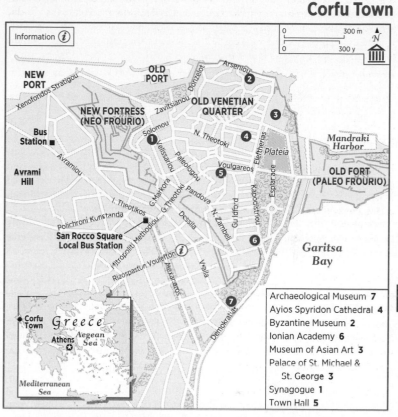

Information ⓘ

0 — 300 m
0 — 300 y

N

NEW PORT
Xenofondos Stratigou

OLD PORT
Arseniou

Zavitsianou
Donzalot

NEW FORTRESS (NEO FROURIO)

OLD VENETIAN QUARTER

2

3

Bus Station ■
Solomou
Velissariou

N. Theotoki

4

Eleftherias

Plateia

Mandraki Harbor

Avramiou

Avrami Hill

Paleologou

Voulgareos

5

Esplanade

Kapodistriou

OLD FORT (PALEO FROURIO)

I. Theotikos
G. Markora
G. Theotoki
Pandova
Gilfordi
N. Zambeli
Dessila

Polichroni Kunstanda

San Rocco Square Local Bus Station

Mitropoliti Methodiou

Alexandros

Rizospastun Vouleftun ⓘ

Vralia

6

Garitsa Bay

7

Demokratias

1

● Corfu Town
Greece
✪ Athens
Aegean Sea
Mediterranean Sea

Archaeological Museum **7**
Ayios Spyridon Cathedral **4**
Byzantine Museum **2**
Ionian Academy **6**
Museum of Asian Art **3**
Palace of St. Michael & St. George **3**
Synagogue **1**
Town Hall **5**

on or off at main points along the way, such as Ioannina. The buses are comfortable enough, but be prepared for many hours of winding roads. The **KTEL office** (📞 **26610/39-627**) is located along Leoforos Avramiou, up from the new port.

VISITOR INFORMATION   In previous years there have been municipal tourist information stations on the Esplanade and down at the new port but you cannot count on these to be there in any given year. The best sources of information are in fact the private travel agencies such as **Corfu Holidays Travel Agency,** at 12 Mantzarou (near the Municipal Theater in the New Town), 📞 **26610/23-523** or www.corfuholidays.com.

GETTING AROUND   By Bus   The dark-blue public buses service Corfu town, its suburbs, and nearby destinations. The semiprivate green-and-cream KTEL buses offer frequent service to points all over the island—Paleokastritsa, Glifada, Sidari, and more. The **KTEL office** (📞 **26610/39-627**) is located along Leoforos Avramiou, up from the new port.

By Taxi   Taxis are of no use inside Corfu Town—distances are short and streets clogged—but are handy for getting to and from the harbor and the airport. Although taxi drivers are supposed to use their meters, many don't, so you should agree on the

15

THE IONIAN ISLANDS

Corfu (Kerkira)

fare before setting out. You may also decide to use a taxi to visit some of the sites outside Corfu town; again, be sure to agree on the fare beforehand.

By Car   You'll find car-rental agencies all over Corfu. Even so, in high season it can be difficult to get a vehicle at the spur of the moment. If you're sure of your plans on Corfu, make arrangements before departing home. Otherwise, try **Corfu Holidays Travel Agency** (see "Visitor Information," above); or **Avanti Rent A Car,** 12A Ethnikis Antistasseos, along the new port (© **26610/42-028**).

By Moped   It's easy to rent mopeds, scooters, and motorcycles, but the roads are so curving, narrow, and steep that you should be very experienced before taking on such a vehicle. And insist on a helmet.

FAST FACTS   The official **American Express** agent for Corfu is Greek Skies Travel Agency, 20A Kapodistriou (© **26610/33-410;** fax 26610/36-161). There are numerous **banks** in both the old town and new town; you'll find ATMs at most of them. The **British Consul** is at 1 Menekrates (© **26610/30-055**), at the south end of the town, near the Menekrates monument. There is no U.S. consulate in Corfu. The **hospital** is out on Julius Andreatti, and directions are signposted around town.

There are several **Internet cafes:** I've always used the Online Cafe, 28 Kapodistriou, along the Esplanade (café_online1@yahoo.com); there's also the Cyber Café Corfu, 3 Gardikioti, down by New Port (cybercafecorfu@hotmail.com). Both are open daily from late morning to late evening. The **police station** (© **26610/39-575**) is at 19 Leoforos Alexandros (near the post office). The **post office** (© **26610/25-544**) is at 26 Leoforos Alexandros. It's open Monday through Friday from 7:30am to 8pm; in July and August, it's also open for a few hours on Saturday. The main **telephone office (OTE)** is at 9 Mantzarou; it's open Monday through Friday from 7am to midnight, and 7am to 10pm on Saturday and holidays.

What to See & Do
THE TOP ATTRACTIONS

Archaeological Museum ★   Even if you're not a devotee of ancient history or museums, you should take an hour to visit this small museum. On your way to see its master work, you'll pass a **stone lion** dating from around 575 B.C. (found in the nearby Menekrates tomb, along the waterfront by the museum). Go around and behind it to the large room with arguably the finest example of Archaic temple sculpture extant, the **pediment from the Temple of Artemis.** (The temple itself was south of Corfu town and dates from about 590 B.C.; the remains do not interest most people.) The pediment features the **Gorgon Medusa,** attended by two pantherlike animals. You don't have to be an art historian to note how this predates the great classical works, such as the Elgin marbles—not only in the naiveté of its sculpture but also in the emphasis on the monstrous, with the humans so much smaller in scale. Interesting for comparison is the fragment from another Archaic pediment found at Figare, Corfu. In an adjoining room, it shows Dionysos and a youth on a couch. Only a century younger than the Gorgon pediment, the humans have reduced the animal in size and placed it under the couch.

1 P. Armeni-Vraila (on the corner of Demokratias, the road along the waterfront). © **26610/30-680.** Admission 4€; free Sun. Tues–Sun 8:30am–2:30pm. Wheelchair accessible. Parking on adjacent streets.

Kalypso Star ☺   This glass-bottomed boat takes small groups offshore and provides fascinating views of marine life and undersea formations.

Old port, Corfu town. ✆ **26610/46-525.** www.greeka.com (search for Corfu, then for "kalypso star"). Admission 15€ adults, 8€ children. In high season, trips leave daily on the hour 10am–6pm, and at 10pm. Call for the off-season schedule. Parking along waterfront.

Museum of Asian Art   The building itself, an impressive example of neoclassical architecture, was constructed between 1819 and 1824 to serve as the residence of the lord high commissioner, the British ruler of the Ionian Islands; to house the headquarters of the Order of St. Michael and St. George; and to provide the assembly room for the Ionian senate. When the British turned the Ionian Islands over to Greece, they gave this building to the king of Greece. As the king seldom spent much time here, it fell into disrepair until after World War II, when it was restored and turned into a museum. The centerpiece of the museum is the collection of Chinese porcelains, bronzes, and other works from the Shang Dynasty (1500 B.C.) to the Ching Dynasty (19th c.). Go, too, to see the impressive Japanese works: woodblock prints, ceramics, sculpture, watercolors, and *netsuke* (carved sash fasteners). You may not have come to Greece to appreciate Asian art, but this is one of Corfu's several unexpected delights.

The Palace of St. Michael and St. George, north end of Esplanade. ✆ **26610/38-124.** protocol@hepka culture.gr. Admission 4€. Tues–Sun 8am–2:30pm. No parking.

Old Fort (Paleo Frourio)   Originally a promontory attached to the mainland, now separated by a moat, this area is known for its two peaks (*koryphi* in Greek), which gave the town and the island their modern names. A castle crowns each peak; you can get fine views of Albania to the east and Corfu, town and island, to the west. The promontory itself, for a long time, was the main town, and it appears as such in many old engravings. The Venetians dug the moat in the 16th century; it successfully held off several attempts by the Turks to conquer this outpost of Christianity. What looks like a Greek temple at the south side is in fact a British church (ca. 1830). In summer, a **sound-and-light** show is held several nights a week (in different foreign languages, so be sure to check the schedule).

The Esplanade (opposite the Liston). Admission 4€ adults, 2€ students and E.U. seniors over 60. Tues–Fri 8am–8pm; Sat–Sun and holidays 8:30am–3pm.

An Excursion to Albania   During high season, several travel agencies and ship lines (I can recommend Corful Holidays or the Petrakis Lines) offer 1-day excursions to Albania. The excursion is becoming popular even though it doesn't go to the capital; the fare for a day trip now costs about 80€, which should include visas, port fees, and a midday meal. Most interesting is to take a brief visit to the major archaeological site of **Butrint,** a UNESCO World Heritage Site. Travel agents in Corfu or at the Albanian port of Saranda, where you land, will set you up with a guide; prices vary depending on your wants, but in general, Albania is still cheap.

Corfu Holidays, 6 Lavrentiou Vrokini. ✆ **26610/23-523.** www.corfuholiday.com. Petrakis Line, 9 Venizelou, new port, Corfu town. ✆ **26610/31-649.** petrakis@hol.gr.

A STROLL AROUND CORFU TOWN ★

This is a browser's town, where as you're strolling in search of a snack or souvenir, you may serendipitously discover an old church or monument. To orient yourself, start with the **Esplanade area** bounded by the Old Fort (see above) and the sea on one side. The small haven below and to the north of the Old Fort is known as **Mandraki Harbor,** while the shore to the south is home port to the **Corfu Yacht Club.**

Dousmani bisects the Esplanade; at the far side is the monument that honors the union of the Ionian Islands with Greece. You might catch a cricket game at the **Plateia,** the northern part of the field. At the north side of the Esplanade, the Palace of St. Michael and St. George is the home of the **Museum of Asian Art** (see above). If you proceed along the northwest corner of the palace, you'll come out above the coast and can make your way around Arseniou above the *mourayia* (medieval sea walls). On your left you will pass the house of Dionysus Solomos, the 19th-centry poet laureate of Greece.

On your way, you will pass (on the left, up a flight of stairs) the **Byzantine Museum** in the **Church of Antivouniotissa.** Even if you're not a particular fan of Byzantine art, you should enjoy the small but elegant selection of icons from around Corfu; of particular interest are works by Cretan artists who came to Corfu, some of whom went on to Venice. The museum is open Monday from 12:30 to 7pm, Tuesday through Saturday from 8am to 7pm, and Sunday and holidays from 8:30am to 3pm. Admission is 3€.

Proceed along the coast road and descend to the square at the old port. Above its far side rises the **New Fortress,** and beyond this is the new port. Off to the left of the square is a large gateway, what remains of the 16th-century Porta Spilia. Go through it to get to the Plateia Solomou.

If you go left from Plateia Solomou along Velissariou, look on the right for the green doors of the 300-year-old **synagogue,** with its collection of torah crowns. It's open on Saturday from 9am until early evening. To gain entry during the week, call the Jewish Community Center at ✆ **26610/38-802.**

Continue on to the part of old Corfu known as **Campiello ★,** with its stepped streets and narrow alleys. You may feel as if you are in a labyrinth—and you will be—but sooner or later you'll emerge onto one or another busy commercial street that will bring you down to the Esplanade.

Heading south on the Esplanade, you'll see a bandstand and, at its far end, the **Maitland Rotunda,** which honors Sir Thomas Maitland, the first British lord high commissioner of the Ionian Islands. Past this is the statue of Count Ioannis Kapodistrias (1776–1836), the first president of independent Greece.

Head south along the shore road from this end of the Esplanade, and you'll pass the Corfu Palace Hotel (see below) on your right; then the **Archaeological Museum** (see above), up Vraila on the right. After 2 more blocks, off to the right on the corner of Marasli, you'll see the **Tomb of Menekrates,** a circular tomb of a

---

📷 Sitting Still

One of the great pleasures of traveling about Greece is just occasionally to sit still—that is, to plunk yourself down on a cafe chair and enjoy a drink, while you observe the passing scene. And the ideal place to do that in Corfu is at one of the cafes that set out their tables and chairs between the Liston and the Esplanade. **The Liston,** the impressive arcade, is a Greek version of "the List," referring to a list of upper-class and privileged individuals who were the only ones allowed to frequent this site after it was erected in the early 1800s. Today we can all sit here and enjoy such pleasures as watching a game of cricket being played on the Esplanade (Spianada, in Greek), the large greensward. Cricket is a vestige of the island's years under British rule, as is ginger beer, which you might consider sipping while you sit there.

notable who drowned about 600 B.C. Proceeding to the right here onto Leoforos Alexandros will bring you into the heart of new Corfu town.

Back at the Esplanade, the western side of the north half is lined by a wide tree-shaded strip filled with cafe tables and chairs, then a street reserved for pedestrians, and then arcaded buildings patterned after Paris's Rue de Rivoli. Begun by the French and finished by the British, these arcaded buildings, known as the **Liston ★★** provide a great backdrop for a cup of coffee or a dish of ice cream.

At the back of the Liston is **Kapodistriou;** perpendicular from this extend several streets that lead into the heart of old Corfu—a mélange of fine shops, old churches, souvenir stands, and other stores in a maze of streets, alleys, and squares that seem like Venice without the water. The broadest and most stylish is **Nikiforio Theotoki.** At the northern end of Kapodistriou, turn left onto Ayios Spiridon and come to the corner of Filellinon and the **Ayios Spiridon Cathedral,** dedicated to Spiridon, the patron saint of Corfu. Locals credit Spiridon, a 4th-century bishop of Cyprus, with saving Corfu from famine, plagues, and a Turkish siege. Inside the church is the saint's embalmed body in a silver casket, as well as gold and silver votive offerings and many fine old icons. Four times a year, the faithful parade the remains of St. Spiridon through the streets of old Corfu: Palm Sunday, Holy Saturday, August 1, and the first Sunday in November.

Proceeding up Voulgareos, behind the southern end of the Liston, you'll come to the back of the **Town Hall,** built in 1663 as a Venetian loggia; it later served as a theater. Turn into the square it faces and enter what seems like a Roman **piazza ★,** with steps and terraces, a Roman Catholic cathedral on the left, and, reigning over the top, the restored Catholic archbishop's residence (now the Bank of Greece).

From here, finish your walk by wandering up and down the streets of old Corfu.

SHOPPING

Corfu town has so many shops selling jewelry, leather goods, olive wood objects, and handmade needlework that it is impossible to single out one or another. If you're looking for needlework, the stores along **Filarmonikis** (off N. Teotoki) may have something that pleases you; prices are generally fair and uniform.

I would never recommend a trip to Corfu *just* for the **kumquat liqueur,** but this Chinese fruit has been cultivated on the island since the late 1800s, and the liqueur makes a unique treat—or gift, if it doesn't appeal to you!

Standing out from the many souvenir-gift shops is **Antica,** 25 Ayios Spiridon, leading away from the north end of Liston (✆ **26610/32-401**), offers unusual older jewelry, plates, textiles, brass, and icons. **Gravures,** 64 Ev. Voulgareos, where the street emerges from the old town to join the new town (✆ **26610/41-721**), has a fine selection of engravings and prints of scenes from Corfu, all nicely matted. Originals (taken from old books or magazines) can cost 150€, reproductions as little as 10€. And for something special, visit the **Patounis Soap-Making Factory** on I. Theotaki (✆ **26610/39-860**) and try some of their olive oil soap.

There's no dearth of ceramics in Corfu, but I favor the **Pottery Workshop,** 15km (10 miles) north of Corfu on the right of the road to Paleokastritsa (✆ **26610/90-704**), where you get to observe Sofoklis Ikonomides and Sissy Moskidou making and decorating all the pottery on sale here. Two kilometers (1¼ miles) farther along the road, on the left, is the **Wood's Nest,** offering a large selection of olive wood objects just slightly cheaper than in town

Where to Stay

The island of Corfu has an apparently inexhaustible choice of accommodations, but in high season (July–Aug), package groups from Europe will book many rooms. Reservations are recommended for that time, especially for Corfu town. And those considering renting a villa or apartment for a more extended stay should contact the **Corfu Holidays Travel Agency,** at 12 Mantzarou (near the Municipal Theater in the New Town) www.corfuholidays.com, © **26610/23-523.**

IN TOWN
Very Expensive
Corfu Palace Hotel ★★   This grand hotel combines the most up-to-date features of an international enterprise (it is owned by the Aquis Hotel Group) with Greek hospitality. In addition to its splendid surroundings, superb service, and grand meals, the hotel provides restful isolation above the bay, even though it is near the city center. The comfortable guest rooms, while not exceptionally large, are well appointed; the marbled bathrooms are large. Every balconied room enjoys views of the sea—insist on one. The hotel's two restaurants, the **Scheria** (a grill room on the poolside terrace) and the **Panorama** (with a view of the bay), serve Greek and international menus; both vie to claim the finest cuisine on Corfu. Guests can use the facilities of the nearby (night-lit) Corfu Tennis Club and Yacht Club and the Corfu Golf Club, 14km (9 miles) away.

2 Leoforos Demokratias, 49100 Corfu. www.corfupalace.com. © **26610/39-485.** Fax 26610/31-749. 115 units. High season 210€–320€ double; low season 170€–225€ double. Children 12 and under stay free in parent's room (without meals). Rates include buffet breakfast; half-board available. AE, DC, MC, V. Free parking. A 5-min. walk from Esplanade, along Garitsa Bay, just south of town center. **Amenities:** 2 restaurants; 3 bars; babysitting; Internet; 3 pools (1 for children); room service; smoke-free rooms. *In room:* A/C, TV, hair dryer, minibar, Wi-Fi.

Moderate
If you prefer old-fashioned period hotels, consider **Astron Hotel,** 15 Donzelot (waterfront road down to old harbor), 49100 Corfu (© **26610/39-505**). It offers up-to-date bathrooms and other facilities while retaining touches of its original charm.

Arcadion Hotel ★   If you like to be at the center of a city, you can't get much closer than this: When you step out the door, the Esplanade and the Liston are only 15m (50 ft.) away. Admittedly, this also means that on pleasant evenings there will be crowds in front of the hotel, but ask for a room off the front. (All windows are double-glazed for sound control.) It's hard to beat for location and comfort. In the evening, you can sit in the roof garden and enjoy a cool drink with a fabulous view.

44 Kapodistriou, 49100 Corfu. www.arcadionhotel.com. © **26610/30-104.** Fax 26610/45-087. 33 units. 120€ double. Rates include buffet breakfast. AE, MC, V. Free public parking nearby. Diagonally across from south end of Liston, facing the Esplanade. **Amenities:** Restaurant; bar; health club; room service; Wi-Fi. *In room:* A/C, TV, hair dryer, Internet, minibar.

Bella Venezia ★🗡   Like the gold-medal winner of the decathlon, this hotel may not win in any single category, but its combined virtues make it the first choice of many. The building is a restored neoclassical mansion (with a major updating in 2006), with character, if not major distinction. The location is a bit off center and lacks fine views, but it's quiet and close enough to any place you'd want to walk to; a decent beach is 300m (1,000 ft.) away. Although not luxurious or large, the guest rooms have some old-world touches; the showers, however, are cramped. There is no restaurant, but there's a colorful patio-garden for breakfast and an enclosed kiosk for light snacks.

4 N. Zambeli (approached from far south end of Esplanade), 49100 Corfu. www.bellaveneziahotel.com. ✆ **26610/46-500.** Fax 26610/20-708. 31 units. High season 200€ double; low season 115€ double. Rates include buffet breakfast. AE, DC, MC, V. Parking on adjacent streets. Within walking distance of old and new towns. **Amenities:** Patio for breakfast and snacks; bar; babysitting. *In room:* A/C, TV, hair dryer, Internet, minibar.

Cavalieri ★   If you like your hotels in the discreet old European style, this place is for you. For glitz, look elsewhere—the main lounge is done in "Italian velvet." The Cavalieri is in an old building with a small elevator. Service is low key, rooms are spare, and bathrooms standard. Ask for one of the front rooms on the upper floors, which boast great views of the Old Fort. Another draw is the **rooftop garden,** which, after 6:30pm, offers drinks, sweets, and light meals along with a spectacular view; even if you don't stay here, it's a grand place to pass an hour in the evening. Because of the hotel's appealing location, advance reservations are required much of the year.

4 Kapodistriou, 49100 Corfu. www.cavalieri-hotel.com. ✆ **26610/39-041.** Fax 26610/39-283. 50 units. High season 142€ double; low season 110€ double. Rates include buffet breakfast. AE, DC, MC, V. Parking on adjacent streets. Within easy walking distance of old and new towns, at far south end of Esplanade. **Amenities:** Breakfast room; bar; room service. *In room:* A/C, TV, hair dryer, minibar.

OUTSIDE TOWN
Expensive
Corfu Holiday Palace ★ ★   Formerly the Hilton (now in the Aquis chain), this is a grand hotel in the contemporary manner—more like a resort, if you consider the range of its facilities. It boasts of all the celebrities it's hosted, but I've always found the staff friendly. Guest rooms are standard Greek-hotel-size, with comfortable beds and state-of-the-art bathrooms. The grounds create a semitropical ambience. In addition to the pools, a lovely private beach below beckons. Kanoni, an island landmark, is nearby (see below). The island's airport is off in the middle distance—not a major problem unless your windows are open, but I advise you to ask for a room facing the sea. Patrons get a generous discount at Corfu Golf Club (18km/12 miles away). Perhaps the biggest surprise of all: One of Greece's major **casinos** is on the premises.

P.O. Box 124, Nausicaa, Kanoni, 49100 Corfu. www.corfuholidaypalace.gr. ✆ **26610/36-540.** Fax 26610/36-551. 266 units. High season 170€–220€ double; low season 100€–125€ double. Rates include buffet breakfast. Half-board includes a fixed-price menu. Special packages available for extended stays. AE, DC, MC, V. Free parking on grounds. About 5km (3 miles) south of Corfu town. **Amenities:** 2 restaurants; 2 bars; babysitting; billiards; bowling; casino; health club; Internet; jogging track; 2 pools; room service; shuttle bus to town; table tennis; lit tennis courts; watersports equipment/rentals; Wi-Fi. *In room:* A/C, TV, hair dryer, minibar.

Inexpensive
Fundana Villas ★ ★ ☺   I predict this will be greatly appreciated by some as a delightful alternative to the other hostelries listed for Corfu—bungalows off in a natural setting. The 12 bungalows vary in size, accommodating from two to seven people, but all have kitchenettes. You are surrounded by fruit trees and the Greek countryside, and you can imbibe the pure spring water. Twice a week, the proprietors prepare traditional Corfiot dinners; for other meals, you have to drive into Corfu town or Paleokastritsa. You will also have your choice of beaches, none of which is much more than about 15km (9 miles) away; the island's golf course, horseback riding, and a water park are also nearby. Some may recognize the main house as the residence in the BBC-TV version of Gerald Durrell's *My Family and Other Animals.*

1 Odysseos, 49100 Corfu. www.fundanavillas.com. ✆ **26630/22-532.** Fax 26630/22-453. 15 units. High season 80€ per couple. Self-catering breakfast 8€. MC, V. Parking on grounds. 17km (11 miles) from

Corfu center, about same to Paleokastritsa. Pets accepted. **Amenities:** Bar; Internet; 2 pools; table tennis. *In room:* A/C, TV, hair dryer, kitchenette.

Where to Eat

IN TOWN
Expensive

Venetian Well ★ MIDDLE EASTERN/INTERNATIONAL/GREEK   For a special dining experience, this remains my top pick in Corfu town. Diners sit at a candlelit table, in a rather austere little square, with a Venetian wellhead (ca. 1699) and a church opposite. When the weather changes, guests sit in a stately room adorned with a mural. There is no printed menu—you learn what's available from a chalkboard or from your waiter—and there's no predicting what the kitchen will offer on any given evening. To some degree, then, the fare can be uneven. Main courses may range from standard Greek dishes such as beef *giouvetsi* (cooked in a pot) to chicken prepared with exotic ingredients. Because the chef uses seasonal vegetables, salads vary from month to month. The wine list is more extensive than in most Greek restaurants.

Plateia Kremasti (on the small square, up from old harbor, behind Greek Orthodox cathedral). ☎ **26610/44-761.** Reservations recommended in high season. Main courses 10€–26€. No credit cards. Mon–Sat noon–midnight.

Moderate

If you want to dine in town yet along the coast, consider **Antranik,** 19 Arseniou (☎ **26610/22-301**), under the awnings on the sea side of the road leading from north of the Esplanade down to the new port. **Faliraki,** at the corner of Kapodistrias and Arseniou, down below the wall (☎ **26610/30-392**), also has a wonderful location right on the water, although the food is standard Greek fare.

Aegli Garden Restaurant ★ GREEK/CONTINENTAL   The tasty and varied menu of this longtime favorite attracts both residents and travelers to its several dining areas—indoors, in the Liston arcade, under awnings across from the arcade, or along the pedestrian mall of Kapodistriou. Try the selection of *orektika* (appetizers) with the wine or beer on tap. The staff takes pride in their Corfiote specialties, several of which are traditional Greek foods with rather spicy sauces: filet of fish, octopus, *pastitsada* (baked veal), *baccala* (salted codfish), and *sofrito* (veal). If spiciness isn't your thing, try the swordfish or prawns. Everything is done with great care, including a delicious fresh-fruit salad—just perfect when you don't feel like a full meal.

23 Kapodistriou. Also entered from Lison Arcade. ☎ **26610/31-949.** Fax 26610/45-488. Main courses 8€–20€. AE, DC, MC, V. Daily 9am–1am. No parking.

Bellissimo GREEK/INTERNATIONAL   This restaurant has become a welcome addition to the Corfu scene—unpretentious but serving tasty food. Located on a central and lovely town square, it's run by the hospitable Stergiou family, Corfiots who returned from Canada. They offer a standard Greek menu with some "exotics," including hamburgers and chicken curry. Especially welcome is their modestly priced "Greek sampling plate"—*tzatziki* (yogurt-cucumber salad), tomatoes-and-cucumber salad, *keftedes* (meatballs), fried potatoes, grilled lamb, and pork souvlaki.

Plateia Lemonia (just off N. Theotoki). ☎ **26610/41-112.** Main courses 6€–18€. No credit cards. Daily 10:30am–11pm. No parking.

Corfu Town After Dark

Corfu town has a nightlife scene, though many people are content to linger over dinner and then, after a promenade, repair to one of the cafes at the Liston, such as the

Capri, Liston, Europa, or Aegli—all of which have similar selections of light refreshments and drinks. Others are drawn to the cafes at the north end of the Esplanade, just outside the Liston—**Cafe Bar 92, Magnet,** or **Cool Down.** For a special treat, ascend to the rooftop cafe/bar at **Cavalieri** hotel (see "Where to Stay," above). Another choice is **Lindos Cafe,** overlooking the beach and facilities of the Nautical Club of Corfu. It's approached by steps leading off Leoforos Demokratias, just south and outside the Esplanade. And one of the best-kept secrets of Corfu town is the little **Art Cafe,** to the right and behind the Museum of Asian Art; its garden provides a wonderful, cool, quiet retreat from the hustle and bustle of the rest of the town.

If you enjoy more action—loud music and dancing—several nightspots are along the coast to the north, between Corfu town and the beach resort of Gouvia. They include **Ekati,** a typical Greek nightclub; **Esperides,** featuring Greek music; and **Corfu by Night,** definitely touristy. Be prepared to drop money at these places.

The youngest night crawlers find places that go in and out of favor (and business) from year to year. Among the more enduring, up around the Esplanade, are the relatively sedate **Aktaion,** just to the right of the Old Fort, and clubs featuring the latest music, such as **Hook** and **Base,** along Kapodistriou (before the Cavalieri Hotel). Young people seeking more excitement go down past the new port to a strip of flashy discos. These clubs charge a cover (about 10€, including one drink).

In summer, frequent **concerts** by orchestras and bands are held on the Esplanade; most of them are free. Corfu town boasts the oldest band in Greece. The **sound-and-light** performances are described in the listing for the Old Fort (see "What to See & Do," earlier in this chapter). September brings **Corfu Festival,** with concerts, ballet, opera, and theater performances, by a mix of Greek and international companies. **Carnival** is celebrated on the last Sunday before Lent, with a parade and the burning of an effigy representing the spirit of Carnival.

Still another possibility would be to take one of the boat cruises that go out each night and provide both a refreshing atmosphere and a view of the glittering island. Any travel agency will be able to sign you up for one of these.

For those who like to gamble, the **casino** at the **Corfu Holiday Palace** (see above) is a few miles outside of town. Open nightly (8pm–3am) to individuals 23 years or older (ID required), it may not have the glamour of Monte Carlo, but it attracts an international set during the high season.

Side Trips from Corfu Town
KANONI, PONDIKONISI & ACHILLEION

Although these sites and destinations are not next door to one another and have little in common, they are grouped here because they all lie south of Corfu town and all could be combined in less than a full day's outing. Everyone who comes to Corfu town will want to visit these places, even if you go nowhere else on the island.

Kanoni is approached south of Corfu town via the village Analepsis; it's well signed. Ascending most of the way, you arrive after about 4km (2½ miles) at the circular terrace (on the right). The area is known as Kanoni (after the cannon once sited here). Make your way to the edge and enjoy a wonderful view. Directly below in the inlet are two islets. If you want to visit one or both, you can take a 10-minute walk down a not-that-difficult path from Kanoni; with a vehicle you must retrace the road back from Kanoni a few hundred yards to a signed turnoff (on the left coming back).

One islet is linked to the land by a causeway; here you'll find the **Monastery of Vlakherna.** To get to the other islet, **Pondikonisi (Mouse Island),** you must go by

Achilleion: A Villa with Many Tales to Tell

The Achilleion has enough back stories to support a TV miniseries. To begin with, the personal life of the Empress Elizabeth, who built it, is one of extravagant eccentricities; look her up in an encyclopedia or online. She was the mother of Rupert, the young prince who in 1889 was found dead at his hunting lodge at Mayerling, Austria, along with his mistress; it was assumed to have been a double suicide, though many questions about their deaths were never answered. In any case, Elizabeth identified Rupert with Achilles, and so the villa is really a memorial to him—you'll see many statues and motifs associated with Achilles (including the dolphins, for Achilles' mother was the water nymph Thetis). In 1898, Elizabeth was assassinated by an anarchist—for no other reason than she was a royal. The villa sat unused until 1907, when Kaiser Wilhelm II of Germany bought it as a summer home. It was appropriated by the Greek government after World War I; the Germans used it during their World War II occupation; it then reverted to the Greek National Tourist Organization, which, in 1962, allowed the top floor to be used as a casino (seen in the 1981 James Bond film *For Your Eyes Only*). This closed in 1992, when the casino was moved to the Corfu Holiday Palace (see above). Now it remains a destination for tourists, with more than its share of tales to tell.

small boat, which is always available (3€ round-trip). Legend has it that this rocky islet is a Phaeacian ship that turned to stone after taking Odysseus back to Ithaka. The chapel here dates from the 13th century, and its setting among the cypress trees makes it most picturesque. Many Corfiotes make a pilgrimage here, in small boats on August 6, for the Feast of the Transfiguration. It's also the inspiration for the Swiss painter Arnold Boecklin's well-known work *Isle of the Dead*, which, in turn, inspired Rachmaninoff's music of the same name.

A causeway across the inlet to Perama, on the main body of the island (the Kanoni road is on a peninsula) is for pedestrians only. So to continue on to your next destination, a villa known as **Achilleion ★,** you must drive back to the edge of Corfu town and then take another road about 8km (5 miles) to the south, signed to Gastouri and the villa of Achilleion. The villa is open daily from 9am to 4pm. Admission is 6€. Bus no. 10, from Plateia San Rocco, runs directly to the Achilleion several times daily.

Empress Elizabeth of Austria-Hungary built this villa between 1890 and 1891. Approaching the villa from the entrance gate, you will see a slightly Teutonic version of a neoclassical summer palace. Take a walk through at least some of the eclectic rooms. Among the curiosities is the small saddle-seat on which Kaiser Wilhelm II of Germany sat while performing his imperial chores.

The terraced gardens that surround the villa are lush. Be sure to go all the way around and out to the back terraces to see the most famous of the statues Elizabeth commissioned, *The Dying Achilles,* by the German sculptor Herter; also, you cannot miss the 4.5m-tall (15-ft.) Achilles that the Kaiser had inscribed, TO THE GREATEST GREEK FROM THE GREATEST GERMAN, a sentiment removed after World War II. But for a truly impressive sight, step to the edge of the terrace and enjoy a spectacular view of Corfu town and much of the eastern coast to the south.

If you have your own car, you can continue on past the Achilleion and descend to the coast between **Benitses** and **Perama;** the first, to the south, has become a popular beach resort. Proceeding north along the coast from Benitses, you come to Perama (another popular beach resort), where a turnoff onto a promontory brings you to the pedestrian causeway opposite Pondikonisi (see above). The main road brings you back to the edge of Corfu town.

PALEOKASTRITSA ★

If you can make only one excursion on the island, this is certainly a top choice. The drive here is northwest out of Corfu town via well-marked roads. Follow the coast for about 8km (5½ miles) to Gouvia, then turn inland. (It is on this next stretch that you pass the **Pottery Workshop** and the **Wood's Nest;** see "Shopping," earlier.) The road eventually narrows but is asphalt all the way as you gradually descend to the west coast and **Paleokastritsa** (25km/16 miles). There's no missing it: It's been taken over by hotels and restaurants, although some of the bays and coves that make up Paleokastritsa are less developed than others. Tradition claims it as the site of **Scheria,** the capital of the Phaeacians—so one of these beaches should be where Nausicaa found Odysseus, though no remains have been found to substantiate this.

Continue on past the beaches to climb a narrow, winding road to the **Monastery of the Panagia** at the edge of a promontory. (The monastery is about 1.6km/1 mile from the beach, and many prefer to go by foot, as parking is next to impossible once you get there.) Although founded in the 13th century, the monastery has no remains that old. It's worth a brief visit, especially at sunset. The monastery is open daily April through October from 7am to 1pm and 3 to 8pm.

More interesting in some ways, and certainly more challenging, is a visit to the **Angelokastro,** the medieval castle that sits high on a pinnacle, overlooking all of Paleokastritsa. Only the hardiest will choose to walk all the way up from the shore, a taxing hour at least. The rest of us will drive back out of Paleokastritsa (2.5km/1½ miles) to a turnoff to the left, signed for Lakones. **Warning:** Don't attempt to drive this road unless you are comfortable pulling over to the very edge of narrow roads—with sheer drops to let trucks and buses by, something you will have to do on your way down. There commences an endless winding ascent that eventually levels out and provides spectacular views of the coast as the road passes through the villages of Lakones and Krini. Keep going until the road takes a sharp turn to the right and down, and you'll come to a little parking area. From here, walk up to the castle, only 200m (656 ft.) away but seemingly farther because of the trail's poor condition. What you are rewarded with, though, is one of the most spectacularly sited medieval castles you'll ever visit, some 300m (1,000 ft.) above sea level.

If you've come this far, reward yourself with a meal and the spectacular view at one of the restaurants or cafes on the road outside Lakones: **Bella Vista, Colombo,** or **Casteltron.** At mealtimes in high season, these places are taken over by busloads of tour groups. If you have your own transport, try to eat a bit earlier or later.

On your way back to Corfu town from Paleokastritsa, you can vary your route by heading south through **Ropa Valley,** the agricultural heartland of Corfu. Follow the signs indicating Liapades and Tembloni, but don't bother going into either of these towns. If you

---

Taking a Dive on Corfu

All of the bays and coves that make up Paleokastritsa boast clear, sparkling turquoise waters. Both **Korfu Diving** (www.dive-centers.net; ✆ 26630/41-604) and **Achilleion Diving** (www.diving-corfu.com; ✆ 69327/29-011) offer courses for beginners, as well as day excursions for advanced divers.

have time for a beach stop, consider going over to **Ermones Beach** (the island's only golf club is located above it—an 18-hole course) or **Glifada Beach.**

WHERE TO STAY & EAT   If you want to spend some time at Paleokastritsa, it's good to get away from the main beach. I've enjoyed the unpretentious 70-unit family-run **Hotel Odysseus** (www.odysseushotel.gr; ✆ **26630/41-209**), high above the largely undeveloped cove before the main beach. A double in high season goes for 75€; in low season, the rate is 55€. Rates include buffet breakfast, and the hotel has a pool. The Odysseus is open May to mid-October. I've not had occasion to eat there, but guests have recommended its restaurant.

On its own peninsula and both fancier and pricier is the 127-unit **Akrotiri Beach Hotel** ★ (www.akrotiri-beach.com; ✆ **26630/41-237**)—completely renovated between 2008 and 2010; an air-conditioned double in high season goes for 120€ to 150€, including buffet breakfast. Half board can also be arranged. All rooms have balconies and sea views. In addition to the adjacent beaches, it has two pools and a tennis court and offers Wi-Fi in the lobby. It's open May through October.

The restaurants on the main beach in Paleokastritsa are definitely touristy. The **Vrahos** is probably the most stylish. However, if you like to eat where the action is, the best value and most fun at the main beach is at the **Apollon Restaurant,** in Hotel Apollon-Ermis (✆ **26630/41-211**). Main courses are 6€ to 16€. I prefer someplace a bit removed, such as **Belvedere Restaurant** (✆ **26630/41-583**), just below Hotel Odysseus, which serves solid Greek dishes at reasonable prices. Main courses range from 5€ to 16€. The restaurant is open mid-April to late October from 9am to midnight.

KEFALONIA (CEPHALONIA) ★

Here is a Greek island the way they used to be: It pretty much goes its own (Greek) way, while you (foreigner) travel around and through it. That said, Kefalonia does have a full-service tourist industry, with fine hotels, restaurants, travel agencies, car-rental agencies along with its natural wonders, a few historical buildings, archaeological sites, and many fine beaches. Because Kefalonia was all but demolished by the earthquake of 1953, most structures on this island are fairly new. And it has long been one of the more prosperous and cosmopolitan parts of Greece, thanks to its islanders' tradition of sailing and trading in the world at large. The filming of the 2001 movie *Captain Corelli's Mandolin* also gave a temporary boost to tourism here, but don't come to Kefalonia for glamour. Come to spend time in a relaxing environment, and to enjoy handsome vistas and a lovely countryside.

Essentials

GETTING THERE   **By Plane**   From Athens, there are usually two flights daily on **Olympic Air;** fares in high season can vary from 60€ to 110€. The Argostoli office is at 1 Rokkou Vergoti, the street between the harbor and the square of the Archaeological Museum (✆ **26710/28-808**). **Kefalonia Airport** is 8km (5 miles) outside Argostoli. As there is no public bus, everyone goes to Argostoli by taxi, which costs about 15€.

By Boat   As with most Greek islands, it's easier to get to Kefalonia in summer than in the off-season, when weather and reduced tourism eliminate the smaller boats. Ferries to Kefalonia are operated by at least four lines: **Strintzis, Agoudimos, Endeavour,** and **Ionian;** check out their schedules at **www.gtp.gr** or **www.ferries.gr**. If you don't make arrangements with a travel agent, you can buy tickets dockside. Throughout the year, a car-passenger ferry leaves daily from Patras to Sami (about 2½ hr.). There is also at least

Kefalonia & Ithaka

To Vassiliki · To Nydri · To Meganisi

Greece
Athens · Aegean Sea
KEFALONIA & ITHAKA
Mediterranean Sea

ATOKOS

Fiskardo · Frikes
Stavros · Kioni
Anogi
To Astakos

Assos
ITHAKA

Myrtos Beach
Divarata · Aetos · Ithaka (Vathy)
Ay. Evthimia

Kardakata

Melissani Cave
Sami
Drogarati Cave
To Patras

Paliki
Havdata · Dilinata
Lixouri
Argostoli · Lassi
KEFALONIA
Tsarkassianos

Ionian Sea

Platis Yialos · Peratata
Mt. Enos
Poros

Metaxata · Tzanata
Svorotata · Pessada
Markopoulo

Katelios · Skala
To Kyllini

Airport ✈
Ferry Route ‑ ‑ ‑

To Kyllini · To Agios Nikoloas (Skinari)

one car-passenger ferry daily (1½ hr.) from Killini (on the northwest tip of the Peloponnese) to one of several ports of Kefalonia—Argostoli, Sami Lixouri, or Poros. To give some idea of the cost, a round-trip Patras-Kefallonia-Patras trip for a couple with their own cabin would be about 150€.

Beyond these more or less dependable services, during the months of July and August, there are alternatives—ships to and from Corfu, Ithaka, Levkas, Brindisi (Italy), or other ports—but they do not necessarily keep the same schedules every year.

VISITOR INFORMATION   The **Argostoli Tourism Office,** in Argostoli, is at the Port Authority Building, on Ioannis Metaxa, along the harbor (© 26710/22-248). It's open in high season daily from 7:30am to 2:30pm and 5 to 10pm; in low season, hours are reduced to Monday through Friday from 8am to 3pm.

GETTING AROUND   **By Bus**   You can get to almost any point on Kefalonia—even remote beaches, villages, and monasteries—by **KTEL bus** (© 26710/22-276 in Argostoli). Schedules, however, are restrictive and may cut deeply into your preferred arrival at any given destination. KTEL also operates special tours to major destinations around the island. The **KTEL station** is on Leoforos A. Tritsi, at the far end of the harbor road, 200m (656 ft.) past Trapano Bridge.

15

THE IONIAN ISLANDS

Kefalonia (Cephalonia)

By Taxi If you don't enjoy driving on twisting mountain roads, taxis are the best alternative. In Argostoli, go to Vallianou (Central) Square and work out an acceptable fare. A trip to Fiskardo, with the driver waiting for 3 to 4 hours, might run to 200€— with several passengers splitting the fare, this isn't unreasonable for a day's excursion. Everyone uses taxis on Kefalonia, and although drivers are supposed to use their meters, many don't; settle the fare before you set off.

By Car There are literally dozens of car-rental firms, from the well-known international companies to hole-in-the-wall outfits. In Argostoli, I've found **Auto Europe,** 3 Lassis (✆ **26710/24-078**), and **Euro Dollar,** 3A R. Vergoti (✆ **26710/23-613**), to be reliable. In high season, rental cars are scarce, so don't expect to haggle. A compact will come to at least 75€ per day (gas extra); better rates are usually offered for rentals of 3 or more days.

By Moped & Motorcycle The roads on Kefalonia are asphalt and in decent condition but are often narrow, lack shoulders, and twist around mountain ravines or wind along the edges of sheer drops to the sea. Having said that, many travelers choose to get around Kefalonia this way. Two-seater mopeds and motorcycles rent for about 30€ to 40€ per day.

FAST FACTS There are several **banks** with ATMs in the center of Argostoli. The **hospital** (✆ **26710/22-434**) is on Souidias (the upper road, above the Trapano Bridge). **Internet access** is available at **Internet Point,** 8 A. Metaxa (www.f2d.gr; ✆ **26710/22-227**) or at **Excelixis Computers,** 3 Minoos (✆ **26710/25-530;** xlixis@otenet.gr). Argostoli's **tourist police** (✆ **26710/22-200**) are on Ioannis Metaxa, on the waterfront across from the port authority. The **post office** is in Argostoli on Lithostrato, opposite no. 18 (✆ **26710/22-124**); its hours are Monday through Saturday from 7:30am to 2pm. The main **telephone office (OTE)** is at 8 G. Vergoti. It's open daily, April through September, from 7am to midnight, and October through March, from 7am to 10pm.

What to See & Do

Staying in Kefalonia's capital and largest city, **Argostoli,** allows you to go off on daily excursions to beaches and mountains, yet return to the comforts of a city. It has the island's most diverse offering of hotels and restaurants, and it feels urban. For those who find that Argostoli doesn't offer enough in the way of old-world charm or diversions, we point out some of the other possibilities on Kefalonia.

Argostoli's appeal does not depend on any archaeological, historical, architectural, or artistic particulars. It's a city for observers—travelers who are content strolling or sitting and observing the passing scene: ships along the waterfront, locals shopping in the market, children playing in the squares. Head to **Vallianou (Central) Square ★** or the **waterfront** to find a cafe where you can nurse a coffee or ice cream. **Premier Cafe,** on the former, and **Hotel Olga,** on the latter, are as nice as any.

The best nearby **beaches** are just south of the city in **Lassi,** which now has numerous hotels, pensions, cafes, and restaurants much loved by package groups.

Historical and Folklore Museum of the Corgialenos Library ★ I recommend
this museum over the dry archaeological museum. Many so-called folklore museums, little more than typical rooms, have sprung up in Greece in recent years, but this is one of the most authentic and satisfying. Meticulously maintained and well-labeled displays showcase traditional clothing, tools, handicrafts, and objects used in daily life across the centuries. Somewhat unexpected are the displays revealing a stylish upper-middle-class

THE IONIAN ISLANDS | Kefalonia (Cephalonia)

Odysseus, the hero of Homer's epic, came from the island of Ithaka. Over the centuries, a few scholars debated which island this was—some even arguing that, in any case, it was all a fiction—but in general, it came to be accepted that Odysseus's island was the same as the one we know today by that name. In 2005, however, several Englishmen announced that they had established that the true Ithaka of Homer's Odysseus is the **Paliki** peninsula, which hangs down along the northwestern coast of Kefalonia. As to the objection that Homer's Ithaka was an island, they claimed that Paliki had been an island but that seismic forces had since joined it to Kefalonia. As of this writing, there is little archaeological evidence to support this claim—and no remains to visit. But for those who relish Homer, it might be worth the few hours it would take to drive over to Paliki and check out the land. (There is also a frequent ferry that cuts down the travel time; but when you disembark, you would need to get wheels to explore the peninsula.) In any case, you might consider packing a paperback translation of the *Odyssey.*

life. Also engaging is a collection of photographs of pre- and post-1953 earthquake Kefalonia. The gift shop has a fine selection, including handmade lace.

Ilia Zervou. (*26710/28-835.* Admission 3€. Apr–Oct Mon–Sat 9am–2pm; off season by arrangement. 2 blocks up the hill, behind public theater and Archaeological Museum square.

SHOPPING

Interesting ceramics are for sale at **Hephaestus,** on the waterfront, at 21 May, **Alexander's,** on the corner of Plateia Museio (the square 1 block back from the waterfront); and **the Mistral,** 6 Vironis, up the hill opposite the post office, offering the work of the potter/owner.

For a taste of the local cuisine, consider Kefalonia's prized Golden Honey, tart quince preserve, or almond pralines. Another possibility is a bottle of one of Kefalonia's highly praised wines. You can visit **Calliga Vineyard** (selling white Robola and red Calliga Cava) or **Gentilini Vineyard** (with more expensive wines), both near Argostoli; or **Metaxas Wine Estate,** south of Argostoli. The tourist office (see "Visitor Information," above) on the waterfront will tell you how to arrange a tour.

Where to Stay

Accommodations on Kefalonia range from luxury hotels to basic rooms. **Ainos Travel,** 14 G. Vergoti (www.ainostravel.gr; (*26710/22-333*), can help with reservations during high season.

EXPENSIVE

White Rocks Hotel & Bungalows ★★   This low-key place is where travelers catch up on the reading they've meant to do all year. Although not the most elaborate, it is probably the most elegant hotel on Kefalonia. On arriving, you descend a few steps from the main road to enter an almost tropical setting. The lobby is subdued and stylish, a decor that extends to the hotel's guest rooms, which are modest in size but have first-rate bathrooms. Pay the extra for the sea-view rooms; they're worth it. Guests have use of their own small beach, as well as a larger one that is open to the public. White Rocks is a couple of miles south of Argostoli, just above the two beaches. It's a quiet retreat that may appeal more to the older set.

Platys Yialos, 28100 Argostoli. At the beach at Lassi, outside Argostoli. www.whiterocks.gr. © **26710/28-332.** Fax 26710/28-755. 162 units. 190€ double; 200€ bungalow for 2. Rates include breakfast and dinner. AE, DC, V. Closed Nov–Apr. Private parking. Occasional public buses go from the center of town to and from Yialos, but most people take taxis. **Amenities:** 2 restaurants; 2 bars; pool; room service; Wi-Fi. *In room:* A/C, TV, hair dryer, minibar.

MODERATE

In addition to the following, consider the 60-unit **Hotel Miramare,** 2 I. Metaxa, at the far end of shore road (© **26710/25-511;** fax 26710/25-512); it's removed from the town's hustle, yet within walking distance of anyplace you'd want to go.

Cephalonia Star   I don't want to oversell this hotel, but it's just the place for those travelers who are never happier than when they are on the waterfront. For such, its location along the bay and the balconied front rooms with fine views compensate for its rather undistinguished accommodations. The white-walled rooms are a bit austere—along the lines of American motel rooms—but adequate. Bathrooms are standard issue, but all are clean and well serviced. There's a **cafeteria-restaurant** on the premises, but except for breakfast, you'll probably want to patronize Argostoli's many fine eateries, all within a few minutes' walk. In August, a mobile amusement park has been known to set up on the quay just opposite, but then August all over Greece is a carnival.

60 I. Metaxa, 28100 Argostoli. © **26710/23-181.** Fax 26710/23-180. 40 units, some with shower or tub. High season 90€ double; low season 70€ double. Rates include breakfast. MC, V. Street parking along waterfront, across from the port authority. **Amenities:** Restaurant; bar. *In room:* A/C, TV.

Hotel Ionian Plaza ★   Although it doesn't quite qualify as a grand hotel, this is the class act of "downtown" Argostoli, and it's also a fine deal. The lobby, public areas, and guest rooms share a tasteful, comfortable, natural tone. Individual details in the furnishings and decor convey the sense of visiting a fine mansion rather than a commercial hotel. Guest rooms are larger than most, while bathrooms are modern if not mammoth. Breakfast takes place under the awning, and the evening meal could well be at the hotel's adjacent **Il Palazzino** restaurant, where the menu has a strong Italian flavor and prices are surprisingly modest. Stay here if you like to be in the heart of a city; the front rooms overlook the Central Square, but because no vehicles are allowed there, most of the noise comes from children playing in the square.

Vallianou Sq. (Central Sq.), 28100 Argostoli. www.ionianplaza.gr. © **26710/25-581.** Fax 26710/25-585. 43 units. High season 120€ double; low season 90€ double. Rates include buffet breakfast. AE, MC, V. Street parking nearby. **Amenities:** Restaurant; bar; room service. *In room:* A/C, TV, fridge, hair dryer, Wi-Fi.

INEXPENSIVE

Mouikis Hotel   Completely upgraded, this once bare-bones hotel now offers many of the amenities of more expensive places and could make a decent choice for those with limited budgets. The rooms and bathrooms are standard for the class. It's on a quiet side street and close to all points in town. It's popular with groups but usually has a few rooms available for individuals. One unusual service: A minibus takes patrons to a swimming pool that belongs to a nearby resort, also owned by Moukisis's owners.

3 Vironis, 28100 Argostoli. www.mouikis.kefalonia.com © **26710/23-281.** 39 units. High season 75€ double; low season 65€ double. Rates include buffet breakfast. AE, MC, V. Street parking. **Amenities:** Bar. *In room:* A/C, TV, fridge.

Where to Eat

Try the two local specialties: *kreatopita* (meat pie, with rice and a tomato sauce under a crust) and *crasato* (pork cooked in wine). The island's prized wines include the Robola, Muscat, and Mavrodaphne.

EXPENSIVE

Captain's Table ★ GREEK/INTERNATIONAL   This is generally conceded to be the best restaurant in Argostoli, especially for seafood—but be sure you go to the original just off the Central Square. Some guests dress up a bit, and there's a touch of celebration to meals at this slightly upscale restaurant. Specialties include the Captain's Soup (fish, lobster, mussels, shrimp, and vegetables), filets of beef, delicate squid, and fried *courgette* (small eggplants). Go early, order a bottle of wine, and enjoy!

Leoforos Rizopaston. ☎ **26710/23-896.** Main courses 8€–20€. MC, V. Daily 6pm–midnight. Just around corner from Central Sq.; identifiable by its boat-model display case.

MODERATE

Consider **Old Plaka Taverna,** 1 1. Metaxa, at the far end of the waterfront (☎ **26710/24-849**), for modest prices and tasty Greek dishes. It's a local favorite.

La Gondola GREEK/ITALIAN   Everyone should take at least one meal on the main square to experience the "dinner theater," with Argostoli's citizens providing the action. All of the restaurants on the square are about the same in quality and menu, but I've enjoyed some special treats at this one. It offers a house wine, literally made by the house, and serves a special pizza-dough garlic bread, zesty chicken with lemon sauce, and cannelloni that stands out with its rich texture and distinctive flavor. Staff and diners always seem to enjoy themselves here, so we think you will, too.

Central Sq. ☎ **26710/23-658.** Main courses 6€–18€. AE, MC, V. Daily 6pm–2am.

Patsouras ★ GREEK   Patsouras continues to live up to its reputation as the favorite of travelers seeking authentic Greek taverna food and ambience. Dine under the awnings on the terrace, across from the waterfront, and try either of the local specialties, *kreatopita* (meat pie) or *crasto* (pork in wine). Such standards as the *tzatziki* and moussaka have a special zest. Greeks love unpretentious tavernas, and you'll see why if you eat at Patsouras.

32 I. Metaxa. ☎ **26710/22-779.** Main courses 5€–16€. V. Daily noon–midnight. A 5-min. walk from Central Sq., along the waterfront.

INEXPENSIVE

Portside Restaurant GREEK   This unpretentious taverna is what the Greeks call a *phisteria*, a restaurant specializing in meats and fish cooked on the grill or spit. Run by a native of Argostoli and his Greek-American wife, it offers hearty breakfasts, regular plates with side portions of salads and potatoes, and a full selection of Greek favorites. On special nights outside the high season, the restaurant roasts a suckling pig. It's popular with Greeks as well as foreigners, and you've got a front-row seat for harborside activities.

58 I. Metaxa. ☎ **26710/24-130.** Main courses 6€–17€. MC, V. Apr–Oct daily 10am–midnight. Along the waterfront, opposite the port authority.

Argostoli After Dark

Free outdoor concerts are occasionally given in the Central Square. At the end of August, the **Choral Music Festival** hosts choirs from all over Greece and Europe. The grand new **Kefalos Public Theater** stages plays, almost always in Greek and seldom in high season. Young people looking for a bit more action can find a number of cafes, bars, and discos on and around the Central Square; they change names from year to year, but **Cinema Music Club, Rumours, Prive, Stavento, Daccapo,** and **Traffic** have been fairly steady. **Bass,** up by the museum, is a favorite club. If your style runs more to lounging with classic rock, try the **Pub Old House,** off Rizopaston, the palm-tree lined avenue leading away from the main square. At the beach resort of Lassi, **So Simple Bar** is popular.

Side Trips from Argostoli

FISKARDO, ASSOS & MYRTOS BEACH ★

I'd advise this excursion if you only had 1 day for a trip outside Argostoli. The end destination is **Fiskardo ★★,** a picturesque port village that is the only major locale on Kefalonia to have survived the 1953 earthquake. Its charm comes from its surviving 18th-century structures and its intimate harbor, which attracts yachts from all over.

You can make a round-trip from Argostoli to Fiskardo in a day on a **KTEL** bus (10€). But with a rental car, you can detour off the main road to the even more picturesque port and village of **Assos** (it adds about 10km/7 miles), and then reward yourself with another detour down to **Myrtos beach,** one of Greece's great beaches.

Plenty of restaurants dot Fiskardo's harbor. I can recommend **Tassia's, Vassos, Nicholas Taverna** (up on the hillside), and **Panormos** (around the bend). The latter two offer rooms as well. For advance arrangements, contact **Fiskardo Travel** (© **26740/41-315;** ftravel@kef.forthnet.gr). If you think you might like to stay for as long as a week and can afford something special, contact the (British) **Greek Islands Club,** which offers waterfront apartments and houses (**www.gicthevilla collection.com**).

SAMI, MELISSANI GROTTO & DROGARATI CAVE

When you arrive in Kefalonia, you may come first to Sami, an unexceptional town on the east coast and the island's principal point of entry before tourism put Argostoli in the lead. Sami is still a busy port. Besides the unusual white cliffs seen from the harbor, travelers are drawn by **two caves** to the north of Sami, both of which can be visited on a half-day excursion from Argostoli. Of the two, the Drogarati is the more rewarding.

Spili Melissani, about 5km (3 miles) north of Sami, is well signposted. Once you're inside, you will be taken by a guide in a rowboat around a small, partially exposed, partially enclosed lake, whose most spectacular feature is the play of the sun's rays striking the water, which creates a kaleidoscope of colors. It's open daily from 9am to 6pm. Admission is 6€.

On the road that leads west to Argostoli (4km/2 miles from Samiles), there's a well-signposted turnoff to **Drogarati Cave ★.** Known for its unusual stalagmites, its large chamber has been used for concerts (once by Maria Callas). You walk through it on your own; the cave is well illuminated but can be slippery. It's open daily from 9am to 6pm, with an admission of 4€.

ITHAKA

Despite the recent claims that Oysseus's Ithaka is a peninsula off Kefalonia, Ithaka continues to attract those who are willing to go along with the traditional linkage of several sites to Homer's epic. Such associations aside, Ithaka appeals to many visitors: It may be small and not easily approached, but its rugged terrain and laid-back villages reward those who enjoy driving through unspoiled Greek countryside.

Although there are (infrequent) ferry connections to Ithaka from Patras (Peloponnese), Astakos (mainland, opposite Ithaka), and Kefalonia (Fiscardo), I'd strongly recommend that you approach Ithaka with a rented car from Argostoli. The boat connecting Kefalonia to Ithaka (its little port shows up as Pissaetos on websites) sails not from Argostoli but from Sami, the port on the east coast of Kefalonia; to make a bus connection with that boat, and then to take a taxi from the tiny isolated port where you disembark on Ithaka, costs far too much time. Rather, in your rented car, drive the 40 minutes from Argostoli to Sami; the boat fare for the car is 12€, for each individual 3€. Once on Ithaka, you can drive to **Vathy,** the main town, in about 10 minutes, and you'll have wheels with which to explore Ithaka and return to Argostoli, all within a day. Most visitors will be able to see what they want of Ithaka in 1 day before driving back to the little port where the last ferryboat to Kefalonia leaves, usually at 5pm—but ask!

Vathy itself is a small port, a miniversion of bigger Greek ports, with their bustling tourist-oriented facilities. For help in making any arrangements, try **Polyctor Tours,** on the main square (www.ithakiholidays.com; ℭ **26740/33-120**). You might enjoy a cold drink or coffee and admire the bay stretching before you, but otherwise there's not much to do or see here. Instead, drive 16km (10 miles) north to **Moni Katheron;** the 17th-century monastery itself is nothing special, but the bell tower offers a spectacular view over much of Ithaka. For a more ambitious drive, head north via the village of **Anogi,** stopping in its town square to view the little church with centuries-old frescoes and the Venetian bell tower opposite it. Proceed on via Stavros, and then down to the northeast coast to **Frikes,** a small fishing village. Finally, take a winding road along the coast to **Kioni,** arranged like an amphitheater around its harbor; this is the place to stay if you want to give some time to Ithaka.

As for the sites associated with the *Odyssey,* what little there is to be seen is questioned by many scholars, but that shouldn't stop you; after all, it's your imagination that makes the Homeric world come alive. From the outskirts of Vathy, you'll see signs for the four principal sites. Three kilometers (2 miles) northwest of Vathy is the so-called **Cave of the Nymphs,** where Odysseus is said to have hidden the Phaeacians' gifts after he had been brought back (supposedly to the little **Bay of Dexia,** north of the cave). Known locally as Marmarospilia, the small cave is about a half-hour's climb up a slope.

The **Fountain of Arethusa,** where Eumaios is said to have watered his swine, is about 7km (4 miles) south of Vathy; it is known today as the spring of Perapigadi. The **Bay of Ayios Andreas,** below, is claimed to be the spot where Odysseus landed in order to evade Penelope's suitors. To get to the fountain, drive the first 3km (2 miles) by following the signposted road to the south of Vathy as far as it goes; continue on foot another 3km (2 miles) along the path.

About 8km (5 miles) west of Vathy is the site of **Alalkomenai,** claimed by Schliemann to be the site of Odysseus's capital; in fact, the remains date from several centuries later than the official dates of the Trojan War. Finally, a road out of Stavros leads down to the **Bay of Polis,** claimed by some as the port of Odysseus's capital; in the nearby cave of Louizou, an ancient pottery shard was found with the inscription "my vow to Odysseus," but its age suggests that this was the site of a hero-cult.

For lunch back in Vathy, I would recommend **Gregory's Taverna** (aka Paliocaravo) on the far northeast corner of Vathy's bay (keep driving, with the bay on your left, even after you think the road may give out). Ideally, you will find a table on the water, where you can look back at Vathy, while enjoying a fresh fish dinner (not cheap, but fresh fish never is in Greece). And if you are so enamored of Ithaka and its Homeric associations, you could spend a night or two at the **Perantzada 1811 Hotel ★★,** in Vathy (**www.arthotel.gr/perantzada**). As its name indicates, it is a converted early-19th-century mansion, but the amenities (and price) are both luxurious and the most up-to-date (including A/C and Internet access). A more moderately priced choice would be the **Hotel Mentor** (**www.hotelmentor.gr**) right on the harbor.

HIGHLIGHTS OF NORTHERN GREECE

by Sherry Marker

For years, most visitors to Greece ignored Thessaloniki, thinking of it—if at all—as a poor second to Athens. That began to change in 1997, when Thessaloniki—the capital of Macedonia, the second-largest city in Greece, and the emotional heart of northern Greece—was named the European City of Culture. Since then, word has gotten out about Thessaloniki's varied charms and more and more visitors are coming here.

The city has had an explosion of renovations, restorations, and innovations. Old warehouses in the waterfront Ladadika district have been smartened up and transformed into cafes, restaurants, and galleries. Museums of photography, cinema, and contemporary art have appeared, along with what may be Greece's liveliest avant-garde music scene.

Increasingly, Thessaloniki is a popular destination city for weekending Greeks and jet-setting Europeans—many from Eastern Europe—who've already "done" Prague and Barcelona. In addition, Thessaloniki has an increasingly large semi-permanent population of immigrants and migrants from throughout the Balkans and the former Soviet Union. In some neighborhoods, in many restaurants and cafes, on street corners and in buses, you'll hear much Russian spoken—and much, much more Russian than English, French, or German. Visitors here—wherever they hail from—can still visit the wonderful Byzantine churches for which Thessaloniki has always been famous, but also enjoy the rhythm of today's Thessaloniki, with its varied cuisine, multiplicity of galleries and museums, and virtually all-night-every-night cafe life. When Athenians cough and complain about pollution and the evil *nefos* (smog) that blankets the capital city every summer, Thessalonians enjoy the cool breezes off the sea as they take evening promenades beside the Gulf of Thessaloniki.

The National Road from Athens to Thessaloniki was considerably improved in 2010–11. It's possible to drive between Greece's two most important cities in 6 hours with a couple of brief stops for snacking and stretching along the way. If you're not pressed for time, break your trip between the two cities by taking in the lively port town of Volos and the wooded villages of Mount Pelion (see "Volos & Mount Pelion" in chapter 12, p. 498). Good roads link the archaeological sites of Vergina, Pella, and

Dion—once homes of the mighty warrior Philip II of Macedon and his famous son, Alexander the Great—both to the National Road and to Thessaloniki. Even Mount Athos and its monasteries are linked to Thessaloniki by a good road—although only men are allowed to visit the Holy Mountain.

In July of 2009, the Via Egnatia, which links Igoumenitsa, in northwest Greece, with the borders of Albania, the former Yugoslav Republic of Macedonia (FYROM), Bulgaria, and Turkey was opened. In theory, the new highway cuts travel time between, for example, Ioannina (see chapter 14) and Thessaloniki from 5 to 2½ hours. Like the National Highway, the Via Egnatia has very heavy truck traffic.

Strategies for Seeing Thessaloniki

My suggestions for exploring Thessaloniki (100,000 and still growing) are really just that: suggestions. Unlike Athens, with its Acropolis, Thessaloniki has no one "must-see" sight. In fact, it's the city of Thessaloniki itself that's the "don't miss" attraction.

What I like best about Thessaloniki are the endless opportunities for what I think of as focused wandering—heading off, perhaps, for the splendid **Archaeological Museum** and **the Museum of Byzantine Culture** (conveniently located side-by-side) and being pleasantly surprised when en route I come across a previously unnoticed small Byzantine church, or a restored Turkish bath, or a cluster of shoe shops with stunning window displays of knockoff Manolos and Jimmy Choos.

Wander along Thessaloniki's main drags, such as **Aristotelous and Egnatia streets,** and you'll suddenly realize you're passing (or just around the corner from) the city's main markets, the ancient agora, the clutch of old-fashioned shops and tavernas in Athonos Square, several small churches and Turkish baths, the Alatza mosque, the city's main church, St. Demetrius—and too many small cafes to count. Don't miss the jumble of old-fashioned shops and chic cafes in little Athonos Square, just off bustling Egnatia. From Athonos, it's only a few steps to wide squares built around churches and Roman palaces, and to harborside promenades with non-stop cafes filled with Thessalonians non-stop talking and texting on their cell phones (*kineta*).

To get a view of the whole show, climb (slowly, and not in the midday sun) up to **Ano Poli (Upper City),** the old Turkish Quarter where many tumble-down wooden houses are being restored as boutique dwellings, with enough cafes thrown in for you to find a place to rest. *One warning:* While you're meandering, don't completely relax. Thessalonians with motorcycles, like Athenians, regard sidewalks as ideal spots to drive and park. And one helpful piece of information to keep in mind while you explore Thessaloniki: As in most Greek cities, there are almost no visible street numbers, nor do Greeks use street numbers when giving directions. Ask for what you want by name or crossroads, not by any street number. Following are some suggestions on how to get to know Thessaloniki (also known as Salonica).

Thessaloniki Culture

The next **Thessaloniki Biennale** (www. thessalonikibiennale.gr) will be held in 2013. If you're in town then, keep an eye out for exhibits. The Macedonian Museum of Contemporary Art, 154 Egnatias (© 2310/240-002; www.mmca.org.gr) is usually a good place to pick up a program with the schedule of events.

IF YOU HAVE 1 DAY

The city's two major museums—the **Archaeological Museum** and the **Museum of Byzantine Culture**—are handily located side by side near the fairgrounds. Decide whether you'd rather start with artifacts from antiquity

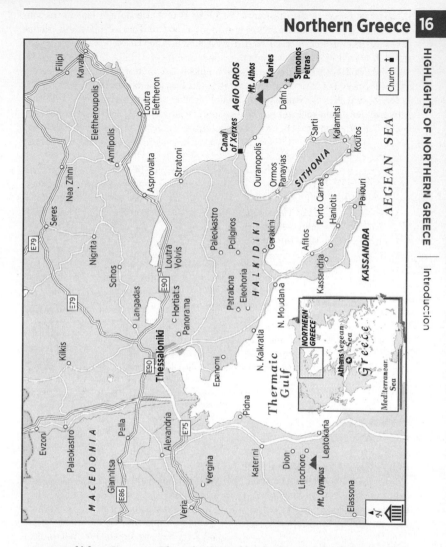

Church †■

or images of life in Byzantine Thessaloniki, and be the first one through the door at the museum you choose. After visiting the museums (with a break at the excellent cafe in the Byzantine Museum), stroll back along the harbor past the White Tower to the center of town for lunch. If you feel energetic, hop a bus or take a taxi to the old-fashioned **Upper City** (known locally both as Ano Poli and Tsinari). Then grab a bite, perhaps at **Tsinari's Ouzeri,** which has been serving up ouzo and mezedes (snacks) since 1859. Once you're fortified, wander back downhill to the center of today's Thessaloniki. *Reminder:* Most of the churches you want to see throughout Thessaloniki are open morning and early evening, but closed during the midafternoon siesta period (roughly 2–5pm).

After your own siesta, you might visit some of the Roman monuments and the churches of **Ayia Sofia** and **Ayios Dimitrios** in the city center, remembering that plenty of cafes are nearby, as well as the famous sweet shop **Terkenlis** (www.terkenlis.gr) in Ayia Sofia Square. When you're ready for dinner, head to one of the cheek-by-jowl restaurants in the **Ladadika,** the restored warehouse district that takes its name from the olives and olive oil once stored here. Another not-to-be-missed dinner choice is the justly famous **Thanasis,** in the rambling Modiano Market.

Note: This makes for a very full day, and you'll certainly enjoy Thessaloniki a lot more if you have more than a day here. Byzantine churches take time to find, to see, and to enjoy. Many of the frescoes and mosaics are high up on walls, or faded by time (a strong flashlight and binoculars are invaluable).

IF YOU HAVE 2 DAYS

If you have more than a day, abbreviate your first day, so you don't feel obligated to see the city in one fell swoop. You might begin your second day with the **Upper City** and work your way downhill. Start at the impressive but overly-restored **Vlatadon Monastery** and then head down, stopping at the appealing churches of **Osios David, Nikolaos Orphanos,** and **Profitias Elias.** Even if church architecture, mosaics, and frescoes are not your thing, you'll enjoy walking through the narrow streets lined with a mixture of tumble-down and restored two-story wood houses dating from the Turkish period. If you didn't see them on your first day, take in the churches of Ayia Sofia and Ayios Dimitrios when you get back down to the city center, and stroll past the Alatza Imaret and Yeni and Bey Hamami Baths, relics of the city's Turkish past.

Then, for a change of pace, take in the city's markets that blur one into another: the **Modiano,** the open-air food market on **Athonos Square,** the **Kapani (Vlali),** and **Bezesteni** markets. If you visit all these, you can buy anything from a copper bucket for milking sheep to the sheep itself. Along the way, you can nibble on souvlaki, pastry, or whatever seasonal fruit catches your fancy—and get a bunch of flowers at the **Louloudadika** (flower market) in a 16th-century Turkish bath, the **Yahudi Haman.** If you haven't already seen the **Arch of Galerius,** the **Rotunda,** and the **Roman agora,** try to take them in during an evening *volta* (stroll), with frequent breaks along the way at some of Thessaloniki's myriad cafes.

IF YOU HAVE 3 DAYS OR MORE

Everyone in Thessaloniki seems to be rushing. Take advantage of being on vacation and spend some time strolling, wandering, and browsing through some of the shops and galleries along **Egnatia, Tsimiski, Aristotelous, Ayias Sofias,** and pedestrianized **Dimitriou Gounari streets.** In the evening, if you want to see young Thessalonians working at relaxing, take in some of the bars at harborside **Aristotelous**

Enjoying Macedonian Wine

One of the many pleasures of Macedonia is its wine. *Mavromatina retsina* and the reds and whites of the Boutsaris winery in Naoussa are famous throughout Greece—and, increasingly, abroad. Check out www.wineroads.gr for information on the vineyards and wineries of Macedonia; www.greekwine.gr is also helpful, as is Miles Lambert-Gocs's paperback, *The Wines of Greece.* You can even plan your visits to the Philip and Alexander sites around your visits to local vineyards!

Square, in and just off **Plateia Athonos** (between Egnatia and Ermou sts.), or at the famous **Mylos** complex on Andreou Georgou.

When you've had your fill of city pleasures, you may want to head out of Thessaloniki to see some of the sites associated with Philip and Alexander, such as **Vergina, Dion,** or **Pella.** If you'd like to avoid a lot of driving, sign up for one of the efficient day trips that take in these sites. (See "Organized Tours" and "In the Footsteps of Philip & Alexander the Great," later in this chapter.)

THESSALONIKI (SALONIKA) ★★★

516km (320 miles) N of Athens

When a Greek tells you he's from Athens, he might sound a bit apologetic, and quickly tells you what village he or his parents came from to live in Athens. Greeks from Thessaloniki, on the other hand, sound very pleased to be from Greece's "Second City." Thessaloniki may be second to Athens in political importance and population, but in popular songs, Thessaloniki is celebrated as "the mother of Macedonia," "the most blessed of cities," "beautiful Thessaloniki," and "the city whose praises are sung."

You, too, may be tempted to sing this city's praises when you take in its wonderful location along the broad expanse of the Thermaic Gulf. You're never far from the sea here; when you least expect it, you can catch a glimpse of waves and boats in the distance. Alas, especially in the summer, you may also notice signs of the harbor's pollution, including a ripe odor. If you're lucky, you'll see Mount Olympus while you're here: Pollution has increasingly obscured even that imposing landmark.

Greeks are fond of reminding foreigners that when their ancestors were painting themselves blue or living in rude huts, Greeks were sitting in the shade of the Parthenon, reading the plays of Sophocles. Similarly, Thessalonians like to remind Athenians that when Athens languished in the long twilight of its occupation by the Romans and Ottomans, Thessaloniki flourished. It's true: Thessaloniki's strategic location on the main land route from Europe into Asia made it a powerful city during the Roman Empire. Many monuments built here date from the 4th century A.D., from the Emperor Galerius's rule.

During the Byzantine Empire (the 4th–15th c. A.D.), Thessaloniki boasted that it was second only to the capital, Constantinople. Thessaloniki's greatest pride—its superb and endearing churches—were built then. After the Turks conquered the Byzantine Empire, Thessaloniki continued to flourish as an important commercial center and port. In the 18th and early 19th centuries, the city's Jewish community was so strong and so prosperous that some called Thessaloniki the "second Jerusalem."

Then, in August 1917, a devastating fire destroyed 80% of the city. Phoenix-like, Thessaloniki rose from the ashes. Unfortunately, only part of the city was rebuilt according to the grand plan of the French architect Ernest Hébrard. More than 130,000 Greek refugees from Asia Minor flooded into Thessaloniki between 1922 and 1923, almost doubling the city's population and leading to enormous unregulated development. Despite this, Thessaloniki has enough tree-lined boulevards and parks to make it feel much greener than Athens.

After World War II, and again in the 1960s, two more growth spurts left much of the city's outskirts crowded and ugly—and all too much of the city center lined with bland apartment buildings. Still, Thessaloniki has none of the horizon-blocking skyscrapers that have proliferated in Athens; earthquake regulations forbid this. The last

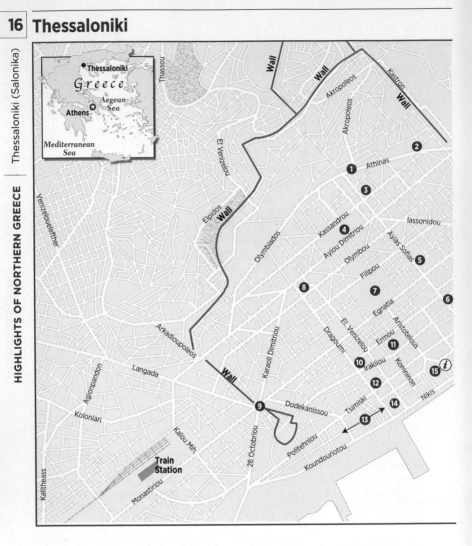

major earthquake was in 1978. In recent years, the narrow lanes and old-fashioned houses of the Upper City (Ano Poli) became sought after for restoration, first into bohemian pads and now into chic urban homes, art galleries, and restaurants.

Glimpses of the sea, tree-lined streets, magnificent Byzantine churches—all these make visiting Thessaloniki special. The food is also more varied and inventive than in most other parts of Greece. The long traditions of Macedonian cuisine are infused with zesty flavors of the Pontus (the area around the Black Sea where most of the city's refugees had lived). And, there's another reason that the food here is so good: The restaurants cater to local customers; none of them make their living off tourists.

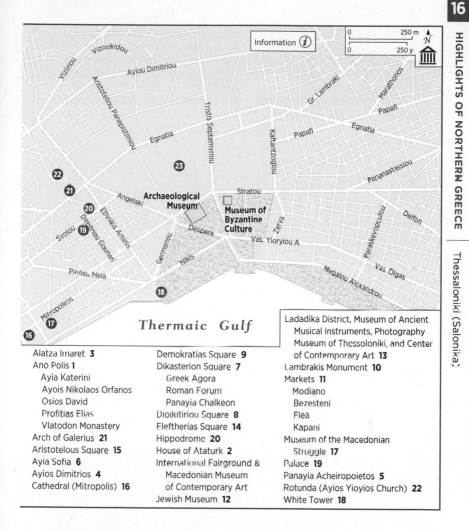

Information ⓘ

Alatza Imaret **3**	Demokratias Square **9**	Ladadika District, Museum of Ancient
Ano Polis **1**	Dikasterion Square **7**	Musical Instruments, Photography
Ayia Katerini	Greek Agora	Museum of Thessoloniki, and Center
Ayois Nikolaos Orfanos	Roman Forum	of Contemporary Art **13**
Osios David	Panayia Chalkeon	Lambrakis Monument **10**
Profitias Elias	Dioikitiriou Square **8**	Markets **11**
Vlatodon Monastery	Eleftherias Square **14**	Modiano
Arch of Galerius **21**	Hippodrome **20**	Bezesteni
Aristotelous Square **15**	House of Ataturk **2**	Flea
Ayia Sofia **6**	International Fairground &	Kapani
Ayios Dimitrios **4**	Macedonian Museum	Museum of the Macedonian
Cathedral (Mitropolis) **16**	of Contemporary Art	Struggle **17**
	Jewish Museum **12**	Palace **19**
		Panayia Acheiropoietos **5**
		Rotunda (Ayios Yioyios Church) **22**
		White Tower **18**

Essentials

GETTING THERE **By Plane** Thessaloniki's **Macedonia International Airport** (℃ **2310/473-212**), 17km (11 miles) south of town, is served from Athens International Airport (www.aia.gr) by **Olympic Air** (℃ **810/114-4444** or 210/966-6666, official Greek phone numbers that never answer; www.olympicair.com) **Aegean Airlines** (℃ **810/112-0000**; www.aegeanair.com) also has several flights daily between Athens and Thessaloniki. From the U.S., there are no direct flights to Thessaloniki. Connections can be made at a number of European cities, including Athens, Amsterdam, Brussels, Frankfurt, London, Munich, Vienna, and Zurich

The busiest time of the year in Thessaloniki is not summer but fall, when the **International Trade Fair** and **Festival of Greek Songs** takes place in September, followed by the **Demitria** celebrations of the city's patron saint continuing into October and November. There is also a film festival in November. If you come between September and November, be sure to book a hotel in advance—and be prepared to pay dearly: Price hikes of more than 50% are usual during convention and festival season, although Greece's wobbly economy may keep prices down.

The airport is a 30-minute drive from the city center. Bus no. 78 runs from the airport into central Thessaloniki in about an hour (usually stopping in Aristotelous Sq. and at the train station) daily from about 6am to 11pm and costs 4€. A taxi ride runs about 15€.

By Train   Five daily trains officially make the trip from Athens to Thessaloniki in about 6 hours, but most are crowded, without air-conditioning, and subject to unexplained delays; nonetheless, they are cheap, at around 50€ round trip coach. If you must take a train, choose the fast **InterCity,** preferably the overnight sleeper, which has first-class compartments for four to six passengers and sleeper compartments for two to six passengers. Make reservations for sleeping compartments well in advance at the Larissa train station in Athens (✆ **210/323-6747;** www.ose.gr).

In Thessaloniki, you can purchase tickets at the **OSE Thessaloniki Train Station,** 28 Monastiriou, the western extension of Egnatia (✆ **2310/599-421**). InterCity coach tickets from Athens to Thessaloniki cost from 120€ round trip, sleeper service from 150€ round-trip. A taxi ride from the station to Aristotelous Square takes about 10 minutes and costs about 8€. *Tip:* Avoid the trek to the train station to get information and buy tickets, and use the **OSE** (train) office instead, at 18 Aristotelous Sq. (✆ **2310/598-120;** www.ose.gr), 9am to 9pm Tuesday to Friday; 9am to 3pm Monday and Saturday.

By Bus   Ten air-conditioned buses from Athens usually make the trip daily to Thessaloniki in about 7 hours (includes one 20-min. stop at a roadside restaurant with toilet facilities). Buses usually arrive on time. Make reservations in advance at the Athens bus terminal, 100 Kifissou (✆ **210/512-4910** or 210/512-9233). A one-way fare costs about 45€. Many buses arrive in Thessaloniki at the station at 65 Monastiriou (✆ **2310/510-834**) opposite the train station, where there are taxis. Some buses stop at the newer bus station at 194 Iannitsou (✆ **2310/595-408**), west of the train station. For general information on Athens–Macedonia schedules and fares, call ✆ **210/512-4910** or go to **www.ktel.org**.

By Car   From Athens, take the 516km (320-mile) National Road, a four-lane highway that's the best in Greece, although stretches are always being repaired or widened, which leads to frequent delays. The road, a major truck route, is also often the scene of serious accidents. Plan on at least 6 or 7 hours, if you stop en route. Gas stations are common along the National Road, but you often must exit to reach them. Much of the road skirts the mountains and goes through the plains of central and northern Greece. In other words, it's not the most stunning drive.

If you're driving to Northern Greece from **Europe,** you'll probably take the ferry from the Italian ports of Bari, Ancona, or Brindisi to Igoumenitsou on the northwest coast of Greece, and then drive across the Pindus Mountains to Thessaloniki. The trip is spectacular; allow at least 5 or 6 hours. The southern route (via Ioannina and Kalambaka to Larissa and the National Rd.) is much less treacherous than the northern alternative (through Kozani)—particularly in winter, although snow can close both routes. The southern route also passes Kalambaka and the monasteries perched on the awesome pinnacles of the Meteora (see chapter 12). You will almost certainly encounter continuing roadwork on the National Highway (called the Via Egnatia, after its Roman predecessor) designed to link Patras (in the Peloponnese) with Central Greece and continue on to Macedonia and the Turkish border. The road was officially completed in June of 2009, but work will continue for some time.

CITY LAYOUT   Thessaloniki sits on the northern coast of the Thermaic Gulf like a lopsided turban tilted to the northwest. Central Thessaloniki is bounded on the south by its deep harbor and on the north by the heights of the **Ano Poli (Upper City).** Thessaloniki's most important square—the equivalent of Athens's Syntagma Square—is **Aristotelous Square,** which runs almost into the harbor. The city's best-known landmark—but no rival to Athens's Acropolis—is the White Tower, a remnant of the massive walls that once encircled the city. The great walls—begun in antiquity and extended and expanded by the Byzantines, Venetians, and Turks—were torn down as the population grew and the city expanded in the late 19th and early 20th centuries. Today, Thessaloniki continues to sprawl along the Thermaic Gulf. To the east are the expanding residential districts, while to the west, there are rail and ship yards and neighborhoods as yet unreclaimed and transformed into galleries and restaurants.

The heart of Thessaloniki, with its most important shops, banks, hotels, restaurants, archaeological remains, and churches lies between the heights of the Ano Poli and the harbor. This is also where you will find (to the east) the campus of several universities, the grounds of the International Trade Fair and the **Archaeological and Byzantine museums;** to the west, there are streets lined with warehouses—many now converted into the chic restaurants and galleries of the **Ladadika district.** Ladadika blurs into **Ksiladika,** the woodworkers' district, which is beginning to lay claim to its own chic restaurants and shops, in addition to the carpenter's workshops that originally gave the district its character.

Central Thessaloniki is dominated by four main streets running from the southwest to the northeast. The largest, **Egnatia,** runs across the northern side of the commercial district. Egnatia is home to discount shops, cheap hotels, and affordable restaurants. The city's second-most important commercial route, **Tsimiski,** parallels Egnatia 2 blocks to the south and runs one-way from east to west. Unpronounceable Tsimiski street (if you make a slight sneeze and you try to say Tsimiski, it may help) has lots of hotels and many of the city's best shops and department stores. One block south of Tsimiski and running one-way from west to east is **Mitropoleos,** with its namesake the Metropolitan Cathedral. Like Tsimiski, Mitropoleost has lots of good shops, boutiques, and sweet shops—Thessalonians adore sweets. The seaside promenade **Leoforos Nikis** is 1 block south of Mitropoleos, runs from the shipping yards to the White Tower, and has virtually non-stop outdoor cafes and bars.

Stand in **Aristotelous Square** at almost any time of the day or night and you'll realize this is the heart of downtown Thessaloniki. Ringed with outdoor cafes and restaurants, it is also the backdrop for the city's major political rallies and demonstrations. Aristotle Street runs to Thessaloniki's other important central square, **Dikasterion,** where most city buses begin and end their runs. The square overlooks the partially excavated Roman marketplace and has a clutch of shady trees, the Byzantine church Panagia

Chalkeon (Virgin of the Copper Workers), and a restored Turkish bathhouse. Some-times, there's an informal street market here run mainly by migrant workers from Eastern Europe, the former USSR, and Africa. Thessaloniki's main market areas, where you can find anything from fresh fish to curtain hooks, spill around the square.

Ayias Sofias Street, another of the city's main drags, named after one of the city's most important churches, is east of Aristotelous Street. This was once Thessaloniki's most fashionable residential square, similar to Athens's chic Kolonaki Square. Just off the square is pedestrianized **Dimitriou Gounari,** whose shop-lined length sits on top of a major Roman thoroughfare that went from the Galerius's palace to his monumental arch. The palace area, now partially excavated, opens onto the tree-shaded park of **Navarino Square,** which is crowded with outdoor cafes, bars, and tavernas, and second only to Aristotelous as the city's major gathering place—although many of the artists and intellectuals who gather here would place it first.

The old **Turkish Quarter** has lots of names: **Ano Poli (Upper City), Eptapir-giou (Seven Gates),** and **To Kastro (Fortress).** This is where you'll find some of the finest Byzantine churches—and, increasingly, some elegant restored town houses. This is easily the most pleasant part of Thessaloniki to explore—but walking all the way up is, well, a *very* steep uphill walk. Your reward is the delights of visiting all those small churches and exploring the winding streets around Kalitheas Square, such as Irodotou, as well as pleasant squares such as Romfei Square, in the district known as Koule Kafe, and Tsinari Square, at the juncture of Kleious and Alexandras Papado-poulou. *Note:* Remember that most churches are closed from about 1 to 5pm.

If you are driving in and out of Thessaloniki, you'll probably use the **Ring Road,** just to the north of the Upper City, that loops around Thessaloniki and connects the National Road from Athens with highways to Thrace and Halkidiki and to the airport at Mikras along the sea to the east.

FINDING AN ADDRESS Buildings almost never have visible numbers; ask for what you want by name, not by number. If possible, have someone write down, in Greek, what you are searching for so that you can show the name to a local. Even with a good map, and helpful locals, you'll probably have trouble finding some of the churches in Ano Poli, but take it, as the Greeks say, *"Siga, siga"* ("Slowly, slowly"), and you'll find your way.

VISITOR INFORMATION The Thessaloniki office of the **Greek National Tourism Organization** is at 136 Tsimiski (© **2310/221-100;** www.visitgreece.gr), 2 blocks inland and 2 blocks east of the harborside White Tower.

MAPS City maps and two excellent guides to the city (*The Thessaloniki Handbook* [with section-by-section maps], by Christos Zafiris; and *Monuments of Thessaloniki* [with an excellent city-center map], by Apostolos Papagiannopoulos) are usually avail-able at bookstores, including **Ianos,** 7 Aristotelous (© **2310/277-164**); **Traveller Bookstore,** 41 Proxenou Koromila (© **2310/275-215**); **Malliaris,** 9 Aristotelous (© **2310/276-926**); and **P. Kyriakides,** 40 Agias Sophias St. (© **2310/241-613**).

GETTING AROUND In the city center, a 20- to 30-minute walk will take you to most attractions, restaurants, and shops. Taxis are usually easy to find, unless you're going to the Upper City. Many taxis are reluctant to make this trip because there is little guarantee of a return fare down, and they may—unlawfully—refuse. But if you're in the cab before you state your destination, there's little the driver can do but take you there. Otherwise, if you don't want to walk up, you can hop on bus no. 23, which leaves from Eleftherias Square.

By Bus Bus tickets cost .50€ from kiosks (*periipetera*) or .60€ on board (exact change required). A price hike is in the offing, so check these prices upon arrival. Keep your ticket in case a conductor boards the bus to check them; fines of 30€ are standard for tickletless riders.

By Taxi This is your best bet except, as noted under "Getting Around" above, when you want to go to the Upper City. Have someone write out your destination in Greek, so that you can show the driver where you want to go. Most hotels will call a taxi for you, or try **Macedonia** (② 2310/550/599) or **Lefko Pyrgos** (② 2310/214/900).

By Car There is little reason to have a car in Thessaloniki. Traffic is terrible and legal parking spots are almost impossible to find, even at the large public parking lot in Plateia Eleftherias. But having a car for excursions into northern Greece will allow you to see and enjoy a lot more than you would either from a bus or on a guided tour. Keep in mind that if you take a day trip, you'll spend at least an hour getting out of and another hour getting back into the city. It makes much better sense to see what you want outside of town on your way in, or out, of Thessaloniki.

Most car-rental agencies—including **Avis** (www.avis.com), **Budget** (www.budget.com), **Eurocar** (www.eurocar.com), and **Hertz** (www.hertz.com)—have offices at the airport. A car with unlimited mileage costs from 60€ per day in high season. (*Reminder:* High season is during the Sept–Oct trade and other festivals.) Be sure to ask if the price quoted includes all taxes and insurance—and be sure to take full insurance if your credit card does not provide it. *Tip:* It is almost always cheaper to book a car with an international agency from abroad, not from within Greece.

By Boat It's possible to take ferries and boats from Thessaloniki to a number of Aegean islands (including Crete, Santorini, and Mykonos) and to the Sporades (Skiathos, Skopelos, and Alonissos). Many travel agents around Plateia Eleftherias and Aristotelous Square sell ferry tickets. Centrally located agencies include **Polaris Travel,** 81 Egnatiou (② 2310/276-051), and **Zorpidis Travel,** 4 Salaminos (② 2310/555-955; www.zorpidis.gr). The harbor police/port authorities can be reached at ② 2310/531-504 (to -507). The website for Greek Travel Pages (**www.gtp.gr**) is also useful for boat schedules.

[FastFACTS] THESSALONIKI

Currency Exchange & ATMs All banks exchange currency, as do most hotels and the central post office. The major banks along Tsimiski and Aristoteleos Square have ATMs. Remember that ATMs are often not stocked on holidays lasting several days and during bank strikes.

Embassies & Consulates The **U.S. Consulate** (② 2310/242-905 or 2310/260-716) is at

43 Tsimiski. It offers a bare minimum of services. The **UK/Commonwealth Honorary Consul** is at 8 Venizelou (② 2310/278-006 or 2310/269-984), by appointment only.

Emergencies The **police hot line** is ② 100; for non-urgent help, call ② 2310/863-393. For **first aid,** call ② 166. For **car breakdowns,** call ② 104 (the Greek Automobile Touring Club, or ELPA). Also try

the **tourist police,** 4 Dodekanisou, near the eastern end of Tsimiski (② 2310/554-870 or 2310/554-871).

Hospitals The main hospital is the **Ippokration** (② 2310/892-2000 or 2310/837-921) at 50 Papanastasiou; doctors who speak some English are usually available.

Internet Access Thessaloniki has many Internet cafes, including centrally located **e-Global,** 117 Egnatia (🕭 **2310/887-711**), and **Meganet,** 5 Plateia Navarino (🕭 **2310/269-591**). By the time you visit, much of the city center should have Wi-Fi.

Newspapers & Magazines English-language publications are available at several kiosks in Aristotelous Square and along Tsimiski.

Pharmacies Pharmacies alternate late-night hours. Lists and addresses of the ones open on a particular night can be found in the local newspapers and the windows of all pharmacies.

Police The 24-hour emergency number is 🕭 **100.** The tourist police number is 🕭 **2310/554-870** or 2310/554-871.

Post Office The main post office is at 26 Aristotelous (🕭 **2310/278-924**). Hours are Monday through Friday from 7:30am to 8pm, Saturday from 7:30am to 2pm, and Sunday from 9am to 1:30pm.

Restrooms All but the smallest eateries and bars have restrooms that you can request to use without embarrassment. Carrying some tissues with you is always a good idea.

Safety Thessaloniki is a very safe city, although the influx of a rough element in recent years means that obvious tourists should exercise the usual big-city caution, especially at night, or if surrounded by a group asking directions (often pickpockets). The only area absolutely to avoid is around Vardaris (Dimokratias) Square, which attracts some shady characters.

The Top Attractions: Museums

Archaeological Museum ★★★   This museum reopened in 2008 after several years of renovations. The displays illuminate how life was lived through the ages, rather than documenting the development of artistic styles and genres. They give us a glimpse of life in Macedonia from about 350,000 B.C. through the early Christian era—an amazingly long period. Several excellent videos (Greek and English) look at how archaeologists interpret what they find and how ancient Macedonia developed and the city of Thessaloniki grew. In addition, exhibits give us a peek behind the scenes at how some objects were found, perhaps when a building was torn down, or when tunnels were dug in the ongoing excavations for Thessaloniki's eventual Metro. If you've visited this museum in past years, you may miss some of its former stars—finds from the tombs at Derveni and the Royal Tombs at Vergina—which are now on display at Vergina. Don't let the absence of these gold treasures keep you from enjoying what is here, including the 4th-century-B.C. **Derveni Krater** with its elaborate and sensual scenes of the marriage of Dionysos and Ariadne. The krater and gold found in a 4th-century tomb near Thessaloniki are on display in the Gold of Macedon room, up several steps and to the right as you enter the museum. (The Gold of Macedon room is indicated on the brochure you should get with your ticket, but is usually quite dark and not signposted in

---

💬 **Catching a Local Festival**

If you are in Salonika in September, check with the GNTO for details on the weeklong wine festival usually held in Anhialos, a village 15km (9 miles) northwest of Thessaloniki. Traveling around May 21? Check out the celebrations in the village of Langadas, 20km (9 miles) northeast of Thessaloniki. It's one of only a few places in Greece and Bulgaria where the devout walk on fire (coals, actually). No one is really sure why the *anastenarides* (firewalkers) do this: Theories include the survival of a pagan custom or the commemoration of an occasion when the devout saved icons from a church conflagration without suffering any burns.

the museum itself.) The Derveni krater and the gold are memorable, but almost more amazing are the paper-thin Hellenistic glass vessels and delicate Roman mosaics from private houses that were used daily in antiquity. That they have survived in such superb condition seems miraculous. And don't miss the portrait bust of 4th-century-A.D. Emperor Galerius, which shows him as the tough brawler he was. Galerius entered the army as a lowly recruit and fought his way up, ending up as the emperor who built many of Thessaloniki's surviving ancient monuments.

This severe, low museum was built in 1962, and is considered to be the best example of "architectural modernism" in Thessaloniki—a sad commentary on that tedious genre. The museum shop has postcards, guidebooks, and a number of souvenirs featuring the 16-point star of Macedon. The museum toilet facilities are good; the cafe has snacks and soft drinks but does not hold a candle to the cafe/restaurant at the nearby Byzantine Museum. Allow several hours here. If you're interested, inquire about the guided tours in English given several times a week.

6 Manoli Andronikou (opposite the south side of the International Fairgrounds). ℂ **2310/830-538.** Fax 2310/861-306. www.amth.gr. Admission 6€; combined admission to Archaeological and Byzantine museums 9€. Mon noon-7pm; Tues-Sun 8am 7pm. Hours subject to change. Bus: 58 from Dikasterion Sq., or 11 heading east from anywhere on Egnatia.

Museum of Byzantine Culture ★★★ With the possible exception of the Byzantine and Christian Museum in Athens, this is Greece's finest collection of Byzantine art. I think the most impressive—and magical—exhibits here are the 4th- to 6th-century barrel-vaulted tombs found in Thessaloniki, with frescoes showing Old and New Testament scenes as well as scenes in Paradise. You'll see Daniel in the Lions' Den, Christ as the Fisher of Men, and blissful scenes of Paradise, where fruit, fowl, and wine are shown in abundance. The text accompanying the exhibit looks at the transition from the ancient image of the Afterworld as the Elysian Fields to the Christian images of Paradise. Not surprisingly, the museum has a number of important icons, including a terrific 12th-century icon of the Virgin and Christ child. A display of bright mosaics and elaborately carved marble panels salvaged from the church of Ayios Dimitrios after the great fire of 1917 brings home just how splendid that church once was.

Exhibits cover the development of Byzantine culture from its early beginnings in the Roman world through the fall of Constantinople in 1453; the final exhibits focus on the lasting influence of Byzantine culture in Greece. As at the Archaeological Museum, the exhibits here attempt to tell the story of Thessaloniki and look at its social history through art and artifacts, including such down-to-earth items as drain pipes and cooking pots. The museum shop usually has a range of books on Byzantine culture, as well as museum reproductions and postcards. The **cafe/restaurant** is so appealing that it has become a popular meeting place for local ladies who lunch. Allow several hours.

2 Leoforos Stratou (just west of the Archaeological Museum). ℂ **2310/868-570.** Fax 2310/838-597. Admission 6€; combined admission to both the Byzantine and Archaeological museums 9€. Mon noon-7pm; Tues-Sun 8am-7pm. Hours subject to unannounced changes. Bus: 58 from Dikasterion Sq., or 11 heading east from anywhere on Egnatia.

The Top Attractions: Monuments

Arch of Galerius ★ If you need directions here, try asking for *ee kamara* (the arch), which is what Thessalonians call this hefty monument built by Galerius around A.D. 305 to celebrate a victory over the Persians. Originally, the arch was even larger: Almost half—another entire arch—is missing. Look for the Persians, some in the peaked caps and trousers that the Greeks and Romans found so effeminate and absurd, in the carved panels that tell the story of Galerius's battles. Until 1953, the tram line ran under this arch. Air pollution steadily erodes many sculptural details. You can take this place in with a glance, or spend a pleasant half-hour admiring the detail.

Just below the Rotunda on Egnatia and Dimitriou Gounari.

Greek Agora & Roman Forum ★   In the 1960s, workmen digging to lay the foundations of new law courts for Thessaloniki came across the remains of the city's ancient Greek agora, which later became the Roman forum. Archaeologists took over and excavated the sprawling complex you see today. As in Athens, this agora/forum was the heart of the ancient city, its commercial, governmental, social, and artistic center—and, as with the Athenian agora, the remains are not easy to identify.

When the Romans came here, they inevitably expanded the Greek agora, creating a two-level forum. You can see the arched remains of the **cryptoporticus,** a retaining wall that supported part of the upper forum. The best-preserved ruin here, the large **Odeum,** or Odeon, is a theater where Romans enjoyed watching both musical performances and fights to the death between gladiators and wild beasts. The Odeum is sometimes still used for summer concerts.

In modern times, the most famous ancient monument here was the stoa with a series of statues facing the Via Egnatia, known as the *Incantadas* (Enchanted Idols), the name given them by Thessaloniki's then-flourishing community of Sephardic Jews. By the 19th century, much of the colonnade was lost, but a segment remained, incorporated into the courtyard of a Jewish home. When the French scholar Emmanuel Miller saw the colonnade, he knew he had to have it—and got permission to cart the remaining *incantadas* off to the Louvre, where they are to this day. Browse in the few book and print shops in Thessaloniki, and you'll probably see reproductions of a charming engraving of the colonnade by the 18th-century English antiquarians Stuart and Revett. There's almost no shade here, so you may want to stroll about a bit and then take in the sights while polishing off an ice cream from one of the cafes overlooking the site.

If things Turkish interest you, stop by the Bey Hamami, Thessaloniki's first and once Greece's largest Turkish bath, built on Egnatia in 1444 from the remains of Christian churches destroyed after the Turkish conquest. The multidomed "Paradise Baths" now function as an exhibit hall, with irregular hours, but is most often open Monday through Friday 8:30am to 3pm (no address, no phone). The Ministry of Culture shop just beyond the Bey Hamami has museum reproductions and bored clerks; officially open daily 8:30am to 2:30pm.

Dikasterion Sq., bounded by Filipou, Agnostou Stratiotou, Olimbou, and Makedonikis Amnis sts.

Hippodrome   We know that the ancient Hippodrome, where chariot races took place, lies under the square of the same name, because of finds made when modern apartments were built. There are almost no aboveground remains of this ancient racetrack where, in A.D. 390, Emperor Theodosius the Great ordered the slaughter of about 7,000 spectators. The reason: Galerius was furious when a mob lynched a close friend of his who had banned a popular charioteer from an important race. After that terrible day, people abandoned the Hippodrome, and it was gradually covered by buildings from successive eras. In 1566, the Turks executed St. Cyril here for not converting to Islam. The charming little church of St. Anthony here was, during the

Turkish Occupation, a lunatic asylum. In the church, you can still see some of the manacles with which "patients" were imprisoned. Allow half an hour here.
Ippodromou Sq.

Galerius's Palace ★   The emperor Galerius built himself a palace in Thessaloniki. After all, his co-emperor Diocletian was building himself a splendid palace at Split, on the Dalmatian coast. Little remains of Galerius's royal home, but even these low ruins give you an idea of the size of the two-story palace with its large central courtyard—fit, in short, for an emperor. The best-preserved part of the complex is the **Octagon,** the building that some archaeologists think may have been Galerius's throne room. The Octagon, opulent and richly decorated with a multicolored marble floor, had two interior recesses. One, a good deal larger than the others, would have been ideal for a throne. That said, it should be noted that a very similar structure built by Diocletian in Spoleto, Italy, was not a throne room but a mausoleum. Allow half an hour here.
Navarino Sq.

Rotunda (aka Ayios Yioryos) ★★   Some say that Galerius built this massive brick-and-stone structure as his immodest mausoleum, while others think he intended it to be a temple, perhaps of Zeus. Later in the 4th century, the Byzantine emperor Theodosius the Great converted the Rotunda into Ayios Yioryos (Church of St. George), and began the ornamentation of its 6m-thick (20-ft.) walls with mosaics. When the Turks conquered Thessaloniki in the 15th century, they converted the church into a mosque (you'll see one minaret left from this period) and destroyed many of the mosaics.

The Rotunda reopened in 1999 after more than a decade spent repairing the damage done by the earthquake of 1978. Artisans and archaeologists worked with literally millions of tesserae, or tiles, to restore the mosaics. Now you can see (especially if you bring binoculars) indigo peacocks, garlands of flowers and fruit, and blond, curly-haired saints and martyrs (and martyred saints) in the mosaics that cover the walls. Try to visit on a Wednesday, when the neighborhood street market stretches for blocks around, and ask about special exhibits or concerts. Allow an hour to explore.
Ayios Yioryos Sq. at Filipou (1 block north of the juncture of Egnatia and Dimitriou Gounari, just above the Arch of Galerius). © **2310/213-627.** Free admission except for special events. Daily 8:30am-3pm. Bus: 10 or 11 heading east from anywhere on Egnatia.

White Tower ★   What Big Ben is to London, and the Eiffel Tower is to Paris, the 16th-century White Tower is to Thessaloniki. It is the city's most famous landmark, although the tower is no longer white; a 1985 restoration (as part of the celebrations of the 2,300th anniversary of Thessaloniki's founding) removed its whitewash. Due to ongoing restoration, the tower is sometimes closed, but it is well worth seeing up close even if only from outside. The tower, first built as part of the city's defense walls, then became an Ottoman prison and place of execution (when it was known as the Bloody Tower). Today, several floors house the Museum of the History and Art of Thessaloniki; the artifacts within give an idea of life here through the centuries. That said, the most fun here comes from climbing the steep winding staircase that takes you up six floors and leads to terrific views of the city and harbor. Each floor has a round room with alcoves, some of which were once prison cells. At the top of the staircase, a cafe on the roof rewards you for the climb. Allow an hour here.
Nikis and Pavlou Mela, on the seaside promenade just south of the Archaeological Museum. © **2310/267-832.** Free admission. Officially, daily 8:30am-3pm. Bus: 58 from Dikasterion Sq., or 11 heading east from anywhere on Egnatia.

Churches ★★★

Thessaloniki's churches are a clear case of the whole being greater than the sum of its parts. Although Ayia Sofia and Ayios Dimitrios are the two best known, and so important to the city that we give each two stars, the smaller, less well-known churches may give you the greatest pleasure. Most Greek Orthodox churches are built either in the **basilica** style, which is a rectangle with side aisles or the domed **cross-in-square** form, which is just what its name says.

Many of these churches keep irregular hours, often closing from about 1 to 5pm. The best way to see them is on one or more morning excursions. You can easily spend a week visiting these churches. Alternatively, you can visit the better-known ones in a rigorous day. Admission to all churches is free. A small donation in the alms box is appreciated; it is usually found near the door or where votive candles are sold. Greeks move around fairly freely in church during many services, but it's not a good idea to be an obvious sightseer during a service.

CHURCHES IN DOWNTOWN THESSALONIKI

Ayia Sofia ★★   It's a pity that Thessaloniki's two most important churches—Ayia Sofia (Holy Wisdom) and Ayios Dimitrios (St. Demetrios)—are both heavily restored. Still, each is worth visiting for its importance in the city's history and for its fine mosaics, although both lack the pleasantly dusty ambience and odor of sanctity found in Thessaloniki's less heavily restored churches.

Thessaloniki's 7th-century Ayia Sofia was inspired by the emperor Justinian's famous 6th-century church of Ayia Sofia in Constantinople, although there may have been a modest 4th-century church here. Like the majestic Ayia Sofia in Constantinople (today's Istanbul), Salonika's namesake has an impressively large—in fact, an astonishingly large and astonishingly technical—dome. The ornately carved marble columns supporting the dome were pillaged from earlier monuments (as they were so often in antiquity and throughout the Byzantine era).

Fortunately, some of Ayia Sofia's original mosaics have survived. The Ascension, with an oddly foreshortened Christ (supported by young angels), and the Virgin Mary with the infant Jesus are especially fine. Look carefully at the mosaics, and you'll notice that some show only crosses and stars and have no human representations. These date from the 8th-century Iconoclastic period, when there was a ban on showing the human figure in religious art. The Iconoclasts destroyed many earlier works of art, including sacred icons, and left us with the word "iconoclast" to describe someone who destroys the past or challenges tradition.

Ayia Sofia Square is one of Thessaloniki's most important, squares. Many of its finest houses were destroyed in the fire of 1917, which damaged Ayia Sofia church as well. Others suffered extensive damage during World War II. A service of thanksgiving was held here when the Allies liberated the city on November 2, 1944. Today, much of Thessaloniki heads here for Easter and other important services. Keep an eye out for the "red house" at 31 Ayias Sofias, built in

---

Dress Appropriately & Keep an Eye on the Time!

Casual attire such as short skirts on women, shorts or sleeveless shirts on men or women, is generally considered disrespectful in Greek churches, which are, of course, primarily places of worship. Most churches both in downtown Thessaloniki and in the Upper City (Ano Poli) close from about 1 to 5pm.

1925 for a wealthy industrialist; across the street is the **Terkenlis** pastry shop, which also has sandwiches and a wide variety of delicious ice creams. The pastry shop is an excellent spot to rest and refresh yourself after you see the church; until then, you can check out the goodies and pinpoint other Terkenlis branches in Thessaloniki at **www.terkenlis.gr**.

Ayia Sofia Sq., btw. Tsimiski and Egnatia. ✆ **2310/270-253.** Daily 8am–9pm (but often closed 1–5pm).

Ayios Dimitrios (aka Church and Crypt of Ayios Demetrios) ★★

Like Ayia Sofia, Ayios Dimitrios was heavily restored—in fact, almost entirely rebuilt—after the fire of 1917. Consequently, this is a church with an imposing history, some fine mosaics, but very little soul. That's a shame, because the story of Dimitrios is stirring: In the 4th century A.D., this site was occupied by a Roman bath, a corner of which was used as a makeshift jail. In A.D. 303, one of the prisoners, young Dimitrios, got into trouble by preaching the Gospel. Dimitrios not only refused to renounce his faith but seems to have converted another prisoner, a gladiator who fought and killed Emperor Galerius's favorite gladiator. Galerius was furious and had Dimitrios executed. Soon, a shrine here commemorated the martyred Dimitrios; then a small church was built, and in the 7th century A.D., the church was enlarged into its present five-aisled basilica form. After the 1917 fire, the church was rebuilt on and off from 1926 to 1949. You can still see scorch marks from the 1917 conflagration on some of the interior walls.

Almost all the mosaics here are restorations of what was lost in 1917, but a cluster from the 5th to 7th centuries A.D. survives. Look for the lovely, original portrait of the boyish saint with two young children, and the representation of Demetrios with the church founders. (You can see other mosaics salvaged after the fire on display in the Museum of Byzantine Culture.) The crypt, which is down a narrow, twisting staircase, reveals several small anterooms and remains of Roman baths; the crypt sometimes functions as a small gallery. Particularly venerated are the spot where Dimitrios is believed to have been martyred (and where a vial of blood, believed to be the saint's, was found) and the spot with a holy-water font. For centuries, the faithful noted a sweet scent at the font, and believed that myrrh, or perfumed fluid, flowed from the saint himself. As you leave the church, have a look at the chapel of St. Euthymius, built into the wall of Ayios Dimitrios. The 14th-century frescoes in the little chapel have all the verve lacking in Ayios Dimitrios's heavily restored mosaics.

Corner of Ayiou Dimitriou and Ayiou Nikolaou, 1 block north of the Roman market, at the base of the Upper City. ✆ **032/0213-627.** Church and crypt usually Mon 12:30–7pm; Tues–Sat 8am–8pm; Sun 10:30am–8pm. Bus: 22 or 23 leaves about every 10 min. from the stop near the church at the southeast side of Eleftherias Sq.

Ayios Panteleimon ★

This 14th-century church, dedicated to one of the physician saints, is a popular place to light a candle and say a prayer for good health. The church, all that remains of a large monastery, is usually closed, but its elaborate brick-and-stonework makes even a glimpse a delight. If you get inside, note how the central dome is supported by four barrel vaults, characteristic of Macedonian churches.

Corner of Egnatia and Iassonidou.

Panagia Acheiropoietos (Church of the Virgin Made Without Human Hands) ★

This 5th-century basilica is the only church from Thessaloniki's early Christian days to have survived pretty much intact, without the restorations and renovations that have changed the characters of Ayia Sofia and Ayios Dimitrios. The church's name comes from an early Christian icon of the Virgin which the faithful believed was made by divine, not human, hands. At some point, the icon was lost, but the church's name still commemorates it. Due to the inexorable rise in street level over the centuries, the church now sits well below the level of today's roads. The marble columns, with their elaborate "perforated" acanthus-leaf decorations, give you a good idea of the Byzantine love of the elaborate—achieved here by vigorous drill work. There are mosaics of floral and vine motifs interspersed with birds and 13th-century frescoes showing some of the 40 martyrs. The missing martyrs were probably obliterated when the church was converted to a mosque in the 15th century after Salonika fell to the Turks

Ayias Sofia, north of Egnatia. No phone.

Panagia Chalkeon (Virgin of the Copper Workers) ★ This tiny church with its three domes looks as if it would fit nicely into a miniature village. It has some fine frescoes, but its real glory is its facade, with windows piled above windows, domes above domes. Like the Panagia Acheiropoietos, the 11th-century Panagia Chalkeon now sits considerably below Thessaloniki's modern street level. Some of the copper-workers' shops, from which this church took its name centuries ago, survive nearby. Locals call this the "red church" for its rosy bricks.

Dikasterion Sq. No phone.

CHURCHES IN THE UPPER CITY (ANO POLI) ★★★

Visiting these churches has a real bonus: You get to explore the narrow streets and lanes of the oldest section of Thessaloniki, once the home of many of its Turkish residents. In fact, many Thessalonians still call Ano Poli by the name Tsinari, the Turkish name of a massive plane tree that once grew here. The neighborhood is a maze of cobbled streets, with streetside fountains, old-fashioned corner groceries, cafes, some neighborhood hangouts, and some chic destination spots. Many of the wooden houses have upper floors that project out over the ground floor and overhang the street. This was a clever way of getting as much space into a house on as little land as available. In the 1960s, Ano Poli was practically falling down and might easily have been torn down and "modernized"—a fate that befell many of the old-fashioned small houses in Athens's once charming narrow streets on the slopes of Mount Lykabettus. Fortunately, before the property developers pounced, young artists and students, along with many foreign residents of Thessaloniki, moved into Ano Poli. These settlers were lured up to the heights above town both by the neighborhood's charm and by its low housing costs. Today, an Ano Poli address is considered very chic.

When you visit the churches of Ano Poli, be prepared to get lost at least once. Don't fret: You'll probably discover a wonderful little cafe, a church tucked away in a nicely tended garden, or a courtyard with a marble fountain while you try to find your way. If you like fortifications, you'll love the remains of the massive Byzantine Eptapirigion (Seven-Gated) Walls that girdle Ano Poli. The walls, built and rebuilt between the 4th and 15th centuries, are often flood-lit at night.

Taking the bus (no. 22 or 23 from Eleftherias Sq.) to the Upper City is an easy ride. You can then wander back downhill.

Ayia Katerini ★ Another of Thessaloniki's 14th-century churches, built with a central dome flanked by four cupolas, is surrounded by apartment buildings and old homes. With elegant brick and stone work, it is a reminder of one of the city's finest artistic periods. Inside, look for the painting showing the healing of the blind.

Corner of Sachini and Tsamadou, near the Byzantine walls.

Ayios Nikolaos Orfanos ★★   Like Osios David (see below), this seemingly unprepossessing brick-and-stone church holds an astonishing treasure: well-preserved frescoes from the 14th century, the zenith of Thessaloniki's artistic excellence. You can pick out haloed St. Nikolaos himself, standing at the helm of the little boat he's guiding across stormy waters. The other frescoes, as is usual in such cycles, show scenes from the Old and New Testaments, as well as saints and prophets. Next to the church, part of its once-flourishing monastery with an attractive veranda has been restored, and makes visitors envy those lucky enough to live here. You may acquire a retinue of curious neighborhood children; most drift away in time, but some have hopes of sweets or even money and can be unpleasantly persistent.

Apostolou Pavlou.

Osios David (Latomou Monastery) ★★★   I manage to get lost almost every time I come here, but eventually find my way to this charming 5th- or 6th-century church, with its comfortable, shaded courtyard. Indeed, what a tempting fantasy to think of taking over the caretaker's job, sitting with a book in the little shelter in the courtyard, tending the flowers, and unlocking the church for visitors—who are bound to be impressed, because nothing about Osios David's simple exterior can prepare you for the glorious mosaic of the vision of Ezekiel inside. The vision shows Christ surrounded by the symbols of the four apostles (the angel, eagle, lion, and bull). If there's a more moving mosaic in Thessaloniki, I've yet to see it! According to local lore, this mosaic spent several centuries hidden beneath a calf's skin, which prevented the Turks from finding and destroying it. Osios David was built over (and used building blocks from) the remains of a once flourishing Roman bath, yet another example of the architectural recycling so popular throughout Greece. According to legend, the first chapel here honored the emperor Galerius's daughter Theodora, who converted to Christianity, and hid a tiny Christian shrine in the tumbledown bath complex. When Galerius learned of her deceit, he first imprisoned her in her own chapel and later had her put to death when she would not renounce her new faith. If you wish to see the mosaics more clearly, ask the caretaker to turn on the lights—and slip her something for her troubles.

Timotheou, off Ayias Sofia.

Profitias Elias ★   This 14th-century church has an elaborate brick exterior well worth seeing. Women, who cannot visit Mount Athos, will get an idea from Profitias Elias of the cross-in-square style (with central dome) that is similar to many of the churches on Mount Athos. If you head back into town from here, you will get good views over the city if you plunge downhill on the narrow street that takes off below the church's courtyard.

Olympiados.

Vlatodon Monastery (aka Vlatades) ★   As you toil uphill, you'll keep seeing the overhanging walls of the Vlatodon Monastery, founded in the 14th century. In the last few years it has been renovated and expanded, and has lost its "old" feeling. Still, the inner courtyard is a cool spot to rest for a moment. Cool, but not quiet: the resident peacocks are usually in good voice. The peacocks are here because they are an early Christian symbol of resurrection, perhaps because it was believed that their flesh did not decay after death. If the main church is locked, don't be disappointed; the Turks damaged the frescoes badly and they have not been restored. By tradition, the little chapel of Sts. Peter and Paul was built on the spot where St. Paul preached when he visited Thessaloniki in A.D. 50.

By the gate to the Acropolis.

Markets ★★

Thessaloniki's markets are a bit of Levantine exotica that knock the socks off anything in Athens. And "anything" is what you can find here, whether it's knockoff designer bags, copper pots, piles of black-and-white postcards, and sheep's bells (or sheep's heads, for that matter). It's a great place to stroll, get lost, and have a snack or a meal.

The Bezesteni ★   It would be wonderful to have a bird's-eye view of the Bezesteni's six domes and four entrances, one on each side. This covered market, built in the 15th century by Sultan Bayezid II, is one of the best-preserved Turkish monuments in Thessaloniki. Now, it specializes in textiles and jewelry—making it a terrific place to browse and feel transported into an Asian bazaar. While you're in the neighborhood, stroll over to the intersection of Egnatia and Venizelou streets, where restoration work began on Thessaloniki's oldest mosque, the 15th-century **Hazma Bey Mosque,** in the summer of 2007. There are plans that the mosque will eventually be a museum housing artifacts found during the excavations for Thessaloniki's Metro.

Venizelou and Solomou. Usually Mon–Sat 9am–7pm.

Flea Market ★   Just what its name implies, this market, which sprawls along Tositsa, sells everything from genuine junk to genuine antiques (much more of the former than the latter). Of late, many eastern European sellers have been plying their wares here: usually leather jackets, fake cameras and designer watches, and an odd assortment of alarm clocks, mirrors, and socks.

Tositsa. Usually Mon–Sat 8am–7pm.

Kapani (Vlali) Market ★   This market sells foods, dry goods, fabrics, and just about everything else you can think of, in a hodgepodge of ramshackle shops crowded one next to the other as far as the eye can see. There's been a market here at least since Turkish times, and probably long before that.

Bounded by Komninon, Egnatia, Aristotelous, and Menexe sts. Mon–Sat about 8am–5pm.

Modiano Market & the Mansions of Vas. Olgas & Vas. Sophias Blvds. ★★
Gypsies with dancing bears once played music in the Modiano Market. The bears are gone, but street musicians still stroll the area. You can easily spend a morning in the glass-roofed market that covers an entire square block, happily wandering from stall to stall and eyeing the fish, meat, fruit, vegetables, flowers, spices, and baked goods on sale. When hunger calls, look for the delicious food at **Thanasis,** or find a seat in one of the other cafes or restaurants. The roofed market was built in 1922 by the wealthy Jewish merchant Eli Modiano, whose family mansion (at 68 Vas. Sophias) is now the home of the intermittently open **Folklore and Ethnography Museum of Macedonia.** Many of Thessaloniki's surviving 19th-century mansions still stand along Megalou Alexandrou and along Vas. Olgas and Sophias; Vas. Olgas was once known as the "Boulevard of the Châteaux" for its imposing town houses. The **Pinakothiki (Municipal Gallery;** www.thessalonikicity.gr), with an extensive collection of works by Macedonian artists, is in an early-20th-century mansion at 162 Vas. Olgas; its usual hours are Tuesday to Friday 9am to 1pm and 5 to 9pm, Saturday 5 to 9pm, and Sunday 8am to 3pm.

The block bounded by Aristotelous, Ermou, Vasileos Irakleiou, and Komninon sts. Mon–Sat about 7am–5pm.

More Attractions

Alatza Imaret ★ Along with the Bezesteni, the Alatza Imaret, a former 15th-century mosque with a poorhouse, or almshouse, is one of the best-preserved Turkish buildings in Thessaloniki. *Alatza* (many-colored) refers to the tiles and stones that covered the mosque in its glory days. If you're lucky, it may be open for an exhibition when you visit; in that case, allow half an hour.

Dimitrion Sq., just off Ayiou Nikolaou, half a block north of Kassandrou, 1½ blocks north of the church of Ayios Dimitrios. (*C*) **2310/278-587.** Free admission. Open intermittently for exhibitions.

Atatürk's Birthplace It's a sign of Salonika's rich Turkish past that Mustafa Kemal (Atatürk), the man who created the modern Turkish state and was its first president, was born here in 1881. You can get permission to visit Ataturk's modest birthplace by applying at the Turkish consulate at 151 Ayiou Dimitriou. Greece gave the house to the Turkish government as a gesture of goodwill in 1933; often a Turkish official will show you through the house, which has been restored and furnished to reflect the way it must have been at Atatürk's birth. An English-language booklet (with photos) explains many of the photos and documents on view. Allow an hour here for the tour.

17 Apostolou Pavlou (8 short blocks east of the church of Ayios Dimitrios). (*C*) **2310/248-452.** Free admission, but passport or ID card necessary. Daily 10am-5pm. Bus: 22 or 23 from Eleftherias Sq.; also stops along El. Venizelou north to Ayiou Dimitriou. Enter through the front gate of the Turkish consulate.

International Fairgrounds If you're in Thessaloniki during the September Trade Fair, you may want to take in some of the exhibits. Notices of special exhibitions or events are usually posted throughout the city. If you're interested in the contemporary Greek art scene, stop in at the sleek modern building housing the **Macedonian Museum of Contemporary Art** (*C* 2310/240-002; www.mmca.org.gr). The museum has frequent special exhibits, as well as a good cafe and shop.

Entrances at the corners of Angelaki and Tsimiski, and Angelaki and Egnatia. Admission 3€. June-Sept Tues-Sun 9am-5pm; Oct-May Tues-Sun 10am-2pm and 5-9pm.

Jewish History Museum (aka Museum of the Jewish Presence in Thessaloniki) ★ The first thing to know about this museum is that if you ask for it by address (13 Agios Mina), you will be directed to the small church of Agios Mina across from the museum. Because many more locals are familiar with the church than the museum, ask for the church and then look across the street for the sign for the Jewish Museum. The museum uses photographs and artifacts to portray Jewish life through the centuries in Thessaloniki. Thessaloniki Jews established the city's first printing press in the early 1500s and founded the city's first newspaper, *El Lunar,* in 1865. The museum is in the 19th-century building which once was home to *L'Independent,* one of Thessaloniki's many Jewish newspapers. The community thrived under the Ottoman Empire, and in 1900, 80,000 of Thessaloniki's 173,000 inhabitants were Jews. Just before World War II, 60,000 Jews lived here; fewer than 2,000 survived the death camps. Museum staff can give you directions if you wish to see the Holocaust Monument, unveiled in 1997 at the corner of Egnatia and Papanastiou streets. Today's Jewish community in Thessaloniki numbers about 1,000. When I was here in May of 2009, a group of Jewish women from Argentina whose grandparents had left Thessaloniki just before the war were visiting. It was a moving experience for them, and for those also visiting when they recognized family members in some of the photographs on display.

Hitting the Beach near Thessaloniki

Any beaches within the bay of Thessaloniki are too polluted to be pleasant, or even safe, although people do swim at them. Beaches in the communities of **Perea** and **Ayia Triada**, 16 to 24km (10–15 miles) along the bay east of the city, are considered reasonably safe. Just past Ayia Triada, on the headland of the bay, is the Greek National Tourism Organization facility of **Akti Thermaikou**, which has a children's playground, changing cabins, snack bars, and tennis courts.

If you're interested in learning more about the Jewish community in Greece, check the publications in the museum store; the locally published *Jewish Community of Thessaloniki* and Niko Stavroloulakis's books *The Jews of Greece* and *Jewish Sites and Synagogues of Greece* are excellent. The museum's website is also very thorough, especially the section under History on the Jews of Thessaloniki. In addition, **www. jewishtours.gr** offers 1-week Jewish heritage tours of Greece that include Thessaloniki. Allow at least an hour for your visit to the museum.

13 Agios Mina.℃ **2310/250-406.** Fax 2310/270-407. www.jmth.gr. Free admission. Tues, Fri, Sun 11am–2pm; Wed–Thurs 11am–2pm and 5–8pm.

Lambrakis Monument　On May 22, 1963, right-wing forces ran down and killed Grigoris Lambrakis, a leftist member of the Parliament, who had been speaking at a peace meeting. Vassilis Vassilikos based his novel *Z* on Lambrakis's death; Costa-Gavras then adapted the novel for his film starring Yves Montand. Lambrakis's assassination and the protests that followed were part of a long series of events culminating in the dictatorship of the colonels in the late 1960s. The bronze monument shows a figure with arms upraised, flanked by a dove of peace.

Intersection of Venizelou, Ermou, and Spandoni.

Museum of Ancient Greek, Byzantine, and Post-Byzantine Musical Instruments ★　What is it about music museums? The small one in Athens is one of that city's finest, and Thessaloniki has its own appealing music museum. The three floors of this one house beautifully displays reproductions of stringed and wind instruments, along with marvelous photographs of instruments from ancient vase paintings or Byzantine manuscripts. Purists may object to the predominance of reproductions here, but the reproductions give a good sense of what the actual instruments looked like. Music sometimes plays softly in the background, the cafe is sometimes open, and if you're lucky, a concert will be scheduled here during your time in Salonika. Allow an hour.

12–14 Katouni, Ladadika.℃ **2310/238-391.** Admission 5€. Tues–Sun 9am–3pm and 5–10pm.

Art Galleries

Thessaloniki's best galleries often have exhibitions worth taking in, although most keep irregular hours. Find out about them from posters in town, from the Greek National Tourism Organization office at 136 Tsimiski St., and from the listings published on Tuesday in *Kathimerini,* the English-language supplement to the *International Herald Tribune.* The weekly publication *City* is in Greek, but has enough information in English to be useful for non-Greek readers. As you explore the city, feel free to step inside any of the galleries; questions about exhibits are usually welcome.

One not-to-miss place is the **Teloglion Foundation of Art,** 159A Ayiou Demetriou, on the Aristotle University campus (© **2310/247-1111;** www.tf.auth.gr/teloglion). The gallery displays the collections of a number of prominent Greek art collectors and also holds important exhibits. If that's not enough reason to visit, consider this: Chef Ektoras Botrini's Mediterranean cuisine at Art02-Ristorante Botrini, the in-house restaurant, won *Athinorama* magazine's "value for money" award in 2009

Check out **Apothiki,** on Nikis by the waterfront (© **2310/240-877**); **Foka,** 17 Foka (© **2310/240-362**); **Kalfayan,** 43 Proxenou Koromilia (© **2310/231-187**); and **Metamorfosis,** 128 Tsimiski (© **2310/285-071**). **Terracotta,** 13 Chrysostomos (aka Chrys.) Smirnis and 76 Mitropoleos (© **2310/235-689**), features works by some of Greece's best-known contemporary artists as well as works by the up and coming.

In addition to these galleries, several museums and other galleries, open most days during normal business hours, emphasize the art and life of Thessaloniki and Macedonia, with particular reference to the lively pre– and post–World War II art scene. These include the **Municipal Art Gallery,** 162 Vas. Olgas (© **2310/425-531**), with a collection of 19th- to 21st-century works by Greek artists, many from Thessaloniki, the **Gallery of Fine Arts,** 1 Nicephorus; **Germanou,** inside the National Theater Building (© **2310/238-601**); the **State Museum of Contemporary Art in Thessaloniki,** 21 Kolokotroni, in the Lazariston Monastery (© **2310/589-140;** www.greekstatemuseum.gr), with a collection of 20th- and 21st century Russian art; and the **National Bank's Thessaloniki Cultural Center,** 108 Vas. Sophias St. (© **2310/586-123**). Two museums in the art complex housed in renovated waterfront warehouses in the Port of Salonika are reached through Gate A off Koundouriotou St.: the **Museum of Photography,** Warehouse A (© **2310/566-716;** www.thmphoto.gr), and the **Center of Contemporary Art,** Warehouse B1 (© **2310/546-683;** www.cact.gr). Galleries are free; museum admissions are usually 3€.

Organized Tours

Zorpidis Travel, 4 Salaminos (© **2310/555-955;** www.zorpidis.gr), is a reliable Thessaloniki-based tour operator.

Strolling or Cruising in Thessaloniki

Taking what the Greeks call a *volta* (stroll) along the seaside promenade, particularly at sunset or under a full moon, is one of the greatest pleasures of being in Thessaloniki. It's also a great way to unwind after visiting the Archaeological and Byzantine museums, inland from the east end of the promenade. Around the **White Tower,** you'll see lots of peanut vendors, balloon sellers, pony rides for the children, and at least one horse-drawn carriage, all yours for no more than a few euros.

You might also decide to take an hour (or longer) to **cruise** the harbor on one of the small excursion boats (one dolled up as a pirate ship, another as Jason's Argonaut) that dock near the tower. Posted signs advertise cruises of different lengths and prices. *One warning:* The harbor can smell pretty ripe in hot weather. If possible, take your cruise on a slightly chilly day with a brisk wind.

Spectator Sports

Like most Greeks, Thessalonians are keen soccer and basketball fans, rooting for the home teams. (Confusingly, the Aris and PAOK stadiums are home to both basketball *and* soccer teams.) Your best bet if you don't speak or read Greek and want to catch a game is to check with the concierge at your hotel. In general, soccer games are in spring and fall, basketball year-round. **Aris Stadium** is in the suburb of Harilaou (✆ **2310/305-402**), while the much-easier-to-reach **PAOK Stadium** is on Ayios Dimitrios, 2 blocks northeast of the International Fairgrounds (✆ **2310/238-560**).

Shopping

Lots of Greeks think that their second-largest city offers better shopping than Athens, in part because the compact city center makes it easy to explore the major shopping districts. Also, because Thessaloniki is relatively tourist-free, you won't be overwhelmed here by streets lined with garish souvenir and T-shirt shops, as is the case in much of Athens, especially the Plaka district. Keep in mind that in Thessaloniki—as throughout Greece—most chic boutiques stock imported goods from Europe and the States, usually with a hefty import duty that is passed on to the customer. If you shop the winter (Jan) and summer (late July and Aug) sales, you may find some bargains.

Some shops still sell crafts by local artists, including coppersmiths. Not surprisingly, many of these shops are near the church of Panagia Chalkeon (Virgin of the Copper Makers) in **Dikasterion Square.** The website **www.virtualtourist.com** has *lots* of Thessaloniki shopping suggestions, but keep in mind that prices at most boutiques listed will be well in excess of what you would pay in the USA or Great Britain.

ANTIQUES

You'll find a number of antiques shops on Mitropoleos and Tositsa streets. *Tip:* Reputable shops will explain that you'll need an export license to take out of Greece any item more than 100 years old. The Wednesday street market area around the Rotunda (Agios Yiorgos Church) has a number of stalls with pseudo and genuine antiques, as well as a lot of, well, junk.

Relics Offering high-quality antiques, from silver- and glassware to jewelry, ceramics, prints, Art Nouveau lamps, and Victorian-era dolls, this is a serious shop with serious prices. It's located a block east of the Mitropoleos Cathedral off Mitropoleos (closed Sun). 3 Yioryio Lassani. ✆ **2310/226-506**.

BOOKS, NEWSPAPERS & MAGAZINES

Ianos, 7 Aristotelous (✆ **2310/277-164**); **Travel Bookstore** (✆ **2310/275-215**); and **Malliaris,** 9 Aristotelous (✆ **2310/276-926**), have wide selections of Greek and foreign books, as well as other publications. **Molho** long the oldest and finest bookstore in Thessaloniki, closed early in 2009.

Apostolic Diakonta Bookstore ★ Although this handsome bookstore specializes in books on religious matters, it also carries a wide selection on Greece (in English and French, as well as Greek). This is a wonderful place to browse. Even if you can't afford one of the superb photography books of Greece, you can find wonderful cards as well as good reproductions of icons. 9A Ethnikis Aminis, near the Archaeological and Byzantine museums. ✆ **2310/275-126**.

COPPER

Adelphi Kazanzidi At this family-run shop, copper-working skills have been passed down from generation to generation. The shop sells finely crafted copperware

More About Shopping

In Thessaloniki, old-style, pre–European Community **shopping hours,** unfathomable to foreigners, still predominate. Stores open at about 9am and close around 1:30 or 2pm for the afternoon siesta. On Tuesday, Thursday, and Friday evenings, some (but not all) reopen from about 5:30 to 8:30pm.

In July, however, almost all shops close for the evening. The best time to shop is morning. Note that some of these stores will take major credit cards, but almost all, especially the smaller ones, prefer not to. As a Greek friend reminds me, "If we don't have the money in our wallet, we don't buy something."

items such as wine carafes, skillets, water heaters, and trays, all handmade on the premises. There are also many copper shops around the Panagia Chalkeon church. 12 Klissouras, off the western side of Dikasterion Square, a block north of Egnatia. ℂ **2310/262-741.**

DEPARTMENT STORES

Lambropoulos The best department store in the city (now also known as Notos Galleries) has five floors of everything and anything you might want, from cosmetics to basketballs. It's a block west of Aristotelous, in the Stoa Hirsch, at the corner of Komninon. 18 Tsimiski. ℂ **2310/269-971.**

FASHION

For both men's and women's fashions, try the department stores such as Lambropoulos (see above) or the chic—and expensive—boutiques on Tsimiski and on pedestrian walkway Dimitriou Gounari. But, remember: nearly anything here will be more expensive than in London or New York.

GIFTS & SOUVENIRS

Almost all the museums have gift shops with some excellent museum reproductions; Athonos Square, off Egnatia, has some handicraft shops and Nikis Street, along the harbor, has a sprinkling of small shops with souvenirs.

Tanagrea You'll find a wide selection of handcrafted items by a stable of artisans employed by this well-known chain of stores, which also has outlets in Athens, Crete, and Spetsai. Offerings include ceramics, pewter, silver, leather goods, paintings, glassware, and jewelry. On Vogatsikou a block east of the Metropolitan Cathedral btw. Mitropoleos and Proxenou Koromila.

ZM Pronounced *Zee-*ta *Mee,* this store offers three floors of expensive but well-crafted Greek souvenir items such as worry beads, pottery, folk art, rugs, toys, handcrafted caiques, prints, and a few antique silver place settings and jewelry. It's an extremely tempting gallerylike place to browse. 1 Proxenou Koromila, a block east of Aristotelous Sq. ℂ **2310/240-591.**

LEATHER

If you want good-quality leather, resist the eastern European leather vendors who set up stalls on many street corners.

Falli One of the best of several leather-goods shops in the area is Falli on the southwest corner of the outdoor market, near Ermou and El. Venizelou. It makes and sells shoulder bags, backpacks, attaché cases, and sandals. Try to bargain by looking downcast and disappointed when you hear the price. 11 Askitou. ℂ **2310/229-197.**

MUSIC

Blow Up: The Music Stores, 8 Aristotelous, on the east side of the street a block north of Tsimiski (✆ **2310/233-255**); **Patsis,** 39 Tsimiski, at the corner of Aristotelous (✆ **2310/231-805**); **Studio 52,** 46 Dimitrious Gounari (✆ **2310/271-301**), and **En Chordes,** 3 Ipodromiou (✆ **2310/282-248**), sell many kinds of musical instruments and CDs, including Byzantine music.

SHOES

Pak This store carries a wide selection of high-quality Greek shoes—from hiking boots to high heels—at decent prices. The foreign brands here are much more expensive. 3 Ayias Sofias Sq., opposite the north side of the church. ✆ **2310/274-863**.

SWEETS

In a city where sweetness is next to godliness, the venerable **Agapitos,** 53 Tsimiski (✆ **2310/279-107**), gets rave reviews, as does **Hatzi,** 50 Venizelous (✆ **2310/279-058**). All are made with great, mouthwatering, high-caloric care. One of the branches of the excellent sweet shop, **Terkenlis** (✆ **2310/271-148;** www.terkenlis.gr), is nearby at 30 Tsimiski, so you can easily compare and contrast. Both are closed on Sunday. Don't panic: **Averof,** 11 Vas. Georgiou (✆ **2310/814-284;** www.averof.gr), Thessaloniki's famous kosher bakery, is usually open 365 days a year.

Where to Stay

The price range we quote is for the touristic high season, **not** Thessaloniki's convention high season. Due to the depressed economy and poor tourist season, most hotel prices dropped in 2011. If things improve, they will go back up in 2012. Thessaloniki is a major convention center, not just in Greece, but for the entire Balkans. Almost every Greek businessman, doctor, politician, lawyer—well, you get the idea—attends a convention in Thessaloniki at least once. Understandably, many of the city's hotels focus on its commercial visitors, not on tourists. The recommendations below avoid the large, expensive hotels that appeal more to business travelers than to independent travelers (good location and pleasant accommodations). We also omit the okay but not appealing hotels near the railroad station; these hotels are a long uninteresting hike from anything you want to see.

Much more appealing to independent travelers are the newer hotels either in the Ladadika (the trendy restored harborside area) and reliable favorites on and around the main squares and thoroughfares. Sprinkled throughout Ladadika and the town center are a number of "boutique" hotels, notably the Capsis Bristol Hotel, Andromeda, Luxembourg and Daios. In addition, some old standbys, such as the Tourist, Le Palace, the Olympia, and the Plaza Art Hotel have undergone extensive renovations.

One out-of-the-way hotel I will mention, since it consistently makes **Odyssey** magazine's annual list of the Best Hotels in Greece: the 74-room **Les Lazaristes,** 16 Kolokotroni, (www.domotel.gr; ✆ **2310/647-400**), in a restored tobacco factory, with big rooms, lavish bathrooms, a spa, and pool, good restaurant—the works. But, you'll be in unappealing location, either taking a taxi wherever you want to go or waiting for their shuttle bus (about 10 min. to the center); doubles from 100€.

It makes sense to reserve in advance year-round to avoid difficulties during Thessaloniki's many trade fairs, festivals, and associated cultural events. Bookings peak in September and October, when the International Trade Fair is quickly followed by the month-long Demetria cultural festival (not to mention the Festival of Greek Songs and the Film Festival). Hotel prices can be especially confusing, with online booking often advertising, but not always producing, prices much lower than those quoted by the hotels. **Tip:** Expect a hefty surcharge (sometimes 50% or more) on the summer high-season rates that we list below during the autumn fairs and festivals.

In addition to the following well-established options, here are three relatively new centrally located hotels to consider that were offering surprisingly reasonable rates in 2011. Most rooms are ornately themed at the elegant five-star **Andromeda,** 5 Komninon St. (www.andromeda-hotel.gr; ✆ **2310/254-760;** doubles from 85€–140€), with a Jacuzzi in the Tokyo Room, stark white decor in the Italian minimalist room, rose-colored brocades in the Viennese room, and so forth—the so forth including at least one suit of armor. The adjacent **Luxembourg,** 6 Komninon St. (www.hotelluxembourg.gr; ✆ **2310/252-600**), has more traditionally elegant rooms (soothing pastels, heavy curtains and bedspreads), with doubles from 85€. Both are small, with personable staff and great locations steps from the action on seafront Nikis Street. If these two keep their prices this low, they will be very good choices, indeed. The **Daios Hotel,** 59 Nikis St. (www.daioshotels.com; ✆ **2310/250-200;** doubles from 120€), has a seaside location near the White Tower, steps from more cafes than you can count (including their own elegant one) and minimalist rooms in beige and blonde tones. I find the public rooms here engaging and the bedrooms boring. A big plus: excellent soundproofing on the windows and sea views from many rooms.

VERY EXPENSIVE

Capsis Bristol Hotel ★★ The Capsis Bristol just may be *the* place to stay, with a great location in the lively waterfront Ladadika neighborhood. You'd never guess that this small, elegant boutique hotel occupies a 19th-century building that was once an Ottoman post office. Most of the guest rooms are painted deep, rich colors, all are decorated with antiques and paintings—and named after Macedonian heroes. (You might choose the Alexander Room.) Unusually for Greece, some rooms are handicap accessible. Unless you want a larger hotel, it's hard to find anything to fault here. **Tip:** Be sure not to confuse this hotel with the massive (serviceable, but not charming) 415-unit Capsis Hotel, also in the Capsis group, out of the city center near the train station.

2 Olimpiou and Katouni, 54626 Thessaloniki. www.capsisbristol.gr. ✆ **2310/506-500.** 20 units. 180€–220€ double. AE, DC, MC, V. **Amenities:** Restaurant; bar; babysitting; concierge; room service. *In room:* A/C, TV, hair dryer, minibar, Wi-Fi.

Classical Makedonia Palace (aka Makedonia Palace) ★ ☺ This hotel almost always makes it onto *Odyssey* magazine's prestigious list of Greece's best hotels—and, if you are here on business or traveling with children for whom pools are always a big plus, this could be the place for you. If you're here to see and experience Thessaloniki, you may find this—like many luxury hotel enclaves—too isolated from all that you've come here to see. The clientele includes lots of Greek families on holiday and a fair number of eastern European gamblers. (Europe's largest casino is next door.) In the usual manner of Greek hotel decor, the serious glitz is concentrated in the lobby and the guest rooms are rather bland. All units have balconies and picture windows, but if you stay here, insist on a seaside room. (Why pay all that money and not have the view?) The three **restaurants** include a sushi bar and rooftop restaurant, serving international cuisine with splendid views over the city and Gulf.

2 Leoforos Megalou Alexandrou (on the seafront promenade 1km/½ mile east of the White Tower), 54640 Thessaloniki. www.classicalhotels.gr. ✆ **231/089-7197.** Fax 231/089-7211. 284 units. 300€–500€ double. Discounts sometimes available off season. AE, DC, MC, V. **Amenities:** 3 restaurants; 2 bars;

airport pickup arranged; playground; concierge; health club and spa; 2 outdoor pools (saltwater and freshwater); room service; smoke-free rooms; tennis courts. *In room:* A/C, TV, hair dryer, minibar, Wi-Fi.

Mediterranean Palace Hotel ★★★ In 1997 the Mediterranean Palace opened in the Ladadika district, with its tempting restaurants and cafes; its location, comforts, and service continue to make it Thessaloniki's best large centrally located hotel. Everyone I know who has stayed here agrees that this is *the* place to stay in Thessaloniki—but not if you want a minimalist approach to decor. This hotel is self-consciously old-fashioned and elegant. Balconied front rooms overlook the harbor, and almost every unit is large and furnished with comfortable beds (with elegant silk and brocade coverlets), spiffy wall-to-wall carpeting, and cozy chairs, including leather recliners. Many of the guest rooms have especially nice touches, such as decorative moldings and large walk-in closets—and if you want to make a phone call from your bathroom, this is the place to do it. As for the suites, with their large living rooms, kitchenettes, and bedrooms, I could happily live in one for months. The hotel consistently appears in *Odyssey* magazine's list of the best hotels in Greece. Check for special packages.

3 Salaminos and Karatassou, 54626 Thessaloniki. www.mediterranean-palace.gr. ✆ **2310/552-554.** Fax 2310/552-622. 120 units. 110€–200€ double. American-style buffet breakfast 15€. AE, DC, MC, V. **Amenities:** 2 restaurants; 2 bars; concierge; exercise room; pool (indoor); room service; smoke-free rooms. *In room:* A/C, TV, hair dryer, kitchenette (suites), minibar, Wi-Fi.

EXPENSIVE

Electra Palace Hotel ★★ Overlooking Thessaloniki's main square, the Electra Palace, with its curved, arcaded facade, has the best location in town—except when there are demonstrations in Aristotle Square. The Electra also has a rooftop pool and **restaurant.** If you stay here, insist on one of the fourth- or fifth-floor rooms with a balcony overlooking the square; some of the interior rooms are astonishingly small.

9A Aristotelous Sq., 54624 Thessaloniki. www.electrahotels.gr. ✆ **2310/232-221.** Fax 2310/235-947. 70 units. 110€–180€ double. Rates include American-style buffet breakfast. AE, DC, MC, V. **Amenities:** 2 restaurants; 2 bars; concierge; health club and spa; outdoor rooftop pool; room service; smoke-free rooms. *In room:* A/C, TV, hair dryer, minibar, Wi-Fi.

MODERATE

City Hotel ★★ The City's heart-of-town location is excellent—steps from the appealing restaurants on Kominon Street in the Louloudadika. Rooms and bathrooms are generously proportioned. City is home to the excellent **Elenis Spa** (✆ **2310/269-421**), which offers everything from a quickie "taster facial" (50€) to a full "day of tranquillity" (300€). There are often spa specials for hotel guests. The City gets lots of tour groups, but still manages to give independent travelers individual attention.

11 Komninon St., 54642 Thessaloniki. www.cityhotel.gr. ✆ **2310/269-421.** 125 units. 100€–150€ double. Rates include America-style buffet breakfast. AE, DC, MC, V. **Amenities:** Bar; room service; smoke-free rooms; spa. *In room:* A/C, TV, hair dryer, minibar, Wi-Fi.

Hotel Olympia ★ Well-traveled Greek friends who stayed here loved the central location, praised the restaurant, and liked their stylish room. Most rooms are decent size with good beds and—still a pleasant surprise in a Greek hotel—many have good reading lights. The Olympia's location, at the northern end of the Roman market, near St. Demetrios Church and the flea market, is quieter than some of the nearby main drags. The website is not helpful.

65 Olympou, 54631 Thessaloniki. www.hotelolympia.gr. ⓒ **2310/235-421.** Fax 2310/276-133. 111 units. 110€–160€ double. Compulsory breakfast 10€. AE, DC, MC, V. **Amenities:** Restaurant; bar. *In room:* A/C, TV, minibar, Wi-Fi.

Le Palace Hotel ★★ This small hotel with a central location has high ceilings, Art Deco touches, and a contemporary room style that includes both fairly minimalist doubles and more swish triples and suites. Many Thessaloniki fans make a point of returning year after year, drawn by the Palace's tasteful and cozy ambience; most bathrooms have a tub as well as a shower, not standard in Greek hotels. The in-house restaurant provides lunch and dinner with advance notice, and the breakfast buffet is lavish. In fact, Le Palace makes it into British hotel critic Alastair Sawday's upmarket *Special Places to Stay in Greece* on the basis of the breakfasts alone.

12 Tsimiski, 54624 Thessaloniki. www.lepalace.gr. ⓒ **2310/257-400.** Fax 2310/256-589. 58 units. 100€–180€ double. AE, DC, MC, V. **Amenities:** Bar. *In room:* A/C, TV, Internet.

Mandrino Hotel ★ 💧 A complete renovation turned this centrally located hotel into a fine choice at a good price. Egnatia Street is a main thoroughfare and shopping street, so don't expect tranquillity; rear rooms are less noisy than those facing Egnatia. Bathrooms and rooms are small and simple. One plus: The Mandrino does have nonsmoking rooms, which is still unusual in modest hotels in Greece.

29 Egnatia, 54624 Thessaloniki. www.mandrino.gr. ⓒ **2310/526-321** to 325. Fax 2310/526-321. 72 units. 100€ double. Discounts usually offered for booking through the hotel's website. AE, MC, V. **Amenities:** Bar; lounge; Internet. *In room:* A/C, TV, minibar, Wi-Fi.

Plaza Art Hotel ★ 💧 With a great location in Ladadika, close to scads of restaurants and cafes, the Plaza offers excellent value. The rooms are not my idea of restful: Some have red curtains and bedspreads, others red-and-white-striped walls, and at least one has a circular bed with a Hollywood film noir black satin spread. As for the art—there are lots of reproductions and some pieces by contemporary Greek artists.

5 Paggeou, 54631 Thessaloniki. www.hotelplaza.gr. ⓒ **2310/520-120.** 35 units. 65€–100€ double. MC, V. **Amenities:** Breakfast room. *In room:* A/C, TV, minibar, Wi-Fi.

INEXPENSIVE

Hotel Orestias Castorias ★★ 💧 This formerly modest little hotel has undergone a considerable face-lift in the last few years and is now one of the best buys in town. The location, near the Roman Forum, is quiet; the (small) rooms have balconies (no. 27 overlooks a quiet garden; front rooms overlook the Forum); the staff is welcoming. Many guests are budget-conscious eastern Europeans, often travelling in groups, sometimes in high spirits. One possible drawback: There is no elevator.

14 Agnostou Stratiotou, 54631 Thessaloniki. www.okhotel.gr. ⓒ **2310/536-280.** Fax 2310/276-572. 28 units. 55€–70€ double. MC, V. **Amenities:** Lounge; Internet. *In room:* A/C, TV.

Hotel Tourist ★ 💧 This longtime favorite has a great location, helpful staff, but some absurdly small bedrooms, and a good deal of street noise. Renovations have spiffed up much of the Hotel Tourist's dingy decor. The gold-gilt borders of the high ceilings gleam, the crystal chandeliers sparkle, and the breakfast room is a welcome addition. Some of the smaller rooms are *very* small and gloomy, with just about enough room for a double bed, with a bathroom (showers only) small enough to make me resolve (again) to take up yoga. I cherish my memory of the time I stayed here and when I asked where to park my car, the clerk gestured expansively to . . . the sidewalk.

21 Mitropoleos, 54624 Thessaloniki. www.touristhotel.gr. ℭ **2310/270-501.** Fax 2310/226-865. 37 units. 65€–85€ double. Discounts usually offered for booking through the hotel's website. Inquire about reduced rates. DC, MC, V. **Amenities:** Breakfast room; lounge. *In room:* A/C, TV, fridge.

JUST OUTSIDE THESSALONIKI

When I'm in Thessaloniki, I want to be *in* Thessaloniki. But if you are just passing through and changing planes at the Thessaloniki airport, you may want to collapse at the nearby **Hyatt Regency Casino Thessaloniki** (ℭ **2310/401-234**), which has a large casino, pools, tennis courts, spas, restaurants—everything, in short, to pass the time between flights. The casino is popular year-round, mostly with foreigners, and often draws charter flights filled with gamblers from the Balkans. This casino is open 24 hours, and the 25€ entrance fee is often waived between 8am and 6pm.

Where to Eat

Some people come to Thessaloniki to see its Byzantine monuments, some to enjoy its art galleries and night life, but just about everyone agrees that you can eat better in Thessaloniki than anywhere else in Greece. If you have skirts or slacks with elastic waistbands, be sure to pack them when you come here!

You can combine culture with cuisine if you have a snack at the excellent restaurant at the Byzantine Museum or the Teloglion Foundation (p. 589 and p. 599). Most restaurants and tavernas offer cuisine of a distinctly Thessalonian character (see "The Food of Thessaloniki," below), including game, while ouzeries specialize almost exclusively in *mezedes* (appetizers). The *mezedes* are so good and so varied that you may be tempted to make a meal of these alone, although many ouzeries offer more substantial main courses.

THE food OF THESSALONIKI

It's a vexing question: To what extent has Thessaloniki's cuisine been influenced by Turkish cuisine? Certainly, the use of spices, the delicate hand with fish, the wide variety of vegetable dishes, and the extravagantly rich pastries so popular in Thessaloniki are not unknown in Turkey. As any Greek will tell you, this is because the Turks, during their long occupation of Greece, absorbed—stole, actually—the secrets of Greek cuisine. Some might argue that when the Turks withdrew from Greece, they took many of those secrets with them. Others would simply say that in some parts of Greece—such as Thessaloniki—a love of cuisine and a devotion to spices lives on.

In fact, it's the spices that set Thessaloniki's cuisine apart from the rest of Greece. Take the peppers: the most famous Macedonian peppers are the red *florines,* originally grown in the town of Florina, but now raised throughout Macedonia. These can be sweet or so hot that they lift off the top of your head. I like both varieties, but I'd be a lot more relaxed when taking that first bite if I knew for sure whether any individual *florina* were going to be sweet or pyrotechnic.

In addition to the *florines,* there are some *really* hot peppers traditionally grown in the Macedonian town of **Piperia** (the Greek word for "pepper"). These peppers are dried, then flaked, and the result, called *boukovo,* is sprinkled liberally into just about everything. *Tip:* In some Thessaloniki restaurants, in addition to the salt and black pepper on your table, you'll find another shaker of red pepper. Treat it with respect.

Sadly, the increased pollution in the bay has reached a point that makes me avoid most fish here; mussels are popular at many restaurants and almost always brought in from outside the area. If you insist on fish, here are some suggestions. As you might guess from its trendy name, **Entryfish,** 5 Pavlou Mela (© **2310/230-031**), caters to the smart set that knows its fish (and eel and mussels), and expects the best.

If you want to get out of town for a meal, head to the suburb of Nea Krini, a 20-minute taxi ride from the center of town. Noted food writer and critic Diana Farr Louis has recommended **Archipelasos** (© **2310/435-800**) and **Hermodrakas** (© **2310/447-947**); others praise **Miami** (© **2310/447-996**) and **Porto Marina** (© **2310/451-333**), both serving fresh fish that is not from the bay. With even the humblest fish usually selling for more than 40€ a kilo in the market, all these restaurants are expensive—and the price of fish continues to go up.

Even in the most expensive establishments, the dress code in Thessaloniki is studiedly casual for men; ties and jackets are rare, but designer shoes are de rigueur, as are designer name jackets and sweaters. Twentyish women are partial to low-cut designer jeans and tops with lots of cleavage and sequins, whereas most older women are resolutely chic, in little black dresses or more conservative trouser suits, but always with freshly styled hair, elegant handbags, and high-heeled shoes or boots that add inches to their height. Most restaurants don't take reservations, but you'll almost always get a table if you arrive for lunch before 1pm and for dinner no later than 9pm.

Warning: Most Thessaloniki restaurants—even the fanciest—do not accept credit cards.

RESTAURANTS & TAVERNAS
Expensive/Moderate

Draft ★★ GREEK/INTERNATIONAL   Back in 1997, Draft was one of the first Ladadika spots to renovate an old brick warehouse and capitalize on the seemingly endless local love of ouzo, beer, and *mezedes*. Today, it's still one of the best places in town for beer (46 bottled and 4 draft beers available) and munchies, in either the casual ground floor bar area, or one of the more elegant lounges upstairs. In summer, you can sit out in the garden. What could be more pleasant than to let the evening slip away while listening to some low-key jazz while nibbling on salmon rolls with caviar, vegetable dips and fritters, and shrimp in hot sauce? I've never ordered an entree here, but always end up making my way through as many *mezedes* as possible.

3 Lycourgous and Salaminos, Ladadika. © **2310/555-518.** www.draft.gr Main courses 12€-25€. DC, V. Mon-Sat noon-1am.

Kioupia ★ GREEK   This trendy taverna with brick walls and wood floors in the old warehouse district has excellent *stifada* (stews), *keftadakia* (meatballs), and spicy *gardoubitsa* (liver and garlic); wild boar is sometimes on the menu, which also has a number of tasty pork dishes. If you like *spanakopita* (spinach pies), try the wide range of phyllo-wrapped vegetable (eggplant, zucchini, cheese) and meat (minced lamb or beef with cheese) snacks usually available. Dessert brings a range of Greek and Turkish sweets, the house retsina is excellent, and the wine list is extensive. The same management runs the nearby **Amorgos,** 4 Panaiou and **Doxis,** Ladadika (© **2310/ 557-161**), which specializes in fresh fish.

3-5 Morihovou Sq., Ladadika. © **2310/553-239.** Fax 2310/553-579. www.kioupia.gr. Reservations recommended after 9pm. Main courses 15€-25€. AE, MC, V. Mon-Sat 1pm-1am.

Krikelas ★★ GREEK   In 1999, Krikelas, a Thessaloniki institution since the 1940s, opened a branch in the Ladadika district, just across from the Mediterranean Palace Hotel. For visitors, the Ladadika Krikelas is conveniently located, and the food continues to be as good as ever. The specialties: a mouthwatering variety of *mezedes* and whatever game is in season (including quail, pheasant, rabbit, boar, and partridge). A regional specialty, *spetzofai,* combines seasonal vegetables with a pungent country sausage. For dessert, try the homemade halva with almonds. The wine list at both branches is serious, although you can get a decent bottle for around 15€. There's another location at 32 Eth. Antistaseos (℃ **2310/451-289;** same hours apply, except in summer when the Ladadika branch is sometimes closed in July and August, but the Eth. Antistaseos branch may be open).

6 Salaminos, Ladadika. ℃/fax **2310/501-600.** Fax 2310/451-690. Reservations usually not accepted. Main courses 15€–25€. No credit cards. Mon–Sat 11:30am–2am. Usually closed July–Aug (but the Ladadika branch may be open then).

Tiffany's ★ GREEK/CONTINENTAL   This popular place, with wood paneling and pictures of old Salonika on the walls, seats about 100 and attracts an interesting mix of people: regulars who drop in every night for a quick bite, and then the gaggles of 20-somethings who sit at the window tables and wait to be seen. I like the atmosphere here more than the food: two of the house specialties—*bifsteki Tiffany's* (steak stuffed with cheese and tomatoes) and *hanoym borek* (casserole of roasted chicken, ham, veal, and cheese)—both strike me as rather bland. On the other hand, I've had fun trying to figure out the principle behind the music here, which can include everything from Harry Belafonte and Greek golden oldies to Philip Glass.

3 Iktinou (on the walkway btw. Tsimiski and the church of Ayia Sofia). ℃ **2310/274-022.** www.tiffanys. gr. Reservations recommended after 10pm. Main courses 10€–20€. DC, MC, V. Daily 11:30am–2am.

Wolves ★ GREEK   This warm, dark-wood, old-fashioned restaurant, established in 1977, serves up basic Greek fare including *pastitsio* and moussaka, and somehow makes these old standbys seem fresh. Try the roasted red peppers from Florina as one of your starters. For the main course, sample the house moussaka, the oregano-flavored stewed pork or lamb, or the batter-fried codfish in garlic sauce—or take a look at the day's special on the kitchen's display counter.

6 Vas. Olgas (1 block in and 2 blocks east of the Makedonia Palace Hotel). ℃ **2310/812-855.** Main courses 10€–18€. No credit cards. Mon–Sat 12:30pm–1am; Sun 12:30–5pm. Usually closed Dec 12–Feb and Aug 5–15.

Zythos ★★ GREEK/CONTINENTAL   This was one of the first restaurants to open in the restored warehouse district, and it's still very popular with ladies who lunch, young lovers, harried businesspeople, and groups of golden youths. The decor is wood and brick, as you'd expect in a former warehouse, although the slim young waiters in their chic outfits hardly suggest warehouse workers. I always like the fluffy croquettes of vegetables, the zesty *saganaki* (fried cheese), and veggie pasta. Usually one of the two daily specials is a vegetarian choice. Reservations are a good idea on weekends. If you like Zythos, try its branch, **Dore Zythos,** 7 Tsirogianni (℃ **2310-279-010**), by the White Tower, which sometimes has live music.

5 Katouni, Ladadika. ℃ **2310/540-284.** Main courses 10€–18€. No credit cards. Daily 11am–1am.

Inexpensive
Kentrike Stoa ★ GREEK/CONTINENTAL   This snacks-and-drinks place in the Central Market is up a winding metal staircase from the market itself. The ceiling is

covered with parachute cloth, jazz contends with shouts from the market below, and the languid local 20-something crowd tolerates outsiders gracefully—and can be fun to watch as they vie to impress one another.

32 Vas. Hrakleiou. ℂ **2310/278-242.** Snacks 5€–15€. No credit cards. Mon–Sat noon–1am.

Loutros ★★ 🍴 GREEK   A Saloniki favorite, Loutroslong occupied part of an old Turkish bath, before moving to new quarters across from the Bezesteni, the old Turkish market still in use. The menu still includes mountains of crispy fried minnows (which you eat whole), spicy *florines* (red peppers), spicy mussels with pilaf, shrimp and cheese in (you guessed it) spicy red sauce, and a pungent house retsina. The music here is usually very Levantine-sounding—which, in Greece, is a polite way of saying that it sounds absolutely Turkish. The retsina, from the barrel, is memorable, especially now that real retsina has been almost entirely washed away in the bland sea of rosé wines available most places.

5 M. Kountoura (opposite the Bezesteni), just past the Ouzerie Melathron (see below). ℂ **2310/228-895.** Main courses 8€–15€. MC, V. Mon–Sat 11am–midnight.

Thanasis (Myrobolos Smyrnis) ★★★ 🍴 GREEK   For 47 years, Thessalonians have beat a path to this taverna that serves zesty home-style cooking—including stuffed squid and mussels (both fried or steamed). In fact, the first customer through the door in the new millennium was then-Greek Prime Minister Simitis. The sign over the door reads H MYPOBOLOS SMYRNH (Fragrant Smyrna), but everyone knows it as well by the name of its original owner, Thanasis. Usually quiet from around 7 to 9pm, at lunch and dinner this place is packed. The potato salad, cheese croquettes, spicy peppers with cheese, squid stuffed with cheese and rice, grilled fish and meats, and *bakaliaro* (batter-fried cod) are wonderful, as is the atmosphere when this restaurant with photos and old prints on the walls reverberates to the wails of Balkan music.

Ermou and 32 Komninon (just inside Modiano Market). ℂ **2310/274-170.** Fax 2310/347-062. Reservations necessary after 10pm. Main courses 8€–15€. No credit cards. Mon–Sat about 10am–3am.

Xenophon ★★ 🍴 GREEK   There's been a Xenophon restaurant on Komninon, the little street that runs past an old Turkish bath and flower market, since 1942. In 2008, Xenophon got a complete face-lift, with sleek black tables and white chairs inside and out. Inside, prepared dishes are helpfully on view in a display case just inside the door where the chef grills to order. This is a perfect place to come for a big lettuce and tomato salad (with a terrific sesame seed dressing) and grilled *bifstekakia* (zippy hamburgers) or *soutoukakiai* (cigar-shaped beef and lamb patties). There are also stews and chops, but the *bifstekakia* and *soutoukakiai* are so good I have yet to try them. If you want a more varied menu than the Xenophon's, try another slightly more expensive longtime favorite, the excellent **Louloudadika,** which often has live music in the evening, a few steps away at 20 Komninon.

18 Komninon. ℂ **2310/272-870.** Main courses 8€–10€. No credit cards. Mon–Fri noon–midnight; Sat noon–5pm.

OUZERIES

Ouzeries specialize in ouzo and the *mezedes* that go with them—and make it possible to consume more than a sip or two of the high-voltage ouzo! Still, you need not drink ouzo, or any kind of alcoholic beverage, to enjoy the marvelous variety of foods ouzeries offer: octopus, meatballs, shrimp, squid, taramosalata (fish roe puréed with oil and bread), *tzatziki* (cucumber, yogurt, and garlic), *melitzanosalata* (eggplant purée), cheeses, and salads of potatoes, beets, or beans. If you're uncertain about what to chose, ask if you can go with your waiter to look at the offerings and point to what you want. The prices below is for an ouzo and a selection of two or more *mezedes*; you can eat very cheaply at these places or run up an impressive tab, depending on how many snacks and ouzos you want to try. Ouzeries, like so many places in Greece, are great places to take things *siga, siga* (slowly, slowly.)

Aproopto Light ★ GREEK   Highly popular with professionals of the nearby State Theatre and other artistic types, this place serves excellent *mezedes* as well as mussels with spinach, leeks a la Parisienne, and *saganaki* (fried cheese). Its relatively small, convivial, well-decorated sidewalk and interior dining areas are usually packed.

6 Zevksidos (a pedestrian walkway off the eastern end of the church of Ayia Sofia). 🕻 **2310/241-141.** 10€-25€ for several *mezedes* and ouzos. No credit cards. Daily noon-1:30am.

Aristotelous ★★★ GREEK   After all these years, Aristotelous is still packed during the peak lunch and dinner hours, and remains popular with writers, artists, and everyone else in the know, so you should come either early or late or you'll end up waiting at least 20 minutes. Indoor and outdoor seating areas between high-rise office buildings contribute to the crush and, somehow, the charm. You can and should linger for hours, which is why it's often so hard to get a table. The variety of *mezedes* is sumptuous. Try the fried zucchini and eggplant, the *ktipiti* (feta cheese mashed with hot peppers and olive oil) and, for something more substantial, the *soupia* (stuffed cuttlefish). Also delicious is homemade halva for dessert.

8 Aristotelous (in a cul-de-sac btw. office buildings on the east side of Aristotelous, just north of Tsimiski). 🕻 **2310/230-762.** Reservations not accepted. 15€-25€ for several *mezedes* and ouzos. No credit cards. Mon-Sat 10am-2am; Sun 11am-6pm.

Ouzerie Melathron ★ GREEK   This is one of a chain of ouzo and *mezedes* places, most of which are in northern Greece. You'll find a wide choice of ouzos, good house wine, and *mezedes*, including the popular *saganaka* (a slab of fried cheese with a crispy exterior and a melty interior), *keftedes*, grilled hot or cold octopus, sprats, and local olives.

23 Eleftherious Venizelou and Ermou. 🕻 **2310/220-043.** 15€-25€ for several *mezedes* and ouzo. No credit cards. Usually closed July-Aug. Daily from 11am till at least midnight.

Tsinari's ★ GREEK   A very welcome place to plop down for a rest from sightseeing in the Upper City, this ouzeri started life as a Turkish coffeehouse, and may be the only such spot to have survived the great fire of 1917. There's a wide variety of *mezedes* and, in my experience, somewhat capricious hours.

72 Papadopoulou. 🕻 **2310/284-028.** 10€-20€ for several *mezedes* and ouzos. No credit cards. Opening hours vary; call ahead.

Thessaloniki After Dark

If you think that everyone in Thessaloniki is rushing somewhere all day, just wait until nightfall. It seems like everyone in town stops at a favorite cafe on the way home from work and then heads out to dinner—this, before or after taking in a play or concert at one of the city's many theaters, concert halls, and nightclubs with live entertainment. Though many publications list events and posters splattered everywhere announce them, almost all will all be Greek (or possibly Russian or Japanese) to you. Ask for information at your hotel, or stop by the office of the **Greek National Tourism Organization (EOT),** 136 Tsimiski (🕻 **2310/221-100;** www.mintour.gr).

Meanwhile, the city seems festooned with enough bars and clubs to serve a population twice its size, yet all of them are crowded to the bursting point—and more open every year. For some of the liveliest nightlife in town, try one of the cafes in the waterfront Ladidika district, or along the harbor on Nikis Street, or head inland to Athoonos Square, or sample the cafes on pedestrianized Zefxidos and Iktinos streets.

THE PERFORMING ARTS

Kratiko Theatro (State Theatre of Northern Greece) has two venues. In winter, it stages plays in the **Royal State Theatre,** next to the White Tower (© **2310/860-966**); in summer, it stages plays at **Theatro Dasous (Forest Theatre),** an open-air amphitheater in the forested hilltop area east of the Upper City (© **2310/245-307**). The company presents ancient and modern Greek plays, as well as Greek translations of foreign plays by authors as varied as Christopher Marlowe and Arthur Miller.

In summer, the **Forest Theatre,** which has a marvelous view of the city, also hosts lively, well-attended concerts by popular Greek singers and composers, as well as performances by visiting ballet companies.

Thessaloniki's splendid **Megaron Mousikis (Concert Hall),** 25 Martiou and Paralia (© **2310/895-800;** www.tch.gr), opened in 2000; in 2009, the excellent Thessaloniki State Orchestra celebrated its 50th anniversary. Check with your hotel concierge or at the hall for a concert schedule. **Aristotle University Concert Hall** also hosts concerts (it's on Nea Egnatia, opposite the northern entrance of the International Trade Fairgrounds) September through May (© **2310/283-343**).

FESTIVALS

DEMETRIA FESTIVAL October 26, St. Dimitrios's day is celebrated all over Greece, but in Thessaloniki, the celebration lasts for weeks. The festival, which gets bigger every year, started with a Greek film festival and now includes many theatrical and musical events.

THE FEAST OF STS. CONSTANTINE & ELENI (MAY 21) On or around the feast of the first Christian emperor and his mother, villagers in **Ayia Eleni** (80km/50 miles northeast of Thessaloniki) and at **Langadas** (12km/7 miles northeast of Thessaloniki) engage in *pirovassia* (fire dancing). Crowds come from all over Macedonia to see the faithful dance over a bed of hot coals. When they're done, they feast on the roasted black bull sacrificed earlier in the day. In case you're wondering—yes, much of what's done here preserves pre-Christian rites.

INTERNATIONAL TRADE FAIR FESTIVAL This takes place every year during the first 2 weeks in September and draws businesspeople from around the world. The international fairgrounds have lots of exhibits, so hotel rooms are hard to find—and expensive (often double normal prices).

THE BAR, CLUB & MUSIC SCENE

In July and August, many of Thessaloniki's best bars and clubs shut down. Some immediately reopen branches along a section of the road leading east along the coast, about a mile before the airport. This, plus the fact that new or newly decorated and renamed venues are constantly opening while others go out of fashion and close, makes it virtually impossible to recommend any with certainty. No one ever answers the phone at these places and most addresses are not visible, so I am not listing either.

Most of these places are open virtually 24 hours a day; some have gaggles of unattached but alert singles looking for action in its many manifestations. Others are teeming with more staid locals. In short, take a stroll; start with harborside Nikis Street and you'll eventually spot the bar scene that suits you best.

In town, in the summer of 2011, Greek friends of mine were heading to bars like **Urban** and the improbably named **Pasta Flora Darling!** on Zefxidos Street, but they were pretty sure they'll be looking for new spots in a year or two. On the Ladadika waterfront, by the State Museum of Contemporary Art (**www.greekstatemuseum. gr**; housing a surprising collection of contemporary Russian paintings), you can begin or end your revels with breakfast at the **Kitchen Bar** in Warehouse B.

A couple of neighborhoods churn out new favorites in nightlife year after year. In Ladadika, try the spots along Katouni Street and around Agia Sophia Square, check out Zefkidos Street. Keep going west and you pass from Ladadika into the neighborhood of Xyladika, where lots of warehouses and shops around the old railroad station are being converted into bars and galleries. You'll probably enjoy exploring Xyladika more with Greek friends than on your own. Along Nikis Street, check out **Elvis,** which often has a D.J, **Tribeca, DaDA, Thermaikos,** the oddly named **Pollock,** and the drop-dead understatedly elegant **Daios** (often with jazz Fri–Sat). Best of all, get a local with similar tastes to give you some tips.

Milos ★★★ In the midst of all the clubs and bars that come and go, this place seems eternally popular. Not only is it a permanent fixture of Thessaloniki nightlife year-round, but it manages to include the best of the bar, music, and club scenes in the city. Within the grounds of a restored flour-mill complex, the Milos (*Mee*-los) complex contains a club for blues, folk, jazz, and pop groups; a nightclub featuring Greek singers and comedians; a bar/disco; an outdoor concert stage and movie theater; several exhibition rooms and art galleries; a cafe; and an ouzeri that serves more than 30 kinds of *mezedes*. Almost as soon as it opened in 1990, Milos became one of the top musical venues in the country. Check out the website and you'll see how busy it is each summer, when performers from around the world (and from throughout Greece) appear and perform everything from golden oldies to neo-grunge. If you want to be sure of a seat, it's a good idea to arrive before the clubs open at 10pm. The ouzeri, cafe, and galleries open from about noon. Go west on Tsimiski to its end and turn left onto 28 Octobriou. At the first traffic light, turn right onto Andreadou Yioryiou and continue to the end of the street. This is quite a hike from the center, and you may want to take a cab. 56 Andreadou Yioryiou. ✆ **2310/551-838** or 2310/525-968. www. mylos.gr. Cover varies: usually no more than 40€; drinks from around 10€.

IN THE FOOTSTEPS OF PHILIP & ALEXANDER THE GREAT ★★

In 338 B.C. King Philip of Macedon conquered Greece; a few years later, his son Alexander—whom history remembers as Alexander the Great—set off to conquer the world. Today, more and more visitors are heading north to see Pella, Vergina, and Dion, the cluster of ancient sites most closely associated with these two famous Macedonians. If you can only visit one of these sites, head for Vergina if you like monumental tombs and glittering gold, Pella, if you'd like to try to decipher the remains of a now landlocked ancient port town, and Dion, if you want to wander around a lush green site that seems more like a picnic spot than the enormous army training ground where young Alexander himself bivouacked. Of the three, Vergina is usually by far the most crowded, due to its close connection with King Philip.

Greek interest in Macedonia has been intense since 1991 when, just across the border, the former Yugoslavian district of Macedonia proclaimed itself a republic.

How dare these non-Greeks take the name of Macedonia, Greeks asked—forgetting that their own ancestors had not considered Philip of Macedon a Greek! Most Greeks remain furious that Philip's best-known royal symbol—a star with 16 rays—was put on the new Former Yugoslav Republic of Macedonia's flag. Things calmed down after the new Republic of Macedonia (FYROM) changed its flag, but this issue has not gone away: When President Obama and Prime Minister Karamanlis met in 2009, discussion of rights to use the name of Macedonia was on the agenda.

Greece's ongoing determination to prove that there is only one Macedonia, and that it is Greek, has led the Greek Archaeological Service to redouble its efforts to excavate the Macedonian royal sites and build museums. And that, of course, means that there's much more to see aboveground than there was even a few years ago.

Essentials

GETTING THERE The only enjoyable and efficient ways to see the places where Philip of Macedon (382–38 B.C.) and Alexander the Great (356–23 B.C.) lived and reigned are by car or with a tour. (*Tip:* Prices on rental cars from international agencies are almost always lower when the car is booked in advance from outside Greece.) **Budget Rent-A-Car** has offices at the airport (© **2310/471-491**) and in the city at 15 Angelaki, opposite the International Fairgrounds (© **2310/274-272** or 2310/229-519). Other rental offices are **Avis**, 3 Leoforos Nikis, at the western end of the harbor, opposite the docks (© **2310/227-126** or 2310/683-300); **Europcar**, 5 Papandreou (© **2310/836-333**), and **Hertz**, 4 El. Venizelou, on Eleftherias Square (© **2310/224-906**).

Several Athens-based companies, such as **CHAT** (www.chatours.gr) and **Dolphin-Hellas** (www.dolphin-hellas.gr) offer **tours** of Central and Northern Greece that take in the most important Macedonian sites; 5 days from about 500€. **Zorpidis Travel**, 76 Egnatia(© **2310/244-400**; www.zorpidis.gr; website only in Greek, English information on Zorpidis's Facebook page), is an established Thessaloniki company offering tours of the Philip and Alexander sites. A day trip to Pella, Edessa, Veria, and Vergina, or to Philippa, Kavala, and Amphipolis, costs from 150€. It is vital to make an advance reservation. Avoid visiting on summer weekends, when Greeks flock to these sites. Be prepared to encounter school groups throughout the year.

By Bus If you try to visit these sites by local bus, you may feel that it takes you longer to see them than it took Alexander to conquer the world. Still, if you have lots of time and love buses, you can visit the following sites by bus from Thessaloniki. For **Pella,** there are sometimes direct buses; failing that, take a bus to Edessa and ask to be let off at Pella. For **Vergina,** take a bus to Veria, and then a local bus to the site of Vergina. To travel from Pella to Vergina, take the Thessaloniki bus from Pella to Halkidona, where you can get a bus to Veria. This may involve a substantial wait. For **Dion,** take a bus to Katerini and then a local bus to Dion. For information on bus schedules and departure points, check with the **Greek National Tourism Organization,** 136 Tsimiski St., in Thessaloniki (© **2310/221-100;** www.mintour.gr); the bus information line (© **2310/512-122**) is unlikely to have English-speaking staff.

VISITOR INFORMATION If you stop in Athens or Thessaloniki before visiting these sites, the free brochure *Greece/Macedonia* should be—but may not be—available at the **Greek National Tourism Organization (www.gnto.gr)** in Athens at 7 Tsohas (© **210/870-7000**) or in Thessaloniki at 136 Tsimiski (© **2310/252-170**).

Pella ★

Pella, once the capital of the Macedonian kingdom and the birthplace of Philip II of Macedon in 382 B.C. and his most famous son, Alexander the Great, in 356 B.C., is easy to spot. The **archaeological site** and **museum** are right beside the highway (a 40km/24-mile drive west of Thessaloniki on the E86 Hwy. to Edessa).

The first thing to know about Pella is that what you see today bears no resemblance to what you would have seen when Philip and Alexander lived here. Then, you would not have looked out on a dusty plain, but on an inlet to the sea, with ships docked near the palace. The navigable inlet ran all the way from Pella to the broad Thermaic Gulf that borders Thessaloniki. Over the centuries, the inlet silted up, leaving Pella landlocked, but in Philip and Alexander's day, ships would have bobbed in the waters of today's flat plain. The city itself is thought to have covered at least 13 sq. km (5 sq. miles), of which only a fraction has been excavated.

There's more than enough of Pella above ground to give you an idea of this stylish city, with its large, square agora (market and civic center) bordered by colonnaded stoas and flanked by streets lined with shrines, sanctuaries, temples, and private homes. The lovely frescoes that once adorned house walls are gone, but a number of handsome **pebble mosaic floors** remain, both on the site and in the museum. These gaily painted houses with sheltered inner courtyards must have been exceptionally pleasant. Long ago, families might have passed an evening discussing the Athenian playwright Euripides's *The Bacchae*, which had its premiere here around 408 B.C. in the as-yet-undiscovered theater.

Unfortunately, the dwelling you'd probably most like to see—the **palace** where both Philip and his son Alexander were born—is not open to the public. Not to worry: You can drive or walk to the hilltop north of the site and peer over the wire fence to get an idea of how large this royal home was. In fact, the palace covered 60,000 sq. m (645,835 sq. ft.). Somewhere in this vast complex, Aristotle tutored the young Alexander. The view from the hill is still tremendous, but it must have been truly breathtaking in antiquity, when the palace overlooked both the plain and the channel down which ships sailed, bringing supplies from around the Mediterranean.

Pella's small **museum** is superb, especially the glorious pebble mosaics found in the excavated 4th-century-B.C. homes. The two best-known mosaics show a lion hunt and the god of wine, Dionysos, riding a leopard. The lion hunt is especially tantalizing. It's a powerful depiction of a lion and two youths—one of whom may be Alexander. Some scholars suggest that the mosaic records an incident when the young Alexander was saved by a friend from a lunging lion. Others suspect that this is merely a genre scene of a hunt. You can compare the marble bust of Alexander in the museum with the youth under attack in the lion hunt and decide for yourself. Be sure to see whether the gold and jewelry from 25 6th-century-B.C. tombs discovered here in 2005 and the remains of a vast eight-chamber Hellenistic tomb discovered in 2006 (the largest known such tomb) are on view yet. Allow at least 2 hours to visit the site and museum.

ⓒ **23820/31-160** or 23820/31-278. Combined museum and site admission 6€. Summer Mon 1:30–8pm, Tues-Sun 8am–8pm; winter Mon 1:30–3pm, Tues-Sun 8am–3pm.

WHERE TO STAY & EAT

After you visit the site, you may want to take in **Edessa,** 45km (27 miles) west of Pella, a scenic cliff-top town with bubbling waterfalls and pleasant, small cafes and restaurants. **O Stathmos,** near the train station, comes highly recommended by Greek-American food critic Diana Farr Louis. **Paeti,** on 18 Oktobriou, serves hearty

HISTORY 101: PHILIP & ALEXANDER

When Philip was born in 382 B.C., most Greeks thought of Macedonians—if they thought of them at all—as one of the rude northern tribes who lived in the back of beyond. Macedonians, after all, were not even allowed to participate in the Panhellenic Games at Delphi. Clearly, this irritated Philip. By 346 B.C., after conquering a number of Athenian colonies and allied cities, Philip had won a place on Delphi's governing board. A few years later, in 338 B.C., despite Demosthenes's best oratorical efforts to alert the Athenians to Philip's intentions, the Macedonian king had conquered all of Greece. Two years later, Philip was dead, cut down as he strolled to see a performance in the theater at his capital city of Vergina. Some said that his young son Alexander was behind the assassination, while others wondered how the unproven youth could rule Macedonia, let alone Greece.

No one, except perhaps Alexander himself, could have imagined that by the time he died at 33, he would have conquered much of the known world as far east as India. Alexander's early death makes it impossible to know what he would have done with the rest of his life, once he had no new worlds to conquer. Some scholars think that Alexander was a visionary bent not only on conquering but also on uniting the world into a "brotherhood of man." This, they suggest, is why Alexander contracted so many foreign marriages and accepted conquered princes into his retinue. Other scholars, more cynical, think that Alexander's marriages and his use of former enemies were simply shrewd political moves. The truth probably lies between the two theories.

In any event, after Alexander's death, his former comrades turned on one another and destroyed his empire. Within a few generations, Macedon was once more a northern kingdom in the back of beyond, living on memories of its brief period of international importance.

---

meals that include game in season. Note that Edessa is almost always crowded on summer weekends, when many Thessalonians come here to escape the heat.

If it's the weekend or if you're rushed after visiting Pella, you can grab a bite at one of the small roadside restaurants by the fountain beside the (signposted) remains of Baths of Alexander, a Hellenistic fountain incorporated into a Roman bath about 1km (½ mile) from Pella on the Edessa road.

As far as overnighting here, keep in mind that Edessa is a popular year-round destination for Thessalonians. It has only about 200 hotel/B&B rooms, and on summer and holiday weekends, most are taken. The nicest places in town are two small hotels run by the same family. The **Varosi** (www.varosi.gr [Greek only]; ✆ **23810/21-865**), is in a carefully restored 18th-century stone town house; the 10-room **Varosi Four Seasons** (www.varosi.gr; ✆ **23810/51-440**) is very popular with Greeks, more up-to-date, and styles itself a "boutique" hotel; doubles at both go from 70€–80€.

Vergina & Environs: The Tombs at Leukadia, the Town of Veria & Vineyards ★★★

Vergina is 20km (12 miles) south of Pella and 62km (38 miles) west of Thessaloniki, just outside the hamlet of Palatitsia. It's well signposted off the main road and poorly signposted as you approach from Thessaloniki. If you're short on time, head for the museum. If not, explore the **Vergina site (Palace of Palatitsa)** and the **Royal Tombs Museum** (✆ **23310/92-347**). Combined museum and site admission is

8€. Summer hours for both are Monday from noon to 7pm and Tuesday through Sunday from 8am to 8pm; in the off season, the site and museum close at 5pm. Allow at least 3 hours to visit both.

Vergina (known as Aigai in ancient times) is the most important of the royal Macedonian sites; the museum contains some of the most spectacular gold objects found in ancient Greece. King Philip lived here when not at Pella and in 336 B.C. died here. Preliminary excavations suggest that the palace was enormous, with an inner courtyard about 14 sq. m (147 sq. ft.). Around the courtyard ran a Doric colonnade; the bases of some of its 60 columns are still in place and give you a sense of the courtyard's size. The palace also had a long, airy, colonnaded veranda running the length of its north side, overlooking the theater. It's quite possible that the royal family watched spectacles in the theater from the comfort of the palace veranda.

HISTORY 101: PHILIP'S TOMB

Vergina's first excavator, the French archaeologist Leon Heuzey, prophesied in 1876 that when Vergina was fully excavated, "the importance of its ruins for Macedonia will be comparable to Pompeii." The Greek Archaeological Service began to work here in the 1930s and uncovered several tombs that looked like small temples. For years, the excavators nibbled away at the largest burial mound of all, the **Great Tumulus,** measuring 110m (361 ft.) across and 12m (39 ft.) high, containing a number of burials. One tomb they found was almost totally destroyed, another well preserved but robbed. Still, head excavator Manolis Andronikos remained convinced that he was excavating ancient Aigai, Philip's capital city, and might yet find Philip's own tomb.

Finally, in 1977—on the last day of the excavation season—Andronikos and his workers opened the massive marble gates of the final remaining tomb. As Andronikos later wrote in *Vergina: The Royal Tombs:*

We saw a sight which it was not possible for me to have imagined, because until then such an ossuary (a container for bones) had never been found—all-gold—with an impressive relief star on its lid. We lifted it from the sarcophagus, placed it on the floor, and opened it. Our eyes nearly popped out

of our sockets and our breathing stopped; there unmistakably were charred bones placed in a carefully formed pile and still retaining the color of the purple cloth in which they had once been wrapped. If those were royal remains, then, had I held the bones of Philip in my hands?

Andronikos—and virtually all of Greece—answered his question with a resounding yes, in large part because of the other objects found in the tomb. The gold wreaths, Andronikos felt, were too fine to belong to anyone but a king. And surely the little ivory portrait heads were the spitting images of Philip and Alexander themselves. And, most persuasive of all, what about the unequally sized bronze greaves (shin guards) found in the tomb? Philip was known to have legs of different length, due to an early injury.

It is difficult to overestimate the Philip fever that swept through Greece when Andronikos announced that he had found Philip's tomb and identified Vergina as ancient Aigai, Philip's capital city. Although some spoilsport scholars have questioned whether this is, in fact, Philip's tomb, those scholars are not Greek. Greeks regard with horror any suggestion that this splendid tomb may have belonged to Arrhidaeos, the son of Philip known only for his lack of distinction.

Unfortunately for Philip, that's not what he did on the fatal day in 336 B.C. when he was assassinated en route from the palace to take in a performance at the theater. Some scholars surmise that Alexander was behind the assassination. Others said that the young prince was not noticeably grief-stricken by his father's death, and left it at that. You can sit in the **theater,** the only really impressive remains, and contemplate the moment when Philip realized that he was about to be struck down.

As you drive from the site to the Royal Tombs Museum, notice the hundreds of low mounds on the gentle hills of the Macedonian plain. Some of the more than 300 **burial mounds** found here date from as long ago as the Iron Age, although many are from the time of Philip himself. Robbers looted most of these graves in antiquity. Fortunately—and almost miraculously—the tomb identified as Philip's lay undisturbed for almost 2,000 years. How it was found is one of the great stories of archaeology, deserving a place beside accounts of how Schliemann found Troy and excavated the Tomb of Agamemnon at Mycenae.

The arched roof of the **Royal Tombs Museum** re-creates a sense of the Great Tumulus itself, as does the passageway leading into the tomb area. A helpful video (Greek and English) is shown throughout the day. Each of the tombs is protected by a glass wall, but seeing the tombs this way is the next best thing to standing inside them. Give your eyes time to get accustomed to the darkness, then enjoy the decorative paintings on the sculptured facades of the templelike tombs and the spectacular gold objects found in the frescoed chambers. Most Greek (and fewer non-Greek) archaeologists think that the gold *larnax* (box) with the 16-pointed star held the bones of Philip II of Macedon, that the small ivory head is his portrait, and that the bronze greaves—of different lengths, just like the king's injured legs—were part of his armor.

The monumental tomb paintings here are among only a handful to have survived from antiquity. Don't miss the dramatic scene of Hades's abduction of Persephone. Hades carried the maiden off to live with him in the underworld, but Persephone's mother Demeter persuaded the evil god to let her daughter live in the world for 6 months of each year. The ancient Greeks believed that this was the origin of the seasons: When Persephone is in Hades, barren winter rules the earth; when Persephone is aboveground, crops grow and flourish.

VERIA (VEROIA) & ITS BYZANTINE, JEWISH & TURKISH REMAINS ★

The hill town of Veria (Veroia), rich in medieval remains, is 15km (9 miles) northwest of Vergina. The **Municipal Culture Office,** at the corner of Pavlou Mela and Bizantiou in the center of town (© **23110/27-914**), has helpful maps and brochures. The Veria, in the throes of development, still has a number of old streets, wood houses with overhanging bay windows, more than 50 small Byzantine churches (usually locked), a 15th-century cathedral, and a good number of buildings from the Ottoman period, including a former mosque and *hamam* (bath). Most will want to stop here for a coffee and a stroll; devotees of small Byzantine churches, ramshackle Turkish houses, and winding lanes may wish to spend longer. If you're here in winter, you'll encounter skiers who come to the **Veria Ski Center** on Mount Vermion at Souli (© **23310/49-226;** www.seli-ski.gr).

Don't feel bad if you don't have time for Veria's small museums; you'll have much more fun wandering the streets of this old town, with its Turkish remains and old Jewish quarter. The synagogue (in Greek, sin-ah-go-*gay*), not open and not easy to find, is in the Barbouta district, off Kentrikis and Merarchias streets. At the corner of Anixeos and Pasteur, the 1930s Vlachoyiannis town house displays the collection of the restored Museum of Modern History and Art; it also has a cafe. If you combine visits to the museum exhibits with a stroll past a cluster of nearby 20th-century houses, "eclectic" in style, you'll get a sense of how people in Veria lived in the first half of the 20th century. Nearby, the **Byzantine Museum** is in the restored Markos mill on Mylos Markou Street (✆ **23310/25-847**). Admission is 2€; official hours are Tuesday to Sunday 8:30am to 3pm. Only the truly devoted will wish to visit the **Archaeological Museum,** 47 Anoixeos (✆ **23310/24-972**), which features finds from local sites. Admission is 2€; hours are Tuesday through Sunday from 8:30am to 3pm.

THE NAOUSSA VINEYARDS

About halfway between Veria and Edessa, on the slopes of Mount Vermion, you'll see roadside signs for several vineyards open to the public. At Naoussa, a region famous for its wine, **Stenimachos Winery,** run by the well-known Boutari vintners, offers tours (sometimes in English) of the winery most work days. For information, call ✆ **23320/41-666** or go to www.boutari.gr.

WHERE TO STAY & EAT FOR VERGINA & VERIA

The 10-unit **Dimitra** (✆ **23310/92-900**) and the 10-unit **Vergina Pension** (✆ **23310/92-510**), both near the Vergina site, are both reasonably priced small family-run hotels; the Dimitra has studios with full kitchenettes. Neither takes credit cards, and staff is not absolutely comfortable in English; doubles run from 65€ at the Vergina, from 75€ at the Dimitra. Of the local restaurants, the **Filippion** (also spelled Philippion), with cafeteria-style lunch service, is reliable.

In Veria, the 37-unit **Hotel Makedonia,** 50 Kontogeorgaki (www.makedoniahotel. gr; ✆/fax **23310/66-902** or 23310/66-946), has the bland ambience of a businessperson's, rather than a traveler's, hotel. Rooms come with air-conditioning and TVs. The new **Veria,** Km 6.5 on the Veria-Naousa Hwy. (www.veriahotel.gr; ✆ **23310/93-112**), gets a fair amount of tour business. The hotel is set back from the highway just enough to make traffic noise manageable. Although staying here makes exploring Veria itself a miniexcursion, you may find the pool so welcoming that you never leave. The rooms are standard Greek-hotel quality, but most have balconies as well as air-conditioning and TVs. Both the Makedonia and the Veria usually offer doubles from 60€ to 100€. Two Veria tavernas, **Vergiotiko** and **Katafugio,** are usually excellent; ask for directions in town, as the streets are not signposted. Katafugio is in a nicely restored old building and sometimes has game on the menu.

Dion ★★

The **Dion Archaeological Site and Museum** (✆ **23510/53-206**) has an idyllic site just beyond the Vale of Tempe, in the foothills of Mount Olympus. The site is on the fringes of the village of Dion, about 8km (5 miles) west of the DION sign on the E75, the main Athens-Thessaloniki highway (and 78km/48 miles south of Thessaloniki). Combined admission to the site and museum is 6€. Hours are Monday from 1:30am to 8pm and Tuesday through Sunday from 8:30am to 8pm; both close at 3pm in the off season. Allow at least 2 hours for your visit.

This is an unusually green spot, with pine groves and farm fields watered by springs fed by the melting snow that clings to Olympus's peaks year-round.

According to legend, Dion was founded as a religious sanctuary back in the mists of time, but its constant water supply led both Philip and Alexander to change the character of the sacred site and establish military training camps here. Philip bivouacked at Dion before he marched south to conquer Greece, while Alexander drilled his men here before heading east to conquer Asia.

According to a story preserved by the 2nd-century-A.D. biographer Plutarch, it was at Dion that Alexander, then only 8 years old, first saw Bucephalos, the handsome black stallion soon to be his favorite mount. Philip bought the horse but found that neither he nor any of his men could ride it. Alexander asked his father if he could have a go at taming the creature. Muttering that if *he* could not tame the horse, an 8-year-old hardly could, Philip nonetheless agreed to give Alexander a chance. Immediately, Alexander turned Bucephalos so that he could not see his shadow, leapt up, and galloped away. When the young prince returned from his ride, Philip said, "My son, look for a kingdom equal to you. Macedonia is too small."

Although Dion—which sits by a narrow pass between Thessaly and Macedonia—was an important military camp first for the Macedonians and then for the Romans, it is much more than the Fort Bragg of antiquity. The Romans adorned Dion with a **theater** (bigger and better than the Hellenistic one, as was the Roman habit) and built **sanctuaries** to the healing god Asclepius, the nurturing goddess Demeter, and the Egyptian goddess Isis. In addition, of course, the Romans built **baths**—and baths being large structures, a good deal remains for you to explore. The site sprawls on both sides of a through road and it is not hard to get somewhat disoriented here, despite helpful information signs beside many of the ruins. Copies of statues found in the sanctuaries have been erected at the site; the originals are tucked away safely in the museum.

There's a lot to see at Dion, but I have to confess that some of my happiest visits have been spent picnicking under the trees—especially in spring, when the Greek wildflowers more than live up to their reputation. From your shady spot, you can make excursions through the site, following the course of a stoa, admiring the statue of Isis seemingly admiring her reflection in a pool, and imagining the day that Alexander, all of 22 years old, mounted Bucephalos and set off to conquer the world.

The Dion **museum** is a heartening example of a well-funded and well-cared-for provincial museum. An English-language video and the English-language museum labels help foreign visitors understand the importance of what they are seeing, while models of the ancient site make the Dion of Philip and Alexander easy to visualize. Exhibits include statues of the children of Asclepius (lined up as though posing for a family photo), grave monuments, votive offerings, mosaics and, best of all, a wonderful copper water organ probably made in the 2nd century A.D.; today it would be the hit of any music hall. A 1st-century-B.C. music critic described the tone of water organs as "sweet and joyful."

In July and August, the **Olympos Festival** (© 23510/76-041) presents concerts and plays at the ancient site.

WHERE TO STAY & EAT

Choose from several cafes and restaurants in the village near the Hotel Dion and also along the road that bisects the site and museum. An archaeologist friend reports eating well at the **Dionysos,** across from the museum, which serves good roast goat, *loukanika* (sausages), and the usual chops and salads. Expect to pay about 15€ for lunch or dinner unless you go overboard on the roast goat, which is priced by the kilo and will raise your tab a few more euros. For accommodations, see also accommodations in Litochoro (especially the Dion Palace Spa Hotel) and Ambelakia in chapter 12. An appealing place to stay in Dion is the little **Safeti** (www.safetis.gr; © 23510/46-272);

unfortunately, the Safeti's four cozy and well-appointed self-contained apartments (from 65€) are usually snapped up well ahead of time for longish winter and summer visits to the Mount Olympos area by Greeks.

Hotel Dion ★   The rooms here are good size, economically furnished, and pleasant; most have balconies. When I stayed here, the town was quiet all night—except for a few late-night motorcycles and some early-morning roosters. One problem: The owners are not always around, so if you stop here without a reservation, it may take some time to find them.

Dion, 60200 Macedonia. ✆ **23510/53-682.** 20 units. 70€. double. Rates include breakfast. Considerable reductions possible off season. MC, V. **Amenities:** Breakfast room/bar. *In room:* TV.

MOUNT ATHOS (THE HOLY MOUNTAIN) ★★★

130km (80 miles) SE of Thessaloniki

The most important thing to know about Mount Athos is that you can't just come here. And if you're a woman, you can't come here at all. In 1926, Athos was declared a Theocratic Republic. Although part of Greece, it is self-governing—hence, the need for an entry permit. Up-to-date information on permits should be available at two websites (**www.macedonian-heritage.gr/Athos** [make sure you use a capital "A"] and **www. ouranoupoli.com**) and at the **Holy Executive of the Holy Mount Athos Pilgrim's Bureau,** 14 Karamanli, Thessaloniki (✆ **2310/861-611**). Recently, there have been mutterings that antidiscrimination regulations of the European Common Market may force Athos to open its doors to women; to avoid potential complications, however, Mount Athos has refused any Common Market funds for restoration of its monasteries and it is highly unlikely that the bureaucrats of the Common Market will prove a match for the monks of Athos and their centuries of tradition.

Ouranopolis is the jumping-off point for Mount Athos, but it is an increasingly unappealing little town filled with souvenir shops. However, the handsome tower immortalized in Joyce Nankivell Loch's *A Fringe of Blue* still stands. Joyce Loch and her husband, Sydney, both Quakers, lived in Ouranopolis on and off from the 1920s to the 1960s and worked with villagers and refugees from Asia Minor. For some years, the tower was both the Lochs' home and a weaving school; today it houses exhibits.

There is almost always at least one boat a day at 9:45am from Ouranopolis to Mount Athos. In summer, additional departures are often scheduled.

If you can't go to Athos itself from Ouranopolis, take one of the **excursion boats** that cruise around the peninsula (tickets cost about 25€). The **Ouranopolis Port Authority** (✆ **23770/71-248**) usually has information on the excursion boats. (When Prince Charles visited Athos in 2004, Camilla Parker-Bowles circled the Holy Mount on the Royal Yacht.) The views of the rugged, pine-clad mountain promontory are superb, and you'll be able to see a number of the monasteries, most of which were built between the 9th and 19th centuries. Most look like villages from the outside, perched on astonishingly high and sturdy stone foundations and surrounded by massive walls.

The first, and still the most important, monastery, the **Great Lavra** or **Meyistis Lavras** (*lavra* means a community of monks), was founded around 960, and others quickly followed. In 1060, an imperial decree barred "every woman, every child, eunuch, smooth faced person, and female animal" from Athos, which suggests that

If you visit Mount Athos, you will walk almost everywhere, and stay and eat at the monasteries you have come to visit, which certainly simplifies things. "Simple" is a key word here—both your accommodations and food (Athos is a vegetarian's paradise) will be very basic, and usually only one meal a day is served. You may be cheered to know that the wine made on Athos and sold throughout Greece, including Tsantali white (not all of which is made here, despite its labels) is particularly refreshing. The Metochi Mylopotamou vintage made at the Great Lavra Monastery is also well regarded. Keep in mind that although most monasteries will not accept direct payment in cash for food and lodgings, you are expected to make a donation in the monastery's church.

As always, when walking in Greece, keep in mind the danger of fires, and be sure to dispose of any matches or cigarettes with care. Also, do not show up at the monasteries in the afternoon, when the monks are taking their siestas.

there had been incidents of inventive nonchastity over the years. In recent years, hens have been allowed onto Athos to produce eggs, and cats to catch vermin.

Today, there are 20 active monasteries, many visible from the sea, with at least that many again closed over the centuries. Solitary hermits still live on Athos, but most monks follow a communal rather than an isolated life. In fact, monastic life has had something of a revival; Father Gabriel, gardener at the Iviron Monastery, was quoted in the July 28, 1998, Athenian newspaper *Kathimerini* as saying, "More are interested in becoming monks than we are ready to accept." According to the same story, Father Gabriel has added to his gardening duties the preparation of a computer catalog of manuscripts and icons. When asked if this would take a very long time, he replied, "We've got all eternity."

The Most Important Monasteries on Mount Athos

The Great Lavra The first (about A.D. 960) monastery founded on Athos and hence the foremost, the Great Lavra has the red-painted katholikon characteristic of Athos's monasteries. Its 15th-century frescoes, especially those showing exuberant singers and dancers in the Chapel of Koukouzelissa, are delightful. Call ✆ **23370/23-758** to make a reservation to spend the night.

The Monastery of Chelandariou This monastery was founded in the 12th century by St. Sabbas of Serbia. Fortunately, Sabbas's father was the king of Serbia, which guaranteed a handsome endowment. Some scholars think that the lovely frescoes in the church here were done by the same painter who decorated the walls of Ayios Nikolaos Orfanos in Thessaloniki (p. 595). You can try to make a reservation here by calling ✆ **23370/23-797.**

The Monastery of Dionissiou This 14th-century monastery seems to grow right out of a rock above the sea. Its dizzily overhanging balconies are braced by precarious-looking wood supports. Favored by the emperor Alexios III Komnenos, Dionissiou has a superb collection of manuscripts, as well as an icon said to be the oldest on Athos. You can try to make a reservation by calling ✆ **23370/23-687** or by faxing 23370/23-686.

The Monastery of Iveron   Iveron, founded in the 10th century, looks from the sea like a medieval hill town—only the hill is actually the monastery's solid foundation. Call ✆ **23370/23-643** for overnight reservations.

The Monastery of Vatopedi   Founded only a decade after the Great Lavra, Vatopedi's long outline of red-and-white-tile-roofed buildings is clearly visible from the sea. Call ✆ **23370/23-219** for overnight reservations.

Where to Stay in Ouranopolis

Xenia ★★   The Xenia offers all the creature comforts you may have missed while visiting Athos, including several restaurants, fresh- and saltwater pools, riding, tennis, and its own beach, about 8km (5 miles) outside Ouranopolis. The large guest rooms have balconies, most have desks with good reading lamps, and all have excellent bathroom facilities; ask for one of the 40 rooms added in 2007 and 2008, most of which have sea views. The Xenia website sometimes offers greatly reduced rates, especially in winter.

Ouranopolis, 63075 Macedonia. www.xeniaouranoupolis.com. ✆ **23770/71-412.** Fax 23770/71-362. 886 units, including 28 bungalows. 130€–150€ double or bungalow. Rates include breakfast buffet. AE, DC, MC, V. **Amenities:** 2 restaurants; 2 bars; 2 pools; spa; tennis. *In room:* A/C, TV, hair dryer, minibar, Wi-Fi.

THE NORTHEASTERN AEGEAN ISLANDS

by John S. Bowman

Looking for a new or different experience with Greek islands, one that gives a sense that this is how Greeks live? The three covered in this chapter—Samos, Hios (Chios), and Lesvos (Mitilini)—might be the destination for you. Far removed from the Greek mainland and dispersed along the coast of Turkey, these islands are still relatively untouched by tourism. Vacationers here tend to be concentrated in a few resorts, leaving the interiors and much of the coast open to exploration.

Along their coasts, you'll find some of the finest beaches in the Aegean, and within the interiors richly forested valleys, precipitous mountain slopes, and exquisite mountain villages. These agricultural islands produce olives, grapes, and honey in abundance, providing the basis for excellent local cuisine.

The influence of Asia Minor is not as evident as you might expect, given the proximity of the Turkish coast. What you may notice is the sizable Greek military presence—certain areas of each island are occupied by the military and are off limits, which shouldn't bother you unless you're hiking or biking in the area. Travel between Greece and Turkey remains unrestricted, and relations between the two countries on a personal level seem amicable. Many travelers use the Northeastern Aegean islands as jumping-off points for Turkey; in particular, Samos (only 3km/2 miles away at the closest point) offers easy access to **Ephesus.**

Strategies for Seeing the Islands

Because the distances between islands are substantial, island-hopping by boat can be costly and time-consuming. Add to that the fact that each island is quite large, and it becomes clear that you're best choosing one or two islands to explore in depth rather than attempting a grand tour. Both **Olympic Air** and **Aegean Airlines** offer some interisland flights that are relatively inexpensive, frequent, and fast. If you travel by ferry, you'll find that departure times are more reasonable for travel from north to south, whereas traveling in the opposite direction usually involves departures in the middle of the night. Fly to Lesvos (Mitilini) if you insist on seeing all three. The islands are too large and the roads often too rough for mopeds to be a safe option; you'll find that if you want to get around it's necessary to rent a car.

SAMOS

322km (174 nautical miles) NE of Piraeus

The most mountainous and densely forested of the Northeastern Aegean isles, Samos appears wild and mysterious as you approach its north coast by ferry. The hills plunging to the sea are jagged with cypresses, and craggy peaks hide among the clouds. Samos experienced a series of wildfires during the summer of 2000, which briefly brought the island to the attention of the international press, but effects of that event have faded.

In recent years, Samos has played host to that form of mass tourism involving "package" groups from Europe. This is mostly confined to the eastern coastal resorts—Vathi, Pithagorio, and Kokkari—all of which have developed a generic waterfront of hotels, cafes, and souvenir shops. The rugged splendor of the island's interior continues to hide the most interesting and beautiful villages. Difficult terrain and a remote location made these villages an apt refuge from pirates in medieval times; in this age, the same qualities have spared them from tourism's worst excesses.

Although Samos has several fine archaeological sites, the island is most noted for its excellent beaches and abundant opportunities for hiking, cycling, and windsurfing. Those who remember nothing from studying geometry except the Pythagorean Theorem may be pleased to know that Pythagoas was born on Samos, about 580 B.C. Also, Samos is the best crossover point for those who want to visit **Ephesus ★★,** one of the most important archaeological sites in Asia Minor.

GETTING THERE   Although ferries connect Piraeus to Samos, the trip is long. The best way to get here is to fly.

By Plane   Both **Olympic Air** and **Aegean Airlines** offer several flights daily between Athens and Samos. Contact Olympic Air in Athens (🕿 **210/966-6666;** www. olympicair.com). Contact **Aegean Airlines** (🕿 **801/112-0000;** www.aegeanair.com). **Athens Airways** (**www.athensairways.com**) has also been listing some flights to Samos. The Samos airport is 3km (2 miles) from Pithagorio, on the road to Ireon; from the airport, you can take a taxi to Vathi (30€) or Pithagorio (20€).

By Boat   The principal port of Samos is **Vathi,** also called Samos; the other two ports are **Karlovasi** and **Pithagorio.** Ferries from the Cyclades usually stop at both Vathi and Karlovasi: Take care not to get off at the wrong port! There are daily boats (sometimes two) from Piraeus to Karlovasi (11–14 hr.) and Vathi (8–14 hr.); in the opposite direction, ferries travel daily or nearly daily from Samos to Mykonos (5½ hr.). Boats to Hios from Vathi via Karlovasi (5 hr.) travel three times per week; there is also a once-weekly Rhodes-Vathi-Lesvos-Alexandroupoli run. Boats (mostly hydrofoils) to the Dodecanese islands depart regularly from Vathi and Pithagorio. If you want to travel one-way to Turkey, Turkish ferries depart daily (Apr–Oct; less regular off-season); a visa is required for all American, Canadian, British, and Irish citizens who intend to stay for more than 1 day. Be sure to inquire in advance about current visa regulations with a local travel agency. For more information on visas, see "A Side Trip to Turkey: Kusadasi & Ephesus," below.

The Northeastern Aegean Islands

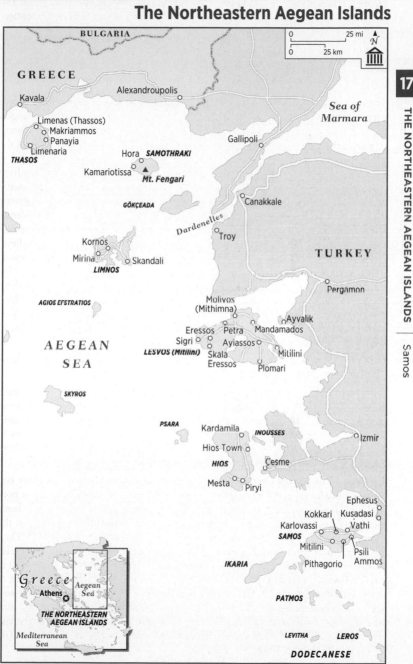

BULGARIA

GREECE

Kavala

Alexandroupolis

Sea of
Marmara

Limenas (Thassos)
Makriammos
Panayia
Limenaria

THASSOS

Gallipoli

Hora *SAMOTHRAKI*

Kamariotissa

▲ Mt. Fengari

GÖKÇEADA

Canakkale

Dardenelles

Troy

TURKEY

Kornos
Mirina
Skandali

LIMNOS

Pergamon

AGIOS EFSTRATIOS

Molivos
(Mithimna)

Ayvalik

AEGEAN

Eressos Petra Mandamados
Sigri
Ayiassos

SEA

LESVOS (Mitilini) Skala
Eressos
Plomari

Mitilini

SKYROS

PSARA

Kardamila

INOUSSES

Izmir

Hios Town

HIOS

Çesme

Mesta Piryi

Ephesus

Kokkari Kusadasi

Karlovassi Vathi

SAMOS

Mitilini

Pithagorio

Psili
Ammos

IKARIA

PATMOS

Greece

Aegean
Sea

Athens ✪

*THE NORTHEASTERN
AEGEAN ISLANDS*

*Mediterranean
Sea*

LEVITHA *LEROS*

DODECANESE

Vathi, Karlovasi & the Northern Coast

Vathi (aka Samos town), on the northeast coast, and **Karlovasi,** to the northwest, are the two principal ports of Samos and the island's largest towns. Neither is particularly exciting, and we recommend both as bases rather than as destinations in themselves.

Vathi becomes a slightly overextended resort town in high season but is beautifully situated in a fine natural harbor. An extensive development project in Pithagora Square and along the *paralia* (beachfront road) allows visitors to walk on a pedestrian pathway along the water and take in open-air concerts at the bandstand. The old town, **Ano Vathi,** rises to the hilltops in steep, narrow streets that hide a few tavernas and cafes.

Karlovasi is even less interesting as a town. Although it's adjacent to several of the best beaches on the island, it's spread out and offers fewer amenities than Vathi, although nearby is the recently opened, luxurious **Marnei Mare ★★** "retreat" (www.marneimare.gr)—three villas set in a natural and secluded estate. Most tourist facilities are clustered along the water at the west end of town, forming a tiny beach resort with several hotels, restaurants, grocery stores, and souvenir shops. The old town hovers above the lower town on the slopes of a near-vertical pillar of rock; the lovely small chapel of **Ayia Triada** is at the rock's summit.

The **north coast** of the island is wild and steep, with mountains rising abruptly from the water's edge. One of the most interesting areas to explore is the **Platanakia** region, known for its rushing streams, lush valleys, and picturesque mountain villages. A sequence of excellent **beaches** between Kokkari and Karlovasi includes the two finest beaches on the island, **Micro Seitani** and **Megalo Seitani;** you can reach them via a short boat ride or a somewhat long hike to the west of Karlovasi.

ESSENTIALS

VISITOR INFORMATION   There is an official **tourist office** at 107 Themistioklis Sofouli (© 22730/28-582), but it is easier to go directly to private travel agencies for information. Try one of the major travel agencies in Samos: **Rhenia Tours,** 15 Themistoklis Sofouli (© 22730/88-800; www.diavlos.gr/rhenia); and **Samina Tours,** 67 Themistoklis Sofouli (© 22730/87-000; www.samina.gr). Here you can make arrangements for accommodations and excursions (including excursions to Turkey, Patmos, and Fourni, as well as tours of Samos), rent cars, and so on. The **Diavlos** website (**www.diavlos.gr**) has information on ferries, attractions, and accommodations. Another website with useful information is **www.samos-travel.com**.

GETTING AROUND   By Bus   There's good public bus service on Samos throughout the year, with expanded summer schedules. The **Vathi bus terminal** (© 22730/27-262) is a block inland from the south end of the port on Kanari. The bus makes the 20-minute trip between Vathi and Pithagorio frequently. Buses also travel to Kokkari, the inland village of Mitilini, Pirgos, Marathokambos, Votsalakia beach, and Karlovasi. Schedules are posted in English at the bus terminal.

By Boat   From Karlovasi, there are daily excursion boats to **Megalo Seitani,** the best fine-sand beach on the island. A once-weekly around-the-island tour aboard the *Samos Star* is a great way to see the island's remarkable coastline, much of it inaccessible by car. The excursion boat departs from Pithagorio at 8:30am (a bus from Vathi departs at 7:30am), currently on Tuesday, and returns to Pithagorio at 5:30pm; the fare is 75€. Book with one of the travel agencies listed above. Most excursions depart from Pithagorio, although many offer bus service from Vathi an hour prior to departure; for descriptions, see "Pithagorio & the Southern Coast," below.

Samos

THE NORTHEASTERN AEGEAN ISLANDS

Vathi

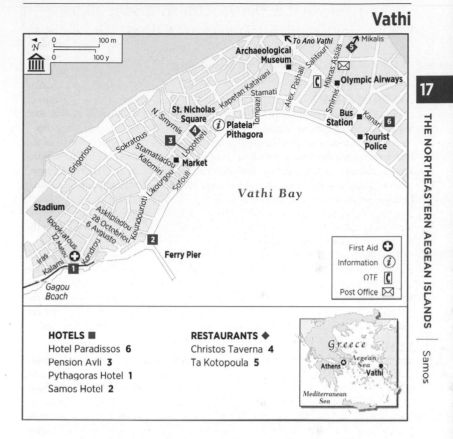

By Car & Moped **Autoplan,** 17 Themistoklis Sofouli (℗ **22730/23-555;** autoplan@internet.gr), and **Aramis Rent a Car,** at the pier in Vathi (℗ **22730/23-253;** www.samos-rentacar.com), offer good prices and selections. The least expensive car in high season is about 70€, including insurance and 100 free kilometers (62 miles). Mopeds go for 20€ to 30€ per day. But there are other agencies, so shop around.

By Taxi The principal taxi stand in Vathi is on Plateia Pithagora, facing the *paralia.* The fare from Vathi to Pithagorio is about 16€. To book by phone, call ℗ **22730/23-777** in Vathi, or 22730/33-300 in Karlovasi.

Bicycling For renting a bicycle, go online to **www.samos-travel.com**, where you will find that InterHermes, in Vathi (℗ **22730/28-833**), and AutoLand, in Kokkari (the beach resort just west of Vathi; ℗ **22730/92-825**), offer this service.

FAST FACTS The **banks** in Vathi are on the *paralia,* in the vicinity of Plateia Pithagora, and are open Monday through Thursday from 8am to 2pm, Friday from 8am to 1:30pm; most have ATMs. Most travel agents change money, sometimes at bank rates, and they're open later. The island's **hospital** (℗ **22730/83-100**) is in Vathi. **Internet access** his been available at Diavlos Internet Cafe (**www.diavlos.gr**) on the *paralia,* next to the police station; Diavlos is open daily from 9:30am to 11pm

May through October, but mornings only November through April. The **post office** (© **22730/27-304**) is on the same street as the Olympic Air office, 1 block farther in from the *paralia,* and 2 blocks from the bus station. The **telephone office** (**OTE;** © **22730/28-499**) is down the street from the Olympic Air office, in the direction of the archaeological museum. The **tourist police** (© **22730/81-000**) are on the *paralia,* by the turn into the bus station.

ATTRACTIONS

Archaeological Museum ★   This fine museum is two buildings at the south end of the harbor, near the post office. The newest building houses sculpture—the island's best sculptors traveled all over the Hellenistic world to create their art. The most remarkable work is a *kouros* (statue of a boy), which stands 5m (16 ft.) tall. The large and varied collection of bronze votives found at the Heraion is also impressive.

Kapetan Yimnasiarhou Kateveni (near park and behind town hall). © **22730/27-469.** Admission 3€, E.U. seniors 2€. Tues–Sun 8:30am–3pm. No parking.

Moni Vronta   The 15th-century fortified monastery of Moni Vronta is on a mountain overlooking the sea and the hilltop village of Vourliotes. Few if any monks live there these days, but a caretaker is usually about; if the gate is locked, try knocking—one of the soldiers from a nearby post may be around to let you in. Ask to see the *spileo* (cave), an old chapel, built into the thickness of the outer wall that holds a collection of ancient objects, some from the time of the monastery's founding.

Vourliotes. No phone. Free admission. Daily 8am–5pm. 23km (15 miles) west of Vathi; continue driving uphill about 2km (1 mile) past the village of Vourliotes (see below).

THREE HILL TOWNS ON THE NORTH COAST

Amid the densely wooded valleys, cascading streams, and terraced slopes of Samos's Platanakia region, hide many villages that sought to evade the pirates, who repeatedly ravaged all settlements visible from the sea. Three of the most picturesque of the surviving hill villages in this region are Manolates, Vourliotes, and Stavrinides.

Manolates is a 4km (2½-mile) drive uphill from the coast road. The village, until recently, was inaccessible by car, but once the paved road was built, many more visitors have come here to explore the steep, narrow cobblestone streets. There are several tavernas, numerous shops, and *kafenions* (coffeehouses, where the locals go).

Vourliotes, about 21km (14 miles) west of Vathi, was settled largely by repatriated Greeks from the town of Vourla, in Turkey. It's the largest producer of wine in the region, and the local wine is among the best on the island. Walk from the parking lot at the Moni Vronta turnoff to the charming central square. Try **Manolis Taverna,** on the left as you enter the square (© **22730/93-290**), which has good *revidokeft-edes,* a delicious local dish made with chickpea flour and cheese. Also on the square, across from Manolis, is a small market whose displays seem not to have changed in the past 50 years. Be sure to visit the monastery of **Moni Vronta** (aka Vrontiani), 2km (1 mile) above the town (see "Attractions," above).

Stavrinides, perched on the mountainside high above Ayios Konstandinos, is the least touristic of the Platanakia villages. Here the tavernas and the few shops cater primarily to the villagers. **Taverna Irida,** in the first square of the village, offers good, simple food. A walking path between Stavrinides and Manolates makes an exceptional outing; the route out from Stavrinides is signposted.

The easiest way to visit these towns is by car. The island buses are an option, if you don't mind the steep 4- to 6km (2½–3¾-mile) walk from the coastal road to the villages.

A Side Trip to Turkey: Kusadasi & Ephesus ★★

In high season, two boats a day make the run between Vathi and Kusadasi, Turkey, itself a popular resort, but of interest here as the gateway to the magnificent archaeological site at **Ephesus**. Although it's in Turkey now, Ephesus was a Greek city, famous, among other things, for its Temple of Artemis, one of the Seven Wonders of the Ancient World. A major city in the eastern Mediterranean, it fell to the Romans, and it was under their rule that an important Christian community and church were established here. Excursion boats depart from Vathi, and on certain days, an excursion also departs from Pithagorio. A round-trip ticket to Kusadasi that includes the boat fare, port fees, and the guided tour with the entrance fee costs about 100€. If you're not returning the same day, you'll need to investigate visa requirements. These are granted without difficulty at time of sailing and cost about $20 for Americans, C$50 for Canadians, £15 for U.K. citizens,10€ for Irish citizens, and A$25 for Australians; New Zealanders don't need a visa. The travel agencies recommended above will help you with arrangements.

An abundance of footpaths connect these villages—ask for routes. **Ambelos Tours,** in Ayios Konstandinos (☎ **22730/94-442;** folas@otenet.gr), operated by the friendly and knowledgeable Manolis Folas, is a useful resource.

BEACHES

The closest decent beach to Vathi is **Gagou,** 2km (1 mile) north of the pier. But the best beaches on Samos are found along the north coast, the most beautiful and rugged part of the island. The busy seaside resort of **Kokkari,** 10km (6 miles) west of Vathi, has several beaches in rock coves as well as the crowded stretch of sand running parallel to the town's main road. To find the smaller cove beaches, head seaward from the main square. Just west of Kokkari is **Tsamadou,** a short walk down from the coast road, which offers sufficient seclusion for nude sunbathing. Continue west past Karlovasi to find **Potami,** an excellent long pebble-and-sand beach with road access.

The two best beaches on the island, **Micro Seitani ★** and **Megalo Seitani ★**, are accessible only by boat or on foot. Boat excursions depart daily from the pier in Karlovasi. To get here on foot, continue past the parking lot, on a dirt road, for the beach at Potami; walking time to the first beach is 45 minutes. After about 5 minutes of uphill walking, the road splits—turn right, continuing to follow the coast. After another 5 minutes of walking, three obvious paths turn off to the right in close succession. Take the third, marked by a cairn, and follow the well-worn path another half-hour to Micro Seitani, a glorious pebble-and-cobble beach in a rocky cove. On the beach's far side, a ladder scales the cliff to the trail, which will take you, after an additional 30 minutes of walking, to Megalo Seitani, as incredible a stretch of sea sand as any in the Aegean. At the far end of Megalo Seitani are a few houses and a taverna.

OUTDOOR PURSUITS

BICYCLING   Samos has many dirt roads and trails perfect for mountain biking. The only obstacles are the size of the island, which limits the number of routes available for day trips, and the fact that much of the backcountry is off limits due to Greek military operations. Bike rentals, information about trails, and guided mountain-bike tours are available in Vathi, at **Bike** (✆ **22730/24-404**). The shop is open daily from 8:30am to 2pm and 5 to 9pm; it's behind the old church, opposite the port, on the market street. The bikes are high quality, and the rental includes helmet, pump, and repair kit; clipless pedals and shoes are also available for an extra charge. A basic aluminum-frame bike is 25€ per day; a full-suspension bike is 35€.

WALKING   Some of the best walking on the island is in and around the Platanakia region of Samos's north coast, where well-marked trails connect several lovely hilltop villages. Manolates and Vourliotes are among the villages on this network of trails. A trail goes from Manolates to the summit of Mount Ambelos, the second-highest peak on Samos at 1,153m (3,780 ft.); the demanding round-trip takes about 5 hours. Those seeking a more "professional" exploration of the truly natural Samos might try one of the outfits listed at "Tours/Special-Interest Trips in chapter 2.

WHERE TO STAY
Vathi

Hotel Paradissos   Despite a central location just off the *paralia* and a block away from the bus station, the walled garden and pool terrace here seem a world away from the traffic and dust of Vathi. Drinks and simple Greek foods are available all day at the poolside **bar.** The pool invites lingering, with lounge chairs and umbrellas for sunning, and shaded tables for meals or drinks. All guest rooms have balconies, although the views aren't great. Bathrooms are small, but they do have full tubs. Note that although there is air-conditioning in every room, it isn't turned on until sometime in July.

21 Kanari, Vathi, 83100 Samos.✆ **22730/23-911.** Fax 22730/28-754. 51 units. 95€ double. Rates include continental breakfast. MC, V. Closed Nov–Mar. **Amenities:** Restaurant; bar; pool; room service. *In room:* A/C, TV, hair dryer, minibar.

Pension Avli ✦   Although you won't find any luxuries here, you may enjoy the most charming, romantic pension on the island. Abundant bougainvillea fills the arcaded courtyard of this former 18th-century convent. Most rooms have been reno-vated within the last few years, but they are spartan, with minimal furnishings. Each tiny bathroom is encased entirely in a plastic shell, making a shower a surreal experi-ence. This is a place for those with big imaginations and small budgets.

2 Areos, Vathi, 83100 Samos.✆ **22730/22-939.** 20 units. 50€ double. No credit cards. Turn in from the *paralia* at Agrotiki Trapeza (down from Aeolis Hotel), turn left on town's market street, and you'll see the Avli's unassuming sign directly ahead. *In room:* No phone.

Pythagoras Hotel   This plain but comfortable family hotel, on a hill overlooking Vathi Bay, offers the best views in town from its nine seaside units and from the restaurant terrace. Guest rooms facing the road can be noisy—book ahead to ensure a unit on the water. Rooms and bathrooms are small, clean, and minimally furnished. The **cafe/restaurant** downstairs serves a good, inexpensive breakfast, light meals, and snacks from early morning to midnight. Hotel staff will meet you at the port or airport at any time, a generous offer given the frequency of early morning ferry arrivals.

12 Kallistratou, Kalami, Vathi, 83100 Samos. On the coast road, 600m (1,968 ft.) north of the pier. ✆ **22730/28-422.** Fax 22730/28-893. 19 units. From 50€ double. MC, V. **Amenities:** Restaurant; bar. *In room:* TV, Internet.

Samos Hotel   For travelers who want a modern hotel on the harbor with all (well, most of) the amenities, this is *the* place in Vathi. Right along the *paralia*, the hotel is subject to a certain amount of harbor noise. But the hotel is air-conditioned, making it somewhat insulated. Rooms are nothing special in size or decor, but beds and bathrooms are comfortable; most have balconies overlooking the harbor. Only about a 20-minute walk from Gagou Beach, this hotel is not for those seeking atmosphere.

11 Themistoklis Sofouli, 83100 Vathi. www.samos-hotels.com. © **22730/28-377.** 100 units. High season 90€ double; low season 70€ double. Rates include continental breakfast. MC, V. Parking by hotel. **Amenities:** 2 restaurants; 2 bars; Jacuzzi; pool; room service. *In room:* A/C, TV, fridge, hair dryer.

Ayios Konstandinos

This coastal town in the heart of the Platanakia region is a great base for touring the north coast of Samos. Ask Manolis Folas, of **Ambelos Tours** (folas@otenet.gr; © **22730/94-442**), about traditional houses for rent; each unit sleeps three and costs about 50€ per night.

Daphne Hotel ★ The Daphne is the finest small hotel on the island. Artfully incised into the steep hillside in a series of terraces, the hotel commands a fine view of the stream valley leading to Manolates and a wide sweep of sea. All rooms are moderate in size and have balconies with the same great view; bathrooms have both shower and tub. This is a good location for walkers, with many trails nearby to Manolates and other hill towns. Make your reservations well in advance, as this hotel is filled through much of the summer by European tour groups. There is free transportation to and from the airport or the port, due to the somewhat remote location, you'll probably want a car during your stay here.

Ayios Konstandinos, 83200 Samos. www.daphne hotel.gr. © **22730/94-138.** 35 units. 80€ double. Rates include breakfast. V. Take the 1st right after turning onto the Manolates road, 19km (12 miles) from Vathi. Closed Nov–Apr. **Amenities:** Restaurant; swimming pool w/bar; TV lounge. *In room:* A/C.

WHERE TO DINE
Vathi

The food along the *paralia* in Vathi is mostly tourist quality and mediocre; you'll find the best restaurants in the small towns away from the harbor. The local wines on Samos, for a long time, have been known for their excellence. (As Byron exclaimed, "Fill high the bowl with Samian wine!") **Samaina** is a good, dry white; **Selana,** a relatively dry rosé. The Greeks here also like sweet wines, with names such as Nectar, Doux, and Anthemis. Almost any restaurant will serve one or all of these choices.

Christos Taverna GREEK   This simple little taverna, under a covered alleyway decorated with odd antiques, is to the left off Plateia Pithagora, as you come up from the port. The food is simply prepared and presented; it comes in generous portions and is remarkably good. Try the *revidokeftedes,* a Samian specialty that is made with cheese fried in chickpea batter.

Plateia Ayiou Nikolaou. © **22730/24-792.** Main courses 7€–16€. No credit cards. Daily 11am–11pm. Parking on streets around a square.

Ta Kotopoula GREEK   Ta Kotopoula is on the outskirts of Vathi, somewhat hard to find but worth the trouble. From the harbor's south end, walk inland past the Olympic Air office and the post office, bearing right with the road as it climbs toward Ano Vathi. Where the road splits around a large tree, about 700m (2,296 ft.) from the harbor, you'll see the vine-sheltered terrace of this taverna on the left. The food is basic Greek fare, but the ingredients are exceptionally fresh—chicken being the specialty, as the name suggests. Local wine is available by the carafe.

Vathi. © **22730/28-415.** Main courses 7€–17€. No credit cards. Daily 11am–11pm. Parking near restaurant.

Ayios Konstandinos

Platanakia Paradisos GREEK   Paradisos is a large garden taverna at the Manolates turnoff from the coast highway; it has been in the Folas family for nearly 30
years and has been operating as a taverna for more than 100. Manolis Folas, the
owner, makes his own wine from the excellent Samian grapes. Mrs. Folas's *tiropita* is
made from local goat cheese wrapped in a flaky pastry. Live traditional music is performed Wednesday and Saturday nights in summer.

Ayios Konstandinos. © **22730/94-208.** Main courses 6€–17€. No credit cards. Daily 3–11pm. Parking
near restaurant.

VATHI AFTER DARK

"In" places change from year to year, but one of the hottest discos in Vathi has been
Metropolis, behind the Paradise Hotel. For bouzoukia, there's **Zorba's,** out of town
on the road to Mitilini. Various kinds of bars line the lanes just off the port. **Number
Nine,** at 9 Kephalopoulou, beyond the jetty on the right, is one of the oldest and best
known. For more sedate setting and music, try **Nefeli** bar/cafe along the harbor.

Pithagorio & the Southern Coast

Pithagorio, south across the island from Vathi, is a charming but overcrowded seaside
resort built on the site of an ancient village and harbor. Although this is a convenient
base for touring the southern half of Samos, the town exists primarily for the tour
groups that pack its streets in the summer. We recommend staying only for a day or
two to explore the nearby historic sites, then moving on to the more interesting and
authentic villages of the north coast.

ESSENTIALS

GETTING THERE   By Plane   The Samos airport is 3km (2 miles) from Pithagorio; from the airport, you can take a taxi into town for 20€.

By Boat   Ferries from the Cyclades typically don't stop at Pithagorio, so you'll need to
take a taxi or bus from Vathi. Near-daily hydrofoil service links Pithagorio and Patmos
(60–90 min.), Lipsi (1½–3 hr.), Leros (1½–3 hr.), Kalymnos (3–6 hr.), and Kos (3–4 hr.);
there are also excursion boats to Patmos four times weekly. Check the most current ferry
schedules at the **Pithagorio Municipal Tourist Office** (© **22730/61-389** or
22730/61-022; www.gtp.gr), or at **Pithagorio Port Authority** (© **22730/61-225**).

By Bus   Buses depart frequently for the 20-minute trip between Vathi and Pithagorio. Contact the **Vathi bus terminal** (© **22730/27-262**) for current schedules.

VISITOR INFORMATION   The **Pithagorio Municipal Tourist Office**
(© **22730/61-389** or 22730/61-022) is on the main street, Likourgou Logotheti, 1
block up from the *paralia*; its hours are daily from 8am to 10pm. Here you can get
information on ferries, buses, island excursions, accommodations, car rental, and just
about anything else. Pick up the handy *Map of Pithagorion,* which lists accommodations, attractions, and other helpful information.

GETTING AROUND   By Bus   The Pithagorio **bus terminal** is in the center of
town, at the corner of Polykrates (the road to Vathi) and Likourgou Logotheti. The
bus makes the 20-minute trip between Vathi and Pithagorio frequently. There are also
four buses daily from Pithagorio to Ireon (near the Heraion archaeological site).

By Boat   Summertime **excursion boats** from the Pithagorio harbor go to **Psili
Ammos beach** (on the east end of the island) daily, and to the island of **Ikaria** three

times weekly. A popular day cruise goes to **Samiopoula,** a small island with a single taverna and a long sandy beach. Boats leave daily at 9:15am and return to Pithagorio at 5pm; the fare of 35€ includes lunch. Four times a week, the *Samos Star* sails to **Patmos,** departing from Pithagorio at 8am and returning the same day at 4pm; travel time to Patmos is 2 hours, and the fare is 50€. A Sunday excursion to the tiny isle of **Fourni,** also aboard the *Samos Star,* gives you 6 hours to check out the beaches and sample the island's renowned fish tavernas; the boat leaves Pithagorio at 8:30am and the cost is 35€ per person. A once-weekly **around-the-island tour** aboard the *Samos Star* is a great way to see this island's coastline, much of it inaccessible by road. The excursion boat departs from Pithagorio at 8:30am (a bus from Vathi departs at 7:30am) on Tuesday and returns to Pithagorio at 5:30pm; the fare is 60€.

By Car & Moped   **Aramis Rent a Car** has a branch near the bus station in Pithagorio (© **22730/62-267;** www.samos-rentacar.com). It often has the best prices, but shop around.

By Taxi   The taxi stand is on the main street, Likourgou Logotheti, where it meets the harbor. The fare from Vathi to Pithagorio is 25€. To book by phone, call © **22730/ 61-450.**

FAST FACTS   **National Bank,** opposite the bus stop (© **22730/61-234**), has an ATM. A small **clinic** on Plateia Irinis, next to the town hall (© **22730/61-111**), is located 1 block in from the beach, near the port police. Access the Internet at **Nefeli** (© **22730/61-719**), a cafe on the *paralia's* north side (left, if you're facing the harbor), open from 11am to 2am daily. The rate is 5€ per hour for use of one of the two computers. The **post office** is several blocks up from the *paralia,* on the main street, past the bus stop. The **telephone office (OTE)** is on the *paralia,* near the pier (© **22730/61-399**). The **police** (© **22730/61-100**) are a short distance up Polikrates, the main road to Vathi.

ATTRACTIONS

Efpalinion Tunnel ★★   One of the most impressive engineering accomplishments of the ancient world, this 1,000m (3,280-ft.) tunnel through the mountain above Pithagorio was excavated to transport water from mountain streams to ancient Vathi. The great architect Efpalinos directed two teams of workers digging from each side, and after nearly 15 years they met within a few meters of each other. You descend into the tunnel, and then if you can muster the courage to squeeze through the first 20m (66 ft.)—the tunnel is a mere sliver in the rock for this distance—you'll see that it soon widens considerably, and you can walk another 100m (328 ft.) into the mountain. Even though a generator supposedly starts up in the event of a power outage, you might be more comfortable carrying a flashlight.

Pithagorio. © **22730/61-400.** Admission 4€ adults, 1.50€ students and E.U. seniors, free for youths 17 and under. Tues–Sun 8:45am–2:45pm. 3km (2 miles) northwest of Pithagorio; signposted off the main road to Vathi.

Heraion   All that survives of the largest of Greek temples is its massive foundation, a lone reconstructed column, and some copies of the original statuary. A forest of columns once surrounded this temple, so many that rival Ionian cities were so impressed that they rebuilt many of their ancient temples in similar style. The Temple of Artemis, in Ephesus, is a direct imitation of the great Samian structure. The Heraion was rebuilt and greatly expanded under Polycrates, in the 6th century B.C. It was damaged during numerous invasions and finally destroyed by a series of earthquakes.

Ireon. © **22730/95-277** or 22730/27-469 (the Archaeological Museum in Vathi). Admission 4€ adults, 1.50€ students and E.U. seniors, free for youths 17 and under. Tues–Sun 8am–2:30pm. 9km (5½ miles) southwest of Pithagorio; signposted off the road to Ireon.

BEACHES

In Pithagorio, the local beach stretches from Logotheti Castle, at the west side of town, several kilometers to Potokaki and the airport. Expect this beach to be packed throughout the summer. Excursion boats depart daily in the summer for **Psili Ammos,** 5km (3 miles) to the east. The daily boats also leave Pithagorio for **Samiopoula,** an island off the south coast with two good beaches.

On the south coast of the island, the most popular beaches are on Marathokambos Bay. The once-tiny village of **Ormos Marathokambos** has several tavernas and a growing number of hotels and pensions. Its rock-and-pebble beach is long and narrow, with windsurfing an option. A couple of kilometers farther west of Ormos Marathokambos is **Votsalakia,** a somewhat nicer beach.

WHERE TO STAY

Rooms in Pithagorio are quickly filled by tour groups, so don't count on finding a place here if you haven't booked well in advance. You can find a long listing of hotels in Pithagprio at **www.samos-hotels.com**, but you are advised to check them out on tripadvisor.com as many of the expensive ones are found wanting. I can recommend two of the more moderate.

Georgios Sandalis Hotel 🍴   Above Pithagorio, this homey establishment has a front garden bursting with colorful blossoms. The tastefully decorated rooms all have balconies with French doors. Back rooms face quiet hills and another flower garden, while the front units face a busy street and can be noisy. All rooms have kitchenettes, but only some have air-conditioning (there's an extra charge, if you use it). No meals are served on the premises, but breakfast can be had at reduced rates at family-owned **Enplo Café,** which is nearby, on the harbor. The friendly Sandalises are gracious hosts; they spent many years in Chicago and speak perfect English.

Pithagorio, 83103 Samos. http://samos-hotels.com/en/index.htm. © **22730/61-691.** 12 units. 50€ double. No credit cards. Head north on Polykrates (the road to Vathi); hotel is on your left, about 100m (328 ft.) from the bus station. Parking on adjacent streets. *In room:* A/C (in some), TV, kitchenette.

Hotel Zorbas 🍴   This place is more pension than hotel, but the rooms are comfortable. Seven units have great views of Pithagorio Harbor. The atmosphere is decidedly casual and friendly—the hotel lobby doubles as the Mathios family's living room. The hotel is on a steep hill on the north side of town, a healthy climb from the *paralia,* at the port police station. Rooms facing the sea have spacious balconies, with views over the rooftops to fishing boats docked in the harbor, while streetside rooms are a bit noisier and have no views. Breakfast is served on a terrace facing the sea.

Damos, Pithagorio, 83103 Samos. © **22730/61-009.** Fax 22730/61-012. 12 units. 55€ double. Breakfast extra 6€. No credit cards. Parking on adjacent streets.

WHERE TO EAT

Esperides Tavern INTERNATIONAL   This pleasant restaurant with a walled garden is a few blocks inland, and west of the main street. You'll find uniformed waiters and a dressier crowd. The Continental and Greek dishes are well presented and will appeal to a variety of palates—try the baked chicken with vegetables in season.

Pithagorio. © **22730/61-767.** Reservations recommended in summer. Main courses 7€–20€. No credit cards. Daily 6pm–midnight. No parking.

Varka ★ GREEK/SEAFOOD   This ouzeri/taverna is in a stand of salt pines at the south end of the port. Delicious fresh fish, grilled meats, and a surprising variety of *mezedes* (appetizers) are produced in the small kitchen. The grilled octopus, strung up on a line to dry, and the pink *barbounia* (clear gray mullet), cooked to perfection over a charcoal grill, are the true standouts of a meal here. The cafe pavilion by the water is a cool, breezy location for a drink or dessert.

Paralia, Pithagorio. ✆ **22730/61-088.** Main courses 7€–20€. MC, V. Daily noon–midnight. Closed Nov-Apr. Parking on adjacent streets.

HIOS (CHIOS)

283km (153 nautical miles) NE of Piraeus

"Craggy Hios," as Homer dubbed it—and he should know, as this is said to be his native home—remains relatively unspoiled, and that's why I continue to recommend it. Those seeking just to relax will find the black-pebble beaches on the southeast coast of the island well attended, but white-sand beaches on the west coast see far fewer people. The majestic mountain setting of **Nea Moni**—an 11th-century Byzantine monastery in the center of the island—and the extraordinary mosaics of its chapel make for an unforgettable visit. The mastic villages on the island's south side are among the most unusual medieval towns in Greece; the towns get their names from tree resin used in chewing gum, paints, and perfumes that grow nowhere else in the world.

The *paralia* of **Hios town** is likely to be your first glimpse of the island, and admittedly, it isn't an especially appealing sight—modern buildings and generic cafes have taken over what must once have been a fine harbor. Thankfully, a few pockets of the original town farther inland have survived earthquakes, wars, and neglect. The kastro, the mosque on the main square, the mansions of Kampos, and the occasional grand gateway (often leading nowhere) are among the signs of a more prosperous and architecturally harmonious past.

Essentials

GETTING THERE   By Plane   Both **Olympic Air** and **Aegean Airlines** offer several flights daily between Athens and Hios. Contact Olympic Air in Athens (✆ **210-966-6666;** www.olympicair.com) or **Aegean Airlines** (✆ **801/112-0000;** www.aegeanair.com). Olympic also offers flights once or twice a week from Lesvos (Mitilini) and Thessaloniki. If you arrive by plane, count on taking a cab into town at about 15€ for the 7km (4¼-mile) ride.

By Boat   From Piraeus, there's one daily Hios-bound car ferry (8–9 hr.); there's also a daily connection with Lesvos (3 hr.). Three ferries weekly serve Limnos (9 hr.) and Thessaloniki (16–19 hr.), two ferries weekly to Samos (5 hr.), and one weekly to Siros (5 hr.). Check with **Hios Port Authority** (✆ **22710/44-434;** www.gtp.gr) for current schedules.

VISITOR INFORMATION   The **Tourist Information Office,** on 18 Kanari (✆ **22710/44-389**), stocks free brochures, including maps; it's located on the second street from the north end of the harbor, between the harbor and the Central (Plastira) Square. In summer, it's open Monday to Friday from 7am to 2:30pm and 6:30 to 9:30pm, Saturday and Sunday from 10am to 1pm; the off-season sees reduced hours. Ask here (or at any travel agency) about free guided tours to some of Hios's major sites, sponsored by the island's government.

📎 **Have a Driver's License on Hios**

Anyone not carrying a driver's license from a country in the European Union must have an international driver's license to rent a car in Greece; but in most places, they will accept valid US and other national licenses. On Hios, however, car-rental agencies and the police tend to be strict about enforcing this. If you expect to rent a car on Hios, get an international driver's license before you leave your home country—the police here do enforce this regulation. Relatively easy and cheap to obtain, it can be issued through national automobile associations.

Another mine of information is **Chios Tours,** 4 Kokkali (✆ **22710/29-444;** www. chiostours.gr). The office is open Monday through Saturday from 8:30am to 1:30pm and 5:30 to 8:30pm. The staff will assist you with a room search, often at a discount.

GETTING AROUND **By Bus** All buses depart from one of the two bus stations in Hios town. The **blue buses** (✆ **22710/23-086**), which leave from the blue bus station, on the north side of the public garden by Plateia Plastira, serve local destinations such as Karfas, to the south, and Daskalopetra, to the north. The **green long-distance KTEL buses** (✆ **22710/27-507**) leave from the green bus station, a block south of the park, near the main taxi stand. Six buses a day depart to Mesta, eight a day to Piryi, five to Kardamila, and four to Emborio, but only two buses a week go to Volissos and Nea Moni. Fares are 2€ to 7€.

By Car Hios is a large island to explore, so I recommend a car. For advance reservations, try **Pangosmio Rent a Car** (✆ **2810/811-750;** www.pangosmio.gr). On the scene, try **Vassilakis Rent-A-Car** at 3 Evangelos Chandrs (✆ **22710/29-300**).

By Taxi Taxis are easily found at the port, though the taxi station is beyond the OTE, on the northeast corner of the central square. You can call ✆ **22710/41-111** or 22710/43-312 for a cab. Fares from Hios town run about 25€ to Piryi, 30€ to Mesta, and 40€ round-trip to Nea Moni.

Bicycling/Moped Hios is too large, and the hills too big, for most bicyclists; rent a motorbike, and if you're inexperienced with these, you're better off with a car.

FAST FACTS **Commercial Bank (Emboriki Trapeza)** and **Ergo Bank** are located at the harbor's north end, near the corner of Kanari. Both have ATMs and are open Monday through Thursday from 8am to 2pm, Friday from 8am to 1:30pm. The **hospital** is 7km (4¼ miles) from the center of Hios town (✆ **22710/44-301**). **Internet access** is available daily from 9am to midnight at Enter Internet Cafe, 98 Aegeou (✆ **22710/41-058**), at the *paralia*'s south end. One hour online costs 5€. The **post office** is at the corner of Omirou and Rodokanaki (✆ **22710/44-350**). The **telephone office (OTE)** is across the street from the tourist office, on Kanari (✆ **131**). The **tourist police** are headquartered at the harbor's northernmost tip, at Neorion 35 (✆ **22710/44-427**).

Hios Attractions

Argenti Museum and Koraï Library ★ Philip Argenti was the great historian of Hios, a local aristocrat who devoted his life and savings to the recording of island history, costumes, customs, and architecture. The museum consists largely of his personal collection of folk art, costumes, and implements, supplemented with a gallery of family portraits and copies of Eugene Delacroix's *Massacre of Hios,* a masterpiece depicting the Turkish massacre of the local population in 1822. The library is excellent, with much of its collection in English and French. If you're interested in local architecture and village life, ask to see the collection of drawings by Dimitris Pikionis (a renowned 20th-c. Greek architect). The drawings of the Kampos mansions and village houses are beautiful, and have yet to be published.

Koraï, Hios town. © **22710/44-246.** Museum admission 3€; free admission to library. Mon–Fri 8am–2pm; also 5–7:30pm on Fri; Sat 8am–12:30pm. Parking on adjacent streets.

Nea Moni ★★   The 11th-century monastery of Nea Moni is one of the great architectural and artistic treasures of Greece. The monastery is in a spectacular setting in the mountains overlooking Hios town. Its grounds are extensive—the monastery was once home to 1,000 monks—but the population has dwindled to several elderly nuns. The focus of the rambling complex is the *katholikon,* or principal church, whose square nave has eight niches supporting the dome. Within these niches are sequences of extraordinary mosaics, among the finest examples of Byzantine art. You can see the portrayals of the saints in the narthex, and a representation of Christ washing the disciples' feet. The museum contains a collection of gifts to the monastery, including several 17th-century icons. Also of interest is the cistern, a vaulted room with columns (bring a flashlight); and the small Chapel of the Holy Cross at the entrance to the monastery, dedicated to the martyrs of the 1822 massacre by the Turks (the skulls and bones displayed are those of the victims themselves). The long barrel-vaulted refectory is a beautiful space, its curved apse dating from the 11th century.

The bus to Nea Moni is part of an island excursion operated by KTEL, departing from the Hios town bus station Tuesday and Friday at 9am and returning at 4:30pm. The route takes you from Nea Moni to Anavatos to Lithi beach to Armolia and back to Hios town; it costs 25€ per person. A taxi will cost about 40€ round-trip from Hios town, including a half-hour at the monastery.

Nea Moni, 17km (11 miles) west of Hios town. No phone. Free admission to monastery grounds and katholikon; museum admission 3€ adults, 1€ students and E.U. seniors. Monastery grounds and katholikon daily 8am–1pm and 4–8pm; museum Tues–Sun 8am–1pm.

A Day Trip to the Mastic Villages: Piryi, Mesta & Olimbi ★

The most interesting day trip on Hios is the excursion to the **mastic villages** in the southern part of the island, which offer some of the best examples of medieval town architecture in all of Greece. Mastic is a gum derived from the resin of the mastic tree, used in candies, paints, perfumes, and medicines. It was a source of great wealth for these towns in the Middle Ages, and it is still produced in small quantities. All the towns were originally fortified, with an outer wall formed by an unbroken line of houses with no doors and few windows facing out. You can see this distinctive plan at all three towns, although in Piryi and Olimbi, the original medieval village has been engulfed by more recent construction.

Piryi is known for a rare technique of geometric decoration used on buildings, known as *ksisti.* In the main square, this technique reaches a level of extraordinary virtuosity. The beautiful **Ayioi Apostoli ★** church and every available surface of every building are banded with horizontal decorations in a variety of motifs. At the town center is the tower for which the village was named, now mostly in ruins. It was originally the heart of the city's defenses, and a final place of refuge during sieges.

Mesta ★ is the best-preserved medieval village on Hios, a maze of narrow streets and dark covered passages. The town has two fine churches, each unique on the island. **Megas Taxiarchis,** built in the 19th century, is one of the largest churches in Greece, and it was clearly built to impress. The arcaded porch, with its fine pebble terrace and bell tower, create a solemn and harmonious transition to the cathedral precinct. The other church in town, **Paleos Taxiarchis,** is located a few blocks below the main square. As the name suggests, this is the older of the two, built in the 14th century. The most notable feature here is the carved wooden iconostasis, whose surface is incised with miniature designs of unbelievable intricacy. If either church is closed, you can ask for the gatekeeper in the central square.

Olimbi is the least well known of the three. Though not as spectacular as Piryi, nor as intact as Mesta, it contains many medieval buildings. It has a central tower similar to that of Piryi, and stone vaults connect the houses.

Piryi is the closest of the three villages to Hios town, at 26km (16 miles); Olimbi and Mesta are within 10km (6 miles) of Piryi. The easiest way to see all three is by car. Taxis from Hios to Piryi cost about 25€. KTEL buses travel from Hios to Piryi eight times a day, and to Mesta five times a day. The bus to Piryi is 6€, and to Mesta 7€.

Beaches

There's no question that Hios has the best beaches in the Northeastern Aegean. They're cleaner, less crowded, and more plentiful than those of Samos or Lesvos, and would be the envy of any Cycladic isle.

The fine-sand beach of **Karfas,** 7km (4¼ miles) south of Hios town, is the closest decent beach to the town center; it can be reached by a local (blue) bus. The development of tourism in this town, however, ensures that the beach will be crowded.

The most popular beach on the south coast is **Mavra Volia (Black Pebbles),** in the town of Emborio. Continue over the rocks to the right from the man-made town beach to the main beach. Walking on the smooth black rocks feels and sounds like marching through a room filled with marbles. The panorama of the beach, curving coastline, and distant headland is a memorable sight. Buses from Hios town or Piryi (8km/5 miles away) run regularly to Emborio. A short distance south is the south coast's best beach, **Vroulidia** ★, a 5km (3-mile) drive in from the Emborio road. This white-pebble-and-sand beach, in a rocky cove, offers great views of the craggy coastline.

⊙ An Epic Experience

Little has been made of one of Hios's greatest claims to fame—as the birthplace and home of **Homer**—but knowing he is associated with this island adds a special buzz to your visit. In fact, it is one of several islands or cities around the eastern Mediterranean that lay claim to this honor, but Hios's is probably the oldest and strongest. In any case, Hios has been adopted as the home by a group of modern scholars in Homeric studies, and each year this **Academia Homerica** holds a weeklong session on Hios, where students and scholars gather to lecture, study, and learn more about Homer. Because most visitors will not be able to spend a week with Homer, I have a suggestion: Bring a paperback copy of the *Iliad* or the *Odyssey* to read here—on a beach or in a cafe. It's an experience you will treasure.

The west coast of the island has a number of stunning beaches. **Elinda Cove** shelters a long cobbled beach, a 600m (1,968-ft.) drive in from the main road, between Lithi and Volissos. Another excellent beach on this road is **Tigani-Makria Ammos,** about 4km (2½ miles) north of Elinda; turn at a sign for the beach, and drive in 1.5km (1 mile) to this long white-pebble beach. There's also a small, cove-sheltered cobbled beach about 300m (984 ft.) before the main beach. There are three beaches below Volissos, the best of which is Lefkathia, just north of the harbor of Volissos (Limnia).

South of Elinda, the long, safe beach at **Lithi Bay** is popular with families. Of the several tavernas, I can recommend **Ta Tria Adelphia** (**The Three Brothers;** ✆ **22710/73-208**). It's the last taverna you come to as you're walking along the beach.

The beaches of the north coast are less remarkable. **Nagos** (4km/2½ miles north of Kardamila) is a charming town in a small, spring-fed oasis, with a cobble beach and two tavernas on the water. This beach can get very crowded—the secret is to hike to the two small beaches a little to the east. To find them, take the small road behind the white house near the windmill.

Where to Stay

CHIOS TOWN

Chios Chandris Hotel   For those who prefer an in-town modern hotel with resort-type facilities within walking distance of the town's attractions, this is the place to be. Rooms are of standard size and decor, but there are suites and studios for those who want something a bit roomier; almost all units have views overlooking the port of Hios town. During the summer, you can take your meals or drinks at the poolside cafe. What recommends this place is the fact that after a day of enjoying other places in town or around the island, you can stroll back in about 10 minutes and be in the pool.

2 Euyenias Handri (in the port), 82100 Hios. www.chandris.gr. ✆ **22710/44-401.** 139 units. 125€ double; 190€–200€ suite or studio. DC, MC, V. Rates include breakfast. Parking adjacent to hotel. **Amenities:** Restaurant; 2 bars; pool; room service; tennis courts nearby; Wi-Fi in public areas. *In room:* A/C, TV, hair dryer, Internet, kitchenette (in some), minibar.

Voulamandis House ★ ☺   Although about 6.4km (4 miles) from the center of Chios Town, this is such a delightful place that many would feel it is well worth the short trip. (Free parking would make it worthwhile to rent a car to take excursions around the island.) It's a mansion on a 4.8-hectare (12-acre) estate—in fact, a working farm that provides many of the ingredients for the breakfasts and meals served here. The Voula-mandis family makes you feel like a guest at their country home, not at a hotel. You're only 3.2km (2 miles) from the Karfas beach (see above), and boat trips to the beaches on the island's south coast can be arranged. Ideal for a family, and with free Wi-Fi and free parking, this can provide a true bargain as well as a most pleasant stay on Chios.

117 Fragovouni, 82100 Kampos. ✆ **22710/44-500.** Fax 22710/44-600. 10 units. 60€ double; 70€ apt. Rates include breakfast. AE, DC, MC. Dogs accepted. **Amenities:** Restaurant; babysitting; room service for breakfast. *In room:* A/C, TV, fridge, hair dryer; Wi-Fi.

KARFAS

Karfas, 7km (4½ miles) south of Hios town, around Cape Ayia Eleni, is a resort area exploding with groups in summer. It has a fine-sand beach lined with resort hotels.

Golden Sand Hotel ☺   For those who prefer to be on a beach, away from the bustle of a city, Karfas offers numerous accommodations, of which this is the finest. Built in 1989, it's been well maintained and offers many of the activities of the typical Greek resort hotel—Greek music/folk-dancing nights, weekly barbecue, and theme nights. Almost all rooms have views overlooking the sea—insist on one. Drinks and meals can be enjoyed poolside. As Greek luxury resorts go, this is low key, and all the more enjoyable for being so.

Karfas Beach, 7km (4½ miles) from Hios center, 82100 Hios. www.goldensand.gr. ✆ **22710/32-425.** 108 units. 125€–145€ double. Rates include buffet breakfast. AE, MC, V. Parking on premises. **Amenities:** 2 restaurants; 2 bars; children's playground; pool; room service. *In room:* A/C, TV, hair dryer, Internet, minibar.

KARDAMILA

Kardamila, on the northeastern coast, is our choice among the resort towns because it's prosperous, self-sufficient, and not at all touristy.

Hotel Kardamila ★ This modern, and moderate, resort hotel was built for the guests and business associates of the town's ship owners and officers, and it has its own small cobbled beach. The guest rooms are large and plain, with modern bathrooms and balconies overlooking the beach. It is under the management of another good local hostelry, the Hotel Kyma, so the service is good.

Kardamila, 82300 Hios. ✆ **22710/23-353.** Fax 22710/23-354. (Contact kyma@chi.forthnet.gr for reservations.) 32 units. 120€ double. Rates include breakfast. No credit cards. Closed Nov–Apr. *In room:* A/C.

VOLISSOS

This hilltop village is one of the most beautiful on the island. A fine Byzantine castle overlooks the steep streets of the town, which contain numerous cafes and tavernas. Volissos is too far north to be a convenient base for touring the whole island, but if you want to get to know part of it, you couldn't choose a better focus for your explorations.

Volissos Traditional Houses ★ The care with which these village houses have been restored is unique on this island, if not in the whole northeastern Aegean. The beamed ceilings, often supported by forked tree limbs—a method of construction described in the *Odyssey*—are finely crafted and quite beautiful. Built into the stone walls are niches, fireplaces, cupboards, and couches. The houses and apartments are distributed throughout the village of Volissos, so your neighbors are likely to be locals rather than fellow tourists. Each apartment and house has a small kitchen, a spacious bathroom, and one or two bedrooms. The largest units (on two floors of a house) have two bedrooms, sitting rooms, kitchens, and large terraces. Most have views of the sea. There are shops in the village that can satisfy most basic needs.

Volissos, Hios. volissos@otenet.gr. ✆ **22740/21-421** or 22740/21-413. 16 units. 60€–100€ double. Closed Nov–Apr. No credit cards. *In room:* A/C (in some), TV (in some), no phone.

MESTA

The best-preserved medieval fortified village on Hios, Mesta is a good base for touring the mastic villages (see above) and the island's south coast.

Pipidis Traditional Houses ★ These four homes, built more than 500 years ago, have been restored and opened by the Greek National Tourism Organization as part of its Traditional Settlements program. The houses have a medieval character, with vaulted ceilings and irregularly sculpted stone walls (covered in plaster and whitewash). One unfortunate aspect of these dwellings is the dearth of natural light: If a room has any windows, they're small and placed high in the wall. Each house comes equipped with a kitchen, a bathroom, and enough sleeping space for two to six people.

Mesta, Hios. ✆ **22710/76-029.** 4 units. 65€ 2 persons; 90€ 4 persons. No credit cards. Closed Nov–Apr. *In room:* Kitchen; no phone.

Where to Eat

HIOS TOWN

If you're just looking for a cheap midday snack, go to the large Platea Vounakiou, at the far end of the Hios waterfront, where vendors set up tents and sell souvlaki and other finger foods—a most enjoyable (and frugal) way to take a meal in Hios town.

Hios Marine Club GREEK   This simple taverna serves the standard Greek dishes, pasta, grilled meats, and fish—but it's good. Don't be put off by the ugly yellow-and-white concrete facade. It's on the bay at the edge of town, just south of the port, 50m (164 ft.) beyond Hotel Chandris.

1 Nenitousi. ☎ **22710/23-184.** Main courses 6€–19€. MC, V. Daily noon–2am. Park on adjacent streets.

Hotzas Taverna GREEK   Hotzas is a taverna that offers a basic but well-prepared selection. It's the best option in a town not known for its restaurants. The summer dining area is a luxuriant garden, with lemon trees and abundant flowers. There's no menu; you choose from a few unsurprising but delicious offerings each night. Many of the dishes are meat-based, but some are fish-based—and squid is always available. This place isn't easy to find: Take Kountouriotou in from the harbor, and look for Kondili, the first right turn after a major road merges at an oblique angle from the right; after this it's another 50m (164 ft.) before the taverna appears on your left.

3 Yioryiou Kondili. ☎ **22710/42-787.** Main courses 6€–20€. No credit cards. Mon–Sat 6–11pm. Park on adjacent street.

LANGADA

Yiorgo Passa's Taverna ★ GREEK/SEAFOOD   Langada is a fishing village with a strip of five or six outdoor fish tavernas lining the harbor. Our favorite of these is Yiorgo Passa's Taverna, the first on the left, as you approach the waterfront. As in most Greek restaurants, fish is priced per kilogram. At first it sounds expensive, but divided among two or four diners, it's about what you'd expect to pay at home. And you can't put a price on the warm and friendly ambience. *Note:* There are evening dinner cruises to Langada from Hios; check with Chios Tours (see "Visitor Information," earlier) for details.

Langada. ☎ **22710/74-218.** Fish from 50€ per kilo. No credit cards. Daily 11am–2am. 20km (12 miles) north of Hios town, on the Kardamila road.

MESTA

Messaionas Taverna ★ GREEK   You will almost certainly have come to Mesta to visit the 14th-century Paleos Taxiarchis church, with its remarkable carved wooden iconostasis, so while you're here, take a meal at this taverna on the main square, long a favorite. The menu features a variety of *mezedes*, many with variations on traditional dishes. The stuffed tomatoes with pine nuts and raisins are delicious, as are the fried dishes such as *domatokeftedes* (tomatoes with herbs) or *tiropitakia* (cheese balls).

Mesta. ☎ **22710/76-050.** Main courses 6€–18€. No credit cards. Daily 11am–midnight. Parking on adjacent streets.

LESVOS (MITILINI)

348km (188 nautical miles) NE of Piraeus

Roughly triangular Lesvos—now called Mitilini in many Greek publications—is the third-largest island in Greece, with a population of some 120,000. As a large, bustling island, it long failed to bother itself with attracting tourists, but in recent years, it has been developing as a destination. In particular, it has been promoting itself as the birthplace of Sappho, the ancient poet.

The three principal towns—**Mitilini, Molivos,** and **Eressos**—are near the corners of the triangle. Mitilini and Molivos are about as different as two towns on the same island could possibly be. Mitilini is a working port town, low on sophistication or pretension, with little organized tourism but lots of local character. Molivos is a picture-postcard seaside village, a truly beautiful place; but in the summer, it exists only for tourism. Due to its remote location, Eressos is a good destination for a day trip, but not a recommended base for touring the island.

Not to be missed are the Archaeological and Theophilos museums, in Mitilini; the town of **Mandamados** and its celebrated icon (the east-coast road, btw. Mandamados and Mitilini, is the most scenic on the island); the 1.5km-long (1-mile) beach of **Eressos;** and the labyrinthine streets of Molivos's castle-crowned hill.

Getting around on Lesvos is complicated by the presence of two huge tear-shaped bays in the south coast, which split the island at its center. Because bus schedules are not designed for day-trippers, this is one island where you'll want a car to get around.

GETTING THERE   By Plane   Both **Olympic Air** and **Aegean Airlines** offer several flights daily between Athens and Lesvos (Mitilini); both also offer occasional flights to Thessaloniki. Contact Olympic Air, in Athens (ⓒ **210/966-6666;** www. olympicair.com) or **Aegean Airlines** (ⓒ **801/112-0000;** www.aegeanair.com). **Athens Airways** (www.athensairways.com) has also been listing some flights to Mitilini. The **airport** (ⓒ **22510/61-490** or 22510/61-590) is 7km (4 miles) south of Mitilini. There's no bus to the town; a taxi will cost about 15€.

By Boat   The principal port of Lesvos is Mitilini, from which almost all the ferries arrive and depart, although there is some ferry traffic through the west-coast port of Sigri. There's one ferry daily to Mitilini from Piraeus, stopping at Hios (10–12 hr.); there are also several ferries weekly from Rafina to Sigri (9 hr.). There are daily boats, in both directions, between Mitilini and Hios (3 hr.). Two boats call weekly at Mitilini from Kavala (10 hr.) and Thessaloniki (10–13 hr.), stopping at Limnos on the way. There's also one ferry a week from Siros (9 hr.). Check schedules with a local travel agent,

---

Remembering Sappho in Lesvos

In recent years, Lesvos—because of its associations with the poet Sappho (ca. 612 B.C.?)—has become a favorite destination of lesbians from many parts of the world. Although little is known about Sappho's life, it is accepted that she was born here; Eressos, in the far west corner, is now the favored site, and as such, has become a popular destination. It is also accepted that she was the leader of some sort of circle of young women; certainly some of her finest verses express warm feelings toward females. But it is not really clear that she was herself a lesbian—she married and had a daughter. Little of her poetry survives, but what there is has retained the admiration of readers and critics. So by all means, come to Lesvos in tribute to Sappho, but don't make a big deal with the locals out of associating the island with modern lesbians—the locals are not especially pleased about this. And don't forget that the tribute that authors really want is that their works be read.

Greek Travel Pages (www.gtp.gr), the **Mitilini Port Authority** (✆ **22510/28-827**), or **Sigri Port Authority** (✆ **22530/54-433**).

Once you get to Lesvos, double-check the boat schedule for your departure, as the harbor is extremely busy in the summer, and service is often inexplicably irregular.

Mitilini & Southeast Lesvos

With an ambience more like that of a big mainland city than a Greek island port, Mitilini isn't to everyone's taste. Your first impression is likely to be one of noise and traffic. Commercial development has resulted in a modern generic beachfront; the only signs of a more auspicious past are the cathedral dome and the considerable remains of a hilltop castle. Still, once you leave the *paralia,* there's little or nothing in the way of amenities for tourists, which can be refreshing for those who enjoy seeing how others actually live. In the vicinity of Ermou (the market street), Mitilini's crumbling ocher alleys contain a mix of traditional coffeehouses, artisans' studios, ouzeries, stylish jewelry shops, and stores selling antiques and clothing. Although good restaurants are notably absent in the town center, a few authentic tavernas lie on the outskirts of town.

ESSENTIALS

VISITOR INFORMATION The Greek National Tourism Organization (EOT) has turned its functions over to the **North Aegean Islands Tourism Directorate.** Its office is at 6 James Aristarchou, 81100 Mitilini (✆ **22510/42-511;** fax 22510/27-601). Primarily an administrative center, the office is not especially set up to provide hands-on help for tourists. It's open daily from 8am to 2:30pm, with extended hours in the high season. The **tourist police** (✆ **22510/22-276**) may also be helpful, but private travel agencies are your best bet for information.

GETTING AROUND   By Bus There are two bus stations in Mitilini, one for local and the other for round-the-island routes. The **local bus station** (✆ **22510/28-725**) is near the harbor's north end, by the (closed) Folklife Museum and across from the Commercial Bank (Emporiki Trapeza). Local buses on Lesvos are frequent, running every hour from 6am to 9pm most of the year. The destinations covered are all within 12km (7½ miles) of Mitilini, and include Thermi, Moria, and Pamfilla to the north, and Varia, Ayia Marina, and Loutra to the south. The most expensive local fare is 6€. The schedule is hard to read, but ticket sellers can decipher it. You can catch the **round-the-island KTEL buses** (✆ **22510/28-873**) in Mitilini, at the port's south end, behind Argo Hotel. There's daily service, in summer, to Kaloni and Molivos (four times), Mandamados (once), Plomari (four times), and Eressos and Sigri (once each).

By Car Rental prices in Mitilini tend to be high, so shop around. There are many choices, but for those more comfortable with a well-known brand, try the **Avis Agency** at the airport, or in town, at 99 Koundouriotou (along the left arm of the harbor; ✆ **22510/42-910**). Summer daily rates start at around 100€, with unlimited mileage.

By Taxi Lesvos is a big island. The one-way taxi fare from Mitilini to Molivos is about 50€; from Mitilini to Eressos or Sigri, it's about 70€. The main taxi stand in Mitilini is on Plateia Kyprion Patrioton, a long block inland from the port's southern end; there's a smaller taxi stand at the port's north end, near the local bus station.

FAST FACTS The **area code** for Mitilini is 22510, for Molivos (Mithimna) and Eressos 22530, and for Plomari 22520. There are **ATMs** at several banks on the port, including the Ioniki Trapeza and Agrotiki Trapeza (both south of the local bus station). **Vostani Hospital** (✆ **22510/43-777**), on P. Vostani, southeast of town, will take care of emergencies. **Glaros Laundry** (✆ **22510/27-065**), opposite the tourist police, near the ferry pier, is open from 9am to 2pm and 6 to 8pm; the turnaround time is usually 24 hours. The **post office** and the **telephone office (OTE)** are on Plateia Kyprion Patrioton, 1 block inland from the town hall, at the south end of the port. The principal **taxi stand** is also on Plateia Kyprion Patrioton. The **tourist police** (✆ **22510/22-776**) are located just east of the ferry quay.

ATTRACTIONS

Archaeological Museums of Mitilini ★ The excellent Mitilini archaeological museum has been augmented by a large new museum a short distance up the hill toward the kastro. The museums have the same hours, and the price of admission includes both locations. The new museum presents Roman antiquities of Lesvos and some finds from the early Christian basilica of Ayios Andreas, in Eressos. The highlight of its collection is a reconstructed Roman house, from the 3rd century B.C., whose mosaic floors depict scenes from comedies of the poet Menander, and from classical mythology. The exhibits are thoughtfully presented, with plenty of explanatory notes in English. A rear building houses more marble sculpture and inscribed tablets, while the main museum contains figurines, pottery, gold jewelry, and other finds from Thermi, the Mitilini kastro, and other ancient Lesvos sites.

7 Eftaliou, Myrina. ✆ **22510/28-032.** Admission 4€ adults, 1€ students and E.U. seniors. Tues–Sun 8:30am–3pm. A block north of the tourist police station, just inland from the ferry pier.

Kastro Perched on a steep hill north of the city, the extensive ruins of Mitilini's castle are fun to explore and offer fine views of city and sea from the ramparts. The kastro was founded by Justinian, in the 6th century A.D., and was restored and enlarged, in 1737, by the Genoese. The Turks also renovated and built additions to the castle during their occupation. In several places, you can see fragments of marble columns in the castle walls—these are blocks from a 7th-century-B.C. Temple of Apollo, taken by the Genoese. Look for the underground cistern at the north end of the castle precinct: This echoing chamber is a beautiful place, with domed vaults reflected in the pool below. In summer, the castle is sometimes used as a performing-arts center.

8th Noemvriou, Mitilini. ✆ **22510/27-297.** Admission 3€ adults, 1€ students and E.U. seniors. Tues–Sun 8am–2:30pm. Just past the new Archaeological Museum, turn right on the path to the kastro.

Theophilos Museum ★ One of the most interesting sights near Mitilini is this museum in the former house of folk artist Hatzimichalis Theophilos (1868–1934). Most of Theophilos's works adorned the walls of tavernas and ouzeries, often painted in exchange for food. Theophilos died in poverty, and none of his work would have survived if it weren't for the efforts of art critic Theriade (see below), who commissioned

---

📷 Excursion to a Mountain Village

An enjoyable destination for a day trip is the hamlet of **Ayiassos**, 23km (14 miles) west of Mitilini. The town, built on the foothills of Mount Olympus, consists of traditional gray-stone houses (with wooden "Turkish" balconies, often covered in flowering vines), narrow cobblestone lanes, and small churches. Here, local craftspeople still turn out their ceramic wares by hand. Excursion buses can bring you from Mitilini, or you can share a taxi (about 70€ for the ride and a reasonably moderate wait).

A Side Trip to Pergamum in Turkey

From Mitilini, there's a direct connection to Turkey via its port of Ayvalik, a densely wooded fishing village that makes a refreshing base camp from which to tour the ancient Greek site of **Pergamum.** The acropolis of Pergamum is sited on a dramatic hilltop, with substantial remains of the town on the surrounding slopes. The complex dates back to at least the 4th century B.C., and there are remains from this period through Roman and Byzantine times. It is one of Turkey's most important archaeological sites. All-inclusive 1-day tours to Pergamum—including round-trip boat fare, bus ride to the site, and guided tour—cost about 100€; inquire at Mitilini travel agencies such as **Dimakis Tours,** 73 Koundouriotou (℃ 22510/27-865), or **Aeolic Cruises Travel Agency,** 47A Koutouriotou (℃ 22510/46-601). Ships to Turkey usually sail three times a week, more often in high season, if the demand is there. A passport is required, but no visa is required for a 1-day visit. However, U.S., British, Irish, Canadians, and Australians need a visa for even an overnight; it costs between 45€ and 55€, but is good for 90 days in Turkey. Your visa is issued at the Customs House upon your arrival in Ayvalik.

the paintings on display here during the last years of the painter's life. These primitive watercolors depicting ordinary people, daily life, and landscapes are now celebrated and have been exhibited at the Museum of Folk Art, in Athens. Be sure to take in the curious photographs showing the artist dressed as Alexander the Great. As the museum may be closed for renovations, you should call before setting out to visit it.

Varia. ℃ **22510/41-644.** Admission 3€. Tues-Sun 9am-1pm and 4:30-8pm. 3km (2 miles) south of Mitilini, on airport road, next to Theriade Museum.

Theriade Library and Museum of Modern Art   The Theriade Library and Museum of Modern Art is in the home of Stratis Eleftheriadis, a native of Lesvos who emigrated to Paris and became a prominent art critic and publisher. (Theriade is the Gallicized version of his surname.) On display are copies of his published works, including *Minotaure* and *Verve* magazines, as well as his personal collection of works by Picasso, Matisse, Miró, Chagall, and other modern artists.

Varia. ℃ **22510/23-372.** Admission 3€. Tues-Sun 9am-1pm and 5-8pm. 3km (2 miles) south of Mitilini, on airport road, next to Theophilos Museum.

WHERE TO STAY
Moderate

Theofilos Paradise Boutique Hotel ★★   This is bit pricey and showy for this corner of the Aegean, but not compared to such hostelries elsewhere, and for some who have come this far, it may be a welcome bargain. Originally an early 1900s mansion, it has now expanded to include two adjacent buildings—if you can reserve early enough, insist on the mansion. Furnishings are more decorator's bourgeois than traditional Greek but all kinds of creature comforts are provided—a spa, hydromassage shower, flatscreen TV in rooms, pool with its bar, underground parking. It has rooms and facilities for travelers with disabilities and is also specifically gay friendly. (And pets are accepted on prior request.) Finally, it is in the neighborhood of Kioski, with its many traditional and fine old homes and away from the town's hustle and bustle.

7 Skra, Mitilini, located in 81000 Lesvos. www.theofilosparadise.gr. ✆ **22510/43-300.** 24 units. 85€–110€ double. Rates include breakfast. MC, V. **Amenities:** Restaurant; bar; pool; sauna;. Wi-Fi. *In room:* A/C, TV, hair dryer, minibar.

Inexpensive

Hotel Erato   On a busy street leading away from the port, this hotel offers convenience, cleanliness, a friendly and helpful staff, and a noise level marginally below that in many portside hotels. Most of the small, bright rooms have balconies facing the street, some with a view over the traffic to Mitilini Bay; there is also a fine park in front of the hotel. The four-story hotel was converted from a medical clinic and retains an atmosphere of institutional anonymity; on the positive side, it's well maintained. *Note:* If you intend to pay by credit card, inform the desk well in advance of your planned departure.

2 P. Vostani, Mitilini, 81000 Lesvos. www.filoxenia.net/hotels/erato.htm. ✆ **22510/41-160.** 22 units. 90€ double. MC, V. **Amenities:** Bar. *In room:* A/C, TV, minibar.

Hotel Sappho   The Sappho is a no-nonsense but conveniently located hotel, offering simple accommodations at moderate rates. Nine rooms have balconies facing the port (and can be a bit noisy in the morning); the rest have no balconies and face a sunny rear courtyard. All units have wall-to-wall carpets, white walls, minimal furnishings, and tiny bathrooms with showers. A breakfast room, on the second floor, has an outdoor terrace with a fine port view.

31 Palou Kountourioti, Mitilini, 81000 Lesvos. www.filoxenia.net/hotels/sappho.htm. ✆ **22510/28-415.** 29 units. 70€ double. Continental breakfast 7€. No credit cards. **Amenities:** Restaurant; bar; Internet; room service. *In room:* A/C.

WHERE TO EAT

Mitilini has more portside cafes than your average bustling harbor town. A cluster of chairs around the small lighthouse at the point heralds the most scenic (as well as the windiest) of the many small ouzeries that specialize in grilled octopus, squid, shrimp, and local fish. Some of the best restaurants are a short taxi ride outside the city.

Averof 1841 Grill   GREEK   This taverna, located midport, near the Sappho Hotel, is one of the better grills around, and one of the only restaurants in Mitilini center worth trying. Its beef dishes are particularly good. Try any of the tender souvlaki dishes or the lamb with potatoes.

Port, Mitilini. ✆ **22510/22-180.** Main courses 6€–19€. No credit cards. Daily 7am–5pm and 7–11pm.

O Rembetis   GREEK   Kato Halikas is a hilltop village on the outskirts of Mitilini, and although this simple taverna might be hard to find, it's well worth the effort. At the south end of the terrace you can sit beneath the branches of a high sycamore and enjoy a panoramic view of the port. The food isn't sophisticated or surprising, but it's very Greek, and the clientele is primarily local. There's no menu, so listen to the waiter's descriptions or take a look in the kitchen—there's usually fresh fish, in addition to the taverna standards. The wind can be brisk on this hilly site, so bring a jacket, if the night is cool. The best way to get here is by taxi; the fare is about 10€ each way.

Kato Halikas, Mitilini. ✆ **22510/27-150.** Main courses 6€–18€. No credit cards. Daily 8pm–midnight.

Salavos   GREEK   Despite its location on the busy airport road, this small taverna is one of the best in Mitilini. A garden terrace in back offers partial shelter from road noise. The seafood is fresh and delicious; try the calamari stuffed with feta, vegetables, and herbs. The restaurant is popular with locals, who fill the place on summer nights. As you travel south from Mitilini toward the airport, it's about 3km (2 miles) from town, on the right. Taxi fare is about 8€ each way.

Mitilini. ℂ **22510/22-237.** Main courses 5€–18€. No credit cards. Daily noon–1am.

MITILINI AFTER DARK

In Mitilini, there's plenty of nightlife action at both ends of the harbor. Several of the cheaper and more informal such as **La Notte** and **Hott Spott** are found on Koundouriotou, the street facing the harbor at the east side (left looking seaward). The more sophisticated places are off the harbor's south end. Outdoor **Park Cinema,** on the road immediately below the stadium, and **Pallas,** on Vournazo (by the post office), are both open May through September. Summer occasionally brings professional entertainment to the Kastro.

Molivos & Northeast Lesvos

Molivos (aka Mithimna) is at the northern tip of the island's triangle. It's a highly picturesque, castle-crowned village, where mansions of stone and pink-pastel stucco are capped by red-tile roofs. Balconies and windowsills are decorated with geraniums and roses.

The town has long been popular with package-tour groups, especially during the summer months. Souvenir shops, car-rental agencies, and travel agents outnumber local merchants, and the restaurants are geared toward tourists. Despite this, it is a beautiful place to visit and a convenient base for touring the island.

ESSENTIALS

GETTING THERE   By Bus   KTEL buses (ℂ **22510/28-873**) connect Molivos with Mitilini four times daily in the high season. The Molivos bus stop is just past the Municipal Tourist Office, on the road to Mitilini.

By Taxi   The one-way taxi fare from Mitilini to Molivos is about 50€.

VISITOR INFORMATION   The **Municipal Tourist Office,** 6 J. Aristarchou, on the road heading down to the sea (ℂ **22530/71-347**), is housed in a tiny building next to the National Bank. It's open Monday through Friday. **Panatella Holidays,** 2 Possidons (ℂ**2530/715-20;** www.panatella-holidays.com) can book car rentals, accommodations, and excursions. Both the tourist office and Panatella are open daily in summer from 8:30am to 9:30pm.

GETTING AROUND   By Car   There are numerous rental agencies in Molivos, and rates are comparable to those in Mitilini.

By Boat   Boat taxis to neighboring beaches can be arranged at the port or in a travel agency (see Panatella Holidays under "Visitor Information," above).

By Bus   Tickets for day excursions by bus can be bought in any of the local travel agencies. The destinations include Thermi/Ayiassos (60€), Mitilini town (35€), Sigri/Eressos (60€), and Plomari (65€); the excursions are offered once or twice each week in the summer.

FAST FACTS   An ATM can be found at the **National Bank,** next to the Municipal Tourist Office, on the Mitilini road. The **Internet** can be accessed at **Communication and Travel** (ℂ **22530/71-900**), on the main road to the port. The **police** (ℂ **22530/71-222**) are up from the port, on the road to the town cemetery; the **port police** (ℂ **22530/71-307**) are—where else?—on the port. The **post office** (ℂ **22530/71-246**) is on the path circling up to the castle—turn right (up), past the National Bank.

ATTRACTIONS

Kastro   The hilltop Genoese castle is better preserved than Mitilini town, but it's much less extensive and not as interesting to explore. There is, however, a great view from the walls, worth the price of admission in itself. There's a stage in the southwest corner of the courtyard, often used for theatrical performances in the summer. To get here by car, turn uphill at the bus stop and follow signs to the castle parking lot. On foot, the castle is most easily approached from the town, a steep climb no matter which of the many labyrinthine streets you choose.

Molivos. No phone. Admission 3€ adults, 1€ students and E.U. seniors. Tues–Sun 8:30am–3pm.

Mandamados Monastery ★   Mandamados is a lovely village on a high inland plateau, renowned for the remarkable icon of the Archangel Michael in the local monastery. A powerful story is associated with the creation of the icon: It is said that during a pirate raid, all but one of the monks were slaughtered. This one survivor, emerging from hiding to find the bloody corpses of his dead companions, responded to the horror of the moment with an extraordinary act. Gathering the blood-soaked earth, he fashioned in it the face of man, an icon in relief of the Archangel Michael. This simple icon, its lips worn away by the kisses of pilgrims, can be found at the center of the iconostasis, at the back of the main chapel.

Mandamados. Free admission. Daily 6am–10pm. 24km (15 miles) east of Molivos, 36km (23 miles) northwest of Mitilini.

BEACHES

The long, narrow town beach in Molivos is rocky and crowded near the town, but becomes sandier and less populous as you continue south. The beach in **Petra,** 6km (3¾ miles) south of Molivos, is considerably more pleasant. The beach at **Tsonia,** 30km (19 miles) east of Molivos, is only accessible via a difficult rutted road, and isn't particularly attractive. The best beach on the island is 70km (44 miles) southwest of Molivos, in **Skala Eressos,** on the southwestern coast.

SHOPPING

Molivos is dominated by tacky souvenir shops. To find more authentic local wares, you'll have to explore neighboring towns. **Mandamados,** known as a center for pottery, has numerous ceramics studios. **Eleni Lioliou** (✆ **22530/61-170**), on the road to the monastery, sells brightly painted bowls, plates, and mugs. **Anna Fonti** (✆ **22530/61-433**), on a pedestrian street in the village, produces plates with intricate designs, in brilliant turquoise and blue. Also in Mandamados is the diminutive studio of icon painter **Dimitris Hatzanagnostou** (✆ **22530/61-318**), who produces large-scale icons for churches and portable icons for purchase.

WHERE TO STAY
Moderate

Delphinia Hotel and Bungalows ★ ☺   Often rated the best hotel on Lesvos, one of the major attractions of this white-stucco and gray-stone resort is its panoramic setting above the Aegean, but for families it will be the many activities. A path leads 200m (656 ft.) from the hotel to a fine-sand beach and a recreation complex with saltwater swimming pool, snack bar, and tennis courts (the latter illuminated for night games). The hotel rooms are simple, with small, shower-only bathrooms. The 57 bungalows are more spacious: The living room has a couch that pulls out to provide an extra bed, most bathrooms include a bathtub, and each unit has either a large terrace or a balcony. Breakfast at the hotel is served on a terrace, while the bungalows include free room service for breakfast only. The second-floor rooms in the bungalows are the most spacious, have the best views, and cost a bit more.

Molivos, 81108 Lesvos. www.greekhotel.com. © **22530/71-373.** 125 units. 95€–115€ double; 130€–150€ 2-person bungalow. Rates include buffet breakfast. AE, DC, V. Parking adjacent. 1.6km (1 mile) from town center. **Amenities:** 2 restaurants; 2 bars; babysitting; basketball; children's playground; pool; room service; table tennis; 3 night-lit tennis courts; volleyball; free Wi-Fi in public areas. *In room:* A/C, TV, fridge, hair dryer, minibar.

Hotel Olive Press   This charming hotel is—you guessed it—an old converted olive press and, as such, is not much to look at from the outside. But its great attraction is its location, right on the beach. The rooms are on the small side but comfortable, with terrazzo floors, handsome furnishings, and bathtubs. Some of the units have windows opening onto great sea views, with waves lapping beneath. The inner courtyard has several gardens. Staff is gracious and friendly. On the downside is that the rear rooms can be noisy in July and August, when young people gather at a popular bar nearby.

Molivos, 81108 Lesvos. www.olivepress-hotel.com. © **22530/71-205.** 50 units. 100€) double; 140€ studio. Rates include buffet breakfast. AE, DC, V. Closed Nov–May. **Amenities:** Restaurant; bar; small pool. *In room:* Fridge (in studios), kitchenette.

Inexpensive
Sea Horse Hotel   Set among a cluster of relatively new Class C hotels below the old town, right along the port, is this smaller, homier hotel. Rooms are tidy, if fairly basic. All units come with a balcony facing the sea; four also have minimal kitchen facilities. On-site are a restaurant and an in-house travel agency.

Molivos, 81108 Lesvos. www.seahorse-hotel.com. © **22530/71-630.** 16 units. 80€. Continental breakfast 7€. No credit cards. **Amenities:** Restaurant; travel agency. *In room:* A/C, TV, fridge (in some), hair dryer.

WHERE TO EAT
Captain's Table ★ SEAFOOD/VEGETARIAN   Right on the harbor at Molivos, this is many visitors' favorite restaurant in the area. It's run by Melinda, an Australian, and her Greek husband, Theo. Although the emphasis is now on fresh grilled fish, the menu still offers some of Melinda's excellent trademark vegetable dishes, or Theo's roast lamb or pork fillets wrapped in bacon. There are even curries, Italian gnocchi, and fresh mussels with house white, if some variety is to your taste. Live bouzouki music is played 3 nights a week. Needless to say, the restaurant is crowded in high season.

The Harbor, Molivos. © **22530/71-241.** www.lesvosvacations.com/captainstable.htm. Main courses 8€–22€. V. Daily 11am–1am.

Octopus SEAFOOD   One of the oldest restaurants on the harbor of Molivos, the Octopus has had to serve tasty food in order to survive the tides of fashion. It specializes in grilled fish and meats but offers a selection of other dishes, such as peppers stuffed with spicy cheese, for instance. And your waiter can not only help you assemble your meal, but he can also advise you about the island's attractions.

The Harbor, Molivos. © **22530/71-317.** Main courses 6€–19€. No credit cards. Daily 11am–1am.

Tropicana ★ CAFE/ICE CREAM   Stroll up into the old town to sip a cappuccino or have an ice cream at this outdoor cafe, which offers classical music and a relaxed ambience. Owner Hari Procoplou, learned the secrets of ice creamery in Los Angeles.

Molivos. © **22510/71-869.** Snacks/desserts 3€–16€. No credit cards. Daily 8am–1am.

MOLIVOS AFTER DARK

Those seeking a bit of culture should ask at the Tourist Office about the occasional theatrical performances at the kastro looming over the town. Young travelers will have no trouble finding clubs and music to their taste, but those seeking something more indigenous will want to head for **Vangelis Bouzouki** ★ (no phone), Molivos's top acoustic bouzoukia club. It's located west from Molivos, on the road to Efthalou, past the Sappho Tours office. After about a 10-minute walk outside of town, you'll see a sign that points to an olive grove. Follow it for another 500m (1,640 ft.) through the orchard until you reach a clearing with gnarled olive trees and a few sheep. When you see the circular cement dance floor, surrounded by clumps of cafe tables, you've found the club. Have some ouzo and late-night *mezedes*, and sit back to enjoy the show.

PLANNING YOUR TRIP TO GREECE

Greece remains one of the world's oldest and premier destinations for travelers and a visit there should be an occasion for sheer enjoyment—even exultation. There is no denying, however, that as this guidebook goes to press, the news and images coming out of Greece have been unsettling, and remain unsettled. Greece's finances, economy, government, and society all appear to be in turmoil.

Most museums and archaeological sites have remained open, but often with reduced hours (and even days of closure). If Greece's economic difficulties continue, it is possible that some stores, restaurants and hotels may change the times that they are open, or even close. Not to worry: there are more than enough other hotels, restaurants and shops that we recommend to help you have a great trip. Assuming that Greeks do adopt the necessary reforms by the time this guide is in your hands, we believe that most visitors will be able to go about their travels without being unduly inconvenienced. Our best advice is to go to **www.frommers.com** and click your way through to the Online Update for Greece.

Planning ahead has always been advisable for any trip, but with the economic crisis that Greece has been experiencing since 2009, a new layer of warnings comes into play: Many prices of hotels in particular and hours of admission to museums and archaeological sites have been in more than usual flux. Although we have tried to account for these changes, we are not oracles (so to speak).

Still, as with any destination, the ease, comfort, and pleasure of your time in Greece will be greatly improved with some planning ahead. This chapter provides a variety of planning tools, including information on how to get there; tips on accommodations;

Strike While the Museum Is Open!

Remember that **strikes** can close museums and archaeological sites without warning. Decide what you want most to see, and go there as soon as possible after you arrive. If possible, phone the site or museum you are about to visit just before you head there; much information given out by hotels, websites, and even Greek National Tourism offices is wrong.

and quick, on-the-ground resources. One constant we cannot stress enough: If you are planning to visit Greece during the peak season—from July through August, and even from mid-May to mid-September—you are advised to make reservations for airline fights, hotels, and even major cultural events well in advance.

GETTING THERE

By Plane

The vast majority of travelers reach Greece by plane, and most arrive at the Athens airport—officially **Eleftherios Venizelos International Airport** (ATH), sometimes referred to by its new location as "the Spata airport." **Thessaloniki International Airport** (Macedonia; SKG) in northeastern Greece is an alternative for those who might like to make their way south but it has far fewer connecting flights to foreign cities.

Four airlines offer direct flights from North America to Athens: Continental, Delta, Olympic Air and USAir (Many airlines these days belong to an "alliance" or code-sharing group so you might be able to use or earn frequent-flyer miles with one of the other members.) All the other airlines make stops at some major European airport, where a change of planes is usually required. Once you're on the Continent, you'll find that nearly all the major European airlines fly to Greece. There are also countless airlines from countries all over the world that provide direct or indirect connections. Ryanair, the bargain airline based in Dublin, makes some flights to Greece, as does Belleair, with its home base in Tirana, Albania.

By Car

Many Europeans drive down into Greece—and some North Americans may wish to bring rented cars in. (Make sure a car rented in another country is allowed to be taken to Greece.) Drivers often come from Italy via ferry, usually disembarking at Patras; the drive to Athens is about 210km (130 miles). Others enter from the Former Yugoslavian Republic of Macedonia, or FYROM. (The road from Albania, although passable, doesn't attract many tourists.) There are no particular problems or delays at the border crossings, providing all your papers are in order.

If you come through Skopje, FYROM, the road via Titov Veles to the southeast leads to the border, where it picks up an expressway down to the edge of Thessaloniki (242km/150 miles). Over to the west, there is a decent-enough road via Vitola, FYROM, that leads to Florina, Greece (290km/180 miles); that road then continues east to Thessaloniki (another 161km/100 miles) or south to Kosani (another 89km/55 miles). A long day's drive!

DRIVING YOUR OWN VEHICLE   To bring your own vehicle into Greece, valid registration papers, an international third-party insurance certificate, and a driver's license are required. Make sure you have adequate insurance, because many Greek drivers do not. Valid E.U. drivers' licenses are accepted in Greece. as are most United States and Canadian licenses, but technically you should have an International Driver's License and you are advised to get one so as to forestall any problems at the border. (National automobile associations issue them.) A free entry card allows you to keep your car in the country up to 4 months, after which another 8 months can be arranged without you paying import duty. Check with your own car insurance company to make sure you are fully covered.

In any case, arm yourself with a good up-to-date map such as the ones published by Baedeker, Hallwag, Michelin, or Freytag & Berndt. For information on car rentals, prices of gasoline (petrol), unusual conditions and other matters peculiar to driving in Greece, see "By Car" in the "Getting Around" section

By Train

There is train service to Greece from virtually all major points in Europe, although the trains tend to be slow and uncomfortable in the summer. A Eurailpass is valid for connections all the way to Athens or Istanbul and includes the ferry service from Italy. Endless types of passes are now offered—long stays, short stays, and combinations with airlines, among others. Note that North Americans must purchase their Eurailpasses before arriving in Europe. For information, see **www.raileurope.com**.

By Ship

Probably most people traveling to Greece from foreign ports these days are on cruise ships, but there are still many who come on other ships—mainly from Italy. There is also occasional service from Cyprus, Egypt, Israel, and Turkey. Brindisi, Italy, to Patras is the most common ferry crossing, about a 10-hour voyage, with as many as seven departures a day in summer. There is also regular service, twice a day in summer, from Ancona and Bari, once daily from Otranto, and two or three times a week from Trieste or Venice. Most ferries stop at Corfu or Igoumenitsa, often at both; in summer, an occasional ship will also stop at Kefalonia.

If you want to learn more about the ferry services between Greece and foreign ports, the best website is Paleologos Agency's **www.ferries.gr**. Britons might try the London-based agency **Viamare Travel,** Graphic House, 2 Sumatra Rd., London NW6 1PU (© **0870/410-6040;** www.viamare.com). The **Superfast Ferries Line,** 157 Leoforos Alkyonidon, 16673 Athens (© **210/969-1100;** www.superfast.com), offers service between Ancona and Patras (17 hr.), or between Ancona and Igoumenitsa (15 hr.); also between Bari and Patras (12 hr.) or between Bari and Igoumenitsa (8 hr.). Not all these so-called superfast ferries actually save that much time if you take into consideration boarding and debarking. In addition, their fares are almost twice as much as those of regular ferries.

On the regular ferries, one-way fares during high season from Brindisi to Patras at press time cost from about 75€ for a tourist-class deck chair to about 135€ per person to share an inside double cabin. Vehicles cost at least another 75€ to 150€. **Note:** The lines usually offer considerable discounts on round-trip/return tickets. Fares to Igoumenitsa are considerably cheaper, but are by no means a better value unless your destination is nearby. Because of the number of shipping lines involved and the variations in schedules, we're not able to provide more concrete details. Consult a travel agent about the possibilities, book well ahead of time in summer, and reconfirm with the shipping line on the day of departure.

GETTING AROUND
By Plane

Compared to the cheaper fare classes on ships and ferries, air travel within Greece can be expensive, but we recommend it for those pressed for time and/or heading for more distant destinations (even if the planes don't always hold strictly to their schedules). Until the late 1990s, **Olympic Air** maintained a monopoly on domestic air travel and had little incentive to improve service. Eventually it declared bankruptcy, and it was not until 2009 that it was purchased by the Greek-based Marfin Investment Group, which is proceeding with a major overhaul and improvement of services—better computerized booking, reducing delays, and more hospitable flight attendants. It should be said that Olympic has had one of the best safety records of any major airline.

Book as far ahead of time as possible (especially in summer), reconfirm your booking before leaving for the airport, and arrive at the airport at least an hour before departure; the scene at a check-in counter can be quite hectic.

Olympic Air has offices in Athens, though most travel agents sell tickets. (For online booking, **www.olympicair.com**) It offers **mainland** service to Aktaion Preveza, Alexandroupolis, Ioannina, Kalamata, Kavala, Kastoria, Kozani, and Thessaloniki. As for **islands,** Olympic services Astipalea; Corfu (aka Kerkira); Iraklion, Chania, and Sitia, Crete; Hios (aka Chios); Ikaria; Karpathos; Kassos; Kastellorizo; Kefalonia; Kos; Kithira; Leros; Limnos; Milos; Mykonos; Mitilini (aka Lesvos); Naxos; Paros; Rhodes; Samos; Santorini (aka Thira); Skiathos; Skyros; Siros; and Zakinthos.

Olympic's domestic flights leave from the new international airport at Spata. Most flights are to or from Athens, although during the summer there may be some inter-island service. The baggage allowance is 15 kilos (33 lb.) per passenger, except with a connecting international flight; even the domestic flights generally ignore the weight limit unless you are way over. Smoking is prohibited on all domestic flights.

A round-trip ticket costs double the one-way fare. To most destinations within Greece from Athens, round-trip fares (including taxes) at this writing have been about 180€. From Athens to the nearer destinations, fares drop to about 130€. As you can see, such fares are not especially cheap, but there's no denying that for those with limited time, air travel is the best way to go. Ask, too, if Olympic still offers reduced fares for trips Monday through Thursday and trips that include a Saturday-night stay.

Only one other airline provides a real alternative to Olympic: **Aegean Airlines.** Check **www.aegeanair.com**, which allows you to order e-tickets. Its prices now pretty much match those of Olympic but are sometimes significantly cheaper. Their service is limited, but includes Alexandroupolis, Chania, Chios, Corfu, Ioannina, Iraklion, Kavala, Kos Mitilini, Mykonos, Patras, Rhodes, Samos, Santorini, and Thessaloniki. They also offer direct flights to London, Paris, Rome, Brussels, Barcelona, Madrid, Milan, Moscow, Bologna, Cyprus, and several major German cities. Foreign travel agents and travel booking websites may not be aware of Aegean Airlines, so visit the airline's actual website. People who have been flying Aegean for several years now find the airline reliable, safe, and hospitable.

In recent years, two other airlines have started up: **Athens Airways** (www.athens airways.com) and **Sky Express** (www.skyexpress.gr). Both offer limited service between Athens and various major cites and islands. Sky Express actually seems to be more like a charter airline. You are invited to look into their respective websites, but we must state that we cannot yet recommend these airlines based on either our own or friends' personal experience.

Note: Most Greek domestic tickets are nonrefundable, and changing your flight can cost you up to 30% within 24 hours of departure and 50% within 12 hours.

By Car

Driving in Greece is a bit of an adventure, but there's no denying that it's the best way to see the country at your own pace. By and large, the public transportation system outside of the main cities simply doesn't arrange its schedules for the convenience of tourists. **Note:** Greece has one of the highest accident rates in Europe, probably due somewhat to treacherous roads, mountain terrain, and poor maintenance of older cars as much as to reckless driving—although Greeks are certainly aggressive drivers. Athens is a particularly intimidating place in which to drive at first, and parking spaces are practically nonexistent in the center of town. (Main routes in and out of cities are sometimes signed by white arrows on blue markers.) A few of the major cities are linked to Athens by modern expressways with tolls; as these highways are currently being upgraded—and sections are to be privatized—it is difficult to tell the exact toll charges, but the toll for Athens to Thessaloniki, for instance, has been about 5€ and may well go up. Accidents must be reported to the police for insurance claims.

If you intend to do a fair amount of driving, acquire a good, up-to-date map before you set off. The best source is a British shop that allows for online ordering, **www. themapstore.com**.

The **Greek Automobile Touring Club (ELPA)**, 395 Mesoyion, 11343 Athens (© **210/606-8800**), with offices in most cities, can help you with all matters relating to your car, issue **International Driver's Licenses,** and provide **maps and information** (© **174,** 24 hr. daily). ELPA's emergency road service number is © **104.** Though the service provided by the able ELPA mechanics is free for light repairs, definitely give a generous tip.

The price of gasoline fluctuates considerably from week to week and from service station to service station, but as of the time this guide went to press it was about 1.75€ per liter—which works out to about US$9.75 for an American gallon. There is no shortage of gasoline stations in all cities, good-size towns, and major tourist centers, but if you are setting off for an excursion into one of the more remote mountain areas or to an isolated beach, fill up on gas before setting out.

CAR RENTALS   You will find no end of car-rental agencies throughout Greece, both the familiar international ones and many Greek firms. There is considerable variation in prices, although rates in high season are shockingly high. But we'd be wary of renting from some local agency just because it seems a bit cheaper: if anything goes wrong with your car while out in the countryside, they will probably not be able to do much to help you.

Many cars have a standard shift; if you must have an automatic, make sure in advance that one is available (and be prepared to pay extra). In high season you are

---

📎   **Warning on Car Rentals & Licenses**

Legally, all non-E.U. drivers in Greece are required to carry an International Driver's License. In practice, most car-rental agencies will rent to Americans and other non-E.U. drivers with their national driver's licenses, although they usually have to have been licensed for at least 1 year. (One major exception is on the island of Hios, where the International Driver's License is usually required.) This is fine as long as you

don't get involved in an accident—especially one involving personal injury. Then you could discover that your insurance is voided on a technicality. Meanwhile, you run the risk of an individual policeman insisting that you must have the international license. Best, then, is to obtain one before leaving home (from your national automobile association) or from the **Greek Automobile Touring Club** (EPLA; see above).

TAXI tips: FARES, ZONES & SURCHARGES

Certainly in Athens and several other large cities, travelers may prefer a **taxi** to driving themselves. Here are some tips that will help you understand and navigate the taxi system as you travel in Greece:

○ Taxi rates are in constant (upward) flux, so the rates you see here are the ones in effect as we go to press. First, (if it's before midnight), check to see that the number next to the Euro display on the meter is **"1"** and not **"2"**—the latter is the setting for rates for midnight to 5am or outside the city limits (about double the regular rate). If that's not the case, indicate that you notice.

○ All fares are subject to change (by law, that is), but at the time this guide went to press, the meter is allowed to start at the basic 1.20€ as you set off—check to see if this is the case. Drivers have been known to start with a higher number already registered; or they leave the meter off, then try to extort a larger fare from you. Even if you don't speak a word of Greek besides "taxi,"

point at the meter and say "meter." The basic rate is higher between midnight and 5am.

○ The fare from and to the airport in Athens has been fixed at 35€ except between midnight and 5am when it is 50€. (The fare depends on the *arrival* time at the destination.) The minimum fare for any trip in and around Athens and Piraeus is 3.10€ and 4€ for the rest of the country. But you shouldn't pay much more than 15€ for a trip within Athens itself.

○ At least in the major cities you should be able to ask for receipt from the meter—if not printed, you can ask the driver to write one out. By the way, the taxi should also have the A/C on when the weather calls for it—and do not let the driver charge you extra for it.

○ For a group, a driver may insist that each person pay the full metered fare. Pay only your proportion of the fare if all of you have the same destination. Pairs or groups of tourists should have a designated arguer; the others

strongly advised to make your reservation before leaving home and well in advance. Always ask if the quoted price includes insurance; many credit cards make the collision-damage waiver unnecessary, but you will find that most rental agencies automatically include this in their rates. You can sometimes save by booking at home before you leave; this is especially advisable in summer. If you are shopping around, let the agents see the number of competitors' brochures you're carrying.

Most companies require that the renter be at least 21 years old (25 for some car models). There are occasional reports that some car-rental agencies will not rent to drivers 75 or over—or even 70—but this does not seem to be an issue in Greece. If in doubt, inquire beforehand of the rental company. Technically you should possess an International Driver's License, but many car-rental agencies do accept a valid Australian, Canadian, E.U. nation, or U.S. driver's license. You must also have a major credit card (or be prepared to leave a *very* large cash deposit).

The major car-rental companies in Athens are **Avis** (© 210/322-4951), **Budget** (© 210/349-8700), **Hertz** (© 210/922-0102), **National** (© 210/349-3400), and **AutoEurope** (© 00800/11574-0300); all have offices in major cities, at most airports, can write down names and numbers, stick with the luggage, or look for help—from a policeman, maitre d', or desk clerk.

o Late at night, especially at airports, ferry stops, and bus and railroad stations, a driver may refuse to use his meter and demand an exorbitant fare. Smile, shake your head, and look for another cab; if none are available, start writing down the driver's license number and he will probably relent.

o Again, these may change, but at press time, legal surcharges include: 2.80€ for the Thessaloniki airport, and 2.30€ for other major airports; .95€ pickup at ports, bus terminals, or train terminals; .35€ per piece of luggage over 10 kilos (22 lb.). (Road tolls are charged to the passengers—for example, you will pay 2€ for the new road from the airport to Athens.) Radio taxis (called from hotels, for instance) get a 2.50€ surcharge, 5€ for a fixed appointment.

o A driver may say that your hotel is full, but that he knows a better and cheaper one. Laugh, and insist you'll take your chances at your hotel.

o A driver may want to let you off where it's most convenient for him. Be cooperative if it's easier and quicker for you to cross a busy avenue than for him to get you to the other side, but you don't have to get out until you're ready.

If things are obviously not going well for you, conspicuously write down the driver's name and number and report him to the **tourist police** (© **171**) if he has the nerve to call your bluff. One of the best countertactics is to simply open the door slightly; he won't want to risk damaging it. (Two passengers can each open a door.)

Our final advice: Don't sweat the small change. So the driver is charging you 12€ for a ride you have been told should be about 10€; are you prepared to go to court for 2€? Any difference above 5€ probably should be questioned—but it may have to do with traffic delays when the meter ticks at the rate of 9.60€ per hour. Most cabbies are honest—just be aware of the possibilities. And be sure to reward good service with a tip.

and on most islands. Smaller local companies usually have lower rates, but their vehicles are often older and not as well maintained. If you prefer to combine your car rental with your other travel arrangements, we recommend **Galaxy Travel,** 35 Voulis, near Syntagma Square (© **210/322-2091**; www.galaxytravel.gr). It's open Monday through Saturday during the tourist season.

Rental rates vary widely—definitely ask around. In high season, daily rates with unlimited mileage will be about 65€ for a compact and 135€ for a full-size car; weekly rates with unlimited mileage might run 240€ for a compact and 300€ for a full size. In low season, rates are often negotiable in Greece when you show up in person. The prices quoted should include the various taxes (although there may be a surcharge for pickup and drop-off at airports in high season).

Note: If you intend to take your car on a ferry or into a foreign country, you must have written permission from the car-rental agency.

DRIVING RULES In Greece, you drive on the right, pass on the left, and yield right of way to vehicles approaching from the right except where otherwise posted. Greece has adopted international road signs, although many Greeks apparently haven't learned what they mean yet. The maximum speed limit is 100kmph (62 mph) on open roads, and 50kmph (30 mph) in town, unless otherwise posted. Seat belts are required. The police have become stricter in recent years, especially with foreigners in rental cars; alcohol tests can be given and fines imposed on the spot. (If you feel you have been stopped or treated unfairly, get the officer's name and report him at the nearest tourist police station.) Honking is illegal in Athens, but you can hear that law broken at any odd moment.

PARKING   Parking a car has become a serious challenge in the cities and towns of Greece. The better hotels provide parking, either on their premises or by arrangement with a nearby lot (our hotel reviews include information on where to park). Greece has few public parking garages or lots; follow the blue signs with the white P and you may be lucky enough to find a space. Most city streets have restricted parking of one kind or another. In some cities, signs—usually yellow, and with the directions in English as well as in Greek—will indicate that you can park along the street but must purchase a ticket from the nearest kiosk. Otherwise, be prepared to park fairly far from your base or destination. If you lock the car and remove valuables from sight, you should not have to worry about a break-in.

By Boat

Ferries are the most common, cheapest, and generally most "authentic" way to visit the islands, though the slow roll of a ferry can be stomach-churning. A wide variety of vessels sail Greek waters—some huge, sleek, and new, with TV lounges, discos, and good restaurants; some old and ill kept, but pleasant enough if you stay on deck.

Ferry service (often accommodating vehicles) is available between Athens (Piraeus) and several other Greek ports. There's regular service from Piraeus to Aegina and to Poros in the Saronic Gulf; most of the Cyclades; Chania and Iraklion on Crete; Hios; Kos; Lesvos; Rhodes; and Samos. For the Cyclades, crossing is shorter and less expensive from Rafina, an hour east of Athens. From Patras, there's daily service to Corfu, Ithaka, and Kefalonia. The Sporades have service from Ayios Konstandinos, Kimi, and Volos (and then among the several islands). There's also service between many of the islands, even between Crete and Rhodes, as well as car-crossing to and from Turkey between Hios and Çesme; Lesvos and Dikeli; and Samos and Kusadasi.

There is also frequent ferry service (often also for cars) between several Italian ports (Ancona, Bari, Brindisi, Venice) and Patras (with stops at several major islands en route) But if you intend to continue on with your vehicle into Turkey or Italy or plan to enter Greece from Turkey, or Italy, you should inquire long before setting off for either country, and make sure that you have all the necessary paperwork.)

So-called "Flying Catamarans" and hydrofoils dubbed "Flying Dolphins" (see "By Hydrofoil," below) also serve many of the major islands. Undoubtedly faster, they cost almost twice as much as regular ferries, and their schedules are often interrupted by weather conditions. (Never rely on a tight connection between a hydrofoil and, say, an airplane flight.) Ferries, too, often don't hold exactly to their schedules, but they can be fun if you enjoy opportunities to meet people. Drinks and snacks are almost always sold, but the prices and selection are not that good, so you may want to bring along your own.

The map of Greece offered by the Greek National Tourism Organization (EOT), which indicates the common boat routes, is useful in planning your sea travels. Once you've learned what is *possible,* you can turn your attention to what is *available.* Remember that the summer schedule is the fullest, spring and fall bring reduced service, and winter schedules are skeletal.

There are dozens of shipping companies, each with its own schedule—which, by the way, are regulated by the government. Your travel agent might have a copy of the monthly schedule *Greek Travel Pages,* or you can search online at **www.gtp.gr** or **www.ferries.gr**. When in Greece, it's best to go straight to an official information office, a travel agency, or the port authority as soon as you arrive at the place that you intend to leave via ferry.

Photos can give you some idea of the ships, but remember that any photo displayed was probably taken when the ship was new, and it is unlikely that anyone will be able (or willing) to tell you its actual age. The bigger ferries offer greater stability during rough weather. Except in summer, you can usually depend on getting aboard a ferry by showing up about an hour before scheduled departure—interisland boats sometimes depart before their scheduled times—and purchasing a ticket from a dockside agent or aboard the ship itself, though this is often more expensive.

Your best bet is to buy a ticket from an agent ahead of time. In Athens, we recommend **Galaxy Travel,** 35 Voulis, near Syntagma Square (© **210/322-2091;** www.galaxytravel. gr); and **Alkyon Travel,** 97 Akademias, near Kanigos Square (© **210/383-2545**). During the high season, both agencies keep long hours Monday through Saturday.

Note: Different travel agencies sell tickets to different lines—this is usually the policy of the line itself—and one agent might not know or bother to find out what else is offered. However, if you press reputable agencies, they will at least tell you the options. The port authority is the most reliable source of information, and the shipping company itself or its agents usually offer better prices and may have tickets when other agents have exhausted their allotment. It often pays to compare vessels and prices.

First class usually means roomy air-conditioned cabins and its own lounge; on some routes it costs almost as much as flying. However, on longer overnight hauls, you're on a comfortable floating hotel and thus save the cost of lodging. Second class means smaller cabins (which you will probably have to share with strangers) and its own lounge. The tourist-class fare entitles you to a seat on the deck or in a lounge. (Tourists usually head for the deck, while Greeks stay inside and watch TV.) Hold onto your ticket; crews conduct ticket-control sweeps.

Note: Those taking a ferry to Turkey from one of the Dodecanese islands must submit passport (or E.U. citizens, an ID) and payment to an agent the day before departure.

We include more details on service and schedules in the relevant chapters to the various destinations, as well as suggested travel agencies and sources of local information. To give you some sense of the fares, here are examples for standard accommodations from Piraeus at press time (compare with airfares during this same time): to Crete (Iraklion), 80€–110€; Kos, 60€; Mitilini (Lesvos), 68€; Mykonos, 60€; Rhodes, 100€; Santorini, 60€. And don't be surprised if small taxes get added at the very end.

BY HYDROFOIL Hydrofoils (often referred to as Flying Dolphins, or by Greeks as *to flying*) are faster than ferries and their stops are much shorter. They have comfortable airline-style seats and are less likely to cause seasickness (but they are noisy) but at least smoking is prohibited. Although they cost somewhat more than ferries, are frequently fully booked in summer, can be quite bumpy during rough weather, and give little or no view of the passing scenery, they're the best choice if your time is limited. Everyone should ride one of these sleek little crafts at least once.

There is regular hydrofoil service to many of the major islands; new routes and new schedules appear often. Longer trips over open sea, such as between Santorini and Iraklion, Crete, may make them well worth the extra expense. (A one-way fare from

In the early and late weeks of the tourist season—from April to early May, and September to November—boat service can be unpredictable. Boat schedules, at the best of times, are tentative—but during this time, they are wish lists, little more. Our best advice is that you wait until you get to Greece, then go to a major travel agency and ask for help.

18

Getting Around

PLANNING YOUR TRIP TO GREECE

Heraklion to Santorini in high season, for instance, is 40€–50€.) The forward compartment offers better views but is also bumpy.

The Flying Dolphins are operated by **Hellenic Seaways,** 6 Astiggos, Karaiskaki Square, 18531 Piraeus (📞 **210/419-9000;** www.hellenicseaways.gr). The service from Zea Marina in Piraeus to the Saronic Gulf islands and throughout the Sporades is recommended for its speed and regularity. There is also service from Rafina, on the east coast of Attika, to several of the Cyclades islands.

BY SAILBOAT & YACHT   Many more tourists are choosing to explore Greece by sailboat or yacht. There are numerous facilities and options for both. Experienced sailors interested in renting a boat in Greece can contact the **Hellenic Professional and Bareboat Yacht Owners' Association,** A8–A9 Zea Marina, 18536 Piraeus (📞 **210/452-6335**). Less experienced sailors should consider signing up for one of the flotillas—a group of 12 or more boats sailing as a group led by a boat crewed by experienced sailors; the largest of such organizations is **Sunsail USA,** 93 North Park Place Boulevard, Clearwater FL 33759 (📞 **888/350-3568;** www.sunsail.com). However, travel agencies should be able to put you in touch with other such outfits.

At the other extreme, those who want to charter a yacht with anything from a basic skipper to a full crew should first contact the Hellenic Professional and Bareboat Yacht Owners' Association (listed above) or **Ghiolman Yachts,** 8 Propileon, 11742 Athens (📞 **210/325-5000;** www.ghiolman.com). If you feel competent enough to make your own arrangements, contact **Valef Yachts Ltd.** (📞 **800/223-3845** in the U.S.; www.valefyachts.com). In Greece, you can contact one of these organizations or try a private agency such as **Alpha Yachting,** 67 Leoforos Possidonos, 16674 Glyfada (📞 **210/968-0486;** www.alphayachting.com).

By Train

Greek trains are generally slow but are inexpensive and fairly pleasant. The **Hellenic State Railway (OSE)** also offers bus service from stations adjacent to major train terminals. (Bus service is faster, but second-class train fare is nearly 50% cheaper, and trains offer more comfortable and scenic rides.) If you are interested in special arrangements involving rail passes for Greece (sometimes in combination with Olympic Air flights within Greece), check out **www.raileurope.com** or call 📞 **800/622-8600** in the U.S. or 800/361-7245 in Canada.

For information and tickets in Athens, visit the **OSE office** at 1–3 Karolou (📞 **210/522-4563**), or at 6 Sina (📞 **210/362-4402**), both near Omonia Square. From abroad, visit **www.ose.gr.**

Purchase your ticket and reserve a seat ahead of time, as a 50% surcharge is added to tickets purchased on the train, and some lines are packed, especially in summer. A first-class ticket may be worth the extra cost, as seats are more comfortable and less crowded. There is sleeper service on the Athens-Thessaloniki run. Though the costly sleepers are a good value, you must be prepared to share a compartment with three to five others. Express service (6 hr.) runs twice a day, at 7am and 1pm.

Trains to northern Greece (Alexandropolis, Florina, Kalambaka, Lamia, Larissa, Thessaloniki, Volos, and other towns) leave from the Larissa station (Stathmos Larissis). **Trains to the Peloponnese** (Argos, Corinth, Patras) leave from the Peloponnese station (Stathmos Peloponnisou). Take trolley no. 1 or 5 from Syntagma Square to either station.

The Peloponnese circuit from Corinth to Patras, Pirgos (near Olympia), Tripolis, and Argos is one way to experience this scenic region, though the Athens-Patras stretch is often crowded. The spectacular spur between Diakofto and Kalavrita is particularly recommended for train enthusiasts.

By Bus

Public buses are inexpensive but often overcrowded. Local bus lines vary from place to place, but on most islands the bus stop is in a central location with a posted schedule. Destinations are usually displayed on the front of the bus, but you might have to ask. The conductor will collect your fare after departure.

Note that in Athens and other large cities, a bus ticket *must* be purchased before *and* validated after boarding. Kiosks usually offer bus tickets as well as schedules. The Athens metro ticket's cost is based on the destination, but usually costs about .70€

Note: Save your ticket in case an "inspector" comes aboard. If you don't have a ticket, the fine can be at least 30 times the price of the ticket!

Greece has an extensive **long-distance bus service (KTEL),** an association of regional operators with green-and-yellow buses that leave from convenient central stations. For information about the long-distance-bus offices, contact the KTEL office in Athens (℃ **210/512-4910**).

In Athens, most buses heading to destinations within **Attica** leave from the Mavromate terminal, north of the National Archaeological Museum. Most buses to **Central Greece** leave from 260 Liossion, 5km (3 miles) north of Omonia Square (take local bus no. 024 from Leoforos Amalias in front of the entrance to the National Garden and tell the driver your destination). Most buses to the **Peloponnese,** and to **western** and **northern Greece** leave from the long-distance bus terminal at 100 Kifissou, 4km (2½ miles) northeast of Omonia Square. To get to the long-distance bus terminal, take local bus no. 051 from the stop located 2 blocks west of Omonia, near the big church of Ayios Konstandinos, at Zinonos and Menandrou.

Express buses between major cities, usually air-conditioned, can be booked through travel agencies. Make sure that your destination is understood—you wouldn't be the first to see a bit more of Greece than bargained for—and determine the bus's schedule and comforts before purchasing your ticket. Many buses are not air-conditioned, take torturous routes, and make frequent stops. (NO SMOKING signs are generally disregarded by drivers and conductors, as well as by many older male passengers.)

Organized and guided **bus tours** are widely available. Some of them will pick you up at your hotel; ask the hotel staff or any travel agent in Athens. We especially recommend **CHAT Tours,** the oldest and probably most experienced provider of a wide selection of bus tours led by highly articulate guides. Almost any travel agent can book a CHAT tour, but if you want to deal with the company directly, contact them through their website, www.chatours.gr; in Athens, the CHAT office is at 9 Xenofontos, 10557 Athens (℃ **210/323-0827**). Then there is the longtime favorite, **American Express,** with offices all over North America and Europe; the Athens office (📞 **210/325-4690**) is located at 31 Panepistimiou, right on the corner of Syntagma Square.

Note: Readers have complained that some bus groups are so large they feel removed from the leader; inquire about group size if this concerns you.

TIPS ON ACCOMMODATIONS

Greece offers a full spectrum of accommodations ranging from the extravagant to the basic. Within a given locale, of course, not all options are available, but most readers will find something that appeals to them.

 Ask for Discounts

If you're watching your budget (and who isn't?), ask for the cheapest room at hotels and inquire about special offers. If tourism continues to decline, and the Greek economy remains troubled, many hotels may offer seriously discounted prices. Still, expect weekend hotel prices to be much higher than during the week, due to weekend travel by the Greeks themselves.

Hotels used to be required to publicize a grading system imposed by the Greek government. Classes still exist and are indicated by stars, but these are based more on facilities such as public areas, pools, and in-room amenities than on any comfort or service ratings. (Each room's rate should be posted on the inside of the door.) Basically it is a market economy, for hotels know better than to ask for too much because competitors will undercut them. Frommer's own rating system of stars and icons for special features takes care of all such differences.

International travelers will be familiar with some of the major chains—the Westin, Hilton and Best Western, for example. A number of Greek chains, such as Louis and Chandris, also own numerous hotels, while several hotels now belong to the Luxury Collection of Starwood Hotels and Resorts. These latter tend to be extremely upscale hotels. However, most Greek hotels are independent lodgings run by hands-on owners.

Be aware that a **double room** in Greece does not always mean a room with a double bed, but *might* be a room with twin beds. Double beds in Greece are called "matrimonial beds," and rooms with such beds are often designated "honeymoon rooms." This can lead to misunderstandings.

RENTALS (APARTMENTS & HOUSES)   An increasingly popular way to experience Greece is to rent an apartment or a house; the advantages include freedom from the formalities of a hotel, often a more desirable location, and a kitchen that allows you to avoid the costs and occasional crush of restaurants. Such rentals do not come cheap, but if you calculate what two or more people might pay for a decent hotel, not to mention all the meals eaten out, a rental can turn out to be a good deal. (Cost per person per day in a really nice apartment runs about 100€; a fancier villa with two bedrooms might cost about 200€ per person per

 Climate Control in Greek Hotels

Most of the Greek hotels recommended now promise air-conditioning in the hot season and heating in the colder months. The equipment is indeed there, but you should be aware that except in the most expensive hotels, neither will necessarily be as adequate as you might like.

Try to make reservations **by fax** so that you have a written record of the room and the agreed–upon price. If you booked **by e-mail**, bring a printout of your confirmed reservation.

Note that in a few instances—usually at the most expensive hotels—the prices quoted are **per person**. (We indicate this in our recommendations.) Note, too, that room prices, no matter what people say officially, are often negotiable, especially at the edges of the season. Because of Greek law and EOT regulations, hotel keepers are often reluctant to provide rates far in advance and often quote prices higher than their actual rates. When you bargain, don't cite our prices, which may be too high, but ask instead for the best current rate. Actual off-season prices may be as much as 25% lower than the lowest rate given to us for this book.

day.) Any full-service travel agency in your home country or in Greece should be able to put you in touch with an agency specializing in such rentals.

The fact is that the British dominate this field in Greece, in terms of both experience and sheer numbers of offerings. So via the Internet, anyone can now see what's offered and contact such outfits as **Simply Travel Ltd.,** Columbus House, Westwood Way, Coventry CV4 8TT (℃ **0871/231-4050;** www.simplytravel.co.uk); or **Pure Crete,** Bolney Place, Cowfold Road, Haywards Heath, West Sussex RH17 5Q7 (℃ **1444/881-402;** www.purecrete.com). Among those in the United States are **Villas International,** 17 Fox Lane, San Anselmo CA 94960 (℃ **800/221-2260;** www.villasintl.com); and **Villas and Apartments Abroad,** 183 Madison Ave., Suite 201, New York, NY 10016 (℃ **212/213-6435;** www.vaanyc.com). In Canada, try **Grecian Holidays,** 1315 Lawrence Ave. East, Toronto, Ontario M3A 3R3 (℃ **800/268-6786;** www.grecianholidays.com).

For apartment, farmhouse, or cottage stays of 2 weeks or more, **Idyll Untours** (℃ **888/868-6871;** www.untours.com) provides exceptional vacation rentals for a reasonable price—which includes air/ground transportation, cooking facilities, and on-call support from a local resident. Best of all: Untours—named the "Most Generous Company in America" by Newman's Own—donates most profits to provide low-interest loans to underprivileged entrepreneurs (see website for details).

Another option is to rent a traditional house in one of about 12 relatively rural or remote villages or settlements throughout Greece. These small traditional houses have been restored by the Greek National Tourism Organization (GNTO or EOT); to learn more about this possibility, contact the GNTO office nearest you (see "Visitor Information," in "Fast Facts" later).

[Fast FACTS] GREECE

Area Codes All phone numbers in Greece are 10 digits long. Area codes range from three digits in Athens **(210)** to as many as five digits in less populated locales; the phone numbers themselves range from five digits to eight but all must add up to a total of ten including the area code. All numbers provided in the text start with the proper area code. Also see "Telephones," later in this section.

Business Hours Greek business and office hours take some getting used to, especially in the afternoon, when most English-speaking people are accustomed to getting things done in high gear. Compounding the problem is that it is nearly impossible to pin down the precise hours of opening. We can start by saying that almost all stores and services are closed on Sunday—except, of course, tourist-oriented shops and services. Supermarkets, department stores and chain stores are usually open 9am to 9pm, Monday through Saturday. On Monday, Wednesday, and Saturday, smaller retail shops' hours are usually 9am to 3pm; Tuesday, Thursday, and Friday, it's 9am to 2pm and 5 to 7pm. The afternoon siesta is generally observed from 3 to 5pm, though many tourist-oriented businesses have a minimal crew on duty during naptime, and they may keep extended hours, often from 8am to 10pm. (In fact, in tourist centers, shops may be open at all kinds of hours.) Most government offices are open Monday through Friday only, from 8am to 3pm. Call ahead to check the hours of businesses you must deal with, and try not to disturb Greek friends during siesta hours. Final advice: Anything you really need to accomplish in a government office, business, or store should be done on weekdays between about 9am and 1pm.

Banks are open to the public Monday through Thursday from 8am to 2:30pm, Friday from 8am to 2pm. Banks at a few locations may be open for some services such as foreign currency exchange into the evening and on Saturday. All banks are closed on the long list of Greek holidays. (See "When to Go," p. 28.)

Customs Passengers from North America arriving in Athens aboard international flights are generally not searched, and if you have nothing to declare, continue through the green lane. (Because of the continuing threat of terrorism, baggage is X-rayed before boarding domestic flights.) Citizens of the United States, Canada, Australia, New Zealand, and other non-E.U. countries do face a few commonsensical restrictions on what you can bring into Greece. Clearly, no narcotics: Greece is *very* tough on drug users. No explosives or weapons—although upon application, a sportsman might be able to bring in a legitimate hunting weapon. Only medications for amounts properly prescribed for your own use are allowed. Plants with soil are not. Dogs and cats can be brought in, but they must have proof of recent rabies and other health shots.

What You Can Take Out of Greece:

(All Nationalities): Exportation of Greek antiquities is strictly protected by law. No antiquities may be taken out of Greece without prior special permission from the **Archaeological Service,** 3 Polignotou, Athens. Also, you must be able to explain how you acquired your purchase—in particular, icons or religious articles. A dealer or shopkeeper must provide you with an export certificate for any object dating from before 1830. In general, **keep all receipts** for major purchases in order to clear Customs on your return home.

For further information on what you're allowed to bring into your country of residence, contact one of the following agencies:

U.S. Citizens: U.S. Customs & Border Protection (CBP), 1300 Pennsylvania Ave. NW, Washington, DC 20229 (© **877/227-5511;** www.cbp.gov).

Canadian Citizens: Canada Border Services Agency (© **800/461-9999** in Canada, or **204/983-3500;** www.cbsa-asfc.gc.ca).

U.K. Citizens: HM Revenue & Customs © **0845/ 010-9000** (from outside the U.K., 020/8929-0152), or consult their website at www.hmce.gov.uk.

Australian Citizens: Australian Customs Service at © **1300/363-263,** or log on to www.customs.gov.au.

New Zealand Citizens: New Zealand Customs, the Customhouse, 17–21 Whitmore St., Box 2218, Wellington (© **0800/428-786;** www.customs.govt.nz).

Travelers with Disabilities Increasingly, people with physical disabilities who travel abroad will find more options and resources than ever before. However, few concessions exist for travelers with disabilities in Greece. Steep steps, uneven pavements, almost no cuts at curbstones, few ramps, narrow walks, slick stone, and traffic congestion can cause problems. Archaeological sites are, by their very nature, difficult to navigate, and crowded public transportation can be all but impossible.

The new airport and the Athens Metro system are wheelchair accessible, and thanks to the 2004 Olympics, an elevator now takes individuals in wheelchairs to the top of the Acropolis; but even this requires that the wheelchair be pushed up a lengthy path. More modern and private facilities are only now beginning to provide ramps, but little else has been done. Increasingly, hotels are setting aside rooms that they advertise as "disability-friendly" or "handicap accessible," but that may mean nothing more than handrails in the bathtub. Nonetheless, foreigners in wheelchairs—accompanied by companions—are becoming a more common sight in Greece. Several travel agencies now offer customized tours and itineraries for travelers with disabilities; one is the British-based **Makin' Tracks: www.makintracks.eu**. A number of agencies offer customized tours and itineraries for travelers with disabilities. Among them are **Flying Wheels Travel** (© 877/451-5006; www.flyingwheelstravel.com) and **Accessible Journeys** (© 800/846-4537; www.disabilitytravel.com).

There is now one particular establishment in Greece that should have a special appeal to those with physical disabilities: the **Eria Resort Hotel** on Crete, designed, built, and dedicated to provide as convenient, comfortable, and active a stay in Greece as possible. For a full description, see p. 318.

Organizations that offer a vast range of resources and assistance to travelers with disabilities include **MossRehab** (© 800/CALL-MOSS [225-5667]; www.mossresourcenet.org); the **American Foundation for the Blind** (**AFB**; © 800/232-5463; www.afb.org); and **SATH** (Society for Accessible Travel & Hospitality; © 212/447-7284; www.sath.org). **AirAmbulanceCard.com** is partnered with SATH and allows you to preselect hospitals in case of an emergency.

British travelers should contact **Holiday Care** (© 0845-124-9971 in the U.K. only; www.holidaycare.org.uk) to access a wide range of travel information and resources for the elderly and people with disabilities.

Doctors   Any foreign embassy or consulate can provide a list of area doctors who speak English. If in a town without these offices, ask your hotel management to recommend a local doctor—even his or her own.

Drinking Laws   The minimum age for being served alcohol in public is 18. Wine and beer are generally available in eating places, but not in all coffeehouses

or dessert cafes. Alcoholic beverages are sold in food stores as well as liquor stores. Although a certain amount of high spirits is appreciated, Greeks do not appreciate public drunkenness. The resort centers where mobs of young foreigners party every night are tolerated as necessary for the tourist trade, but such behavior wins no respect for foreigners. Do not carry open containers of alcohol in your car and don't even think about driving while intoxicated.

Electricity   Electric current in Greece is 220 volts AC, alternating at 50 cycles. (Some larger hotels have 110-volt low-wattage outlets for electric shavers, but they aren't good for hair dryers and most other appliances.) Electrical outlets require Continental type plugs with two round prongs. U.S. travelers will most likely need an adapter plug and a transformer/converter. Laptop computer users will want to check their requirements; a transformer may be necessary, and surge protectors are recommended. But increasingly various appliances—including laptops and hair dryers—allow for a simple switch to the 220 volts.

Embassies & Consulates   In Athens: **Australia,** Thon Building, Corner Kifias and Alexandras avenues (© 210/870-4000); **Canada,** 4 Ioannou Yenadiou (© 210/727-3400); **Ireland,** 7 Leoforos Vasileus (© 210/723-2771); **New**

Zealand, 268 Leoforos Kifissias, Halandri (© **210/6874-
700**); **United Kingdom,** 1
Ploutarchou (© **210/727-
2660**); **United States,** 91
Leoforos Vas. Sofias
(© **210/721-2951**).

Emergencies If there is
no tourist police officer
available (© **171**), contact
the local police, © **100**. For
fire, call © **199**. For medical emergencies and/or first
aid and/or an ambulance,
call © **166**. For hospitals,
call © **106**. For automobile
emergencies, put out a triangular danger sign and
call © **10400**. Embassies,
consulates, and many
hotels can recommend an
English-speaking doctor.

Family Travel If you
have enough trouble get-
ting your kids out of the
house in the morning, drag-
ging them thousands of
miles away may seem an
insurmountable challenge.
But family travel can be
immensely rewarding, giv-
ing you new ways of seeing
the world through smaller
pairs of eyes.

Set goals for your family
for your travels in Greece.
The whole family can head
for the beaches. At the other
extreme, however, think
twice about taking younger
kids along on a full-day
exploration of museums and
archaeological sites. Travel
with infants and young children—say, up to about age
5—can work; most children
ages 6 to 16 become restless
at historical sites. If you're
lucky, your children may tune
into history at some point in
their teens.

There are some kid-
friendly distractions in
Greece: playgrounds all
over the place, water parks
here and there, and zoos.
Greeks boys now play
pickup basketball even in
small towns—if your kids go
for that, it's a great way to
be quickly accepted.

To make it easy to pick
out those accommodations,
restaurants, and attractions
that are particularly kid-
friendly, we mark them with
the "Kids" icon in this guide.

Most hotels allow chil-
dren 5 and under a free bed
or cot in your room, and
reduced prices for children
11 and under. Some muse-
ums have children's prices,
but by and large Greece is
not set up to offer reductions at every turn.

As for passport require-
ments for children, see
"Passports," later (or go to
the State Department's
website, **www.travel.state.
gov**). If you are traveling
with children other than
your own, you must be sure
you have full identification
as well as notarized autho-
rization from their parents.

Health If you suffer from
a chronic illness, consult
your doctor about your
travel plans before your
departure. If you have special concerns, before heading abroad you might check
out the United States **Centers for Disease Control and
Prevention** (© **800/232-
4636**; www.cdc.gov/travel).

Greeks have national
medical insurance. Citizens
of other E.U. nations should

inquire before leaving, but
your policies will probably
cover treatment in Greece.
Non-E.U. travelers should
check your health plan to
see if it provides appropriate
coverage; you may want to
buy **travel medical insurance** instead. (See **www.
frommers.com/planning**.)
Bring your insurance ID card
with you when you travel.
Although you will receive
emergency care with no
questions asked, make sure
you have coverage at home.

Drugstores/Chemists:
These are called *pharmikon*
in Greek; aside from the
obvious indications in windows and interiors, they are
identified by a green cross.
For minor medical prob-
lems, go first to the nearest
pharmacy. Pharmacists usually speak English, and
many medications can be
dispensed without prescription. In the larger cities, if it
is closed, there should be a
sign in the window direct-
ing you to the nearest open
one. Newspapers also list
the pharmacies that are
open late or all night.

Common Ailments: Diarrhea
is no more of a problem in
Greece than it might be any-
time you change diet and
water supplies, but occasionally visitors do experience it.
Common over-the-counter
preventatives and cures are
available in Greek pharmacies, but if you are con-
cerned, bring your own.

If you expect to be tak-
ing sea trips and are
inclined to get **seasick,**
bring a preventative.

Allergy sufferers should carry antihistamines, especially in the spring.

Sun Exposure: Between mid-June and September, too much exposure to the sun during midday could well lead to sunstroke or heatstroke. High-SPF **sunscreen** and a hat are strongly advised.

Hospitals In Greece, modern hospitals, clinics, and pharmacies are found everywhere, and personnel, equipment, and supplies ensure excellent treatment. Dental care is also widely available. Most doctors in Greece can speak English (many having trained in North America or the U.K.).

You can also try the emergency room at a local hospital. In addition, many hospitals have walk-in clinics for emergency cases that are not life threatening; you may not get immediate attention, but you won't pay the high price of an emergency room visit. For major cities in Greece, the phone numbers and addresses for hospitals or medical centers are given in the relevant "Fast Facts" section in each destination chapter. In an emergency, call a **first-aid center** (✆ **166**), the nearest **hospital** (✆ **106**), or the **tourist police** (✆ **171**).

Emergency treatment is usually given free in state hospitals, but be warned that only basic needs are met. The care in outpatient clinics, which are usually open mornings (8am–noon), is often somewhat better; you can find them next to most major hospitals, on some islands, and occasionally in rural areas, usually indicated by prominent signs.

Insurance Given the sometimes unstable conditions in Greece in recent years, some might consider purchasing travel insurance. But it is vital to understand just what you are paying for—that is, exactly what kind of incident or situation would allow you to cancel and collect. Your own last-minute fears about strikes in Greece would not qualify, nor would a canceled flight within Greece.

For information on traveler's insurance, trip cancellation insurance, and medical insurance while traveling, please visit **www.frommers.com/planning**.

Internet & Wi-Fi

Internet connection with or without Wi-Fi is now available virtually anywhere a visitor is apt to be. Some hotels do charge for either or both services (and this will be indicated at each appropriate listing). To find cybercafes in your destination you might start by checking **www.cybercaptive.com** and **www.cybercafe.com**. But frankly, these lists are by no means thorough or up-to-date when it comes to Greece. All decent-size cities now have Internet cafes in their centers; if you are having trouble finding one, ask a young person or a shop-owner.

Language

Language is usually not a problem for English speakers in Greece, as so many Greeks have studied it and find it necessary to use in their work worlds—most particularly, in the tourist realm that visitors encounter. Many Greeks have also lived abroad where English is the primary language. Young people learn it in school, from Anglo-American–dominated pop culture, and in special classes meant to prepare them for the contemporary world of business. Several television programs are broadcast in their original languages, and American prime-time soaps are very popular, nearly inescapable. Even advertisements have an increasingly high English content. Don't let all this keep you from trying to pick up at least a few words of Greek; your effort will be rewarded by your hosts, who realize how difficult their language is for foreigners and will patiently help you improve your pronunciation and usage.

There are several books and audio courses on learning Greek, including *Berlitz's Greek for Travelers*, *Passport's Conversational Greek in 7 Days*, and *Teach Yourself Greek Complete Course* (book and CD pack). In recent years, Rosetta Stone has been heavily promoting its courses as the best way to learn a foreign language: based on my own experience, this is not the best way for those who simply want to learn some basic and functional Greek for traveling there. It is, rather, for those who intend to learn the language for long-term usage.

Legal Aid If you need legal assistance, contact your own or another English-speaking embassy or consulate; their addresses and phone numbers are provided at "Embassies & Consulates," above or in the "Fast Facts" sections of major cities. If these institutions cannot themselves be of help, they can direct you to local lawyers who speak English and are willing to help.

LGBT Travelers

Greece—or at least parts of it—has a long tradition of being tolerant of gay men, and in recent years these locales have extended this tolerance to lesbians. Bars and such places especially open to and frequented by LBGT travelers are identified in the relevant locales. But although Greeks in Athens, Piraeus, and perhaps a few other major cities may not care one way or the other, Greeks in small towns and villages—indeed, most Greeks—do not appreciate flagrant displays of dress or behavior. Among the best-known hangouts for gays and lesbians are Mykonos, Mitilini (Lesvos), and Chania, Crete, but gays and lesbians travel all over Greece without any particular issues. The age of consent for sexual relations with homosexuals is 17, and this can be strictly enforced against foreigners.

Mail The mail service of Greece is reliable—but slow. (Postcards usually arrive after you have returned.) You can receive mail addressed to you c/o Poste *Restante,* General Post Office, City (or Town), Island (or Province), Greece. You will need your passport to collect this mail. Many hotels will accept, hold, and even forward mail for you; ask first. American Express clients can receive mail at any Amex office in Athens, Corfu, Iraklion, Mykonos, Patras, Rhodes, Santorini, Skiathos, and Thessaloniki, for a nominal fee and with proper identification. For the fastest service, try FedEx or one of the other major private carriers; travel agencies can direct you to these.

Postage rates have been going up in Greece, as they are elsewhere. At press time, a postcard or a letter under 20 grams (about .7 oz.) to foreign countries costs .75€; 20 to 50 grams (up to 1.75 oz.), 1.30€; 50 to 100 grams (3.5 oz.), 1.75€. Rates for packages depend on size as well as weight, but are reasonable. *Note:* Do not wrap or seal any package—you must be prepared to show the contents to a postal clerk. If you are concerned about some particular item, you might consider using one of the well-known international commercial delivery services. Your hotel or any travel agency can direct you to the nearest local office.

Medical Requirements

There are no immunization requirements for getting into Greece, though it's always a good idea to have polio, tetanus, and typhoid covered when traveling anywhere. See "Health," above.

Mobile Phones The three letters that define much of the world's wireless capabilities are **GSM (Global System for Mobile Communications),** a big, seamless network that makes for easy cross-border cellphone use throughout Europe—including Greece—and indeed most countries around the world. In the U.S., T-Mobile, and AT&T Wireless, use this quasi-universal system; in Canada, Microcell and some Rogers customers are GSM, and most Australians use GSM.

GSM phones function with a removable plastic SIM card, encoded with your phone number and account information. But some phones are "locked" and must be unlocked; go to your phone's website and get information as to how to unlock your phone. If your cellphone is on a GSM system, and you have a world-capable multiband phone such as many Sony Ericsson, Motorola, or Samsung models, you can make and receive calls around much of the globe. Just call your wireless operator and ask for "international roaming" to be activated on your account. Unfortunately, per-minute charges can be high—usually $1 to $1.50 in Greece. But the reassuring point is that cellphone services are generally available wherever you go in Greece.

An alternative way if you intend to make many phone calls in Greece is to bring your unlocked cellphone to Greece and buy a SIM card in the national telephone office (OTE) center in major cities or a commercial phone store. These cards—actually a tiny chip inserted into your phone—cost about 20€ and include a Greek phone number and a number of prepaid minutes; when you have used up these minutes, you can purchase a phone card at a kiosk that gives you more minutes. But it must be said that any calls outside of Greece by this system are very expensive.

For many, **renting** a phone in Greece is a good idea. You can rent a phone from any number of places in Greece—including kiosks at major airports, OTE offices, and cellphone stores. But if you expect to be abroad for more than a brief time, and/or to be visiting more than one country, **buying a phone** can make economic sense. Numerous companies now sell phones with a SIM card included

and with a U.S. or U.K. phone number assigned to it—so-called global roaming services that offer relatively cheap per minute rates for both outgoing and incoming calls: Typical would be 90¢ from Greece to the U.S. and 25¢ from the U.S. to Greece. (U.K. rates are much cheaper.) Google "global roaming SIM card" to compare various services and charges or look into **www.cellularabroad.com**.

You can buy a phone in Greece in either the national telephone office (OTE) in any decent-size city or a retail electronics store. If you take the cheapest package; you'll probably pay less than $100 for a phone and a starter calling card. Local calls may be as low as 10¢ per minute, and in many countries incoming calls are free.

Money & Costs Frommer's lists exact prices in the local currency (the euro). The conversion rate

provided was correct at press time. However, rates fluctuate, so before you leave, check a website like **www.oanda.com/currency/converter** online for the latest rates The currency in Greece is the **euro** (pronounced *evro* in Greek), abbreviated "eu" and symbolized by €. (If you still own the old drachmas, it is no longer possible to exchange them.)

The euro comes in seven paper notes and eight coins. The notes are in different sizes and colors. They are in the following denominations: 5, 10, 20, 50, 100, 200, and 500. (Considering that each euro is worth over $1, those last bills are quite pricey!) Six of the coins are officially "cents"—but in Greece they have become referred to as *lepta,* the old Greek name for sums smaller than the drachma. They come in different sizes and their value is 1, 2, 5, 10,

THE VALUE OF THE EURO VS. OTHER POPULAR CURRENCIES

EURO€	Aus$	Can$	NZ$	UK£	US$
1	A$1.35	C$1.34	NZ$1.80	£ .85	$1.45

WHAT THINGS COST IN ATHENS

Taxi from the airport to downtown Athens	35–50€
Double room, moderate	90–110€
Double room, inexpensive	65–85€
Three-course dinner for one without wine, moderate	12–20€
Bottle of beer	2.50–4€
Cup of coffee	1.50–3.50€
1 gallon/1 liter of gas	6.70/1.75€
Admission to museums and archaeological sites	2–12€

THREE warnings ABOUT DEBIT & CREDIT CARDS

As part of banks' and credit card companies' increasing concern about fraud, it is our experience that they are apt to deny your cards if you go to use them too far out of your normal circuit of use. It's a wise idea to contact your cards' customer service department by phone and inform them of your travel plans.

Meanwhile, perhaps you have been reading about the new Chip-and-PIN (aka "Smart Cards") credit cards that are being introduced throughout much of the world. Unlike the long-standard credit cards that have only a magnetic strip, these have a small chip embedded in them and then require the user to enter a PIN. The European Union has required all its member nations to introduce these, but as of this writing, most American issuers of credit cards have not adopted them. This means that Americans abroad may face a problem when presenting their standard magnetic strip cards: some places may claim that they are no longer acceptable. In fact, they are: If the individual rejecting your card doesn't know this, he must punch in your card number manually—and you must provide them with that card's PIN. So, if you do not know your card's PIN, you must call your card issuer and obtain one (for **MasterCard,**

call *C* **800/622-7747;** for **Visa,** *C* **800/857-2911**). Allow some time for this as it may involve sending mail from and back to the issuer. *Note:* This problem does not arise if you are using a card as a debit card, which already requires its PIN.

Credit cards are accepted throughout Greece in the better hotels and at most shops. But even many of the better restaurants in major cities do *not* accept credit cards, and certainly most restaurants and many smaller hotels in Greece do not. Some hotels that require a credit card number when you make advance reservations will demand payment in cash; inquire beforehand if this will be the case.

Beware of hidden credit card fees while traveling. Check with your credit or debit card issuer to see what fees, if any, will be charged for overseas transactions. Recent reform legislation in the U.S., for example, has curbed some exploitative lending practices. But many banks have responded by increasing fees in other areas, including fees for customers who use their cards while out of the country. Fees can amount to 3% or more of the purchase price. Check with your bank to avoid any surprise charges on your statement.

20, and 50. There are also 1€ and 2€ coins. Although one side of the coins differs in each of the member E.U. nations, all coins and bills are legal tender in all countries using the euro.

Warning: The 1€ and 2€ coins look similar to a 1 lira Turkish coin—worth less than half the 1€, so count your change carefully.

It's a good idea to exchange at least some

money—enough to cover airport incidentals and transportation to your hotel—before you leave, so you can avoid lines at airport ATMs. You can exchange money at your local American Express or Thomas Cook office or at some banks.

For many decades after World War II, Greece was one of the great bargain destinations for tourists. But since the 1990s, it can no

longer be described this way. It may not be in the category of London or New York or Paris or Tokyo, but in the major cities and hot spots, hotels are no longer bargains and the upscale restaurants are comparable to restaurants in most other developed countries. Admission to major museums and archaeological sites is comparable to fees in other major cities. Flights within Greece are expensive, as are car rentals—especially in high season. But it is still possible to have a reasonably modest holiday in Greece. You can start by visiting outside the high season—July and August. Pick midprice hotels and restaurants—and make sure breakfast is included in your hotel price. Look for deals on car rentals. Fly off-peak hours, and avoid expensive services such as spas or purchases such as jewelry. As noted frequently throughout this book, the current economic flux in Greece *may* lead to discounted rates at hotels and restaurants—it's always worth asking.

For help with conversions, tip calculations, and more, download Frommer's Travel Tools app for your mobile device. Go to **www.frommers.com/go/mobile** and click on the Travel Tools Icon.

ATMs

In commercial centers, airports, all cities and larger towns, and most tourist centers, you will find at least a couple of machines accepting a wide range of cards. Smaller towns will often have only one ATM—and it may not accept your card. **Commercial Bank (Emboriki Trapeza)** services Plus and Visa; **Credit Bank (Trapeza Pisteos)** and **AlphaBank** accept Visa and American Express; **National Bank (Ethiniki Trapeza)** takes Cirrus and MasterCard/Access.

But for all the prevalence of ATMs, you should keep at least some actual cash on you for those occasions when all the ATMs you can locate are out of order or out of cash. Keep enough euros or your own currency to get you through at least 24 hours.

Note: Greek ATMs accept only a four-digit PIN—you must change yours before you go. And since Greek ATMs use only numeric PINs (personal identification numbers), before you set off for Greece be sure you know how to convert letters to numerals as the alphabet will be in Greek.

Credit Cards

In Greece, Visa and MasterCard are the most widely accepted cards. Diners Club is less widely accepted. And American Express is still less frequently accepted because it charges a higher commission and is more protective of the cardholder in disagreements.

Multicultural Travelers

Greece has an age-old tradition of welcoming peoples from around from the world and there is no expectation that "people of color" would be treated any differently than other foreigners. However, it should be said that people of African descent—that is to say, native Africans, U.K.-Africans and African-Americans—have not made Greece a particular "destination.". Likewise, Greeks have not set up any special network of hotels, resorts, or restaurants to cater to individuals of African descent—or for that matter, any people of color. But I would

like to believe that all people of color are treated like all other guests in Greece, and in my (albeit limited) encounters with African-Americans in Greece, I have always found this to be true. What people might experience, however, is being stared at by some individuals in communities not accustomed to seeing people of color.

As for making any special travel arrangements, again, it must be said that agencies that do specialize in servicing African-Americans or U.K.-Africans probably have little experience in making arrangements in Greece. One exception is the black-owned agency in Philadelphia **Rodgers Travel** (*(Ⓒ)* **888/823-1775;** www.rodgerstravel.com), which handles clients of all colors. So the best advice is to go to any travel agency that handles arrangements for Greece and expect to be treated like everyone else.

Newspapers & Magazines All cities, large towns, and major tourist centers have at least one shop or kiosk that carries a selection of foreign-language publications; most of these are flown or shipped in on the very day of publication. English-language readers have a wide selection, including most of the British papers (*Daily Telegraph, Financial Times, Guardian, Independent, Times*), the *International Herald Tribune* (with its English-language insert of the well-known Athens newspaper, *Kathimerini*), and *USA Today. Kathimerini,* by the way, has an online English edition that is quite adequate for keeping up with Greek news (**www. ekathimerini.com**).

Packing As most visitors to Greece tend to be there between the first of May and the end of September, light jackets and sweaters should suffice for any overcast days or cool evenings—unless, of course, you are planning to spend time in the mountains. Except for the really high-class hotels and resorts, casual dress is accepted in almost all restaurants and facilities. But Greeks remain uncomfortable with beach-wear or too-casual garb in villages and cities. And females are expected—indeed, often required—to cover their arms and upper legs before entering monasteries and churches. Some priests and monks are stricter than others and may flatly bar men as well as women if they feel that the men are not dressed suitably.

Passports For entry into Greece, citizens of Australia, Canada, New Zealand, South Africa, the United States, and almost all other non-E.U. countries are required to have a **valid passport,** which is stamped upon entry and exit, for stays up to 90 days. All U.S. citizens, even infants, must have a valid passport, but Canadian children under 16 may travel without a passport if accompanied by either parent.

Citizens of the United Kingdom and other members of the European Union are required to present a valid ID (driving licenses do not qualify) for entry into Greece; you may stay an unlimited period (although you should inquire about this at a Greek consulate or at your embassy in Greece). Children under 16 from E.U. countries may travel without an ID if accompanied by either parent. All E.U. citizens are reminded that they should check the requirements for non-E.U. countries through which you might travel to get to Greece.

For stays longer than 90 days, all non-E.U. citizens will require visas from the Greek embassies or consuls in their home countries. If already in Greece, arrangements must be made with the **Bureau of Aliens,** 173 Leoforos Alexandras, 11522 Athens (✆ **210/770-5711**). See **www.frommers.com/ planning** for information on how to obtain a passport.

For Residents of Australia Contact the **Australian Passport Information Service** at ✆ **131-232,** or visit the government website at www.passports.gov.au.

For Residents of Canada Contact the central **Passport Office,** Department of Foreign Affairs and International Trade, Ottawa, ON K1A 0G3 (✆ **800/567-6868;** www.ppt.gc.ca).

For Residents of Ireland Contact the **Passport Office,** Setanta Centre, Molesworth Street, Dublin 2 (✆ **01/671-1633;** www. irlgov.ie/iveagh).

For Residents of New Zealand Contact the **Passports Office** at ✆ **0800/ 225-050** in New Zealand, or 04/474-8100, or log on to www.passports.govt.nz.

For Residents of the United Kingdom Visit your nearest passport office, major post office, or travel agency or contact the **United Kingdom Passport Service** at ✆ **0870/521-0410** or search its website at www.ukpa.gov.uk.

For Residents of the United States To find your regional passport office, either check the U.S. State Department website or call the **National Passport Information Center** toll-free number (✆ **877/487-2778**) for automated information.

Police To report a crime or medical emergency, or for information or other assistance, first contact the tourist police (✆ **171**), where an English-speaking officer is more likely to be found. If there is no tourist police officer available, contact the local police at ✆ **100.** Tourists who report petty thievery to the local police will probably feel that they are not being taken all that seriously, but it is more likely that the Greek police have realized there is little they can do without solid identification of the culprits. As for the other side of the coin—police being exceptionally hard on foreigners, say, when enforcing traffic violations—although there is the rare reported incident, it does not seem to be widespread. Drugs, however, are a different story: The Greek authorities and laws are extremely tough when it comes to foreigners with drugs—starting with marijuana. Do *not* attempt to bring any illicit drug into or out of Greece.

Safety   Crime directed at tourists was traditionally unheard of in Greece, but in more recent years there are occasional reports of cars broken into, pickpockets, purse snatchers, and the like. Normal precautions are called for. For instance, if you have hand luggage containing expensive items, whether jewelry or cameras, never give it to an individual unless you are absolutely sure it will be safe with him or her. Lock the car and don't leave cameras or other such gear visible. Don't leave your luggage unattended when entering or leaving hotels. Also, it is probably safer not to leave valuables unattended at beaches. And young women should observe the obvious precautions in dealing with men in isolated locales.

One other thing that might be of concern to some: Greece is undeniably exposed to earthquakes, but there are almost no known instances in recent decades of tourists being injured or killed in one of these. Of far more potential danger are automobile accidents: Greece has one of the worst vehicle accident rates in Europe. You should exercise great

caution when driving over unfamiliar, often winding, and often poorly maintained roads. This holds true especially when you're driving at night. As for those who insist on renting motorbikes or similar vehicles, at the very least wear a helmet.

Senior Travel   Greece does not offer too many discounts for seniors. Some museums and archaeological sites offer discounts for those 60 and over, but the practice is unpredictable, and in almost all instances the discount is restricted to citizens of an E.U. nation.

Try mentioning the fact that you're a senior when you make your travel reservations. Many hotels continue to offer discounts for seniors.

Members of **AARP,** 601 E St. NW, Washington, DC 20049 (© **888/687-2277;** www.aarp.org), get discounts on hotels, airfares, and car rentals. AARP offers members a wide range of benefits, including *AARP The Magazine* and a monthly newsletter. Anyone over 50 can join.

Many reliable agencies and organizations target the 50-plus market. **Road Scholar** (formerly **Elderhostel;** © **800/454-5768;** www.roadscholar.org) arranges study programs for those ages 55 and over (and a spouse or companion of any age) in the U.S. and in more than 80 countries around the world. Most courses last 5 to 7 days in the U.S. (2–4 weeks

abroad), and many include airfare, accommodations in university dormitories or modest inns, meals, and tuition. In Greece, groups typically settle in one area for a week or so, with excursions that focus on getting to know the history and culture. Canada-based **ElderTreks** (© **800/741-7956;** www.eldertreks.com) offers small-group tours to off-the-beaten-path or adventure-travel locations, restricted to travelers 50 and older. Britons might prefer to deal with **Saga Holidays** (Saga Building, Folkestone, Kent CT20 1AZ; © **800/096-0084** in the U.S. and Canada, or 0808/ 234-1714 in the U.K.; www. saga.co.uk), which offers all-inclusive tours in Greece for those ages 50 and older.

Single Travelers   Single travelers are usually hit with a "single supplement" to the base price for package vacations and cruises, while the price of a single room is almost always well over half that for a double. To avoid such charges, you might consider agreeing to room with other single travelers or to find a compatible roommate before you go from one of the many roommate locator agencies.

Travel Buddies Singles Travel Club (© **800/998-9099;** www.travelbuddies worldwide.com), based in Canada, runs small, intimate, single-friendly group trips and will match you with a roommate free of charge. **TravelChums** (© **212/787-2621;**

www.travelchums.com) is an Internet-only travel-companion matching service with elements of an online personals-type site, hosted by the respected New York–based Shaw Guides travel service.

Many reputable tour companies offer singles-only trips. **Singles Travel International** (✆ 877/765-6874; www.singlestravelintl.com) offers escorted tours to places like the Greek Islands. **Backroads** (✆ 800/462-2848; www.backroads.com) offers "Singles + Solos" active-travel trips to destinations worldwide.

Smoking

In recent years the Greeks have imposed no-smoking regulations on airplanes, on areas of ships, and—as of July 1, 2009—all public locations (banks, post offices, and so on); also small restaurants, tavernas and cafes must declare whether they allow smoking or not; larger such establishments are supposed to set aside smoking areas. But Greeks continue to be among the most persistent smokers and, except on airplanes, many Greeks—and some foreigners—feel free to puff away at will. Hotels are only beginning to claim that they have set aside rooms or even floors for nonsmokers, so ask about them, if it matters to you. If you are really bothered by smoke while eating, about all you can do is position yourself as best as possible—and then be prepared to leave if it gets really bad.

Student Travel

In Greece, students with proper identification (ISIC and IYC cards) are given reduced entrance fees to archaeological sites and museums, as well as discounts on admission to most artistic events, theatrical performances, and festivals. So you'd be wise to arm yourself with an **International Student Identity Card (ISIC),** which offers substantial savings on rail passes, plane tickets, and entrance fees. It also provides you with basic health and life insurance and a 24-hour help line. The card is available for $22 from **STA Travel** (✆ 800/781-4040; www.statravel.com), the biggest student travel agency in the world.

The **International Student Travel Confederation** (**ISTC;** www.istc.org) was formed in 1949 to make travel around the world more affordable for students. Check out its website for comprehensive travel services information for students.

If you're no longer a student but are still under 26, you can get an **International Youth Travel Card (IYTC)** from the same people, which entitles you to some discounts. **Travel CUTS** (✆ 800/592-2887; www.travelcuts.com) offers similar services for both Canadians and U.S. residents. Irish students may prefer to turn to **USIT** (✆ 01/602-1906; www.usit.ie), an Ireland-based specialist in student, youth, and independent travel.

A Hostelling International membership can save students money in some 5,000 HI hostels in 70 countries (including Greece), where sex-segregated, dormitory-style sleeping quarters cost about $15 to $35 per night. In Greece, an International Guest Card can be obtained at the **Greek Association of Youth Hostels (OESE),** in Athens at 75 Dhamereos, Athens 11633 (✆ 210/751-9530; www.athens-yhostel.com).

Taxes & Service Charges

The **Value Added Tax** (VAT) has in response to Greece's economic crisis been greatly increased—it now stands at 23% for many purchases and services, including restaurants and car rentals; food and medicine and certain other "vital goods" tend to have a VAT of 11% while books and newspapers have 5.5%. You may sometimes be given a printed receipt that shows these percentages but the point to realize is that the taxes have been included in the price quoted and charged. In addition to the VAT, hotel prices usually include a service charge of up to 12% and a "community tax," about 4% to 5%. (By the way, don't confuse any of these charges with many restaurants' "cover charge" that may be .50€–2€ per place setting.) Also see "Tipping," below.

If you have purchased an item that costs 100€ or more and are a citizen of a non–European Union nation, you can get most of the VAT refunded (provided you export it within 90 days of purchase). It's easiest to shop at stores that display the sign tax-free for tourists. However, any store should be able to provide you with a Tax-Free Check Form, which you complete in the store. If you use your charge card, the receipt will list the VAT separately from the cost of the item. As you are leaving the country, present a copy of this form to the refund desk (usually at the Customs office). Be prepared to show both the goods and the receipt as proof of purchase. Also be prepared to wait a fair amount of time before you get the refund. (In fact, the process at the airport seems designed to discourage you from trying to obtain the refund.)

Telephones Until the late 1990s in Greece, most foreigners went to the offices of the Telecommunications Organization of Greece (OTE, pronounced oh-*tay*, or *Organismos Tilepikinonion tis Ellados*) to place most of their phone calls, especially overseas. But because phone cards are now so widespread throughout Greece, this is no longer necessary, once you get the hang of using them. You must first purchase a phone card at an OTE office or at most kiosks. (If you expect to make any phone calls while in Greece, buy one at the airport's OTE office upon arrival.) The cards come in various denominations, from 3€ to

25€. The more costly the card, the cheaper the units. The cost of a call with a phone card varies greatly depending on local, domestic, and international rates. A local call of up to 3 minutes to a fixed phone costs about .10€, which is three units from a phone card; for each minute beyond that, it costs another .06€, or two units off the card (so that a 10-min. local call costs 17 units, or .52€). All calls, even to the house next door, cost Greeks something, so if you use someone's telephone even for a local call, offer to pay the charges.

In larger cities and larger towns, kiosks have telephones from which you can make local calls for .10€ for 3 minutes. (In remote areas, you can make long-distance calls from these phones.) A few of the older public pay phones that required coins are still around, but it's better to buy a phone card. If you must use an older pay phone, deposit the required coin and listen for a dial tone, an irregular beep. A regular beep indicates that the line is busy.

Note: All phone numbers in Greece are 10 digits long, including the area code; the area code may range from 3 to 5 digits, and the number itself may range from 5 to 8 digits, but the total will always be 10. All (except for cellphones—see below) also precede the city/area code with a 2 and end that with a 0. For example, since the Athens city code was originally 1, it is now 210, followed by a seven-digit number,

but most other numbers in Greece are six digits with a four-digit area code. In all cases, even if you are calling someone in the same building, you must dial all 10 digits.

Calling a **cellphone** (mobile) in Greece requires substituting a 6 for the 2 that precedes the area code.

Long-distance calls, both domestic and international, can be quite expensive in Greece, especially at hotels, which may add a surcharge of up to 100%, unless you have a telephone credit card from a major long-distance provider such as AT&T, MCI, or Sprint. But if possible, avoid making long-distance calls from a hotel.

If you prefer to make your call from an OTE office, these are centrally located in all decent-sized cities. At OTE offices, a clerk will assign you a booth with a metered phone. You can pay with a phone card, international credit card, or cash. Collect calls take much longer.

To Call Greece from the United States, Canada, U.K., Australia, or New Zealand:

1. Dial the international access code: 011 from the U.S or Canada.; 00 from the U.K., Ireland, or New Zealand; or 0011 from Australia
2. Dial the country code: 30
3. Dial the city code (three to five digits) and then the number. *Note:* All numbers in Greece must have 10 digits, including the city code.

To Make International Calls from Within Greece The easiest and cheapest way is to call your long-distance service provider before leaving home to determine the access number that you must dial in Greece. The principal access codes in Greece are: AT&T, ✆ 00800-1311; MCI, ✆ 00800-1211; and Sprint, ✆ 00800-1411.

If you use the Greek phone system to make a direct call abroad—whether using an OTE office, a phone that takes cards, or a phone that takes coins—dial the country code plus the area code (omitting the initial zero, if any), then dial the number. Some country codes are: Australia, 0061; Canada, 001; Ireland, 00353; New Zealand, 0064; United Kingdom, 0044; and United States, 001. Thus, if you wanted to call the British Embassy in Washington, D.C., you would dial 001-202-588-7800.

Note that if you are going to put all the charges on your phone card (that is, not on your long-distance provider), you will be charged at a high rate per minute (at least 3€ to North America), so you should not make a call unless your phone card's remaining value can cover it.

For Operator Assistance: If you need operator assistance in making a call, dial ✆ **139** if you're trying to make an international call and ✆ **169** if you want to call a number in Greece.

Toll-Free Numbers: Numbers beginning with **080** within

Greece are toll-free, but calling a 800 number in the States from Greece is not toll-free. In fact, it costs the same as an overseas call.

Rechargeable Phone Cards: One of the newest, easiest, and cheapest ways to make calls while abroad is to sign on for a phone card that can be used in most countries and can be recharged (that is, money and therefore minutes added from your charge card account). To learn more about this card and its various other feature, see **www.ekit.com**.

Time The European 24-hour clock is used to measure time, so on schedules you'll see noon as 1200, 3:30pm as 1530, and 11pm as 2300. In informal conversation, however, Greeks express time much as we do—though noon may mean anywhere from noon to 3pm, afternoon is 3 to 7pm, and evening is 7pm to midnight.

Greece is 2 hours ahead of Greenwich Mean Time. In reference to North American time zones, it's 7 hours ahead of Eastern Standard Time, 8 hours ahead of Central Standard Time, 9 hours ahead of Mountain Standard Time, and 10 hours ahead of Pacific Standard Time. Note that Greece does observe daylight saving time, although it may not start and stop on the same days as in North America. For help with time translations, download our convenient Travel Tools app for your mobile device. Go to **www.frommers.com/ go/mobile** and click on the Travel Tools icon.

Tipping Restaurant bills no longer include a service charge or tip and it is customary to leave 10% to 15%; also consider "rounding off" on larger bills; to the nearest 1€. Good taxi service merits a tip of 5% to 10%. (Greeks rarely tip taxi drivers, but tourists are expected to.) Hotel chambermaids should be left about 2€ per night per couple. Bellhops and doormen should be tipped 1€ to 5€, depending on the services they provide.

For help with tip calculations, currency conversions, and more, download our Travel Tools app for your mobile device. Go to **www.frommers.com/go/mobile** and click on the Travel Tools icon.

Toilets Most Greek establishments—hotels, restaurants, museums, and so on—now provide flush toilets, but especially in villages, you may still be asked to deposit toilet paper in a container beside the toilet. In cheaper and more remote restaurants, however, you may find that there is no water at the hand bowl or a shortage of toilet paper so you might consider keeping some tissues with you.

Public restrooms are generally available in any good-size Greek town, and though they are sometimes rather crude, they usually do work. (Old-fashioned stand-up/ squat facilities are still found.) If there is an attendant you are expected to leave a small tip. In an emergency, you can ask to use the facilities of a restaurant or shop; however, near major attractions, the facilities are denied to all but customers, because traffic is too heavy. If you use any such facilities, respect its sponsor and give an attendant a tip.

Visas Travelers bearing passports from the European Union countries, the USA, Canada, Australia and New Zealand do not need visas, nor do citizens of many other countries. But to be sure, check with the nearest Greek consulate. And allow several weeks to get such a visa.

Visitor Information

The **Greek National Tourism Organization (GNTO** or **EOT** in Greece—and increasingly referred to as the Hellenic Tourism Organization) has offices throughout the world that can provide you with information concerning all aspects of travel to and in Greece. Look for them at **www.gnto.gr** or contact one of the following GNTO offices:

United States Olympic Tower, 645 Fifth Ave., 5th Floor, New York, NY 10022 (☏ **212/421-5777;** fax 212/826-6940).

Australia & New Zealand 37–49 Pitt St., Sydney, NSW

2000 ((☏ **29/241-1663;** fax 29/241-2499).

Canada 1500 Donmills Rd., Toronto, ON M3B 3K4 ((☏ **416/968-2220;** fax 416/968-6533).

United Kingdom & Ireland 4 Conduit St., London W1S 2DJ ((☏ **207/495-9300;** fax 207/495-4057).

Among the sites we've used for broad-based searches on Greece are:

○ **www.mfa.gr** (official Greek matters)

○ **www.gtp.gr** (ship and air travel in Greece)

○ **www.phantis.com** (current news about Greece)

○ **www.culture.gr** (official site for Greek's cultural attractions)

○ **www.perseus.tufts.edu** (classical Greek texts)

But probably the best source for up-to-date on-the-ground travel information is on **www.frommers.com**, both its Updates and its Community Forums.

Water The public drinking water in Greece is safe to drink, although it can be slightly brackish in some locales near the sea. For that reason, many people prefer the bottled water available

at restaurants, hotels, cafes, food stores, and kiosks. The days when Greek restaurants automatically served glasses of cold fresh water are gone; you can ask for the tap or house water—be sure to do so before the waiter opens bottled water. If you do order bottled water, you will have to choose between natural or carbonated *(metalliko)*, and domestic or imported. Cafes, however, tend to provide a glass of natural water.

Women Travelers

Young women—especially singles or small groups—may well find Greek males coming on to them, especially at beaches, clubs, and other tourist locales in a rather forward manner. But our informants tell us that, in general, Greek males (a) do not attempt any physical contact; and (b) sooner or later respect "No." One tactic said to work for women is to say, "I'm a Greek-American." The other advice is not to leave well-attended locales with someone you don't really know. Women should also be aware that some cafes and even restaurants are effectively male-only haunts; the males will not appreciate attempts by foreign women to enter these places.

THE GREEK LANGUAGE

This chapter offers you a few aids to help you make your way in Greek. First: Remember that literacy is nearly universal in Greece. The table below will help you move from Greek letters or words to a sense of how they should sound. This transliteration of modern Greek is used throughout this book, except with names that have become household words in English, like Athens, Socrates, Olympus, and so on. Generally, all you have to say is what you are looking for, raising your voice at the end of the word to let your listener know it's a question, and bingo!—someone will help.

Alphabet		Transliteration	Pronunciation
A α	álfa	a	father
B β	víta	v	viper
Γ γ	gámma	g before α, o, ω, and consonants	get
		y before αι, ε, ει, η, ι, οι, υ	yes
		ng before κ, γ, χ, or ξ	singer
Δ δ	thélta	th	the (not as the th- in "thin")
Ε ε	épsilon	e	set
Ζ ζ	zíta	z	lazy
Η η	íta	i	magazine
Θ θ	thíta	th	thin (not as the th- in "the")
Ι ι	ióta	i	magazine
		y before a, o	yard, yore
Κ κ	káppa	k	keep
Λ λ	lámtha	l	leap
Μ μ	mi	m	marry
Ν ν	ni	n	never
Ξ ξ	ksi	ks	taxi
Ο o	ómicron	o	bought
Π π	pi	p	pet

Alphabet	Transliteration	Pronunciation
P ρ	ro	r	*r*ound
Σ σ/ς	sígma	s before vowels or θ, κ, π, τ, φ, χ, ψ	*s*ay
		z before β, γ, δ, ζ, y before λ, μ, ν, ρ	la*z*y
T τ	taf	t	*t*ake
Y υ	ípsilon	i	magaz*i*ne
Φ φ	fi	f	*f*ee
X χ	chi	h	*h*ero (before e and i sounds; like the *ch*- in Scottish "loch" otherwise)
Ψ ψ	psi	ps	colla*ps*e
Ω ω	ómega	o	b*ou*ght

USEFUL WORDS & PHRASES

When you're asking for or about something and have to rely on single words or short phrases, it's an excellent idea to use "*sas parakaló*," meaning "please" or "you're welcome" to introduce or conclude almost anything you say.

English	Greek
Airport	Aerothrómio
Automobile	Aftokínito
Avenue	Leofóros
Bad	Kakós, -kí, -kó*
Bank	Trápeza
Breakfast	Proinó
Bus	Leoforío
Can you tell me?	Boríte ná móu píte?
Cheap	Ft(h)inó
Church	EkklIssía
Closed	Klistós, stí, stó*
Coffeehouse	Kafenío
Cold	Kríos, -a, -o*
Dinner	Vrathinó
Do you speak English?	Miláte AnglIká?
Excuse me.	Signómi(n).
Expensive	Akrivós, -í, -ó*
Farewell!	Stóka-ló! *(to person leaving)*
Glad to meet you.	Chéro polí.**
Good	Kalós, lí, ló*

English	Greek
Goodbye.	Adío or chérete.**
Good evening.	Kalispéra.
Good health (cheers)!	Stín (i)yá sas or Yá-mas!
Good morning or Good day.	Kaliméra.
Good night.	Kaliníchta.**
Hello!	Yássas or chérete!**
Here	Ethó
Hot	Zestós, -stí, -stó*
Hotel	Xenothochío**
How are you?	Tí kánete or Pós íst(h)e?
How far?	Pósso makriá?
How long?	Póssi óra or Pósso(n) keró?
How much does it cost?	Póso káni?
I am a vegetarian.	Íme hortophágos.
I am from New York.	Íme apótí(n) Néa(n) Iórki.
I am lost or I have lost the way.	Écho chathí or Écho chási tón drómo(n).**
I'm sorry.	Singnómi.
I'm sorry, but I don't speak Greek (well).	Lipoúme, allá thén miláo elliniká (kalá).
I don't understand.	Thén katalavéno.
I don't understand, please repeat it.	Thén katalavéno, péste to páli, sás parakaló.
It's (not) all right.	(Dén) íne en dáxi.
I want a glass of beer.	Thélo éna potíri bíra.
I want to go to the airport.	Thélo ná páo stóaerothrómio.
I would like a room.	Tha íthela ena thomátio.
Left (direction)	Aristerá
Lunch	Messimerianó
Map	Chártis**
Market (place)	Agorá
Mr.	Kírios
Mrs.	Kiría
My name is . . .	Onomázome . . .
New	Kenoúryos, -ya, -yo*
No	Óchi**
Old	Paleós, -leá, -leó* (pronounce palyós, -lyá, -lyó)
Open	Anichtós, -chtí, -chtó*
Patisserie	Zacharoplastío**
Pharmacy	Pharmakío
Please or You're welcome.	Parakaló.
Please call a taxi (for me).	Parakaló, fonáxte éna taxi (yá ména).
Point out to me, please . . .	Thíkste mou, sas parakaló . . .
Post office	Tachidromío**

English	Greek
Restaurant	Estiatório
Restroom	Tóméros *or* I toualétta
Right (direction)	Dexiá
Saint	Áyios, ayía, *(plural)* áyi-i *(abbreviated* ay)
Show me on the map.	Díxte mou stó(n) chárti**
Square	Plateia
Station (bus, train)	Stathmos (leoforíou, trénou)
Stop (bus)	Stási(s) (leoforíou)
Street	Odós
Thank you (very much).	Efcharistó(polí).**
Today	Símera
Tomorrow	Ávrio
Very nice	Polí oréos, -a, -o*
Very well	Polí kalá *or* En dáxi
What?	Tí?
What's your name?	Pós onomázest(h)e?
What time is it?	Ti óra ine?
Where am I?	Pou íme?
Where is . . . ?	Poú íne . . . ?
Why?	Yatí?

*Masculine ending -os, feminine ending -a or -i, neuter ending -o.

**Remember, *ch* should be pronounced as in Scottish *loch* or German *ich*, not as in the word *church*.

NUMBERS

English	Greek
0	Midén
1	Éna
2	Dío
3	Tría
4	Téssera
5	Pénde
6	Éxi
7	Eftá
8	Októ
9	Enyá
10	Déka
11	Éndeka
12	Dódeka
13	Dekatría
14	Dekatéssera

Index